Computer Service and Repair

Sixth Edition

Chuck Easttom • Richard M. Roberts

Correlates to CompTIA A+ 220-1101/220-1102 Objectives

Publisher
The Goodheart-Willcox Company, Inc.
Tinley Park, IL
www.g-w.com

Library of Congress Control Number: 2023940632

ISBN 979-8-88817-184-4

1 2 3 4 5 6 7 8 9 – 25 – 28 27 26 25 24 23

Image Credits. Front cover: raigvi/Shutterstock.com
Figure 3-9: Used under the Creative Common Attribution 3.0 Unported (CC BY 3.0)
https://creativecommons.org/licenses/by/3.0/deed.en; no changes made
Figure 6-6: Used under the Creative Common Attribution-ShareAlike 4.0 International (CC BY-SA 4.0)
https://creativecommons.org/licenses/by-sa/4.0/deed.en; no changes made
Figure 8-20: Used under the Creative Common Attribution-ShareAlike 4.0 International (CC BY-SA 4.0)
https://creativecommons.org/licenses/by-sa/4.0/deed.en, Attribution-ShareAlike 3.0 Unported (CC BY-SA 3.0)
https://creativecommons.org/licenses/by-sa/3.0/deed.en, Attribution-ShareAlike 2.5 Generic (CC BY-SA 2.5)
https://creativecommons.org/licenses/by-sa/2.5/deed.en, Attribution-ShareAlike 2.0 Generic (CC BY-SA 2.0)
https://creativecommons.org/licenses/by-sa/2.0/deed.en, and Attribution-ShareAlike 1.0 Generic (CC BY-SA 1.0)
https://creativecommons.org/licenses/by-sa/1.0/deed.en; no changes made
Figure 8-26: Used under public domain; no changes made
Figure 11-14: Used under public domain; labels added
Figure 17-2: Used under CC0 1.0 Universal (CC0 1.0) Public Domain Dedication
https://creativecommons.org/publicdomain/zero/1.0/deed.en; Photo cropped

Preface

Support for PCs and mobile devices has evolved into one of the largest service industries in the world, and the demand for skilled technicians to maintain, support, and upgrade PCs and mobile devices is ever-growing. Working as a PC technician is a rewarding and challenging career that can take you anywhere in the world and is the perfect place to start if you wish to learn computer networking, programming, administration, or any of the computer sciences. A good foundation in computer technology provides a base of knowledge that will assist you in other technical areas, such as networking and cybersecurity.

Computer Service and Repair provides an introduction for becoming a certified support professional in the IT industry. The text focuses on configuration, troubleshooting, repair, maintenance, and support for desktop computers, mobile devices, operating systems, application software, and printers. In addition, it provides critical content for becoming a professional, courteous, and successful support technician.

The text is aligned to CompTIA A+ Certification 220-1101 (Core 1) and 220-1102 (Core 2) Exam Objectives. The CompTIA A+ Certification Exam is an industry-recognized certification and starting point for a career in IT. The CompTIA A+ Certification is also a CompTIA Core Skills Certification, meaning it provides a groundwork for future career growth by going beyond just PC repair to prepare candidates for troubleshooting and problem-solving for a wide variety of scenarios, including those associated with networking, operating systems, mobile devices, and security.

By studying *Computer Service and Repair* and using the ancillary Study Guide and Lab Manual, you can improve your level of preparation to earn an industry-recognized certification. Upon completing this course, you should able to

- recall and identify essential components of a personal computer (PC);
- differentiate between operating system releases and understand how they interact with the computer on which they are installed;
- understand how motherboards operate and how they interact and work with individual components;
- compare, select, troubleshoot, and install a central processing unit;
- troubleshoot, replace, and understand the functionality of power supplies;
- upgrade, install, and understand the construction and operation of memory;
- list and identify common input devices and their interactions with computers;
- compare, troubleshoot, and install monitors and video adapter cards;
- describe characteristics of audio data and install sound cards;
- differentiate, troubleshoot, and replace both magnetic and solid-state storage devices;
- compare, contrast, and comprehend the construction and operation of optical storage technologies;
- troubleshoot and explain the operation principles of various printer types;
- compare, contrast, troubleshoot, and replace laptop and mobile device components;
- understand the differences among Internet-connection methods and troubleshoot modems;
- discuss methods for physically securing a workstation and enforcing authentication;
- categorize malware and list common security applications;
- diagnose a variety of commonly encountered PC symptoms, differentiate between Windows diagnostic utilities, and apply preventive maintenance procedures;
- differentiate among and apply various data recovery techniques;
- discuss the benefits of a computer network and differentiate among common network devices;

- understand the communication process between networks and identify network media and tools;
- manage administration functions of a network;
- recall network operation;
- design and install a SOHO network;
- apply communication, professionalism, and customer-support skills;
- actively and efficiently prepare for and pass the CompTIA A+ Certification Exam; and
- understand employment options and requirements for a professional career.

Studying *Computer Service and Repair* will provide you with the knowledge for earning professional credentials for technical support and operational roles, help you learn to connect users to the data they need to do their jobs, and prepare and validate your foundational skills required as an IT professional.

About the Authors

Dr. Chuck Easttom is the author of 41 books, including several on computer security, forensics, and cryptography. He is also an inventor with 25 patents and the author of over 70 research papers. He holds a D.Sc. in cybersecurity; a Ph.D. in Nanotechnology; a Ph.D. in computer science; and master's degrees in applied computer science, education, and systems engineering. He is a senior member of both the IEEE and the ACM. He is also a Distinguished Speaker of the ACM and a Distinguished Visitor of the IEEE. Dr. Easttom is currently an adjunct professor for Georgetown University and for Vanderbilt University.

Richard M. Roberts has designed curriculum; taught electricity, electronics, and computer technology; and supervised technical teachers for nearly 50 years. He was an adjunct instructor at South Florida State College. He has divided his time between consulting, teaching students and instructors, and writing instructional materials. He also coauthored the *Networking Fundamentals* textbook and the *Electricity and Electronics* textbook. He holds active CompTIA A+, Network+, and Security+ certifications.

Reviewers

The author and publisher wish to thank the following industry and teaching professionals for their valuable input into the development of *Computer Service and Repair*.

Dr. Marsha Craig, Ed.D.
Calhoun Community College
Decatur, Alabama

Franklin Fondjo Fotou
Langston University
Langston, Oklahoma

Julie Hester
Northeast Alabama Community College
Rainsville, Alabama

Steven R. Hultgren
Johnson County Community College
Parkville, Missouri

Valeria McLain
Lake Superior College
Duluth, Minnesota

Stephen Paduhovich
York County School of Technology
York, Pennsylvania

Veronica Pulido, A+, CCNA
San Elizario High School
San Elizario, Texas

Kenneth Schaffer
Southwest Technical Institute
Sioux Falls, South Dakota

Brian Volkmuth
St. Cloud Technical and Community College
St. Cloud, Minnesota

Anthomy Zampino
Kent State University Trumbull
Warren, Ohio

CompTIA A+ Certification

How to Become CompTIA Certified

This training material can help you prepare for the CompTIA A+ Certification 220-1101 (Core 1) and 220-1102 (Core 2) Exams. The Computing Technology Industry Association (CompTIA) is a nonprofit information technology (IT) trade association, and its certifications are designed by subject-matter experts. Each certification is vendor-neutral, covers multiple technologies, and requires demonstration of skills and knowledge widely sought after by employers in the IT industry. There are four general steps to achieving CompTIA certification:

1. Choose the desired IT certification from CompTIA
2. Familiarize yourself with the exam, its objectives, and the types of questions used
3. Begin studying, learning, and preparing for the exam
4. Register for the exam, read and sign the Candidate Agreement, and take and pass the exam

For more information about CompTIA certifications, such as industry acceptance, benefits, or updates, visit certification.comptia.org.

CompTIA A+ Correlation Charts

Complete mappings (correlation charts) of the CompTIA A+ Exam Objectives to the content of the *Computer Service and Repair* textbook are located on the G-W website at www.g-w.com. On this website, you will find one correlation chart per exam:

- CompTIA A+ 220-1101 (Core 1)
- CompTIA A+ 220-1102 (Core 2)

Each chart lists the exam objectives and corresponding page numbers where you can find the related content.

How to Use This Text

The *Computer Service and Repair* text and accompanying resources will help you prepare for the CompTIA A+ Certification Exam by teaching you the basics of PC maintenance, troubleshooting, repair, and component replacement. Additionally, you will learn about networking, have access to an A+ practice exam, and understand qualities employers seek in job candidates while maintaining realistic expectations about employment. These are concepts that you will need to understand for not only the certification exam, but also your career as an information technology professional.

Each chapter in *Computer Service and Repair* begins with a set of Learning Outcomes that outline the goals you should focus on accomplishing by the time you complete each chapter. For each outcome, there is a corresponding top-level heading, review question, and set of summary bullet points to help ensure you understand the topics covered in the chapter. There is also a list of CompTIA A+ Certification Exam Objectives in the beginning of each chapter that outlines the CompTIA content to be discussed.

In addition to Learning Outcomes, the chapter-opening material also lists a set of key terms discussed throughout the material. These terms are in boldface when they appear in the content to make them easily distinguishable from the rest of the text. There are also important words or phrases printed in italic text to which you should pay special attention and consideration. Studying these terms will help you understand the material and better prepare you for certification and employment.

Each chapter concludes with a summary of important points to remember, organized by level-one headings. This summary will help you review important topics from each section of the chapter.

The following suggested guidelines will help you make the most of your introduction to computer maintenance and repair.

- Read the Learning Outcomes listed in the chapter opener. Each outcome is tied directly to a heading within the content as well as a set of summary bullet points and end-of-chapter review questions. The connection of Learning Outcomes throughout the content helps you focus and apply important information as you read each chapter.
- Read the list of CompTIA A+ Objectives in the chapter-opening material. These objectives are also noted in the margin with an icon where the material is covered. Use the list of objectives in the chapter opener as a checklist to take inventory of CompTIA standards you understand as well as information you need to review. The icons in the margins are there to direct you to the coverage of each objective for review.
- Pay attention to the illustrations. Each illustration is strategically created to highlight important information. By studying these, you will extend your learning and improve retention and application of the content.
- Read all A+ Note, Tech Tip, and Caution features as you progress through the material. This information helps supplement your learning by highlighting study tips, providing useful industry information, and helping you ensure personal and machine safety when working with computing devices.
- Review the summary at the end of each chapter. This will help you retain important information from the chapter.
- Answer the review questions and sample A+ questions in the end-of-chapter material. These questions provide exposure to the types of questions likely to be on the CompTIA A+ Certification Exam. By practicing these questions, you increase your chances of successfully earning CompTIA A+ certification.

New to This Edition

The sixth edition of *Computer Service and Repair* was revised to align to current CompTIA A+ Exam Objectives. Additionally, updates were made in each chapter to provide coverage of the newest operating systems and recent technological developments in computing and mobile devices.

- **Chapter 1 Introduction to a Typical PC** was reorganized and streamlined to present data in a more logical fashion. Similar topics now appear closer together than in the previous edition and outdated or irrelevant material has been removed from the chapter.
- **Chapter 2 Operating Systems** underwent significant changes in this edition. Not only were Windows 7 and Windows 8 removed, but short introductions to Windows 11 were also provided in anticipation of wider adoption. Additionally, the macOS and Linux handbook that appeared as an appendix in the previous edition has been relocated and included in this chapter. As a result, the existing macOS and Linux sections of this chapter have grown.
- **Chapter 3 Motherboards** was reorganized to streamline the chapter and group similarly related topics together.
- **Chapter 4 Central Processing Unit (CPU)** received a general update to reflect today's technological advancements in processing. Like other chapters, Chapter 4 was also reorganized to streamline the reading and group similar topics under one heading.
- **Chapter 5 Power Supplies** received updates to both content and visuals. Additionally, the chapter was reorganized in an effort to group similar topics closer together.
- **Chapter 6 Memory** was updated to include details about DDR5 memory. Additionally, outdated types of memory were truncated or removed as necessary.
- **Chapter 7 Input Devices** received a general update to remove references to outdated operating systems and devices. Additionally, a new section dedicated to managing mobile device hardware and components was added.
- **Chapter 8 Video Systems** received substantial reorganization to group similar topics together and reduce the number of top-level headings and objectives. Additionally, outdated topics such as CRTs were removed from the chapter.
- **Chapter 9 Audio Systems** received a minor update, largely to the content and visuals. Examples of new content include a dedicated Windows Control Panel section as well as information about audio capture cards.
- **Chapter 10 Magnetic and Solid-State Storage Devices** received a general update to place greater emphasis on solid-state media. Additionally, information about partition systems and disk-centric commands was revised to reflect today's technology.
- **Chapter 11 Optical Storage Technology** was updated to reflect advances in optical technology and add material about digital information rights.
- **Chapter 12 Printers** was updated to reflect modern aspects in printing, specifically information about 3D printing and printing languages.
- **Chapter 13 Laptops and Mobile Devices** received extensive updates to reflect today's technological landscape. Much of the new information added was about mobile devices, including new operating system information, security topics, and troubleshooting. Additionally, the symptoms listed at the end of the chapter content were reorganized to merge similar symptoms and make space for additional symptoms.
- **Chapter 14 Modems and Transceivers** was revised to begin phasing out discussion of outdated equipment. While legacy topics such as dial-up connectivity have been retained for historical and comparative reasons, these obsolete topics have been pared down substantially to provide space for current topics such as cable access and 5G.
- **Chapter 15 Physical Security and Authentication** was revised to provide expanded information about topics such as physical security measures, including bollards and access control vestibules. Additionally, a significant amount of authentication information was added, including a discussion of HSMs. The content about passwords was also expanded to include new information such as rainbow tables. Finally, the social engineering section was relocated to a location where it makes more sense for the reader.
- **Chapter 16 Security Applications and Malware** was updated to include information about additional malware types, social engineering attacks, and web-based threats according to the CompTIA A+ Certification objectives.

- **Chapter 17 PC Troubleshooting** was updated to include expanded discussion of the DiskPart utility. Other areas were revised to provide more general discussion of some troubleshooting tips. Additionally, information about installing and upgrading operating systems has been merged with appropriate sections of existing content as opposed to being a small, standalone section.
- **Chapter 18 Data Recovery** was updated to reflect the current menu and utility names in Windows 10 and remove references to outdated operating systems.
- **Chapter 19 Introduction to Networking** was reorganized to group similarly related items together. Additionally, some top-level headings were renamed to better reflect the content contained within them. Some material, such as DNS, was introduced to provide foundational material for the student that can be helpful in upcoming networking chapters. Finally, much of the visuals have been updated to provide students with contemporary examples of devices.
- **Chapter 20 Network Communication, Media, and Tools** received numerous content updates, including discussion of coaxial RG-8 and Category 8 cabling. Concepts such as DSL and cable modems, optical network terminals, and software-defined network were also added to make content easier to understand without having to look to a different chapter. Finally, additional protocols were added to the discussion of protocol suites.
- **Chapter 21 Managing Networks**, previously titled *Network Administration*, underwent an extensive reorganization to provide a more logical flow of information and reduce redundancy. Similar topics are now grouped under top-level, overarching headings instead of having multiple sections of tangentially related material.
- **Chapter 22 Network Operation and Connectivity**, previously titled *Wide Area Network (WAN)*, was revised to be more generalized, which is reflected in the new title. In previous editions, this chapter focused on WAN management, but many of the concepts were applicable to other network types. Additionally, outdated cloud services and methods, such as those specific to Windows 7, were removed from this edition.
- **Chapter 23 Small-Office/Home-Office (SOHO) Networking** was updated to reflect new information in SOHO networking and provide fresh screen captures. Specifically, the material about cloud services was expanded to include discussion of topics such as VDI and remote access.
- **Chapter 24 Customer Support, Communication, and Professionalism** underwent light revisions, including the addition of ticketing systems and an expanded section about document types. Additionally, the change-management section was updated to include example risk levels.
- **Chapter 25 CompTIA A+ Certification Exams Preparation** was updated to reflect the domain percentages of the 220-1101 and 220-1102 exams. Both practice exams within the chapter were revised to match those percentages.
- **Chapter 26 Employment and Advanced Education** received a general content update to reflect new certifications and remove outdated certifications. Additionally, the section on professional attire was revised to be more gender-neutral. Finally, information about job searches was unified to one section.

Focus on Certification

Computer Service and Repair is designed with certification in mind. In addition, it guides students through upgrading, configuring, troubleshooting, and networking desktop and mobile computers and devices.

This text has been updated to reflect current programs, systems, and practices in the information technology industry. It adheres to the CompTIA A+ 220-1101 and 220-1102 Exam Objectives, ensuring students are up to date with the most recent testing domains.

Chapter Opening Materials

At the beginning of each chapter, a list of outcomes guides your learning as you read the material presented. Each outcome is aligned with a content heading, as well as with a summary bullet point and review question at the end of the chapter. This alignment provides a logical flow through each page of the material so you may build on individual knowledge as you progress through the chapters.

A+ Objectives

CompTIA A+ Exam Objectives are listed in the opening of each chapter to engage learning and highlight important testing points presented in the content. Use the list of objectives as a checklist to verify your understanding of the A+ standards as presented in the material. In addition, objectives are noted by an icon in the margin where material is covered and provides a visual clue as to where each objective is met.

Tech Tip

The Tech Tip feature highlights supplemental information about practical application of networking concepts. These tips vary in their scope, ranging from simple synonyms or definitions of discussed material to real-world advice that provides you with insight that will help in your assignments and careers.

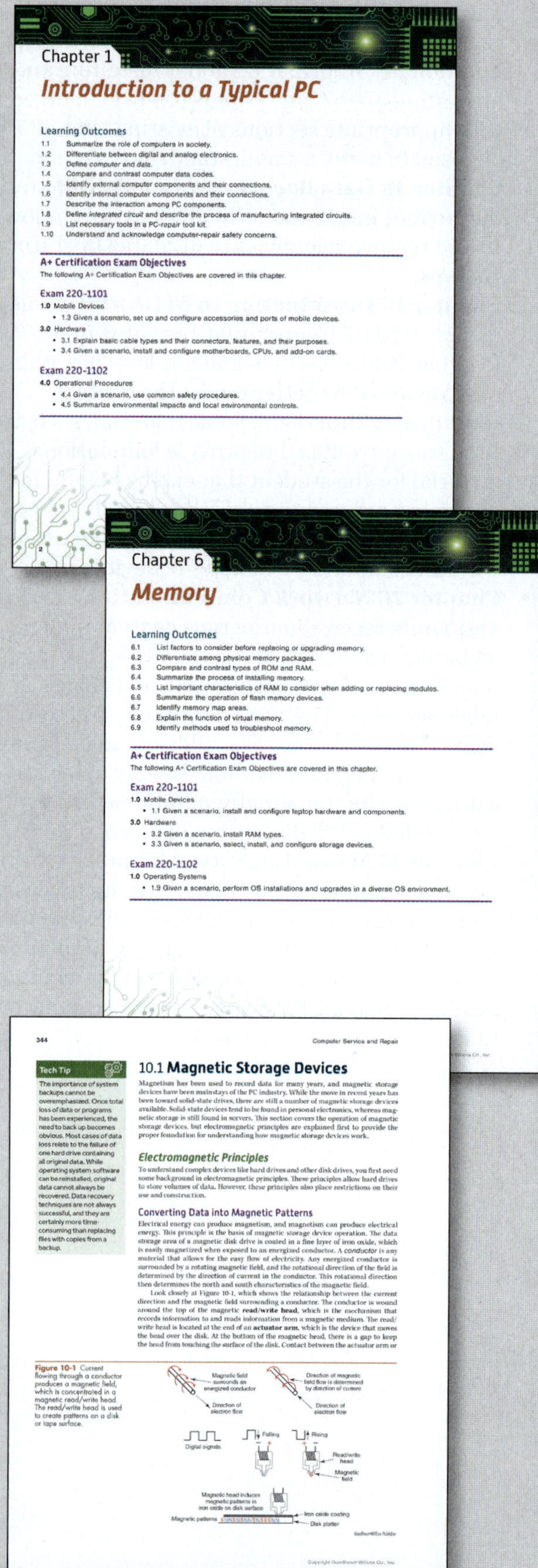
Chapter 1

Introduction to a Typical PC

Learning Outcomes

1.1 Summarize the role of computers in society.
1.2 Differentiate between digital and analog electronics.
1.3 Define computer and data.
1.4 Compare and contrast computer data codes.
1.5 Identify external computer components and their connections.
1.6 Identify internal computer components and their connections.
1.7 Describe the interaction among PC components.
1.8 Define integrated circuit and describe the process of manufacturing integrated circuits.
1.9 List necessary tools in a PC-repair tool kit.
1.10 Understand and acknowledge computer-repair safety concerns.

A+ Certification Exam Objectives

The following A+ Certification Exam Objectives are covered in this chapter.

Exam 220-1101

1.0 Mobile Devices
- 1.3 Given a scenario, set up and configure accessories and ports of mobile devices.

3.0 Hardware
- 3.1 Explain basic cable types and their connectors, features, and their purposes.
- 3.4 Given a scenario, install and configure motherboards, CPUs, and add-on cards.

Exam 220-1102

4.0 Operational Procedures
- 4.4 Given a scenario, use common safety procedures.
- 4.5 Summarize environmental impacts and local environmental controls.

Chapter 6

Memory

Learning Outcomes

6.1 List factors to consider before replacing or upgrading memory.
6.2 Differentiate among physical memory packages.
6.3 Compare and contrast types of ROM and RAM.
6.4 Summarize the process of installing memory.
6.5 List important characteristics of RAM to consider when adding or replacing modules.
6.6 Summarize the operation of flash memory devices.
6.7 Identify memory map areas.
6.8 Explain the function of virtual memory.
6.9 Identify methods used to troubleshoot memory.

A+ Certification Exam Objectives

The following A+ Certification Exam Objectives are covered in this chapter.

Exam 220-1101

1.0 Mobile Devices
- 1.1 Given a scenario, install and configure laptop hardware and components.

3.0 Hardware
- 3.2 Given a scenario, install RAM types.
- 3.3 Given a scenario, select, install, and configure storage devices.

Exam 220-1102

1.0 Operating Systems
- 1.9 Given a scenario, perform OS installations and upgrades in a diverse OS environment.

344 Computer Service and Repair

Tech Tip

The importance of system backups cannot be overemphasized. Once total loss of data or programs has been experienced, the need to back up becomes obvious. Most cases of data loss relate to the failure of one hard drive containing all original data. While operating system software can be reinstalled, original data cannot always be recovered. Data recovery techniques are not always successful, and they are certainly more time-consuming than replacing files with copies from a backup.

10.1 Magnetic Storage Devices

Magnetism has been used to record data for many years, and magnetic storage devices have been mainstays of the PC industry. While the move in recent years has been toward solid-state drives, there are still a number of magnetic storage devices available. Solid-state devices tend to be found in personal electronics, whereas magnetic storage is still found in servers. This section covers the operation of magnetic storage devices, but electromagnetic principles are explained first to provide the proper foundation for understanding how magnetic storage devices work.

Electromagnetic Principles

To understand complex devices like hard drives and other disk drives, you first need some background in electromagnetic principles. These principles allow hard drives to store volumes of data. However, these principles also place restrictions on their use and construction.

Converting Data into Magnetic Patterns

Electrical energy can produce magnetism, and magnetism can produce electrical energy. This principle is the basis of magnetic storage device operation. The data storage area of a magnetic disk drive is coated in a fine layer of iron oxide, which is easily magnetized when exposed to an energized conductor. A *conductor* is any material that allows for the easy flow of electricity. Any energized conductor is surrounded by a rotating magnetic field, and the rotational direction of the field is determined by the direction of current in the conductor. This rotational direction then determines the north and south characteristics of the magnetic field.

Look closely at Figure 10-1, which shows the relationship between the current direction and the magnetic field surrounding a conductor. The conductor is wound around the top of the magnetic **read/write head**, which is the mechanism that records information to and reads information from a magnetic medium. The read/write head is located at the end of an **actuator arm**, which is the device that moves the head over the disk. At the bottom of the magnetic head, there is a gap to keep the head from touching the surface of the disk. Contact between the actuator arm or

Figure 10-1 Current flowing through a conductor produces a magnetic field, which is concentrated in a magnetic read/write head. The read/write head is used to create patterns on a disk or tape surface.

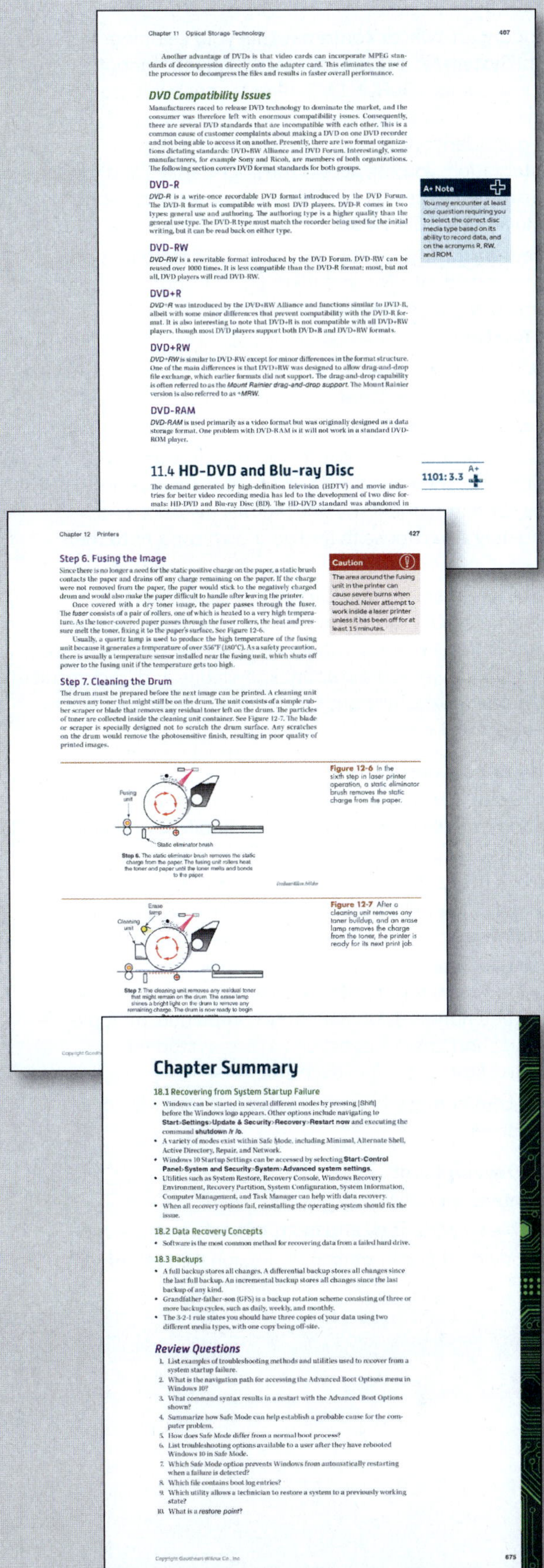

A+ Note

The A+ Note feature provides tips and facts regarding the CompTIA A+ Certification Exams. These tips will help you as you study for the A+ Certification Exams.

Caution!

The Caution! feature highlights important personal- and machine-safety information you need to know before performing specific tasks. These features alert you to actions that may cause personal injury or damage to a computer or electronic device.

End-of-Chapter Content

End-of-chapter material provides an opportunity for review and application of concepts.

- A concise **Summary** reiterates the Learning Outcomes and provides a brief review of the content for your reference. This helps you focus on important concepts presented in the text.
- **Review** questions highlight basic concepts presented in the chapter so you can evaluate your understanding of the material.
- **Sample A+ Exam Questions** challenge you to answer questions similar to those you will face on the CompTIA A+ Certification Exam, providing a sample of what to expect on the exam.

TOOLS FOR STUDENT AND INSTRUCTOR SUCCESS

Student Tools

Student Text

Computer Service and Repair presents the fundamentals of computer maintenance and repair as well as introductory networking theory and concepts to prepare students for the 220-1101 and 220-1102 CompTIA A+ Certification Exams.

Lab Workbook

- Hands-on practice includes questions and activities.
- Projects offer students opportunities to work on various computer troubleshooting and administration challenges.

Study Guide

- Practice exercises reinforce concepts and skills learned in the corresponding textbook chapters.
- A CompTIA A+ Reference Guide helps students study and prepare for the CompTIA A+ Exam.

G-W Digital Companion

For digital users, e-flash cards and vocabulary exercises allow interaction with content to create opportunities to increase achievement.

Online Learning Suite

- Online student text, study guide, and lab manual, along with rich supplemental content, bring digital learning to the classroom.
- All instructional materials are accessible at home, at school, or on the go.

G-W EduHub®

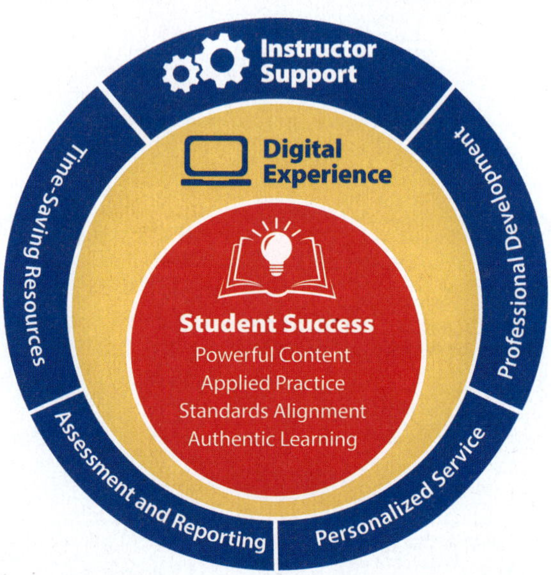

Instructor Tools

LMS Integration

Integrate Goodheart-Willcox content within your Learning Management System for a seamless user experience for both you and your students. EduHub LMS–ready content in Common Cartridge® format facilitates single sign-on integration and gives you control of student enrollment and data. With a Common Cartridge integration, you can access the LMS features and tools you are accustomed to using and G-W course resources in one convenient location—your LMS.

G-W Common Cartridge provides a complete learning package for you and your students. The included digital resources help your students remain engaged and learn effectively:

- **Digital Textbook**
- Online **Lab Manual content**
- Online **Study Guide content**
- **Drill and Practice** vocabulary activities

When you incorporate G-W content into your courses via Common Cartridge, you have the flexibility to customize and structure the content to meet the educational needs of your students. You may also choose to add your own content to the course.

For instructors, the Common Cartridge includes the Online Instructor Resources. QTI® question banks are available within the Online Instructor Resources for import into your LMS. These prebuilt assessments help you measure student knowledge and track results in your LMS gradebook. Questions and tests can be customized to meet your assessment needs.

Online Instructor Resources

- The **Instructor Resources** provide instructors with time-saving preparation tools such as answer keys, editable lesson plans, and other teaching aids.
- **Instructor's Presentations for PowerPoint®** are fully customizable, richly illustrated slides that help you teach and visually reinforce the key concepts from each chapter.
- Administer and manage assessments to meet your classroom needs using **Assessment Software with Question Banks**, which include hundreds of matching, completion, multiple choice, and short answer questions to assess student knowledge of the content in each chapter.

See www.g-w.com/computer-service-repair-2025 for a list of all available resources.

Professional Development

- Expert content specialists
- Research-based pedagogy and instructional practices
- Options for virtual and in-person Professional Development

Brief Contents

Contents

Chapter 1

Introduction to a Typical PC

Learning Outcomes

1.1 Summarize the role of computers in society.
1.2 Differentiate between digital and analog electronics.
1.3 Define *computer* and *data*.
1.4 Compare and contrast computer data codes.
1.5 Identify external computer components and their connections.
1.6 Identify internal computer components and their connections.
1.7 Describe the interaction among PC components.
1.8 Define *integrated circuit* and describe the process of manufacturing integrated circuits.
1.9 List necessary tools in a PC-repair tool kit.
1.10 Understand and acknowledge computer-repair safety concerns.

A+ Certification Exam Objectives

The following A+ Certification Exam Objectives are covered in this chapter.

Exam 220-1101

1.0 Mobile Devices

- 1.3 Given a scenario, set up and configure accessories and ports of mobile devices.

3.0 Hardware

- 3.1 Explain basic cable types and their connectors, features, and their purposes.
- 3.4 Given a scenario, install and configure motherboards, CPUs, and add-on cards.

Exam 220-1102

4.0 Operational Procedures

- 4.4 Given a scenario, use common safety procedures.
- 4.5 Summarize environmental impacts and local environmental controls.

Key Terms

American Standard Code for Information Interchange (ASCII)
analog electronics
antistatic wrist strap
binary number system
bit
byte
central processing unit (CPU)
computer
device bay
digital electronics
driver
electromagnetic interference (EMI)
electrostatic discharge (ESD)
expansion card
firmware
hard drive
hexadecimal number system
integrated circuit (IC)
motherboard
parallel transfer
peripheral
power supply
radio frequency interference (RFI)
random access memory (RAM)
serial transfer
solid-state drive (SSD)
surge protector
word

Overview

This chapter introduces many basic concepts you need to understand computer hardware and software. These concepts are expanded into complete chapters later in the textbook. Much of this text presents the personal computer based on the IBM-compatible computer architecture, better known as the PC, and prepares you for CompTIA A+ Certification.

CompTIA is a not-for-profit, vendor-neutral organization that certifies the competency level of technicians through examinations written to test specific areas. The CompTIA association has prepared the examinations to test individuals with approximately 12 months of PC repair, installation, and support experience. The certification awarded on successful completion of the exams is called *A+ Certification*. It is recognized throughout the industry as a certification of basic PC repair and support skills. The combination of this textbook and its accompanying Laboratory Manual and Study Guide prepares you for the certification exams. There is more information about preparing for CompTIA certifications in a later chapter. You can also visit the CompTIA website for the latest certification information.

A+ Note

Some of the very basic questions on the A+ Certification Exams deal with cable and connector identification, component handling, and safety procedures. Connector identification can be difficult for students new to PC technology, but anyone who has worked with a PC for some time will be able to answer these types of questions. As a student, you can prepare by looking at the end of the cable and noting if it uses pins or a socket. Do the same for the connection on the PC.

1.1 The Role of Computers

Computers are found in every aspect of our lives, including banking, business, military equipment, automobiles, televisions, communication systems, home appliances, satellites, submarines, and police stations. Computers can vary in size from a small, simple microprocessor found in a coffee maker or a clock radio to huge mainframe systems that are used in research and governmental agencies. Figure 1-1 shows a microprocessor along with a typical home or business PC and a large mainframe-type computer system.

At first, the makeup of a computer can seem intimidating. However, as you progress through this text, you will see that the mechanics of a computer are quite simple. The difficulty is overcome by understanding the interaction of hardware and software, grasping different operating systems, and recognizing upgrade and compatibility issues. Replacing a damaged or defective part is easy; the challenge is in determining whether the problem is from a software or hardware issue and what hardware is damaged or defective.

This chapter introduces the major components of a typical PC as well as basic computing concepts such as computer data and software. As your studies progress through the text, each part and concept will be covered in greater depth; for now, it is best to have an overall view of the PC system. No component can be fully understood without realizing how it interacts with the other components in the system. This chapter covers introductory-level knowledge of the computer system before going in-depth at a technician level.

1.2 Digital Electronics

All electronic components fall into one of two categories: *digital* or *analog*. **Digital electronics** are those that only have two states: on or off. It is a system best represented by a simple switch. There can only be two conditions in the switch circuit: on or off. Look at Figure 1-2, which shows a typical switch wired to a lamp. The switch controls power to the lamp, which can be turned on or off. No other electrical condition can exist for this simple circuit. Digital electronics in computers use on and off conditions. There is either full voltage or no voltage applied to the circuit.

Analog electronics are those that use and produce varying voltage levels. Analog electrical circuits can be represented with a dimmable light switch, such as the one illustrated in Figure 1-3. In this circuit, the intensity of the lamp varies as the dimmer switch is turned. The light from the lamp has different intensities based on the variation of electrical energy reaching the lamp from the dimmable switch.

A Skrypnykov Dmytro/Shutterstock.com B Oleksiy Mark/Shutterstock.com C Timofeev Vladimir/Shutterstock.com

Figure 1-1 Computers vary in size from small microprocessors (A) to typical home PCs (B) to large mainframe-type computer systems for research and data centers (C).

A computer is constructed of some very complex digital circuits that are combined into modules such as circuit board cards. As a PC technician, you will usually only be responsible for replacing the module, not repairing the digital circuits. As such, you do not need an extensive electronics background to repair a PC.

1.3 What Is a Computer?

A **computer** is an assembly of electronic modules that interact with computer programs known as *software* to create, modify, transmit, store, and display data. The computer has rapidly evolved from a simple electronic device able to perform basic mathematical functions into a sophisticated technology able to perform highly complex data automation.

Processing power, memory, and storage continue to increase at a rapid rate, and new types of computing such as quantum computers are being researched. While computing technology continues to advance, the basic purpose is the same: automating data processing. For the A+ Certification, and for working with computers, you will need to know basic terminology, concepts, and components.

At the core of their functionality, computers process *data*, which is information in a multitude of forms. Data can be text (such as *ABC* or *123*), graphics (pictures), or other media, such as audio recordings (music or voices) and video.

Data inside the computer is represented electronically as high and low voltages. The voltages are pulsed through the system to create what is called a *digital signal*. These pulses allow data to be displayed on a computer monitor or stored in memory or storage media such as a hard drive or flash drive. When written to a traditional magnetic hard disk drive, the electrical pulses are converted to magnetic patterns on the surface of the disk.

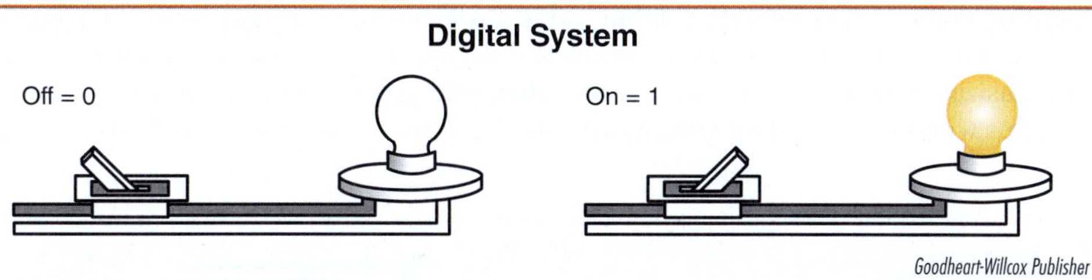

Figure 1-2 Digital electronics are those that only have two states, on or off, much like a simple light switch.

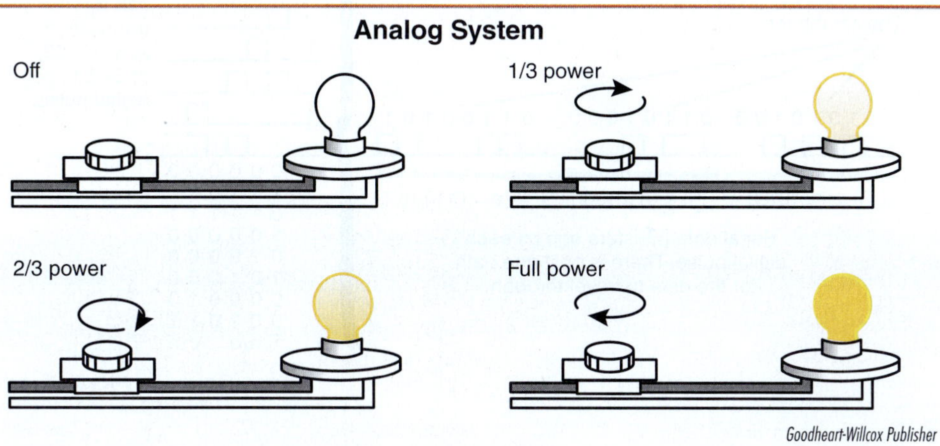

Figure 1-3 Analog electronics are those that use and produce varying voltage levels, much like a dimmable light switch.

Data in a computer system is represented as a pattern of ones and zeros known as the *binary system*. You will be introduced to the binary system later in this chapter. Some digital patterns represent words, pictures, and sounds; other patterns represent commands, such as load file, find file, and save file. Remember, computers do not contain any intelligence. Rather, they simply manipulate, store, and display data.

A+ 1001: 1.3

Serial and Parallel Data Transfer

In a computer system, data is transferred in one of two modes: series or parallel. Ports on a computer are similarly classified as serial or parallel. In a **serial transfer**, data is sent through a port one bit at a time in successive order over a serial cable. For example, modems are used to communicate with other computers over telephone lines. Because of the limited capacity in a telephone line, data is transferred through modems in a serial fashion. Other examples of serial data transfer include data sent to and from a keyboard and mouse.

In **parallel transfer**, eight bits of data are sent side-by-side at one time. This enables data to transfer at a much higher rate through a parallel port than a serial port. Data is transferred in parallel on the computer bus system between devices such as the hard drive, RAM, and the CPU. Figure 1-4 shows a comparison between serial and parallel data transfer.

A+ Note

Being able to differentiate between serial and parallel data transmission is an important skill for the A+ Certification Exams.

1.4 Computer Data Codes

Computer data and functions are expressed in a variety of ways, including voltage levels, numeric systems such as binary and hexadecimal, and symbolic codes such as ASCII. Although computer data and commands can be expressed in many different forms and still have the same meaning, the form selected should be the one that is easiest to grasp for the given material. For example, it is much easier to express memory locations as hexadecimal values rather than binary values, although the memory location could be expressed in either value. As a computer technician, you must be very familiar with each of these forms of data expression. The A+ Exam no longer emphasizes number systems and codes. However, you will encounter these number systems when working with computers, making it important for you to learn.

Figure 1-4 Data is transferred in one of two modes: serial or parallel.

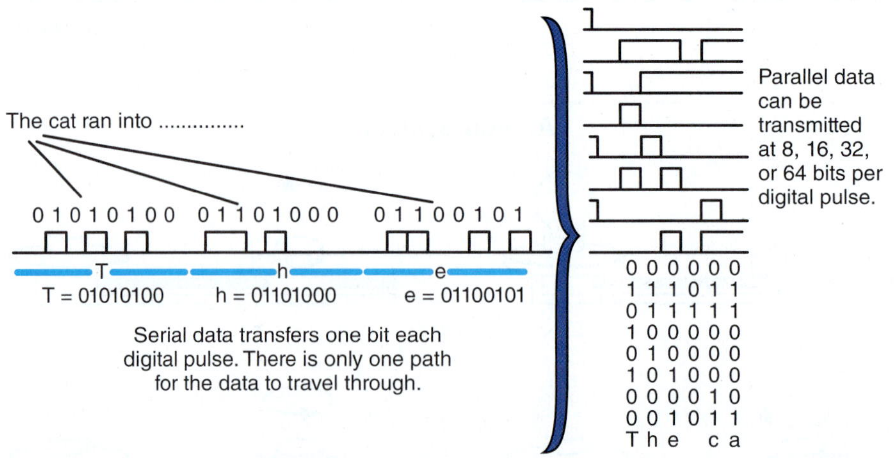

Goodheart-Willcox Publisher

Binary Number System

The **binary number system** consists entirely of ones and zeros. It is the perfect numbering system to represent digital electronic systems. Just as a digital device has only two states (on and off), the binary system uses only two numbers: *0* and *1*. Look at Figure 1-5 to see how the binary number system is used to express different values from 0 to 15. The ones and zeros of the binary system are used to represent the high and low voltage signals that travel throughout the computer system, as well as data stored on disks or in memory chips.

Like digital electronics, binary can be compared to a switch. Look back to Figure 1-2. When the switch is closed, the lamp is on; when the switch is open, the lamp is off. These two states correspond to the binary digits *1* and *0*. The lamp being on correlates to a binary value of *1*, and the lamp being off correlates to a binary value of *0*.

This may seem like an oversimplification of representing data in a computer, but consider the Morse code system. The Morse code system also consists of only two states represented by tones: a short beep and a long beep. These sounds are referred to as a *dot* and a *dash*, respectively. Figure 1-6 illustrates an example of Morse code. Notice how the two conditions of Morse code resemble those from the binary system. The dots and dashes can be combined in sequences that represent the alphabet and the numerals *0* through *9*. A more recent example would be scanning a photo into a computer. Light and dark areas of a graphic are represented by the presence or absence of voltage, mirroring the binary system.

Binary and Decimal Equivalents

Binary	Decimal
0000	0
0001	1
0010	2
0011	3
0100	4
0101	5
0110	6
0111	7
1000	8
1001	9
1010	10
1011	11
1100	12
1101	13
1110	14
1111	15

Goodheart-Willcox Publisher

Figure 1-5 The binary number system consists entirely of ones and zeros and can be used to represent any integer in the decimal system.

Bits, Bytes, and Words

Bit, byte, and word are basic computer units of data based on the binary number system. Short for *b*inary dig*it*, a **bit** is a single binary unit of either a one or zero. A **byte** is equal to eight bits. Most computers process data in bit patterns of eight digits, forming 8-bit bytes.

A **word** is the total number of bytes a computer can process at one time. Consequently, the length of a word can vary from computer to computer. For example, many computer systems process either 32 or 64 bits at one time. Hence, a word in those machines consists of 32 bits (4 bytes) or 64 bits (8 bytes), respectively. Computers are often compared by the size of the word they can process. A comparison of a bit, byte, and word is shown in Figure 1-7.

Hexadecimal Number System

The **hexadecimal number system** is a numbering system that uses 16 characters, as shown in Figure 1-8. It is based on the number base 16, similar to how the binary code is based on the number base 2.

The hexadecimal system uses numerals *0* through *9* from the decimal number system and six additional characters from the alphabet: *A* through *F*. Binary numbers are too long and awkward to be used to express computer values such as memory locations, so hexadecimal numbers are often used instead. The hexadecimal code uses less space.

The hexadecimal system best matches the hardware system of most computers. As you will learn, data lines in a computer are 8, 16, 32, or 64 lines wide. They use increments of 8 and 16, which work beautifully with a hexadecimal system. Additionally, the number values you will encounter that are used to express memory sizes (such as 256, 512, and 1,024) are also in increments of 16. As you can see, a number system based on 16 is used to best match the digital electronic system of computers.

Both the binary and hexadecimal number systems will be used to express values and illustrate computer operation many times throughout the study of computer systems.

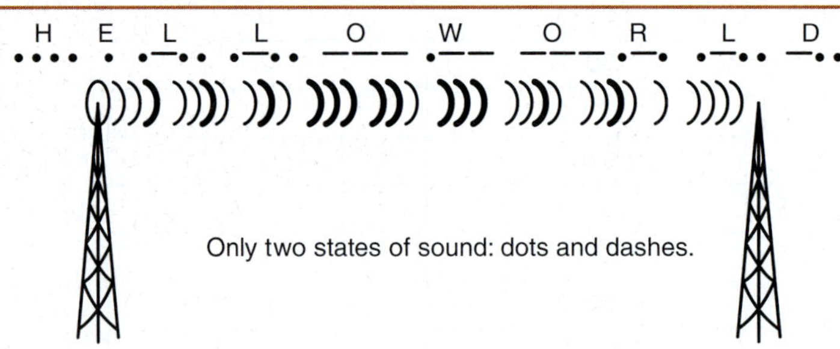

Figure 1-6 Morse code transfers letters between two antennas using a combination of two states: dots and dashes.

Goodheart-Willcox Publisher

Figure 1-7 Bit, byte, and word are basic computer units of data based on the binary number system. A bit is a single binary unit of either a one or zero. A byte is equal to eight bits. A word is the total number of bytes a computer can process at one time.

Comparison Between Bits, Bytes, and Words

Unit	Size	Binary Equivalent
Bit	0 or 1	1
Byte	8 bits	01011110
Word	1–8 bytes	10010010 11110000 00110011 10101010

Goodheart-Willcox Publisher

Hexadecimal and Decimal Equivalents	
Hexadecimal	**Decimal**
0	0
1	1
2	2
3	3
4	4
5	5
6	6
7	7
8	8
9	9
A	10
B	11
C	12
D	13
E	14
F	15

Goodheart-Willcox Publisher

Figure 1-8 Hexadecimal numbers include the digits *0* through *9* and the letters *A* through *F*.

ASCII Code

The **American Standard Code for Information Interchange (ASCII)** was the first attempt to standardize computer character codes among the varieties of hardware and software. When a key on a computer keyboard is pressed (for example, [M]), all computer systems display the letter *M* on the monitor. When the letter *M* is sent to the printer, the letter *M* is printed as expected. Figure 1-9 is an abridged listing of character codes and their ASCII code representatives.

The ASCII system was a great attempt to standardize the computer coding system, but it had limitations. The extended character set is unique to certain systems, such as IBM or equivalent machines, and must be used with a compatible software system; otherwise, unexpected characters will be generated. In addition, the standard form of ASCII does not allow for common requirements of word-processing packages such as **bold**, *italic*, underline, or variations in fonts. ASCII was meant for symbol compatibility used for basic data files. ASCII is still used today, especially when data needs to be transferred between two different software programs.

Computer Numerical Values

Metric prefixes are commonly used to express the speed and size of computer systems and hardware. Prefixes are usually used in combination with the word bit (b) or byte (B). For example, speed is usually expressed in *bits* while storage space is usually expressed as *bytes*. See Figure 1-10 for a listing of commonly used metric prefixes.

Metric prefixes can cause confusion when expressing computer sizes due to the possibility of two possible values for a large expression such as a megabyte. For example, the nominal value for megabytes using the base-10 number system is equal to 1,000,000. However, in computer systems, a 1-megabyte item such as

Figure 1-9 ASCII (pronounced as *as-key*) was the first attempt to standardize computer character codes among the varieties of hardware and software.

Table of Standard ASCII Characters		
Code	**Character**	**Description**
0	NUL	Null
1	SOH	Start of header
2	STX	Start of text
3	ETX	End of text
4	EOT	End of transmission
5	ENQ	Enquiry
6	ACK	Acknowledgment
7	BEL	Bell
8	BS	Backspace
9	HT	Horizontal tab
10	LF	Line feed
11	VT	Vertical tab
12	FF	Form feed
13	CR	Carriage return
14	SO	Shift out
15	SI	Shift in
16	DLE	Data link escape
17	DC1	Device control 1
18	DC2	Device control 2
19	DC3	Device control 3
20	DC4	Device control 4
21	NAK	Negative acknowledgment
22	SYN	Synchronous idle
23	ETB	End of transmit block
24	CAN	Cancel
25	EM	End of medium
26	SUB	Substitute
27	ESC	Escape
28	FS	File separator
29	GS	Group separator
30	RS	Record separator
31	US	Unit separator
32	SP	Space

Goodheart-Willcox Publisher

memory is 1,048,576 (2^{20}) bytes (the power of 2 raised to the 20th). The large values expressed for computer systems are based on the binary number (base-2) system. Figure 1-11 compares the values of the base-10 number system and the base-2 number system.

Metric Expressions					
Metric Prefix	Symbol	Number Base 10	Number Base 2	Common Name	Numeric Equivalent for the Base-10 Number System
Pico	p	10^{-12}	2^{-40}	trillionth	0.000 000 000 001
Nano	n	10^{-9}	2^{-30}	billionth	0.000 000 001
Micro	μ	10^{-6}	2^{-20}	millionth	0.000 001
Milli	m	10^{-3}	2^{-10}	thousandth	0.001
Base unit	N/A	1	2^{1}	N/A	1
Kilo	k	10^{3}	2^{10}	thousand	1,000
Mega	M	10^{6}	2^{20}	million	1,000,000
Giga	G	10^{9}	2^{30}	billion	1,000,000,000
Tera	T	10^{12}	2^{40}	trillion	1,000,000,000,000
Peta	P	10^{15}	2^{50}	quadrillion	1,000,000,000,000,000
Exa	E	10^{18}	2^{60}	quintillion	1,000,000,000,000,000,000

Goodheart-Willcox Publisher

Figure 1-10 Metric prefixes are usually used to express the speed and size of computer systems and hardware.

Base-2 and Base-10 Values		
Measurement	Base-2 Number System	Base-10 Number System
Kilobyte	1,024	1,000
Megabyte	1,048,576	1,000,000
Gigabyte	1,073,741,824	1,000,000,000
Terabyte	1,099,511,627,776	1,000,000,000,000
Petabyte	1,125,899,906,842,624	1,000,000,000,000,000
Exabyte	1,152,921,504,606,846,976	1,000,000,000,000,000,000

Goodheart-Willcox Publisher

Figure 1-11 There are two possible values for a large expression: base 2 or base 10.

1.5 Outside the Computer Case

A basic workstation consists of a computer connected to both input and output devices. The computer itself is composed of a case that houses the motherboard, CPU, memory, hard drive, power supply, and other associated electronics parts and modules that make up the computer system. The typical input devices found at a workstation are a keyboard and mouse, but there are many other devices that can be used for input. An *input device* is any piece of equipment used to communicate with the PC system and provide the PC with data. Conversely, an *output device* is any piece of equipment used to display, print, or otherwise report data from a computer. Typical output devices found at the workstation are the computer monitor, printer, and speakers.

Peripherals

The keyboard, mouse, monitor, printer, and speakers are classified as peripherals. A **peripheral** is an optional piece of equipment used to display or input data. The keyboard is used to enter alphanumeric text and issue commands using special-purpose keys, such as the function keys and key combinations. The mouse is used to interact with coordinates on the display. When an area on the display is selected with a left mouse click, a command is entered. The monitor displays data in the form of words and pictures. A touch screen monitor is both an input and output device; the screen is used to display data as output and to input commands by touching the screen. The printer displays data in printed form on paper. The speakers convert data into sound such as music and spoken language. All these devices will be covered in detail later in the textbook.

Case Style

Many different case styles are used to contain and protect the electronic parts of a computer. Some of the most common case styles are referred to as desktop, tower, mini tower, micro tower, laptop, and notebook. Case selection is usually based on individual taste. There will be more about cases in a later chapter.

A+ Note

Be sure you can identify PC exterior ports and connections.

Exterior Connections

A+ 1001: 1.3

The outside of the computer allows access to the electronic parts inside. Data can be entered into the computer system through the hard drive, optical (CD/DVD) drive, or one of the input/output (I/O) ports in the back. Be aware that not all computers have the same input and output options, and it can vary depending on the purpose of the computer. Figure 1-12 shows the I/O ports of a newer desktop PC with multiple USB and HDMI ports. Other models may only have one HDMI with a different video output, such as VGA, DVI, or DisplayPort.

The exterior connections to a computer are well worth a closer look. The connectors discussed in this section are some of the more common connectors you will find on a PC. More information is given on these connectors in the sections detailing the components with which they work. For the most part, adapters can be used whenever you encounter legacy technology. This allows a technician to user newer technology without having to replace older components, for example. Common adapters include DVI to HDMI, DVI to VGA, and USB to Ethernet.

FireWire

FireWire is no longer being used in new devices. It was used in Macintosh products but has been phased out as of the writing of this text. However, you are likely to encounter older devices that may still have FireWire connections. The FireWire connection, also known as the IEEE-1394 connector, could connect up to 63 hot-swappable devices. The term *hot-swap* means to connect or disconnect a device while the PC is running. FireWire was designed for Apple computers by Lucent Technologies and was proprietary. As such, FireWire was seen more often on Apple equipment than on PC equipment. It was designed for high-speed data transfers such as those required for video equipment or uploading images from a

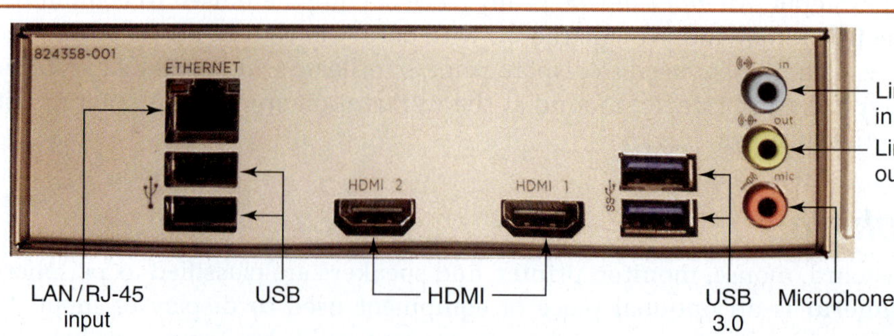

Figure 1-12 A PC's backplane allows access to the electronic parts inside.

Goodheart-Willcox Publisher

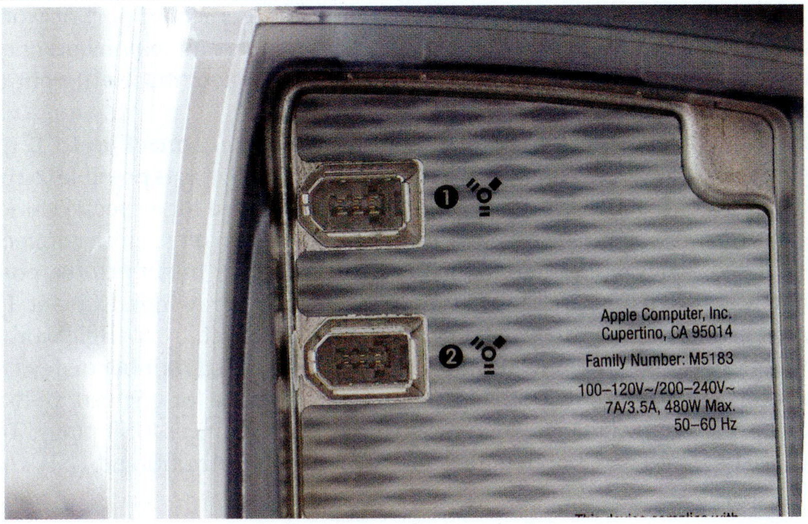

Goodheart-Willcox Publisher

Figure 1-13 FireWire was a proprietary Apple connection designed for high-speed data transfers such as those required for video equipment or uploading images from a digital camera to a computer.

digital camera to a computer. FireWire was also used for other equipment connections such as hard drives, optical drives, and printers. Figure 1-13 shows a pair of FireWire connectors on an Apple desktop computer.

Lightning

1001: 1.3 A+

Lightning is a proprietary connection type for Apple products introduced with the iPhone 5 in 2012. Lightning has a reversible male-type connector with exposed contacts and originally featured speeds comparable to USB 2.0. However, new versions of Lightning can work up to 5 GB/s. This interface can be found on newer iPhones and iPads. It should be noted that Apple has received criticism for the use of the proprietary Lightning connector. For example, in 2020, the European Union passed legislation requiring all computer manufacturers, including Apple, to support common connectors such as USB-C.

Thunderbolt

1001: 3.1 A+

Thunderbolt is a type of interface developed by Intel Corporation for connecting external devices to a computer. The goal was to support multiple common interface protocols used for video and audio as well as data via a single connection and was originally planned as an optical interface. However, electrical-cable interface was instead selected as the standard when Thunderbolt was first introduced in 2011. Thunderbolt technology combines PCI Express and DisplayPort (DP) into a single meta-protocol that can be transmitted over a single cable. There are now three versions: Thunderbolt 1, 2, and 3. The first two versions use cables with Mini DisplayPort (MDP) at either end. Thunderbolt 3 adopts the Type-C connector the same as USB 3.0.

USB

1001: 1.3, 3.1 A+

The Universal Serial Bus (USB), as shown in Figure 1-14, is a standard type of connection used on PCs. The USB port is a multipurpose connection that allows many different devices to connect to the PC in a daisy-chain fashion or using a hub. USB replaced the legacy mini-DIN ports used up until the late 1990s as the default for keyboard and mouse. While almost all mouse and keyboard inputs are USB today, some older legacy computers may still be encountered on the job that use the mini-DIN interfaces. On such older systems with only few or no USB ports, a mini-DIN to USB converter may be used so standard USB keyboards and mice may be connected to legacy computers that utilize DIN ports. The USB design allows for connections to peripheral devices that formerly may have required a dedicated port or would even have required a technician to open the PC case to insert an expansion card. Since USB was introduced, the need to open the case to connect most different types of devices has been eliminated.

Another desirable advantage of USB is that you can connect up to 127 devices through the USB port in a daisy-chain fashion. Before USB, it was possible to run out of ports to support all of the equipment that might be needed for a special workstation. For example, a workstation used by a graphics designer might require connections to a scanner, digital camera, microphone, laser printer, color inkjet printer, poster-size plotter printer, and a digital graphics tablet for freehand drawings. USB and FireWire ports are capable of supporting numerous devices required by a single workstation. Legacy workstations could only be used to support a limited number of devices.

In addition to standard USB type-A and type-B ports for USB 1.0, USB 2.0, and USB 3.0, a technician will also encounter mini-USB and micro-USB plugs, as shown in Figure 1-15. While both are significantly smaller than traditional USB, they have

Figure 1-14 Universal Serial Bus (USB) is a standard type of connection used on PCs.

Goodheart-Willcox Publisher

Figure 1-15 While both mini-USB and micro-USB are smaller than traditional USB, they have fundamental differences.

Goodheart-Willcox Publisher; (photo credit) Tuomas Lehtinen/Shutterstock.com fundamental differences. Mini-USB connections feature a fifth pin known as an ID pin. The ID pin has no real functionality but was included to allow for upgrades. The micro-USB is the smallest connector for USB 1.0, 2.0, and 3.0 and has a wider connection face. Micro-USB is the most common interface for small or mobile devices.

USB 3.0 most often uses a blue-colored type-A connector on the system side of the connection and a micro-USB on the device end. There are other types of connectors compatible with USB 3.0, but the symmetrical type-C connector is the most common on devices since 2018. USB-C connectors are 24-pin, rounded-edge connectors. They appear similar to the Apple Lightning connector. You will most likely encounter these used with smartphones or other mobile devices.

USB 4.0 specification was made public in August 2019. USB 4.0 is based on the Thunderbolt 3 protocol and supports 40 Gbit/s throughput. It is also backward compatible with USB 2.0 and 3.0. USB 4.0 is not yet included on the A+ Exam, but you should be aware of its existence.

Device Bay

The **device bay** is a drive bay designed to accommodate the easy hot-swap of devices such as hard drives, tape drives, and optical drives. The device bay is prewired for either USB or FireWire and allows devices to slide into or out of the PC case easily. An example of an external, network-attached device bay is shown in Figure 1-16. By installing the device into the device bay, the problem of long cords running across and around valuable desk space can be eliminated.

RJ

A+ 1001: 3.1

Registered Jack (RJ) refers to a standardized telecommunication connection for voice and data transfer. There are two types of RJ connectors commonly used with a PC: RJ-45 and RJ-11. RJ-45 is used for network connections, while RJ-11 is used for modem telephone connections. They look nearly identical, but RJ-45 connectors are significantly larger. This is because RJ-45 uses eight conductors and eight pins, while RJ-11 uses four conductors and four pins, as seen in Figure 1-17.

DB

A+ 1001: 1.3

Common DB connectors look similar in shape to the letter *D*, as shown in Figure 1-18. The DB connector comes in various sizes based on the application and type of signals carried. They are typically classified as 9-, 15-, or 25-pin, and they generally adhere to the RS-232 standard. The DB connection occasionally found at the back of some

Lost_in_the_Midwest/Shutterstock.com

Figure 1-16 A device bay is a drive bay designed to accommodate the easy hot-swap of devices such as hard drives, tape drives, and optical drives.

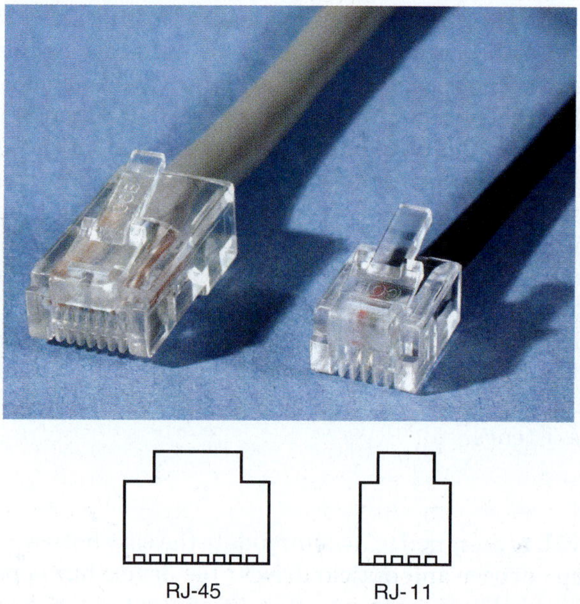

Figure 1-17 Two types of RJ connectors commonly used with a PC are RJ-45 and RJ-11.

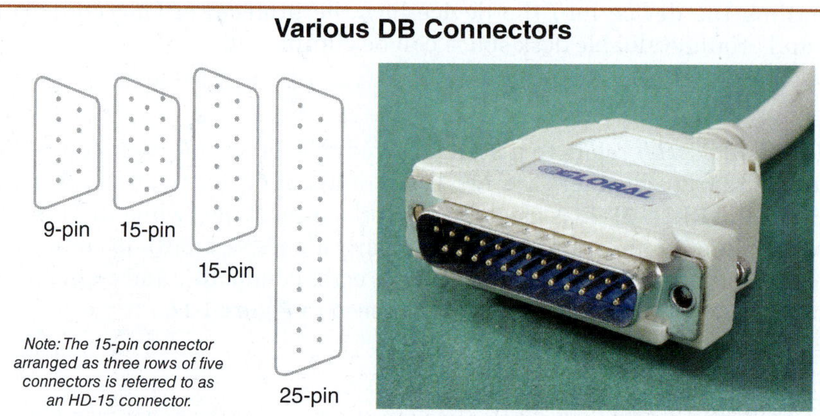

Figure 1-18 DB connectors are used for both serial and parallel connections and come in a variety of sizes.

sound cards is also referred to as a ***game port***. When a 15-pin D-shell connector is arranged with three rows of five connections, it is referred to as an ***HD-15***. The HD represents ***high density*** and is used for monitor connections. Three-row DB-15 connectors are also referred to as DB-15HD and DE-15. Technically speaking from an electronics point of view, DE-15 is the correct term to describe a DB-15 connector designed for computer video ports. The DB connector was once commonly used to connect items such as a joystick, monitor, or printer but has since been supplanted by more universal connections such as USB and HDMI.

Most current computers do not have DB or mini-DIN connections, as USB has become the standard peripheral connection type. You may, however, still encounter DB connections on legacy PCs while doing repair work for customers.

A+ **1001: 3.1, 3.4**

VGA, DVI, and HDMI

You may encounter a variety of video connections, including VGA, DVI, and HDMI, on the back of a PC, as shown in Figure 1-19. Video Graphics Array (VGA) is an analog port, while Digital Visual Interface (DVI) and High-Definition Multimedia Interface (HDMI) are digital ports. There will be much more about these connections in a later chapter. The connections shown in Figure 1-19 are built into an older-type motherboard and may not appear on newer models. In fact, most new models of computers do not include DVI or VGA. You may, however, still encounter them in the field.

As previously referenced, not all computers have the same external connections. Often, the external connections are dictated by the use of the computer. For example, if the computer has a high-performance motherboard, there may be a number of USB, or even legacy eSATA ports, instead of video ports, as shown in Figure 1-20. Motherboards such as these are designed for a video card to be installed in an expansion slot.

External SATA

1001: 3.1, 3.4 A+

Another major difference in the computer in Figure 1-20 is the legacy external SATA port and the power eSATA port. Today, you will only find eSATA on much older computers, as USB 3.0 has replaced the eSATA as the standard for connecting external disks. The *external SATA (eSATA)* port provides a data connection to an external SATA device but does not provide power to the device. The *power eSATA* port, also called *eSATAp*, is needed to provide power to an external SATA device with a data connection and electrical power.

There will be more detailed information about ports and motherboards in a later chapter. This chapter is intended only to familiarize you with the exterior connections and help you develop the ability to identify each port type visually.

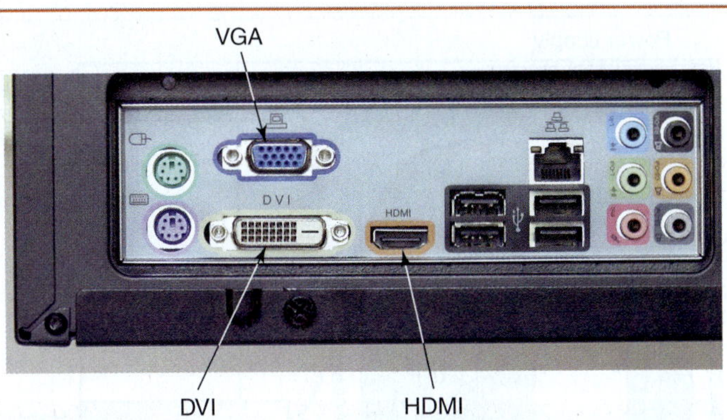

Goodheart-Willcox Publisher

Figure 1-19 Most PCs, especially those with older motherboards, feature a variety of video connections.

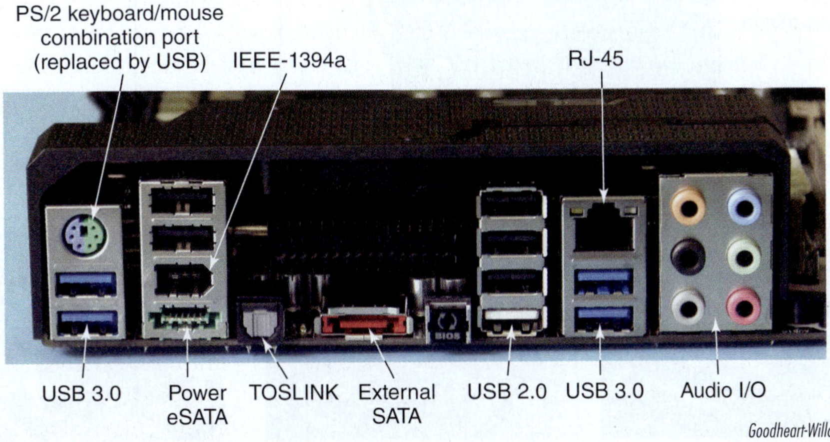

Goodheart-Willcox Publisher

Figure 1-20 High-performance PCs typically have a multitude of external connection options.

1.6 Inside the Computer Case

The inside of a PC is filled with a number of standard components and expansion slots that allow each computer to be customized with a tremendous variety of interesting tools, as demonstrated in Figure 1-21. The equipment that follows details only the common computer components.

CPU

In the simplest of terms, the **central processing unit (CPU)** is the brain of the computer where the actual instructions are executed. Individual components of a CPU are shown in Figure 1-22. The CPU consists of millions of tiny electronic components called *transistors.* Inside a CPU chip, these transistors are individually printed onto a single piece of silicon known as a *wafer* and electrically interconnected to form an *integrated logic circuit* or *IC.* The circuits are designed in a way that enables them to perform the logic of computer programs and process data.

All the other computer components depend on the actions of the CPU. The CPU controls the data in the computer. Commands are issued to the CPU via software. The CPU translates the commands into actions, such as save the data on the screen to memory, open a new file, and locate a file.

Within the CPU are arithmetic logic units, control units, and input/output units. The *control unit (CU)* directs activities of the processor. The *arithmetic logic unit (ALU)* handles bitwise logic operations. The *input/output unit (IO)* is used to move data into and out of the CPU. The CPU will also usually have a cache that is

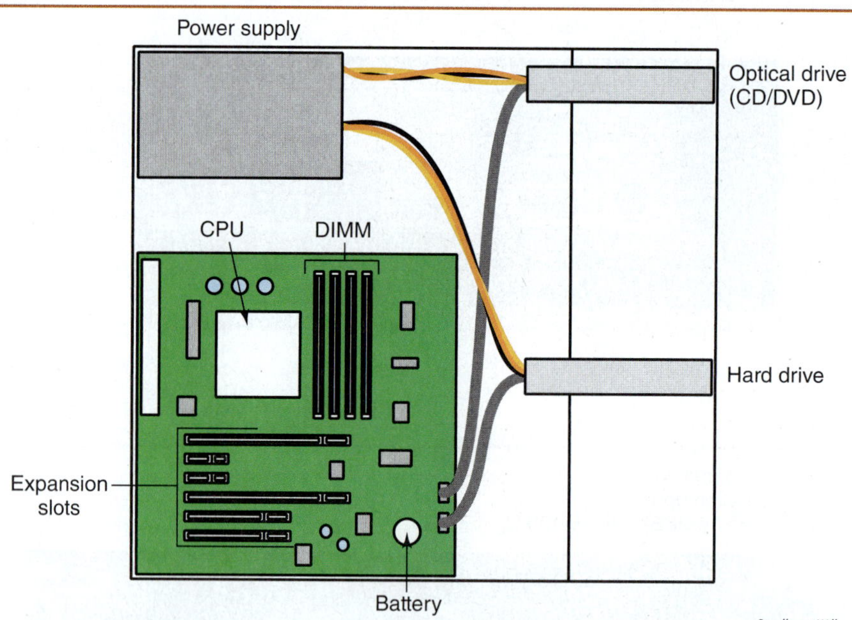

Figure 1-21 While the arrangement and number of components varies from one PC to another, some components are common to most PCs.

Goodheart-Willcox Publisher

Figure 1-22 The CPU is the brain of the computer and consists of three parts: the motherboard socket (A), the CPU chip that is inserted into the motherboard (B), and the heat sink or cooling fan that sits on top of the chip (C).

Goodheart-Willcox Publisher

basically smaller, faster memory used by the CPU rather than having to always use the main memory of the computer. The CPU itself is made up of sub-components, which will discussed in detail in a later chapter.

Power Supply

The **power supply** is an electrical device that converts the 120-volt AC power from the wall outlet to DC voltage levels used by the various computer components. A power supply is shown in Figure 1-23. Once the 120 volts of AC power is converted to a lower DC voltage—usually 3.3, 5, or 12 volts—cables carry the electrical energy to the motherboard, hard drive, and other major components. There will be extensive coverage of power supplies in a later chapter.

Hard Drive

The **hard drive** (also called the *internal drive* or *hard disk drive*) is the main storage device where a computer system stores programs and data. Two hard drives are

Goodheart-Willcox Publisher

Figure 1-23 The power supply converts 120-volt AC power from the wall outlet to DC voltage levels used by various computer components.

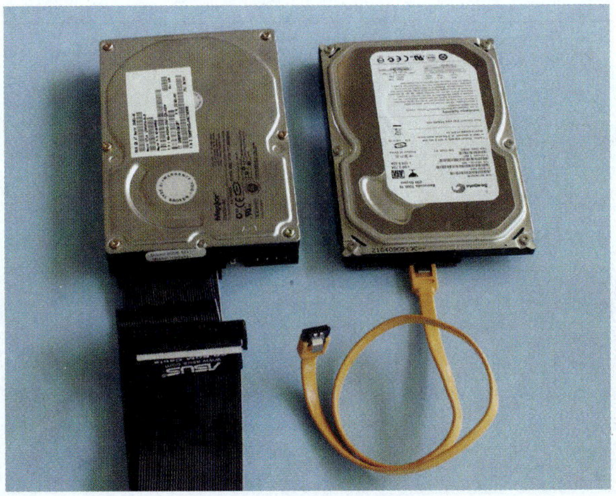

Goodheart-Willcox Publisher

Figure 1-24 Hard drives are the most common storage device used with a PC.

shown in Figure 1-24, each with a specific connection type that will be explored in detail in a later chapter. A hard drive is made up of several disks called *platters* arranged in a stack inside a sealed box. Computer programs and data are stored on the hard drive as magnetic patterns, which are read and written using a floating arm with a magnetic head, called a *read/write head*. Data is accessed as the platter spins under this magnetic head. There is always a slight delay, known as the *seek time*, in accessing data from a hard drive. The seek time corresponds to the wait while the read/write head aligns to the exact location on the platter where the data is located. Data is transmitted to and from the hard drive through a data cable that attaches the hard drive to the motherboard. The hard drive is connected to the power supply by several brightly colored wires that supply the electrical energy needed to run the hard drive system. Platter-based hard drives are not used in newer computers, but you are likely to encounter them while performing PC repair tasks. There will be more discussion about hard drives in a later chapter.

Solid-State Drive

Like a hard drive, a solid-state drive can store programs and data. A **solid-state drive (SSD)** is a storage system designed with no moving parts and instead stores data in nonvolatile memory chips, as shown in Figure 1-25. Typically, solid-state drives are faster and more reliable than hard drives. Newer computers utilize SSDs rather than hard drives. Despite SSDs not having any moving parts, you will often hear people use the term *hard drive* colloquially to refer to any nonvolatile storage, whether it is actually a platter-based hard drive or an SSD. Solid-state drives are faster due to the elimination of seek time as the data is directly accessed electronically rather than physically located on a spinning platter. Additionally, since there are no moving parts in a solid-state drive, there are no motors or other components to wear out and fail, making SSDs more reliable than hard drives. Data can be transmitted to and from SSDs through the same data cables and interfaces as hard drives, making them interchangeable in most systems where hard drives are used. There will be more discussion on SSDs in later chapters.

Motherboard

The **motherboard** is a typically rectangular-shaped type of circuit board covered with many conductors that provide electrical energy paths to computer components and expansion slots, as seen in Figure 1-26. It provides a way to distribute the digital signals used for carrying data, sending control instructions, and providing

Figure 1-25 A solid-state drive (SSD) is a storage system designed with no moving parts and instead stores data in nonvolatile memory chips.

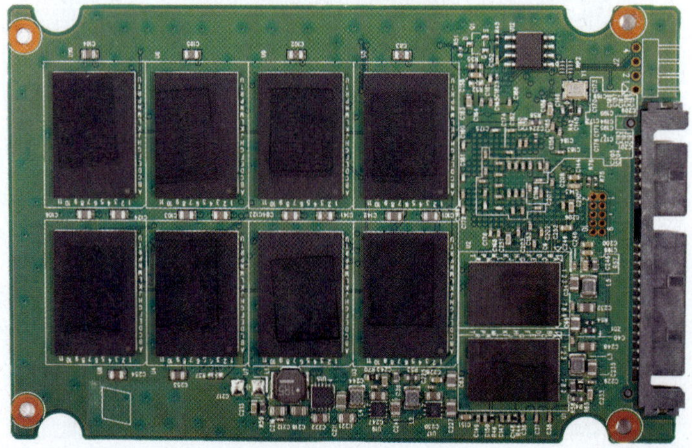

Peter Gudella/Shutterstock.com

small amounts of electrical power to the many different components mounted on the board. The electrical system of pathways for various functions are referred to as computer *buses*. Motherboards come in a variety of sizes, known as the *form factor*. To fit into established form factors, motherboards are scaled to fit inside different types of computer enclosures. It is essential to match the form factor and enclosure type to ensure the two are compatible and the system will correctly operate. There will be more discussion about motherboards and form factors in a later chapter.

RAM

Random access memory (RAM) is a type of fast data storage where computer programs are loaded to and from the hard drive for quicker access by the CPU. Figure 1-27 shows two different styles of RAM modules. RAM is classified as a *volatile* memory system, meaning the data and programs loaded in RAM are lost when power is turned off. All data stored in RAM is therefore considered temporary. If data needs to be retained once the computer is turned off, it must be written to a hard drive or other permanent storage method. Every time a computer is started, all information must be reloaded from permanent storage into RAM.

Increasing the amount of computer RAM is one of the most common types of upgrades performed. RAM is usually mounted into several parallel slots on the motherboard near the CPU. The amount of RAM in a low-end home PC or laptop

Naumov S/Shutterstock.com

Figure 1-26 A motherboard is circuit board, often rectangular in shape, covered with many conductors that provide electrical energy paths to the computer components and expansion slots.

Figure 1-27 Random access memory (RAM) is a type of fast data storage where computer programs are loaded to and from the hard drive for quicker access by the CPU. RAM modules can come in a variety of styles, including plain modules (A) and those with heat sinks (B).

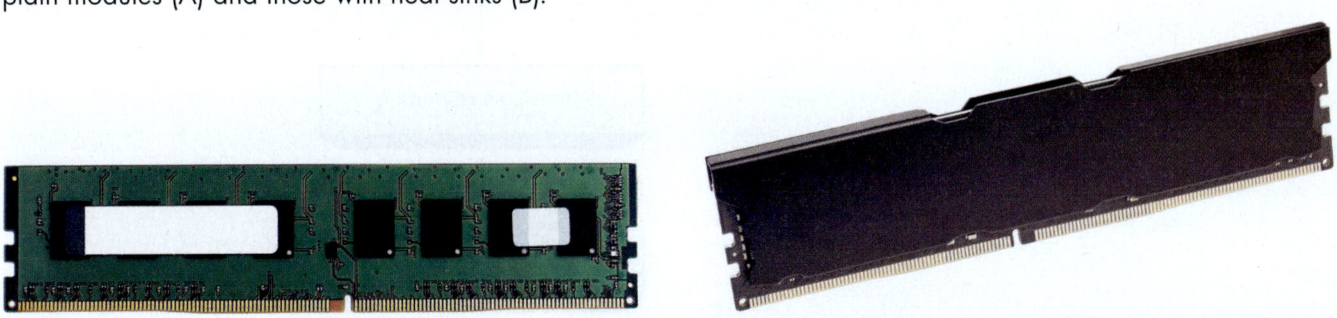

A B

Goodheart-Willcox Publisher; (A) Fmax/Shutterstock.com; (B) monte_a/Shutterstock.com today will be at least 8 GB, but you will likely encounter less in older computers. With newer computers, it is not uncommon to find memory in sizes ranging from 16 GB to 32 GB or even more. Depending on the type of applications to be run, the amount of RAM required will vary. The more data an application uses, the more RAM that is required for that application to perform effectively on the system. For text and graphics to be displayed on a computer screen, that data must first be copied from RAM into the memory of the display controller or graphics card. Graphics take much more memory than written text due to the volume of information required to represent captured images. There will be more discussion about RAM in a later chapter.

Firmware

Firmware is hardware-specific software required to boot the computer and support communication between the operating system and hardware devices. Firmware interprets commands of higher-level software programs, such as operating systems, and translates the commands into actions understandable by hardware devices, such as the hard drive, memory, keyboard, and mouse. Figure 1-28 shows the relationship of firmware to hardware, application software, and the operating system.

Firmware is not only found on the motherboard; it is also incorporated into many computer devices such as graphic cards, hard drives, and SCSI drive controllers. Firmware works hand in hand with drivers. A **driver** is a small software program written specifically for a hardware device that allows the operating system to communicate with the device properly. For example, a printer requires a specific driver to be installed on the computer before the operating system can successfully use the printer. Without the driver, the printer will not function properly.

The terms *firmware*, *BIOS*, and *CMOS* (pronounced *c-moss*) are often interchanged but are actually distinct concepts. *Firmware* is a combination of a special type of memory chip and software programs that support communication and compatibility. It includes the setup utility, which is responsible for setting and storing the date and time and information about the computer hardware. *CMOS* is an integrated circuit where the setup utility stores information about the computer's hardware, date, and time. CMOS stands for *complementary metal oxide semiconductor*

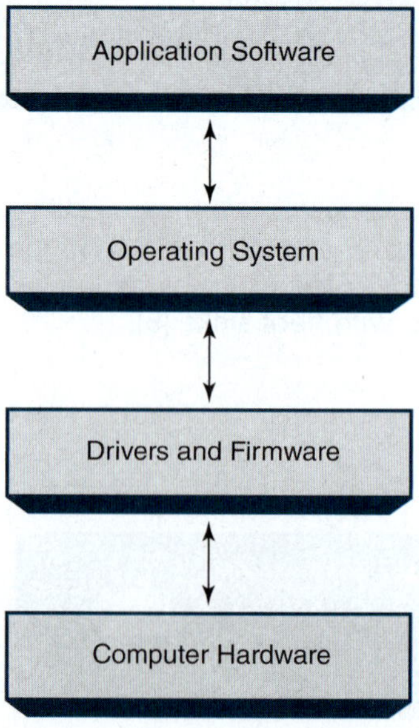

Figure 1-28 Firmware is hardware-specific software required to boot the computer and support communication between the operating system and the hardware devices.

Goodheart-Willcox Publisher

and is a type of low-power semiconductor chip technology. In the electronics field, there are many different types of devices designed from CMOS technology; however, in computing, it is understood that it refers to the location where the BIOS settings or data are stored.

Originally, firmware software was permanently etched into a read-only memory (ROM) chip. ROM firmware was permanent and could only be changed by replacing the ROM chip. Today, firmware software is stored in an electrically erasable programmable read-only memory (EEPROM) chip, which is reprogrammable and often referred to as flash ROM. Flash ROM retains data when electrical power to the computer is disconnected or turned off, and it can be erased electrically and reprogrammed with an updated version of a software program.

BIOS (Basic Input/Output System) is a type of firmware. It is a small software program written in *machine language*, which is a language that uses hexadecimal codes to write a program and is understood by computers. It is many times faster than other programming languages, but it is much more difficult to write. BIOS is typically 64 kB (kilobytes) in size and has limitations on the amount of RAM it can use. Because there is no single BIOS standard, BIOS systems are diverse. This has led to hardware compatibility problems that require BIOS upgrades. Even with these disadvantages, BIOS firmware is the most prevalent firmware in use.

EFI or UEFI is a type of firmware created to replace BIOS. *EFI (Extensible Firmware Interface)* was introduced in the late 1990s but was not standardized until 2005, at which time, it became known as *UEFI (Unified Extensible Firmware Interface)*. In contrast to BIOS, UEFI has a standard set of boot programs and configuration data, which enables hardware manufacturers, software companies, and operating systems to use the firmware in a consistent manner and achieve similar results without compatibility problems. This consistency makes it much easier to develop new hardware drivers and to support hardware devices. Soon, UEFI will be the most common firmware used in computers and related hardware.

Battery

The CMOS battery is installed on the motherboard and supplies voltage to the CMOS, which contains the firmware setup data. Without the battery, the computer would lose the date, time, and all the important information about the hardware components when the computer power switch is turned off. Figure 1-29 shows a photo of a CMOS battery.

Figure 1-29 Without the CMOS battery, the computer would lose date, time, and any important information about hardware components when the computer is powered down.

Goodheart-Willcox Publisher

Expansion Cards

An **expansion card**, sometimes called an *interface card* or *host adapter*, is a small circuit board that can be easily installed in a computer to enhance or expand its capabilities. An expansion card allows the computer to be custom designed to meet the needs of different consumers. A given computer may have video circuitry integrated into the motherboard or a separate video card that only allows for minimal video performance. The performance of this video system would be adequate for accounting or word-processing functions, but it would be substandard for computer-aided drafting or game applications. To remedy this, a new video card, or video expansion card, can be added to the computer system.

Expansion cards are used for such devices as TV tuners, video cards, sound cards, and telephone modems. They can also provide additional USB ports for connecting external devices such as hard drives, as shown in Figure 1-30. Many devices that were designed as expansion cards for internal installation have been redesigned as exterior devices that connect to the computer, typically through a USB port.

Expansion Card Slots

An expansion card fits snugly into an expansion card slot, shown in Figure 1-31. The *expansion card slot*, also called an *expansion slot*, is a port that allows the expansion card to connect directly to the electronic circuitry in the motherboard and communicate directly or indirectly with other components on the motherboard

Figure 1-30 An expansion card is a board that can be easily installed in a computer to enhance or expand its capabilities.

MMXeon/Shutterstock.com

Figure 1-31 Expansion card slots enable an expansion card to communicate with the motherboard or CPU by providing direct access to the electronic circuitry.

Goodheart-Willcox Publisher

or with the CPU. There are several types of expansion slots, but the most popular type for modern desktops is *Peripheral Component Interconnect Express (PCIe)*. To retain backwards compatibility, PCI expansion slots are still provided on many motherboards. Expansion cards and slots are discussed in detail in a later chapter.

Cooling Fans

A *cooling fan* is a computer part that supplies a constant stream of air across the computer components to keep them at a safe operating temperature. Electronic components can be permanently damaged by excessive heat, so all computers come equipped with a fan mounted on the CPU attached to the motherboard to assist in the cooling process, as shown in Figure 1-22C. Additional cooling fans may be found inside the power supply and on some higher-end graphics cards. Cooling fans can also be found mounted directly on the computer case to add additional airflow internal airflow. These fans are critical to maintain proper cooling of the rest of the components. It is important to keep all cooling fans in good working condition because fans can fail if they get fouled by dust buildup or if the bearings inside the fan motor give out. Any fan that is not functioning should be replaced promptly to prevent heat damage and extend the life of electronic components.

Cables

1001: 3.1 A+

There are several types of cables commonly used inside the PC case to connect the motherboard to devices such as the hard drive and optical drive. Figure 1-32 shows two types of cables used to connect a hard drive and optical drive to the motherboard: *Serial ATA (SATA)* and *Parallel ATA (PATA)*. These cables are also visible in Figure 1-24. Hard drives and optical drives originally used an ATA cable, which looks similar to the PATA cable in that it consists of many parallel conductors. Some of the conductors in an ATA and PATA cable are used to transfer data, while others are used to transmit control signals between the motherboard and the device.

SATA cables use fewer individual wires to achieve much higher data rates than PATA. The individual wires in a SATA cable are twisted together, which enables higher frequencies and data rates. The design is based on electronic engineering principles. A great deal of study is required to fully understand the principles applied to the cable design. For now, consider any cable designed with twists to be able to achieve a higher data rate than a cable designed without twists.

Electrical power for SATA and PATA devices can be transmitted through the cable conductors, but many devices consume more electrical power than the cables and motherboard are designed to carry safely. When a large volume of electrical power is required for a device, a separate power cable that runs directly from the power supply is used.

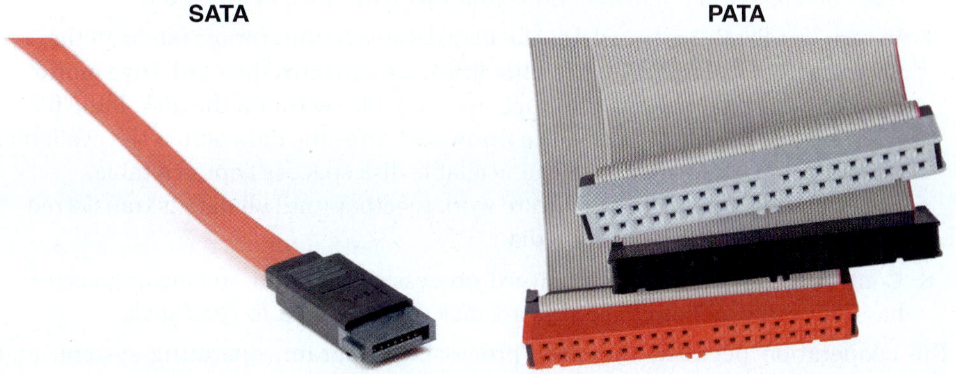

Figure 1-32 SATA (A) and PATA (B) cables connect the motherboard to devices such as the hard drive and optical drive.

Cables for external SATA (eSATA) devices connect external hard drives and optical drives. The technology in eSATA cables is slightly different from that found in SATA. PATA, SATA, and eSATA technologies are discussed in detail in a later chapter.

1.7 How the Major Parts Work Together

The following scenario traces how a sequence of events occurs in a typical PC system. In this example, a user moves from turning on the computer through saving text data. Please note that there are many different PCs, and they all have unique start-up features and program interactions.

1. When the power switch is turned to the *on* position, electrical power from the wall outlet moves through the power supply where it is converted to a much lower DC voltage (or voltages). This stepped-down power is used to run the major components of the computer system including the motherboard, hard drive, and expansion cards. Additionally, the fan starts up, providing a rush of cool air across the components.
2. Next, the firmware system activates and performs a power-on self-test (POST). The POST checks the components in the computer such as RAM, ROM, hard drive, and keyboard to ensure they are in proper working order. Information such as the type and model number of the firmware and the amount of memory, will flash across the computer's monitor, providing information.
3. After the firmware checks the computer components, the operating system takes control. There are many different types of operating systems, but for our example, Windows software will be used.
4. The CPU now waits for activity to be generated by the mouse, keyboard, modem, or other input device. The CPU constantly checks if a key is pressed, or the mouse is moved or clicked. The CPU checks these items thousands of times per second.
5. The user moves the mouse pointer to an icon and clicks the left mouse button to activate a program, such as a word-processing program. The software represented by the icon is activated and shares control of the computer with the CPU.
6. Some typing is done, and then the save command is issued by clicking the save icon in the word-processing program. The program now attempts to save to the Documents folder. When the word-processing program saves, the operating system takes over in conjunction with the firmware. The operating system interprets the command issued from the word-processing program and translates it to a set of instructions that the firmware can interpret.
7. In turn, the firmware translates the instructions to the storage media. If the file is saving to a hard disk drive, the firmware activates the hard drive motor and actuator arm, moving it to the next available sector on the disk. If the file is saving to a solid-state drive, the firmware writes the data across the available memory chips. Information about available disk space is kept in a table. The operating system and firmware work together until all data is transferred and recorded on the storage media.
8. Control is then returned to the word-processing program, so long as an error has not occurred. Possible errors are *disk full* or *unable to read disk*.

The cooperation between the word-processing program, operating system, and firmware goes unnoticed by the user.

1.8 Integrated Circuits

The term *chip* is often used in the computer industry. A chip is actually the final product of the manufacturing of an integrated circuit. An **integrated circuit (IC)** is a collection of transistors, resistors, and other electronic components reduced to an unbelievably small size. In fact, hundreds of millions of transistors can be manufactured as an integrated circuit and made to fit into an area the size of a US dime. Chips are also commonly found on many types of circuit boards; they are the black square and rectangular devices with silver or gold electrical contacts on the edges.

Manufacturing an Integrated Circuit

Manufacturing an IC is not on the A+ Exam. However, it is useful information for someone working with PCs. The manufacturing process that creates an IC consists of many hundreds of steps in a process covering a period of several months. The first step in the manufacturing of a chip is the design of the circuit. The circuit is drawn on a very large scale. When the design is completed and all drawings are finished, the drawings are photographed. The negative of the drawing's photograph is used as a template in the manufacturing process.

An *ingot*, or block, of pure silicon is made and then sliced into thin wafers to serve as the base of the IC. Silicon is the same as most common beach sand, but it is extremely pure. The material cannot contain any impurities that might cause adverse effects in the manufacturing of the IC. A series of layers are produced over the surface of the silicon wafer using a process called *photolithography*.

Photolithography is described in the following sequence of events. First, a heat process vaporizes silicon dioxide. Then, various other chemicals are used to form many extremely thin layers over the surface of the wafer. After each layer is formed, the entire surface of the wafer is coated with a chemical called *photoresist*, which reacts when exposed to ultraviolet light.

The negative from the circuit drawing photograph, called a *photomask*, is used as a stencil. When ultraviolet light shines through the mask, it causes the photoresist to leave a pattern of soft and hard surfaces in the exact pattern of the designed circuit. The soft photoresist is then washed away, leaving an etched pattern of valleys and ridges on the surface of the wafer. These valleys are filled with conductive materials in a process called *doping* or *implantation*. This process is repeated many more times until 20 or more layers are developed over the surface of the entire wafer. A single wafer consists of many integrated circuits that are then cut into individual ICs and packaged. The IC manufacturing process is illustrated in Figure 1-33.

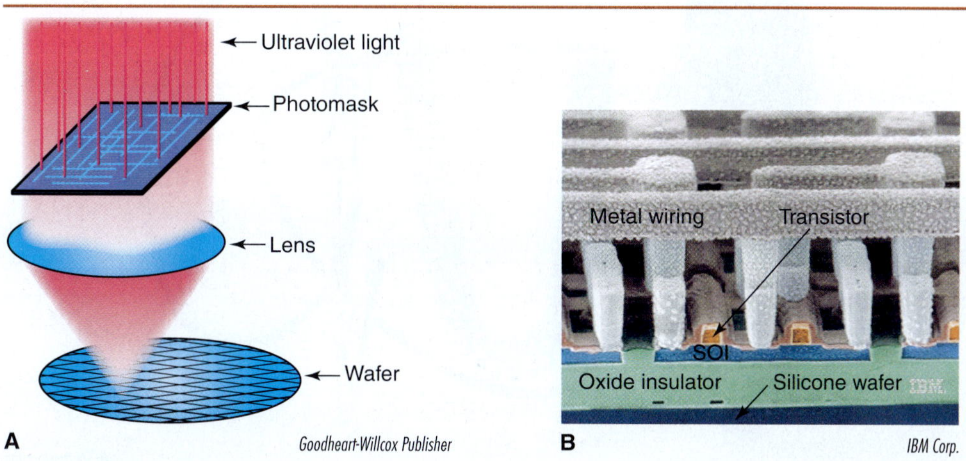

Figure 1-33 Once an integrated circuit is created (A), layers of silicon are controlled to create millions of transistors and other electronic components (B).

One of the most difficult parts of packaging the integrated circuit is connecting the fine wires between the wafer circuits and the much larger pins on the outside of the package. The entire wafer and thin connection wires are encapsulated in a hard insulating material resembling black plastic.

Modern computer technology would not be possible without the techniques used in building integrated circuits. The ICs used in computers have many specialized purposes. For example, the CPU is the most complex IC within a computer system and controls all PC activities. Computer modems, used to communicate across telephone lines, have specialized chips that change computer data into a stream of various voltage levels that represent the data. They also convert the stream back into digital data at the receiving end. Various other chips on the motherboard have special purposes. Some assist the CPU with data flow across the motherboard; others control devices such as the hard drive and optical drive. The RAM used in computers is nothing more than a group of ICs mounted on an insulated circuit board.

A+ 1002: 4.4

Electrostatic Discharge (ESD)

In the world of computer maintenance, **electrostatic discharge (ESD)** is best defined as the transfer of static electrical energy from one object to another. ESD can destroy the miniature circuits inside a computer chip. Static charges are usually created by friction created from two dissimilar materials rubbing together and producing an electric charge. Static buildup is always greatest when the air is dry and cool.

A common example of static electricity buildup and discharge is when you walk across a rug and reach out to touch a doorknob. You feel a sharp snap as the electrical charge of your body discharges to the doorknob. This is ESD.

Understanding how ICs are manufactured, you can appreciate the small scale of the circuit and how damaging electrostatic discharge can be to the tiny circuits inside the chip. To prevent static discharge between two objects, you must create a condition where both objects are at the same static voltage level or the same potential. When two objects have the same static voltage level, static discharge will not occur.

Technicians typically wear an antistatic wrist strap, such as the one shown in Figure 1-34, when handling static-sensitive devices to avoid ESD. An **antistatic wrist strap**, also known as a *ground strap*, is a device designed to create an equal static voltage level between your body and the object to which the strap is connected. To prevent ESD damage to sensitive components, connect the alligator clip to the bare metal on the computer case or power supply. These straps are often used in conjunction with antistatic mats.

Tech Tip

There may be times when an antistatic wrist strap is not available. You can avoid ESD by touching the bare metal inside the computer case with your hand.

Figure 1-34 Antistatic wrist straps create equal static levels between the technician's body and the object to which the other end of the strap is clipped.

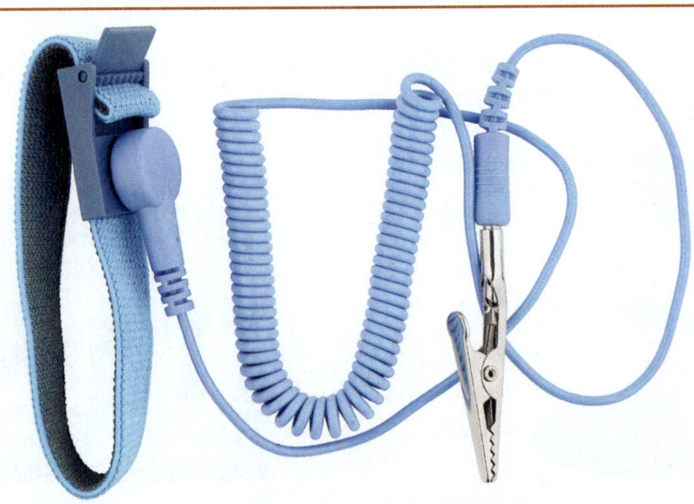

MNI/Shutterstock.com

To prevent ESD, electronic parts and devices are shipped inside antistatic bags, similar to the one shown in Figure 1-35. When removing parts from a computer, place the parts on an antistatic mat or inside an antistatic bag. You will accumulate plenty of antistatic bags while working as a computer technician. Every time you install a part, such as a hard drive or a motherboard, you will end up with an empty antistatic bag. Save the bag for temporarily storing static-sensitive components that you remove from a computer.

A+ Note

Be familiar with antistatic procedures, specifically the use of straps, mats, and bags.

Electromagnetic Interference (EMI)

Electromagnetic interference (EMI) is interference or damage to components caused by magnets and magnetic fields. Any device that operates on magnetic principles should not come in contact with or close proximity to a magnetic field. In the early days of electronics and computers, power magnets and magnetic devices called *bulk erasers* were used to wipe data from data storage devices such as tapes and floppy disks.

The most common source of magnetic fields in computer repair is the presence of magnetic tools, such as screwdrivers with a magnetic tip. Outdated technology such as floppy disks were wildly susceptible to destruction from magnetic fields. However, floppy disks are seldom encountered today, so views have changed about the use of magnetic tools, though there is still some debate. Some say the hard drive can be corrupted by magnetism, but this is not necessarily true. The case surrounding a hard drive is metallic and generally acts as a shield to protect the disks inside from a magnetic field. Some types of computer chips can be damaged by strong magnetic force, but most are designed with some form of magnetic shielding.

There are computer technicians who do use magnetic-tipped tools such as screwdrivers and have never encountered a problem. However, it is considered best practice not to use magnetic tools inside a computer case.

Radio Frequency Interference (RFI)

Radio frequency interference (RFI) is interference produced by electronic devices that use radio waves. In general, radio waves are very weak and do not damage electronic components, but they can interfere with radio transmissions between electronic devices. Wireless network devices can fail or operate erratically because of radio frequencies broadcast by other devices. For example, a wireless network

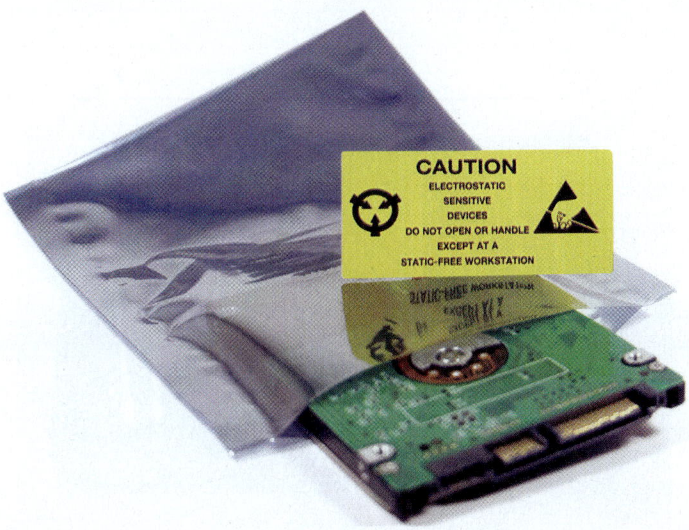

Sawangkaew/Shutterstock.com

Figure 1-35 Antistatic bags help prevent accidental ESD during shipping and handling of electronic components.

device can be temporarily affected by a running microwave oven. Some common devices that generate RFI include baby monitors, cell phones, cordless phones, wireless network components, and microwave ovens.

A+ 1002: 4.5

1.9 Tool Kit

Computer repair requires a minimum number of tools, as shown in Figure 1-36. A standard tool kit can vary from a small pouch to a more elaborate tool case. A variety of flat tip, Phillips, and star drivers are needed. Additional helpful tools include cans of compressed air, chip pullers, antistatic wrist straps, a multimeter, extra screws, and a star-shaped driver set. Additionally, some type of extraction tool for retrieving dropped screws and other parts is definitely needed.

You will find that a software tool kit is just as important as a hardware tool kit. You will probably depend more on your skills using software than hardware to troubleshoot, diagnose, and repair PCs. As you progress through the textbook, there will be many suggestions about software to add to your tool kit. There will also be many references to third-party suppliers and shareware available for your use.

Shareware is software that is freely distributed, usually by downloading from the Internet. Shareware is not always free for your unlimited use. It is usually intended for use on a trial basis only. The distributor expects the subscriber to purchase the software later.

1.10 Safety

Safety is the responsibility of all personnel in classroom, laboratory, and workplace areas. This includes students, instructors, employees, and managers. A general understanding of common safety practices is a must to help avoid classroom, laboratory, and on-the-job injuries. Safety is best practiced as a habit, not as a written test because developing safety habits helps avoid possible injury. This section covers safety as related to the computer repair environment. Detailed safety information is provided later in this textbook as it relates to specific topics. For example, concepts related to power supplies such as grounding will be covered later after you are more familiar with the relevant technologies.

Figure 1-36 Antistatic bags help prevent accidental ESD during shipping and handling of electronic components.

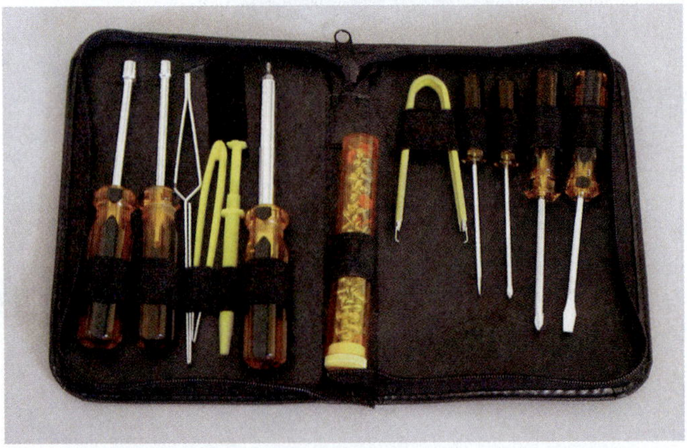

Sawangkaew/Shutterstock.com

Physical Safety

A+ 1002: 4.4

One of the most common physical dangers in the classroom or work environment is cables, such as power cords and network cables, lying across the floor. Cables cause a tripping hazard, which can result in injury. Avoid running cables across pathways. When cables must be laid across a floor, the pathway should be blocked to prevent pedestrian traffic, or the cable should be taped to the floor with duct tape. You can also use a cable floor runner or cord protector designed specifically for running cables across a floor, as demonstrated in Figure 1-37.

When working with computers, there is a real possibility of burns caused by electronic components. Common high-temperature components are the CPU and some associated motherboard chips. These components reach high temperatures due to the high-frequency electrical power passing through them, so you should avoid touching or handling them while the computer has power or soon after the computer is turned off. Laser printers also have high-temperature parts capable of causing skin-surface burns.

Loose clothing and inappropriate footwear—such as open-toed shoes—should not be worn in the computer repair environment. Dropping a computer or backup power supply on an unprotected foot can cause severe injury. Loose clothing can snag on a computer case or computer parts, causing the computer or parts to fall to the floor. This can possibly damage the items or cause injury, and many insurance companies will not cover employees who willfully disobey safety practices specifically stated in the company insurance policy.

Technicians often lift and move computers and battery backup power supplies, both of which can be quite heavy. One of the most common work-related injuries is back injuries caused by improperly lifting heavy objects. However, most physical injuries can be avoided when safety standards are followed. A comprehensive source of safety information for all occupations is regulated by the Occupational Safety and Health Administration (OSHA). OSHA is part of the Department of Labor that enforces safety standards as well as trains, educates, and assists employers and employees. Because there are a great many work-related back injuries, OSHA has developed a formula to determine the maximum weight a person can lift without causing physical injury. The formula includes factors such as the height of the object being lifted, the distance it is moved, and how many times the movement is repeated within a given period. Most employers restrict their employees to a maximum lift

Goodheart-Willcox Publisher

Figure 1-37 Cable floor runners or cord protectors are used when running cables across a floor to prevent a tripping hazard.

of 50 pounds. When the weight of an object exceeds 50 pounds, you should wait for assistance from coworkers or special equipment designed for lifting and hauling heavy objects. Figure 1-38 shows a typical cart used to transport heavy equipment.

OSHA also provides standards for such areas as ladders, electrical cords, grounding, working surfaces, adequate lighting, and computer workstation-related injuries. Chances are, you spend a lot of time at a computer workstation as a student and computer technician. Check out the OSHA website to learn how to avoid computer workstation-related injuries; you may be surprised at some bad habits you have developed over the years.

There may come a time when airborne particles or hazardous gases are released during the maintenance or repair of a computer component. For example, many types of solder are made with lead, which produces hazardous fumes if you have to solder a new chip into a motherboard. In a situation where airborne particles or hazardous gases will be released, consider working in an enclosure to prevent the spread of the particles or gases, and always wear an air filter or mask and goggles to protect your respiratory system and eyes.

There are other issues that are often overlooked, such as dust. Excessive dust can lead to damage to electronic components and poses a fire hazard. Cans of compressed air can be useful in removing dust. Generally, the cleaner a work area is, the safer it is.

A+ 1002: 4.4

Electrical Safety

Students who first enter a computer course typically do not have an electronics background that would enable them to fully understand the electrical hazards in a computer laboratory environment. As you progress through this course, you will gain more knowledge about potentially hazardous practices and devices. At this point, the best practice to follow concerning electrical safety is the following: *Do not attempt to open, inspect, or repair any electronic device that you have not been trained on by your instructor or if you have not received your instructor's permission.*

Figure 1-38 When the weight of an object exceeds 50 pounds, a cart should be used to move the item to prevent physical injury.

Goodheart-Willcox Publisher

In general, before opening the case to begin work, disconnect the electrical power from the computer. The recommended practice is to unplug the AC power cord from the computer's power supply because many motherboards and power supplies maintain a small electrical current to some critical parts when the computer is turned off. For example, after powering off a computer with the on/off switch, you may see LEDs lit on the motherboard, indicating the presence of electrical current.

Removing jewelry before working inside a computer case is also recommended. Jewelry can snag on electronic components, damaging the component. Additionally, if the component were accidentally energized, the jewelry could make an excellent electrical path, causing electric shock.

Surge protectors are also an important way to protect your electronic components. As implied by its name, a **surge protector** is an electrical device intended to dissipate voltage spikes to protect downstream devices. A voltage surge or spike usually lasts much less than a second but can carry high voltages of 1,000 volts or more and can damage electronics. A good surge protector can protect your electronic equipment from most surges. Surge protectors are also called by other names such as *surge protection device (SPD)*, *transient voltage surge suppressor (TVSS)*, and *surge suppressor*, among others. When selecting a surge protector, there are several specifications to consider. The clamp voltages specify what voltages will cause the surge protector to activate or "clamp." When a surge protector *clamps*, it redirects the electrical energy away from the devices attached to it. The lower the clamping voltage, the better the protection. Response time is also important. There will be some delay, but the lower the delay, the better. A third specification is the joule rating. A *joule* is a unit of measurement for energy. As such, a *joule rating* determines how many joules of energy the surge protector can absorb in a single event. The larger this rating is, the better the protection.

Fire Safety

A+ 1002: 4.4

The possibility of fire is always a threat in a computer laboratory as well as on the job or in your home. Good fire preparedness requires you to have a basic understanding of fire extinguisher types and how to use them. Pay particular attention to the information related to electrical fires, and always follow your teacher's instructions concerning fire safety procedures and fire safety in the classroom and lab.

Fire extinguishers are divided into five classes and assigned letters to represent the classification, as listed in Figure 1-39. Some fire extinguishers are designated with a combination of letters, which means they are suitable for each classification indicated by those letters. For example, a fire extinguisher with the letters *A*, *B*, and *C* would be suitable for a Class A, B, or C fire.

Fire Extinguisher Classes

Class	Description
A	Ordinary materials, such as paper, wood, cardboard, most plastics, and similar items
B	Flammable liquids, such as gasoline, kerosene, oil, and common combustible solvents
C	Energized electrical equipment, appliances, fuse boxes, electrical power tools, wiring, and other electrical devices
D	Combustible metals, such as magnesium, sodium, potassium, and titanium
K	Kitchen fires caused by cooking grease and oils

Goodheart-Willcox Publisher

Figure 1-39 Fire extinguishers are divided into five classes to distinguish the type of fires for which each class should be used.

A+ Note

The A+ Exams often have at least one question related to fire safety.

Obviously, a computer lab should be equipped with a Class C fire extinguisher or one that is designated with a combination of letters, as long as the letter *C* is clearly marked.

Water extinguishers are only appropriate for Class A fires and should never be used on a Class B, C, D, or K fire. Class A uses water or a liquid that reacts violently with Class B, C, D, and K fires and could cause the fire to spread rather than extinguish.

The handy acronym P.A.S.S. is used to remember the proper procedure for using a fire extinguisher. This acronym was developed to match the recommended procedures by the National Fire Protection Agency (NFPA) for fire extinguisher use. While standing approximately six to eight feet from the fire, follow the procedure as outlined.

P = Pull the pin.

A = Aim at the base of the fire.

S = Squeeze the handles together slowly to discharge the fire extinguisher.

S = Sweep the nozzle from side to side, moving carefully toward the fire while keeping the discharge aimed at the base of the fire.

Be sure you know the location of all fire extinguishers in your classroom and lab area. Also, know the fire exit procedure and the designated regroup area. It is beneficial to understand not only the appropriate class and procedure for fire suppression, but also the appropriate parts of the extinguisher itself. Figure 1-40 shows the fire extinguisher parts with which you should be familiar before attempting to use it.

A+ **1002: 4.4, 4.5**

Chemical Safety

As a computer technician, you will be exposed to potentially hazardous materials to some extent. For example, toner used in the laser printers can cause irritation to skin and eyes and may cause respiratory issues if accidentally inhaled. A *material safety data sheet (MSDS)* is required by federal law for such hazardous materials. An MSDS provides information such as proper handling, storage, and disposal of the material as well as information about health effects or harmful effects from breathing and contact with the skin or eyes. Material safety data sheets are used by emergency response personnel, such as firefighters and emergency medical technicians, and workers who commonly encounter the chemicals.

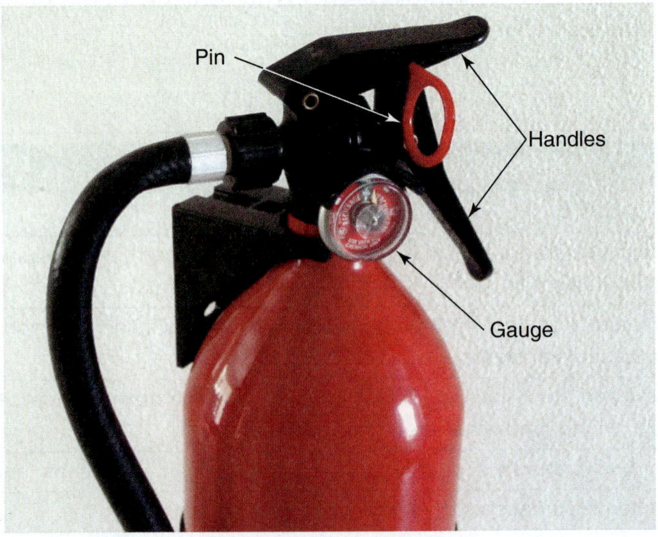

Figure 1-40 To use a fire extinguisher, pull the pin and squeeze the handles together. The gauge on the side shows if the extinguisher is safe to use.

Goodheart-Willcox Publisher

Electronic devices often contain material considered harmful to the environment. The Environmental Protection Agency (EPA) provides information about how to properly dispose of and recycle electronic equipment. Cities, counties, and states often have additional regulations concerning the disposal of computer and electronic equipment that exceed those of the federal government. Always check your local regulations on proper disposal. Consult the EPA website to learn more about environmental regulations.

An electronic device that causes the most concern is the monitor. Monitor displays are typically composed of a liquid crystal display (LCD) or light-emitting diodes (LEDs). Each of these needs to be disposed of properly.

Batteries are also an issue for disposal. It does not matter what sort of battery you are using, disposing of it properly is important. The EPA provides specific guidelines for specific types of batteries, which are shown in Figure 1-41.

Toner is also an issue. Hewlett Packard (HP), a major manufacturer of printers and toners, highly recommends recycling old toner and provides shipping materials for sending used toner cartridges back to HP for recycling. Many office-supply retail stores also offer recycling services.

Whether it is monitors, toner, or batteries, the issue is the same. Do not simply throw them in the trash. In many cases these items can be recycled, and simply throwing them in the trash may violate environmental laws and will probably introduce harmful chemicals into the environment.

Figure 1-41 Proper disposal of batteries varies from one battery type to another.

Proper Battery Disposal	
Battery	**EPA-Recommended Disposal**
Lithium Single-Use	Place each battery in separate plastic bags or place non-conductive tape (e.g., electrical tape) over the battery's terminals or around the entire button. A lithium battery may spark and cause fires if damaged or the terminal ends touch. If the battery becomes damaged, contact the manufacturer for specific handling information.
Lithium-Ion (Li-ion), Nickel-Zinc (Ni-Zn), Nickel Metal Hydride (Ni-MH), and Nickel Cadmium (Ni-Cd)	Removable rechargeable batteries can be brought to specialized battery recyclers.

Goodheart-Willcox Publisher; Source: EPA.gov

Chapter Summary

1.1 The Role of Computers

- Computers are used in every aspect of daily life and in all industries.
- Computers vary in size from small microprocessors to large research systems.
- The mechanics of a computer are quite simple; the difficulty in understanding them is overcome by understanding the interaction of hardware and software, grasping different operating systems, and recognizing upgrade and compatibility issues.

1.2 Digital Electronics

- All electronic components fall into one of two categories: digital or analog.
- Digital electronics work on a simple switch. Similar to a basic light switch, there are only two conditions: on or off.
- Analog electronics produce varying voltage levels, similar to a dimmable light switch.

1.3 What Is a Computer?

- A computer is an assembly of electronic modules that interact with computer programs known as software to create, modify, transmit, store, and display data.
- At the core of their functionality, computers process data, which can be text, graphics, and other media.
- Data is represented in the computer electronically as high and low voltages, which are pulsed through the system to create a digital signal.
- Data is transferred in one of two modes: series or parallel.
- Serial data transfer sends one bit at a time in successive order.
- Parallel data transfer sends eight bits of data side-by-side at one time.

1.4 Computer Data Codes

- The binary system consists of only two numbers: 0 and 1.
- The binary system is the basis for binary digits (bits), bytes, and words. A bit consists of either a single 0 or 1. A byte consists of a string of eight bits. A word is the number of bytes a given computer architecture can process at one time.
- The hexadecimal system has sixteen characters: 0–9 and A–F.
- ASCII (pronounced *as-key*) was the first attempt to standardize computer character codes among the varieties of hardware and software.
- Computer speed is usually expressed in bits.
- Storage space is usually expressed in bytes.
- Metric prefixes are used to express both speed and size but can cause some confusion due to the possibility of two values existing for a large expression.

1.5 Outside the Computer Case

- A basic workstation consists of a computer connected to input and output devices.
- Peripherals are optional pieces of equipment used to display or input data.
- Some common external connections on a typical PC are video, USB, FireWire, RJ-45, and audio.

1.6 Inside the Computer Case

- A computer case houses standard components such as a motherboard, CPU, power supply, storage device, cooling fan(s), RAM, expansion cards, and cables.
- Firmware is hardware-specific software required to boot the computer and support communication between the operating system and hardware devices.
- Without the CMOS battery installed on the motherboard, the computer would lose the date, time, and important information about the hardware components.

1.7 How the Major Parts Work Together

- When a command in a software program is initiated, the operating system interprets the command and translates it into a set of instructions that the firmware can interpret, and then control is returned to the software program.

1.8 Integrated Circuits

- An integrated circuit (IC) is a collection of transistors, resistors, and other electronic components reduced to an unbelievably small size. Hundreds of millions of transistors can be manufactured as a single integrated circuit the size of a US dime.
- Electrostatic discharge (ESD) is a static charge of electricity that can damage integrated circuits.
- Electromagnetic interference (EMI) is interference or damage to components caused by magnets and magnetic fields.
- Radio frequency interference (RFI) is interference produced by electronic devices that use radio waves.

1.9 Tool Kit

- Typical tools used in computer repair are flat tip screwdriver, Phillips screwdriver, star drivers, compressed air, antistatic wrist strap, multimeter, extraction tool, and extra screws.

1.10 Safety

- Some common safety practices related to computer repair are to disconnect electrical power from the computer before beginning repair and to avoid touching electronic components while the computer is energized or soon after the computer has been turned off.
- Use a cable runner or cord protector if cabling must be run across a walking area.
- Loose clothing and open-toed shoes should never be worn in a computer repair environment.
- There are five classes of fire extinguishers, each with its own specific type of usage: Class A, Class B, Class C, Class D, and Class K.
- Refer to a material safety data sheet (MSDS) for disposal of hazardous material.

Review Questions

1. Summarize the role of computers in society.
2. Differentiate between digital and analog electronics.
3. What is a computer?
4. Distinguish between serial and parallel data transfers.
5. List and describe three computer data codes.

6. In what way is the binary system similar to a light switch?
7. Explain the difference between *bits*, *bytes*, and *words*.
8. Which data coding method best matches the computer hardware system and why?
9. Explain how metric prefixes can cause confusion when discussing speed or storage measurements.
10. What types of devices are commonly found outside the computer case?
11. What common internal components are in almost every computer system?
12. List and describe the units that exist within a CPU.
13. What is the difference between a magnetic hard disk drive and a solid-state drive?
14. Describe the sequence of events that occurs between turning a computer on and saving text data in a word-processing program.
15. Describe the process of *photolithography*.
16. Differentiate between ESD, EMI, and RFI.
17. List tools commonly found in a PC-repair tool kit.
18. What is *shareware*?
19. Who is responsible for safety in classroom, laboratory, and workplace areas?
20. List each fire extinguisher class and its intended usage.

Sample A+ Exam Questions

1. Which type of cable connector is used by an analog display monitor?
   A. DB-9
   B. DB-15
   C. 9-pin serial
   D. 25-pin parallel
2. Which type of cable connector is used by a hard drive?
   A. SATA/PATA
   B. DB-15
   C. RJ-45
   D. UDB
3. Which type of cable connector is used by a telephone modem to connect to the telephone line?
   A. RJ-45
   B. DB-9
   C. RJ-11
   D. SATA or PATA
4. The maximum number of devices that can be connected to an IEEE-1394 connector is _____.
   A. 7
   B. 24
   C. 63
   D. 127

5. The maximum number of devices that can be connected using a USB connector is _____.
   A. 7
   B. 24
   C. 63
   D. 127
6. Which of the following items is associated with firmware?
   A. RAM
   B. BIOS
   C. DVD
   D. Speaker amplifier system
7. Which two are the most commonly encountered slot types? (Select two.)
   A. ISA
   B. PCI
   C. EISA
   D. PCIe
8. The acronym CMOS represents which of the following answers?
   A. Complementary mechanical operating system
   B. Complementary metal oxide semiconductor
   C. Complementary media operating system
   D. Complementary metallic opposition semiconductor
9. Which is the accepted method for a technician to manage ESD?
   A. Always use insulated hand tools.
   B. Place the PC on a rubber mat before disassembly.
   C. Disconnect the ground before servicing a PC.
   D. Always wear an antistatic wrist strap before touching PC components.
10. Which type of fire extinguisher is used on electrical fires?
    A. Class A
    B. Class B
    C. Class C
    D. Class A and Class B

Chapter 2

Operating Systems

Learning Outcomes

2.1 Explain the purpose of an operating system.
2.2 Describe the common characteristics of all operating systems.
2.3 Compare Windows operating systems.
2.4 List different types of Windows installations.
2.5 Summarize the Windows boot sequence.
2.6 Describe characteristics, tools, and features of Apple's macOS.
2.7 Identify characteristics of Linux OS.
2.8 List and explain best practices for Linux and macOS.
2.9 Provide examples of common mobile devices and tasks.
2.10 Define common operating system terminology.

A+ Certification Exam Objectives

The following A+ Certification Exam Objectives are covered in this chapter.

Exam 220-1101

1.0 Mobile Devices

- 1.4 Given a scenario, configure basic mobile-device network connectivity and application support.

3.0 Hardware

- 3.4 Given a scenario, install and configure motherboards, CPUs, and add-on cards.

Exam 220-1102

1.0 Operating Systems

- 1.1 Identify basic features of Microsoft Windows editions.
- 1.2 Given a scenario, use the appropriate Microsoft command-line tool.
- 1.3 Given a scenario, use features and tools of the Microsoft Windows 10 operating system.
- 1.4 Given a scenario, use the appropriate Microsoft Windows 10 Control Panel utility.
- 1.5 Given a scenario, use the appropriate Windows settings.
- 1.6 Given a scenario, configure Microsoft Windows networking features on a client/desktop.
- 1.7 Given a scenario, apply application installation and configuration concepts.
- 1.8 Explain common OS types and their purposes.
- 1.9 Given a scenario, perform OS installations and upgrades in a diverse OS environment.
- 1.10 Identify common features and tools of the macOS/desktop OS.
- 1.11 Identify common features and tools of the Linux client/desktop OS.

2.0 Security

- 2.4 Explain common social-engineering attacks, threats, and vulnerabilities.
- 2.5 Given a scenario, manage and configure basic security settings in the Microsoft Windows OS.
- 2.10 Given a scenario, install and configure browsers and relevant security settings.

Key Terms

boot sequence
bug
cold boot
command-line interface (CLI)
configuration files
cooperative multitasking
directory
dual-boot system
file system
file table
flag
graphical user interface (GUI)
kernel
multiple-boot system
multitasking
multithreading
operating system (OS)
pathname
power-on self-test (POST)
preemptive multitasking
registry
root directory
software driver
software patch
subdirectory
virtual machine
warm boot

Overview

This chapter introduces you to the Microsoft Windows 10 operating system and provides overviews of both macOS and Linux OS. Troubleshooting a PC requires a basic understanding of operating system functionality, and in order to gain in-depth knowledge of an operating system, you must use its various options. It is imperative that you supplement textbook studies through hands-on practice with current Windows operating systems. The Laboratory Manual associated with this textbook will give you the necessary skills and first-hand knowledge required to pass the A+ Certification Exams and to become a proficient PC technician.

A+ Note

You must know the system requirements for Windows operating systems and be familiar with the features of each operating system. You should also know basic text-based commands such as **cmd**, **dir**, **rd**, **md**, **del**, **fdisk**, **format**, **copy**, **xcopy**, **robocopy**, **diskpart**, **sfc**, **attrib**, **defrag**, **edit**, and **ckdsk**. Many of these commands are covered in more detail in later chapters of this textbook. Even with an excellent knowledge of Microsoft Windows operating systems, the lack of sufficient knowledge of text-based commands can result in failure on the CompTIA A+ Certification Exams.

In addition, be sure you can define *multitasking*, both preemptive and cooperative. You should know how to navigate a directory structure from Windows Explorer and from the command-line interface and how to create and manage files and directories.

A+ 1102: 1.9

2.1 What Is an Operating System?

Tech Tip

All operating systems are subject to a product life cycle. In most cases, the life cycle consists of four stages: *market introduction*, which correlates to high costs, slow sales, and little competition and demand; *growth*, which correlates to reduced costs, increased sales, profitability, and increased competition and demand; *maturity*, which correlates to peak sales, dropping prices, brand differentiation, and decreased profits; and *saturation and decline*, which correlates to a decline in cost efficiency, sales, and profitability.

An **operating system (OS)** is the underlying software that provides a computer user with all the basic services of resource management on the machine, including a file system structure for data storage and a means of communicating with all the various computer hardware. The operating system controls input and output (I/O) from disk storage units, monitors, printers, memory, and other computer components. It is also the job of the operating system to make sure programs running on the computer do not interfere with each other when competing for system resources. In the early days of computing, before operating systems were devised, users had to write code for all of the common tasks. For example, if you wanted to save data, you had to write the code that told your computer how to do so.

Each operating system has its individual strengths and weaknesses, and like every aspect of computing, OS software has evolved over the years. Think of the evolution of computer software and hardware as a group of inventors constantly building a better mousetrap; what is considered a cutting-edge or industry-leading operating system one day may not be the next day. In fact, an OS will likely become obsolete only a few years after its release. The constant evolution of computers makes this concept confusing.

The core of any operating system is referred to as the **kernel**. Just as a plant buds and grows from a single seed or kernel, so does operating system software. The core program is enhanced by other software applications that refine the computer system. Associated with the kernel can be programs that provide for user interface style, security, and specialized file systems. The OS enables these additional programs to communicate with the BIOS, which translates the software requests into instructions the hardware can understand, as outlined in Figure 2-1.

A user can give instructions directly to the operating system, or a user can give instructions via application software such as spreadsheets, word-processor, or game software. The operating system communicates with the BIOS, which then communicates with the computer hardware and peripherals.

For laptops, desktops, and workstations, the main operating systems in use today are Microsoft Windows, Apple macOS, and Linux. The latter two are derivatives of the Unix operating system originally developed by Bell Labs in the late 1960s. Linux first appeared in 1991 as an alternative to commercial operating systems and quickly gained popularity, in part because of its open-source model. There are

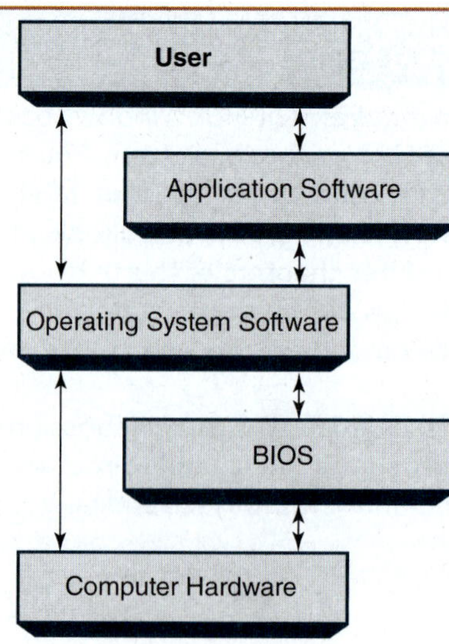

Figure 2-1 Operating systems allow application software to communicate with the BIOS, which translates application software requests into instructions the hardware can understand.

Goodheart-Willcox Publisher

many versions of Linux OS available today, both free and commercial distributions, to meet computer users' needs.

There are varieties of ways in which an operating system can be installed. At one time, the most common installation method was bootable installation OS images stored on a CD or DVD. However, many new systems, especially mobile computers, do not include an optical drive reader. In these situations, the OS can be installed locally via USB or flash drive, solid-state drive, removable or hot-swappable drive; via network connection or network server; or remotely through a preboot execution environment (PXE). For these to install correctly, the bootable and installation images of the operating system are stored on the respective device, which is loaded into the desired machine. When the computer starts, the user enters the BIOS and selects the desired device from the boot media options. The operating system could also be loaded onto a partition of the internal hard drive, but these are often reserved as recovery or repair installations.

2.2 Operating System Characteristics

Operating system characteristics refer to the ways an operating system handles activities, such as storing data, interfacing with the user, and presenting information on the screen. Most operating systems appear similar when judged by their screen display. However, there are many differences in the way they handle activities, especially data storage. Common characteristics among operating systems include multitasking, multithreading, architecture version (32 or 64 bits), interface, file systems and their structures, and configuration files.

Multitasking

Multitasking is the ability of an operating system to simultaneously support two or more running programs. When multitasking, it seems to the user that both programs are running simultaneously even though they are not. The computer simply switches control between the programs, giving the illusion they are running at the same time. For example, imagine you printed a file while browsing the Internet, streaming music, and checking your e-mail. It may appear as though all these programs are running simultaneously, but in reality, the computer runs the software in between sending packets of data to the printer.

Most operating systems support multitasking, but not all hardware does. Systems designed with minimal hardware, such as tablets and smartphones, do not support multitasking very well. If you attempt to perform more than one task, either the system will not allow you to run an additional program or the system will run sluggishly because of the shared resources (CPU, RAM, and chipset). There are two major classifications of multitasking: preemptive and cooperative.

Preemptive Multitasking

Preemptive multitasking, sometimes referred to as *time slicing*, is a process that allows multiple programs to share control of the operating system. For example, two or more programs can share the CPU for processing information, but no single program can totally take charge of a computer system. All programs running in preemptive mode are allowed to run for a set period of time, called the *time slice*, by an operating system process known as the *scheduler*. At the end of the time slice, a process is interrupted so the next process in line can run. This way, all the processes on the computer can share the CPU fairly. Since each time slice is brief (around 20 milliseconds in Windows), the processes appear to be running parallel to each other. Beginning with Windows 95, all versions of Windows OS, including Windows

10 and Windows Server, use preemptive multitasking. Most other modern operating systems, including OS/2, macOS, Unix, and Linux also use a preemptive kernel.

Cooperative Multitasking

Cooperative multitasking allows one program to dominate the CPU but will allow another program to run while it is idle. This is a legacy multitasking classification. It was common in early macOS versions up to version nine. It was also used in DOS and Windows versions before Windows 98. Although it is rarely used in commercial operating systems today, it can still often be found in embedded systems with memory constraints used for specific applications.

Multithreading

You may have heard the term *thread* or *threads* used when referring to computer processing. These terms refer to passing small portions of a computer program through the core of the processor. **Multithreading** refers to the sharing of data and parts of a program between two or more CPUs or between the cores of a single CPU. Note the difference between multithreading and multitasking, which is the ability of an operating system to support two or more programs running at the same time.

A+ 1102: 1.7

32-Bit and 64-Bit

A+ Note

For the A+ Exams, be sure to know the difference between hardware recommendations for 32-bit, 64-bit, and mobile versions.

Operating systems, hardware devices, and software applications are identified using the terms *32-bit* and *64-bit*, which describe the amount of data that can be stored or processed. In other words, *32-bit* and *64-bit* refer to how much data the CPU can process at once or how much total memory the operating system can access. All modern PCs run 64-bit because it is faster and more efficient as well as backward compatible with 32-bit programs. This has been the case for many years, and you are quite unlikely to find a 32-bit system today.

The maximum amount of memory a 32-bit Windows operating system can access is 4 GB. Even if the computer contains more than 4 GB of RAM, only 4 GB will be accessible by the 32-bit operating system, and the amount of memory dedicated for video will further reduce the actual usable RAM to the 2.6–3.5 GB range. On the other hand, a 64-bit Windows desktop operating system recognizes a maximum of 8–512 GB of memory depending on the version and operating system edition.

When upgrading an operating system from one edition to another without a full reinstall, you are usually required to stay at the same bit level. For example, you can only directly upgrade a 32-bit operating system to another 32-bit operating system or a 64-bit operating system to another 64-bit operating system. Upgrading directly from a 32-bit operating system to a 64-bit operating system will delete all data files (documents, photos, music, etc.) stored on the computer. Thus, you first need to back up all files, then perform the upgrade from 32-bit to 64-bit, and finally restore the software applications and user data files. This is the recommended approach unless the system has less than 2 GB of RAM. Since all 64-bit versions of Windows come with DOS support via NT DOS Virtual Machine (NTDVM), there is no reason to run a 32-bit OS solely for the sake of software compatibility.

A+ 1102: 1.1

User Interface

There are two dominant user interfaces used to issue commands on a computer system: graphical user interface and command-line interface. Graphical user interface is referred to as GUI (pronounced *gooey*). The command-line interface is commonly referred to by Microsoft as the *command prompt*.

Graphical User Interface

A **graphical user interface (GUI)** is a visual interface that allows the user to perform functions by selecting on-screen icons rather than issuing text-based commands. Although DOS and DOS-like systems controlled over 80 percent of the early PC market during the 1980s, the user-friendly GUI of Macintosh soon gained popularity. Creating GUIs for the PC in the form of Windows 3.1 and Windows NT helped Microsoft retain control of the operating system market.

In most operating systems used today, the GUI displays the file system consisting of folders, icons, and names. In Windows versions, this file system interface is called File Explorer or, more often, Explorer. One great advantage of using the GUI is that the entire file structure is easily displayed and interpreted. Figure 2-2 shows a typical GUI display of a file system organization as well as the default desktop view. Although this is a Windows 10 desktop, all Windows GUIs are very similar.

Command-Line Interface

1102: A+
1.2, 1.11

The **command-line interface (CLI)** is a text-based interface that allows a user to issue commands by entering text at the command prompt, as shown in Figure 2-3. Under normal circumstances, the command window has a black background with white text. However, this window has been modified to make it easier to read in this text. Some common commands are **dir**, **cd**, and **copy**, which call up a directory, change directories, and copy a file or disk, respectively. Several common commands that you should know for both Windows and Linux are described in Figure 2-4.

This is not a comprehensive list of command-line commands, but it does provide a good basic set of commands. Most commands have flags. A **flag**, also referred to as a *switch*, is an addition to a command that modifies its function. You can find out the flags for any command by typing the command name followed by /?. For example, the command syntax dir /? returns the possible flags for the **dir** command.

Navigating drives is simple in a command interface and can be accomplished in most cases simply by entering the drive letter. For example, if you are currently on the **c** drive and wish to navigate to the **e** drive, just type e: and press [Enter]. You can also format a drive using the **format** command. You can simply enter format *drive letter*, for example format d:, or you can use format/? to learn the flags of the **format** command. Note that formatting can also be accomplished via the GUI by right-clicking on any drive letter and selecting **Format** from the shortcut menu.

Figure 2-2 A graphical user interface (GUI) provides a more user-friendly method of file management than issuing text-based commands (A). The desktop GUI for all Windows operating systems is similar in look and feel (B).

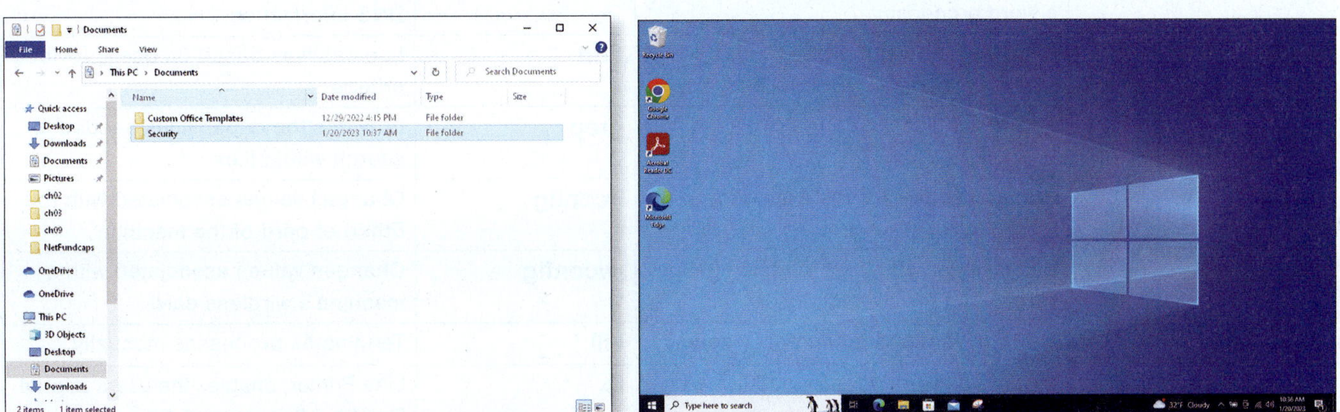

A

B

Goodheart-Willcox Publisher

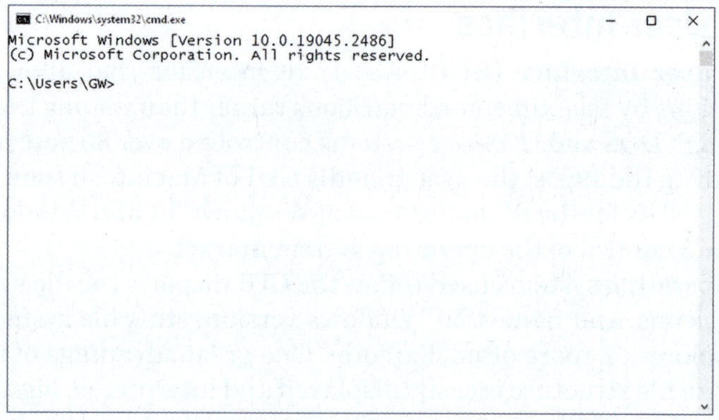

Goodheart-Willcox Publisher

Figure 2-3 The command-line interface is a text-based interface that allows a user to issue commands by entering text at the command prompt.

Figure 2-4 There are many commands that can be issued at the command prompt, but some are more commonly used than others.

Commonly Used Commands			
Windows Command	**Description**	**Linux Command**	**Description**
..	Used as part of a command to reference the parent directory	**apt-get**	Retrieves, installs, or removes packages
cd (or **chdir**)	Changes from the current location in a directory to another directory	**cat**	Concatenate; reads files sequentially and prints their contents into an output stream
chkdsk	Checks a disk for errors and displays results	**cd**	Same as Windows; changes the current location in a directory to another directory
copy	Copies data from one location to another	**chmod**	Changes the mode of a file via their permissions
date	Displays the date	**chown**	Changes the ownership of a file
del	Deletes a file	**cp**	Copies a file
dir	Displays a list of files, directories, and subdirectories	**dd**	Used to back up data to drives, CDs, or DVDs
DISM	Deployment Image Servicing and Management; prepares a Windows image for deployment	**df**	Displays amount of disk space available
edit	Starts a text-editor program similar to a word processor	**dig**	Domain Information Groper; gathers DNS information
exit	Exits the command prompt window and returns to the Windows desktop	**find**	Locates files based on user-provided criteria
fc	Compares files	**grep**	Provides the capabilities needed to search within files
format	Prepares a disk for first-time use	**ifconfig**	Changes values associated with the Ethernet card of the machine
gpresult	Displays Resultant Set of Policy (RSoP) information for a remote user	**iwconfig**	Changes values associated with a machine's wireless card
gpupdate	Modifies Windows group policy settings	**kill**	Terminates processes manually
ipconfig	Returns network adapter details	**lp**	Line Printer; enables the users to print files from the command-line interface

(continued)

Figure 2-4 continued.

Commonly Used Commands (cont.)			
Windows Command	**Description**	**Linux Command**	**Description**
md (or **mkdir**)	Creates a directory	**ls**	Displays a listing of the Present Working Directory/Directories (PWD)
netstat	Displays network connections and statistics	**man**	Displays user manual for Linux commands
ping	Tests network connectivity	**mv**	Moves a file to another destination or renames it
print	Prints a text file to a printer	**nano**	Open-source text editor with basic functionality
rd (or **rmdir**)	Deletes a directory	**passwd**	Changes the password of a user account or directory access
ren (or **rename**)	Changes the name of a file	**ps**	Displays running commands and the Process ID of all users
robocopy	Robust file copy for mirroring directories	**pwd**	Displays the Present Working Directory
SFC	System File Checker; used with DISM to repair or replace missing or corrupted system files	**rm**	Deletes a file
shutdown	Change running OS state to shut down, reboot, hibernate, etc.	**shutdown**	Performs the halt and shutting down of the system
taskkill	Terminates one or more tasks or processes	**su**	Allows a user to change to another user's account
time	Displays the time	**sudo**	Allows users to insert superuser commands
tree	Displays tree structure of a directory	**top**	Displays information about CPU and memory usage in real time
ver	Displays the software version running on the computer	**vi**	Opens the vi text editor
winver	Displays the Windows version running on the computer	**yum**	Yellowdog Updater Modified; enables users and administrators to install, update, remove, or search for software

Goodheart-Willcox Publisher

A+ 1102: 1.11

Most Windows and macOS users prefer the GUI for navigation, but many Linux users opt to use the Shell/Terminal for carrying out certain actions or providing basic commands. The *Shell* is the program where the commands are inserted, and the *Terminal* runs a Shell or multiple Shells. Be aware that there are some commands that can only be run by a user with administrative privileges.

Disk Operating System (DOS) was the major operating system used by many PCs from 1980 to the late 1990s. However, because DOS was command-line based, it was not considered a user-friendly OS since users had to memorize many different commands to become productive with the operating system. Today, text-based commands are still used, especially by system administrators and when troubleshooting. Text-based commands are particularly important when a PC fails to complete its startup process and take the user to the GUI. When troubleshooting with system recovery tools, the Windows admin can use the command window to enter text-based commands to check for disk and file system errors. It is important that the technician be familiar with command-line options to be able to use the command prompt effectively.

A+ Note

Text-based commands are still very much part of the A+ Certification Exams. To pass the exams, you must be familiar with each command's function.

Modern Windows systems no longer use DOS and are instead based on the NT kernel. For backward compatibility, a DOS emulator is provided with the look, feel, and functionality of a real DOS prompt. Many of the restrictions or limitations of DOS are not found in the virtual DOS machine (NTDVM); for example, many of the restricted characters not allowed in DOS file names can be used in the modern Windows command line or DVM because they are supported by the underlying NT kernel.

When a computer system fails during the startup process, there is no access to a graphical user interface. The best means of communicating with the computer system is by using a recovery CD or booting to built-in OEM recovery partition. Most of the commands used in Recovery Console look and work exactly like the original DOS commands. Figure 2-5 lists the most commonly used Recovery Console commands.

There are also newer text-based commands that complement today's more sophisticated operating systems. There will be much more about command-line support in a later chapter.

File Systems

No introduction to operating systems would be complete without mentioning file systems. A **file system** refers to the method of organizing files on a storage device. It is an indexing system used by the operating system to keep track of all files on the disk. The file system maintains a file table of all areas on the disk, and it tracks which areas are being used for data and which are free and available at any given time. A **file table** is a component of a file system used to organize files on a storage device.

A+ 1102: 1.8

Legacy file systems with which you should be familiar are FAT12, FAT16, and FAT32. Beginning with Windows NT, the default file system used by Windows operating systems has been NTFS. The basic FAT and FAT16 were options for Windows 7

Figure 2-5 Many of the commands used in Recovery Console look and work exactly like the DOS commands and DOS emulator.

Commonly Used Recovery Console Commands

Recovery Console Command	Function
attrib	View or set the attributes of a file or directory
cd	View or change the current directory
chkdsk	Check and display the status of a hard drive
copy	Copy a file
del	Delete a file
dir	Display the files, directories, and subdirectories of the current working directory
disable	Disable a service or a driver
diskpart	Partition a hard drive
enable	Enable a service or a driver
exit	Exit Recovery Console
fixmbr	Repair the master boot record
format	Format a hard drive
help	Display a list of Recovery Console commands
md	Create a directory
ren	Rename a file
rd	Delete a directory

Goodheart-Willcox Publisher

when formatting flash drives. In Windows 10 and 11, FAT and FAT16 are only supported for reading older devices, and USB media can only be formatted as FAT32, exFAT, or NTFS. It is important to note that the FAT file system is no longer supported for formatting or installing the OS on internal storage as of the latest Windows 10 release. As you study operating systems more in-depth, you will learn about other types of file systems, such as Apple File System (APFS). The Linux OS has support for many different file system types including ext2, ext3, ext4, Btrfs, XFS, and JFS. Each type of file system has its own features and advantages, so it is important to understand these features in order to select the best choice for a given application. File systems will be covered in greater depth in a later chapter.

File System Structure

A+ 1102: 1.6

Programs and user files are stored as data on computers via the file system, which manages the formatting and organizing of storage devices, such as hard drives, solid-state drives, CDs, and USB sticks. There are many different file system types supported by modern desktop and mobile operating systems, and many have similar or common characteristics for managing storage. The basic structure is made of data repositories called directories, subdirectories, and files. A **directory** is a special type of file used to group or contain other files together in a hierarchical file structure. A **subdirectory** is a file that subdivides the content of a directory. *Directory* and *subdirectory* are relative terms found in Unix, Linux, and macOS, while Windows uses the terms *folder* and *subfolder* to mean the same thing. A *file* is a program or a collection of data that forms a single unit. Examine Figure 2-6, which shows a typical directory and file structure. It shows the relationship of the root directory, directories, subdirectories, and files.

In both Unix and Windows OS, the **root directory** is at the top of the directory structure. Windows uses letters to label disk drives. By default, the C:\ appears at the top for the OS or system drive in Figure 2-6; thus, the root directory is C: (the hard drive). Next, there are directories or folders stemming from the root directory, for example, Games and School. Looking at the example again, you will see that English is a subdirectory to School. Both English and School are directories, but the placement in the structure determines if it is a subdirectory. Both directories and subdirectories can contain files. Under the directory Games, you can see several game files, such as Hearts and Solitaire.

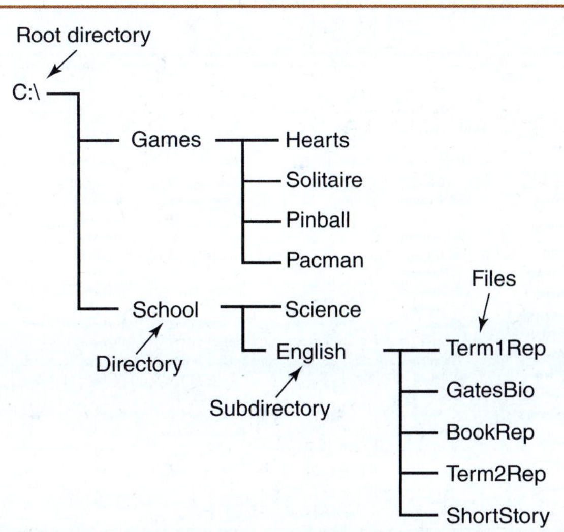

Goodheart-Willcox Publisher

Figure 2-6 The basic file structure used in many file systems is made of directories, subdirectories, and files.

A+ 1102: 1.6

A **pathname** is a unique address used to identify the precise location of a specific file. Pathnames are also known as *File Explorer navigation paths* or *network paths*. Look at Figure 2-7. The Windows pathname for the file is **This PC>C:>Users>GW**. The **This PC** in the directory structure identifies the local user computer or workstation. **C:** is the root directory, **Users** is the first directory, and **GW** is a subdirectory of **Users**. The bottom subdirectory reveals a collection of additional subfolders, which are subdirectories such as **Contacts**, **Favorites**, and **Music**, to give a partial listing.

Most of the Windows operating system files are located by default in the **Windows** folder on the **C:** partition or drive. The pathname for this location is **C:\Windows**. In reality, this folder can be located on any partition. In Microsoft technical literature, the exact location of the Windows folder is indicated as **%systemroot%** rather than **C:\Windows**. The **%systemroot%** variable is used in the path to represent the location of the Windows folder.

A+ 1102: 1.3

Configuration Files

When a computer system is configured, the type of hardware and software the system has planned for use is recorded in a configuration file. **Configuration files** contain information such as the amount of memory and the type of video adapter present in the system. Configuration information is stored in the **config.sys** file of DOS systems, which is still used today but only to support legacy software applications.

Early Windows systems stored configuration information in the **win.ini** and **system.ini** files. Software applications also stored configuration setting in **.ini** files. These configuration files are replaced by the Windows registry settings beginning with Windows 95. Many computer systems still contain **.ini** files to maintain a downward compatibility with some software programs.

The OS configuration file found in the Windows operating systems is called a registry. The **registry** is a hierarchical database that stores configuration information. The major sections of the registry are referred to as HIVES and are listed as follows with their contents:

- **HKEY_CLASSES_ROOT**: object linking and embedding (OLE) information and how files are associated with each other
- **HKEY_CURRENT_USERS**: information for the current user of this workstation
- **HKEY_LOCAL_MACHINE**: information specific to the local computer
- **HKEY_USERS**: information for each user of this workstation
- **HKEY_CURRENT_CONFIG**: display and printer settings

Note in the previous list, the **HKEY** is short for *Hive Key*.

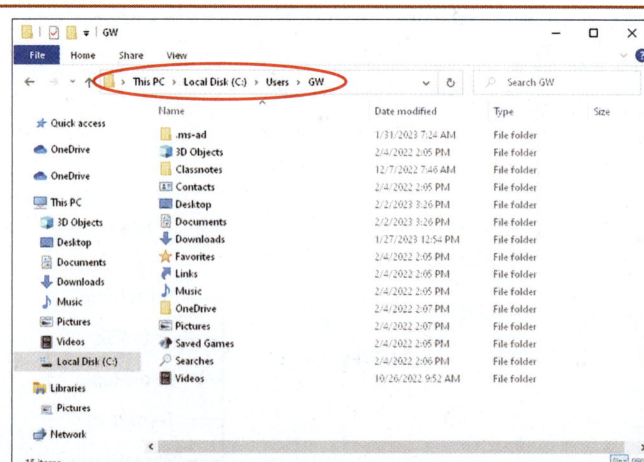

Figure 2-7 A pathname indicates the precise location for a file on a computer or across a network system.

Goodheart-Willcox Publisher

The registry is accessed by entering regedit in the **Run** dialog box found in the **Start** menu or by entering regedit at the command prompt. Figure 2-8 shows the Windows 10 Registry Editor. The Windows 11 Registry Editor looks precisely the same; the only changes have been the addition or alteration of a few registry keys.

There are two main registry files: **system.dat** and **user.dat**. The **system.dat** file contains information about the computer settings. The **user.dat** file contains information about individuals who use the computer. Registry files can be copied to disk, installed on another computer, backed up, and modified. The registry is repaired through the System Restore utility. Rarely does a technician need to access the registry files directly, and when a technician does access the registry files, it is usually as part of repair steps outlined by Microsoft on its TechNet website. Direct modification of the registry should be a last-resort effort.

A+ 1102: 1.3

Tech Tip

Changes in the registry can completely disable your computer operating system. Do *not* experiment with registry settings unless you fully understand the change or are under the supervision of your instructor.

2.3 Microsoft Windows Operating System

A+ 1102: 1.8

The most widely used desktop operating system is Microsoft Windows, and most desktop users are likely running Windows 10 or Windows 11. On servers, you will find a mix of Windows, Linux, and legacy Unix versions. This section references Windows operating system versions Windows 7 and later, and differences among operating systems are pointed out when appropriate.

In October 2009, Microsoft released the Windows 7 operating system and announced the end of extended support to be January 14, 2020, meaning the commercial life for that OS lasted just over a decade. In October 2012, Microsoft introduced Windows 8 with an entirely new look and feel. In this OS, Microsoft made the attempt to make the user interface in the style of emerging mobile devices and in the process, eliminated many popular and familiar features of earlier versions of Windows. A large number of users were so unhappy, Microsoft released Windows 8.1 a year later and restored many of the missing features. Windows 10 was released in July 2015, containing both the tablet style and the traditional look and feel of a graphical user interface—allowing users to decide which style to run. By default, Windows 10 looks more like Windows 7 rather than Windows 8. Windows 11 has a similar look and feel to Windows 10, though the organization of the taskbar is slightly different. By default, it is centered on the bottom of the GUI rather than aligned to the left margin. This can be changed by the user, but the option to move the taskbar to a different side of the screen entirely was removed. Many of the

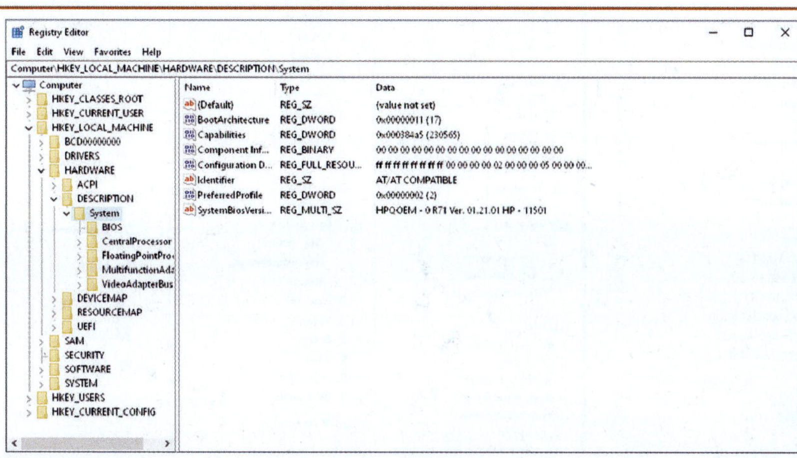

Goodheart-Willcox Publisher

Figure 2-8 The Windows registry is accessed by entering regedit in the **Run** box for the command prompt. Users should not experiment with registry settings without cause or knowledge of the action they are taking.

differences between these operating systems will be covered in the following sections as the major features of the Windows operating systems are reviewed.

Windows OS Directory Structure

The Microsoft approach to software is like constantly trying to improve a mousetrap; they keep reinventing existing features. Nowhere is there a better example of this process than comparing the directory structure of the various Windows operating system versions. As new solutions to old problems are discovered and new technologies are introduced, changes are reflected in the directory structure.

A directory structure consists of files, folders, documents, and items such as hard drive partitions, CD/DVD drives, and network locations. To make a quick comparison of the Windows 7, Windows 8, Windows 10, and Windows 11 directory structures, look at Figure 2-9.

The Windows XP directory was simple in comparison to Windows Vista, which introduced the concept of a Public folder to make sharing easier for users. The Windows 7 directory structure was even more complex, having introduced Libraries and HomeGroup into the directory structure. HomeGroup was an improved sharing feature, and Libraries allowed easier access to files and folders located in multiple locations. Changes in the directory structure is one of the biggest reasons people have trouble locating their files after upgrading to a new operating system or buying a computer with a newer version of an operating system. In Windows 10, the Quick Access view was added in File Explorer that shows a list of recently accessed objects and was retained for the release of Windows 11. Quick Access objects are not duplicates; rather, they are simply shortcut links to the same files and folders under **This PC** and the **C:** drive views. Users will need to understand this new feature and how it works to avoid confusion.

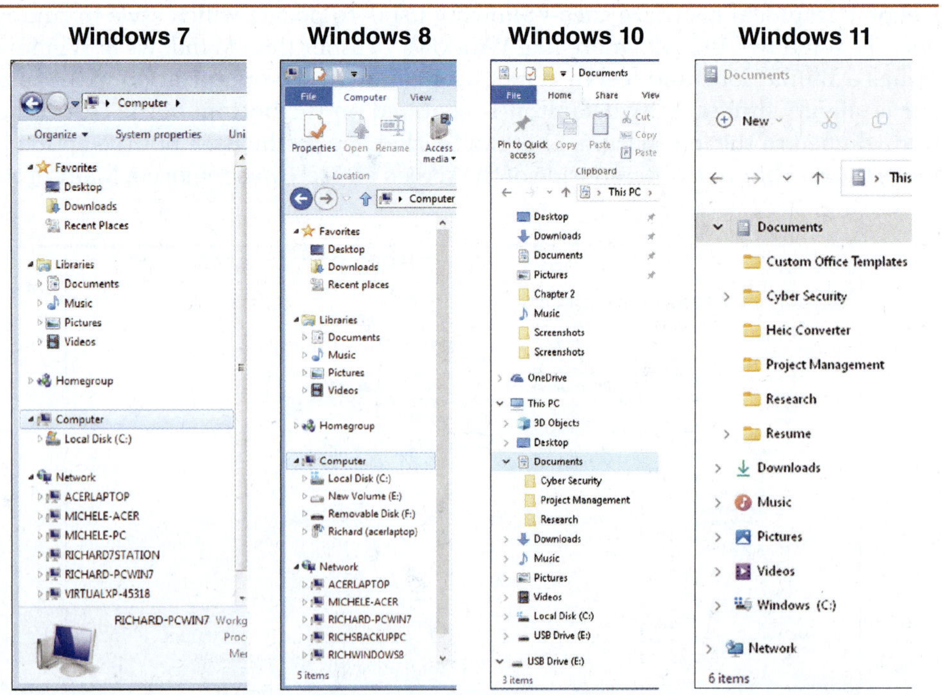

Figure 2-9 The Windows directory structure has remained relatively unchanged since Windows 7.

Goodheart-Willcox Publisher

Windows File Names

File names originally had to conform to DOS standards, which required that file names be no more than eight characters followed by a period and a file extension. A *file extension* is an identification consisting of three additional characters that allows Windows to recognize the file type. Commonly encountered examples include **.doc** or **.docx** for Microsoft Word documents, **.jpg** for JPEG images, and **.pdf** for PDF files. In modern operating systems, the file extension is not necessary but still helps with file identification and mapping to a default application assigned to handle a given file type. The table in Figure 2-10 lists common file extensions and the type of program to which they are related.

Modern operating systems utilize a standard known as *long file names*, which allows names up to 255 characters. Long file names allow for the content of the file to be described in some detail. This provides relief from brief, cryptic, eight-character file names. For example, a file could be saved as Term1 Science Paper The Factors Affecting Ocean Tides.

While long file names provide room for additional characters, some characters or symbols still cannot be used in the file name. The following characters are not allowed in the long file name system:

| * > < ? : \ / "

These characters have unique meanings within the operating system and will produce errors or unwanted results when used. As you can see in Figure 2-11, Windows displays an error message when the user attempts to use a restricted character in the folder file name. Restricted characters also provide backward compatibility to legacy operating systems.

Common File Extensions	
File Extension	**Description**
.avi	Audio video file
.bmp	Bitmap graphics file
.com	Executable file
.doc	Document file
.exe	Executable file (a program that runs when the file name is entered at the command prompt)
.ini	File containing configuration data
.jpg	Picture file
.log	File listing actions that have occurred or containing a brief record or collection of data
.mpg	Video file
.tmp	Temporary file (typically associated with Internet downloads and software installations)
.txt	Text file
.wav	Wave audio file
.wmv	Windows media video file
.wps	WPS Office for Windows word-processor document

Goodheart-Willcox Publisher

Figure 2-10 A file extension is an identification consisting of three additional characters that allows Windows to recognize the file type.

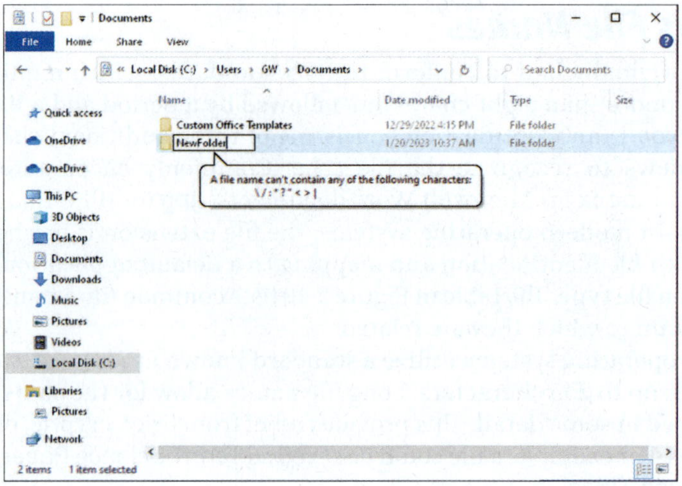

Figure 2-11 Windows displays an error message when a user enters a file name that contains a restricted character.

Goodheart-Willcox Publisher

Windows Desktop

The Windows desktop has maintained a similar user interface from Windows XP to Windows 11. The lone exception was Windows 8, which used a tiled interface and did away with the popular **Start** menu. As mentioned previously, negative feedback from the Windows user base resulted in the **Start** menu being reintroduced in a point release to Windows 8 called Windows 8.1. The **Start** menu located at the bottom-left corner of the desktop has remained relatively uniform since its introduction. From this menu, users can launch programs, access folders such as **Documents** and **Pictures**, and initiate commands such as **Shut down**.

Due to the incorporation of a tablet-style interface, Windows 8 did not support the **Start** menu feature. The Windows 8.1 default screen was named Start and contained a set of objects called *Tiles*, which represented shortcuts to Windows 8 program applications, referred to as *apps*. The Tiles were similar to icons used on earlier Windows desktop operating systems and could easily be added or removed. The new design was made for devices with touch screens, such as the tablet and smartphone, but users could still use a mouse to navigate.

Windows 8 also included an alternate desktop that resembled the traditional Windows desktop except that it did not have a **Start** menu icon. Instead, a taskbar was displayed across the bottom of the desktop with familiar icons displayed, and users could create desktop shortcuts or pin programs to the taskbar for quick access to commonly used software applications.

Windows 10 reintroduced the **Start** menu, but it uses Windows 8-style Tiles for the menu format, as shown in Figure 2-12. Users can customize how many of the Tiles they see by selecting **Settings**>**Personalization**>**Start**. In place of Control Panel, there is now a gear icon to access a setting window. The Control Panel application is still available and can be found using Windows search located to the right of the **Start** menu icon. It can also be accessed directly through the Most Used portion of the **Start** menu or through **Start**>**Settings**>**Control Panel**. Windows 10 also introduced an AI personal assistant called Cortana, which accepts voice commands in addition to typed search commands.

Windows 11 only has minor changes to the GUI from Windows 10. In fact, the Windows 11 desktop looks identical to the Windows 10 desktop. The only real changes of note are small adjustments to the taskbar, as shown in Figure 2-13A. By clicking on the small Windows icon, you will see apps, the power button, and more, including recommended applications or files, as shown in Figure 2-13B.

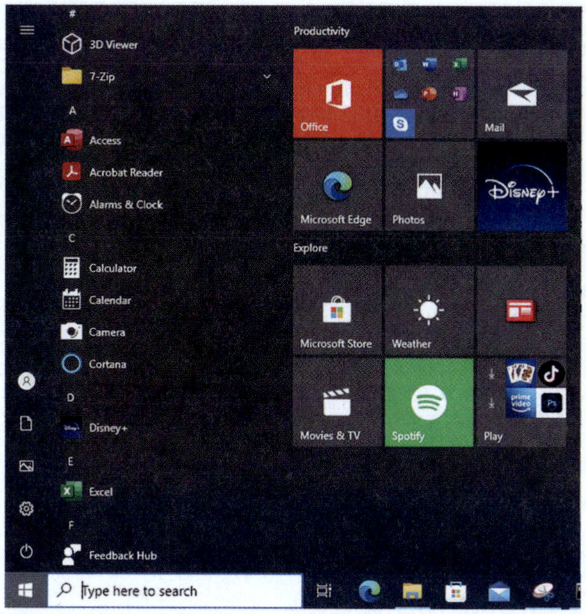

Goodheart-Willcox Publisher

Figure 2-12 Windows 10 reintroduced the **Start** menu but includes Windows 8-style Tiles for the menu interface and format.

Figure 2-13 Windows 11 made only minor changes to the GUI from what was in Windows 10. The taskbar (A) includes a button for the **Start** menu and a dedicated **Search** button instead of a Cortana search bar. The inside of the **Start** menu (B) omitted Tiles and instead shows recommended files, a power button, and applications.

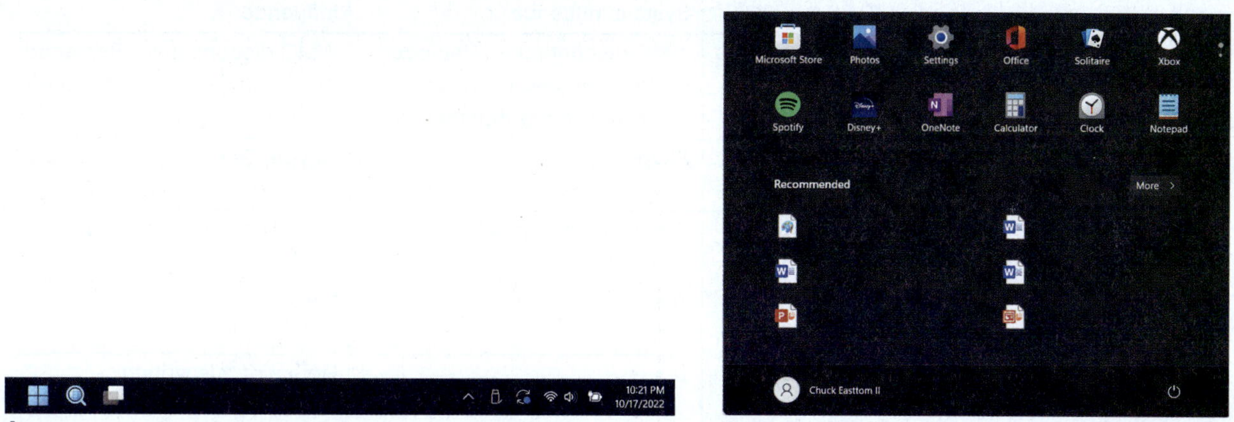

A B

Goodheart-Willcox Publisher

Windows Features and Tools

1102: 1.9 A+

Tech Tip

A feature update is one that contains revisions not only to security and user experience but also feature additions and changes. These updates are typically released as soon as they are available, and it is highly encouraged that they are installed in a timely fashion.

The most important Windows features are introduced in this section. Not all features are available in all versions of Windows. You can use Figure 2-14 to quickly identify in which version of Windows each feature is integrated. Features unique to Windows 10 are also covered in the following sections.

Figure 2-14 Some features are common from one Windows OS to another.

Comparison of Windows OS Features

Windows Feature	Windows 10	Windows 11
Encryption	BitLocker (Professional and Enterprise editions only)	BitLocker (Pro, Enterprise, and Education editions only)
Mobile Device Encryption	BitLocker To Go (Professional and Enterprise editions only)	BitLocker To Go (Pro, Enterprise, or Education editions only)
Cortana Personal Assistant	Yes	Yes
DOS Compatibility	32-bit Yes 64-bit Yes, via NTDVM	No
Libraries	Yes	Yes
Microsoft User Account	Yes	Yes
Network Discovery	Yes	Yes
Picture Password	Yes	Yes
Recovery, Refresh, and Reset	Recovery Drive, System Restore, and Reset PC	Recovery Drive, System Restore, and Reset PC
Sync Your Settings	Yes	Yes
Tablet PC Settings	Yes	Yes
Windows Look and Feel	Microsoft Fluent Design System influence	Microsoft Fluent Design System influence
Desktop Multimedia Support	WMC discontinued. Replaced by streaming services and other third-party applications.	WMC discontinued. Replaced by streaming services and other third-party applications.
Collaboration Software	Skype	Skype, Teams
Windows Mobility Center	Yes, disabled by default	Yes, disabled by default
Windows ReadyBoost	Yes	Yes
Windows Shadow Copy and Previous Versions	Yes	No, as of this writing
Windows To Go	Enterprise and Education editions only	No

Goodheart-Willcox Publisher

A+ Note

The A+ Certification Exams require knowledge of a variety of Windows operating systems and features. Always check the CompTIA website for a list of operating systems that are covered on the exam.

For a more detailed list of Windows operating system features, check the Microsoft website. You can conduct an online search using the key terms Microsoft Windows feature comparison. Be sure to add the operating version or edition names in the search key terms.

Control Panel

1102: 1.4 A+

Windows Control Panel is a menu accessible from the **Start** menu that contains several utilities used to manage hardware, software, user and system settings, and troubleshooting. Users can also adjust general folder options, such as viewing hidden files, hiding or showing file extensions, changing folder icons, and customizing how files and folders appear in searches. Three important utilities found in Control Panel include, among many others, Date and Time, Internet Options, and System.

Date and Time

1102: 1.5 A+

One example of a utility in Control Panel is Date and Time, which allows you to set the date, time, and time zone for the installed Windows operating system. This dialog box also allows you to select an Internet clock with which to synchronize your computer.

Internet Options

1102: 1.4, 1.5 A+

Another example of a useful tool in Control Panel is Internet Options, which allows users to adjust the properties of their Internet connections. The Internet Options dialog box includes seven tabs:

- **General**: allows users to change options for home page, startup, tabs, history, and appearance
- **Security**: allows users to change options for security settings and security levels
- **Privacy**: allows users to adjust privacy options, such as location and pop-ups
- **Content**: allows users to view or clear certificates, change AutoComplete settings, and customize web feeds
- **Connections**: allows users to customize their connection configuration
- **Programs**: allows users to manage add-on programs and file associations
- **Advanced**: allows users to customize their web browser experience further

System

1102: 1.4, 1.5 A+

The System window provides a wealth of useful information to the user. This window is where users can view performance statistics; the type of OS installed, such as 32-bit or 64-bit; and the amount of memory installed, including virtual memory. The System window is also where users can adjust settings for various system components, including the display, sound, notifications, battery, and multitasking, among others. For example, if you wanted to establish a time frame during which you want notifications silenced, you can navigate to the System settings and select the **Focus assist** option. The **System** settings is also the location for configuring multiple displays and power options. This page can also be accessed by navigating to **Start**>**Settings**>**System**.

Mail

1102: 1.4 A+

As with previous versions of Microsoft Windows, you may install any e-mail client you wish. Many users will choose to use Microsoft Outlook since it is the default option. However, Microsoft Windows 10 and 11 both come with a mail app, which can be used to sign into any e-mail account including Microsoft Outlook, Google, iCloud, Live, Hotmail, or MSN address. Selecting the **Add account** option launches a wizard that walks you through the process of adding an e-mail account.

Indexing

1102: 1.4 A+

Users who have utilized Windows search may have found the search can be rather slow. This has led to a number of third-party apps being developed to enable faster Windows searches. The process of indexing involves examining the metadata in files and preparing an index so future searches go faster. The initial indexing process can be slow. However, after you have completed the indexing, you will notice a substantial improvement in future searches. Windows 10 and 11 have built-in indexing options, as shown in Figure 2-15. These options can be accessed through the Control Panel, though you may have to change the view in order to see **Indexing Options** as a selection. Alternatively, you can enter indexing into the **Search** pane and select **Indexing Options** from the results. You can then select any folders or drives you wish to be indexed, including entire drives or specific folders that you happen to frequently search.

A+ 1102: 1.4

Programs and Features

The **Programs and Features** menu lists all programs and applications installed on the PC. From this menu, a user can repair, change, or uninstall an application or program. The best way to access this menu is by opening **Control Panel** and selecting **Programs**. Note, this menu is titled **Programs** when viewing categories and **Programs and Features** viewing an icon-based arrangement. Though technically separate, you can perform the same basic actions from the **Apps & features** setting menu, which can be opened by searching for programs and selecting **Add or remove programs** from the results list.

Notepad

Notepad is a plain-text editor built into Windows operating systems. It was initially released in MS-DOS as a mouse-based program and is one of the few features that has been incorporated in every version of Microsoft Windows since the initial release in 1985. Files saved in Notepad have a **.txt** file extension, unless otherwise specified by the user. A common use for Notepad is coding HTML by hand and saving the file with a **.html** extension.

Windows Look and Feel

Windows Aero (Authentic, Energetic, Reflective, and Open) was an enhancement to the graphical user interface look and feel introduced in Windows Vista. Aero was designed to have a glass-like appearance (sometimes called Windows Glass) with various degrees of transparency similar to popular Linux GUIs of the late 1990s. The downside to the attractive look and feel is that it used more system resources and video memory to run. As a result, it was common for users to disable the feature in exchange for performance. The Windows Aero feature was one of the main reasons a greater amount of RAM and a quality 3D graphics card or motherboard was required. The glass-like look and feel of Aero was phased out after Windows 7 and not included in releases beginning with Windows 8.

Another GUI feature phased out after Windows 7 were Gadgets. Gadgets were introduced in Windows Vista as mini-software programs that provided services, such as an online dictionary, clock, calendar, weather report, and CPU monitor. Gadgets were continued through Windows 7 but dropped for Windows 8 and later.

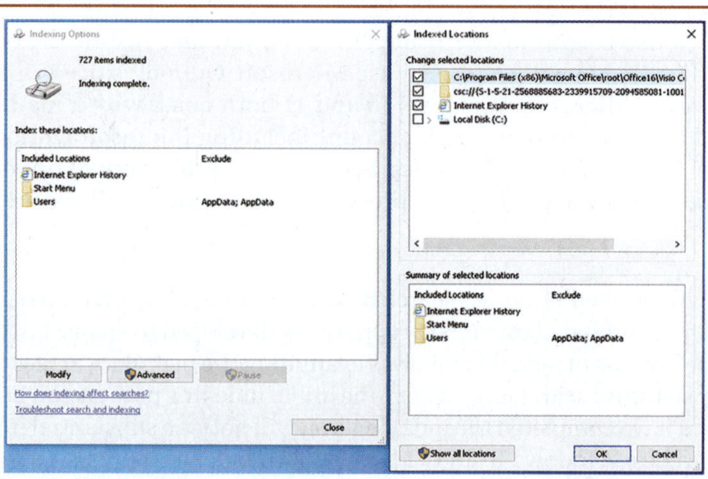

Figure 2-15 The process of indexing involves examining the metadata in files and preparing an index so future searches go faster.

Goodheart-Willcox Publisher

Windows 10 has a similar basic look and feel to Windows 7 without the Aero styling and with the addition of the Tile-based **Start** menu from Windows 8. Windows 10 users see a look and feel influenced by Microsoft Fluent Design System created to establish common appearance and behavior across the OS and applications. Microsoft created *UWP (Universal Windows Platform)* to support implementation of Fluent Design standards. The Windows 11 appearance of individual Windows, including the Control Panel, is nearly identical to Windows 10.

Drive Encryption

1102: 1.1, 2.5 A+

BitLocker Drive Encryption is an encryption feature that is available as part of many versions of the Windows OS. *Encryption* is the process of rendering the contents of a file and folder unreadable by people other than those who hold the key and are allowed to read it. BitLocker differs from earlier versions of file encryption in that it encrypts the entire volume, including the system files required for startup and logon, rather than just data files. BitLocker ensures that data remains encrypted even when the operating system is not running. For example, if someone removes a hard drive and then attempts to access the data from another computer using a different operating system or software utility, BitLocker prevents the data from being accessed because the data remains encrypted.

BitLocker is transparent to the user after it is activated. It is designed to be used with a computer that has a Trusted Platform Module (TPM) or firmware that can read a USB flash drive. The TPM is a microchip that ensures encryption is intact throughout the boot sequence of the computer. If the TPM is missing or has changed, the user is required to supply a password to access the encrypted data. If BitLocker is configured on a system that does not have a TPM, a startup key is required when it is first configured. A typical startup key is a software program loaded on a USB flash drive. The software program contains the encryption key used to access the encrypted drive. For Windows 7, BitLocker was a downloadable option. In Windows 10 and 11, it is a bundled option only available with Pro and Enterprise editions.

BitLocker To Go is an enhanced version of the BitLocker application first introduced in Windows 7 that allows encryption of USB storage devices. As the name implies, you can encrypt files on a USB drive, remove the drive, and take it to another computer. Microsoft provides the BitLocker To Go Reader as a free download that allows a user to read the contents of an encrypted flash drive. BitLocker To Go, when enabled, is automatically added to the USB flash drive or storage media by default. Starting with Windows 10, the Used Space Only encryption feature allows removable devices to be encrypted in seconds rather than minutes in most cases. There will be more discussion about BitLocker and BitLocker To Go in a later chapter.

Desktop Multimedia Support

Windows Media Center (WMC) was a collection of media manipulation utilities and tools that was part of Windows Vista and Windows 7. WMC was popular with users; however, it was discontinued in 2015 due to changes in the market and multimedia technologies. WMC was not included with either Windows 8 or Windows 10, but it was supported as a paid add-on for Windows 8.1. With Windows Media Center, you could edit digital movies; modify or adjust digital photos; and record, copy, and create DVDs. If your PC ran Windows 7 or 8 and had a television tuner card installed, you could also watch live television.

WMC is not officially supported on Windows 10 because streaming services and third-party media applications provide similar feature sets to WMC that have replaced the need for Microsoft to provide a dedicated tool. If you are upgrading a system from Windows 7 to Windows 10, Windows Media Center will be removed, and Windows DVD Player will be downloaded and installed in its place. With the advent of modern streaming services and third-party multimedia applications,

Microsoft chose not to continue with a dedicated media tool suite for Windows 10. Windows Media Center was not included in Windows 11, but early adopters have reported that one can download the Windows 7 or 8 Windows Media Center, which will work on Windows 11.

Windows Mobility Center

Windows Mobility Center provides a central location for accessing the most commonly used features for laptops, such as presentation configurations for a projector and energy conservation configurations. It also automatically configures common network connections, such as for home, office, or work locations. Windows Mobility Center, as viewed in Windows 10, can be seen in Figure 2-16.

The Windows Hot Start feature allows a laptop to start a selected program with the touch of a single button. There is no need to wait long periods of time while the program is located, opened, and loaded into memory. It will start an application directly out of sleep mode or hibernation and even when the computer has been turned off. The feature was designed specifically for mobile PCs.

Collaboration Tools

For collaboration, the older Windows Meeting Space has been replaced by Skype and Skype for Business. Skype is designed for video and text collaborating over a network with features such as instant messaging, voice, video chat, screen sharing, and conference calls. Windows 7 supported another collaboration tool, People Near Me, but that was phased out for Windows 8. Since its 2011 acquisition by Microsoft, Skype has replaced Meeting Space and other legacy solutions for collaboration. The main difference between Skype and Skype for Business is that the former is designed for individual users and the latter has additional features for enterprise and business users.

Microsoft Teams is a business communication and collaboration program developed as part of Microsoft 365. Similar to Slack, Microsoft Teams provides instant messaging, videoconferencing, and file storage options. Recently, Teams has been replacing Skype and Microsoft Classroom in many cases. It gained quite a few new users during the 2020 COVID-19 pandemic. Teams can be installed on Windows, macOS, and Linux devices, as well as both Android and Apple mobile devices.

A+ 1102: 1.5

Network and Internet

The **Network & Internet** menu is essentially the same information as what appears in the traditional **Network and Sharing Center** available in Control Panel. From this menu, you can view your current connectivity status and configure network adapters and connections. This menu is accessible by navigating to **Start**>**Settings**>**Network & Internet**.

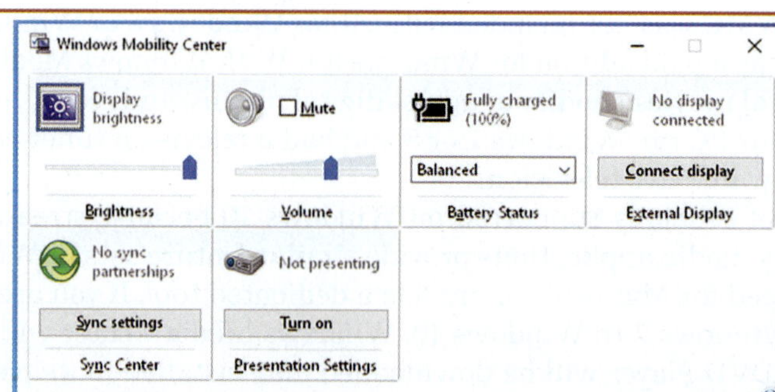

Figure 2-16 Windows Mobility Center provides a central location for accessing the commonly used features for laptops, including projector, display, and energy-saving settings.

Goodheart-Willcox Publisher

Network Discovery

Network Discovery was introduced with Windows Vista and has continued to be supported by subsequent Windows versions, including Windows 10 and 11. It makes setting up and configuring a network easy as it automatically detects and configures a network and sets up a share and Internet connection. It also allows files to be shared much easier in a peer-to-peer network, while still providing security from the Internet. The main exception arises if there is a router or gateway being used that is not compatible with the automatic networking features.

Figure 2-17 shows the **Advanced sharing settings** menu, which is accessed from the Network and Sharing Center. Notice the **Network discovery** option in the **File and printer sharing** sections of the menu. These options let you enable and disable the respective features. The Advanced Sharing options look the same in Windows 11.

Windows Shadow Copy and Previous Versions

The Windows Shadow Copy feature automatically makes a copy of files that have changed and been saved. This feature allows a user to open an earlier version of a file using the Previous Versions feature. To restore a file using the Previous Versions feature, right-click the folder that held that file or the current version of that file and select **Properties** from the shortcut menu. Next, select the **Previous Versions** tab to view available versions of the file. Select the desired file and then click **Restore**. Windows Shadow Copy was first introduced in Windows Server 2003 and has been available in all Windows versions since Windows 7, although the features vary slightly from one version to another.

Windows ReadyBoost

Many software programs require a great deal of RAM to operate efficiently. Otherwise, the program responds slowly, may not work at all, or the system will seem to freeze up. Operating systems typically use the hard drive to store limited amounts of program information when the RAM is full. For example, a computer with 1 GB of RAM may use 500 kB of memory, referred to as a ***page file***, to store information temporarily. This keeps the program working reasonably well when the RAM is full. It should be noted, however, that the hard drive is notoriously slow when accessing and manipulating data compared to RAM.

Windows ReadyBoost is a great improvement to overall performance when a computer system is overworked. It allows a flash drive to store page files temporarily,

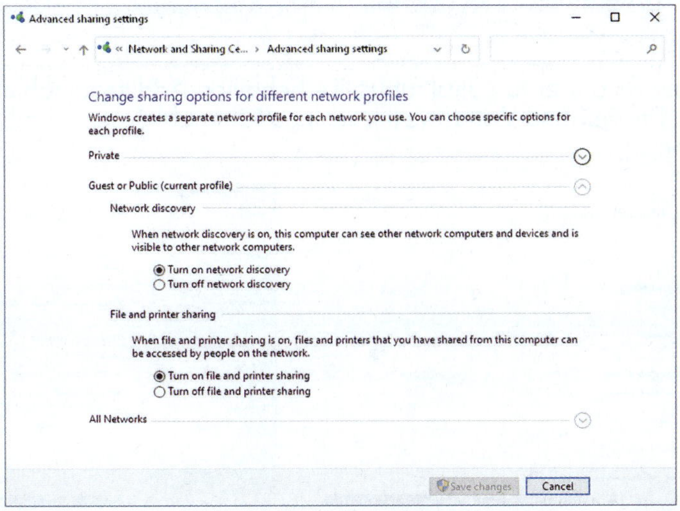

Goodheart-Willcox Publisher

Figure 2-17 Network Discovery can be accessed by selecting **Change advanced sharing settings** from the Network and Sharing Center in Windows 10.

which is faster because data on a flash drive can be accessed and manipulated much faster than data on a hard drive. Windows ReadyBoost is also an excellent feature for legacy laptops, which typically have much less memory than desktop computers.

Windows Defender

Windows Defender works directly with web browsers to protect the computer from spyware. Originally introduced to interface with Internet Explorer 7, it scans files as they are downloaded to the computer through the Internet browser, identifies what appears to be spyware, and allows the user to decide what action to take. The possible actions are ignore, allow, quarantine, and always allow. ***Quarantine*** isolates and stores the suspected spyware file, allowing the user to install it later if it is found not to be spyware. Windows Defender is fully integrated with the operating system for Windows 10 and works with Microsoft Edge, the replacement for Internet Explorer.

Tablet PC Settings

Tablet PC Settings were introduced in Windows XP Service Pack 2 (SP2), and they continue through Windows 10, albeit with some modifications. The enhancement to tablet settings that enabled touch screen entry was introduced in Windows Vista, enabling users to input commands with a finger or stylus and text with an on-screen keyboard. Windows 8 was designed primarily as an enhanced tablet mode GUI and eliminated the classic Windows desktop mode. This change was reverted for Windows 10, which integrates support for both desktop and tablet mode, giving the user the ability to easily transition between the two modes. Windows 10 also introduced touch screen gestures similar to keyboard shortcuts for touch screens.

Windows 10 tablet settings allow the user to adjust the tablet mode behavior, such as which mode to use by default and whether to ask when automatically switching tablet mode on or off. Figure 2-18A shows the **Tablet** settings menu. In Windows 10, touch screen and pen functionality are supported in both desktop and tablet mode so the settings for these features are no longer part of the tablet settings. Additional tablet settings are shown in Figure 2-18B. The settings to configure the pen and touch display and calibrate pen input now have their own menus under **Settings**. The menu for Pen and Windows Ink settings is shown in Figure 2-18C. There is also a calibration feature to convert handwriting into text associated with typing from a keyboard. After handwriting calibration is configured, handwriting can be converted to a typed document. Tablet devices commonly have their own configuration software application and may not use the Microsoft Windows version. Windows 10 has continued feature-rich support of tablet mode. These look essentially the same in Windows 11.

Figure 2-18 Windows 10 tablet mode (A) allows a user to adjust tablet-like behavior. Additional tablet settings (B) further customize the tablet mode experience. The Pen and Windows Ink settings (C) enable users to adjust features such as handwriting calibration and conversion.

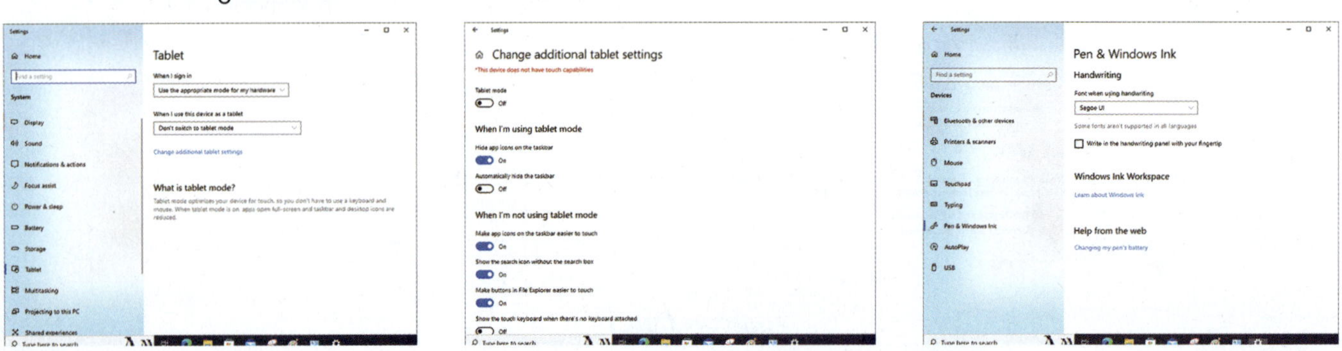

A B C

Goodheart-Willcox Publisher

Windows Services Manager

1102: 1.3 A+

Windows Services are applications that most often start when the computer is booted. They typically run in the background without the user having to interact with them. In Windows 10, the easiest way to access this menu is to enter services.msc into the **Run** dialog box. Once the Services menu opens, users can start, stop, or disable specific services.

Libraries

Libraries were introduced in Windows 7 as alternatives to the My Documents and Documents folders in older Windows operating systems. A *library* is a virtual container of user content, such as documents, music, and pictures, that can be located on the local computer, remote locations, and on external storage devices. Libraries serve as pointers to content that is stored in one central virtual storage location.

Libraries consist of four default folders: Documents, Music, Pictures, and Videos. Libraries are not the only way folders can be organized on Windows 7 and later computers, however. The Public folders, which were first introduced in Windows Vista, can also be used. Libraries are supported under Windows 10, but must first be enabled in File Explorer. To enable, open File Explorer and select **This PC**. Next, select **View**>**Navigation pane**>**Show libraries.** Once enabled, the four default library folders will appear, as shown in Figure 2-19.

BranchCache

BranchCache is a feature of Windows that allows remote, or branch, network users to download desired files to a central cache. When multiple users across a WAN are repeatedly requesting materials, the available bandwidth on the network decreases. BranchCache solves this by storing copies of the requested content, essentially creating a cache at the remote location. When other users from the same branch of the network request the same content, they receive information from the local cached data.

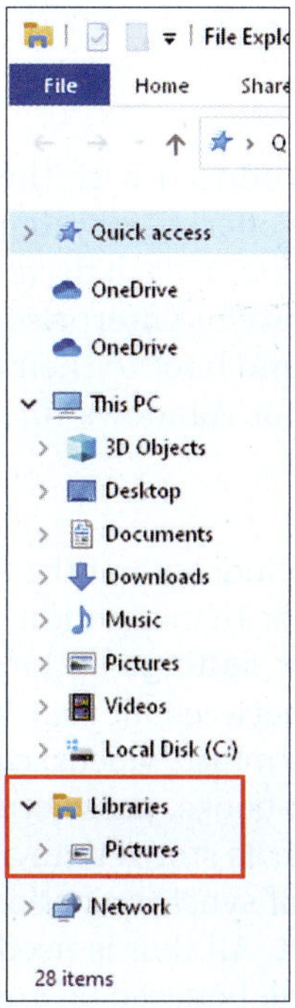

Goodheart-Willcox Publisher

Figure 2-19 To enable Libraries in Windows 10, open File Explorer and select **This PC**. Next, select **View>Navigation pane>Show libraries**.

A+ 1102: 1.3

Task Manager

Task Manager provides a resource for users to find detailed information about a computer's applications, processes, performance, networking statistics, and user data. Users can use Task Manager for a variety of reasons, including setting processor affinity, starting and stopping services, and forcibly ending processes, among others. Task Manager can be launched by searching task manager, or by using the [Ctrl][Shift][Esc] keyboard combination.

A+ 1102: 1.3

Task Scheduler

Task Scheduler is an administrative tool in Windows. As the name implies, it can be set to run tasks or programs at a future time. A common example of a task programs schedule for startup is to look for software or firmware updates. The easiest way to open Task Scheduler is to search task scheduler or enter taskschd.msc in the **Run** menu. Once open, you can view groups and subgroups that match the folder structure of a corresponding area in Explorer. Users can view information about each task, such as what triggers the task, the actions performed, history of this task's past actions, and related settings.

Microsoft User Account

There are two general user account types associated with Windows: the *Microsoft account* and the *local user account*. The Microsoft account is a combination of your e-mail address, such as Student1481@email.com, and a password. The local user account name is simply a username such as *Student1481* and a password. Any e-mail address can be used for the Microsoft account, not necessarily a Microsoft e-mail account. For example, you could use your Gmail account or the account provided by your Internet service provider without issue.

The Microsoft account is configured during installation of the operating system or creation of a user account. When you log on using your Microsoft account, you automatically connect to the Internet. If configured, you will also automatically connect to your e-mail account, Facebook, Twitter, LinkedIn, and an assortment of other accounts. When you log on using the local user account, you do not automatically connect to the Internet.

Windows To Go

Windows To Go was a feature introduced with the Windows 8 Enterprise edition that allowed a Windows Enterprise operating system and desired files and folders to run from a USB storage device, such as a flash drive or external hard drive. The idea is to allow technicians in a corporate or enterprise environment to plug their USB storage device into any computer and boot to their own personal computer configuration. This feature was retained for Windows 10.

A+ 1101: 1.4
1102: 2.10

Sync Your Settings

File synchronization is not new to Windows, but the **Sync your settings** option introduced in Windows 8 was redesigned with many additional features. The screen capture in Figure 2-20 shows the **Sync your settings** options in Windows 10. Notice the list of items that can be synchronized between all your Windows devices, including contacts, applications, e-mail, pictures, music, videos, calendar, bookmarks, documents, location data, social media data, e-books, passwords, and more. You can also synchronize your browser settings, such as stored data and sign-in details. This is a great improvement over earlier versions of synchronization because it requires little effort or technical skills on the user's part. All that is needed is for a user to log on with a Microsoft account so the settings will be saved on any of the Microsoft cloud services. This means that when you use a device that automatically connects to cloud services using your Microsoft account, your personal settings will match on each device.

Picture Password

Windows 8 introduced two authentication methods for logging on to a Windows 8 device. The new authentication methods were designed to better accommodate touch screen devices, such as tablets and phones, by authentication using either a PIN or picture. The PIN is a four-digit number created by the user. When using the picture authentication method, you first select a picture. Then you draw directly on the touch screen creating a combination of circles, straight lines, and taps locations. The size, direction, and location of your gestures become your picture password. Additionally, you can still log on to your PC using a standard password. Windows 10 retained the picture password method. To configure it, navigate to **Start>Settings>Accounts>Sign-in options** and scroll to the Picture password section. Selecting the **Add** button launches a wizard that walks you through the process of configuring a picture password.

Recovery, Restore, and Reset

Windows 8 changed the traditional System Recovery feature from previous versions of Windows by introducing two new wizards: **Refresh** and **Reset.** However, these features were replaced again in Windows 10 with options such as **Create a recovery drive**, **Open System Restore**, and **Configure System Restore**, as shown in Figure 2-21.

The recovery drive is used for major issues such as hardware failure. Creating a recovery drive is quite simple.

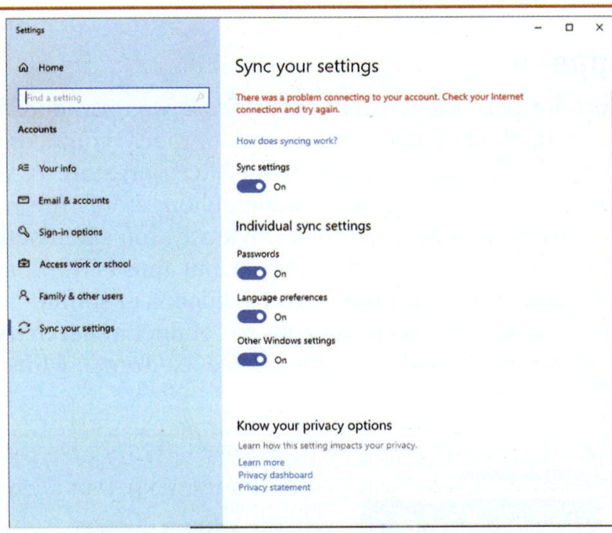

Goodheart-Willcox Publisher

Figure 2-20 The **Sync your settings** option enables a user to synchronize all their devices, including PCs and mobile devices.

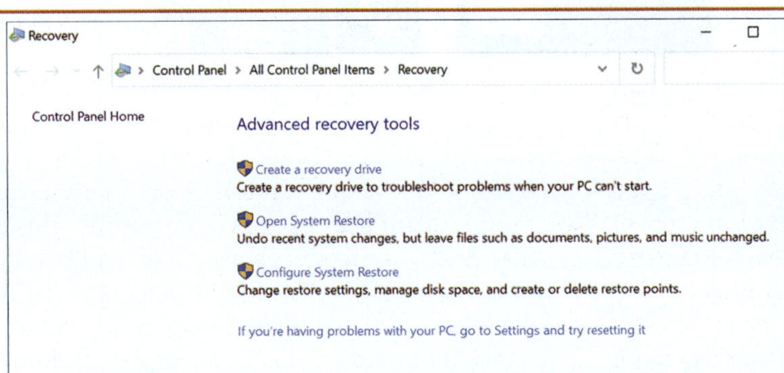

Goodheart-Willcox Publisher

Figure 2-21 Windows 10 Recovery options include **Create a recovery drive**, **Open System Restore**, and **Configure System Restore**. There is also a **Reset the PC** option in **Start>Settings>Update & Security>Recovery**.

- First, conduct a search using the phrase create a recovery drive, and select the appropriate option from the results list. You may have to run it as an administrator, enter an admin password, or confirm your choice, depending on your individual computer's settings.
- When the tool opens, be sure to choose the option that allows you to backup system files to the recovery drive before clicking **Next**.
- Connect a USB drive to your PC, select it, and click **Next**.

It should be noted that when creating a recovery drive, many files need to be copied, so it might take a while for the initial creation.

Resetting a PC can be accomplished from the recovery screen shown in Figure 2-21, or you can navigate to **Start**>**Settings**>**Update & Security**>**Recovery**>**Reset this PC**> **Get Started.** This will launch the **Reset the PC** wizard, which will allow you to keep your files, choose cloud or local storage, change settings, and set preinstalled apps.

The Windows 10 and Windows 11 System Restore is used to return to a previous restore point. Restore points are typically created when an app, patch, driver, update, or something similar has caused an issue.

A+ 1102: 1.5, 1.9

Personalization

Windows 10 and 11 both offer multiple ways to personalize your Windows experience. The easiest way to personalize is to right-click anywhere on the desktop and select **Personalize** from the shortcut menu. Once the **Personalization** menu opens, you can change the background, font size, and degree of zoom on the screen. You can also change language packs and other aesthetic settings such as themes and colors. The **Personalization** menu is shown in Figure 2-22.

A+ 1102: 1.5, 1.9

Windows Apps

The *Microsoft Store*, formerly known as *Windows Store*, was introduced with Windows 8 and is the primary method of distributing apps for the Windows operating system, as shown in Figure 2-23. The biggest change to the Microsoft Store for Windows 10 was its merger with the Xbox, Windows, and Windows Phone stores. It functions similarly to the Google Play store and Mac App Store. Obviously, you can install apps that you purchase at a store or download from the Internet, but apps in the Microsoft Store are vetted and far less likely to have any malware, backdoors, or similar issues.

The easiest method for downloading apps to conduct a search using the phrase Microsoft Store. Apps you already own are labeled as Owned, while available apps

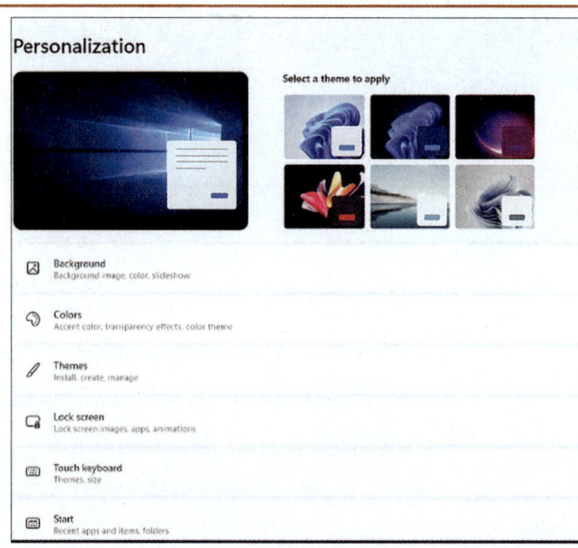

Figure 2-22 Windows offers a variety of ways for users to personalize their Windows experience.

Goodheart-Willcox Publisher

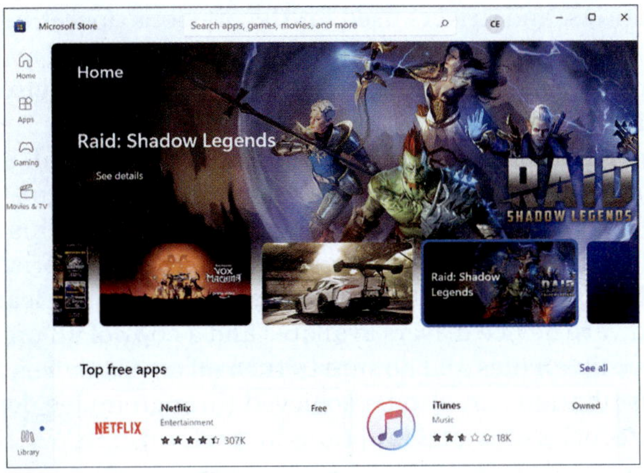

Goodheart-Willcox Publisher

Figure 2-23 The Microsoft Store is the primary method of app distribution for the Windows operating system.

are labeled by price (or as Free). Notice there are app categories, such as **Gaming** and **Movies & TV**.

1102: 1.5 A+

Microsoft-brand games can be purchased and installed from the **Gaming** category and optimized through the **Gaming** setting (**Start>Settings>Gaming**), which allows users to enable options such as screenshots, recording, turning microphone on and off, broadcasting, and whether to show or hide the camera during a broadcast.

The **Apps & features** menu (**Start>Settings>Apps**) functions similarly to the **Programs and Features** menu in Control Panel. The main difference between the two is that uninstalling or changing a program is in a separate menu than establishing default programs in Control Panel, whereas the **Apps & features** menu includes both options on one screen.

Devices

1102: 1.5, 1.9 A+

The **Devices** menu (**Start>Settings>Devices**) enables a user to configure peripherals such as Bluetooth devices, printers, scanners, mice, touchpads, keyboards, digitizer pads, and USB devices. This menu also allows users to adjust AutoPlay settings. In many cases, the options are not as robust as if you were adjusting settings through Device Manager or Control Panel, but it is arguably more convenient, as most devices appear in one place.

2.4 Microsoft Windows Installation

1102: 1.1, 1.9 A+

When installing Windows, you can perform an upgrade or a clean install. An *upgrade* means that you can install Windows on an existing operating system and retain files, settings, and applications. A *clean install* means that either there was no OS on the hardware, or you are completely relacing the previous installation and overwriting all files, settings, and applications. Similar to clean installations are *repair installations*, which use various installation media to overwrite an existing operating system that has become corrupt or damaged. The main difference between a clean install and a repair install is that repair installations keep applications, user files, and settings. Microsoft uses the term *custom* to refer to a clean install on top of an existing Windows partition. Before performing a clean install or custom installation, you must back up all data. After the installation process, the data can be restored to the system.

Sometimes, upgrading from a previous version of a Windows operating system to a newer version requires a clean install, such as when upgrading to Windows 10 from a system already running Windows 7, 8, or 8.1. For all older versions of Windows, one would need to do a custom install, which wipes out all data on the hard drive, and perform a clean installation of Windows 10. Be aware that hardware,

A+ 1102: 1.9

software applications, and drivers used for the previous operating system may not be supported in a newer version of Windows. Before performing an upgrade or clean install, it is always a good idea to run the Windows Upgrade Advisor to ensure compatibility, especially on older hardware.

It is recommended that in most cases, you do a clean install after partitioning and reformatting the hard drive. This will eliminate any file fragments and most registry corruption from the previous operating system version. This also provides an opportunity to format the hard drive properly with the appropriate partitions and formatting needed for your installation. Before you perform a clean install, be sure you have all hardware device drivers available and a copy of all previously installed applications. Back up all files and be sure to turn off any antivirus programs.

Windows installation can also be achieved through image deployment, which refers to three categories of available options for performing a Windows installation:

1. *Modern deployment* is the preferred method for enterprise management using Windows autopilot to install OS and applications or using Windows Setup to do an *in-place upgrade*. This method supports using enterprise tools such as Microsoft Deployment Toolkit and System Center Configuration Manager.
2. *Dynamic deployment* methods provide tools to customize the OS installation for a specific purpose like mobile devices using either subscription activation, Active Directory and Mobile Device Management (MDM), or Windows Imaging and Configuration Designer tool with provisioning packages.
3. *Traditional deployment* methods use standard tools and methods to deploy operating system images.

There will be much more about disk images and image deployment in a later chapter.

Tech Tip

Always back up the entire computer before performing an upgrade or custom install. Anything might go wrong. Without a complete backup, you may not be able to restore the system files or data files.

A+ 1102: 1.1, 1.9

Windows Upgrade

If one is still using Windows 8.1, there are specific upgrade paths to Windows 10, as shown in Figure 2-24. Upgrading from Windows 10 to Windows 11 is typically much easier, provided the system meets the minimum requirements. In many cases, Windows will notify you if your device can be upgraded, but you can also conduct a manual search through the Windows Update tool by navigating to **Start**>**Settings**>**Update & Security**>**Windows Update**>**Check for updates**. If the computer is Windows 11-ready, a message will appear on screen, as shown in Figure 2-25. The minimum requirements for Windows 11 are

- a dual-core 1-Ghz or faster processor;
- 4 GB RAM;
- 64 GB storage;
- UEFI Secure Boot capabilities;
- Trusted Platform Module 2.0; and
- a graphics card compatible with Direct X 12 or later.

Figure 2-24 Windows 8 has specific upgrade paths to Windows 10.

Upgrade Paths from Windows 8 to Windows 10

Windows 8 Edition	Windows 10 Home	Windows 10 Pro	Windows 10 Pro Education	Windows 10 Education	Windows 10 Enterprise
Core	✓	✓	✓	✓	✓
Connected	✓	✓	✓	✓	✓
Pro	–	✓	✓	✓	✓
Pro Student	–	✓	✓	✓	✓

Goodheart-Willcox Publisher

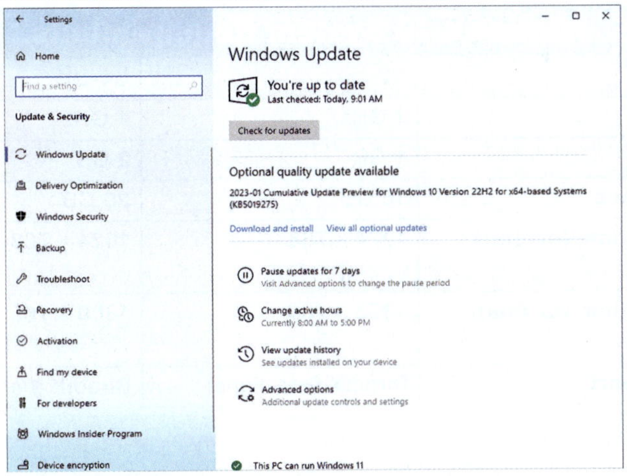

Goodheart-Willcox Publisher

Figure 2-25 The Windows Update utility is a good tool for determining whether a Windows 10 computer is capable of installing and running Windows 11.

Additionally, if you wish to use Client Hyper-V, then the PC needs a processor with second-level address translation (SLAT) capabilities (available in Windows Pro and above editions).

When contemplating a PC, it is best to bear in mind that minimum requirements are precisely that: the minimum for the machine to be able to boot up. These are not ideal parameters. For performance reasons, it is best to have 8 GB RAM and of course when it comes to storage, more is almost always better.

Windows Versions and Editions

1102: 1.1, 1.7 A+

Not every copy of Microsoft Windows is the same. Windows is available in different versions and editions. A *version* of Windows most often refers to the major operating system releases, such as Windows 10, and an *edition* is a specific type of version, such as Home, Pro, and Enterprise. You can think of versions and editions like makes and models of vehicles. The brand, or make, of the vehicle is equal to a Windows version, and the model of the vehicle is equal to a Windows edition. Every version of Windows has various editions and requirements unique to itself. This section will discuss the differences among editions.

Windows 10 Editions

1102: 1.1 A+

Windows 10 is available in 12 different editions, each with various features and intended usage. Baseline editions of Windows 10 include Home, Pro, and Pro for Workstations, all of which have gone through multiple release versions. With each release update, the OS changes in a variety of ways. For example, in release version 1803, HomeGroup was replaced with a new feature called Nearby Sharing. This can make it difficult to stay up to date on features and requirements. Windows 10 is also available in organizational editions, including Education, Pro Education, Enterprise, and Enterprise Long-Term Servicing Channel, as well as device-specific editions, such as IoT and Team. Figure 2-26 lists the Windows 10 minimum system requirements.

A+ Note

The A+ Exams often ask questions requiring you to match which operating system edition can be upgraded to another. Be sure you can answer those types of questions.

Windows 11 Editions

Windows 11 is available in two editions:

- Home edition is intended for consumer users.
- Pro edition contains additional networking and security features (such as BitLocker), as well as the ability to join a domain.

To learn more about any particular operating system, visit the Microsoft website or conduct a search using the key terms Microsoft features followed by the name of the edition, such as Windows 10 Home.

Figure 2-26 Windows 10 requirements are the same as those for Windows 8, making for an easy upgrade.

Windows 10 System Requirements		
Hardware	**32-bit**	**64-bit**
CPU	1 GHz	1 GHz
RAM	1 GB	2 GB
Hard drive space	16 GB	20 GB
Screen resolution, for Start interface	1024 × 768	1024 × 768
Screen resolution, for Snap feature	1366 × 768	1366 × 768
Graphics support	DirectX 9 or higher	DirectX 9 or higher

Goodheart-Willcox Publisher

Windows Easy Transfer

Windows Easy Transfer tool is designed to assist during a custom install to back up and transfer user accounts, files, and settings to a USB storage drive, similar to performing a backup. Then, after performing a custom install, use Windows Easy Transfer tool to reinstall the files and settings to the new operating system. You can also use this tool to transfer data from an old computer to a new computer. Windows Easy Transfer was available for Windows 7, 8, and 8.1, but support was not continued in Windows 10. Windows 10 users will instead need to use a third-party tool to replicate the functionality of Windows Easy Transfer.

Tech Tip

When possible, always use the latest version of WinPE to deploy Windows.

Windows PE

Windows Pre-installation Environment (WinPE) is a minimal 32-bit Windows operating system that prepares a disk storage system before the complete operating system is installed. In addition, Windows PE supports CD, DVD, and USB flash drives, all of which may be required for the complete operating system installation. Windows PE supports the Remote Installation Services (RIS), which allows an operating system to be installed from across a network. Windows PE is part of the Windows installation program when performing a complete installation from a Windows DVD.

The latest version at the time of this writing is based in the Windows 10 environment, in which Windows PE functions as a small operating system used to install, deploy, and repair Windows 10 for Home, Pro, Enterprise, and Education editions. It can also be used for Windows Server and other Windows operating systems.

In addition to preparing a computer for operating system installation, Windows PE can be used to recover a failed computer or for troubleshooting purposes. Windows PE is part of the *Windows Automated Installation Kit (WAIK)*, which is a set of installation tools available for free download from the Microsoft Support website. The tools included in the WAIK allow a computer technician to create disk images, deploy operating systems automatically to computers that have no operating systems, manage existing systems by automatically installing new device drivers, and create a Windows Pre-installation Environment on a disk or flash memory device.

2.5 Microsoft Windows Boot Sequences

This section serves as an introduction to the Windows boot sequence. A **boot sequence** is the step-by-step process of bringing a computer to an operational state. This involves a combination of hardware and software control to initialize hardware and load operating system files. An in-depth understanding of boot sequences is essential to troubleshooting startup problems, and a more detailed description is presented in a later chapter.

Warm and Cold Booting

When the boot sequence is initiated, it is called *booting the computer.* There are two styles of booting a computer: cold boot and warm boot. A **cold boot**, also called a *hard boot,* means that the electrical power switch is used to turn on the computer. A **warm boot**, or *soft boot,* is used to restart a computer that is already running. A warm boot can be initiated by a software program as part of a typical installation, such as installing a game; by using the [Ctrl][Alt][Delete] keyboard combination; or by selecting **Start**>**Power**>**Restart**, as shown in Figure 2-27.

POST

All operating systems start with a power-on self-test. The **power-on self-test (POST)** is a simple diagnostic program that is initiated when electrical power is applied to the computer system. It is common to all operating systems, including macOS and Linux. The POST does a quick system check to determine if all major hardware components, such as the CPU, RAM, keyboard, mouse, video system, and storage devices, are in proper working order. The devices checked may vary slightly from computer to computer depending on the firmware.

The test it performs is not as sophisticated as diagnostic software, but it will check for major problems. When the POST is finished, it usually makes one "beep" sound to let you know that the POST is complete, and everything is in working order. If an error is detected during the POST, an error code is usually displayed on the screen and a series of beeps is heard that match the code. The codes and beep pattern vary according to the different BIOS or UEFI chip manufacturers, and a list of error codes and beep codes can often be obtained from the website of the manufacturer.

A+ Note

The A+ Certification Exams usually stress knowledge of the boot sequence. When answering questions about boot sequences, remember that Windows 10 uses the Windows Boot Loader file, **winload.exe**, not the legacy ntldr. Exercises in the accompanying Lab Manual will help you understand the boot process better.

BIOS

1101: 3.4 A+

In a BIOS-based system, the POST is initiated by the bootstrap program in the firmware. The *bootstrap program* is a short program that runs the POST, searches for the Master Boot Record (MBR)—typically located on the first section of the hard drive, loads into

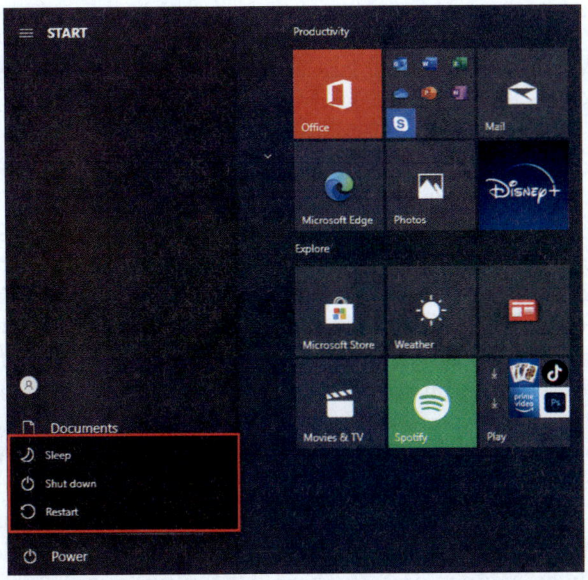

Goodheart-Willcox Publisher

Figure 2-27 The **Restart** command can be used to perform a warm boot.

memory some basic files, and turns the boot operation over to the operating system. The word *bootstrap* comes from the expression "to pull oneself up by one's bootstraps."

A+ 1101: 3.4

UEFI

The boot sequence is slightly different for a computer equipped with UEFI or EFI. The Unified Extensible Firmware Interface (UEFI) is a modern approach to the BIOS system and an enhancement to the boot process. When a device equipped with UEFI completes POST, control is turned over to a built-in boot manager program rather than the MBR, which contains the bootstrap program. The UEFI firmware uses an improved hard drive technology known as the GUID partition table. There will be more about UEFI and GUID later in this textbook when you have a better understanding of data storage and system files.

Some computers have a UEFI boot manager and an MBR to ensure backward compatibility with devices and software that require BIOS firmware. The UEFI firmware directly supports BIOS features using a compatibility support module (CSM), which is programmed into the UEFI. The CSM emulates the BIOS features. For example, when a computer system that has BIOS firmware is upgraded to a new operating system that uses UEFI firmware and supports the GUID partition table, the UEFI technology will use CSM to support a BIOS MBR partition. This way, backward compatibility is maintained. Windows operating systems began support for EFI and UEFI with the release of Windows Vista. Windows operating systems must be 64-bit versions to use UEFI.

Windows 8 was designed with a secure boot sequence to prevent malware and unauthorized changes to the operating system. By default, Windows 8 installed the boot sequence for the use of UEFI firmware. Windows 8 had the ability to run on computers designed with BIOS, but some of the security features would not be installed because BIOS could not implement these features. UEFI firmware protected the computer before the start of the Windows 8 operating system by allowing an antimalware program to begin before the operating system starts. The early start of antimalware software helped to prevent attacks on the computer before the operating system was loaded. Also, Windows 8 only allowed the installation of Microsoft preapproved software applications to prevent malware applications from altering or damaging the system configuration. There will be much more about UEFI protection in later chapters.

Tech Tip

Because the term *BIOS* is so ingrained in computer technician jargon, it will still be used for many years to represent the correct terms *firmware* and *UEFI*. Although not technically accurate, this is the way technical language commonly evolves. You will often encounter terms that are not always correct when reading resource materials and talking to other technicians.

Boot Sequences by Version

After the Windows 10 POST completes, the firmware boot loader boots the UEFI instead of using the BIOS, which shortens boot times and supports more options than BIOS such as loading OEM UEFI applications.

The next phase for Windows 10 and Windows 11 is the Windows Boot Manager phase, during which the Windows Boot Manager (bootmgr) reads a registry-type file called the Boot Configuration Data (BCD) file. The BCD file stores boot configuration information, such as the names of the operating systems to list in a boot menu, the amount of time the boot menu should be displayed while waiting for user input, and the default operating system to load if no user input is entered.

The Windows Boot Manager (bootmgr) replaces **bootcfg.exe** used by older Windows NT-based operating systems. The Windows Boot Manager will not display a selection of operating systems if there is only one operating system on the computer, but if there are two or more operating systems, the Windows Boot Manager appears for approximately 30 seconds to allow the user to select which operating system to boot. If no selection is made, the default operating system is started.

When the Windows Boot Manager phase completes, the Windows Boot Loader (**winload.exe**) phase begins. First, the kernel (**ntoskrnl.exe**) is loaded into memory but is not executed. The **hal.dll** file and registry data are also loaded into memory. The Windows Boot Loader phase ends by executing the kernel and beginning the kernel-loading phase.

In this phase, the kernel starts the Session Manager (**smss.exe**), which creates the system environment. Up until now, the operating system has been in a text-based mode; however, with **smss.exe** loaded, the operating system switches to graphic mode by loading the GUI. It is at this point that the familiar progress bar appears at the bottom of the screen.

The kernel interacts with **hal.dll** and the registry information in memory to load hardware drivers and other files necessary to complete the boot operation. The last phase in the boot sequence is the logon phase, which is initiated by the loading of the Logon Manager (**winlogon.exe**). After a successful user logon, the desktop appears, and the user can start using the various software applications.

Certain files are automatically loaded into RAM after a successful user logon. These files are generally referred to as *startup programs*. They will start quickly after they are selected from the **Start** menu or from a shortcut icon because they are already loaded into RAM. If a program is not a startup program, it will need to be loaded to RAM before it starts, thus causing a short delay in program response when selected. The following steps detail the Windows 10 and Windows 11 boot sequences:

For Windows 10 and 11

1. Firmware performs the POST.
2. Firmware boot loaders bootstrap the UEFI environment (think mini-OS).
3. Run any SoC vendor, Microsoft, or OEMs UEFI-level applications.
4. UEFI finds the boot location via the GUID partition table (GPT).
5. UEFI launches the Windows Boot Manager (bootmgr).

Common Steps for Windows 10 and 11

1. Windows Boot Manager reads the BCD file and displays the boot menu.
2. Windows Boot Manager starts the Windows Boot Loader (**winload.exe**) when Windows 10 or Windows 11 is selected or if started automatically.
3. The Windows Boot Manager loads **ntoskrnl.exe** and **hal.dll** into memory and scans the registry for device drivers to load. It then passes control to the kernel.
4. The kernel loads the device drivers and **hal.dll** and initializes the computer settings using the values stored in the system registry.
5. The kernel starts the Session Manager (**smss.exe**), which creates the system environment.
6. The operating system switches to graphics mode and the **winlogon.exe** file is loaded, thus starting the Logon Manager (**winlogon.exe**).
7. The Logon Manager allows the user to begin the logon process.

Dual-Boot and Multiple-Boot Systems

When two operating systems are installed on a single computer, it is referred to as a **dual-boot system**. For example, Windows 10 and Windows 11 can both be installed on the same computer, resulting in a dual-boot configuration. The Windows Boot Manager or a third-party boot loader such as GRUB allows the user to select which operating system to start. If no selection is made, the default operating system will start.

You could also configure a **multiple-boot system**, also known as a *multiboot system*, which contains more than two operating systems. For example, you could have Windows 8, Windows 10, and Windows 11 installed on the same computer. You could also add a non-Microsoft operating system, such as Linux.

Tech Tip

You can create a dual-boot system with Windows 10 by making a spare partition on your system drive and loading it with any legacy versions of Windows, such as Windows 7, Windows 8, or Windows 8.1.

Virtual Machine

When a computer is configured as a dual-boot or multiple-boot system, you can only run one operating system at a time. However, a virtual machine can be created using a special software application that allows more than one operating system to run at the same time. A computer that runs two operating systems at the same time is referred to as a **virtual machine** or *virtual PC*. The Microsoft application for creating a virtual machine is called *Windows Virtual PC*. There are also third-party vendors that market virtual machines, such as *VMware* and *VirtualBox*.

When two operating systems are running at the same time, they must share the CPU and RAM. Sharing the CPU and RAM negatively impacts computer performance when compared to a dual-boot or multiple-boot system.

A+ 1102: 1.8, 1.10

2.6 Apple Macintosh OS

MacOS is the operating system developed by Apple, Inc. to run on their Macintosh line of computer systems. A major change that Apple made to macOS was in the Mojave release, which included a redesigned App Store and a *dark mode* feature, which was an inverse of the classic white background in the GUI. Generally, the macOS system includes many popular applications from Apple's mobile operating system, iOS.

The current version is macOS Ventura, which was released in October 2022. MacOS Ventura added new apps and features, including a standalone weather app. Prior to this, the weather app in macOS directed to the Weather Channel website. There is also a whiteboard app named Freeform, which is used for collaboration. There is also an app named Stage Manager used for organizing windows on the desktop. In addition to new apps, some existing features have been improved. As one prominent example, FaceTime now allows a user to hand off FaceTime calls between Apple devices. For example, a user running FaceTime on a MacBook can now hand the conversation off to their iPhone to continue it on the go.

A+ 1102: 1.10

Regardless of which version of MacOS you are using, the Apple ID is key. The *Apple ID* is how you access iCloud, App Store, iMessage, and the Find My app. This is the key to any user account in the Macintosh world. A corporate version, called *Managed Apple IDs*, is used in business settings and is unique to each company. Professionals can associate a Managed Apple ID with their personal phone number and e-mail address, but IT administrators from their workplace are able to manage the services accessible by a Managed Apple ID. Managed IDs typically include the phrase appleid in the company e-mail address. For example, an employee at XYZ Corporation with a Managed Apple ID may have an e-mail address such as firstnamelastname@appleid.xyzcorp.com.

A+ 1102: 1.10

The iCloud storage drive is more important with each version of macOS and iOS. Apple introduced iCloud in 2011 as a straightforward, cloud storage service and has continued to expand it. There are now multiple services tied to iCloud, including iCloud photos, iWork, and iCloud drive. Additionally, data, including e-mail, and messages, among other types, can be synchronized across devices using iCloud and the user's Apple ID. An example of data that can be synchronized is files associated with the iWork suite of office applications, which includes the presentation application Keynote, the word- and desktop-publishing application Pages, and the spreadsheet application Numbers.

To understand the feature set behind macOS, one should look at the history of the company. In 1996, Apple purchased a second computer company called Next Computer, which was also founded by Steve Jobs. That purchase included rights to the Next operating system known as NextSTEP.

MacOS is derived from NextSTEP, which itself was based off the Mach kernel from CMU and the Berkeley Software Distribution (BSD) of the Unix operating system. NextSTEP is also the foundation for the operating systems that run other Apple devices such as iOS and watchOS. Because of the common code base behind all of its operating systems, Apple can provide a high level of integration among their various families of products.

Macintosh computers tend to have a higher price point than standard, Windows-based PCs, but they tend to have more advanced features when it comes to creative work. Often, Macs are not found in traditional office-type work environments, but they are used almost exclusively in industries that fit their creative features, such as graphic design and video production.

System Preferences

A+ 1102: 1.10

System Preferences, more commonly called System Settings, is the main configuration menu for macOS. It is launched by either selecting the **Settings** icon from the Dock or by opening the Apple menu and selecting **System Settings**. Once open, you will be able to configure a variety of aspects, including your displays, network, printers and scanners, privacy settings, and accessibility settings, among others.

Displays

When selected from the System Settings pane, the **Display** page provides insight into how items appear on the screen. You can choose which display to use, as well as adjust how large text appears. You can also adjust the brightness of the screen as well as toggle True Tone on or off. For those familiar with the **Night Shift** feature in iOS and iPadOS, the **Display** page allows macOS users to establish a similar schedule. When Night Shift is set to turn on, the screen colors will automatically shift to the warmer end of the color spectrum to help you get more restful sleep.

Networks

The **Network** page provides an overview of network connects and firewall settings, similar to the Windows **Network and Sharing Center** and **Network & Internet** screens. From here, users can connect to a wireless network, establish firewall options, and manage services such as VPNs and USB docks.

Printers & Scanners

The **Printers & Scanners** page provides just what the name suggests: options for configuring printers and scanners. Available options include connecting and establishing default devices as well as setting a default paper size. Users can also open specific devices to customize that device's settings further, for example updating drivers, sharing a device, and even ordering supplies.

Privacy & Security

The **Privacy & Security** page lists various apps and utilities installed on a Mac and informs the user as to which apps have requested access to it. For example, users will commonly see their calendars or contacts in the Privacy portion of this window. When a user selects on of them, a window will open that lists the apps that have requested access to the user's contacts or calendar. The Security portion of the window enables users to establish security settings, such as from where applications can be downloaded, access to FileVault, and whether they want to activate **Lockdown Mode**, which locks out much of the computer so it operates in an extremely limited mode.

Accessibility

The **Accessibility** page offers accessibility options. It is organized into four areas:

- Vision provides options for those with vision issues. Options include screen readers, zoom options, descriptive audio, and a shortcut to the **Display** page.
- Hearing provides options for those who are hard of hearing. These options include real-time text (RTT) for phone calls, captions for streaming media, live captions for live TV, and a shortcut to the **Audio** page.
- Motor provides options for those with physical difficulty working on a computer. These options include voice control, pointer control, switch control, and a shortcut to the **Keyboard** page.
- General provides options for Apple's virtual assistant, Siri, as well as the location where accessibility shortcuts can be toggled on or off.

This is fundamentally the same as the Ease of Access menu in Windows.

A+ 1102: 1.10

Tools and Features

It is common for operating system vendors to load their products with unique and practical tools and features, and Apple is no exception. Just like with Windows, Macintosh computers come with a variety of proprietary tools and features. Some tools are simply renamed versions of utilities encountered in other operating systems. For example, Macintosh's Force Quit is fundamentally the same as Linux's **kill** command or Microsoft's **End Task** button. However, Macintosh computers also have a number of tools that are unique to the macOS environment. Examples of these tools and features include the App Store, Boot Camp, screen sharing, Spotlight, Quick Look, and other cross-platform programs. Additional examples of features are listed in Figure 2-28.

A+ 1102: 1.10

Tech Tip

Users of macOS can use the Force Quit feature to close unresponsive apps. To use Force Quit, open the Apple menu, and select Force Quit from the list of options. This opens the **Force Quit Applications** window, in which you should select the app you want to close before selecting **Force Quit**. If you want to close multiple apps, hold the [Command] key while selecting them. You will then be prompted to confirm by selecting **Force Quit** again. The keyboard shortcut used to open the **Force Quit Applications** window is [Option][Command][Esc].

A+ 1102: 1.10

App Store

Similar to the Microsoft Store, Apple's App Store is an app marketplace from which users can download apps that have already been vetted and confirmed to be compatible with Apple devices. Accessible from macOS, iOS, and iPadOS, the App Store also provides lists of trending downloads and most popular downloads. In most cases, the App Store appears as a default application on Apple devices. Once a user signs in using their Apple ID, they can purchase and download applications. Important app updates are also pushed through the App Store.

A+ 1102: 1.10

Installing apps on macOS is relatively simple. For apps you have downloaded from the Internet, simply open the **Downloads** folder and double-click the disk image or package file, which should look like an open box. If the app is on a disc, then insert the disc (or USB drive) and look for the image or package. Apple's macOS supports three types of images to install: **.dmg**, **.pkg**, and **.app**. DMG files are containers for apps in macOS. You open them, drag the app to your **Applications** folder, and then eject them. PKG files, as the file extension suggests, are packages containing all that a given app will need to execute. APP files are simply applications. Each of these

Common macOS Features	
Feature Name	**Description**
Spaces	Allows users to create multiple virtual desktops; was moved to Mission Control in 2011
Mission Control	Suite of three separate features: • *Dashboard* provides accommodation of widgets, which are simple applications that launch quickly and do not consume much memory. • *Exposé* allows users to view all windows in use by a given app or switch between recently opened documents, windows, or apps. • *Spaces* provides the ability to create multiple virtual desktops.
Keychain	Password-management system that stores and synchronizes passwords, private keys, certificates, and secure notes
Gestures	Provides touch screen-like functionality to a trackpad; depending on the number of fingers used and motion on the trackpad, users can scroll, click, right-click, zoom, drag, swipe, rotate, show the desktop and access Mission Control, among other options
Finder	Default file manager and GUI shell of macOS; similar to Windows File Explore
Remote Disc	Allows the user to access a CD or DVD installed in a separate computer on the same network
Dock	Apple equivalent of the Windows Taskbar

Goodheart-Willcox Publisher

Figure 2-28 Apple's macOS comes with a variety of features and tools. Many are similar to the features and tools found in Windows, but some are exclusive and unique to macOS.

file extensions allows you to install apps on macOS; however, the **.dmg** files are the most common. To uninstall an app, use the **Finder** icon to find that app. If it is in a folder, you can look to see if there is an uninstall app in that folder, which is common with professionally developed apps. You can also simply drag that app to the **Trash**. It should be noted, however, that dragging an app to the Trash may not remove all supporting files, so uninstalling, if available, is the best option.

Installing Windows Operating System via Boot Camp

Windows operating systems allow users to partition their hard drives; however, users who are operating macOS will likely need to create a *parallel*, which serves the same purpose as a partition in a Windows operating system. Once a user has created a parallel, they will be able to install Boot Camp, which is used to install a Windows operating system on their Macintosh personal computer.

Sharing Screens and Files

Users may share their screen and files to other users, similar to a Windows operating system feature. If a user wants to share screens, files, or allow other users to control his or her machine, the user may do so by selecting the specified user from his or her contacts list and providing the permission(s) to obtain access to the user's machine. This requires that the user and the contact who is being granted access both use macOS. However, a user may also share files only by utilizing share discs. The share disc, or *Remote Disc*, must have one user's files and settings sent to a USB, CD, or DVD, which is then installed onto the other user's Macintosh personal computer. In the event a user wants to use more than one screen, he or she may utilize the Mission Control feature to do so.

A+ 1102: 1.10

Searching with Spotlight

The macOS Search with Spotlight feature allows users to search for current news, sports, weather, or files. This operation can be completed by selecting the magnifying glass icon in the upper-right corner of the menu bar or pressing [Command][Spacebar] on the keyboard. When the Spotlight tool opens, users may input what they are searching for, and the tool will search for the inserted content request and present itself in the **Finder** utility.

Macintosh Quick Look

The Quick Look feature was first added to Mac OS X Leopard (version 10.5). It allows the user to preview a file without opening it. Quick Look previews files such as HTML, videos, PDFs, and Office documents, among others. There are several ways to launch Quick Look, including selecting a file and using keyboard shortcuts such as [command][Y], [space bar], and [option][space bar] and text-based commands such as qlmanage -p *filename*.

A+ 1102: 1.10

Disk Utility

Similar to the Disk Management utility in Windows, Apple's Disk Utility performs various tasks associated with the primary storage device in a macOS installation. Disk Utility is most commonly used for

- creating, converting, and backing up disk images;
- mounting, unmounting, and ejecting storage devices;
- enabling or disabling journaling;
- verifying disk integrity and repairing damaged disks;
- erasing, formatting, or portioning disks;
- secure erasure of data;
- manipulating the partition table;
- restoring disks via images; and
- checking the S.M.A.R.T status of a disk.

Disk Utility can be accessed by the macOS GUI, but it also can be launched through the **diskutil** and **hdiutil** commands.

A+ 1102: 1.10

FileVault

FileVault is a disk encryption program in macOS similar to the Windows BitLocker utility. Originally introduced in Mac OS X Panther (version 10.3), FileVault uses XTS-AES-128 encryption with a 256-bit key to encrypt the hard disk. It also provides a master password and recovery keys for forgotten passwords. FileVault can be accessed by launching the Apple menu and selecting **System Settings**>**Privacy & Security**>**FileVault**.

A+ 1102: 1.10

Terminal

Terminal is the macOS equivalent of Windows Command Prompt. It provides a command-line interface for macOS users. Each window opened in Terminal is an individual instance of a shell process. It can be launched in one of two ways:

- Select the Launchpad icon from the Dock and conduct a search using the keyword Terminal
- Open the Finder; then navigate to **Applications/Utilities**>**Terminal**

In the event you wish to close one shell process, open the window running the process you want to quit and execute the **exit** command. This closes all commands issued in this specific shell. In the event any commands are still running, a dialog box will appear prompting the user to confirm they want to quit.

Cross-Platform Tools and Features

Additional tools and features allow macOS users to understand the functionality of all Macintosh personal computer hardware. For example, Mac-based laptops, called *MacBooks*, have multi-touch gestures that are the same across all platforms and generations. This means the default settings of the touchpad are the same and will perform the same functions regardless of the generation of the hardware or software of the MacBook. Similar to this hardware feature, most versions of macOS have virtual docking stations to connect peripherals and have cross-platform software such as iCloud to save your settings and files. Another cross-platform feature is Keychain, which saves all a user's passwords across all Apple or Macintosh devices.

Updating macOS

1102: 1.9 A+

One common way to update the macOS is through **System Settings**. Navigate to **System Settings>General>Software Update** to open the **Software Update Pane**, which will automatically check for updates. In versions of macOS before OS X version 10.8), there was a separate application that performed updating, but that was merged into the App Store application with the release of Mountain Lion. The Software Update utility has been the primary updating tool since the release of macOS Mojave (version 10.14). For those who prefer command-line terminals, the **softwareupdate** command can also be employed to update the computer system.

2.7 Linux OS

1102: 1.8 A+

Linux is an open-source Unix-like operating system developed originally by Linus Torvalds. Similar to the different versions of Windows, Linux exists in variations called *distributions*, or *distros*. Information about most distributions can be found on the DistroWatch website, which is a website dedicated to discussing, reviewing, and providing information about open-source operating systems, including links and lists of the most popular distributions. The list of the most popular distributions typically includes Mint, Fedora, Ubuntu, and Debian Linux.

Directories

The Linux operating system, regardless of the distribution, has common directories with which you should be familiar. These directories include the following.

- The /root directory is the home directory for the root user, which is the administrator in Linux and Unix systems. This is a rather important directory because it represents the path to all data and files stored on that partition.
- The /bin directory holds binary or compiled files. For this reason, you will find many programs in this directory.
- The /etc folder contains configuration files. Most applications require configuration when they start up, and those configuration files will be found in this directory.
- The /usr directory contains all the subdirectories, and thus all the files, for all users on the system. Each user has their own sub-directory in this directory.
- The /var directory contains data that is changed when the system is running normally. This will usually include log files.

A+ 1102: 1.11

Linux Command Line

In Linux, the command line is referred to as a *shell*. Commands are executed, similarly to what you saw in the Windows command line. As with Windows commands, Linux commands have a variety of flags, which can be found by appending a given command with **-?** or **/?**. Alternatively, you can use the **man** command followed by the command for which you desire more information. For example, if you want to know more details about the **ps** command, you can enter man ps. The **man** command launches the manual and will display details about the requested command. In addition to those listed in Figure 2-4, additional basic commands are described in the following.

- The **ls** command lists the contests of the current directory. This is similar to the Windows **dir** command.
- The **cd** command is used to move father up or down the directory tree, very much like the **cd** command in Windows. When followed by a tilde (cd ~), the command changes the active directory to the root directory. When followed by two periods (cd ..), the command changes the directory by moving one level up.
- The **dd** command, following by a directory name, changes the active directory to whatever is specified in the command syntax. For example, dd usr changes the active directory to the user directory.
- The **ps** command is used to list processes that belong to the current user and have a controlling terminal. One of the flags for the **ps** command is **-e**. When executed, the **ps -e** command displays all processes on the system regardless of user or terminal. The **pstree** command shows processes listed in tree fashion.
- The **mkdir** command is used to create directories, and **rmdir** is used to remove them. These function similarly to the Windows **md** and **rd** commands.

Graphical User Interface

While Linux users tend to rely on the command line/shell much more frequently than Windows users, Linux does provide a graphical user interface. There are several popular GUIs for Linux, including GNOME (GNU Network Object Model Environment). GNOME is the default GUI for Ubuntu distributions, and can be researched more thoroughly at http://www.gnome.org. Plasma is another popular Linux GUI. This was originally called KDE, but has evolved into the current Plasma desktop, causing some sources to call it *KDE Plasma*.

GNOME and Plasma are very common, but there are numerous Linux GUIs one can use. Examples include MATE, which is based on GNOME 2 and is one of the official GUIs for Ubuntu Linux. There is also LXDE (Lightweight X11 Desktop Environment), which—as the name suggests—uses less CPU and RAM than some other GUIs.

A+ 1102: 1.11

Samba

Even the most ardent Linux fan must agree that Windows is still very prevalent on workstations. For this reason, it is important that a Linux machine be able to communicate with Windows machines. This means more than just sending an e-mail; it also means sharing files and network resources. Since 1992, this has been most often accomplished with Samba. Samba handles file and print services, authentication, service discovery, browsing, and name resolution. All of these are accomplished in such a way that both Linux and Windows computers can use the aforementioned services.

Samba uses the Server Message Block (SMB) protocol to accomplish its goals. SMB is actually a Microsoft protocol, which is why Samba can facilitate Linux-Windows interoperability. As of this writing, the current version of Samba is version 4.17 and was released September 2022.

2.8 Best Practices for Linux and macOS

1102: 1.10, 1.11 A+

Technicians should be aware that macOS, and Linux-based operating systems, have precautions and best practices similar to those for Windows-based computers. While these precautions are similar, they are usually implemented differently in macOS- and Linux-based systems. These precautions include scheduled backups, system updates, and the installation of antivirus or antimalware software and updates.

Scheduled Backups

1102: 1.9, 1.10, 1.11 A+

As you know, Windows includes restoration and recovery features by default, and Apple computers are no different. The macOS software provides a utility called Time Machine Backup, which allows a user to determine the day(s) and time(s) they wish to have their machine and its data perform a backup via a Snapshot. If a Snapshot is not available in the Machine Backup of macOS, a user may utilize an image recovery to create an Apple Disk Image file (**.dmg**) that will bring the computer state and settings that match when the image was generated. This is similar to System Restore and Restore Points in Windows operating systems. Furthermore, an image recovery may also be used on other Macintosh computers if a user wants to transfer settings to another machine. Users should also consider utilizing the Run Disk Utility, which provides disk maintenance similar to the Windows defragmentation and Disk Cleanup tools.

Linux backups are often performed through the Shell. Commands such as **BACULA**, **RSYNC**, and **BackupPC** all provide users with options for determining what data and settings are stored as a backup. It is recommended that users perform backups regularly, just as with any other operating system.

System Updates

1102: 1.9, 1.10, 1.11 A+

Linux-based updates are accessed through Terminal by executing the command syntax sudo apt-get update. However, updates for macOS are obtained similarly to those for Windows and Apple's iOS platforms. Apple typically notifies a user when updates are available and advises immediate installation. The user may have to access device settings or the App Store to install manually if they do not wish to install at the time of the notification.

Antivirus and Antimalware Updates

1102: 1.10, 1.11 A+

While users may have the perception that Linux and macOS are not vulnerable to malware, viruses, and other forms of malicious code, it is not recommended to operate any operating system that has a connection to the Internet without antivirus protection. Antivirus programs are updated on a consistent basis and can quarantine a file that appears to be of a malicious threat to a user's computer and data. Therefore, users need to install an antivirus program and run scans on a consistent basis for their own protection.

2.9 Common Mobile Devices and Operating Systems

1102: 1.8 A+

In general, mobile operating systems are designed for portable devices with limited hardware resources, such as cell phones or smartphones, tablets, and some gaming hardware. Although some mobile operating systems do appear on larger devices, such as laptops and tablets, they are typically designed with limited CPU and memory support. For example, they will not support extensive graphics associated with games or sophisticated graphic design programs, such as some web design software or computer-aided drafting and engineering software. In general, the mobile operating system is designed to provide the widest assortment of popular user applications on limited hardware with a minimal amount of software required to perform a task. Common portable device tasks are Internet access and collaboration activities, such as instant messaging, texting, social media, taking photos, and sharing music and photos. As mobile device operating systems and mobile devices evolve, it will soon be difficult to discern between what is and is not considered a mobile device.

Perhaps the most important thing to remember when working with mobile devices and their respective operating systems is that they are generally not compatible with one another. For example, iPhones manufactured by Apple are likely not going to be able to run Android, or Chrome and vice versa. Currently, the most commonly encountered mobile platforms are Android OS, iOS, and iPadOS.

A+ 1102: 1.8

Android OS

The Android OS was introduced by Google in 2008 to power mobile phones from various manufacturers and compete with Apple's iOS. The platform is promoted by the open handset alliance—a group of technology and mobile companies that integrate the Android OS into their products. Chrome OS is another mobile operating system developed by Google. Derived from the Linux operating system, it is designed to run on a range of mobile devices other than smartphones.

A+ 1102: 1.8

iOS and iPadOS

iOS is a proprietary mobile operating system created by Apple Inc, exclusively for Apple hardware. It is the operating system used in iPhones and, for many years, in iPads. This operating system was first announced in January 2007 and is based on using touch for interaction. Touch consists of specific gestures such as tap, swipe, and pinch. The Home screen of iOS is handled by SpringBoard, an internal Apple app. Multitasking was introduced to iOS in 2010.

Eventually, Apple separated the iPad into its own operating system named iPadOS, which was released in 2019. While it is now different from iOS, it is remarkably similar. As time progresses, it is likely there will be increasing divergence in the iOS and the iPadOS. As of this writing, while the two interfaces look similar, iPadOS has some features not present in iOS. For example, iPadOS supports the ability to run multiple apps simultaneously and supports picture in picture. Starting with iPadOS 14, an app called Scribble is included to convert text written by an Apple Pencil into typed text.

A+ 1102: 1.8

Tech Tip

The phrase *end of life* refers to a product that is supplied to consumers that has reached the end of its utility, according to the vendor. In response, the vendor stops marketing and selling the product, and they will eventually end or limit support for it, resulting in fewer or limited updates.

2.10 Common Operating System Terminology

There is a tremendous amount of operating system terminology common to all operating systems. A few terms should be mastered early, such as application software, software driver, and software patch. There will be many more terms introduced throughout the textbook and your instruction. Be sure to master these three for now.

Application Software

1102: 1.7 A+

Application software, also referred to as *end-user software*, is designed for a specific purpose, such as creating databases or spreadsheets, word processing, producing graphics, or just for entertainment. It is not an operating system.

Typical application software relies on the operating system to communicate with PC hardware such as the hard drive or CD-ROM drive. When a word-processing program issues a save command, the command is interpreted by the operating system, which in turn passes it through the CPU and on to the hardware. While most 32-bit software applications will run on a 64-bit computer system, some will not. Antivirus programs are a classic example of software applications that must match the system type: 32-bit or 64-bit.

Software Driver

A **software driver** is a small package of programs that allows proper communication between the computer and a peripheral device. Common devices that require drivers are printers, modems, monitors, and storage devices. Software drivers act as translators, converting common commands issued from the CPU to the device in use.

PC and software systems are constantly evolving, but not necessarily in the same time frame. For example, you may install a printer that is much newer than the software installed on a computer. The computer may not have the software programs necessary to communicate correctly with the printer. A typical scenario is when a new printer is installed on a PC and the self-test runs perfectly. However, when a file you have created on the PC is sent to the printer, it prints out a garbled set of meaningless symbols or an endless stream of blank pages. This is a classic case of incorrect driver software.

Software drivers are typically classified as 32-bit or 64-bit and are not interchangeable. You must match the driver to the type of operating system. Microsoft operating systems require 64-bit driver software to be digitally signed, meaning it contains a security code that identifies and verifies the developer of the software driver. Because the driver is verified, Microsoft recognizes it as a driver from a legitimate software vendor that does not contain malware.

Windows operating systems incorporate options to allow you to run legacy software applications and legacy drivers. The screen capture in Figure 2-29 shows the options for configuring a program to run as if it were installed on a previous version of Windows. In this example, the Google Chrome web browser installed in Windows 10 is configured to run as if it were installed on a Windows 8 version of the operating system. Microsoft provides a compatibility wizard launched via the Control Panel, as shown in Figure 2-30. The Program Compatibility Troubleshooter automatically detects possible compatibility problems associated with various legacy programs, Figure 2-31.

Software Patch

1102: 1.5, 1.9, 2.4 A+

A **software patch** is a fix for operating systems and application software that have already been released. It also contains security updates when the operating system or software has been compromised. Although operating systems and software go through countless hours of testing, many have errors in programming referred to as **bugs**. Patches for software programs can assist in correcting bugs and are readily available for download off the Internet. Periodically, a large collection of patches is released at once and referred to as a *service pack*.

Figure 2-29 Windows operating systems provide compatibility options for configuring legacy software applications.

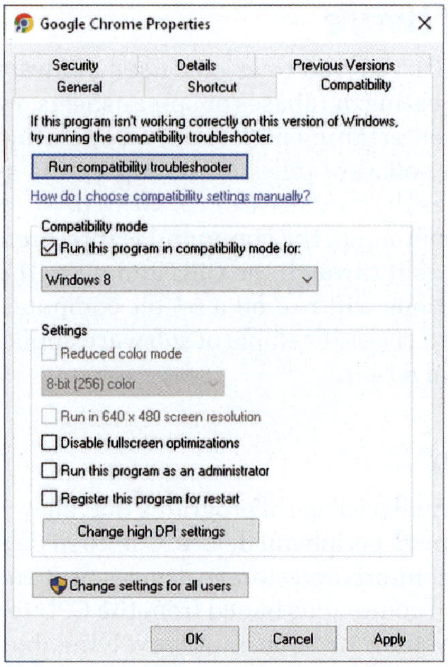

Goodheart-Willcox Publisher

Figure 2-30 Microsoft provides a compatibility wizard launched via the Control Panel.

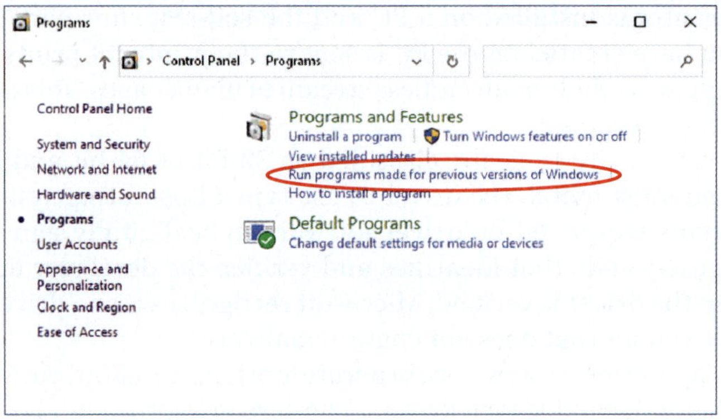

Goodheart-Willcox Publisher

Figure 2-31 The Program Compatibility Troubleshooter detects possible compatibility problems associated with legacy software applications.

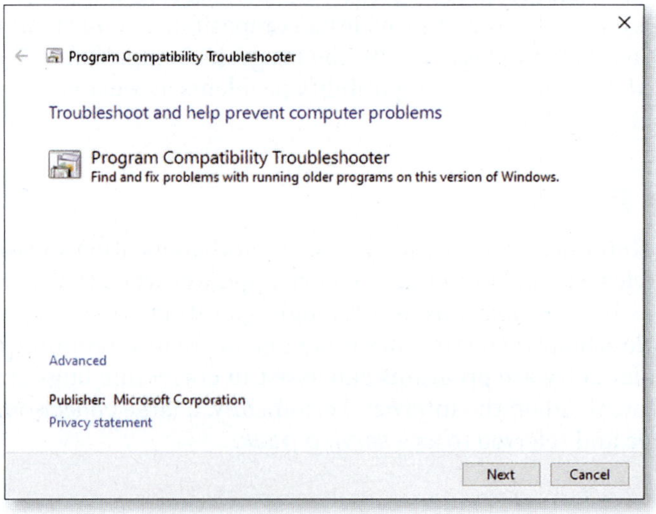

Goodheart-Willcox Publisher

Patch management takes place when an operating system is in need of an updated driver or another form of a patch that is needed to allow the operating system and its software to operate properly. If a patch is needed, it is normally installed onto a machine automatically to avoid any urgency in the operation of the machine. Although patches are typically installed automatically, users are able to download patches manually. Furthermore, patch management implementation is the same for all operating systems.

Windows normally notifies the user of updates and patches through the Windows Update utility. Similarly, both macOS and Linux operating systems use patch management utilities to install and attempt to repair any hardware or software that could cause interruption of the operating system's functionality. These installation and repairs are performed in a way so the user is not interrupted from their personal use and can be performed without any knowledge of the user. However, users can download driver and firmware updates and install them manually if they wish to do so. Some patches may require the user to restart the computer to take effect.

Chapter Summary

2.1 What Is an Operating System?

- An operating system is the underlying software that provides a computer user with all the basic services of resource management on the machine, including a file system structure and a means of communicating with the computer hardware.
- The core of any operating system is referred to as the *kernel*.
- Operating systems are installed in a variety of ways, including via CD/DVD, USB drive, network connection, and remotely through preboot execution environments.

2.2 Operating System Characteristics

- Multitasking is the ability of an operating system to simultaneously support two or more running programs.
- There are two types of multitasking: preempting, which allows multiple programs to share control of the OS, and cooperative, which allows one program to dominate the CPU and allows another program to run while the first program is idle.
- Multithreading refers to the sharing of data and parts of a program between two or more CPUs or between multiple cores within a single CPU.
- Operating systems, hardware devices, and software applications are identified using the terms *32-bit* and *64-bit*, which describe the amount of data that can be stored or processed.
- There are two dominant user interfaces: a graphical user interface (GUI), which allows the user to perform functions by selecting on-screen icons rather than issuing text-based commands, and command-line interface, which allows a user to issue commands by entering text at the command prompt.
- A file system refers to the method of organizing files on a storage device. File systems include FAT12, FAT16, and FAT32, which are all legacy systems. Currently, only FAT32, exFAT, and NTFS are used for Windows. Additional types include Apple File System (AFS) and Linux-based systems such as ext2, ext3, ext4, Btrfs, XFS, and JFS.
- File system structure typically involves directories and subdirectories.
- Configuration files contain information such as the amount of memory and type of video adapter present in the system.

2.3 Microsoft Windows Operating System

- Microsoft Windows is the most widely used operating system.
- There have been significant changes from Windows Vista to Windows 11, including Windows 8 removing the **Start** menu and Windows 10 bringing it back, albeit with Windows 8 tiles.
- The Windows directory structure is regularly evolving, though it has remained relatively consistent since Windows Vista.
- Windows 7 introduced Libraries to the directory, which can still be enabled in Windows 10.
- A file extension is an identification consisting of three characters that allows Windows to recognize the file type.
- The Windows desktop has maintained a similar user interface from Windows XP to Windows 11, with the exception of Windows 8 removing the **Start** menu.
- Most versions and editions of Windows have a similar set of features.

2.4 Microsoft Windows Installation

- An *upgrade* means that you can install Windows on an existing operating system and retain files, settings, and applications. A *clean install* means that the previous operating system is completely replaced and you will lose all files, settings, and applications.

- Carrying out a Windows installation calls for knowledge of an operating system's hardware requirements and determining whether an upgrade or clean install should be performed.
- A Windows *version* refers to major releases, for example Windows 10 and Windows 11. An *edition* is a specific type of version, such as Home, Pro, and Enterprise. Windows 10 is available in 12 different editions, but baseline editions are Home, Pro, and Pro for Workstations. Windows 11 has only two editions: Home and Pro.

2.5 Microsoft Windows Boot Sequences

- A boot sequence is the step-by-step process of bringing a computer to an operational state.
- A cold boot, also called a *hard boot,* means that the electrical power switch is used to turn on the computer. A warm boot, or *soft boot,* is used to restart a computer that is already running.
- All operating systems start with a simple diagnostic program called a power-on self-test (POST).
- The boot sequence for UEFI/EFI computers is slightly different from those with BIOS due to the addition of a built-in boot manager.
- Windows 7, Windows 8, Windows 10, and Windows 11 share a similar boot sequence: POST, initial startup phase, Windows Boot Manager phase, Windows Boot Loader phase, kernel-loading phase, and logon phase. Windows 10 supports the UEFI in place of the BIOS for a faster, more flexible boot process.
- A dual-boot system is one in which two operating systems are installed on a single computer. A multi-boot, or *multiboot,* system contains more than two operating systems.
- Virtual machines, also known as virtual PCs, are capable of running two operating systems at the same time.

2.6 Apple Macintosh OS

- macOS is the operating system developed by Apple, Inc. to run on their Macintosh line of computer systems.
- macOS is derived from NextSTEP, which itself was based off the Mach kernel from CMU and the Berkeley Software Distribution (BSD) of the Unix operating system.
- Often, Macs are not found in traditional office-type work environments, but they are used almost exclusively in industries that fit their creative features.
- Tools and features included in most macOS versions include Boot Camp, screen sharing, Spotlight search, Quick Look, and cross-platform functionality.

2.7 Linux OS

- Linux is an open-source Unix-like operating system.
- Linux exists in variations called distribution, or distros.
- The /root directory is the home directory for the root user, which is the administrator in Linux and Unix systems.
- The Linux command line is called the shell.
- There are multiple GUIs available for Linux distros.
- Samba enables Windows and Linux systems to communicate.

2.8 Best Practices for Linux and macOS

- Similar precautions and practices exist for Linux and macOS as in Windows, including scheduled backups, system updates, and installation and update of antivirus and antimalware software.
- For macOS, the Time Machine Backup utility can be used to create backups via Snapshots. Linux commands **BACULA**, **RSYN**, and **BackupPC** perform a similar function.

- Linux updates can be performed with the command syntax sudo apt-get update. Updates for macOS are distributed similarly to those for Windows in that the user is notified of an update and prompted top install immediately.

2.9 Common Mobile Devices and Operating Systems

- Common mobile devices are cell phones, tablets, and some gaming hardware; common portable device tasks are Internet access and collaboration activities.
- Android OS was introduced by Google in 2008 to power mobile phones from various manufacturers and compete with iOS.

2.10 Common Operating System Terminology

- There is a tremendous amount of operating system terminology common to all operating systems. Application software, also referred to as *end-user software,* is designed for a specific purpose. A software driver is a small package of programs that allow proper communication between the computer and the peripheral device. A software patch is a fix for operating systems and application software that have already been released.
- Most 32-bit software applications will run on a 64-bit computer system, but some will not; 32-bit and 64-bit drivers will only run on the system for which they were designed.

Review Questions

1. What does an operating system do?
2. What is a kernel?
3. List common characteristics of all operating systems.
4. Differentiate between preemptive multitasking and cooperative multitasking.
5. What are two main advantages of 64-bit systems over 32-bit systems?
6. List and describe two dominant user interfaces used to issue commands on a computer.
7. Compare Windows versions from Windows 7 to now.
8. What is included in a directory structure?
9. Regarding Windows installation types, what is the difference among upgrades, clean installs, and custom installs?
10. What is a POST and what does it do?
11. Summarize the Windows 10 boot sequence.
12. During which phase of the Windows boot sequence does the operating system switch from the text mode to the graphic mode?
13. Describe characteristics, tools, and features of Apple's macOS.
14. Identify characteristics of Linux OS.
15. What precautions should be taken in Linux and macOS as a form of best practices?
16. What macOS utility is provided to enable a user to determine the day and time their machine performs a backup?
17. What command syntax accesses Linux updates via Terminal?
18. Provide examples of common mobile devices and tasks.
19. List examples of mobile-specific operating systems.
20. Differentiate between application software, a software driver, and a software patch.

Sample A+ Exam Questions

1. What is the maximum RAM supported for a Windows 10 Pro 64-bit installation?
   A. 128 GB
   B. 4 GB
   C. 512 GB
   D. 2 GB

2. The operating feature that allows two programs to appear to be running simultaneously is called _____.
   A. multiprocessing
   B. multitasking
   C. program coordination
   D. kernel sharing
3. When entered at the command prompt, which command grants a user access to the registry?
   A. cmd
   B. help
   C. regedit
   D. registry32
4. What is the maximum amount of RAM supported by a 32-bit Windows 7 system?
   A. 1 GB
   B. 2 GB
   C. 4 GB
   D. 8 GB
5. Which device would contain the POST program?
   A. Hard drive
   B. RAM
   C. USB flash drive
   D. BIOS chip
6. Which of the following are no longer required by Windows? Select two.
   A. **ntdetect**
   B. **ntoskrnl**
   C. **boot.ini**
   D. POST
7. Which command entered into the **Search** box will produce the command prompt?
   A. prompt
   B. msdos.sys
   C. cmd
   D. doscom.com
8. Which program is executed first during the boot process?
   A. **ntldr**
   B. POST
   C. **bootcfg**
   D. **ntdetect**
9. Which Microsoft security feature is used to encrypt an entire hard disk drive?
   A. Sync
   B. BitLocker
   C. VPN
   D. Windows Defender
10. Which of the following allows DOS programs to run on newer 64-bit operating systems?
   A. Dual-boot
   B. Multiple-boot
   C. NTDVM
   D. Tablet mode

Chapter 3

Motherboards

Learning Outcomes

3.1 Recall motherboard buses.
3.2 Identify common motherboard form factors.
3.3 Explain motherboard bus architecture.
3.4 Summarize the importance of ensuring RAM compatibility.
3.5 Identify architectures of expansion card slots.
3.6 Identify system resources using Device Manager and System Information.
3.7 List and describe common administrative tasks associated with motherboards.
3.8 Identify major components of a motherboard.

A+ Certification Exam Objectives

The following A+ Certification Exam Objectives are covered in this chapter.

Exam 220-1101

3.0 Hardware

- 3.1 Explain basic cable types, features, and their purposes.
- 3.2 Given a scenario, install the appropriate RAM.
- 3.4 Given a scenario, install and configure motherboards, CPUs, and add-on cards.

Exam 220-1102

1.0 Operating Systems

- 1.3 Given a scenario, use features and tools of the Microsoft Windows 10 operating system.
- 1.4 Given a scenario, use the appropriate Microsoft Windows 10 Control Panel utility.
- 1.5 Given a scenario, use the appropriate Windows settings.
- 1.9 Given a scenario, perform OS installations and upgrades in a diverse OS environment.

Key Terms

backplane
bus
chipset
direct memory access (DMA)
expansion card slot
flash BIOS
form factor
I/O port address
IRQ (Interrupt Request)
memory address range
northbridge
PCI Express (PCIe, PCI-E)
plug-and-play
southbridge
traces
Universal Serial Bus (USB)

Overview

The *motherboard* is the most important element and the core of a computer system. All major components connect to and transmit data across the motherboard. The motherboard is the communication center for input and output to critical components such as the memory, CPU, keyboard, mouse, monitor, and network connection. The motherboard also provides the connection points required by the fans, speaker, power switch, LED indicator lights, and CMOS battery.

The motherboard provides a means for expanding and customizing the system by inserting expansion boards into slots, which support a direct connection to the bus architecture. Various special-purpose chips control communication between the different buses and devices mounted on the motherboard. The motherboard is also referred to as the *system board*, *main board*, and *planar board*. The lines are blurred somewhat with newer mini-systems such as Raspberry Pi and other small single-board computers, which do not typically have expansion slots. The newer micro devices utilize system boards that may or may not include expansion connectors.

A+ Note

This chapter covers many of the objectives on the CompTIA A+ Certification Exams. Be sure you can access the setup utility for several different computer systems and understand the terminology associated with the settings. Motherboard technical manuals are available on the Internet and provide detailed setup utility information. Be sure to look at several manuals thoroughly. Typical questions on the exam will address upgrading the firmware and changing the setup utility configuration and its password. There may also be questions related to motherboard expansion architecture, such as the data rate of PCI, PCIe, USB, SATA, and eSATA, as well as questions to test basic knowledge of form factors.

3.1 Motherboard Construction

The *motherboard* provides a physical surface on which to mount electronic components such as resistors, capacitors, chips, slots, and sockets. The motherboard is a combination of insulating material and electronic circuit paths constructed of thin conductors. The motherboard insulation material does not conduct electrical energy, which prevents the electrical energy from contacting the case and creating an electrical short circuit. It also prevents electrical energy from flowing directly between motherboard **traces**, which are the electrical circuits that run across the surface of the motherboard and provide the paths between all the different components mounted on the motherboard. Traces confine the flow of electrical energy to distinct paths and provide a means of sending and receiving data between the components connected to the motherboard. Motherboard traces are shown in Figure 3-1.

The thin conductors also provide electrical energy to low-power devices. High-power consumption devices, such as disk drives, are powered directly from the power supply through much thicker conductors. Many of the thin conductors on the motherboard are grouped together to make up what is referred to as a bus. A **bus** is a collection of conductors that works together for a specific purpose. There are many bus types, including the following.

- The *data bus* is used to move data between components. The data is moved between components in groups of 8, 16, 32, or 64 bits, known as the *bus width.*
- The *control bus* is used by the CPU to communicate with and activate other devices such as hard drives.
- The *memory bus* connects the processor directly to the memory.
- The *I/O bus*, also called an *expansion bus*, connects the processor to the expansion slots.
- The *internal bus* is part of the integrated circuit inside the CPU.
- The *local bus*, or *system bus*, connects directly to the CPU and provides communication to high-speed devices mounted closely to the CPU.
- The *address bus* connects the CPU with the main memory module. It identifies memory locations where data is to be stored or retrieved.
- The *power bus* is used to send electrical power to low-consumption devices such as speakers, lights, and switches. Recall that high-consumption devices, such as disk drives, connect directly to the power supply using much larger conductors.

Figure 3-1 The motherboard is a physical surface to which electronic components are mounted. Traces are the electrical circuits that run across the surface of the motherboard.

Goodheart-Willcox Publisher

A bus may also refer to a collection of bus types. For example, the *local bus* consists of power, data, control, and memory bus lines. For this reason, the local bus may be referred to by other names such as the *system bus*. Intel has coined the local bus as the *front-side bus (FSB)*, a term used quite often when specifying motherboard bus speeds. It is also often used to describe any motherboard bus that connects directly to the CPU. The term *backside bus* is used to describe an internal bus inside the CPU.

Most motherboard designs come with different types of expansion slots to accommodate system customization by connecting additional hardware to various system buses. These expansion slots, also called *bus slots*, provide access for expanded memory and input/output devices by plugging expansion hardware into the motherboard using the appropriate expansion slot. It is important to ensure the expansion component and the bus slot are compatible for the system modification to function properly.

3.2 Form Factors

1101: 3.4 A+

The **form factor**, also called the *footprint*, is the physical shape or outline of a motherboard and the location of the mounting holes. A motherboard form factor must be considered when upgrading a PC because it determines whether the motherboard will fit the PC case style you intend to use. Compatible form factors are often stamped into the inside of a computer case, as shown in Figure 3-2. The power supply must also match the form factor of the case and motherboard.

The form factors that have been developed over the years are AT, Baby AT, ATX, Micro-ATX, Flex-ATX, Mini-ITX, Nano-ITX, Pico-ITX, Mobile-ITX, LPX, NLX, BTX, Micro-BTX, Nano-BTX, Pico-BTX, and backplane. ATX is the most common form factor used for full-size computers. The motherboard and power supply are installed into the appropriate cabinet by aligning the screw holes on the component with the screw sockets on the computer case. Incompatible hardware with the wrong form factor will be obvious because the fittings will not line up correctly between the component and the cabinet.

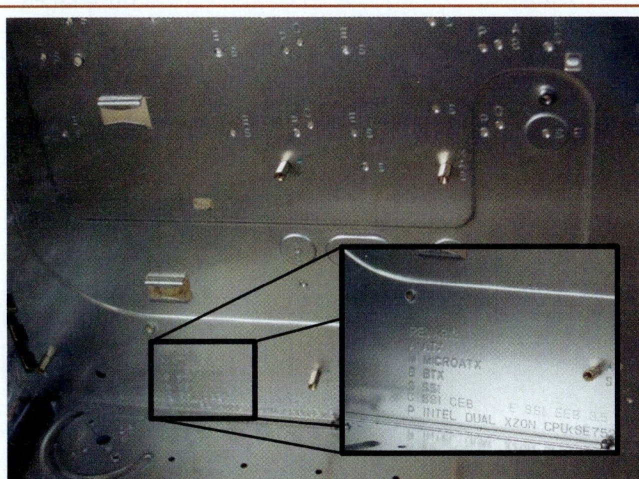

Goodheart-Willcox Publisher

Figure 3-2 The form factor refers to the physical shape or outline of a motherboard and the location of the mounting holes. It determines if the motherboard will fit in a given PC case.

AT and Baby AT

One of the earliest standard sizes was the AT (Advanced Technology) form factor. It provided a 16-bit data bus. As chip technologies have advanced, it has become possible to reduce the size of the motherboards over time. For example, after AT, a smaller 16-bit motherboard was introduced called the *Baby AT*, referenced in Figure 3-3.

A+ 1101: 3.4

ATX

The Baby AT remained popular until 1996 when the ATX gained popularity. The ATX board looks similar to a Baby AT board that has been turned 90 degrees inside the computer case. Due to this shape, it requires a particular power supply shape so both the motherboard and power supply will fit in the case. ATX is incompatible with most other motherboard form factors but is available in three common sizes, as shown in Figure 3-4:

- *ATX* is 12″ × 9.6″
- *Micro-ATX* is 9.6″ × 9.6″
- *Flex-ATX*, also referred to as *Mini-ATX*, is 7.5″ × 9.6″

The overall size of the ATX motherboard is reduced by decreasing the total number of adapter slots for each ATX form factor.

The most welcomed feature of the ATX form factor is the supply connector mounted on the motherboard. The connector is designed to prevent the power supply from being plugged into the motherboard with the polarity reversed, which would result in a blown motherboard.

Power supplies and power supply connections will be discussed with more detail in a later chapter. For quick identification, an ATX form factor motherboard uses a 20-pin power supply connector, and an AT form factor motherboard uses a 12-pin connector. A newer style of the ATX form factor, called ATX12V, uses a 24-pin connector.

A+ 1101: 3.4

Mini-ITX

The *Mini-ITX* was developed by Via Technologies in 2001 and is a smaller version of the Micro-ATX. It provides for a compact system using the same standard components as the ATX form factors. Figure 3-5 shows the size relationship of the ATX, Micro-ATX, and Mini-ITX form factors.

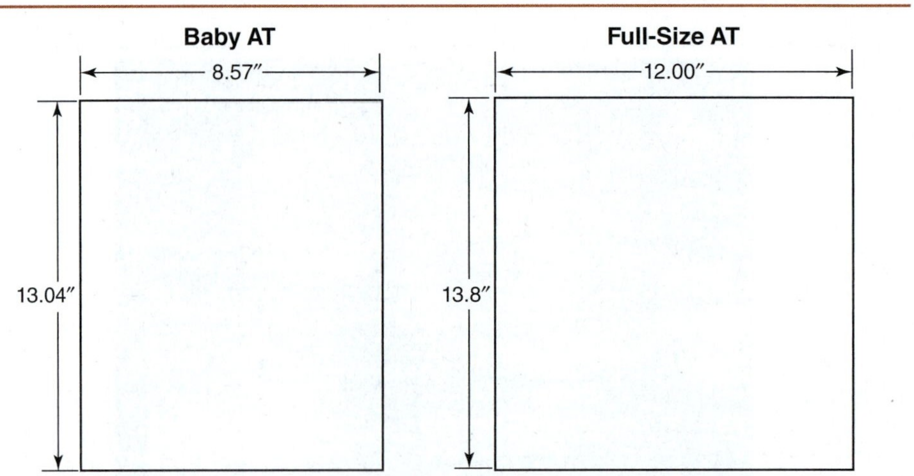

Figure 3-3 The Baby AT motherboard form factor is smaller than the full-size AT form factor but allows for a 16-bit data bus.

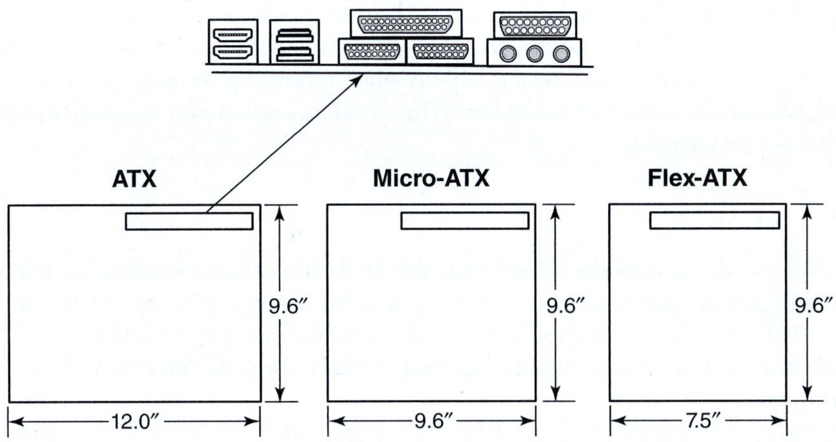

Goodheart-Willcox Publisher

Figure 3-4 The ATX form factor has three distinct sizes.

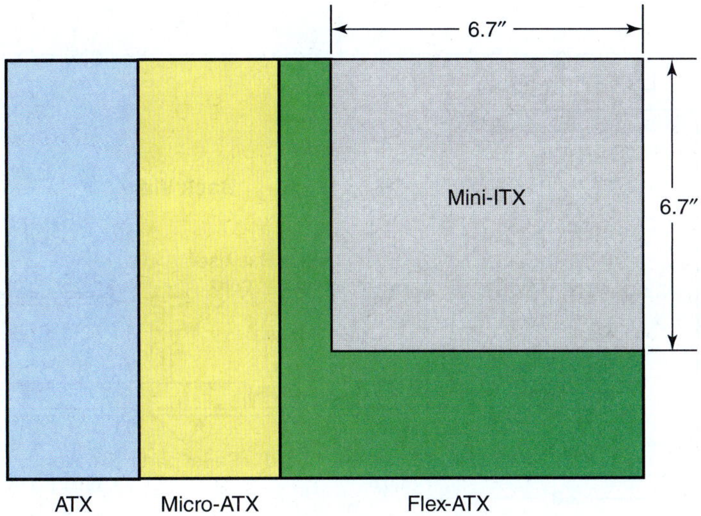

Goodheart-Willcox Publisher

Figure 3-5 The Mini-ITX form factor provides for a compacter system without sacrificing typical computing components.

The Mini-ITX form factor is used for small desktop computers, but there are even smaller ITX form factors used for mobile devices:

- The *Nano-ITX* is 4.7″ × 4.7″.
- The *Pico-ITX* is 3.94″ × 2.83″.
- The *Mobile-ITX* is 2.36″× 2.36″.

Many proprietary small form factors (SFF) exist to be used for a wide variety of mobile devices.

LPX

The *LPX* form factor was designed for a low-profile desktop computer or a slim tower. It is also popular with low-priced computer systems. This motherboard does not have expansion slots like a typical motherboard and instead has a single expansion slot usually mounted in the middle of the motherboard. This expansion slot hosts a bus riser card, as illustrated in Figure 3-6. Expansion cards are plugged into the bus riser card at right angles so they are parallel to the motherboard. This is what allows for a low-profile computer case.

The LPX is not considered a true standard and cannot be easily upgraded. Rather, it is a proprietary style, and as a result, the bus riser card is not always located in the same spot. This variation can be a problem when changing or upgrading the motherboard. Obtaining a motherboard from the same manufacturer is usually required to get the correct layout.

NLX

The *NLX* form factor uses the same principle as the bus riser-card design. However, rather than placing the bus riser card in the middle of the motherboard, it is located at the end of the board, and expansion cards jut out above and parallel to the motherboard. In fact, the edge of the motherboard plugs directly into the riser card, as diagrammed in Figure 3-7.

The major advantage of the NLX board over the LPX is that the NLX is standardized in the industry, meaning you can replace or upgrade any NLX board with any other NLX board. The board width is a standard 9.0″, while the length can vary from 10.0″ to 13.6″. Even though the length may vary, it is still considered a standard. NLX

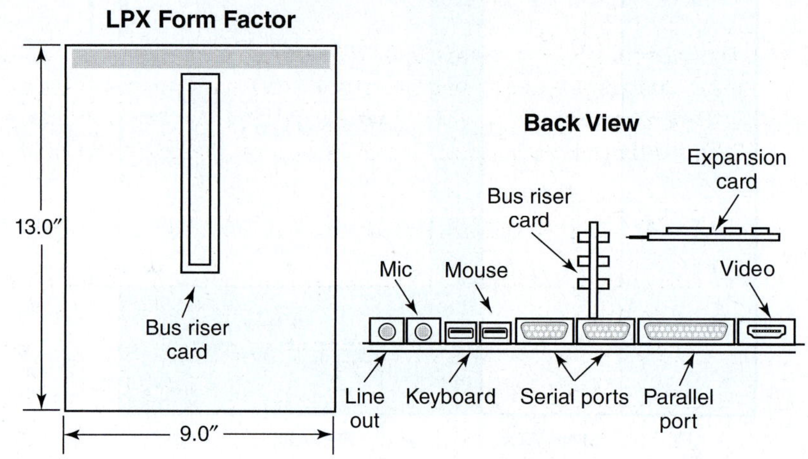

Figure 3-6 The LPX form factor does not have expansion card slots. Instead, cards are plugged into a bus riser card at right angles parallel to the motherboard. This enables a low-profile case design.

Goodheart-Willcox Publisher

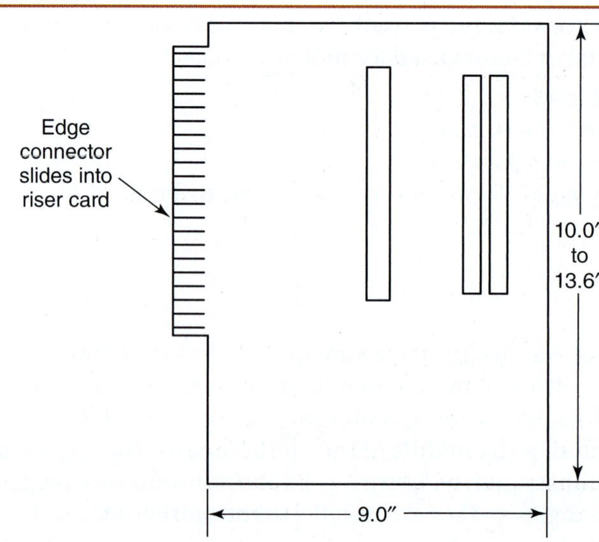

Figure 3-7 The NLX form factor uses a riser card at the edge of the motherboard for expansion cards.

Goodheart-Willcox Publisher

was popular among leading PC manufacturers such as Gateway, Hewlett-Packard, IBM, NEC, and Micron. In fact, ATX and NLX continue to be the most popular designs used by computer manufacturers.

BTX

BTX (Balanced Technology Extended) was designed for improved system cooling and acoustics. Many PC components, such as CPUs, chipsets, and graphic cards, operate at a much higher frequency than their predecessors do and, as a result, require a superior cooling system. The BTX form factor allowed for a direct stream of air across the CPU and other heat-generating components.

Another key aspect of the design was the ability to reduce the noise level of PC cooling system fans. The BTX design was not compatible with the ATX case design, but the BTX could use a typical ATX power supply and any standard device that is not form-factor dependent, such as hard drives, CPUs, and expansion cards.

The BTX motherboard had four form factor sizes, as illustrated in Figure 3-8:

- BTX was 10.5″ × 12.8″.
- Micro-BTX was 10.5″ × 10.4″.
- Nano-BTX was 10.5″ × 8.8″.
- Pico-BTX was 10.5″ × 8.0″.

Like the ATX form factors, the width of the BTX form factor was shrunk by reducing the number of expansion slots. For example, standard BTX had up to seven expansion slots, Micro-BTX had four expansion slots, Nano-BTX had two expansion slots, and Pico-BTX had only one expansion slot. BTX is now obsolete as a form-factor case design.

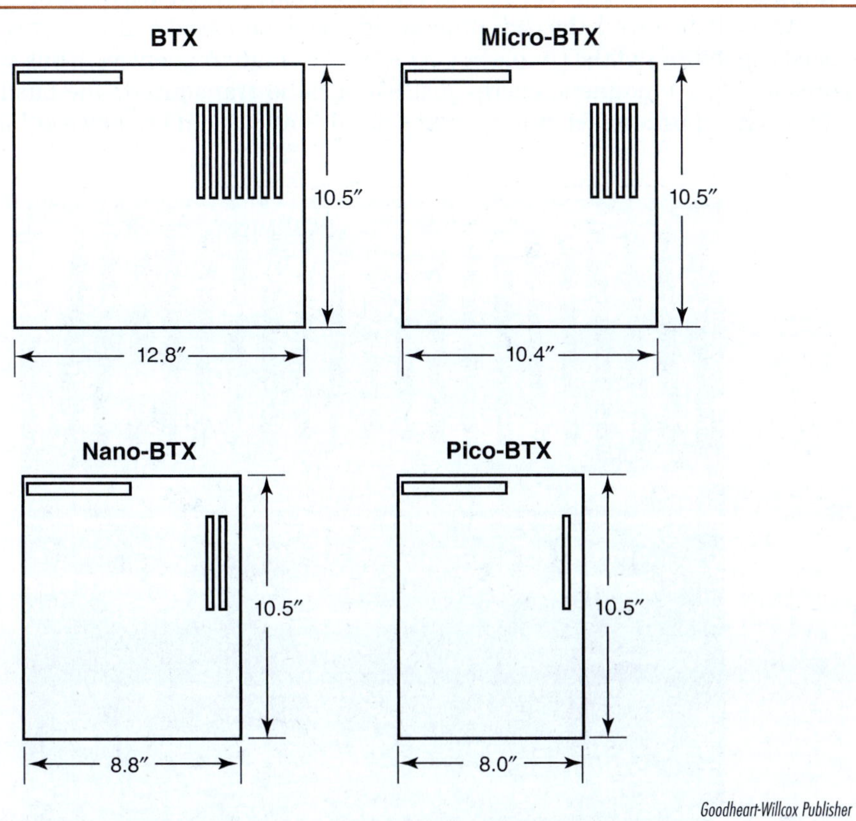

Figure 3-8 The BTX form factor has four sizes: BTX, Micro-BTX, Nano-BTX, and Pico-BTX.

Backplane

A **backplane** is a circuit board with an abundance of slots along the length of the board. While not a true form factor design, backplanes must be considered with a discussion on form factors and motherboards because they function similarly. The main difference between the two is that a backplane does not accommodate for on-board processing and storage like a motherboard does. Instead, a backplane simply joins multiple cards. Figure 3-9 shows a backplane in the top portion of the image, and the traces for the expansion slots are shown in the bottom portion. Expansion cards, and even a CPU, slide into the expansion slots. The main idea of the design is to ensure easy upgrades of all components. This style is very popular in heavy industry. The backplane is considered proprietary.

There are two main classifications of backplane boards: passive and active. In a *passive* design, all typical motherboard circuits and chips are located on the expansion cards and not on the backplane. An *active* backplane design contains the usual circuitry found on any typical motherboard except for a main processor. The processor is usually installed into an expansion slot to allow for an easy upgrade as more advanced processors come on the market.

3.3 Motherboard Bus System Architecture

The original PC had a simple bus architecture in which one bus connected all major components to the RAM and CPU. The CPU transmitted data to and from components on the motherboard at the same speed, as diagrammed in Figure 3-10. The original bus architecture consisted of one bus, and its speed matched the processor speed.

As the PC evolved, the CPU processing speed increased and soon surpassed the speed capabilities of the simple bus structure. At high frequencies, a bus system can transmit electromagnetic energy just like a radio transmitter. The bus inside the CPU is very short; in fact, it is microscopic. This allows data to move at high speeds

Figure 3-9 A backplane is a circuit board with an abundance of expansion slots.

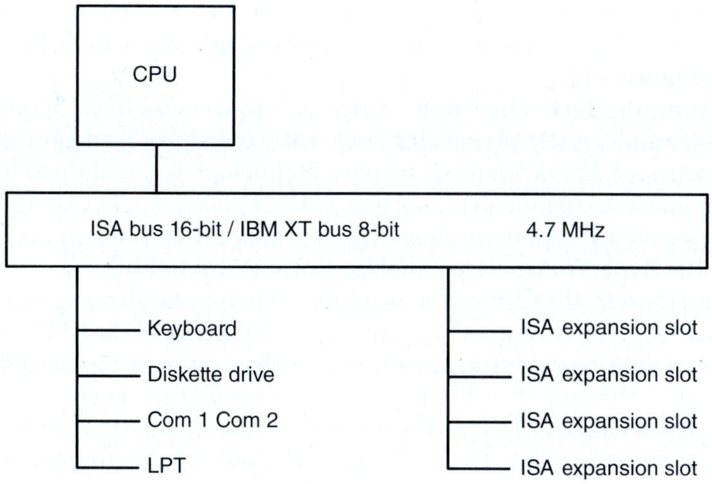

Figure 3-10 The original PC had a simple bus architecture in which one bus connected all major components to the RAM and CPU.

without generating electromagnetic interference. The bus outside the CPU is a great deal longer, and interference is a significant problem. This is the main reason for limited data transmission speed on a bus system.

The electrical occurrence of *inductive reactance* limits the speed of electrical energy flow through a conductor and results in a choking effect on the flow of electrical energy. The amount of choking effect is directly related to the speed of data transmission (frequency) and the length of the conductor (bus wire length); it increases in direct proportion with the speed of data transmission and the length of the data path.

A PC motherboard is designed with many different bus speeds. For example, it may have PCIe, USB, SATA, and eSATA ports and buses of different bandwidths (data rates) connecting to the CPU and RAM. Because there are different bandwidths, there must be a way of joining the different systems together and making them compatible with each other. This is the main function of a chipset. A **chipset** is a collection of integrated circuits that connects the motherboard buses and ports that run at different speeds. It supports the flow of data and control signals of different bus technologies to and from the CPU, RAM, hard drive, and video system.

Originally, chipsets consisted of two discrete chips referred to as the northbridge and southbridge. The **northbridge** was a chipset used to connect high-speed devices to the CPU, such as RAM and PCI slots, and was placed near the CPU. The **southbridge** was a chipset that was previously used to connect slower devices, such as the keyboard, mouse, printer, hard drive, and USB ports, and was placed farther from the CPU. Today, motherboards have only one chipset, but the terminology still lingers. While the single chipset is often referred to as the *southbridge*, it is technically just a chipset. The high-speed devices that originally connected to the northbridge, such as RAM and the PCIe slots designed for video, connect directly to the CPU.

Intel phased out the northbridge and southbridge and replaced them with a bus they refer to as the *Intel QuickPath Interconnect (QPI)*, as illustrated in Figure 3-11. Devices that demand high-speed connections, such as PCI Express (PCIe) 3.0 slots used for video cards and DDR3 RAM, connect directly to the CPU. The Intel chipset connects slower devices—such as WiMAX/Wi-Fi, Serial ATA (SATA), USB 2.0 and 3.0, audio, networking, and BIOS—to the CPU. There can also be a digital display bus connecting to the chipset used when there is no high-performance video card installed in the high-performance PCIe slot(s).

AMD invented and developed *HyperTransport Technology* to improve the performance of the front-side bus, northbridge, and southbridge. HyperTransport Technology allows devices to connect directly to each other using bidirectional

Tech Tip

The terms *northbridge* and *southbridge* are still used by many technicians when describing motherboard features, even though it is technically incorrect.

communication and to negotiate data transfer speed. It does not use a northbridge chip or an FSB. It connects directly to the southbridge, additional CPUs, and other devices. See Figure 3-12.

HyperTransport Technology only works with processors that support the technology. For example, AMD processors work with the HyperTransport bus system, but Intel processors do not. HyperTransport Technology is maintained by a consortium of computer-related industries, such as AMD, NVIDIA, Apple, Cisco Systems, and Sun Microsystems. To learn more about HyperTransport Technology and the organization, visit the HyperTransport Technology Consortium website.

Without chipsets, the CPU would be required to handle all computer data operations through its own core, greatly reducing the efficiency of the CPU. For example, if every byte of data representing a picture transferring from the hard drive to the RAM had to pass through the CPU, the computer would run slowly.

There are also chipsets designed to handle additional functions such as enabling motherboard expansion slots to work with RAM and other computer components with minimal CPU intervention.

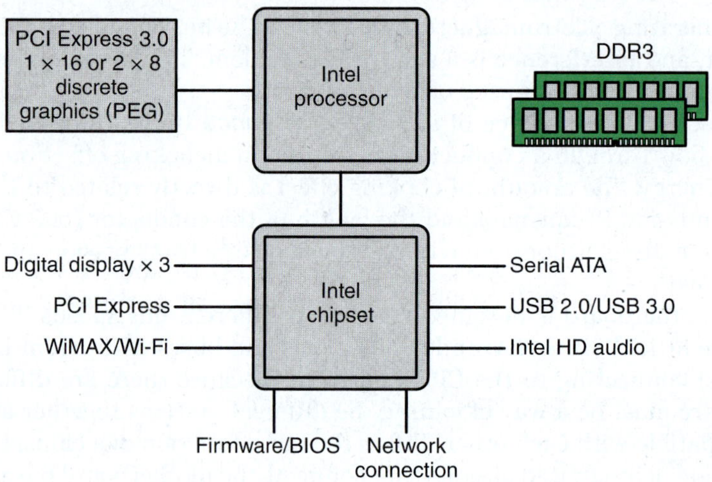

Goodheart-Willcox Publisher

Figure 3-11 Intel phased out the northbridge and southbridge and replaced them with a bus they refer to as the Intel QuickPath Interconnect (QPI), which connects slower devices to the CPU.

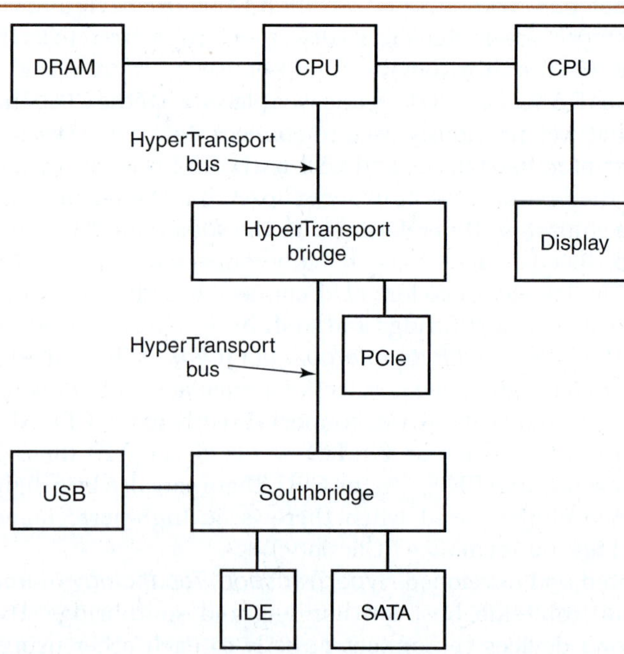

Goodheart-Willcox Publisher

Figure 3-12 AMD's HyperTransport Technology allows devices to connect directly to each other using bidirectional communication and to negotiate data transfer speed. HyperTransport Technology only works with processors that support the technology.

Chipset specifications vary a great deal in what they can support, such as maximum amount of memory, type of memory, number and type of USB and SATA ports, type of video (DVI, VGA, HDMI), type of audio, type of firmware support (EUFI, BIOS, or both), and type of processor. As technology evolves, chipsets also evolve to support the newer technologies. For example, when a newer version of SATA or USB technology is released, a new chipset will also be released to support it. Some major chipset manufacturers include Intel, SIS, and VIA.

Chipsets are an integral part of the motherboard and not field replacement units. A *field-replaceable unit (FRU)* is a component that can be quickly or easily replaced by a technician at the point of inspection. You cannot change the chipset. Instead, you must replace the entire motherboard.

3.4 RAM Compatibility

1101: 3.2 A+

Previous sections have briefly mentioned a few types of RAM. In this section, we will focus on the various RAM types and their usage. When someone talks about computer memory, they are generally referring to *Random Access Memory* or *RAM*. It is important to know the type of RAM you plan to use as well as the type of motherboard because RAM is not always interchangeable. For example, in many cases, the keyed notch at the bottom of a RAM module is compatible with specific ports on a motherboard. There will be much more about RAM in a later chapter. This section is merely to introduce the concept as it is a significant aspect of and important port on a motherboard.

Throughout the years, there have been numerous technologies used to implement RAM. These have included static RAM (SRAM), dynamic RAM (DRAM), and synchronous dynamic RAM (SDRAM). The last type, SDRAM, is what has been used for many years now.

When naming RAM, the primary focus has been on capacity. This began with *DDR*, or *Double Data Rate*, and continues today with DDR5. Each version of DDR improves the capacity of the previous. *Capacity* refers to both speed and amount of memory. In the last fifteen years, RAM has evolved through three iterations of DDR:

- DDR3 was released in 2007.
- DDR4 was released in 2011 and had begun to spread in the market by 2013.
- DDR5 was released in 2020.

DDR2 had clock rates of 200 to 800 MHz. Initially, DDR3 had clock rates of 400 to 533 MHZ, but those increased to 2,800 MHZ. DDR4 initially had rates of 2,133 MHz, but that increased over time to 4,266 MHz. Additionally, DDR4 uses less power than its predecessor, using only 1.2 volts compared to the 1.4 volts of DDR3.

DDR5 doubled bandwidth while again reducing power requirements. It also introduced a feature called *Decision Feedback Equalization (DFE)* that supports higher speeds and bandwidths. Like all version of DDR since DDR3, DDR5 offers a low-power version of the standard.

All RAM has to account for possible errors. As data is written to and read from RAM, errors can occur, requiring some sort of error-correction code (ECC). In general, ECCs work by containing redundant information with the actual message. This redundant information allows the detection of any errors. The very first error-correcting code was invented in the 1950s by Richard Hamming and is called the *Hamming (7,4) code*.

Another aspect of RAM is the channel configuration. Assuming the motherboard supports the RAM configuration you are using, a single RAM chip is *single channel*, two RAM chips is *dual channel*, and four RAM chips is *quad channel*. Three RAM chip configurations are very uncommon. It should be noted that these configurations are not always based on the number of chips, however. There are four chip configurations that operate with *single channel.* This is an important compatibility concern you should be aware of when purchasing a motherboard.

Beyond the configuration issues, there is a performance advantage for some configurations. Essentially, a single channel has one pathway for memory where a dual channel has two, and thus twice the memory transfer capacity. A quad channel has four times the pathways and thus four times the capacity.

A+ Note

You may encounter information about legacy expansion card slots such as ISA, EISA, MCA, and VESA. You do not need to study these particular expansion card slots for the CompTIA A+ Certification.

3.5 Expansion Card Slots

Recall from Chapter 1 that an **expansion card slot** is a port that allows an expansion card to connect directly to the electronic circuitry in the motherboard and communicate with other components on the motherboard or with the CPU. Expansion card slots, or *bus slots*, provide a quick and easy method of system customization by connecting devices directly into the motherboard bus system. They are designed to hold inserted cards called *adapters*, *expansion cards*, *interface cards*, and *daughter boards*. This allows a technician to modify the existing computer system for additional hardware such as network cards, which allow communication with a network, and video graphics cards, which supplement or upgrade the PCs, graphics capabilities.

The most common expansion slot encountered is the *PCI Express*, or *PCIe*. USB and IEEE-1394 are not physically designed as traditional slots. However, they are a type of hardware expansion architecture and are therefore covered in this section.

A+ 1101: 3.4

PCI

Peripheral Components Interconnect (PCI) was introduced in the early 1990s and was the best choice for general-purpose expansion cards. An example of a PCI-based Ethernet card is shown in Figure 3-13. PCI has a 32-bit data width that transfers data at a rate of 132 MBps. The original PCI adapter had a frequency of 33 MHz, which was later increased to 66 MHz with the PCI 2.0 standard.

PCI incorporates a chipset with a buffer, which is used for a temporary data storage area. The buffer makes it possible to communicate with a slow motherboard bus by providing a place to store data until the bus becomes available.

PCI dominated the motherboard adapter design for over 10 years. However, demands for even greater data transfer rates spurred faster versions of PCI.

Figure 3-13 Peripheral Components Interconnect (PCI) was introduced in the early 1990s and was the best choice for general-purpose expansion cards.

Pakpoom Phummee/Shutterstock.com

PCI-X

PCI Extended (PCI-X) was designed as a replacement for PCI. It had a 64-bit data width and was capable of operating at a higher frequency (speed) than PCI. Fully backward compatible with PCI, you could install a PCI or PCI-X in the same expansion slot because they used the same pin assignments and voltages. The only difference was the higher-frequency capability of PCI-X, which caused high data transfer rates. PCI-X 2.0 introduced the double data rate (DDR), which operates at 266 MHz, and the quad data rate (QDR), which operates at 533 MHz. These speeds are high enough to support data transfers to gigabit Ethernet network cards as shown in Figure 3-14.

PCI-X was not widely accepted in desktop models of computers and was limited to network servers and high-end desktop models. As a result, PCI-X was quickly replaced by the PCI Express standard.

PCI Express

1101: 3.3, 3.4 A+

Often confused with PCI-X, **PCI Express (PCIe, PCI-E)** is a high-speed expansion bus designed to replace PCI and PCI-X. PCI Express was introduced in 2004 as an expansion card technology designed to replace earlier versions of adapters such as PCI, PCI-X, and AGP. An example of a PCI-E graphics card is shown in Figure 3-15.

While the original PCI adapter is based on parallel data transfer, PCIe uses serial data transfer. Ordinarily, data transferred in parallel moves much more data than a serial connection, but when it comes to electronics, you must understand electronic principles to see the advantage of serial data transfer over parallel.

At lower frequencies, parallel data transfer is better than serial, but serial data transfer is better than parallel at high speeds. As the speed of computers has increased over the years, serial has become the preferred method of data transfer

PCI-X Transfer Speeds

Bus Type	Speed	Capacity
PCI-X 1.0	133 MHz	8.5 Gbps
PCI-X 2.0 (DDR)	266 MHz	17 Gbps
PCI-X 3.0 (QDR)	533 MHz	34 Gbps

Goodheart-Willcox Publisher

Figure 3-14 The main difference between PCI and PCI-X was the higher data transfer rates in PCI-X, which were capable of supporting gigabit Ethernet.

Evan-Amos/Public Domain

Figure 3-15 PCI Express was introduced in 2004 as a replacement for PCI and PCI-X.

because at high frequencies, there are electrical limitations imposed by the parallel data bus design. There are two main circuit construction principles that must be followed to achieve high data rates:

- All circuit conductors need to be the same length.
- All conductors need to be bundled together, or in close proximity, to reduce the effects of inductive reactance.

The simple PCIe design meets both design principles and results in higher data rates. All PCIe conductors are the same length and are in close proximity. There are some variations of PCI Express such as PCI Express 2.0 and PCI Express 3.0. As of June 2022, the latest version is PCI Express 7.0, which provides a 128-GT (giga transfers) per second raw bit rate.

Conductor Length

When conductors have the same length, data transferred across the bus system arrives at the same time. Parallel bus design involves right-angle turns, which cause the length of the outside conductor to be many times longer than the inside conductor, as illustrated in Figure 3-16. Notice how the outside conductor length in Figure 3-16A is drastically longer in comparison to the inside conductor. This means that if data were sent in parallel over the conductors, the data would arrive at the ends of the conductors at different times. However, when conductors are run in pairs, as shown in Figure 3-16B, the overall length is more closely matched, and a higher data rate can be achieved.

Conductor Proximity

All conductors have a degree of inductive reactance when functioning as an electrical path, which reduces the ability of the conductor to achieve high data rates. When the conductors are bundled together, inductive reactance is reduced to a minimum or nearly canceled, thus allowing for higher data rates than a flat ribbon data cable.

Since PCIe uses a pair of conductors in close proximity to each other, most of the effect of inductive reactance is cancelled. This same principle of conductor pairs is used for IEEE-1394, USB, and SATA cables. These cables have all but replaced original flat ribbon-cable designs.

PCIe is designed from serial links referred to as *lanes*. The simplest PCIe, identified as PCIe, ×1 consists of a single lane with two pairs of conductors, or four conductors total. PCIe is bidirectional, meaning it can send and receive data at the same time. One conductor of each pair is used to send data, and the other conductor of each pair is used to receive data. A collection of lanes is referred to as a *link*.

The number of lanes used for PCIe is represented by the symbol "×" followed by a number. The symbol "×" represents the word "by." For example, *PCIe ×16* means *PCIe by 16* and represents a PCIe adapter with 16 lanes, or pairs of conductors. There is a

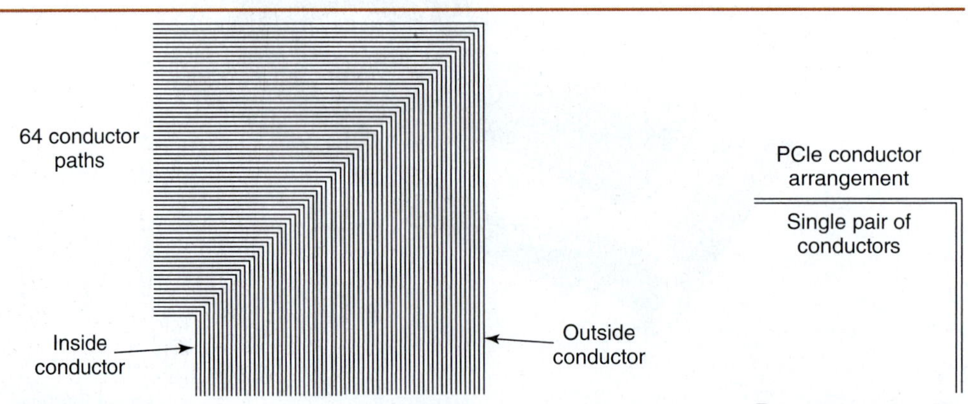

Figure 3-16 When conductors have the same length, data transferred across the bus system arrives at the same time. Parallel bus design involves right-angle turns (A), which cause the length of the outside conductor to be longer than the inside. Higher data rates can be achieved by running conductors in pairs (B).

PCIe ×32 specification, but it is seldom found in desktop motherboard designs because of space requirements. Relatively speaking, the PCIe 32-bit wide bus is so rare because it takes an enormous amount of motherboard real estate to implement. Figure 3-17 compares the design of PCIe ×1 conductors to traditional parallel conductors.

PCIe Specifications

The original PCIe specification, PCIe 1.1, typically runs at 2.5 GHz and transfers data at a rate of 250 Mbps per lane. In January of 2007, the PCI Express 2.0 specification was released with an increase that doubled the throughput of data. The PCIe 2.0 specification raised the bandwidth to 5.0 GHz and raised the data rate to 500 Mbps. The PCIe 3.0 standard further raised the data rate to 1 Gbps, while PCIe 4.0 is 2 Gbps and PCIe 5.0 is almost 4 Gbps. Figure 3-18 compares these specifications as well as other specifications you may encounter.

Figure 3-18 shows the transfer rate per lane, expressed in Gb/s, which is also the total number of bits transferred across the data bus, including control and timing signals, which is commonly referred to as ***overhead***. You may also see this figure expressed in ***GT/s (giga-transfers per second)***. The final five columns of the table indicate how many lanes each given version of PCIe supports. Thus, the value for an ×16 link is the total data rate when using all 16 lanes to transfer data.

A+ Note

The CompTIA A+ Certification Exams may contain several questions based on expansion card speeds. You should memorize the total bandwidth values of PCIe 1.1, PCIe 2.0, PCIe 3.0, PCIe 4.0, and PCIe 5.0. Always check the CompTIA website for the latest exam objectives.

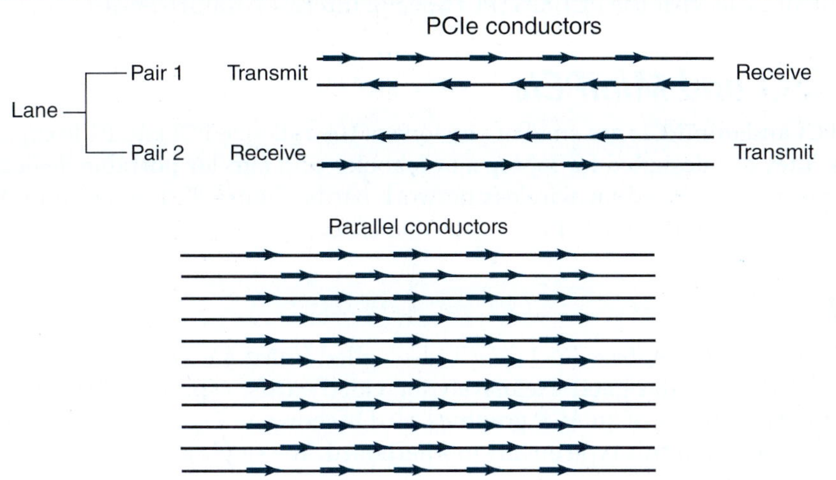

Goodheart-Willcox Publisher

Figure 3-17 A PCIe lane consists of two pairs of conductors, with each pair forming a single communication pair. These pairs cancel most of the effect of inductive reactance. Parallel conductors, however, carry data in the same direction and do not cancel the effect of inductive reactance.

Figure 3-18 Data rates for PCIe have steadily increased since its inception.

PCIe Throughput (Unencoded Bandwidth) by Specification

Version	Year Introduced	Transfer Rate per Lane (Encoded Serial Bit Rate)	×1	×2	×4	×8	×16
1.0	2003	2.5 Gb/s	0.25 GB/s	0.50 GB/s	1.0 GB/s	2.0 GB/s	4.0 GB/s
2.0	2007	5.0 Gb/s	0.50 GB/s	1.0 GB/s	2.0 GB/s	4.0 GB/s	8.0 GB/s
3.0	2010	8.0 Gb/s	0.985 GB/s	1.969 GB/s	3.938 GB/s	7.877 GB/s	15.754 GB/s
4.0	2017	16 Gb/s	1.969 GB/s	3.938 GB/s	7.877 GB/s	15.754 GB/s	31.508 GB/s
5.0	2019	32 Gb/s	3.938 GB/s	7.877 GB/s	15.754 GB/s	31.508 GB/s	63.015 GB/s
6.0	2022	64 Gb/s	7.563 GB/s	15.125 GB/s	30.25 GB/s	60.50 GB/s	121.0 GB/s
7.0	2025 (planned)	128 Gb/s	15.125 GB/s	30.25 GB/s	60.5 GB/s	121.0 GB/s	242.0 GB/s

Goodheart-Willcox Publisher

Parallel circuits are most often expressed in bytes (B), and serial are expressed in bits (b), which can add to the confusion when comparing various bus technologies. The bus data width must also be considered. For example, early PCI and PCI-X used 32-bit and 64-bit data bus widths, but the bus width for PCIe is 2—based on two pairs of conductors per lane. The chart in Figure 3-19 compares the data speed of PCI, PCI-X, and PCIe standards. Notice the performance difference between PCIe and earlier adapter technologies, such as PCI.

The PCIe standard maintains physical and electrical backward compatibility. This means you can install a legacy PCIe card into a PCIe 4.0 slot or install a PCIe 5.0 or PCIe 4.0 device into a PCIe 1.1 slot. However, when you mix two versions of PCIe slot and hardware devices, the device will only operate at the lower of the two bandwidths. In other words, if you install a PCIe 5.0 device with a bandwidth of 4 Gb/s into a PCIe 1.1 expansion slot with a bandwidth of 250 Mb/s, the much faster device will be stepped down to only operate at 250 Mb/s to match the legacy bus speed.

PCIe expansion cards are somewhat compatible, but some physical limitations exist. For example, a PCIe ×1 card can be inserted into a PCIe ×4 slot and perform without a problem, but you cannot insert a PCIe ×4 card into a PCIe ×1 slot because the PCIe ×4 card is much bigger than the PCIe ×1 slot. A variety of PCIe and PCI expansion slots on a motherboard are shown in Figure 3-20. PCIe provides better video performance than AGP and can be used for more devices than just video cards, but AGP is only used for video cards. To learn the latest up-to-date information about PCIe, visit the PCI-SIG (PCI Special Interest Group) website.

A+ 1101: 3.1, 3.4

MiniPCI and MiniPCIe

MiniPCI and miniPCIe are smaller versions of the full-size PCI and PCIe expansion cards. They are designed for laptops, notebooks, and similar portable devices and are typically employed for wireless network cards. Figure 3-21 shows a miniPCIe card next to a standard-size PCIe expansion card.

AGP

The *Accelerated Graphics Port (AGP)*, also called *Universal Accelerated Graphics Port (UAGP)*, was designed exclusively for video cards, especially for 3D graphic support. An example of an AGP graphics card is shown in Figure 3-22. There is usually only one slot of this type on any motherboard. The slot is designed to fit as close

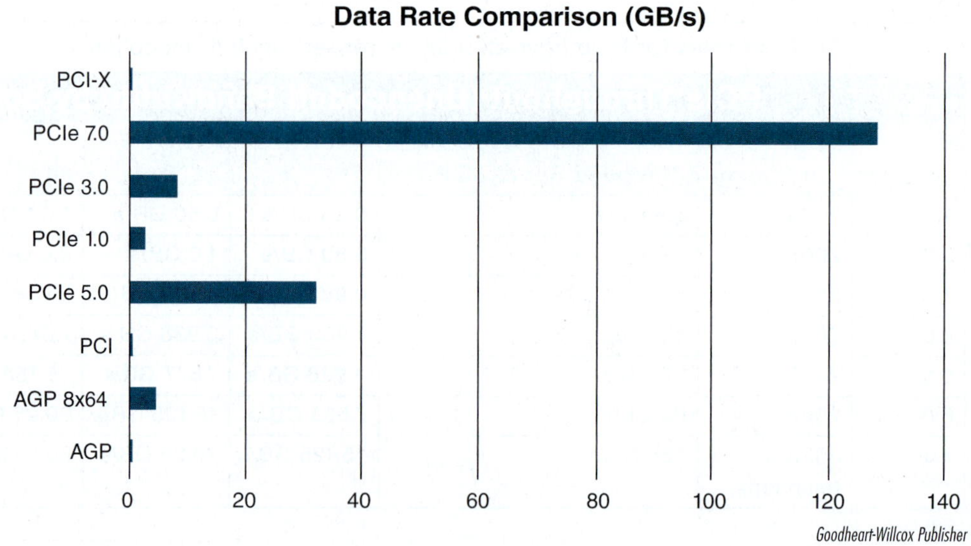

Figure 3-19 A tremendous amount of performance difference exists between early technologies, such as PCI, and new advancements, such as recent PCIe versions.

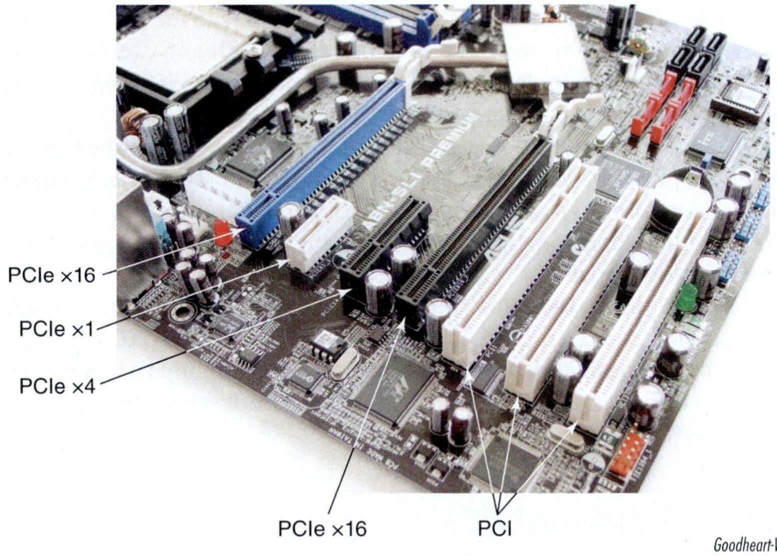

Goodheart-Willcox Publisher

Figure 3-20 A variety of PCIe and PCI expansion slots are available on most motherboards.

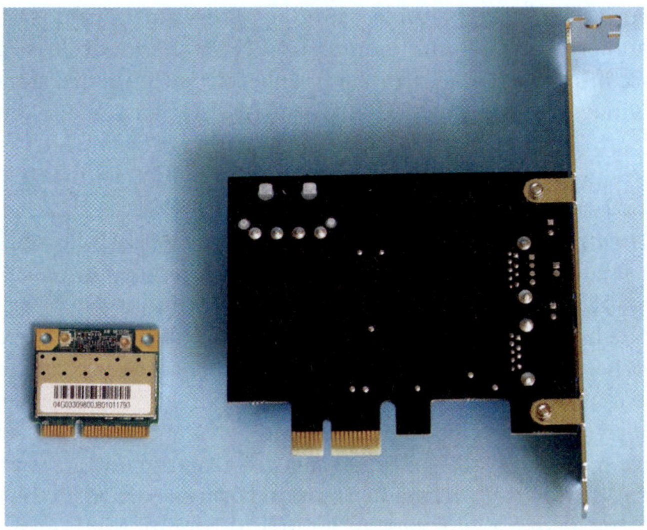

Goodheart-Willcox Publisher

Figure 3-21 MiniPCI and miniPCIe are smaller versions of full-size PCI and PCIe cards.

S.Dadhkevych/Shutterstock.com

Figure 3-22 The Accelerated Graphic Port (AGP) was designed exclusively for 3D graphic support.

as possible to the CPU and RAM to allow for high data transfer rates. The bandwidth for transferring data to and from the AGP can be significantly faster than PCI. AGP supported 32-bit data transfers at speeds ranging from 266 MBps for AGP 1.0 to 2133 MBps for AGP 2.0, as shown in Figure 3-23.

AGP offered excellent support for graphics programs until the introduction of PCIe. The most powerful feature of AGP is *Direct Memory Execute (DIME)*, which is the direct access to main memory used strictly to support video. This means the video card can use large portions of RAM rather than only the memory modules located on the video card.

AGP is almost obsolete at the time of this writing, and most video cards are now PCIe. You may still need to replace an AGP video card when repairing a legacy PC, so there will be much more about AGP, PCI, and PCIe as applied to video cards later in the textbook. For now, be able to identify these technologies and explain what they are used for most commonly.

Combined Functionality

Many devices are commonly used in a standard desktop computer. By combining the functions of several separate technologies into a single unit, a more economical device can be produced. For example, manufacturers can combine the functions of audio, USB, modem, DSL, network connection (Ethernet), wireless access technologies, and more into one device. Three examples of motherboard slot specifications that meet this need are Audio/Modem Riser (AMR), Advanced Communications Riser (ACR), and Communications and Networking Riser (CNR). The combined technologies are incorporated into one riser board, which is inserted into a slot on the motherboard.

The AMR technology was released first and was closely followed by CNR. AMR was later replaced by ACR, which maintained backward compatible with AMR. ACR is an organization that developed the ACR standard supported by 3COM, AMD, Lucent Technologies, VIA Technologies, Motorola, Texas Instruments, ACER, PCTEL, and others. ACR is now obsolete due to discrete components mounted directly on the motherboard.

CNR was originally developed by Intel and is the more popular choice by computer hardware manufacturers because it is royalty free and uses the same space as the PCI slot. With CNR sharing a PCI slot on the motherboard, the manufacturer does not need to make a major design change in the motherboard structure and circuitry the way they would for an AMR slot. On a single card, the Intel CNR board supports up to four different devices out of a possible seven types of devices. The slot is typically located at the edge of the motherboard, far away from components that produce interference. The riser cards incorporate audio devices. Audio can be corrupted by stray electromagnetic interference generated by other high-speed components. Figure 3-24 shows an example of a CNR slot.

Figure 3-23 AGP supports 32-bit data transfers at a variety of speeds based on the standard being used.

AGP Data Rates by Standard

Standard	Speed	Data Rate
AGP 1.0	1×	266 MBps
AGP 1.0	2×	533 MBps
AGP 2.0	4×	1066 MBps
AGP 3.0	8×	2133 MBps
AGP 3.5	8×	2133 MBps

Goodheart-Willcox Publisher

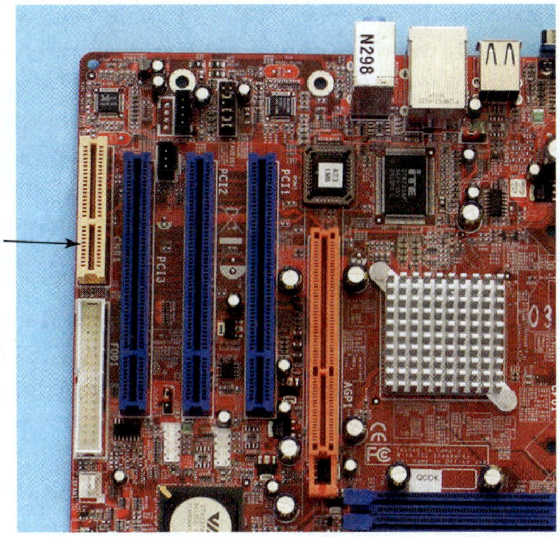

Goodheart-Willcox Publisher

Figure 3-24
Communications and Networking Riser (CNR) is a royalty-free standard developed by Intel corporation that supports up to four different devices.

Riser board technology is favorable for development of low-cost motherboard manufacturing, but there are two problems. First, if one or more of the devices incorporated into the riser board goes bad, the entire board will need to be replaced at a higher cost than if replacing a single item such as a modem card. Second, the cost of a replacement board is higher because you need to go through the original manufacturer.

Some Apple products have used *GeoPort*, a serial data system that allows for communication between internal and external devices. This technology is older and has largely been replaced by USB, but you may see it in the course of PC repair.

Common Expansion Cards

Given the wide variety of expansion slots available on motherboards, it should not come as a surprise that there are numerous expansion cards used to provide additional functionality to a motherboard. In most cases, these cards are used to add additional ports to the back of a computer. For example, many PCs are built with minimal ports in an effort to cut down weight, production time, and cost. As a result, the end-user may opt to increase the number available I/O options. Common examples of expansion cards are USB, external SATA, and IEEE-1394.

USB

A+ 1101: 3.1

Universal Serial Bus (BUS) is an industry standard for external serial bus ports and cables that function as connection, communication, and power for computers, peripherals, and networked devices. The USB system was designed to replace the existing variety of ports and expansion slots, such as serial and parallel ports and any expansion slot type, with the exception of high data-rate video expansion slots. USB is designed as a port rather than a traditional slot and connects many different types of input and output peripherals, up to 127 devices. It is accessed by plugging a USB device or cable into the bus at a port opening in the case. Inside the case, an internal USB connection is provided on the motherboard that feeds the system's external USB ports. For USB 1.0 and USB 2.0, there is a keyed 2×5 connection cable that slips over nine pins arranged in two rows on the edge of the motherboard. USB 3.0 utilizes a wider 19-Pin/20-Pin IDC male connector on the motherboard since it is reversible. In all cases, the USB connector attaches to a cable that feeds the external USB ports on the outside of the computer cabinet. External USB devices using USB cables are simply daisy-chained, so there is no need to open the computer case. Figure 3-25 shows a variety of USB 1.1 and 2.0 cable end connectors.

USB is designed so devices connected to the port are automatically detected, and communication between the computer system and the device begins. USB technologies conserve the use of IRQ assignments because each port only requires one IRQ, no matter how many devices are connected to it. For example, when two or more devices are connected to a USB port, they automatically share the same IRQ address without creating a conflict. Each device that connects to the USB port is assigned an address for identification purposes, and the devices alternate communicating through the USB port. Data moves along data lines as packets of information, similar to how networks communicate.

For USB to work properly, an operating system and a dedicated chipset must be used. For example, when a new USB standard is released, existing motherboard chipsets do not automatically support the new standard, even when the operating system does by using a software patch. The chipset and motherboard may not be designed for the improvements.

Figure 3-26 lists the names associated with each USB standard and its data rate. The USB names, Low-Speed, Full-Speed, Hi-Speed, SuperSpeed, SuperSpeed+, and Double SuperSpeed+, were designated by the USB Implementers Forum (USB-IF), which is responsible for developing the USB specifications.

Figure 3-25 USB cables connect many different types of peripherals and devices. One USB port can support up to 127 devices.

Daniele Mezzadri/Shutterstock.com

Figure 3-26 USB data rates vary based on the USB standard employed.

USB Standards and Data Rates

Name	USB Standard	Data Rate	Date Introduced
Low-Speed	1.0	1.5 Mbps	Jan. 1996
Full-Speed	1.1	12 Mbps	Aug. 1998
Hi-Speed	2.0	480 Mbps	Apr. 2000
SuperSpeed	3.0	5 Gbps	Nov. 2008
SuperSpeed+	3.1	10 Gbps	Jan. 2013
Double SuperSpeed+ (speed for USB-C)	3.2	10 Gbps plus 20 Gb over USB-C connectors	Jul. 2017
USB4 20 Gbps	4 Gen 2X2	20 Gbps	Mar. 2019
USB4 80 Gbps	Gen 4 Symmetric	80 Gbps	Sep. 2022

Note: The USB Implementers Forum (ISB-IF) refers to high-speed USB as "Hi-Speed" USB.

Goodheart-Willcox Publisher

USB 3.0, also known as SuperSpeed USB, made many improvements over the USB 2.0 standard. For example, the USB 3.0 standard provides much higher data transfer rates, raising the previous 2.0 standard from 480 Mbps to 5 Gbps—providing approximately 10 times more bandwidth. USB 3.0 also increased the output electrical power to 900 mA (milliamps) from the previous 500 mA associated with the USB 2.0 standard. The 3.0 standard specifies that data can be transferred in both directions at the same time. This is technically referred to as ***full duplex***. USB 2.0 is limited to half-duplex transmissions, which means data can only be transferred in one direction at a time. For example, two devices connected by USB 2.0 must take turns when communicating.

Another improvement of USB 3.0 is less power consumption. USB 3.0 devices use less power because the port is not constantly "polled" as it is with previous USB versions to see if a device is attached. The other major power-saving factor is the transfer speed. While USB 3.0 requires approximately twice as much power while performing data transfers, it transfers 10 times as much data. This is a net result of one-fifth total power consumed when transferring the same amount of data as USB 2.0. The last power-saving factor is data transfer overhead. USB 3.0 sends larger packets than USB 2.0, thus requiring less packet overhead (control signals). No polling, faster data transfer, and less data transfer overhead result in less power consumption. This is good for devices that use batteries, such as cell phones and tablets.

USB 3.1 introduced SuperSpeed+, which runs at 10 Gbit/s—double the rate of USB 3.0. The USB 3.2 standard brought yet another doubling bandwidth option for Type-C connectors via multi-lane operations over extra wires, which enable flip-flop reversible capabilities of the plug.

In August 2019, the USB-IF released the standards for USB 4, which is based on the Thunderbolt 3 protocol and supports 40 Gbit/s throughput. USB 4 2.0 was released in October 2022, but support for USB 4 is still lagging. There are a number of new Apple products that support USB 4, as do the Windows 11 operating system and the Linux kernel version 5.6.

USB Cables and Connectors

1101: 3.1 A+

Cables for USB 2.0 and earlier consist of four wires or conductors: two data lines (D+ and D–), a voltage bus (Vbus), and a ground (GND), as illustrated in Figure 3-27. The combination of the Vbus and GND carry power to each device connected to the USB port. Since the actual amount of electrical power carried on the electrical power lines is low, devices requiring additional power use their own electrical power supply.

USB carries commands and data on the two twisted data lines. The twist in the data pair reduces the amount of inductive reactance and helps achieve high data rates. This technique is also incorporated in some other high data-rate computer cables like SATA and network cables.

Typical USB 1.0 and USB 2.0 cables have various types of connectors on either end that are ***keyed***, which means they can only be inserted one way. On the computer end is a flat, rectangular plug known as a Type-A connector. Most computers have multiple Type-A interfaces for connecting various peripherals. On the other

Tech Tip

You must use high-speed USB 3.0 cables when connecting to USB 3.0 ports to achieve the 5-Gbps bandwidth. If you use a USB 2.0 cable with a USB 3.0 port, you will only achieve the USB 2.0 standard bandwidth.

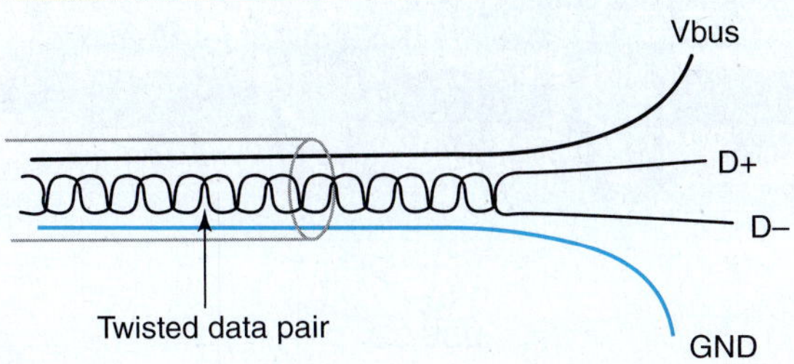

Goodheart-Willcox Publisher

Figure 3-27 Cables for USB 2.0 and earlier consist of two conductors, a voltage bus, and a ground.

end of USB 1.0 and USB 2.0 cables are various other styles of connectors specific to the type of peripheral being interfaced, including the following.

- Type-B: an almost square-shaped connector commonly used for printers and other powered devices
- Mini-USB: a somewhat flat plug that was the early standard for smaller devices
- Micro-USB: a nearly flat plug smaller than Mini-USB

Micro-USB is the most common standard for mobile and small, portable devices compatible with USB 1.0 and USB 2.0.

USB 3.0 increased the number of conductors and connection pins to achieve high bandwidth. Figure 3-28 compares the USB 2.0 motherboard connections with the USB 3.0 connections. Notice the increased pin count for USB 3.0 compared to USB 2.0. Figure 3-29 lists and describe the pin identification for USB 3.0 and earlier. Notice that USB 3.0 has an additional two pairs of data transmission wires labeled TX–, TX+, RX–, and RX+ beyond the single pair of USB 2.0 data lines labeled D– and D+. The additional USB 3.0 data lines enable USB 3.0 to have a higher data rate than USB 2.0. Also, notice how the first four pins of the USB 3.0 pinout perfectly match the USB 2.0 and earlier pinouts.

USB 2.0 has a specified cable length of five meters. USB 3.0 has no specified length but is generally three meters long. There are two general variations of USB connectors: Type A and Type B. Type-A USB connectors and ports are found on almost every full-size desktop computer, and Type-B USB connectors and ports are found mostly on printers, scanners, and external storage devices. The micro and mini styles are most often found on portable devices, such as cell phones, cameras, tablets, and GPS devices.

Figure 3-30 shows the general shape and number of connection pins for each USB 2.0 and USB 3.0 connector, Type A and Type B. Not included is USB 1.0, which is obsolete but has the same physical shape as USB 2.0. There are also several proprietary connector shapes not included that are similar to the micro and mini connector shapes.

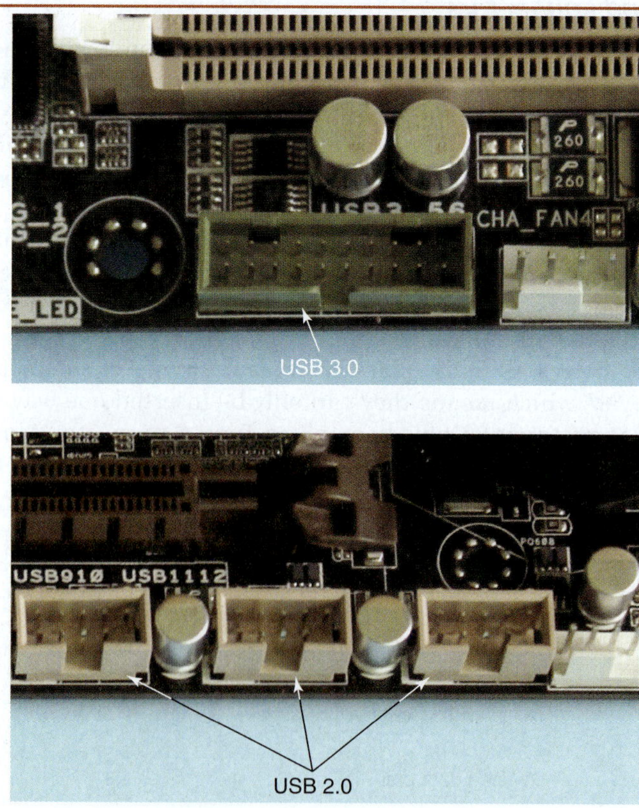

Figure 3-28 USB 3.0 provides additional pins to achieve higher bandwidth than USB 2.0.

Goodheart-Willcox Publisher

USB Pin Identification			
Generation	**Pin Number**	**Identification**	**Purpose**
1.0–2.0	1	Vbus	Electrical, 5 volts
1.0–2.0	2	D–	Data
1.0–2.0	3	D+	Data
1.0–2.0	4	GND	Electrical ground
3.0	1	Vbus	Electrical, 5 volts
3.0	2	D–	USB 2.0 data
3.0	3	D+	USB 2.0 data
3.0	4	GND	Electrical ground for power
3.0	5	RX–	USB 3.0 signal receive
3.0	6	RX+	USB 3.0 signal receive
3.0	7	GND	Electrical ground for signals
3.0	8	TX–	USB 3.0 signal transmit
3.0	9	TX+	USB 3.0 signal transmit
3.0	10	GND	Connection shield ground

Goodheart-Willcox Publisher

Figure 3-29 USB 3.0 has an additional two pairs of data transmission conductors labeled TX–, TX+, RX–, and RX+ when compared to USB 1.0, 1.1, and 2.0.

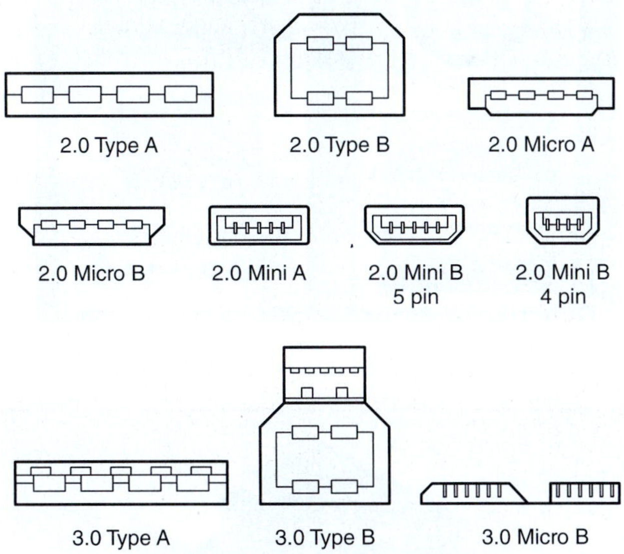

Goodheart-Willcox Publisher

Figure 3-30 USB connectors come in a variety of shapes and sizes (connectors not drawn to scale).

The USB Type A for 2.0 and 3.0 are physically the same shape, but they have a different number of pins: USB 2.0 has four pins, and the USB 3.0 has nine pins. The USB 2.0 mini–Type B comes in two varieties—five pin and four pin—and even though they share the same name, they are physically different. Other similar USB connectors exist that are proprietary and typically found on mobile devices such as cell phones.

Since USB 2.0 and USB 3.0 are visually similar, USB 3.0 ports are typically identified with a blue connector when both USB 2.0 and USB 3.0 exist on the same computer, as shown in Figure 3-31. The USB 3.0 standard does not specify that the color blue be used, but blue has been widely accepted as a de facto standard, meaning most people accept blue as the appropriate standardized color. Also, most computers use some type of port shield with markings, indicating the location of the USB 3.0 and USB 2.0 ports.

If a person attaches a USB 3.0 device to a USB 2.0 port, the device will not achieve the expected bandwidth. The same problem could occur if the user attaches a USB 3.0 device to a USB 3.0 port but uses a cable designed for USB 2.0 or older. When USB 3.2 is transmitted over a cable with USB-C connecters on both ends, the user can achieve the fastest possible connection to date at 20 Gb/s.

A+ 1101: 3.1

Upgrading to and Adding Extra USB 3.0 Ports

Upgrading a computer from USB 2.0 to 3.0 is easy. In fact, most new computers may not even need to be upgraded because Windows versions began support for USB 3.0 in Windows 8, and Windows 10 has built-in support for USB 3.0. However, if you need to add additional ports, you can do so with an expansion card such as the one shown in Figure 3-32. USB expansion cards install into PCIe slots and are powered by the computer's power supply. When installing a USB card, be sure to search for and install the most recent drivers. Without proper drivers, the USB 3.0 data speeds cannot be achieved, and the ports would behave like USB 2.0 or not function at all.

Figure 3-31 The USB 3.0 port is typically identified with a blue connector.

Goodheart-Willcox Publisher

Figure 3-32 Upgrading a computer or adding additional USB ports requires the installation of a USB expansion card and installation of drivers.

MZinchenko/Shutterstock.com

Notice the white connector on the expansion card in Figure 3-32. This is a typical Molex power connector. USB 3.0 is designed to provide up to 900 mA of current to USB 3.0 devices, which almost one full ampere of electrical current. The PCIe bus is not designed to supply this amount of current, so a separate power connection is provided to the expansion card.

Another option is to install exterior ports using an adapter, which installs into an empty slot in the back of the PC case and is powered by a port on the motherboard. There are also adapters made to fit into the front of the PC case. If you are just looking to add more USB ports, a simpler approach is to utilize a USB hub, such as the one shown in Figure 3-33. A ***USB hub*** is a peripheral device that plugs into a USB port and provides multiple access ports for additional devices. Note the blue USB 3.0 ports on the hub in Figure 3-33.

External SATA

1101: 3.1, 3.4 A+

While SATA technology was originally limited to internal PC connections used for hard drives and solid-state drives, external SATA (eSATA) allows devices to be connected outside the PC case. Figure 3-34 shows a comparison between SATA and eSATA connections. Many times, these cables and ports are often confused with USB cables and ports. Upon a closer examination you will notice that SATA and eSATA both have physical differences when compared to USB Type-A ports and connectors. If you look back to Figure 3-31, you will see an example of an eSATA port. Do not confuse SATA and eSATA among themselves, either. Note the distinct L-shape of the SATA connector shown in Figure 3-34. Since USB 3.1 SuperSpeed+ 10 Gb is nearly twice as fast as 6 Gb eSATA, this makes the latter standard mostly obsolete as external drives can efficiently connect via USB with better performance. There will be much more about SATA in a later chapter.

IEEE-1394

Specification ***IEEE-1394*** was first introduced by Apple computer systems and branded by the trade name ***FireWire***, though other manufacturers call their similar systems names such as ***i.link*** and ***Lynx***. FireWire is no longer supported by any newer devices. However, the nature of PC repair involves, at least occasionally, working with older devices. For that reason, it is important to know about FireWire.

Bborriss.67/Shutterstock.com

Figure 3-33 A USB hub is a peripheral device that plugs into a USB port and provides multiple access ports for additional devices.

Goodheart-Willcox Publisher; (SATA) macro lens/Shutterstock.com; (eSATA) Vincente Barcelo Varona/Shutterstock.com

Figure 3-34 SATA devices are internal, such as hard drives or optical drives. External SATA (eSATA) allows devices to be connected outside the PC case.

There are two IEEE-1394 standards associated with this specification: IEEE-1394a and IEEE-1394b. The IEEE-1394a standard provides a high rate of data transfer at 400 Mbps, and IEEE-1394b is twice as fast at 800 Mbps. FireWire was historically used for devices requiring a high data rate, such as video cameras. A single IEEE-1394 port can serve up to 63 external devices in daisy-chain fashion.

With the introduction of USB and IEEE-1394, manufacturers began reducing the number of slots available on the motherboard. In fact, the use of USB and IEEE-1394 has all but eliminated the need for expansion slots and parallel and serial ports as USB and IEEE-1394 can be used to connect any device that presently uses motherboard adapter-slot technology.

A+ 1102: 1.4

3.6 System Resources

System resources must be assigned and made available for peripheral devices such as printers, hard drives, and sound cards. The major system resources to consider are the I/O port address, memory addresses, IRQ, and DMA settings. Typically, system resources are automatically assigned by the operating system and device drivers. A PC technician rarely has to configure a hardware device manually but must be prepared to do so if needed.

A+ 1102: 1.3, 1.4

Windows Device Manager

A+ Note

Be sure you know the various ways to access Device Manager and modifications that can be made to hardware devices from that menu.

System resource assignments can be viewed in Windows Device Manager. To see the system resources assigned to a Windows 10 or 11 computer, open the **Start** menu, right-click **Computer**, and select **Properties** from the shortcut menu. From the System dialog box, select the **Device Manager** option. However, the easiest way to access Device Manager is through the **Search** box. This can be accomplished by entering Device or Device Manager into the **Start**>**Search** box or the **Search** box on the taskbar. You can also use the keyboard combination [Windows][X] and select **Device Manager** from the menu. You should see a screen similar to the one shown in Figure 3-35.

Device Manager presents a list of hardware devices installed in the computer system. The general hardware items listed can be expanded to show individual hardware devices identified by name.

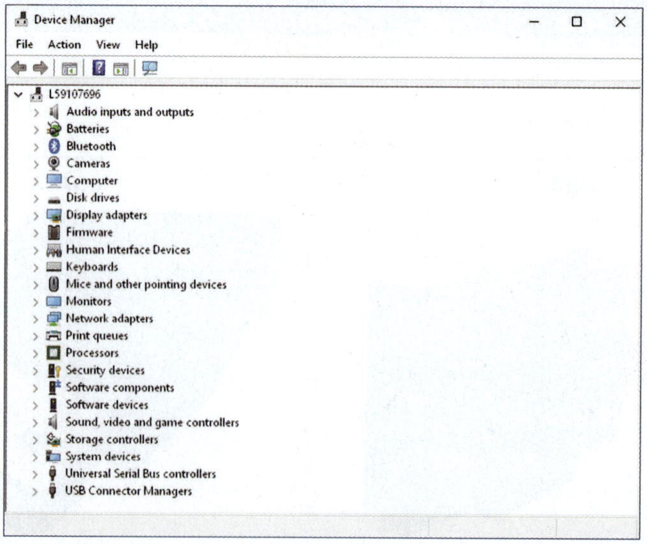

Figure 3-35 Device Manager is used to view hardware devices in the computer system and to configure or modify device resources and hardware drivers.

Goodheart-Willcox Publisher

To access the Properties menu for a specific hardware device, you can either right-click the device and select **Properties** from the shortcut menu or select **Action>Properties** from the menu listed at the top of Device Manager. The Properties menu displays information about the hardware configuration and resources, including options to make changes to the hardware device driver. Figure 3-36 shows the information revealed by each of the six tabs associated with the Properties menu of an Intel USB 3.1 host controller. Notice that you can view driver details as well as update the driver, disable the hardware device, uninstall a driver, and roll back a driver to an earlier version if a driver has been installed previously. The **Resources** tab reveals the system resources assigned to the hardware device. The **Events** tab was added in Windows 8 and continues through Windows 11. The **Power Management** tab enables a user to decide whether the device can be turned off by the computer and whether the device should be able to wake up the computer.

System Information

System resources can also be viewed from the System Information program, shown in Figure 3-37. This program is accessed by running **msinfo32.exe**. To run this file, you can enter msinfo32 or System Information in the **Search** box and then select the appropriate result.

Figure 3-36 The Properties menu displays information about the hardware configuration and resources.

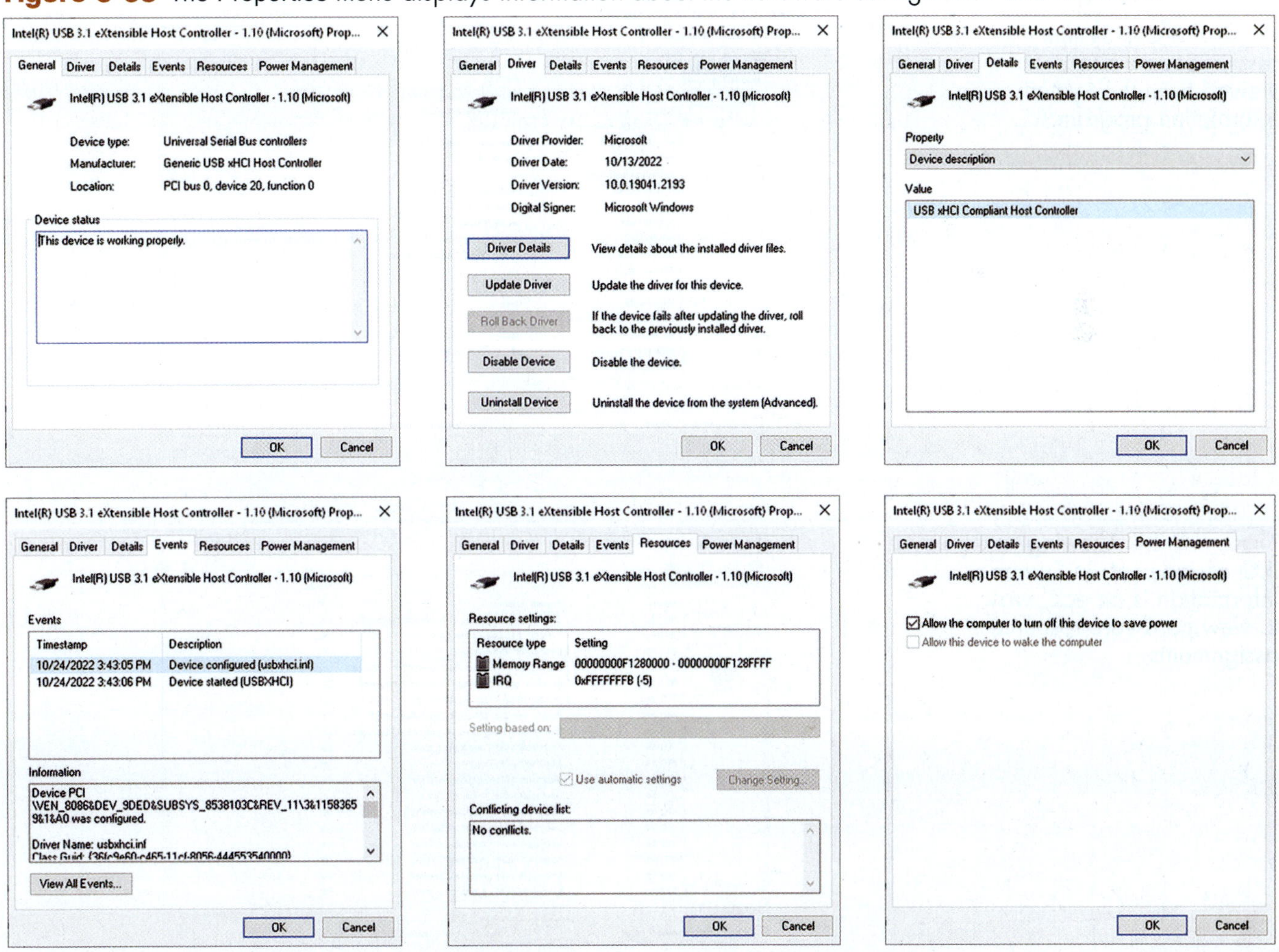

Goodheart-Willcox Publisher

The left pane lists the categories of information that can be viewed. When a category or subcategory is selected, the related information is displayed in the right pane. When **System Summary** is selected, information such as the operating system name and version, system (computer) name, username, processor type, and BIOS version is displayed. The system resources are located in the subcategories under the **Hardware Resources** category, including **Conflict/Sharing**, **DMA**, **Forced Hardware**, **I/O**, **IRQs**, and **Memory**. To view the subcategories, click the plus (+) sign next to **Hardware Resources**. In Figure 3-38, the **IRQs** subcategory is selected, and information about the assigned IRQs is shown in the right pane. You can see which IRQs are assigned to each device. This is a convenient way to view the hardware resource assignments. Additionally, a user may save the system information into a text file format or print the summary from the menu options.

I/O Port and Memory Address Range

Hardware components require part of the computer system's memory to be used for temporary data storage, and each device has a unique memory address range. A **memory address range** is an assigned section of memory used as a temporary storage area for data before it is transferred. Each device also has an **I/O port address**, which is an address assigned to a device for identification and communication purposes. Both the I/O port and the memory address are expressed as a range

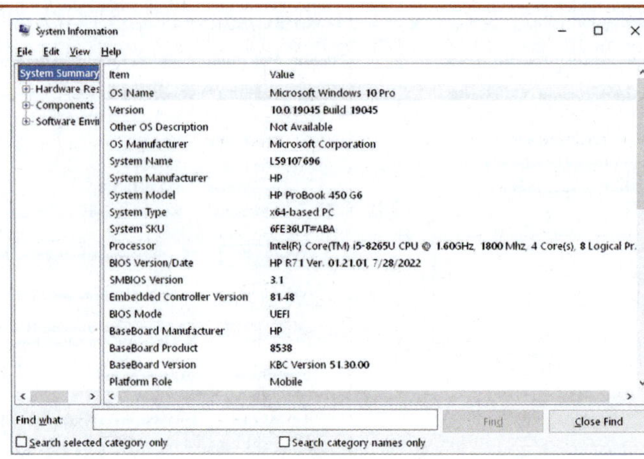

Figure 3-37 System resources can also be viewed from the System Information program.

Goodheart-Willcox Publisher

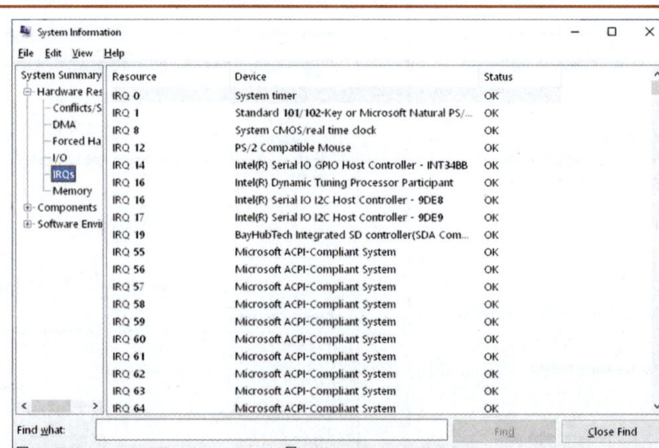

Figure 3-38 Viewing IRQ assignments in System Information is an easy way to view hardware resource assignments.

Goodheart-Willcox Publisher

and in hexadecimal notation, such as 03B0–03BB. Some devices have an I/O port address and a name.

A memory address is often mistaken for an I/O port address because a memory address also uses hexadecimal numbers for its assignments. Look at the resources assigned to a bus controller in Figure 3-39. The memory address range is the area used to store large amounts of disk information, and the I/O port is used to control communication between the PCI bus and the CPU. For example, if a command is issued on the bus for I/O port address number 2050–205F, then the device that is assigned port number 2050–205F accepts the command. Not all hardware devices have an assigned memory range, but most do have an assigned I/O port address range. Video cards, for example, require a large amount (range) of memory. If a large amount of video information is sent to the video card, the information is temporarily stored in the device's memory location range.

IRQ Settings

At some point, all devices connected to a motherboard will need the attention of the CPU, and the only way to share the attention of the CPU is through an orderly system of IRQ settings. An **IRQ (interrupt request)** is a signal that interrupts the processes taking place in the CPU to give attention to a device such as a keyboard or printer. Interrupts can refer to both hardware and software interrupts. Hardware interrupts are physically wired to the computer bus, whereas software interrupts are programmed into the software and call for the CPU's attention.

Figure 3-40 shows a listing of typical hardware IRQ assignments. Early PC designs used only eight IRQs, numbered 0 through 7, but today there are 16 IRQ settings used, numbered 0 through 15. Many of the IRQ settings are standard, such as the system timer, keyboard, COM1, LPT, primary IDE, and secondary IDE. However, computer systems are not limited to 16 hardware IRQ assignments. An unlimited number of IRQ assignments can be assigned through software. When an IRQ assignment is created using software, it is a logical or virtual assignment, which allows for flexibility and solves system conflicts much more easily. Look again at Figure 3-38 to see IRQ assignments higher than IRQ 16.

IRQs are also assigned priorities. A lower number for an IRQ means a higher priority. Look again at the system timer in Figure 3-40. It is assigned to IRQ 0, giving it the highest priority. The system timer is responsible for the timing of all devices, including the CPU, so this should always have an assignment of 00.

Tech Tip

When the IRQ design evolved from 8 to 16 IRQs, IRQ 2 was cascaded with IRQ 9. This means that IRQ 2 should never be assigned to any device, because IRQ 2 communicates with IRQ 9.

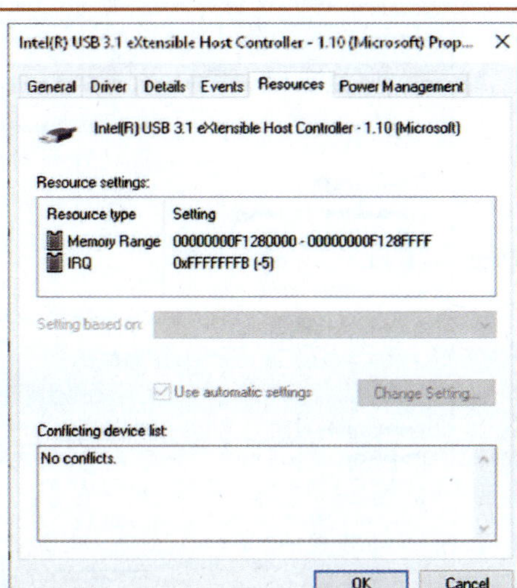

Goodheart-Willcox Publisher

Figure 3-39 A memory address range is an assigned section of memory used as a temporary storage area for data before it is transferred and is noted in hexadecimal form.

Another important aspect of IRQ assignments is ***IRQ conflicts*** that arise when two or more devices assigned the same IRQ setting try to access the CPU at the same time. When this happens, the conflicting request for attention can cause strange occurrences. Usually, only one of the two devices will have access to the CPU, giving the other device an appearance of being dead.

Two IRQ assignments can be shared if the devices are not going to be used at the same time, for example a scanner and camera. A digital camera can share an IRQ assignment with a scanner because it is highly unlikely both would be used at the same time. However, if the mouse and an optical drive were assigned the same IRQ setting, a problem would arise. If a mouse were identified first by the CPU, then the optical drive would appear disabled, and vice versa. Today, many chipsets are identified by IRQs and are shared with other chipsets and devices. Plug-and-play technology remedies most of the assignment problems, which will be discuss later in this chapter.

Examine Figure 3-41, which shows an interrupt request assignment viewed through the Properties menu for a system device. This dialog box is often used to verify or change IRQ settings. To view these settings for a device, open Device Manager and double-click the device in which you are interested; alternatively, you can also right-click the device and select **Properties** from the shortcut menu.

Figure 3-40 IRQ assignments may not match on all computers. Many IQRs will have more than one device assignment to them, especially controller chips.

Typical IRQ Settings

00 System timer
01 Keyboard
02 Cascade to 09
03 Com2
04 Com1
05 Sound card
06 Floppy disk controller
07 LPT1
08 System CMOS time clock
09 Network card (also cascade from IRQ2)
10 USB
11 SCSI
12 Mouse
13 Math coprocessor
14 Primary IDE
15 Secondary IDE

Goodheart-Willcox Publisher

Figure 3-41 Interrupt requests can be viewed through the Properties menu of a system device.

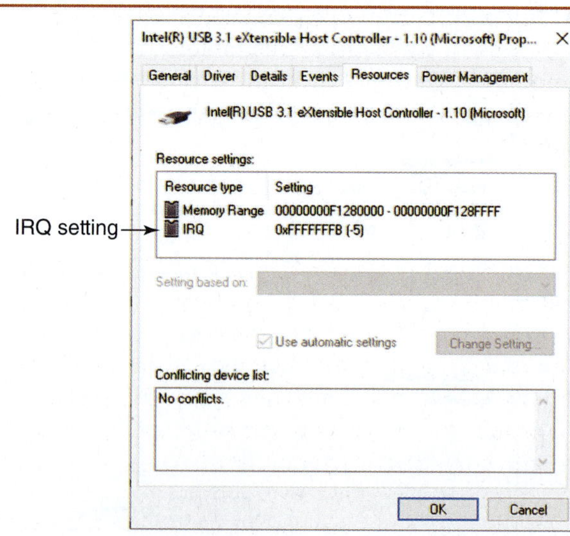

Goodheart-Willcox Publisher

DMA Channels

In the early days of computers, the CPU was designed to control all devices and their functions. For example, when data was moved from the hard drive to the RAM memory, each bit would have to be transferred to the CPU, and then the CPU would transfer the data to the memory location. **Direct memory access (DMA)** is a combination of hardware and software that allows the hard drive to transfer all data directly to memory without involving the CPU. Waiting for the CPU to take action caused a bottleneck for the transfer of data in the computer system. If the data did not need the CPU's attention, a device that has DMA could transfer the data directly into memory via the DMA controller.

The *DMA controller* is a chip that connects certain devices directly to memory, bypassing the CPU. Each DMA controller has four channels with one connected device per channel. A motherboard with a DMA controller has eight channels available for devices. DMA settings, like IRQ and I/O settings, can be viewed through the Properties menu for a system device.

DMA technology was used mainly for PATA hard drives, legacy printers, and floppy drives. Today, DMA assigned to a device is seldom encountered because chipsets eliminate the need for DMA assignments. The DMA controller still exists on modern computers to ensure backward compatibility with legacy devices, and you can still see DMA assignments for floppy drives, some types of PATA hard drives, and legacy printers using RS232-type connections.

Bus Mastering

Bus mastering is another method of control that allows data to be transferred directly between two devices without the intervention of the CPU. Control of the bus is usually taken while the CPU is busy with a task that does not require the use of the bus system.

The main difference between bus mastering and DMA is the intent of the device. Bus mastering takes control of the bus system to which it is attached, while DMA is used to access the memory system. DMA is designed to allow devices to communicate directly to and from the memory (RAM) without the intervention of the CPU. Bus mastering technology allows devices to carry out specific tasks such as communicating with each other without direct intervention of the CPU, allowing devices to carry out their individual tasks without using the CPU for every bit transfer. While the CPU is busy with other tasks such as calculations, the bus master controller handles the communication between two devices on the bus system.

Both DMA and bus mastering were designed to speed up the common operations involving data flow. To use either technology, the device, BIOS, operating system software, and motherboard chipset must be designed to support the technology. The function of bus mastering and DMA has been incorporated into modern motherboard chipsets.

Plug-and-Play

Plug-and-play refers to the automatic assignment of system resources such as DMA channels, interrupts, memory, and port assignments. As the name implies, with plug-and-play, you simply plug a device into the computer, and the system software automatically assigns the system resources; there is no need to configure the system resources manually. USB devices, such as keyboards, mice, and flash drives, are common examples of plug-and-play technology at work. For plug-and-play to work, the BIOS, hardware, and operating system must all support it. Before plug-and-play, expansion cards required the installer to set jumpers or dip switches into specific configurations to identify such things as the card's IRQ setting and port address.

Plug-and-play works well most of the time, but not for every case. There are times when the user must intervene. For example, you may encounter some difficulty when installing a device that incorporates newer technology than when the operating system was developed.

A+ 1102: 1.5, 1.9

3.7 Administrative Tasks

When it comes to motherboard functionality, there may be times when administrative intervention is needed. Often, this starts as a hardware device not behaving as expected or some type of utility not functioning correctly. In these cases, a technician or administrator may need to perform some type of corrective action. Generally, these tasks involve installing or updating drivers, upgrading the BIOS, utilizing the setup utility, or troubleshooting the actual motherboard.

Installing Software Drivers

In Windows 10 and 11, many device drivers, such as those for network adapters, monitors, printers, and video cards, are automatically downloaded and installed through **Windows Update**. Occasionally a download may still be required, but Windows has gotten efficient in terms of finding and loading the correct driver, especially in Windows 10 and 11. For older versions of Windows, many hardware device manufacturers recommended installing the software drivers before installing the device so the OS can use the correct drivers. Otherwise, the OS may choose a generic driver or incorrectly identify the device. When this happens, the device may not function properly. Software drivers, also called *device drivers*, are typically downloadable or available on an accompanying CD/DVD.

Device Manager has two options for changing a driver:

- The **Roll Back Driver** option can be used to replace the current driver with an earlier version.
- The **Update Driver** option automatically searches for a newer version of the driver.

These options are convenient, but there is a risk involved. Recall that an operating system may incorrectly identify a device or install an incorrect driver. If this occurs, visit the website of the hardware manufacturer and manually download and install the most recent driver for your device.

Motherboard chipsets also require software drivers. A common mistake made by novices when building a computer system or replacing the motherboard is not installing the motherboard drivers, which can result in a failure of the system to support hardware devices connected to the motherboard. Historically, motherboard drivers were located on a setup CD/DVD that typically accompanied the motherboard, but with optical drives appearing on fewer devices, you may have to download these drivers to a flash drive prior to installation. Note, the drivers for the motherboard are not the same as the firmware software in the BIOS or UEFI.

When installing the motherboard drivers using the setup CD/DVD, it is important to read all the information provided on the disc and to perform a custom install rather than a default install. The default install will typically install all software that comes on the disc, which likely includes trial versions of commercial products such as web browser software, security suites, antivirus software, and computer utilities. When a custom install is selected, you can choose exactly which products you wish to install. If you install a security suite from the motherboard disc and then install another security suite or antivirus program, computer performance will be greatly decreased. Additionally, multiple security system software on the same computer is not a good practice. There will be more about this issue later in the textbook.

Upgrading the BIOS

Upgrading the BIOS is a common task performed when upgrading hardware systems on older computers, but it is not exclusive to hardware. Certain software programs can require an upgraded version of the BIOS. For example, problems arose when plug-and-play was introduced to consumers. The appropriate operating system may have been available with a plug-and-play device installed, but the system could not detect or support the device until the BIOS was upgraded.

To upgrade the BIOS program on early computer motherboards, a technician had to either replace a physical BIOS chip or use an ultraviolet light to erase the program on the chip before reprogramming it. The first BIOS programs were electrically etched into the microscopic circuitry inside a programmable read-only memory (PROM) chip. These chips were programmed once by the manufacturer and could not be reprogrammed and simply had to be replaced.

Another variation of the BIOS chip called the erasable programmable read-only memory (EPROM) was developed with a transparent window usually covered by a foil sticker with the BIOS manufacturer name and part identification on it. When the sticker was removed, a window exposing the circuitry inside the chip was revealed. If an ultraviolet light were shone through the exposed window, the program in the chip would be erased, allowing it to be reprogrammed. These past techniques are no longer used.

Modern PCs use **flash BIOS**, which is a reprogrammable BIOS stored in an electrically erasable programmable read-only memory (EEPROM) module. Flash BIOS is reprogrammed using software available through the motherboard manufacturer's website and an updated BIOS program file. Today, most PC manufacturers also offer utilities to install firmware upgrades on the system, such as bug fixes and security patches.

The following are general instructions for upgrading flash BIOS. Be sure to follow the manufacturer's instructions for upgrading a specific BIOS. Note, if not done correctly, flashing the BIOS can result in an operable machine.

1. Download the BIOS upgrade program and updated BIOS program file from the motherboard manufacturer's website.
2. Copy the BIOS upgrade program and the updated BIOS program file onto a USB flash drive.
3. Boot the PC with the USB flash drive inserted into a USB port.
4. Run the BIOS upgrade program.
5. When the BIOS upgrade program asks for the name of the BIOS program file, enter the exact name of the BIOS program file.
6. If the BIOS upgrade program asks you if you want to back up the contents of the BIOS, answer "yes." Having a backup of the BIOS is vital if you need to return the BIOS to its original state. The BIOS upgrade program will then back up the original contents of the BIOS, erase the contents from the BIOS, and write the new BIOS program file to the BIOS.
7. When the procedure has successfully completed, reboot your PC, and enter the setup utility. Do not be alarmed if you do not see the new BIOS date and information in the setup utility screen.
8. Enter the setup utility and set it to its default settings.
9. Save the changes and reboot the computer again.
10. When the computer is rebooting, enter the setup utility again. You should see the date of the new BIOS program.
11. Enter the correct settings for your system.
12. Save the changes and reboot the computer.

A+ 1101: 3.4

Tech Tip

Upgrading the BIOS can render the PC inoperable. Visit the manufacturer's website first and read all information pertaining to BIOS upgrades before attempting to perform. Follow the manufacturer's instructions for upgrading your particular BIOS, and always ensure a laptop is plugged in before attempting to upgrade.

Tech Tip

Details vary somewhat for different motherboards and BIOS upgrade procedures. For detailed steps on upgrading a particular BIOS, consult the manufacturer's website.

On most current motherboards, the BIOS can be automatically upgraded through the Windows operating system. For example, the Intel Express BIOS Update utility can be downloaded via the Internet and saved as an executable file (**.exe**) in the default **Downloads** folder. To start the upgrade process, you simply double-click the executable file, and the familiar InstallShield Wizard followed by the typical license agreement will display. When you click **Finish**, the computer will automatically reboot and start the upgrade process. The status of the upgrade process will appear on the screen in text format. The computer will restart once again when the BIOS upgrade process is complete.

Some ASUS-brand motherboards include a USB BIOS Flashback button, often found on the back of the motherboard, as shown in Figure 3-42. These buttons enable a PC technician to update the system BIOS. The technician must first download the newest version of firmware to a USB flash drive and then insert the drive into the white USB 2.0 port beside the USB BIOS Flashback button. Next, the technician presses the button, and the firmware is automatically upgraded.

The BIOS determines any interface configurations or restrictions that have occurred to assure effective operation of hardware. It also permits the appropriate resources to allow a computer to run the operating system. However, a technician can enter a computer's CMOS Setup to adjust interface configurations and other base-level settings, such as those for USB, serial, and parallel port interfaces, as well as the boot order of the personal computer. CMOS Setup is stored in nonvolatile random-access memory (NVRAM), which means that the changes to the settings are not lost if or when a machine loses its power.

Tech Tip

The exact process and terminology of clearing the CMOS data varies among motherboard manufacturers.

Setup Utility

To store a computer's date, time, and information about its hardware in CMOS, the setup utility is used. The setup utility allows you to

- identify the type of hard drive and other storage systems installed;
- identify the type of chipset installed;
- establish a password for accessing the setup utility;
- select power-management features; and
- configure the boot order of the hard drive, CD/DVD drive, USB flash drive, and solid-state drive (SSD).

The setup utility is activated by a special set of keystrokes during the boot-up period. The instructions for accessing the setup utility are often displayed on the screen, but when they are not, accessing a computer's setup utility can be difficult. There are many ways to access the setup utility, some of which are listed in Figure 3-43. These key combinations could prove helpful for the troublesome computer. Keep in mind that what works for a particular brand one day may not work in the future. Another way to find the right key combination is to check the manufacturer's website. You may have to open the computer case and look at the brand and model number on the BIOS chip.

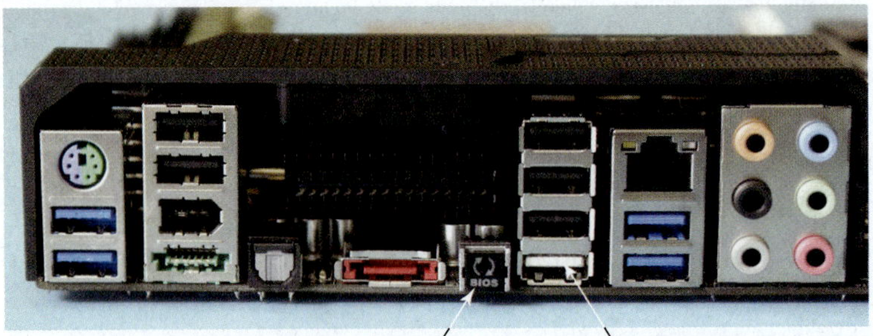

Figure 3-42 The USB Flashback button and white USB 2.0 port on some motherboards allow for an easy method for updating the BIOS.

Goodheart-Willcox Publisher

Figure 3-44 shows an illustration of a typical setup utility screen. Not all setup utility screens look the same, but they are similar in appearance and function. The most obvious difference between traditional BIOS and UEFI setup utilities is the appearance. UEFI firmware has a true high-resolution GUI and allows for the use of a mouse or similar pointing device, whereas the traditional BIOS setup utility is a text-based interface that only allows keyboard input. The traditional BIOS setup utility may use graphic images to display during the boot process, but the images are low resolution. The text-based interface at times appears to be graphic, but on closer examination, you can see that the graphics, such as lines, boxes, and shading, are really made from ASCII characters. UEFI firmware uses graphics consisting of drawn lines and shapes.

The usual default setting for the boot sequence is the hard drive followed by the CD/DVD drive. You may also see an option for a floppy drive since older computer systems may present the floppy drive as a choice whether the drive is installed or not. Modern computer systems often present a floppy drive as a choice only if it is physically installed and detected. Sometimes, computers are set to boot from the hard drive first as a time-saving measure or for security reasons.

Another interesting feature is password protection for the setup utility. By protecting the setup program with a password, unauthorized personnel cannot change

Setup Utility Access	
BIOS or Computer Manufacturer	**Key(s) to Press**
AMI	[Del] or [Esc] during POST
Award, Phoenix	[Ctrl][Alt][Esc] or [Ctrl][Alt][S] or [F2] during POST
Dell	[Ctrl][Alt][Enter]
Compaq	[F2] or [F10] or [Ctrl][Alt][F2]
DTK	[Esc]
IBM PS/2	[Ctrl][Alt][Del] followed by [Ctrl][Alt][Insert]
Gateway 2000	[F1]
Sony PC	[F3] while booting, followed by [F1] at Sony logo
NEC	[F1] when cursor flashes on screen

Goodheart-Willcox Publisher

Figure 3-43 Accessing a computer's setup utility can be accomplished in various ways.

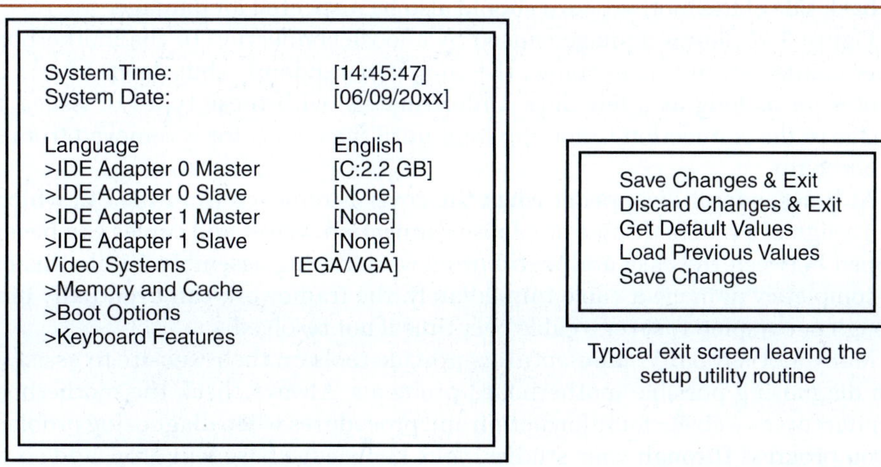

Above is a typical first screen display of the setup utility program.

Goodheart-Willcox Publisher

Figure 3-44 Not all setup utility screens look the same, but they are all similar in appearance and function.

the settings. Curious PC users often inadvertently change the system settings, and having a password prevents accidental changes.

If the setup utility is password protected and the password is forgotten, the CMOS will have to be erased to allow a new password to be programmed. Some motherboards are equipped with a jumper for erasing the data in CMOS. Moving the jumper to the "clear CMOS" position erases all CMOS data, even the password, and moving it back to its original location allows settings to be reentered.

Troubleshooting Motherboards

The motherboard is one of the most expensive parts to replace, and problems with it are some of the most difficult to diagnose. Understanding all the peripheral devices associated with the PC is required for diagnosing a defective motherboard. Many times, the process of diagnosing a problem requires third-party diagnostic software or hardware.

The difficulty in diagnosing a motherboard fault is that all major components use the motherboard circuitry. For example, imagine you are troubleshooting a problem with a Wi-Fi card. First, you would examine the Wi-Fi card and its connections. After all methods of diagnosing the card have been exhausted, the motherboard chipset or circuitry could be at fault. Unfortunately, the entire motherboard must be changed to be sure.

Issues with the CPU are even more problematic. Substitution can be expensive when trying to determine if the CPU or motherboard is at fault because both parts are expensive. Before replacing the motherboard, always start with a simple inspection of some common failure points; many times, electronic equipment failures are nothing more than loose connections. All the jumpers and connections associated with the motherboard should be checked. A detailed drawing of the component layout (from the manufacturer's website) will help locate all possible connections and jumpers. Many times, the simple act of reconnecting jumpers and connections will remedy the problem.

Sometimes a computer can be repaired simply by removing and reinstalling the CPU. The connection pins can become oxidized and stop the flow of electrical energy. Removing and reinserting often clears enough of the thin coating of oxidation to clear the fault. It is important to follow proper procedures when pulling a CPU, including using a grounding strap. When cleaning or upgrading a CPU on the motherboard, be sure to apply new thermal paste or silver silicone thermal conductive compound grease to the top of the chip before replacing the heat sink and fan.

Look for obvious signs of lightning or high-voltage surge damage. A small, burnt area on the motherboard bus at the connection to a component is a sure sign. The back side of the motherboard should also be inspected for damage.

Figure 3-45 shows damage caused by a loose connection to the motherboard power connector. In this example, the computer randomly shut down after a few minutes for as long as a few days. Unfortunately, with these types of issues, the damage to the connection is not apparent until the connector is removed from the motherboard.

At times, a fault disappears when the cover is removed from the PC, which is often a sign of a pinched cable or a loose connection. Wires and cables can become trapped between the case and metal framework during assembly. While this may not completely damage a cable immediately, the framework can eventually pinch through or completely sever a cable over time if not resolved.

Many motherboard manufacturers provide tools on their website to assist you with diagnosing possible motherboard problems. Always check the motherboard manufacturer's website for information and procedures when diagnosing problems. As you progress through your studies, your knowledge base will grow and so will your troubleshooting skills.

3.8 Identifying Motherboard Components

There are many motherboard manufacturers, each with their own unique designs. As a result, the process of identifying jumper and connection locations, chips, and other major components can be very confusing. Motherboard manufacturers often include a drawing of the motherboard in the motherboard user guide to help with identifying the approximate locations of all common connection points on the motherboard, such as the USB ports, power, fan power ports, CPU socket, PCI slots, and PCIe slots. The parts in the drawing are numbered, and the numbers are correlated to their related component name and listed in a table. A motherboard user guide comes with a motherboard when purchased or it can be downloaded from the manufacturer's website.

A+ 1101: 3.4

Figure 3-46 shows a photo of the motherboard with the components labeled. Most motherboard components can be easily identified by their relative position

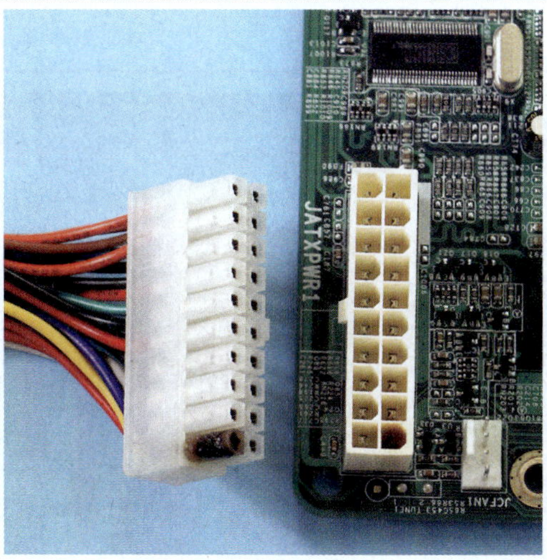

Goodheart-Willcox Publisher

Figure 3-45 A loose power connector can damage the power supply connector and its motherboard connection.

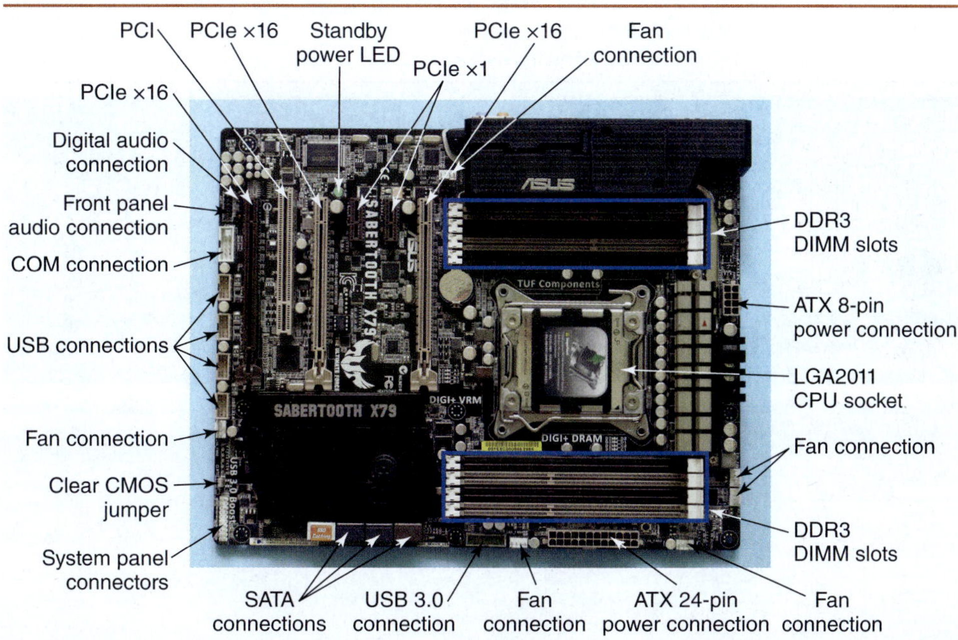

Goodheart-Willcox Publisher

Figure 3-46 Motherboard components can be easily identified by their relative position and outline on each motherboard.

and outline on each motherboard. The pin locations for the front-panel connection on this same motherboard are shown in Figure 3-47. These pins provide a connection point for the power switch, system reset switch, power-on LED, hard drive activity LED, and simple speaker, which is used to sound out diagnostic beeps. Also shown are connections for a system fan and USB 2.0 port.

Front-panel connection wires are usually quite small, and it can be difficult to get the conductor onto the correct motherboard connection pin. To make this process easier, some motherboards provide a front-panel connector kit, such as the one shown in Figure 3-48. You simply insert the front-panel conductors into the appropriate slot of the connection kit; then attach the kit to the front-panel pins located on the motherboard. The connector kit adapter slips easily over the connection pins (sometimes referred to as the ***header***) on the motherboard, ensuring each conductor is on the correct pin. As you can see, the connection pins are clearly marked, which is much easier than trying to read the connection pin locations on the motherboard. Notice that the electrical polarity plus (+) and minus (–) is indicated on the connector. Electrical devices such as LED lights must connect with the correct polarity, or they will not work properly.

Figure 3-47 The front-panel connection is used to provide a connection point for a variety of devices, including USB, power fans, and power and reset buttons. They also allow a user to clear the CMOS through the placement of a jumper.

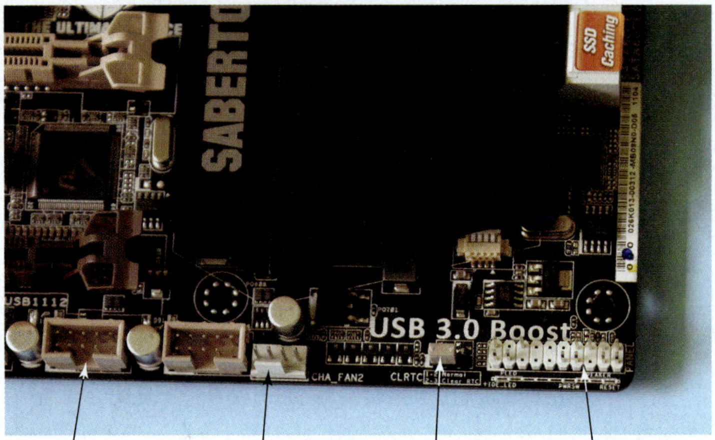

Goodheart-Willcox Publisher

Figure 3-48 Front-panel connector kits can be used to make connections between cables in the front of the PC and front-panel pins on the motherboard.

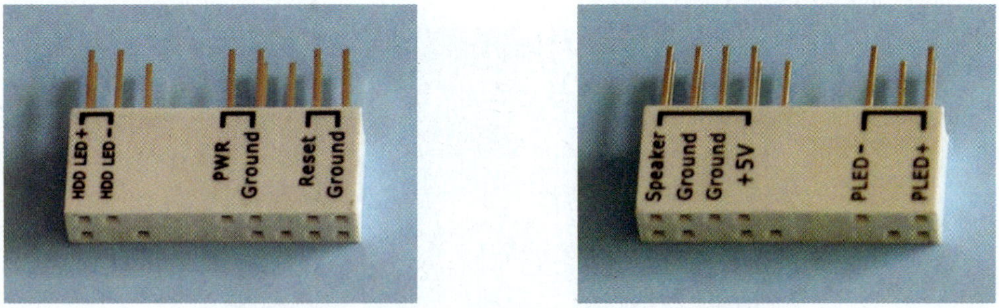

Goodheart-Willcox Publisher

Chapter Summary

3.1 Motherboard Construction

- The motherboard provides a physical surface on which to mount electronic components such as resistors, capacitors, chips, slots, and sockets.
- The electrical circuits that run across the surface of the motherboard are called *traces*.
- Conductors are grouped together to make up what is called a bus. Common motherboard buses include the data bus, control bus, memory bus, I/O bus, internal bus, local bus, address bus, and power bus.

3.2 Form Factors

- The form factor is the physical shape or outline of a motherboard and the location of the mounting holes.
- There are multiple form factors, including AT, Baby AT, ATX, Micro-ATX, Flex-ATX, Mini-ITX, Nano-ITX, Pico-ITX, Mobile-ITX, LPX, NLX, BTX, Micro-BTX, Nano-BTX, Pico-BTX, and backplane.

3.3 Motherboard Bus System Architecture

- A motherboard chipset is a collection of integrated circuits that connects the motherboard buses and ports that run at different speeds.
- Chipsets are an integral part of the motherboard and not field replacement units. You cannot change the chipset. Instead, you must replace the entire motherboard.
- Originally, chipsets consisted of two chips referred to as the northbridge and southbridge. The northbridge connected high-speed devices and was located near the CPU. The southbridge connected slower devices and was placed farther away from the CPU.
- Today, motherboards only have one chipset, but the terminology remains. Intel replaced the northbridge and southbridge with the Intel QuickPath Interconnect (QPI).

3.4 RAM Compatibility

- It is important to know the type of RAM you are using because not all types are compatible with all motherboards.
- There have been numerous technologies used to implement RAM, including DDR, DDR2, DDR3, DDR4, and DDR5.
- Each version of DDR improved on the clock speeds and, in many cases, power consumption of its predecessor.
- RAM types have various channel configurations, which usually—but not always—match the number of chip configurations.

3.5 Expansion Card Slots

- Expansion card slots provide a quick and easy method of connecting devices directly into the motherboard bus system.
- There are several types of motherboard slots available, such as PCI, PCI-X, PCIe, Mini-PCI, Mini-PCIe, AGP, CNR, ACR, and AMR. PCIe is the most common.
- Using the expansion card slots, a user can add a variety of additional I/O ports to the computer, including USB, eSATA, and IEEE-1394.

3.6 System Resources

- System resource assignments must be assigned for peripheral devices such as printers, hard drives, and sound cards. These assignments can be viewed in Windows Device Manager or System Information.
- Each device has a unique memory address range and I/O port address.
- IRQ assignments determine where the CPU's attention is directed.
- Direct memory access (DMA) channels allow the hard drive to transfer data directly to memory without involving the CPU.

3.7 Administrative Tasks

- Administrative tasks related to motherboard maintenance include installing or updating drivers, upgrading the BIOS, utilizing the setup utility, and troubleshooting the motherboard.
- Device Manager allows you to replace drivers with earlier versions or update drivers to new versions.
- Manufacturers typically recommend that software drivers for a device be installed before installing the device.
- Upgrading the BIOS is common when upgrading hardware systems on older computers.
- BIOS upgrade procedures vary somewhat for different motherboards; therefore, you should always consult the manufacturer's website for detailed steps on upgrading a particular BIOS.
- The setup utility allows users to identify the type of hard drive and other storage systems installed; identify the type of chipset; establish a password for accessing the setup utility; select power-management features; and configure the boot order of the hard drive, CD/DVD drive, USB flash drive, and solid-state drive (SSD).
- The setup utility is used to view and modify system settings and can be accessed by a special set of keyboard strokes during the boot-up period.
- The motherboard is one of the most expensive parts to replace, and problems with it are some of the most difficult to diagnose.
- When troubleshooting a motherboard, look for pinched cables, loose connections, oxidation, and high-voltage damage.

3.8 Identifying Motherboard Components

- Motherboard manufacturers include a drawing of the motherboard in a user guide, which can be used to identify the major parts of a motherboard.
- Some motherboards provide a front-panel connector kit to make it easier when connecting front panel cables to the motherboard.

Review Questions

1. What is a *trace*?
2. List and describe eight types of buses found on a motherboard.
3. What does a motherboard's form factor identify?
4. List form factors that have been developed over time.
5. What is unique about the LPX and NLX form factors?
6. Explain motherboard bus architecture.
7. Explain *inductive reactance*.

8. Summarize the importance of ensuring RAM compatibility with a motherboard.
9. Identify architectures for expansion card slots.
10. What are the four major system resources used by computer devices?
11. Explain the purpose of Device Manager.
12. What type of information can be found in the Properties menu for a component listed in Device Manager?
13. Differentiate between a memory address range and an I/O port address.
14. Which IRQ assignment has the highest priority?
15. List common administrative tasks associated with motherboards.
16. Explain how to perform a software driver installation.
17. Summarize the process for performing a BIOS upgrade in a recent Windows operating system.
18. What types of actions can be performed in setup utility?
19. When troubleshooting a motherboard, what are some things a PC technician should check?
20. What can a PC technician use to aid in component identification on a motherboard?

Sample A+ Exam Questions

1. Which is the smallest motherboard form factor?
   A. AT
   B. Mini-ATX
   C. Flex-ATX
   D. Mini-ITX
2. Which technology supports the fastest transfer speeds?
   A. PCI
   B. USB 3.0
   C. PCIe
   D. IEEE-1394b
3. Which slot design is exclusively used for video cards?
   A. PCI
   B. AGP
   C. USB
   D. IEEE-1394
4. IRQ settings can be accessed and modified in Windows through the _____.
   A. Device Manager
   B. System Resource icon in Control Panel
   C. IRQ icon in Control Panel
   D. System Resources dialog box
5. Which program will display information about all the system resource assignments at once?
   A. Internet Explorer
   B. Device Manager
   C. System Information
   D. Event Viewer

6. With which of the following is the UEFI standard concerned?
   A. Software drivers
   B. Motherboard ports
   C. System firmware
   D. System video
7. Where does the computer store information about the type of hard drive installed?
   A. At sector 2 of the hard drive
   B. In the CMOS
   C. In the system ROM chip
   D. In the system RAM chip
8. What is required for plug-and-play technology to work correctly? Select all that apply.
   A. Plug-and-play BIOS
   B. An operating system that supports plug-and-play
   C. Plug-and-play enabled through Device Manager
   D. Plug-and-play supported by a device being installed

9. What is the name of the executable file that produces the System Information window?
   A. **msinfo32.exe**
   B. **32.exe**
   C. **system32.exe**
   D. **information32.exe**
10. Which of the following items controls the speed of data flow across different bus architectures on a motherboard?
   A. BIOS
   B. Motherboard chipsets
   C. DMA channels
   D. IEEE-1394

Chapter 4

Central Processing Unit (CPU)

Learning Outcomes

4.1 Recall the purpose of an instruction set.
4.2 List the components of a CPU that work together to perform basic operations.
4.3 List technologies used to enhance CPU operation.
4.4 List features and terms used to explain, identify, and compare CPUs.
4.5 Identify top CPU manufacturers and discuss recent CPU evolution for each.
4.6 Differentiate between multicore and multi-socket CPUs.
4.7 Summarize the installation process of a CPU.
4.8 Differentiate among processor-cooling technologies.

A+ Certification Exam Objectives

The following A+ Certification Exam Objectives are covered in this chapter.

Exam 220-1101

3.0 Hardware

- 3.4 Given a scenario, install and configure motherboards, CPUs, and add-on cards.

Exam 220-1102

1.0 Operating Systems

- 1.3 Given a scenario, use features and tools of the Microsoft Windows 10 operating system.
- 1.7 Given a scenario, apply application installation and configuration concepts.

Key Terms

Advanced RISC Machine (ARM) processors
arithmetic logic unit (ALU)
assembly language
cache
compiler
complex instruction set computer (CISC)
control unit
decode unit
dual independent bus (DIB)
dynamic execution
floating-point unit (FPU)
instructions
instruction set
integrated memory controller (IMC)
interpreter
L1 cache
L2 cache
multicore processor
multiple branch prediction
overclocking
pipelines
processor affinity
processor throttling
reduced instruction set computer (RISC)
registers
register unit
simultaneous threading
superscalar execution
thread
zero insertion force (ZIF) socket

Overview

CPU stands for *central processing unit*, and it does exactly what its name implies. It is *central* in that all other components are dependent on the CPU. It is a *processor* in that it processes data. It is a *unit* in that it is very much a self-contained device that is modular in design. The CPU is considered the brain of a PC because it carries out all actions and instructions. In short, everything that happens goes through the CPU. If a CPU fails, it cannot be repaired. Instead, it is replaced as an entire unit.

A+ Note

The CompTIA A+ Certification Exams ask basic questions about the CPU, sockets, terminology, and cooling methods. Be prepared to answer questions such as the following:

- How is CPU performance measured?
- Which CPU fits which socket?
- What effect does overclocking have on a CPU?
- What is the difference between 32- bit and 64-bit processing?
- What is the purpose of thermal compound?
- What purpose does processor throttling serve?

4.1 Instructions and Data

The CPU is the closest thing to a brain that a computer has. It has evolved over the years from a simple chip composed of only 27,000 transistors in early 1978 to a highly sophisticated integrated chip. In today's technological landscape, the important measurement is not the number of processors but the size of the trace. Recall that a *trace* is an electrical circuit that runs on a printed circuit board or a chip. On chips, the trace width is extremely small, below 14 nm.

The CPU follows **instructions**, which are commands in machine language used to process data. The data is normally stored in RAM or introduced into the system by some device such as a keyboard, mouse, microphone, hard drive, or optical drive. All components in a computing system depend on the CPU, as illustrated in Figure 4-1. Every processor runs from a set of basic commands called the **instruction set**, which is the lowest language level used to program a computer, although some processors have an even lower level called *microcode*. The instruction set is written in **assembly language**, which is one step above machine language. When code is written in a high-level language such as BASIC or C++, it must be compiled or interpreted before it can run on the computer as a standalone or executive program. A **compiler** is a program that translates the higher-level language into machine language based on the CPU's instruction set. An **interpreter** is a program that performs on-demand translation of higher-level language into machine language and generally runs more slowly than compiled code. The instruction set contains commands such as add; subtract; compare; add one to; subtract one from; get the next one, two, or four bytes from; and put the next one, two, or four bytes at.

The CPU has several **registers**, which are small pockets of memory used to temporarily store data that is being processed by the CPU. For example, when adding two numbers together, one number is stored in register A and the other number is stored in register B. The *add* command adds the contents of register A to the contents of register B and places the result in register C. Next, the contents can be moved from register C to a RAM address. With *orthogonal registers*, any register can serve any function as with the IBM 360/370 mainframe architecture of old. The Intel CPUs say they are designed for general purpose, but by no means can they be orthogonal; each register has a specific function.

Assembly language programs are translated into machine code, which is usually a one-to-one translation from the assembly code symbol to the corresponding machine code. The assembly program is written as a series of commands and bytes of data to be acted on, one byte at a time. Writing code in assembly is often painstakingly difficult,

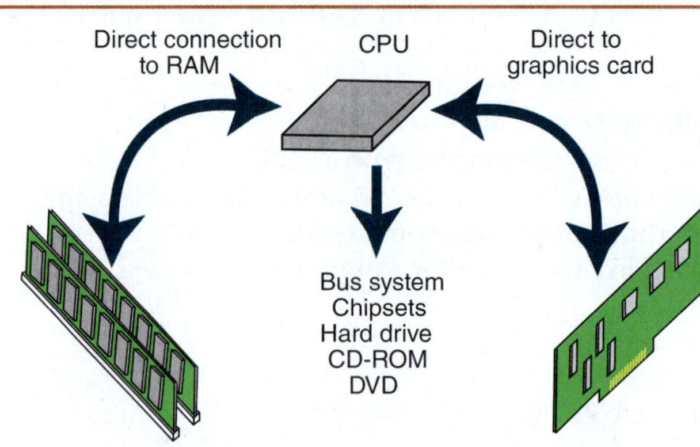

Figure 4-1 The CPU is considered the brain of the computer, and all other components rely on it for instructions.

Goodheart-Willcox Publisher

but it produces the fastest execution possible if the programmer codes proficiently. Assembly language translated into machine code is used when speed or compact size is a necessity. The kernel code of operating systems and BIOS programs are usually written to some degree in assembly language. Most other common programs are written for computers using a higher-level language that is then translated from the higher-level language to machine-like code. However, using a higher-level language and then compiling the code results in a larger, slower program.

Machine-level programs are lengthy but appear transparent to the user because of the sheer speed at which the instructions are carried out by the computer. Programming in machine language is an entire science, but only needs to be briefly explained to give you the necessary insight on how a CPU functions with data.

4.2 CPU Operation

A CPU is in a state of constant operation. When not processing commands to process data, the CPU is

- refreshing memory;
- checking for communication from other devices through the system of hardwired IRQs and software IRQs;
- monitoring system power; and
- performing any other programmed duties.

Look at Figure 4-2 to see how a CPU performs the simple operation of addition. This series demonstrates how the registers are used to manipulate data. To add the numerical value of two numbers, three registers are used. The value 3 is placed in register A, and the value 4 is placed in register B. The contents of the two registers are then added together and stored in register C. While this action seems simple, there are many other activities occurring simultaneously that are controlled by the CPU. For example, the CPU is refreshing the RAM, checking IRQ status (checking for keyboard input, mouse input, and other such input), and displaying the contents of the registers on the monitor.

CPU Parts

The following is a simplified discussion of CPU operation, but it should give you some idea of how the major parts work together to perform operations on data. CPUs are generally composed of bus units, cache, decode units, control units, arithmetic logic units, and register units. Recall that a *bus* is a collection of conductors that work together for a specific purpose, such as connecting major components, accepting data, and sending data through the input and output bus sections. CPUs have two general types of caches: an instruction cache and a data cache. The term **cache** (pronounced *cash*) refers to a small area of temporary memory storage. Cache is used to separate and store incoming data and instructions. Most CPU's have a hierarchy of caches including L1, L2, and L3. In a multicore CPU, each core has its own L1 cache, but the cores share L2 or higher-level caches. There also may be any number of specialized caches. For example, a *trace cache* is used in the Intel Pentium 4 and increases the bandwidth for fetching instructions.

A **decode unit** decodes instructions sent to the CPU and sends the data to other areas in an understandable format. It works under the direction of a control unit. The **control unit** controls the overall operation of the CPU by taking instructions from the decode unit, directing command instructions to the arithmetic logic unit,

Figure 4-2 Three registers are used to add the numerical value of three numbers. The value 3 is placed in register A; the value 4 is placed in register B. The contents of the two registers are added together and stored in register C.

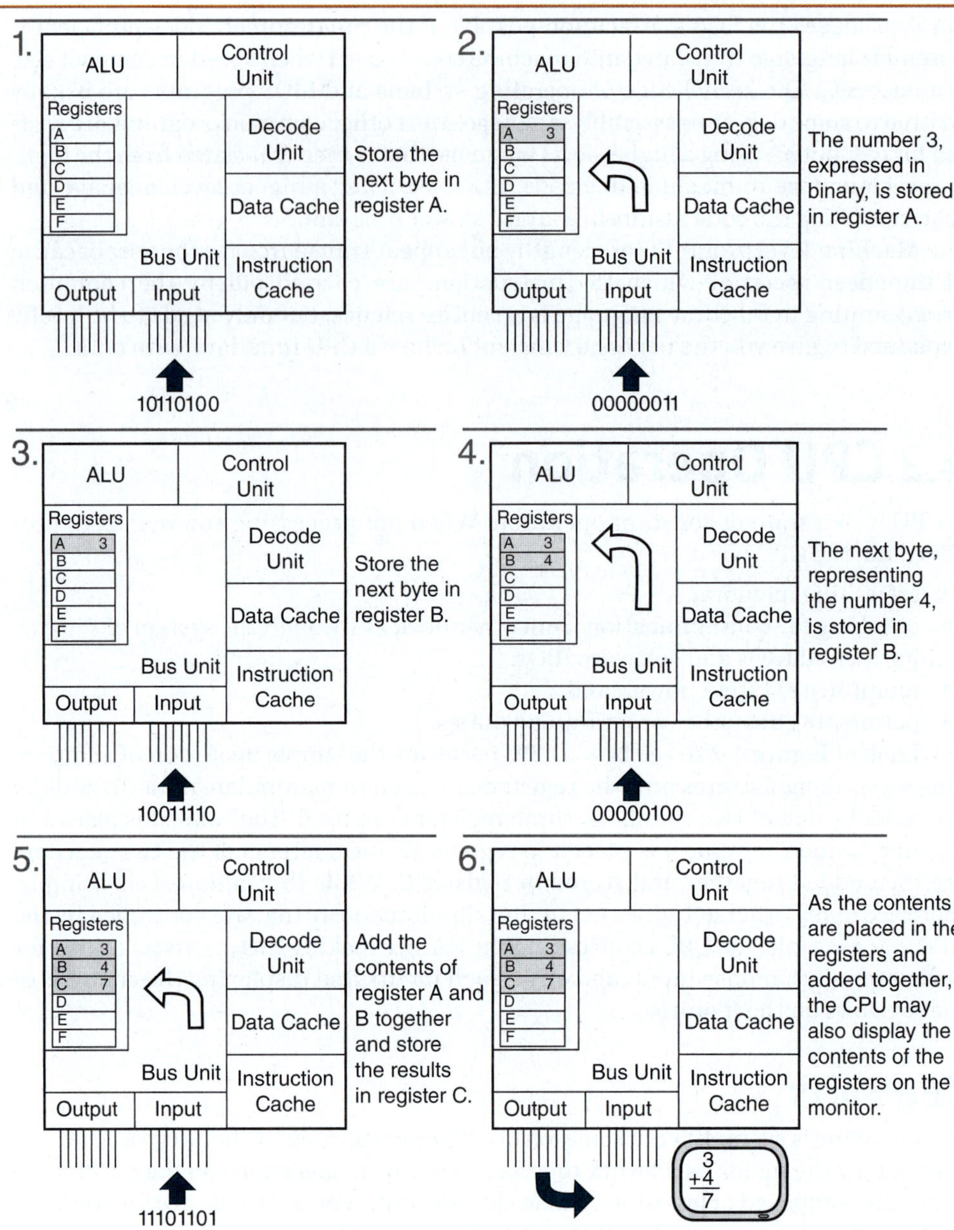

Goodheart-Willcox Publisher

and directing data to be manipulated to the register area. The **arithmetic logic unit (ALU)** performs mathematical functions on data stored in the register area and performs data manipulations such as comparing two pieces of data stored in the registry unit. It can perform comparisons such as "equal to," "greater than," and "less than." The ALU also performs manipulations on the data stored in registers, such as adding or subtracting the contents of register A to or from the contents of register B. The ALU can also compare the contents of A or B, such as determining which is larger.

The **register unit** is composed of many separate storage units smaller than cache. Each register has a unique identity. In Figure 4-2, each register unit is labeled with a letter of the alphabet. The main difference between register storage and cache is that registers contain a single data element, such as a number or a letter, whereas the data and instruction cache can each hold multiple pieces of data and commands.

Manipulating a list of words in alphabetical order is an example of a comparison of the contents of two or more registers. Each letter is given a numeric value, processed through the CPU in pairs, and then stored in either cache or RAM in the appropriate order. The series of comparisons can consist of over a thousand repetitions. The CPU operates at such a high speed that the process appears very brief, which is the great value of the computer. A computer can perform repetitive tasks such as sorting the addresses of 2,000,000 names for a phone book in a few minutes or even seconds. Performed manually, the same operation would take weeks or even months to perform. Animation on the screen of the display unit has also been made possible because of the great speed of the control unit, the ALU, and the registers. See Figure 4-3 for an illustration of this process.

CPU Power

Not all business conducted with a PC requires the use of a powerful CPU; it really comes down to how demanding a program is. For example, a simple word-processing package will work with most any CPU, but extreme software gaming, computer-aided drafting or manufacturing, scientific simulations and research, and large corporate financial record calculations require powerful CPUs.

CPU power can be taken even further. Many sophisticated operations, such as weather prediction and medical research, have requirements well beyond a standard PC and must use a mainframe or a supercomputer. In recent years, artificial intelligence software that performs a collection of tasks known as ***machine learning*** can often use the multiple cores (small processors) typically present on graphics-processing hardware.

Animation, especially those involving three-dimensional images, is CPU intensive. Imagine manipulating a CAD drawing of a shopping center in which people walk through a virtual mall as though they were actually shopping, or imagine popular game scenarios as you navigate through a maze of hallways. One form of animation technology requires the redrawing of every line in the image for each display change, as shown in Figure 4-4. Before redrawing each line, a calculation is made based on the X, Y, and Z coordinates of each end of the line. The distance and angle of the new location is used as part of the algorithm. An ***algorithm*** is similar to a recipe: you simply insert the X, Y, and Z coordinates of the existing position of each line end and then input the new X, Y, and Z coordinates.

Rather than inputting the exact coordinates manually, they can be "implied" using a mouse, keyboard, or game control device. To give a realistic feeling, an illustration containing up to thousands of lines must be computed in a fraction of a

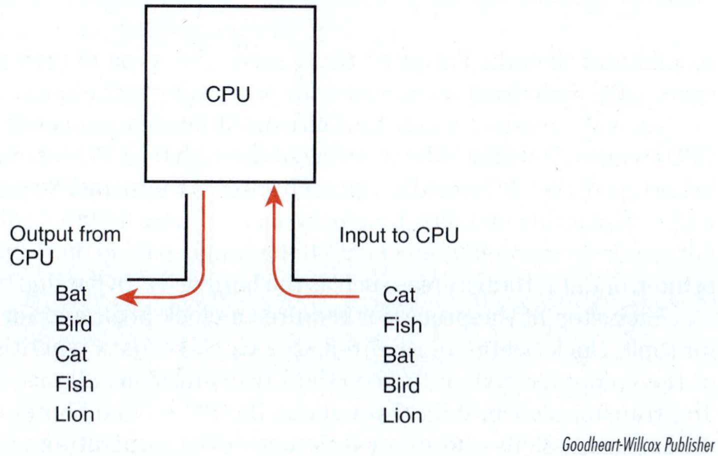

Figure 4-3 The CPU operates at such a high speed, complex processes appear brief. For example, a list of words is entered into the CPU and stored in cache. The control unit sends pairs of words to the registry, broken down by the letter, and compares each pair until all possible combinations are exhausted. The result is an alphabetically sorted list of words. Doing the same process manually would take significantly more time.

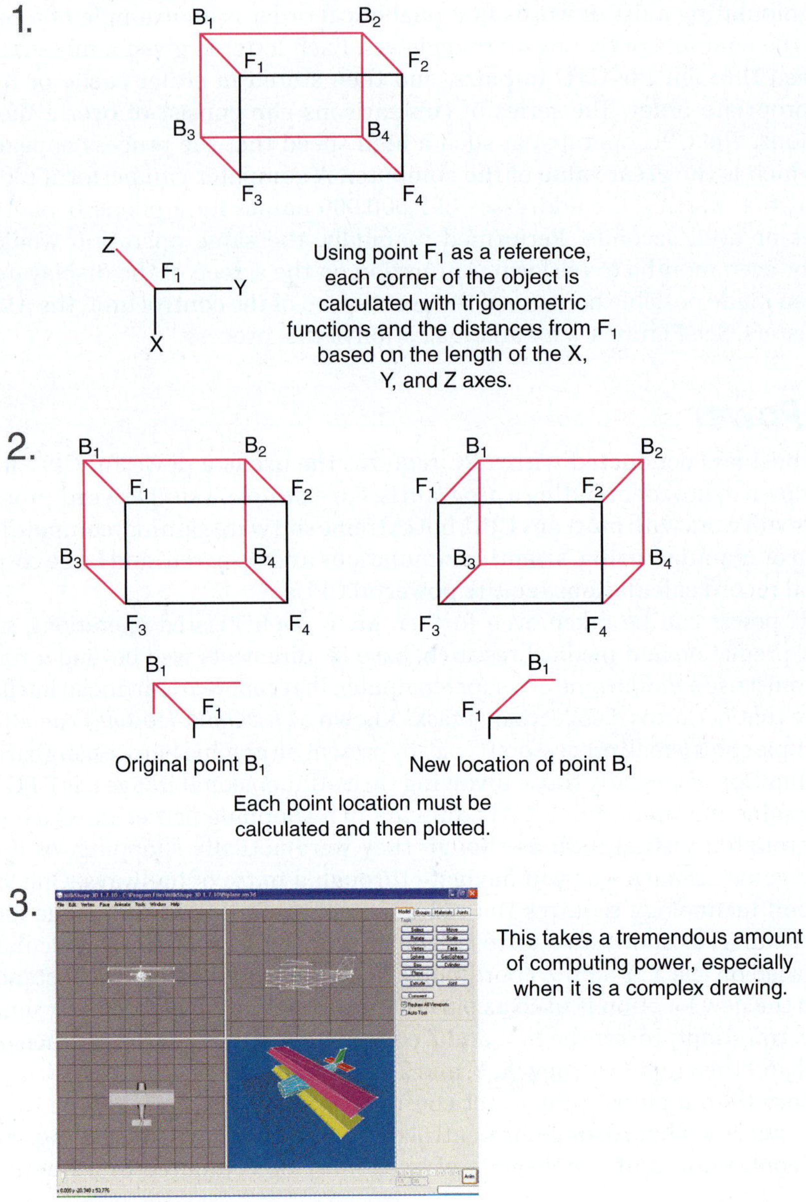

Figure 4-4 One form of animation technology requires the redrawing of every line in the image for each display change. Before redrawing each line, a calculation has to be made based on the X, Y, and Z coordinates of each end of the line.

Goodheart-Willcox Publisher

second and then displayed on the screen. This type of operation requires a high-speed CPU with many advanced data-processing techniques.

The CPU receives a constant stream of alternating commands and data. Early CPUs required all data to be transferred through the CPU; for example, if a memo were being typed, the CPU would act on each letter in the memo. Now, modern systems allow for bus mastering and direct memory access. These additions allow repetitive actions not requiring manipulation of data to be simply passed on to memory, the screen, the printer, or data storage areas such as the hard drive, bypassing the CPU entirely.

Each step of the processor requires a clock beat, and for complex processors, multiple clock beats are required. The clock sends a repetitive signal to all parts of the computer system to keep data transmissions aligned with the other parts. The transmission of data throughout the PC is a combination of serial and parallel transmissions and many different devices operating at different speeds. For example, the keyboard is a serial device, so keyboard data must first be converted to parallel data and then transmitted in step with the other parts of the computer.

CPU Speed

The CPU has been progressively made to operate faster and more efficiently. Modifications to data-processing methods are given special names to describe their actions, such as RISC, superscalar technology, dynamic execution, and additional cache. In the next section, we will take a closer look at processor speed and these unique modifications to the CPU.

CPU comparison is usually based on speed and bus width. The *speed* is how quickly the CPU can process information. The *bus width* is how many bits can be passed simultaneously on parallel circuits, for example, 8, 16, 32, and 64 bits simultaneously.

The CPU or processor speed is measured in hertz (Hz), or cycles per second (frequency). The term *frequency* is used to express the number of cycles in one second. Thus, if there were 25 complete digital cycles in one second, the frequency is 25 hertz (25 Hz). A digital signal is a fluctuation of electrical energy. In digital electronics, a complete cycle is one complete sequence of the digital signal shape. Look at Figure 4-5 to see an illustration of one complete cycle of a digital signal.

A CPU that runs at 1 MHz (megahertz) carries out instructions and data movement at one million digital pulses per second. To determine the speed of a CPU, multiply the bus width by the data flow, as demonstrated in Figure 4-6. In the example shown, a 5-MHz data has a bus width of 16 bits. Therefore, the CPU speed is 80 Mbps (16 bits × 5 MHz = 80 megabits per second).

As computer systems shifted from text-based command operating systems to graphical user interface systems, speed became an extremely important factor. For example, the intense graphics of Windows requires a faster computer system

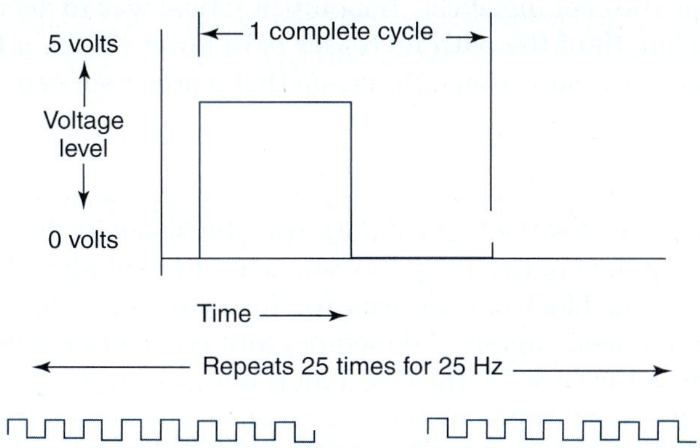

Goodheart-Willcox Publisher

Figure 4-5 A complete cycle of a digital signal includes a signal rising to a 5-volt level and falling back down to a 0-volt level. The number of times it repeats the pattern in one second is the *frequency* of the signal.

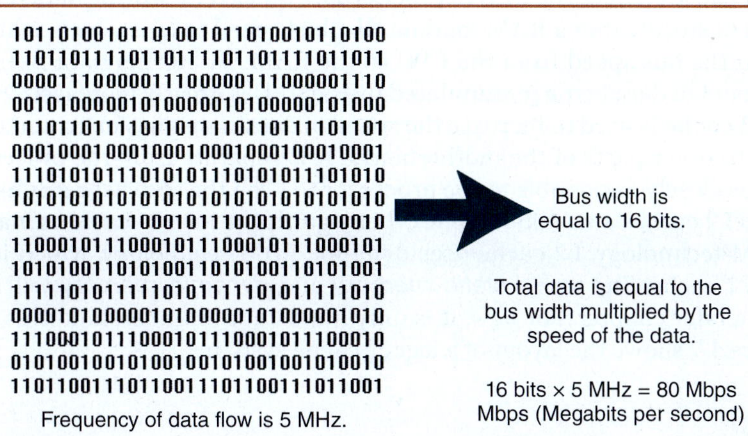

Goodheart-Willcox Publisher

Figure 4-6 The rate of data transfer is based on the width and speed of the bus system.

than what was needed for DOS machines. Graphics functions demand much processor attention, and each release of Windows makes additional demands on the processor that are more complex.

A+ 1101: 3.4

4.3 Enhancing CPU Operation

A+ Note

Make sure you are able to identify which features most influence a processor's ability to process data quickly.

Processors are continually gaining speed and power, and each new generation of CPU can operate on shorter clock cycles. However, a CPU's abilities can be enhanced in ways besides simply producing faster chips. These improvements include changing the local bus; adding cache or a math coprocessor; use of multiple branch prediction, superscalar execution, dynamic execution, integrated memory controllers, and integrated graphics processing; usage of a dual independent bus; simultaneous threading; and overclocking.

Local Bus

The *local bus* is connected directly to the CPU and is always the highest-speed bus in the entire computer system. The local bus is the bus system connecting certain components directly to the CPU. For example, RAM and video card slots are connected directly to the CPU to better enhance performance. The local bus is also referred to as the *system bus* or the *front-side bus*. Recall that much of the terminology used is dependent on the product manufacturer or on the generation of the technology.

The shorter the distance between two devices, the higher the data transfer rate. It is not the length the data has to travel, but the effect of inductive reactance that causes a choking effect on the electrical impulses. As the length of the data path increases, so does the choking effect. The only practical way to decrease this choking effect as the length of the path increases is to lower the data flow rate. Thus, the inductive reactance slows down the speed that a processor can run.

Cache

The processor bus speed is the highest data-transfer speed in the entire computer system. The development of the 486 processor sought to enhance the speed of data processing, so a special block of RAM was developed and manufactured as an integral part of the processor. This special memory unit is called a *cache*.

The **L1 cache** is the cache in the CPU and is designed to run at the same speed as the CPU. It is the most costly memory to produce when compared on a per-byte basis. As design engineers must create a CPU and computer system that will work at high speeds while staying within a reasonable cost that the customer can afford, the L1 cache is smaller on less expensive processors.

The L1 cache enables the CPU to process data quickly by storing data temporarily instead of storing it in a RAM module. The bus speed to L1 cache is many times faster than the bus speed from the CPU to the RAM. By storing data in L1 cache, the movement of data being manipulated by the CPU is greatly increased.

The **L2 cache** is used to increase the speed of data transmission to and from the processor to other parts of the motherboard. It is separate from the processor but mounted as closely as possible to the processor to keep the transfer rates high.

L1 and L2 caches also differ in one other significant way. L1 cache is made from static RAM technology. L2 cache uses dynamic RAM technology, which is slower than the L1 cache. The terms *static memory* and *dynamic memory* will become clearer in a later chapter. For now, it is only important to understand this distinction. Figure 4-7 shows the layout of a legacy cache system.

Today, CPU architecture incorporates L1, L2, and L3 caches within the CPU unit. See Figure 4-8, which shows the architecture of an Intel Core i7 CPU. Notice that each core has two L1 caches: one for data and the other for instructions. Each core also has its own L2 cache, and all cores share a common L3 cache. Every core supports two threads, which is equal to two logical processors. The CPU has a DDR3 controller that connects directly to three channels of DDR memory mounted on the motherboard. There are two Intel QuickPath Interconnect (QPI) controllers incorporated into the CPU. An Intel QPI controller connects to a high-speed I/O controller mounted directly on the motherboard in close proximity to the CPU. The combination of the QPI controller and high-speed I/O controller has replaced the front-side bus.

The latest processors also have an integrated memory controller (IMC) and integrated graphics processing unit (GPU) incorporated into the processor die. Originally, the IMC was a separate chip mounted on the motherboard, and they communicated across a bus on the motherboard. The incorporation of the IMC into the processor improved access to RAM.

Floating-Point Unit

The **floating-point unit (FPU)** is a set of circuits incorporated into the processor that is used for mathematics computation. Originally, computer systems had a special chip on the motherboard called the *math coprocessor* that served as the mathematical computation unit. Incorporating the mathematical computation unit into the processor produces more computation speed when compared to a separate chip on the motherboard.

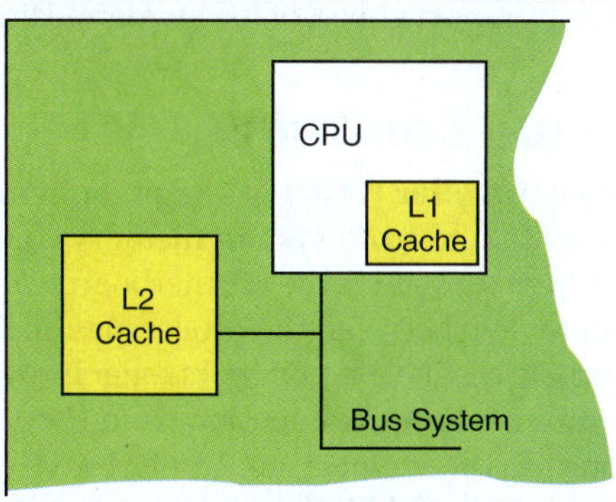

Goodheart-Willcox Publisher

Figure 4-7 Beginning with the 486 processor, L1 cache was incorporated into the CPU, and L2 cache was mounted on the motherboard close to the CPU.

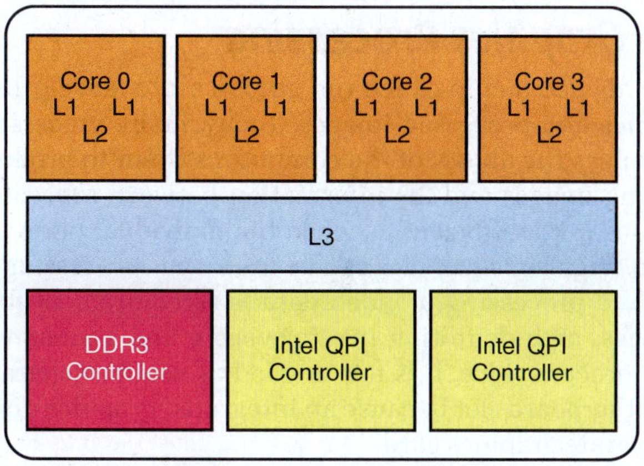

Goodheart-Willcox Publisher

Figure 4-8 CPU architecture has evolved to incorporate L1, L2, and L3 caches.

Multiple Branch Prediction

Multiple branch prediction is a technique that guesses what data element will be needed next rather than waiting for the next command to be issued. It is especially accurate in repetitive tasks and can significantly speed up CPU operations. Multiple branch prediction has proven to be over 90 percent accurate.

Superscalar Technology

The 486, and all processors before it, could only process one instruction at a time. Beginning with the Pentium, processing multiple instructions at the same time became possible. The act of processing more than one instruction at the same time is called **superscalar execution**. All modern processors use superscalar technology, and CPUs are now designed with two pipelines. **Pipelines** are parallel paths on which data travel to the CPU sections. This parallel path concept is what makes the CPU capable of performing two data manipulation functions at the same time. Superscalar technology is dependent on not only a new physical design of the processor, but also on an additional set of instructional commands to operate the twin pipelines while still maintaining backward compatibility with previous processors.

Dynamic Execution

Dynamic execution is a term coined by Intel to describe the enhanced superscalar and multiple branch prediction features associated with the Pentium II processor. Dynamic execution is a combination of new physical features and additional instruction set commands manufactured into the processor. It also looks ahead at instructions coming to the processor. If an instruction can be carried out faster than the instruction preceding it, it is moved ahead of its current position and then executed.

Integrated Memory Controller

The **integrated memory controller (IMC)** is a digital circuit built into the processor that manages data flow to and from system memory. The memory controller for early processors was a chip mounted on the motherboard close to both the CPU and RAM, and it controlled data flow between the processor and RAM over the front-side bus. Current processors integrate the memory controller into the processor via a short motherboard bus that makes a direct connection from the processor to the motherboard RAM. By incorporating the memory controller into the processor and providing a direct connection to system RAM, the performance of the computer system is greatly enhanced.

A+ 1102: 1.7

Integrated Graphics Processing

Early motherboards had a chip called the *graphics processing unit (GPU)*, which supported graphics and processed images. Today, many processors integrate the GPU, which enhances the ability of the computer system to produce video and 3D images. Processing images and 3D information between separate devices across the motherboard is not as efficient as when the individual parts are incorporated into the same die. Higher frequencies can be used, thus processing video data more quickly. High-speed processing of video data is a requirement for streaming live video, DVD movies, high-definition live television, and similar video. While this is a good way to process video, it is not as good as using a separate graphics card mounted in a motherboard slot because an integrated graphics unit is not nearly as powerful as a separate graphics card.

It is not unusual to find separate graphics cards each with their own processors, especially on systems designed for computer gaming. Some GPU models have thousands of cores that are relatively simple compared to CPU cores, but they provide a powerful platform for artificial intelligence techniques such as neural networks.

Dual Independent Bus

Dual Independent Bus (DIB) refers to a bus architecture introduced with two separate or independent bus systems incorporated into the processor chip. The first DIB was introduced with the Pentium Pro and Pentium II. One bus connects to the main memory, and the other connects with the L2 cache. Both buses can be used simultaneously rather than individually to increase program execution speed. Today, DIB has been replaced by Intel QuickPath Interconnect and AMD HyperTransport Technology.

Simultaneous Threading

1101: 3.4 A+

In software programming, a **thread** is part of a software program that can be executed independently of the entire program. When two or more threads are executed at the same time, it is called **simultaneous threading** or, sometimes, *multithreading*. On most processors, a thread is defined to be a lightweight process and will generally run with shared memory with other threads, whereas processes receive their own memory space. Intel uses the term *Hyper-Threading* to describe this technology. Hardware and software companies often coin new terminology to describe computer technology in their advertisement campaigns. Sometimes the technology is new, but often only the marketing term is new.

Intel Hyper-Threading Technology was introduced many years ago and is still a vital part of the Intel processor design. The Intel Core series of multicore CPUs uses two threads per core, resulting in twice the processing power for the number of cores. For example, a quad-core processor in which each core has the capability of supporting two threads has the logical processing power of eight processors. The processing power of the quad-core is doubled as a direct result of simultaneous threading.

In Figure 4-9, Windows Task Manager shows the performance of an Intel Core i7 processor, which has two cores. Notice the data for the threads and processes is displayed as a graph within a table. Additionally, CPU statistics, such as utilization, speed, and number of processes, are listed under the graph.

A+ Note

To prepare for the CompTIA A+ Certification Exams, you should be able to explain the concepts of virtualization, cache, Hyper-Threading, and integrated GPUs as they relate to processing and CPUs.

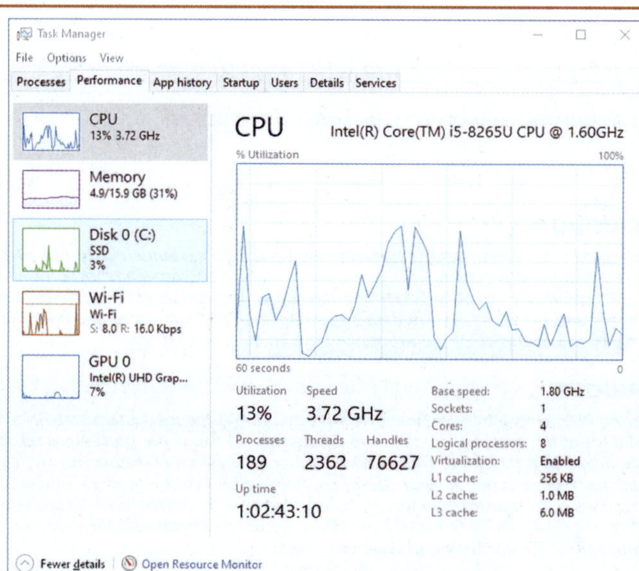

Goodheart-Willcox Publisher

Figure 4-9 Windows Task Manager displays statistics of CPU performance.

Overclocking

Processors have design specifications that indicate their maximum frequencies. Applying a higher-than-specified frequency results in excessive heat, which can damage a processor. Processors can withstand short periods of time under excessive heat conditions without damage, but this condition should be monitored closely.

Overclocking is the intentional application of frequencies higher that a processor's design specification to obtain enhanced performance. In other words, overclocking allows a processor to accomplish more tasks in a shorter time because the number of tasks performed by a processor is directly related to the applied frequency. The frequency applied to a processor can be controlled by software or BIOS configuration.

Excessive electrical power consumption damages a processor in the same way any electrical device is damaged by excessive electrical current. Electrical devices are protected by fuses, which blow when a predetermined value of electrical current is reached. Processors, however, have no fuses or equivalent circuitry, so the only practical solution is monitoring the amount of electrical current flowing through to the processor. When a predetermined current value is reached, overclocking is halted by returning the applied frequency to its specified value.

The practice of overclocking is generally not supported by the processor-manufacturing industry and voids the warranty status of the processor due to damage that may incur as a result. The CPU may freeze and come to a complete stop with or without a fatal error message. This is because fatal error messages are issued by normally working processors that have a software or hardware problem.

Intel provides the Overclocking Assistant for the Intel Desktop Board, which serves as a guide to overclocking. Even though Intel provides information about how to overclock the system and provides the software application to perform the overclocking, it also provides a disclaimer in the guide, as shown in Figure 4-10. Intel warns that altering the frequency or voltage levels of a system processor and memory can cause failure or damage and it does not warranty the operation of the Intel processor beyond its specification. The same disclaimer applies to other manufacturers' memory modules.

A user might attempt to overclock the CPU and cause the system to fail or lock up during POST. You can usually correct this problem by resetting the BIOS to its default settings. Resetting the BIOS is typically performed by using the jumper located near the CMOS battery, but some motherboard manufacturers include a button labelled *Back-to-BIOS*, which reboots the system and opens the setup utility.

Figure 4-10 Intel provides information about how to overclock a system but also issues a warning and disclaimer about doing so.

Overclocking Assistant for the Intel® Desktop Board DZ87KLT-75K

⚠ WARNING

Altering clock frequency and/or voltage may (i) reduce system stability and useful life of the system and processor; (ii) cause the processor and other system components to fail; (iii) cause reductions in system performance; (iv) cause additional heat or other damage; and (v) affect system data integrity. Intel has not tested and does not warranty the operation of the processor beyond its specifications.

⚠ WARNING

Altering PC memory frequency and/or voltage may (i) reduce system stability and useful life of the system, memory and processor; (ii) cause the processor and other system components to fail; (iii) cause reductions in system performance; (iv) cause additional heat or other damage; and (v) affect system data integrity. Intel assumes no responsibility that the memory included, if used with altered clock frequencies and/or voltages, will be fit for any particular purpose. Check with the memory manufacturer for warranty and additional details.

Goodheart-Willcox Publisher

A third method of resetting the BIOS is the watchdog timer embedded into the motherboard circuitry. The watchdog senses a boot system failure and then automatically opens the setup utility, allowing the technician to make changes. A *watchdog timer* works by requiring itself to be reset by the system—when the reset does not occur, the watchdog timer will then open the utility. The availability of each method is determined by the motherboard chipset and BIOS.

4.4 Processor Features

Processor features are a collection of terms used to explain, identify, and compare CPUs. Among other topics, these terms refer to CPU architecture, instruction, and performance. It is important for computer technicians to be familiar with these terms because while you may not encounter all of them in the field, it is likely you will encounter some. Important topics that describe processor features are RISC, CISC, MMX, 32- or 64-bit technologies, compatibility, virtualization, SMM, throttling, SpeedStep technology, voltages, and processor size.

A+ Note

The CompTIA A+ Certification Exams require knowledge of basic processor technologies.

RISC

A **reduced instruction set computer (RISC)** is a type of CPU architecture that is designed for faster processing. It is a common myth that RISC processers have fewer instructions. In fact, the PowerPC RISC processor had instruction sets as large as CISC instruction sets. The term *reduced* actually refers to the amount of work a given instruction accomplishes, not the number of instructions. The term *RISC* was developed at the Berkeley National Laboratory as part of the Berkeley RISC project. Many sources cite the first RISC design being the IBM 801 from 1980.

CISC

Complex instruction set computer (CISC) is a CPU designed so the die can accept many machine-language commands that manipulate or process complex mathematical formulas and instruction sets. An increased number of transistors are required to produce a CISC-based CPU. The added complexity causes an increase in clock cycles to carry out an expanded and more complex set of programming instructions. This type of system is best used for complex programming techniques.

MMX

In 1997, the MMX processor was introduced by Intel with the Pentium P5 chip. *MMX* is a single instruction, multiple data (SIMD) instruction set architecture. The MMX processor was based on a standard processor with the addition of 57 commands that enhanced its abilities to support graphics technology. Many of the commands replaced functions normally carried out by the sound and video card. This allowed for faster processing of video and sound data. The L1 cache was made larger to assist in speeding up the processing of video frames. The initials MMX represent a trademarked name owned by Intel and not an acronym; however, a number of unofficial meanings have been proposed, including *MultiMedia eXtension* and *Matrix Math eXtension*.

32-Bit and 64-Bit Technology

1101: 3.4 A+
1102: 1.7

CPUs and other computer devices, as well as software, are often referred to as 32-bit or 64-bit, which describes the amount of data that can be processed in parallel during one cycle or clock beat. This is also referred to as the *data width*. You will often see 64 bit simply designated as X64 and 32 bit as X86. The 64-bit technology provides data paths twice as wide as 32-bit technology, meaning large volumes of data can be transferred much quicker with a 64-bit processor than with a 32-bit processor. The 64-bit technology is superior to 32-bit technology when large amounts of program storage are required. It is very unlikely that you will encounter 32-bit technology today, but a brief description of 32-bit is included for historical purposes and to provide a perspective on 64-bit technology.

The 64-bit technology provides access to vast amounts of memory for programs that require it, such as CAD/CAM, digital image creation and manipulation, in-depth financial analysis, computer games with rich graphic content, or any application requiring a great deal of memory and processor throughput.

For a computer system to take full advantage of 64-bit technology, four things are required in addition to a 64-bit processor:

- A BIOS that supports a 64-bit processor
- A 64-bit operating system
- 64-bit device drivers
- Software applications written for 64-bit

Take note that for data to transfer using 64-bit technology, the 64-bit operating system requires 64-bit device drivers, otherwise data will be transferred as 32-bit. Also, keep in mind that a software program designed as a 32-bit system will not show any significant increase in performance when running on a 64-bit CPU using a 64-bit operating system because the main processor was designed to be backward compatible with 32-bit software.

A+ 1102: 1.7

Software Compatibility

The principal method used by Windows 10 or 11 to achieve software compatibility with older applications uses files with a designation of *WoW*, which stands for *Windows 32-bit on Windows 64-bit.* Current approaches yield satisfactory performance of 32-bit applications without compromising the 64-bit architecture. Be aware that this kind of compatibility does not automatically assure compatibility across Windows operating systems.

A+ 1101: 3.4

Virtualization

Virtualization makes a single physical processor appear as multiple processors to the computer software system and the user. This allows a single computer to run multiple operating systems, software applications, and users simultaneously. Virtualization for multiple users is typically applied to network server systems rather than to desktop systems.

Both Intel and AMD processors support virtualization and have trademarked names for their virtualization technologies: Intel Virtualization (VT-x) and AMD Virtualization (AMD-V). Some virtualization programs occupy the entirety of the CPU and operating memory. To avoid conflicts, ensure you maximize the amount of CPU cores and RAM, especially if you intend to run multiple virtual workstations. There will be more about virtualization and virtual machines in a later chapter.

System Management Mode

System Management Mode (SMM) is a CPU operating mode in which execution is suspended and an alternate system is executed. SMM was first developed for laptop computers to save electrical energy when using a battery. SMM was introduced in the 486SL processor and became a standard for all Pentium and later processors.

The power management is controlled by software, usually the setup utility. Power management puts the CPU and the computer system into a state of rest or sleep and can shut down the computer.

Throttling

Processor throttling is a method of controlling processor frequency to conserve portable computer battery life. The frequency of the CPU is directly proportional to the demand of the software applications running on the system. If no software applications are running, the frequency of the processor is automatically lowered to conserve battery life and produce less heat. This feature is commercially known as *Power Now*, *Precision Cooling*, and *Cool 'n' Quiet*.

Enhanced Intel SpeedStep Technology

Intel originally developed Enhanced Intel SpeedStep Technology for its line of portable computers. This technology is designed to change the applied system voltage and CPU frequency under certain conditions. For example, when a laptop is connected to an AC source, the CPU frequency is 2.6 GHz, the applied system voltage is 1.3 volts, and the overall power consumed is 30 watts. When the same laptop is run on battery power, the CPU frequency is reduced to 1.2 GHz, the applied system voltage is reduced to 1.2 volts, and the overall power consumed is 20.8 watts—a reduction of almost 10 watts. To take advantage of this technology, the computer's operating system, BIOS, and chipset must support it. Enhanced Intel SpeedStep Technology is already incorporated into Windows operating systems. It can be accessed on a portable computer under the **Power Options** icon in Control Panel.

Figure 4-11 shows the Windows 10 **Power Options** menu. The Windows 11 **Power Options** menu appears the same. This allows the user to select specific devices and control device performance as related to power consumption. The **Processor power management** item is designed to be easy to use; in fact, Windows 10 settings for power are much simpler than previous versions of Windows. SpeedStep has evolved to include extensions such as SpeedStep II and SpeedStep III.

AMD has a similar technology named AMB Turbo Core, which uses dynamic frequency scaling to allow the processor to adjust the processor operating frequency. Essentially, when extra processing power is needed, the process can increase its speed temporarily. This can achieve up to a 900 MHz of additional clock speed.

CPU Voltages

CPU operating voltage has decreased over the years to reduce the amount of heat generated by the CPU when processing data. Starting with the Pentium processor, applied voltage from the motherboard was reduced from 5 volts to 3.3 volts. Today, processor core voltage can be less than 1 volt, especially on laptops. Lowering a

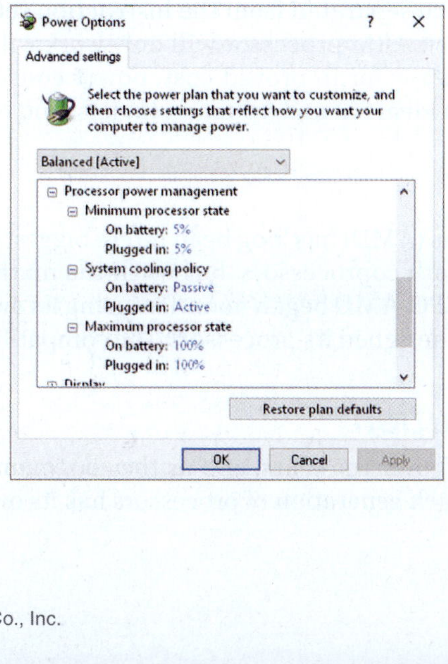

Goodheart-Willcox Publisher

Figure 4-11 Windows 10 settings for power are much simpler than previous versions of Windows.

processor's core voltage results in less wattage, and thus, less heat. Motherboards are designed in different ways to achieve different CPU voltage levels. Some boards are equipped with a set of jumpers located beside the CPU, and various voltage levels can be achieved by moving the jumper position. This is especially common on third-party motherboards. Another method is the use of a voltage regulator. A voltage regulator is installed on the motherboard beside the CPU and is usually equipped with its own small heat sink, making it easy to identify. Additionally, some overclocking software can manipulate the voltage level of the processor.

Processor Size

The physical size of processors has not changed significantly over the years, but the electronics inside the chip have become more compact. There are many more transistors packed into the processor chips, and the density of transistor circuits in a CPU is expressed in nanometers (one billionth of a meter). This measurement is applied to processors by expressing half the distance between two distinct electronic surfaces, such as traces, inside a processor. For example, the trace spacing in the first generation of Intel Core processors is 45 nm, and the trace spacing in the third generation is 22 nm.

A+ 1101: 3.4

4.5 Processor Manufacturers and Evolution

While there are many past and present CPUs to choose from, two companies have produced most of these chips. These competitors are Intel and AMD, both of which manufacture excellent CPUs.

Intel

Intel is the dominant force in the manufacturing of CPUs for both Microsoft and Apple computers. Intel has been at the top in sales since introducing the 8086 processor to the market in the 1970s. Sales of Intel's 8088 chip were great enough to propel Intel into the Fortune 500.

Intel has continued to dominate the computer processor manufacturing market through the years. Today, Intel controls the vast majority of computer chip manufacturing and manufactures not only CPUs but also chipsets, motherboards, wireless devices, and networking devices. However, with the rise of smartphone manufacturing, the number of ARM processors has surpassed the number of Intel processors produced.

A+ 1101: 3.4

Advanced RISC Machine (ARM) processors are processors with a microarchitecture that cannot be separated from the instruction set. This means that software designed for a given ARM processor will only work with that processor. Their size and architecture allow for improved cost, power consumption, and heat distribution, making them ideal for smartphones, tablets, and other portable devices.

AMD

Advanced Micro Devices (AMD) has long been Intel's biggest competitor. Originally, AMD manufactured math coprocessors, but when the math coprocessor began to be integrated into the CPU, AMD began manufacturing its own CPU. AMD began its series with the 486 and designed its processor to be compatible with the Intel series.

A+ 1101: 3.4

Processor Evolution

Processors have evolved over the years, and as they do, manufacturers reinvent the way processors work. Each generation of processors has its own unique technologies that make them run more powerfully than their predecessors. Manufacturers continue to develop processors with more and more transistors and other electronic components. In this section, we will take a brief look at some of the most significant processors used in computing. Major emphasis is on the very latest processors.

Tech Tip

If you are unsure of the compatibility between a processor and motherboard, consult an online compatibility guide. Many online retailers provide compatibility checkers as part of the purchasing process.

Intel

Nearly all modern Intel processors run in some multiple of gigahertz (GHz). Laptop computers are often slower than desktops, although this is not always the case. In most situations, the speed of the CPU does not exert as much effect on perceived speed as does the presence of significant amounts of memory. Figure 4-12 shows a table of the speeds and introduction dates for Intel processors beginning with the Xeon.

Intel Celeron

The Intel Celeron was introduced in 1999 as a budget-minded processor designed for general-purpose applications. The limited size of the Celeron's L1 and L2 caches counters the high speed of the processor, resulting in reduced overall performance when compared to other Intel processors. Motherboards designed for the Intel Celeron and Pentium processors use front-side bus (FSB) technology. Even today, Intel Celeron processors are not uncommon on budget Chromebooks.

Intel Atom

The Intel Atom is a specialized processor designed for low power consumption and low heat production. It is available in 32-bit and 64-bit and in single-core and dual-core. The Atom is limited to applications requiring minimal processor performance; as such, it is used in tablets, smartphones, and similar devices. The Atom is soldered to the motherboard, which makes replacement difficult and requires the motherboard to be replaced if the processor were defective.

Core i3

The Intel Core i3 is designed for minimal computing power and is not intended for high-performance applications. It will perform word-processing functions, e-mail services, and web-browsing applications. This processor is ideal for a computer that uses cloud services, because these services provide the processing power needed for more intense software applications. Compared to the Core i5 and i7, the Core i3 has

Intel Processors over Time

Processor	Bus Speed	Introduced
Intel Xeon	100 MHz, 133 MHz, 400 MHz, 533 MHz, 667 MHz, 800 MHz, 1066 MHz, 1333 MHz, 1600 MHz, 4.8 GT/s, 5.86 GT/s, 6.4 GT/s	1998–present
Intel Celeron	66 MHz, 100 MHz, 133 MHz, 400 MHz, 533 MHz, 800 MHz	1999–present
Intel Atom	400 MHz, 533 MHz, 667 MHz, 2.5 GT/s	2008–present
Intel Core i7	4.8 GT/s, 6.4 GT/s	2008–present
Intel Core i3	1066 MHz, 1600 MHz, 2.5–5 GT/s	2009–present
Intel Core i5	2.5–5 GT/s	2009–present
Intel Core i7 (Extreme Edition)	2.5 GT/s–6.4 GT/s	2011–present
Intel Core i9	8 GT/s	2017–present

Goodheart-Willcox Publisher

Figure 4-12 There are many Intel processors available, each with varying degrees of speed and capabilities.

the smallest L3 cache size. In addition, Turbo Boost 2.0 Technology and Performance Tuning are not available for the Intel Core i3.

Core i5

The Intel Core i5 processor is designed as an intermediate processor with performance between the Core i3 and i7. The Core i5 does not support Intel Hyper-Threading Technology, but it does have many of the other processor features such as performance tuning. The addition of Performance Tuning enhances overall system performance for gaming, video editing, and computation but not to the level expected from a Core i7 processor. The L3 cache of the Core i5 is bigger than that of the Core i3 but smaller than that of the Core i7, meaning the processor performs better than the Core i3 but less than the Core i7. This processor is perfect for users looking for an average computer system with limited multimedia-editing capabilities.

Core i7

The Intel Core i7 processor comes in two versions: Intel Core i7 and Intel Core i7 Extreme. Both processors have the most processor cores and threads as compared to Core i3 and i5. Additionally, both versions of Core i7 have the most desirable features for high performance such as Intel Turbo Boost 2.0 Technology, Intel Hyper-Threading Technology, Performance Tuning, and the largest L3 cache.

The main difference between the Core i7 and Core i7 Extreme edition is the Extreme edition provides better graphics performance than the Core i7. The Intel Core i7 Extreme processor is the best Intel processor designed for high-performance software applications, such as gaming with intense 3D graphics. This processor supports up to 32 GB of DDR3 memory. The Core i7 Extreme has additional cache and is capable of higher clock speeds when compared to the Core i7.

A+ 1101: 3.4

Core i9

The Core i9 has 10–18 cores, depending on the model. They have high power consumption, high thermal output, extremely high performance, and a special socket: LGA 2066. In general, the i9 class is aimed at users such as high-intensity game players. The mobile version using the BGA1440 socket appeared in 2018 and featured six hyper-threaded cores and 12 MB of onboard cache. These processors may achieve speeds of up to 5 GHz. As of this writing, Intel Core i9 is still the most advanced Intel processor, but they have added code words for specific improvements. For example, Tiger Lake was the Intel code name for the 11th generation processors. These depend on the Willow Cove architecture. The most recent iteration, Tiger Lake H35, was launched in January 2021.

Raptor Lake

Raptor Lake is the code name for the latest, 13th generation, of Intel Core processors. This technology was launched in October 2022 and depends on Raptor Cove performance cores working along with Gracemont power-efficient cores. This processor can support up to a 36-MB L3 cache, DDR5-5600 RAM, and up to 6.0 GHz. There are versions based on Core i5, Core i7, and Core i9. This processor was developed largely to compete with AMD's Ryzen 7000 series.

AMD

As previously mentioned, AMD has long been Intel's biggest competitor. The two companies' processor production and evolution can be thought of as mirror images of one another. As one company makes strides in creating faster, more efficient processors, the other company must stay competitive. Pay close attention to Figure 4-13, which lists AMD processor architectures, their speeds and families, and when they were released.

AMD Processors over Time			
Family	**Speed (MHz)**	**Released**	**Architecture**
Athlon 64	2000–2800	2003	K8
Athlon 64 FX	2200, 2400, 2600, 2800	2003	K8
Mobile Athlon 64	1600–2600	2004	K8
Mobile Sempron	1600–2200	2004	K8
Sempron	1800–2300	2004	K8
Athlon 64 X2	2000–3200	2005	K8
Turion 64	1600–2400	2005	K8
Turion 64 X2	1600–2400	2006	K8
Opteron	1400–3200	2006	K8
Athlon	2400–2700	2007	K10
Athlon X2	2300–2800	2007	K10
Opteron	1700–2500	2007	K10
Sempron	2700	2007	K10
Phenom	1800–2600	2008	K10
Turion II	2000–2700	2008	K10.5
Athlon II	2200–3600	2009	K10.5
Phenom II	2600–3700	2009	K10.5
Llano	2100–3000	2011	K10.5
Sempron	2600–2900	2011	K10.5
Ryzen	3200–3800 (3800–4000 boost)	2017	Zen

Goodheart-Willcox Publisher

Figure 4-13 Similar to Intel, AMD produces a number of processors for different types of computing.

Athlon 64

The AMD Athlon 64, introduced in 2002, is an extremely powerful desktop CPU. As the name implies, it uses both 32-bit and 64-bit processing technology. L1 and L2 caches are integrated into the CPU, and an L3 cache is mounted on the motherboard. The Athlon 64 is designed to mount in a 940-pin socket; normally, an increased number of pins would increase the overall dimensions of the CPU socket, but the Athlon 64 CPU uses the Socket 940 micro PGA. The micro PGA reduces the socket pin grid-array area, reducing the overall size of the CPU socket, even with an increase in the number of pins.

Opteron

1101: 3.4 A+

The AMD Opteron, introduced in 2003, is a high-end processor designed and developed for network servers. The Opteron eliminated the 4-GB memory address barrier associated with earlier processors. The 4-GB memory access limitation is a trait of the 32-bit design, but the Opteron uses a 64-bit memory address design, allowing for greater memory capacity. Total possible accessible memory is 256 TB, but that number is impractical for now. The typical core processor speeds range from 800 MHz to 2.6 GHz, and the processor can produce a throughput of 19 GB or more by using multiple paths to process data. The 64-kB L1 cache and the 1,024-kB (1 MB) L2 cache are both integrated into the CPU chip. Like the Athlon 64, the Opteron mounts into a Socket 940 micro PGA.

Sempron

AMD Sempron, introduced in 2004, is the successor to the AMD Duron processor and is designed for use in low-cost computer systems much like the Intel Celeron is. The Sempron requires a socket 754 on the motherboard. The interesting thing about the Sempron is that it comes in two very different styles: front-side bus with a north-bridge chipset and HyperTransport. To maintain compatibility, you must be sure of which Sempron you are going to install or replace.

For CPUs that use HyperTransport, speed is represented by megatransfers per second (MT/s), not frequency (Hz). AMD claims 2,000 MT/s is equal to 4 GBps in each direction of the bus. The transfer speed can also be measured as gigatransfers per second (GT/s), but AMD has chosen to represent the transfer speed in MT/s. To a casual reader with no real computer expertise, 2,000 MT/s looks much more impressive than 2 GT/s.

Athlon 64 X2

The AMD Athlon 64 X2, introduced in 2005, is a dual-core processor that incorporates a new technique of accessing frequently used data. The Athlon 64 X2 cores are capable of higher data throughput than the single-core Athlon 64. The Athlon 64 X2 is intended to be used in all computer systems except in high-end or high-performance models.

Athlon 64 FX

In 2006, AMD introduced the Athlon 64 FX and a new socket design called *AM2*. However, the Athlon 64 FX processor is physically and electrically compatible with the socket 939 and socket 940, meaning the Athlon 64 FX can be used to upgrade an older computer that uses the previous CPU version mounted in a socket 939 or socket 940. The AM2 socket, however, is not compatible with previous versions of AMD processors that fit into the socket 939 and socket 940. The Athlon 64 FX is comparable to the Intel Core 2 Extreme, as both are intended for use in high-end or high-performance computer systems that require intense processing performance.

A+ **1101: 3.4**

Ryzen

AMD Ryzen was introduced in early 2017 for desktop, mobile, and embedded platforms. It is the first AMD processor to utilize AMD's Zen microarchitecture, which provides better energy efficiency and a significant increase in instructions per cycle. The Ryzen processor is an AM4 socket type and supports DDR4 memory. Depending on the model, the base clock rate ranges from 3.1 GHz to 3.8 GHz and offers boosted rates ranging from 3.4 GHz to 4.0 GHz. Ryzen processors are marketed for mainstream users and enthusiasts. As of this writing, the Ryzen 8000 is AMD's latest chip.

In November 2020, AMD released the Zen 3 series of CPUs. Zen 3 uses two core complex dies with a total of 8 CPU cores and a shared L3 cache. These chips are commercially branded as Ryzen 5, Ryzen 7, and Ryzen 9. Ryzen 9 can have up to 16 cores.

A+ **1101: 3.4**

4.6 Multicore and Multi-Socket CPUs

Multiprocessor systems have become rather common in recent years. This includes both single processors that have multiple processor cores and machines that have multiple sockets for separate processors. The physical installation of either multicore or multi-socket systems does not differ from that of single-core or single-socket systems. In fact, from the outside of the chip, there is no clear difference between a single core and a multicore CPU.

A **multicore processor** is a type of processor with two or more cores constructed on the same die. It consists of a single integrated circuit that has two or more processing units, which work separately. However, they will usually share the same front-side bus and L2 cache since they are in the same integrated circuit. Multicore processors demonstrate a substantial increase in performance over a single core processor as increased data throughput is achieved mainly by using a dual core.

Multi-socket systems have two or more CPU sockets that can have entirely separate CPUs. This means each CPU has its own L2 cache and front-side bus. Clearly, this provides a performance advantage over even multicore processors. However, the greatest advantage comes when one uses processor affinity, which is the use of operating system features to direct some portion of the machine's activities to a specific processor. For example, if one has a dual processor database server, one can set the database management system to have affinity for the second processor. That way, the first processor manages all operating system functionality, and the second processor is only concerned with running the database.

Multicore Processors

1101: 3.4 A+

Figure 4-14 compares the internal architecture of an AMD Athlon 64 processor and an AMD Athlon 64 FX processor. The AMD Athlon 64 processor in Figure 4-14A contains a single core and two L1 caches. One L1 cache is used to store processing instructions and commands temporarily, and the other L1 cache is used to temporarily store data being processed. The two L1 caches make data processing twice as fast as processors with a single L1 cache. L1 cache is typically smaller and faster than L2 cache. The AMD Athlon 64 uses an L1 cache of 64 kB while L2 cache is typically 1 MB or more. The DDR memory controller connects directly with RAM, and the HyperTransport link connects to other devices and buses across the motherboard.

As you can see in Figure 4-14B, the AMD Athlon 64 FX processor consists of two complete AMD Athlon 64 processors on the same die. Each processor has its own set of L1 caches, and each has its own L2 cache. The two processors share the DDR memory controller and the HyperTransport link.

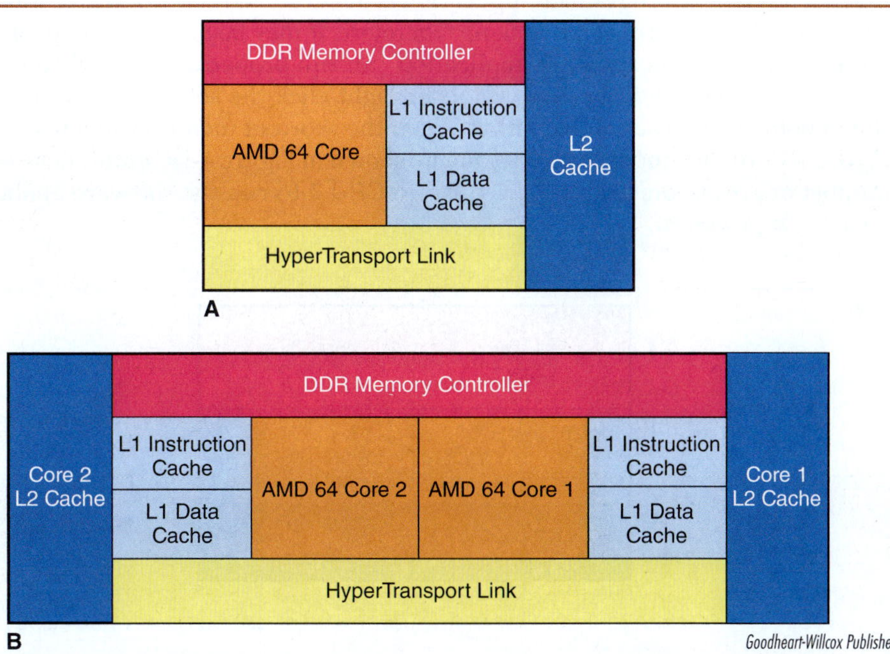

Figure 4-14 The internal architecture of a single-core processor differs from that of a dual-core processor. The additional cores enable faster data processing.

As illustrated in Figure 4-15, the Intel Core Duo has two L1 caches per core, just like the AMD Athlon 64 FX processor. The big difference between the AMD and Intel multicore processors is the L2 cache design. The AMD Athlon 64 FX processor has an L2 cache for each core; the Intel Core Duo has one L2 cache, which is shared by each core. The reason Intel decided to share the L2 cache is in order for the amount of L2 cache used by each core to be directly proportional to the processing demand of each core. For example, if only one core is used, then that one core will use the entire L2 cache. If one core is running at 25 percent and the other at 75 percent, the L2 cache will also be split at 25 percent and 75 percent. This means that the entire L2 cache is always used, whereas in the AMD design, the L2 cache can only be used by the corresponding processor core.

Another significant difference between the Intel Core Duo and the AMD Athlon 64 FX is the AMD multicore design makes use of HyperTransport Technology instead of a northbridge chip. The data throughput using the HyperTransport Technology is used to connect directly to the southbridge, additional CPUs, or other devices. The AMD multicore processor also connects directly to the RAM and does not have a front-side bus as the first Intel multicore designs did. The FSB design of Intel multicore system requires that the RAM share the FSB with the northbridge. See Figure 4-16.

AMD and Intel both introduced newer multicore technologies that are designed with the individual core processors communicating directly with each other and directly to memory. In earlier versions of processor and motherboard architecture, the processor had to communicate with memory through chipsets mounted on the motherboard. Also, early versions of multicore processors communicated with each other through the processor L3 cache rather than directly. The AMD version is called Direct Connect Architecture, and the Intel version is called QuickPath Technology.

A+ 1102: 1.3

Processor Affinity

Processor affinity is the ability to select the number of CPU cores to apply to a software application. To take advantage of multicore processors, the operating system and software application must be designed to operate in a multicore environment. If a software program or application is not designed to work with a multicore processor, the software could lock up. Therefore, it may be necessary to disable the multiple cores so the software application can run properly. To disable one of the cores, you simply open the Task Manager, right-click the software program under the **Details** tab, and select **Set affinity** from the shortcut menu, as demonstrated in Figure 4-17. In the Processor affinity menu, shown in Figure 4-18, simply deselect any number of processors from CPU 0 through CPU 7 to run the software application on a single processor.

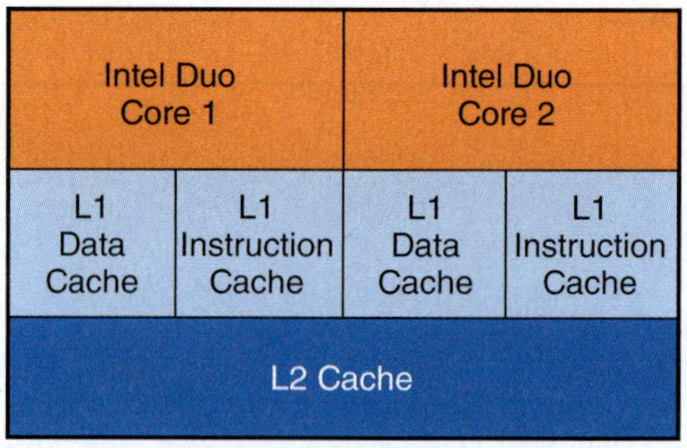

Figure 4-15 In an Intel Core Duo processor, the L2 cache is shared by each core.

Goodheart-Willcox Publisher

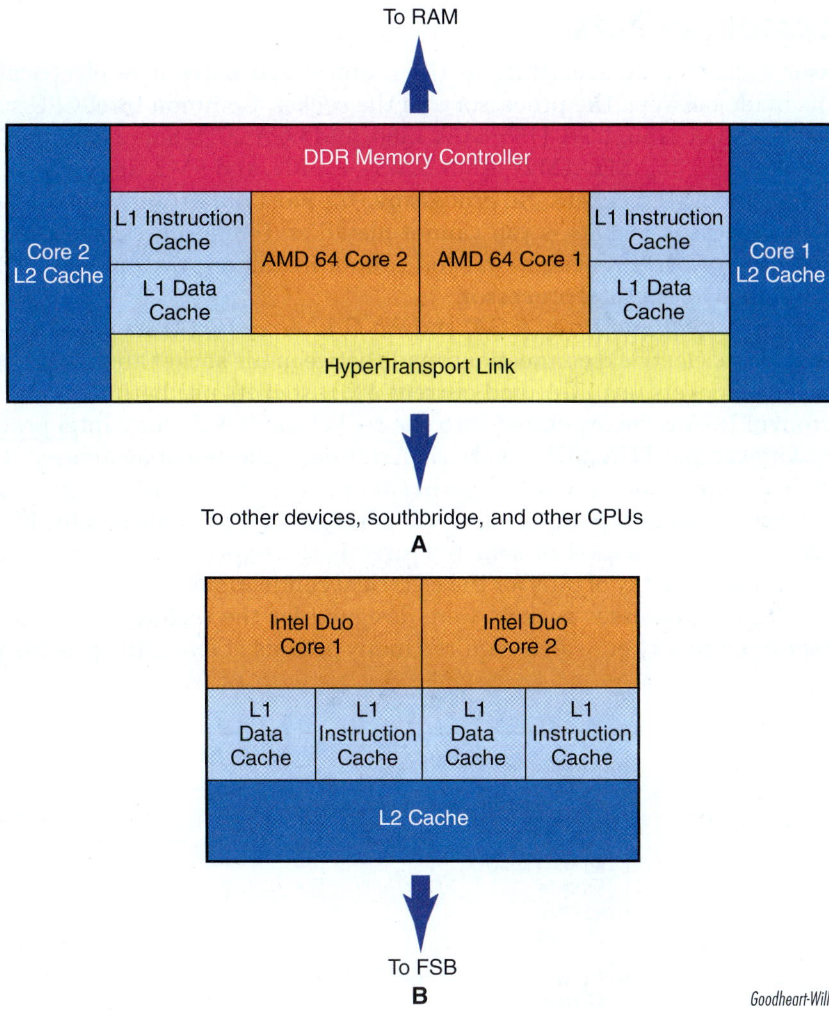

Goodheart-Willcox Publisher

Figure 4-16 An AMD multicore processor and an Intel multicore processor interface differently with motherboard devices, chipsets, and other CPUs. The AMD 64 processor (A) uses a HyperTransport link, which connects it directly to the southbridge, other devices, and other CPUs. It also has a DDR memory controller to connect directly to RAM. The Intel Duo Core (B) instead connects to a front-side bus, which shares RAM with the northbridge.

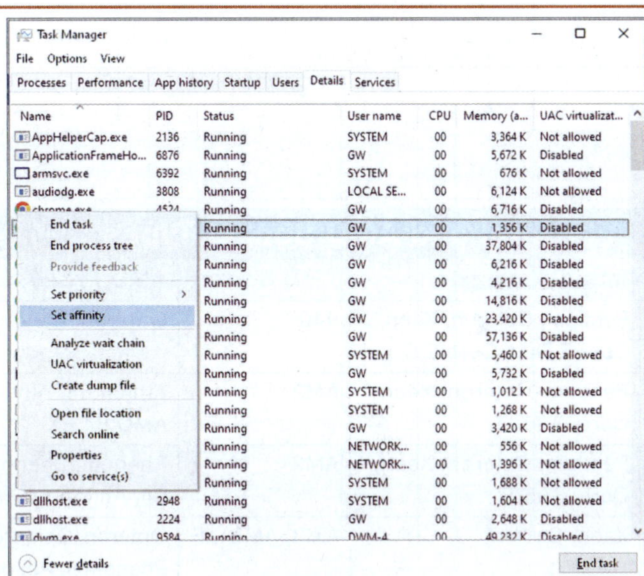

Goodheart-Willcox Publisher

Figure 4-17 To access the Processor affinity menu, open **Task Manager**, select the **Details** tab, right-click the program in question, and select **Set affinity** from the shortcut menu.

A+ 1101: 3.4

Processor Sockets

Processor sockets vary according to the number and pattern of electrical connections made between the processor and the socket. Common Intel CPU sockets are LGA 775, LGA 1155, LGA 1156, LGA 1366, and LGA 2011. Some common AMD CPU sockets are 940, AM2, AM2+, AM3, AM3+, F, FM1, and FM2. See Figure 4-19 to match Intel and AMD sockets and processors. The most important thing to remember about processor sockets is you cannot install an Intel processor into a socket designed for an AMD processor, and you cannot install an AMD processor into a socket designed for an Intel processor.

The terms *Land Grid Array (LGA)* and *Pin Grid Array (PGA)* are used to identify the physical and electrical connections made between the socket and the processor. Current Intel sockets use LGA, and current AMD sockets use both PGA and LGA. The acronym LGA is incorporated into the socket name for many Intel processor sockets, for example, LGA 2011. Land Grid Array uses a design or an array of "lands" as electrical connection points. The term *land* refers to the small flat area used as an electrical connection point on the back of the processor. Additionally, LGA can either be used with a socket or soldered directly to the printed circuit board. Pin Grid Array uses an array of pins for the electrical connections.

The original processor sockets were designed for the technician to press the processor into the socket, which required many pounds of force. The processor had

Figure 4-18 The **Processor affinity** menu allows you to select the CPUs you wish to use for a given program.

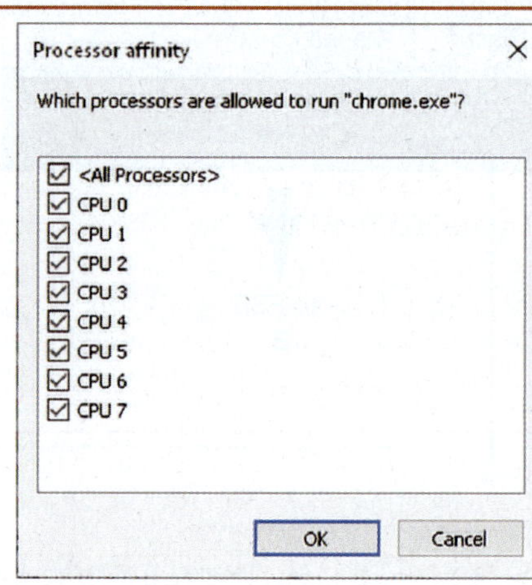

Goodheart-Willcox Publisher

Figure 4-19 Intel and AMD processors have varying socket types.

Intel and AMD Socket Types

Intel Socket	Intel Processor	AMD Socket	AMD Processor
LGA 775	Pentium, Celeron, Xeon, Core 2 Duo, Core 2 Quad	940	Opteron, Athlon 64 FX
LGA 1155	Pentium, Celeron, Xeon, Core i3/i5/i7	AM2	Athlon 64, Athlon 64 X2, AMD 64 FX
LGA 1156	Pentium, Celeron, Xeon, Core i3/i5/i7	AM2+	Phenom, Phenom II, Athlon 64, Athlon 64 X2
LGA 1366	Xeon, Core i7	AM3, AM3+, F	Opteron, Sempron, Phenom II, Athlon II, FX, Llano
LGA 2011	Xeon, Core i7	FM1, FM2	A4, A6, A8, A10, E2

Note: The table contains only a partial list of sockets and processors. Check the manufacturer's website for the latest information about sockets and processors.

Goodheart-Willcox Publisher

an array of long pins on the back that were forced into the socket. If the processor pins were misaligned with the processor socket, the force of the insertion would bend some of the pins. When the pins were straightened back out, they would sometimes break off, resulting in a processor that could not be repaired. In order to alleviate the use of severe force, the zero insertion force (ZIF) socket was designed. A **zero insertion force (ZIF) socket** is a type of socket for mounting a CPU that is designed not to cause stress or damage during insertion. ZIF sockets have a lever to assist in the installation of the CPU. This type of socket requires practically no force at all to insert the CPU into the socket while the lever arm is raised. Once the CPU is inserted into the socket, the lever is lowered, which causes each pin to fit tightly into the socket. The ZIF socket literally clamps each pin into place.

Intel identifies its processor sockets with numbers. For example, an Intel LGA 2011 socket has 2,011 locations or connection points. In contrast, an LGA 775 socket has 775 connection points. This means the socket and the motherboard are only compatible with a specific set of processors. AMD identifies its processor sockets with numbers and letters. AMD is moving away from number identification and is now using more letters.

1101: 3.4 A+

AMD features two sockets: socket 939 and socket 940. They appear almost identical except for a difference of one pin. The one-pin difference is very significant. The socket 939 does not require registered RAM, but socket 940 does. *Registered RAM* is typically used for servers and mission-critical computers. Most desktop PCs do not require registered RAM, so you will find that most AMD desktop PCs use a socket 939.

The AMD AM2 socket closely resembles the 939 and 940 sockets, but it is not electrically or physically compatible with CPUs designed for 939 and 940 sockets. The reason for the change is the HyperTransport interface on an AM2 socket processor. AMD CPUs that use the HyperTransport technology are no longer compatible with motherboards that use a northbridge chip in the chipset. The AMD Athlon 64 FX will physically fit into a 939, 940, and AM2 socket, but it can only take advantage of the larger L2 cache design when installed in an AM2 socket.

The AM2 socket also supports direct data transfers to DDR2 RAM, while the 939 and 940 sockets do not. DDR2 RAM is a high-performance RAM that is covered in detail in a later chapter. The original name of the AM2 socket was simply M2 but later was changed because it was confused with the M2 socket introduced by Cyrix.

Processor Performance

Tech Tip

A software utility that identifies the processor, motherboard, and memory specifications is a valuable asset to a PC technician's tool kit.

Since the physical designs of processors are so different from one manufacturer to another, they cannot be evaluated by their specific features. Both AMD and Intel claim superior performance based on their CPU designs, so the only way to evaluate CPU performance fairly is when it is running software applications.

The true performance of a CPU can only be measured by evaluating the performance of two different computer systems using similar hardware. However, it is nearly impossible to match the two systems exactly because of the motherboard chipset and bus system. Rather than attempting to evaluate a specific CPU, you are better off evaluating a complete computer system and the performance of the same software application programs on each computer system. A CPU analyzer can also be used to evaluate a processor's performance. A free CPU analyzer, called CPU-Z, can be downloaded from CPUID and will identify the CPU, size of the L1 and L2 caches, socket type, core speed, bus speed, and more.

The CPU-Z utility shown in Figure 4-20 has identified four cores for the processor and additional related information. This is an excellent tool for obtaining processor specifications as well as motherboard and memory specifications without opening the computer case and looking for part numbers. Intel and AMD also provide similar software utilities to inspect the processor. Figure 4-21 shows the Intel Processor Identification Utility.

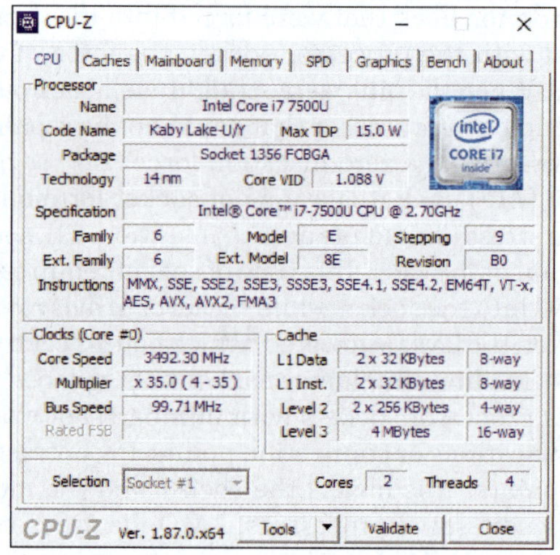

Goodheart-Willcox Publisher

Figure 4-20 The CPU-Z utility available from CPUID can be used to identify the CPU, size of L1 and L2 caches, socket type, core speed, bus speed, and more.

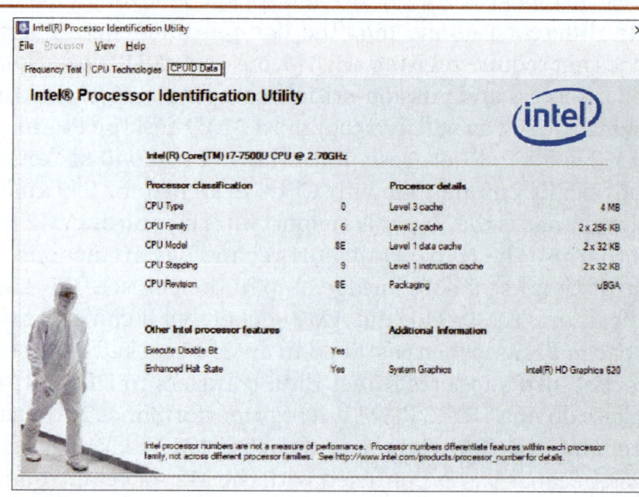

Goodheart-Willcox Publisher

Figure 4-21 The Intel Processor Identification Utility identifies data about the installed processor, such as the processor name, model number, cache sizes, and socket type.

A+ 1101: 3.4

4.7 Installing a Processor

Installing or replacing a processor is not a difficult task. If it is your first time installing a particular processor, you need to do your research before beginning, especially when matching the correct cooling device to the processor. Processor installation has always been an easy task, but installing a cooling device has been known to be much more difficult. The information presented in this section is to serve as a general guide for installing a processor and cooling device. You should always consult the manufacturer's website before performing a complete processor installation or replacement.

A CPU socket is designed as a mechanical assembly with a mounting plate and lever(s) that secure the processor in the socket. Figure 4-22 shows the LGA 2011 and LGA 775 sockets for comparison. The LGA 775 has a single lever called a load plate lever. The LGA 2011 has two socket levers: the active lever and the hinge lever. These levers are designed to place equal physical pressure on both ends of the loading plate, ensuring that the processor is firmly mounted in place. Having an additional lever helps secure the processor in place when a heavy cooling unit is mounted on the socket.

The LGA 2011 socket has been designed to accommodate heavy processor cooling devices. The socket is made of a heavy-duty metal frame, which is securely fastened to the motherboard. The metal frame has four threaded mounting studs used to secure the cooling device. The cooling device can be a simple, lightweight heat sink and fan combination, a heat sink and heat tube combination, or a radiator and liquid cooler pump combination. The lightweight heat sink and fan combination is used for the average processor, but high-performance processers and those used in overclocking applications typically require a heat sink and tube combination or a radiator and liquid cooler pump combination.

The major parts of an LGA 2011 socket are identified in Figure 4-23. The entire socket assembly is fabricated on a metal frame, which is mounted to the motherboard. The motherboard typically has a plate on its reverse side that is in direct alignment with the socket mounting plate, as shown in Figure 4-24. Motherboards without a backplate require one to be installed when using certain types of cooling devices.

When a motherboard is removed from the shipping box, the socket will have a cover over it held in place by the load plate. The cover is designed to keep foreign objects out of the socket and protect the electrical connections from accidental physical damage. The levers must be released to remove the cover from under the loading plate.

The two levers on the LGA 2011 have a specific sequence for opening and closing. To open the socket load plate, the hinge lever must be released first, followed by the active lever. When closing the load plate, the operational sequence is reversed; the active lever is closed first, and then the hinge lever is closed. The hinge lever is designed to keep the active lever from being opened first, as illustrated in Figure 4-25. After both the hinge lever and the active lever are released, the load plate can be tilted back and the cover removed, thus exposing the processor socket.

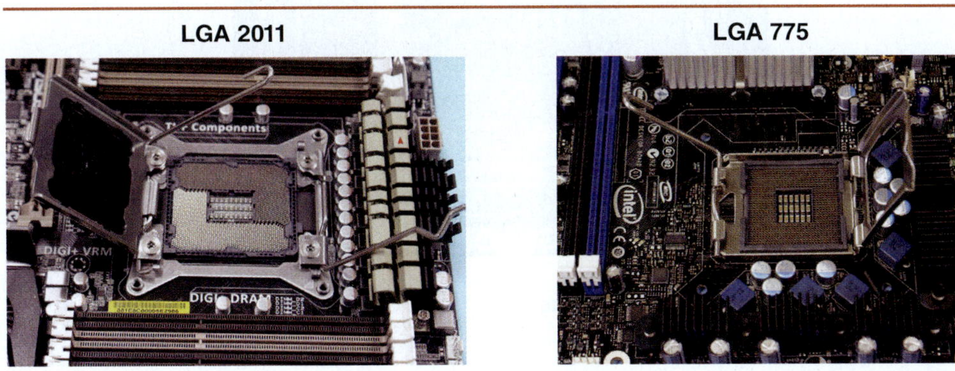

Goodheart-Willcox Publisher

Figure 4-22 A CPU socket is designed as a mechanical assembly with a mounting plate and lever(s) that secure the processor in the socket.

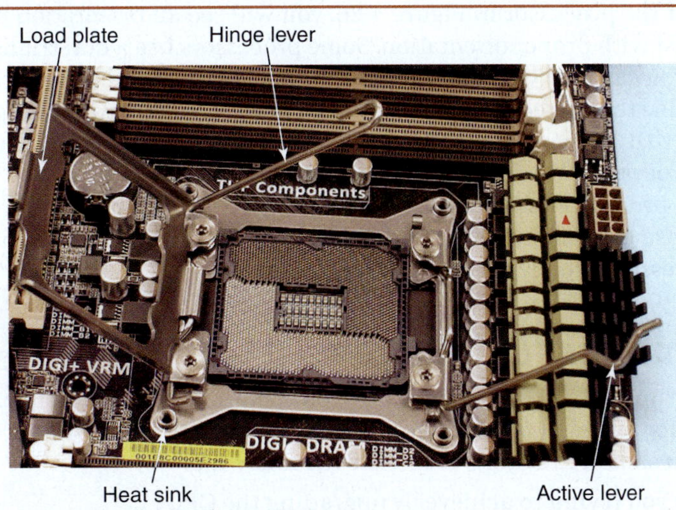

Goodheart-Willcox Publisher

Figure 4-23 Many CPU sockets include a load plate, hinge lever, active lever, and heat sink mounting stud.

Figure 4-24 Motherboards typically have plates on the reverse side that align almost directly with the socket mounting plate.

Goodheart-Willcox Publisher

Figure 4-25 Sockets with two levers have a specific sequence for opening and closing.

Goodheart-Willcox Publisher

After the processor socket is exposed, the processor can be installed. There is only one way to install the processor correctly; it must be aligned with the socket. If you look closely at the processor in Figure 4-26, you will see an orientation mark on the corner to assist with proper orientation. Some processors use a dot, triangle, or some other mark. You can also visually compare the pin pattern on the socket and processor to determine the correct orientation or use the notches provided along the edge of the processor that align with the notches along the edge of the socket. There is no need to force the processor into the socket. Simply drop it into place, gently.

After the processor is installed, close the active lever and then the hinge lever to snuggly close the loading plate over the processor and secure it into the socket. Now the processor is ready for the cooling system.

Considerations for Upgrading a CPU

The process of upgrading a CPU can range from easy to nearly impossible. The degree of likelihood for a logical upgrade is based on several computer system conditions. Questions you should first answer include the following:

- What are you trying to achieve by upgrading the CPU?
- Is the upgrade processor compatible physically with the motherboard?

Goodheart-Willcox Publisher

Figure 4-26 Processors are keyed so there is only one correct way to install them.

- Will the chipset and BIOS support the upgraded processor?
- Does the motherboard bus speed and chipset, rather than the CPU speed, limit the increase in speed you desire?
- Does the motherboard chipset support the desired features of the new CPU, such as a new 3D technology?

You may wish to upgrade from a low-end processor such as an Intel Celeron or Intel Core i3 to a Core i7, but the higher performance expected may not be encountered because the motherboard chipset is most likely matched to the processor. Simply replacing the existing processor with a much better one may not achieve your desired purpose.

Upgrading a CPU will not solve all speed-related issues. Transferring data to and from the hard drive is mostly an issue involving the motherboard bus speed and port speeds and not the speed of the CPU. If an increase in the speed of downloading information from the Internet is the challenge, a new processor is not likely to help. Download speed is more dependent on the cabling system between the downloading site and the computer as well as the modem speed. In addition, modern computer systems are dependent for speed based on the amount of RAM, which will often control perceived speed more than the speed of the processor.

As you can see, upgrading a processor may not meet your desires. If you process a lot of data or play games that contain intensive graphics and sound, you may very well improve the performance of the computer system by upgrading the CPU. Often, it is more practical to replace the CPU and the motherboard to achieve the desired results.

4.8 Cooling the Processor

1101: 3.4 A+

As the CPU evolved to higher data speeds, the heat generated by the processor circuits also increased. Electrical circuits generate heat in proportion to the speed of data flow, and integrated circuits start to break down at approximately 160°F (71°C). There are two main choices of cooling the processor:

- Simple heat sink and fan assembly
- Liquid cooling system

A simple heat sink and fan assembly is most common. Heat sinks are attached to the CPU by heat conductive paste, also called *thermal compound* or *thermal paste*, which has the dual function of adhesion as well as heat transfer. Thermal paste is essentially a grease or paste that is thermally conductive but electrically insulating. It is quite common to find thermal paste being used between the CPU case and a heat sink. Thermal adhesive is quite similar to thermal paste, except the thermal adhesive also acts like a glue to ensure a good fit between the surface of the processor and heat sink. Without the paste, the heat sink could warp slightly, resulting in poor physical contact between the surfaces and causing the CPU to heat up to a dangerous level. While heat sinks, fans, and liquid cooling systems are common, there are other methods of cooling the CPU.

A+ Note

When preparing for the A+ Certification Exams, remember that overclocking, even when using a liquid cooling device, generally voids the processor warranty.

A heat-pipe cooling system is more expensive than a simple heat sink and fan and is generally much heavier. A liquid cooling system is the most expensive. Both the heat pipe and the liquid cooling systems are commonly used in overclocking applications but reduce the heat from the processor much more efficiently than a simple heat sink and fan assembly.

The difficulty of installing a cooling system ranges from simple to complicated, depending on the type of system you choose to install. Additionally, some of the assembly kits can contain many parts, and the instructions are not always as clear. Experience is a great help when installing cooling kits. The cooling kit manufacturer typically provides detailed instructions at their website. There are also several YouTube videos designed to show how to install a cooling system for a particular type of CPU and motherboard combination.

A+ 1101: 3.4

Heat Sink and Fan Assembly

For general purpose computer systems, you will most likely use a heat sink and fan assembly. The simple heat sink and fan assembly are the least expensive of the three cooling systems. The fan assembly screws into place on an LGA 2011 socket. Another type of fan assembly used with a different physical socket does not use threaded screws and instead uses plastic legs that are pushed through the physical connection points. Figure 4-27 shows both installation methods.

After the heat sink and fan assembly are physically installed over the processor, you must connect the fan wiring to the motherboard. A typical motherboard has several fan connections with one usually designated as the CPU fan connection, as shown in Figure 4-28. The CPU fan connection can be monitored by the BIOS, which will warn the user when the fan is running too slowly or when the CPU is generating excessive heat. The motherboard manual usually contains all information needed for proper installation of a simple heat sink and fan.

When a motherboard manual is not available, you can check the motherboard manufacturer's website or processor manufacturer's website to match the cooling device to the processor and motherboard socket correctly. The website or manual will contain detailed instructions for the correct installation of the processor and the cooling system. An illustrated manual usually accompanies a nonstandard cooling device. Again, you can consult the manufacturer's website for detailed instructions on how to install the cooling device. YouTube commonly has videos posted by other technicians or the manufacturer that explain the correct installation procedure.

A B

Goodheart-Willcox Publisher

Figure 4-27 A heat sink and fan assembly is most often used for most general-use computer systems. The fan assembly is screwed into the mounting studs of the socket assembly (A), or the fan assembly's plastic mounting legs are inserted and twisted into the mounting holes (B).

Liquid Cooling System

A liquid cooling system is by far the most expensive of the three cooling systems. The pump and a heat sink are mounted directly on the processor. The heat generated by the processor is absorbed by the heat sink and transferred to the liquid, which is circulated by the pump mounted on the processor heat sink. The liquid is circulated to a radiator where the heat is released. A fan is mounted on the radiator to assist with the removal of the heat. See Figure 4-29.

The cooling system can be monitored by the BIOS, and the computer system will automatically shut down if a predetermined temperature is reached or if the cooling system fails, such as a fan going below a preset rpm. To monitor the cooling system, a three- or four-wire fan connection is required. To simply power a cooling fan, only a two-wire fan connection is required.

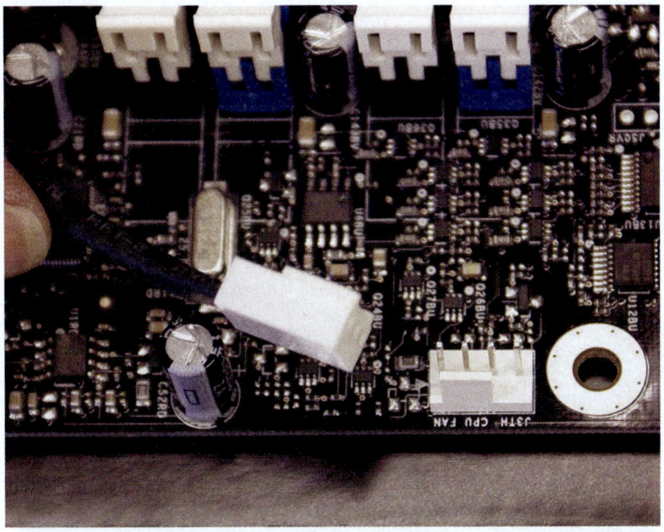

Goodheart-Willcox Publisher

Figure 4-28 A typical motherboard has several four-pin CPU fan connections.

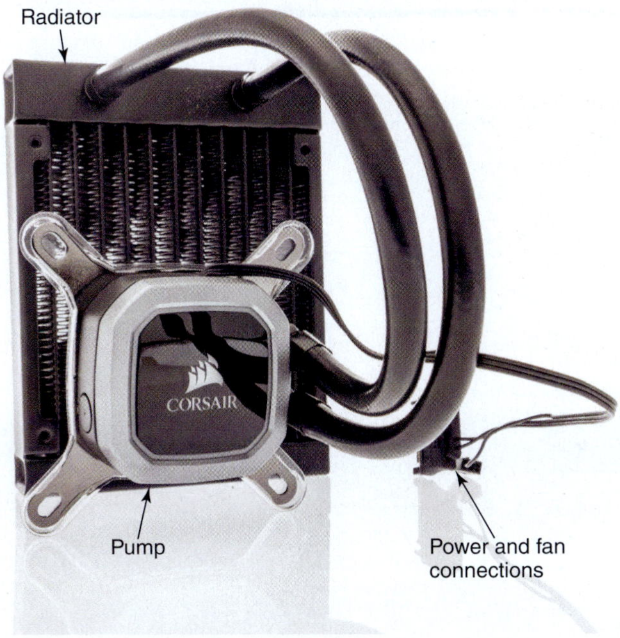

Keith Homan/Shutterstock.com

Figure 4-29 A liquid cooling system consists of a pump and radiator. The pump circulates the liquid, and the radiator releases the heat generated by the processor.

Look again at Figure 4-29. Notice that the liquid cooling pump uses two different electrical connections. One is a typical fan connection, which provides power to the fan and transmits monitoring information. The other is a power connection, which provides electrical power to the pump.

After installing the liquid cooling unit, the computer can be booted. If a problem occurs, the computer BIOS will automatically stop the boot process. Figure 4-30 shows the ASUS UEFI BIOS monitoring the computer system. The system was halted because of a cooling fan problem detected.

The information for the fan at fault is displayed in red. The BIOS detected that the CPU cooling fan rpm is too low and stopped the boot process. A high-performance CPU can rapidly generate excessive heat and lock up during the boot process. After the problem is corrected, the computer can be safely booted. There is also an option that will allow you to ignore the problem. Not all computers have this type of monitoring; its availability depends on the motherboard BIOS system.

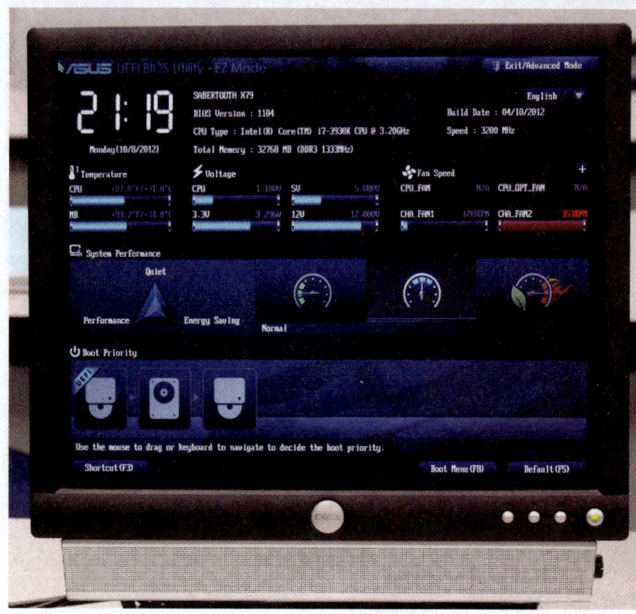

Figure 4-30 Some BIOS programs halt the boot process in the event of a cooling problem.

Goodheart-Willcox Publisher

Chapter Summary

4.1 Instructions and Data

- The CPU is the closest thing to a brain that a computer has. It follows commands called instructions and processes data.
- An instruction set is the lowest language level used to program a computer. It is written in assembly language, which is one step above machine language.
- A compiler is a program that translates higher-level language into machine language based on the CPU's instruction set. An interpreter is a program that performs on-demand translation of higher-level language into machine language.
- A CPU contains several registers, which are small pockets of memory used to temporarily store data being processed.

4.2 CPU Operation

- A CPU is constantly in operation. It processes commands and data, refreshes memory, checks for communication from system devices, monitors the system power, and performs other programmed duties.
- A bus unit is a network of circuitry that connects all the other major components together, accepts data, and sends data through input and output bus sections.
- A decode unit decodes instructions sent to the CPU and works under the direction of the control unit, which controls the overall operation of the CPU.
- The control unit controls the overall operation of the CPU, the arithmetic logic unit (ALU) performs mathematical functions on the data in the registers, and the register unit is composed of many separate storage units smaller than cache.

4.3 Enhancing CPU Operation

- Some of the technologies used to enhance CPU operation are local bus, cache, floating-point unit, multiple branch prediction, superscalar technology, dynamic execution, integrated memory controllers, integrated graphics processing, dual independent bus, simultaneous threading, and overclocking.
- The local bus is the highest-speed bus in the computer system.
- CPUs have L1, L2, and sometimes, L3 caches.
- The floating-point unit (FPU) is a set of circuits incorporated into the processor that is used for mathematics computation.
- Multiple branch prediction is a technique that guesses what data element will be needed next rather than waiting for the next command to be issued.
- Superscalar execution is the act of processing more than one instruction at the same time.
- Dynamic execution is a term coined by Intel to describe the enhanced superscalar and multiple branch prediction features associated with the Pentium II processor.
- The integrated memory controller (IMC) is a digital circuit built into the processor that manages data flow to and from system memory.
- Dual Independent Bus (DIB) is a bus architecture introduced with two separate or independent bus systems incorporated into the processor chip. The first DIB was introduced with the Pentium Pro and Pentium II.
- In software programming, a thread is part of a software program that can be executed independently of the entire program. When two or more threads are executed at the same time, it is called simultaneous threading.

- Overclocking is the intentional application of frequencies higher that a processor's design specification to obtain enhanced performance.

4.4 Processor Features

- A reduced instruction set computer (RISC) is a type of CPU architecture that is designed with fewer transistors and commands.
- Complex instruction set computer (CISC) refers to a CPU designed so the die can accept many machine language commands that manipulate or process complex mathematical formulas and instruction sets.
- MMX is a single instruction, multiple data (SIMD) instruction set architecture. The MMX processor was based on a standard processor with the addition of 57 commands that enhanced its abilities to support graphics technology.
- The terms 32-bit and 64-bit refer to the data width, which is the amount of data that can be processed in parallel during one cycle or clock beat.
- The principal method used by Windows 10 or 11 to achieve software compatibility with older applications uses files with a designation of *WoW*, which stands for *Windows 32-bit on Windows 64-bit*.
- *Virtualization* makes a single physical processor appear as multiple processors to the computer software system and the user.
- System Management Mode (SMM) is a CPU operating mode in which execution is suspended and an alternate system is executed.
- Processor throttling is a method of controlling processor frequency to conserve portable computer battery life.
- Enhanced Intel SpeedStep Technology is designed to change the applied system voltage and CPU frequency under certain conditions.
- CPU operating voltage has decreased over the years to reduce the amount of heat generated by the CPU when processing data.
- The physical size of processors has not changed significantly over the years, but the electronics inside the chip have become more compact. The density of transistor circuits in a CPU is expressed in nanometers.

4.5 Processor Manufacturers and Evolution

- There are many CPUs, but two companies have produced most of them: Intel and AMD.
- Processors have evolved over the years, and as they do, manufacturers reinvent the way processors work.
- Intel and AMD processors often follow a similar timeline in terms of evolution, capabilities, and release dates.
- The Intel Core i9 is among the most recent CPUs. It has 10–18 cores, depending on the model, and high power consumption. Raptor Lake is the code name for the latest generation of Intel processors.
- AMD's Ryzen was introduced in 2017. At the time of this writing, the Ryzen 8000 is AMD's latest CPU.

4.6 Multicore and Multi-Socket CPUs

- A multicore processor is a type of processor with two or more cores constructed on the same die.
- The individual cores in AMD and Intel multicore processors communicate directly with each other and directly with memory.

- Another difference is that AMD utilizes HyperTrasnport Technology instead of a northbridge chip. HyperTransport Technology connects the CPU directly to the southbridge, additional CPUs, and other devices.
- Processor affinity is the ability to select the number of CPU cores to apply to a software application.
- To take advantage of multicore processors, the operating system and the software application must be designed to operate in the multicore environment.
- Common Intel CPU sockets are LGA 775, LGA 1155, LGA 1156, LGA 1366, and LGA 2011; some common AMD CPU sockets are 940, AM2, AM2+, AM3, AM3+, F, FM1, and FM2.
- Zero insertion force (ZIF) sockets have a lever to assist in the installation of the CPU. ZIF sockets were designed to alleviate the use of severe force.
- Since the physical designs of processors are so different from one manufacturer to another, they cannot be evaluated by their specific features.
- The true performance of a CPU can only be measured by evaluating the performance of two different computer systems using similar hardware.
- The CPU-Z utility is an excellent tool for obtaining processor specifications as well as motherboard and memory specifications without opening the computer case and looking for part numbers.

4.7 Installing a Processor

- Processor installation has always been an easy task, but cooling device installation has been known to be much more difficult.
- Consult the manufacturer's website before performing a complete processor installation or replacement.
- There is only one way to install the processor correctly; it must be aligned with the socket.
- An orientation mark is used to assist with proper orientation. This mark is often a dot, triangle, or some other mark. You can also compare the pin patterns on the socket and processor to determine the correct orientation.
- If multiple levers are included in the socket, be sure to use them in the correct order.
- Before upgrading a CPU, a series of questions should be asked relating to what is to be achieved by the upgrade and whether the new CPU will be compatible with the motherboard.
- Upgrading a CPU will not solve all speed-related issues.

4.8 Cooling the Processor

- Common choices of cooling the processor are a simple heat sink and fan assembly and a liquid cooling system.
- A simple heat sink and fan assembly is most common. Heat sinks are attached to the CPU by heat conductive paste, also called *thermal compound*, which has the dual function of adhesion as well as heat transfer.
- A heat-pipe cooling system is more expensive than a simple heat sink and fan and is generally much heavier.
- A liquid cooling system is the most expensive option. The pump and a heat sink are mounted directly on the processor. The heat generated by the processor is absorbed by the heat sink and transferred to the liquid, which is circulated by a small pump mounted on the processor heat sink. The liquid is circulated to a radiator where the heat is released. A fan is mounted on the radiator to assist with the removal of the heat.

Review Questions

1. What is the *instruction set*?
2. Differentiate between a compiler and an interpreter.
3. What is the function of registers?
4. List the components of a CPU that work together to perform basic operations.
5. Describe the cache hierarchy in a CPU as well how those caches are shared among CPU cores.
6. What is the unit of measure for CPU or processor speed?
7. List technologies used to enhance CPU operation.
8. Differentiate between the L1 cache and L2 cache.
9. What is a Dual Independent Bus?
10. In terms of software programming, what is a *thread*?
11. What does it mean to overclock a CPU?
12. List features and terms used to explain, identify, and compare CPUs.
13. Differentiate between RISC and CISC.
14. What is processor throttling?
15. What is the relationship between CPU voltage, energy, and heat?
16. Identify top CPU manufacturers and the recent evolution of their products.
17. Differentiate between multicore and multi-socket CPUs.
18. Differentiate between a Land Grid Array and Pin Grid Array.
19. Summarize the installation process of a CPU.
20. Differentiate among methods for cooling a processor.

Sample A+ Exam Questions

1. Which of the following are true statements concerning the L1 cache? Select all that apply.
   A. It is generally incorporated into the CPU.
   B. It generally transfers data faster than external cache.
   C. It is usually much larger in storage size than motherboard RAM.
   D. It is a form of temporary memory storage.
2. Which of the following best describes a CPU register?
   A. Cache memory used to store hardware information
   B. Temporary memory storage unit
   C. CPU clock signal generator
   D. Trademark associated with the brand of CPU
3. What does the acronym GPU represent?
   A. Graded Processor Unit
   B. Graphics Processor Unit
   C. Grounded Physical Unit
   D. Graphics Production Utility

4. What is the relationship between CPU frequency, temperature, and performance?
   A. Raising the applied processor frequency results in faster processor performance and increased processor heat.
   B. Raising the applied processor frequency results in faster processor performance and makes the fan run faster, which results in lower overall processor temperature.
   C. Raising the applied processor frequency results in slower processor performance and lower processor heat.
   D. Raising the applied processor frequency results in no change in processor performance and no change in processor temperature.
5. Which processor is commonly used in tablet PCs?
   A. Intel Core i7
   B. AMD A8
   C. Intel Atom
   D. Intel Pentium Xeon
6. When upgrading a CPU, which three items should be given consideration? Select three.
   A. BIOS version
   B. CPU socket/slot type
   C. Size of the RAM
   D. Motherboard chipset
7. Which CPU cooling method is most commonly used for Intel processors?
   A. Heat sink and fan assembly
   B. Passive heat pipe
   C. Heat pipe and fan assembly
   D. Liquid cooling and fan assembly
8. Which processor is compatible with an AM2+ socket?
   A. Core i7
   B. Pentium
   C. Celeron
   D. Athlon 64
9. Which factors directly affect the speed of data manipulation by the CPU? Select two.
   A. Clock frequency
   B. Bus width
   C. Voltage level
   D. System temperature
10. What should always be done when replacing or upgrading the CPU?
   A. Leave the fan assembly off and run the system for a while to be sure the new CPU is operating correctly.
   B. Move the jumpers on the motherboard to test for the highest overclocking speed that the CPU can safely handle.
   C. Check the manufacturer's website for the latest upgrade or replacement information.
   D. Replace the BIOS as a matter of routine practice.

Chapter 5

Power Supplies

Learning Outcomes

5.1 Define the terms *voltage*, *current*, *resistance*, and *power* in relation to electrical energy.
5.2 Summarize the procedures for using a multimeter.
5.3 Describe characteristics of branch circuits.
5.4 Describe the function and replacement of a PC power supply.
5.5 Explain the operation of surge-protection devices.
5.6 Use the appropriate guidelines for safe usage and disposal of a battery.
5.7 Summarize Windows Power Options for controlling PC power consumption.
5.8 Differentiate among backup types.

A+ Certification Exam Objectives

The following A+ Certification Exam Objectives are covered in this chapter.

Exam 220-1101

3.0 Hardware

- 3.1 Explain basic cable types and their connectors, features, and purposes.
- 3.4 Given a scenario, install and configure motherboards, central processing units (CPUs), and add-on cards.
- 3.5 Given a scenario, install or replace the appropriate power supply.

5.0 Hardware and Network Troubleshooting

- 5.2 Given a scenario, troubleshoot problems related to motherboards, RAM, CPUs, and power.

Exam 220-1102

1.0 Operating Systems

- 1.4 Given a scenario, use the appropriate Microsoft Windows 10 Control Panel utility.

4.0 Operational Procedures

- 4.3 Given a scenario, implement workstation backup and recovery methods.
- 4.4 Given a scenario, use common safety procedures.
- 4.5 Summarize environmental impacts and local environmental controls.

Key Terms

- Advanced Configuration and Power Interface (ACPI)
- alternating current (AC)
- amperes (A)
- backfeed
- blackout
- brownout
- continuity
- current
- dedicated circuit
- direct current (DC)
- electronic vaulting (e-vaulting)
- fuse
- memory effect
- ohm
- power
- rails
- resistance
- surge
- uninterruptable power supply (UPS)
- voltage
- volt-amperes (VA)
- volts (V)
- watts (W)

Overview

This chapter introduces you to the basic concepts of electrical energy. It will not turn you into an electronics technician, but it *will* familiarize you with the basic electrical terminology and concepts needed to ensure success as a computer technician and success on the A+ Certification Exams. You will learn how to use a multimeter to test voltage and resistance and to test the standard features of computer power supplies. The basis of this chapter is the discussion and illustration of the PC power supply unit. The power supply is easy to understand and simple to replace, but improperly installing a power supply can damage the motherboard. This would be a very expensive mistake.

A+ Note

Expect some basic questions about meters and reading the resistance values of wires and fuses. There may also be questions related to power supplies, such as wattage, connector identification, and voltage levels, as well as items related to UPS systems, battery disposal, and power management.

5.1 What Is Electrical Energy?

Electrical energy is best defined as the flow of electrons, which can be described in terms of electrical values, such as *voltage*, *current*, *resistance*, and *power*. Each term will be explained individually and in relation to each other. The details of electrical energy have been de-emphasized on the latest CompTIA A+ certification, so you should not expect to see many questions about these topics. However, it is still essential knowledge when working in PC repair.

Voltage and Current

Voltage and current are two measurements of electrical power tested by technicians when diagnosing problems related to the PC. **Voltage** is the amount of electrical pressure present in a circuit or power source. The scale used in measuring electrical pressure is **volts (V)**. **Current** is the amount of electron flow. In other words, it is the measure of electrical energy flowing through the system. The scale used to measure the volume of electron flow in a current is **amperes (A)**. Do not mistake the ampere measurement of electrical energy as speed. These measurements are usually taken with a universal multimeter, which will be discussed later in this chapter.

The measurement of electrical energy can be compared to the measurement of water in a pipe. Water flow is measured in gallons per minute (GPM) as well as pounds per square inch (PSI). GPM describes the rate of flow or volume of water while PSI describes the amount of pressure used to produce the flow. Electrical energy is similar. The voltage of the electrical source produces the force for moving electrical energy through the wires and devices, and the amount of electrical energy, or current, moved depends on the amount of voltage applied and the amount of resistance in the path.

Direct Current and Alternating Current

Direct current (DC) refers to electrical energy that flows in one direction, from negative to positive. A DC power source has two terminals: positive and negative. The positive terminal is indicated by the color red and a plus (+) sign, and the negative terminal is indicated by the color black and a minus (–) sign. See the left side of Figure 5-1 to see how DC electrical energy flows steadily from negative to positive.

Alternating current (AC) has no negative or positive markings because it is in a state of constant change or alternating polarities, as illustrated in Figure 5-1. The current in an AC circuit flows in one direction and then in the opposite direction. The completed sequence of flow, first in one direction and then in the other, is called a *cycle*. Current flows in one direction during the first half cycle and then flows in the opposite direction the next half. Figure 5-2 illustrates a complete AC cycle.

Figure 5-1 Direct current (DC) refers to electrical energy that flows in one direction, from negative to positive. Alternating current (AC) has no negative or positive markings because it is in a state of constant change or alternating polarities.

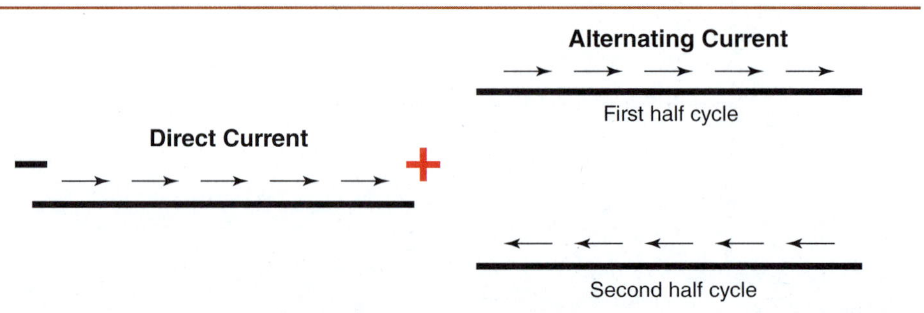

This pattern is repeated as long as power is applied to the circuit. The frequency of how often the cycle is repeated is expressed in hertz (Hz) and is based on a period of one second. Standard household electrical energy is 60 Hz, meaning the direction of the current changes at a rate of 60 times per second, or 60 Hz. See Figure 5-3.

Resistance

Electrical components that manipulate the voltage and current levels in a circuit have measurable resistance values. **Resistance** is the opposition to the flow of electrical energy. The unit of measurement for resistance is the **ohm** and is expressed with the letter *R* or the symbol omega (Ω). Computer technicians are rarely required to take accurate resistance readings, and the resistance readings taken by PC technicians are usually to check for electrical continuity. **Continuity** is the ability of a device or component to allow an unobstructed flow of electrical energy.

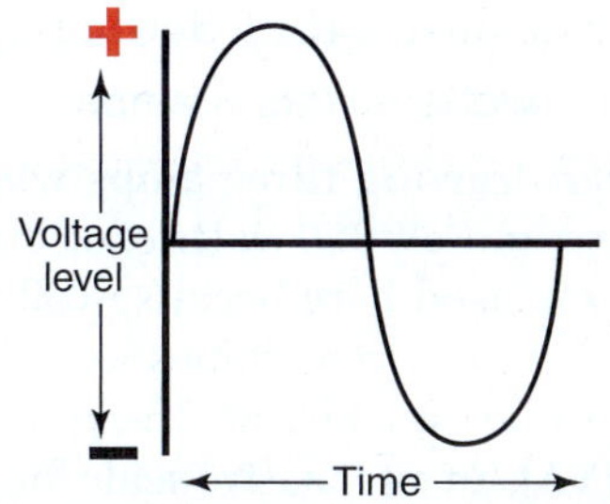

Goodheart-Willcox Publisher

Figure 5-2 Alternating current voltage is commonly drawn as a graph with the voltage level plotted along the vertical axis and the time plotted along the horizontal axis.

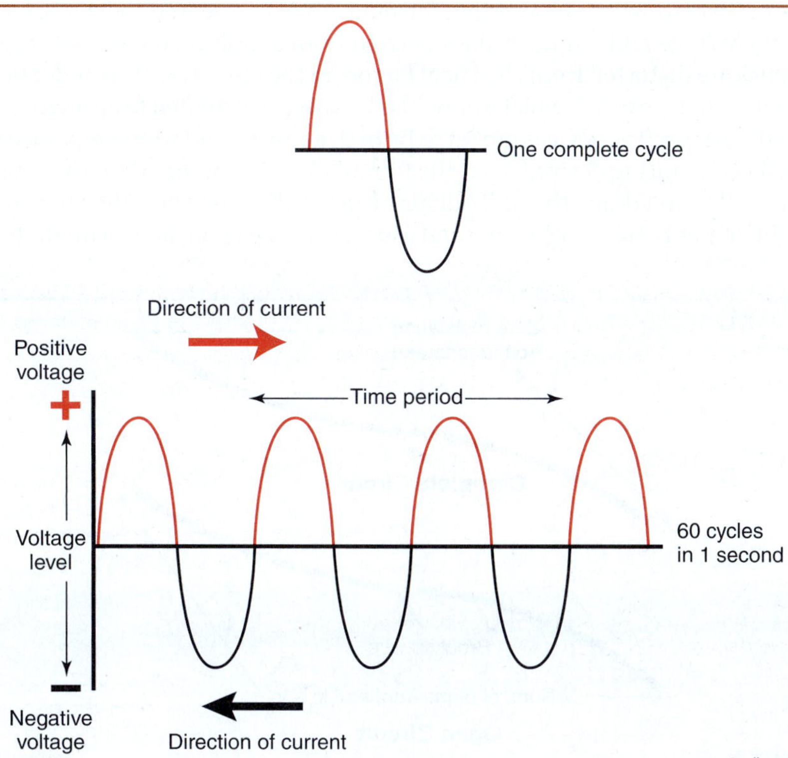

Goodheart-Willcox Publisher

Figure 5-3 The cycle pattern represents the rise and fall of a voltage level. This pattern repeats 60 times in one second (60 Hz) for standard household electrical energy.

Turn your attention to Figure 5-4. In the illustration, there are two electrical wires, which are referred to as *conductors* in electrical terminology. A complete conductor, one that has no breaks, will have a resistance reading of zero because there is no significant resistance to be measured. When a conductor has a break in its path, referred to as an *open*, there is an immeasurable amount of resistance. This extreme condition of high resistance is referred to as *infinity*, implying that the reading is so high, it is beyond the capability of the multimeter to read it. It is imperative that you learn these two readings, what they mean, and the conditions that cause them. This is the key to using the ohmmeter function to troubleshoot certain PC items. Checking the resistance values of fuses, cables, and switches is covered later in this chapter.

A+ 1101: 3.5

Power

Power is the amount of electrical energy provided or used by equipment, and the scale used in measuring electrical power is called **watts (W)**. *Wattage* is the product of voltage and current. In other words, to determine the wattage that a DC circuit is using, the electrical pressure measured in volts is multiplied by the electrical current measured in amps, as shown in the following equation:

$$\text{watts} = \text{volts} \times \text{amps}$$

For example, a computer drawing three amps when connected to a 120-volt source would consume approximately 360 watts of electrical energy (120 × 3). Notice that the term *approximately* is used here because voltage level in an AC circuit is not constant. When calculating wattage values associated with AC power, there are other electrical factors to be considered. The power value of an AC circuit is expressed in **volt-amperes (VA)**, an alternative scale for measuring electrical power.

A power supply's capacity can be rated in both watts and VA. However, when AC power is used, watts and VA are not the same expression and wattage is considered the "true" power rating of a device. Wattage can be measured with a very expensive wattmeter or calculated with a more exact formula. VA is considered the *apparent power* because the voltage and ampere values derived from a multimeter are not true values. These values are distorted from electrical factors in the circuit, such as induction. Turn your attention to Figure 5-5, which shows the total load calculated from a group of computers and a printer. The devices are rated by both amperes and wattage. Notice that the calculated power rating derived from the formula V × A is higher than the total power rating derived from adding the individual wattage values, which is the true power rating. The difference between VA rating and wattage rating has an approximate 1:1.4 ratio.

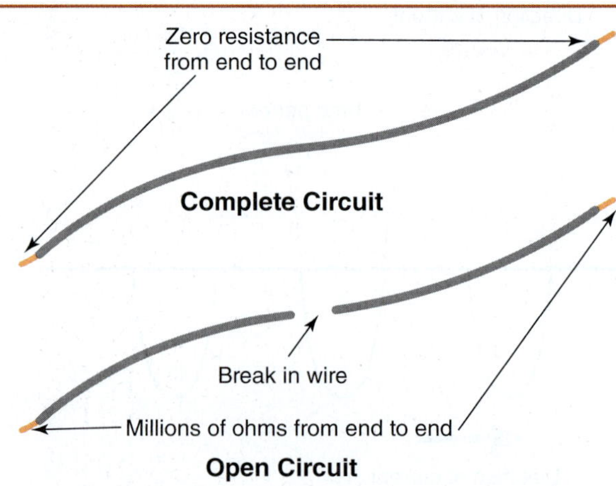

Goodheart-Willcox Publisher

Figure 5-4 A complete conductor will have a resistance reading of zero. When a conductor has a break in its path, there is an immeasurable amount of resistance.

Each Monitor = 140 Watts 140 W + 140 W + 140 W + 140 W + ⇨ 560 Watts
Each CPU = 180 Watts 180 W + 180 W + 180 W + 180 W + ⇨ 720 Watts
One Printer = 300 Watts 300 W 300 Watts
Total = 1,580 Watts

Each Monitor = 1.6 Amps 1.6 Amps + 1.6 Amps + 1.6 Amps + 1.6 Amps + ⇨ 6.4 Amps
Each CPU = 2.0 Amps 2.0 Amps + 2.0 Amps + 2.0 Amps + 2.0 Amps + ⇨ 8.0 Amps
One Printer = 3.5 Amps 3.5 Amps 3.5 Amps
Total = 17.9 Amps

Volts × Amps = VA
120 volts × 17.9 Amps = 2,148 VA

Volt-amperes (VA) equal 2,148 while watts equal 1,580.

Always use the equipment wattage rating when sizing power supplies. Do not calculate wattage based on volts and amps. The result will be volt-amperes (VA), not true watts.

Goodheart-Willcox Publisher; (workstation icons) romvo/Shutterstock.com; (printer icon) VectorShow/Shutterstock.com

Figure 5-5 It is not unusual for the calculated wattage (volts × amps) to be larger than the wattage totals.

When sizing the load capacity of a computer configuration, there are two choices. All the watt values can be added together to arrive at the total load in watts, or all the ampere loads can be added together and then compared to the amperage rating of the power supply.

1102: 4.4 A+

Wattage measurements are used in two primary ways: power consumed and power supplied. The amount of power consumed by devices is expressed in watts, meaning that when wattage is written on a device that uses or *consumes* electrical power, such as monitors or hard drives, the watts label is used to express the amount of power used or consumed by that device. When watts are used as a label on a device that *supplies* electrical energy, such as a generator or power supply, it represents the amount of power that can be safely provided from that unit. The amount of power a device can safely produce or consume is referred to as its *power handling specification.*

Be aware that power supplies and generators can supply more power than the amount for which they are rated. However, when excess amounts of power are taken from a power supply, excessive heating occurs, which can permanently damage the power supply.

When changing power supplies, the replacement power supply must have a wattage equal to or greater than the original supply. A power supply with less wattage capability may work for a while, but it will surely burn up after a period of time. Additionally, consider the number and types of existing devices to be powered, as well as any future additions, to size the power supply needed. It is recommended to allow an additional 30 percent capacity to accommodate variations and future expansions in power requirements.

To determine how much equipment can be connected to a power strip, the wattage ratings of each piece of equipment should be added together. A typical power strip should not connect to a total of over 1,600 watts of equipment, and power strips should *never* be in a daisy-chain arrangement as shown in Figure 5-6 because when daisy-chained, the first strip carries the total load of both strips.

Another consideration when using extension cords is wire size. A cord with smaller than 16-gauge wire should not be used. Wire smaller than 16-gauge can pose a fire hazard. Wire gauge is used to indicate the size of wire and how much current it can safely handle without excessive heat. Remember, the larger the number, the smaller the wire. Figure 5-7 shows a wire size chart with current ratings.

Clean Electrical Power

Clean power is a term that refers to a steady commercial electrical supply without any voltage spikes. Do not confuse this with *clean energy*, which refers to renewable power such as wind or solar. Clean power can be difficult to obtain without additional equipment added to the supply system. Switching between high-voltage power lines, lightning, cars hitting electrical utility poles, or routine line maintenance can cause voltage spikes. When a spike occurs, an abnormally high level of voltage is sent through the electrical system. See Figure 5-8 for an illustration of a line spike in relation to normal AC voltage pattern.

Line voltage spikes can be reduced or eliminated with line-conditioning equipment. A common method of ensuring a constant supply of clean power is the use of an uninterruptible power supply (UPS). The UPS system will be discussed later in this chapter.

Figure 5-6 Power strips should never be daisy-chained, because the first strip carries the total load of both.

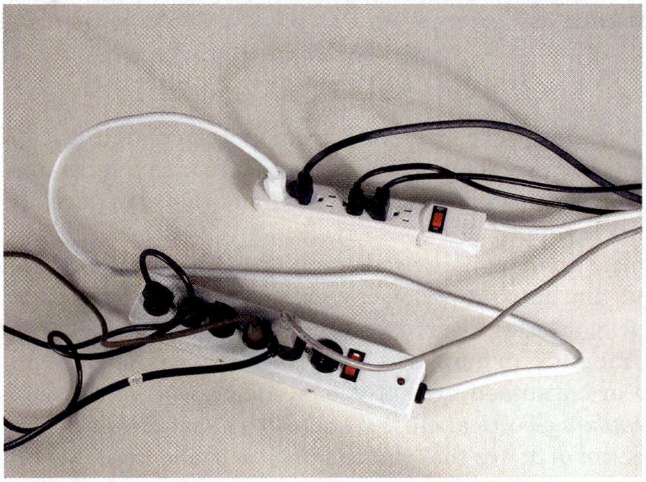

Goodheart-Willcox Publisher

Figure 5-7 Wire gauge is used to indicate the size of wire and how much current it can safely handle without excessive heat.

Ampere Ratings by Wire Gauge	
Wire Gauge	**Ampere Rating**
12	20
14	15
16	7
18	5

Goodheart-Willcox Publisher

Figure 5-8 When a spike occurs, an abnormally high level of voltage is sent through the electrical system.

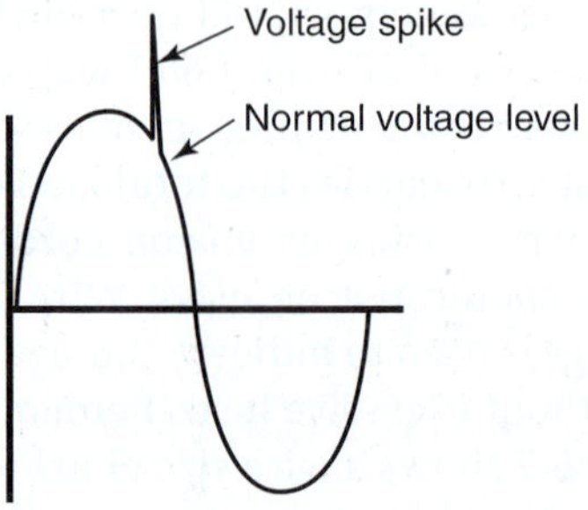

Goodheart-Willcox Publisher

5.2 Using a Digital Multimeter

A digital multimeter is an all-in-one type of meter used to measure current, resistance, and voltage values. As the name implies, the meter is constructed from digital circuits, and it is used in place of multiple meters. Specifically, one multimeter replaces the use of individual volt, ohm, and amp meters. Due to this, the terms *multimeter*, *ohmmeter*, and *voltmeter* are often used interchangeably. See Figure 5-9, which shows a typical digital multimeter with major parts labeled.

Probes and Test Leads

The meter is equipped with two test leads, each with probes at the end used for touching test points. These leads follow a universal color combination in which the black lead is used for the negative side of a reading and the red lead is used for the positive side. The black lead plugs into the meter at the jack that is marked in black, has a negative sign, or both. The jack may also be marked with the word "COM," as it is on the meter in Figure 5-10. The red lead plugs into the jack with the red marking or the plus sign for voltage and resistance readings. There is usually a different position in which to plug the red lead for measuring current.

A+ Note

You will most likely encounter a scenario-type question asking you to choose the most appropriate test instrument for an application. For example, you may be asked to select the appropriate tool for testing wall outlet voltage. The answers may include multimeter, crimper, cable tester, tone probe, or similar type of equipment. As such, you should know the basic tools for performing common tests and tasks.

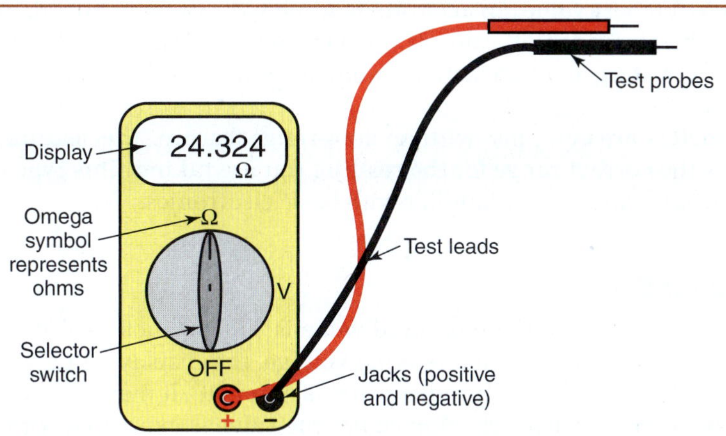

Goodheart-Willcox Publisher

Figure 5-9 A digital multimeter is used to measure current, resistance, and voltage values.

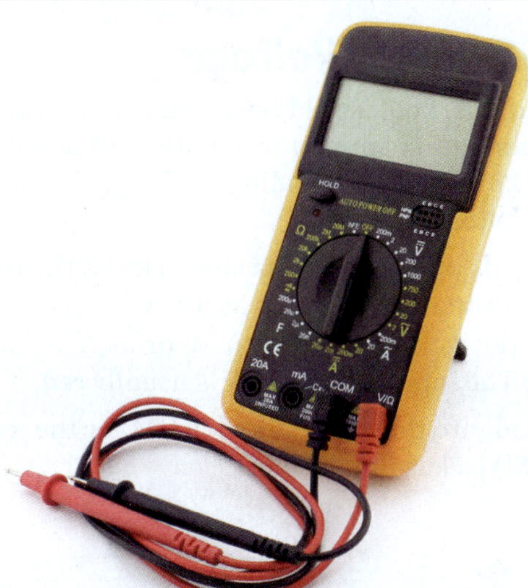

Mihancea Petru/Shutterstock.com

Figure 5-10 A meter is equipped with two test leads with probes at the end of each used for touching test points. The black lead is for the negative side; the red lead is for the positive side.

As a PC technician, you typically never need to measure current. Current readings are much more complicated and require knowledge of electronic components to connect the meter correctly. However, voltage readings and occasionally resistance readings are required.

Forming safe habits is essential. *Never* touch the probes with your fingertips when taking readings, even when the voltage is low. If you touch the bare tip of the probe during routine checks of low voltage where there is not sufficient voltage to harm you, you may create a bad habit, leading to touching the tips when reading dangerously high voltages. Low voltages (below 50 volts) will not normally harm you, and you normally do not feel any electrical sensation. However, touching a 120-volt AC line is entirely different. You will not only feel the sensation of electrical energy, but it is also possible to incur a permanent injury or even death. Remember, safety is a habit. Develop safe habits when reading low voltages and you will automatically use the same habits when reading a much higher voltage.

Range Selector

The range selector is used to choose the appropriate value to be read: voltage, current, or resistance. The dial indicator should be placed in the lowest range that is greater than the value to be read. For example, a meter with voltage ranges of 5, 50, and 500 should be set to 50 to take an expected 12-volt reading. If it is placed higher than the next-highest value, an accurate reading will not be obtained; instead, the reading will be a rounded-off value. If you go below the desired level, you will probably not get a reading at all. In fact, most meters will likely display a warning in the display area.

Some meters are equipped with an auto-range feature. This feature automatically selects the correct range for the reading you are taking. This type of meter is recommended for anyone not familiar with basic electronics.

Display Area

The display area is where the measured value is shown, such as voltage, current, or resistance. For example, when reading voltage, the display will give a numeric value of the voltage and possibly indicate if it is AC or DC. It may also indicate if you are out of the correct range selection value. The value is expressed with a decimal point when appropriate and is coordinated with the range selector setting and the jacks into which the leads are inserted.

Procedure for Reading Voltage

Before taking any readings, you should have some idea of the level of voltage you expect to read. For example, a common wall outlet is 120 volts AC. A power supply unit might be 12, 5, or 3.3 volts DC depending on the exact power supply connection.

To read AC or DC voltages:

1. Insert the meter leads into the appropriate jacks on the meter. The red lead is inserted into the jack marked with the letter "V" or plus (+) symbol. (Generally, you will never use the jacks marked with "A" or "mA" as they are used for current readings.) The input voltage jack is usually red.
2. Insert the black lead into the jack marked "COM" or the minus (–) symbol. The common (COM) jack is usually black.

Caution

Never wear an antistatic wrist strap or ground strap while taking meter readings. The strap makes you an excellent conductor of electricity, which can result in fatal injury.

3. Turn the selector switch to voltage AC. On some meters, this can require the use of two separate switches. One switch selects AC or DC voltage, and the other switch selects the voltage range. If you do not have an auto-range meter, set the range selector to the next-highest voltage level over what you expect to read.
4. Touch the test locations with the probes. Keep your fingers away from the tips of the probes.
5. Read the display and record the voltage. It should be within 10 percent of the expected voltage level.

Procedure for Reading Resistance

To read resistance:

1. Ensure the power is *off* before attempting to read resistance.
2. Insert the meter leads into the appropriate jacks on the meter. The red lead is inserted into the jack marked with the letter "V" or plus (+) symbol.
3. Insert the black lead into the jack marked with "COM" or the minus (–) symbol. The common (COM) jack is usually black.
4. Set the selector switch to the highest value of resistance.
5. Touch the test probes together to see if the meter is working properly. The reading should be zero. If not, the battery inside the unit could be weak. The ohmmeter portion of a multimeter depends on battery power to take a resistance reading. Most multimeters produce a beeping sound to indicate a zero reading, and older, analog multimeters may allow a calibration for a precise resistance measurement by manually adjusting the dial reading to zero as the test probes are touching each other.
6. Touch the probes to the part (fuse or cable) to be tested.
7. When checking resistance of a fuse or a cable, you should read either zero resistance or infinity. A good fuse will cause a reading of zero resistance, as will a good cable. A bad fuse will cause a reading of infinity, as will a cable that is not complete from end to end.

Caution

Electrical voltage can damage a meter if the meter is set to read resistance.

Checking Fuses, Cables, and Switches

When checking fuses, cables, and switches, there are only two resistance values that are typically displayed on a digital meter: zero ohms and infinity. A typical low-ampere fuse found in electronic equipment is simple in construction. A **fuse** is a cylinder shape of glass or ceramic with a metal cap on each end and a fuse link on the inside. A *fuse link* is a thin metal wire that burns and splits into two parts at a predetermined ampere value.

The easiest way to tell if the fuse is good (or not) is to remove it from the fuse holder and take a resistance reading across the fuse, as shown in Figure 5-11. Since the fuse is made of a thin metal wire, it will have very low resistance, and when tested with an ohmmeter, the meter will indicate zero resistance. If the fuse is burned open, it will have a resistance value too high to read. You would be trying to read through the air or space inside the tube; thus, the reading is shown as *infinity*, meaning it is beyond the capabilities of the meter's range.

The same principle applies to cables and switches. Before reading a switch or cable with an ohmmeter, it must be removed from the PC. A cable should read zero resistance from one end to the other, but a cable with a broken wire will read infinity. See Figure 5-12 for an illustration of a cable with a meter attached, showing both good and bad cable readings.

Tech Tip

Remember that a fuse must be removed from the circuit before taking a resistance reading.

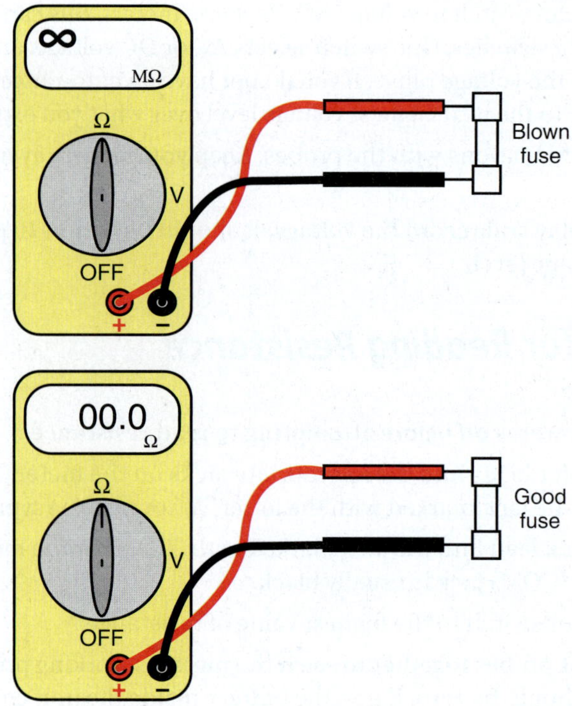

Figure 5-11 A meter is equipped with two test leads with probes at the end of each, which are used for touching test points. The black lead is for the negative side; the red lead is for the positive side.

Goodheart-Willcox Publisher

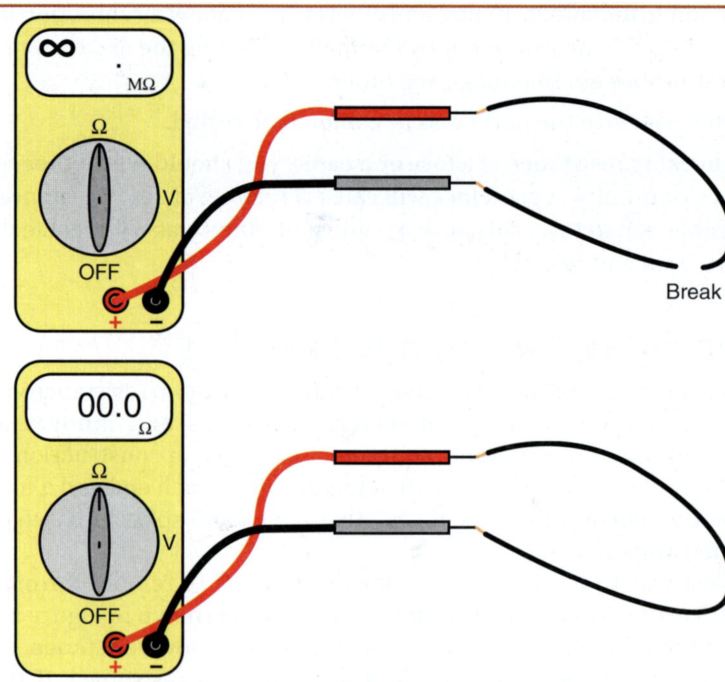

Figure 5-12 A good conductor will read zero resistance; a conductor with a break or open will read infinity, the highest possible resistance reading.

Goodheart-Willcox Publisher

Testing switches is very similar to testing fuses. An open switch will show an infinite resistance, and a closed switch should show zero ohms of resistance, as illustrated in Figure 5-13. As with testing a fuse, make sure the switch is removed from the PC.

A switch can be difficult to remove from the circuit, and the type of switch present must be identified. Some switches are capacitor-type switches. These switches are usually very small in comparison to the physical size of mechanical switches and cannot be adequately diagnosed with an ohmmeter. If a switch is suspected as the problem, it may be best to replace the switch with a known good switch rather than attempt to diagnose it with a meter.

Resistance values can fool an untrained technician. Situations may arise where a resistance reading taken on a circuit component gives false information. For example, an open switch can have what appears as a resistance value other than infinity. In this case, the meter may be reading through the electronic components mounted in the system and indicate a value anywhere between zero and infinity.

Look at the drawing in Figure 5-14. In the illustration, the ohmmeter is reading resistance through the circuit components even after the switch is opened. This is referred to as backfeed. **Backfeed** refers to a common condition in which electrical power originates from a part of the circuitry. To avoid backfeed situations, the component to be read should be removed from the circuit whenever possible. This is not always practical, however, and at times, it is more appropriate to take voltage readings to indicate the condition of fuses, breakers, and switches.

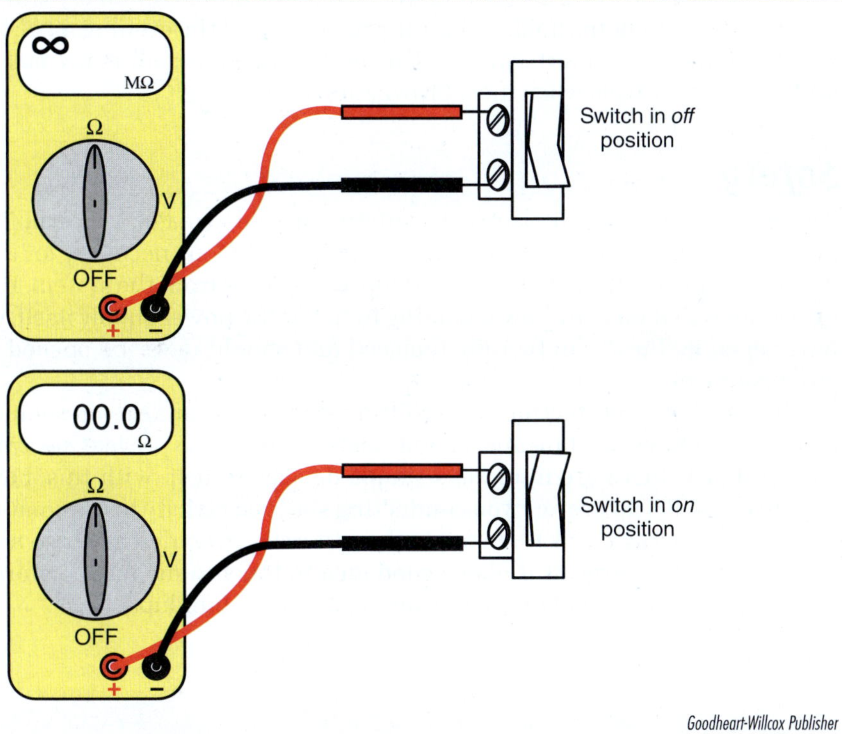

Figure 5-13 A closed switch has zero resistance, while an open switch has infinite resistance.

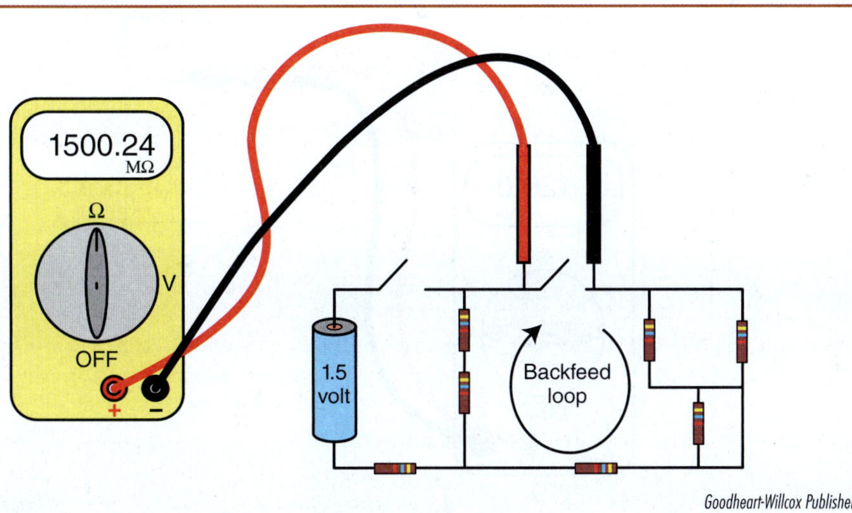

Figure 5-14 A backfeed occurs when an ohmmeter reads resistance through circuit components even after the switch is opened.

Caution

Never touch the tips of meter leads when taking readings.

Tech Tip

When checking for low voltage, it is best to have the air-conditioning or heating system operating at maximum, so you can see the system under maximum strain. This is especially important when checking an intermittent problem and a low-voltage condition is suspected.

Checking Power Outlets

Checking a power outlet is a very common task. As shown in Figure 5-15, the meter probes are simply inserted into a wall outlet to check for electrical power. There is no polarity when reading AC voltage sources, so the polarity markings on the meter need not be observed. A good voltage reading is considered to be plus or minus 10 percent of the 120-volt rating. In actuality, the voltage can drop or rise considerably more before affecting a PC.

Two other important considerations when taking voltage readings are the weather and the time of day. Low voltage is common on extremely hot or cold days when electrical heat or air-conditioning help maintain a building's internal temperature. Heating and air-conditioning call for a large demand on the electrical system inside a building, and the highest demand for electrical power is usually between the hours of 4:00 p.m. and 6:00 p.m. During this period, most households are actively using power because of those coming home from school or work. As such, the demand for heating or cooling increases and often combines with the power consumption of a household, including preparation of the evening meal, homework, web browsing, and entertainment. During the same period, many businesses are still operating. This is when most brownouts occur.

Safety

Anytime one deals with electricity, safety must be a major concern. This means proper handling of power. While electricity is an obvious necessity for a computer, it is also a danger. The first rule is to remove all power from the system. Do ***not*** work on a system that has any power coming to it. For the power supply itself, you should never open it. These can be fully replaced and should never be opened under any circumstances.

In addition to protecting yourself from electrical damage, you should also protect the computer. That means having safety measures to prevent electrostatic discharge (ESD). There are numerous simple devices to help with this. For example, ESD straps will help prevent you conducting static electricity to the computer. There are also grounding cords that ensure the system is grounded and also help prevent electrostatic discharge. It is also a good idea to touch some metal before touching the computer, which will discharge any electrostatic buildup.

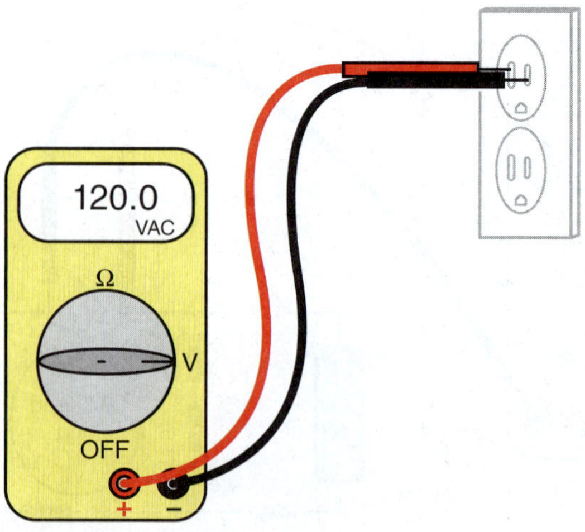

Figure 5-15 When checking a power outlet, the meter probes are simply inserted into a wall outlet to check for electrical power.

Goodheart-Willcox Publisher

5.3 Branch Circuits

Many computer problems can be generated by the electrical system inside a home or small business. The electrical power in a home setting and in some businesses originates from an electrical panel. ***Branch circuit*** is the technical name for the wiring from an electrical panel to the final outlet on that circuit. Put simply, branch circuits originate at the electrical panel and service all outlets in a building, similar to branches on a tree. Electrical equipment running anywhere within these circuits can cause a power problem for a computer system. See Figure 5-16 for a drawing of a typical home distribution system.

For example, the operation of a vacuum cleaner or a power tool can generate voltage spikes that can disrupt the computer process. The computer can be damaged, develop a glitch, or simply lock up. It is imperative that a surge protector be installed at the computer location.

A typical commercial installation uses two electrical distribution panels: one panel for lighting and the other panel for distributing power to equipment. Figure 5-17 is an illustration showing side-by-side panels. One panel is for lighting and the other is for power.

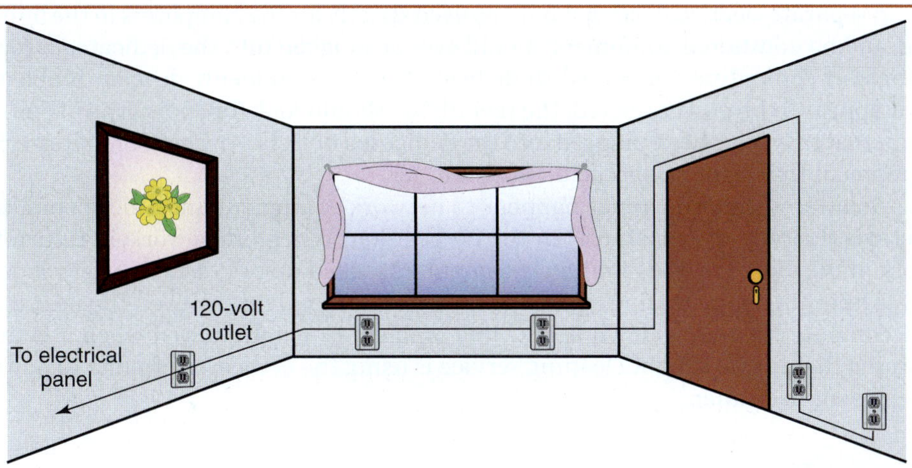

Goodheart-Willcox Publisher

Figure 5-16 The electrical power in a home setting originates from an electrical panel.

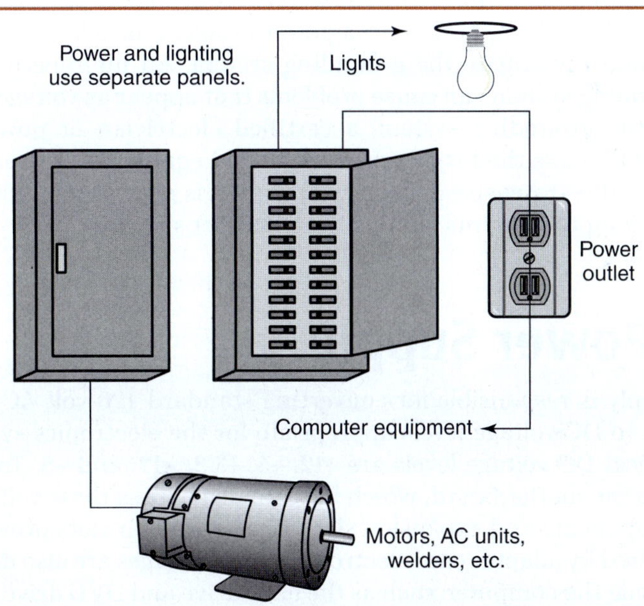

Goodheart-Willcox Publisher

Figure 5-17 A typical commercial installation uses two electrical panels: one for lighting and one for power.

Computers are in every type of business location, so it is important to know the type of equipment the company operates and the electrical distribution panel that serves the computer stations. The type of electrical distribution and the equipment connected to that electrical system is of major concern to reliable computer operation. An office located in a large industrial building can be misleading to a technician. While the immediate environment may look like a typical office setting, the same electrical circuits in the office can be serving heavy printing press equipment directly behind the office wall. A surge-protector power strip may not be adequate in this type of location. A more reliable device is a quality uninterruptible power supply (UPS) system. UPS systems are covered later in this chapter.

Dedicated Circuit

A **dedicated circuit** is an electrical power distribution system designed to serve *only* computer equipment. It is wired separately from other electrical circuits and typically uses an isolation transformer to separate the computer electrical power from other power circuits. An *isolation transformer* converts electrical energy to magnetic energy and then back to electrical energy to help buffer the circuit against voltage spikes generated inside and outside the building.

A separate electrical panel should be used strictly for the computers in the building, and no additional equipment should ever be plugged into the dedicated circuit outlets. If computers connected to dedicated circuits suddenly develop problems that appear to be power related, the technician should look for some type of equipment that may have been plugged into the dedicated outlets. Any noncomputer-type equipment that is found should be removed.

An interesting occurrence happens to network equipment and office computer systems that are left constantly in the *on* position. When office workers return to work in the morning, they find their computers locked up or crashed. After rebooting, everything appears fine again. However, a few days later, or even the next day, the computer system is down again. This problem is usually solved when it is discovered that the overnight cleaning service is using the dedicated circuits to power their vacuum cleaners.

A+ 1102: 4.4

Grounding

Improper grounding conditions can cause serious problems to computer equipment. After all other attempts to solve a power problem have been exhausted, the technician should investigate the grounding system. An improperly installed or damaged grounding system can cause problems that appear as voltage problems.

To check the grounding system, a certified electrician or power company technician should make the inspection. Specialized equipment is used to perform grounding tests. It is expensive and special training is needed to use it. This is one time when the computer technician must call another specialist.

Tech Tip

When upgrading a computer, always consider the effect on the power supply. For example, many high-performance video cards consume large amounts of electrical power. Video card manufacturers will recommend a minimum power supply size for a given video card.

5.4 PC Power Supply

The power supply is responsible for converting standard 120-volt AC power from the wall outlet to DC voltage levels appropriate for the electronics systems of the computer. Typical DC voltage levels are +12, +5, +3.3, –12, and –5. These voltages are provided to the motherboard, which in turn, distributes these voltage levels to connected components and expansion slots. The expansion slots provide the voltage levels required by adapter card electronic parts. Voltages are also distributed to peripherals inside the computer, such as the hard drive and DVD drive.

Power supplies have form factors just as motherboards do. The power supply must fit into the case and allow room for the motherboard. Some of the standard form factors are named after the motherboard form factors, such as AT, Baby AT, LPX, ATX, ATX12V, and NLX. In addition, they can be broken down further to tower or desktop models. Other power-supply form factors found in the industry include ATX Large, ATX-EPS, FlexATX, CFX12V, SFX12V, TFX12V, and LFX12V. For more information about form factors, review Chapter 3.

You should be aware of a variety of nonstandard, proprietary power supplies. The color-coding on the wiring for these types of power supplies are not truly standard. In fact, any implied standardization should not be taken for granted. Always check with the manufacturer's specifications for definitive information about color and voltages.

Main Power Connectors

A+ 1101: 3.5

To assist in making the proper voltage level connections, power plugs have a special shape that matches the voltage level required by the motherboard or peripheral. Figure 5-18 illustrates two styles of motherboard main power connections: ATX and ATX12V. Notice that both connectors have a PWR_OK connection, which refers to the power good signal. The ***power good signal*** is used during POST to verify the power supply is working properly. This signal is transmitted from the power supply to the motherboard and on to the CPU.

The +5VSB (standby) connection provides voltage even when the power switch is set to *off* and allows the computer to "wake up" on an event. The exception is when the AC plug is physically unplugged from the wall outlet or the power supply. The ***standby power connection***, also called ***soft power***, provides power to the keyboard when the computer system is in sleep mode. Power is reduced to the entire system, but some power must remain to reactivate or wake the system. The power-on and standby power connections are also used jointly by Windows operating systems to turn the computer off using software commands rather than a physical switch. For example, the +5VSB connection can provide electrical power to a network card so that the computer can be activated when a network event occurs. The BIOS/UEFI setup utility is used to configure the computer to "wake up on LAN," which means network activity can awaken or start the computer system. This is a common feature of all modern computer systems.

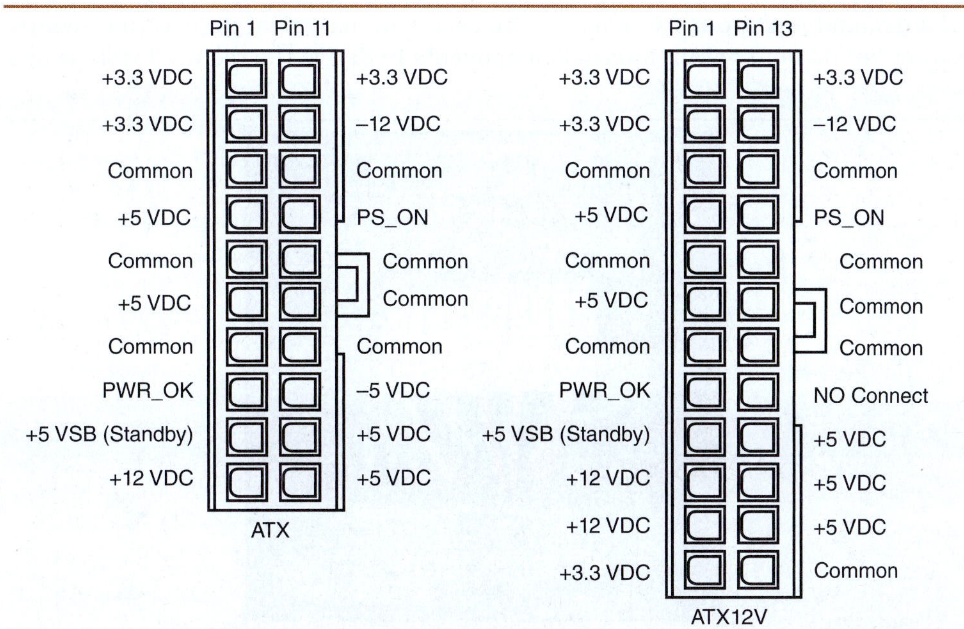

Figure 5-18 Two common motherboard power connections are ATX and ATX12V.

The ATX and ATX12V form factors also have 3.3-volt power connectors. The addition of 3.3 volts at the power connection has eliminated the need for a voltage regulator located at the CPU. The regulator was used to convert the 5 volts from the power supply to the lower voltage required by the new CPU units.

ATX is one of the most popular power-supply form factors on the market, and the ATX12V power supply is simply a redesign of the ATX power supply. Changes to the design were made to accommodate new power requirements such as those for PCIe devices and power-hungry video cards. If you look closely at Figure 5-18, you will notice that the ATX12V connector added four additional pins for a total of 24. These pins can be found at the bottom of the connector in the figure. These four additional pins on the ATX12V are used to supply additional electrical power required by the more modern motherboards.

Most ATX motherboard designs will accept an ATX12V connector, and the ATX12V standard is backward compatible with older motherboards. This is useful when purchasing an ATX12V power supply to replace a defective ATX power supply. Additionally, conversion kits are available to change a 20-pin connector into a 24-pin connector and vice versa. Many motherboards have no problem with a pin conversion kit, which is typically two connections, one 24-pin and one 20-pin joined by wires. If you study the pin assignments carefully in Figure 5-18, you will see that the first set of 20 pins of an ATX power supply connector closely match the first 20-pins of the 24-pin ATX12V power supply.

Figure 5-19 and Figure 5-20 show the ATX and ATX12V power connectors, respectively. The plastic of these plugs is molded so the connector can connect to the motherboard in only one way to prevent an improper connection that will destroy the motherboard. However, this does not make incorrect connections *impossible*. If sufficient force is applied, it can be plugged in backward. Be cognizant when connecting power supplies to motherboards. The connector should attach easily; if it does not, do not force it.

External Power Supply (AC Adapter)

Most mobile devices, such as laptops, phones, and tablets, use an external power supply, commonly referred to as an ***AC adapter*** due to the fact that they convert AC power to DC. Other common names include ***plug pack***, ***plug-in adapter***, ***adapter block***, ***domestic mains adapter***, ***line power adapter***, ***power brick***, ***power adapter***, ***charger***, and ***recharger***. AC adapters are used with electrical devices that require power but do not contain internal components to derive the required voltage and

Figure 5-19 An ATX motherboard power connector is design to fit an ATX motherboard in only one way.

Goodheart-Willcox Publisher

Goodheart-Willcox Publisher

Figure 5-20 Most motherboards designed to work with a 20-pin ATX power supply will also work with a 24-pin ATX12V power supply.

power from mains power. The internal circuitry of an external power supply is very similar to the design that would be used for a built-in or internal power supply.

The use of an external power supply allows for portability of equipment powered by either mains or battery without the added bulk of internal power components. This makes it unnecessary to produce equipment for use only with a specified power source; the same device can be powered from 120-VAC or 230-VAC mains, vehicle or aircraft battery, or other storage devices by using a different adapter. The connector used to attach the external power supply to the mobile device is often called a *DC jack* or *DC connector,* which may be a proprietary type or belong to common industry standards, such as USB-C, EIAJ, or DIN.

Modular Power Supply

A+ 1101: 3.5

A *modular power supply* is simply a power supply with detachable cables. Fully modular power supplies are those with no cables attached, and *nonmodular power supplies* have all cables permanently attached. There are also *semi-modular power supplies* that have the most important cables attached and others detachable.

Redundant Power Supplies

A+ 1101: 3.5

Computers may be built with redundant power supplies, meaning there are two different power supplies in the computer case. This is usually only found in servers but could theoretically be installed in any computer with the space and resources to operate it. In normal operation, each power supply provides half of the power needed, and if one of the power supplies fails, then the other will temporarily supply all of the needed power. Many of these redundant power supplies are hot-swappable, meaning you can replace one while the system is running.

Other Power Connectors

A+ 1101: 3.4

A wide assortment of power connectors besides the main motherboard connection can be used with a computer power system. Figure 5-21 shows two of the more common connections you will encounter. The +12-volt power connector, Figure 5-21A, is also referred to as a 2 × 2, 12-volt connector. The designation *2 × 2* represents the pin configuration as two pins in two rows. The 2 × 2 designation is a way to differentiate it from the four-pin peripheral power connector, Figure 5-21B. The four-pin peripheral power connector would be designated as 1 × 4. Power supply main motherboard connectors are referred to in the same fashion. For example, a 20-pin ATX connector is referred to as a 2 × 10 connector, while the 24-pin ATX12V connector is referred to as a 2 × 12 connector.

Tech Tip

Always check your motherboard manual or support documentation to determine the location and type of power connections to use.

The 2 × 2, 12-volt power connector in Figure 5-21A is used to supply 12 volts to newer high-performance CPUs. There are also 2 × 4, 12-volt power connectors on many power supplies. Figure 5-22 shows a power splitter cable with 2 × 4 and 2 × 2, 12-volt connectors. The voltage applied to the processor was raised from 5 VDC to 12 VDC. Therefore, the ATX12V power supply uses a connector with four or more pins attached directly to the motherboard near the processor rather than through the main motherboard power connector. Figure 5-23 shows an auxiliary power connector.

The ATX style could only carry voltage and higher current to the CPU through motherboard traces, which are limited in the amount of current that they can carry. Power connections made directly to locations on the motherboard as well as directly to devices overcome the current limitations of motherboard traces. The power connection near the CPU is critical on motherboards with high-performance processors, and without the direct connection, the computer will not boot.

Figure 5-21 There is a wide assortment of power connectors besides the main motherboard power connectors that can be used with a computer power system.

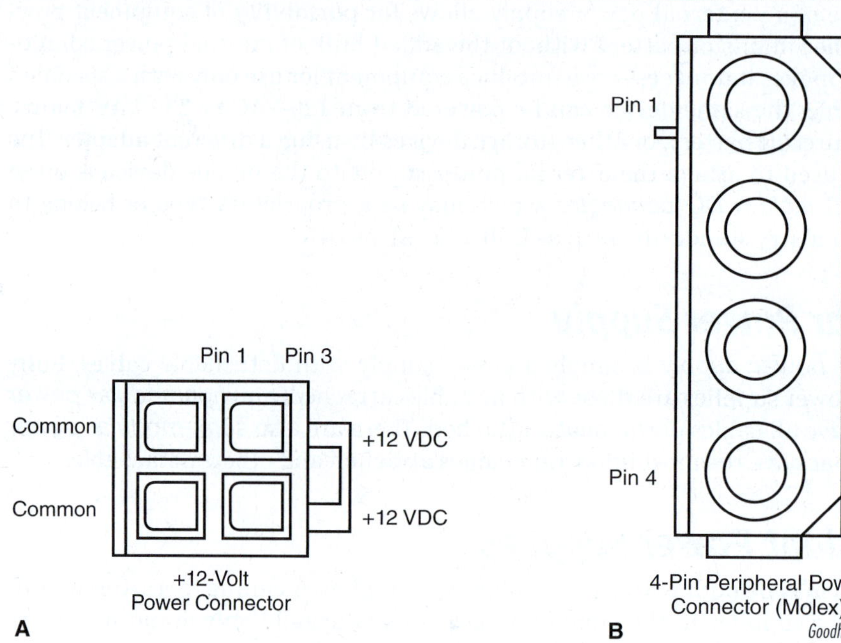

Goodheart-Willcox Publisher

Figure 5-22 Many power supplies use a 2 × 4 12-volt connector, which requires the use of a power splitter.

Goodheart-Willcox Publisher

The *four-pin peripheral power connector* is used to connect to ATA hard drives, CD-ROM drives, and DVD drives. It is also commonly referred to as a *Molex connector*. These devices typically use the +12-volt level from the connector. Figure 5-24 shows a picture of the four-pin peripheral power connector.

There are also power connectors designed to connect directly from the power supply to a PCIe card. For example, video cards with high-performance processors require a separate power supply connected directly to the card. Graphics cards can consume a wide range of power, from just a few watts to over 500 watts. Typically, a 2 × 3 or 2 × 4 power connector is required to provide ample power directly to the video card. Some power supply manufacturers identify which power connector is designed especially for use with a video graphics card. Look at the connector in Figure 5-25. It shows the letters "PCI-E" on the side of a 2 × 3 connector, identifying it for use with a PCI Express graphics card.

Serial ATA (SATA) hard drives use a SATA power connector, shown in Figure 5-26, which has 14 pins at three different voltage levels. Adapter wiring kits are available so that you can connect a SATA hard disk drive to a power supply that does not have a SATA power connector.

1101: 3.1 A+

Tech Tip

The term *Molex* is commonly used and universally accepted to identify the four-pin connector, although this is incorrect. Molex is the name of the company that designed and markets this type of connection. The technical name is *four-pin peripheral power connector*.

Goodheart-Willcox Publisher

Figure 5-23 An auxiliary power connector is used to supplement power connections.

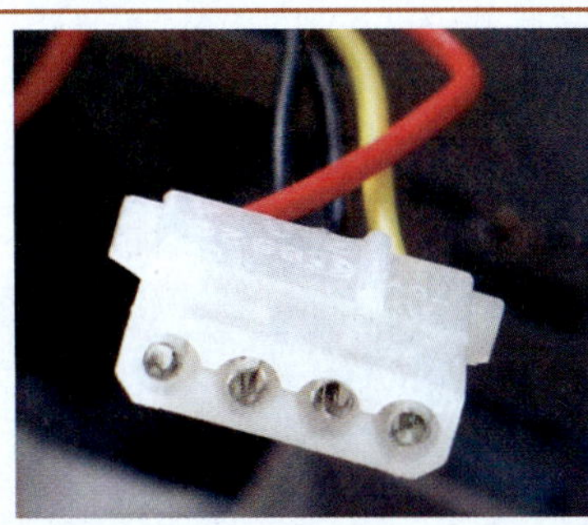

Goodheart-Willcox Publisher

Figure 5-24 The four-pin peripheral power connector is used to connect to ATA hard drives and optical drives. It is also called a *Molex connector*.

Goodheart-Willcox Publisher

Figure 5-25 A power-supply connector labeled with PCI-E is intended for use with a PCIe video card.

External SATA (eSATA) devices can connect to a power supply using a connector called *eSATAp*. Additional names for eSATAp include *Power over eSATA*, *Power eSATA*, *eSATA/USB Combo*, and *eSATA USB Hybrid Port/EUHP*. The eSATAp connector combines the functionality of an eSATA and a USB port, as well as a source of power in a single connector. It can supply power at 5V and 12V. On a desktop computer, the port is simply a connector, usually mounted on a bracket at the back of the case and accessible from outside the machine. It is connected to motherboard sources of SATA, USB, and power at 5V and 12V. On many notebook computers, only a limited amount of power at 5V is available, and none at 12V. Cables are available to both connect and power a SATA device from an eSATAp port (including 12V power, if available).

A+ 1101: 3.5

Input and Output Voltage Levels

Input voltage levels are specified by the Form Factors Organization, which makes a set of recommended nonbinding specifications that are used as a guideline for power supply manufacturers, as shown in Figure 5-27. Since computers are used worldwide, they are typically designed with two available voltage levels, either through use of a switch or by automatic electrical sensing and switching circuitry. Most countries in the world use 50-Hz electrical power rated at 230 volts. Some use 115 volts at 50 Hz. The United States is one of the few countries that use a 115-volt and 230-volt, 60-Hz electrical system. While a computer will run on 230 volts at 50 Hz, the 120-volt, 60 Hz standard electrical plug will not physically fit into the 230-volt, 50-Hz wall outlet. In addition, countries with the same voltage and frequency specifications may use different plugs and outlets, referred to as types A through M. In such situations, a special adapter must be used to make the computer power supply physically compatible. This is especially relevant for power adapters used in mobile computers. Always check the foreign country that the client or customer is going to so you can best advise them as to the electrical requirements. A universal adapter kit that will allow connection to all plug types used in the world is often found useful by frequent travelers.

Figure 5-26 Serial ATA (SATA) hard drives use a SATA power connector, which has 14 pins at three different voltage levels.

Goodheart-Willcox Publisher

Figure 5-27 Input voltage levels are specified by the Form Factors Organization.

Power Supply Voltage Guidelines			
Input	**Minimum VAC**	**Nominal VAC**	**Maximum VAC**
115 VAC	90	115	135
230 VAC	180	230	265
Frequency (Hz)	47	50/60	63

Goodheart-Willcox Publisher

To learn more about specific countries throughout the world, visit the Europlugs website. This site has a comprehensive list of countries and their standard electrical power systems, voltages, frequencies, and power plug and socket types.

The DC output levels of an ATX12V power supply are +12, –12, +5, and +3.3 volts. These voltage levels are needed to supply power to various internal and peripheral devices found in modern computers. Figure 5-28 lists the tolerance levels for these voltages. Thus, a connection that is designated to output +12 volts may actually output anywhere from +11.40 volts to +12.60 volts.

All power supplies use a transformer that converts the voltage levels identified in the table. These voltage levels are distributed by **rails**, which is the electrical term used to describe the conductor paths inside the metal power supply case. It was introduced with the ATX12V power supply. There is one rail for each voltage level, and each rail supplies the electrical voltage level to all connectors that require that specific voltage. In other words, every connector that requires +5 volts will connect to the same +5 rail inside the power supply.

Some power supplies use a dual rail for a specific voltage. For example, a power supply designed to provide large amounts of wattage would have dual +12-volt rails, each supplying 18 to 20 amperes. When you look at a set of manufacturer specifications for a specific power supply, the voltages available will be stated by rail.

Power Supply Label

Power supplies include a label that informs the user of its electrical power, including the output voltages and the power in watts the unit can deliver. See Figure 5-29 for an example. Notice that the power supply label indicates a +5VSB entry. The acronym VSB represents "Volts Standby." The +5VSB is the electrical power present when the power supply is plugged in but not turned on. It is used to keep the computer in standby mode. For example, it allows the computer to "wake up" when a signal is sent to the network card from the network. The VSB is also used to keep devices powered at a minimum level during sleep mode.

ATX12V DC Output Tolerances			
Output VDC	**Range**	**Minimum**	**Maximum**
+12	+/– 5 percent	+11.40	+12.60
+5	+/– 5 percent	+4.75	+5.25
+3.3	+/– 5 percent`	+3.14	+3.47
–12	+/– 10 percent	–10.80	–13.20

Goodheart-Willcox Publisher

Figure 5-28 The DC output levels of an ATX12V power supply are +12, –12, +5, and +3.3 volts.

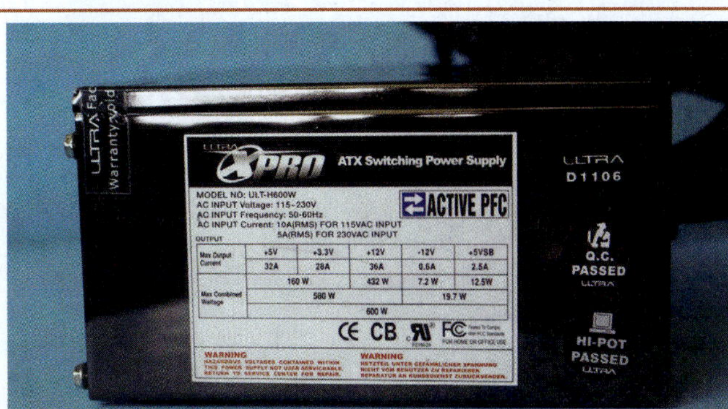

Goodheart-Willcox Publisher

Figure 5-29 The typical information found on a power supply label includes the output voltages and the power in watts the unit can deliver.

Troubleshooting the Power Supply

In general, there are no serviceable parts inside the power supply. Although it is possible to repair a power supply, it is not cost-effective. The cost of most power supplies does not come near the cost of having an electronic technician repair the unit. The time taken to diagnose the power supply, locate the component, and replace the defective component is simply cost-prohibitive, and replacing the defective component is difficult due to space constrictions, as shown in Figure 5-30. It is always much quicker and more economical to replace rather than repair. As such, it is considered a field replacement unit. In fact, power supplies are often sealed to make them difficult to open. Power supplies are low-cost components because the only real cost factors are the cost of labor and availability of replacement parts.

Power supply failure is quite frequent when compared to the failure of other computer components. Although some of the indicators can be caused by other system components, it is most likely that the power supply has caused the occurrence. The following are the common signs of a defective power supply:

- **Inoperable cooling fans:** Cooling fans that are not running are a consistent sign that the power supply has failed, because they receive their power directly from the power supply.
- **No indicator lights**: No lights or lit LEDs is a good sign that the power supply has failed.
- **Smoke**: Smoke coming from the power supply is an indicator of electronic component or circuit board damage. Electronic components usually burn up from an overload condition. This usually results in excessive heat, which generates the smoke.

A+ 1101: 5.2

- **Burnt smell:** The distinctive smell of a burnt electrical device in the proximity of a failed computer is an indication that the power supply is defective. The smell can linger for hours after a system failure.
- **Circuit breaker tripping:** If a circuit breaker is tripped, it is most likely caused by the power supply unit in the computer. With the exception of the monitor, no other component will generate a condition to trip the breaker. To verify that the problem is with the power supply, unplug the monitor to isolate the computer power supply.
- **Automatic rebooting:** If the computer reboots automatically while on standby or during normal operation, it is a good indication of a bad power supply. The power level dropping and rising is a common occurrence as the power supply breaks down. This fluctuating voltage level causes the computer system to reboot for no apparent reason.

Figure 5-30 The typical information found on a power supply label includes the output voltages and the power in watts the unit can deliver.

Goodheart-Willcox Publisher

- **Electric shock:** Any electric shock received from the computer case is a sign of a bad power supply or one that is breaking down. *Always use extreme caution when troubleshooting a suspected power supply unit. Remember that 120-volt AC power can be deadly.*
- **Excessive heat:** This troubleshooting diagnosis is made through experience. Even a normally functioning power supply will produce a certain amount of heat, as heat is a normal by-product of electrical equipment. However, excessive heat is a sure sign that complete failure of an electronic component is imminent, especially if it presents in combination with other signs. The power supply should never be so hot that you cannot touch it. Electronic components usually start to break down at 160°F (71°C).

Figure 5-31 shows a typical ATX power tester with the cover removed to expose the LED indicators better. The LEDs light up to indicate the presence of +12, +5, +3.3, –12, and –5 voltage levels corresponding to the ATX main motherboard connection. This is the preferred method of checking power. Also, notice that the two large white rectangular areas at the top corners of the device These are resistors used to simulate an actual electrical load. To measure a true voltage output level, some electrical load must be used. Many times, a false good reading is indicated on a voltage power-supply output when there is no electrical load. This is one of the shortcomings of using a digital voltmeter to check the power-supply output voltage.

Replacing a Power Supply

It should be noted that power supplies are frequently replaced. Remember, you should *never* open one to attempt to repair or replace components inside the power supply, because the power supply has enough electricity to cause death. When discussing replacing a power supply, the focus is on simply replacing the entire unit. Replacing a power supply is an easy task, but you must make sure the replacement is an acceptable form factor to match the case and motherboard. You must also make sure there is an adequate wattage capacity provided by the replacement unit. *The wattage capacity should either match or exceed the unit being replaced.*

The steps for power supply replacement are as follows:

1. Ensure the power is off. (Do *not* use an antistatic wrist strap for this operation.)
2. Open the PC case and sketch or take photos of all the connections between the old power supply unit and the other computer components. (This will save you a great deal of time later.)

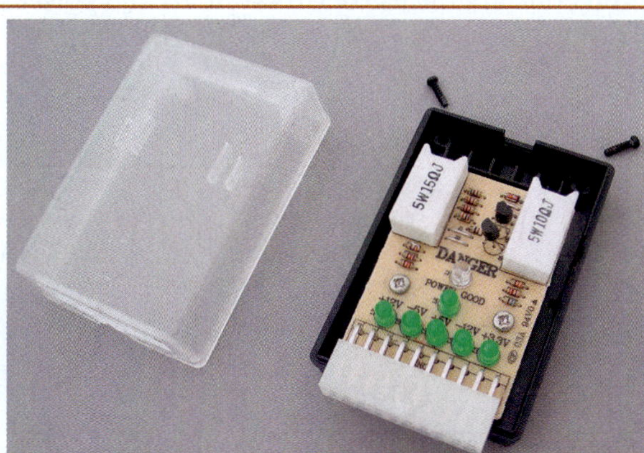

Goodheart-Willcox Publisher

Figure 5-31 A typical ATX power checker will have LEDs that light up to indicate the presence of +12, +5, +3.3, –12, and –5 voltage levels.

3. Remove the power connections carefully. Try not to disturb other cable connections on the motherboard or other devices. Also, remove the power cord attached to the power supply.
4. Remove the retaining/mounting screws from the case that secure the power supply in place.
5. Place the new power supply into the case and secure the retaining/mounting screws.
6. Reconnect the power connections to the motherboard and devices using the reference created in Step 2 as a guide.
7. Place any unused connections from the power supply in a neat bundle, keeping the loose connectors away from the motherboard. A loose connector could easily slip over a motherboard bare jumper, causing destruction during power-on. It can also catch in the fan blades, thus stopping the fan and causing the CPU to overheat.
8. Take one last look at the connections. Verify that they are all correct and secure, and then power on the computer before replacing the case cover. The cover should be left off until you are satisfied the PC is working properly. Any error messages at this time could be generated by a loose or improper connection during installation.
9. If everything is fine, replace the case cover and, if needed, power on the PC once more. When replacing the case cover, be careful not to pinch any of the cables between the case frame and cover.

A+ 1102: 4.5

5.5 Surge-Protection Devices

An electrical surge, brownout, or blackout can happen at any time. A **surge** is the presence of higher-than-desired voltage in the electrical system. A **brownout** occurs when low voltage is present. A **blackout** is a condition in which no voltage is present. Blackouts can happen at any time and go entirely unnoticed, but they can also cause a computer to crash or lockup in the absence of one electrical cycle of power or less. Figure 5-32 shows a series of cycles with one flat-lined cycle. Below it is a series of digital signals with a large group of flat digital pulses in relation to the one cycle. This represents a blackout condition.

Surge protection devices are designed to protect computer and other electronic devices against harmful surges of electrical energy. Two of the most common methods of providing protection are the use of UPS systems and power strips.

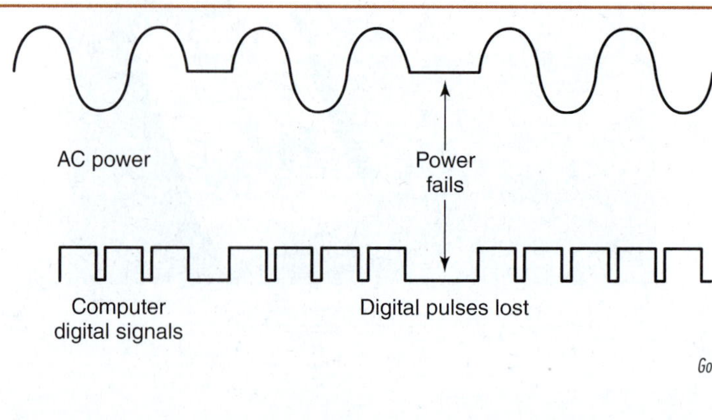

Figure 5-32 Blackouts can happen at any time and go entirely unnoticed, but they can also cause a computer to crash or lockup in the absence of one electrical cycle of power or less.

Goodheart-Willcox Publisher

UPS Systems

An **uninterruptible power supply (UPS)** is an electrical device designed to ensure a constant supply of quality electrical power to the computer system. *Quality power* means a power supply that eliminates surges, low voltage, and complete power outage conditions. UPS systems also protect against brownouts and blackouts. Figure 5-33 illustrates a typical UPS system showing outlets, surge protection, batteries, and chargers.

A UPS system monitors the power input to the computer while maintaining a fully charged battery. An AC/DC inverter is used to convert some of the 120 VAC from the outlet to 12 VDC used to keep the batteries fully charged. When commercial power fails, the inverter changes the 12 VDC from the battery back into 120 VAC, which is used to maintain power to the computer until the PC can be properly shut down, preventing the loss of data. Without the UPS system, the PC would crash when the power failed, and all data in RAM would be lost. Figure 5-34 shows the internal batteries of a UPS system.

Even though low-voltage situations and brownouts are common occurrences in electrical distribution systems, be aware that even a few milliseconds of low voltage can create problems for computers and networks. Remember that the digital traffic in a computer is traveling at megahertz speeds. Many commands can be issued, or thousands of bits of data sent, in a few milliseconds, all of which could be lost during the momentary voltage loss. Many computer system lockups are caused by momentary low-voltage conditions that can be prevented only by using a UPS.

Power Strips

Not all power strips protect against power surges. Some are designed only as a strip of convenient outlets into which someone can plug equipment. Power strips that are designed for power surge protection have a metal oxide varistor (MOV) connected

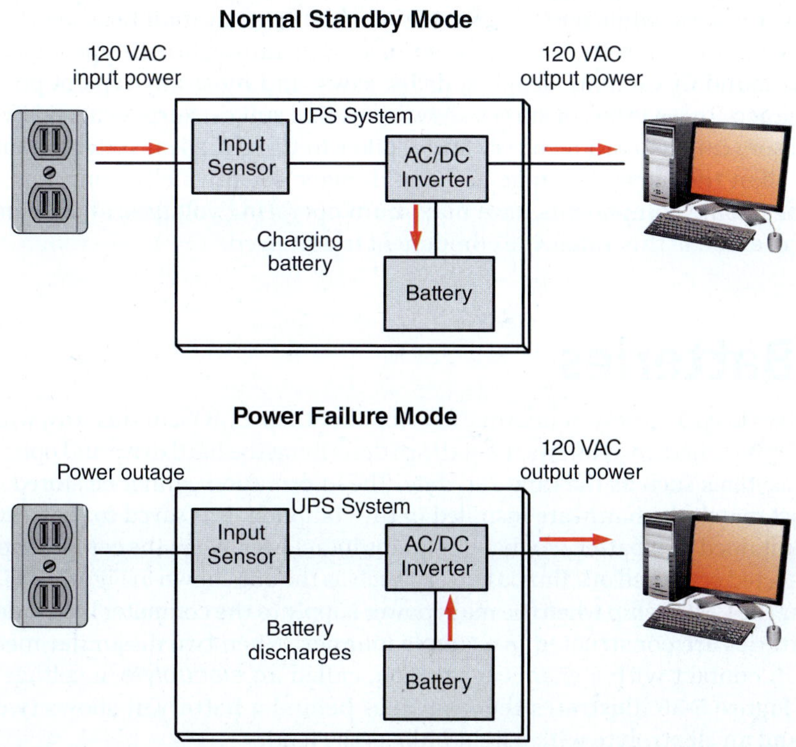

Goodheart-Willcox Publisher; (workstation icon) romvo/Shutterstock.com

Figure 5-33 A typical UPS monitors the 120-VAC input. When power is normal, the battery is kept fully charged and AC power is supplied to the computer. When the 120-VAC input fails, the battery discharges through the inverter to create 120-VAC for the computer.

xfilephotos/Shutterstock.com

Figure 5-34 An AC/DC inverter is used to convert some of the 120 VAC from the outlet to 12 VDC used to keep UPS batteries fully charged. When commercial power fails, the inverter changes the 12 VDC from the battery back into 120 VAC.

across the internal electrical line. The *metal oxide varistor (MOV)* does not normally conduct electricity until a certain voltage level is reached and then acts like a direct short, providing an alternate path for current. This diverts the current from the path through the electronic equipment plugged into the strip.

Power strips offer some degree of protection against power surges. While there is no true protection against extreme power surges, such as those generated by a direct hit from a bolt of lightning, a surge protector *does* protect against lower forms of power surges. A power surge can occur naturally many times a day in high-voltage power distribution systems and while most go unnoticed, some are quite severe. Surges are produced in the normal course of events, such as in the opening and closing of electrical switchgear. For this reason, electrical distribution systems are normally rerouted while performing routine or emergency maintenance.

Other sources of voltage surges are caused by running brush-type motors, such as those found in vacuum cleaners, drills, saws, and most any type of power tool or appliance. These types of surges show up as line spikes. Surges caused by brush-type motors can also produce very large spikes in the electrical system many times greater than the normal voltage and can damage sensitive electronic equipment. Many electronic components have maximum operating voltages, and when a voltage surge exceeds this value, the component is damaged.

5.6 Batteries

Computers keep a variety of information stored in their CMOS. In this way, when your computer is turned on, it knows the settings describing the hard drive and optical drive as well as items such as the time and date. The information cannot be stored in ROM and must match the hardware installed in the computer. It is saved to the CMOS chip and maintained by a battery so that it remains intact even when the computer power is disconnected or turned off. Thus, a battery, such as the one shown in Figure 5-35, is used to power the CMOS chip when the main power supply to the computer is shut down.

Batteries are constructed in a simple manner. When two dissimilar metals are placed in contact with a chemical solution, called an *electrolyte*, a voltage is produced. Figure 5-36 illustrates the principles behind a battery. It shows two metal plates and an electrolyte with a light bulb as the load.

The most common types of batteries used for motherboards are alkaline, nickel metal hydride, nickel cadmium (also called NiCad), and lithium, all of which are rechargeable. The charge on a lithium battery lasts longer than the other three types of battery, so lithium is the preferred choice, especially for laptop computers.

A sure sign of failure of the CMOS battery is the PC's failure to correctly keep the date and time. Battery failure can also cause the system to fail to recognize the hard drive and other devices that store information in CMOS. A typical PC battery should last five to seven years, but they have been known to fail sooner. You can reset and save the information with the setup utility and use the computer as normal until the battery is replaced.

The batteries used for a UPS system are usually lead-acid or a gel-type. These batteries can provide power for a substantial period of time. The biggest advantage of gel-type is the lack of regular maintenance required as compared to lead-acid, but newer lead-acid batteries should also be maintenance-free. Both types should be periodically inspected for corrosion on the battery terminals.

Batteries have evolved over the years, and the types of batteries used in computers, laptops, and smartphones have improved. Nickel cadmium (NiCd) batteries are now considered old technology and suffer from **memory effect**, which is a reduction in the lifespan and charge of a rechargeable battery caused by incomplete discharges. As a result, NiCd batteries were supplanted by nickel metal hydride (NiMH) batteries. They are fundamentally the same as nickel cadmium batteries but can contain higher energy and can run for 30 to 40 percent longer.

Goodheart-Willcox Publisher

Figure 5-35 A battery is used to power the CMOS chip when the main power supply to the computer is shut down.

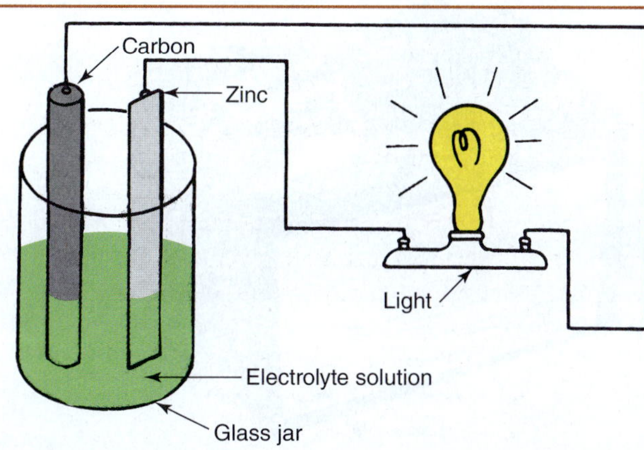

Goodheart-Willcox Publisher

Figure 5-36 Batteries can be constructed in as simple a manner as placing two dissimilar metals in contact with an electrolyte.

Lithium ion (Li-Ion) batteries are the most popular batteries used in cell phones, as they are light and portable. However, newer battery technology has been gaining popularity. Lithium polymer (Li-Poly) batteries have all the attributes of a lithium-ion battery with the added benefits of ultra-slim geometry and simplified packaging. Li-Poly batteries now represent the latest technology but are currently found in few mobile devices.

A+ 1102: 4.4, 4.5

Battery Disposal

Batteries must be disposed of in the manner outlined by the Environmental Protection Agency (EPA). Most manufacturers will readily accept an old battery in return for the purchase of a new one because they have the proper means of disposal at hand that the typical technician does not. You cannot simply throw an old battery in the trash, especially large UPS batteries, due to environmental protections. More information on battery recycling can be found on the EPA website. Also, you should always check your local jurisdiction, such as your county and city, to see if they have their own set of regulations on battery disposal.

A material safety data sheet (MSDS) is required for batteries that contain hazardous materials such as lead, zinc, magnesium chloride, mercury, and cobalt. When requested, manufacturers must supply an MSDS that contains information about how to handle the product safely, what to do if a person is contaminated by the product, and how to dispose of the product properly. A complete list of material safety data sheets for the most common batteries can be found online. As new battery technologies are developed using different chemicals, regulatory agencies frequently update their definition of hazardous materials and MSDS forms should be updated accordingly.

Battery Safety

Some battery manufacturers print information about safety and proper disposal on their labels. The APC battery in Figure 5-37 lists the following safety warnings:

- **Do not charge in gas-tight container.** The gases could accumulate and then a spark would cause an explosion.
- **Do not short battery terminals.** Short-circuited battery terminals cause excessive current flow. This can cause severe flash burns and possible explosion.
- **Do not incinerate.** Incineration can cause battery cells to expand and explode. In addition, burning some types of batteries causes toxic materials to be released into the atmosphere.
- **Flush with water at once if contaminated with electrolyte (acid).** The acid in this type of battery can cause skin irritation. When splashed or rubbed into the eye area, it can cause blindness.

Figure 5-37 Safety and disposal information is often printed on a label and affixed to the side of a battery.

Goodheart-Willcox Publisher

5.7 Power-Management Standards

1102: 1.4 A+

Power management is a critical issue when it comes to power consumption of desktops, laptops, and servers. Controlling power consumption on laptops is critical for battery life before charging is required. Power consumption for desktops and servers can result in significant electrical energy costs, especially in an environment of several hundred or even thousands of computers. Even just turning off computer displays and putting the computer into hibernation can save thousands of dollars in energy costs. These savings are not just directly related to electrical energy consumed by the computer system, but also to electrical energy consumed by air conditioning because computers and displays generate a lot of heat.

The original implementation of computer power management is Advanced Power Management (APM), which was designed for the BIOS to control power-management features of the computer system. APM was configured in the BIOS setup utility and determined the amount of time before the display screen and hard disk drive would be turned off. It was later replaced by ACPI. **Advanced Configuration and Power Interface (ACPI)** is an open industry power-management standard for desktops, laptops, and servers that allows the operating system to control the power-management features.

ACPI is enabled in the BIOS/UEFI setup utility but not controlled or configured by it. It is configured through the operating system. The operating system then determines when to implement the energy-saving features.

ACPI defines the interfaces between firmware (such as UEFI) and the operating system and system hardware. The ACPI standard is closely related, and in fact central to Operating System-directed configuration and Power Management (OSPM) operating system standard. When an OSPM-compliant system activates ACPI, the operating system then has full control over power management and device configuration.

Recent versions of Windows, including Windows 10 and Windows 11, provide three general power options: **Balanced**, **Power saver**, and **High performance**. Figure 5-38 shows these options in Windows 10. To the right of each option, you can see the relationship of energy savings to computer performance. For example, the **Power saver** option would be the best choice for the maximum life of a laptop battery charge. There will be much more about power saving and laptops in a later chapter. The **Power Options** dialog box is accessed through **Control Panel> Hardware and Sound>Power Options** in both Windows 10 and Windows 11.

Windows uses dynamic processor throttling to control the processor when in certain processor management modes. The Windows operating system can automatically throttle CPU performance to conserve electrical energy. Figure 5-39 lists the various modes.

A+ Note

You will likely see a question concerning power options for desktop and laptop computers. Be sure you can identify which power options are available for all current Windows operating systems.

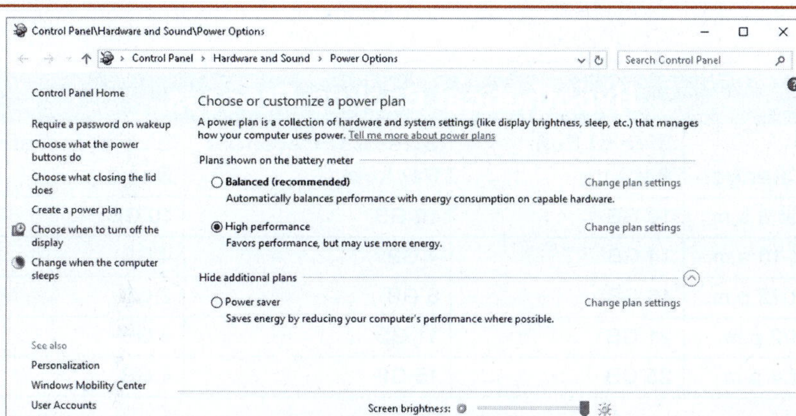

Goodheart-Willcox Publisher

Figure 5-38 Windows 10 has three power options: **Balanced**, **High performance**, and **Power saver**. These options are also available in Windows 11.

A+ 1102: 4.3

5.8 Backup and Recovery

Backups are important for computer security. There are many types of backups, but there are three main backups that cover most needs:

- **Full:** backs up all files
- **Incremental:** backs up all files that have changed since the last backup, regardless of the type of backup it was
- **Differential:** backs up only the files that have changed since the last *full* backup

To illustrate the differences, consider the table in Figure 5-40, which demonstrates how much data is backed up in a given hypothetical backup process—assuming the first backup is a full backup. For example, assume you will be performing a full backup at noon, by which time a total of 16 GB has been added to the system (10 GB at 8 a.m., 4 GB at 10 a.m., and 2 GB at noon). The entire 16 GB will be backed up despite the fact that only 2 GB is new. This is because a full backup includes everything each time it is performed.

Now, assume the system in Figure 5-40 system crashes at 4:15 p.m. What you do depends on the type of backup you performed:

- If you performed only full backups, you only must restore the 4 p.m. backup.
- If you performed differential backups, you must restore the 8 a.m. full backup and the 4 p.m. differential backup.
- If you performed incremental backups, you must restore the 8 a.m. full backup, as well as (in order) the 10 a.m., 12 p.m., 2 p.m., and 4 p.m. incremental backups.

Electronic vaulting (e-vaulting) is the idea of sending all changes to a file to a remote site using non-backup methods. This can be accomplished in real time or in batches. *Write once read many (WORM)* storage is a special type of electronic vaulting that automatically writes and protects data as soon as it is saved to the system. Large scale WORM implementations allow for large amounts of data to be stored in a write-protected environment.

Figure 5-39 Windows uses dynamic processor throttling to control the processor when in certain processor management modes.

Windows CPU Throttling Modes	
Mode	**Description**
Non	Run at highest performance possible
Constant	Always run at lowest possible performance to conserve maximum energy
Adaptive	Performance-based on demand
Degrade	Always run at lowest performance state; used mainly for laptops to conserve maximum amount of energy

Goodheart-Willcox Publisher

Figure 5-40 There are three types of backups: full, incremental, and differential. Full backups save everything. Incremental backups save all files that have changed since the last backup, regardless of type. Differential backups save everything that has changed since the last full backup.

Hypothetical Backup Process			
Data Change	**Size of Full Backup**	**Size of Differential Backup**	**Size of Incremental Backup**
10 GB at 8 a.m.	10 GB	10 GB	10 GB
4 GB at 10 a.m.	14 GB	4 GB	4 GB
2 GB at 12 p.m.	16 GB	6 GB	2 GB
5 GB at 2 p.m.	21 GB	11 GB	5 GB
4 GB at 4 p.m.	25 GB	15 GB	4 GB

Goodheart-Willcox Publisher

Chapter Summary

5.1 What Is Electrical Energy?

- Voltage is the amount of electrical pressure present in a circuit or power source. The scale used in measuring electrical pressure is volts (V). Current is the amount of electron flow. The scale used to measure the volume of electron flow in a current is amperes (A). In other words, it is the measure of electrical energy flowing through the system.
- Direct current (DC) refers to electrical energy that flows in one direction, from negative to positive. Alternating current (AC) has no negative or positive markings because it is in a state of constant change or alternating polarities.
- Resistance is the opposition to the flow of electrical energy. The unit of measurement for resistance is the ohm and is expressed with the letter *R* or the symbol omega (Ω). Continuity is the ability of a device or component to allow an unobstructed flow of electrical energy.
- Power is the amount of electrical energy provided or used by equipment, and the scale used in measuring electrical power is called watts (W). Wattage is the product of voltage and current.

5.2 Using a Digital Multimeter

- A digital multimeter is an all-in-one type of meter used to measure current, resistance, and voltage values.
- The meter is equipped with two test leads, each with probes at the end used for touching test points. These leads follow a universal color combination in which the black lead is used for the negative side of a reading and the red lead is used for the positive side.
- The range selector is used to choose the appropriate value to be read: voltage, current, or resistance. The dial indicator should be placed in the lowest range that is greater than the value to be read.
- A good fuse or cable produces a zero resistance reading, and an open fuse or cable produces an infinity reading.
- When testing outlets, take the weather and time of day into consideration.

5.3 Branch Circuits

- Many computer problems can be generated by the electrical system inside a home or small business.
- *Branch circuit* is the technical name for the wiring from an electrical panel to the final outlet on that circuit.
- A dedicated circuit is an electrical power distribution system designed to serve *only* computer equipment.
- Improper grounding conditions can cause serious problems to computer equipment.

5.4 PC Power Supply

- The power supply is responsible for converting standard 120-volt AC power from the wall outlet to DC voltage levels appropriate for the electronics systems of the computer (+12, +5, +3.3, –12, and –5).
- Power plugs have a special shape that matches the voltage level required by the motherboard or peripheral.

- Most mobile devices use an external power supply, commonly referred to as an *AC adapter.* The use of an external power supply allows for portability of equipment powered by either mains or battery without the added bulk of internal power components.
- Modular power supplies are those with detachable cables.
- Redundant power supplies are additional supplies installed in the event one fails.
- Since computers are used worldwide, they are typically designed with two voltage levels available either through use of a switch or by automatic electrical sensing and switching circuitry.
- Power supplies include a label that informs the user of its electrical power, including the output voltages and the power in watts the unit can deliver.
- The signs that a power supply is bad are inoperable cooling fans, no indicator lights, smoke, burnt smell, circuit breaker tripping, automatic rebooting, electric shock, and excessive heat.

5.5 Surge-Protection Devices

- A surge is the presence of higher-than-desired voltage in the electrical system; a brownout is when low voltage is present; and a blackout is a condition in which no voltage is present.
- Blackouts can happen at any time and go entirely unnoticed, but they can also cause a computer to crash or lockup in the absence of one electrical cycle of power or less.
- A UPS system provides protection against power surges, low voltage, and temporary power outages.
- Not all power strips protect against power surges. Those designed for power surge protection have a metal oxide varistor (MOV) connected across the internal electrical line.

5.6 Batteries

- The most common types of batteries used for motherboards are alkaline, nickel metal hydride, nickel cadmium (also called NiCad), and lithium, all of which are rechargeable.
- NiCd batteries were supplanted by nickel metal hydride (NiMH) batteries. They are fundamentally the same as nickel cadmium batteries but can contain higher energy and can run for 30 to 40 percent longer.
- Lithium ion (Li-Ion) batteries are the most popular batteries used in cell phones, as they are light and portable. However, newer battery technology has been gaining popularity. Lithium polymer (Li-Poly) batteries have all the attributes of a lithium-ion battery as well as ultra-slim geometry and simplified packaging.
- Information on battery recycling can be found on the Environmental Protection Agency's website and material safety data sheets.

5.7 Power-Management Standards

- Advanced Configuration and Power Interface (ACPI) is an open industry power-management standard for desktops, laptops, and servers.
- The Windows **Power Options** dialog box located in **Control Panel** can be used to control PC power consumption.

5.8 Backup and Recovery

- There are many types of backups but there are three main types that cover most needs.
- A full backup backs up all files.
- An incremental backup backs up all files that have changed since the last backup.
- A differential backup backs up all files that have changed since the last full backup.
- Electronic vaulting (e-vaulting) is the idea of sending all changes to a file to a remote site using non-backup methods.
- *Write once read many (WORM)* storage is a special type of electronic vaulting that automatically writes and protects data as soon as it is saved to the system.

Review Questions

1. Differentiate between voltage, current, resistance, and power.
2. Differentiate between DC and AC.
3. Summarize the procedure for reading voltage with a digital multimeter.
4. Summarize the procedure for reading resistance with a digital multimeter.
5. A wall outlet is determined to have sufficient voltage if it is within 10 percent of what voltage rating?
6. What resistance measurement identifies a good cable or fuse?
7. What resistance value identifies a blown fuse?
8. Describe characteristics of branch circuits.
9. What is the difference between a branch circuit and a dedicated circuit?
10. Describe the function of a PC power supply.
11. Summarize the procedure for replacing a PC power supply.
12. What are the typical DC voltage levels from a PC power supply unit?
13. What is the difference between an ATX and an ATX12V motherboard main power connection?
14. Explain the operation of a UPS.
15. How does a surge-protecting power strip protect devices from electrical spikes?
16. What is the difference between a surge, brownout, and blackout?
17. How does one properly dispose of a battery?
18. Summarize Windows Power Options for controlling PC power consumption.
19. Summarize the difference between APM and ACPI.
20. Differentiate among backup types.

Sample A+ Exam Questions

1. Select the best definition of a PC power supply.
   A. A power supply converts 120 VAC power into +/–3.3, 5, and 12 VDC levels that are used by the motherboard and various components.
   B. A power supply converts 120 VDC power into +/–3.3, 5, and 12 VDC levels that are used by the motherboard and various components.
   C. A power supply converts 120 VAC power into +/–5, 12, and 18 VDC levels that is used by the motherboard and various components.
   D. A power supply converts 120 VDC power into +/–5, 12, and 18 VDC levels that is used by the motherboard and various components.

2. Which unit below is used to express electrical pressure?
   A. Ampere
   B. Volt
   C. Watt
   D. Ohm
3. Which electrical characteristics does a digital multimeter measure? Select all that apply.
   A. Voltage
   B. Resistance
   C. Amperes
   D. Wire size
4. Which item ensures a steady and clean supply of electrical energy during power outages?
   A. VOM
   B. DMM
   C. UPS
   D. APC
5. Which letter usually expresses electrical power?
   A. V
   B. A
   C. W
   D. R
6. What is the maximum electrical load that may be connected to a typical 120-VAC power strip supplying computer equipment?
   A. 1,000 W
   B. 1,600 W
   C. 2,000 W
   D. 2,400 W
7. Which of the following is the closest to the resistance reading of a blown fuse?
   A. 0 Ω
   B. 120 volts
   C. 10 MΩ
   D. Infinity
8. Which is a typical procedure when a power supply is suspected to be bad?
   A. Open the power supply unit and replace the fuse.
   B. Check the output voltage levels of the wall outlet.
   C. Run **msinfo32** from **Run** in the **Start** menu to diagnose the power output.
   D. Put on an antistatic wrist strap and then open the power supply box to replace the fuse.

9. Which system is controlled by the operating system to conserve electrical energy?
   A. ACPI
   B. APM
   C. DDR
   D. DMA
10. Which DC voltage levels are associated with a typical ATX power supply?
    A. +/–3.3, 5, 12
    B. +/–5, 12, 18
    C. +/–3.3, 5, 12, 18
    D. +/–12, 18, 24

Chapter 6

Memory

Learning Outcomes

6.1 List factors to consider before replacing or upgrading memory.
6.2 Differentiate among physical memory packages.
6.3 Compare and contrast types of ROM and RAM.
6.4 Summarize the process of installing memory.
6.5 List important characteristics of RAM to consider when adding or replacing modules.
6.6 Summarize the operation of flash memory devices.
6.7 Identify memory map areas.
6.8 Explain the function of virtual memory.
6.9 Identify methods used to troubleshoot memory.

A+ Certification Exam Objectives

The following A+ Certification Exam Objectives are covered in this chapter.

Exam 220-1101

1.0 Mobile Devices

- 1.1 Given a scenario, install and configure laptop hardware and components.

3.0 Hardware

- 3.2 Given a scenario, install RAM types.
- 3.3 Given a scenario, select, install, and configure storage devices.

Exam 220-1102

1.0 Operating Systems

- 1.9 Given a scenario, perform OS installations and upgrades in a diverse OS environment.

Key Terms

buffer
column address selection (CAS)
conventional memory
dual in-line memory module (DIMM)
dual-channel mode
dynamic RAM
electrically erasable programmable read-only memory (EEPROM)
erasable programmable read-only memory (EPROM)
error-correction code (ECC)
even parity checking
expanded memory standard (EMS)
extended memory system (XMS)
flash memory
flash ROM
flex mode
heap
high memory area (HMA)
MicroDIMM
odd parity checking
page file
parity
programmable read-only memory (PROM)
quad-channel mode
read-only memory (ROM)
registered memory
row address selection (RAS)
serial presence detect (SPD)
single-channel mode
small outline DIMM (SO-DIMM)
small outline RIMM (SO-RIMM)
stack
static RAM
triple-channel mode
upper memory area (UMA)
virtual memory

Overview

The memory in a computer is one of the most difficult components to explain and understand. It is imperative that you carefully examine the illustrations provided in this chapter while studying the concept of memory. You may also need your instructor's help to grasp this concept completely. While memory is, without question, one of the easiest upgrades that can be made to a PC, understanding system memory and its evolution is complex and can be confusing.

This chapter covers memory types, terminology, diagnostics, and management used by the various Microsoft operating systems. It will also help you understand the complexity of PC memory and develop troubleshooting strategies. A large part of the A+ Certification Exams is dedicated to questions regarding memory terminology. The terminology associated with memory can be confusing, but with a little concentration and effort, you will master the subject of PC memory.

A+ Note

For the CompTIA A+ Certification Exams, you should be familiar with compatibility issues among the various types of DDR memory. You should also master the terminology and acronyms presented in this chapter.

A+ 1102: 1.9

6.1 Factors to Consider before Upgrading Memory

Before you begin purchasing and upgrading memory modules, you must first consider a number of issues. Novices simply plug memory modules into motherboards and expect the amount of memory and performance to increase, but this will not always be the result. Improperly identified memory modules and improper installation can decrease PC performance and possibly damage the motherboard, so the following questions should be answered before upgrading memory:

- **Compatibility:** With which type of memory is the motherboard compatible?
- **Quantity:** What is the total amount of RAM desired? Are you adding to existing RAM or replacing it?
- **Speed:** Will the existing chipset support the speed (frequency) of the memory module?
- **Pairings:** Must the memory modules be installed in pairs? If so, must the size and latency match when installed in pairs?
- **Miscellaneous:** Are there any other specifications that must be followed?

These questions should all be answered before attempting a memory upgrade on a PC, and making a determination on these issues will save time and money.

Generally, the maximum memory on a computer is defined by the size of the address space, physical size of the computer, availability of appropriately sized memory cards, and cost. The rest of this chapter assists with answering these questions, while also exploring important concepts that will aid in your understanding of technical manuals and memory issues.

Tech Tip

An operating system's bit type has a significant impact on the amount of supported memory. For example, a 32-bit address scheme can address up to 4 GB of memory, but the usable space is around 3.3 GB due to OS requirements. However, a 64-bit OS can support up to 16 exabytes of memory.

6.2 Physical Memory Packages

Physical size of the memory package is important when assessing an upgrade or a replacement. PC memory chips are packaged in several different physical styles. Some of these are SIP, DIP, SIMM, and DIMM.

SIP

A *single in-line package (SIP)* is a memory chip with a single row of connections that run along the length of a chip, as shown in Figure 6-1. SIPs are sometimes referred to as *single in-line pin packages (SIPPs)* because the row of connections along the modules are pins. This type of module is not often used today because it has a high physical profile, and the pins are easily bent.

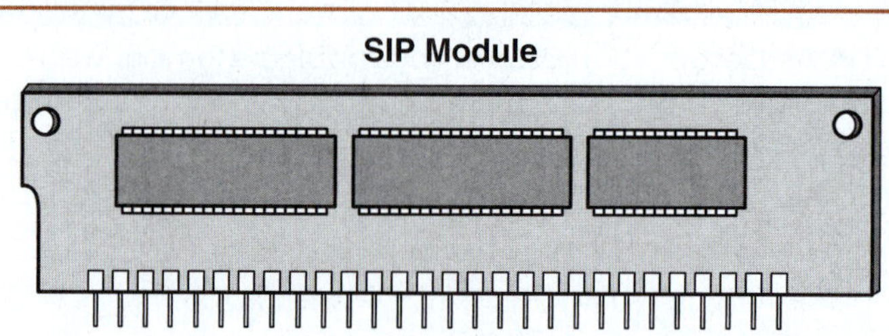

Figure 6-1 Early memory modules were almost exclusively SIPs.

Goodheart-Willcox Publisher

DIP

A *dual in-line package (DIP)* is a chip that has two rows of connections, one row per side of the chip, as illustrated in Figure 6-2. This style is commonly used for *cache* memory, which is temporary, or for memory that must be mounted permanently on a circuit board. Memory of this type is typically found on older-model motherboards mounted in rows near the CPU.

SIMM

A *single in-line memory module (SIMM)* is a memory module containing a row of DIP memory chips mounted on a circuit board and flat contacts that run along both sides of the bottom edge. This type of connection is called an *edge connector*. The circuit board is then inserted into a SIMM memory slot on the motherboard. The SIMM is designed so when it is plugged into the memory socket, each side of the edge connector is the same circuit. This eliminates easily damaged pins. SIMMs come in 30-pin and 72-pin packages. SIMM chips have not been used since the early 2000s, but you may still encounter them doing PC repair.

DIMM

A **dual in-line memory module (DIMM)** is a memory module constructed much like a SIMM but has edge connectors located directly across the circuit board from each other that do not connect electrically. DIMMs were originally created in the 1990s as an upgrade and replacement for SIMMs. The main difference is in the fact that DIMM edge connectors are not the same electrical connection as they are on SIMM boards. The DIMM design allows for more electrical connections per inch than the SIMM design, as shown in Figure 6-3. DIMMs come in 168-pin, 184-pin, and 240-pin packages.

SO-DIMM and SO-RIMM

1101: 3.2 A+

Small outline DIMM (SO-DIMM) and **small outline RIMM (SO-RIMM)** are small-outline packages of regular memory modules. They are used especially for laptop applications where space is compact. The small outline package is designed to fit easily into the small confines of a laptop computer.

MicroDIMM

MicroDIMM is a more compact version of the standard SO-DIMM package. KINGMAX Semiconductor coined the term "MicroDIMM" to distinguish it from the already existing SO-DIMM package and to emphasize its smaller size. Other

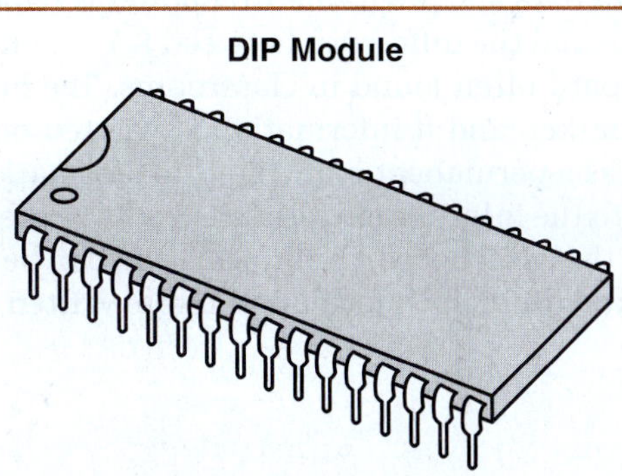

Goodheart-Willcox Publisher

Figure 6-2 Another early form of PC memory was the DIP.

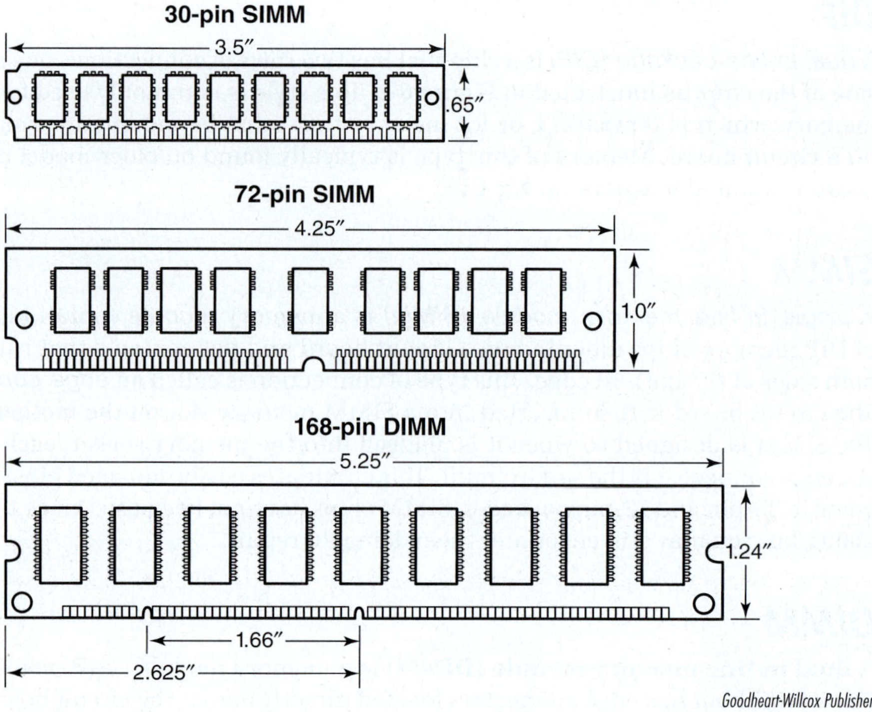

Figure 6-3 The various packages of memory can be easily identified by size. Shown here are two SIMMs and a 168-pin DIMM.

memory manufacturers, such as Kingston, use SO-DIMM as the name of the smaller module. Either way, the module is quickly identified because of the overall smaller dimensions and pin count. Where the SO-DIMM has 200 pins, the MicroDIMM has only 172 pins. This makes MicroDIMM perfectly suited for use in many notebook and laptop computers, but not in desktops.

6.3 ROM and RAM

Computer systems contain both read-only memory (ROM) and random access memory (RAM) memory. **Read-only memory (ROM)** is designed to store program information in a nonvolatile fashion, while *random access memory (RAM)* is designed to store data or programs temporarily. The terms *volatile* and *nonvolatile* are often used to differentiate among types of computer memory. RAM is considered volatile memory because it loses data when power is removed from the computer. ROM chips are nonvolatile, meaning they retain their information even when the power is removed from the computer. Content in RAM can be repeatedly erased and reloaded, but all programming and data in RAM is lost when power is removed from the chip. On the other hand, ROM retains data and programs after power is removed.

To help you understand the difference between RAM and ROM, think of a typical white dry-erase board often found in classrooms. The board requires the use of a specific type of marker, and if information is written on a whiteboard using something else—such as a permanent marker—the information will remain on the board forever, similar to the information written in a ROM memory chip. If an erasable marker is used on the whiteboard, the information can be wiped clean from the board, allowing new and different information to be written on the board. This is similar to RAM.

Types of ROM

There has been a good deal of innovation involving ROM memory. Not all ROM chips have permanently embedded programs; many variations of ROM chips can actually be reprogrammed with different data or programs. They are still classified as ROM chips because, in normal applications, they retain their information even after power is removed from the computer.

PROM

Originally, ROM chips were manufactured with a program etched into the chip. The technically correct term for this type of ROM chip is *mask ROM* because the manufacturer uses a mask to create the circuitry. Recall the discussion from Chapter 1 about the chip-manufacturing process. This circuitry represents the program when the chip is manufactured, and the programs in these chips cannot be altered.

Programmable read-only memory (PROM) is similar to mask ROM but is used extensively in computer program development. Blank ROM chips are purchased and programmed using a device called a PROM burner. The PROM burner connects to the PC, where programs and data are written before being transferred to the burner and burned into the blank PROM chip. The PROM chip retains the program indefinitely, but it cannot be reprogrammed. PROM chips are common with embedded automotive software.

EPROM

Erasable programmable read-only memory (EPROM) was an advancement from PROM that allowed chips to be programmed, erased, and then reprogrammed. The ability to reprogram chips is a huge advantage since the code can be upgraded over time to fix bugs or add features, but the number of rewrites is limited. The EPROM has a small window that exposes the miniature circuitry inside the chip. By shining an ultraviolet light through the window, you can erase the program and return the EPROM to its original blank state. EPROMs are often installed on a motherboard in a removable socket so they can be easily swapped out by field technicians performing upgrades. The old chip is removed and can be reprogrammed, and the new chip is installed in its place.

EEPROM

Electrically erasable programmable read-only memory (EEPROM) is similar to EPROM in that it can be reprogrammed, but it uses a high electrical charge instead of ultraviolet light to erase the chip. The charge used for reprogramming must be higher than the original charge used to program it. The EEPROM was designed to be erased one bit at a time so part of a program could be erased rather than the entire program at one time. EEPROMs are common during the development phase of embedded software.

Flash ROM

Flash ROM is a type of ROM that behaves similarly to RAM, meaning it is possible to replace its memory contents. It functions similarly to EEPROM, but it uses a much higher voltage to erase the chip and also erases the entire block of memory at one time.

It is important to note that EEPROM and flash ROM can only be reprogrammed a limited number of times. At some point, the chip will become damaged by the application of the higher-than-normal voltage used in the erase operation. Software developers often develop complex algorithms to detect damage and find ways to use other portions of the memory.

A+ 1101: 3.2

Types of RAM

Random access memory is a matrix of individual storage areas where information can be stored as bits. The name *random access* means that the CPU can access any bit anywhere in the memory; put simply, the CPU does not have to go through the memory in sequential fashion. Early computer systems did not have the advantage of RAM chips or disk drive systems; instead, they used ROM chips and stored data on magnetic tape. The data on the tape was stored sequentially, bit by bit, along the entire length of tape. To access any information on the tape, the tape would have to play back each bit sequentially until the desired information could be retrieved.

Dynamic RAM vs. Static RAM

There are two basic forms of RAM. One type, dynamic RAM, uses capacitors to store the information. The second type, static RAM, uses devices called flip-flops.

Dynamic RAM (referred to as DRAM and pronounced *dee-ram*) is a type of integrated circuit that uses capacitors to assist in storing data in the transistors. Capacitors are capable of storing electrical charges, the presence or absence of which represents the binary data being stored. Because of their microscopic size, the capacitors in the integrated circuit lose their charge over a short period of time. To retain the charge, the capacitors must be constantly refreshed (recharged) with electrical energy, which reduces the amount of time available for writing and reading the contents of the chip. Dynamic RAM is used in the CPU because it is very small and is low cost when compared to static RAM.

The basic DRAM is a typical memory chip installed in older PCs. When someone says a computer has 2 GB of RAM, they are generally saying that the computer has DRAM. DRAM memory chips must be refreshed periodically to retain the information stored on them.

Static RAM (referred to as SRAM and pronounced *es-ram*) is an integrated circuit technology based on digital flip-flop components. The flip-flop does not use a capacitor to hold the data condition as dynamic RAM does, which results in faster data transmission than dynamic RAM because it does not have to be constantly refreshed. To take advantage of the faster data transfer speed, most PC cache systems use static RAM as opposed to dynamic RAM. However, SRAM is approximately four times larger than DRAM, and it is considerably more expensive. Consequently, the bulk of a computer's RAM will be some variant of DRAM.

EDO DRAM

Extended Data Output DRAM (EDO DRAM) is faster than conventional DRAM. Conventional DRAM accesses only one block of memory at a time and then passes the data completely on to the next component before it transfers in new data. EDO DRAM is designed to access and transfer in new data before the previous data stored on the chip is transferred out. This technique greatly improves the transfer rate of memory.

BEDO DRAM

Burst Extended Data Output DRAM (BEDO DRAM) is an improved version of EDO DRAM. It can transfer data in groups (or "bursts") of four memory addresses at one time. BEDO DRAM cannot keep up with a motherboard bus that runs faster than 66 MHz, however. Consequently, there are few current applications for this type of memory.

SDRAM

Synchronous dynamic RAM (SDRAM), shown in Figure 6-4, is much faster than conventional DRAM. SDRAM can transfer data at speeds exceeding 100 MHz and synchronizes the data transfer with the CPU chip, which increases data transfer rates. This is because the chip does not have to wait for the next tick of the CPU clock system to begin transferring data. SDRAM can be found on video cards because of its high-speed transfer rate.

DDR1

Double Data Rate-SDRAM, or simply *DDR1,* was designed to replace SDRAM. DDR1 was originally referred to as DDR-SDRAM, or simply DDR. It was not until DDR2 was introduced that DDR became referred to as DDR1. As a result, both *DDR* and *DDR1* are used interchangeably. Names of components constantly change as newer technologies are introduced, especially when the newer technology is based on a previous one.

The principle applied in DDR is exactly as the name indicates: it doubles the rate at which data is transferred by using both the rising and falling edges of a typical digital pulse. Earlier memory technology, such as SDRAM, transferred data after one complete digital pulse. DDR transfers data twice as fast by transferring data on both the rising and falling edges of the digital pulse, as illustrated in Figure 6-5.

DDR2

DDR2 was the next generation of memory developed after DDR. It has a greater data transfer rate (bandwidth) than DDR1, which is achieved by increasing its operational frequency to match the front-side bus (FSB) frequencies and doubling the prefetch buffer data rate. The memory prefetch buffer data rate is discussed in detail later in this chapter.

Goodheart-Willcox Publisher

Figure 6-4 The original SDRAM had exposed memory chips. Today, SDRAM used in high-performance memory applications has heat spreaders to dissipate heat created by high frequencies.

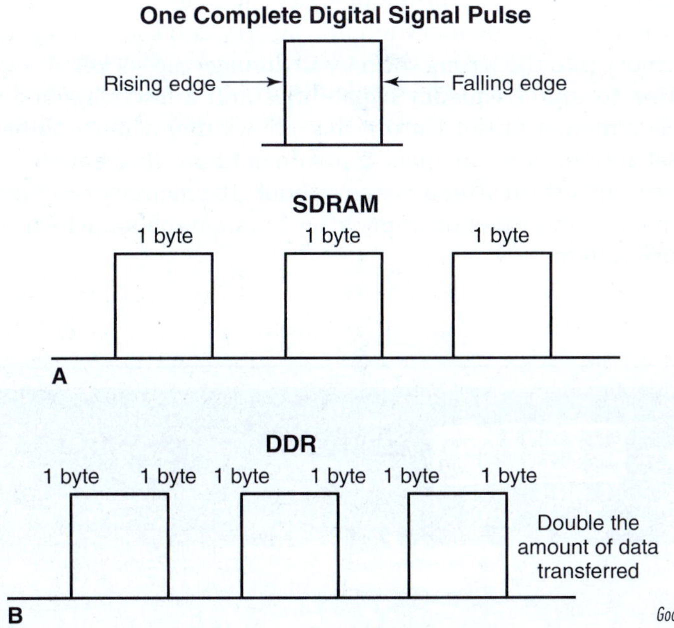

Goodheart-Willcox Publisher

Figure 6-5 SDRAM transfers data on a complete digital signal pulse (A), while DDR transfers data on the rising edge and falling edge of a digital signal pulse (B), thus transferring twice as much data as SDRAM.

DDR2 is a 240-pin DIMM design that operates at 1.8 volts. The lower voltage counters the heat effect caused by high-frequency data transfer. DDR1 operates at 2.5 volts and is a 184-pin DIMM design. DDR2 uses a different motherboard socket than DDR1, meaning it is incompatible with motherboards designed for DDR1. The DDR2 DIMM key does not align with the DDR DIMM key slot, so forcing a DDR2 module into a DDR1 socket will damage the socket and expose the memory to a high voltage level.

A+ 1101: 3.2

DDR3

DDR3, shown in Figure 6-6, was introduced in the summer of 2007 and was the natural successor to DDR2. DDR3 increased the prefetch buffer size to 8 bits and increased the operating frequency, resulting in higher data transfer rates than DDR2. In addition, the voltage level was lowered to 1.5 volts to counter the heating effects of the high frequency. By now, you can see the trend of memory is to increase the prefetch buffer size, increase the operating frequency, and lower the operational voltage level to counter the effects of heat.

In 2009, the Joint Electron Devices Engineering Council (JEDEC), an organization that develops and distributes specifications for memory modules, modified the DDR3 standard to further decrease the voltage levels to 1.35 volts (identified as DDR3L) and 1.25 volts (identified as DDR3U). The new identifiers represent "low voltage" (L) and "ultra-low voltage" (U), respectively.

Lowering the operational voltages also lowers the amount of current as well as the amount of wattage consumed by the memory module. Lower wattage also results in less heat. When applied to portable devices such as laptops, it means a slightly longer battery life between charges. When used in server applications, it means greatly reduced heat and electrical consumption. Think of a large server facility such as at Google; the total number of memory modules for all the servers would collectively be in the thousands. Not only is there a direct savings in energy costs due to less wattage consumed by the servers, but there is also direct energy savings for cooling and air-conditioning because less heat is generated. The computer system firmware detects the presence of the memory module and then automatically configures the voltage level to be compatible with the detected module.

DDR3 is designed with 240 pins like the DDR2, but the notch is in a different position to prevent insertion into a DDR2 socket. DDR3 is both electrically and physically incompatible with other versions of DDR RAM. See the location of the notch placed along the bottom edge of the memory modules in Figure 6-7. The notch is used to ensure the proper memory module inserts into the correct socket because inserting memory into the wrong socket will damage the socket.

In addition to high-frequency capabilities and a lower applied voltage level, the DDR3 has a memory reset feature that allows the memory to be cleared by a software reset action. Other memory types do not have this feature, and thus their memory state is uncertain after a system reboot. The memory reset feature ensures that the memory will be clean or empty after a system reboot, which creates a more stable memory system.

Figure 6-6 DDR3 was introduced in the summer of 2007 with an increased prefetch buffer size and operating frequency.

Kjerish/CC BY-SA 4.0

DDR4

1101: 3.2 A+

The JEDEC standard for DDR4 was released in late 2012. DDR4 has 288 pins (256 on the SO-DIMM version) and an operating voltage of 1.2 volts. DDR4 has a greater bandwidth than DDR3; in fact, the lowest bandwidth rate of DDR4 overlaps the DDR3 bandwidth rate. Voltage of DDR4 varies from 1.2–1.4 V depending on the standard in question. Low-voltage standards are estimated to be approximately 1.05 V, and DDR4 allows for nearly four times the total capacity of DDR3.

Figure 6-8 lists the PC classification, memory chip classification, and bandwidth of various SDRAM and DDR memory modules. The memory chip classification correlates to the memory-chip frequency design. For example, a DDR2-400 is designed to operate at 400 MHz. The memory-module PC classification correlates to the memory-module frequency times eight. For example, a DDR2-400 would be identified as a PC2-3200 because 3,200 is equal to 8 times 400.

The memory-module bandwidth is a theoretical amount of data that can be transferred, even though it is expressed as an exact value, such as 12.8 GB. The table in Figure 6-8 is based on theoretical throughputs, meaning it does not take the

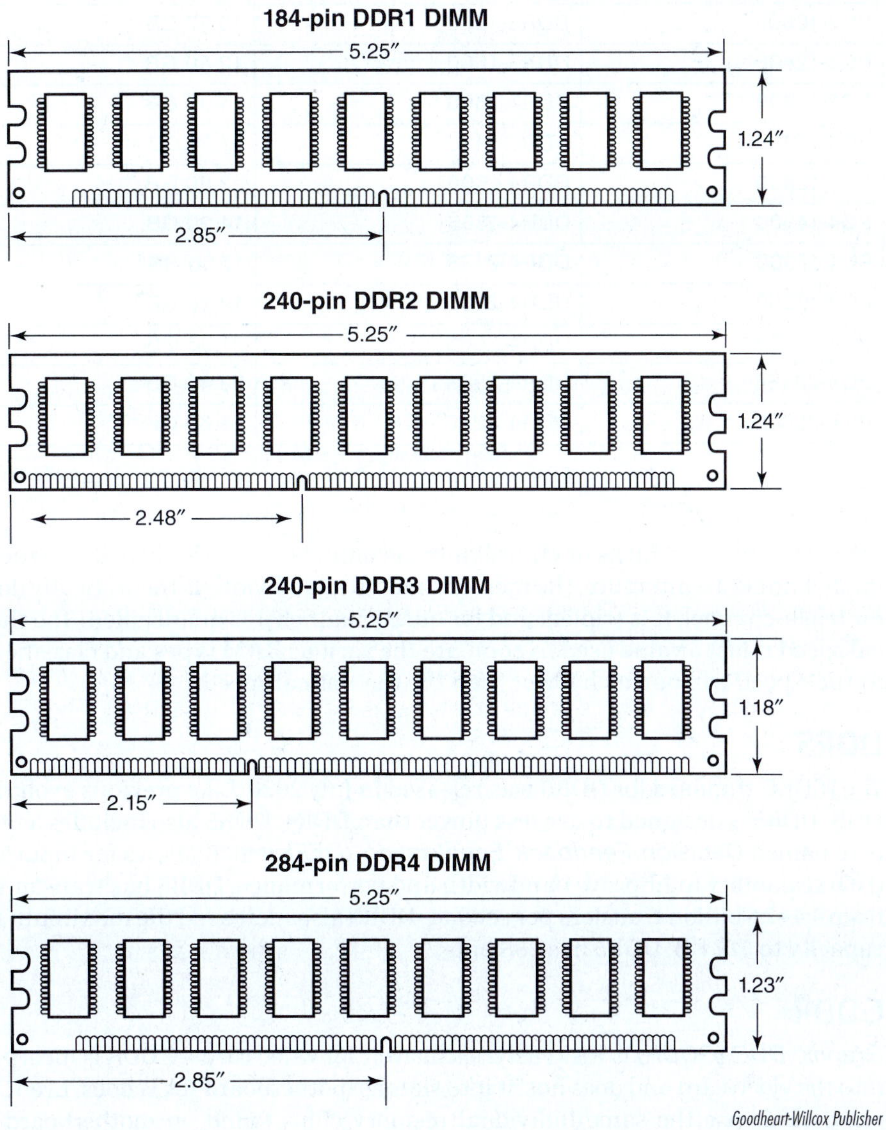

Figure 6-7 Variations in the design of DDR1, DDR2, DDR3, and DDR4 DIMMs prevent users from inserting a module into the wrong socket.

Figure 6-8 The memory-module PC classification equates to the frequency of the memory module multiplied by eight.

DDR Bandwidths by Classification		
Memory-Module PC Classification	**Memory Chip Classification**	**Memory-Module Bandwidth**
PC100	SDRAM	800 MB
PC133	SDRAM	1.10 GB
PC1600	DDR1	1.60 GB
PC2100	DDR1	2.10 GB
PC2700	DDR1	2.70 GB
PC2-3200	DDR2-400	3.20 GB
PC2-4200	DDR2-533	4.20 GB
PC2-5300	DDR2-667	5.30 GB
PC2-6400	DDR2-800	6.40 GB
PC2-8500	DDR2-1066	8.50 GB
PC3-6400	DDR3-800	6.40 GB
PC3-8500	DDR3-1066	8.53 GB
PC3-10600	DDR3-1333	10.67 GB
PC3-12800	DDR3-1600	12.80 GB
PC3-14900	DDR3-1866	14.90 GB
PC3-17000	DDR3-2133	17.00 GB
PC4-12800	DDR4-1600	12.80 GB
PC4-14900	DDR4-1866	14.90 GB
PC4-17000	DDR4-2133	17.00 GB
PC4-19200	DDR4-2400	19.20 GB
PC4-21333	DDR4-2666	21.33 GB
PC4-23466	DDR4-2933	23.46 GB
PC4-25600	DDR4-3200	25.60 GB

Goodheart-Willcox Publisher

memory controller, BIOS, or chipset into account. For a motherboard designed with dual-channel architecture, the memory-module bandwidth is theoretically doubled; for triple-channel, it is tripled; and for quad-channel, it is quadrupled. The theoretical speed is just a value used to compare the various RAM types and classifications. Actual speed will be much lower than the theoretical speed.

A+ 1101: 3.2

DDR5

The JEDEC standard for DDR5 was released in July 2020. Like previous evolutions of DDR, DDR5 is designed to use less power than DDR4. DDR5 also includes a new feature named *Decision Feedback Equalization (DEF)*, which allows for input/output (I/O) scalability to improve bandwidth and performance. DDR5 has transfer speeds from 4.4–7.6 billion transfers per second. DDR5 also increased the maximum DIMM capacity to 512 GB. DDR5 has 288 pins.

Tech Tip

Memory chip technology is rapidly changing. New memory types are often developed and released roughly every year or two.

GDDR

Graphic DDR (GDDR) is RAM used exclusively for video cards. GDDR is incorporated into the video card and does not fit into slots as motherboard RAM does. Even though video cards use the same individual memory chips found on motherboard RAM, the electronic specifications are different from motherboard RAM. GDDR is designed to transfer data to and from the video processor directly at much higher frequencies than motherboard RAM. Since the video RAM runs at higher frequencies, it generates more heat than motherboard RAM. As a result, cooling fans are incorporated into high-performance video cards that use high-performance RAM. Video RAM generations are sequential just like DDR, for example GDDR3, GDDR4, GDDR5, and GDDR6. The latest generation, GDDR6 has several variations such as GDDR6X and GDDR6W.

Cache

Cache is a temporary storage location for data, where it remains until the bus system is ready to transfer it to another component. Cache can be found throughout the computer system. For example, the CPU has cache (small pocket of RAM), as do hard drives, modems, and video cards. A hard drive uses cache (RAM chip) to store data temporarily during a disk read/write operation. A typical modem uses cache to store data while waiting to transfer data into the computer bus system. Anywhere data transfer is taking place, you can be sure there is a cache system designed in the circuit board. All caches are designed to improve system performance by moving frequently accessed data into quicker memory. Cache memory will generally hold anticipated data or frequently accessed data in a memory form that is much faster than sources like a mechanical hard drive, which will increase the throughput.

The size of cache directly affects the rate of data transfer. The larger the cache, the more data can be transferred. This results in a higher data rate, which is interpreted as high data speeds. Speed of data are based on how much data can be transferred in a given time period. Discussion of L1, L2, and L3 cache can be found in Chapter 4.

SPD

Serial presence detect (SPD) is a technology that identifies the type of RAM installed on a computer. It involves the presence of an extra chip on the memory module, which contains technical information about the module. The information provided by SPD is used by the BIOS to configure the BIOS RAM settings automatically to match the installed RAM. You can still change the RAM settings manually with the setup utility, but this is inadvisable.

Increasing the RAM access clock speed is commonly performed by PC enthusiasts, often called *overclockers*, who wish to increase the performance of their computer. This action is often performed to the CPU as well as the RAM. Remember, when you manually override the automatic SPD detection and configuration with the setup utility, you run the risk of overheating the memory chips and causing a system failure or lockup. After failing to tweak the speed of the RAM, the computer BIOS must be reset, thus allowing the SPD to reconfigure the BIOS RAM configuration correctly. In short, the SPD capability is there for a reason; it allows the computer system to protect itself.

6.4 Installing RAM Modules

1101: 1.1 A+

Adding memory is one of the easiest upgrades you can make to a computer. You simply insert the module and the computer's BIOS recognizes the new memory when you start your computer. However, the memory and the slots on the motherboard can be damaged if you are not careful, so there are a few important facts to keep in mind when installing memory.

Memory modules are extremely sensitive to static discharge. Always wear an antistatic or grounding wrist strap when handling memory chips, and never touch the edge of the module where the electrical circuit connections are located. Touching the exposed electrical connections could cause electrostatic discharge

Caution

Do *not* force a memory module into a socket. Doing so may damage the memory module or socket.

(ESD) damage. Notice in Figure 6-9, the technician is holding the memory module by the heat spreader.

Each memory type has a notch that is used to orient the memory module with the memory slot and to ensure the correct type of memory is used to match the motherboard system, as shown in Figure 6-10. The slot has a corresponding key that fits into the notch. After properly aligning the memory notch with the slot key, press the module firmly into the slot using your thumbs, similar to what is shown in Figure 6-11. When the memory is firmly seated in the slot, the clips at each end of the slot will clamp onto the module, thus holding it securely in place.

To insert a memory module into a laptop, ensure the laptop is powered down and disconnected from the outlet. On the underside of the laptop should be an access panel secured with one or more screws. Remove the screw(s) and access

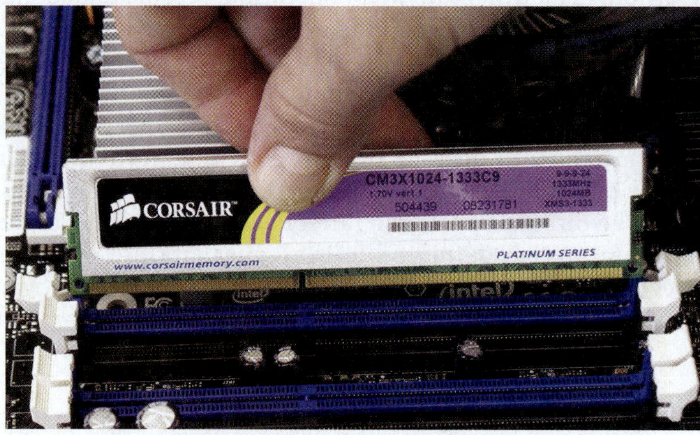

Figure 6-9 Do not touch the electrical connections running along the bottom of the module, and align the notch on the bottom of the module with the key in the memory socket before inserting it.

Goodheart-Willcox Publisher

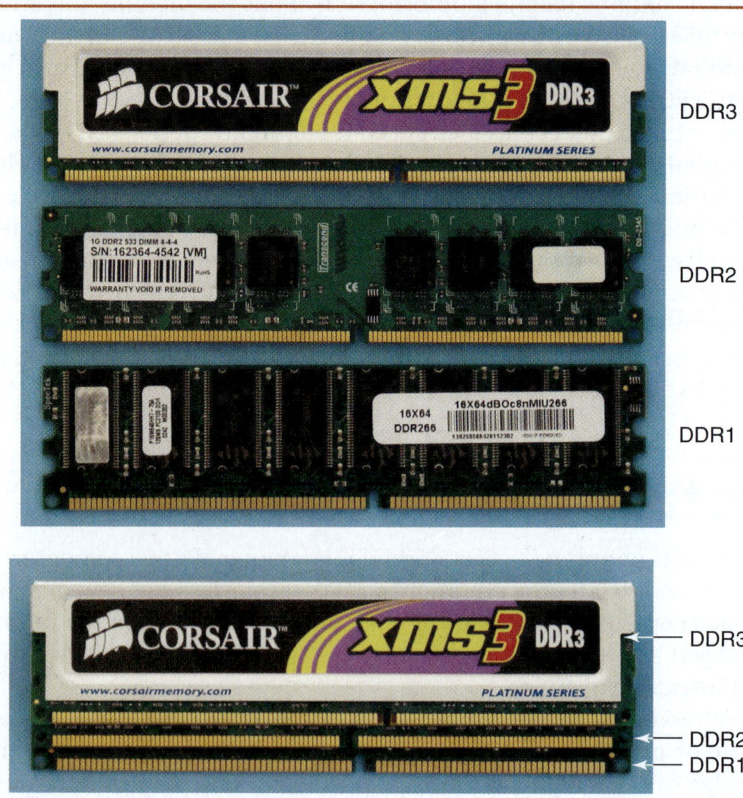

Figure 6-10 Each type of DDR memory module has a different notch location.

Goodheart-Willcox Publisher

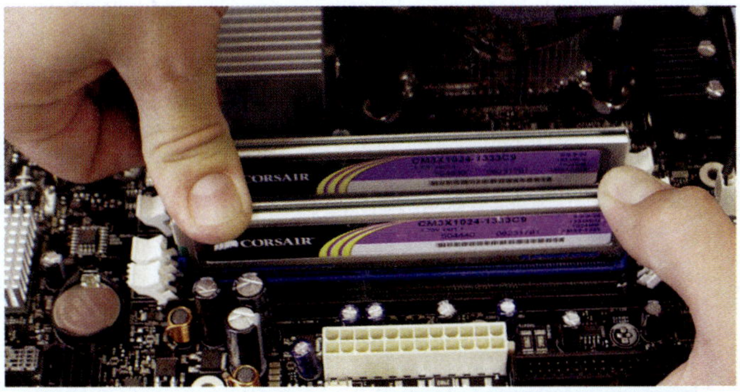

Goodheart-Willcox Publisher

Figure 6-11 Press the memory module down into the slot until the clips at each end close, locking down the module.

panel. Memory modules for laptops do not stand upright; rather, they lie flat and slide into the socket. If you have to remove existing memory modules, release the latches on the side of the module, and lift the module at an approximate 30-degree angle to unlock it. The module should slide out. To insert RAM, reverse this process by sliding the new module into place and gently pushing down to secure it. Then, replace the access panel and screw(s).

To achieve better performance, install DIMMs in sets as prescribed by the technology. For example, to achieve dual-channel capability, the modules must be installed in pairs. The following section covers various DIMM installation arrangements.

DIMM Physical Arrangements

Motherboards are capable of many different DIMM physical arrangements. The five DIMM arrangements you should be familiar with are

- single-channel mode;
- dual-channel mode;
- triple-channel mode;
- quad-channel mode; and
- flex mode.

To determine the correct arrangement for a specific motherboard, you need to consult the motherboard manual or the motherboard or computer manufacturer's website. In addition, memory manufacturers provide online resources for matching memory to motherboards or computers.

Caution

The drawings in this section are made solely as an aid for explanation of the way the various channel modes are configured. Do *not* use these drawings as a practical example to be copied.

Single-Channel Mode

1101: 3.2 A+

Single-channel mode, also referred to as *asymmetric mode,* is when a single DIMM is installed, or multiple DIMMs of different memory capacity are installed in the motherboard memory slots. Figure 6-12 shows an example of single-channel mode with one DIMM, and Figure 6-13 shows an example of single-channel mode with DIMMs of different values. In the latter example, the different-value DIMMs may have a total memory capacity of 6 GB or less depending on the motherboard and whether the DIMM has been installed in the correct sequence as specified by the motherboard manufacturer. If the DIMM arrangement is incorrect, the computer may fail to boot or not all of the memory may be detected.

When different memory modules have different speed specifications, the memory performance will be based on the slowest speed. For example, when installing a 400-MHz memory module with a 533-MHz memory module, the performance will be based on 400 MHz. Also, most motherboards require that memory modules be placed in a specific order of arrangement. Random arrangement will most likely generate an error message and the computer may not boot properly.

Tech Tip

You will see memory kits advertised such as "16 GB (8 GB × 2)." This means it contains two identical 8-GB memory modules.

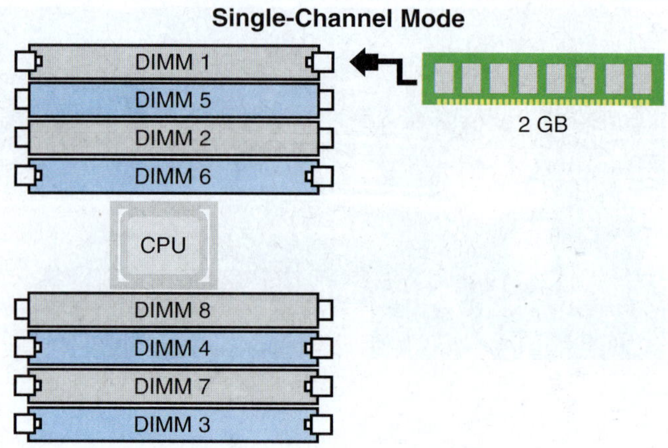

Figure 6-12 Single-channel mode refers to a single DIMM installed. It is also referred to as *asymmetric mode*.

Goodheart-Willcox Publisher

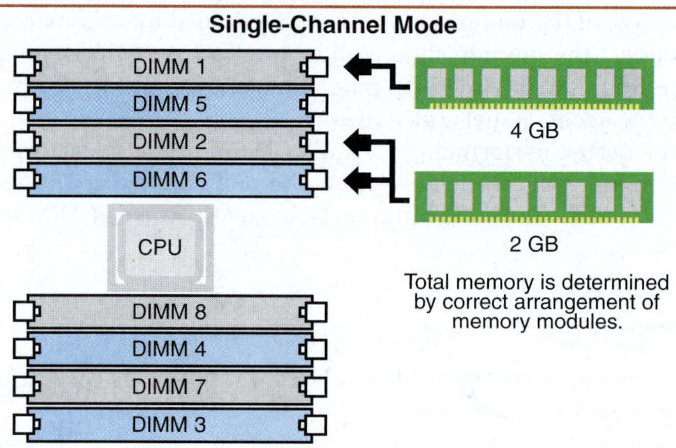

Figure 6-13 For asymmetric mode to function, the memory modules must be installed in correct sequence. If not, the computer may fail to boot or will not have the full capacity of the memory installed.

Goodheart-Willcox Publisher

A+ 1101: 3.2

Dual-Channel Mode

Dual-channel mode, also known as *interleaved mode*, is when the DIMMs are arranged as a pair and in a specific way according to the motherboard manual. *Dual-channel DDR* memory takes advantage of dual-channel technology developed by Intel in 2003. The RAM bus system, also known as the front-side bus (FSB), consisted of a single bus system. The Intel Corporation redesigned the motherboard to provide two memory buses between the RAM and the northbridge chipset, as shown in Figure 6-14. In this design, the northbridge chipset contains the memory controller, which controls the flow of data between the RAM and CPU. Today, computers incorporate the memory controller into the CPU chip and the northbridge is eliminated. Dual-channel technology greatly increased the data flow between the processor and the RAM. It is important to note that dual-channel technology does not actually double the data rate to the CPU, but the data rate is increased significantly.

To implement dual-channel mode, you must install DRAM as a pair. The pair does not necessarily need to match, but matching is highly recommended for best performance. When the pair does not match, the module with the least amount of memory will be matched by the other module. For example, a 2-GB memory module and a 4-GB memory module paired in a dual-channel arrangement will result in the same effect as two 2-GB modules. Also, be aware that the worst latency will apply to both modules as a pair.

When installing pairs of memory in dual-channel mode, the size, speed, and latency should be matched; otherwise, unexpected and intermitted problems could occur. Latency is covered later in this chapter.

Triple-Channel Mode

A+ 1101: 3.2

Triple-channel mode is interleaved in the same way as dual-channel mode except triple-channel mode uses three channels to support memory access. To configure a triple-channel mode of operation, three identical memory modules are inserted into the three identified memory slots, as illustrated in Figure 6-15. If only two memory modules are installed, the mode of operation will be dual channel, not triple channel. If a single memory module is installed, the mode of operation will be single channel.

When configured for triple-channel mode, the memory size is equal to adding the three separate memory capacities together. For example, three 2-GB memory modules would equal 6 GB of total memory. The speed is greatly increased, but not actually tripled.

Quad-Channel Mode

A+ 1101: 3.2

As the name implies, **quad-channel mode** supports four identical memory modules into the designated quad-channel slots. Again, the speed is greatly increased, but is not necessarily four times faster. Figure 6-16 shows two different quad-channel mode arrangements. In Figure 6-16A, four 2-GB DIMMs are arranged in quad-channel mode for a total of 8 GB. In Figure 6-16B, eight 2-GB DIMMs are arranged in quad-channel mode for a total of 16 GB of RAM.

A quad-channel motherboard can also be configured for the triple-channel, dual-channel, and single-channel modes of operation. Quad-channel is not yet common in PC systems, except for in some high-performance systems, such as network servers. These systems often contain large amounts of memory to perform better while being accessed by multiple clients.

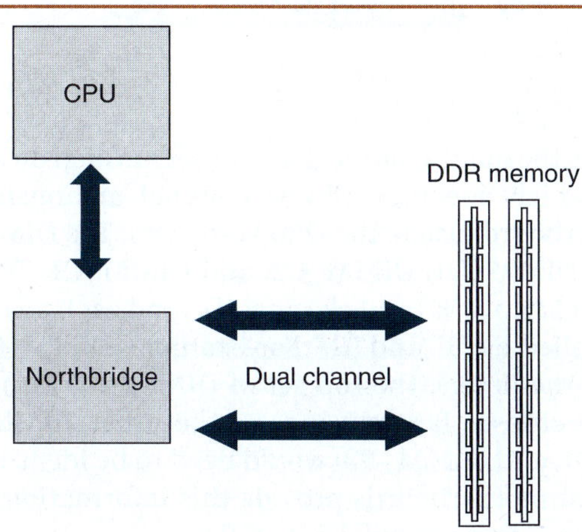

Goodheart-Willcox Publisher

Figure 6-14 The Intel dual-channel DDR memory motherboard architecture significantly increases the data throughput from the RAM to the northbridge.

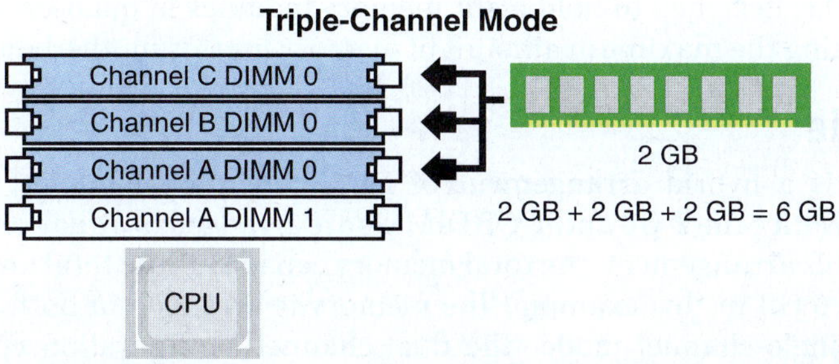

Goodheart-Willcox Publisher

Figure 6-15 Triple-channel mode is interleaved in the same way as dual-channel mode, only triple-channel mode uses three channels to support memory access.

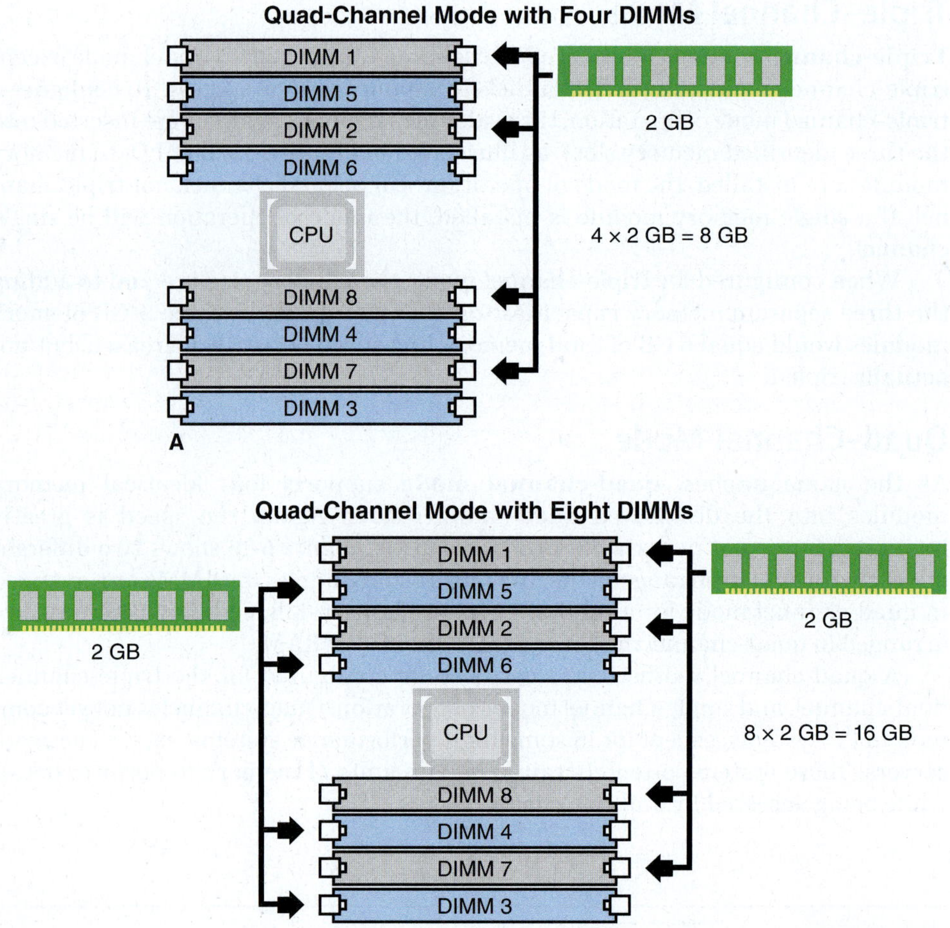

Figure 6-16 Quad-channel mode supports four identical memory modules in designated quad-channel slots.

Goodheart-Willcox Publisher

Figure 6-17 shows the quad-channel locations identified on an ASUS Sabertooth X79 motherboard, which specifies DIMM channel arrangements through text printed on the motherboard beside the DIMM sockets. The DIMM sockets are identified as DIMM_D2, DIMM_D1, DIMM_C2, and DIMM_C1. This means the channels are identified as channel "C" and channel "D," and each channel consists of two DIMM sockets identified as "1" and "2." For example, DIMM_C1 identifies DIMM channel C, slot 1. In the image, the top set of DIMM slot identification markings are obscured by the chipset fan housing, so the other DIMM slots (DIMM_A1, DIMM_A2, DIMM_B1, and DIMM_B2) would need to be identified using the motherboard manual. Most motherboards provide this information, but the location of the printed circuit board imprint will likely differ.

Memory slot pairs are also identified with color. For the motherboard shown in Figure 6-17, the pairs are identified with the colors brown and tan. This particular motherboard is designed to hold eight memory modules in quad-channel configuration, meaning the maximum amount of memory for this motherboard is 64 GB.

Flex Mode

Flex mode is a hybrid arrangement of DIMM memory modules, as shown in Figure 6-18. Notice the 2-GB and 4-GB DIMMs are arranged in a dual-channel configuration. In this arrangement, the total memory capacity is the total amount of RAM installed, or 6 GB in this example. The memory is arranged in both dual-channel mode and single-channel mode. The dual-channel configuration consists of the single 2-GB memory module and the first 2 GB of the 4-GB module. The remaining 2 GB of the 4-GB module operate in single-channel mode. In other words, this example is operating in dual-channel and single-channel mode at the same time.

To understand how the speed is increased by the various modes of operation, look at Figure 6-19. Notice that the bandwidth for single-channel operation is 64 bits wide, meaning there are 64 separate paths to and from the memory controller and the processor. As the channel number increases, so does the number of paths. For example, when dual-channel mode is configured, the number of paths is doubled from 64 to 128. In triple-channel mode, the bandwidth is tripled, and in quad-channel mode, the bandwidth is quadrupled.

Goodheart-Willcox Publisher

Figure 6-17 The quad-channel memory location identification labels are in close proximity to the DIMM slots, and the slots are color-coded to help identify the different channel pairs.

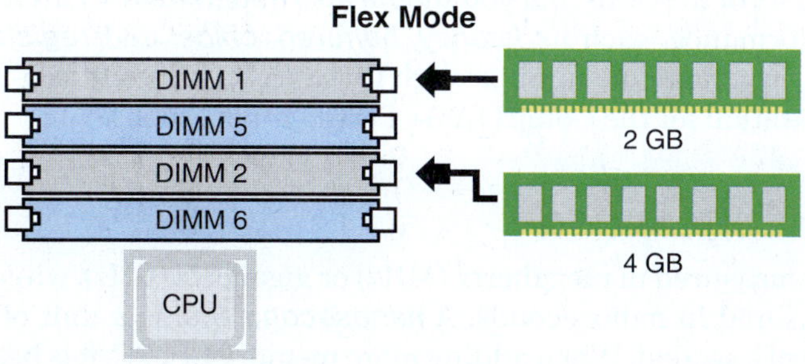

Goodheart-Willcox Publisher

Figure 6-18 In a flex-mode DIMM configuration, the 2-GB module and 2 GB of the 4-GB module operate in dual-channel mode. The remaining 2 GB from the 4-GB module operate in single-channel mode.

Operational Mode Bandwidths

Channels	Bandwidth in Bits
Single	64
Double	128
Triple	192
Quad	256

Goodheart-Willcox Publisher

Figure 6-19 Bandwidth for single-channel operation is 64 bits wide. As the channel number increases, so does the number of paths.

The speed of data transfer is theoretical, meaning it is not actually doubled, tripled, or quadrupled. In actual application, factors such as computer hardware and software reduce the speed from the theoretical speed to actual speed. For example, data is not transferred continuously with every beat of the processor frequency. The processor does not strictly communicate with the DIMM; it communicates with all the devices in the computer system. Data transferred to and from the processor and memory is held in cache for an undetermined amount of time, which also reduces the theoretical transfer rate of the memory read or write operation.

Memory Overclocking

Just as some processors can be overclocked to increase performance, so can some types of memory. Some memory modules have two speed ratings: standard and maximum. The *standard memory frequency* is the speed at which the memory is designed to be used. The *maximum speed* is the maximum speed for which the memory has been tested in actual applications and typically requires additional cooling just as overclocked processors require additional cooling. Cooling devices are available, such as fans that attach to the memory modules and eliminate excessive heat. When memory is normally installed in a computer system, it is automatically detected and configured for the standard speed. However, to maximize memory throughput, you need to configure the memory speed manually and ensure adequate cooling is installed to handle the extra heat. This process is not usually needed any more given the advances in memory technology.

6.5 Matching RAM Characteristics

When adding or replacing RAM modules, it is important that certain characteristics of the modules are matched. Important characteristics of RAM to consider when adding or replacing modules include memory chip speed, latency, buffering, prefetch buffers, registered memory, data integrity, and whether RAM is single or double sided. The two most important characteristics of RAM chips are the speed and the integrity of the chips, but you should also understand terms used to describe memory performance, such as *latency*, *buffered chips*, and *registered memory*. Additionally, you should be familiar with these terms not only as a technician, but also for preparation for the CompTIA A+ Certification Exams.

Memory Chip Speed

CPU speed is measured in megahertz (MHz) or gigahertz (GHz), while memory chip speed is measured in nanoseconds. A *nanosecond (ns)* is a unit of time equal to one-billionth of a second. When adding more memory to a PC, it is best to match the speed of the existing memory chips. If faster memory chips are added to an existing slower memory chip bank, the faster chips will run at the same speed as the existing chips. The chips will run successfully, but they are unlikely to be cost-effective since they will run at a slower speed. While faster RAM will slow down to run on a computer with a slower bus speed, RAM modules with a speed slower than that of the motherboard bus will not run at all.

Another consideration is the maximum speed the motherboard system bus and chipsets can support. You must check the PC, chipset, and BIOS documentation before attempting to upgrade RAM, especially if the PC you are attempting to upgrade is several years old.

Latency

To understand latency, you must first understand how computers locate and transfer data stored in memory locations. The RAM can be thought of as a matrix of storage bins, with each bin containing a bit of information in a binary format. Each location corresponds to a specific column and row identification, as illustrated in Figure 6-20.

Reading or writing to a memory location takes time. The time required to complete a memory read or write operation is measured in *clock signals*, which occur when the voltage level switches between high and low. There are two main and several minor measurements of read-write access. The two main measurements are RAS and CAS.

Row address selection (RAS) describes the time it takes to start a memory read or to write the row location in the memory matrix. RAS is the first step of a memory access operation and is followed by CAS.

Column address selection (CAS), also called *column address strobe*, is a term that describes the time it takes to access the exact column location in the memory matrix after RAS. There is a minimum amount of time the CAS must remain active to complete the read operation. For example, a *CAS 3* means that three clock signals will occur before the CAS can complete the read of the memory location.

CAS is considered by most experts as the most important number when expressing latency. You will find that in most cases, CAS is the primary latency measurement. In other words, when a publication or review states that a memory module's latency is five, they are generally basing the latency measure on the CAS.

Other latency measures are used when memory latency is expressed as a series of numbers. For example, it may be expressed as 3-3-3-5, which represent tCL, tRCD, tRP, and tRAS, respectively. Figure 6-21 describes each term.

Tech Tip

Be aware that most computers will develop memory errors if the latency of the memory modules paired does not match. This is an important consideration for memory upgrades or replacements.

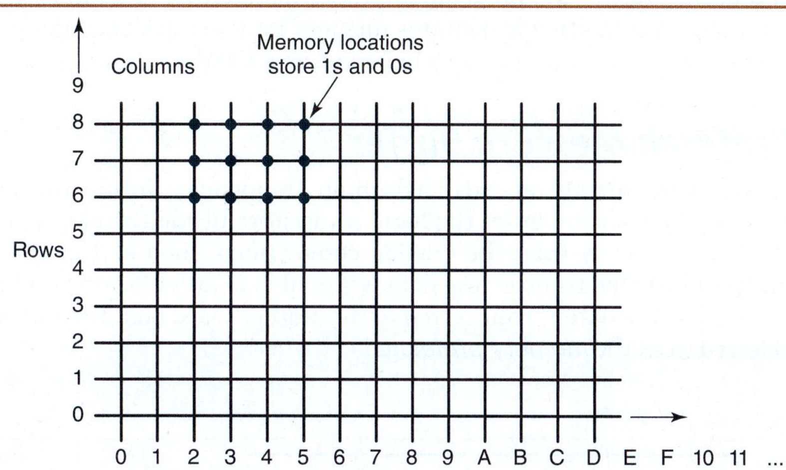

Goodheart-Willcox Publisher

Figure 6-20 Each memory location corresponds to a specific column and row identification.

Additional Latency Measurements

Term	Description
tCL	Equal to CAS
tRCD	The amount of delay between the RAS and CAS
tRP	How long it takes to precharge the RAS
tRAS	The delay to precharge the RAS

Goodheart-Willcox Publisher

Figure 6-21 In addition to RAS and CAS, latency measurements can be based off the tCL, tRCD, tRP, or tRAS.

In general, the lower the number used to describe the latency, the better the performance. There is an exception to this rule, however. You must compare latency between similar DDR technologies for a fair comparison because as frequencies rise, memory latency also rises. For example, latency measurements for each generation of DDR are as follows:

- DDR1 has latencies in the range of 1.5 to 3.
- DDR2 has latency range from 2 to 5.
- DDR3 has latency from 9 to 11.
- DDR4 has latency from 13 to 22.
- DDR5 has latency of approximately 40.

While DDR5 has the largest latency number compared to earlier DDR models, it provides much better system performance. If you double the memory frequency, you will of course double the latency.

Buffered Chips

The term *buffer*, in relationship to a PC, can be likened to a temporary waiting or holding area. A **buffer** is used to store data temporarily before transferring it to a device. Remember that there are several different bus systems on the computer motherboard, and all of them are running at different speeds. In addition, many of the devices attached to the computer have speeds much slower than memory chips. For this reason, fast memory requires buffering when exchanging data with other components in the PC.

The buffer area can be provided in the motherboard chipset or as an additional chip on the memory module. DIMM memory modules have specific notch patterns that match the memory-module slots on the motherboard as a form of mistake-proofing. This design prevents improper installation of a buffered DIMM into a motherboard that already contains memory buffer chips. See Figure 6-22 to view a drawing of the variance in notch locations on a DIMM.

DDR Prefetch Memory Buffer

Memory chips can operate at extremely high frequencies inside the memory chip structure. The frequencies of the logic transistors inside the chip operate at a much higher frequency than the outside connections, such as the FSB or the HyperTransport bus. The transferring data is stored in a buffer located on the chip. At the proper time, the data is transferred to the motherboard bus. This entire operation is referred to as the *memory prefetch*.

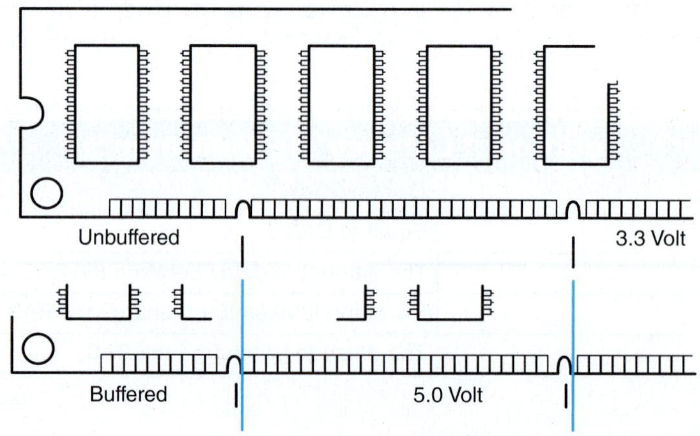

Figure 6-22 Buffering and voltage can be identified by the position of the notch at the bottom of the DIMM. This is how manufacturers ensure the correct type of DIMM is installed on the motherboard when replacing or upgrading memory modules.

Goodheart-Willcox Publisher

The term *prefetch* is followed by the lowercase letter *n* and a number that represents the number of data bits as a power of two. For example, DDR1 has a prefetch 2n, which means it can store 2 bits of data in each prefetch buffer. DDR2 uses a prefetch 4n, or 4-bit buffer, thus doubling the amount of data transferred from the buffer as compared to DDR1. DDR3 uses a prefetch 8n, double the size of the prefetch used in DDR2. Look at Figure 6-23 and compare the prefetch buffer, voltage level, and FSB data rates of DDR1, DDR2, DDR3, DDR4, and DDR5. Note that the power of two concept does *not* hold for DDR4. Increasing the size of the prefetch buffer and the memory bus operational frequency allows each generation of DDR to increase the overall throughput. Additionally, the prefetch buffer size for DDR4 could theoretically increase to 16 bits if that standard is revised.

Registered Memory

Registered memory, sometimes referred to as *buffered memory*, is a memory module that incorporates a registry chip to drive and synchronize the memory without depending on the motherboard. Typical motherboards incorporate chipsets with functions to drive and synchronize the memory units with the motherboard bus systems. Some computer systems incorporate a memory register or buffer on the motherboard. The important thing to remember is that registered and nonregistered memory modules *cannot* be mixed. Registered memory is not typically found on standard PCs but is commonly encountered on high-end PCs and network servers. Additionally, registered memory often consumes time, which is another reason you will likely find it on servers, where data integrity is a priority.

Memory Data Integrity

Data can become corrupted while waiting in memory, often due to electrical voltage leaking from the memory module, electrical interference, power surges, and electrostatic discharges. Even weather phenomena such as cosmic rays and solar flares can corrupt data. Think for a moment about a 16-MB SIMM memory module. It is composed of 128 million memory cells, so there is always a possibility for the transmission of corrupted data. Corrupt data processed through the RAM can result in mathematical computation errors as well as program run errors that can cause a computer system to lock up. There are two common methods for checking the integrity of data transferred in and out of memory: parity and error-correction code.

Parity

As you have learned, all data transmitted through a PC system consists of ones and zeros together in groups of eight called bytes. **Parity** is simply the counting of either odd or even bits of the bytes transmitted. To understand the role of parity, we must first look at how memory is constructed. A memory chip consists of millions of tiny

DDR Buffers, Voltages, and Data Rates			
DDR Type	**Prefetch Buffer**	**Voltage Level**	**Data Rates (in MHz)**
DDR1	2 bits	2.5 V	200, 266, 333, 400
DDR2	4 bits	1.8 V	400, 533, 677, 800
DDR3	8 bits	1.5 V	800, 1,066, 1,330, 1,600
DDR4	8 bits	1.2 V	1,600, 2,133, 2,400, 2,667
DDR5	16 bits	1.1 V	4,400, 4,800, 5,200, 5,600, 6,000, 6,400, 6,800, 7,200, 7,600

Goodheart-Willcox Publisher

Figure 6-23 Increasing the size of the prefetch buffer and the memory bus operational frequency allows each generation of DDR to increase the overall throughput.

cells that store data, and each cell contains either a one or zero. The ones and zeros represent the state of electrical charge in the cell. Typically, a 5-volt electrical charge represents a one, while no electrical charge represents a zero. The cells within a memory chip are grouped together in sets of eight cells totaling one byte.

When memory chips and data transfer techniques were first developed, they were not as reliable as they are today. Out of the millions of cells designed in the memory module, a few of the individual cells might be flawed, and as a result, they tend to lose their electrical charge, or *leak*. If a single cell changes its charge state from 5 volts to 0 volts while it is stored, then the data it represents also changes. For example, the stored binary number 00001010 represents the decimal number 10. If one cell loses its charge, the binary format of the data could look like 00000010, which now represents the decimal number 2. As a result, the data stored also changes from decimal 10 to decimal 2. Data stored in a changing byte is not limited to data that represents numbers. The stored byte could represent letters, sound, part of an illustration, or even a program command.

Data can also change while being transferred from one module to another. Remember that data is processed through a PC. The information could be loaded from a disk to the memory and then moved to the CPU to be manipulated and then routed simultaneously to the screen and to RAM. While the data is transferred around the PC system, any of the bits that form a complete byte could be changed by outside electrical interference or by a slightly defective part such as a circuit board trace that is starting to fail.

Parity was developed to ensure data received by RAM and transferred to other parts is still valid. Instead of just the usual eight bits being stored to represent one byte, an additional bit, called a *parity bit*, was added to make a total of nine bits.

The parity bit reflects the number of ones and zeros contained in the data byte. For example, assume the number of ones being transmitted to or from the memory is counted. Based on the number of bits counted, the parity bit will be either even or odd. **Odd parity checking** is a mode of parity checking in which a parity bit is included whenever a transmission contains an odd number of bits. **Even parity checking** is a parity checking mode in which an extra bit is included whenever there is an even number of bits in the byte being transmitted. See Figure 6-24 for additional explanation. Parity checking is not solely limited to memory; it is also used for transmitting data across telephone and network lines.

The only problem with a parity check using this method is it assumes that only one bit will change. If two bits change, the parity will not change, and the error will go undetected. In other words, parity is a "weak" correctness check.

SIMMs usually contain eight chips to store memory and a ninth chip to check parity. The only way to be certain if a memory module uses fake parity checking or not is to check the part number, followed by research. All information needed about the chip is usually listed on the company website.

Figure 6-24 For odd parity checking, a parity bit of one is generated whenever the number of ones in a byte is odd. In even parity checking, a parity bit of one is generated whenever the number of ones in a byte is even.

Odd Parity Checking

Data bit value is odd	Parity bit is added
1 0 0 0 1 0 1 0	1
Data bit value is even	No parity bit is added
1 0 1 0 1 1 1 1	0

Even Parity Checking

Data bit value is odd	No parity bit is added
1 0 0 0 1 0 1 0	0
Data bit value is even	Parity bit is added
1 0 1 0 1 1 1 1	1

Goodheart-Willcox Publisher

Error-Correction Code

1101: 3.2 A+

Another form of checking the integrity of data is an error-correction code. An **error-correction code (ECC)** not only checks for, but also corrects, most errors. Parity checking simply generates an error code, which displays on the screen and stops the program. An error-correction code requires an additional chip designed especially for this type of error checking and correcting. ECC cannot correct all errors, only the usual corrupt single bit. If multiple bits are corrupt, the ECC chip cannot correct the data. ECC is not often found in desktop PCs. It is usually only found in high-end computers such as servers.

Single-Sided and Double-Sided

According to Intel, double-sided memory modules contain two rows of SDRAM, and single-sided memory modules contain one row of SDRAM. Single-sided memory modules are identified as *SS*, while double-sided modules are identified as *DS*. This memory designation is unique to Intel motherboards.

Single-sided and double-sided memory is often referred to as *ranked modules*. Single-sided memory refers to modules with chips on one side of the printed circuit board, and double-sided memory refers to modules with chips on both sides of the circuit board. Most Intel motherboards work with either single-sided or double-sided memory modules. However, you must consult the motherboard manual or manufacturer's website to verify the type of memory module that is compatible with a particular motherboard.

Tech Tip

Always check the motherboard documentation for the memory type that is compatible with the motherboard and motherboard chipset.

6.6 Flash Memory Devices

1101: 3.3 A+

Flash memory is a solid-state, reusable data storage device that can retain data even when the electrical power is disconnected. It is derived from EEPROM technology, taking advantage of the EEPROM's ability to be programmed and reprogrammed. However, unlike the original EEPROM, flash memory originally only stored data, not computer programs. Current flash devices can run portable software and software installation files. Like the EEPROM, flash memory does not require a power source to retain data, which results in significantly reduced size and weight.

Flash memory devices are often referred to as hot-swappable, meaning they plug into or unplug from a computer system while the computer is running. This is especially convenient in a situation that requires multiple devices or drives. A technicians can simply unplug or switch from one device from another without having to shut down the computer.

Some typical devices that use flash memory technology are miniature data drives, global positioning system (GPS) devices, digital cameras, smartphones, electronic instruments, MP3 players, and personal computer systems. Note that the discussion of flash memory in this chapter is limited directly to computer memory and storage applications even though there are numerous other applications of flash memory.

USB Flash Drives

USB flash drives, such as the one shown in Figure 6-25, are reusable storage systems that connect to the computer system via a USB port. The electrical power for energizing the USB flash drive is delivered by the USB port, so there is no need for an external power supply. A typical flash drive is constructed from EEPROM chips. Data is flashed to the EEPROM chip similarly to how BIOS chips are flashed. There are many different names used for the EEPROM memory devices such as pen drives, jump drives, micro drives, thumb drives, micro vaults, stick drives, and more. In this textbook, the term *USB flash drive* is used.

A+ Note

You may be asked to identify types of boot media that can be used to contain an operating system and boot a PC. Remember that a flash drive, CD, or DVD can be used as bootable media.

After data is transferred to the USB flash drive, the drive can be removed from the system while still retaining the data for a long time. The data on the USB flash drive can also be transferred to another computer or to a similar device. The USB flash drive can have additional data added to it or it can be completely erased like most other storage media.

At the time of this writing, USB flash drives range from a modest 16 GB up to 1 TB. For perspective, a 16-GB USB flash drive stores an incredible amount of data for such a compact device. This is the same storage capacity as approximately twenty-four standard 650 CD-RW discs or approximately four 4.7-GB DVDs. In terms of size, USB flash drives compete with traditional hard drives and have already replaced compact discs for most storage applications. The main advantage of the USB flash drive is it has no moving parts to wear out or misalign since the entire system is designed from integrated chip technology.

When connected to a computer system through the USB port, the USB flash drive is recognized as a removable hard drive, as shown in Figure 6-26. The USB flash drive is listed beneath **Devices and drives** and is identified as **USB20FD (D:)**.

The operating system automatically detects and configures a USB flash drive when it is inserted into the computer system's USB port. As a precaution, the USB flash drive should be deactivated, or *ejected,* before removing it from the port. This is especially true while data is being transferred to or from the USB flash drive. Figure 6-27 shows a Windows 10 **Safely Remove Hardware and Eject Media** dialog box.

The **Safely Remove Hardware and Eject Media** dialog box identifies the USB flash drive as a USB 2.0 FD with the appropriate reference letter. The user simply clicks the device name and then proceeds to unplug the USB flash drive from the port after receiving notification. Many users simply unplug the USB flash drive, unaware of the possible damage that could occur to the drive because the write buffers have not yet been flushed. It is always recommended to disable a USB drive before disconnecting it.

Figure 6-25 USB flash drives are reusable storage systems that connect to the computer system via a USB port.

SpelaG91/Shutterstock.com

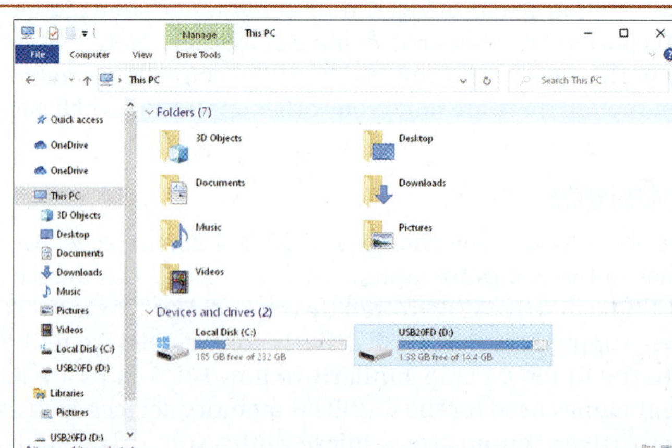

Figure 6-26 Removable storage devices, such as USB flash drives, are automatically detected when inserted into the computer system's USB port and are listed under the Devices and drives heading of **This PC**.

Goodheart-Willcox Publisher

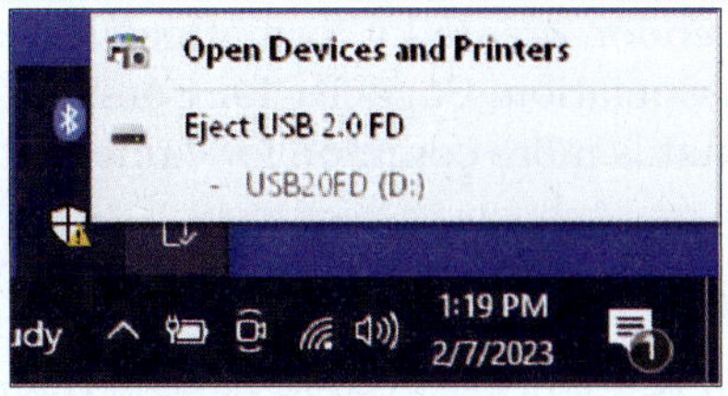

Goodheart-Willcox Publisher

Figure 6-27 The USB flash drive, as with any other removable computer device, should first be stopped with the **Safely Remove Hardware and Eject Media** function.

Flash Memory Cards

A+ 1101: 3.3

Flash memory cards hold text, image, and sound data. Flash memory technology has been incorporated into many digital systems, such as music players, laptop computers, smartphones, electronic test equipment, MP3 players, and video recorders. Some cards, such as the now-obsolete xD Picture Cards, were designed to be used solely in digital imaging equipment, while others are designed especially for security systems. Cards designed for security systems contain user passwords required to log on to the computer system, and they support data encryption.

Flash memory cards go by many different names, such as SmartMedia, CompactFlash, MultiMediaCard, Memory Stick, Secure Digital, and SDXC. The names vary because of the individual competing companies who developed and marketed the flash memory cards. Although they are all designed on the same principles of flash memory technology, they differ in their overall physical design, electrical characteristics, and software system requirements for reading and writing to the media. Because they have different attributes, you must either match the card type to a particular reader or use one of the readers that supports multiple card formats.

The Secure Digital (SD) card is a form of nonvolatile memory and is classified by both physical and memory size. The following physical designations adhere to the standard set by the SD Card Association:

- SD: 32 mm × 24 mm
- MiniSD: 21.5 mm × 20 mm
- MicroSD: 11 mm × 15 mm

MicroSD cards are often sold with a full-sized SD carrier. The user slides the microSD into the carrier for use with computers that only have SD ports. The memory designations, which come after the size designations, are as follows:

- SD (no extension): Less than 2 GB, although a few go up to 4 GB
- HC: Greater than 2 GB to 32 GB
- XC: Greater than 32 GB to 2 TB
- UC: Greater than 2 TB to 128 TB

In addition to physical and memory sizes, the cards also have different transfer rates:

- Standard bus: 12.5 megabytes/second
- High-speed bus: 25 megabytes/second
- UHS – I bus: 50 to 104 megabytes/second
- UHS – II bus: 156 to 312 megabytes/second
- UHS – III bus: 312 to 624 megabytes/second
- SD Express: 985 megabytes/second

All the designations expressed so far are based on the SD Association standards. Vendors may add other designations, such as "Class 10" that generally apply to SDHC cards. The minimum speeds for these designations are as follows:

- Class 2: 2 MB/s
- Class 4: 4 MB/s
- Class 6: 6 MB/s
- Class 8: 8 MB/s
- Class 10: 10 MB/s

SanDisk, a well-known vendor, created a format called CompactFlash, which has its own CompactFlash Association. Capacity for CompactFlash cards ranges from 2 MB to 512 GB. This format is more common for cameras than computers.

Solid-State Drives

A ***solid-state drive (SSD)*** is a storage system designed with no moving parts and that consists entirely of DRAM chips. You may recall from Chapter 1 that instead of disks and platters, SSDs store data in nonvolatile memory chips. The SSD is also referred to as a ***RAM drive***. The SSD is very advantageous to laptop designs because it requires less electrical power, is much lighter than mechanical drives, boots faster, and does not generate noise the way mechanical drives do. It is also not as easily damaged as mechanical drives when dropped, nor does it experience mechanical shock.

SSDs were originally designed mainly for laptops and other forms of portable equipment. The cost to produce SSD drives has dropped, and they are now more common on desktop models of computers, often supported by a separate traditional spinning hard drive. There will be more information about SSDs in later chapters.

6.7 Memory Map Structure and Development

Memory mapping is no longer covered on the CompTIA A+ Certification Exams. However, this section will provide you with a more detailed understanding of how memory works. ***Memory map structure*** is a description of the way memory is allocated in the PC. Due to the issue of backward compatibility in the PC industry, the development of the memory structure has become complex and confusing. The desire for the latest computer system to be compatible with ancient 8-bit system technology has created the evolution of a difficult memory structure. There have been many different software attempts to overcome these structural limitations.

The terminology of memory structure dates back to the original PC and the oldest DOS operating system. The early PC could theoretically only access 640 kB of memory (1,024,000 bytes) using segmented memory access, a peculiarity of Intel

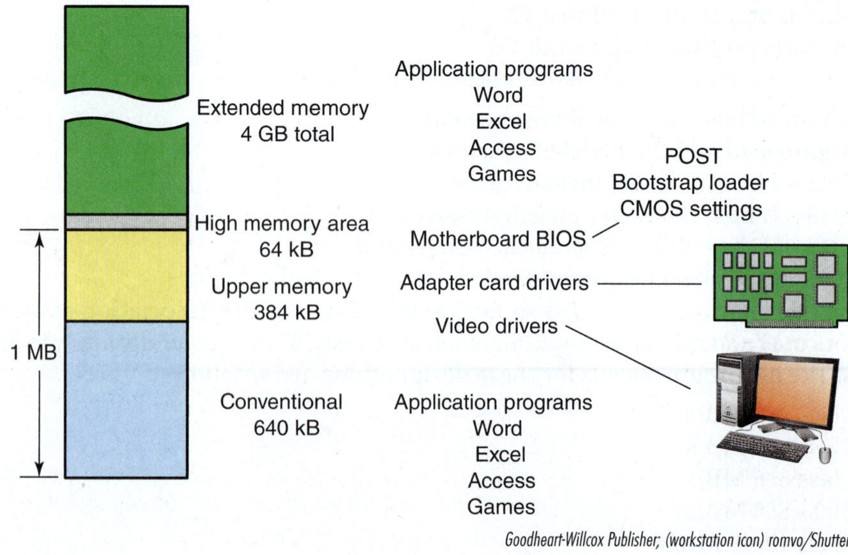

Figure 6-28 Each layer of memory deals with specific programs, or functions.

Goodheart-Willcox Publisher; (workstation icon) romvo/Shutterstock.com

processors of the 1980s. The restrictions to less than 1 MB of memory are DOS and Windows 3.x restrictions and do not apply to Windows 95 or later operating systems. Windows 95 and later follow the DOS memory pattern *only* when dealing with legacy cards or 16-bit software programs. Windows NT and later are not affected at all by the DOS memory structure since these operating systems handle individual memory areas as one big block. The block of allocated static memory is referred to as the **stack**, and the block of allocated dynamic memory is referred to as the **heap**. The memory is then portioned out as needed. The only exception is during the POST when using a BIOS type of firmware. The BIOS limits access of memory to the first 1 MB of RAM. For further clarity, it is important to consider how the memory system structure was designed and labeled.

Conventional Memory

Examine Figure 6-32. This illustration diagrams the relation of the various areas in RAM and how they developed. **Conventional memory** is a term given to the first 640 kB of memory. Note the memory structure illustrated in Figure 6-28, which shows the layout of conventional, upper, high, and extended memory. The original PC was limited to 1 MB (1,024 kB) of RAM. This first memory was originally divided in half (512 kB each) with segments of 64 kB each, although the theoretical 1 MB could be available, as shown in Figure 6-29A. After the original PC was on the market for a short time, the memory system was redesigned into parts that were no longer equal. The bottom part was given 640 kB and was called *conventional memory*, and the top part was given 384 kB and called *upper memory*, or *reserved memory*. This division of the first 1 MB of memory into two unequal parts—conventional (640 kB) and reserved (384 kB)—became the industry standard for computers with Intel-based processors, as showin in Figure 6-29B.

Conventional memory was where application programs were loaded. The reserve memory was allocated for use by the video system, expansion cards, and BIOS. The reserved memory is dedicated (or reserved) for hardware drivers and cannot be used by application programs. For many years, conventional memory (640 kB) was referred to as the *memory barrier* because early computer programmers were required to write programs that could fit into the 640 kB space of conventional memory.

The term *conventional memory* is still in use, but 32-bit operating systems of newer models easily work around the 640 kB barrier. Programs, as well as drivers, can be loaded into memory well beyond the first 1 MB. Of course, 64-bit operating systems go beyond this limitation.

The lowest 64 kB could be used to run small executable files with an extension of **.com**. These files could only use data and code in that segment of memory.

Upper Memory Area (Reserved Memory)

The **upper memory area (UMA)**, or *reserved memory*, is the 384 kB of memory remaining after the first 640 kB of conventional memory, as shown in Figure 6-29B. The term *reserved* means that only the PC system software drivers used to run and interface with the system hardware components can be loaded into this area. The reserved memory cannot be used for application software such as word-processor programs, gaming, or other software.

The upper memory is divided into sections that are determined by their function. The first part of the UMA (128 kB) is used for the video system, meaning information about the computer monitor is stored in this area. The next part of the UMA (128 kB) is used for adapter boards mounted in slots on the motherboard, such as modem or network cards. VGA adapter cards sometimes utilize the first 32 kB of this area of memory. The last part of the UMA (128 kB) is used for the motherboard BIOS, CMOS settings, POST program, and bootstrap program.

Figure 6-29 As RAM has evolved, so has its usage.

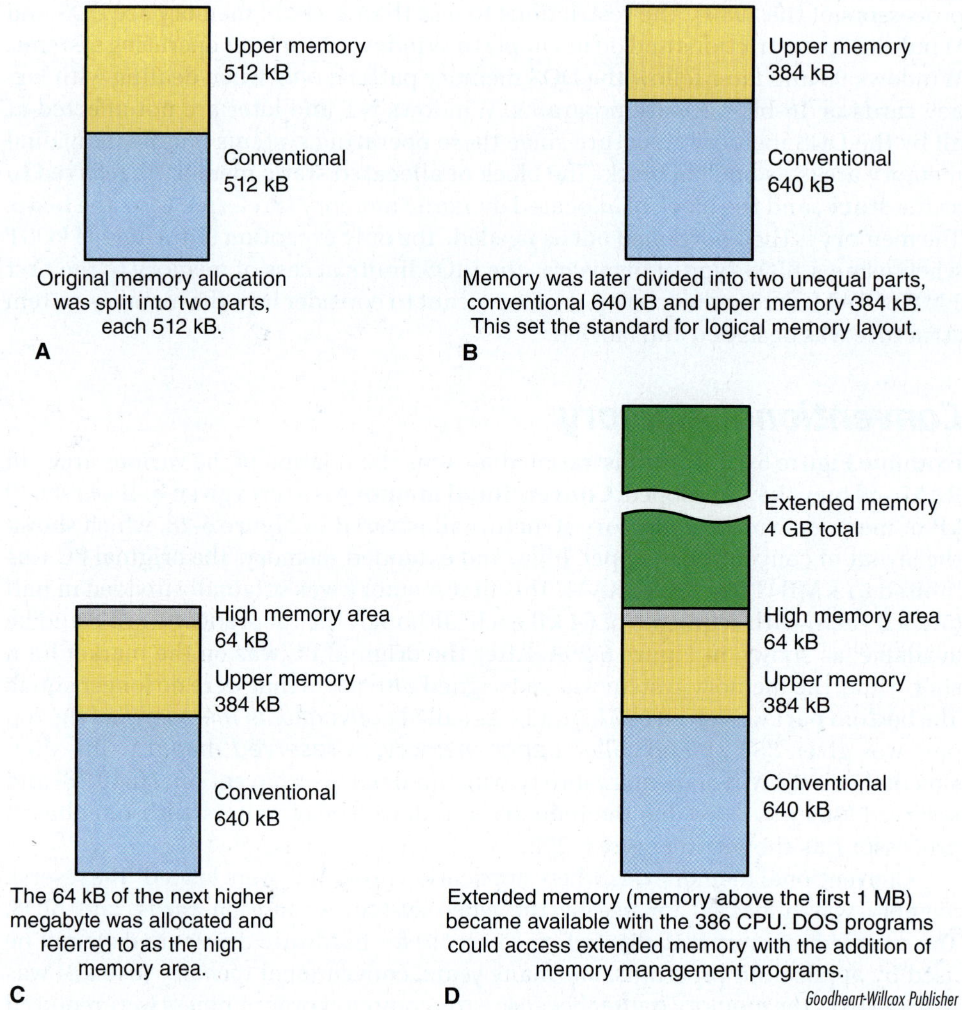

Many types of device drivers are also loaded into the UMA. A section of UMA can also be occupied by a memory manager program, which permits certain programs to use memory beyond the 1 MB barrier. Again, modern operating systems have no problem accessing RAM beyond the first 1 MB. This was a restriction of earlier operating systems.

High Memory Area

It is easy to confuse a high memory area with upper memory. The **high memory area (HMA)** is the first 64 kB of the extended memory area, as shown in Figure 6-29C. In truth, it is 16 bytes short of a full 64 kB.

This area was first discovered as a design flaw in the memory-access data lines, but it soon became the standard method to gain more conventional memory space. Conventional memory holds not only application programs, but also basic DOS files needed to operate the PC, such as the kernel. The DOS kernel file is approximately 45 kB in size. Transferring a DOS kernel to the high memory area releases 45 kB of conventional memory space for use by application programs. To use the HMA, the line DOS=HIGH is added to the **config.sys** file.

In DOS 5.0 and later versions, the DOS=HIGH syntax loads the DOS program kernel into the high memory area. The high memory area can also be used to store a software driver instead of the DOS kernel, but note that only one program can be stored in the high memory area.

Expanded Memory

Expanded memory was an early method to move past the 1 MB memory barrier. **Expanded memory standard (EMS)** was designed to increase the amount of data memory available for applications. An expanded memory adapter board loaded with memory chips was inserted into a motherboard expansion slot. Unlike RAM, the expanded memory adapter board was not accessed directly by the CPU, but rather by a software-driver program, which was loaded into reserved memory. The software-driver program transferred data to and from the memory adapter board to the 64-kB EMS window established in upper memory. See Figure 6-30 for a memory map illustrating the 64-kB EMS window and expanded memory available on the expanded memory adapter board. The transfer rate of data with EMS is extremely slow because it is limited to the speed of the motherboard bus slot. Due to this, EMS is obsolete, and the memory boards are no longer manufactured.

Extended Memory

Shown in Figure 6-29D, the **extended memory system (XMS)** includes all of the PC's memory beyond the first 1 MB when the CPU is running in real mode. As operating systems evolved over time, the CPU was designed to access more memory than the early predecessors did. Today, a 32-bit operating system can access 4 GB of RAM. A 64-bit operating system can theoretically access 16 TB (terabytes) of RAM. However, the 64-bit upper memory access limit is not realistic at this time as no hardware is designed to allow for 16 TB of memory. A more realistic maximum RAM value of 8 GB to 128 GB can be expected for desktops.

Real Mode, Protected Mode, and Safe Mode

The terms *real mode* and *protected mode* are used by programmers to describe the boundaries of memory as related to programming code and structure of memory. *Real mode* is designed on the DOS system of memory access in which only the first 1 MB of RAM can be accessed. *Protected mode* includes all of real mode plus extended memory. Multitasking can only occur in protected mode or when more than the first 1 MB is accessed by the system. The limitations of protected mode also depend on the firmware installed. The BIOS typically follows the DOS guidelines and limits access to the first 1 MB of RAM. UEFI can exceed the 1-MB limit during the POST.

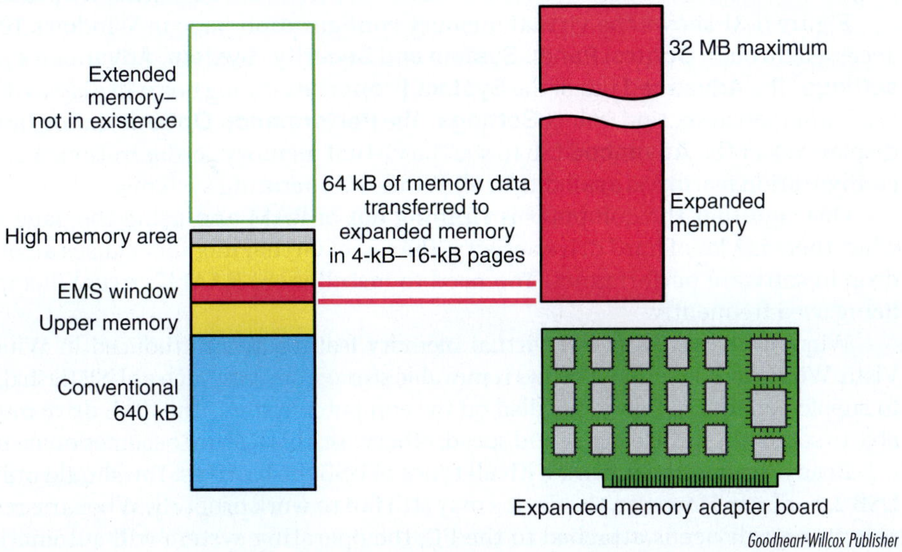

Figure 6-30 Expanded memory is provided by a memory adapter board inserted into a motherboard expansion slot. A small EMS window is set up in the upper memory area and transfers data to and from the expanded memory in increments of 4 kB to 16 kB pages of data, totaling 64 kB.

The term *Safe Mode* is used by technicians to describe starting the computer in protected mode. Usually, Safe Mode is accessed in Windows by pressing the [F8] key during the startup or boot operation for all Windows operating system versions. Today's computer systems boot very fast, and it is almost impossible to press the [F8] key at the exact time between the POST finishing and the operating system loading. The best way to enter Safe Mode is to repeatedly press [F8] during the boot operation, starting during the POST and continuing until the **Advanced Boot Options** menu appears. You should research the Safe Mode access key for your specific system, as the access methods and functionality can vary from one system to another.

Putting Windows 10 into Safe Mode can be a great deal more complicated and difficult. The combination of the Windows 10 operating system and more modern computers has greatly increased the boot speed. There is an extremely short period of time between the POST and the loading of the operating system. Thus, it can be difficult to access Safe Mode. To access Windows 10 Safe Mode, press and hold the [Shift] key while quickly tapping the [F8] key. You also have an option to hold down the [Shift] key while rebooting the computer.

Windows 10 is designed to detect errors during the boot process and then present a screen with an option to go into Safe Mode when an error is automatically detected. There is also an option to start the computer in Safe Mode automatically. This will be covered in detail in a later chapter.

Starting Windows in Safe Mode is a very common troubleshooting technique. Safe Mode loads only minimal drivers and limits the memory access to the first 1 MB of RAM, thus eliminating any problems caused by 32-bit or 64-bit drivers and software applications. If the computer successfully starts in Safe Mode, then it is a good indication that the problem is software related rather than hardware based. Many troubleshooting features are available while in Safe Mode, often including the ability to run antimalware software.

A+ 1101: 3.2

6.8 Virtual Memory

Virtual memory is memory that supplements physical RAM. Virtual memory is located in a reserved portion of a hard disk referred to as a **page file**, sometimes called a *swap file*, which is divided into units called *pages*. RAM is used to hold data content as well as the software application, and if data or sections of an application program are not accessed for a period of time, then the data or application section is transferred to virtual memory as a page of information. The transfer to the page file is called *paging* or *swapping*. When needed, the data is transferred back to RAM from the hard drive page file.

Figure 6-31 shows the virtual memory configuration page in Windows 10. It is accessed through **Control Panel**>**System and Security**>**System**>**Advanced system settings**. The **Advanced** tab of the **System Properties** dialog box will display. Under the Performance section, select **Settings**. The **Performance Options** dialog box will display. Select the **Advanced** tab to see the virtual memory configuration. A similar configuration feature is available in all Windows operating systems.

One sign that the computer is running out of RAM and using the page file is when there is a lot of hard drive activity. The use of virtual memory causes an overall drop in software performance. You need to install more RAM if virtual memory is being used frequently.

Windows ReadyBoost is a virtual memory feature first introduced in Windows Vista. Windows ReadyBoost allows removable storage devices, such as USB flash drives, to supplement the memory installed on the computer system. The flash drive must be able to support a sufficient size and speed; otherwise, this feature becomes unavailable.

ReadyBoost will not work with all types of USB flash drives. You should only use USB 2.0 or later. However, the device may still fail to work properly. When the removable storage device is attached to the PC, the operating system will automatically detect it and display a menu option for ReadyBoost. The option **Speed up my system using Windows ReadyBoost** is located at the bottom of the **AutoPlay** dialog box. If the removable flash drive is compatible with the ReadyBoost feature, a dialog box will appear after choosing the **Speed up my system using Windows ReadyBoost** option. However, if the computer has a large amount of RAM, ReadyBoost may be unavailable, as shown in Figure 6-32. The device in the example is limited to only 15 GB, so it would not provide sufficient space to supplement the 2 GB of RAM already installed on a small PC. You could delete files from the removable device to free up space, which would allow more space to be usable by ReadyBoost.

Microsoft recommends the space on the removable drive be one to three times the amount of installed physical RAM. For example, if the system has 512 MB of RAM,

Figure 6-31 Windows allows users to configure virtual memory (paging file) settings. Users can access this resource from **Control Panel> System and Security> System> Advanced system settings> Settings>Advanced** tab.

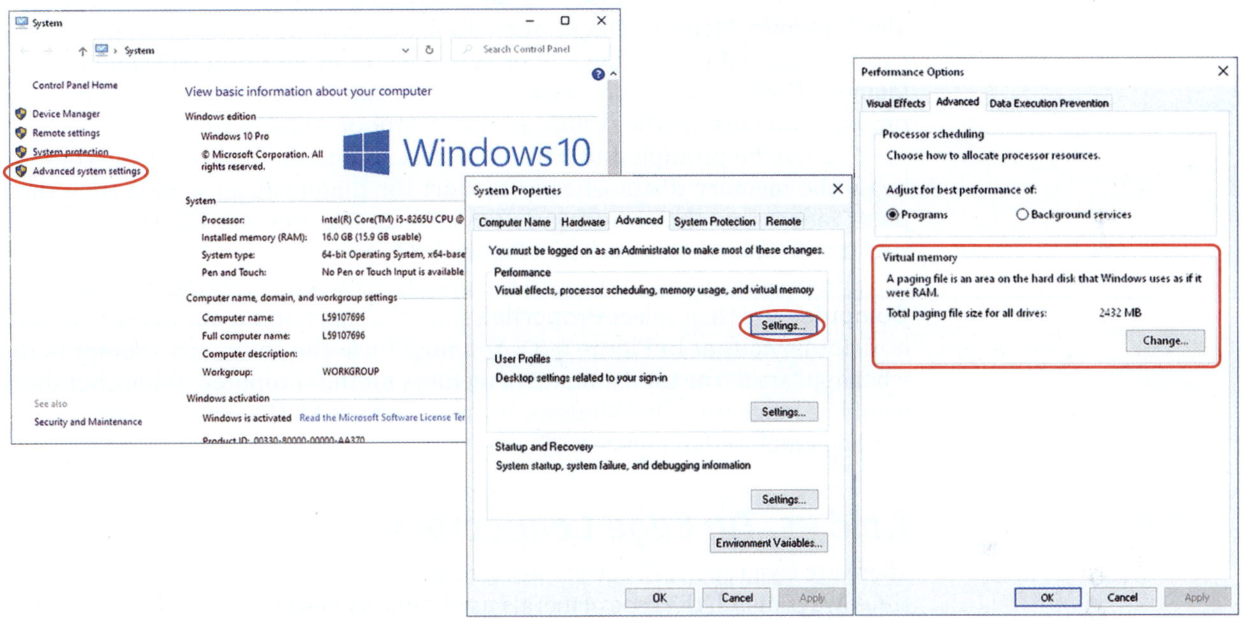

Goodheart-Willcox Publisher

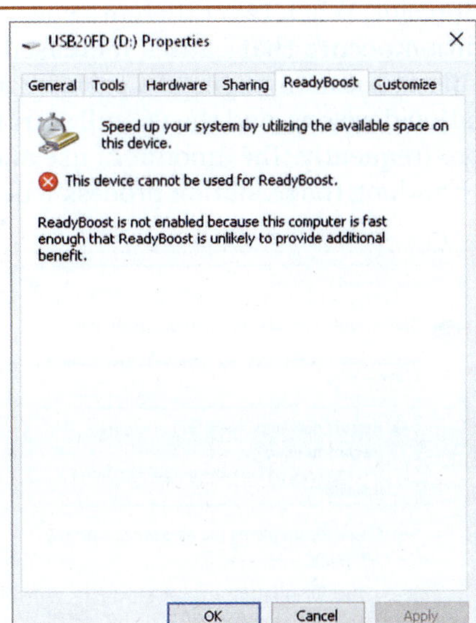

Figure 6-32 Computers with high volumes of RAM are often not able to utilize the ReadyBoost feature in Windows.

Goodheart-Willcox Publisher

the recommended maximum amount of USB flash memory is 1.5 GB. ReadyBoost will perform faster than the page file system that uses space on the hard disk drive since the USB flash drive has a faster read and write rate than the hard drive.

6.9 Troubleshooting Memory

Memory problems can be quite difficult to diagnose, especially intermittent problems. Fortunately, Microsoft provides a memory diagnostic tool as part of the operating system. In this section, you will learn about general methods used to troubleshoot memory, including the Windows Memory Diagnostics Tool, monitoring edge connectors for signs of oxidation, and monitoring the computer and memory for excessive heat.

Windows Memory Diagnostics Tool

The Windows Memory Diagnostics Tool was introduced in Windows Vista and can be accessed in Windows 10 or Windows 11 by entering mdsched or Windows Memory Diagnostics in the **Search** box on the **Start** menu or at the command prompt. You must be the system administrator or equal to run it.

You will be prompted to have Windows automatically restart the computer to begin the memory diagnostics or to start the diagnostics the next time the computer reboots, as shown in Figure 6-33. When the Memory Diagnostics Tool does run, it will look similar to that in Figure 6-34.

For an overview of how much memory is installed in a Windows PC, right-click **Computer** and then select **Properties** from the shortcut menu. You will see a dialog box similar to that in Figure 6-35. You might use the command prompt to display what appears as the total amount of memory for the computer system, but the result would be inaccurate. In Windows 10 and Windows 11, the simplest way is to use the method employed in Figure 6-35.

Gold vs. Tin Edge Connectors

There are two types of edge connector finishes used on memory modules: gold and tin. Always match the type of metals used. Quality systems match gold to gold, which is a good reason why old systems should be retired for recycling of precious metals. The memory-module (SIMM or DIMM) edge connector should match the connector finish inside the expansion slot. When two different types of metal are in contact with each other, a condition occurs that causes increased oxidation. When first installed, the memory will not show any signs of a problem and will work perfectly, but as time goes by, oxidation develops, and the PC will start to generate error codes such as parity errors more frequently. The amount of use and the conditions of the environment determine how long the oxidation process will take. Once it reaches a

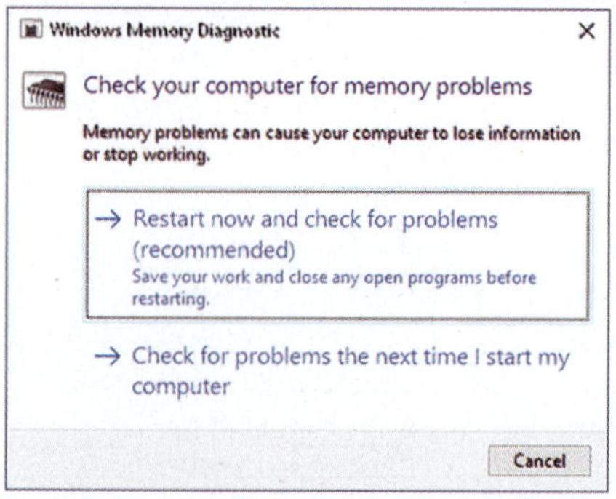

Figure 6-33 When the Windows Memory Diagnostic window appears, you can select to restart the computer now and begin diagnostics or check for problems the next time you start the computer.

Goodheart-Willcox Publisher

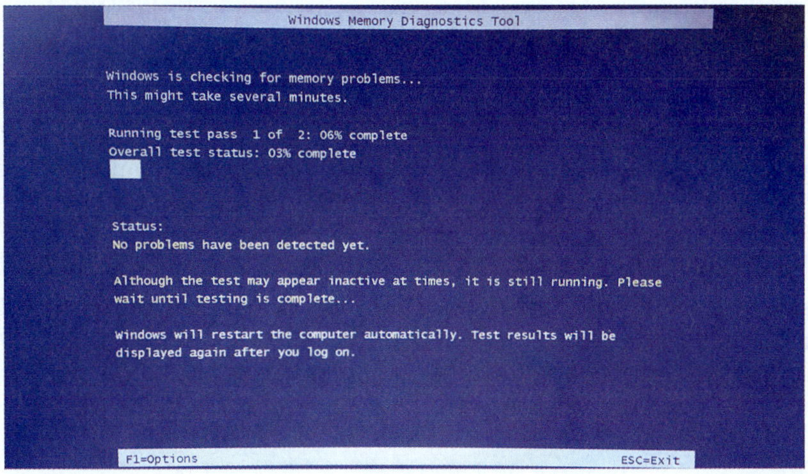

Goodheart-Willcox Publisher

Figure 6-34 The Windows Memory Diagnostics Tool is a comprehensive memory testing utility available through Windows.

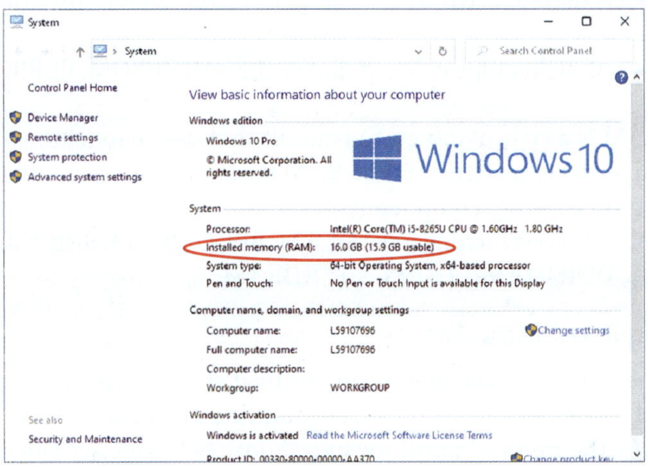

Goodheart-Willcox Publisher

Figure 6-35 You can quickly check the amount of installed RAM by accessing the **System** window.

point that the electrical connection between the memory edge connector and the slot connector has totally degenerated, errors will constantly occur.

Some oxidation can be removed by simply removing and reinserting the memory module or gently cleaning the memory card contacts with a microfiber cloth. This action alone may correct the error; however, the condition can be so bad, it renders the motherboard slot useless.

Memory and Heat

Heat will destroy a chip or cause temporary chaos in a computer. A common symptom of excessive heat causing memory problems is when a PC works fine for a short period of time (20 minutes) and then locks up. At the time the PC locks up, a sufficient level of heat has been generated to cause a circuit problem inside one of the memory chips. This causes the PC to fail. Fans should be checked, filters cleaned, and dirt and dust removed to prevent heat buildup.

High-performance memory modules generate a lot of heat, the amount of which is directly related to the operational frequency of the memory module. The higher the frequency, the higher the temperature generated. One cooling method is using a heat spreader, but another, more effective method is to add a fan that is especially designed for cooling memory modules. Cooling fans for memory are used in many overclocking systems.

Chapter Summary

6.1 Factors to Consider before Upgrading Memory

- Before upgrading RAM, questions related to compatibility, quantity, speed, pairings, and other memory specifics should be answered.

6.2 Physical Memory Packages

- Physical size of a memory package is important for confirming compatibility.
- Memory chips are packaged in several different physical styles such as SIP, DIP, SIMM, DIMM, SO-DIMM, SO-RIMM, and MicroDIMM.

6.3 ROM and RAM

- Read-only memory (ROM) is designed to store program information in a nonvolatile fashion.
- Random access memory (RAM) is designed to store data or programs temporarily.
- Various types of ROM chips exist, including PROM, EPROM, EEPROM, and Flash ROM.
- Dynamic RAM is a type of integrated circuit that uses capacitors to assist in storing data in the transistors. Static RAM is an integrated circuit technology based on digital flip-flop components.
- Additional RAM types include EDO DRAM, BEDO DRAM, SDRAM, DDR1, DDR2, DDR3, DDR4, DDR5, GDDR, and RDRAM.

6.4 Installing RAM Modules

- To install memory, hold the module by the heat spreader, properly orient the module in the slot, and firmly press the module into place.
- Depending on the motherboard, you can choose between five DIMM arrangements, including single-channel mode, dual-channel mode, triple-channel mode, quad-channel mode, and flex mode.
- Some types of memory can be overclocked but doing so often requires additional cooling.

6.5 Matching RAM Characteristics

- Typical memory characteristics to consider when adding or replacing RAM modules relate to chip speed and integrity.
- Specific characteristics to consider include chip speed, latency, buffering, registered memory, data integrity factors such as parity and ECC, and whether modules are single or double sided.

6.6 Flash Memory Devices

- Flash memory is a solid-state, reusable data storage device that can retain data even when the electrical power is disconnected.
- Flash memory is derived from EEPROM technology.
- Examples include USB flash drives, flash memory cards, and SSDs.

6.7 Memory Map Structure and Development

- The logical areas of RAM are conventional memory, upper memory area (reserved memory), high memory, expanded memory, and extended memory.

- Real mode is designed on the DOS system of memory access in which only the first 1 MB of RAM can be accessed.
- Protected mode includes all of real mode plus extended memory.
- Safe Mode is a term used by technicians to describe starting the computer in protected mode.

6.8 Virtual Memory

- Virtual memory is memory that supplements physical RAM.
- Virtual memory is located in a reserved portion of a hard disk referred to as a page file and is used to supplement available RAM.
- Windows ReadyBoost allows a USB flash drive to supplement RAM.

6.9 Troubleshooting Memory

- Memory problems can be difficult to diagnose.
- The Windows Memory Diagnostics Tool makes diagnosing memory issues easier.
- Always match the type of metal used on edge connectors.
- Oxidation on memory-module contacts can generate error codes.
- Excessive heat can cause a PC to lock up.

Review Questions

1. List factors to consider before installing or replacing memory.
2. Differentiate between physical memory packages.
3. List the three pin packages available for DIMM constructions.
4. What is the difference between ROM and RAM?
5. Compare and contrast types of ROM.
6. Compare and contrast types of RAM.
7. List the number of pins for each DDR type.
   A. DDR2
   B. DDR3
   C. DDR4
   D. DDR5
8. Briefly summarize how to install RAM modules into a desktop computer.
9. Briefly summarize how to install RAM modules into a laptop.
10. List and describe five DIMM physical arrangements.
11. A technician installs one 4-GB and one 2-GB memory module into a dual-channel mode system. How much memory will operate in interleaved mode, and how much memory will operate in asymmetric mode?
12. List important characteristics of RAM to consider when adding or replacing modules.
13. What is the difference between RAS and CAS?
14. Regarding a DDR memory module, what does *prefetch 2n* mean?
15. What is flash memory?
16. Summarize the operation of flash memory devices.
17. Identify memory map areas.
18. Differentiate between the terms *real mode*, *protected mode*, and *Safe Mode*.
19. What is the function of virtual memory?
20. Identify methods used to troubleshoot memory.

Sample A+ Exam Questions

1. During the system boot, the following error message is displayed: "Parity check failure!" To what particular system component would the message be referring?
   A. RAM
   B. ROM
   C. HDD
   D. USB
2. In the Windows 10 operating system, how would you display the amount of RAM installed on a PC?
   A. Open the **Start** menu, right-click **Computer**, and select **Properties** from the shortcut menu.
   B. Open the **Start** menu, right-click **Computer**, and then select **System Status** from the shortcut menu.
   C. Select **Start**>**Control Panel**>**RAM**.
   D. Select **Start**>**Control Panel**>**System and Security**>**System**>**View amount of RAM and processor speed.**
3. Which command will evoke a memory diagnostic routine for Windows 7?
   A. **mdsched**
   B. **sysconfig**
   C. **msinfo32**
   D. **memprob**
4. Which memory module is compatible with DDR3?
   A. DDR2
   B. DDR5
   C. DDR4
   D. No other memory module is compatible with DDR3.
5. Which type of memory must constantly be refreshed to retain the stored data?
   A. SRAM
   B. PROM
   C. DRAM
   D. C-RIMM
6. What effect will adding more RAM have on a desktop PC?
   A. Improve the Internet connection speed
   B. Improve overall computer performance
   C. Increase HDD storage capacity
   D. Reduce the overall POST time
7. How can you access the **Advanced Boot Options** menu when using the Windows 10 operating system?
   A. Hold down [F1] during the POST.
   B. Press [F8] immediately after the POST.
   C. Press [Ctrl][Alt][Delete] at the same time.
   D. Select **Start**>**Settings**>**Update & security**>**Recovery**>**Restart now.**
8. A memory chip's speed is measured in which standard unit?
   A. Megahertz
   B. Gigahertz
   C. Nanoseconds
   D. Cycles per second

9. Which memory module is designed with DDR4 memory chips?
   A. PC2100
   B. PC2-6400
   C. PC4-19200
   D. PC3-12800
10. Which items listed below should be practiced to ensure correct installation of additional memory? Select all that apply.
   A. Use an antistatic wrist strap.
   B. Put the PC into real mode to prevent accessing the upper memory area until after the installation is complete.
   C. Turn off all electrical power to the system.
   D. Disconnect all peripheral components until after complete memory installation has been verified by system setup.

Chapter 7

Input Devices

Learning Outcomes

7.1 Summarize the function of the USB Implementers Forum and the standards it has developed.

7.2 Explain how a keyboard operates.

7.3 Detail the operation of an optical mouse.

7.4 List other commonly encountered input devices.

7.5 Differentiate between the characteristics of major touch screen technologies.

7.6 List other examples of wireless input devices, technologies, and protocols or standards.

7.7 Compare and contrast utilities in Microsoft Windows that troubleshoot or enhance input devices.

7.8 Summarize the unique challenges presented by managing mobile device hardware and components.

A+ Certification Exam Objectives

The following A+ Certification Exam Objectives are covered in this chapter.

Exam 220-1101

1.0 Mobile Device

- 1.1 Given a scenario, install and configure laptop hardware and components.
- 1.2 Compare and contrast the display components of mobile devices.
- 1.3 Given a scenario, connect and configure accessories and ports of other mobile devices.

2.0 Networking

- 2.3 Compare and contrast wireless networking protocols.

3.0 Hardware

- 3.6 Given a scenario, deploy and configure multifunction devices/printers and settings.

5.0 Hardware and Network Troubleshooting

- 5.5 Given a scenario, troubleshoot common issues with mobile devices.

Exam 220-1102

1.0 Operating Systems

- 1.4 Given a scenario, use the appropriate Windows 10 Control Panel utility.

Key Terms

active tablet
bar code reader
Bluetooth
charge-coupled device (CCD)
digital camera
digitizer pad
game pad
human interface device (HID) standard
keyboard-video-mouse (KVM) switch
optical character recognition (OCR)
optical mouse
passive tablet
protocol
scanner
touch screen display
trackball
Ultra-Wideband (UWB) standard
USB standard
virtual keyboard
webcam
Wi-Fi standard
Wireless USB (WUSB)

Overview

An input device is any piece of equipment used to communicate with the PC system and provide the PC with data. The keyboard is one of the most common and useful input devices, but there is a broad spectrum of input devices for computers. Some devices, such as the mouse, find widespread use in a variety of different computer applications. Other input devices, like bar code scanners, have more specific uses.

While specific plugs and jacks are common to certain input devices, you may encounter a keyboard, mouse, or other device that installs in some unique way. Some devices have standard connections on the back of the motherboard. Most input devices, however, connect to the PC through the USB port. Other devices require a card to be inserted into a motherboard expansion slot.

A+ Note

Basic input devices are usually a source of questions on the A+ Certification Exams. Some of the devices include touch screens, microphones, KVM switches, webcams, and scanners. Always check the CompTIA website for the latest list of input devices that you may encounter.

7.1 USB Implementers Forum

The *USB Implementers Forum (USB-IF)* consists of industry experts with a common interest in creating a standard guideline for the development of drivers for USB input and output devices. This forum designates hardware devices into groups and refers to the groups as *classifications*, each of which has a specific set of standards to follow for software programming. With a system of standards in place, companies can develop and distribute software templates of code for their device, thus ensuring the device works correctly with different operating systems and other devices. For example, all keyboards are designed to interpret keystrokes and convert them to digital signals that are transmitted to the PC for interpretation by the operating system and a software application, such as Microsoft Word.

The USB-IF provides example software driver programs as a guide to follow when writing drivers for each device. Manufacturers are free to add additional features to the driver program if they so desire. The USB-IF is responsible for the development of the USB standard and human interface device (HID) standard. For more information about the USB-IF, visit their website at https://www.usb.org.

USB Standard

Most input and many output devices are based on the **USB standard**, which describes how different classifications of devices should communicate with a PC. It was developed by the USB Implementations Forum. Common device classifications are keyboards, mice, joysticks, bar code readers, magnetic card readers, game pads, printers, and digital cameras.

The USB standard supports bidirectional communication, which means data can flow to and from the PC and USB device, Figure 7-1. For example, a digital camera can transmit digital photos to a software application on the computer. In turn, the corresponding file explore or software application can delete the data located on the digital camera. Another example of bidirectional communication is an Internet connection provided through a modem with a USB port. The USB port supports data flow both to and from the Internet.

The USB standard is not limited to USB-wired devices. The standard also has a provision for USB wireless devices—a combination of USB, Bluetooth, and Wi-Fi standards. Wireless USB is covered later in this chapter.

General advances in USB involve improvements in bandwidth and speed. For example, USB 3.0 was released in November 2008 and was followed with the release of USB 3.2 September 2017. USB 3.2 is essentially just an improvement over 3.0. USB 4.0 was released in August of 2018 and is based on the Thunderbolt 3 protocol.

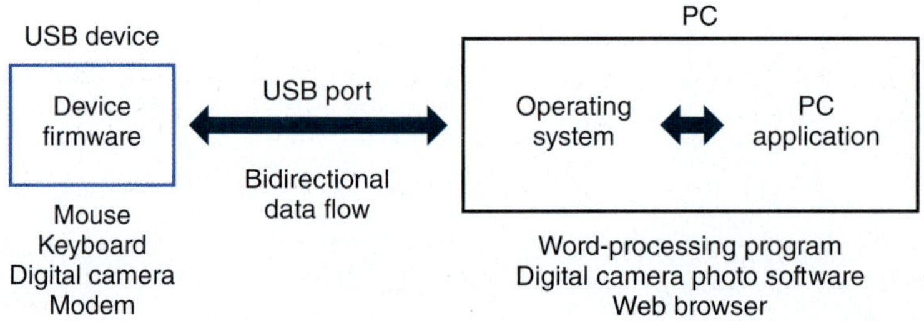

Figure 7-1 The USB standard allows for bidirectional communication between a USB device and a PC.

Goodheart-Willcox Publisher

HID Standard

The USB Implementers Forum also developed the **human interface device (HID) standard**, which is a classification of USB devices as well as a set of standards for device drivers to ensure compatibility between devices and computers. It describes the programming for human input devices, identifies variable names, and provides a set of coding standards so HID software drivers are the same for all input devices except for the features unique to a particular input device.

Before the HID specification, each company that produced a USB input device had to write their own driver code. Now, they simply use the example code, adjust it for unique features, and leave the required code that ensures compatibility with all PCs and operating systems.

7.2 Keyboard

There has been a substantial de-emphasis on keyboards over the past several versions of the CompTIA A+ Certification Exam. While you should expect only a few basic questions, this section provides additional details beyond the scope of the exams. The standard keyboard is a common input device that changes keystrokes into data. The typical keyboard has a small microprocessor installed as a keyboard controller, shown in Figure 7-2. The keyboard controller is not as powerful as the PC processor; rather, it is a limited processor used for small device applications such as telephones, automobiles, and appliances. A circuit board contains the keyboard controller that connects to the keyboard circuit traces and to the USB cable port.

Another keyboard input can occur with a ***chording keyboard***, which allows the user to press a small number of keys in various combinations to generate the standard codes. Chording presents a unique alternative to the typewriter-derived keyboards that are the most common. They can also provide quicker input in the hands of an experienced user.

Several types of switches are used under the keys in keyboards. The most common types of switches are mechanical, membrane, rubber dome, and capacitor. Refer to Figure 7-3 for an illustration of each switch type.

The mechanical switch, Figure 7-3A, is constructed from a set of electrical contacts that are normally open (separated). When the key is pressed, the contacts close and send a signal to the keyboard controller to produce the correct code for input.

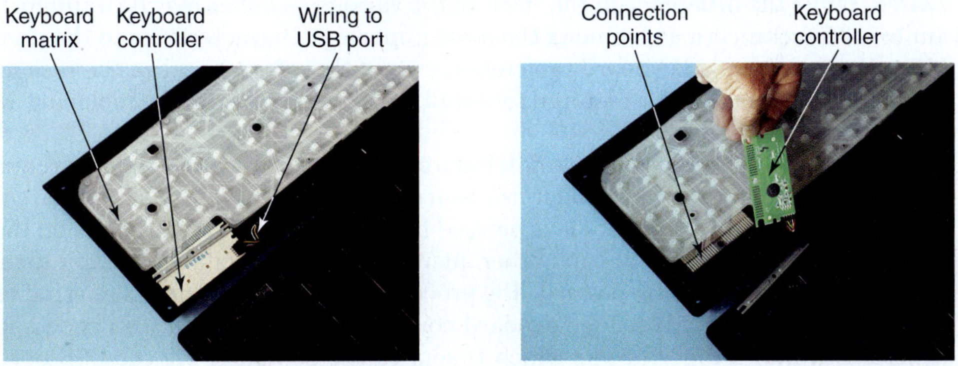

Figure 7-2 The keyboard controller is connected between the circuitry for the keys and the USB port wiring. It converts electrical signals generated from scan codes to numbers represented by digital signals.

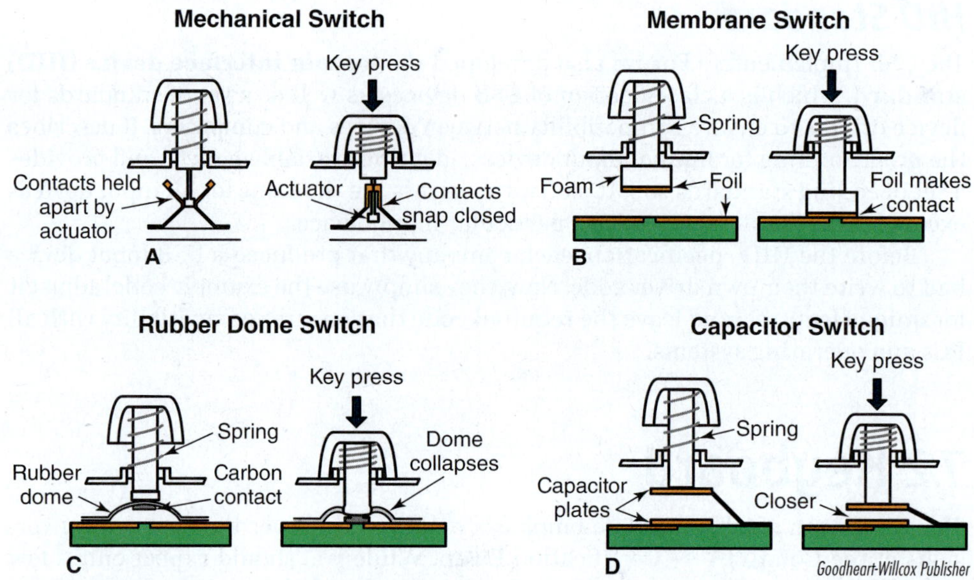

Figure 7-3 There are four common types of keyboard switches: mechanical, membrane, rubber dome, and capacitor.

A membrane switch, Figure 7-3B, is constructed differently than the typical contact switch. A piece of foam with foil on one side is attached to the switch actuator. A circuit board acts as the base of the switch and has a pair of contact points on its surface. When the key is pressed, conductive foil located on the foam completes the circuit across the circuit board contact points.

The rubber dome switch, Figure 7-3C, is constructed with a small rubber dome under the actuator. When the key is pressed, the rubber dome folds down, causing a small carbon contact to complete the circuit. The rubber dome switch makes it unlikely for dirt particles to accumulate between the carbon contact and the circuit board contact, which makes the switch more reliable.

The last type of switch is the capacitor switch, Figure 7-3D. The capacitor switch operates on the principle of an electronic capacitor, which is simply two plates of conductive material near each other. The distance between the plates affects the strength and electrical characteristics of the capacitor. When the key is pressed on the capacitor switch, the plates move close together, but they never touch. The capacitor switch is the most reliable type of keyboard switch. The other three types of switches are susceptible to corrosion, which causes an open circuit. However, capacitor switch keyboards are less likely to be affected by corrosion.

When comparing types of switches, the first difference is the tactile feel of the switch. While the difference in the "feel" of the various switches may be unimportant to a PC technician, it is among the most important characteristics to the user. Most PC users have a keyboard preference, even if they do not realize the reason. Because of this, you may be required to install an older keyboard when replacing an old PC with a newer one.

The rubber dome-type keyboard in Figure 7-4 has two layers of printed circuits on clear plastic. The two printed circuit boards have a pattern, or *matrix*, of circular points. When the rubber dome is pressed by the keys, the circular points on the circuit boards come close to each other, increasing the capacitance and, in turn, identifying the key(s) being pressed. The process of key identification is referred to as generating a *scan code*. The keyboard controller interprets the scan code and translates it into a digital code, which is sent to the computer via the USB port, illustrated in Figure 7-5.

Goodheart-Willcox Publisher

Figure 7-4 Keyboards typically have two layers of printed circuits on plastic.

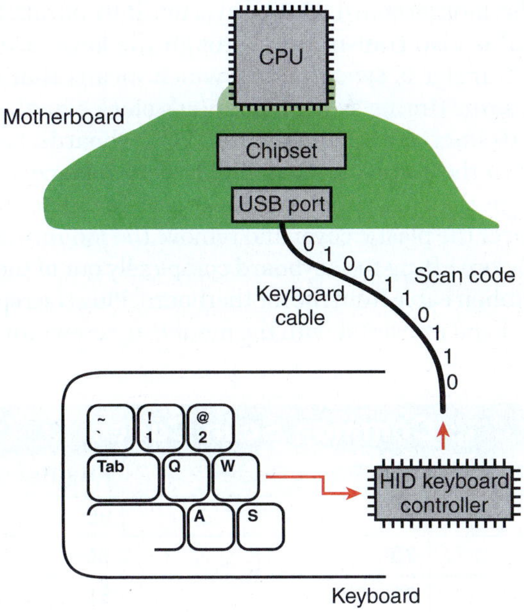

Goodheart-Willcox Publisher

Figure 7-5 When a key is pressed, the scan code is interpreted by the keyboard controller and then translated into a digital code, which is sent to the computer via USB port.

Keyboard Scan Codes

Keyboard scan codes are no longer covered on the CompTIA A+ Certification Exams, but this information is often useful if one is repairing a keyboard. The keyboard is a matrix of electrical connections, and each junction in the matrix is a key location. Each position on the matrix has an assigned number, and when a key is pressed, the electrical signal (digital binary) is sent to the keyboard controller as a scan code. The scan code is interpreted by the system BIOS and application software and is turned into an ASCII character. The scan code represents the position of the pressed key, and another scan code is generated when the same key is released.

The scan code is not the ASCII code or Unicode, nor is it the printed letter, number, or symbol on the physical key. Instead, the scan code is used to identify the exact symbol to be displayed on the screen or to be printed on the printer. Keyboards can have multiple sets of scan codes. Programmers use the scan codes to convert the action of a certain key being pressed into an action by the computer. Usually, that action is the conversion of the scan code into an ASCII or Unicode character, but not always. The scan codes allow multiple languages to be assigned to a particular computer. The scan code from the key is converted into the letter symbol of the language for which the system has been configured.

Look at Figure 7-6 for a listing of scan codes for several keys. Note that the codes for key press and key release are expressed in hexadecimal values. Most coding systems apply to the standard QWERTY keyboard, though other key code interpretations can be implemented in software for other keyboard layouts such as Dvorak.

A+ 1101: 1.1

Keyboard Connectors

Tech Tip

If a customer complains that a new USB keyboard does not work with an old computer, they are most likely using the wrong type of USB adapter.

Most computers use USB ports for keyboard connections. A keyboard can connect to a USB port by wire or wirelessly. Legacy PS/2 connections still exist on many computers, but this type of port is almost entirely obsolete. Some people will purchase or work on a computer that has no PS/2 port and still want to use an existing PS/2 mouse or keyboard. In this case, a USB-PS/2 adapter, such as the one shown in Figure 7-7, can be used to connect a PS/2 device to a USB connection.

In a PS/2 connection, data is sent through only one of the five pins. The keyboard is a serial device, meaning the data sent to the motherboard is sequential. After the data reaches the motherboard, it is converted into parallel form, usually two bytes. A clock signal is also transmitted through the keyboard connector wiring. The keyboard data transfer is ***synchronous***, which means that the data are transferred based on the same timing as the computer's clock signal.

Laptop keyboards interface differently from PC keyboards. Laptop keyboards are physically mounted to the computer, meaning that to replace a defective keyboard, there are far more steps than just simply unplugging it. To replace the keyboard, a technician must disconnect the plastic cover and remove the mounting screws holding the keyboard in place. Before lifting the keyboard completely out of the casing, disconnect the small, flat data ribbon cable from the motherboard. Plug the replacement keyboard into the motherboard and reinsert it with the mounting screws and casing unit.

Figure 7-6 Key press and release codes are expressed in hexadecimal values.

Common Scan Codes

Key	Key Press Code	Key Release Code
A	1E	9E
B	30	B0
Esc	01	81
F2	3C	BC
Home	E047	E0C7
Delete	E053	E0D3
Page Down	E051	E0D1
Spacebar	39	B9
4 $	05	85

Goodheart-Willcox Publisher

Figure 7-7 USB-PS/2 adapters are used to convert an older PS/2-type keyboard or mouse to a newer PC that may not have those connection ports.

Goodheart-Willcox Publisher

Ergonomic Keyboards

Ergonomics is the science concerned with designing and arranging things a person uses so they can be used efficiently and safely. Hence, *ergonomic keyboards* are keyboards shaped for comfort and injury prevention, as shown in Figure 7-8. Many people suffer from *carpal tunnel syndrome*, an inflammation of the tendons in the hands and wrist, caused by repetitive motion without proper rest or support. An example of this type of repetitive movement, and a common cause of carpal tunnel syndrome, is inputting data at a keyboard day after day.

It is believed that by shaping a keyboard so the user's hands and fingers contact the keyboard in a more natural alignment, carpal tunnel syndrome can be prevented. A variety of different designs for keyboards has been developed.

Virtual Keyboard

A **virtual keyboard** is a software-based keyboard that allows the input of data without physical keys, which can be accomplished through a touch screen, such as a smartphone, or through projection of light. Virtual keyboards work with PCs, smartphones, and any application where an input device might be required.

The keyboard shown in Figure 7-9 functions with an infrared light source and pattern projector working together to create an image of a keyboard, which can be projected onto any surface. The light of the keyboard image is reflected off the surface to a set of light sensors. The user simply types on the projected image as though it were a real keyboard. The user's finger motions interrupt the light pattern representing the keyboard. The light sensors detect interruptions in the reflected light, and the light sensor module converts the interruptions into digital signals that represent the keys touched by the user.

Dmitry Melnikov/Shutterstock.com

Figure 7-8 Some keyboards are designed ergonomically to reduce the risk of repetitive-motion injuries.

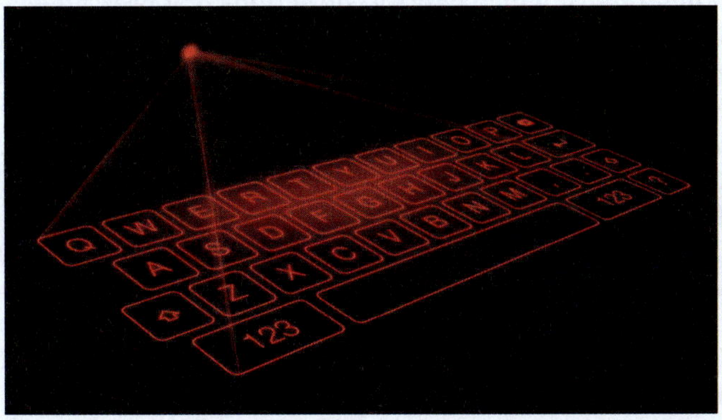

dolphfyn/Shutterstock.com

Figure 7-9 A virtual keyboard is a software-based keyboard that allows the input of data without physical keys. The user's finger movements interrupt the light pattern representing the keyboard. These interruptions are detected by a light sensor module, which converts them into digital signals representing the keys touches by the user.

It is rarely cost-effective to repair damaged keyboards. They are usually less expensive to replace than to fix. However, preventive maintenance extends the life of a keyboard.

Caution

Be careful when disassembling a keyboard. Many styles of keyboards are assembled at the factory in ways that make them nearly impossible to reassemble.

Preventive Maintenance

Most of the problems with keyboards are associated with grime and debris in and around the keys. Keyboard keys can easily be disabled by dirt or corrosion. A keyboard should be cleaned on a regular basis. A small vacuum cleaner or a can of dry compressed air can be used to clean the keyboard.

When using vacuum cleaners, remember that they emit a lot of static and electrical noise that can cause high-voltage spikes. If the vacuum is plugged into the same outlet as the computer being cleaned, be sure the computer is off. Do not equate a suspended state, such as sleep or hibernate, with a computer being off. Also, remember that computers other than the one being cleaned might be connected to the same circuit. A battery-operated vacuum is the safest choice, provided it contains enough power.

Additionally, be careful of static electricity, a common and hazardous by-product of the plastic parts on a vacuum cleaner. Be sure to follow all antistatic procedures to prevent damage to equipment. Vacuum cleaners will also affect voltage.

Most computer users understand the hazards of keeping liquids near computer equipment. If a liquid is spilled on the keyboard, the keyboard should be flushed with distilled water as soon as possible after disconnecting it from the PC. Be sure to use distilled water, as it does not contain any minerals that will cause corrosion. Residue from soft drinks or any other liquid containing sugar will leave a sticky film when dry. This film will quickly collect dirt and dust and the keys will begin to stick. Additionally, certain drinks contain materials that are very corrosive to electrical parts. In the case of a spill on a laptop computer, the computer should be turned off and disconnected from the power source, including the battery if possible, before attempting to remove and clean the keyboard.

Keys on the keyboard can be easily removed using a chip puller. A paper clip can also be improvised to hook under the individual keys. Care should be used when attempting to remove the spacebar, as these keys are notoriously difficult to reconnect to the keyboard after removal.

A+ Note

A question may appear on the A+ Certification Exam asking for the correct path to an option or dialog box. Be sure to learn important paths for the most current operating systems.

Adjusting Keyboard Properties

Certain keyboard properties can be adjusted for preference in the **Keyboard Properties** dialog box. In Windows 10, access it through **Control Panel>Keyboard.** All Windows operating systems use a very similar **Keyboard Properties** dialog box. You can easily change the repeat delay and the repeat rate as well as the cursor blink rate, Figure 7-10. Under the **Speed** tab, you will find the **Repeat delay** and **Repeat rate** adjustments, which control the actions of a pressed key. These adjustments control the length of a pause after pressing a key and the delay for holding a key in place until it repeats a character. A typical application of this timing method is when a user holds the spacebar down to move the cursor across the screen. The number of times per second a character can be typed is expressed as characters per second (CPS). The **Cursor blink rate** adjustment modifies how fast the cursor blinks. It does not affect your typing.

The computer can also be configured to allow a different language to display on the screen. As shown in Figure 7-11, the **Language** screen allows you to add and change the language entered by the keyboard. There are keyboards for all major languages in the world. In Windows 10, you access language options through **Settings>Time & Language>Language.** You can also change how the date and time are shown by adjusting regional settings in **Settings>Time & Language>Region.**

7.3 Optical Mouse

An **optical mouse** traces cursor movement by transmitting a light beam to a surface, such as a desk. See Figure 7-12 for an example of an optical mouse with its light source visible. The light beam is reflected from the surface to a built-in receiver in

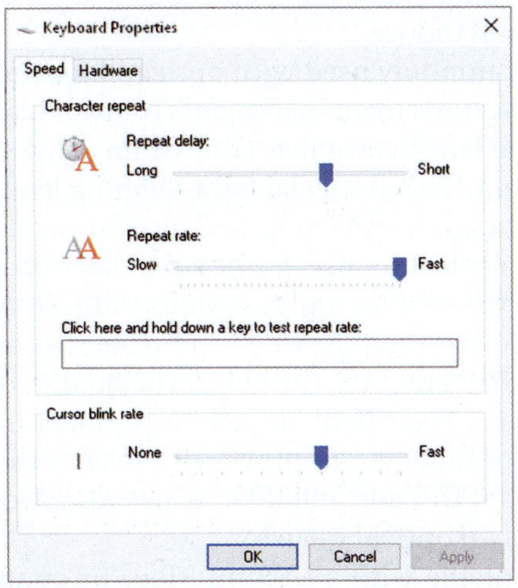

Goodheart-Willcox Publisher

Figure 7-10 The Keyboard Properties dialog box allows you to adjust settings such as **Repeat delay**, **Repeat rate**, and **Cursor blink rate**.

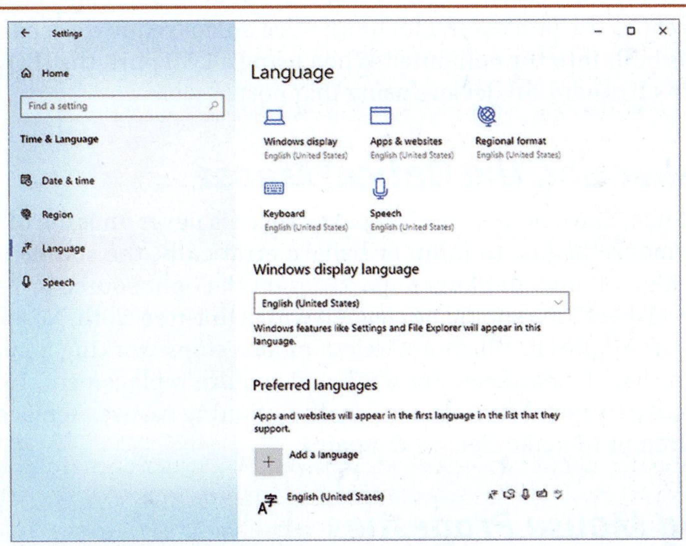

Goodheart-Willcox Publisher

Figure 7-11 Keyboards and languages can be changed through the Windows 10 **Settings** menu or **Control Panel**.

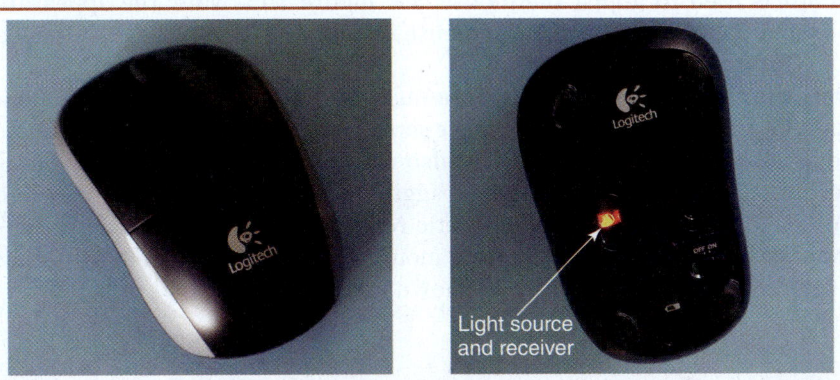

Goodheart-Willcox Publisher

Figure 7-12 An optical mouse traces movement by transmitting a light beam to a surface and picks up the reflection in a built-in receiver.

the mouse. The mouse operates best when used on a reflective surface. Therefore, optical mice are not ideal on clear plastic or glass surfaces. The receiver contains a CMOS digital camera, which captures the image of the surface that is directly under the mouse. The images are taken in rapid succession and compared to one another to determine the direction of motion. The optical mouse may take thousands of images per second. A microprocessor inside the mouse compares the images and translates them into relative direction of movement and speed. There are no mechanical moving parts as found in a ball mouse.

Two light sources commonly used with optical mice are laser and LED. A laser can produce more precise movement increments than an LED because LED depends on a light-shaping optical lens to produce a fine beam of light. A laser has a naturally fine beam of light and requires no special light-shaping lens.

Mouse quality is measured and compared by frames per second (FPS) and dots per inch (DPI). With an optical mouse, *frames per second* translates to how often the mouse sensor reads the surface and transmits data. *Dots per inch* is the degree of accuracy that a mouse can produce when sliding across a surface. The higher the number represented by DPI and FPS, the better the quality of the mouse system.

It is not unusual for a laser light mouse to produce increments of 1,600 DPI and transfer 6,000 FPS or more, an improvement over earlier versions of ball mice movement of less than 100 DPI and 100 FPS. A special reflective surface or pad can enhance performance of an optical mouse.

Today, mice are available with a USB interface or connect wirelessly through radio or Bluetooth transmission. A wireless mouse may also use a USB receiver that plugs into a USB port, receives signals from the mouse, and converts them into a signal to be sent to the processor. Bluetooth mice do not require a separate receiver if Bluetooth is built into the computer. When using a USB port, the IRQ assignment is shared with all other USB devices using that port.

Troubleshooting the Optical Mouse

Since optical mice have no mechanical parts, there is never an issue of worn parts. If an optical mouse begins to jump or behave erratically, the source of trouble is usually a buildup of dust and foreign particles on the light source or light receiver surfaces. The suspect area should be cleaned with a lint-free cloth. No special chemical cleaners are required. When a wireless mouse stops working completely, it is usually a sign that the batteries are weak and require replacement. However, it is not cost-effective to spend time fixing a malfunctioning mouse. Replace the mouse and do not attempt to make electrical repairs.

Adjusting Mouse Properties

Some properties of the mouse can be adjusted for preference. The **Mouse Properties** dialog box is used to adjust the mouse. See Figure 7-13. Note, the appearance of this box may vary depending on the mouse installed. In Windows 10, it is accessed through **Control Panel>Mouse.**

Once the properties window for the mouse is open, adjustments to functionality, such as speed of pointer travel across the screen and the speed used to double-click, are adjustable. The type of mouse is also selectable. One special change allows you to reverse the features (such as dragging) associated with the right and left buttons. Adjustments for purely aesthetic reasons can be performed here as well. For example, the length of the trailing mouse tail can be adjusted, as well as the style, color, and size of the pointer, as shown in Figure 7-14.

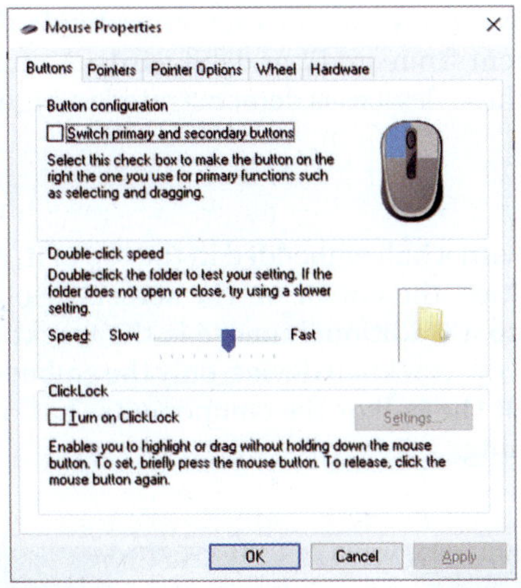

Goodheart-Willcox Publisher

Figure 7-13 The **Mouse Properties** dialog box in Windows 10 allows you to adjust mouse settings.

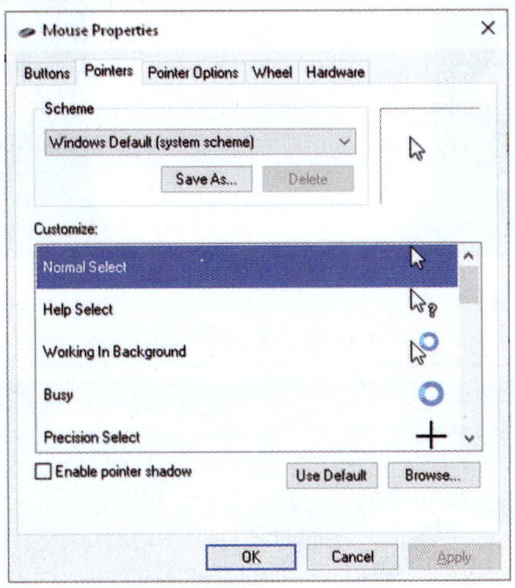

Goodheart-Willcox Publisher

Figure 7-14 The **Mouse Properties** dialog box also allows you to adjust the mouse for purely aesthetic reasons in addition to functionality.

7.4 Other Input Devices

There are many other types of input devices used with computers. In this section, we will limit the instruction to the most commonly encountered input devices as well as those you might encounter on a typical A+ Certification Exam. Commonly encountered input devices include magnetic and chip readers, trackballs, game pads, digitizer pads, bar code readers, scanners, digital cameras, and webcams.

Magnetic Reader and Chip Reader

Historically, magnetic card readers were exclusive to retail establishments. However, as transactions have grown increasingly more mobile-friendly, magnetic and chip card readers have become part of both desktop and mobile computer systems. Companies like Square and Stripe have made it easy to attach a card reader to any computer, laptop, or even a smartphone.

These types of devices can be inserted into a USB or Lightning port, and in some cases, the device can be inserted into the headphone jack of a smartphone or tablet, as shown in Figure 7-15. The consumer then swipes or inserts their card into the reader and completes the transaction by signing on the touch screen interface on the device. This makes it easy for small, independent companies; businesses without one set location, such as food trucks; or even an individual performing a side job or favor to accept payment from credit or debit cards. An example of how a card is swiped through one of these devices is demonstrated in Figure 7-16.

Trackball

A **trackball** is a mouse with a ball embedded in the top of it, as shown in Figure 7-17. The ball is used to position the cursor on the screen display. The advantage of a trackball as compared to a traditional mouse is the trackball remains stationary. You do not need to move the trackball device, only the embedded ball. The disadvantage of a trackball is that the ball or the components that recognize its movement may need periodic cleaning.

Figure 7-15 Magnetic or chip card readers such as those manufactured by Square can be inserted into a computer or mobile device.

Dave Nelson/Shutterstock.com

Figure 7-16 The ability to accept card-based payments through a mobile device makes it possible for businesses to operate virtually anywhere.

Rommel Canlas/Shutterstock.com

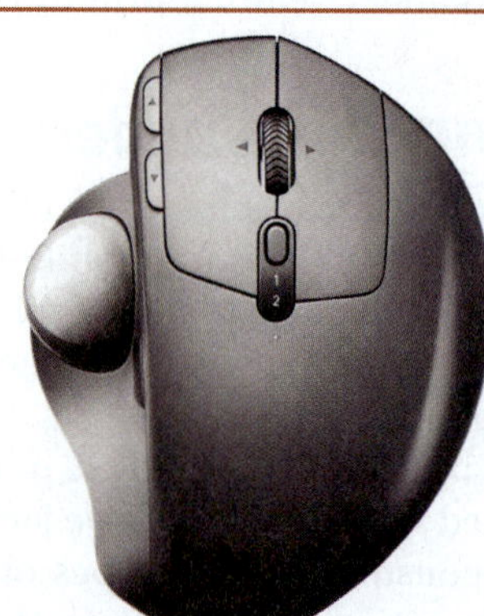

Figure 7-17 A trackball is equipped with a ball embedded into the top of the device. The ball is spun using the fingertips, which results in cursor movement.

AmaPhoto/Shutterstock.com

Game Pad

The term **game pad** applies to any device used as an input for a game application. This includes joysticks, steering wheels, or specialty items. Game pads are physically designed as an ergonomic device for many hours of constant use and generally include buttons or keys as well as a flexible joystick that allows for steering. Some controllers have more than one joystick. What all game pads have in common is their ability to allow keys to be programmed to perform specific tasks such as run, jump, or perform an action. The most commonly used keys included in game pads are [W], [A], [S], [D] as well as function keys. Game pads are generally wireless devices, although some can be attached with a USB cable. Game pads for those with physical impairments have large surfaces and very large controls.

To connect a game pad, the device drivers must be installed. The drivers are provided either on the CD or DVD that comes with the game pad or on the manufacturer's website. Without proper drivers, the game pad will likely fail to operate as intended. It is not uncommon for a game pad to be configured automatically by the operating system but without the latest drivers. In this case, some features may not work correctly.

Digitizer Pad

1101: 1.2, 1.3 A+

A **digitizer pad**, also known as a *trackpad* or *drawing pad*, is a virtual drawing surface that allows the user to create or modify drawings or modify photos. Digitizer pads, such as the one shown in Figure 7-18, serve as input devices for graphic software applications such as Adobe Photoshop, AutoCAD, or most paint or drawing programs. The pen used with the digitizer is also referred to as a *stylus* or *touch pen*. It is used as a virtual pencil, paintbrush, or ink pen. When you draw on the digitizer pad using the stylus, a line or brushstroke appears on the screen in a similar fashion to using a pencil or paintbrush with art medium. These are also sometimes called a digital art board, pen tablet, or similar name.

Figure 7-19 shows a close-up of commonly encountered buttons on a digitizer pad. Often, these pads have *express keys*, which act similarly to function keys on a keyboard, and a touch ring. The exact function of the keys and touch ring depend on the software application used with the digitizer pad. For example, some of the functions of the express keys can produce special menus, control drawing precision, and pan or scroll the image. The touch ring is typically used for zooming in or out of an image, modifying line thickness, rotating the drawing, and cycling through drawing layers. The toggle button in the center of the touch ring is used to select assigned functions.

Evgeny Rukavitsyn/Shutterstock.com

Figure 7-18 A digitizer pad is used as an input device for graphic software applications.

A group of four LEDs along the edge of the touch ring is used to indicate the activation of specific functions associated with the touch ring and toggle button. In Figure 7-19, only one LED is lit.

These pads can be classified based on their functionality. **Passive tablets** use electromagnetic induction with horizontal and vertical lines operating, transmitting, and receiving coils. **Active tablets** use self-powered electronics to transmit signals. These two are the most common, though there have been other variations.

An extension of the digitizer pad concept is the signature pad, most commonly seen in retail stores and used for buyers to sign off on their purchases. The buyer writes on the signature pad using a special stylus, producing a digital facsimile of their signature.

Problems associated with a digitizer pad are like any other input device. The manufacturer provides the latest software drivers and user manual, explaining the use and configuration of the digitizer pad.

Bar Code Readers

A **bar code reader** simply converts bar code images into data. The operation of a bar code scanner is relatively simple, as illustrated in Figure 7-20. It is designed with a light source transmitter and a light source receiver. The light source transmitter projects a light beam across the bar code. The bar code is made up of dark lines of varying width and spacing. The widths of the dark lines combine with the white spaces to form a code that represents ASCII letters and numbers.

The light from the source is reflected by the white spaces and absorbed by the dark lines. The receiver converts the reflected light into electrical pulses representing the data contained in the bar code. The electrical pulses are then passed along as ASCII data to the PC through either a wireless or a wired connection. The PC has software driver programs that use the ASCII data for application programs that manage inventory or drive a cash register program.

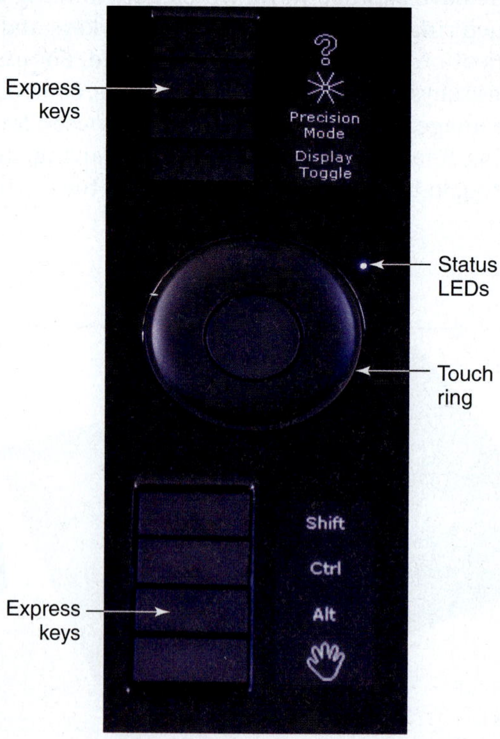

Figure 7-19 Controls are often located on the left side of the digitizer pad and provide common key functions and more.

Goodheart-Willcox Publisher

Scanners and Digital Cameras

1101: 1.2, 1.3, 3.6 A+

A **scanner** is a tool that takes in an optical image and digitizes it. This process is illustrated in Figure 7-21. Scanners can be used to read text into a computer or to create a digital version of an image. To read text into a format that can be used with word-processing software, a scanner uses **optical character recognition (OCR)**, which is software that determines which letters, numbers, and symbols match with images taken by the scanner. The output is an accurate text version of a printed document.

Though film-based cameras still exist and are popular among enthusiasts and professionals, most photos are now taken with digital cameras. A **digital camera** takes pictures by capturing and storing images as digital data instead of on photographic film. Digital cameras can range drastically in their components, abilities, and features. Simple, less-expensive models are designed for everyday use, while more advanced—and far more expensive—digital single-lens reflex (DSLR) cameras provide professional-quality photos. Both types are shown in Figure 7-22.

Another type of digital camera is called a webcam. A **webcam**, also referred to as a *web camera*, is a peripheral device that is commonly used for video conferencing and video chatting. These cameras are often built into a computer monitor or, in the case of laptops, into the computer itself. They are also available as separate peripheral devices connected via USB cable. These devices are often used for video phone calls using utilities such as Skype, Teams, Zoom, FaceTime, or Google Hangouts for web-based meetings or for general conversations. Webcams can be installed and managed from the Control Panel of a Windows 10 operating system. Both scanners and digital cameras rely on either the charge-coupled device (CCD) or CMOS technology to capture digital images.

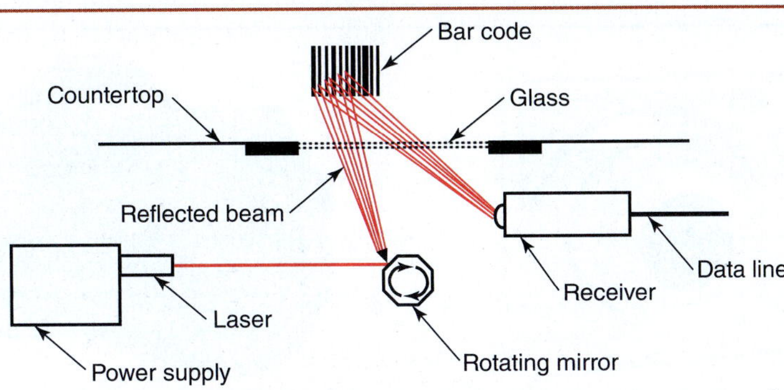

Goodheart-Willcox Publisher

Figure 7-20 Shown here are the workings of a bar code reader that can be found at the checkout counter of most retail stores. Using these fixed readers, bar codes dragged across the glass can be read.

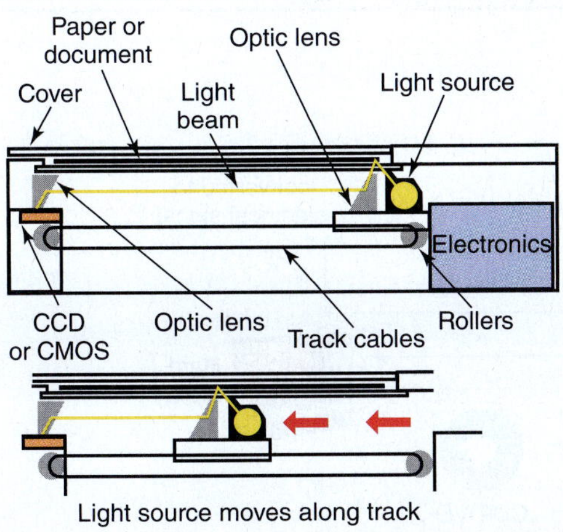

Goodheart-Willcox Publisher

Konstantin Shevstov/Shutterstock.com

Figure 7-21 A scanner changes reflected light into digital signals.

CCD

Think of a **charge-coupled device (CCD)** as a series of light-activated capacitors contained in a single chip. These capacitors convert light into electrical energy. When light strikes the CCD, a voltage is produced in direct proportion to the intensity of the light.

The voltage produced is analog, which means the voltage level is a variable signal. To be used by a computer system, the voltage must be converted to a digital signal, a sequence of discrete voltages. A special chip called an *analog-to-digital converter (ADC)* receives the analog electrical charge from the CCD and converts it to a series of digital signals that represents the light intensity of the image. The digital pulses are stored in memory to be accessed by graphical software programs. See Figure 7-23. CCDs are used in most imaging devices, including scanners and digital cameras.

A flatbed scanner uses a cable to move the light beam along the image placed on the bed of the scanner, capturing the image one line at a time. After a line of the image is captured, the CCD is moved down the image a fraction to capture the next line. This process continues until the entire image has been captured.

The CCD in a camera consists of an array of tiny windows. The entire image is captured at once rather than line by line as in the scanner application. Color filter lenses are used for color images, and each color is captured separately by incorporating a set of color filters into the lens units.

CMOS

A second type of imaging technology used for cameras and scanners is CMOS. CMOS imaging devices get their name from the fact that they are composed of CMOS transistor technology. Both CCD and CMOS convert light into electronic signals that

Figure 7-22 Digital cameras take pictures by capturing and storing images as digital data instead of on photographic film. They can vary drastically in price and quality.

Masalski Maksim/Shutterstock.com

Peter Gudella/Shutterstock.com

Figure 7-23 A charge-coupled device (CCD) produces voltage in analog, which is converted to a digital signal.

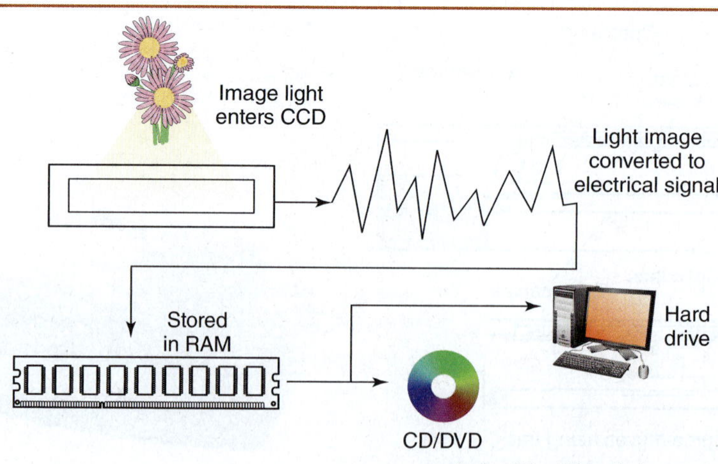

Goodheart-Willcox Publisher; (workstation icon) romvo/Shutterstock.com

can be transmitted to a computer or storage device for retrieval or manipulation. The main difference is CMOS imaging devices can be produced in a smaller package than CCD imaging devices. At the time of this writing, neither technology has dominated the imaging device market.

7.5 Touch Screens

A+ 1101: 1.2

A **touch screen display** is a computer display modified to accommodate input information by touch. The input area on the touch screen is activated by a touch, as the name implies, or by using a stylus. This is especially true for tablets and smartphones.

A touch screen system requires a touch screen panel assembly, controller, port connector, and software driver. The controller, sometimes referred to as a *digitizer*, can be a separate unit attached by cable to the touch screen or incorporated into the edge of the touch screen frame. The typical connection to the computer system is made through a USB port, as illustrated in Figure 7-24. Special PCI cards may be used in place of a USB port because the PCI card can serve as a port connection to the computer and incorporate the necessary electronics to act as the system controller.

A device driver must be installed in the computer system during the installation of the touch screen to provide support for interpreting the digital signal sent by the controller. Installing the necessary driver is like installing a driver for any other computer input device.

A+ 1101: 5.5

In the event a touch screen becomes unresponsive, it is possible the digitizer has malfunctioned. The best course of action is to start by using a keyboard and mouse to close unneeded apps running in the background. Clearing out additional memory can help restart the digitizer. If this does not work, conduct a touch screen calibration, and restart the device. If the touch screen is still unresponsive, it is possible that the display or digitizer will need to be replaced.

Touch screens are often incorporated into a computer system as a convenience for users or when a mouse or keyboard would not be a practical input device. Touch screen applications have been applied to interactive computer communication such as information panels in hotel lobbies, manufacturing assembly-line controls, hospital operating rooms, and the food service industry. They are also used as the

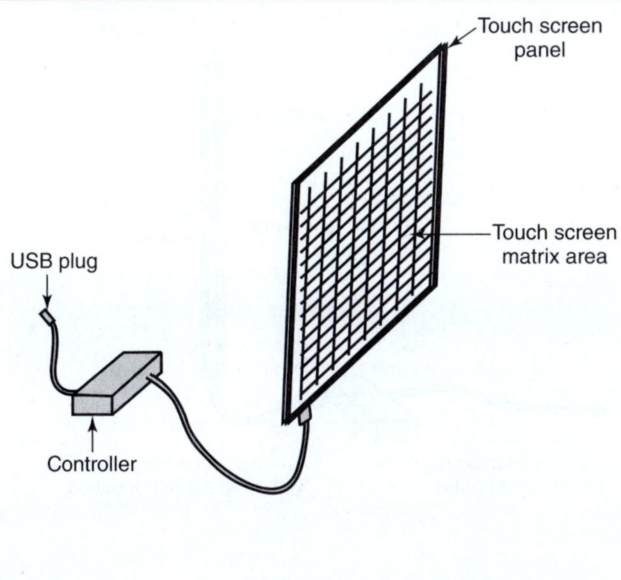

Goodheart-Willcox Publisher

Figure 7-24 Touch screens typically connect to the USB port of a PC. The controller is a separate unit attached to the cable. Touch screens were originally added to the surface of a computer display. Today, the touch screen is incorporated into the monitor, so no exterior connection is required.

main input for tablets, smartphones, and similar devices. Touch screen technology falls into five major sensor categories:

- resistance
- capacitance
- near-field effect
- infrared
- acoustical wave

All touch screen technologies operate in a similar manner. The main difference is in the surface construction of the touch screen and the type of electronic transmitters and receivers or sensors used.

Resistance

Touch screens that utilize the electronic principle of resistance are one of the most common and inexpensive to design. The touch screen consists of two layers of conductors separated by very tiny spacers. The first layer is a series of vertical translucent electrical conductors, and the second layer is a series of horizontal translucent electrical conductors. The two layers combine to form a matrix. The two layers are assembled into a flexible transparent cover, which fits neatly over the monitor display.

The monitor typically displays command buttons or similar graphics, which represent menu commands such as open, save, view files, and exit. When the screen is touched, a connection is made at that point in the matrix, Figure 7-25. Each area on the resistance touch screen produces a unique electrical resistance value. The electrical resistance value is interpreted by the screen controller and then passed to the computer operating system as a screen location. The digital signal is sent into the computer system through a USB port or through a PCI card designed for this purpose. Resistance touch screens work well in dusty or humid environments.

Capacitance

Some touch screens operate on the principle of capacitance, as shown in Figure 7-26. The touch screen is coated with a transparent metal oxide and carries a slight electrical charge, which creates an equally distributed electrical field across the inside of the touch screen. When the screen is touched, the electrically charged field is disturbed. A drop in the electrical potential at that point in the screen is transmitted to the touch screen controller. Capacitance touch screens do not work well in a humid environment.

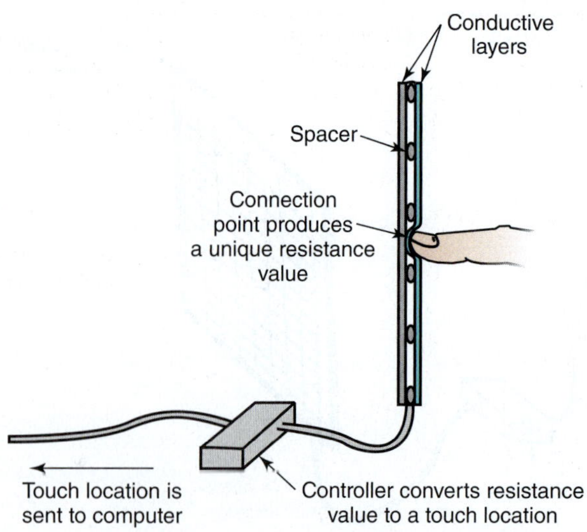

Figure 7-25 In a resistance touch screen, the screen consists of two layers of conductors separated by very tiny spacers. When the screen is touched, a connection is made.

Goodheart-Willcox Publisher

Near-Field Effect

Near-field touch screens also operate on the principle of capacitance. However, a near-field touch screen is constructed from two laminates of glass, each with a pattern of transparent metal oxide coating. The main difference between the two technologies is that for near-field touch screens, you only need to place your finger near the screen area; you do not have to contact the screen. A finger or any other pointing device near the screen area is enough to disturb the electrical field between the two screen plates. Near-field touch screens are excellent solutions for industrial or medical applications where the user may have gloved hands.

Infrared

Infrared touch screens operate by forming a matrix created by a row of infrared transmitters and receivers along the edges of the screen, as illustrated in Figure 7-27. The infrared transmitters are specially designed LEDs that transmit infrared light to the receivers. The receivers are light-activated transistors, which act like switches being turned on and off by the presence or absence of the infrared light beam. When a touch interrupts the infrared beam, the receivers in that matrix area send a signal to the controller, which determines the touch location and sends this location to the computer.

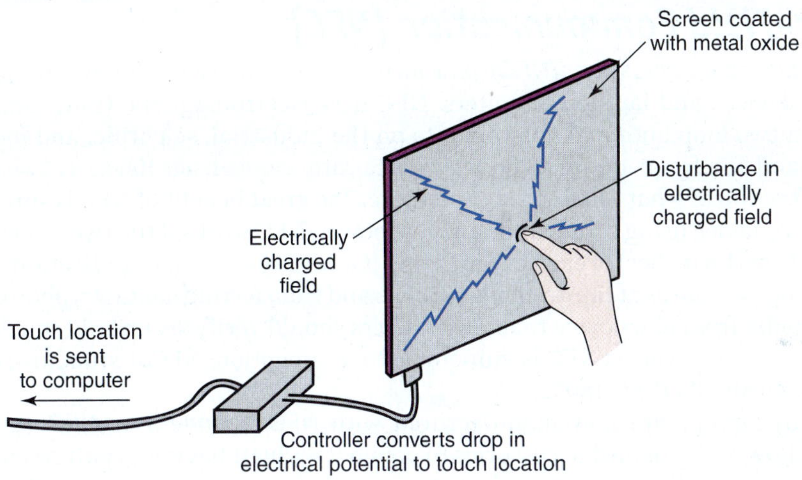

Goodheart-Willcox Publisher

Figure 7-26 In a capacitance touch screen, the screen is coated with a transparent metal oxide, which has a slight electrical charge. This creates an equally distributed electrical field across the touch screen.

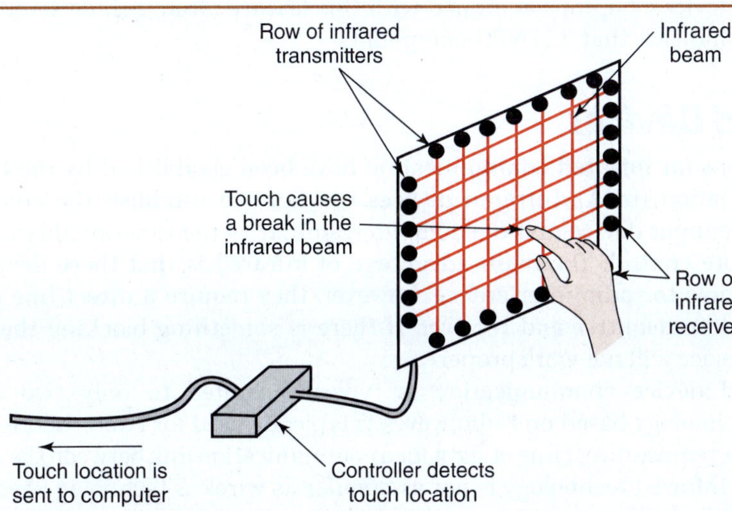

Goodheart-Willcox Publisher

Figure 7-27 An infrared touch screen works by registering interruptions in infrared beams generated from the outside of the screen.

Acoustical Wave

The acoustical wave touch screen is similar in design to the infrared screen, but the primary difference between the two is that the acoustical touch screen uses a matrix of sound waves. The edges of the panel are lined with acoustical sound wave transmitters and receivers. When an object such as a finger interrupts the sound wave, the location of the interruption is transmitted to the screen controller. Acoustical touch screens, as well as infrared screens, do not work well in dusty environments.

7.6 Wireless Input Devices

Modern computing typically involves numerous wireless input devices, such as mice, keyboards, microphones, game input devices, webcams, and digitizer pads. These devices use either radio frequency (RF) or infrared (IR) light to transfer information between an input device and a computer system. The information in this section will be limited to how wireless input device technology correlates to common PC wireless input devices. Other wireless technologies will be introduced in later chapters.

A+ 1101: 1.3

Near-Field Communication (NFC)

Near-field communication (NFC) is a form of input most commonly used with mobile devices and laptop computers. NFC uses electromagnetic (EM) induction between two loop antennas that operate on the industrial, scientific, and medical (ISM) band at a frequency of 13.56 MHz. Data rates range from 106 to 424 kbit/second, a fraction of what Bluetooth can achieve. The great benefit of NFC is simplicity and convenience using short range and low power. NFC works if the two devices are within 4 cm (1.6 inches) of each other, giving it a variety of unique applications, such as making purchases at tap-to-pay terminals and transferring contacts, photos, and other media from one device to another. Users should verify security is enabled on their device, however, as NFC is vulnerable to interception. NFC is standardized in ECMA-340 and ISO/IEC 18092.

A+ 1101: 1.1

Many laptops are now manufactured with *NFC scanners* or *NFC readers*, which allow NFC-enabled accessories to connect without having to pair or connect them. If equipped, users can perform tasks such as sharing photos or other data with a simple tap, play embedded games with friends, and receive information from other NFC devices. Laptops equipped with this feature often include some type of marking to indicate that it is NFC-compliant.

Infrared Devices

Specifications for infrared communication have been established by the Infrared Data Association (IrDA). Infrared devices use light to establish the connection between the input device and the computer, similar to the functionality of a television remote control. The main advantage of infrared is that these devices are not susceptible to radio interference; however, they require a direct line of sight between the transmitter and receiver. If there is something blocking the line of sight, the device will not work properly.

Infrared device communication is typically limited to only two devices. Wireless technology based on radio waves is typically used for two or more devices and does not require direct line of sight for a communication link between the devices. As a result, infrared technology is not as popular as wireless technology because of the required direct line of sight for successful transmission and reception.

Infrared connections occur automatically when devices are brought within one meter of each other. Microsoft operating systems use ActiveSync technology to automatically establish and synchronize a connection between infrared devices such as a PC and a personal digital assistant. Infrared devices are configured in Control Panel or Device Manager of Windows operating systems. However, if the infrared device does not exist, you will not see an option to configure the device. You can access the infrared setup and configuration wizard in Windows by typing irda in Windows **Help and Support** or **Search**.

You can only establish one infrared link between two devices, but the two devices can support more than one software application at the same time. For example, you can transfer the contents of a calendar program, business card program, and e-mail program in one session using one common infrared link.

Several data transfer speeds are associated with infrared technology, as shown in Figure 7-28. Notice that Gigabit Infrared (Giga-IR) has a data rate range from 512 Mbps to a maximum of 1 Gbps. This is because some devices that are less than 1 Gbps but higher than 512 Mbps are classified as Giga-IR. Each generation of IrDA infrared specifications is backward compatible with the previous version. For example, a VFIR device can communicate with an SIR device at the SIR data rate of 115.2 kbps.

RF Devices

Radio frequency (RF) devices use radio waves to communicate between the remote device and the receiver. Early radio remote control devices used the 27-MHz frequency, which is the same frequency used by remote-control planes, cars, and other toys. The use of specific radio frequencies for devices is controlled by the Federal Communications Commission (FCC), which assigns radio frequencies and enforces rules regulating the devices using radio waves.

Unlike infrared, radio frequency does not require line of sight and can transmit through solid material within limits. RF can easily pass through wood, sheetrock, glass, concrete blocks, and other common building materials. However, if the material is very dense, the RF may not pass through. For example, a thick concrete wall containing steel reinforcement may totally block the RF signal. Do not expect RF to pass through metal, such as metal walls or a wall covered with metal file cabinets, as the metal will most likely block the RF signals.

Many RF devices are designed as proprietary devices, meaning the technology was designed by a specific company and may not be used by other manufacturers without the original manufacturer's permission. One of the drawbacks to a proprietary design is that it may not be compatible with other devices that perform a similar function. For example, a mouse designed by Logitech that uses a 27-MHz radio frequency may not be compatible with another brand of mouse receiver. This means that when you replace a 27-MHz Logitech mouse, you must use another 27-MHz Logitech mouse. You cannot use a Microsoft or a Bluetooth mouse.

Infrared Transfer Speeds	
IR Technology	**Data Rate**
Serial Infrared (SIR)	115.2 kbps
Fast Infrared (FIR)	4 Mbps
Very Fast Infrared (VFIR)	16 Mbps
Ultra Fast Infrared (UFIR)	96 Mbps
Gigabit Infrared (Giga-IR)	512 Mbps–1 Gbps

Goodheart-Willcox Publisher

Figure 7-28 Infrared technology has a variety of data transfer speeds.

A+ 1101: 3.6

Wireless Technology Standards

As you study the characteristics of wireless devices, be aware that there are many overlapping RF standards, which can create a lot of confusion. For example, Logitech Fast RF is not a radio frequency standard; rather, it is a Logitech proprietary standard developed for their brand of input devices. Fast RF is not intended to be compatible with devices produced by other manufacturers.

A+ Note

You will most likely be asked questions about wireless technology frequencies and speeds. Keep in mind that standards for computer and electronic devices constantly change. You should always check the manufacturer's website for the very latest information about assigned RF and bandwidth.

The IEEE organization developed and released a set of wireless standards for networking, which is referred to as the IEEE 802.11 wireless standard. The IEEE 802.11 standard specifies how 2.4-GHz and 5-GHz RF are used for networking devices.

ZigBee is a wireless standard used for home entertainment systems. Wireless USB (WUSB) is a standard developed by the Wireless USB Promoters Group to replace wired USB devices with wireless USB devices. Ultra-Wideband (UWB) is an International Standards Organization (ISO) radio standard that has been adopted by several other organizations that are responsible for their own individual set of radio standards.

As technology evolves, some standards are absorbed into other original standards, which adds to the confusion. The wireless technology standards covered in this section are Bluetooth, Wi-Fi, Wireless USB, and Ultra-Wideband.

A+ 1101: 1.3, 2.3

Bluetooth

Bluetooth refers to a standard developed for short-range radio links between portable computers, smartphones, and other mobile devices. It was developed by a special interest group of electronics manufacturers who wanted to produce a standard way to connect low-powered devices over a short distance using the assigned 2.4-GHz frequency. Anyone can use the 2.4-GHz frequency for a wide assortment of devices. The Bluetooth organization was interested in developing a standard to be followed by manufacturers to share communication with each other's devices. For example, as a result of such technology, a cell phone could automatically transfer information between it and a computer. Bluetooth was originally designed only for low-power devices that would transmit data over the 2.4-GHz frequency. As the demand for wireless devices expanded, so did the list of available Bluetooth-enabled products. For example, wireless keyboards and mice conform to the Bluetooth standard.

The Bluetooth technology is slow compared to some other wireless technologies. To stay competitive, Bluetooth is constantly revising their specifications to increase data transfer speeds. The latest version, Bluetooth 3.0, can produce theoretical data transfer rates as high as 24 Mbps.

Bluetooth is often confused with other 2.4-GHz RF devices. The main difference is Bluetooth is a design standard for how a device should operate using the 2.4-GHz radio band. When manufacturers apply the Bluetooth standard to their devices, it is possible for those devices to communicate with any other Bluetooth standard devices no matter who manufactured it. For example, a PC that uses the Bluetooth standard can communicate with any cell phone that uses the Bluetooth standard.

The Bluetooth standard specifies that all Bluetooth devices should use the same protocol when communicating between devices. As defined for use with computer and network communication, a **protocol** is a set of rules used to govern communication between two devices. The rules outline information about how to organize the data that is to be exchanged between the two devices. A protocol sets the standards for such items as the following:

- How devices are to be identified (by numbers or letters) and the exact number of characters
- The maximum amount of data that can be transmitted at one time
- The speed at which each of the electronic devices should operate
- Whether information should be encrypted, and if so, by what method

There are over 1,200 pages in the current Bluetooth standard that manufacturers must follow to ensure compatibility with other Bluetooth devices. The Bluetooth specification as well as many other wireless specifications must adhere to regulations set by the FCC. There are three general wireless power classifications described by the FCC, as shown in Figure 7-29.

The classes are labeled Class 1, Class 2, and Class 3, and the amount of power of each classification is directly related to the maximum distance an RF device can transmit. The power output of radio devices is measured in milliwatts (mW), which is very little energy as compared to other electronic devices.

Most common short-range RF input devices are rated as a Class-3 device with a maximum range of one meter, though there are some instances of Class-2 input devices. In general, the maximum distances indicated in Figure 7-29 reflect ideal conditions. If there is a significant amount of radio interference, the maximum distance will be reduced, and if the radio interference is excessive, the wireless device will fail to operate entirely.

Wireless devices operate in either the 27-MHz range or the 2.4-GHz Bluetooth range, though there are 2.4-GHz devices that are not Bluetooth. Remember, Bluetooth is a standard, not a specific frequency, although it is assigned to use a specific frequency. When Bluetooth is used to connect to the computer receiver, the typical maximum range is approximately six feet (1.8 meters). When using the 27-MHz frequency, the range can be significantly farther. Both the 27-MHz and the 2.4-GHz radio frequencies can be interfered with by other devices, such as cordless phones, microwave ovens, garage door openers, and baby monitors.

Wireless devices are incorporated into many portable devices such as laptops, tablets, smartphones, and cameras. If the device does not have built-in wireless, such as most desktop computers, the wireless connection is provided by connecting a wireless device to any available USB port. Alternatively, a wireless card can often be installed in a PCI slot.

Wi-Fi

The **Wi-Fi standard** was developed by the Wi-Fi Alliance to produce a specification for interfacing with 2.4-GHz networking devices and network applications. It closely follows the IEEE 802.11 standard. Since the original Wi-Fi standard was released, it has expanded to include cameras, webcams, laptops, phones, printers, game consoles, and many other devices that were once dominated by Bluetooth. Interestingly, Microsoft and Logitech have chosen not to include Wi-Fi as a choice for their mice and keyboard communication. Wi-Fi has similar power limitations as Bluetooth, mainly because all radio equipment used in the United States must meet the FCC regulations.

Be aware that both Bluetooth and Wi-Fi devices operate at the same 2.4-GHz frequency and can interfere with each other if they are close in proximity. In addition, Wi-Fi devices may operate at 5 GHz, but 5-GHz devices are not commonly used for short-range input.

FCC Bluetooth Power Classifications

Class	Power in Milliwatts (mW)	Maximum Range in Meters (m)
1	100	100
2	10	10
3	1	1

Goodheart-Willcox Publisher

Figure 7-29 There are three general wireless power classifications described by the FCC.

Wireless USB

One of the latest wireless specifications is the WUSB standard. **Wireless USB (WUSB)** is a wireless standard developed by the Wireless USB Promoters Group to replace the traditional USB2 connections using radio frequencies between 3.1 GHz to 10.6 GHz. The WUSB standard is intended for communication between the PC and many common PC devices such as cameras, projectors, printers, scanners, and MP3 players.

In general, WUSB devices transfer more data per second than Bluetooth and Wi-Fi products. The WUSB data rate is 480 Mbps at three meters and 110 Mbps at 10 meters. As the distance between the wireless devices increases, data throughput decreases.

There are two organizations that sponsor Wireless USB specifications: WiMedia Alliance and Wireless USB Promoters Group and. The *WiMedia Alliance* is an independent industry group sharing a common interest in developing a high-bandwidth, short-range, wireless medium specification. The *Wireless USB Promoters Group* is part of the USB Implementers Forum. This group requests that their standard users identify their products as "Certified Wireless USB" rather than with the acronym WUSB, which can lead to confusion. Both standards are similar and achieve the same data rates. Visit the USB Implementers Forum website to learn more about the USB wireless device standard.

Ultra-Wideband

The **Ultra-Wideband (UWB) standard** is a standard developed by the WiMedia Alliance and describes short-distance (10-meter) radio communication. The UWB standard specifies the use of the 3.1-GHz to 10.6-GHz radio frequencies. The USB and FireWire cable technologies base their wireless media on the UWB specifications. Ultra-Wideband (UWB) was originally an International Standards Organization (ISO) radio standard that was adopted by several other organizations responsible for their own individual set of radio standards.

Other Wireless Protocols

There are a number of protocols that have been developed in recent years. Many of these are commonly used with Internet of Things (IoT) devices. These are not emphasized on the test, but it is possible you might encounter them in the field. Some common, newer wireless protocols are described in this section. In addition to the following, there will be additional wireless technologies discussed in later chapters when subjects such as laptop computers and networking are presented.

ANT+

ANT+ is a wireless protocol often used with sensor data such as in bio sensors or exercise applications. The name is an acronym for *Adaptive Network Topology*. It operates at 2.4 GHZ and is similar in concept to Bluetooth low energy. It is primarily used in sensors, so it has built in power consumption modalities. It can be configured to stay in low power or sleep mode and wake up just to communicate before returning to sleep mode. Each ANT channel has one or more transmitting nodes and one or more receiving nodes. Note that the channels are bidirectional, so any channel can send or receive.

RuBee

RuBee is the common name of IEEE standard 1902.1, which is a two-way wireless protocol designed for harsh environments. It uses long-wave magnetic signals to send short data packets of roughly about 128 bytes. RuBee's bandwidth is low compared to other wireless protocols, but it is not blocked by liquid or even steel. It has been approved for use in the US Department of Defense for high explosive areas, and it is also approved by the US Department of Energy for secure facilities.

MQTT

MQ Telemetry Support (MQTT) is an ISO Standard (ISO/IEC PRF 20922) that functions as a network protocol for transporting messages between devices. It often works with TCP/IP but can work with any protocol that is lossless and bidirectional. It was first designed in 1999 for applications with low network bandwidth and was first used to monitor oil pipelines. An MQTT control message can be as little as two bytes of data, making it attractive in industrial settings.

Synchronizing the Wireless Device

A typical wireless mouse and keyboard are normally ready to use after installing the batteries because the products are usually synchronized at the factory before shipping them to retailers. *Synchronizing* is the operation of matching a pair of devices to each other so that they recognize each other and no other wireless devices in the same general area of use.

After a few months of use, the device batteries may fail, or radio interference from a device other than the matched keyboard and mouse may interfere. In this case, the keyboard or mouse must be resynchronized with the receiver. Synchronization typically requires that a button on the wireless device and receiving unit be pressed so the two devices can identify each other and connect using the same frequency and assigned channel. Figure 7-30 shows the instructions printed on the back of a keyboard.

The diagram shown in Figure 7-30 instructs users to press the button on the receiving unit first and then to press the button on the bottom of the mouse. The two devices will establish a link if they are in range. The diagram indicates to wait 20 seconds for the synchronization to occur and then to repeat the process for the wireless keyboard. Some devices do not have a synchronization button or special sequence to follow to synchronize the receiver and keyboard or mouse. They automatically synchronize when turned on.

Most mice and keyboards have at least two possible channels for communication. For example, Microsoft uses the assigned channels and frequencies indicated in Figure 7-31 to match the receiver with the keyboard and mouse.

Goodheart-Willcox Publisher

Figure 7-30 The back of this particular Logitech keyboard displays instructions for synchronizing the receiving unit with the mouse and keyboard.

Microsoft Wireless Channels		
Device	**Channel 1**	**Channel 2**
Keyboard	27.095 MHz	27.195 MHz
Mouse	27.045 MHz	27.145 MHz

Goodheart-Willcox Publisher

Figure 7-31 Microsoft-brand wireless keyboards and mice use specifically assigned channels and frequencies.

Wireless Device Failure

The most common reason for wireless input device failure is battery failure. A battery will last six months on average, but you can expect variations in battery life based on how much the device is used each day. Also, some batteries provide energy longer than others do. For example, rechargeable batteries last much longer and can often be used for up to five or more years before requiring replacement.

You may encounter device-specific problems. For example, an optical mouse may require cleaning as a routine maintenance or troubleshooting problem. First, clean the optical lens area using a dry lint-free cloth or use dry compressed air designed for this purpose. If this fails to clean the unit, check the manufacturer's website or product literature to see what chemical cleaners, if any, are safe to use on the unit.

Another common reason for failure is radio interference. Many other electronic devices use the same radio frequency that is assigned to wireless devices. For example, baby monitors, garage door openers, microwave ovens, wireless phones, and many other devices may interfere with wireless devices.

Many times, you can counter the effects of radio interference by using a different channel assignment. Some wireless devices have several channels to choose from when configuring the device. If radio interference is suspected as a cause for wireless connection failure or very low data rates, you may want to change the assigned channel. You can locate the exact method to change an assigned channel by checking the device documentation or the manufacturer's website. There will be much more about wireless technology in later chapters, but the following are general steps to take when troubleshooting wireless input devices.

1. Turn the device off and then back on.
2. Plug the USB receiver into another USB port.
3. Restart the computer.
4. Replace the batteries.
5. Download and reinstall the device driver or check for an updated driver.

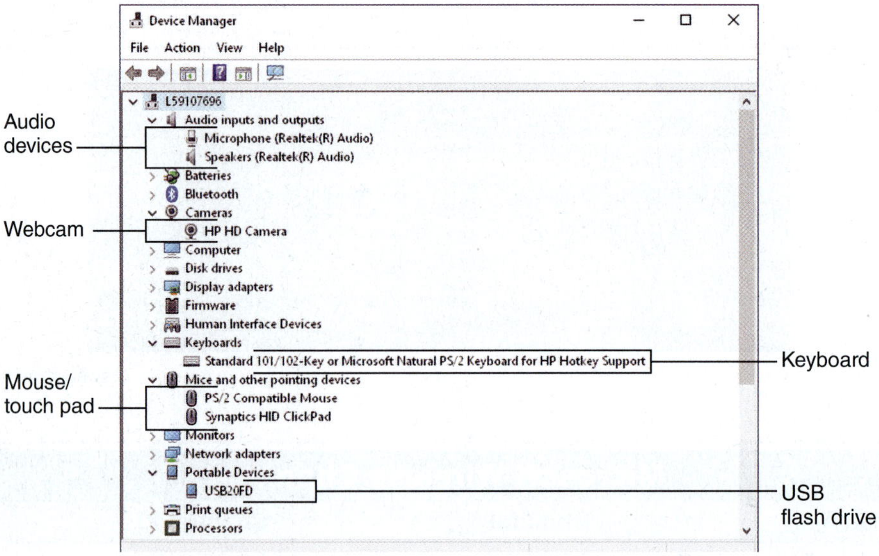

Figure 7-32 Device Manager is a great place to start troubleshooting an input device.

Goodheart-Willcox Publisher

7.7 Managing Input Devices

Input devices can and will fail. When they do, there are several quick and easy ways to investigate the possible reason for failure. The most common Microsoft tool used to inspect input devices is **Device Manager. Devices and Printers** can also be used.

Device Manager

1102: 1.4 A+

Device Manager provides information about input devices and other hardware, as shown in Figure 7-32. It is an excellent tool to determine if an input device is properly installed. A problem with an input device is indicated by special symbols such as a red *X* or yellow exclamation point. **Device Manager** also allows you to obtain driver details and update the driver.

To view the properties of a device, right-click the device name and select **Properties** from the shortcut menu. Select the **Driver** tab, which includes the options **Driver Details**, **Update Driver**, **Roll Back Driver**, **Disable**, and **Uninstall**, as shown in Figure 7-33. Notice that the option to roll back the driver appears dimmed as compared to the other options. This is because you cannot roll back the driver for this device. You can only roll back a device driver when a previous driver has been installed. Windows 8 added a new tab for HID-compliant devices called **Events**, which displays a historical log of activities related to a specific device. For example, the events log might contain the date and time of when a device was configured, stopped, started, or failed. Having a record of events that directly affect a device is invaluable when attempting to solve a device problem.

Devices and Printers

1102: 1.4 A+

Devices and Printers provides a centralized location to add or remove devices, select a default printer, view device properties, and more. Figure 7-34 shows a list of options that are available after right-clicking a device in Windows 10. The Devices and Printers menu can be accessed through **Control Panel>Hardware and Sound>Devices and Printers.** The **Devices and Printers** menu in Figure 7-35 shows icons of the devices associated with a Windows 10 laptop. Though not shown in Figure 7-35, some icons may appear dimmed. This means the device was installed and used in the past but is not currently connected to the computer. You may also see an icon for a *USB Composite Device*, which is two or more USB devices configured through the same input device. For example, a wireless keyboard and mouse may be attached through the same receiver, which would constitute a USB Composite Device.

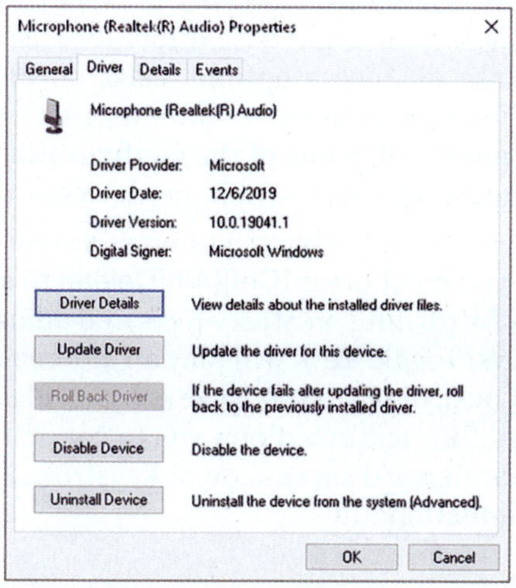

Goodheart-Willcox Publisher

Figure 7-33 The **Device Properties** dialog box includes information about the device and the ability to modify or update drivers for the device.

Figure 7-34 A list of device-related options is revealed when right-clicking a device in **Devices and Printers**.

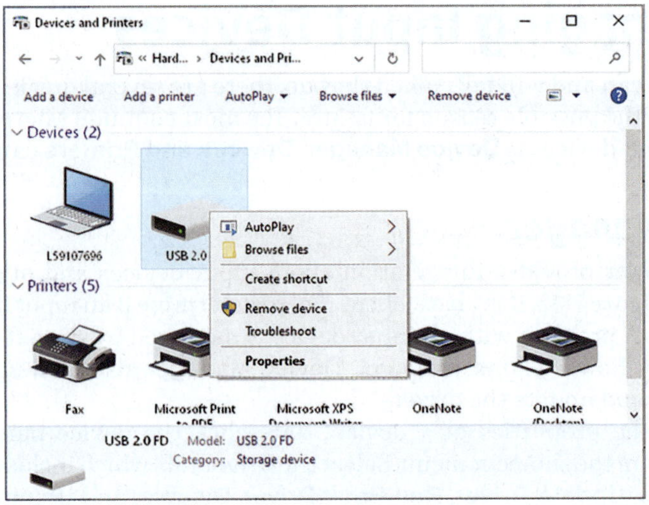

Goodheart-Willcox Publisher

Figure 7-35 Devices and Printers provides a centralized location to add or remove devices.

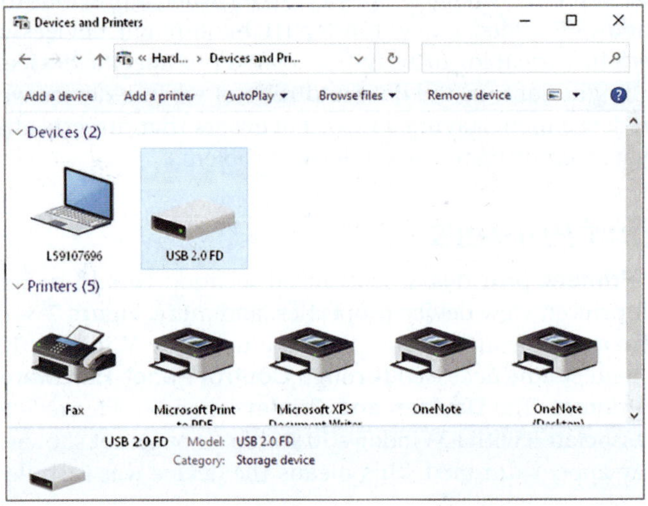

Goodheart-Willcox Publisher

A+ 1102: 1.4

Tech Tip

Sticky keys are often turned on by accident by users who hold a key down for a certain amount of time or press a key a certain number of times in a short period.

Ease of Access

The Ease of Access feature is designed to make the user experience better for people with disabilities, or for those who might have difficulties using a mouse or keyboard or viewing a screen. Ease of Access options exist on all editions of Microsoft Windows. Figure 7-36 shows the options available for user configuration in the Ease of Access Center for Windows 10. Some of the configuration options available that are directly related to mouse and keyboard input devices include the following:

- **Turn on Sticky Keys:** Instead of having to press a combination of keys all at once, such as when you must press [Ctrl][Alt][Delete] to access Task Manager, you can use one key by turning on Sticky Keys and adjusting the settings.
- **Turn on Toggle Keys:** Toggle Keys will play an alert each time you press the [Caps Lock], [Num Lock], or [Scroll Lock] keys by accident.
- **Turn on Filter Keys:** This feature allows you to configure Windows to ignore keystrokes that occur in rapid succession or keystrokes that are held down for several seconds unintentionally.

- **Underline keyboard shortcuts and access keys**: This option makes keyboard access in dialog boxes easier by highlighting the access keys for the commands or options in them.

Several visual and audio enhancements will be discussed in later chapters.

KVM Switch

A **keyboard-video-mouse (KVM) switch** is a device used to share a keyboard, monitor, and mouse with two or more computers or servers. KVM switches are typically found in server rooms, and without a KVM switch, each computer or server would require its own mouse, keyboard, and monitor. The switch allows administrators to toggle from one device to another without having to move to use different input devices. The individual computers are connected through special cables designed for the KVM switch or with standard USB cables using a manually switchable USB hub. Some variations of KVM switches can also share devices such as speakers.

Figure 7-37 shows a VGA-compatible KVM switch that includes USB, video, and audio connections. The black connections are USB and used for the mouse and keyboard. The green connection is for audio, and the blue connection is for a 15-pin VGA connector, which is used for video.

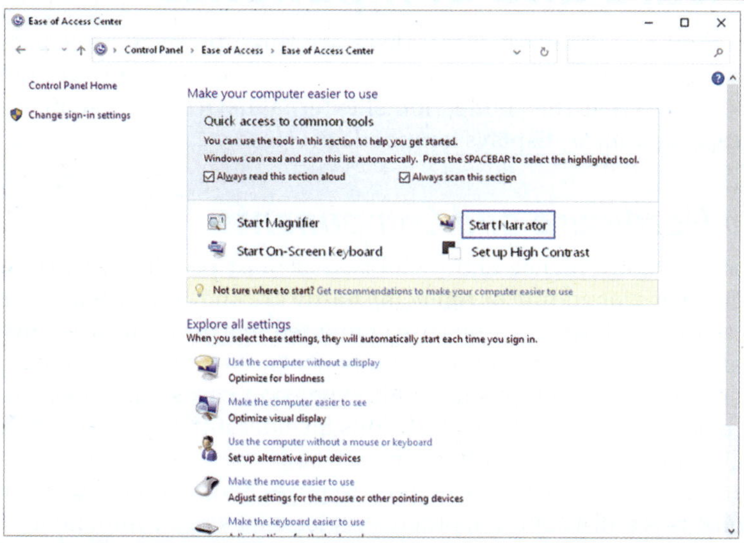

Goodheart-Willcox Publisher

Figure 7-36 The Ease of Access feature is designed to make the user experience better for people with disabilities, or for those who might have difficulties using a mouse or keyboard or viewing a screen.

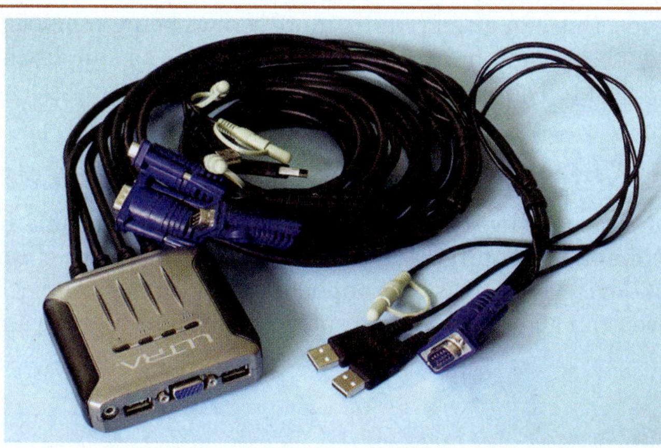

Goodheart-Willcox Publisher

Figure 7-37 A keyboard-video-mouse (KVM) switch is used to share a keyboard, monitor, and mouse with two or more computers or servers.

Tech Tip

The 15-pin VGA connector is also referred to as *DB-15*, *HDB-15*, and *HDDB-15*. The *HD* in these connector names represents *high density*, not *high definition*.

KVM switches are designed for VGA technology when connected to high-definition monitors. These monitors sometimes use pins to exchange information with the computer. These pins are not assigned between the HDMI and DB-15 connections and may not support special video functions, but basic video is still supported. There are special adapters made to correct these video problems by simulating the missing connection pins.

Switching from one computer to the next with a KVM switch is accomplished either through push buttons located on the switch, a rotary switch, or via assigned key combinations on the keyboard.

A special KVM switch called KVM over IP (iKVM) uses a network to exchange commands from a centralized keyboard and mouse with individual computers and servers located on the network. Each computer or server has a specialized video capture card installed, which captures the screen display at each location and transmits the image back to a centralized iKVM-designated computer. The computer can then send keyboard and mouse instructions to each computer via the network connection.

7.8 Managing Mobile Device Hardware and Components

When one thinks of mobile devices, there are three primary categories: laptops, tablets, and smartphones. Each type of device can require hardware replacement or upgrading as well as the connection of external devices. This section will cover these concepts as well as displays for mobile devices.

Laptop Hardware and Components

Laptops provide convenience and mobility that most people enjoy. However, they do pose challenges for adding or replacing hardware and components. There simply is much less space within a laptop case compared to a desktop case. This generally means that if one wishes to add new components, they must be added externally. In the past, this was accomplished with expansion cards, but today, all external devices can be connected utilizing USB. This includes input devices as well as external drives, printers, and many other components.

While adding components to a laptop requires adding them externally, replacing components is still a common practice, at least for some components. Generally, cards such as video and sound cards are built into the laptop motherboard and thus cannot be replaced. However, laptop hard drives can be replaced with very little difficulty. Much like a desktop or server hard drive, the issue will be removing the case. With laptops, this can often require more screws being removed, but once the case is removed, changing a hard drive or RAM chip is as simple and straightforward as it is in a desktop computer.

Tablet and Smartphone Hardware and Accessories

For tablets and smartphones, there is almost no field-replaceable hardware. The only real component you can replace is a SIM card, which will change the phone number for that device. Note, this only applies to smartphones and cellular-enabled tablets. SIM cards can also contain data such as contacts and even apps.

While components are generally not field replaceable, there are a number of accessories that can be attached and replaced, such as the credit card readers discussed in a previous section. Recall that these devices attach to a device via USB, audio, or other type of input port similarly to any other mobile device accessory.

Styluses, also called touch pens, are popular accessories for both smartphones and tablets. In some cases, the stylus also functions as a remote control, often used as a timer or remote for taking photos. If the stylus came with the device, chances are it has already been synchronized. If not, most work via Bluetooth, so all that is needed is to pair the stylus with your device.

1101: 1.3 A+

Mobile Device Display

While a display is not normally considered an input device, display components of mobile devices function as both monitor and input since the touch screen is the only form of user interaction available. Display components of mobile devices have advanced substantially in recent years. Early mobile devices utilized *liquid crystal displays (LCDs)*, which was supplanted by *light-emitting diode (LED)* displays in recent years. There have been many improvements to LED. For example, *organic light-emitting diode (OLED, organic LED)* is a widely used improvement to the previous LED display. OLED displays contain a film of organic compounds that emit light when subjected to electric current and are used in smartphones and tablets, among other devices.

There are two general types of OLED displays: passive-matrix OLED (PMOLED) and active-matrix OLED (AMOLED). Active-matrix OLED exists in a wide array of variations found on specific devices. For example, Super Retina HS is an AMOLED variation used for iPhone 11 and Samsung Galaxy S6 and S7, Dynamic AMOLED is used in Samsung Galaxy S10, and Super Retina XDR Display is used in iPhone 14. There will be more about video and display types in a later chapter.

Like touch screen displays discussed earlier in this chapter, tablets and smartphone displays rely on a touch screen controller or digitizer. Often, the controller or digitizer within a touch screen malfunctions, typically due to a drop or other type of damage to the screen. When this happens, the user will be able to see the display, but their touch input will go unrecognized. In most cases, a damaged digitizer will have to be replaced by the manufacturer. However, there are some basic troubleshooting steps for determining whether a digitizer is damaged or simply unresponsive, such as the following:

1101: 5.5 A+

- Memory issues can cause a digitizer to stop responding. If you can, close out unused or unneeded apps currently open or running on your device to free up additional memory.
- Restart the device.
- If available, perform a touch screen calibration.

Note, if the touch screen is unresponsive, you will likely not be able to perform many of these steps. If possible, connect your device to a dock that has a keyboard and mouse and close the apps that way. In the event you are unable to get your touch screen to continue functioning, you will likely have to replace the display, digitizer, or both.

Chapter Summary

7.1 USB Implementers Forum

- The USB Implementers Forum (USB-IF) consists of industry experts with a common interest in creating a standard guideline for the development of drivers for USB input and output devices.
- The USB standard describes how different classifications of devices should communicate with a PC.
- HID is a set of standards written for hardware device drivers to ensure compatibility between hardware devices and computers.

7.2 Keyboard

- The typical keyboard has a small microprocessor installed as a keyboard controller, which is not as powerful as the PC processor and instead used for small device applications such as telephones, automobiles, and appliances.
- The keyboard controller connects to the keyboard circuit traces and to the USB cable port.
- Switches used under keyboard keys are typically one of mechanical, membrane, rubber dome, or capacitor types.
- Keyboard scan codes are interpreted by the BIOS and sent to the CPU as an ASCII character.
- Ergonomic keyboards are keyboards shaped for comfort and injury prevention.
- A virtual keyboard is a software-based keyboard that allows the input of data without the use of physical keys.
- Most of the problems with keyboards are associated with grime and debris in and around the keys. Keyboard keys can easily be disabled by dirt or corrosion. A keyboard should be cleaned on a regular basis.
- Certain keyboard properties can be adjusted for preference in the **Keyboard Properties** dialog box.

7.3 Optical Mouse

- An optical mouse uses a light beam, receiver, CMOS digital camera, and microprocessor to derive its relative direction of movement and speed.
- Two light sources commonly used with optical mice are LED and laser.
- Optical mice have no mechanical parts, so there is never an issue of worn parts.
- The **Mouse Properties** dialog box is used to adjust the mouse's functionality, such as speed of pointer travel across the screen and the speed used to double-click, and aesthetics.

7.4 Other Input Devices

- Commonly encountered input devices include magnetic and chip readers; trackballs; game pads; digitizer pads; bar code readers; scanners; digital cameras and webcams; light pens; and virtual reality, augmented reality, and audio headsets.
- Magnetic and chip readers can be inserted via USB, Lightning, or headphone ports.
- A trackball is a mouse with a ball embedded in the top of it.
- The term *game pad* applies to any device used as an input for a game application.

- A digitizer pad is a virtual drawing surface that allows the user to create or modify drawings or modify photos.
- A bar code reader uses a light source transmitter and receiver to read bar codes.
- Scanners and digital cameras both depend on either the CCD or CMOS technology to capture images.

7.5 Touch Screens

- The major touch screen technologies are resistance, capacitance, near-field effect, infrared, and acoustical wave.

7.6 Wireless Input Devices

- NFC uses electromagnetic (EM) induction between two loop antennas when NFC-enabled devices transfer information. Data rates range from 106 to 424 kbit/second, a fraction of what Bluetooth can achieve. NFC has a variety of uses, such as making purchases at tap-to-pay terminals and transferring contacts, photos, and other media from one device to another.
- Infrared devices use light to establish the connection between the input device and the computer. These devices work in similar fashion as a television remote control.
- Radio frequency (RF) devices use radio waves to communicate between the remote device and the receiver.
- Bluetooth, Wi-Fi, and IEEE 802.11 use the 2.4-GHz radio frequency; Wi-Fi and 802.11 use the 2.4-GHz and 5-GHz radio frequencies; UWB and WUSB use the 3.1-GHz to 10.6-GHz radio frequencies.
- Synchronizing is the operation of matching a pair of devices to each other so that they recognize each other and no other wireless devices in the same general area of use.
- The most common reason for wireless input device failure is battery failure.

7.7 Managing Input Devices

- Device Manager, Devices and Printers, and the Ease of Access Center can be used to manage computer input devices.
- A keyboard-video-mouse (KVM) switch is a device used to share a keyboard, monitor, and mouse with two or more computers or servers.

7.8 Mobile Device Hardware and Components

- Laptops provide convenience and mobility but pose challenges for adding or replacing hardware and components. If one wishes to add new components, they must be added externally. Replacing internal components is still a common practice.
- For tablets and smartphones, there is almost no field-replaceable hardware. The only real component you can replace is a SIM card.
- There are a number of accessories that can be attached and replaced, such as credit card readers.
- Styluses are popular accessories for both smartphones and tablets. If the stylus came with the device, chances are it has already been synchronized. If not, most work via Bluetooth, so all that is needed is to pair the stylus with your device.
- While a display is not normally considered an input device, display components of mobile devices function as both monitor and input since the touch screen is the only form of user interaction available.

Review Questions

1. What is the purpose of the USB-IF?
2. List and describe standards developed by the USB-IF.
3. List and describe the functionality of four types of keyboard switches.
4. How is a keyboard scan code generated and interpreted?
5. How does an optical mouse operate?
6. Aside from a keyboard and mouse, list commonly encountered input devices.
7. Summarize how a magnetic or chip reader can be used in a mobile device.
8. What do a scanner and camera use to capture images?
9. What is a CCD?
10. What is the main difference between CMOS and CCD imaging devices?
11. Differentiate between the characteristics of major touch screen technologies.
12. What type of touch screen is best for a dusty environment?
13. List examples of wireless input devices.
14. List and describe examples of wireless input technologies.
15. Differentiate among common wireless protocols and standards.
16. What is the main advantage of RF over infrared technology?
17. What common radio frequency is shared by Bluetooth and Wi-Fi?
18. Compare and contrast utilities in Microsoft Windows that troubleshoot or enhance input devices.
19. What is the function of a KVM switch?
20. Summarize the unique challenges presented by managing mobile device hardware and components.

Sample A+ Exam Questions

1. Which two connection ports are most commonly associated with keyboards? Select all that apply.
   A. 15-pin D shell
   B. PS/2
   C. USB
   D. LPT1
2. Which type of device is most commonly associated with HID?
   A. Laser printer
   B. LCD display
   C. Mouse
   D. Portable device battery
3. A wireless optical mouse was installed properly and worked fine for two months. Now it fails to respond. The user has tried rebooting the computer, but the mouse still does not work. What is *most likely* the cause of failure?
   A. An incorrect driver
   B. A recent Windows update
   C. The battery
   D. Radio interference from the keyboard

4. Which best defines a keyboard scan code?
   A. A keyboard scan code is a signal generated when a key is struck on the keyboard. It determines what symbol is displayed on the monitor.
   B. A keyboard scan code is a signal generated by the keyboard scan generator. It checks what key is being pressed and then generates the corresponding ASCII symbol.
   C. A keyboard scan code is a binary code that records the duration that a key is held down.
   D. A keyboard scan code is generated by the CPU and then sent to the keyboard to identify which key is being pressed.
5. The physical design of a keyboard is referred to as what?
   A. Ergonomics
   B. Ecology
   C. Carpalmatics
   D. Physiology
6. Which of the following items is best for cleaning a keyboard?
   A. Glass cleaner
   B. A solution of 50 percent alcohol and 50 percent water
   C. Dry compressed air
   D. Any vacuum cleaner
7. Which technology does an optical mouse use?
   A. Wireless radio communication model
   B. Magnetic wheel that converts a light signal into digital pulses
   C. CMOS technology similar to digital camera technology
   D. Friction surface detection matrix
8. Which frequency is typically associated with Bluetooth and Wi-Fi devices?
   A. 2.4 GHz
   B. 24 MHz
   C. 5 GHz
   D. 5 MHz
9. Which is the correct path to access the mouse configuration speed setting on a Windows 10 computer?
   A. **Start>Mouse>Settings**
   B. **Start>Control Panel>Mouse**
   C. **Start>Control Panel>Pointing Device**
   D. **Start>Control Panel>Device Manager>Settings**
10. What similar light-sensitive devices do scanners and digital cameras use to acquire an image? Select all that apply.
   A. OCR
   B. CMOS
   C. ADC
   D. CCD

Chapter 8

Video Systems

Learning Outcomes

8.1 Recall common characteristics of all monitors.
8.2 Differentiate between LCD, gas-plasma, and projector displays.
8.3 Define commonly encountered video terminology
8.4 Compare and contrast video adapter card types.
8.5 List techniques for troubleshooting, cleaning, and personalizing a video display.
8.6 Identify computer monitor and home-theater connection types.
8.7 Differentiate among coding methods.

A+ Certification Exam Objectives

The following A+ Certification Exam Objectives are covered in this chapter.

Exam 220-1101

1.0 Mobile Devices

- 1.1 Given a scenario, install and configure laptop hardware and components.
- 1.2 Compare and contrast the display components of mobile devices.

3.0 Hardware

- 3.1 Explain basic cable types, features, and their purposes.
- 3.4 Given a scenario, install and configure motherboards, central processing units (CPUs), and add-on cards.

5.0 Hardware and Network Troubleshooting

- 5.4 Given a scenario, troubleshoot video, projector, and display issues.
- 5.5 Given a scenario, troubleshoot common mobile device issues while adhering to the appropriate procedures.
- 5.7 Given a scenario, troubleshoot problems with wired and wireless networks.

Exam 220-1102

4.0 Operational Procedures

- 4.4 Given a scenario, use common safety procedures.
- 4.5 Summarize environmental impacts and local environmental controls.

Key Terms

active-matrix display
alternating-frame rendering
aspect ratio
color palette
digital-to-analog converter (DAC)
dot pitch
extended graphics array (XGA)
gas-plasma display
High-Definition Multimedia Interface (HDMI)
inverter
LED display
liquid-crystal display (LCD)
native resolution
organic LED (OLED) display
passive-matrix display
pixel
pixel pitch
polarized light
refresh rate
resolution
run-length encoding (RLE)
Scalable Link Interface (SLI)
split-frame rendering
Super VGA (SVGA)
thin-film transistor liquid-crystal display (TFT-LCD)
true color
video graphics array (VGA)

Overview

This chapter covers video systems, including computer displays, video cards, and computer-based home entertainment systems. This understanding is critical to designing and evaluating a high-performance computer system or a computer-based home entertainment system. You will be introduced to common Microsoft operating system tools that will assist you in evaluating and designing a high-performance computer system. The video system is one of the most influential modules for determining computer performance.

A+ Note

The CompTIA A+ Exams require candidates to select components for a customized computer based on customer needs. You should be able to evaluate a computer system and decide if it is best for general computer use, graphic design work, audio and video editing, gaming, and similar applications.

Caution

Do *not* open a computer monitor case for any reason. Inside a computer monitor, you may encounter well over 1,000 volts. A monitor should only be opened by a trained and qualified electronics technician.

8.1 Video System and Display Characteristics

A computer video system consists of two main components: the display (monitor) and the adapter. The video adapter is often called a *video card* or *graphics card*. There are some references made to legacy video systems in this chapter, many of which are no longer manufactured. This brief information, however, will help you understand the development of the computer video system as well as help you identify obsolete systems when you encounter them. There are still a number of these old technologies in existence, and being unable to identify them can be extremely frustrating and embarrassing to any technician.

Before examining monitor types and video cards, you should first understand common characteristics of video systems, specifically color display values and resolution. Resolution greatly affects the quality of the picture produced as well as the price you will pay for the unit.

Color Display Values

The color display quality is determined by the number of bits used to represent the individual colors of red, green, and blue. The number of bits used to represent each color also determines the possible number of color shades. A byte contains 8 bits, which translates to 256 possible combinations of 1s and 0s in a byte. This means that an 8-bit color pattern can reproduce 256 intensities of a specific color. Figure 8-1 lists common standard color display values, expressed in bits. As the number of bits increases, so does the number of possible colors produced. By mixing the intensities of red, blue, and green, other colors can be produced.

The color mix guide in Figure 8-2 shows the application of 256,000 color intensities and the total spectrum of color produced by the monitor. This figure is a screen capture taken from the **Edit Colors** dialog box from Microsoft's Paint program. Paint can be accessed through **Start>All Apps>Windows Accessories>Paint**. Alternatively, you could open the **Start** menu and conduct a search using the keyword Paint. Using the **Edit Colors** dialog box, you can create your own palette of colors beyond the standard default colors by moving your mouse across the sample of colors in the display and varying the amount of red, blue, and green that make up the custom color. In the bottom-right corner are three numeric text boxes, each containing the value of red, green, and blue used to make the color indicated under the cursor. The values correspond to the 8-bit range (0 to 255), which is an example of a 24-bit color system. There are also numeric text boxes showing the hue, saturation, and brightness of the given color.

Figure 8-1 As the number of bits in a color display value increases, so does the number of possible colors produced.

Standard Color Display Values

Color Display Value	Number of Colors
8-bit	256
16-bit (true color)	65,536
24-bit (true color)	167,777,216
32-bit (true color)	4,294,967,296
48-bit (deep color)	281,474,976,710,656

Goodheart-Willcox Publisher

Display Resolution

A+ 1101: 3.1

The term **resolution** refers to the amount of detail a monitor can display. This term is also used to describe the detail produced by printers, digital cameras, and any similar type of graphics equipment. High resolution produces finer, better detail than low resolution. See Figure 8-3 for a comparison of resolution patterns. The image in Figure 8-3A has a higher resolution than that in Figure 8-3B.

Resolution is measured in pixels (picture elements). A **pixel** is the smallest unit of color in a screen display. Think of it as a small dot. A typical VGA system has a resolution of 640 × 480, meaning a VGA display has a screen layout of 640 pixels by 480 pixels, or 307,200 pixels. Some of the most common resolutions are listed in Figure 8-4.

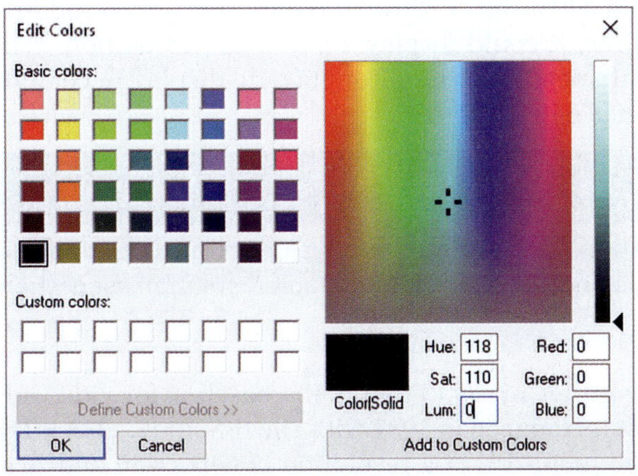

Goodheart-Willcox Publisher

Figure 8-2 The color mix guide in Microsoft's Paint program shows 256,000 color intensities as well as the total spectrum of color produced by a monitor.

A B

Goodheart-Willcox Publisher

Figure 8-3 Resolution refers to the amount of detail a monitor can display. High-resolution monitors (A) produce better detail than low-resolution monitors (B).

Common Resolutions		
Resolution	**Acronym**	**Designation**
640 × 480	VGA	Video graphics array
800 × 600	SVGA	Super video graphics array
1024 × 768	XGA	Extended graphics array
1280 × 1024	UVGA	Ultra video graphics array
1400 × 1050	SXGA	Super extended graphics array
1600 × 1200	UXGA	Ultra extended graphics array
1920 × 1200	WUXGA	Wide ultra extended graphics array

Goodheart-Willcox Publisher

Figure 8-4 Resolution is measured in pixels, the smallest unit of color in a display.

When PCs first came to the marketplace, most displays were monochrome display adapter (MDA) monitors. ***Monochrome*** technology displayed only one color, usually amber or green. The video adapters for these monitors were designed to display text only, not graphics. Graphics required a significant amount of memory, and at that time, large amounts of memory were too expensive for most users. Early computers were used for business and research, not entertainment. The screen resolution was 720 × 350, which presented a very sharp, clear image for text only.

In 1981, IBM introduced the ***color/graphics adapter (CGA)*** video standard, which offered two resolutions: 320 × 200 in four colors (from a choice of sixteen colors) and 640 × 200 in two colors. Another company offered the Hercules adapter card, which had a resolution of 720 × 348 and met the requirements of graphics-heavy programs (such as AutoCAD) that the IBM adapter could not fulfill.

In 1987, IBM introduced the ***enhanced graphics adapter (EGA)***, which could display 16 colors in 640 × 200 or 320 × 200 resolution on a standard IBM color monitor. In monochrome, it could display a 640 × 350 resolution. When the EGA was attached to an enhanced color monitor, it could display 16 colors (from a choice of 64) in a resolution of 640 × 350.

A+ Note

The A+ Certification Exams often contain at least one question referencing VGA resolution. This is because VGA is the default resolution used when booting into Safe Mode.

The **video graphics array (VGA)** is the baseline for video adapters. The VGA standard was first introduced in 1987 with the IBM PS/2. VGA is the true minimum standard for video monitors, at a resolution of 640 × 480 and 16 colors. Up to 256 colors can be displayed, but only when the resolution is reduced to 320 × 200.

The VGA color palette contains 262,144 (256k) different colors. A **color palette** is a collection of possible different colors, usually in degrees or shades, that can be displayed on a monitor. The palette contains a large variety of possible colors, but the total number of colors in the palette cannot be displayed at the same time on a monitor. For example, a video system such as VGA that can display up to 256 colors in the 320 × 200 mode can only use 256 colors from the total 262,144 colors possible in the palette.

Tech Tip

When a computer system detects a malfunction, it will start in Safe Mode, which only supports the minimum video standard of VGA. The VGA mode driver is located in the first 1 MB of memory, while drivers that are more sophisticated require memory above the first 1 MB. For comparison, Windows 10 only requires 800 × 600 resolution, while Windows 8 required 1024 × 768. The Windows 8 requirement was much higher and required more memory. By decreasing the minimum resolution, Windows 10 frees up additional memory for the user.

Think of the color palette as the total number of tubes of color an artist has available to purchase from a supplier. While there may be 262,144 colors in the store, the artist can only afford to buy 256 tubes. Thus, the actual number of colors used for the painting is limited to the 256 colors, assuming the artist does not mix colors. In the same way, while there are 262,144 colors that can be displayed in VGA, the video adapter can only support 256 of the total number at one time.

Also in 1987, the PS/2 display adapter 8514 was also introduced. Compared to VGA, it had a better resolution, offered more colors, and supported up to 1024 × 768 pixels with 256 colors. However, there were some disadvantages. First, the system plugged into IBM micro-channel architecture. Second, to take full advantage of its capabilities, an 8514 color display monitor had to be used. This PS/2 display adapter was replaced by the IBM XGA standard. It is interesting to note that EGA, VGA, and the PS/2 adapter 8514 came out at about the same time. However, only VGA survived the consumer marketplace.

Another standard of the time was the *multicolor/graphics array (MCGA)*. The MCGA adapter could support CGA and provide up to 64 shades of gray when more color variations than the standard CGA were required to be displayed.

Super VGA (SVGA) is a graphics standard that supports 16 million possible colors and various resolutions such as 800 × 600, 1024 × 768, 1280 × 1024, and 1600 × 1200. The exact number of colors that can be displayed at the same time on an SVGA monitor is determined by the amount of memory. The higher the memory, the higher the number of colors produced.

Tech Tip

You will likely see the label *Ultra VGA* used in advertising. Ultra VGA is not a true standard; rather, it is marketing terminology used by manufacturers to describe their video adapters and monitors in an enhanced description.

In 1990, IBM introduced the **extended graphics array (XGA)**, which is a video standard capable of a resolution of 640 × 480 while supporting 65,536 colors and 1024 × 768 with 256 colors. It also supports all of IBM's older graphics standards.

The UVGA, SXGA, UXGA, and WUXGA screen resolutions all evolved naturally from the original VGA and XGA screen resolutions. They are all capable of producing over 16 million colors and supporting the high-definition television (HDTV) resolution standard. When you see a display that is very wide, it will usually be UXGA or WUXGA, as these resolutions are normally used to match the very wide display units.

When the Windows operating system boots in Safe Mode, the screen resolution changes to 640 × 480, the original VGA standard. Compare the 640 × 480 resolution to the screens shown in Figure 8-5. These screens represent the highest and lowest available resolutions for Windows 10. Screen A's resolution is 800 × 600, and the resolution of Screen B is 1366 × 768 (WXGA). The resolution in Screen B is actually a nonstandard resolution derived from widening XGA to a wide-screen ratio. Notice how much larger the desktop icons appear when in the VGA screen resolution.

Figure 8-5 Higher resolutions typically result in smaller icons.

Screen A Screen B

Goodheart-Willcox Publisher

Quad Extended Graphics Array (QXGA) is a graphics standard with a resolution of 2048 × 1536. It has been widely used for many years, most recently in third-generation iPads and the Dell 3008WFP. There are numerous variations on this such as QWXGA (Quad Wide Extended Graphics Array), QSXGA (Quad Super Extended Graphics Array), and WQUXGA (Wide Quad Ultra Extended Graphics Array), among others. More recently, there has been 8K UHD that has a resolution of 7680 × 4320, as well as 16K monitors with resolutions of 17280 × 4320.

A+ 1101: 1.2

8.2 Types of Video Displays

There are a number of different types of display systems for computers. The most common type is the liquid-crystal display (LCD). As the television industry merges computer and television technology into a single display unit, it will no longer be possible to distinguish a computer monitor from a television. Because of this, the gas-plasma display will also be discussed in this chapter. This section covers the basic operation and principles of the displays, technologies, and the terminology with which they are commonly associated.

A+ 1101: 1.2

Liquid-Crystal Displays

A **liquid-crystal display (LCD)** is a flat-panel display that uses liquid crystals and polarizers to produce an image. These types of monitors are the most common. All liquid-crystal displays operate on one of two principles: polarized light and the effect of an electrical voltage applied to a crystalline structure.

Polarized light is light energy composed of light beams with a matching wave angle. A typical light beam consists of numerous waves of light that travel in parallel, but different, wave angles. When a thin slot is cut in a material such as metal, only light waves with an angle matching the slot can travel through the slot. The light that travels through the slot is polarized light.

The second LCD principle is based on the effect of electrical voltage applied to a crystalline structure. When an electrical voltage is applied to a crystal, it changes shape slightly, or twists. The degree of twist is directly related to the amount of voltage applied to the crystal. Light normally passes through the crystal in a straight line. However, when a light is shone through a crystal and voltage is then applied to the same crystal, the angle of the light wave changes as it passes through the crystal.

How Liquid-Crystal Displays Work

To understand how the typical liquid-crystal display works, follow along while referring to Figure 8-6. The LCD panel is constructed of several thin layers of material. A thin fluorescent backlight is used as the source of light energy for the display, and when it strikes through the first polarizing filter, only light waves with an angle matching the slot can pass through the filter.

The polarized light passes through the array of crystals, each of which has a transistor connected to it. The transistors act similarly to a dimmer light switch, which can be turned on in varying degrees. The amount of voltage applied to each crystal by the individual transistors determines the amount of twist in each crystal and, by extension, the amount of change in the light wave. Any crystal that has voltage applied to it causes the angle of the light beam to change as it passes through the crystal.

The second polarizing filter is used to screen out light waves that are no longer polarized. The amount of change in each light wave determines how much of the polarized light can pass through the second filter. For example, a light beam passing through a crystal with a maximum voltage applied will have its angle changed to the extent that none of the light energy will pass through the second filter. This creates a dark pixel image on the display. A light beam passing through a crystal with no voltage applied will not have its angle changed and will therefore pass through the second filter. This creates a pixel image at full brightness. The number of light and dark pixels directly relates to the applied voltage at each crystal.

Backlighting

A+ 1101: 1.2

Liquid-crystal displays require some form of backlighting. The two sources of backlighting are cold cathode fluorescent lamp (CCFL) and light-emitting diode (LED).

A CCFL consists of a glass tube filled with a gas and an electrode at each end. When high voltage is applied to the two electrodes, an electrical circuit is created through the gas in the tube, creating light. Normally, a computer monitor or television has a 120-VAC electrical supply. When no such supply is available and the device is energized by a power source such as a battery, an inverter is required. An **inverter** is an electronic device that converts the low voltage (12–18 VDC) from the portable battery to a much higher voltage required by the CCFL, Figure 8-7. The CCFL may require as much as 1,200 VAC for initial lighting and, on average, as much as 800 VAC to maintain the light. The voltage range during normal operation, including dimming, can be as low as 200 VAC.

Another type of backlight used for portable devices is light-emitting diode (LED). An LED is an electronic device that emits light when a DC voltage is applied to it. Figure 8-8 shows the construction of a single LED light.

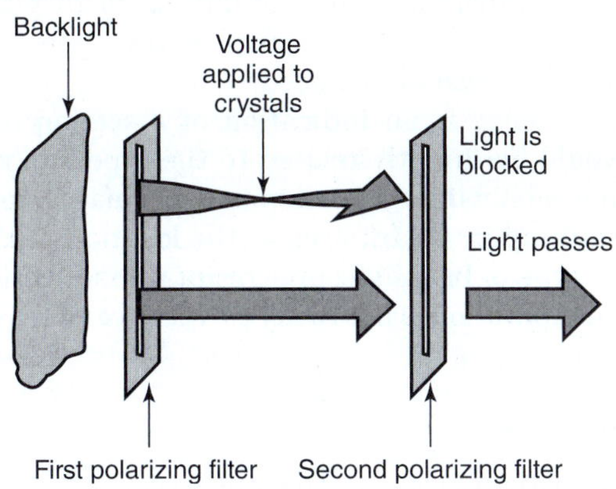

Goodheart-Willcox Publisher

Figure 8-6 Liquid crystals are used to twist light waves produced in an LCD.

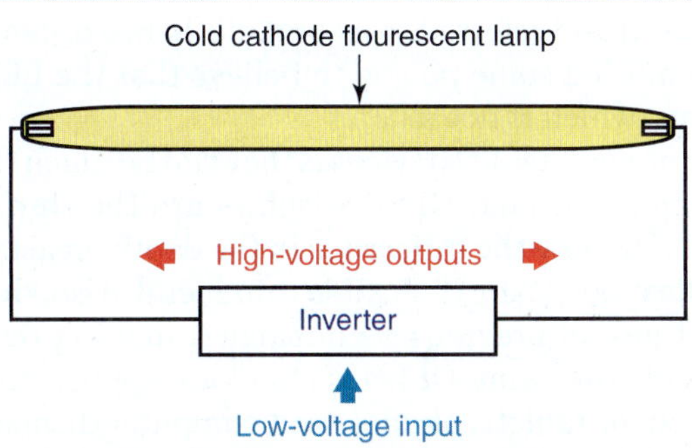

Goodheart-Willcox Publisher

Figure 8-7 High-voltage AC is required to conduct electricity through a CCFL gas tube, thus creating light. An LCD panel for a portable device requires an inverter to change the low-voltage DC battery power to a much higher AC voltage.

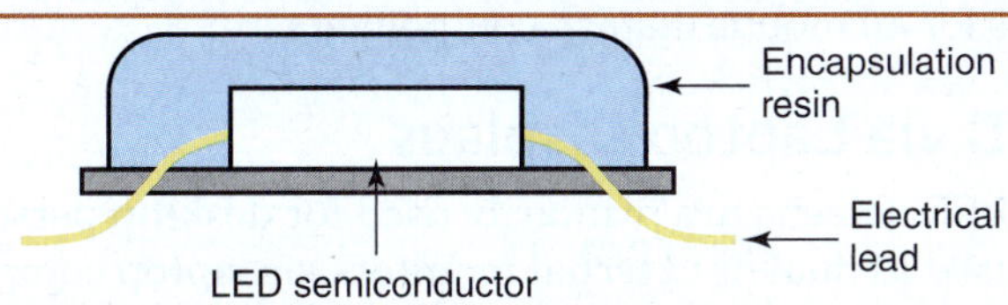

Goodheart-Willcox Publisher

Figure 8-8 An LED backlight is made up of multiple LEDs. An LED is an electronic device that emits light when a DC voltage is applied.

LED Displays

An **LED display**, also known as an *LED monitor* or *LED TV*, is an LCD screen that uses an LED backlight. It is important to note that an LED monitor is still a form of an LCD monitor, and the only difference between an *LCD monitor* and *LED monitor* is that an LED monitor uses a set of LEDs as the source of backlighting rather than a CCFL.

LED backlighting is typically assembled in one of two ways. Either a series of LEDs are located along all four edges of the display, or a matrix of LEDs is spread across the back of the display. CCFL display assemblies typically consist of two CCFLs: one at the top of the display and the other at the bottom, though only one inverter is required for the two CCFLs.

A much thinner display can be created using LED backlighting because the LED assembly is much more compact as compared to a CCFL or inverter assembly. Also, the LED backlighting is less fragile as compared to CCFL because the CCFL uses a glass tube whereas each LED is encapsulated in a resin bubble. The LED is the preferred technology for portable devices such as phones, tablets, and some laptop computers because not only can the display be fabricated much thinner than with CCFL, but it can also better resist physical damage.

When troubleshooting LCD display problems, one of the most common reasons for LCD failure is a bad inverter. The inverter can be replaced, but in most cases, the entire display is simply replaced because of the age of the display unit. Inverter failure is indicated by a black or very dim display that cannot be brightened. Another problem occurs when an individual transistor fails in the display, characterized by a persistent black or white spot on an LCD display. This type of problem cannot be fixed, and the entire display must be replaced.

A dark area on a display is an indication of a section of backlight failure. The exact location would be directly related to the type and arrangement of the backlight. For example, a backlight arrangement in a matrix may have a failure of one small section, resulting in a dark area at the location of the small section of backlighting. An edge type of backlight may result in one section of the edge producing a dark area. This condition is not easily corrected and may result in replacing the entire display.

A+ 1101: 1.2

Organic LED Displays

An **organic LED (OLED) display** is a relatively new type of LED display in which the LED is constructed from carbon-based materials rather than traditional crystalline structures. The term *organic* refers to the use of carbon-based materials. Living things are carbon-based and referred to as organic, hence *organic LED*. The impression of organic LED has led some people to believe that the LED material is made from living organisms, which is not true.

The biggest advantage of OLED devices is they can be much thinner than devices of previous technologies. In fact, OLED displays are the thinnest displays made today. See Figure 8-9 and note the difference in the depth measurements. The OLED can be mounted on flexible plastic or flexible thin metal. Also, the displays are much more durable than those of previous technologies, making the typical protective layer of glass optional. The same OLED technology applied to the television display is also being used for tablets, phones, and computer displays. The flexibility in OLED technology has also allowed smartphone manufacturers to create foldable smartphones, such as those pictured in Figure 8-10. Most recent laptops and mobile devices use OLEDs for all mobile display components.

LED and OLED via Laptop Displays

While LED and OLED screens are primarily used for desktop personal computers, they may also be used as dual or external monitors via laptop computers and other mobile devices. Although various models and displays of both LED and OLED

Goodheart-Willcox Publisher

Figure 8-9 OLED displays can be mounted on flexible plastic or metal. This makes the protective layer of glass optional and allows for a much thinner display.

AronX/Shutterstock.com

Figure 8-10 The flexibility associated with OLED technology allows smartphone manufacturers to create foldable smartphones.

screens will have their own uniqueness, all monitors should be equipped with instructions via a manual to assist during the installation and use of the monitor. Nevertheless, there are key components that need to be adhered to for installation and studied for the A+ Certification Exams.

When installing an LED screen to a laptop or mobile device, it is vital that the screen and device have the proper inputs and outputs for display, such as VGA, DVI, or HDMI. Furthermore, these types of inputs and outputs allow for plug-and-play through operating systems such as Windows 10. As a result, the drivers for the external screen will be downloaded automatically if the device has access to an Internet connection.

OLED screens have similar needs for installation via a laptop or mobile device. However, OLED screens can also be connected via wireless technologies such as 802.11 or Bluetooth connections. The same driver and installation process applies as it does via an LED screen.

Passive-Matrix Display

There are two types of electrical circuitry used to energize the crystal area of a liquid-crystal display: passive and active, as diagrammed in Figure 8-11. A **passive-matrix display** consists of a grid of semitransparent conductors that run to each crystal. The crystals are used as part of the individual pixel areas. The grid is divided into columns and rows, both of which are headed by transistors running along the top and side of the display unit. The combination of a ground applied to a row and a charge applied to a column activates a pixel area. The voltage is applied briefly and must rely on screen persistence and a fast refresh rate. Since current must travel along the row and column until it arrives at the designated pixel, response time is slow.

Active-Matrix Display

In an **active-matrix display**, each pixel in the grid has its own transistor. The active matrix is brighter and provides a better image than the passive-matrix because each cell can have a constant supply of voltage. The most common active-matrix display is the thin-film transistor liquid-crystal display (TFT-LCD). A **thin-film transistor liquid-crystal display (TFT-LCD)**, often referred to as a TFT display, consists of a matrix of thin-film transistors spread across the entire screen. Each transistor controls a single pixel on the display. There are over one million transistors in a display, three transistors at each pixel area, and one transistor for each color pixel, Figure 8-12. The liquid crystals in the TFT display are energized in a pattern representing the data to be displayed.

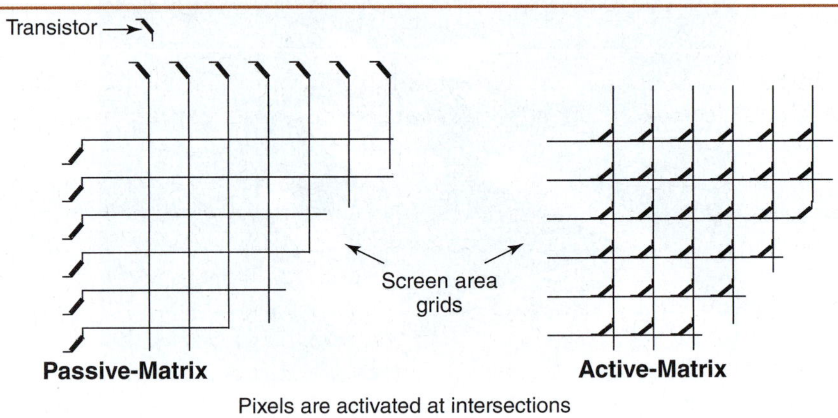

Goodheart-Willcox Publisher

Figure 8-11 In an active-matrix display, each cell in the grid has its own transistor. The active matrix provides a better image than does the passive matrix.

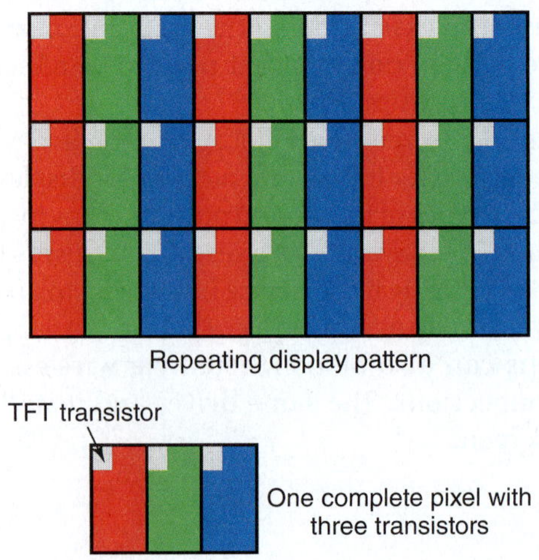

Goodheart-Willcox Publisher

Figure 8-12 Each pixel area on the TFT display consists of three transistor-controlled color fields. The three color fields—red, green, and blue—are combined to form various shades and hues of color.

There have been various advances to active matrix, such as *active-matrix organic light-emitting diode (AMOLED)*, which combines the OLED discussed previously in this chapter with an active-matrix display. This approach to screen design has been commonly used in both mobile phones and televisions.

1101: 1.2 A+

In-plane switching (IPS) is a type of active-matrix LCD monitor that changes the behavior of the liquid crystals, resulting in a sharper image. With IPS, the layer of liquid crystals is between two glass surfaces, and the liquid-crystal molecules are aligned parallel to the surfaces of the glass in specific directions, thus the term *in-plane*. The IPS approach was designed to fix problems with the older *twisted nematic (TN) field effect* LCDs that were widely used in the 1980s. Twisted nematic displays were among the first LCDs on the market and, while inexpensive to produce, had poor color reproduction and were difficult to see at angles. *Advanced fringe field switching (AFFS)* is a similar approach to IPS but offers a wider color display palette as well as greater luminosity. Another type of LCD monitor is *vertical alignment (VA)*. As the name suggests, this approach aligns the crystals vertically to the glass surface when electricity is applied to the monitor.

Gas-Plasma Displays

Gas-plasma displays are flat-panel displays that produce light when a high frequency passes through a gas to a layer of phosphor. This principle is known as *electroluminescence* and works because the frequency passing through the gas to the phosphor layer results in the release of photons, which produces light. A gas-plasma display consists of millions of tiny cells sandwiched between two glass plates. See Figure 8-13. Each cell contains an inert gas and is coated with a phosphorous material of red, blue, or green.

Transparent electrodes run horizontally behind the front panel on top of the cells. Address electrodes run vertically along the rear glass panel beneath the cells. When an address electrode and its corresponding transparent electrode are energized, the gas, in an excited plasma state, releases an ultraviolet light. The ultraviolet light strikes the phosphorus coating inside the cell, causing the cell to release a light corresponding to its color. By varying the pulses of current, the entire light spectrum can be duplicated such as orange, yellow, and brown.

The top electrode is called the *row electrode*, and the bottom electrode is called the *column electrode*. A column and row electrode form a *junction point*, each of which conforms to a memory address. The microprocessor sends information to each memory address and to the monitor, and the junction points become energized in a pattern reflective of the computer memory pattern.

Plasma displays were commonly used in televisions until about 2013, by which time plasma had been largely supplanted by LCD and OLED.

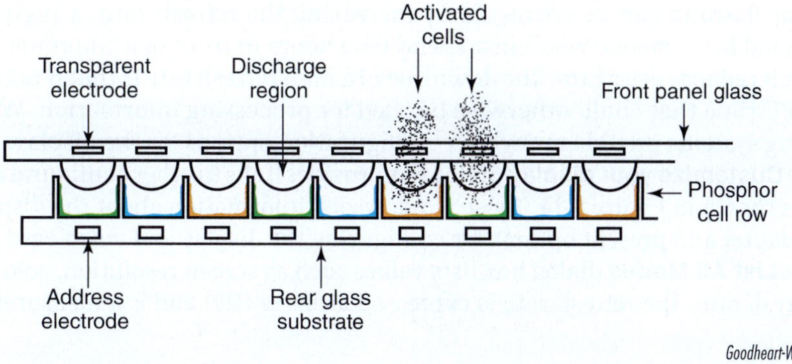

Figure 8-13 Gas-plasma displays operate on the principle of electroluminescence.

A+ 1101: 5.4

Projectors

Although the majority of users obtain their screen output via an LCD, users may also use external displays such as a projector. A *projector* is another form of an LCD and is primarily used as displays in business and home theater settings. However, projectors do not use the traditional technologies of an LCD screen; instead, they mount to a ceiling or wall and use bulbs to project an image onto a projector screen or opposite wall.

Lumens refers to a measurement of how a projector's light is perceived by the human eye rather than the amount of energy or power the projector is using to produce its brightness. The lumens of a projector produce lighting via the amount of ambient light that is produced in a room, and as a result, may diminish a projector's brightness. Although lumens can be predicted by a technician via a projector's screen output, a technician can only be certain of a projector's output once it is installed and generates a display.

It is vital that a technician is sure a projector has cooled down before troubleshooting it. Projectors generate significant heat, so much that they will shut down if they get too hot. When turning the power of a projector off, a technician and user will notice that the fan inside of the device is still running to help cool the unit. Also, it is important that technicians and users understand the price of a projector bulb can range from $50 to $500 and will need to be replaced when errors such as dead pixels or incorrect color patterns occur.

8.3 Display Terminology

Despite the many differences among display types, there are industry terms that apply almost universally. These terms typically refer to functions or operations of the display in question. Examples of terminology that you will need to know when considering new or replacement monitors include dot pitch, refresh rate, contrast ratio, brightness, viewing angle, screen orientation, pixel pitch, native resolution, response time, monitor size, and aspect ratio.

Dot Pitch

Dot pitch is the distance measured in millimeters between two color dots on the screen. It reflects the quality of the image displayed. Generally, the smaller the dot pitch, the higher (sharper) the image quality. An acceptable standard dot pitch is from 0.25 mm to 0.28 mm. The dot pitch cannot be adjusted; it is manufactured into the screen.

A+ 1101: 5.4

Refresh Rate

Originally associated with CRT monitors, the **refresh rate** is the rate at which the entire image is reproduced. The refresh rate of most computer monitors can be adjusted in **Control Panel** using the **Display Properties** dialog box. Often, screen flicker or flashing can be corrected by increasing the refresh rate. A high refresh rate is good for someone who must spend long hours in front of a computer display because it reduces eyestrain. The downside of a high refresh rate is that it takes away from CPU time that could otherwise be used for processing information. Windows operating systems provide many user configuration options for the display.

> **Tech Tip**
>
> The original definition of *refresh rate* referred to CRT monitors, which produced images based on a raster-type display. LCD monitors still use the term *refresh rate*, but the definition has changed.

The **Customize your display** dialog box provides links to other configuration windows, as shown in Figure 8-14. These windows list information about the display and video adapter and present options for configuring the display and video card properties. The **List All Modes** dialog box lists values such as screen resolution, color depth, and refresh rate. The refresh rate is expressed as hertz (Hz) and is a measurement of

Figure 8-14 Windows 10 Display settings allows users to view all modes of screen resolution, color depth, and refresh rate.

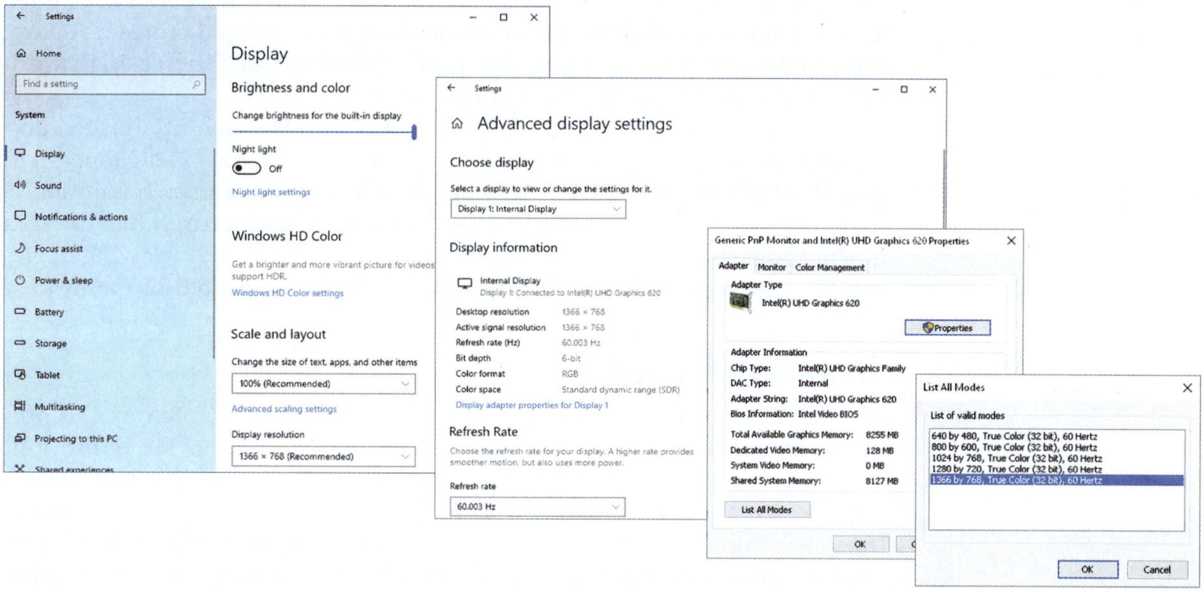

Goodheart-Willcox Publisher

electrical frequency. You can think of hertz as a unit of measurement to express the number of times an electrical characteristic occurs. When used in the **List All Modes** dialog box, hertz expresses the refresh rate of the display and adapter.

Contrast Ratio

Contrast ratio is a numeric expression in the form of a ratio that describes the amount of contrast between the darkest and lightest pixel in the image. The higher the ratio, the better the colors will be represented on the display unit. This is a very important display characteristic that correlates closely to the overall quality of the display. For example, a display with a high contrast ratio will be able to do a better job of displaying finer details of an image. Contrast ratios typically range from 500:1 to 1000:1. A contrast ratio of over 800:1 is considered a high-quality display.

Brightness

Brightness in an LCD is produced by backlighting, which determines the maximum amount of brightness produced in the display. Brightness levels typically range from 200 cd/m^2 (candela per square meter) to 500 or more cd/m^2. A *candela* is a light measurement based on candle illumination. Many people confuse light measurement with watts or wattage, but wattage is a measurement of electrical energy, not light energy. While electrical energy often directly relates to the amount of light produced, there is no direct correlation between electrical energy and light when comparing different light technologies such as the case of incandescent and fluorescent light. For example, a fluorescent light and an incandescent light use two different electrical technologies for generating light. The amount of power consumed measured in watts does not accurately represent the amount of light provided when comparing different technologies. Brightness is also a main factor for determining if the monitor will adequately display an image in a bright environment, such as an outdoor area.

Viewing Angle

The *viewing angle* is a measurement of the angle at which a person can adequately see an image on a display without it looking excessively distorted. As a person's angle to the screen increases, the image displayed becomes increasingly washed out until the image disappears. See Figure 8-15.

The viewing angle of early models of LCD panels was quite limited and could not compete with CRT screens. Today, the viewing angle is of less concern because almost all LCD panels have a very acceptable viewing angle. The actual viewing angle of a display varies from manufacturer to manufacturer, but the minimum viewing angle is typically 150°. Top-of-the-line displays have a viewing angle of 170° or more, which matches or exceeds the viewing angles of old CRT monitors.

Screen Orientation

Personal computers will often have an external monitor, such as the previously mentioned LED or LCD, that may be capable of rotation for either landscape (horizontal) or portrait (vertical) screen displays. However, most laptop computers will have an attached monitor that will be installed primarily for landscape use. Thus, it is important to know how to change a display orientation to match any external monitor(s) that might be connected to it. Generally, the following keyboard combinations can be used to change a display in a Windows operating system:

- [Ctrl][Alt][Up Arrow]: displays the screen(s) normally in landscape orientation
- [Ctrl][Alt][Right Arrow]: rotates the screen(s) 90° clockwise
- [Ctrl][Alt][Left Arrow]: rotates the screen(s) 90° counter-clockwise
- [Ctrl][Alt][Down Arrow]: displays the screen(s) upside-down

If you or a user discovers that the previously mentioned commands do not work, an easy solution can be to right-click the desktop and select **Display Settings** from the shortcut menu. From the **Customize your display** dialog box, select the desired option from the **Orientation** drop-down menu.

Pixel Pitch

Pixel pitch is the distance between two pixels of the same color on the display area, expressed in millimeters (mm). In other words, pixel pitch is the distance between two red pixels, two blue pixels, or two green pixels. It is similar to dot pitch. Each color pixel is composed of three *pels*, one pel for each of the three colors that compose a pixel.

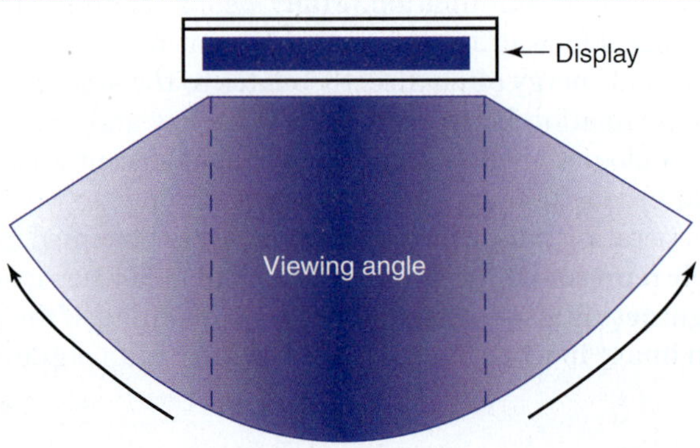

Figure 8-15 The viewing angle defines the locations where the screen can be viewed comfortably without distortion. As the angle of view increases, the image appears increasingly washed out until it disappears completely.

Goodheart-Willcox Publisher

Native Resolution

An LCD is capable of displaying a number of different resolutions. The **native resolution** is the resolution that matches the pixel design of the display. For example, if a display has a native resolution of 1280 × 1024, then it will display images best at 1280 × 1024. If a resolution other than the native resolution is chosen, an image will appear slightly blurred in some areas. Additionally, the monitor may show distorted geometry, where objects are stretched disproportionally. The LCD is manufactured with a set number of pixels, and since a set number of actual pixels are used to generate an image, the display will operate as a bitmap device, blurring when the scale is changed. When a screen resolution other than native is selected, the display controller must either add or remove pixels from the image before it is displayed on the screen, the process of which causes the image to appear slightly blurred. This is especially true when displaying a much higher- or much lower-resolution image.

Turn your attention to Figure 8-16 and compare the screen resolutions. The top image is the recommended, or native, resolution of 1366 × 768. The bottom image is a non-native resolution of 1280 × 720. Notice how much the non-native resolution distorts the images particularly the way the **Display** dialog box enlarges in the non-native resolution. The native resolution produces the sharpest image with the least distortion of the original images and text.

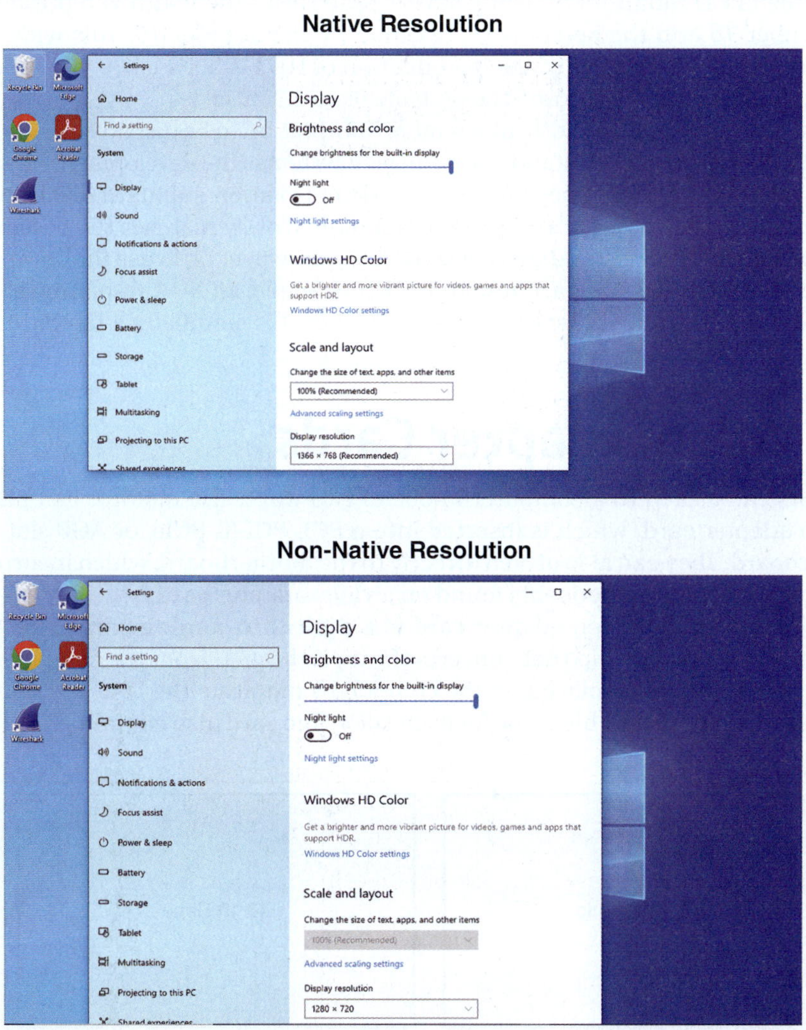

Goodheart-Willcox Publisher

Figure 8-16 Native resolution produces a much sharper image as compared to non-native resolution.

Response Time

The *response time* is the amount of time it takes a TFT pixel to display after a signal is sent to the transistor controlling it. Response time is measured in milliseconds (ms), and a typical response time ranges from 15 ms to 40 ms. The lower the response time, the better the quality of the display unit. A quick response time is required for quality animation. A high response time can cause a slight flicker or breaks in the animation presented on the screen. It is interesting to note that CRTs were historically better at displaying animation or full-motion video than the earlier designs of LCDs. However, modern LCD monitors have response times many times faster than legacy CRT displays and produce much better animation.

Monitor Size

Monitor size is measured in a diagonal line across the front panel of the display. Historically, CRT monitors suffered from lost area since the image display was smaller than the screen size. However, an LCD screen size is the same as the image to be displayed, so there is no display size loss.

Aspect Ratio

Aspect ratio refers to the ratio of the display area's height and width. For example, widescreen LCD monitors typically have a 16:10 ratio. The width is represented by the number *16* and the height is represented by the number *10*. This wide-aspect ratio became a standard with the introduction of HDTV. See Figure 8-17 for a comparison between 16:10 ratio and the now-obsolete 4:3 ratio.

The wide aspect ratio width allows more information to be displayed on the monitor and matches the HDTV standard for display systems. The development of the wide aspect ratio has created a need for newer video resolution standard identifications, which allow a user to select a resolution that more closely matches the design of the monitor. The resolution standards designed for wide aspect ratio use the prefix "W" to describe the modified standard resolution. For example, an XGA resolution based on the traditional 4:3 ratio is identified as WXGA when it is modified for the 16:10 ratio.

A+ 1101: 3.4

8.4 Video Adapter Cards

Monitors can attach to a computer in one of two ways. The monitor can plug into a video adapter card, which is inserted into a PCI, PCI-X, PCIe, or AGP slot on the motherboard. They can also attach directly to the motherboard, which incorporates the same electronic components found on a video adapter card.

The heart of the video adapter card is a **digital-to-analog converter (DAC)**, which is a specialized chip that converts the digital signal from the computer to an analog signal that is displayed on the computer's monitor. The DAC can consist of one single chip or three chips, one for each color. The card also contains RAM, ROM,

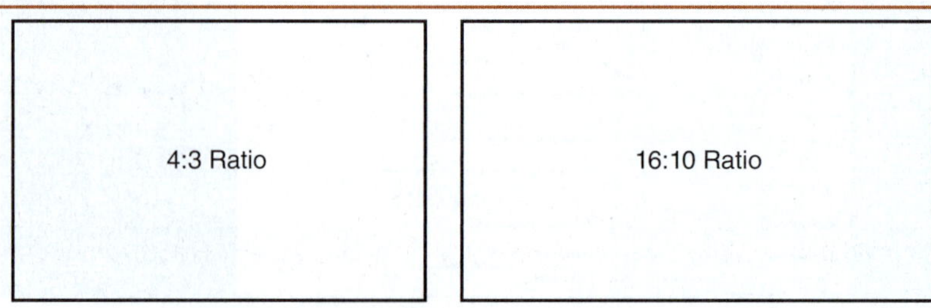

Figure 8-17 The aspect ratio is an expression of height to width of the screen area.

Goodheart-Willcox Publisher

a video processor, and BIOS. The entire video adapter card is similar to a complete computer that has been specialized for video display.

A VGA monitor uses a 15-pin D-shell connector to connect to the video card or to the video port on the motherboard. Figure 8-18 shows a diagram of a standard VGA 15-pin D-shell connector. Note that pin numbers start at the right side of the longer end, counting up as you move left before breaking to the next line, again on the right side. The chart next to the diagram lists the function of each pin on the connector. The 15-pin VGA D-shell is also identified as an HD-15, a DE-15, and a DB-15.

Video adapter cards are installed in PCI, PCI-X, PCIe, or AGP slots on the motherboard. As you can see in Figure 8-19, the PCIe design produces the highest throughput

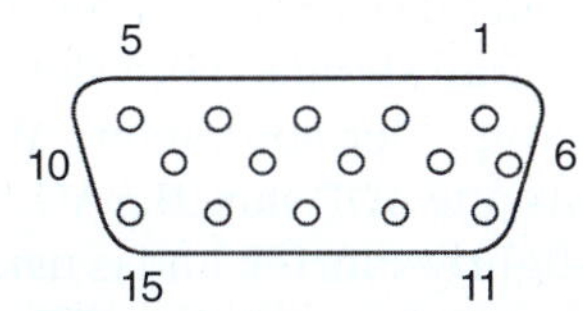

VGA D-Shell Pin Connections

Pin Number	Function
1	Red video
2	Green video
3	Blue video
4	Monitor ID 2
5	TTL ground test pin
6	Red analog ground
7	Green analog ground
8	Blue analog ground
9	Plugged hole
10	Sync ground
11	Monitor ID 0
12	Monitor ID 1
13	Horizontal sync
14	Vertical sync
15	Monitor ID 3

Goodheart-Willcox Publisher

Figure 8-18 In a standard VGA 15-pin arrangement, pin 5 is used for testing the monitor. Some manufacturers use pins 4, 11, 12, or 15 to detect the type of monitor connected to the motherboard. Pin 9 is usually missing by design; others may be missing as well and may vary by the manufacturer.

Bus Speeds and Throughputs

Bus Type	Throughput in MBps	Speed in MHz	Width in Bits
PCI	127.2	33	32
PCI 2.1	508.6	66	64
AGP	254.3	66	32
AGP 2×	508.6	66 × 2	32
AGP 4×	1017.3	66 × 4	32
AGP 8×	2034.4	66 × 8	32
PCI-X 1.0	1060.0	133	64
PCI-X 2.0	2150.0	266	64
PCIe 1.0	2000	NA	NA
PCIe 2.0	4000	NA	NA
PCIe 3.0	8000	NA	NA

Note: The throughput for PCIe is expressed in MBps for comparison to other bus types. PCIe is a serial bus and the other bus types are parallel.

Goodheart-Willcox Publisher

Figure 8-19 The PCIe design of video card slots produces the highest throughput of the three technologies.

of the three technologies. Although, note that because it transfers information in a serial fashion, PCIe is expressed as bits per second (bps), not bytes per second (Bps).

Video performance also depends on the amount of available memory that can be used to create and process images. When the graphics controller is incorporated into the motherboard, the controller uses the RAM installed on the motherboard for video images. This means that the motherboard RAM must be used for all software functions that require RAM as well as for video performance. When a video adapter card is used, the performance is greatly increased. The total effect on video performance is determined by how much RAM is incorporated into the video adapter card. Generally, the more video RAM incorporated into the video adapter card, the better the overall video performance. Other factors that influence video performance are the version of the operating system, the motherboard chipset, and the video adapter card BIOS.

A+ 1001: 3.4

Note that, while related to video adapter cards, ***video capture cards*** are different. These cards take the analog video signal from a television, camcorder, or similar source and convert it to digital video for the computer. However, many of the more expensive graphics cards also support video capture.

AGP

The Accelerated Graphics Port (AGP) is a slot used strictly for AGP adapter cards. It is designed with graphics as a priority, using a computer's memory to work more effectively with graphics. It also operates at a faster bus speed than standard PCI slots.

You will rarely encounter AGP except when servicing older equipment. When AGP is incorporated on a motherboard, there will be only one AGP slot. The AGP slot looks similar in design to the PCI slot, only in reverse, slightly shorter, and is usually a different color. To identify the AGP slot, look for the slot closest to the CPU and offset from the alignment of the PCI slots. As of this writing, the current version of AGP is AGP version 3.5.

PCI-X

PCI Extended (PCI-X) was designed as the successor to the PCI bus. You can see the increase in throughput in Figure 8-19. These are theoretical speeds for PCI-X and can be much slower when the bus is shared with other types of devices. PCI-X is not used by many video card systems but may still be encountered occasionally in older systems.

PCIe

PCIe ×16 is the preferred video card technology. The PCIe standard has evolved from PCIe 1.0 to PCIe 4.0 with each producing faster graphic performance than the previous version. PCIe ×16 provides approximately twice the graphics data throughput as AGP ×8. PCIe ×16 has essentially replaced all other video card standards such as PCI and AGP. You may wish to review the information concerning PCI-X and PCIe bus types in Chapter 3.

Multiple Video Cards

Computers can be configured with two or more video cards to increase overall video performance. This is most desirable for graphics-intensive applications such as games, computer-aided design, and video editing. The increased performance is due to the parallel processing power of joining the two video cards together. The two or more video cards share the workload by using either split-frame rendering or alternate-frame rendering.

A *frame* is a single image, similar to a single digital photo. Video, movie, and game animation consists of a series of frames. When using **split-frame rendering**, each graphics card is responsible for an equal portion of the frame image, based on how many cards are used. For example, if two cards are used, each card is responsible for half of the frame image. If four cards are used, each card is responsible for one-fourth of each image.

The second method is **alternating-frame rendering**, in which each card is responsible for rendering every other frame. For example, if four cards are used, each card is responsible for one-fourth of the total frame image. Some cards are capable of both split-frame rendering and alternate-frame rendering.

SLI

Scalable Link Interface (SLI) is a proprietary video card system owned by the NVIDIA Corporation in which multiple cards work together to produce a single output. The original SLI system required that both cards be identical. This meant that each video card was to have a matching graphics processing unit (GPU) and the same amount of RAM and bus speed. Today, SLI no longer requires identical video cards. However, when the video cards do not match, the best performance is based on the slower of the two cards. Figure 8-20 shows three ASUS video cards installed in an SLI configuration. Notice the SLI bridge connector at the top of the cards.

Originally, the acronym SLI was introduced as Scan-Line Interleave by the 3DFX company. When 3DFX sold the technology to NVIDIA, NVIDIA renamed the acronym to Scalable Link Interface.

AMD CrossFire

AMD CrossFire is multiple-card technology introduced by ATI Technologies Inc., which is now owned by AMD. This is designed as a competitor to NVIDIA's SLI product. With CrossFire technology, two or more cards are configured for the computer. The two cards do not need to match, but they must be compatible with each other. One card is referred to as the *master* or *primary* and the second card is referred to as the *slave* or *secondary*. Both SLI and CrossFire must be installed in matching PCIe slots. For example, you cannot use one card in a PCIe slot and the other in an AGP slot. You must use two PCIe ×16 slots.

In theory, using two video cards would produce an overall video rate of double; in reality, an overall 170- to 180-percent increase is typically achieved at best. There is some software overhead that must be implemented that reduces the theoretical doubling speed and the speed of other processes running in the background.

Coaster J/CC BY-SA 4.0

Figure 8-20 Scalable Link Interface (SLI) is a proprietary video card system in which multiple cards work together to produce a single output.

Videos for installing an SLI video card or a CrossFire system are available on the NVIDIA and ATI or AMD websites, respectively. To access these videos, conduct a search using the keywords, SLI install how to or CrossFire install how to.

A+ 1101: 3.4

Installing a Video Adapter Card

Caution

Before beginning any installation of hardware, *always* back up critical computer files. It is easy to accidentally destroy data on a computer. Sometimes drivers do not work the way they should, causing the computer system to lock up, and anything can happen in the course of recovering the system. The worst-case scenario is losing hard drive data. Always back up the hard drive or critical data before working on a PC.

Installing a video adapter card is easy. The steps that follow are generic in nature, but there should not be much variation in installation among different cards.

1. Back up all computer files.
2. Power off the computer and unplug the power cord from the wall outlet.
3. Read the installation procedures and specification sheet that came with the adapter card. Verify that your new card is compatible with the type of display unit being used.
4. Take normal electrostatic discharge (ESD) precautions.
5. Before attempting to insert the video adapter card into the expansion slot, check for debris in the slot.
6. Insert the card by applying even force to the top of the card. Do *not* rock the card into the slot.
7. Connect the monitor to the new card and turn on the PC. The card will be automatically detected. If not, check the support link at the card manufacturer's website.
8. If Windows cannot find its own driver when the system attempts to detect the card, it will ask you to supply a new driver. The driver may have been packaged with the adapter card as a disc. It is also a good idea to check the card manufacturer's website for any patches or upgrades needed for the driver. Prepackaged drivers will often be out of date, but the most up-to-date drivers can be downloaded from their websites.
9. As the drivers are loading, follow the screen prompts to complete the installation.
10. A message box will display on the screen when the installation is complete. If a problem occurs, a message will appear saying that the installation is not complete. Reread the installation procedures. Also, check for bent pins on the video adapter cable connector. A pin can easily bend when assembling the system. Another area to check is your computer's BIOS. With older systems in particular, you may need to upgrade the BIOS on the motherboard to use your new card. If problems persist, check both the card manufacturer's and the motherboard manufacturer's website. Some motherboards have a video adapter integrated into the circuit board. If this is the case, you may have to disable the integrated system before the new adapter board will work. It is always a good idea to consult the website of the motherboard manufacturer for the latest updates before you begin.
11. If all has gone well, you should be able to close the case and reboot the system.

8.5 Maintaining and Personalizing Video Displays

Displays are not commonly in need of servicing. In fact, there are no field-replaceable parts in most displays. However, with proper care and maintenance, they can last a significantly long time. The following sections present methods for troubleshooting and cleaning video displays as well as personalizing them to suit your particular interests and needs.

Troubleshooting

A+ Note

The A+ Certification Exams usually ask at least one question about how to troubleshoot a display unit and how to clean a display. The tips in this chapter should provide sufficient information to answer most questions concerning these topics.

Troubleshooting displays is quite simple since there are no serviceable parts inside LCD monitors. You simply replace a suspected monitor with another. Before changing the monitor, you should do the following:

- Check that the monitor is turned on
- Check that the power cord is plugged in
- Confirm the wall outlet has voltage
- Confirm the video cable between the computer and the display unit is connected and not loose

If after changing the monitor you still have a problem, you should check the video card. First, reseat the video card in its slot. Sometimes oxidation builds up on the card edge connections. Reseating the card will remove the oxidation, and the card will begin to work again. If reseating the card does not produce the desired results, simply replace the video card.

A+ 1101: 5.4

There are many symptoms of a problem with a display. Older monitors suffered from a problem known as ***burn-in*** or ***image retention***, which occurred when an image is left on a monitor for hours, resulting in the image leaving an impression in the display. Using a screen saver can help prevent this from happening, but it should also be noted that burn-in does not occur with modern LED or OLED monitors.

A+ 1101: 5.4

Another common issue is ***dead pixels***, also known as ***stuck pixels***, which are individual pixels that have stopped working. These often appear as small dots on the display and can be black, white, or a noticeably different color than the rest of the screen. Some dead pixels can be resolved with third-party software, but dead pixels often cannot be fixed without replacing the entire monitor.

A final symptom common to video displays is ***artifacts***, which make the image on the screen appear as if it were split horizontally. This occurs when the video controller is out of sync with the refresh rate of the display. This often means the GPU is overheating. Third-party software can be downloaded and executed to ensure the problem is not with the GPU.

Many motherboards incorporate the video chipset directly on the motherboard, meaning there is no video card in any slot. When this is the case, simply install a video card into any compatible, available slot. This will not always work because when the video chipset is built in as part of the motherboard and it is defective, it may prevent another video card from working. It will mainly depend on the type of electronics failure in the chipset. Also, be aware that items such as a telephone modem or network card could prevent a computer system from completing the

POST and thus make it appear as a video problem. There will be more about this type of scenario in a later chapter.

Before replacing the video card, you should reinstall or update the video card drivers. Drivers often become corrupted, and many times, replacing the drivers or updating the drivers corrects the problem.

A+ 1101: 5.7

When abundant latency is present in a video or audio transmission, jitter can occur. ***Jitter*** consists of small staggers or hesitations in the delivery sequence of audio/video data. For example, news broadcasts that feature a reporter or interviewee broadcasting from a remote location tend to suffer from jitter. You may often notice delays in responses to questions or a disruption in the video feed. This is caused by jitter. One method of reducing jitter is to decrease the sampling rate of the feed. Sampling rate will be discussed in much more detail in a later chapter.

A+ 1101: 5.4

One of the first items you should always check are physical cabling issues. This includes simply verifying that the cable is indeed connected properly. The second cabling issue is to ensure you have the proper cable. A related problem is the incorrect data source. If you have more than one device that can display on a screen, it is important to ensure you are using the correct data source.

A+ 1101: 5.4

A fuzzy or blurry image is often due to improper resolution settings. This will generally require you to go into the operating system and adjust the resolution. Recall that a monitor's native resolution is the resolution at which the monitor functions best.

A+ 1101: 5.4

A burned-out bulb results in replacing either the bulb or the entire monitor. On small devices such as laptops or tablets, it is usually impractical to only replace the bulb. However, that is often an option with a PC monitor. You should first verify the actual symptoms your monitor is showing. For example, a burned-out bulb will lead to a very dim image, while a completely black screen may indicate the monitor itself is not functioning.

A+ 1101: 5.4

A cracked screen is a serious problem but also one that is easy to diagnose and address by replacing the monitor. Black screen or white screen is a more serious video concern. If the screen is a solid monochrome color and you have checked the more basic issues discussed in this section such as cabling issues, then the problem could have a number of possible causes, including hard drive read/write errors, malware, or monitor failure, among others. This is often among the most difficult issues to diagnose and, by extension, correct.

A+ 1101: 5.4

Projectors are commonly encountered in educational and professional settings, and while they are most often used with laptops, they can attach to any computer. In most cases, projectors are relatively simple to diagnose, especially if the problem is related to power. If the projector regularly experiences unexpected or intermittent shutdowns, first check the power connection. This is a common source of this problem. You can also attempt to use the projector with a known good power cord to eliminate the cord as a cause. If you confirm the power connection is sound, next confirm that the projector's buttons are not stuck or locked in place, which can cause seemingly random shutdowns. A common cause of this problem is the projector moving into standby mode, which can be resolved by turning off the standby option.

Cleaning

There is always much debate and conflicting methods for cleaning displays. The following information contains the generally accepted guidelines for properly cleaning displays. However, you should always consult the manufacturer documentation before attempting to clean any display.

Never clean a display while it is energized; always unplug the electrical supply before cleaning the display. Clean the display area using a dry lint-free soft cloth designed for screen display cleaning to remove dust. For more persistent smudges, use a slightly dampened lint-free soft cloth. Avoid using detergents to clean the plastic display case surface because they will often leave a white residue on the surface after drying. Additionally, LCD monitors use a plastic cover and can be easily damaged by chemical solutions, except ones designed specifically for cleaning LCD displays. Never use a paper towel to clean an LCD monitor because paper towels are often made with coarse fibers that can scratch a plastic LCD screen. Instead, use only soft, lint-free cloth.

Never spray liquid directly on the display. Too much spray causes the liquid to run down the display and enter the monitor through the seam along the edge of the screen. When the liquid enters inside the monitor, it can short out the electronic components. Never use acetone, ethyl alcohol, ammonia, or products containing chlorine or chloride to clean a monitor.

A+ 1102: 4.5

Do not place a display unit in direct sunlight, such as in front of a window because direct sunlight can cause excessive heat buildup inside the display, which may damage the electronics. Additionally, direct sunlight can damage plastic cases, resulting in yellowing or fading of colors, or causing the plastic case to become brittle, which may cause the case to crack.

A+ 1102: 4.5

Place the display unit in an area of relatively low humidity. High humidity in the range of 80 to 100 percent can damage electronic components. Avoid moving devices in and out of drastic temperature changes with high humidity present. This is especially true for laptop computers. When moving laptops, try to keep the laptop inside a carrying case designed for the laptop, as it will provide some temperature and humidity control.

Personalizing Display Properties

In the Windows operating system, many adjustments can be made to the appearance of the display. Figure 8-21 shows the **Appearance and Personalization** menu, which allows a user to change the way items appear on the display.

A+ 1102: 1.4

The **Personalization** menu used to be located in this area, but it has since been moved and can now be accessed by right-clicking on the desktop and selecting **Personalization** from the shortcut menu. Similarly, the Display menu also used to be included in Control Panel but was moved to **Start**>**Settings**>**System**>**Display**. The **Taskbar and Navigation** selection allows the user to customize settings for the taskbar, such as auto-hide, button size, and placement locking, as well as window placement and toolbars. The **Ease of Access** dialog box opens the Ease of Access Center, which is used to make Windows easier to use. Recall that Ease of Access was covered in greater detail in Chapter 7. The **File Explorer Options** link opens the **File Explorer Options** dialog box, allowing for adjustment of how windows appear in Explorer. Lastly, the **Fonts** dialog box is where a user would add, remove, or customize installed fonts. These configuration options are very similar in most versions of Windows.

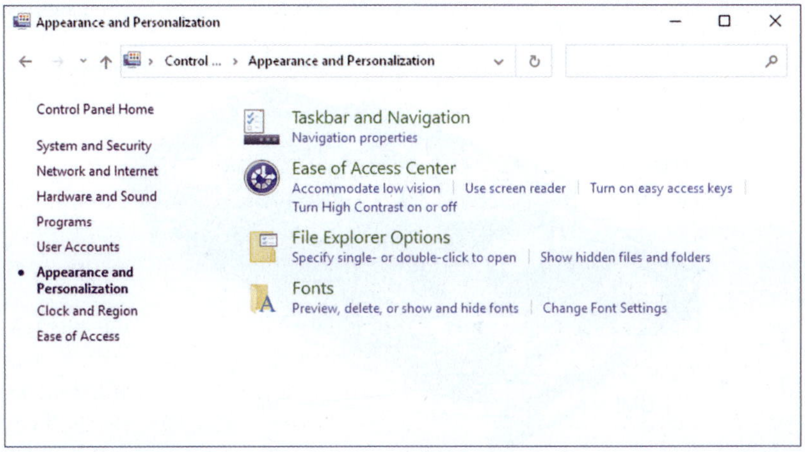

Goodheart-Willcox Publisher

Figure 8-21 In the Windows operating system, many adjustments can be made to the appearance of the display through the **Appearance and Personalization** menu.

8.6 Television and Computers

Computer and television technologies have rapidly merged since the development of high-definition television (HDTV) and the availability of flat-panel display technology such as TFT and gas plasma. It is not unusual for a display unit to be designed to serve as both a television and a computer monitor. The merger of the two technologies has produced many conflicting standards within the television and computer industries, resulting in a variety of connector designs used to connect various displays to computers and television receivers. Figure 8-22 shows some of the connection designs associated with computer and television systems.

A+ 1101: 3.1

All the connection designs carry the acronym DVI, which stands for Digital Visual Interface. The *DVI-I* connector is a combination-type connector designed for both digital and analog connections. The *DVI-D* connector is designed for a digital-only connection. It can be used to connect devices that support compatible digital resolutions. The *DVI-A* connector is used with digital-to-analog conversion and is not commonly used today because of rapid advances in digital video and the fading out of analog systems.

The references to *DVI-D single link* and *DVI-D dual link* relate to the amount of bandwidth that can be transmitted by each connection design. The single link can carry a bandwidth equal to 165 MHz, which is the matching bandwidth for HDTV. It can produce a maximum resolution of 1920 × 1080 at 60 Hz. The dual link can carry twice the bandwidth of the single link and can produce a resolution as high as 2048 × 1536.

A+ 1101: 3.1

Some video adapter cards provide several connection types from which to choose. Both Figure 8-23 and Figure 8-24 show newer video adapter cards with DVI-D, DVI-I, HDMI, and DisplayPort connections. DisplayPort was developed by

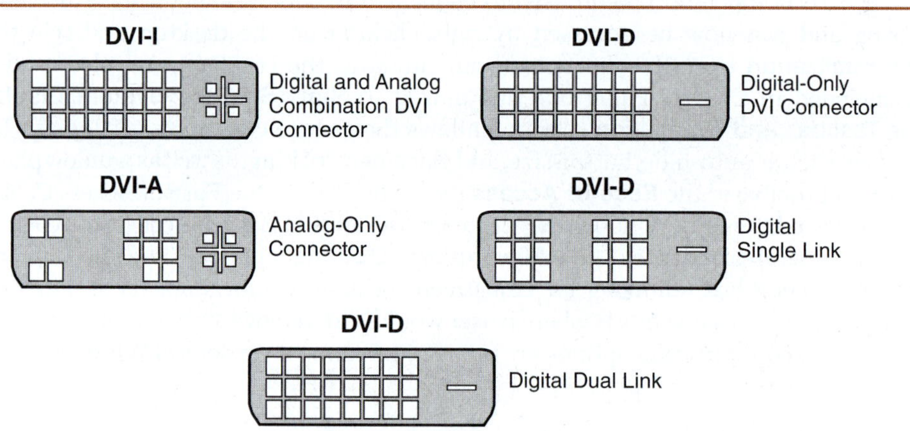

Goodheart-Willcox Publisher

Figure 8-22 A merge between television and computing technologies resulted in a conflict in standards that resulted in a variety of connector designs.

Goodheart-Willcox Publisher; (photo) Billion Photos/Shutterstock.com

Figure 8-23 Video cards are often equipped with a variety of video display ports.

the VESA organization as an open royalty-free display connection. The main advantage of DisplayPort is that it is royalty-free, whereas HDMI charges royalties, such as $10,000 plus $.04 per unit.

Some video adapter cards are manufactured to support two monitors at the same time. Many occupations, such as web-page design, often require more than one display unit while designing web pages. By having more than one display connected to the computer station, they can view the web page they designed at different resolutions. This practice is not exclusive to web design, however. Many jobs that require computers, including those involved with the creation of this textbook, utilize multiple displays for organization and multitasking purposes.

High-Definition Television

High-definition television (HDTV) displays have become the center of home entertainment systems and have created a demand for computer displays that are compatible with the same resolution and aspect ratio as HDTV. The display resolutions and overall physical shape of the viewing area are designed to support HDTV as well as other media center options, such as watching movies and editing video and digital photography.

HDTV Resolution

Original analog television resolution is approximately equal to 720 × 480. The two most common HDTV formats are 720 and 1080. The 720 format is nothing more than an enhanced original analog television resolution of 720 × 480. True HDTV resolution requires a display resolution of at least 1080 × 720. The latest resolution for high-definition television is Ultra high-definition television (UHDTV), which has a resolution four times greater than HDTV and is available in two formats at this time: 4K UHDTV and 8K UHDTV. Figure 8-25 shows a comparison between 4K and 8K. It should be

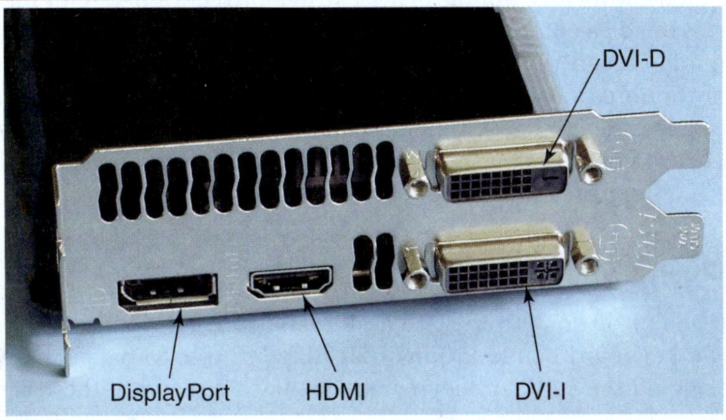

Goodheart-Willcox Publisher

Figure 8-24 Newer video cards typically have ports that represent the latest video technology, such as DVI, HDMI, and DisplayPort.

High-Definition Resolutions

Format	Resolution	Pixels
HDTV	720 × 480	345,600 pixels
True HDTV	1080 × 720	777,600 pixels
4K UHDTV	3840 × 2160	8.3 megapixels
8K UHDTV	7680 × 4320	33.2 megapixels

Note: The 8K UHDTV is also known as the Super High-Definition TV.

Goodheart-Willcox Publisher

Figure 8-25 There are multiple high-definition resolutions currently in use, each building off the previous iteration.

noted that while 16K monitors and displays exist, they are still in their infancy and are not widely used. Nor has there ever been a 16K broadcast as of this writing.

To produce HDTV on a computer system, you must have a monitor resolution of at least 1920 × 1080 pixels. You can display HDTV at other resolution values, but 1920 × 1080 is recommended for the minimal HDTV experience on a digital display such as an LCD monitor.

The original screen resolution for HDTV was based on analog television signals that used raster scans and produced 480 or 720 separate lines counted vertically across the television screen. Today, 1920 × 1080 is considered the native resolution for HDTV and is often referred to as simply *1080 HDTV*, using only the second number of the screen resolution.

A+ 1001: 3.1

VGA vs. Digital Signals

VGA is a legacy analog video signal that uses three separate analog signals to represent the colors red, green, and blue. An analog signal was used for the original television terrestrial signals (radio waves), but the connectors are found on older types of devices.

Digital signals differ from analog signals in that while they are broadcast using similar technology as analog signals, the data is carried in a series of square waves rather than sine waves. The digital (square) signals represent the ones and zeros associated with binary digital code. The progression from analog signals to digital signals was made because digital signals can carry more information than analog signals using the same radio bandwidth.

TV Tuner Cards

Today, more and more computers are being configured as a media center in the home. By adding a television tuner either as an expansion card (internal) or as a USB device (external), the computer can receive analog and digital television signals. Figure 8-26 shows an example of a TV tuner card designed to fit into a PCIe ×1 expansion slot inside a computer case.

Like any add-on card, you will likely have to download drivers so the device functions properly. Some cards may come with a disc containing installation software, but it is always a good idea to check the manufacturer website for up-to-date software. The TV tuner card may also come with a remote control and receiver, which is used to connect the TV tuner card to an antenna or to a television cable box.

Media Playback

The majority of laptop computers with an installation of a Windows operating system will have keyboard combinations that allow a user to pause, play, stop, fast forward, or rewind the audio or video content they are playing. These series of keys

Figure 8-26 A TV tuner card can be installed into a computer and provides a means of receiving television signals through a computer.

Evan-Amos/Public Domain

are typically programmed into the function keys displayed as [F1] through [F12]. These keys are typically found at the top of the laptop computer's keyboard.

Home Theater PC

A *home theater PC (HTPC)* is a customized computer used to enhance the television viewing experience. An HTPC has all the capabilities of a typical PC plus additional software and hardware to support multimedia recording and playback.

Generally, a television has good sound quality, but a user may wish to create a theater-quality sound system by adding a sound card to the HTPC. Additionally, the user must also add enough speakers to create a surround-sound environment for the best possible listening pleasure. In addition to a sound card, you need to use a computer system and Internet access that adequately supports video streaming.

To best understand video streaming, you can compare it to downloading. When you download a file, you establish a connection with a remote resource on the Internet and then download the entire file before opening it to view or hear the contents. With video streaming, you view the contents of the file while downloading the content. The quality of video streaming is based on the ability of the computer system or Smart TV and the quality of the material to be viewed. For video to be streamed smoothly and without interruption, the minimum Internet access speeds should be used:

- 2.3 Mbps for standard-definition (SD) video
- 2.3 Mbps–4.5 Mbps for high-definition (HD) video
- 4.5 Mbps–9 Mbps for HDX video
- 9 Mbps for 3D high-definition (HD) video

High-definition video has a 720p resolution. HDX is full high-definition video, which consists of 1080p video and high-definition audio. Other things that can affect the amount of bandwidth needed for video streaming include the type of *codec (compression and decompression type)* used and the number of users downloading over the same shared Internet connection.

Smart TVs

Smart TVs are televisions with additional built-in features, such as support for Internet access, a Wi-Fi connection, and software applications. The software applications allow Internet browsing and searching, e-mail client services, video conferencing when a webcam is installed, streaming media, and more. The software applications can vary greatly according to the brand of Smart TV, Internet provider, and equipment provided. Smart TVs go by many other names such as *interactive television (iTV)*, *hybrid TV*, and *Internet TV*.

A home theater can be created from many different options and features. Recently, televisions have become something of a sole solution in and of themselves, largely due to the rise in streaming and cloud-based digital video options. Modern televisions are now based on PC technology. In fact, there is very little difference between a television display and a computer. Smart TVs now incorporate full operating systems—often a type of mobile OS, such as Android—as well as high-end video and audio, thus creating a complete entertainment system in one package.

Home Theater Boxes

Home theater boxes are special consumer appliances that provide many of the same services as Smart TVs—such as Internet services, video recording, and software applications—in one specialized box. Other features that may be included are DVD or Blu-ray optical drives, surround sound, and more. The features provided vary by manufacturer and by price. A typical home theater box connects directly to a television and to the Internet.

Home Theater Center Connection Types

A home theater center can consist of many different electronic devices connected together. The system may consist of a high-definition LCD or plasma television, cable TV, antenna or satellite source of signal, speakers, DVR, and a computer. The equipment that comprises a complete home theater center may involve a wide variety of cable connections. You need to be able to identify each type and understand its capabilities.

The signal supplied by the local cable television company or through a satellite dish system typically connects to the initial receiver in the home from a single coaxial cable. Another option is wireless cell access, the same type of connection used for wireless phone service. Original media systems consisted of a single coaxial cable that connected to a cable box and then another single coaxial cable that connected to the television. Today, the single coaxial cable that supplies the cable television signal or satellite dish signal is separated into multiple audio and video signals that are processed by much more sophisticated equipment. The overall product is enhanced audio and video that requires a variety of connections and cables.

It should be noted that audio cables, such as the cable used for speakers, use low frequency—less than 20 kHz and does not require shielding from interference or cause interference the way video signals do. The speaker wiring does not use a carrier wave. It simply transmits the sound pattern as an analog signal.

Video signals are typically either UHF or VHF, each of which is high frequency in the range of hundreds of megahertz. Hence, video cables must be shielded to protect the signal from interference and to prevent the video cable from broadcasting radio wave interference to surrounding devices. Coaxial cable is used for video signals, while unshielded cable is used for speakers. The speaker wires have a much larger core conductor diameter when compared to RG-6 cable, which is a type of coaxial cable. The large diameter ensures less signal loss as the audio signal travels the length of the cable.

Composite Video

Look at the cables in Figure 8-27. Composite video, Figure 8-27A, resembles component video connections and cables, Figure 8-27C. Notice that composite video uses an RCA-type connector similar to component video; however, it uses only one cable for the video signal and two more for stereo sound. The composite video cable uses a larger diameter cable (the one with the yellow connector) for video. The larger diameter cable is an RG-59 coaxial cable. The other two cables are used for audio and do not use coaxial shielding. Composite video provides a better signal than F-type or RF cable connections but does not provide a signal as good as S-Video or component video.

S-video

S-Video, Figure 8-27B, is a round, four-pin connector that delivers separate signals for video signal color and brightness. It is a very simple way to connect components together because there is no way to misconnect the audio and video cables. S-Video supports better signal quality than composite video but not as good as component video.

A nine-pin version of S-Video is used for video-in/video-out (VIVO) configurations, similar to the device shown in Figure 8-28. The nine-pin connector allows video to stream in both directions, while the four-pin connector is used for applications that only require video in one direction. Many video computer cards have the nine-pin S-Video connector, which is used commonly for video editing. The video is copied to the computer from the source, edited on the computer, and then sent back to the source.

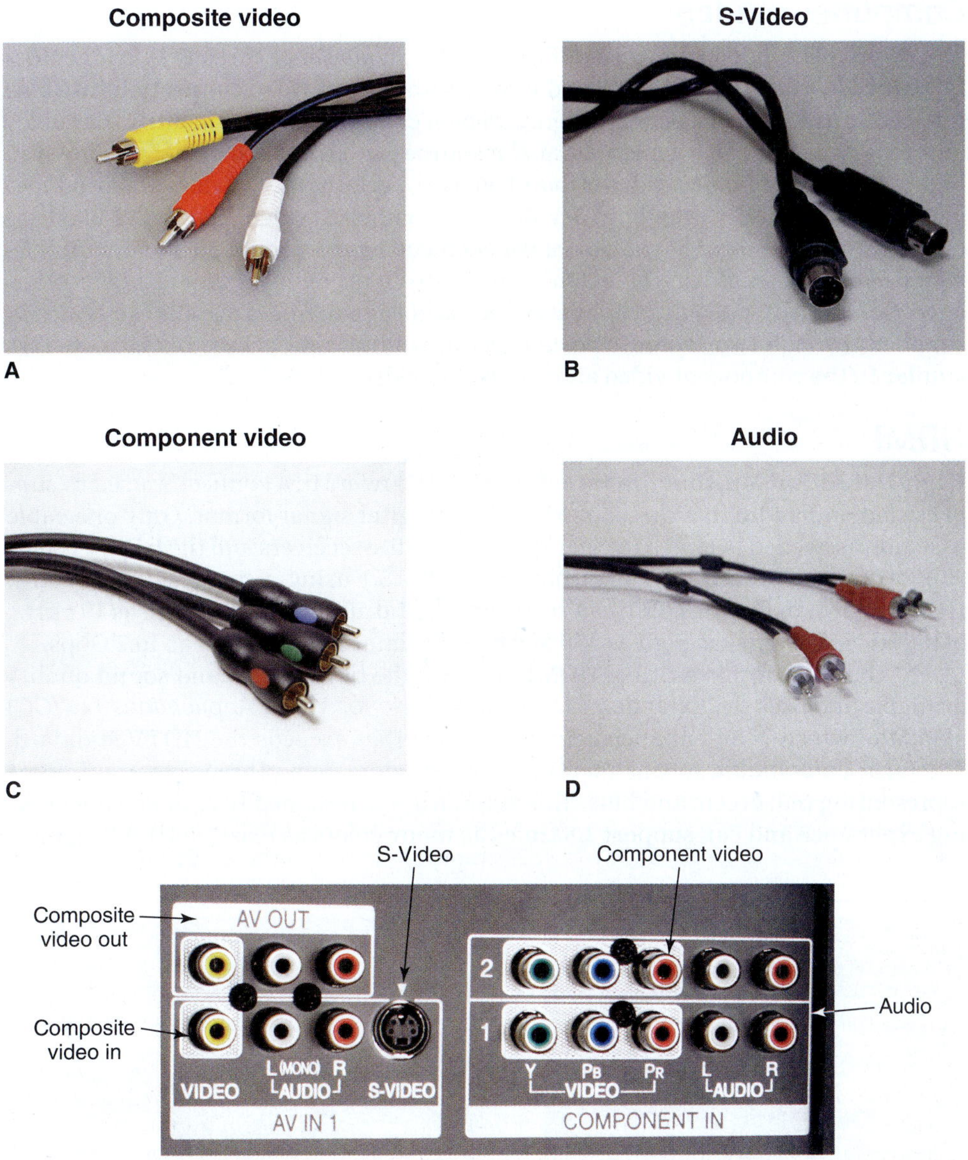

Goodheart-Willcox Publisher

Figure 8-27 Home entertainment centers have various connections and cables, including composite, S-Video, component, and audio.

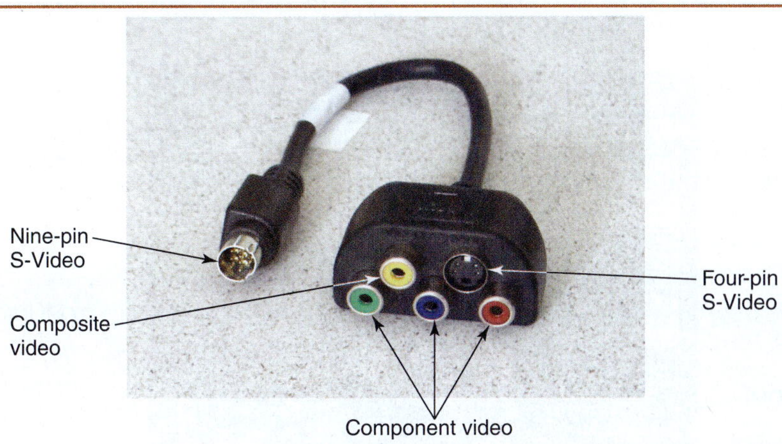

Goodheart-Willcox Publisher

Figure 8-28 A nine-pin S-Video to video adapter allows for video to be streamed in both directions.

Component Video

The component video connection, Figure 8-27C, consists of three RCA connectors typically identified as Y, Pb (Cb), and Pr (Cr). Component video connections are also referred to as RGB because red, green, and blue colors are used to identify the cables and represent the color generated at the source for each video cable, as shown in Figure 8-27E. Component video is found on high-performance devices and produces better picture quality than both S-Video and composite video. The cables used are constructed from flexible coaxial cable, each consisting of a single conductor surrounded by a dielectric and shield to protect it from receiving or generating interference. Component video does not carry the audio signal. Audio signals are typically supplied through two separate ports using an audio cable, shown in Figure 8-27D, similar to the component video and composite video cables.

A+ 1101: 3.1

HDMI

High-Definition Multimedia Interface (HDMI) refers to a connector used to supply video and audio in an uncompressed, all-digital signal format. Only one cable assembly is needed between devices such as satellite receivers and the HDTV. HDMI supports an enhanced HDTV format and Dolby 5.1 using a single shielded cable. HDMI, shown in Figure 8-29A, can support a digital audio signal as high as 192 kHz, a digital video signal as high as 350 MHz, and a data signal as high as 10.2 Gbps.

At the time of this writing, HDMI provides the best picture and sound quality available and uses the *Extended YCC Colorimetric for Video Applications (xvYCC) standard*, which is an enhanced color standard that exceeds the HDTV standard. The term *colorimetric* means identification of colors using three sets of numbers representing red, green, and blue. This standard was designed to enhance the viewing experience and can support 1.8 times as many colors as existing HDTV signals.

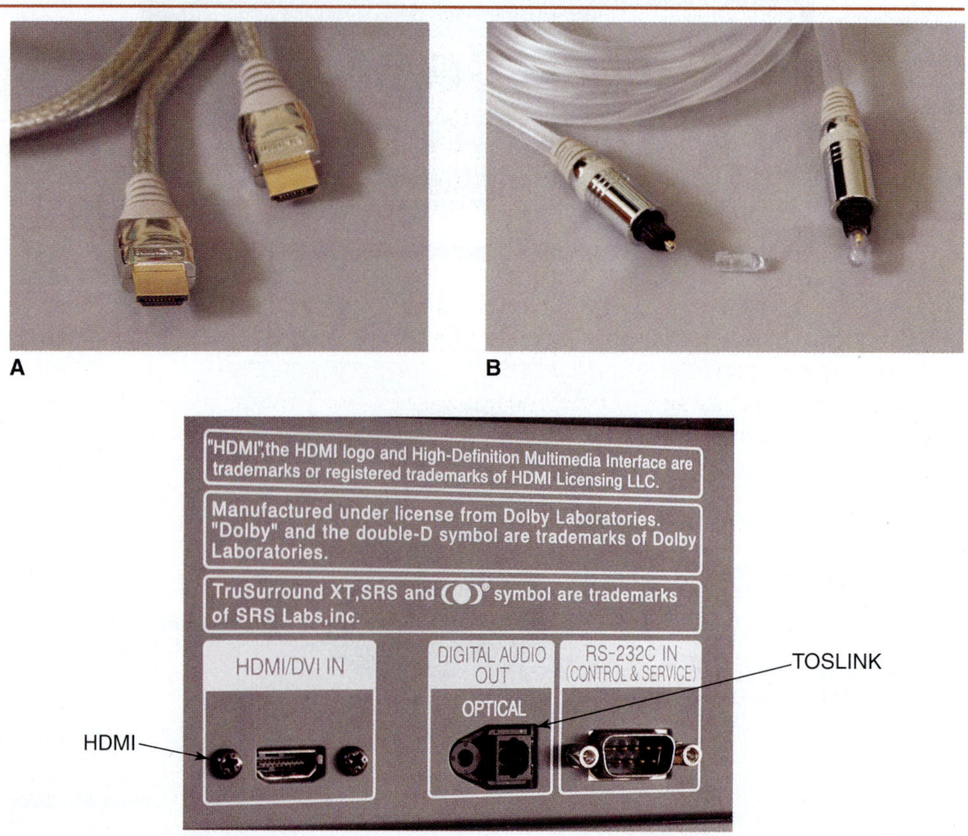

Figure 8-29 HDMI (A) is used to supply video and audio in an uncompressed, entirely digital format. TOSLINK (B) is an optical cable used for home theater equipment (C).

Goodheart-Willcox Publisher

The xvYCC standard is also designed to support Blu-ray technologies for Digital Video Disc (DVD) and the newest video game technology. The HDMI connector is commonly found on many high-end computer video cards.

Mini-HDMI

Although the HDMI connector is perceived to be the most commonly found connector for high-end computer video cards, many laptop computers and mobile devices support a Mini-HDMI display port. Figure 8-30 shows a Mini-HDMI connector next to a standard HDMI connector. The purpose of the Mini-HDMI port is to accommodate HDMI technology in a port smaller than a typical HDMI port. For example, the Mini-HDMI port is primarily connected to laptop computers, mobile devices, and digital imaging devices that do not have large enough hardware to support the full-size HDMI port, yet connect to a device for display purposes, such as a full-size monitor.

Sony/Philips Digital Interconnect Format

Sony/Philips Digital Interconnect Format (S/PDIF) is a special proprietary digital audio connection and cable. S/PDIF can be in one of two formats: coaxial with an RCA connector or fiber-optic with a TOSLINK connector. Fiber-optic connections are sometimes simply identified as "optic" connections rather than S/PDIF or TOSLINK.

TOSLINK

The TOSLINK optical connector, shown in Figure 8-29B, is a proprietary connection developed jointly by Sony and Philips. The TOSLINK cable is used quite often for home theater equipment and is a fiber-optic cable with a glass or plastic core. Fiber-optic cable ensures a high-quality transfer of audio signals because it is immune to radio and magnetic interference emitted from other cables or radio signal sources. Since fiber-optic cable and connectors are susceptible to damage from scratches and dust, the TOSLINK connector includes plastic end pieces to protect it from damage.

RF and F-Type

A+ 1001: 3.1

In general, RF and F-type connections provide the poorest quality video images when used between home entertainment-center devices. They are generally used only with old technologies to support connections between devices. Other cabling technologies, such as component video, S-Video, and HDMI, provide better signal support.

The RF and F-type cables are standard coaxial cables consisting of solid or stranded copper-core conductors, as shown in Figure 8-31. The core conductor is surrounded by a thick insulator material, which is covered by a conductive mesh or foil referred to as the ***shield***. The shield protects the core conductor from outside electromagnetic interference.

Do not confuse the use of transferring a signal between devices with bringing in the raw signal that comes directly from a satellite or broadband cable television. The other types of cabling other than coaxial are not typically used to bring a raw

Kabardins Photo/Shutterstock.com

Figure 8-30 Mini-HDMI is primarily used on laptops and mobile devices that are unable to support standard HDMI but support the video and graphics requirements of high-definition video.

signal into a complete system. The exception is fiber-optic cable, which is now being introduced in many areas to bring raw signals to a final destination. Figure 8-32 compares video connection technologies.

8.7 Graphic Coding

There are many different methods used to code the data of an image. The different coding methods are designed to either compress the content or preserve the quality. Compression is used to reduce file size and the total amount of time it takes for file transfer. Preserving the quality is needed to produce a high-quality final image after file transfer or image manipulation.

Bitmapped Graphics

A *bitmap (BMP)*, also referred to as a *raster image*, is a graphics standard for uncompressed encoding of images. A display screen or printed image is made from thousands or millions of pixels. As discussed earlier, a pixel is the smallest screen element. The number of bits used to encode the pixel determines the color and shades of that color.

For example, an 8-bit code is capable of 256 different binary number patterns, and each binary number pattern can represent a different color or shade of gray. On a color monitor, each pixel is actually a combination of three different colors: red, blue, and green. Each color has an 8-bit binary code that can represent 256 shades of that color. The three individual 8-bit colors combine to form a **true color**, which is a 24-bit code that represents the actual color of the pixel image. When mixed together, true colors can produce over 16 million colors.

Figure 8-31 The RF and F-type cables are standard coaxial cables consisting of solid or stranded copper-core conductors.

Goodheart-Willcox Publisher

Figure 8-32 Video connection types vary drastically in quality of video.

Video Connection Comparison	
Video Connection Type	**Quality Comparison**
HDMI	Best
Component Video	Excellent
S-Video	Good
Composite Video	Poor
RF	Poor

Goodheart-Willcox Publisher

Vector Graphics

Vector graphics are images based on a series of mathematical formulas that can be converted into geometric shapes representing the image to be displayed. Vector graphics are typically produced by drawing programs, not by photographic images. One main advantage of vector images is they can be resized or scaled without losing the quality of the image. When a bitmap image is enlarged or reduced in size, the number of pixels must be increased or decreased accordingly by adding or removing pixels, which distorts the original image. The software program performing the bitmap conversion must decide what color to add as the image is increased. It chooses the pixel color closest to the original pixel. When the image is reduced, the software erases an existing pixel.

Since vector graphic images use mathematical formulas to represent the lines in the figures, the picture retains its original picture quality no matter the size to which it is changed. The lines that compose the image are simply multiplied or divided by the applied scale factor. For example, all the line segments and circle diameters are doubled for a drawing that is to be increased in scale by 200 percent. A vector drawing could scale an infinite number of times and never lose its quality. In comparison, a bitmap image that was resized only a few times would become completely distorted.

Vector image technology is used in critical drawing applications such as computer-aided design (CAD) and in many different animation software programs. Bitmap is mostly associated with photographic images. It is important to note that you can convert a vector image to a bitmap image, but you cannot convert a bitmap image to a vector image.

Graphic Compression

Graphics applications require a lot of memory space for storage. Even a small graphic can require several million bytes of memory, depending on the resolution and the number of colors used to create the graphic. To decrease the amount of memory space needed, image data can be compressed. There are many different compression methods, but they all use similar techniques to accomplish the compression.

A close inspection of a typical graphic reveals the color pixels repeated many times sequentially in an area of the picture. Figure 8-33 shows a series of apple images. Each successive photo in this series looks progressively closer at the apple to expose the pixel pattern of colors. In the first image, you see what appears as very subtle variations of shades of green and red, but as the picture is enlarged, you can see that many of the pixels are the same color. These repeating pixels of the same color are the secret to file compression. Instead of describing every pixel, a compressed file can describe a series of similar pixels with a short piece of code.

For a file compression technique to be effective, it must convert the same information stored in the image but use less memory space. This image was saved as a Windows true color image, meaning that the image pixels are each composed of three 8-bit bytes. Consequently, each picture element shown uses 24 bits to represent the pixel. Look at the magnified images of the apple. Notice several continuous rows of pixels. If a row has 20 pixels, it requires 60 bytes of information.

One compression method worth looking into is run-length encoding. **Run-length encoding (RLE)** is a compression technique that replaces a series of repeated pixels with a single pixel and the length of the series (run). The longer the runs and the greater number of runs there are, the greater the compression that will be achieved. Figure 8-34 shows a comparison of labeled binary codes. The first set of binary codes represents the color white for 20 pixels. The second set of binary codes shows a condensed version of the same information.

Figure 8-33 As images are enlarged, what appears to be finely detailed can be broken down into a series of pixels, some of which repeat.

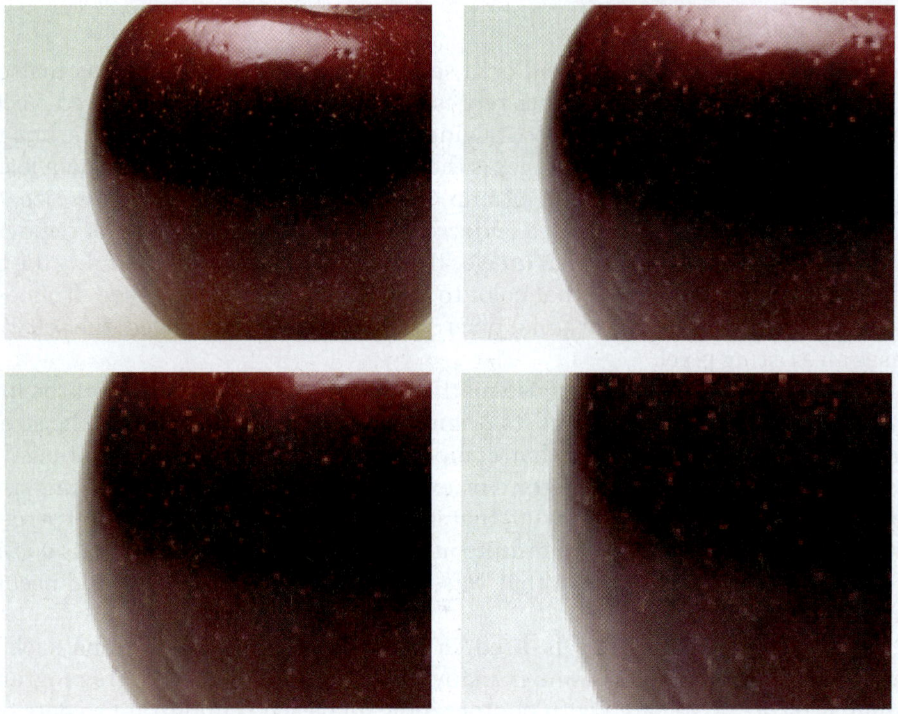

Goodheart-Willcox Publisher

Figure 8-34 Compression techniques can tremendously reduce the amount of code used to store an image or text. Here, repeated data is reduced from 60 bytes to 6 bytes.

The color white is equal to equal color parts of red, green, and blue.

Red	Green	Blue			
11111111	11111111	11111111	11111111	11111111	11111111
11111111	11111111	11111111	11111111	11111111	11111111
11111111	11111111	11111111	11111111	11111111	11111111
11111111	11111111	11111111	11111111	11111111	11111111
11111111	11111111	11111111	11111111	11111111	11111111
11111111	11111111	11111111	11111111	11111111	11111111
11111111	11111111	11111111	11111111	11111111	11111111
11111111	11111111	11111111	11111111	11111111	11111111
11111111	11111111	11111111	11111111	11111111	11111111
11111111	11111111	11111111	11111111	11111111	11111111

Original file information needed for the row of white pixel images

10010011 11100111	11111111 11111111 11111111	00010100
Location of first pixel	The three colors	Repeat (length of run)

Compressed file information for same section

Goodheart-Willcox Publisher

In the compressed file, the first byte gives the location of the first pixel. The next three bytes represent the color white, which is equal to decimal 255 (or binary code 11111111). The color white is composed of equal parts of red, blue, and green. Thus, the color is coded as three bytes, all consisting of eight 1s. The last byte of information contains the number of times necessary to repeat the pattern of white pixels. In the example, the last byte represents the decimal number 20. As you can see, the size of the compressed file, containing only six bytes, is very small in comparison to the original file that required 60 bytes of data.

Looking again at Figure 8-33, you can see many different colors that form a repeating pattern in the image. Each of these areas can be encoded the same way. This is the basic concept of compression. There are many different programs available to compress files, and while they do not all work exactly as demonstrated, they do work in a similar fashion. File compression techniques are used for not only graphics but also for other forms of data such as sound files. Some compression techniques can achieve a compression ratio as high as 12:1.

Tech Tip

The terms *lossy* and *lossless* are used to describe the effect of a file format on the quality of an image file. Lossy loses quality and lossless preserves quality. JPEG is lossy, while formats such as BMP, TIF, and PDF are lossless.

Chapter Summary

8.1 Video System and Display Characteristics

- Color display values and display resolution are aspects common to all monitors.
- Resolution refers to the amount of detail a monitor is capable of displaying.
- A pixel is the smallest unit of color in a screen display.
- The video graphics array (VGA) is the baseline for video adapters. Its color palette contains 262,144 (256k) different colors.

8.2 Types of Video Displays

- An LCD display operates on the principle of polarized light and the effect of an electrical voltage applied to a crystal structure.
- There are two types of backlighting for LCDs: cold cathode fluorescent lamps (CCFLs) and light-emitting diode (LED).
- LED displays are simply LCD screens using an LED backlight.
- Organic LED displays are LED displays in which the LED is constructed from carbon-based materials instead of crystalline structures.
- Passive-matrix displays have semitransparent conductors that run to each crystal. Active-matrix displays include a transistor for each pixel in the grid.
- A gas-plasma display operates on the principle of electroluminescence.
- Projectors do not use the traditional technologies of an LCD screen. Instead, they mount to a ceiling or wall and use bulbs to project an image onto a projector screen or opposite wall.

8.3 Display Terminology

- Important terms to understand when considering new or replacement monitors include dot pitch, refresh rate, raster display, contrast ratio, brightness, viewing angle, screen orientation, pixel pitch, native resolution, response time, monitor size, and aspect ratio.

8.4 Video Adapter Cards

- The PCIe ×16 video adapter card has replaced all other video card standards such as PCI, PCI-X, and AGP.
- A digital-to-analog converter (DAC) is a specialized chip that converts the digital signal from the computer to an analog signal that is displayed on the computer's monitor.
- Computers can be configured with two or more video cards to increase overall video performance. This is most desirable for graphics-intensive applications such as games, computer-aided design, and video editing.
- When using split-frame rendering, each graphics card is responsible for an equal portion of the frame image, based on how many cards are used.
- With alternating-frame rendering, each card is responsible for rendering every other frame.
- Scalable Link Interface (SLI) is a proprietary video card system owned by the NVIDIA Corporation in which multiple cards work together to produce a single output.
- AMD CrossFire is multiple-card technology designed as a competitor to NVIDIA's SLI product.
- Installing a video card involves inserting the card into the proper motherboard slot and installing the latest video card driver.

8.5 Maintaining and Personalizing Video Displays

- Troubleshooting a monitor involves checking power to the monitor and the cable between the computer and the display unit.
- Burn-in, also known as image retention, occurs when an image is left on a monitor for hours, resulting in the image leaving an impression in the display. This does not occur with modern LED or OLED monitors.
- Dead pixels, also known as stuck pixels, are individual pixels that have stopped working. These often appear as small dots on the display and can be black, white, or a noticeably different color than the rest of the screen.
- Artifacts make the image on the screen appear as if it were split horizontally. This occurs when the video controller is out of sync with the refresh of the display.
- Never clean a display while it is energized.
- Clean a monitor display area with a dry lint-free soft cloth.
- Never spray liquid directly on the display.
- Never place a display unit in direct sunlight, such as when placed in front of a window.
- Place the display unit in an area of relatively low humidity.
- **Appearance and Personalization** is used in Windows to change the display properties.

8.6 Television and Computers

- There is abundant crossover between computers and televisions, especially regarding HDTV and TV tuner cards.
- Smart TVs have further blurred the line between computers and televisions.
- Typical home theater connection types are composite video, S-Video, component video, HDMI, S/PDIF, TOSLINK, and RF and F-type.

8.7 Graphic Coding

- Compressing a file is a technique that summarizes redundant information contained in a file.
- A bitmap (BMP) is a graphics standard for uncompressed encoding of images.
- Vector graphics is based on a series of mathematical formulas that can be converted into geometric shapes representing the image to be displayed.
- Run-length encoding (RLE) replaces a series of repeated pixels with a single pixel and the length of the series (run).

Review Questions

1. What determines the possible number of color shades in a color display?
2. How many shades of a specific color can be produced by an 8-bit color pattern?
3. What does the term *resolution* mean in terms of display technology?
4. What is a pixel?
5. Differentiate between LCD, gas-plasma, and projector displays.
6. List two types of backlighting used in LCDs.
7. What is the function of an inverter?
8. What is the difference between an LED and an OLED display?
9. What is the difference between passive and active matrices?
10. List and describe commonly encountered display terminology.
11. Compare and contrast video adapter card types.

12. Differentiate between split-frame rendering and alternating-frame rendering.
13. List steps taken to install a video card.
14. List techniques for troubleshooting video displays.
15. If you are troubleshooting a computer with a video display problem, what should you do before changing the monitor?
16. List techniques for cleaning a video display.
17. List methods used to personalize a display.
18. List monitor and home-theater connection types.
19. Which type of connector is commonly associated with fiber-optic sound port connections?
20. Differentiate among coding methods.

Sample A+ Exam Questions

1. When a legacy PC boots in Safe Mode, which video mode is *most likely* used by the system?
   A. VGA
   B. SVGA
   C. XGA
   D. CGA
2. Which of the following is the best definition of dot pitch?
   A. The distance between two color dots measured in pixels
   B. The distance between two color dots measured in inch fractions
   C. The distance between two color dots measured in millimeters
   D. The distance between the diagonal of the screen corners measured in millimeters
3. Which item may need to be replaced after upgrading the video card in a computer system?
   A. CPU
   B. HDD
   C. Power supply
   D. Motherboard RAM
4. Which component will have the most influence on the performance of a 3D video game?
   A. CPU
   B. Graphics card
   C. HDD
   D. Display unit
5. What is the function of a laptop inverter?
   A. To change black and white images into color
   B. To change the digital data signals into analog data signals
   C. To convert low-voltage DC into high-voltage AC
   D. To convert analog music input into digital data signals
6. The term *codec* best relates to which of the following?
   A. Sound quality measurement
   B. Picture quality measurement
   C. A compression and decompression technique
   D. A sound transmission media type

7. A music file is being downloaded and played at the same time. The music starts, stops, and skips repeatedly. What is *most likely* the reason?
   A. Insufficient amount of RAM. The amount of memory should be increased.
   B. The modem speed needs to be increased to 112 baud.
   C. This is a normal effect caused by low download speeds.
   D. The DMA channels are blocked by too much bus traffic.
8. The smallest picture element on a monitor display is called what?
   A. Raster element
   B. Pixel
   C. Byte mark
   D. Color element
9. When one static image is displayed for an extended period of time, the display is at risk for _____.
   A. artifacts
   B. stuck pixels
   C. burn-in
   D. dead pixels
10. Which of the following refers to an LCD with fluorescent lamps?
   A. LED
   B. DFS
   C. OLED
   D. CCFL

Chapter 9

Audio Systems

Learning Outcomes

9.1 Describe characteristics of sound and factors that contribute to its quality.
9.2 List examples of common audio devices.
9.3 Summarize the steps in a sound card installation.
9.4 Recall common codecs and their purpose.
9.5 List factors to consider when building a custom computer system.

A+ Certification Exam Objectives

The following A+ Certification Exam Objectives are covered in this chapter.

Exam 220-1101

1.0 Mobile Devices

- 1.2 Compare and contrast the display components of mobile devices.
- 1.3 Given a scenario, set up and configure accessories and ports of mobile devices.

3.0 Hardware

- 3.4 Given a scenario, install and configure motherboards, central processing units (CPUs), and add-on cards.

Exam 220-1102

1.0 Operating Systems

- 1.4 Given a scenario, use the appropriate Microsoft Windows 10 Control Panel utility.
- 1.5 Given a scenario, use features and tools of the Microsoft Windows 10 operating system (OS).
- 1.6 Given a scenario, configure Microsoft Windows networking features on a client/desktop.

Key Terms

Advanced Video Coding (AVC)
buffering
codec
frequency response range
Moving Picture Experts Group (MPEG)
multimedia
musical instrument digital interface (MIDI)
sampling
sampling rate
sound

Overview

Audio is the second half of the multimedia experience. All PCs come with a small internal speaker, but that is not enough for most users. High-end sound cards, subwoofers, and microphones have become standard equipment on many systems. The first step in learning audio systems is to understand sound itself and how it is created. The second step is to understand how audio devices interface with the PC.

A+ Note

The CompTIA A+ Exams require candidates to select components for a customized computer based on customer needs. Using information from this chapter, as well as the previous chapter, you should be able to evaluate a computer system and decide if it is best for general computer use, graphic design work, audio and video editing, gaming, and similar applications.

9.1 What Is Sound?

Sound consists of vibrations that are put into motion through a medium, such as air or water. We are most familiar with air as the medium. The air itself carries a vibrating wave action, which can be seen if you place a piece of tissue paper in front of a speaker; the vibration makes the tissue paper move. Additionally, if you are anywhere near large, megawatt speakers turned up very loudly, you are likely familiar with the "feel" of sound.

If all air is removed and only a vacuum exists, sound cannot exist. A vacuum is completely empty, meaning there is no medium to carry the produced vibrations we call sound. This concept can be demonstrated by placing an alarm clock inside a sealed, glass container from which air is removed. When the alarm goes off, it cannot be heard because there is no medium present to transport the pattern of vibrations called sound.

The human ear can only detect sounds within its **frequency response range**, which spans from approximately 20 Hz to 20 kHz. Vibrations above or below this range go undetected by human ears. Other mammals, such as dogs, bats, and whales, have significantly greater frequency ranges, with some species reaching up to 100 kHz.

Sampling

Sampling is the act of measuring an analog signal at regular intervals and is required before converting an analog signal into a digital signal. The quality of any type of analog-to-digital conversion is based primarily on the sampling rate and number of bits used to represent the height or voltage level of the signal. A **sampling rate** refers to the frequency with which samples of an audio signal are taken per second. Sampling rates are incorporated into many different technologies, including weather radar units, security systems based on voice and image identification, and automatic piloting of aircraft, among others.

A high sampling rate (frequent samples taken) results in a better quality of sound. Figure 9-1 shows two different sampling rates taken from the same wave. Notice how the resultant waves differ with high and low sampling rates by comparing the reconstructed analog wave shapes.

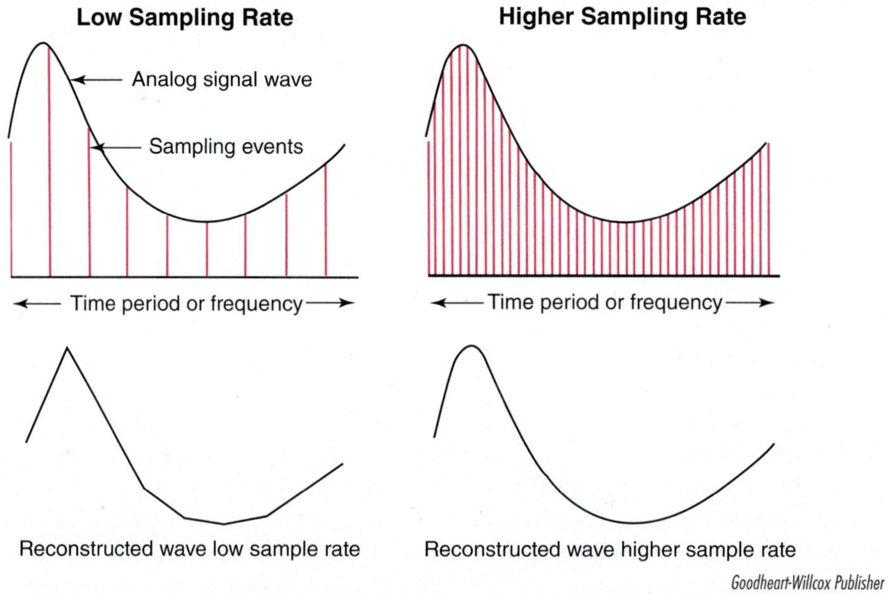

Figure 9-1 A higher sampling rate creates a more accurate reproduction of the original waveform.

A high sampling rate gives a better representation of an analog signal shape. In the illustration, an analog wave shape is sampled at two different rates. When the two wave shapes are reconstructed by connecting the points of sampling, you can see that the higher sampling rate gives a shape closer to the original analog wave shape. The quality of the sampling is directly affected by the sampling rate and by the number of bits used to indicate the height of the signal at the sampling points. The size of the file storing the signal data needed to reconstruct the sound wave also increases proportionately with the sampling rate.

Several factors affect the choice of sampling rates, which vary depending on what is being recorded. For example, music requires a high sampling rate in comparison to a simple voice recording. The quality of sound may not be an issue when leaving a voice mail message, but most listeners are fairly discriminating regarding the quality of their music.

Audio Resolution

A+ 1102: 1.4

The original sound card was an 8-bit card. Today, quality sound cards are 16-bit, 24-bit, or higher. You can record a better image of the original sound using a 16-bit card rather than an 8-bit card. A system based on 8-bit sound is limited to using 256 levels, or binary codes, to store a binary image of the sound wave sample. However, a 16-bit sound card can use 65,536 binary codes to store the sound wave pattern during each sampling, which enables a 16-bit system to save a more detailed representation of the analog sound wave pattern than an 8-bit system because a 16-bit card can capture 65,536 discrete levels of sound. The more bits used to record the audio image of the sound, the better the quality of the sound. For example, a 24-bit card can capture 16,777,216 discrete levels of sound, substantially more than even a 16-bit card.

Think in terms of graphic picture resolution. A better graphic image can be produced using 16 bits per pixel rather than 8 bits per pixel. Look again at Figure 9-1, where sampling rate and reconstructed analog wave shapes are illustrated. In the illustration of sampling rates, the height of the sample is measured in bits. A more detailed graph can be reconstructed by using more bits for the initial readings taken.

Again, audio resolution is based on the sampling rate and the number of bits used to represent the analog sound. The number of bits used to represent the analog sound determines the sensitivity of the analog measurement represented as a voltage level. Together these two quantities determine the quality of the sound captured and played back.

A typical sampling rate for a 16-bit sound card is 44.1 kHz, which is equal to 100 times per second. Most 24-bit sound cards operate at 96 kHz, but a 24-bit sound card with a sampling rate of 99 kHz will record 4 bytes of data 99,000 times a second. A 24-bit 96 kHz sampling rate will result in 33 MB of storage for a one-minute recording. As you can see, audio recordings require a significant amount of data storage.

MIDI Files

Musical instrument digital interface (MIDI) is a file standard developed for music synthesizers. Synthesized music is electronically simulated music sounds rather than recorded sounds. A chip, or set of chips, produces the sounds of many instruments, illustrated in Figure 9-2. To play music, input through the chips is made from a database containing information such as the type of instrument to play, the actual note to play, the length of sound, and any special effects such as an echo chamber effect. The music is actually a sequence of coded instructions sent to the chips that make the sounds. An advantage of MIDI is that it is a universal file format; however, a disadvantage is that many MIDI audio systems sound very much like artificial music to the ear. After all, they are artificial sounds produced by chips rather than real instrument recordings.

MIDI can be created electronically by connecting a PC to a MIDI interface on a sound synthesizer or keyboard, shown in Figure 9-3. The keyboard has selector switches from which the user can select dozens of different instruments. A song can be recorded in MIDI data format to be saved and played back on the PC, and once the soundtrack is saved, it can be manipulated to add special effects. A single musician can create music similar to a complete orchestra of instruments.

9.2 Audio Devices

There are numerous audio devices for the PC. They include both input devices, such as the microphone, and output devices, such as the speaker. Most of these devices are connected to the PC through the sound card.

A+ 1101: 1.2

Microphone

A *microphone* is a simple electronic device used to convert sound waves into electrical energy that is analog in nature. The microphone converts the air vibration that strikes it into voltage levels that are in direct proportion to the strength and frequency of the vibrations. Figure 9-4 shows an illustration of sound waves striking a microphone and their conversion to digital data.

When the signal reaches the sound card, the analog electrical signal is converted to a digital signal, which allows it to be stored in RAM, on a hard drive, or on a CD. When the sound is stored as a digital code, it is often referred to as a *wave* file because it usually has a **.wav** file extension. A one-minute **.wav** file can vary in size from 500 kB to over 20 MB depending on variables, such as the speed of the sampling frequency, whether monophonic or stereo sound is being recorded, whether 8-bit or 16-bit sampling is used, and the compression technique being used (if any).

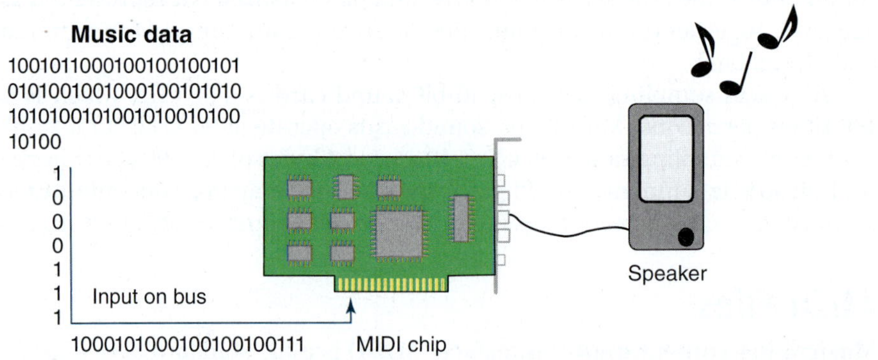

Figure 9-2 A MIDI chip is capable of reproducing sound from a selection of instruments that are stored in its memory.

Goodheart-Willcox Publisher

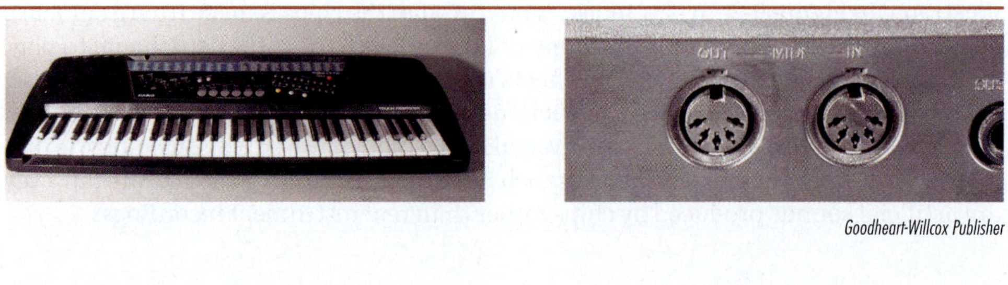

Figure 9-3 MIDI can be created electronically by connecting a PC to a MIDI interface on a sound synthesizer or keyboard.

Goodheart-Willcox Publisher

Speakers

1101: 1.3 A+
1102: 1.4

A speaker converts electrical energy to sound energy. Look at Figure 9-5 to see a digital sound passing through a sound card and out through a speaker. To listen to stored digital code, the code is sent through the sound card and is then converted to an analog electrical signal. As the electrical energy varies in strength, the speaker cone vibrates at a rate proportional to the analog electrical signal.

Take note of the 120-volt power converter, which is used to power the amplifier inside the speaker. The speaker amplifier takes the small analog signal it receives from the sound card and powerfully reproduces it. A typical sound card cannot provide ample power to drive a speaker as most sound cards only produce approximately two watts of energy. This is sufficient to drive only a headphone set, not a desktop speaker. When a speaker has its own built-in amplifier, it is called an *active speaker.* A speaker without amplification is called a *passive speaker.*

A sound system can be installed wirelessly rather than using traditional cabling. A wireless system is typically composed of a set of wireless speakers, a wireless remote control, and a wireless transmitter. The number and type of speakers used depends on the user and application; the user may wish to install a simple two-speaker system or a multiple-speaker system to create a 3D sound system. The wireless transmitter connects to sound devices such as an MP3 player, a television, a CD/DVD system, or any other type of sound device.

Wireless is not always the best choice for high-quality sound systems. All radio wave-based technology can suffer from interference because the operating frequency of a wireless speaker system is also shared by many other types of devices. The federal government assigns radio devices to specific radio frequencies or bands,

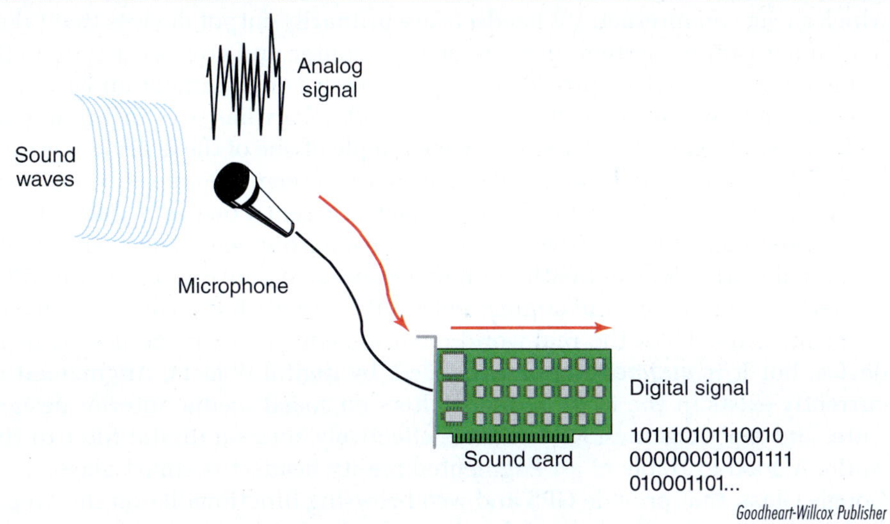

Figure 9-4 An analog sound signal is turned into an analog electrical signal by a microphone and then into a digital electrical signal by a sound card.

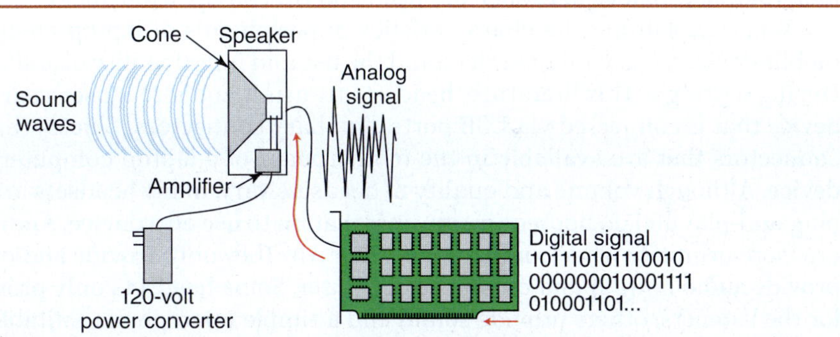

Figure 9-5 A sound card changes a digital signal back into an analog electrical signal. This signal is used to produce sound by a speaker.

also known as *channels*. The 900-MHz radio band is used for such items as wireless microphones, wireless speakers, baby monitors, home security systems, home intercom systems, amateur ham radios, cordless headphones, wireless utility meters, some medical equipment, and many types of industrial equipment used to produce heat for sealing packages and drying items such as glue. As you can see, many different items could interfere with a wireless sound system.

The advertised range for wireless speaker systems is typically 150 feet to 300 feet, but this range is under ideal conditions such as direct line of sight between the transmitter and speaker receivers. Ideal conditions are seldom encountered in application because building materials such as wood, drywall, concrete, and brick reduce radio signal strength. Radio interference also reduces the signal strength and distance the signal can travel. It also distorts the radio signal and causes poor sound quality. There can be many concerns for a wireless speaker system. To ensure the best sound delivery to speakers and other sound devices, cable is the preferred media.

A+ 1102: 1.4

If you are not getting sound from your speakers, the first thing to check, as with most electronic devices, is to ensure it is receiving power and powered on. Next, ensure the volume is up to a level where you would be able to hear it. The next item to check would be the device driver. If the driver is up to date, navigate to **Start>Control Panel>Troubleshooting>Hardware and Sound>Playing Audio.**

Virtual Reality, Augmented Reality, and Audio Headsets

While the CompTIA A+ Certification Exams do not go into these topics, they are becoming more commonplace, and you should be familiar with them. *Virtual reality (VR)* is a computer-generated simulation of a three-dimensional environment with which a user can interact. VR headsets are primarily output devices that take a signal from a gaming system or a personal computer and convert it into audio and visual effects, enough to provide a fully immersive environment and give the user the illusion they are somewhere else. This technology has uses in gaming, design, and even entertainment. A well-known example of one of these devices is the cardboard VR by Google that uses a cell phone for the screen. A far more expensive device is the Oculus and Meta Quest line of products, currently owned by Meta Platforms.

Augmented reality (AR) is an interactive environmental experience that combines real-world elements with computer-generated content. The main difference between virtual reality and augmented reality is that VR is a wholly artificial environment, while AR is the real-world environment in which the user is using the device, but it is *augmented*, or enhanced, by digital objects. Augmented reality currently exists in the form of photo filters on social media, interior design software, and mobile games. AR headsets effectively act as a digital filter to the real world. A good example of an augmented reality headset is smart glasses, such as Google Glass, that provide GPS and web browsing functionality on the eyepiece of the glasses. Another example is a heads-up display (HUD) in aircraft and some automotives that provides data such as speed and GPS on the windshield.

A+ 1101: 1.3

When explaining the characteristics of peripherals of laptop computers and mobile devices, it is vital to understand the use and functionality of audio headsets. During writing of this literature, headsets transmit audio to a user's ear through a device that is connected via USB ports, auxiliary connectors, Bluetooth, and other connectors that are available in the motherboard of a laptop computer or mobile device. Although volume and quality of headsets vary, many headsets are a form of plug-and-play and do not require any installation to use on a device. Audio headsets are more primitive when compared to VR or AR. They only provide audio, but many provide audio both in and out of the computer. Some headsets only provide sound for the listeners; others provide sound and a simple microphone, suitable for game use or with applications such as Skype.

Sound Cards

1101: 3.4
1102: 1.4
A+

Most sound cards purchased today are PCI adapter cards. This means they are plug-and-play technology. Older 8-bit adapter-type cards will most likely require a user to assign system resources manually through software or by setting jumpers or dip switches, and even then, system conflicts are quite common for older cards.

Always check the system resource assignments when problems arise, especially after newer hardware has been installed into an existing system. Software diagnostic programs included in most operating systems can diagnose conflicts. Windows has diagnostic software to assist you with conflicts with system resources. These tools can be accessed through **Start**>**All apps**>**Windows Administrative Tools**>**System Information**. Alternatively, a user could search for msinfo or system information in the search feature. Figure 9-6 shows the Windows 10 **System Information** dialog box, which can assist you when solving system resource conflicts. You can use this window to analyze conflicts arising from system resource assignments. Note that some resources refer to msinfo32. Both msinfo and msinfo32 launch the same utility.

Audio Capture Cards

1101: 3.4
A+

Audio capture cards work similarly to the video capture cards discussed in Chapter 8. They take the analog output of some audio device and convert it to digital format. You can now also purchase audio capture cards that connect via USB. Audio capture cards can be used with microphones, electronic keyboards, and many other sound devices. This allows you to import the sound into a computer then use digital sound-editing software. There are also cards that perform both video and audio capture.

Volume Settings

In addition to adjusting sound settings via System Information, laptop and desktop computers installed with a Windows operating system may have function keys, also known as *shortcut* or *hot keys*, which will provide a user with a combination of keystrokes that allow for the control of a computer's volume. Additionally, these settings can always be found via system settings or the Windows Control Panel. However, most current laptops will also have their own unique volume controls via the laptop's hardware and casing.

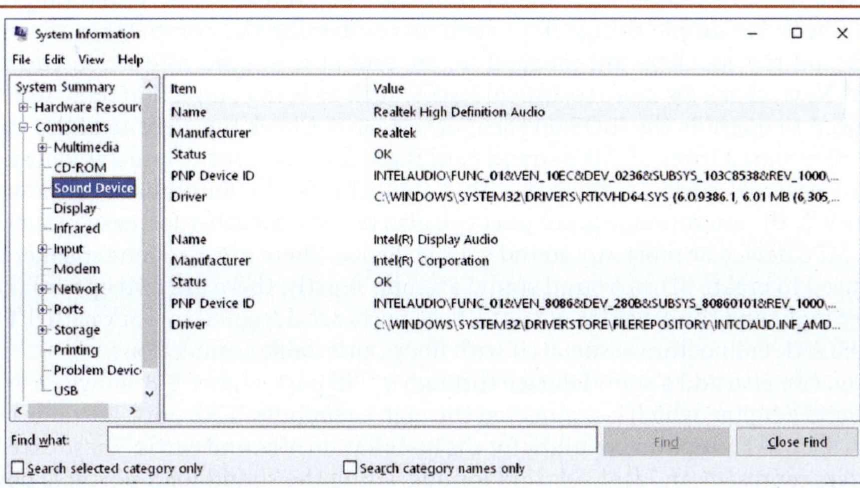

Goodheart-Willcox Publisher

Figure 9-6 The System Information dialog box can be used to help troubleshoot conflicts. It shows the IRQs, DMAs, and I/O port addresses a computer's components are using.

A+ 1101: 3.4

9.3 Installing a Sound Card

Installing a sound card before plug-and-play could be very frustrating. The source of frustration came from system resource assignments. There was almost a guarantee of a system resource conflict appearing with legacy sound cards. Multimedia cards use all areas of system resources. Before installing any legacy sound card, review the IRQs, DMA, memory addresses, and I/O port address topics covered earlier in the textbook.

Although plug-and-play eliminates most conflicts, there can still be problems, especially when upgrades are performed. As new technologies evolve, there will be the need to upgrade current technologies. In other words, plug-and-play operates well now, but a new technology will undoubtedly appear in the future that will also require plug-and-play to be upgraded or redesigned. The following steps are used for the installation of a typical sound card:

1. Back up all computer files before installing a sound card.
2. Power off the computer and unplug the power cord from the wall outlet.
3. Read the card installation procedure and specification sheet.
4. Take normal electrostatic discharge (ESD) precautions.
5. Check for debris in the expansion slot.
6. Insert the card into the slot by applying even force to the top of the card. Do *not* rock the card into the slot.
7. Check if there are any cables that might interfere with the sound card. Voltages can be induced by wires in close proximity to the sound card. This can distort the sound quality. Keep cables away from sound cards.
8. Connect the speakers to the computer and connect the speaker's power supply to the speakers. Turn the speakers on before powering on the computer.
9. Check for the latest drivers at the sound card manufacturer's website.
10. Reboot the computer.

If the new card is plug-and-play compatible, it should be automatically detected, though you may have to supply a driver for the new adapter card when the system detects the card because Windows may not have the correct driver. A driver may be packaged with the sound card on a CD or DVD, but always check the manufacturer's website for the latest patch or upgrade for the driver. Follow the screen prompts to complete the installation.

A+ 1101: 5.4

If all has gone well, you should be able to turn off the power, install the cover, and then reboot the system. If the installation fails, reread the installation procedure. Check for simple things first, such as confirming the computer is receiving power and the speakers are plugged in, on, and at a volume where you can hear sound. Next, check for more technical issues, such as bent connection pins. You may also need to upgrade the BIOS on the motherboard. Check the website of the motherboard manufacturer and the sound card manufacturer for the latest updates.

A variety of ports associated with a typical modern sound card is shown in Figure 9-7. The microphone input port can also be used for other forms of input such as an MP3 device or most any sound source device. There are also four speaker outputs used to create 3D surround sound systems. Lastly, there are two optical ports: one for input and the other for output. These ports are designed to work with S/PDIF or TOSLINK connectors associated with fiber-optic cable connections.

You can also add a sound device through a USB port. Figure 9-8 shows an external sound adapter, which is connected through a computer USB port. Portable computers such as laptops do not allow for the installation of sound cards. These external adapters represent an ideal solution for upgrading the sound for a portable device

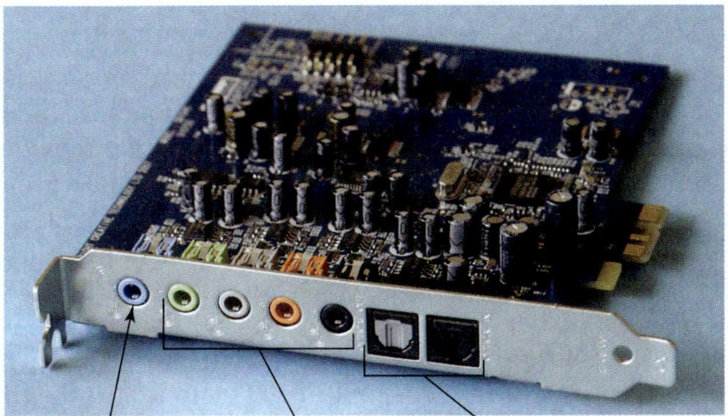

Goodheart-Willcox Publisher

Figure 9-7 A typical sound card has a variety of connection ports that support input and output to and from sound devices.

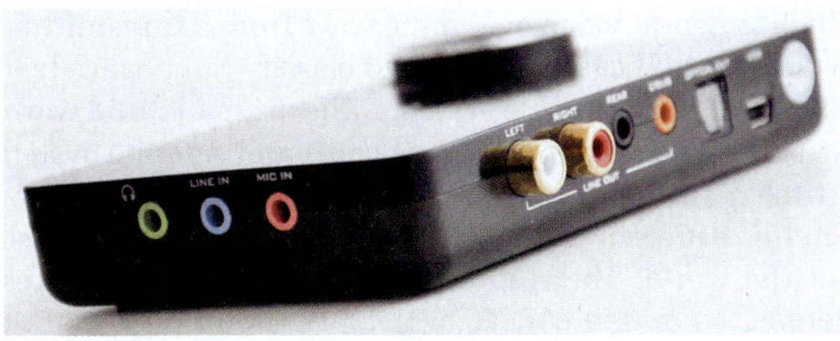

Eviart/Shutterstock.com

Figure 9-8 A sound card can be installed through a USB port on the computer, which eliminates the need to open the computer case. This is ideal for laptops and mobile devices.

such as a laptop. Devices such as this one often come two cables: a USB cable for connection to the computer system and an S/PDIF. The S/PDIF cable can be used in the S/PDIF input or output ports on the side of the sound box. They typically include other ports as well, such as RCA ports for connections to the headphone and speaker ports and an input device port for devices such as a microphone or MP3 player.

9.4 Multimedia

Any file that includes interaction between audio and video is referred to as **multimedia.** Attempts to create and play multimedia files more quickly and clearly have been one of the major driving factors in the computer industry. The computing power needed to render three-dimensional images and the storage needed to store or even play movies have caused the minimum processing speeds of CPUs and the RAM on PCs to increase over the last few years. The greatest recent changes in PC operating systems are those to how they handle multimedia.

Codecs

A term frequently used in compression is *codec*. A **codec** is any hardware, software, or combination hardware and software that can compress and decompress data. The term is a contraction of the two words *compression* and *decompression* and is used most often in the video industry and telecommunication. Some examples of software codecs are MPEG, QuickTime, AVC, ATSC, DVB-T, and many more. When setting up properties for audio and video equipment using Windows, the many compression techniques will be referred to as choosing a method of codec.

MPEG Formats

The **Moving Picture Experts Group (MPEG)**, (pronounced *empeg*), is an organization made up of professionals from all areas of the motion picture industry with the goal of developing a standard format for recording motion picture video and sound. Together, MPEG developed data compression standards and file formats for storing both audio and video data. The two main original formats are MPEG-1 and MPEG-2. MPEG-1 is similar to videotape quality, but MPEG-2 is a higher-quality compression used for PC CD video, Digital Versatile Disc (DVD) (also called Digital Video Disc), and HDTV.

The MP3 standard (short for MPEG layer 3) is used for music and is a derivative of the MPEG-2 standard. MPEG-4 came out in 1999 and is still the main standard used today, though there are several more MPEG standards under development.

Advanced Video Coding (AVC), also referred to as *H.264*, *MPEG-4*, and *MP4*, is a video compression standard used for high-definition video. The AVC standard is used in applications such as digital television, DVD and Blu-ray discs, and Internet video streaming. Codecs use many different broadcast compressions for terrestrial broadcast systems, which transmit video over radio wave from a transmitter to an antenna receiver. The term *terrestrial system* is used to classify radio wave transmission systems that do not use satellite or cable systems. The original radio wave systems were all referred to as terrestrial systems because cable and satellite systems were not in existence at the time of the first radio wave communication systems.

There are many different television standards and compression standards used throughout the world. The standard used in the United States is *Advanced Television Systems Committee (ATSC)*, which is used for high-definition television broadcasts. Additional standards include *Digital Video Broadcasting (DVB)*, which is an open-source set of standards and compression techniques, and *Cable Digital Video Broadcasting (DVB-C)*. Digital Video Broadcasting—Terrestrial (DVB-T) is the primarily standard used in Europe.

Satellite-based video communication is based on Digital Video Broadcasting and is referred to by the acronym DVB-S. The *S*, *C*, or *T* represents the communication media satellite, cable, and terrestrial, respectively. There are many more standards and compression techniques. Each type of media has its own set of standards.

MPEG-7 and MPEG-21 are standards designed to work with existing MPEG standards and do not actually provide enhanced compression. MPEG-7 is used to identify locations of content, thus allowing faster retrieval. For example, think of the last DVD or Blu-ray move you watched. You were likely given the option of choosing a chapter or scene from which to start the film. This is due to MPEG-7. MPEG-21 provides multimedia on demand and protects the digital rights. In other words, MPEG is used to manage the distribution of video while providing copyright infringement protection. Both MPEG-7 and MPEG-21 are open standards so any manufacturer can ensure compatibility of these features for their media and their media players.

Buffering

Buffering is a technique used to play a downloaded file without skips or quiet spots during playback. Recall from Chapter 6 that a *buffer* is used to store data temporarily before transferring it to a device. When downloading music online, it must travel hundreds or even thousands of miles from its source to your PC. Unless you have a high-bandwidth connection such as a fiber, cable, or high-speed wireless, you will have difficulty maintaining a steady stream of data from the other site. There will be additional detailed information about various connection mediums, such as T-Carrier lines and high-speed wireless, in a later chapter.

Data is sent across the Internet to your PC in packets that average 1,500 bytes each. As noted earlier, data for sound is quite large, and a music sample may be constructed from thousands of the 1,500-byte packets. The data does not arrive as a consistent series of packets, and many data packets will even arrive out of their original order since the data route to and from a website is constantly being updated. The Internet is composed of various types of media, both cable and wireless. Much of the media becomes congested with data traffic and, at times, data packets are rerouted to achieve a faster transmission rate. If a quicker route is discovered by the transmission system while data are transferred, the balance of the data will be transmitted through the new route. If another route is discovered or the present one becomes very busy, an alternate route is chosen. As the routes continue to change, some of the packets arrive out of the original order.

In addition, the steady stream of packets can be stopped momentarily due to congestion on the lines. In the last few years, the dramatic increase in video and audio data packets has created a significant increase in traffic on the data lines, resulting in an apparent slowdown of the entire system. A good example of these seemingly slow systems can be seen on many college campuses where scores of students are simultaneously downloading or streaming multimedia files from the Internet.

Since packets are likely arriving out of order, they must be reassembled at their destination. Buffering collects all the downloaded data and reassembles it in its original order, which provides a steady stream of data. In the case of downloading a song, the act of buffering means the song data is downloaded into RAM, where it is then reassembled and transferred to the player. The player plays the song from a steady stream of data located in RAM rather than from the site. With buffering, there are no interruptions in the continuous stream of music.

Audio and Video Players

To access sound and video tracks recorded on the PC or taken from the Internet, you must have a player, which is often called a ***plug-in***. A plug-in is used to decode compressed multimedia files, converting them to audio and video. Players can convert more than one type of compression, but when a new or enhanced compression format is developed, you will need an updated version of the player.

Large varieties of free media players are available through the Internet. Some of the players are only designed to allow you to play through the Internet browser and will not record. The quality of the multimedia presentation is directly related to the quality and capacities of the computer system you use. However, upgrading a single component on an existing system may not show any real improvement. Too often, novices assume that upgrading the CPU or adding more RAM will greatly improve the performance. A system needs to be studied as a whole before a decision is made about enhancing multimedia performance. For example, upgrading the CPU and adding more memory will do little to improve the quality of the multimedia performance if the system uses an 8-bit sound card. A major improvement may result by simply replacing the sound card with a 16-bit PCI sound card.

9.5 Building a Custom Computer System

The CompTIA A+ Certification Exams have de-emphasized building specific custom computer systems, but this is a task you may be required to perform occasionally while working the PC industry. When building a custom computer system, you should keep in mind how performance is affected by the five major components. If you want to build a high-performance system, you need to have a good graphics adapter and plenty of available memory, which means installing a 64-bit operating system. You can use performance information and tools to evaluate a system before making a purchase of similar computers for an office environment or personal use.

The base score generated by the tool will provide information to you concerning the ability of the system to support software applications such as CAD, 3D gaming, or video editing. You can also use this tool to identify problem components that may be upgraded or replaced to improve the system performance.

Selecting PC Components

Selecting components to build a customized computer system is based on the tasks the computer is designed to accomplish. Tasks such as sending and receiving e-mail, web browsing, and word processing can be accomplished by most standard computers whether they are a desktop, laptop, or portable device such as a tablet. But when real performance is needed for media-intensive applications such as CAD, gaming, and multimedia editing, it is common to have a technician design a custom computer system or provide information about which off-the-shelf computer system will meet the performance needs.

The two most important questions to ask first are "How will the computer be used?" and "How much are you willing to spend?" No other computer component is more important than the computer audio/video system when high-performance audio and video is required. A good computer can be upgraded easily by adding a high-performance audio or video card, but these cards require their own electrical power connection. When upgrading to high-performance cards, you may also need to replace the power supply with one that can supply more electrical power. Review the card manufacturer's website for the recommended size of power supply required to support the card. Important factors to consider when building a custom PC are the following:

- **Motherboard/chipset and processor:** Processor and motherboard chipset work as a team
- **Power supply:** CPU and high-performance cards consume the most energy
- **Video card:** Select by amount of video memory and type of video ports needed (DVD-I, HDMI, etc.)
- **Display:** LED, OLED, or gas-plasma; Internet and wireless connections
- **Sound card:** Internal or external, number of channels, S/PDIF ports
- **TV tuner card:** Interior or exterior
- **Mass storage:** Size of disk storage
- **Number and type of ports required on motherboard:** HDMI, S/PDIF, RJ-45, etc.
- **Special application software requirements:** CAD, web-page editors, multimedia editing, and 3D video

Many websites such as Newegg, Intel, AMD, and NVIDIA provide information that can be used to custom design your computer system. There are also countless videos provided on YouTube on this topic.

Performance Information and Tools

Overall, performance is determined by the adapters and RAM used to support audio and video. When the respective cards do not have sufficient dedicated RAM, they will utilize part of the RAM installed on the motherboard. To assist you in evaluating a computer system, Windows provides the Performance Monitor utility, shown in Figure 9-9. This tool determines the overall performance of a computer system and identifies performance capabilities of five major components: processor, RAM, graphics, gaming graphics, and primary hard disk. To access this tool, simply enter perfmon into the **Search** box or select **Start>All apps>Windows Administrative Tools>Performance Monitor**.

Another tool you should be familiar with is the Resource Monitor, or **resmon.exe**. You can launch this tool by entering resmon into the **Search** box and selecting the appropriate utility from the list of results. Figure 9-10 shows the Resource Monitor

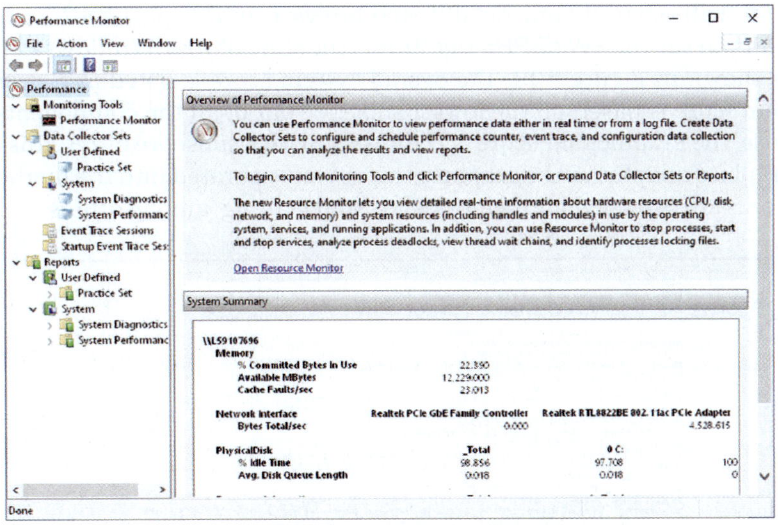

Goodheart-Willcox Publisher

Figure 9-9 Windows Performance Monitor provides a way to determine the overall performance of a computer system.

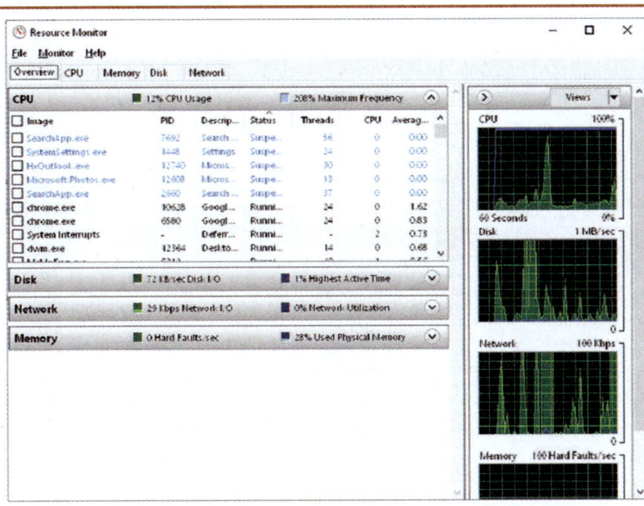

Goodheart-Willcox Publisher

Figure 9-10 The Windows Resource Monitor utility displays information such as running processes and what resources, such as the CPU, memory, and disk utilization, those processes are utilizing.

tool, which displays information such as running processes and what resources, such as the CPU, memory, and disk utilization, those processes are utilizing.

Windows Experience Index

A+ 1102: 1.5

The Windows Experience Index is a numeric rating based on the five major components. The Windows Experience scales are from 1.0 to 7.9. While each component has a subscore, the overall rating or base score is based on the lowest component score. In Windows 10, this score is not as easily found as in previous versions of Windows. In general, you can access your Windows Experience Index through either the Command Prompt and GUI or through PowerShell.

To locate your Windows Experience Index via Command Prompt, enter cmd in the Search bar and select **Run as Administrator** from the list of results. When the **Administrator: Command Prompt** window opens, execute the **winsat formal** command, as shown in Figure 9-11. Note, if you are working on a laptop, you will have to plug it in because the command will not run on battery power. When the command has finished executing, navigate to C:\Windows\Performance\WinSAT\DataStore to find your score. In this folder, you may see multiple files with **.xml** file extensions, as shown in Figure 9-12. Double-click the most recent file.

The file will open in your default web browser and display XML code. Scroll down until you see the <WinSPR> tag. This is the start of your Windows Experience score, as shown in Figure 9-13. The overall system score is listed as SystemScore. The system score is based on the lowest subscore out of all the components tested. In this case, the graphics subscore is the lowest, with a subscore of 7.8. This is based on the graphics adapter or the graphics chipset incorporated into the motherboard. Other scores are provided for memory, CPU, and gaming, among others.

Figure 9-11 The **winsat formal** command is one method of locating a Windows Experience Index rating in Windows 10.

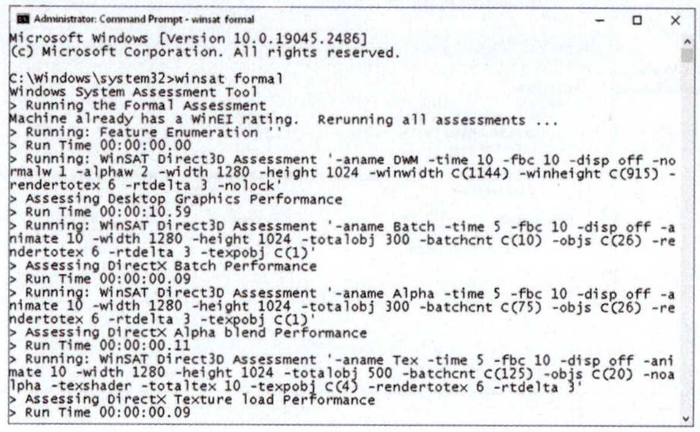

Goodheart-Willcox Publisher

Figure 9-12 Windows maintains a collection of assessments that score a computer based on its performance.

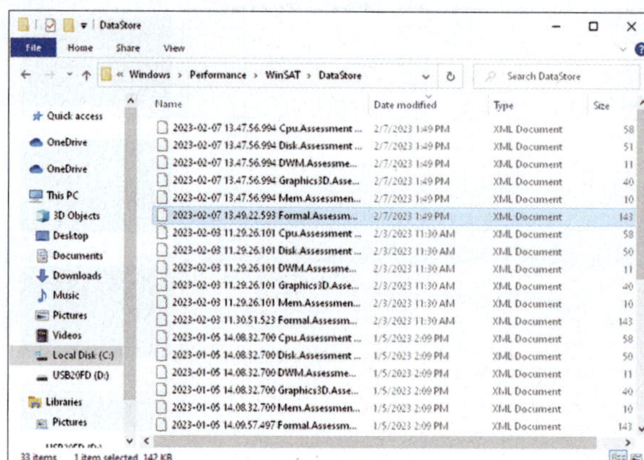

Goodheart-Willcox Publisher

Figure 9-13 A computer's overall score is based on the lowest subscore from all the components tested.

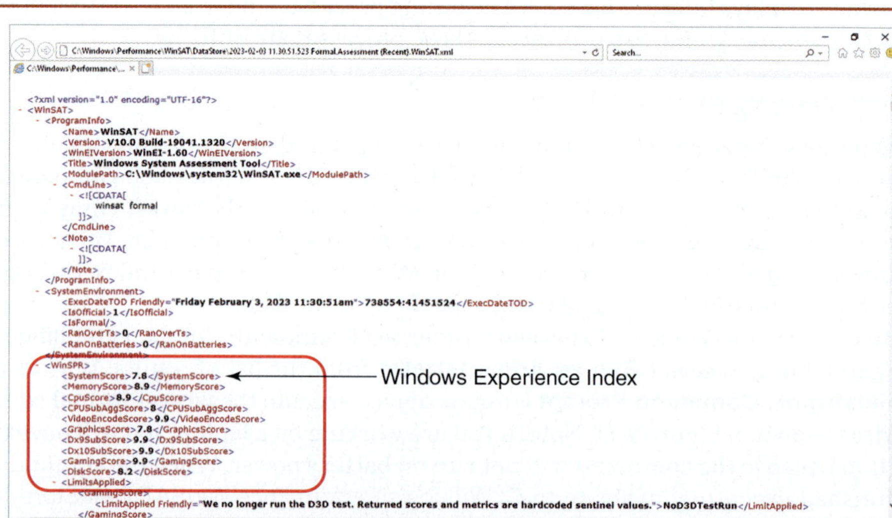

Goodheart-Willcox Publisher

PowerShell provides a much simpler way of identifying your Windows Experience Index. To find your rating via PowerShell, enter powershell in the **Search** bar and select **Run as Administrator** from the list of results. When the **Administrator: Windows PowerShell** window opens, execute the command syn-tax get-ciminstance win32_winsat and press [Enter]. As shown in Figure 9-14, PowerShell will provide a list of results in the window without you having to find a **.xml** file.

The table shown in Figure 9-15 is a guide as to what can be expected from a computer system in regard to the Windows base score. The ranges are approximations. The levels are to serve as a general guide.

DirectX Diagnostic Tool

A+ 1102: 1.5

Microsoft operating system provides the DirectX Diagnostic Tool to perform a quick check of the computer video and audio systems, Figure 9-16. You can run the DirectX Diagnostic Tool either by searching for dxdiag in the search feature, or by issuing the **dxdiag** command from the command prompt. There will be more about DirectX in a later chapter.

Windows Control Panel

A+ 1102: 1.6

There are sound utilities available in the Windows Control Panel that provide an interface to the sound-related features of the Windows operating system. The most basic include the **Sound** settings, shown in Figure 9-17. From this utility, you can select the sound input and output devices, set system volume, and perform basic troubleshooting. You reach this app by simply typing sound settings into the Windows search bar or navigating to **Start>Settings>System>Sound.** From this screen you can select **Sound Control Panel** from the Related Settings portion of

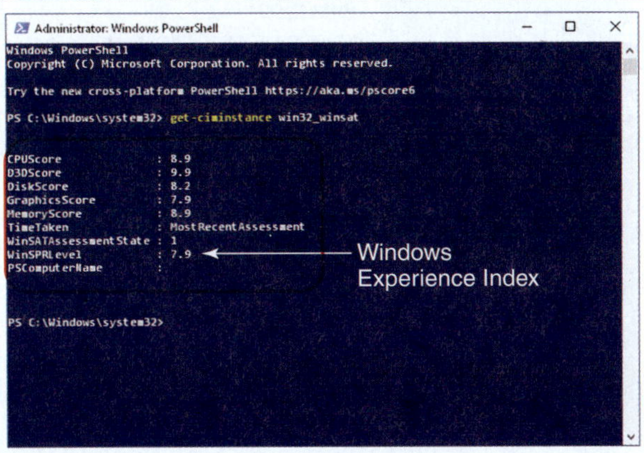

Goodheart-Willcox Publisher

Figure 9-14 PowerShell provides a Windows Experience Index as the result of the **get -ciminstance win32_winsat** command.

Windows Experience Index Capabilities	
Base Score	**Capability**
2.0–2.9	General computing such as business applications, word processing, Internet browsing, and e-mail. Not adequate for most multimedia applications.
3.0–3.9	Can support most, but not all, Windows video features. Can play digital TV but may not support high-definition television (HDTV).
4.0–5.9	Can support all Windows visual features and easily supports running multiple software applications simultaneously.
6.0–7.9	Will support intense graphic applications such as multiplayer games, 3D gaming, and recording and playback of HDTV content.

Goodheart-Willcox Publisher

Figure 9-15 Windows base scores indicate what can be expected from a given computer system.

the window. This will launch the **Sound** menu, as shown in Figure 9-18. From this menu, you can set playback and recording devices, change Windows default sounds, and set communication settings. For example, you can reduce all other computer sounds when you are on a PC phone call.

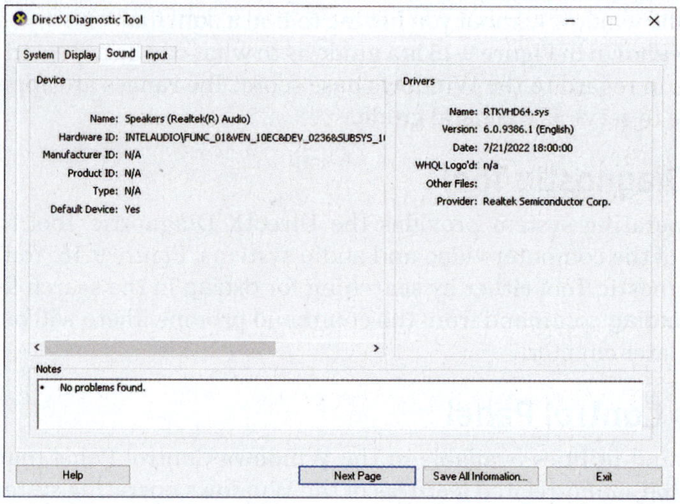

Figure 9-16 The DirectX Diagnostic Tool is used to make simple checks of the computer audio and video systems.

Goodheart-Willcox Publisher

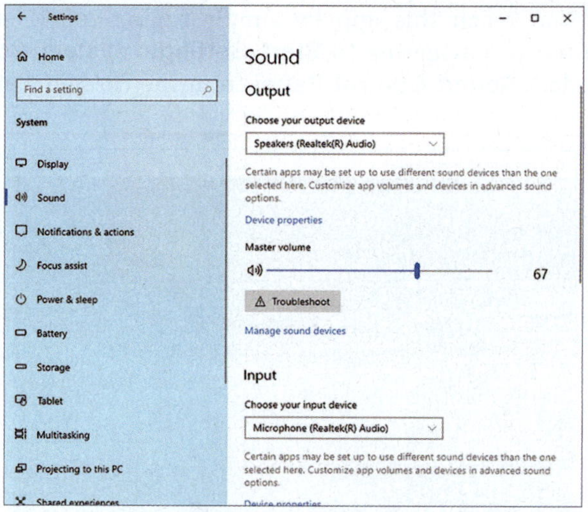

Figure 9-17 The most basic sound-related adjustments can be made in the Windows **Sounds** settings menu, which allows you to select the sound input and output devices, set system volume, and perform basic troubleshooting.

Goodheart-Willcox Publisher

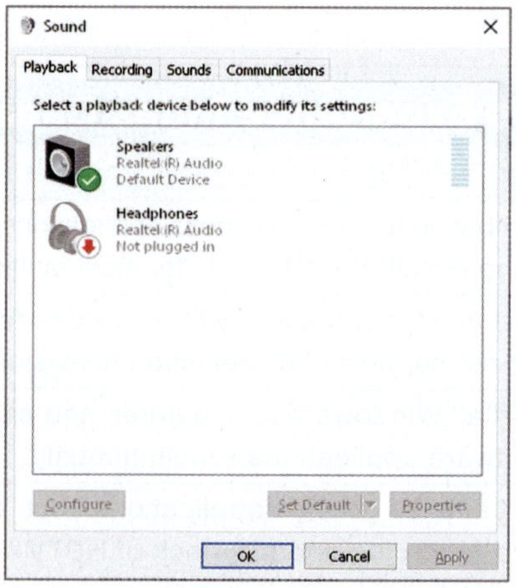

Figure 9-18 The secondary **Sound** menu allows you to set playback and recording devices, change Windows default sounds, and set communication settings.

Goodheart-Willcox Publisher

Chapter Summary

9.1 What Is Sound?

- Sound consists of vibrations that are put into motion through a medium, such as air or water.
- The frequency response range for the human ear spans from approximately 20 Hz to 20 kHz.
- Sampling is the act of measuring an analog signal at regular intervals.
- A sampling rate refers to how frequently samples per second are taken of an audio signal.

9.2 Audio Devices

- A microphone converts sound waves into electrical energy, and a speaker converts electrical energy into sound energy. When the signal reaches the sound card, the analog electrical signal is converted to a digital signal, which allows it to be stored in RAM, on a hard drive, or on a CD, typically as a **.wav** file.
- A speaker converts electrical energy to sound energy. To listen to stored digital code, the code is sent through the sound card and is then converted to an analog electrical signal. As the electrical energy varies in strength, the speaker cone vibrates at a rate proportional to the analog electrical signal. When a speaker has its own built-in amplifier, it is called an active speaker. A speaker without amplification is called a passive speaker.
- Analog-to-digital conversion takes a periodic sample of the voltage levels in an analog signal and stores them in digital format.
- *Virtual reality (VR)* is a computer-generated simulation of a three-dimensional environment with which a user can interact. VR headsets are primarily output devices that take a signal from a gaming system or a personal computer and convert it into audio and visual effects, enough to provide a fully immersive environment and give the user the illusion they are somewhere else.
- *Augmented reality (AR)* is an interactive environmental experience that combines real-world elements with computer-generated content.
- Headsets transmit audio to a user's ear through a device that is connected via USB ports, auxiliary connectors, Bluetooth, and other connectors that are available in the motherboard of a laptop computer or mobile device.
- Most sound cards are plug-and-play PCI adapter cards.
- Audio capture cards take the analog output of some audio device and convert it to digital format. They can be used with microphones, electronic keyboards, and many other sound devices and allow you to import the sound into a computer then use digital sound-editing software.

9.3 Installing a Sound Card

- Installing a sound card involves inserting the card into the motherboard slot, installing the latest drivers, and connecting the speakers to the card and to a power supply.

9.4 Multimedia

- A codec is any hardware, software, or combination hardware and software that can compress and decompress data. The term is a contraction of the two words *compression* and *decompression* and is used most often in the video industry and telecommunication.

- Common codecs are MPEG, QuickTime, AVC, ATSC, and DVB-T.
- The Moving Picture Experts Group (MPEG), (pronounced *empeg*), is an organization made up of professionals from all areas of the motion picture industry with the goal of developing a standard format for recording motion picture video and sound.
- Advanced Video Coding (AVC), also referred to as *H.264*, *MPEG-4*, and *MP4*, is a video compression standard used for high-definition video.
- Buffering is a technique used to play a downloaded file without skips or quiet spots during playback.
- To access sound and video tracks recorded on the PC or taken from the Internet, you must have a player, which is often called a *plug-in*.

9.5 Building a Custom Computer System

- The two most important questions to ask before building a custom PC are "What will the computer be used for?" and "How much are you willing to spend?"
- Performance information can be accessed through the Windows Performance Monitor and Resource Monitor utilities.
- The Windows Experience Index is a numeric rating based on the five major components, each rated from 1.0 to 7.9. You can access your rating through Command Prompt and the GUI or through PowerShell.
- There are sound utilities available in the Windows Control Panel that provide an interface to the sound-related features of the Windows operating system. The most basic include the **Sound** settings. From this screen you can select **Sound Control Panel**, which launches the **Sound** menu, where you can set playback and recording devices, change Windows default sounds, and set communication settings.

Review Questions

1. Describe characteristics of sound.
2. Summarize factors that contribute to audio quality.
3. List and describe examples of common audio devices.
4. Most sound cards purchased today are _____ adapter cards.
5. List steps that should be taken when installing a sound card.
6. Summarize basic troubleshooting steps for a sound card.
7. What is a codec?
8. List common codecs and their purpose.
9. What are the two most important questions to ask before building a customized computer?
10. List factors to consider when building a custom computer system.

Sample A+ Exam Questions

1. Which type of connector port is used for fiber-optic connections carrying sound data?
   A. RJ-45
   B. HDMI
   C. DVI-D
   D. S/PDIF

2. Which example would provide the best quality for a sound recording?
   A. An 8-bit, high-frequency sampling rate
   B. A 16-bit, high-frequency sampling rate
   C. An 8-bit, low-frequency sampling rate
   D. A 16-bit, low-frequency sampling rate
3. Suppose you are asked to build a computer for an audio recording and mixing studio. Which of the following components is most important?
   A. ATX motherboard
   B. High-end graphics card(s)
   C. High-end sound card(s)
   D. Dedicated GPU
4. A recorded sound results in garbled, low-quality audio. You analyze the sound wave and see it is distorted. What is the most likely cause?
   A. Too low of a sampling rate
   B. Faulty speakers
   C. Audio was recorded as MIDI, not MPEG
   D. Bad DAC
5. What is the standard range for a wireless speaker system in ideal conditions?
   A. 20–30 feet
   B. 50–100 feet
   C. 100–120 feet
   D. 150–300 feet
6. What should be done before installing a new sound card?
   A. Disconnect all peripherals.
   B. Back up all computer files.
   C. Create a recording of computer audio for comparison.
   D. Delete all codecs from the computer.
7. Which of the following refers to a common codec?
   A. JPG
   B. MPEG
   C. TIF
   D. BMP
8. Which of the following can be used to perform a check of both audio and video systems?
   A. **msconfig**
   B. **ipconfig**
   C. **dxdiag**
   D. **services.msc**
9. In what range can the human ear detect sounds?
   A. 20 Hz to 20 kHz
   B. 10 Hz to 20 Hz
   C. 20 kHz to 50 kHz
   D. 30 Hz to 90 kHz
10. Which of the following is a file standard for music synthesizers?
    A. MIDI
    B. MPEG
    C. JPG
    D. WAV

Chapter 10

Magnetic and Solid-State Storage Devices

Learning Outcomes

10.1 Explain how magnetic principles are applied to data storage.
10.2 Describe disk geometry in terms of sections used to record data.
10.3 Identify disk partition systems.
10.4 Recall common file systems and their characteristics.
10.5 List utilities used for disk and file maintenance.
10.6 Differentiate between PATA and SATA interfaces.
10.7 Compare SAS and SCSI technologies.
10.8 Recall the uses of solid-state drives and their advantages over disk- and disc-storage devices.
10.9 Discuss the purpose of a virtual hard disk.
10.10 Identify common hard drive symptoms.

A+ Certification Exam Objectives

The following A+ Certification Exam Objectives are covered in this chapter.

Exam 220-1101

1.0 Mobile Devices

- 1.1 Given a scenario, install and configure laptop hardware and components.

3.0 Hardware

- 3.1 Explain basic cable types, features, and purposes.
- 3.3 Given a scenario, select and install storage devices.
- 3.4 Given a scenario, install and configure motherboards, central processing units (CPUs), and add-on cards.

5.0 Hardware and Network Troubleshooting

- 5.3 Given a scenario, troubleshoot and diagnose problems with storage devices and RAID arrays.

Exam 220-1102

1.0 Operating Systems

- 1.2 Given a scenario, use the appropriate Microsoft command line-tool.
- 1.3 Given a scenario, use features and tools of the Microsoft Windows 10 operating system.
- 1.8 Explain common OS types and their purposes.
- 1.9 Given a scenario, perform OS installations and upgrades in a diverse OS environment.

2.0 Security

- 2.5 Given a scenario, manage and configure basic security settings in the Microsoft Windows OS.
- 2.8 Given a scenario, use common data destruction and disposal methods.

3.0 Software Troubleshooting

- 3.1 Given a scenario, troubleshoot Microsoft Windows OS problems.

Key Terms

active partition
actuator arm
AT Attachment (ATA)
basic disk
cluster
cylinder
defragmentation
disk signature
dynamic disk
EFI System Partition (ESP)
encrypted file system (EFS)
extended file allocation table (exFAT)
FAT16
FAT32
GUID Partition Table (GPT)
high-level format
interleave factor
logical drives
low-level format
Master Boot Record (MBR)
Microsoft Reserved Partition (MSR)
multiple zone recording (MZR)
New Technology File System (NTFS)
Parallel ATA (PATA)
primary partition
proprietary recovery partition
protective MBR
read/write head
Resilient File System (ReFS)
sectors
Serial ATA (SATA)
Serial Attached SCSI (SAS)
Small Computer System Interface (SCSI)
solid-state disk caching
tracks
virtual hard disk (VHD)
volume mount point

Overview

This chapter will prove to be one of the most important topics covered in the entire textbook. It will give you incredible insight as to how an operating system organizes, stores, and retrieves data. This information can prove invaluable when troubleshooting system failures. You will also learn about the operation of magnetic storage systems, such as hard drives, as well as solid-state drives. These topics are critical for a computer technician and for CompTIA A+ Certification preparation.

A+ Note

Hard drive installation and replacement is one of the most common jobs for a PC technician and is weighted heavily on the CompTIA A+ Exams. You must also be very familiar with the Disk Management tool in Windows Computer Management as well as with the various actions that can be performed on a hard drive, such as creating a partition, formatting a partition, extending a partition, adding an additional hard drive, and creating a basic or dynamic disk.

Tech Tip

The importance of system backups cannot be overemphasized. Once total loss of data or programs has been experienced, the need to back up becomes obvious. Most cases of data loss relate to the failure of one hard drive containing all original data. While operating system software can be reinstalled, original data cannot always be recovered. Data recovery techniques are not always successful, and they are certainly more time-consuming than replacing files with copies from a backup.

10.1 Magnetic Storage Devices

Magnetism has been used to record data for many years, and magnetic storage devices have been mainstays of the PC industry. While the move in recent years has been toward solid-state drives, there are still a number of magnetic storage devices available. Solid-state devices tend to be found in personal electronics, whereas magnetic storage is still found in servers. This section covers the operation of magnetic storage devices, but electromagnetic principles are explained first to provide the proper foundation for understanding how magnetic storage devices work.

Electromagnetic Principles

To understand complex devices like hard drives and other disk drives, you first need some background in electromagnetic principles. These principles allow hard drives to store volumes of data. However, these principles also place restrictions on their use and construction.

Converting Data into Magnetic Patterns

Electrical energy can produce magnetism, and magnetism can produce electrical energy. This principle is the basis of magnetic storage device operation. The data storage area of a magnetic disk drive is coated in a fine layer of iron oxide, which is easily magnetized when exposed to an energized conductor. A *conductor* is any material that allows for the easy flow of electricity. Any energized conductor is surrounded by a rotating magnetic field, and the rotational direction of the field is determined by the direction of current in the conductor. This rotational direction then determines the north and south characteristics of the magnetic field.

Look closely at Figure 10-1, which shows the relationship between the current direction and the magnetic field surrounding a conductor. The conductor is wound around the top of the magnetic **read/write head**, which is the mechanism that records information to and reads information from a magnetic medium. The read/write head is located at the end of an **actuator arm**, which is the device that moves the head over the disk. At the bottom of the magnetic head, there is a gap to keep the head from touching the surface of the disk. Contact between the actuator arm or

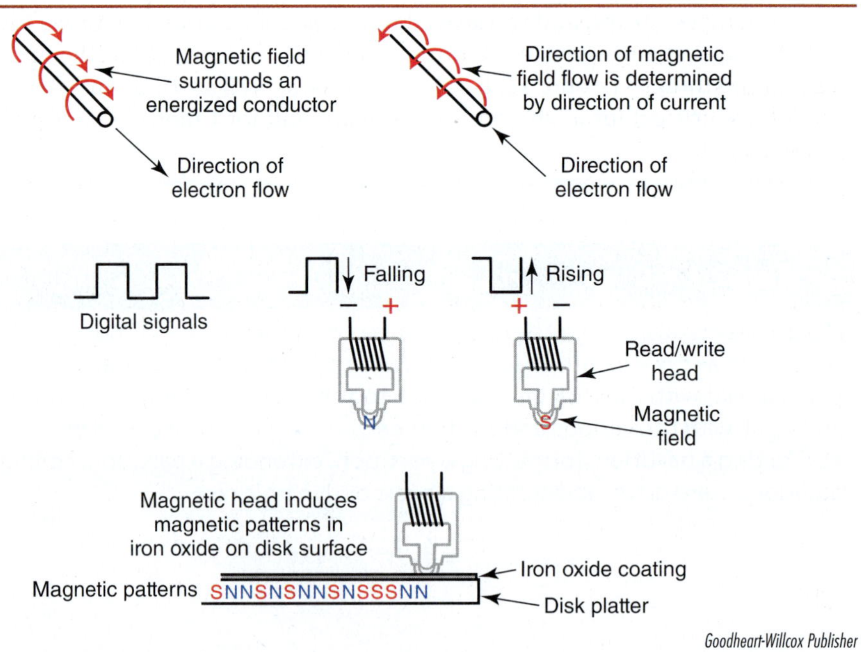

Figure 10-1 Current flowing through a conductor produces a magnetic field, which is concentrated in a magnetic read/write head. The read/write head is used to create patterns on a disk or tape surface.

read/write head and the surface of the disk on a hard drive is called a ***disk crash*** and usually results in loss of data. All magnetic recording devices use this same principle.

A digital signal is composed of rising and falling voltage levels. These rising and falling voltage levels produce a changing current direction. As the current (digital signal) changes direction through the conductor wound around the read/write head, the magnetic field at the gap changes. As the digital signal flows through the read/write head, a magnetic pattern is created on the iron oxide that represents the digital pattern sent to the read/write head. This is how data is stored on a magnetic disk.

Converting Magnetic Patterns into Data

To read the data from a disk, an electrical signal is generated from the magnetic patterns. Electrical energy can be produced by the motion of a magnetic field near a conductor, as illustrated in Figure 10-2. The direction of the current produced in the conductor is directly related to the north and south properties of the magnetic field.

As you now know, a magnetic disk has a magnetic pattern along its surface, and energy is produced in pulses as that magnetic pattern passes rapidly under the read/write head. The electrical pulses that are generated match the pattern on the magnetic code stored on the disk. The pulses of electrical energy are very small, so an amplifier circuit is needed to magnify the electrical energy produced from the magnetic patterns stored on the media to a level high enough to be used by the computer circuitry and components. The amplifier is integrated into the electronic circuitry on the media drive's circuit board.

Hard Disk Drive

A typical hard disk drive, also referred to as a ***hard drive***, consists of several platters in a stack. The platters can be made from glass, aluminum alloy, or even ceramic. The top and bottom of each platter are coated with a thin film of metal oxide, which records the magnetic patterns introduced to the disk platter by the read/write head.

At one time, the read/write head was constructed of very small wire coils. Read/write head technology has now evolved to such microscopic size that the same technology used to manufacture chips is also used to create the head. The read/write head can produce extremely compact magnetic patterns exceeding 10,000 bits per inch.

The hard disk drive is simple in design but impressive when you consider its operational tolerances. The read/write head does not actually touch the platter; instead, it rides over the platter on a cushion of air about 0.001 microns or micrometers (μm) thick, as shown in Figure 10-3. For reference, the average human hair is

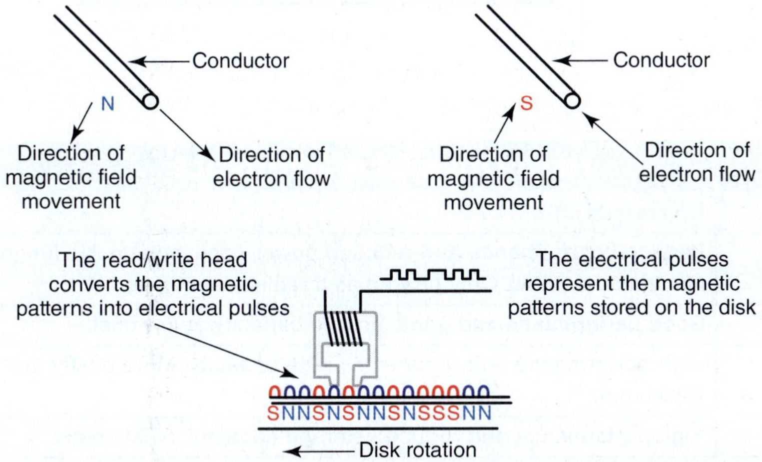

Figure 10-2 Magnetic patterns stored on a disk platter are converted to electrical pulses representing the data stored on a disk. As the platters spin rapidly under the read/write head, the magnetism creates electrical energy in the read/write head.

roughly 50 microns. Since the head travels closely to the platter, the platter must be flat and free of defects, which would destroy the read/write head on contact.

Hard drives have filters to catch any microscopic particles that might be produced during normal read/write operations. Remember that the actuator arm is mechanical and will produce some particles through friction between the moving parts.

A+ 1101: 3.3

Hard drive speeds are listed as 5,400 rpm, 7,200 rpm, 10,000 rpm, and 15,000 rpm. In general, the faster the hard drive, the less storage space and the greater the electrical power consumption. As a drive spins faster, the disk platter encounters more wind resistance and more electrical energy is required to spin it. To overcome the wind resistance, the platter diameter is reduced, resulting in less storage space. Therefore, a faster disk may be compromised by the total amount of storage space available. Additionally, there is a direct correlation between speed and price. In general, a faster drive is usually more expensive.

The 5,400-rpm and 7,200-rpm drives are most commonly encountered in PC devices, but replacements for 5,400-rpm drives must come from existing stock because it is no longer in production. After the existing stocks are gone, 7,200-rpm drives will be used for replacements. The 10,000-rpm and 15,000-rpm drives are the most expensive and can be found in laptop devices. Figure 10-4 summarizes the characteristics of the commonly encountered hard drive speeds.

1.8-Inch Hard Drive

Although you may still encounter them in older devices, the 1.8-inch hard drive faded away in 2014 and has been replaced by solid-state drives. You will sometimes see the term *flash memory* used for the 1.8-inch solid-state drive, but *solid-state* is the term used most often. Given the demise of the 1.8-inch drive, it is likely that when working with magnetic drives, you will interact more often with 2.5-inch or 3.5-inch hard drives.

A+ Note

You may encounter a question related to custom computer design or disk drive replacement. The question will likely relate to disk drive rpm and cost. In general, when the rpm is faster, the performance is better, and the cost is higher. You would want a high-rpm disk for large amounts of storage when cost is not a factor.

Figure 10-3 The read/write head floats just above the spinning disk of a hard drive.

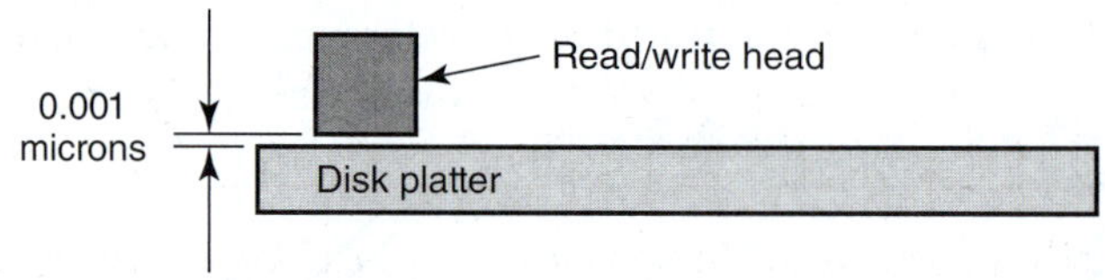

Goodheart-Willcox Publisher

Figure 10-4 In general, the faster the hard drive, the less storage space and the greater the electrical power consumption. However, performance is also usually better.

Hard Drive Characteristics

RPM	Characteristic
5,400	Reduced performance and reduced power consumption. No longer manufactured new. Only offered as a replacement part.
7,200	Good performance and good storage capacity at low cost.
10,000	High performance and reduced storage capacity. More costly than 7,200 rpm.
15,000	High performance and reduced storage capacity. Most costly.

Goodheart-Willcox Publisher

2.5-Inch Hard Drive

A+ 1101: 3.3

This hard drive size has become more common with the popularity of small laptops, largely because the 2.5-inch drive often requires an adapter to fit into a desktop computer's 3.5-inch drive bay. The 2.5-inch mechanical drive is the standard for laptop computers, although extremely thin laptops often only have solid-state drives. Also, note that 2.5-inch drives on laptops usually spin at 5,400 rpm, although higher speeds are possible and more costly.

3.5-Inch Hard Drive

A+ 1101: 3.3

Most modern desktop computers use the 3.5-inch drive, although 2.5-inch drives can be adapted to fit these computers. These drives are capable of spinning at various rates from 5,400 rpm to 15,000 rpm. Basic models often spin at lower rates, and hard drives capable of spinning at rates such as 10,000 or 15,000 rpm are typically used for high-performance servers at the enterprise level.

Hybrid Drives

A+ 1101: 1.1

Hybrid drives have two varieties. The first variety involves two drives, the first of which is often a solid-state drive installed to store the operating system and assigned the letter C: in Windows. The second drive is often a mechanical hard drive, usually assigned the letter D:, used to store all data. These letter assignments will be discussed in a later section. The solid-state drive is used to improve boot time on the system while using the mechanical hard drive as slower, less expensive, mass storage. This approach allows vendors to provide rapid startup with smaller solid-state drives and keep costs down for the user. The second variety of hybrid drive is much less common than the previous example and occurs when the mechanical hard drive is supported by a varying, substantial amount of flash memory attached to the same hardware.

Lightweight, powerful laptops use solid-state drives almost exclusively, although external hard drives can be attached. In fact, laptops can see excellent performance from an external magnetic drive. Magnetic drives provide the most storage for the investment, making it less economical to buy high-capacity solid-state drives with over a terabyte in space. Additionally, hybrid drives provide a compromise between cost and storage for desktop computers, allowing for fast startup with large storage at a reasonable price. Solid-state drives will be discussed at length later in this chapter.

10.2 **Disk Geometry**

The surface of a disk is divided into sections used as data storage areas. The layout of the sections on the disk surface must be recognized by the computer operating systems. The sections used to record data on a disk drive are described in terms such as *tracks*, *sectors*, *clusters*, and *cylinders*, as described in Figure 10-5.

Tracks are composed of a set of concentric circles where data is stored on a disk. The tracks are subdivided into physical sections called **sectors**. The term **cluster**, sometimes referred to as an *allocation unit*, describes file storage space and usually consists of one or more sectors. The smallest sector or cluster size is 512 bytes. A sector is a physical description of a track, whereas a cluster is a logical file storage unit that can span several sectors.

A hard disk drive consists of a stack of platters, each with its own tracks, clusters, and sectors. A **cylinder** is a vertical collection of one set of tracks. There is one cylinder for every stack of tracks, across which the read/write heads move in unison. A hard drive writes to all tracks simultaneously, so data files are often stored in cylinders for fast access.

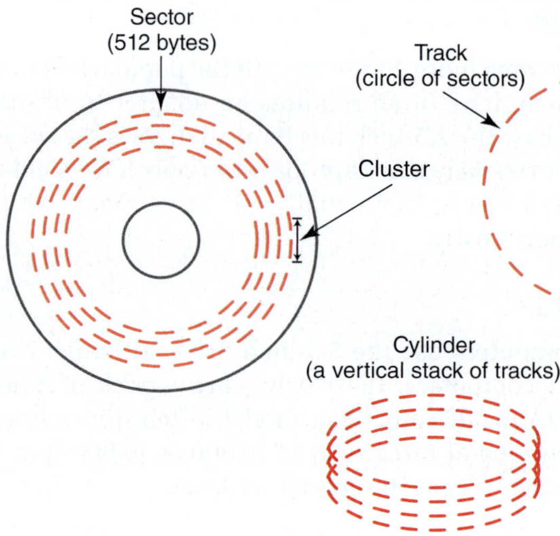

Goodheart-Willcox Publisher

Figure 10-5 Disks are subdivided into sectors, tracks, cylinders, and clusters.

When writing to a disk, each head writes data to the disk sequentially. Head 1 writes data on the first available sector on the top surface of the top platter. When another sector is needed, head 2 writes data on the bottom of that same platter. Head 3 writes data on the top of the second platter, and so on. This scheme of data recording is continued using the read/write heads in sequence until all the data has been recorded. Thus, the data of a single file can be spread over several disk platters.

A typical cluster size range is from 4 kB to 32 kB. It is important to note that the size of the cluster is directly related to the size of the hard disk drive when using certain file systems, such as FAT12, FAT16, FAT32, and NTFS. These file systems are discussed in detail later in this chapter.

Stored data spans many clusters, so there needs to be an organized way to keep track of all the clusters of data on a disk. The computer needs to know where a data group's clusters begin and end and must also distinguish clusters available for storage from those already in use. The GUID Partition Table (GPT) and the Master Boot Record (MBR) both contain information about the disk partition areas, such as the number of bytes per sector, number of sectors per cluster, number of clusters per track, number of tracks, total number of clusters, number of read/write heads, and the type of storage media. They also contain the boot software program used to access or transfer control of the computer system to the operating system. When present, the MBR is located at a hidden, protected area on the first sector of the hard disk drive, and the GPT is located as a hidden, protected area in each individual partition.

Disk geometry is created in three major steps: low-level format, partitioning, and formatting. First, a low-level format is performed on the hard drive at the factory. Next, the hard drive is partitioned. Finally, the disk partition is formatted in what is referred to as a high-level format. Another step, which is unique to the Windows operating system, is *initialization*. When a disk is initialized, the type of partition (MBR or GPT) is selected. There will be more about these topics in this chapter. Some media, such as optical discs, only require formatting and do not require partitioning, which is unique to hard drives.

A+ 1102: 1.9

Low-Level Format

The **low-level format** is a process that determines the type of encoding to be performed on the disk platter and the sequence in which the read/write heads will access stored data. The low-level format also scans to detect bad sectors on the disk platters, which are not used during the high-level format process. The sequence is referred to as the *interleave factor*.

Interleave factor refers to the order in which sectors are laid out on a disk surface. Many times, you will see an illustration showing sectors laid out side by side, which is only half the story. While sectors do physically exist next to each other, they are not sequential. Instead, sequential numbers are staggered across the tracks, as illustrated in Figure 10-6, and information is included at the each of each cluster or sector about where the next cluster or sector is located. If the actual sectors were in sequential order side by side, disk access would be slow, and the read/write head would pass the next sector before the location information could be processed, forcing the disk make a complete revolution before the data could be read from the next sector. Staggering the sectors across the disk track area optimizes a hard drive's data access rate. When the read/write head passes over the end of the sector, all information about the location of the next storage sector can be processed before the read/write head reaches it, meaning the disk read/write head does not need to wait for a complete disk revolution to read the stored data in the next data storage sector.

The interleave factor is unique to each disk design by taking into consideration the disk RPM, speed of data transfer across the bus, and speed of transfer through the chips and read/write head. Since these factors differ greatly from one manufacturer to another, the interleave factor also varies greatly. The interleave factor is only important for performing a low-level format, which arranges the locations of the sectors on the disks. To identify the sector locations and construct the file tables, the high level format is performed after a drive is partitioned. File tables and formatting are covered later in this chapter.

Multiple Zone Recording

Early disk drive geometry provided an equal number of sectors on the innermost and outermost tracks, but since there is more space on the outside of a disk compared to the inside, space was wasted in the outer tracks. To improve the storage capacity of the platters, multiple zone recording was developed as a new method of sectoring tracks to minimize wasted space. **Multiple zone recording (MZR)**, also called *zone bit recording*, provides twice as many sectors in the outermost tracks as compared to the innermost tracks. Turn your attention to Figure 10-7. The disk on the left reflects the older style for setting up sectors on a hard drive in which inner and outer tracks contain the same number of sectors. The disk on the right shows multiple zone recording, which consists of more sectors on outer tracks than inner tracks.

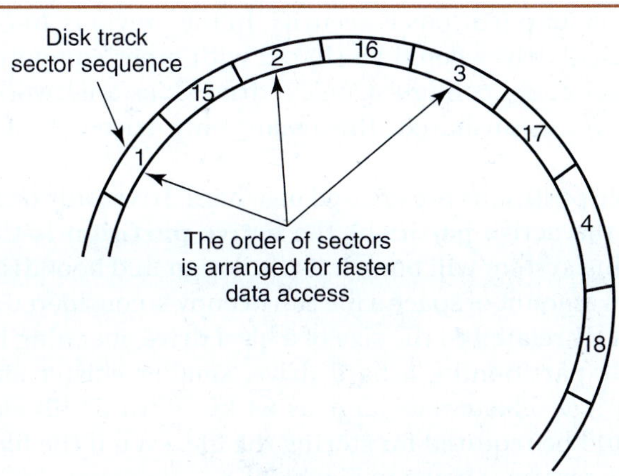

Goodheart-Willcox Publisher

Figure 10-6 The interleave factor describes the pattern in which sectors are laid out on a disk. Sequential sectors are not side by side.

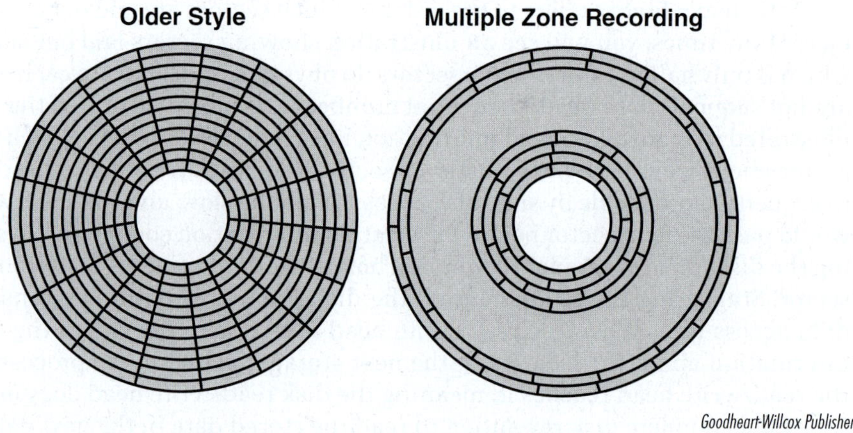

Figure 10-7 Multiple zone recording allows for more sectors on the outer tracks of a disk.

A+ 1102: 1.9

10.3 Disk Partition Systems

Computer technology is constantly evolving, and the hard drive partition system has become complicated in recent years because of the need to accommodate large disk drives and to design a better system of protection for critical boot files. Because of this, there are two different Microsoft disk partition styles used for hard disk drives: Master Boot Record (MBR) and GUID Partition Table (GPT). The **Master Boot Record (MBR)** is a boot sector located at the beginning of a partition that identifies how and where an operating system is located so it can be booted. Similarly, the **GUID Partition Table (GPT)** is a disk partitioning method in which the layout of partition tables within a storage device are identified using *globally unique identifiers (GUIDs)*. The MBR and the GPT identify the location of the partitions on a hard disk drive. The type of partition used is determined when the disk if first initialized and is directly related to the type of firmware designed to work with the motherboard: BIOS or UEFI.

The operating system performs the initialization. When a hard disk drive is initialized, MBR or GPT is selected and configured or written on the hard disk drive so the drive can then be partitioned. Before GPT, partition style was never a choice, so it did not require user input.

When a disk is partitioned, it is divided into **logical drives**, which are separate storage areas created on a hard drive and designated by a letter. A logical drive is not a physically separate drive even though it appears to the user as one. For example, a 10-GB hard drive can be partitioned into several areas. A user could theoretically create five 2-GB logical drives, each with a unique drive designation, such as C:, D:, E:, F:, and G:. These five drives are considered logical because they exist on one physical drive.

Another reason for partitions is security. In the previous 10-GB drive example, some of those logical drives could be shared with other computers on a network. For example, a user could configure logical drive C: as a network share and leave the remaining drives as unshared. This means only drive C: is accessible to other network users.

When multiple partitions are created on a hard drive, only one of the partitions is designated as the active partition. The **active partition** is the partition from which the operating system will boot. It is the designated boot disk for the system.

The minimum amount of space a file can occupy is considered a cluster. The size of clusters is directly related to the size of a hard drive, meaning larger drives have larger clusters. By partitioning a hard drive, smaller cluster sizes can be used. A hard drive can have clusters as large as 64 kB. With 64-kB clusters, the entire 64-kB cluster would be required for storing the file, even if the file size were only a few hundred bytes total, as shown in Figure 10-8.

Tech Tip

Storage devices such as hard disk drives and solid-state drives must be automatically detected by the system firmware. A failure of the firmware to detect and list the device is a symptom of a complete failure of the device's electronic circuitry or a loose cable. Cable failures are resolved by reconnecting or replacing the cable. In the event of circuit board failure, you will have to replace the entire device.

Since the cluster size is directly related to partition size, you can use disk space more efficiently by using more than one partition. For example, a 20-GB hard drive formatted with FAT32 as one partition will contain 16-kB clusters. The same 20-GB hard drive formatted with FAT32 but divided into two equal partitions will contain 8-kB clusters. Partitioning improves the efficiency of disk storage space.

The size of the cluster is also dependent on the file system used. The chart in Figure 10-9 details cluster size in relation to hard drive size and the file system used. Note the NTFS cluster sizes compared to FAT16 and FAT32. The NTFS system uses much smaller cluster sizes than FAT16 and FAT32, resulting in more efficient use of hard disk space.

MBR Partitions

A+ 1102: 1.9

The Master Boot Record (MBR) contains partition information and a small amount of executable code that launches the computer operating system. In a FAT16- or FAT32-formatted system, the file allocation table (FAT) contains information about where each file starts on the disk. In a system formatted as NTFS, a master file table (MFT) contains similar information. See Figure 10-10.

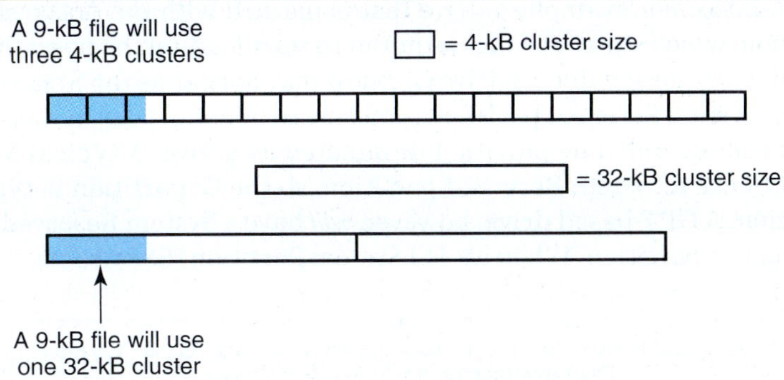

Goodheart-Willcox Publisher

Figure 10-8 For a 9-kB file, the 4-kB cluster wastes only 2 kB of storage space when storing the file. The 32-kB cluster format wastes 23 kB of space.

Partition Sizes by Format Type

Volume or Partition Size	FAT16 Cluster Size	FAT32 Cluster Size	NTFS Cluster Size
7 MB–16 MB	2 kB	NA	512 bytes
17 MB–32 MB	512 bytes	NA	512 bytes
33 MB–64 MB	1 kB	512 bytes	512 bytes
65 MB–128 MB	2 kB	1 kB	512 bytes
129 MB–256 MB	4 kB	2 kB	512 bytes
257 MB–512 MB	8 kB	4 kB	512 bytes
513 MB–1024 MB	16 kB	4 kB	1 kB
1025 MB–2 GB	32 kB	4 kB	2 kB
2 GB–4 GB	64 kB	4 kB	4 kB
4 GB–8 GB	NA	4 kB	4 kB
8 GB–16 GB	NA	8 kB	4 kB
16 GB–32 GB	NA	16 kB	4 kB
32 GB–2 TB	NA	NA	4 kB

Goodheart-Willcox Publisher

Figure 10-9 NTFS allows the smallest cluster for larger partitions.

An MBR-based hard drive can contain up to four primary partitions or three primary partitions and one extended partition, as illustrated in Figure 10-11. The extended partition can contain additional logical drives, but only one extended partition can exist on a disk drive and can only be created on an MBR-based disk.

All hard disk drives must contain at least one **primary partition**, which is the partition that houses the operating system as well as system files, boot files, or a combination of both. According to Microsoft, the Windows *system files* are used to start the computer, and the *boot files* are used to run the operating system after the boot sequence is completed.

There can be a lot of confusion about the locations and purpose of partitions, especially since the development of the UEFI firmware and the System Reserved partition. Early disk systems using the MBR-partition style often used the terms *primary partition*, *active partition*, *system partition*, and *boot partition* to mean the same partition because they were all located on the same partition most of the time. Today, the boot and system partitions can be two different partitions. To determine the exact location of these designated areas on a specific computer, inspect the partition status located in the Disk Management tool of Computer Management.

The *partition status* is how Microsoft identifies the role of specific partitions and the location of some critical files. Typical partition statuses include Primary, Active, Boot, System, Page File, and Crash Dump. Often, the purpose of a partition is identified by the status. For example, a drive that is marked with the Active status is an active partition, which stores the files required to start loading the operating system. It is not necessarily designated as drive C:, but it may appear as the System Reserved partition. The System Reserved partition is discussed in detail later in this chapter.

There is usually only one partition designated as active. A typical MBR-based drive will not have a System Reserved partition, so the C: partition is typically the active partition. A GPT-based drive, however, *will* have a System Reserved partition, and it is the active partition. When an EFI System Partition (ESP) exists, it serves the

Figure 10-10 Three pieces of information are necessary to locate a file on a disk: the drive letter, the name of the file or directory, and the cluster locations of the file.

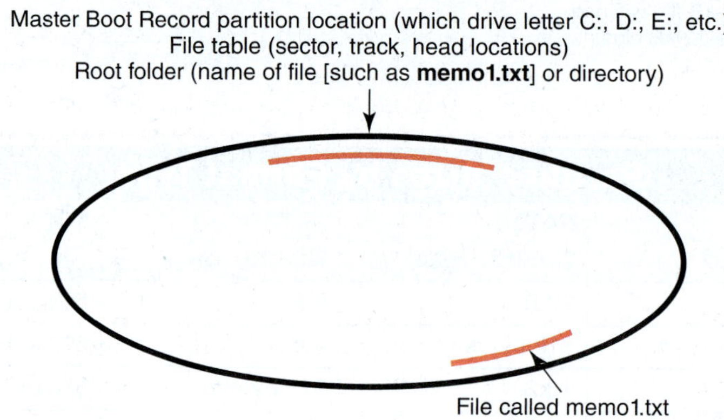

Goodheart-Willcox Publisher

Figure 10-11 An MBR-based hard drive can contain up to four primary partitions or three primary partitions and one extended partition.

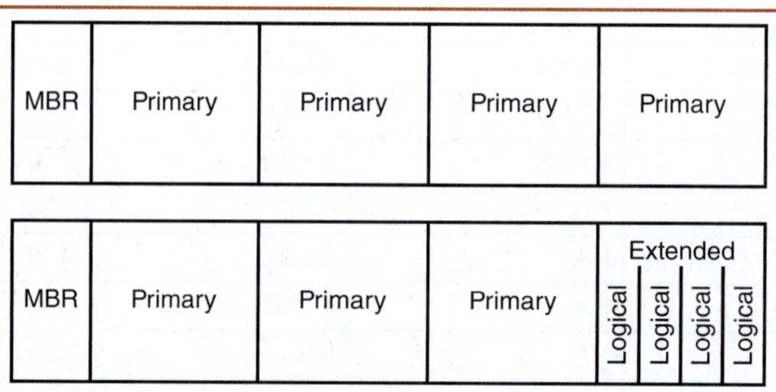

Goodheart-Willcox Publisher

same function as the active partition, but it is not necessarily identified as Active in the partition status. The EFI System Partition (ESP) is covered later in this chapter.

The Page File status indicates the location of the *page file*, which is a portion of the hard drive used to augment the system RAM. The Crash Dump status is the location where the operating system attempts to write information when a system failure happens. The file is also called a *crash dump,* and the default location is the system root, which is drive C: in Windows.

The System status indicates a system partition and is where hardware-specific files needed to load the operating system are located. Some of the information stored on the system partition is directly related to the locations of other partitions, as well as security tools such as BitLocker and, sometimes, recovery tools.

The Boot status indicates the boot partition, which is the location of most of the operating system files as compared to the system partition. Many people and documents use the terms *system partition* and *boot partition* interchangeably because the system and boot files were often located on the same partition in early computer systems. The confusion starts when you have multiple partitions or a System Reserved partition present. In these cases, the files can be located on different partitions.

Tech Tip

One of the most confusing Microsoft naming schemes is the way Microsoft identifies the status of the boot partition and system partition. The DOS operating system designated the boot and system partitions the opposite as they are identified today.

GPT Partitions

A+ 1102: 1.9

GPT partitions rely on Globally Unique Identifiers (GUIDs). You should recall from Chapter 2 that Unified Extensible Firmware Interface (UEFI) firmware uses a GUID Partition Table (GPT). GPT-based partition systems do not have the same limitations as MBR-based partition systems. The primary advantage is that you may create 128 primary partitions on a disk system initialized with GPT.

Another advantage of GPT is that it can handle large hard disk drives better than MBR. The MBR can support hard disk drive storage sizes of up to two terabytes (TB), but GPT is designed to support hard disk drive storage sizes of up to 18 exabytes (EB). An exabyte is equal to approximately one million terabytes. GPT was first introduced with Windows XP 64-bit edition and Windows Server 2003, and it is still used in Windows 10, Windows 11, and Windows Server 2019 and 2022. Figure 10-12 compares MBR and GPT partitions.

GPT uses a process known as *logical block (LB) addressing*, rather than the older *cylinder-head-sector (CHS) addressing* that was used for many years with magnetic devices. The GPT header has a pointer to a partition table, and each entry in that partition table has a size of 128 bytes.

Figure 10-13 illustrates some possible partition arrangements you may encounter. Notice the addition of the Microsoft Reserved Partition (MSR), also called the System Reserved. Added are the proprietary recovery partition which is created by the system manufacturer, and EFI System Partition (ESP), which is created by Extensible Firmware Interface (EFI). The partitions are arranged in Microsoft's recommended sequence, but the exact order may vary according to where the system manufacturer places the proprietary recovery partition. These additional partitions are explored in the following sections.

MBR and GPT Comparison

MBR	GPT
Supports a maximum of four primary partitions	Supports a maximum of 128 primary partitions
Can support a 2-TB partition size	Can support an 18-EB partition size
Has no backup partition table	Has backup partition table

Goodheart-Willcox Publisher

Figure 10-12 GPT offers many advantages over MBR.

> **Tech Tip**
>
> The acronym EFI represents *Extensible Firmware Interface*, and the acronym ESP represents *EFI System Partition*. However, these acronyms are often used interchangeably when discussing disk partitions.

EFI System Partition (ESP)

The **EFI System Partition (ESP)** is a special area of the hard disk drive intended for use solely by the firmware and typically contains files and data required to boot the computer system. This partition is created automatically by a computer system with UEFI firmware, and it requires a GUID Partition Table (GPT). Only one ESP is required per computer, no matter how many physical or logical disks are installed. Not all GPT arrangements show an ESP, however. For example, a computer with BIOS firmware can create an MBR or a GPT partition and will not include an ESP. However, a computer operating with both UEFI and a GPT requires an ESP. In Figure 10-14, an ESP appears in the Disk Management tool in Computer Management and is labeled Disk 0 partition 1.

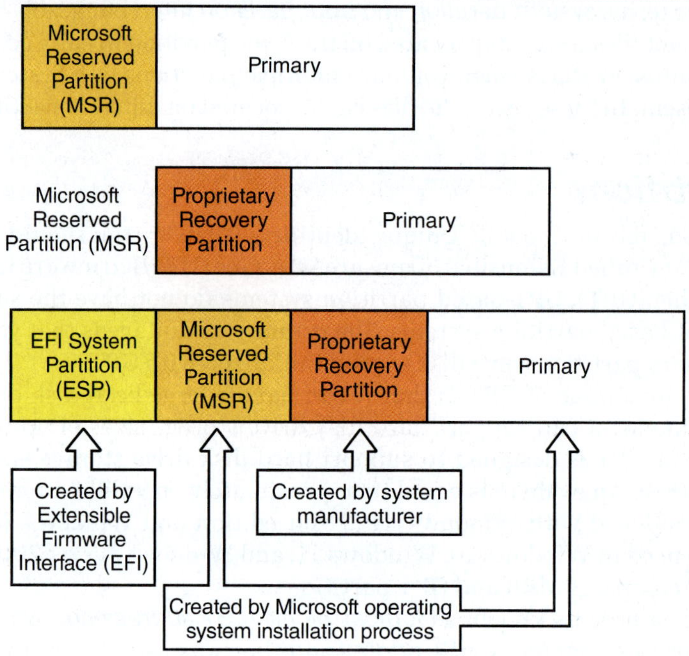

Figure 10-13 There are many possible arrangements of MSR that may be encountered.

Goodheart-Willcox Publisher

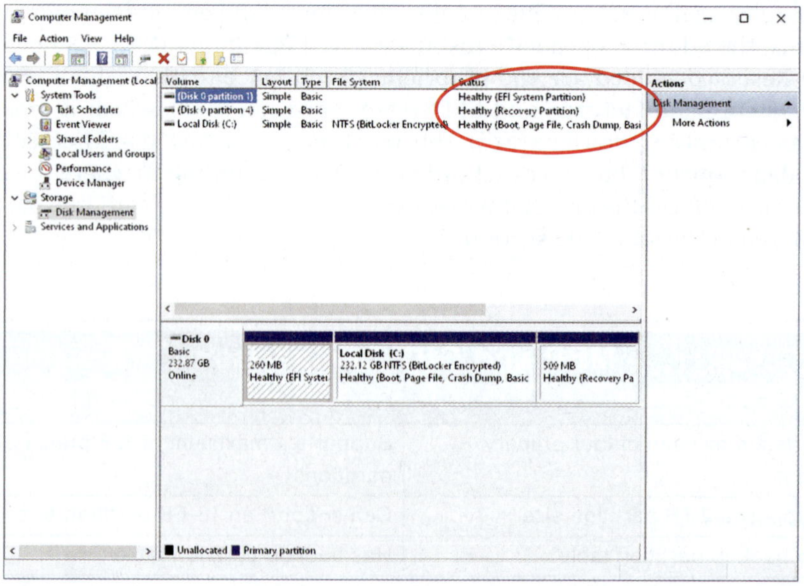

Figure 10-14 The EFI System Partition (ESP) is a special area of the hard disk drive intended for use solely by the firmware and typically contains files and data required to boot the computer system.

Goodheart-Willcox Publisher

The ESP can be created by firmware or the Microsoft DiskPart utility. As of this writing, the ESP cannot be created using the Disk Management tool in Computer Management or in the Microsoft Management Console (MMC). When present, the ESP typically contains the following required boot files: **NTLDR**, **HAL**, and **boot.txt**. Additional files, such as hardware drivers, may also be contained in the ESP. Generally, the ESP is a hidden partition that can only be viewed using the UEFI software-created utilities. The proprietary recovery partition may be hidden as well, but not always.

Microsoft Reserved Partition (MSR)

The **Microsoft Reserved Partition (MSR)**, or *System Reserved Partition*, is a data partition that reserves a portion of disk space for use by the Windows operating system and is required for GUID partition tables. The Windows installation program creates an MSR if one does not already exist. The MSR is usually located on the EFI System Partition (ESP) in any original equipment manufacturer (OEM) partitions.

Primary Partition

When both a primary partition and an MSR are present, the primary partition will contain the boot files, and the MSR will contain the system files. The primary partition is created by the Microsoft operating system during the installation process.

When an EFI System Partition (ESP) is created, it is required for booting and takes priority over both the MSR and primary partitions. The ESP is typically 100 MB, and the MSR is typically 128 GB.

Removing the ESP or the MSR can cause boot failure. The failure is directly related to the fact that the partition table and the required boot files will be missing.

A+ 1102: 3.1

Proprietary Recovery Partition

The **proprietary recovery partition**, also known as the *original equipment manufacturer (OEM) partition* or *factory recovery partition*, is an optional partition created by the system's original equipment manufacturer (OEM). This partition usually contains recovery tools, a copy of the operating system files, and any other program files that the manufacturer selects as necessary to completely recover a computer from a catastrophic failure. For example, all Windows operating system files used for installing the operating system might be placed in the recovery partition, as well as software application files, copies of hardware drivers, and anything else necessary to restore the computer completely to its original condition at the time of purchase.

The recovery partition is used to recover a computer system by the computer owner either through a tech support conversation, e-mail, or with a message textbox displayed at the time of failure. The user simply selects a key such as [F12] to start the automated recovery process. This type of recovery often, but not always, results in the loss of all user files such as documents, pictures, and music.

The proprietary recovery partition is identified as PQSERVICE on some computers. Executing the **DiskPart list** command identifies the partition as Recovery, and the **DiskPart volume** command identifies the same partition as the PQSERVICE volume.

UEFI Specification Partition Terminology

The UEFI standard was developed as a guide for standardizing the way partitions are arranged and where critical files are stored in the partitions. The UEFI standard allows software application tools, utilities, and operating systems to follow a standard way of arranging partitions and locating critical files. See Figure 10-15 for a visual representation of the standard.

Tech Tip

You can convert an MBR disk to a GPT disk or a GPT disk to an MBR disk, but all data on the disk will be lost.

Protective MBR	Primary GPT	EFI System Partition (ESP)	Partition	Partition	Partition	Backup GPT

Goodheart-Willcox Publisher

Figure 10-15 The UEFI specification for disk partitions uses a combination of GPT and protective MBR.

A+ 1102: 3.1

You may see a protective MBR located on a GPT-partitioned hard drive. The **protective MBR** protects the GPT when legacy software tools are used to explore or repair the MBR. The legacy tools could interpret a missing MBR as an unpartitioned disk and restore it, rendering a GPT system unbootable.

The UEFI standard calls for the protective MBR to be located first on the hard drive followed by the primary GPT, which is used by 64-bit systems to identify system partitions. A backup of the GPT partition information is stored in a separate partition called the *backup GPT*. A computer can contain multiple physical disks, which can be a mixture of both GPT- and MBR-based disks, but a single physical hard disk drive cannot have both a GPT and an MBR because the system can only have one place from which to boot.

The EFI System Partition (ESP) contains the boot loader program. After completing the POST, the control of the computer is passed from the UEFI firmware to the boot loader program, which starts the proprietary operating system and then loads the remaining portions of the operating system. After the ESP, there are one or more partitions used to contain operating system files required to run the program and store data files.

Conflicting terminology is used to identify and explain the function and purpose of the disk partition system. This is quite common in computer-related fields when a new technology is released, especially before a standard is adopted by all parties. During the transition, you will encounter hybrids of the new and old technologies, and terminologies will conflict because of different sources of information emerging at the same time. Also, be aware that companies sometimes create their own terminology and present the information in a manner that will lead you to believe that they invented it first. This is a typical marketing technique used by software and hardware companies.

Unfortunately, not all hard disk drives conform to one arrangement, nor do all manufacturers of hardware and software use the same terminology as presented in the standard. Because of the lack of a strict standard adoption, you will encounter several variations of partition arrangements. Variations are caused by the desire of OEMs to install a recovery partition to support system recovery for their computer operating systems.

Another factor for the various partition arrangements that do not adhere to the UEFI standard is the fact that many OEMs released computer systems into the marketplace before the standard was fully adopted by all major OEMs. You will often encounter this lack of total uniformity to a specific standard in the computer industry. In the free marketplace, manufacturers are always rushing to introduce their own improved technology rather than wait for a standard to be fully adopted. As a result, you will encounter many systems that are hybrids of the standard and the legacy technology.

Initializing a Disk

When a new hard disk drive is first installed on a computer that supports UEFI, it must be initialized before it can be partitioned. The Microsoft Support website states that disk initialization writes a signature to the disk. A **disk signature** is a unique identifier for a storage device that identifies the disk type and properties so the Microsoft operating system can utilize the disk. In addition to the disk signature, the type of partition style (MBR or GPT) is selected and created during initialization.

During a clean installation of Windows for a new computer system, the GPT partition is automatically selected. When an additional hard drive is installed in the system and detected, the **Initialize Disk** dialog box will automatically appear, as shown in Figure 10-16. Notice that there are two choices of initialization presented in the dialog box: **MBR (Master Boot Record)** and **GPT (GUID Partition Table).** As the dialog box indicates, the GPT partition style is not recognized by early versions of Windows, and it is recommended for partitions larger than 2 TB.

During your computer laboratory activities, you will often install a hard drive that has been used at least once by previous students. When this is the case, you will not see the **Initialize Disk** dialog box because the hard disk drive has previously been initialized and the partition style (MBR, GPT) has previously been selected.

When a physical disk that has not been initialized is viewed through the Computer Management tool, it will be labeled as Unknown and Not Initialized. Additionally, the System Reserved partition, also called the Microsoft Reserved Partition (MSR), has no assigned partition letter.

The MBR is located at sector one, cylinder zero, head zero. It is created when a disk is initialized as MBR. Figure 10-17 shows the critical files pattern on an MBR-based hard disk for FAT16 and FAT32 file systems. Other compatible systems have followed this design to maintain downward compatibility.

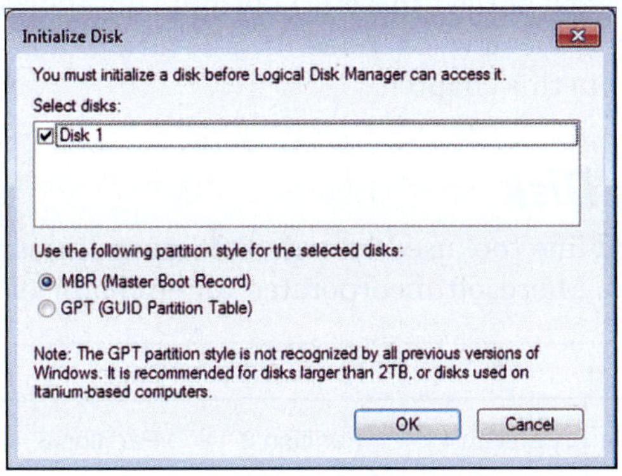

Goodheart-Willcox Publisher

Figure 10-16 A new disk must be initialized with a partition style selected.

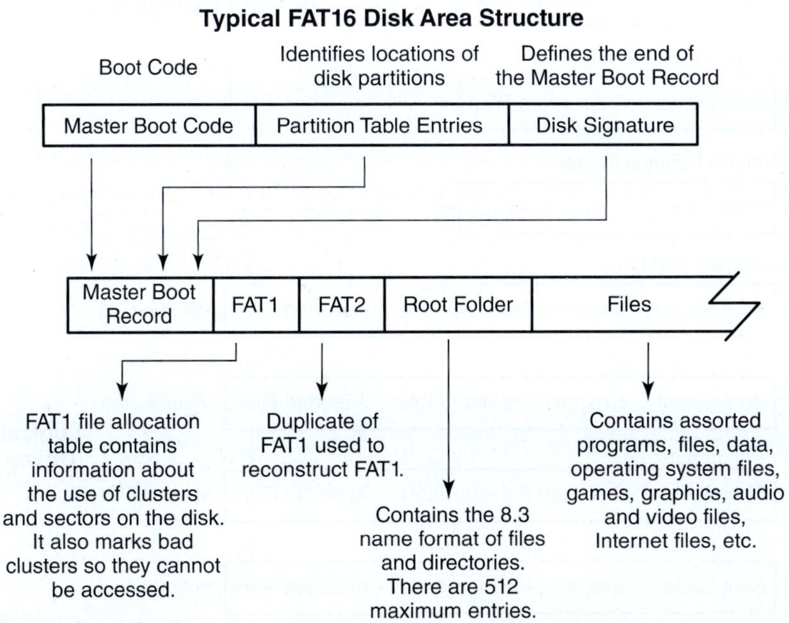

Goodheart-Willcox Publisher

Figure 10-17 The critical files pattern on an MBR-based hard disk is standard for FAT16 and FAT32 systems, as well as other compatible systems.

Tech Tip

There can be a lot of confusion concerning the proper terminology of the Master Boot Record. Often, the MBR is referred to as the boot record, boot sector, master boot sector, and boot program. This text uses terminology as defined by Microsoft in the Microsoft Resource Kit.

As stated previously, a hard drive can be divided into two or more partitions. Having one hard drive with multiple partitions simulates having multiple hard drives. In an MBR-based system, each partition has its own boot record, but the partition used to boot the operating system must contain the Master Boot Record, as diagrammed in Figure 10-18.

A bad sector or cluster anywhere on a disk simply causes a loss of that file. Often, parts of a file can be recovered using third-party utility programs, but when the MBR is corrupted or infected by a virus, access to the entire disk is usually lost. The MBR may be recoverable if precautions have been taken. One method of recovery is to have a copy of the MBR saved on disk or flash memory so that it can be reinstalled to replace the corrupted sector that contains the MBR.

A GPT-based system is much less likely to fail due to corruption as compared to an MBR-based system because of its redundant partition tables. In Figure 10-19, notice that a complete copy of the primary GUID partition table header and GUID partition entries is copied to another location. The backup is used to rebuild the original primary GUID partition header table and GUID partition entries if the primary becomes corrupted. Additionally, notice the protective MBR is included in the partition structure.

To understand the progression to GPT after MBR, one must first look at some of the limitations of MBR. MBR was introduced after the file allocation table (FAT) file system, which used a table to organize and locate files and directories on the disk. While an excellent system at the time, it is now quite obsolete for today's large hard drives. The exception is the new extended file allocation table (exFAT) file system, which is covered later in this chapter.

Partitioning a Disk

Fdisk was a command-line tool used in early DOS operating systems to partition a hard disk drive. Later, Microsoft incorporated an emulator of the **fdisk** command

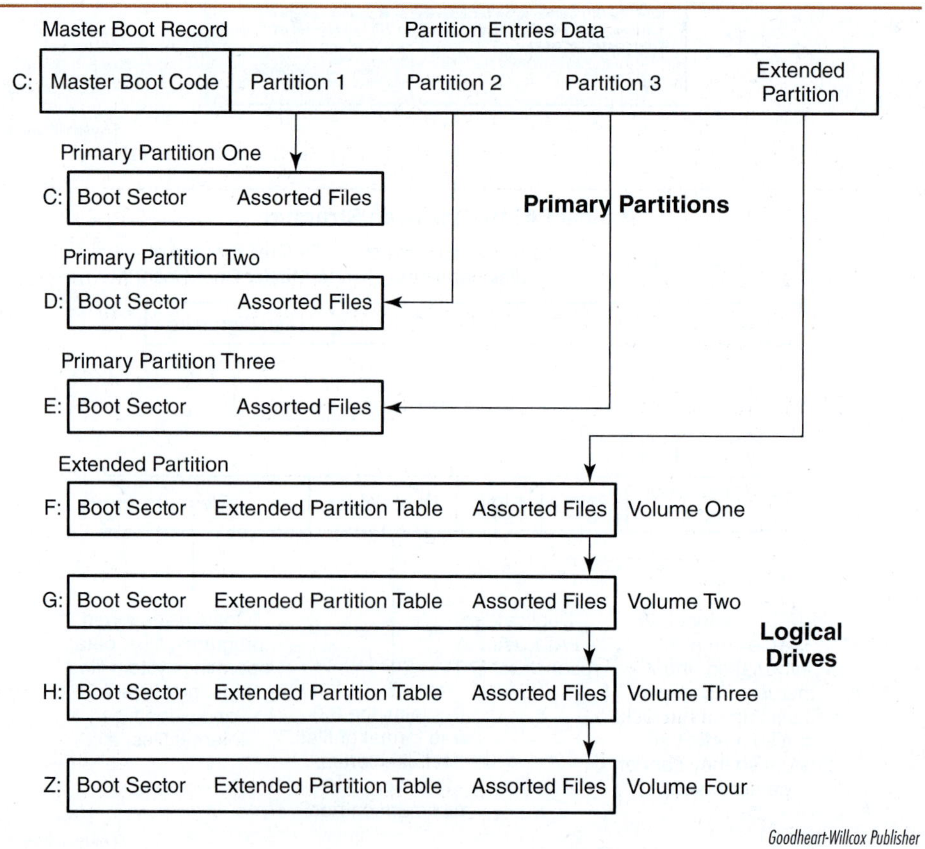

Figure 10-18 A disk drive can be divided into many sections called partitions. Each partition is identified with a drive letter such as C:, D:, E:, up to Z:.

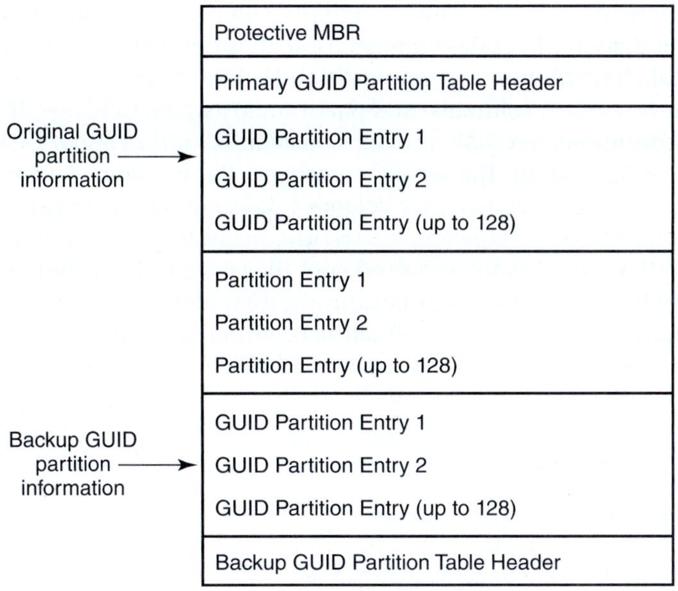

Goodheart-Willcox Publisher

Figure 10-19 A complete copy of the primary GUID partition table header and GUID partition entries is copied to another location.

into the Windows operating systems. The **fdisk** command only works with FAT16 and FAT32 systems, not NTFS systems. Modern operating systems incorporate partitioning and formatting utilities into the operating system. These utilities are accessed either through the command prompt using the DiskPart command-line utility or through Disk Management. Early operating systems required that the hard drive be partitioned and formatted before you ran the operating system installation program. Modern operating systems incorporate the creation of the system partition(s) and formatting the partition(s) as part of the operating system installation process.

DiskPart Utility

A+ 1102: 1.2

The DiskPart utility is used to manage disk partitions and volumes from the command prompt and has replaced the functions served by the **fdisk** command, which was no longer recognized by Windows as of the release of Windows Vista. In both Windows 10 and Windows 11, executing the **fdisk** command launches the DiskPart utility. Disks, partitions, and volumes are managed using the Disk Management tool located in Computer Management, but there will be times when you will need to use the DiskPart utility, especially when you cannot access Computer Management. This may happen, for example, during some troubleshooting operations while trying to recover a failed operating system.

Figure 10-20 lists the commands revealed from the command interpreter after issuing the **DiskPart help** command. It should be noted that only a partial list of commands is shown in the figure.

The DiskPart utility is much more complex than the fdisk utility. Commands typically use two or more words in the command-line syntax. Also, be aware that you must select the partition, disk, or volume before you can carry out many of the commands. Figure 10-21 shows an example of the sequence used to view the details about a selected partition. Notice that the object to be viewed, such as the hard drive, partition, or volume, must first be selected with the **select** command, after which, you can use the **detail** to display information about the object.

In the example shown in Figure 10-21, the user started the DiskPart utility by executing the **diskpart** command, followed by the **select disk 0** command to focus the DiskPart utility on the hard disk drive identified as Disk 0. The DiskPart utility responded with a text message that read, Disk 0 is now the selected disk. Next, the **select partition 1** command was issued, to which DiskPart responded with

Partition 1 is now the selected partition. Finally, the command **detail partition** was entered, which displayed detailed information about partition 1. Note, you can also use the **list disk**, **list volume**, and **list partition** DiskPart commands to reveal information about the disk(s), volume(s) and partition(s) as seen in Figure 10-22.

The first command, **list disk**, provides basic information about Disk 0, the first and only disk in the system. The second command, **list volume**, identifies three volumes that exist on Disk 0. Notice that Volume 1 does not have a drive letter assigned and has been identified or labeled as SYSTEM, or System Reserved disk. The System Reserved disk contains the required boot files used to boot the computer after POST and then load the remaining operating system files located in Volume 0 (drive C:). There is more information about **DiskPart** commands available at the Microsoft

Figure 10-20 Issuing the **help** command in the DiskPart utility displays a list of DiskPart commands.

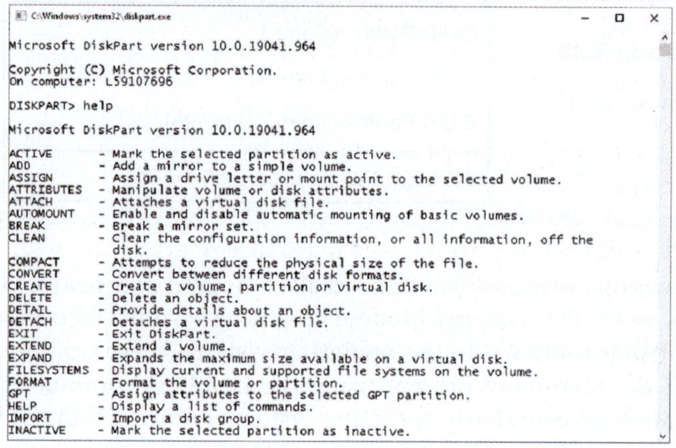

```
C:\Windows\system32\diskpart.exe

Microsoft DiskPart version 10.0.19041.964

Copyright (C) Microsoft Corporation.
On computer: L59107696

DISKPART> help

Microsoft DiskPart version 10.0.19041.964

ACTIVE      - Mark the selected partition as active.
ADD         - Add a mirror to a simple volume.
ASSIGN      - Assign a drive letter or mount point to the selected volume.
ATTRIBUTES  - Manipulate volume or disk attributes.
ATTACH      - Attaches a virtual disk file.
AUTOMOUNT   - Enable and disable automatic mounting of basic volumes.
BREAK       - Break a mirror set.
CLEAN       - Clear the configuration information, or all information, off the
              disk.
COMPACT     - Attempts to reduce the physical size of the file.
CONVERT     - Convert between different disk formats.
CREATE      - Create a volume, partition or virtual disk.
DELETE      - Delete an object.
DETAIL      - Provide details about an object.
DETACH      - Detaches a virtual disk file.
EXIT        - Exit DiskPart.
EXTEND      - Extend a volume.
EXPAND      - Expands the maximum size available on a virtual disk.
FILESYSTEMS - Display current and supported file systems on the volume.
FORMAT      - Format the volume or partition.
GPT         - Assign attributes to the selected GPT partition.
HELP        - Display a list of commands.
IMPORT      - Import a disk group.
INACTIVE    - Mark the selected partition as inactive.
```

Goodheart-Willcox Publisher

Figure 10-21 To view a partition's details, the user must first select the desired disk, then select the desired partition, then request details.

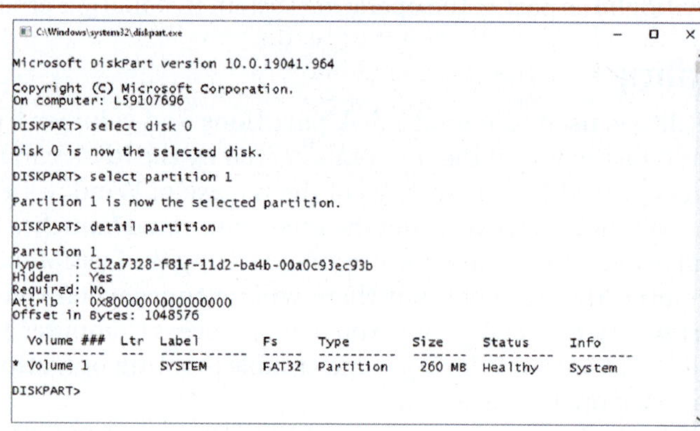

```
C:\Windows\system32\diskpart.exe

Microsoft DiskPart version 10.0.19041.964

Copyright (C) Microsoft Corporation.
On computer: L59107696

DISKPART> select disk 0

Disk 0 is now the selected disk.

DISKPART> select partition 1

Partition 1 is now the selected partition.

DISKPART> detail partition

Partition 1
Type    : c12a7328-f81f-11d2-ba4b-00a0c93ec93b
Hidden  : Yes
Required: No
Attrib  : 0x8000000000000000
Offset in Bytes: 1048576

  Volume ###  Ltr  Label        Fs     Type        Size     Status     Info
  ----------  ---  -----------  -----  ----------  -------  ---------  --------
* Volume 1         SYSTEM       FAT32  Partition    260 MB  Healthy    System

DISKPART>
```

Goodheart-Willcox Publisher

Figure 10-22 Additional commands used in the DiskPart utility include **list disk**, **list volume**, and **list partition**, among others.

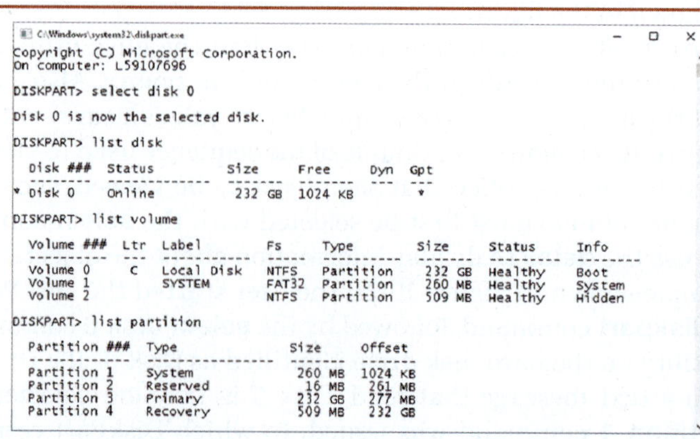

```
C:\Windows\system32\diskpart.exe
Copyright (C) Microsoft Corporation.
On computer: L59107696

DISKPART> select disk 0

Disk 0 is now the selected disk.

DISKPART> list disk

  Disk ###  Status         Size     Free     Dyn  Gpt
  --------  -------------  -------  -------  ---  ---
* Disk 0    Online          232 GB  1024 KB        *

DISKPART> list volume

  Volume ###  Ltr  Label        Fs     Type        Size     Status     Info
  ----------  ---  -----------  -----  ----------  -------  ---------  --------
  Volume 0     C   Local Disk   NTFS   Partition    232 GB  Healthy    Boot
  Volume 1         SYSTEM       FAT32  Partition    260 MB  Healthy    System
  Volume 2                      NTFS   Partition    509 MB  Healthy    Hidden

DISKPART> list partition

  Partition ###  Type              Size     Offset
  -------------  ----------------  -------  -------
  Partition 1    System             260 MB  1024 KB
  Partition 2    Reserved            16 MB   261 MB
  Partition 3    Primary            232 GB   277 MB
  Partition 4    Recovery           509 MB   232 GB
```

Goodheart-Willcox Publisher

TechNet website. You can find this information by conducting an online search using the keywords Microsoft TechNet DiskPart.

Disk Management

1102: 1.3 A+

The preferred, easy-to-use tool is Disk Management, located in Computer Management or through the Microsoft Management Console (MMC). The Disk Management tool provides easy access to all installed disk drives and allows information to be displayed about each drive and its partition(s). You can view the drive type, the file system used, and the status of each drive. Figure 10-23 shows an example of the Windows 10 Disk Management accessed through the Computer Management utility. Notice the items listed in the shortcut menu, which appears when you right-click the mouse on a selected partition.

The Disk Management tool is very similar in all versions of Windows operating systems. In addition to displaying information about the disk system, it contains tools that allow you to extend or shrink the size of a partition, add additional drives and partitions, format the partitions, change the drive letters, allocate the amount of space each user can use (disk quota), convert a basic disk to dynamic disk, and run both the check-disk (chkdsk) and Disk Defragmenter utilities. When an option in the shortcut menu is not available, it will appear in light gray letters, or appear dimmed.

Each of the valid options in the shortcut menu starts a wizard that walks you through the configuration of the hard disk drive or partition. For example, to resize a partition, you simply right-click the partition you wish to resize and then select the **Extend Volume** option. A wizard provides information about the process and requests information about the size to extend the volume. The other configuration options, such as **Format**, **Shrink Volume**, **Delete Volume**, and **Add Mirror**, provide wizards as well, though you should be familiar with the terminology to complete the selected disk configuration option successfully. Computer Management provides an extensive help menu with detailed information about all the Disk Management configuration options. Figure 10-24 shows additional disk configuration options available under the **Actions>Disk Management** menu.

In Windows 10, Computer Management can be accessed through **Control Panel>System and Security>Administrative Tools** (named **Windows Tools** in Windows 11) or by right-clicking **Computer** and selecting **Manage** from the shortcut

A+ Note

To access Computer Management from a command prompt, enter compmgmt.msc. To access the Microsoft Management Console, enter mmc.exe. Be sure you know how to access the Microsoft Management Console and Computer Management from the command prompt as well as through Control Panel before taking the A+ Exams.

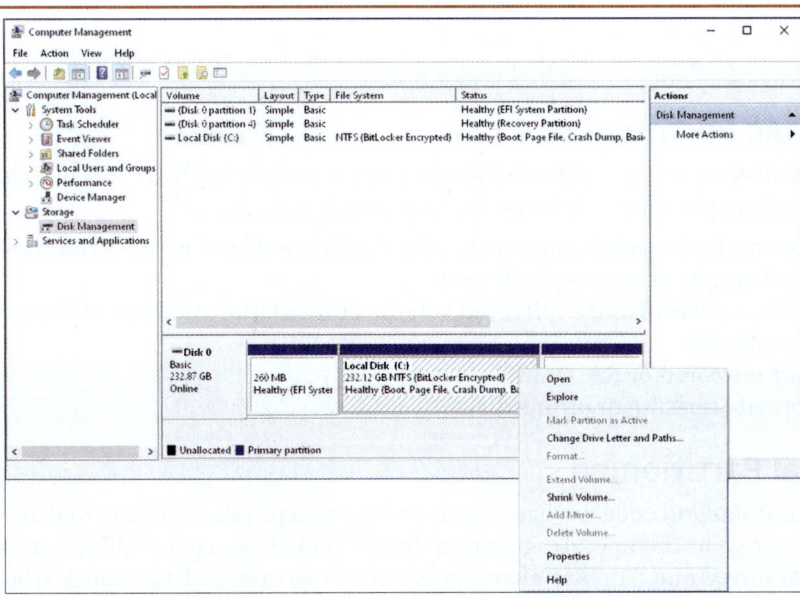

Goodheart-Willcox Publisher

Figure 10-23 The Disk Management tool in Computer Management can be used to display information about the disk system and to perform maintenance-related tasks, such as extend or shrink the size of a volume, delete a volume, and format a partition.

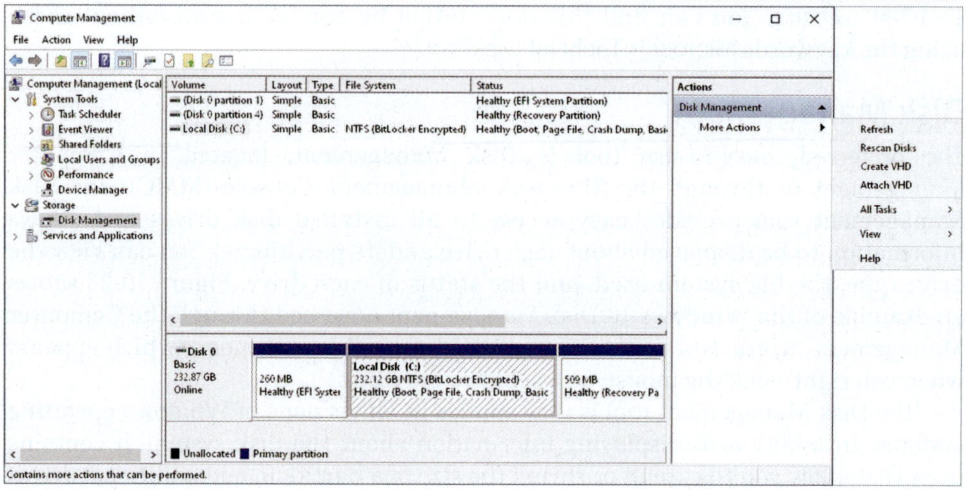

Figure 10-24 Some of the options available under the **Actions>Disk Management** menu include **Refresh**, **Rescan Disks**, **Create VHD**, and **Attach VHD**.

Goodheart-Willcox Publisher

menu. However, the simplest way to access Computer Management is to enter computer management in the **Search** feature of the taskbar.

A customized console can be created with the Microsoft Management Console (MMC). Entering MMC or MMC.exe into the **Search** box will generate a blank MMC that can be customized to include the tools you want. The MMC will be explored more in the related lab activities. There is also a lot of information about the MMC in **Help and Support**, which is located off the **Start** menu. You can also conduct an online search using the key terms Microsoft MMC.

Basic Partitioning

A basic disk is the most common storage format used in Windows. Users can have both primary partitions and logical drives and format these partitions with the appropriate file systems. If the basic volume (drive) needs an extension of a partition, the volume must be in the NTFS format, which is the default format for Windows. The following operations can *only* be performed on basic volumes:

- create an extended partition
- delete an extended partition
- create a logical drive inside an extended partition
- delete a logical drive inside an extended partition
- format a partition and indicate it is active

Dynamic Partitioning

Dynamic disks are required for sophisticated approaches like RAID-5 fault tolerance. The following operations can be performed on dynamic drives:

- create or delete simple, spanned, striped, mirrored, and RAID-5 volumes
- extend simple or spanned volumes
- remove a mirror from a mirrored volume or break the mirrored volume into two volumes
- repair mirrored or RAID-5 volumes
- reactivate missing or offline disks

Logical Partitioning

Logical partitioning occurs when a user configures a physical drive to look like more than one drive to the operating system. Recall that these virtual drives are known as *logical drives* and can help enable a user to categorize and customize storage for their unique needs.

10.4 File System Formats

1102: 1.9 A+

After a hard disk drive is partitioned, it must be formatted, during which the type of file system selected determines the file system format or structure. The most commonly encountered file system formats are NTFS and some variation of FAT, such as FAT16, FAT32, or exFAT. Original FAT file systems, such as FAT12, FAT16, and FAT32, are obsolete and seldom encountered on computer systems, but you may still encounter the FAT and exFAT file systems used for some USB storage devices and small portable electronic device storage systems. FAT and exFAT are used when small storage capacity is required because FAT has less overhead than the NTFS file system. The smaller overhead makes it ideal for small storage systems.

FAT16 and FAT32

1102: 1.8 A+

There are several forms of FAT systems. The original DOS and the original release of Windows 95 used **FAT16**, which used 16 bits to identify stored data and had a maximum storage of 2 GB. As the demand for greater storage capability evolved, the FAT32 system was designed and released with Windows 95 OSR2. **FAT32** used 32 bits to identify stored data, and its upper limit for storage is theoretically 2 TB (terabytes). However, Windows 2000 limits the size to 32 GB. Windows versions after 95 OSR2 can use either FAT16 or FAT 32.

Tech Tip

FAT16 and FAT32 are still used today for flash memory systems such as USB drives or flash memory cards.

FAT16 is limited to 512 files contained in the root directory. The root directory identifies the files and directories by name and identifies files associated with various directories and their location(s) on the disk. It also stores information such as the file extension, file attribute, time, date, and location of the first cluster.

This does not imply that a hard disk storage unit can only contain 512 files; rather, it means that there can be only 512 unique names of files and directories in the root directory of a FAT16 file system. There can be more files on the hard disk using directories and subdirectories. A directory in the root directory appears as a single file, but it can have an unlimited number of files contained under it as files and subdirectories.

exFAT

1102: 1.8 A+

Extended file allocation table (exFAT) is a proprietary Microsoft file system designed for portable devices such as USB flash drives and flash memory cards. The exFAT file system can also be used to format external hard disk drives when attached through a USB port.

The SD Association has chosen exFAT as the default file format for its Secure Digital Extended Capacity (SDXC) memory card, which is used in portable devices such as cameras and tablets. The exFAT file format extends the memory card capacity from the previous 32 GB to 2 TB.

NTFS

1102: 1.8, 2.5 A+

The **New Technology File System (NTFS)** is a file system designed specifically to operate with Windows NT operating systems. Microsoft realized the limitations of FAT, particularly a 2-GB size limit for a volume on a hard drive and for large cluster sizes and designed NTFS to ensure that much larger hard drives could be accommodated. NTFS has a maximum hard drive volume of 16 EB (exabytes) and limits the size of clusters, which results in less wasted space on the hard drive. NTFS also uses a master file table (MFT) similarly to how the FAT file system uses a file allocation table to locate files.

For user convenience, NTFS supports long file names and security access features not available in FAT systems. NTFS is compatible with FAT16 but not FAT32. Windows 2000 further developed the NTFS with additional features and called its file system *dynamic disk*. NTFS was originally more commonly found on file servers or NT workstations than on a typical PC, but since the introduction of Windows XP, Microsoft moved the home user to an NTFS-based file system. NTFS can support volumes as large as 8 petabytes on Windows Server 2019 and 2022 as well as Windows 10, version 1709 and newer.

Since the introduction of the dynamic disk file system, the NTFS name has been changed to NTFS5.0. The original NTFS is now called NTFS4.0. This can lead to a lot of confusion. Technical literature written during and before the year 2000 uses the terms *NTFS* and *dynamic disk*, while literature produced post-2000 uses NTFS4.0 and NTFS5.0. Today, the preferred term is simply *NTFS* for either NTFS4.0 or NTFS5.0. The only distinction is when technical information uses the term *dynamic disk* about NTFS5.0. Microsoft uses the term *dynamic disk* in their own literature when describing NTFS, but publications that originate outside of Microsoft use *NTFS5.0*. In addition, Microsoft refers to FAT16, FAT32, and NTFS4.0 as *basic disk systems*. Figure 10-25 shows the results of executing the **fsutil fsinfo ntfsinfo c:** command. You will note that it returns 3.1 as the NTFS version.

A+ 1102: 2.5

Encrypted File System

The **encrypted file system (EFS)** is the native encryption system used with NTFS. EFS is only available in Windows Professional and Ultimate editions, not in Home editions. NTFS uses a file encryption key (FEK) to encrypt and decrypt file contents, and it allows a single file, folder, or a complete data drive to be encrypted. A common way to use EFS is to create a folder in a directory and then set the properties of the folder to encrypt. After the folder is set for encryption, any file dropped into the folder will be encrypted. The encryption and decryption processes are transparent to the authorized user of the file, making EFS an ideal security measure for preventing confidential data from being accessed by unauthorized users.

The compression and encryption features in Windows operating systems can be accessed by right-clicking the item to be encrypted (file, folder, or data drive), and selecting **Properties>Advanced** from the shortcut menu. This launches the **Advanced Attributes** dialog box, as shown in Figure 10-26.

Tech Tip

Only uncompressed files can be encrypted with EFS.

There is one shortcoming of EFS: it cannot encrypt the entire hard disk drive, including where required system files are located and any hidden partitions. Microsoft now offers BitLocker as an application that permits the encryption of the entire hard disk drive, even the boot files and hidden partitions. The advantage of using BitLocker is that it provides for extreme security by preventing unauthorized access to a disk system. A portable version of BitLocker is available as BitLocker To Go, which allows the entire contents of a flash drive to be encrypted.

```
C:\Windows\system32>fsutil fsinfo ntfsinfo c:
NTFS Volume Serial Number :         0x9802917802915c56
NTFS Version      :                 3.1
LFS Version       :                 2.0
Total Sectors     :                 1,952,239,725  (930.9 GB)
Total Clusters    :                   244,029,965  (930.9 GB)
Free Clusters     :                    43,878,213  (167.4 GB)
Total Reserved Clusters :                 674,203  (  2.6 GB)
Reserved For Storage Reserve :            655,360  (  2.5 GB)
Bytes Per Sector  :                 512
Bytes Per Physical Sector :         512
Bytes Per Cluster :                 4096
Bytes Per FileRecord Segment    :   1024
Clusters Per FileRecord Segment :   0
Mft Valid Data Length :             2.07 GB
Mft Start Lcn  :                    0x00000000000c0000
Mft2 Start Lcn :                    0x0000000000000002
Mft Zone Start :                    0x00000000ab499a0
Mft Zone End   :                    0x000000000ab561c0
MFT Zone Size  :                    200.13 MB
Max Device Trim Extent Count :      512
Max Device Trim Byte Count :        0xffffffff
Max Volume Trim Extent Count :      62
Max Volume Trim Byte Count :        0x40000000
Resource Manager Identifier :       40D3B8FB-0F65-11EC-889D-9A29FE367F75

C:\Windows\system32>
```

Goodheart-Willcox Publisher

Figure 10-25 New Technology File System (NTFS) was specifically designed to operate with the Windows NT operating system, though there is some confusion surrounding the nomenclature relating to NTFS type.

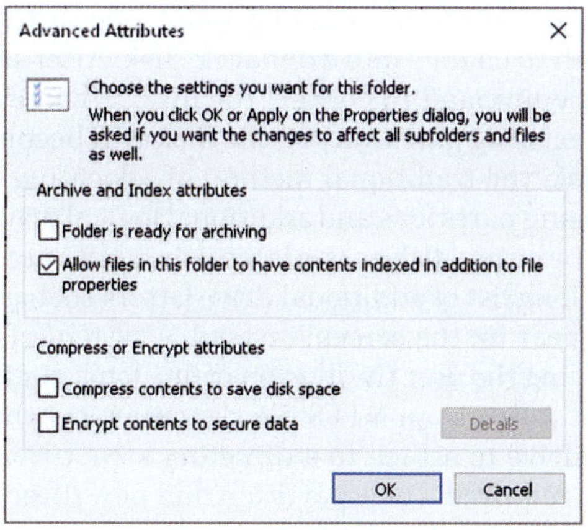

Goodheart-Willcox Publisher

Figure 10-26 The **Advanced Attributes** dialog box can be used to encrypt or compress a file in an NTFS-formatted system.

NTFS Compression

NTFS supports its own file compression system, which allows you to compress a single file, a folder, or entire volume. Like file encryption, file compression is transparent to the user. A compressed file opens and closes in a fashion typical to an uncompressed file. The only time file compression is obvious to the user is during the initial compression of a large folder or volume. An entire volume could take hours to compress, but after compression, the time it takes to open and close is comparable to an uncompressed volume.

Compression does not always achieve the desired effect. For example, if a user is trying to create more disk space by compressing graphics files, they may notice very little difference in file size after compression. Most graphics file formats, such as JPEG and GIF, already use a file compression technique, so additional compression has little-to-no effect on the file size. Also, be aware that compressed files may be difficult or impossible to recover after a complete system failure.

Tech Tip

File systems often derive their names from the amount of available space used to identify the clusters in binary form and to store the value in the file allocation table. For example, FAT12 has 2^{12} entries; FAT16 has 2^{16} entries; FAT32 has 2^{28} entries; and exFAT has 2^{70} entries. It is important to note that FAT32 technically has 2^{32} entries, but it only uses 2^{28} and saves the rest as spares.

Disk Quotas

There are several important advantages to NTFS as compared to FAT file systems, including the ability to set disk quotas. That means when a hard disk drive is shared by several users, each user can be allocated a portion of the disk for storage. However, the user cannot use more space than what he or she has been allocated. This prevents one user from using up all the disk space for photos and such.

Dynamic Disk

Dynamic disk was first introduced with Windows 2000 Professional and provided many more disk configuration options as compared to basic disk. This feature continues with Windows 10 and 11. **Basic disk** refers to the traditional FAT16, FAT32, exFAT, and NTFS file storage system. Dynamic disk is based on NTFS technology but has benefitted from significant improvements, such as improved disk security as well as fewer restrictions normally associated with NTFS.

One of the biggest advantages to dynamic disk as compared to basic disk is that dynamic disk can span a volume (partition) across multiple physical disks, while basic disk cannot. This means that you can keep increasing the size of a volume (partition) by adding additional disk drives.

You can install a basic disk file system on your computer and convert to dynamic disk at any time without losing data, but you will likely not be able to reverse the operation without losing data. Microsoft recommends against reversing the process, though some third-party utilities claim they can do the job. Use these utilities at your own risk.

You can change a basic disk to a dynamic disk either through Computer Management, Microsoft Management Console (MMC), or at the command prompt with the DiskPart utility. At the command prompt, access the DiskPart utility and select the disk you wish to change into a dynamic disk. After selecting the disk, issue the **convert dynamic** command to convert the disk. When converting a basic disk into a dynamic disk, existing partitions on the disk will become simple volumes.

With dynamic disk, the traditional method of allocating additional space on a large disk system by using partitions and additional logical drives is no longer needed. Dynamic disk treats the entire disk as one large volume of data and appears seamless to the user. The usual long list of additional drive letters such as R:, P:, S:, and Z: is no longer required to appear on the screen; instead, a system of volume mount points can be established, giving the user the illusion of one long, continuous file structure.

A **volume mount point** is an NTFS file system object that allows a volume or additional hard disk drive to attach to a directory structure. Traditionally, adding a new hard disk drive required a new partition and new directory assigned, such as E: or F:. With the volume mount-point feature, a new volume or disk can instead be attached to an existing directory.

Instead of assigning a partition or volume letter, NTFS dynamic disk allows you to create a partition and assign it to a folder through the **New Simple Volume Wizard**. When the new volume is created, no partition letter will be assigned; rather, it will be listed as the folder to which it was assigned. For example, if the new volume were assigned to a folder in the C: drive labeled Artwork, the drive path would be C:\Artwork, and it will effectively serve as a shortcut to the Artwork folder.

When the new partition/volume is created, it is spliced into an existing file structure rather than appearing as a separate drive with an individual drive letter. Basic file systems are limited in the number of drives that can be installed and in the maximum number of partitions that can be created. The maximum number of partitions is equal to the letters of the entire alphabet minus the letters used for assignment to existing drives. Since the volume mount-point technology does not require a separate drive letter, there is no practical limitation to the number of drives assigned to a system. This is especially important on network systems.

Storage Spaces

Storage Spaces was introduced in Windows 8 and allows a group of two or more drives to be configured into a pool of storage devices. All data stored on the original storage drive is automatically written to a second or third storage drive within the pool, which prevents the loss of data caused by disk storage failure. The technique of writing duplicate data to separate drives is referred to as *disk mirroring*. You can access Storage Spaces by entering Storage or Storage Spaces in the Windows **Search** box. You can also access it through **Control Panel>System and Security**, as demonstrated in Figure 10-27.

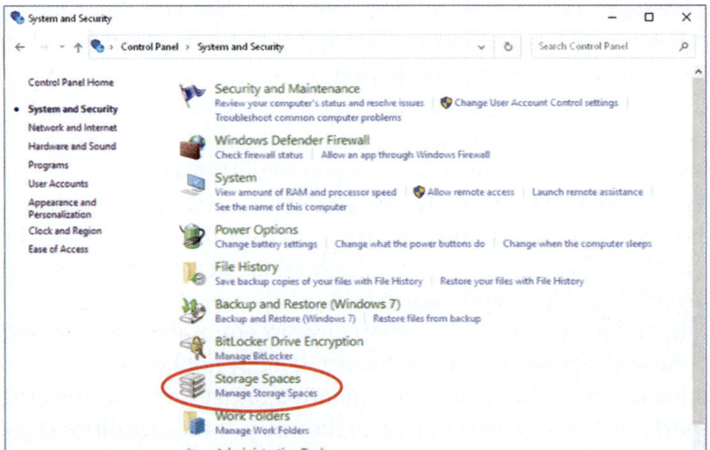

Figure 10-27 Windows Storage Spaces can be accessed through **Control Panel>System and Security**.

Goodheart-Willcox Publisher

The Storage Spaces wizard will prompt for information about the desired configuration, such as the storage name, resiliency type, and storage size. When applied to mass storage, the term *resiliency* refers to the ability of a computer system to recover from data loss caused by a disk or storage system failure.

Windows 10 supports four resiliency types: simple, two-way mirror, three-way mirror, and parity. *Simple resiliency* means that the data is stored as one copy only. A *two-way mirror* means that the data is duplicated across two separate drives. A *three-way mirror* functions like a two-way mirror, only the data is duplicated across three separate drives. *Parity* resiliency is when data is written across all drives but in a special way. The first two drives each contain the actual data, and the third contains a parity bit, which is calculated from the data on the first two drives. If any single drive fails, the parity bit can be used to automatically rebuild the missing data and a new drive after it is installed.

ReFS

A+ 1101: 5.3

Resilient File System (ReFS) is the newest Microsoft file system, which builds off the enhancements made in NTFS. ReFS was introduced in 2012 and remains available today, including in Windows Server 2012 (also known as Windows Server 8) through 2022. It has many improvements over other file systems, but the most outstanding feature is its resiliency and ability to recover after a major catastrophe such as a power outage or system failure. With previous versions of file systems, such as FAT or NTFS, a power failure or a system failure would usually corrupt the file system, especially if the operating were writing data to a file, because the file-writing process would stop before the file is properly closed. Remember that a file can require two or more clusters or sectors to hold its contents, with each cluster or sector reserving its last byte of storage for identifying the location of the next storage segment. Any interruption in the writing process ends the write and leaves the cluster or sector without the address of the next storage segment, thus corrupting the file.

The Resilient File System maintains copies of file contents on two or more disks. When a file corruption error is detected, ReFS replaces the corrupt file with a good copy. The entire process of detecting and replacing corrupt data is transparent and requires no user intervention.

While Microsoft provides other means of duplicating file content, ReFS is the only method that continually runs in the background. You can say that it is continually checking for data errors and making continuous data backups. ReFS is intended primarily for use on a network server designed for data storage only and not intended to be used as a file system for hosting an operating system on a server or personal computer. Due to the continuous data-checking feature used with ReFS, an operating system would be slowed down considerably and would appear too sluggish to a user.

NFS Formatting

NFS formatting was originally a Sun Microsystems implementation of a distributed network. Not surprisingly, this network approach was initially supported using variants of the Unix operating system. Because of its popularity, it is widely available for any personal computer-based operating system, including Windows 10. To use NFS on Windows 10, one must install it as a service and mount the file system so the Unix/Linux drives can be accessed. *Mounting* a file system is similar to what occurs when a user plugs a USB flash drive into a personal computer. When initially mounted, the user will only have read privileges, but these can be modified to include write privileges as well.

A+ 1102: 1.8

Ext3 and Ext4 Formatting

Ext3 and Ext4 are referred to as journaling file systems using the Linux operating system. *Journaling* is a technique designed to improve file system reliability. The journaling approach keeps track of changes to the file system and has been part of NTFS since 1993, meaning all subsequent 32-bit and 64-bit Windows variants possess this capability. Ext4 is the successor to Ext3, though both protocols are used by the Linux kernel. One of the benefits of Ext4 is the support for massive volumes/drives (2^{60} bytes in theory).

HFS and APFS

HFS and HFS plus generally refer to an older Apple Macintosh file system, although confusion can arise due to the use of the same nomenclature by IBM for their z-class systems. It is thanks to HFS that Windows PC users observe file names that look like typical file names accompanied by the same file name with the addition of a period. In Apple terminology, these are known as the data and resource forks, which separate the data from information such as the icon for the files. The purpose of this approach was to provide flexibility for local changes. Apple has since moved to Apple File System (APFS).

A+ 1102: 1.8

APFS was first introduced with macOS Sierra (2016), iOS 10.3, tvOS 10.2, and watchOS 3.2. APFS uses 64-bit iNode numbers, which allows it to address more storage space. Due to the 64-bit iNode, APFS can support up to 2^{63} files on one volume. APFS uses GPT partitioning (GUID Partition Table), and the GPT contains one or more APFS containers with each container holding one or more APFS volumes. APFS supports full disk encryption, which makes it more secure than HFS, and it is also designed to avoid corruption in the event of a system crash.

Swap Partition

All modern personal computer operating systems can use a swap partition when needed. A *swap partition* is a standard partition that is designated as temporary storage and effectively maximizes utilization of RAM. The system will detect which open program has been idle the longest and move it to the swap file/virtual memory. If the user clicks on that program to activate it, it can then be loaded quite quickly. This file used to end in a **.swp** extension, but now it is called **pagefile.sys**, which normally appears in the root directory (C:\). It is also used for memory dumps after blue or black screens of death (BSOD).

Starting with Windows 8 and moving on to Window 10, there have been some changes in **hyberfil.sys**, **swapfile.sys**, and **pagefile.sys**. The **pagefile.sys** file is present all the time, but **hiberfil.sys** is only present if you have fast startup enabled. Additionally, Windows 10 uses a hybrid shutdown by default, which causes a **hyberfil.sys** file to be generated, though it only has the kernel and files needed to boot, so it is smaller.

A+ 1102: 1.9, 2.8

Formatting a Disk

Before a hard disk can be used to store data, it must be formatted. This type of format is referred to as a **high-level format**, which prepares a disk to receive data in a systematic, organized manner; determines the file table type; checks the physical condition of all sectors; marks bad sectors so that they cannot be used to store data; and identifies the operating system being used. A low-level format destroys all data on a disk, and while a high-level format is said to destroy all data, the sectors/clusters still contain the original data. It erases only the contents of the file table so that no file name is associated with the data clusters.

Data *can* be recovered after a high-level format takes place. The collection of clusters that contain the file data can be identified and given a file name using third-party tools. Additionally, certain third-party disk editor utilities can display the ASCII contents of a file after the disk has been formatted or the file deleted.

The **format** command is seldom issued from the command prompt today; instead, when a hard drive requires formatting, the Disk Management tool in Computer Management is typically used. For removable storage such as flash memory, the format process is carried out through a format tool. You can locate the portable storage device using Explorer and then simply right-click on it and select the **Format** option from the shortcut menu.

When formatting storage media, Windows offers two format methods: quick and full. The quick format is used on a disk that has already been formatted once and simply erases the FAT. Rather than prepare the entire disk surface for storage, only the file table and root directory are changed. This is much quicker than the full formatting process, which prepares the entire disk. The full format erases information across the entire disk and checks for bad sectors. The full formatting process would typically be used for an unformatted disk. Since disks are now formatted during manufacturing, this process is not needed as often.

Figure 10-28 shows the available file system choices when formatting a removable disk: NTFS, FAT, FAT32 (Default), and exFAT. FAT is only available for small drives less than 4 GB, so for drives with at least 4 GB of storage, such as the one shown in Figure 10-28, FAT is simply not listed an option.

File systems use part of the storage space for file tables known as *overhead*. NTFS requires much more overhead as compared to the FAT file system. The modern flash memory systems are often formatted with exFAT rather than NTFS because exFAT can theoretically support 64 zettabytes (ZB), or 64,000,000 terabytes, but Microsoft recommends a limit of 512 TB.

Tape uses a format similar to disks. A file allocation table is used to keep track of sectors on the tape, which must also be formatted before it can be used. Formatting a tape is like formatting a disk except that it takes a great deal of time because of the tape's large capacity. Tapes are generally preformatted when they are purchased, saving hours of valuable time. Some of the top-of-the-line tape systems can format a tape as they are being used.

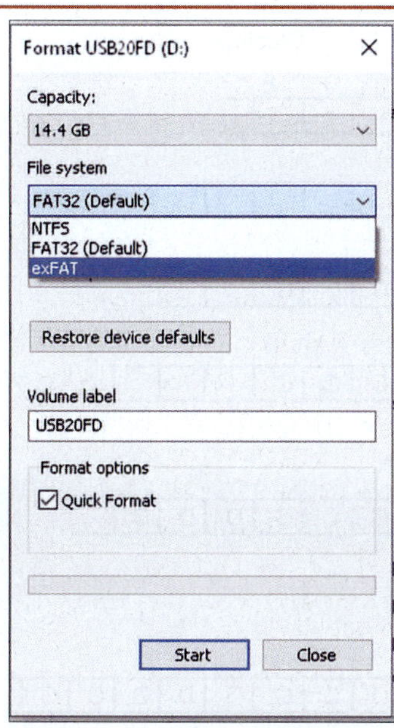

Goodheart-Willcox Publisher

Figure 10-28 The file format selection is directly affected by the size of the USB device. FAT is only available for drives with less than 4 GB of storage.

10.5 Disk and File Maintenance

Disk drives require routine maintenance to enhance performance. Common tools used to perform disk maintenance are Disk Defragmenter, chkdsk, SFC, and various benchmarks such as performance measurements and drive status.

A+ 1102: 1.3

Disk Defragmenter

File fragmentation is a common occurrence on disks. Files are assigned to disks by clusters, and when storage clusters are not consecutive, a file is considered fragmented. File fragmentation occurs through normal disk activities such as saving new files, erasing files, opening files, and adding additional data to files.

Figure 10-29 illustrates a possible sequence of events leading to fragmented files on the hard drive. The first three files saved (A, B, and C) show no file fragmentation. Each file is stored in a consecutive series of clusters. When file B is erased, it creates an opening in the sequence of clusters, which can now be used for the storage of new data. When file D is saved, it uses the two clusters left open by the deletion of file B as well as three additional clusters that exist after file C. File D is a fragmented file because the clusters used to store the data are not sequential. Next, file C is opened and used, causing it to grow in size. When file C is saved back to the disk, it uses its four original clusters plus two additional clusters at the end of the file system, meaning file C is now also fragmented.

The more frequently files are opened, modified, closed, or erased from a disk, the more fragmented the system becomes. Fragmented files take longer to load and use, and it becomes increasingly difficult for a data recovery utility to identify the cluster sequences of fragmented files. As part of routine file maintenance, a hard drive should be defragmented (*defragged*) regularly with the Disk Defragmenter utility. **Defragmentation** is the process of moving clusters so all files have their clusters organized sequentially. Windows 8 introduced a disk defragmenter program called Optimize Drives, which was combined with the defragmenter utility for Windows 10 and renamed Defragment and Optimize Drives. The utility is located at **Start**>**All apps**>**Windows Administrative Tools**>**Defragment and Optimize Drives**.

Figure 10-29
Fragmentation occurs through the repeated saving and deletion of files.

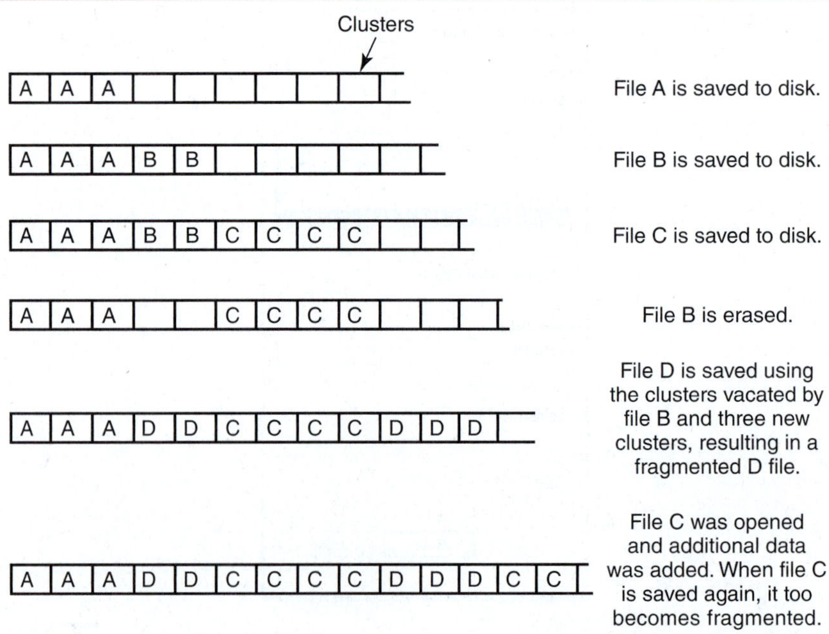

Goodheart-Willcox Publisher

Figure 10-30 shows the Windows 10 **Optimize Drives** dialog box. Notice that it is configured to optimize drives automatically every week. It should be noted that solid-state drives generally do not require defragmentation or optimization.

Chkdsk

1102: 1.2 A+

Chkdsk is a utility that checks and repairs the integrity of the file system on a hard drive. Disk problems such as bad sectors, lost clusters, cross-linked files, and directory structure errors can be detected and repaired automatically. Chkdsk can be run from the command prompt or from the GUI. Figure 10-31 shows the results of the **chkdsk** command run on a Windows 10 computer from the command prompt.

When the chkdsk utility is run from the command prompt, it will identify, but not repair, problems found. To automatically repair problems found, the **chkdsk** command must be run with the **/r** switch.

To run the chkdsk utility as part of a GUI, simply access the Windows Explorer view of the desired drive or partition you wish to test. Then, right-click the partition or drive and select **Properties** from the shortcut menu.

Under the **Tools** tab, click the **Check** button to check the partition or drive, as shown in Figure 10-32A. A dialog box may appear stating that the disk does not have to be scanned since no new errors have been found. This box will still allow the user to scan the disk, however. Additionally, the user can continue using the disk during the scan, and chkdsk will decide what to do about any errors discovered during the scan.

Tech Tip

While chkdsk is often run as a routine attempt to repair a volume, Microsoft recommends backing up your data before running chkdsk with the automatic repair option.

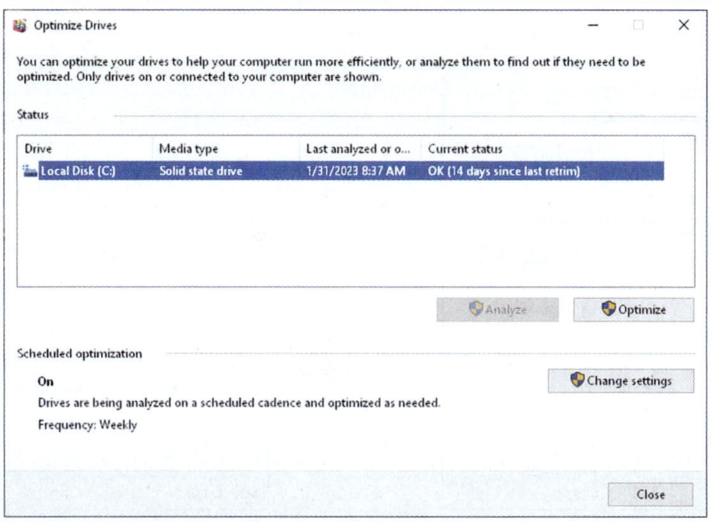

Goodheart-Willcox Publisher

Figure 10-30 Optimize Drives can be accessed through **Control Panel>System and Security>Administrative Tools>Defragment and Optimize Drives**.

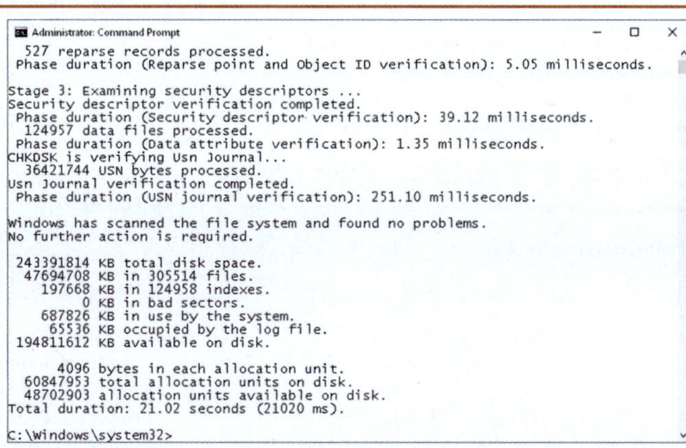

Goodheart-Willcox Publisher

Figure 10-31 The results of the **chkdsk** command typically identify issues such as bad sectors, lost clusters, cross-linked files, and directory structure errors.

The chkdsk utility will run as a GUI, and when completed, the results will be displayed in GUI format similar to the Windows 10 screen capture in Figure 10-32B. If a user were to select the **Show Details** link, Event Viewer would open with full details of the scan that are very similar to when chkdsk is run from the command prompt.

Chkdsk must have exclusive control of the volume it is checking. This is a problem when attempting to run chkdsk on the default boot partition when it contains the complete operating system. A message will appear indicating that chkdsk cannot be run at this time, but it can be scheduled to run automatically when the computer is restarted. When the computer is restarted or shut down and started later, the chkdsk utility will automatically start up and run on the boot partition.

SFC

The *System File Checker (SFC)* is a utility that enables users to scan for and repair corrupted system files and is included in Windows 10 and Windows 11. To run SFC, you need to launch the command prompt as administrator. There are two common commands for the SFC utility:

- **sfc /scannow** This syntax performs a scan and repairs any corrupted files.
- **sfc /verifyonly** This syntax only performs a scan; it does not repair any corrupted files.

Figure 10-33 shows the results of a scan executed with the **sfc /verifyonly** command.

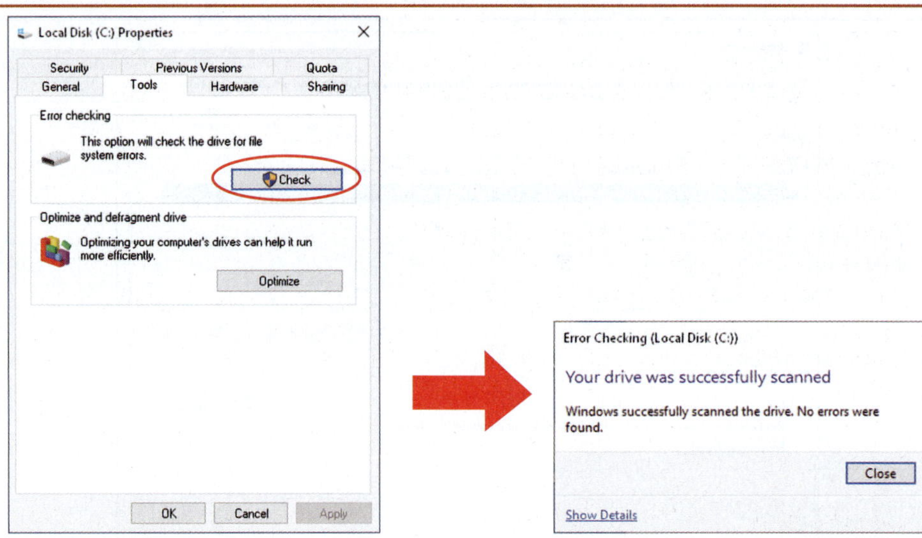

A B

Goodheart-Willcox Publisher

Figure 10-32 Chkdsk can be run from the GUI by right-clicking the drive, selecting **Properties** from the shortcut menu, and choosing **Tools>Check** (A). When completed, the GUI will alert the user to any errors found and provide a link to the full details of the scan (B).

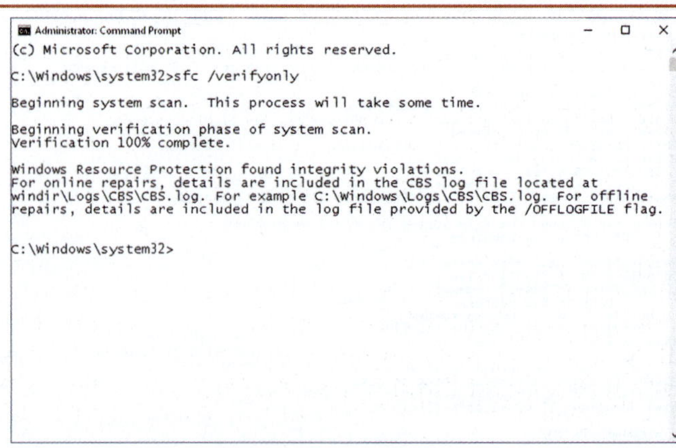

Goodheart-Willcox Publisher

Figure 10-33 The System File Checker (SFC) is a utility that enables users to scan for and repair corrupted system files.

Performance Measures

Benchmark tests are performance tests conducted to compare different hardware and software. Industry journals and third-party organizations often make comparisons to rate the quality of hardware and software, and many times, these same performance tests are conducted by the manufacturer and then used in advertising campaigns. Always check to see who conducted the performance test and review the results of the test with that in mind.

Hard drive performance is typically judged on such items as *access time*, *latency*, or *seek time*, all of which mean the same thing when it comes to performance. These terms refer to the amount of time taken to position the read/write head over the proper sector, usually measured in microseconds.

Another standard of measure is the data transfer rate. This rate refers to the speed of transfer of data to and from the disk. The actual time it takes must include the fact that cache memory is used to give the appearance of higher transfer rates. Disk data transfer rates are usually measured in megabytes per second (MBps).

The fastest and easiest way to compare disk drive systems is to load the two drives that are to be compared with a Windows operating system. Place one or two typical software applications in the system's Startup folder so that they launch when Windows opens. The two systems should then be booted so you can compare the length of time it takes to boot and load the software systems. Any technician can perform this simple test. When comparing two devices, all other hardware must be equal; the only variation can be the actual piece of hardware or software being compared in the test.

A+ 1101: 5.3

Another metric that is gaining popularity is *input/output operations per second (IOPS)*. This metric is used for measuring the performance of nonvolatile storage, as well as storage area networks (SAN). There are several different IOPS metrics:

- *Total IOPS*: total number of I/O operations per second
- *Random Read IOPS*: arithmetic mean of random read I/O operations per second
- *Random Write IOPS*: arithmetic mean of random write I/O operations per second
- *Sequential Read IOPS*: arithmetic mean of sequential read I/O operations per second
- *Sequential Write IOPS*: arithmetic mean of sequential write I/O operations per second

Drive Status

It is important for a technician to be able to assess a drive's status. Typically, one of four methods can be used to achieve this. First, the technician could use a tool developed by the drive manufacturer, assuming it is available. Second, the chkdsk utility can determine drive status, but it does not yield the best information or results. Third, the Windows Management Instrumentation Command-line utility (WMIC) can be run, but this has effectively been replaced by PowerShell cmdlets. Finally, a third-party utility can be purchased and used.

Mounting a Disk

A+ 1102: 1.7

Mounting occurs when a disk format—electronic or magnetic—becomes available to the operating system. Most often, mounting occurs transparently to the user, although the Windows Disk Management tool can be used to change drive letters and paths. This can be accomplished by right-clicking the desired drive in Disk Management and selecting **Change Drive Letter and Paths** from the shortcut menu.

Mounting can also be accomplished with ISO (optical media). The ISO can be on physical media such as a CD or DVD, or it can be a downloaded file. Linux users frequently download an ISO of a given Linux distribution and then mount that disk. Most virtual machine hosts (i.e., VMWare, Oracle Virtual Box, etc.) will allow one to mount the ISO image in the virtualized environment.

Modifying Partitions

The technician can extend, split, or shrink a partition using the Disk Management tool. To extend a partition, open **Disk Management** and select **Extend Volume**. One can only extend a partition when adjoining, unallocated space is available. Alternatively, a user can use the DiskPart utility. When using Disk Management to split partitions, the user may be asked to create a dynamic drive, which may not suit the user's purposes. Additionally, third-party software exists to modify a partition.

The Disk Management tool is also the primary tool for shrinking a partition. Technicians may shrink a partition to improve performance, simplify malware scans, or to provide space for another partition.

Adding Drives

Adding a drive should occur automatically under the Windows operating system. If you dismount a drive, the simplest way to remount it is to reboot the OS. Otherwise, you may have to use the Disk Management tool and Disk Initialization, which will erase all data.

A+ 1101: 3.1, 3.3

10.6 PATA and SATA Hard Disk Interfaces

A+ Note

For the A+ Exams, CompTIA usually asks questions concerning hardware data speeds or bandwidth. Make sure you memorize hardware port speeds and can select the highest or lowest speed when presented with a list of device ports.

IBM introduced the first hard drive in 1957. It was constructed of fifty 24-inch platters with a total storage capacity of 5 MB. IBM would not sell the hard disk, but at that time, it could be leased for approximately $35,000 per year. The entire disk drive system was roughly as large as a refrigerator box, physically enormous by today's standards. Contemporary hard disks have a thousand times more storage space at a fraction of the size and cost.

Early PC hard drive controller circuitry was mounted on an adapter card and installed into an ISA slot. A cable ran from the adapter card to the hard disk drive. A second hard disk drive standard was introduced by IBM and was used with the MCA slot. It was used to interface with the MCA bus system and is now obsolete.

As hard disk drives became popular, the card was integrated into the drive to become one unit. This was the beginning of a third standard called the **AT Attachment (ATA)**, which was a 16-bit data transfer system using a 40-pin cable connector that attached to the motherboard and to the circuit board mounted on the hard drive. It was originally developed for the 80286 model. With the development and release of the SATA standard, ATA is now referred to as PATA.

Parallel ATA (PATA) is an interface standard for the connection of storage devices. PATA is in use today and is referred to as *IDE* or *EIDE*. The term *Integrated Drive Electronics (IDE)* refers to the adapter card being integrated into the hard drive device. *Enhanced Integrated Drive Electronics (EIDE)* was a term introduced by Western Digital Corporation, a major hard drive manufacturer. EIDE hard drives originally used a new ATA standard known as ATA-2, Fast ATA, or Fast ATA-2.

All the different terminology around the ATA/IDE drive connection can prove very confusing. Some manufacturers chose not to wait for new standards to be implemented and came out with similar sounding names, while others have changed the requirements for their standard. The requirements for EIDE have changed many times. Refer to Figure 10-34 for ATA standards.

Some ATA designs use an adapter board inserted into the PCI slot to take advantage of higher data transfer speeds. When using the expansion slot to upgrade to a higher ATA standard, first check that the motherboard chipset supports the higher ATA standard. Otherwise, the desired higher transfer speed of the newer ATA design may not be reached.

When working with computers, be aware that computer repair shops and your own classroom laboratory may have many old devices and cables in supply storage areas. Be sure you are using the correct cable to match the technology. Figure 10-35 shows two types of ATA cable. One has 40 conductors, and the other has 80 conductors. You must use an 80-conductor ATA data cable to support the higher data rates of ATA-5, ATA-6, and ATA-7. ATA-6 reaches 100 MBps. ATA-7, also known as ATA-133, can reach data speeds of 133 MBps.

Serial ATA (SATA) is a transport protocol that determines the amount of data that can be transferred between a motherboard and storage device. It was developed

ATA Standards

Drive Specification	Features
ATA-1	The original ATA design released in 1988 used a 40-conductor ribbon cable and featured a master, slave, and cable select option. It also used a programming technique to automatically identify itself to the BIOS system during setup.
ATA-2	Released in 1996, it allowed other storage devices to be connected to the bus system, not just hard disk drives. It allowed disks up to 8.4 GB to be accessed easily. It was also called Fast ATA because it featued faster DMA data transfer speeds than ATA-1.
ATA-3	A revised ATA-2 that allowed password protection for hard disk drive security and a few other minor changes.
ATA-4	A 1998 revision that allowed data transfer rates as high as 33 MBps. It is also referred to as UDMA/33 and Ultra ATA/33. ATA-4 also introduced an optional 80-conductor ribbon cable for the standard 40-pin connector. This modification reduced electrical effects that limited data transfer rates. The ATA-4 specification also integrated the ATAPI standard, which allows for the attachment of CD-ROM, tape drives, and other forms of mass storage devices that required an ATAPI interface.
ATA-5	Introduced in 1999 with a standard 80-conductor ribbon cable. The 80-conductor ribbon cable allowed for transfer rates as high as 66 MBps as long as the motherboard was designed to take advantage of the ATA-5 design. If not, the transfer rate was only 33 MBps. The ATA-5 is also referred to as UDMA/66.
ATA-6	ATA-6, released in 2000, offers transfer rates as high as 100 MBps. An 80-conductor ribbon cable is again used with this design. If the motherboard is not designed for the ATA-6 specification, then the highest transfer speed will probably be 33 MBps.
ATA-7	ATA-7, also known as ATA/133, is the latest and fastest version of the ATA series. It is capable of producing a transfer data rate of 133 MBps. ATA-7 was introduced in 2005 and uses Ultra DMA 133 and an 80-conductor data cable.

Goodheart-Willcox Publisher

Figure 10-34 Requirements surrounding ATA standards have changed many times.

to overcome the limitations of the ATA drive. The SATA 1.0 maximum transfer rate is 150 MBps and as high as 600 MBps for SATA 3.0, as shown in Figure 10-36. The table expresses the data rates in both gigabits and megabytes. SATA is a serial device, and serial data rates are normally expressed in bits. However, since bytes are the common measure used for parallel devices such as the original ATA hard disk drive, the chart uses both serial and parallel rates so that SATA technology can be more easily compared to other technology data rates. As of July 2020, the latest version is SATA version 3.5.

Note that 3.0 and 3.5 have the same transfer rate, as the changes in 3.5 were to improve other aspects of the drive specification. SATA has a higher performance than ATA because it moves data to the motherboard in a series of packets in a similar fashion to USB and FireWire. The ATA transfer rate is slower because it is limited due to the clock frequency of the motherboard and the effect of induction caused by the design of the flat ribbon cable. The SATA design can achieve a higher data rate because it generates its own frequency for the data transfer, and its cable is designed to reduce the effects of electrical induction. As you recall from earlier chapters, induction can limit the frequency of data traveling through a conductor, reducing data transfer speeds.

A+ Note

It is common for the A+ Exams to include a question related to installing a second PATA drive and the correct primary and secondary jumper settings.

SATA was originally designed for internally connected PC devices. Later, the eSATA standard was developed for connecting external SATA devices. Standards for eSATA have the same data rates as corresponding SATA generations; the primary difference is that eSATA provides a SATA connection and electrical power to an external device. Note, while not on the CompTIA A+ Exams, you should be aware of Fibre Attached Technology Adapted (FATA). FATA is essentially a low-cost SATA disc equipped with a small external converter that bridges the interface to a Fibre Channel connection.

A+ **1101: 1.1, 3.1**

PATA Drive Installation

Figure 10-37 illustrates two drives, one primary and one secondary, connected to a motherboard using an IDE interface connection point. Typical motherboards provide

Figure 10-35 ATA drive cables come with 40 and 80 conductors. You must use an 80-conductor cable to meet the ATA-5, ATA-6, and ATA-7 data rates.

40-Conductor ATA Cable **80-Conductor ATA Cable**

Goodheart-Willcox Publisher

Figure 10-36 Data rates vary tremendously between SATA 1.0 and SATA 3.0.

SATA Transfer Rates

Standard	Gigabit/Second	Megabyte/Second
SATA 1.0	1.5 Gbps	150 MBps
SATA 2.0	3 Gbps	300 MBps
SATA 3.0	6 Gbps	600 MBps
SATA 3.5	6 Gbps	600 MBps

Goodheart-Willcox Publisher

two sets of connections identified as IDE0 and IDE1, which provide two channels of communication to hard drives and to other devices such as optical disc or tape drive systems. Each channel can provide an interface with the computer bus system for two hard drives, creating four separate physical drives. Each channel consists of one drive designated as primary or master and the other designated as secondary or slave. Moving jumper settings on the hard drive sets these designations, as shown in Figure 10-38.

When two or more drives are installed on the same PC system, you must designate one as primary and one as secondary because the two drives share the same communication cable. Failure to configure one device as primary and the other as secondary can result in hard drive failure. Think about the partitions in the hard drive system. When the PC is booted, it must be able to differentiate between the two or more drives. If the BIOS cannot tell the difference between the two drives, it will not be able to locate the active boot partition. By making one the primary and the other the secondary, one drive becomes the extension of the other, and the BIOS system can now differentiate between the two drives and try each one out as it searches for the master boot partition.

Tech Tip

Historically, multiple hard drives have been referred to as *master* or *slave*. You may also see these referred to as *primary* and *secondary* or *default* and *secondary*.

1102: 3.1 A+

SATA Drive Installation

1101: 1.1, 3.1, 3.3 A+

SATA drives use a thin, flat or round cable with seven conductors and a 7-pin cable connector. This is quite a reduction in cable width compared to the width of the 40- and 80-conductor ATA cables. Because of this reduction, the SATA cable is much easier to route inside the computer chassis. During the early implementation of

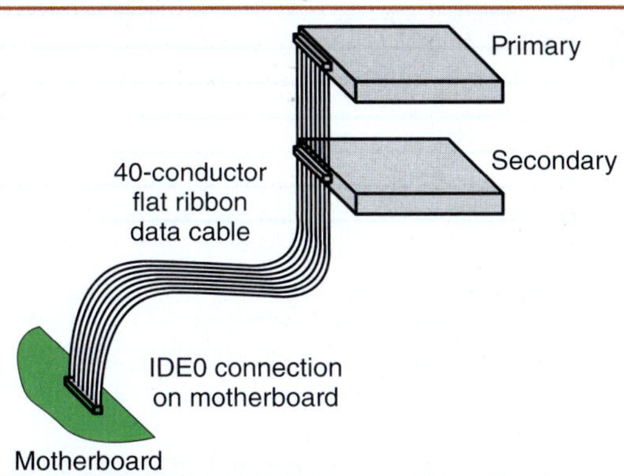

Figure 10-37 When two hard drives are connected to one motherboard, one is configured as the *master* or *primary*, the other as the *slave* or *secondary*.

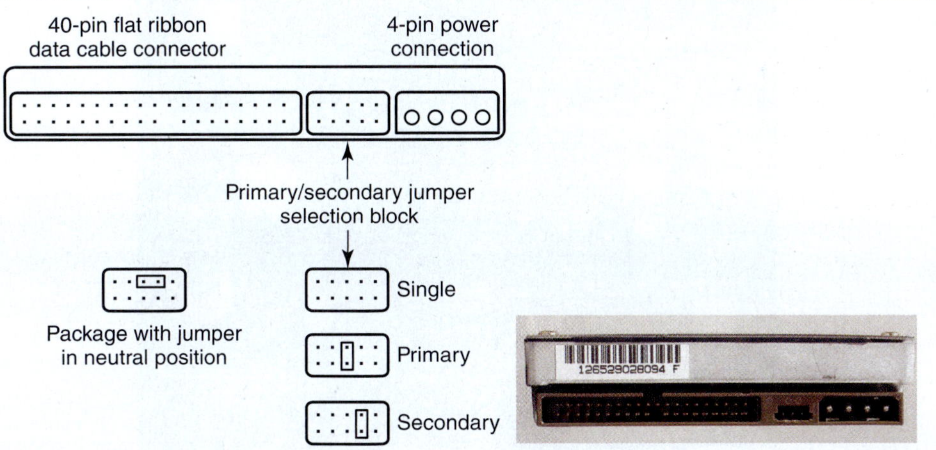

Figure 10-38 Moving jumper settings on the hard drive sets the designation of primary or secondary.

SATA, regular ATA drives were fitted with adapters and a SATA conversion chip at the manufacturer and then marketed as SATA drives.

Turn your attention to Figure 10-39, which shows the conductors inside a SATA cable. Notice that three of the seven conductors in the illustration are identified with the letter *G*, which represents ***ground***. The pair of conductors used to transmit data are marked *DT–* and *DT+*, and the pair of conductors used to receive data are marked *DR–* and *DR+*. Both pairs of cables and the grounds are twisted together to reduce the negative effect of electrical induction on the data transfer rate.

SATA cable connectors are keyed to prevent a user from incorrectly connecting the cable to the motherboard or to the hard drive. The SATA cable is connected to the motherboard at locations identified as SATA 0 and SATA 1, as shown in Figure 10-40.

The SATA drive is designed with only two sets of connectors: power and data, as shown in Figure 10-41. There are no primary/secondary jumper pin connections because each device is automatically set as primary. There is no secondary in the SATA design.

An existing computer system may be upgraded to SATA by using a SATA host adapter card, which installs in an available PCI slot. The SATA drive is then connected to the host adapter card using a SATA cable. When using a host adapter card, you must check that the BIOS and motherboard will support the SATA technology, and even if SATA is supported, the motherboard BIOS may report the SATA drive as a SCSI drive. The SATA system should perform normally even if it is identified as a SCSI drive.

Tech Tip

Always verify a hard drive it faulty before replacing it. Try installing the suspect drive in another PC to verify it is indeed bad. There are many items, such as the data cable, the EIDE on the motherboard, or a boot sector virus, that would make the hard drive appear to be defective.

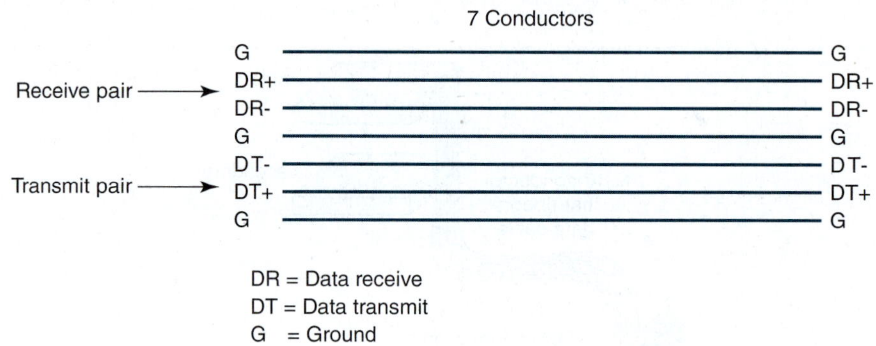

Figure 10-39 The SATA cable consists of seven conductors—two sets of transmitting and receiving pairs and three separate grounds.

Goodheart-Willcox Publisher

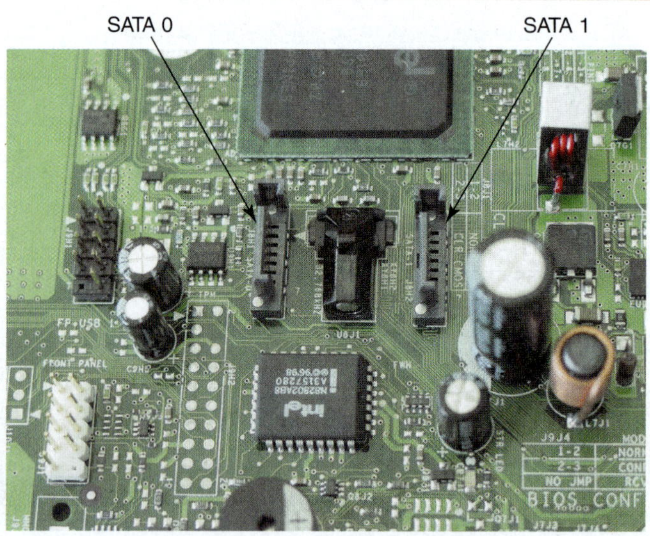

Figure 10-40 The SATA cable is connected to the motherboard at SATA-specific connections, typically identified as SATA 0 or SATA 1.

Goodheart-Willcox Publisher

Note that only one SATA drive can be connected on a SATA cable. This means that each motherboard SATA connection can only support a single SATA device.

eSATA Drive Installation

1101: 3.1, 3.4 A+

SATA drives can also be connected from the exterior through specially designed SATA bays. Figure 10-42 shows a SATA bay used to connect a SATA drive to a computer system from outside the case. SATA bays are also referred to as *hard drive docks*, *docking stations*, and *docking bays*. The SATA drive is simply inserted into the drive bay. You do not need to turn off the computer power before inserting the SATA drive because it is designed as a hot-swap device. SATA bays can be added to an existing computer using any empty drive bay in the front of the computer case. The electronics incorporated into the bay case allow the SATA device to be hot-swappable.

A+ Note

Be able to identify a cable type when presented with a picture or drawing of a connector or port such as PATA, SATA, and eSATA.

The SATA drive adapter kit in Figure 10-43 allows an internal SATA drive to be connected to an external USB port on a computer. A USB-to-PATA or USB-to-SATA 7 adapter can be used to connect any device designed to be installed internally in a computer to an external USB port. For example, a PATA drive can be connected to an external USB port and then accessed by the computer after a reboot. The typical adapter kit comes with a power supply that converts 120-VAC power to the 12 VDC required by the drive. The adapter is designed with a 40-pin PATA connector and a

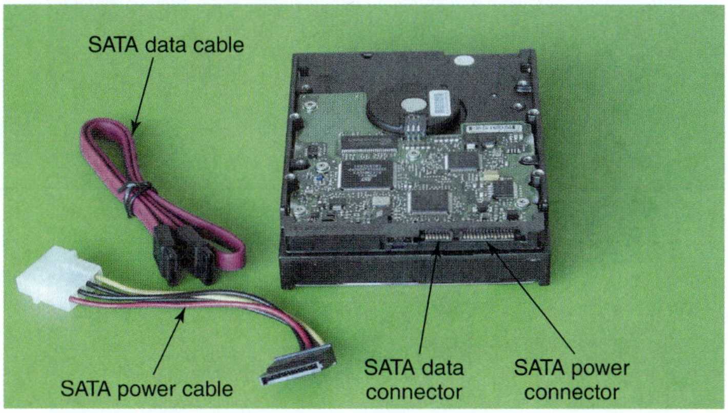

Goodheart-Willcox Publisher

Figure 10-41 SATA drives have only two connectors: one data connector and one power connector.

Figure 10-42 SATA bays allow for the insertion or removal of a SATA drive without having to power down the computer. Often, the bay doors include a notched cutout (A) for thin, laptop-style drives as well as a spring-activated bay door (B) for full-size drives.

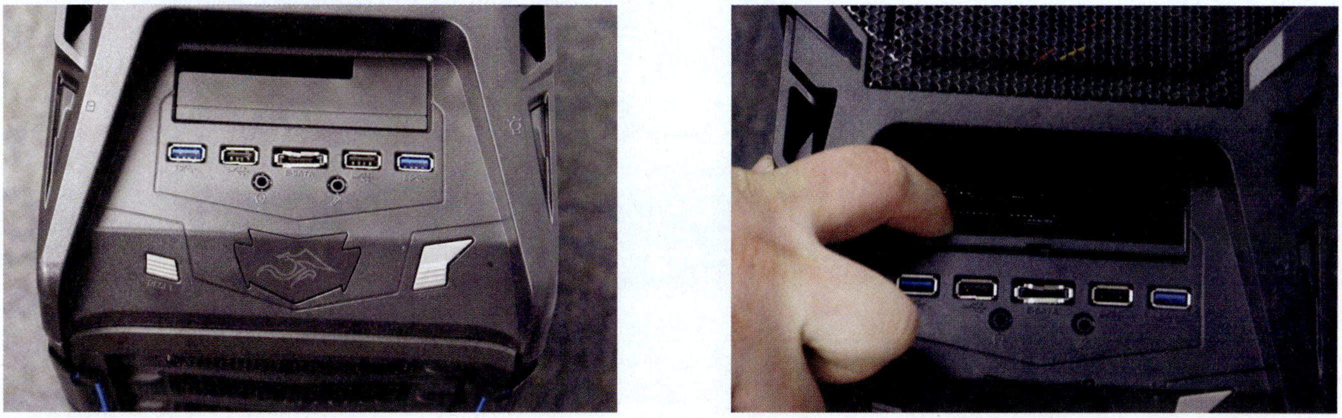

A B

Goodheart-Willcox Publisher

SATA connector, which connect to the computer through a USB port. The adapter is not limited to hard drives and can also be used for internal devices such as an optical drive.

There are also other products designed to support exterior connections of internal devices. In Figure 10-44, you can see how an external port and 12-VDC power supply connector can be added to an exterior slot on the computer case. After the exterior SATA port is installed, a SATA device and power can be connected to the expansion port. The power connection adapter in Figure 10-45 connects SATA devices to a 12-VDC, 4-pin peripheral power connector (Molex connector).

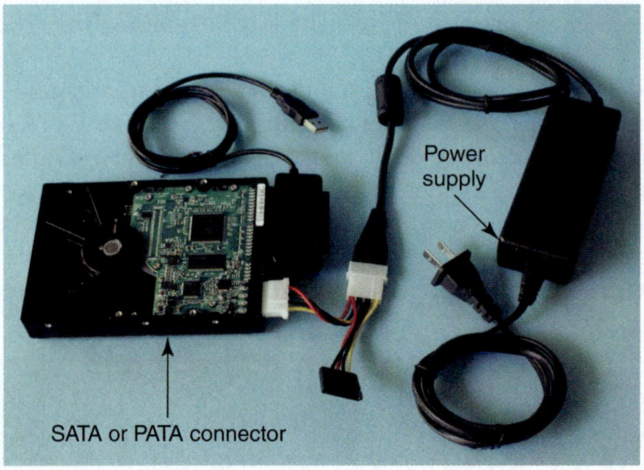

Figure 10-43 SATA adapters allow for internal SATA drives to be connected externally via USB.

Goodheart-Willcox Publisher

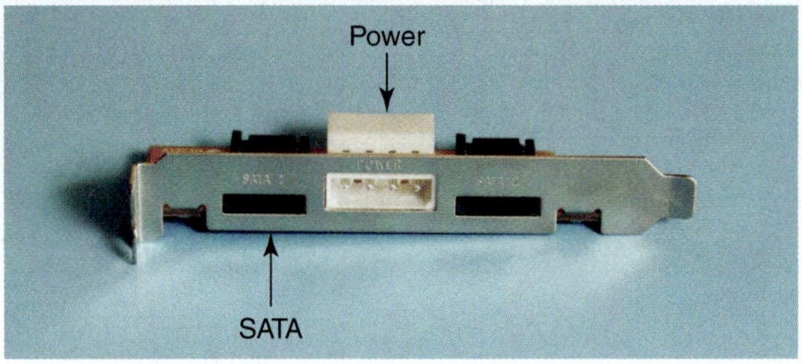

Figure 10-44 External SATA ports can be added as an expansion card inside a computer.

Goodheart-Willcox Publisher

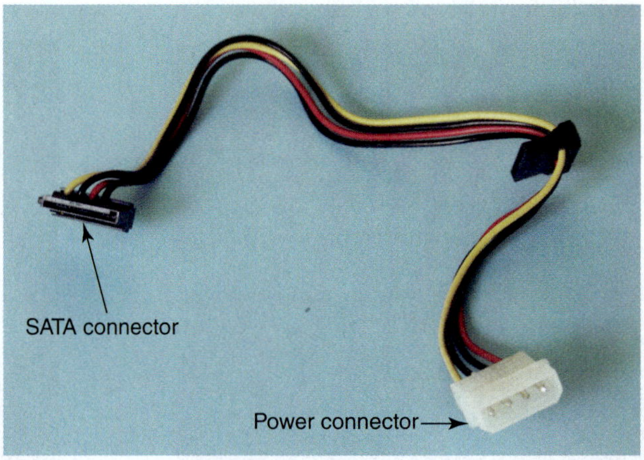

Figure 10-45 An adapter can be used for converting a standard 12-VDC Molex connector to supply power to two SATA devices.

Goodheart-Willcox Publisher

10.7 SCSI System

1101: 3.1

A+ Note

The number of SCSI devices allowed can make for a tricky question on the A+ Certification Exams. When asked how many devices can be connected to a SCSI-1 cable, the correct answer is eight. However, if eight is not one of the choices, the answer is seven. The key is to examine how the question is worded. A SCSI cable can connect to eight devices, but that includes an adapter card. In truth, a SCSI cable connects the adapter card to a maximum of seven devices. In various reference materials, you will see it written that seven devices can be connected to a SCSI-1 cable because the host adapter card is understood to be a necessary part of the installation. Always read and answer the questions carefully.

Small Computer System Interface (SCSI) (pronounced *skuzzy*) refers to a set of standards for connecting up to seven peripheral devices, often storage devices, to a PC using an adapter board and one flat ribbon cable. This is the standard system used by Apple Macintosh and many Unix mainframe systems to connect peripherals. Because it was expensive, SCSI technology was slow coming to the PC market and was first used in the IBM market for file servers that required a lot of disk storage. *File servers* are like super PCs that control network systems. They are covered in more detail in later chapters.

The SCSI standard was developed, in part, to remedy compatibility problems between PCs and aftermarket hardware. Originally, PC manufacturers created proprietary systems, and both upgrading and expansion were challenging due to compatibility issues. SCSI was designed to eliminate some of these issues by creating a standard that was available to all manufacturers.

The SCSI system was also designed to free the CPU from the burden of processing all data transactions. SCSI interfaces with a PC through an intelligent controller card inserted into the expansion bus. A SCSI bus cable connects the SCSI card to a series of devices, which communicate freely along the cable as directed by the controller card, which eliminates the need for the CPU's involvement.

Figure 10-46 shows a typical SCSI-1 installation, which allows for a maximum of eight devices—including the host adapter card—to be connected to a SCSI-1 cable.

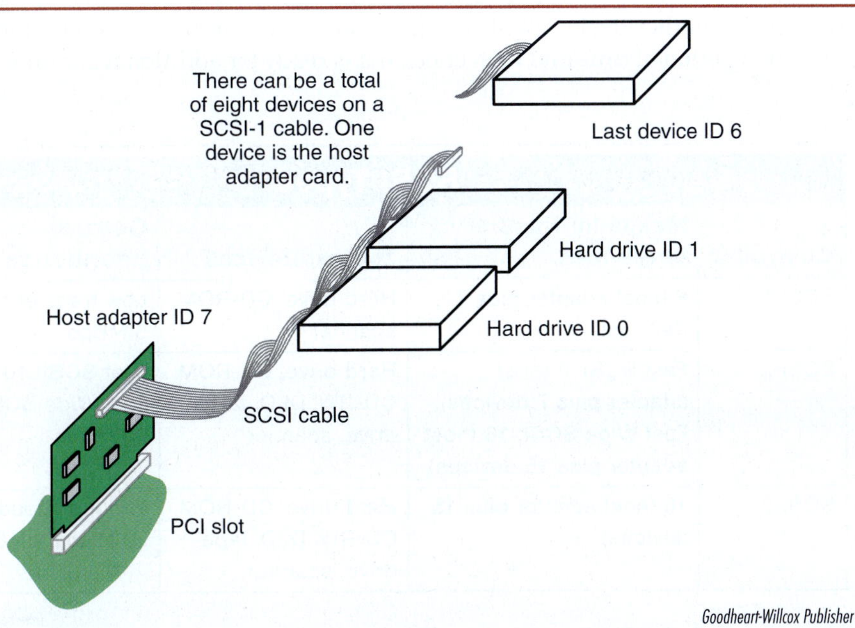

Figure 10-46 There can be a total of eight devices, including the adapter card, arranged in a SCSI-1 setup.

The assigned ID numbers range from zero to seven (eight numbers total). SCSI-2 allows for 16 devices (host adapter included) to be assigned.

Many styles of SCSI have developed over the years. The main three classifications are SCSI-1, SCSI-2, and SCSI-3, as listed in Figure 10-47, but each of these has variations that can cause confusion. Some of the variations are Wide SCSI, Fast SCSI, Fast Wide SCSI, Ultra SCSI, Ultra2 SCSI, and Wide Ultra2 SCSI. When selecting SCSI hardware to install or replace, you must exercise caution. Though SCSI was originally created to help solve compatibility problems, many of the SCSI systems are still not compatible with each other. The problem lies in the many proprietary variations.

You must be careful to match the device to the proper SCSI technology. ***SCSI-1*** uses an 8-bit system and supports data transfer rates as high as 5 MBps. It was the first SCSI technology and uses a 25-conductor flat ribbon cable. ***SCSI-2*** operates similarly to SCSI-1, but it uses a wider 50-conductor connector and only supports up to seven devices on one cable. ***Wide SCSI*** uses a wider cable with 68 conductors and can transfer 16 bits of data at one time. ***Fast SCSI*** uses an 8-bit bus like SCSI-1, but it has a much higher transfer rate of 10 MBps. There are also Fast-20, Fast-40, and Fast-80 SCSI systems. The last two digits of the name reflect the speed of data transfer in megabytes per second (MBps). The speed of each can be doubled by using a Fast Wide device. Hence, a normal SCSI that is 10 MBps will become 20 MBps when employed as a Fast Wide SCSI.

Another variation of SCSI is Serial Attached SCSI (SAS). The current version is SAS-5 which achieves 45 Gbit/s transfer speed. While older parallel SCSI limited connected devices to 8 or 16 devices, serial SCSI allows up to 65,535 devices.

Advantages of SCSI

One advantage of SCSI is that SCSI devices can be connected inside or outside the computer case, allowing some flexibility for the user. SCSI also has very high data transfer rates. Older SCSI hard drives were much faster than IDE hard drives, though newer EIDE drives have closed that gap. Most SCSI devices are also fully compatible with the plug-and-play specification, making installation simple. It should be noted, however, that some older SCSI systems may not be plug-and-play compatible.

A big advantage of SCSI in a multitasking environment is the ability to disconnect the communication between devices when the device is not needed, thus conserving resources. For example, when a tape is rewinding, it does not need to maintain its connection to another device. SCSI can disconnect the communication to and from the tape for a period of time and then check if it is ready for additional communication.

Figure 10-47 There are many styles of SCSI that have been developed over the years.

SCSI Types

Controller	Maximum Number of Devices	Typical Devices	General Information
SCSI-1	8 (host adapter plus 7 devices)	Hard drive, CD-ROM, scanner	Low transfer rate, 5 MBps
SCSI-2	Fast SCSI: 8 (host adapter plus 7 devices); Fast Wide SCSI: 16 (host adapter plus 15 devices)	Hard drive, CD-ROM, CD-RW, DVD, tape drive, scanner	Fast SCSI: 10 MBps; Fast Wide SCSI: 20 MBps
SCSI-3	16 (host adapter plus 15 devices)	Hard drive, CD-ROM, CD-RW, DVD, tape drive, scanner	Various speeds from 20 MBps to 160 MBps

Goodheart-Willcox Publisher

In the SCSI technology system, equipment can be easily exchanged. At most, the driver may need to be upgraded. To a SCSI host adapter, all hard drives look the same, as do other SCSI devices such as printers and optical drives. Of course, the total capacity of the drives may differ. There is no need for primary and secondary arrangements as there is with IDE/EIDE. Each device is given its own unique ID number.

SCSI ID

SCSI devices must have a unique ***SCSI ID number***, which is used to identify a given SCSI device. The ID range for the typical SCSI-1 is from zero to seven (eight total ID numbers). When two devices attempt to control the SCSI bus at the same time, the device with the higher number takes control.

While any device connected on the SCSI cable can have any ID number assignable, there are some common assignments. The host adapter is usually assigned the number *7*, making it the highest priority, and hard drives are usually assigned *0* and *1*. These are normal SCSI assignments, but they are not mandatory nor a recognized standard; it is simply a general practice.

The original SCSI limit of eight devices was first expanded using SCSI bus extenders. The bus extenders were integrated circuit cards that connected as SCSI devices and allowed an additional seven devices to be connected within a SCSI system. See Figure 10-48. As the SCSI-1 system was expanded, an additional system of identification was needed, resulting in the development of logical unit numbers. A ***logical unit number (LUN)*** is a unique identification given to devices connected to a SCSI extender. Like SCSI IDs, LUN IDs range from zero to seven.

Expanders can also be found in some SCSI-2 systems and may be referred to as ***expanders***, ***repeaters***, and ***regenerators***. The use of an LUN ID is not limited to only SCSI storage drives and is often used to identify nonstorage devices connected on a common SCSI cable, such as SCSI-compatible CD-ROM, DVD, and tape drives.

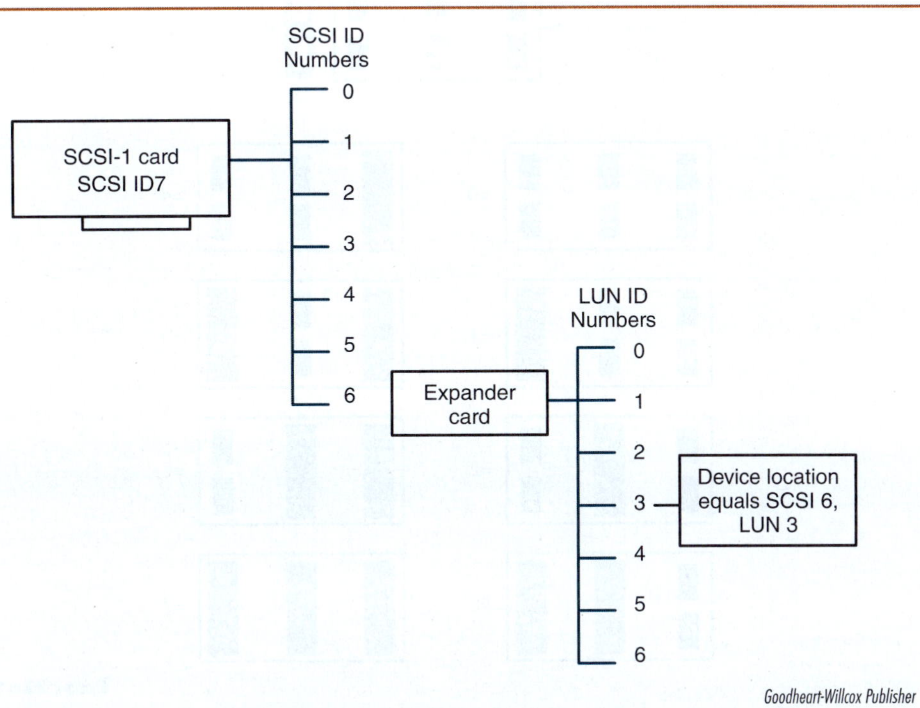

Figure 10-48 The SCSI limit of eight devices can be expanded by using expander cards, which allow an additional seven devices to be connected.

SCSI ID Jumpers

Older SCSI systems used jumpers to identify devices. Figure 10-49 illustrates how a set of pins and jumpers might look on a SCSI device. The pins are actual electrical connections, and the jumpers are used to make an electrical connection across pairs of pins. The jumpers are set in the binary pattern that represents the SCSI ID number. If you have trouble interpreting the jumper patterns, you may wish to review Chapter 1, which illustrates and discusses binary numbers.

LVD and HVD

SCSI systems communicate using two different voltage levels identified as *High Voltage Differential (HVD)* and *Low Voltage Differential (LVD)*. HVD uses 5 volts for a high and 0 volts for a low. LVD uses 3.3 volts for a high and 0 volts for a low. The high- and low-voltage levels are represented by a binary 1 or 0, respectively. The advantage of HVD is that data can be transmitted on cables up to 25 meters long, while LVD is limited to cables 5 meters long.

The SCSI Trade Association website has excellent reference materials, such as detailed charts of SCSI connectors. Additionally, Adaptec and other hard drive manufacturer websites contain SCSI information.

SCSI Commands and Terminology

In the SCSI system, there are two classifications of hardware relating to communication between SCSI devices: *initiators* and *targets*. The SCSI host adapter card is usually the initiator, while the devices connected to the SCSI bus (printers, hard drives, tape drives, and other SCSI devices) are usually the targets.

SCSI has its own set of commands, which is used to control the flow of data and the communication between targets and initiators. There are also nine special control signals used in a SCSI system:

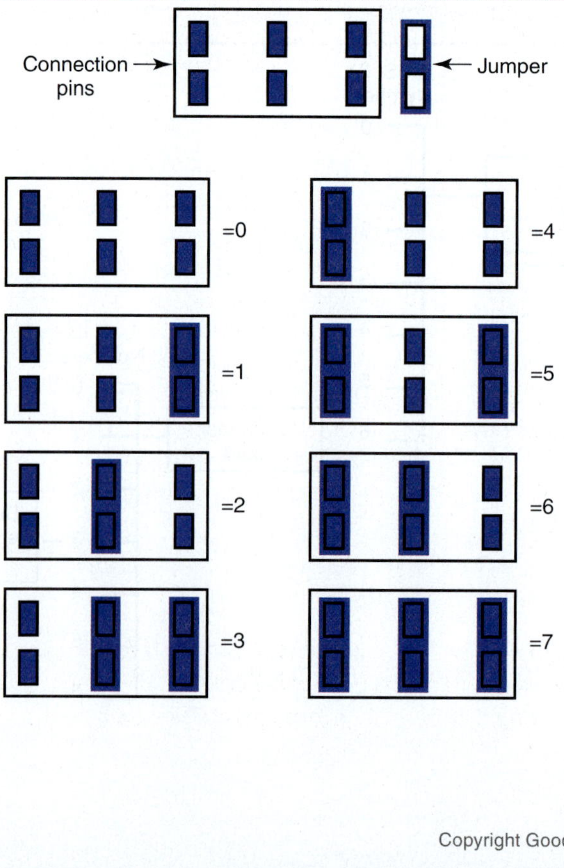

Figure 10-49 Jumpers are set in the binary pattern that represents the SCSI ID number.

Goodheart-Willcox Publisher

- C/D (Control/Data): This control signal allows the target to signal if it will return a command or data to the initiator. The initiator will then wait for the data or command.
- I/O (Input/Output): This indicates whether the target will be sending or receiving on the data bus.
- MSG (Message): The target uses this control signal to send error messages or status conditions back to the initiator.
- REQ (Request): This control signal allows the target to obtain data from the bus.
- ACK (Acknowledge): This is a reply signal sent after the REQ signal. It acknowledges the REQ signal and takes control of the bus.
- BSY (Busy): This control signal lets other devices know that a device is busy.
- SEL (Select): This control signal is used to select a target device.
- ATN (Attention): This control signal informs the target that a message is coming.
- RST (Reset): This control signal resets all devices on the bus system.

These signals are sent on wires inside the complete cable assembly and are invisible to the user. By placing a high- or low-voltage level on the wire, a signal is sent between initiator and target devices. Additional wire in the cable assembly supplies data and power.

SCSI Cable

SCSI cables are either single-ended or differential. A *single-ended* cable simply carries the signal from the initiator to the target. Each wire carries the signal to the target and to a common ground, and there is a terminating resistor located at each end of the cable to absorb stray signals.

In a *differential* design, a pair of wires is used for each transmitted signal. By using a pair, the signal travels simultaneously to and from both the initiator and target, cancelling the effects of electrical noise generation. The system still uses terminating resistors at each end to absorb the signals. The main advantage of the differential design is that it can be used for greater distances, up to 25 meters. In high-speed data transmissions, a single-ended cable may need to be as short as 1.5 meters.

SCSI Termination

Each end of the SCSI cable must be terminated immediately after the last device on the end of the cable; otherwise, data would be distorted. The high-speed transmission of data through the cable would produce an effect similar to radio broadcast waves, and these waves would echo and return to the ends of the cable, causing distortion. Cable termination is classified as either active or passive.

Active termination uses resistors to terminate the cable on each end and is powered through the cable itself and uses voltage regulators that maintain a constant voltage. *Passive termination* uses a single resister and a voltage regulator to control the amount of voltage transmitted inside the cable and to absorb the signals at the end of the cable. Passive termination allows greater lengths of SCSI cable to be used and is typically used for cable runs outside the computer case to connect devices such as flatbed scanners.

SCSI Bus Operation

The first part of communication on the SCSI bus is the control of the bus, which can only be attempted while there is no active BSY or SEL signal; both BSY and SEL must be idle. Only one device can communicate on the bus at a time, so the device

> **Tech Tip**
> When establishing a SCSI system with multiple devices, install the host adapter card first, followed by one device at a time. By using this method, it is easy to isolate a problem with an individual device if it arises during assembly. Also, all devices on your SCSI chain must support (or not support) parity. Some SCSI devices use parity, and others do not.

must gain exclusive control of the bus, and the device that has control is the *initiator*. When a device is attempting to take control of the bus, it is called the *arbitration phase*. Once the initiator has taken control of the bus, it identifies the target device. Identification of the target device is called the *selection phase*.

The individual devices negotiate the control of the SCSI bus. When two devices attempt to take control of the bus at the same time, the device with the higher-assigned ID number wins control. This is the reason that the host adapter is usually assigned the highest number.

The initiator sends a BSY signal and SEL signal. After the initiator has transmitted data or a command, it then releases the BSY signal. The target then receives the data and issues a BSY signal until a reply with data or a command, such as ACK, is transmitted. The following steps are an example of how a typical communication might take place between two devices:

1. The system checks that the bus is idle with no BSY or SEL signal.
2. Arbitration takes place until the chosen initiator takes control.
3. The selection phase occurs.
4. The target device acknowledges the communication link.
5. The target notifies the initiator that it is ready to receive data.
6. The data is transferred to the target device.
7. Status of the data transfer is maintained. For example, are there any errors?
8. A message indicating all the data have been transferred is sent.
9. The bus is released to all devices.

Serial Attached SCSI

Serial Attached SCSI (SAS) is the latest development for SCSI technology and is similar in design to SATA. An SAS host adapter card can connect to two types of drives: SAS and SATA. Many different types of SAS cable designs are mostly proprietary. Some SAS cables look like SATA cables. Figure 10-50 shows an SAS cable that consists of an SAS connector, a SATA connector, and a 4-pin peripheral power connector (Molex connector). The SAS connector connects directly to an SAS hard drive, the SATA connector connects to the motherboard SATA port, and the power connector provides 12 VDC to the drive.

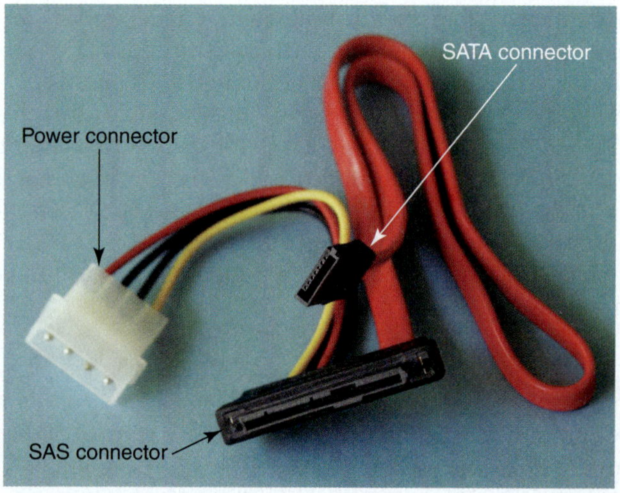

Figure 10-50 SAS cables often consist of an SAS connector, a SATA connector, and a 4-pin Molex connector.

Goodheart-Willcox Publisher

Figure 10-51 shows an SAS cable that supports multiple SATA drives connected to an SAS host adapter. Look closely at the red cable assembly. This cable is equipped with one mini-SAS (mSAS) and four SATA connectors. The four SATA connectors connect to SATA disk drives or to SATA solid-state drives, and the single mSAS connector attaches to an SAS host adapter card located in a PCI or PCIe slot inside the computer. This cable is designed for RAID arrangements, which is a disk configuration that provides redundancy to prevent data loss when a disk device fails. There will be much more about RAID in a later chapter.

SAS can achieve data transfer rates as high as 6 Gbps. Note that SAS data rates are expressed in gigabits per second (Gbps), not gigabytes per second (GBps). Gbps is used as a measurement for serial data transfers, and since SAS transfers data serially, Gbps is technically correct. For comparison to other SCSI standards, 6 Gbps is equal to 375 MBps. This is more than twice as fast as the 160-MBps transfer rate associated with the SCSI-3 standard. While SCSI devices still exist in network storage environments, SAS devices have made SCSI a legacy device.

SAS disk arrays create large storage pools for networks. A typical PC user does not require the use of SCSI or SAS arrays, so these arrays are employed commonly to support network server storage. An SAS switch provides multiple disk connections and one Ethernet port, which allows the switch to be connected to a network system. Mini-SAS cables are often used with SAS switches and connect between the switch and other storage devices or network servers. Advantages of SAS over SCSI include the following:

- Higher data transfer speeds
- Can be used to create arrays containing 65,000 devices with expanders
- Does not require termination like SCSI
- The cost of installation can be reduced because SAS host adapters can connect to SATA storage devices

10.8 **Solid-State Drives**

1101: 1.1, 3.3 A+

As you may recall from previous discussion, a *solid-state drive (SSD)* is a storage system designed with no moving parts that consists entirely of DRAM chips. It uses flash memory in place of disks or discs for storage, which makes for faster data transfer, less power consumption, quieter operation, and no risk of parts wearing out over time. SSDs do not have latency issues when accessing a data location as

Figure 10-51 SAS cables can also be made to support multiple SATA drives, including mini-SAS devices.

Goodheart-Willcox Publisher

A+ Note

You may see a question about a problem installing a new SSD on an older computer system. The correct answer to remedy the problem will most likely relate to upgrading the motherboard BIOS. An old system may not recognize an SSD.

storage devices that use disks or discs do, and computers booting from SSDs boot faster than disk-based systems.

The most common application of SSDs is in portable computers. SSDs weigh less and are much smaller in physical size than traditional laptop storage drives, which helps make laptops and portable devices lighter and thinner. The SSD uses both ATA-6 and SATA data interfaces. Solid-state drives are much quicker than traditional hard drives. To increase the performance of a computer system, an SSD is often used in combination with a hard drive. This allows overall performance to be improved without completely replacing the low-cost hard drive with a much higher-cost SSD.

Additionally, SSDs can be used to augment the hard drive system in desktop computers by providing a temporary storage space for frequently accessed files or programs. When the SSD is used as a temporary storage location for frequently accessed files or programs, it is referred to as **solid-state disk caching**. The SSD is used to store frequently accessed files and programs to allow for quicker loading. The operating system keeps track of which programs and files are commonly accessed, and it stores an up-to-date copy on the SSD. After the computer finishes its boot sequence, the file or program loads much quicker as compared to a system that relies solely on a hard drive for file and program storage. Figure 10-52 shows how an Intel motherboard identifies a SATA port used specifically for solid-state disk caching. Solid-state disk caching is referred to by Intel as Smart Response Technology (SRT).

A+ 1101: 3.4

M.2 Drives

The M.2 format was designed to overcome the limitations of SATA (600 MBps) performance as SSDs have become faster. An M.2 drive can use multiple "lanes" and achieve theoretical transfer rates of up to 4.0 GBps, which is more than six times the performance. Note that the laptop or desktop must have the ability to handle these kinds of speeds. If the system is an older system, it may still be limited to the 600 MBps, making the SSD installation nonproductive. M.2 cards are also smaller by 8 mm than the older mSATA approach.

A+ 1101: 3.3

NVMe

NVMe is a standard created by a consortium of SSD vendors. This standard has "lanes" as with M.2, but a modern PC can have as many as 16 lanes for a theoretical throughput of 16 GBps. These SSDs can use a PCIe slot on the motherboard with an adapter. Older systems with antiquated BIOS may not support this approach. NVMe drives can also use an M.2 slot, but compatibility should be checked first by going to the vendor site.

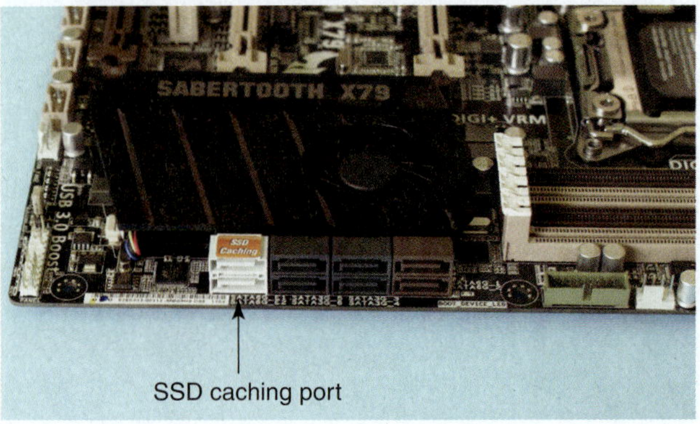

Figure 10-52 Intel motherboards often provide a special SATA port to support SSD caching.

Goodheart-Willcox Publisher

SATA 2.5 and Beyond

SATA 2.5 has been available since 2005, whereas the SATA 3.3 revision has been available since 2016 and represents improved performance. All 3.X variants of the SATA specification doubled the throughput from 3 Gbps to 6 Gbps at a minimum, which is still much slower than M.2 or NVMe.

A+ 1101: 3.3

There have been a number of revisions to the SATA standard over the years. In 2011, SATA version 3.1 was released and included mSATA for solid-state drives, particularly in mobile computing devices. The mSATA standard uses a connector that appears much like a PCI Express mini-card. Version 3.1 also introduced SATA optical drives that do not draw power when idle. Revision 3.2 was released in 2013 and included SATA Express, which has an interface that combines SATA and PCI Express buses. SATA version 3.3 was released in 2018 and included a technology called *Shingled Magnetic Recording (SMR)* that supports a 25-percent increase in hard drive capacity, which is achieved by overlapping tracks on the media.

10.9 Virtual Hard Disk

A+ 1102: 1.7

A **virtual hard disk (VHD)** is a file that behaves exactly like a physical hard disk. The ability to create a VHD from Computer Management was first introduced in Windows 7. Refer to Figure 10-24 to see the **Create VHD** and **Mount VHD** options. Selecting the **Create VHD** option will open the dialog box shown in Figure 10-53.

After creating a VHD, it must be mounted, which makes it available for access. The VHD can be used as a backup location for the existing operating system. For example, the VHD can be used for a complete backup of the entire operating system and important files. If needed, it can later be used to recreate the original operating system and files much in the same way a recovery partition is used to reinstall an operating system after a system failure.

Another way the VHD is used is to run or test another operating system. For example, after a new operating system has been installed on a computer, it is discovered that the new operating system will not support an older software application or hardware device such as a printer. A VHD can be created, and the legacy

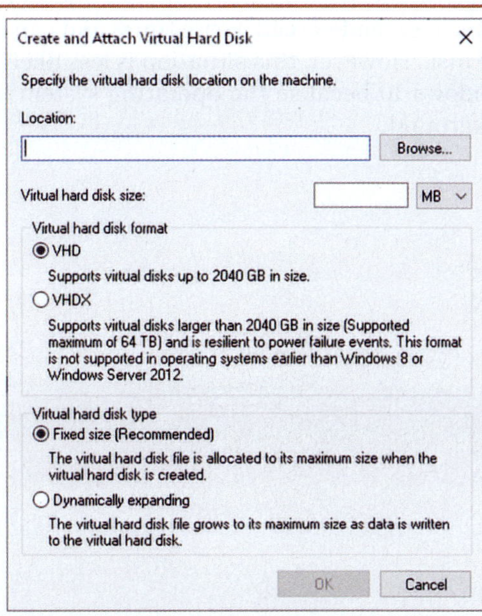

Goodheart-Willcox Publisher

Figure 10-53 Users can create and attach virtual hard disks in Windows by opening Computer Management and selecting **Disk Management>More Actions>Create VHD or Attach VHD**.

operating system can be installed in the VHD, thus allowing the older software application or legacy hardware device to function.

A VHD can also be used to test a new operating system. For example, you can create a VHD, install a newer operating system on a computer system, and test it out before replacing the existing operating system. You could create a VHD on a Windows 10 computer and then install Windows 11 into the VHD. The VHD can be made bootable so that the VHD containing the Windows 11 system becomes the boot partition or drive.

10.10 Troubleshooting Hard Drives and RAID Arrays

When a hard drive is bad, the easiest solution is to replace it. Under normal circumstances, a hard drive is not a component a technician repairs; rather, it is more cost-effective to replace the bad drive with a better one. However, a user could experience symptoms related to a hard drive error that do not require replacement. Common symptoms of hard drive issues include read/write failures, slow performance, loud clicking noises, RAID arrays not working, and S.M.A.R.T. errors.

A+ 1102: 3.1

Read/Write Failure

A *read/write failure* is often the product of the inability of the BIOS to read the first sector of a drive of any kind. Read/write errors on boot should be considered catastrophic, especially for magnetic drives, because the critical portion or portions of the drive have most likely been damaged by a head crash. If the read/write error occurs during normal operation, the chkdsk tool can be used to repair or mark off the sector causing the problem. However, this can also be indicative of progressive drive damage.

A+ 1101: 5.3 1102: 3.1

Slow Performance

Most often, slow magnetic drive performance is the product of degradation caused by fragmentation of files on the drive due to numerous additions and deletions. This typically results in slow or extended read/write times and can normally be resolved by defragmenting the disk. However, this situation is less likely to occur under normal operation of Windows 10 because the operating system takes care of defragmentation in the background.

Loud Clicking Noise

1101: 5.3 A+

If you can verify that the clicking noise arises from the magnetic hard drive, be prepared for a replacement. Loud clicking noises are indicative of a catastrophic condition such as a head crash. The standard method for improving resilience is a vigorous backup philosophy, including SSD, magnetic drives, and cloud-based approaches.

RAID Not Found

1101: 5.3 A+

RAID arrays are commonly found in servers. When a server is having an issue, and the user attempts to access it, they may encounter an error stating that RAID cannot be found. Chances are, the RAID array is present, but the computer or controller is not configured properly. Be sure to check the BIOS settings to ensure it is configured to allow for RAID and that all the motherboard connections are made correctly. Ensure the power and data cables connect securely to the drive, and troubleshoot the hard drive on ports that appear to have an issue. Identifying the faulty port tells you which drive inside the system is behaving improperly. If all devices have already passed through a diagnostics test, chances are either the hard drive or controller is undetected or, possibly, the software is malfunctioning. There will be much more about RAID in a later chapter.

RAID Stops Working

1101: 5.3 A+

RAID 0 uses striping to distribute files across two drives to improve performance. If a RAID 0 failure occurs, the entire volume is lost, suggesting a vigorous backup program is mandatory. If a RAID 1 system loses a drive, the remaining drive can be used because RAID 1 is a redundant system designed to reduce risk. Simply replace the defective drive, synchronize the new drive to the others, and move on. RAID 5 failures will cause the loss of fault tolerance, but they are not initially catastrophic. However, replacement of the bad drive is warranted just as it is with RAID 1. There will be much more about RAID in a later chapter.

S.M.A.R.T. Errors

1101: 5.3 A+

A *Self-Monitoring and Repair Tool (S.M.A.R.T.) drive* can inform the user when troublesome behavior occurs on the drive. Check first to see if your vendor has software that assists in troubleshooting the drive. If that is not the case, a technician can run Windows Management Instrumentation. This is accomplished by entering the **WMIC** command in command prompt. After the directory changes, the technician should enter the command syntax diskdrive get status and press [Enter], which will result in a drive health status displaying.

Chapter Summary

10.1 Magnetic Storage Devices

- Magnetic storage devices operate on the principle that electrical energy can produce magnetism and magnetism can produce electrical energy.
- To read the data back from a disk, an electrical signal is generated from the magnetic patterns. Electrical energy can be produced by the motion of a magnetic field near a conductor.
- The conductor is wound around the top of the magnetic read/write head, which records and reads information on a magnetic medium. The read/write head is located at the end of an actuator arm, which moves the head over the disk.
- A typical hard disk drive consists of several platters in a stack. The top and bottom of each platter are coated with a thin film of metal oxide, which records the magnetic patterns introduced to the disk platter by the read/write head.
- Hard drive speeds are listed as 5,400 rpm, 7,200 rpm, 10,000 rpm, and 15,000 rpm. In general, the faster the hard drive, the less storage space and the greater the electrical power consumption.

10.2 Disk Geometry

- Tracks are a set of concentric circles where data are stored on a disk.
- Tracks are subdivided into physical sections called *sectors*.
- Clusters refer to file storage space and consist of one or more sectors.
- A cylinder is a vertical collection of one set of tracks. There is one cylinder for every stack of tracks.
- The low-level format is a process that determines the type of encoding to be performed on the disk platter and the sequence in which the read/write heads will access stored data.
- *Interleave factor* refers to the order in which sectors are laid out on a disk surface.
- Multiple zone recording (MZR), also called zone bit recording, provides twice as many sectors in the outermost tracks as compared to the innermost tracks.

10.3 Disk Partition Systems

- Hard drives can be divided into multiple partitions to simulate additional drives.
- The Master Boot Record (MBR) is a boot sector located at the beginning of a partition that identifies how and where an operating system is located so it can be booted. Similarly, the GUID Partition Table (GPT) is a disk partitioning method in which the layout of partition tables within a storage device are identified using globally unique identifiers (GUIDs).
- A logical drive is not a physically separate drive even though it appears to the user as a separate drive.
- The active partition is the partition from which the operating system will boot. It is the designated boot disk for the system.
- The Master Boot Record (MBR) contains partition information and a small amount of executable code that launches the computer operating system.
- The primary partition can contain the system files, the boot files, or a combination of both.
- GPT-based partition systems do not have the same limitations as MBR-based partition systems. The primary advantage is that you may create 128 primary partitions on a disk system initialized with GPT.
- The EFI System Partition (ESP) is a special area of the hard disk drive intended for use solely by the firmware and typically contains files and data required to boot the computer system.

- The Microsoft Reserved Partition (MSR), or System Reserved Partition, is a data partition that reserves a portion of disk space for use by the Windows operating system and is required for GUID partition tables.
- The proprietary recovery partition, also known as the original equipment manufacturer (OEM) partition, or factory recovery partition, is an optional partition created by the system's original equipment manufacturer (OEM).
- When a new hard disk drive is first installed on a computer that supports UEFI, it must be initialized before it can be partitioned. The Microsoft Support website states that disk initialization writes a disk signature, which is a unique identifier for a storage device that identifies the disk type and properties so that the Microsoft operating system can utilize the disk.
- The DiskPart utility is used to manage disk partitions and volumes from the command prompt.

10.4 File System Formats

- FAT16, FAT32, exFAT, NTFS, and ReFS are common file systems.
- NFS formatting was originally a Sun Microsystems implementation of a distributed network.
- Ext3 and Ext4 are what is called journaling file systems using the Linux operating system.
- HFS and HFS plus generally refer to an Apple Macintosh file system, although confusion can arise due to the use of the same nomenclature by IBM for their z-class systems.
- Before a hard disk can be used to store data, it must be formatted with a high-level format. A low-level format destroys all data on a disk, and a high-level format only the contents of the file table so that no file name is associated with the data clusters.

10.5 Disk and File Maintenance

- Disk Defragmenter is used when files become fragmented under normal disk operations.
- Solid-state drives generally do not require defragmentation or optimization.
- Chkdsk checks and repairs the integrity of the file system on a hard drive.
- The System File Checker (SFC) is a Windows utility that enables users to scan for and repair corrupted system files.
- Benchmark tests are performance tests that are conducted to compare different hardware and software.
- The technician can extend, split, or shrink a partition using the Disk Management tool.

10.6 PATA and SATA Hard Disk Interfaces

- Parallel ATA (PATA) is an interface standard for the connection of storage devices. PATA is in use today and is referred to as IDE or EIDE.
- Serial ATA (SATA) is a transport protocol that determines the amount of data that can be transferred between a motherboard and storage device.
- When two PATA drives are installed on the same cable, one drive must be designated the primary and the other the secondary.
- SATA drives do not have primary/secondary jumper pin connections, and only one drive can be installed per cable.

10.7 SCSI System

- Small Computer System Interface (SCSI) refers to a set of standards for connecting multiple peripheral devices, often storage devices, to a PC using an adapter board and up to seven devices on one flat ribbon cable.
- SCSI is the standard system used by Apple Macintosh and many Unix mainframe systems to connect peripherals.

- Advantages to SCSI include flexibility for the user, higher data transfer rates, and conservation of resources.
- All SCSI devices must have a unique SCSI ID number.
- SAS technology can achieve higher data transfer rates than SCSI and does not require termination.

10.8 Solid-State Drives

- Solid-state drives transfer data quicker, quieter, and use less power than disk or disc storage devices, and they do not have any moving parts, which can wear out in time.
- SSD formats include M.2, NVMe, and SATA 2.5.

10.9 Virtual Hard Disk

- A virtual hard disk (VHD) is a file that behaves exactly like a physical hard disk.
- The Computer Management utility is used to create and mount a virtual hard disk.

10.10 Troubleshooting Hard Drives and RAID Arrays

- Common symptoms of hard drive issues include read/write failures, slow performance, loud clicking noises, RAID arrays not working, and S.M.A.R.T. errors.

Review Questions

1. Explain how magnetic principles are applied to data storage.
2. Summarize the relationship between disk RPM and energy.
3. Describe disk geometry in terms of sections used to record data.
4. Describe the function and benefit of an interleave factor.
5. Differentiate among disk partition systems.
6. How does the maximum number of primary partitions identified by an MBR-based drive differ from that of a GPT-based drive?
7. Recall common file systems and their characteristics.
8. Summarize the purpose of a high-level format.
9. List utilities used for disk maintenance.
10. What command syntax is used to launch the System File Checker and repair any corrupted files?
11. Differentiate between PATA and SATA interfaces.
12. How many drives are designated as primary on a PC with two channels and four physical hard drives?
13. Compare SCSI and SAS technologies.
14. In terms of SCSI systems, what are initiators and targets?
15. Recall common uses of solid-state drives.
16. List four advantages of solid-state drives over disk- and disc-storage devices.
17. What is a virtual hard disk?
18. How is a VHD used?
19. List common hard drive symptoms.
20. Why are fragmentation-related errors less likely to occur in a Windows 10 system?

Sample A+ Exam Questions

1. You install a new second hard drive to increase the total storage capacity of a PC. Both hard drives are installed on the same PATA data cable. When you boot the system, the computer displays the BIOS information and the RAM test on the screen. After the RAM test is completed and passed, the PC hangs up. What is *most likely* the problem?
   A. The BIOS needs to be upgraded to match the new hard drive.
   B. A virus has been introduced into the system from the new hard drive.
   C. The jumper settings identifying primary and secondary are incorrect.
   D. The two drives' positions are reversed on the data cable.

2. Where in a FAT16 file system is the MBR located?
   A. In the first disk sector
   B. In the last disk sector
   C. Location varies according to the number of cylinders
   D. Only on a hard disk system formatted for NTFS4.0
3. Which of the following file systems is the default file system used for a Windows Vista clean install?
   A. FAT16
   B. FAT32
   C. VFAT
   D. NTFS
4. Which FAT file system is used for flash drives of 32 GB or larger?
   A. FAT12
   B. FAT16
   C. FAT32
   D. exFAT
5. A certain file consists of 12 sectors. The sectors are not contiguous but rather divided into two separate areas on the disk. Which of the following technical terms is used to describe this condition of file storage?
   A. Cross-linked sectors
   B. File fragmentation
   C. Multiple-zone recording
   D. Multiple-sector storage
6. Which of the following technologies is *not* used for disk storage?
   A. ATA
   B. IDE
   C. SCSI
   D. DDS
7. What is the size in bytes of the smallest typical disk sector?
   A. 256
   B. 512
   C. 1024
   D. 2048
8. What is the maximum number of hard drives that can be installed on a Wide SCSI-2 configuration?
   A. 5
   B. 9
   C. 15
   D. 24
9. Which is the correct path to Computer Management on a Windows 10 operating system?
   A. **Start>All apps>Accessories>System Tool>Disk Management**
   B. **Start>All apps>Windows Administrative Tools> Computer Management**
   C. **Start>Control Panel>Hardware and Sound**
   D. **Start>This PC>Properties>Device Manager**
10. What is the maximum number of hard disk drives that can be installed on a single motherboard PATA port?
    A. One
    B. Two
    C. Three
    D. Eight

Chapter 11

Optical Storage Technology

Learning Outcomes

11.1 Explain the manufacturing and operation of CD technology.
11.2 Explain data storage and retrieval using magneto-optical storage devices.
11.3 Compare CD and DVD construction.
11.4 Compare HD-DVD and Blu-ray Disc storage technologies.
11.5 Summarize the installation of an optical disc drive.
11.6 Identify digital rights management technologies.
11.7 Identify the most common problems encountered with an optical storage system.

A+ Certification Exam Objectives

The following A+ Certification Exam Objectives are covered in this chapter.

Exam 220-1101

3.0 Hardware

- 3.3 Given a scenario, select and install storage devices.

Exam 220-1102

1.0 Operating Systems

- 1.7 Given a scenario, apply application installation and configuration concepts.

2.0 Security

- 2.6 Given a scenario, configure a workstation to meet best practices for security.
- 2.9 Given a scenario, configure appropriate security settings on small office/home office (SOHO) wireless and wired networks.

4.0 Operational Procedures

- 4.6 Explain the importance of prohibited content/activity and privacy, licensing, and policy concepts.

Key Terms

access time
Advanced Access Content System (AACS)
Advanced Video Coding High Definition (AVCHD)
AT Attachment Packet Interface (ATAPI)
Blu-ray Disc (BD)
Blu-ray Disc Plus (BD+)
colored books
compact disc read-only memory (CD-ROM)
constant angular velocity (CAV)
constant linear velocity (CLV)
data transfer rate
digital rights management (DRM)
digital versatile disc (DVD)
finalizing
High-bandwidth Digital Content Protection (HDCP)
High Sierra format
ISO 9660
ISO image
lands
magneto-optical (MO) drive
photocell
pits
Ultra High-Definition (HD) Blu-ray
Universal Disk Format (UDF)
Volume Table of Contents (VTOC)

Overview

Optical data storage began with the CD-ROM. It revolutionized the methodology for storing and retrieving data. Great amounts of data could be stored in much smaller physical areas. The CD-ROM paved the way for economical computer storage of music, graphics, and video. Although optical storage devices are being rapidly replaced by solid-state and cloud storage alternatives, the low cost and portability of optical media such as DVDs keep them as a viable option for storage and distribution of digital media. This chapter discusses and explains CD, DVD, and BD technologies associated with computer storage.

A+ Note

For the CompTIA A+ Exams, you should know the differences between CD, DVD, and Blu-ray Discs (BD), and be familiar with the different storage capacities of disc types and disc compatibility. You should also know the various ways optical storage devices can be added to an existing computer system.

A+ 1101: 3.3

11.1 CD

In 1978, Philips and Sony Corporations developed the **compact disc read-only memory (CD-ROM)**, an optical disc able to store large amounts of data. Compact disc (CD) technology was originally developed to replace plastic records and tapes used in the music industry and not directly for computer storage. The first CD-ROMs were large 12-inch platters, and by 1982, the 4.72-inch platter became the standard. While CDs are uncommon today, the successors of CDs, including Blu-ray Discs, are quite common. As you will see later in this chapter, optical drives and discs have continued to evolve since the first CDs.

Tech Tip

Note the spelling difference between *disc* and *disk*. Spelling *disc* with a *c* is a common practice to indicate optical storage media. Spelling *disk* with a *k* is used to indicate magnetic media, such as hard drives.

CDs have layers on which data is stored, as shown in Figure 11-1. CD layers are typically composed of a polycarbonate (plastic) wafer approximately 1.2 mm thick and coated with an aluminum alloy, which is where the actual data is encoded. A final layer of polycarbonate is used to seal the aluminum alloy layer, and a label is then placed on the top of the CD. Data is recorded on (and read from) the aluminum alloy as a series of pits and lands. In terms of optical storage, **pits** are holes etched into the disc to record data, and **lands** are the flat areas between pits that reflect the light of the laser beam. The pits disperse the light rather than reflect it. The pits and lands convey the binary values of 1 and 0; changes from lands to pits or pits to lands create 1s, and the lack of change for defined periods of time creates 0s.

Most CDs are mass-produced using a laser to etch the surface of a disc known as the *master*. The master is then used to "stamp out" copies of the original data pattern onto many more plastic discs. Each disc is then coated with a thin film of aluminum reflective material that follows the pits and lands etched into the plastic. An additional layer of plastic seals the aluminum material, and the outside is given a smooth finish to allow the laser light to pass freely through the surface.

An optical drive uses a laser diode to read the disc, as illustrated in Figure 11-2. The laser diode produces a laser light when energized, which produces a low-energy

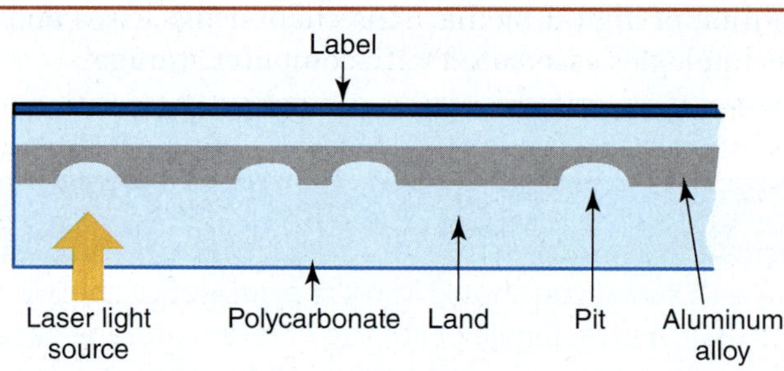

Figure 11-1 A typical CD is composed of a plastic wafer coated with an aluminum alloy, where the data is encoded.

Goodheart-Willcox Publisher

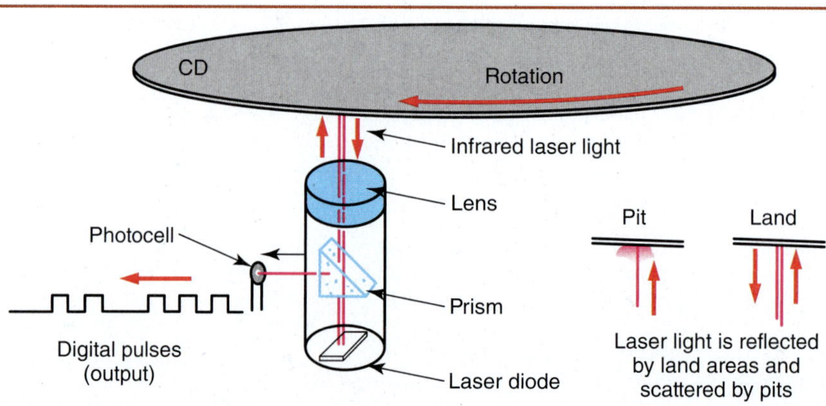

Figure 11-2 A laser diode sends a beam of light through a prism and onto the CD. If the light hits a land, the light is reflected. Pits, on the other hand, disperse the light. The reflected light travels through a prism, sending some of the light to a photocell, which turns the light into digital pulses.

Goodheart-Willcox Publisher

infrared beam. A servomotor in the drive follows commands issued by software to position the beam on the spiral path of pits and lands on the disc. The pits diffuse the light, while the lands reflect the light. The reflected light strikes a **photocell**, sometimes referred to as a *photo detector*, which is an electronic component that changes light energy into electrical energy.

The light reflected off the CD produces a pattern that replicates the data stored on the disc. The light is reflected to the photocell where it generates electrical pulses that are reproduced as a digital signal (on or off), and they represent the binary codes used to encode the data on the CD. Once the information stored on the CD is converted to digital signals, it can be utilized by the computer system. A typical CD-ROM contains between 650 MB and 700 MB of information.

Data on a CD is organized differently than on a hard drive platter. CDs use a spiral technique to record data rather than dividing the platter into separate tracks, Figure 11-3. By using a spiral technique, it is possible to increase storage capacity because there is no wasted space as with conventional hard disk platters.

In addition to a lack of wasted space, another major advantage of optical storage over magnetic storage is the stability of stored data. Magnetic systems such as hard drives maintain data for approximately five to eight years before they must be refreshed (written again). Optical storage does not have this limitation. There is debate over how long a CD can last before it degrades to a point where it cannot be read. Some estimate 10 to 25 years, while others estimate the lifespan of the discs to be over 100 years.

Caution

Working with any laser source can result in permanent damage to your retinas. There are specially designed safety glasses for working on lasers. As a computer technician, you should *never* work directly on the parts inside a CD device, which is considered a field replacement unit.

CD-R

Originally called CD-write once read many (CD-WORM), *compact disc-recordable (CD-R)* is an optical storage media that uses photosensitive reflective dye to simulate the pits and lands of a standard CD, which allows you to write data to a CD. With CD-R, data can be erased, and the disc can be written to again. However, data cannot be written to a previously recorded sector. When an area on the CD is said to be erased, the data is still present but can no longer be accessed. Consequently, every time a file is updated on a CD-R, the existing file is made inaccessible and a new section of the CD-R is used to store the newest version of the file.

A CD-R is designed with a layer of photosensitive, transparent organic dye is placed against an aluminum alloy layer inside the CD. The photosensitive layer reflects light in its natural state; thus, in its natural state, it appears as one long land to the CD reader. Figure 11-4 shows a typical CD-R disc. When exposed to the recording laser light, the photosensitive layer changes from a reflective state to an opaque state. Instead of reflecting light, it absorbs the light from the laser similar to the pits used in the standard CD.

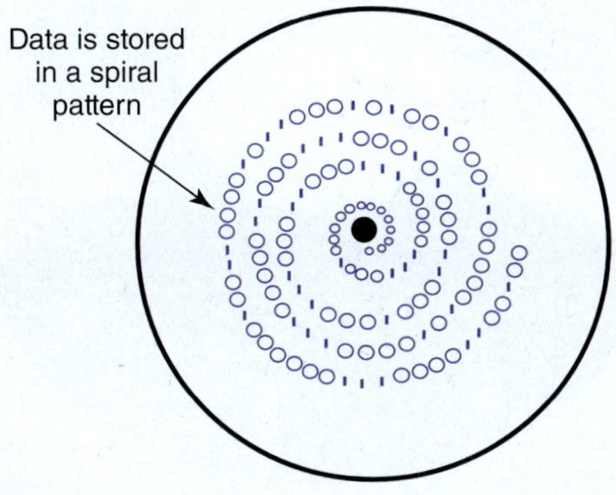

Goodheart-Willcox Publisher

Figure 11-3 CDs store data in spiral patterns, not in sectors.

Note that with these discs, you can see where you have recorded your data. With the mass-produced CDs, the entire disc has universal shine. With CD-R discs, the area that has been recorded reflects light differently than the unrecorded area, as shown in Figure 11-5.

For the most part, CD-R drives have been replaced by CD-RW, DVD, and Blu-ray drives. You will still encounter the CD-R drive in existing PCs for some time, but most new PCs, when equipped, come with combination CD-RW and DVD recordable systems or Blu-ray recorders that can also read and record CDs and DVDs.

CD-RW

Compact disc-rewritable (CD-RW) is an improvement over the CD-R technology, allowing data to be erased and rerecorded. It allows data to be written to the same sections of a CD many times instead of only once by including a special polycrystalline structure inside the plastic platter, as illustrated in Figure 11-6. The polycrystalline is a composite silver-indium-antimony-tellurium layer.

This technology uses a laser beam that has two states of heat intensity: low and high. When the polycrystalline structure is exposed to the high temperatures, roughly 932°F–1,292°F (500°C–700°C), it loses its reflective quality. When the low-power beam of the laser operating at 392°F (200°C) is applied, it changes the surface back to a reflective

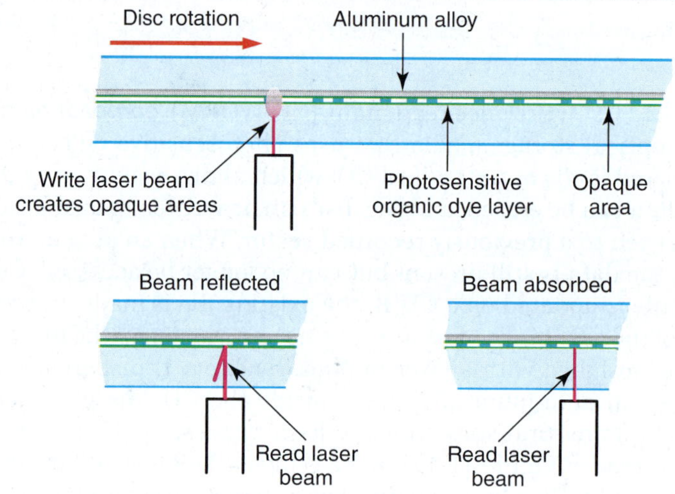

Figure 11-4 To a write to a CD-R, two lasers must be used: one to read, and the other to write.

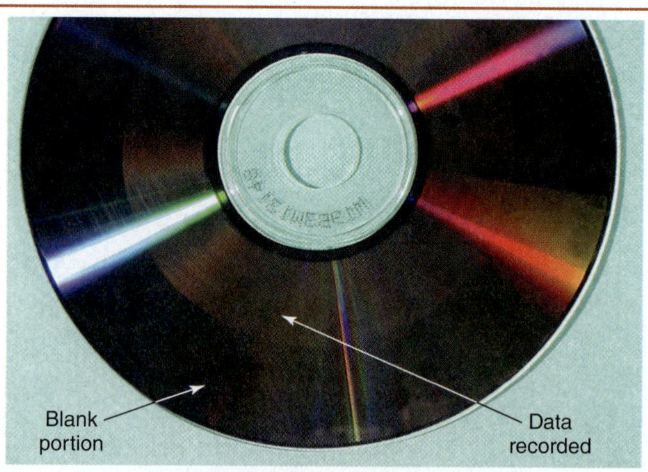

Figure 11-5 Data that has been recorded on a CD-R reflects light differently than the unrecorded area.

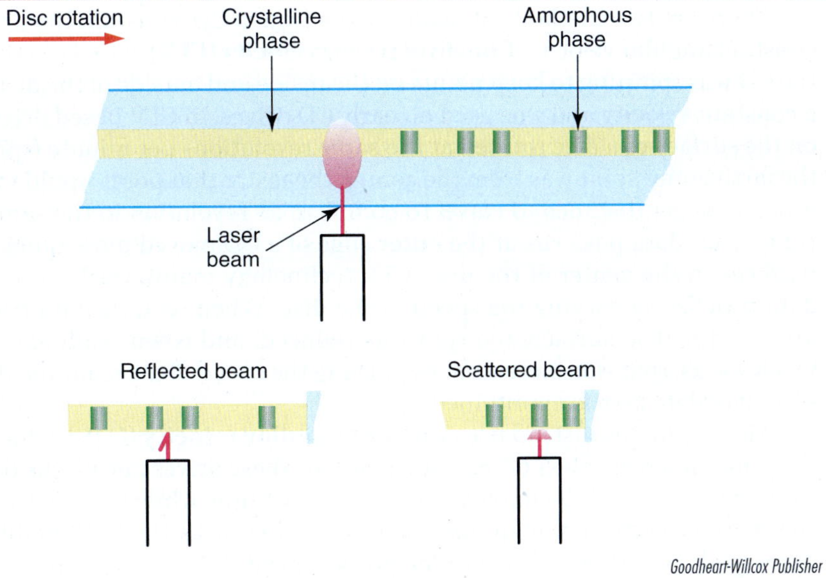

Figure 11-6 In the CD-RW process, a high-intensity laser causes the disc to lose its reflective quality. Then, a low-intensity beam returns the reflective quality to the material.

quality. By applying the high- and low-beam heat effects on the polycrystalline structure, the reflective quality of the disc can be arranged (and rearranged) into a state similar to the land and pit technique. This means that previously recorded areas of the disc can be rewritten, allowing for data recording functionality similar to a hard drive. The CD-RW has become a cost-effective medium for low-volume data backups.

At times, compatibility issues have plagued the CD industry. Older CD players were often not be able to play new CDs, specifically CD-RWs. This lack of recognition was related to the intensity of the light used to represent the lands and pits on newer discs. The original CD standards required that the CD reflect at least 70 percent of the light striking the land and no more than 28 percent of the light reflected in pits. On the modern CD-RW, the land areas reflect no more than 15 to 25 percent of the light striking the surface of the land, well below the early standard of 70 percent.

Today's CD and CD-RW systems can read older technologies and adjust for the various light-reflective intensities. However, the older technologies cannot make these adjustments. Consequently, a CD-RW made on a PC today may not be readable by a CD system that is not CD-RW capable. Typically, only a CD-RW can exchange data with another CD-RW.

CD Specifications

Two of the most common CD specifications are data transfer rate and access time. Like magnetic media, the **data transfer rate** is a measurement of how much data can be transferred from the CD to the PC RAM in a set period of time. This standard is usually given in kBps or MBps. Data transfer rate is especially important if you transfer a lot of data from a CD on a continual basis, such as playing games off a CD.

The access time for a CD is measured in much the same way as it is for a hard disk. The **access time** is the amount of time that passes between the issue of the read command and the point in time when the actual first data bit is read after it has been located on the disc. Since the amount of time delay varies according to where the data is physically located on the CD, the rating is usually an average and is typically measured in milliseconds. If you run applications where you periodically access a CD, access time becomes a more important time factor.

Note that CD drives are commonly advertised as 40X, 48X, or 52X. This naming convention is relative to the speed at which the disc is spinning, with 1X set by the speed at which the early CD-ROM drives turned. This rate corresponds to a data rate of 1,536 kBps, sufficient to play back CD-quality uncompressed audio.

There are two methods of reading data from a CD: constant linear velocity and constant angular velocity. **Constant linear velocity (CLV)** varied the speed at which the CD was spinning to keep points on the inside and outside of the disc spinning at a constant velocity and was used on early CD drives. In CLV-based drives, all points on the surface of a disc rotated at the same revolutions per minute (rpm). However, the farther any point was from the center, the faster that point would move because it had a longer distance to travel to complete its revolution in the same amount of time. Thus, data patterns at the outer edge of a CD moved more quickly than data patterns in the center of the disc. CLV technology maintained the same speed of data transfer by varying the speed of the disc. When reading data from the outer areas of the disc surface, the rpm was reduced, and when reading data from the inside areas, rpm was increased. By varying the speed of the spinning disc, a steady stream of data flow is maintained.

Modern drives instead use **constant angular velocity (CAV)**, which maintains the same rpm regardless of the data location. These drives permit the data flow rate to change. With CAV technology, there is no lost time while the CD drive adjusts its speed. Thousands of revolutions could be wasted with the CLV method while the drive sped up or slowed down to the proper speed.

CD Formatting

Without a standard method for coding CDs, data recorded on one CD device would be unreadable to a CD device made by a different manufacturer. Manufacturers of CD technology foresaw these problems and met to set standards for the industry. The first set of standards became what is known as the *High Sierra format*, which was later modified into ISO 9660: the worldwide standard for CD-ROMs. An additional format, UDF, was developed for packet writing of information. *Packet writing* records data in small blocks similar to the way hard drives store data. This format was developed primarily for the CD-RW and DVD systems.

High Sierra Format

The **High Sierra format** is a standard for compact discs that was created so CDs could be read on any CD device. CD industry representatives were interested in combining their efforts to achieve a common format they could all share so they could use their CDs on any type of CD device.

In High Sierra format, the first section of the spiral path or sector on the CD identifies the CD as the media and synchronizes the CD with the drive mechanism. The disc also identifies the directories of data on the volume. The CD contains a **Volume Table of Contents (VTOC)**, which is a data structure that tells the CD drive how the data is laid out on the disc, similar to the file table on a hard drive.

The spiral path of data on the CD has sectors and clusters, but there is no need for tracks since the disc consists of one long spiral. The CD also contains a directory used for organizing the data stored on the CD.

ISO 9660

In 1988, the High Sierra format was updated to **ISO 9660**, also called *CD-ROM file system (CDFS)*, which includes a file-system structure similar to FAT16, albeit with improvements. The two standards are identical in content, but the exact formatting is different. The ISO 9660 format is the CD format used today. With ISO 9660, there is no limit to the size of the root directory, and it can contain up to eight levels of files and directories. Consider the following file path:

F:\LEV1\LEV2\LEV3\LEV4\LEV5\LEV6\LEV7\LASTFILE.pdf

The root directory is F:\ and there are seven levels of subdirectories ending with the file LASTFILE.pdf.

ISO 9660 supports long file names, but if you intend to use it with an operating system like DOS, you must use the 8.3 file naming convention. The ISO standard for CDs allows only uppercase letters, digits, and the underscore when naming a file or directory. CD files are stored by sectors, but the sectors can be made larger or smaller, and the exact size of a sector can be different depending on whether the disc is providing header information or error correction. Traditionally, the sector data size on a CD is 2,048 bytes, but with header information, it is 2,352 bytes. The sectors are numbered consecutively starting with sector zero.

A+ 1102: 1.7

An **ISO image** is a type of disc image that serves as an exact copy of the contents by copying all sectors containing data and ignores the file system being used. For example, if you need an exact copy of an operating system, creating an ISO image will copy all sectors containing data and will ignore the file system being used. Windows operating systems cannot create an exact ISO image of a disk without the use of a third-party software package. ISO disk images are a common way of distributing software operating systems and an excellent way to back up a computer system.

UDF

The Optical Storage Technology Association (OSTA) was formed by manufacturers to create a file system structure that could be used for CD-RW, magneto-optical, and DVD technology. The file system structure accepted for CD-RW, magneto-optical disc, and DVD technology is **Universal Disk Format (UDF)**. UDF is the successor to the ISO 9660 file structure and defines the new file system structure. A newer version, UDF 2.50, was adopted as a file system for Blu-ray Discs.

The greatest improvement of the UDF file system structure is that it allows for a bootable disc. One of the reasons CD-RW discs cannot be read by CD-ROM technology is the way the UDF file structure is organized.

Disc System Standards

Disc system standards are outlined in a series of specifications referred to as the **colored books**. Each set of specifications is classified by book color. The *red book* specifications describe the physical properties of compact disc audio and graphics. The *yellow book* describes the requirements for using CD technology for data storage systems. The *green book* describes the specifications of interactive CD technology (CD-i). The *orange book* describes recordable CD media. The *white book* is used for video standards. The *blue book* is an expanded version of music standards referred to as *CD Plus* or *Enhanced Music CD*.

The CD standards contain information about the physical description of sectors and overall physical dimensions as well as data formats, data encoding, disc compression, light reflection intensities, and error-correction techniques. The standards allow for compatibility between different manufacturers in the industry.

11.2 Magneto-Optical

A **magneto-optical (MO) drive** combines magnetic and optical principles to store and retrieve data on a CD-like disc. The MO disc is constructed of a magnetically sensitive metal crystal that is manufactured between two plastic discs.

When writing to an MO disc, a laser heats the plastic surrounding the metallic crystal. This allows the crystal to change its orientation on the disc when exposed to the magnetic field of the write head. When the plastic cools, the metallic crystal is aligned along the disc track representing the binary information, Figure 11-7.

To read the data from the disc, the CD is spun while the laser is focused on the track. This time the laser uses much less power and simply provides light to be reflected back to the photodiode. The reflected light is slightly polarized by the magnetic domain, and the direction of the polarization represents the bit pattern stored on the disc. For example, a north-pole orientation may represent a binary 1, while a south-pole orientation may represent a binary 0.

As with all removable storage media, the advent of inexpensive CD/DVD drives and flash memory has made magneto-optical discs largely redundant. MO discs were expensive when new, and while highly reliable, the slow writing time was also a detriment. Magnetic tape formats like linear tape-open (LTO) have far surpassed MO media for high capacity, enterprise-grade backup storage.

A+ 1101: 3.3

11.3 DVD

Digital versatile disc (DVD), also known as *digital video disc (DVD)*, is a standard pushed by the motion picture industry so it could release films on discs instead of tape. DVD obtains its higher storage capacity than CD by using a shorter wavelength of light to record and play data. Look at Figure 11-8 to see a comparison of CD, DVD, HD-DVD, and Blu-ray Disc land and pit spacing. As disc technology advanced from the CD to Blu-ray, the land and pit areas and the distance between the spiral tracks became more compact. Consequently, DVDs can store more data than CDs in the same physical area. Data transfer rates, indicated in multiplication factors such as 1X, 4X, etc. are also significantly higher than CDs. In the case of DVDs, 1X refers to a data rate of 1.385 MB/s for data and 1.25 MB/s for video, sufficient to play back uncompressed SD-quality video at the highest video bit rate.

Another factor to consider is the wavelength of the laser used to record data. As wavelengths become shorter, it is possible to write data in smaller and closer lands and pits. DVD uses a shorter-wavelength red light as opposed to the infrared

Figure 11-7 The crystals on a magneto-optical disc are fixed until the plastic around them is heated with a laser. During the heating process, the crystals are susceptible to having their orientation on the disc changed to store data.

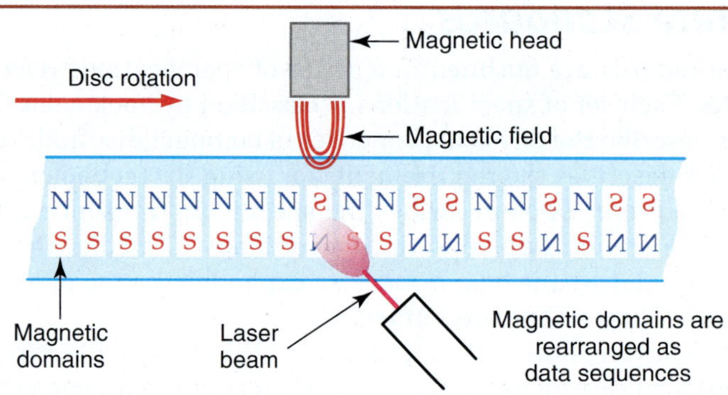

Goodheart-Willcox Publisher

Figure 11-8 By decreasing pit and land areas and track spacing, each evolution of optical technology has successfully increased storage capacities.

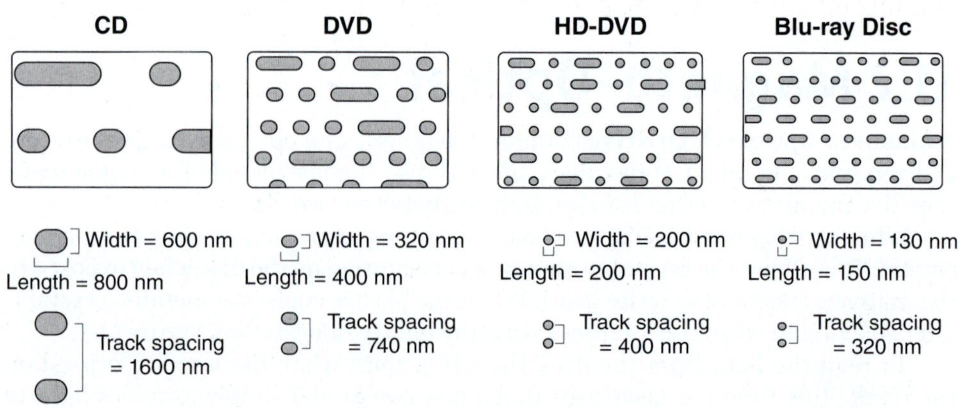

Goodheart-Willcox Publisher

light used by CDs, and the wavelength continues to be progressively shorter until it reaches Blu-ray.

Look at Figure 11-9 to see a comparison of CD, DVD, HD-DVD, and Blu-ray laser wavelengths as well as approximate storage capacity for a single-layer disc and the depth of the laser penetration into the disc. The wavelength of the red CD laser is 780 nm, the red DVD laser is 650 nm, and HD-DVD and Blu-ray Disc both use a blue laser wavelength of 405 nm. However, the depths of HD-DVD and Blu-ray lasers are different at 0.6 mm for HD-DVD and 0.1 for the Blu-ray Disc.

The DVD Forum developed DVD-RW standards, which are not compatible with DVD-RAM developed by manufacturers that did not wait for a standard to be developed. DVD-ROM was developed mainly to focus on multimedia in order to store video and sound on the same disc space. DVD-ROM is a playback-only media and cannot be used to record. DVD-RAM is made to be written to and played back many times. It features the random access of data.

DVD Structures

The DVD comes in several structure styles to increase data storage capacity. In general, the more sides and layers a disc has, the greater the storage capacity. See Figure 11-10 for a drawing of DVD structures. The 4.7-GB single-sided, single-layer

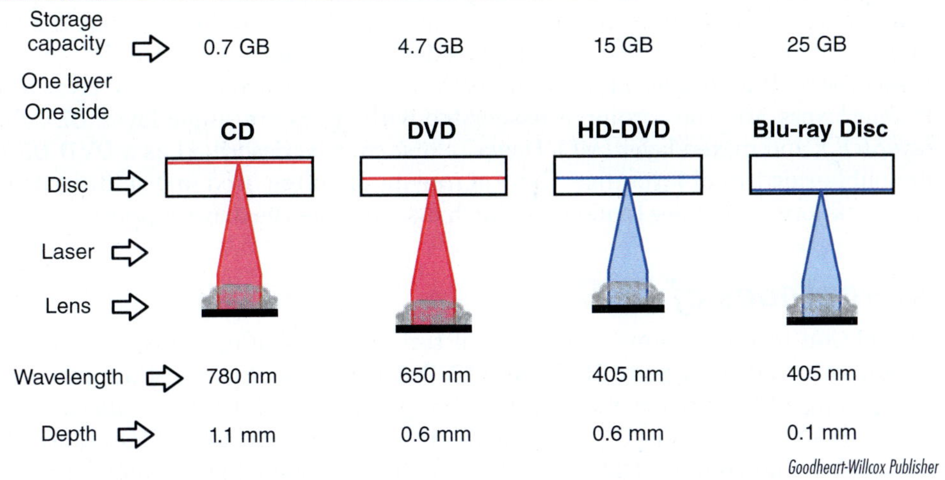

Figure 11-9 Shortening the wavelengths used for disc technology resulted in lesser depth penetration and greater storage capacity.

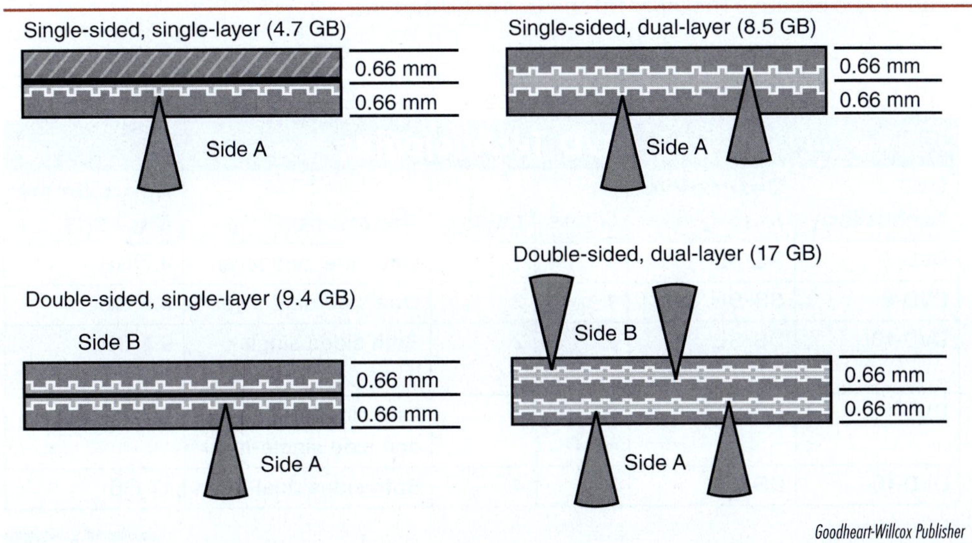

Figure 11-10 Different DVD structures allow for a variety of storage capacities. DVDs can store up to 17 GB of data.

DVD structure consists of a single layer of reflective film that contains the pit and land areas representing stored data. It is similar in construction to the typical CD, but the 4.7-GB DVD storage capacity far surpasses the CD's 650-MB capacity.

The 8.5-GB single-sided, dual-layer structure contains two reflective film layers, a gold layer and a silver layer. For this technology to operate, the laser beam is run at two different intensities. The first layer (the gold layer) is partially transparent to the laser beam at high intensities, which allows the data on the second layer (the silver layer) to be read. When intensity is lowered, it cannot penetrate through the gold reflective layer, allowing the gold layer data to be read.

The 9.4-GB double-sided, single-layer disc structure is accessed from both sides. Think of the 9.4-GB double-sided, single-layer disc as two 4.7-GB discs stacked label to label. The double-sided disc works with a DVD drive that has two lasers, one to read the top and another to read the bottom of the disc. If the DVD drive has only one laser, the disc must be turned over to read the other side.

The 17-GB disc is dual-layer for each disc joined together, creating four layers total. It is similar to two 8.5-GB dual-layer, single-sided discs stacked label to label. The same technology of the gold and silver layers is applied to this disc structure. Again, as with the 9.4-GB double-sided disc, there must be two lasers, or the disc must be turned over to access data on both sides of the disc. A 13.2-GB disc is double-sided with a dual-layer on one side and a single layer on the other side. This type of disc is referred to as a mixed-layer disc.

Look at the table in Figure 11-11. Notice the DVD can record to one or both sides. When both sides are used for recording media, it is referred to as *double-sided*. The acronyms used to describe single-sided and double-sided are *SS* and *DS*, respectively. The number of layers used to record varies from a single layer to up to four layers, and the acronyms associated with layers are single-layer (*SL*), dual-layer (*DL*), and mixed-layer (*ML*). Hence, a disc may be described as a DVD DS/DL or double-sided, dual-layer disc. These acronyms are often used in disc-drive device specifications and tables to identify which disc formats the drive supports.

Advantages of DVD

In addition to the obvious advantage of tremendous storage capacity, there are several other advantages to DVDs and DVD drives. One of the best advantages of purchasing a DVD drive is its backward compatibility with CD technology. A DVD drive will read most older CD technologies in addition to the new DVDs. Most DVD players have no trouble reading CD-ROMs; however, some players may have difficulty with CD-Rs and CD-RWs. Unfortunately, older CD technology drives will not read DVDs because the laser intensities are different.

Figure 11-11 The variance in DVD structures allows for different capacities ranging from 4.7 GB to 17 GB.

DVD Technologies

DVD Technology	Descriptive Acronym	Sides	Layers	Description	Approximate Capacity
DVD-5	SS/SL	1	1	One side, one layer	4.7 GB
DVD-9	SS/DL	1	2	One side dual-layer	8.5 GB
DVD-10	DS/SL	2	2	Both sides single-layer	9.4 GB
DVD-14	DS/ML	2	3	One side dual-layer, one side single-layer	13.2 GB
DVD-18	DS/DL	2	4	Both sides dual-layer	17 GB

Goodheart-Willcox Publisher

Another advantage of DVDs is that video cards can incorporate MPEG standards of decompression directly onto the adapter card. This eliminates the use of the processor to decompress the files and results in faster overall performance.

DVD Compatibility Issues

Manufacturers raced to release DVD technology to dominate the market, and the consumer was therefore left with enormous compatibility issues. Consequently, there are several DVD standards that are incompatible with each other. This is a common cause of customer complaints about making a DVD on one DVD recorder and not being able to access it on another. Presently, there are two formal organizations dictating standards: DVD+RW Alliance and DVD Forum. Interestingly, some manufacturers, for example Sony and Ricoh, are members of both organizations. The following section covers DVD format standards for both groups.

DVD-R

DVD-R is a write-once recordable DVD format introduced by the DVD Forum. The DVD-R format is compatible with most DVD players. DVD-R comes in two types: general use and authoring. The authoring type is a higher quality than the general use type. The DVD-R type must match the recorder being used for the initial writing, but it can be read back on either type.

A+ Note

You may encounter at least one question requiring you to select the correct disc media type based on its ability to record data, and on the acronyms R, RW, and ROM.

DVD-RW

DVD-RW is a rewritable format introduced by the DVD Forum. DVD-RW can be reused over 1000 times. It is less compatible than the DVD-R format; most, but not all, DVD players will read DVD-RW.

DVD+R

DVD+R was introduced by the DVD+RW Alliance and functions similar to DVD-R, albeit with some minor differences that prevent compatibility with the DVD-R format. It is also interesting to note that DVD+R is not compatible with all DVD+RW players, though most DVD players support both DVD+R and DVD+RW formats.

DVD+RW

DVD+RW is similar to DVD-RW except for minor differences in the format structure. One of the main differences is that DVD+RW was designed to allow drag-and-drop file exchange, which earlier formats did not support. The drag-and-drop capability is often referred to as the *Mount Rainier drag-and-drop support*. The Mount Rainier version is also referred to as *+MRW*.

DVD-RAM

DVD-RAM is used primarily as a video format but was originally designed as a data storage format. One problem with DVD-RAM is it will not work in a standard DVD-ROM player.

11.4 HD-DVD and Blu-ray Disc

A+ 1101: 3.3

The demand generated by high-definition television (HDTV) and movie industries for better video recording media has led to the development of two disc formats: HD-DVD and Blu-ray Disc (BD). The HD-DVD standard was abandoned in 2008 because it failed to successfully compete with the Blu-ray standard. **Blu-ray Disc (BD)** is a high-definition video and data format developed by the Blu-ray Disc

Association, which was started by Sony. Blu-ray and other large-capacity DVDs are the preferred formats of the movie industry.

The DVD Forum's approach was to preserve as much previous DVD design technology as possible to ensure backward compatibility while increasing storage capacity. The Blu-ray Disc Association is more concerned with achieving the greatest possible storage capacity while not necessarily ensuring compatibility with previous CD and DVD designs. The Blu-ray Disc Association encourages, but does not require, backward compatibility in its specifications for the design of Blu-ray devices. Modern Blu-ray discs recording devices are compatible with CD and DVD technology and can burn Blu-ray discs, as well as CDs and DVDs.

A standard CD can store approximately 650 MB of data, and a DVD can store 4.7 GB of data, which is far less than what is required to record movies and television programs in HD format. However, single-layer HD-DVD has a capacity of 15 GB, and single-layer Blu-ray Disc has a capacity of 25 GB, both of which double in dual-layer formats. For example, dual-layer HD-DVD can store 30 GB, and dual-layer Blu-ray Disc can store 50 GB. The latest BD-XL formats support a storage capacity of up to 128 GB for quad-layer discs. Consequently, data rates in BD drives are also significantly higher than CDs or DVDs. For BDs, 1X refers to a transfer rate of 36 Mbit/s for data and 54 Mbit/s for video, about three to five times higher than standard DVD rate, to allow playback of HD-quality video. See Figure 11-12 for a comparison of the various disc technologies.

Note that in Figure 11-12, the HD-DVD and Blu-ray data transfer rates are typically specified in bits per second (bps) but are presented in bytes per second (Bps). This was done intentionally to make it easier to compare to CD and DVD transfer rates. HD-DVD has a bit transfer rate of 36.5 Mbps, and Blu-ray has a bit transfer rate of 36 Mbps.

Blu-ray has continued to expand with triple-layer disks being able to support 100 GB and quadruple-layer disks supporting 128 GB. There is also BDXL which allows 100 GB and 128 GB storage, but in write-once disks. Blu-ray 3D is another variation of the Blu-ray format primarily for use with 3D televisions, rather than computers.

The Blu-ray Disc surface is sealed using a much more scratch-resistant material than CDs and DVDs. The harder disc surface is required because scratches would more easily prevent the laser from reading data from the smaller and closer disc tracks used in Blu-ray. As with DVD, there are several different formats of HD-DVD and Blu-ray Disc, as listed and described in Figure 11-13.

A+ 1101: 3.3

The HD DVD-R was a record-only disc that is now obsolete. The HD DVD-R was available in a single-layer capacity of 15 GB or a dual-layer capacity of 30 GB. *Blu-ray Disc Recordable (BD-R)* can only be recorded to once and is available in single-layer 25 GB and dual-layer 50 GB. *Blu-ray Disc Recordable Erasable (BD-RE)* discs are single-sided Blu-ray Discs that allow you to add to and back up your data, music, or video to approximately 1,000 times.

Figure 11-12 As disc technology has evolved, the capacities, transfer rates, and video resolution have increased.

Evolution of Disc Technology

Media Type	Storage Capacity	1X Data Transfer Rate	Video Resolution	Wavelength
CD	0.65 GB	0.153 MBps	Varies	750 nm (infrared)
DVD	4.7 GB	1.384 MBps	720 × 480	650 nm (red)
HD-DVD	15 GB	4.56 MBps	1,920 × 1,080	405 nm (blue-violet)
Blu-ray Disc	128 GB	4.5 MBps	3,840 × 2,160	405 nm (blue-violet)

Goodheart-Willcox Publisher

High-Definition Disc Media Variations		
Formats	**Storage Capacity**	**Description**
HD DVD-R	15-GB, single-layer 30-GB, dual-layer	Record only. Used for distribution of media such as movies. Legacy standard abandoned as a movie media since 2008.
BD-R	25-GB, single-layer 50-GB, dual-layer	The disc can only record once.
BD-RE	25-GB, single-layer 50-GB, dual-layer	The disc can be used to record, erase, and rerecord. Used for distribution of media such as movies.
BD-XL	100-GB, triple-layer 128-GB, quadruple-layer	Suitable for BD rewrite drives in computers.
UHD BD	50-GB with 82 Mbit/sec 66-GB with 108 Mbit/sec 100-GB with 128 Mbit/sec	Suitable for 4K video at 3840 × 2160 resolution and up to 60 fps.

Goodheart-Willcox Publisher

Figure 11-13 There are obvious benefits to Blu-ray Discs over the now-obsolete HD-DVDs.

Ultra High-Definition (HD) Blu-ray, not to be confused with HD-DVD, is an optical data storage format that supersedes Blu-ray. Ultra HD Blu-ray Discs are incompatible with existing Blu-ray players. Designed primarily for media storage and delivery, Ultra HD Blu-ray supports 4K UHD (3840 × 2160 resolution) video at frame rates up to 60 frames per second, encoded using High Efficiency Video Coding (HEVC). The discs support both high dynamic range by increasing the color depth to 10 bits per color and a greater color range than supported by conventional Blu-ray video. The Ultra HD Blu-ray specification allows for three disc capacities, each with its own data rate: 50 GB with 82 Mbps; 66 GB with 108 Mbps; and 100 GB with 128 Mbps. Ultra HD Blu-ray technology was licensed in mid-2015 with the first official release of Ultra HD 4K Blu-ray Discs from four studios following on March 1, 2016. Unlike conventional DVDs and Blu-ray Discs, the new 4K UHD BD format does not have region coding. There will be more information about region coding later in this chapter.

11.5 Disc Drive Interface

1101: 3.3 A+

There are several ways to interface disc drive technology with existing PC technology. PATA and SATA are commonly used for internal connections, while USB and eSATA are used for external connections. The main advantage of an eSATA device is that the device does not need a separate power source. FireWire can be found on legacy computers, but replacement FireWire devices are difficult to find.

The IDE port on a motherboard was designed as a hard drive interface. As CD technology became popular, the IDE system was modified to accept a CD upgrade; hence, the development of ATAPI. **AT Attachment Packet Interface (ATAPI)** is the interface used for standard IBM PC AT and compatible systems for accessing CD devices. ATAPI drives are also referred to as *Enhanced IDE* drives or *EIDE*.

Tech Tip

The technology name *PATA* commonly used today was referred to in the past by several other legacy terms, such as *IDE*, *EIDE*, *ATAPI*, and *ATA*.

The connection points on an optical drive are similar to those found on a hard disk drive with the addition of an audio analog and digital output connection. When connecting to a SATA optical drive, separate audio analog and digital output is not necessary. Figure 11-14 shows the back view of a PATA optical drive, and Figure 11-15

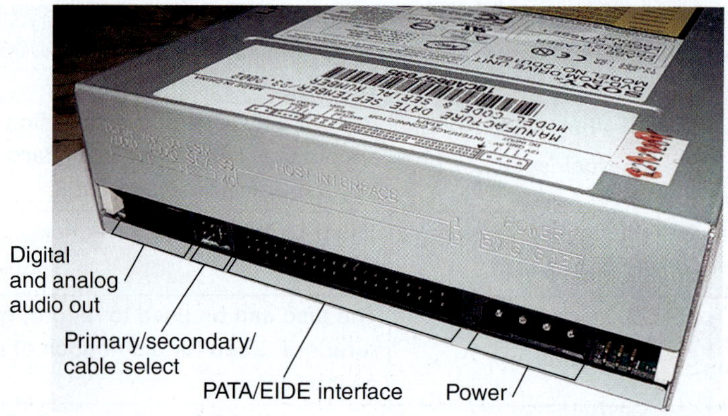

Goodheart-Willcox Publisher; (image) Baran Ivo/Public Domain

Figure 11-14 PATA optical drives are more complicated to install than their SATA counterparts because of the various connection ports required for power, data, and analog or digital audio.

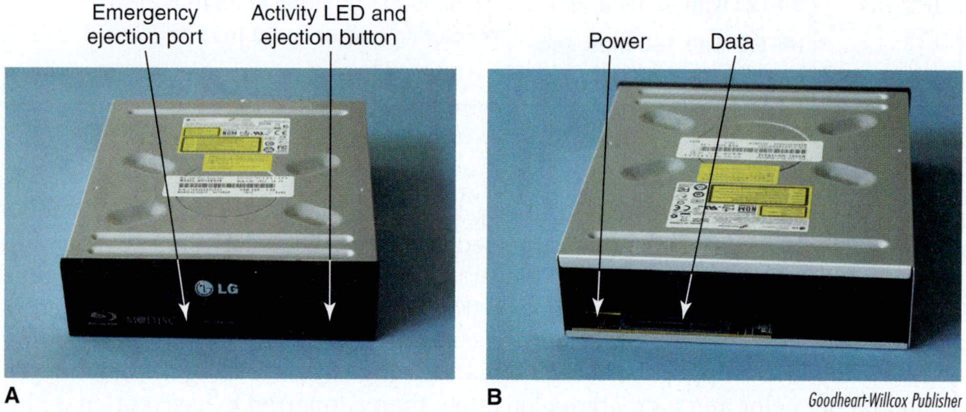

Goodheart-Willcox Publisher

Figure 11-15 Modern SATA drives have limited controls on the front of the drive (A) and use a software interface to control functions such as volume, fast forward, and reverse. Additionally, they are much simpler to install as they only require power and data/control connections (B).

shows the front and back of a SATA optical drive. Notice that the power and data connection cables are similar to the ones found on SATA and PATA hard disk drives.

The difference between legacy optical drives and SATA optical drives is the audio analog and digital output connections. The CD or DVD analog connection connects to the sound card, which provides sound from the disc drive to the sound card. The digital connection can be connected to a recording device for direct data transfer to the device.

Installation of CD and DVD technologies can also be made using SCSI. SCSI was once the preferred method for high data transfer rates but has been surpassed by SATA. SATA is also the preferred and most common method, and it works well for most consumer PCs.

Comparing the SATA optical drive with the PATA optical drive, you see that there is a more complex set of connections required for the PATA optical drive. The PATA drive requires an EIDE connection, also known as an *ATA connection*. Note that primary/secondary selection jumpers must also be installed if the optical drive is to share a channel with another EIDE (PATA) device such as a hard drive or another optical drive. When possible, avoid sharing EIDE channels with an optical drive, as sharing the same channel with the optical drive can cause some unusual problems.

Many legacy motherboards have both PATA and SATA data connectors. You may encounter a problem or conflict when attempting to use both types of devices. Device configurations of motherboards with both PATA and SATA connections depend on the motherboard firmware. Refer to the motherboard documentation to determine if there are any possible conflicts. The computer industry made the transition from PATA to SATA a bit later with optical drives than it did with hard disks, which led to problems when working with older computer systems. One way to resolve an issue with older systems is to use an external optical drive connected through a USB port. For BD drives, it is important to use faster USB 3.0 or SATA interfaces to support much higher data transfer rates.

Installing an optical drive in a laptop can be more difficult than in a desktop PC, mainly due to the size constraints of laptop-compatible optical drives compared to those compatible with a desktop PC. The process will also vary depending on the brand and model of laptop. Generally, to install a CD/DVD/BD drive in a laptop, one first needs to remove the screws that hold the drive in place on the bottom of the laptop enclosure. Once the screws are removed, the drive should slide out from the side of the device. Resistance is normal, as the drive must be disconnected from the laptop interface. Slide the new drive into the existing port, ensuring a connection is made and the drive has been securely inserted, and replace the screws in the enclosure.

Tech Tip

Some SATA optical drives are not detected or automatically configured by the Windows operating system. This is likely because the motherboard firmware may need to be upgraded.

11.6 Digital Rights Management

1102: 4.6 A+

Digital rights management (DRM) is any technology that ensures copyright protection for digital media, such as digital music and video. Online stores and media providers use DRM. Some online stores provide download services that use DRM to prevent illegal copies of media from being distributed. A common example of DRM is an *end-user license agreement (EULA)*, which is a legally binding contract between a software creator and user that specifies the user's right to use the software under specified terms.

It is also important to ensure that licenses are valid. For example, your organization may have four licenses for Windows Server 2019, which will not cover installing Windows 2019 on five servers. Similarly, a license could be expired. As part of sound digital rights management, you must ensure that you have valid, non-expired licenses.

DRM has a specific set of permissions that controls how the media can be used. For example, you can have a permission set to allow two copies of the media to be burned to discs, install the media on two different devices, or synchronize the media between two devices. The number for each of the examples simply refers to how many times the media can be copied or synchronized, when in reality, the media provider determines the maximum number of copies, devices, or number of synchronized devices. The media-user's rights are often referred to as a *media license*. When an individual user purchases software, the EULA will often refer to this as an *individual* or *personal license*, which means only one machine can have the software installed on it. If a company wishes to use software on multiple workstations, it must purchase a *site license* or *enterprise license*.

An exemption to DRM is software and utilities that are open source. *Open source* refers to products that have had their source code freely open and available to the public. This grants anyone permission to download and use the product with no charge or restrictions. Compare this to commercial-license software, which is incredibly limiting in its download, usage, licenses, and modification abilities.

DRM is constantly evolving because it is continually compromised, resulting in unauthorized duplication of media. Since DRM rapidly changes, you need to check for the very latest on a regular basis.

Advanced Access Content System

Advanced Access Content System (AACS) is a standard designed as a digital rights management system for media content distribution. The AACS restricts access to and copying of optical discs, such as CDs, DVDs, and Blu-ray Discs. The specification was publicly released in April 2005, and the standard has been adopted as the access restriction scheme for HD-DVD and Blu-ray Disc.

The AACS standard uses a security system based on a set of encryption keys that must be used to play the media. An *encryption key* is a special series of letters and numbers used to encode content, and a *decryption key* is used to decode the content. Encryption keys are constantly updated to prevent them from being compromised by unauthorized personnel. There will be much more about encryption in a later chapter.

High-Bandwidth Digital Content Protection

High-bandwidth Digital Content Protection (HDCP) is a digital copy-protection system that encrypts the data sent by a high-definition content player such as Blu-ray or HD-DVD to other devices such as a television or computer monitor via a physical connection. The encryption used is Advanced Encryption Standard (AES), a robust symmetric algorithm. The idea is to prevent copying copyrighted media content as it travels across cables. The Blu-ray Disc is reproduced with a lower resolution whenever a full HDCP-compliant link is not used, thus producing a low-quality copy.

Advanced Video Coding High Definition

Advanced Video Coding High Definition (AVCHD) is a proprietary specification developed jointly by Sony and Panasonic in 2006. The AVCHD standard allows using recordable DVDs, memory cards, nonremovable solid-state memory, and hard disk drives as recording media.

The AVCHD format allows high-definition video to be burned to a standard DVD, which can then be played in a Blu-ray Disc player at high-definition resolution. This means that a Blu-ray Disc burner is not required to burn a high-definition recording when using devices compatible with AVCHD format technology such as computers, video recorders, and similar devices. At the time of this writing, only Panasonic and Sony video recorders use AVCHD technology, but many different brands of Blu-ray Disc recording devices can use AVCHD.

Region Code

Region codes have been developed and assigned to specific media discs and disc players to protect digital content on DVD. The region code is configured to only play discs authorized by the content provider for that region. The region code allows the content creator or distributor to control the price and the release date of the media, such as a movie, according to the physical location or country.

To change the current region, right-click the DVD drive located in Windows Explorer and then select **Properties** from the shortcut menu. When the **Properties** dialog box appears, select the **Hardware** tab and then select the DVD drive from the list under **All disk drives.** Click the **Properties** button to open the **Properties** dialog box for the selected CD or DVD drive and select the **DVD Region** tab to access the region codes. Notice in Figure 11-16B that Windows allows you to change the region up to five times. In Windows, the video format that is selected by default is based on the **Region and Language** settings in Control Panel and is selected during the installation of the operating system.

BD+

Blu-ray Disc Plus (BD+) is another standard used with Blu-ray Disc digital rights management systems and performs the same type of protection as DVD region codes. Developed by Cryptography Research Inc., Blu-ray Discs are digitally encoded with a region code (A, B, or C, sometimes referred to as 1, 2, or 3), that allows the disc to play only in a Blu-ray player with the same region code. Windows operating systems do not incorporate a region code for Blu-ray. In fact, Microsoft does not directly support Blu-ray Disc functions. Blu-ray Disc support requires a third-party software application when a Blu-ray device is installed on a computer that uses a Windows operating system.

11.7 Troubleshooting CD, DVD, and BD

There are many reasons for failure of the optical disc system to write or read disc data. This section introduces some of the most common problems encountered with optical disc systems.

Failure to Eject

Optical drives can fail mechanically or physically become jammed and fail to eject disc media properly. For this reason, they are equipped with a small access hole in the front panel of the drive. A paper clip can be inserted into the small hole to release the lock mechanism. The drive tray and disc will be partially ejected, which will allow you to retrieve the disc from the failed system, as shown in Figure 11-17.

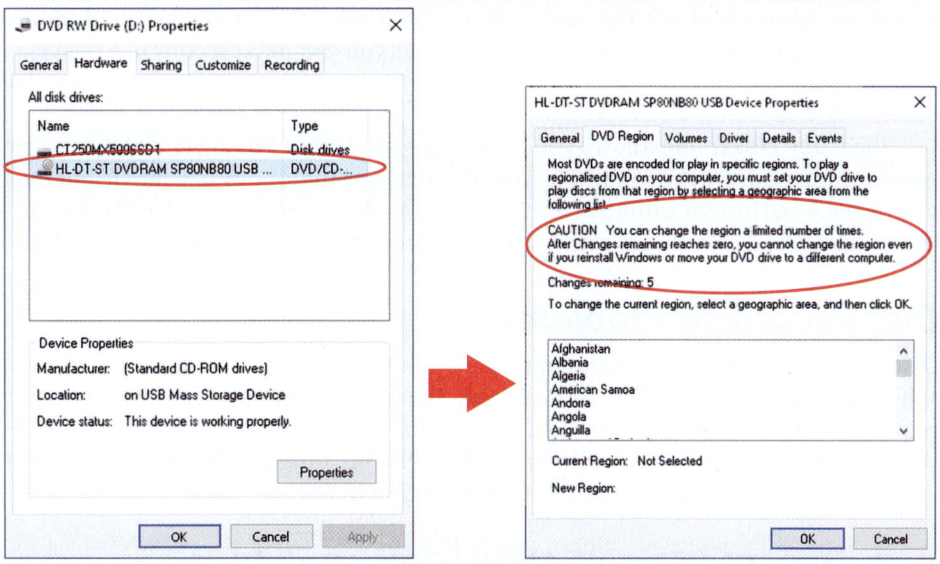

A B

Goodheart-Willcox Publisher

Figure 11-16 CD and DVD players can be encoded to play only in specific regions. Users can navigate to the DVD Drive Properties dialog box (A) to set the region code, which can only be changed a number of times (B).

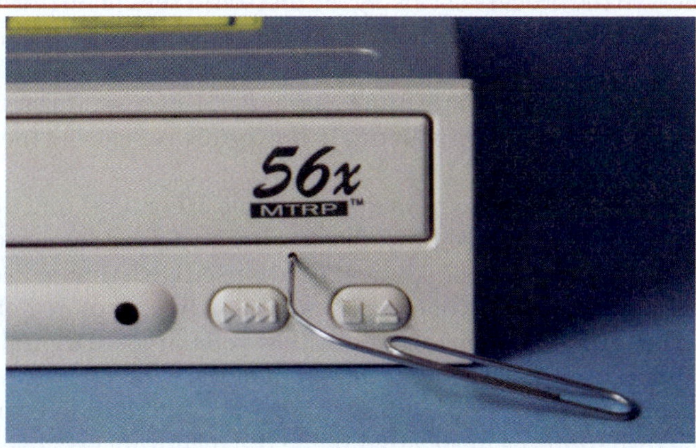

Goodheart-Willcox Publisher

Figure 11-17 Optical storage drives are equipped with emergency ejection systems. You simply insert a paper clip into the emergency ejection hole in the front panel of the drive.

Copy Control Protection Problems

Copy Control is a type of protection used to control the number of copies (if any) that can be made of a disc. For example, television DVD recorders can be designed to allow the user to make a single copy of a movie or some other type of television program only once. The single copy can be played back later but only on the same device or another device that has been equipped with the same type of copy protection. Typically, this code is associated with digital video recorders (DVRs) used with television systems and similar services. Since many entertainment systems use computers as the heart of the system, it is important for you to understand why clients are having what they perceive as a problem moving recorded materials between television DVRs and computer system as well as other devices.

Three common flags are used for Copy Control protection. A *flag* is a short program code that identifies the type of copy protection assigned to the recorded media. The three common Copy Control protection flags are Copy Freely, Copy No More or Copy Once, and Copy Never.

Copy Freely means the content is free to be copied as many times as you desire. When identified with a Copy Freely flag, you can generally record the content on one type of device and play it on another type of device. For example, a Copy Freely flag on a DVR-recorded movie should be able to be viewed on a PC and vice versa.

Copy No More and *Copy Once* mean you can only make a single copy of the media and then play back the media. You cannot copy the media a second time or play the media in a different device. For example, you can make a copy of a television show on your DVR for playback later. That copy cannot be copied or even played on another device that is networked to the DVR.

The *Copy Never* flag allows you to copy the media but has several strict restrictions as far as using it. For example, you may make a single copy of a movie but must play it back within 90 minutes. You can only make a single copy similar to Copy Once. The Copy Never flag is commonly used with Pay-Per-View (PPV) content.

Disc Recording Problems

Disc burning can be affected by computer system resources such as hard disk drive space, memory, and CD/DVD drive speed. The function of burning a disc typically requires RAM and hard disk storage. When using a computer with limited resources, you should not engage in any other activity while burning the disc because operating other activities can cause a disc burn function to fail.

Failure to Finalize or Close a Disc Session

Tech Tip

The Volume Table of Contents (VTOC) is added when a disc is finalized. Without the VTOC, the new device cannot locate data on the disc.

In general, a disc must be finalized before it can be played on another optical device. **Finalizing** refers to the process of closing the disc-burn session to prevent any additional data from being written to the disc. Microsoft uses a disc recording feature known as Live File System, which allows you to continually record on disc media as long as you continue to use it on the same computer. However, if you try to use the disc on another optical device without finalizing the disc or closing the disc session, the disc will fail.

During finalization, data such as a menu or table of contents and directory data have been written to the disc, and the disc has been enabled to play on other systems. Approximately 20 MB of disc storage space is used each time a disc is finalized. In general, once a disc has been finalized, it may not have any more data written on it. There are software applications that will allow you to record digital information again on the disc but only in the unused region of the disc. Closing a disc session means that the current recording has been temporarily stopped and you can access the data on the disc from the device that made the recording because the disc session has not been finalized.

When writing data to a CD/DVD/BD, Windows provides you with two options: **Like a USB flash drive** (Live File System) and **With a CD/DVD player** (Mastered), as shown in Figure 11-18. The **Live File System** allows you to save, edit, and delete files on the disc at any time, but **Mastered** will not allow you to change the contents of the files after burning. **Mastered** is permanent, while **Live File System** is not. When you eject a disc that was written to with the **Mastered** option, it is automatically finalized. When you eject the disc that was written to with **Live File System**, it is not finalized; instead, the session is simply closed, and more data can be added to the CD or DVD.

Before you can use a recordable optical disc formatted with the **Live File System** format in a different computer, you need to close the disc session. The disc session is closed by default when you eject a recordable optical disc, but you can change the close session settings for both multi-session and single-session capable discs by opening **Computer**, right-clicking the disc burner, and selecting **Properties** from the shortcut menu to open the **Properties** dialog box for the drive. Click the **Recording** tab and then select the **Global Settings** button to open the **Global Settings** dialog box, as shown in Figure 11-19.

The options in the **Global Settings** dialog box allow you to finalize a recording session when the disc is ejected. If you do not want to close the recording session automatically when the disc is ejected, simply click the appropriate check box to remove the check mark. The check mark means the session will be finalized.

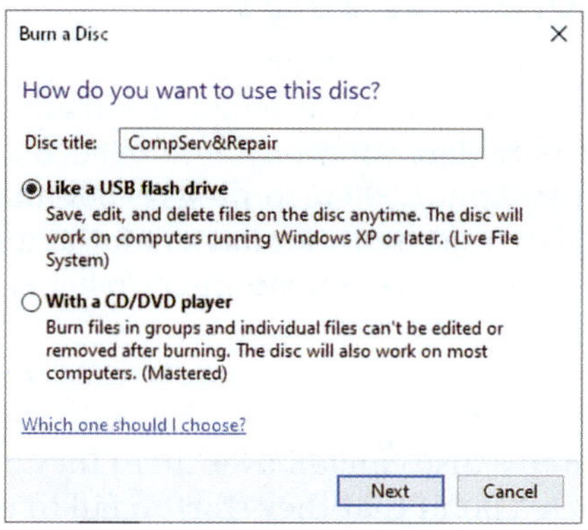

Goodheart-Willcox Publisher

Figure 11-18 Windows provides two choices when writing data to a CD or DVD drive: **Like a USB flash drive (Live File System)** or **With a CD/DVD player (Mastered)**.

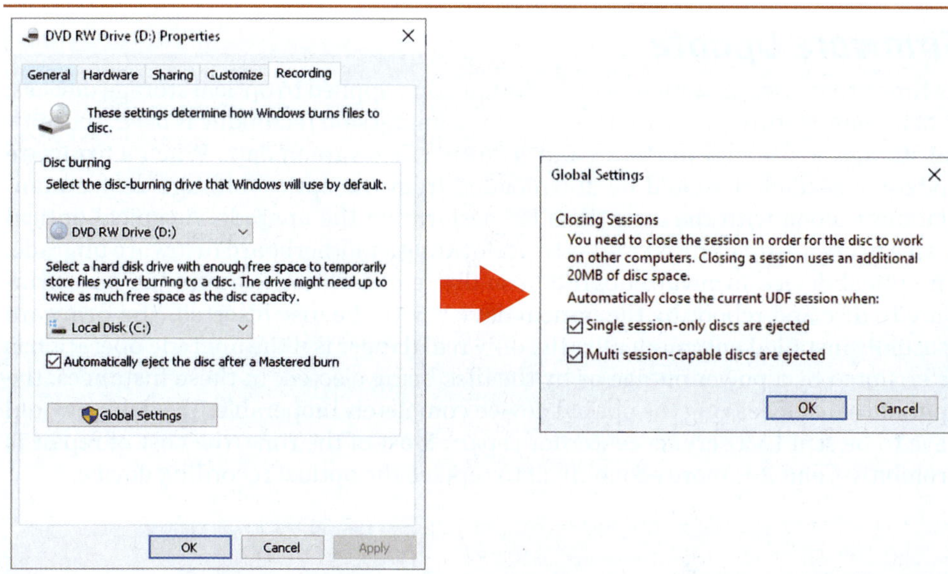

Goodheart-Willcox Publisher

Figure 11-19 A disc session must be closed before it can be read by another computer. The Global Settings dialog box allows you to change if a disc session is automatically closed when ejected.

Physical Defects

Dirt, scratches, or dust on the recording media can prevent a successful burn. Handle recording media by the edges so that you do not leave fingerprints on it. Do not lay the media down on a surface that can scratch the disc.

Wrong Media

A user might attempt to use the wrong type of media in an optical drive, such as inserting a DVD into a CD drive or a Blu-ray Disc into a DVD drive. Most Blu-ray recorders are backward compatible and can write to all DVD and CD formats such as DVD-RW, DVD+RW, DVD-R, and DVD+R.

Burning Speed Too Fast

When burning a disc that is to be used on the same optical device, recording speed is not that critical. However, when burning a disc to be used on another optical device or for distribution, speed can be an issue. You could burn a disc at a recording speed too high to be read by another optical device. To ensure universality, burn at a speed that can be read by most drives.

Too Many Repeated Writings

Rewriteable media has a range of maximum recording events. Most will not record over 1,000 times, and some media have even fewer burning events as a maximum. At first, this sounds like more than you would ever need, but when used in an application such as a security system, 1,000 recordings is not unusual. The disc could be recording video camera data repeatedly for days, months, and even years. Sooner or later, the media will reach its range of maximum number of recordings.

Laser Failure

Lasers used to burn data to a disc can fail over time. They can also become weaker with time until they reach a point that they start to fail to make a successful burn, leaving many points of corrupt data on the disc. There is no economical way to repair a media laser; you simply replace the optical recording device.

A+ 1102: 2.9

Firmware Update

As time progresses, new recording techniques are applied to optical storage devices. When a new feature such as a new codec or compression technique is used, the optical storage device may not work and require a firmware update. When a firmware update is needed, it should be downloaded from the optical storage device manufacturer along with the directions for performing the upgrade. A typical optical device firmware upgrade is similar to performing a motherboard firmware upgrade. An optical device firmware upgrade usually requires downloading the new firmware to disc and rebooting the optical device with the disc inserted. The firmware is usually installed automatically. The only real danger is if the upgrade operation is interrupted by a power outage or by the disc being ejected. In these instances, the upgrade can fail, leaving the optical device completely inoperable. The device would have to be sent to a service center for repair. Most of the time, the cost of repair is prohibitive, and it is more economical to replace the optical recording device.

Failure to AutoPlay Disc

1102: 2.6 A+

The way media such as audio CDs, movie discs, and blank discs react when placed into the optical drive can be configured through **Control Panel>Hardware and Sound>AutoPlay**, as shown in Figure 11-20. The **AutoPlay** dialog box will display and allow you to configure how the media will react when inserted into a drive. Figure 11-21 shows the **AutoPlay** dialog box from a Windows 10 operating system, but it is similar in other versions of Windows.

Options such as **Take no action**, **Burn an Image using ImgBurn**, or **Ask me every time** are just three of the options available. When a third-party software application is installed along with the device driver, other options often appear using the software application name.

Failure to play automatically may be intentional by the owner of the computer. Features such as AutoPlay or AutoRun may be disabled intentionally as a security measure. By disabling AutoPlay or AutoRun, executables on optical media will not run as soon as the media is loaded. This can prevent malware from executing on the computer.

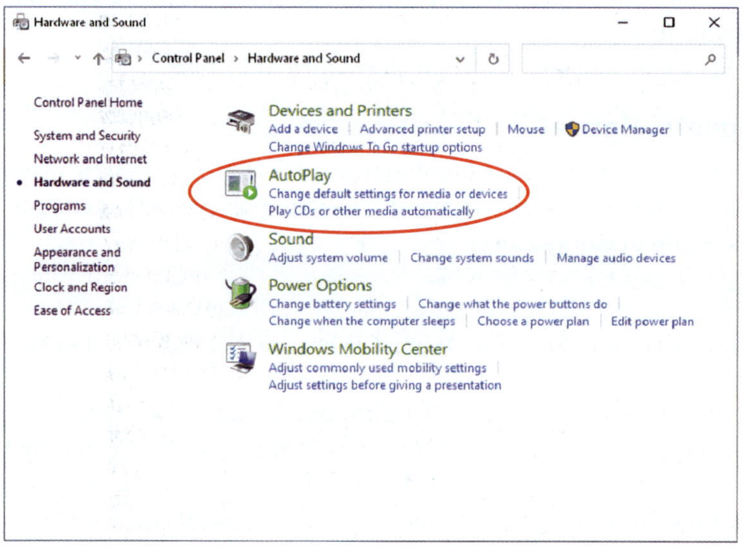

Goodheart-Willcox Publisher

Figure 11-20 The default settings for media can be changed through **Control Panel>Hardware and Sound>AutoPlay**. After selecting **AutoPlay**, you will see a detailed list of options for the different types of media.

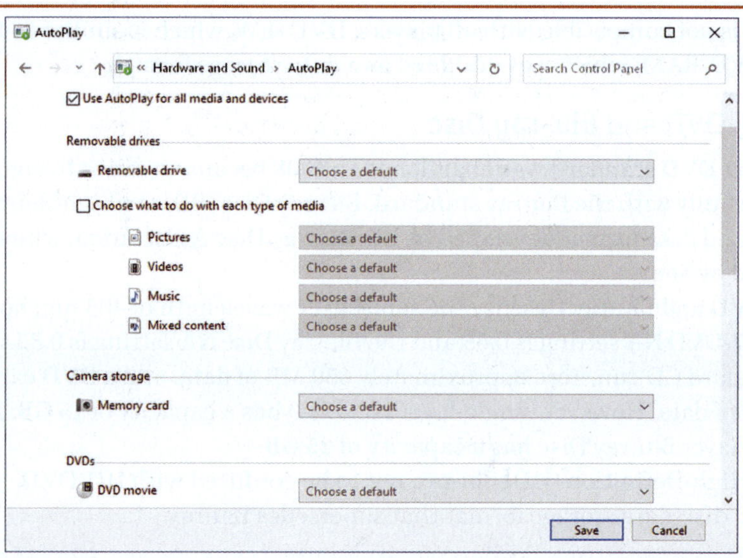

Goodheart-Willcox Publisher

Figure 11-21 The **AutoPlay** dialog box allows you to configure how media, such as a blank disc, reacts when placed into the optical disc drive.

Chapter Summary

11.1 CD

- CD technology uses laser light reflected from the CD to generate electrical pulses that represent the data stored on the disc; patterns known as land and pit areas represent data stored on a CD-ROM.
- In terms of optical storage, pits are holes etched into the disc in order to record data, and lands are the flat areas between pits that reflect the light of the laser beam. The pits disperse the light rather than reflect it. The pits and lands convey the binary values of 1 and 0.
- CD-R allows you to write data but not over a previously recorded sector. CD-RW allows for erasure and rerecording of data over the same sections of the CD.
- Constant linear velocity (CLV) varied the speed at which the CD was spinning to keep points on the inside and outside of the disc spinning at a constant linear velocity. Constant angular velocity (CAV) maintains the same rpm regardless of the data location.
- ISO 9660 format replaced the High Sierra format in 1988.

11.2 Magneto-Optical

- Magneto-optical drives use a combination of laser and magnetic properties to store data; the magnetic properties are used to polarize reflected light from the magneto-optical storage disc.

11.3 DVD

- DVD offers the same flexibility that a CD has, only at much higher storage density.
- Different DVD structure styles offer different storage capacities.
- In addition to the obvious advantage of tremendous storage capacity, there are several other advantages to DVDs and DVD drives, including backward compatibility and the incorporation of MPEG standards directly onto the adapter card.
- DVDs have different format standards as CDs do. Standards include DVD-R, which is a write-once DVD format; DVD-RW, which is rewriteable; DVD+R, which is not compatible with all players; DVD+RW, which is similar to DVD-RW; and DVD-RAM, which was designed as a data storage format.

11.4 HD-DVD and Blu-ray Disc

- The HD-DVD standard was abandoned in 2008 because it failed to compete successfully with the Blu-ray standard. Blu-ray Disc (BD) is a high-definition video and data format developed by the Blu-ray Disc Association, which was started by Sony.
- HD-DVD and Blu-ray Disc use the same laser wavelength of 405 nm; however, the HD-DVD NA setting is 0.65 and the Blu-ray Disc NA setting is 0.85.
- A standard CD can store approximately 650 MB of data, and a DVD can store 4.7 GB of data. However, single-layer HD-DVD has a capacity of 15 GB, and single-layer Blu-ray Disc has a capacity of 25 GB.
- Ultra High-Definition (HD) Blu-ray, not to be confused with HD-DVD, is an optical disc-data storage format that supersedes Blu-ray.

- Designed primarily for media storage and delivery, Ultra HD Blu-ray supports 4K UHD (3840 × 2160 resolution) video at frame rates up to 60 frames per second, encoded using High Efficiency Video Coding.
- Ultra HD Blu-ray specification allows for three disc capacities, each with its own data rate: 50 GB with 82 Mbps; 66 GB with 108 Mbps; and 100 GB with 128 Mbps.

11.5 Disc Drive Interface

- AT Attachment Packet Interface (ATAPI) is the interface used for standard IBM PC AT and compatible systems for accessing CD devices.
- PATA and SATA are commonly used for internal disc drives; USB and eSATA are used for exterior connections.
- The connection points on an optical drive are similar to a hard disk drive with the addition of an audio analog and digital output connection.
- Installation of CD and DVD technologies can also be made using SCSI.

11.6 Digital Rights Management

- Digital rights management (DRM) is any technology used to ensure copyright protection for digital media.
- Examples of DRM include Advanced Access Content System (AACS), High-bandwidth Digital Content Protection (HDCP), Advanced Video Codec High Definition (AVCHD), Region Codes, and Blu-ray Disc Plus (BD+).

11.7 Troubleshooting CD, DVD, and BD

- Some of the most common problems encountered with an optical disc system are failure to eject, Copy Control protection, disc recording problems, not finalizing the disc, physical defects, using the wrong media in an optical device, burning speed is too fast, too many repeated writings, laser failure, firmware updates, and failure to AutoPlay disc.

Review Questions

1. Summarize the manufacturing process and operation of CD technology.
2. Differentiate between CD-R and CD-RW.
3. How does the track on a CD differ from the track arrangement on a hard drive?
4. Differentiate between CLV and CAV.
5. Explain data storage and retrieval using magneto-optical storage devices.
6. From what material is a magneto-optical disc constructed?
7. Compare and contrast CD and DVD construction and operation.
8. Explain how DVDs can have multiple sides and layers.
9. Compare HD-DVD and Blu-ray Disc storage technologies.
10. What is the wavelength of Blu-ray Disc?
11. Differentiate Ultra HD Blu-ray from traditional Blu-ray technologies.
12. List three disc capacities for Ultra HD Blu-ray.
13. What acronyms are used to identify legacy motherboard ports that are similar to PATA?
14. Summarize the difference in connections between legacy PATA optical drives and SATA optical drives.
15. Summarize the installation of an optical disc drive.
16. What is digital rights management (DRM)?

17. Identify digital rights management technologies.
18. What is the purpose of a region code?
19. Which DRM technology used with Blu-ray Discs performs the same protection as a region code?
20. Identify the most common problems encountered with an optical storage system.

Sample A+ Exam Questions

1. After upgrading an existing computer CD drive to a Blu-ray recordable device, the Blu-ray recorder is not detected correctly by the operating system or BIOS. What is *most likely* the cause of the problem?
   A. The Blu-ray recorder has been connected to the wrong type of motherboard port.
   B. The motherboard BIOS needs to be updated.
   C. The Blu-ray recorder is defective.
   D. The Blu-ray recorder drivers have a virus.
2. Which is true about MO disc technology?
   A. The read/write head uses intense magnetic fields to change the arrangement of the magnetic particles embedded in the disc drive.
   B. The read/write process uses laser technology to heat the plastic surrounding the magnetic storage particles being written to.
   C. The laser head is used to melt the reflective material embedded in the plastic disc leaving a bit pattern matching the data.
   D. The read/write head cuts small notches, which represent binary data, into the surface of the plastic disc. The individual notches reflect laser light, which is then interpreted as data by the BIOS system.
3. Which are the standards for CD file storage? (Select two.)
   A. UDF
   B. CDUF
   C. CDRW
   D. CDFS
4. The amount of storage on a typical single-layer Blu-ray Disc is equal to _____.
   A. 650 MB
   B. 15 GB
   C. 25 GB
   D. 50 GB
5. A DVD fails to eject from a DVD recorder because of mechanical failure. After repeatedly attempting to eject the disc through the user interface, how would you proceed to remove the disc from the recorder?
   A. Disassemble the optical disc after removing it from the computer.
   B. Use a small flat-tip screwdriver to pry open the disc tray.
   C. Insert one end of a paper clip into the emergency eject port of the front panel of the optical disc recorder.
   D. Reboot the computer and the disc will be automatically ejected.

6. Which of the following technologies offers the greatest storage capacity?
   A. DVD+R
   B. Dual-layer HD-DVD
   C. Single-layer BD
   D. Dual-layer BD-RE
7. Which two options are available for recording to a DVD-RW in Windows 10? (Select two.)
   A. Mastered
   B. Live File System
   C. Blue book
   D. Yellow book
8. Which type of optical disc requires a third-party software application to record media when using a Windows 7 operating system?
   A. CD+R
   B. DVD+R
   C. DVD RW
   D. BD
9. A couple brings in their laptop computer and complains that when they make a video disc using their Blu-ray recorder on the laptop, they cannot play the video on their older desktop PC that has a CD player. What is *most likely* the cause of the problem?
   A. The Blu-ray is copy protected and cannot be played back on another player.
   B. The Blu-ray player has a much more powerful laser and has burned the disc severely, preventing playback on the older player.
   C. The BIOS on the desktop must be upgraded to match the laptop DVD player/recorder.
   D. The density of the Blu-ray Disc is too high to be read by the older CD player.
10. What is the purpose of the VTOC on an optical disc?
   A. Its function is similar to a FAT. It describes how the data is laid out on the disc.
   B. It controls the volume level on the disc so that it will not blow the speaker system during playback.
   C. It controls the speed of the compact disc to make it compatible with other systems, such as DVD.
   D. It is a special identification data flag that protects against copyright infringements.

Chapter 12

Printers

Learning Outcomes

12.1 Explain the operating principles of various types of printers.
12.2 List various methods for installing a printer.
12.3 Use the print queue window to view and manage print jobs.
12.4 Summarize the process of upgrading printer memory.
12.5 Identify and diagnose common printer faults.
12.6 Differentiate between a bitmap font and a vector font.

A+ Certification Exam Objectives

The following A+ Certification Exam Objectives are covered in this chapter.

Exam 220-1101

3.0 Hardware

- 3.6 Given a scenario, deploy and configure multifunction devices/printers and settings.
- 3.7 Given a scenario, install and replace printer consumables.

5.0 Hardware and Network Troubleshooting

- 5.6 Given a scenario, troubleshoot and resolve printer issues.

Exam 220-1102

1.0 Operating Systems

- 1.3 Given a scenario, use features and tools of the Microsoft Windows 10 operating system.
- 1.4 Given a scenario, use the appropriate Microsoft Windows 10 Control Panel Utility.
- 1.6 Given a scenario, configure Microsoft Windows networking features on a client/desktop.
- 1.9 Given a scenario, perform OS installations and upgrades in a diverse OS environment.

4.0 Operational Procedures

- 4.5 Summarize environmental impacts and local environmental controls.

Key Terms

- bitmap font
- CMYK
- color thermal printer
- dot matrix printer
- dye-sublimation printer
- electrophotographic process (EP)
- font
- HP network re-discovery port monitor
- inkjet printer
- LED printer
- local printer connection
- network printer
- network printer connection
- paper train
- pitch
- points
- print queue
- print spooler
- printer
- printer driver
- solid ink printer
- spooling
- three-dimensional (3D) printer
- vector font
- virtual printer
- Web Services for Devices (WSD)

Overview

PC technicians are responsible for the installation, configuration, modification, and troubleshooting of printer systems. A PC technician is not usually responsible for making physical repairs to the electromechanical parts of the printing engine, but a good knowledge base of the electromechanical operation of printers can prove valuable when troubleshooting a printer system. The electromechanical repair of printers is a specialization area. In this chapter, you will learn the basic operation of the most common styles of printers.

A+ Note

For the A+ Certification Exams, you should be able to discriminate between printer types, such as laser, inkjet, thermal, and impact. The exam usually features a few questions about the function of the major parts of the laser printer, such as the primary corona wire. Study the major parts and the steps of the laser printer process. You should also understand how printer drivers are installed and how to solve common printer problems.

12.1 Printer Types

A **printer** is an electromechanical device that converts computer data into text or graphic images printed to paper or other presentation media. Numerous types of printers are available to install into a computer, each with its own unique operation that allows it to read data and produce a hard copy. Examples of printer types include laser, LED, inkjet, dot matrix, thermal, dye-sublimation, solid ink, all-in-one, and 3D. Depending on the type of work needed, one type of printer may be better suited. Always have a conversation with the user regarding how the printer will be used to determine which printer should be installed.

A+ 1101: 3.6

Many printers, including many laser, inkjet, and solid ink printers, as well as many scanners, include an *automatic document feeder (ADF)*. This is simply a mechanical portion of the printer that feeds paper into the printing. There are two types of ADFs. The first is the *duplexing automatic document feeder (DADF)*, which is a two-sided, or *duplex*, scanning type. A duplex ADF prints or scans both sides of the paper in a single pass. The second type is called a *reversing automatic document feeder (RADF)*, which prints or scans one side of a page at a time. If you want to print or scan the other side, you must turn the paper over and reinsert it.

A+ 1101: 3.7

Laser Printer Operation

Laser printers were invented in the 1970s by Xerox but did not become widely used until well into the 1980s with products such as the HP LaserJet and the Apple LaserWriter. Traditional printing is based on wet ink applied to paper using several different processes, but laser printing uses a process called the electrophotographic process. The **electrophotographic process (EP)** is a combination of static electricity, light, dry chemical compound, pressure, and heat. To better understand this process and the role that the major parts of the laser printer perform in the printing process, view the step-by-step series of illustrations shown in the following sections. In these figures, a black-and-white laser printer is shown.

A+ 1101: 3.6

Step 1. Processing

Processing is sending the data (text or image) to the printer. The processing stage relies on the correct printer driver software being installed. The **printer driver** converts specific file types to electronic signals that control how the image or document is printed on the paper. For example, the electronic signals control the quality of the image or document, number of copies, and overall size of the image or document. In addition to controlling how the document or image is printed, the print driver provides alert messages for low toner or ink, paper jams, and many other functions. See Figure 12-1. When data is sent to a printer, it first passes through a **print spooler**, which is a software program that temporarily stores the data in RAM or an area on the hard drive. Print spooling is discussed later in this chapter.

Caution

The laser-printing process uses extremely high levels of voltage. *Never* attempt to repair or disassemble a laser printer. Repairing a laser printer requires special training and safety precautions. PC technicians do not normally replace laser printer parts other than toner cartridges.

Figure 12-1 The first step in laser printer operation involves the computer and printer exchanging information.

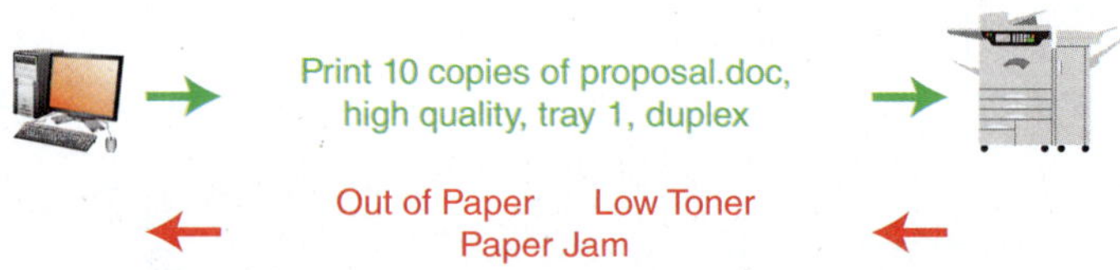

Step 1. Processing involves sending data to the printer and receiving messages from the printer.

Goodheart-Willcox Publisher; (PC icon) romvo/Shutterstock.com; (printer icon) VectorShow/Shutterstock.com

This is also why it is important to be careful and ensure you are using the correct printer driver. That means not just the correct model of printer, but for the correct operating system. There are usually different drivers for the same printer model for Windows, macOS, and Linux operating systems.

Step 2. Charging the Drum

The *primary corona wire* is a wire that is charged to approximately –6,000 volts with the purpose of drawing toner off the drum and onto the paper. The high voltage creates an electrical condition known as a *corona*, which is a static charge surrounding a high-voltage conductor. The primary corona wire is near the drum and applies a large negative charge of approximately –600 volts to –1,000 volts to the surface of the drum. See Figure 12-2.

Step 3. Exposing the Image

The image is *exposed*, or written, to the drum using laser light, which changes intensity according to the light and dark patterns encoded by the data describing the image. A rotating pentagon-shaped mirror reflects the laser beam horizontally across the surface of the drum. See Figure 12-3.

After each horizontal pass, or *trace*, is complete, the drum rotates by a small increment, and the next trace begins. A typical laser printer makes 300 to 1,200 increments of rotation per inch. The drum is coated with a light-sensitive photoconductive material that conducts electricity when struck by intense light. As the laser beam is reflected across the drum, the areas struck by the beam become conductive and lose most of their negative static charge. For example, when a typical image or business letter is to be printed, the white areas of the image are struck by the laser beam while

A+ Note

The printing process for laser printers often appears on the CompTIA A+ Exams. The exact term used to identify the process of using a light beam to create an image on the drum changed from *writing* to *exposing* but could change back again in the future. The exact terminology is determined by a team of subject experts who review and write the objectives, and the next team of subject experts very well could change the term back to *writing*.

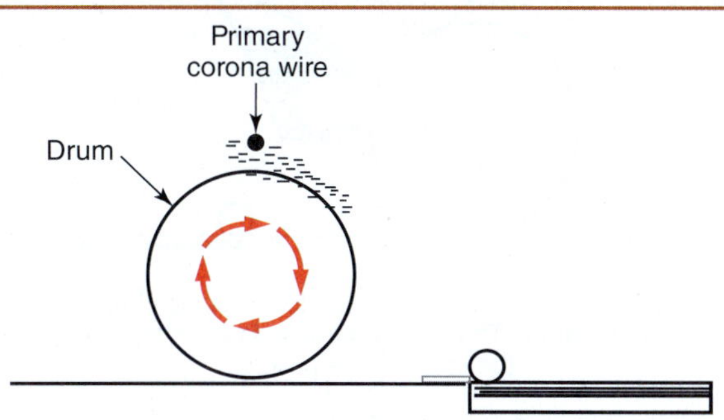

Step 2. The primary corona wire charges the surface of the drum with a negative charge of approximately –600 to –1,000 volts.

Goodheart-Willcox Publisher

Figure 12-2 The second step in laser printer operation involves the primary corona wire charging the printer drum.

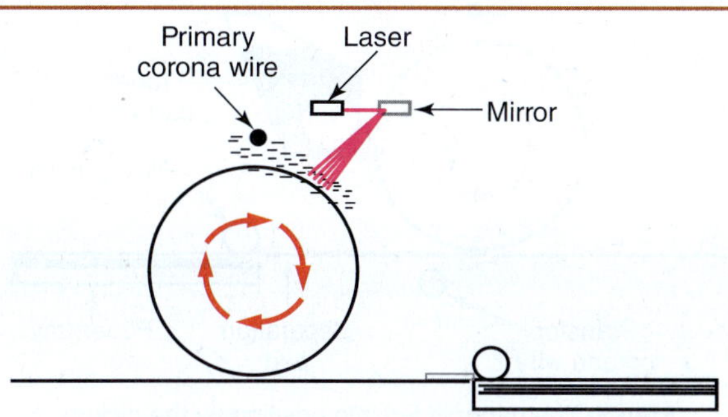

Step 3. A laser beam pulses to a spinning mirror, which reflects light across the negatively charged drum. The laser light draws the outline of the image to be produced.

Goodheart-Willcox Publisher

Figure 12-3 The third step in laser printer operation is the exposure or writing of the image.

the dark areas, such as letters and lines, are not struck by the laser light. The parts of the drum that are not exposed to the light retain the 600- to 1,000-volt negative charge.

Step 4. Developing the Image

As the drum turns, the image created by low and high static charges on the drum pass by the toner cartridge. The toner is attracted to the static charge on the drum. Think of *toner* as a form of very fine plastic dust particles. See Figure 12-4.

A roller is incorporated in the toner cartridge to assist with dispersing the toner from the cartridge. The image to be printed is now formed on the drum.

Step 5. Transferring the Image

As the drum continues to rotate, the paper is fed under it. A set of rollers, called *pickup rollers*, lifts one sheet of paper at a time from the paper tray and feeds it into position under the drum. A device known as a *separator* is located at the edge of the paper tray near the pickup rollers to ensure only one sheet of paper is sent into the drum area at a time.

Just before the paper passes under the drum, it is given a positive charge by the transfer corona wire. See Figure 12-5. The transfer corona wire works much like the primary corona, only using the opposite charge. The paper now has a positive static charge applied to its surface. As the positively charged paper passes under the negatively charged toner on the drum, the toner is attracted to the paper.

Figure 12-4 The fourth step in laser printer operation is the development of the image.

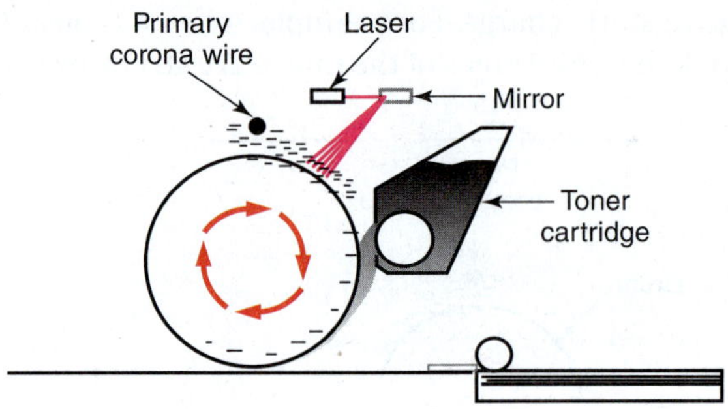

Step 4. The toner is attracted to the static charge on the drum. The static charge is in the shape of the image to be printed.

Goodheart-Willcox Publisher

Figure 12-5 The fifth step in laser printer operation is transferring the image to the paper using a toner drum and a positively charged corona wire.

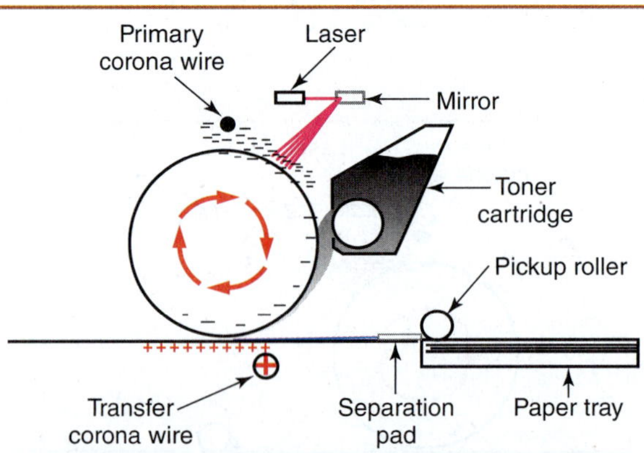

Step 5. The paper is fed into position by the pickup roller. The paper receives a positive charge from the transfer corona wire. The positively charged paper attracts the toner from the drum, creating the image.

Goodheart-Willcox Publisher

Step 6. Fusing the Image

Since there is no longer a need for the static positive charge on the paper, a static brush contacts the paper and drains off any charge remaining on the paper. If the charge were not removed from the paper, the paper would stick to the negatively charged drum and would also make the paper difficult to handle after leaving the printer.

Once covered with a dry toner image, the paper passes through the fuser. The *fuser* consists of a pair of rollers, one of which is heated to a very high temperature. As the toner-covered paper passes through the fuser rollers, the heat and pressure melt the toner, fixing it to the paper's surface. See Figure 12-6.

Usually, a quartz lamp is used to produce the high temperature of the fusing unit because it generates a temperature of over 356°F (180°C). As a safety precaution, there is usually a temperature sensor installed near the fusing unit, which shuts off power to the fusing unit if the temperature gets too high.

Caution

The area around the fusing unit in the printer can cause severe burns when touched. Never attempt to work inside a laser printer unless it has been off for at least 15 minutes.

Step 7. Cleaning the Drum

The drum must be prepared before the next image can be printed. A cleaning unit removes any toner that might still be on the drum. The unit consists of a simple rubber scraper or blade that removes any residual toner left on the drum. The particles of toner are collected inside the cleaning unit container. See Figure 12-7. The blade or scraper is specially designed not to scratch the drum surface. Any scratches on the drum would remove the photosensitive finish, resulting in poor quality of printed images.

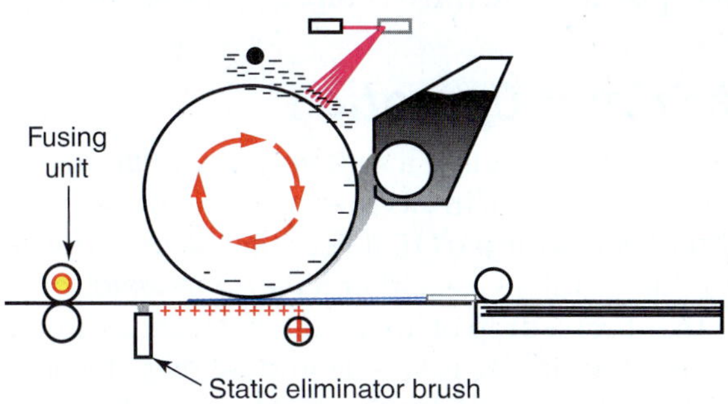

Figure 12-6 In the sixth step in laser printer operation, a static eliminator brush removes the static charge from the paper.

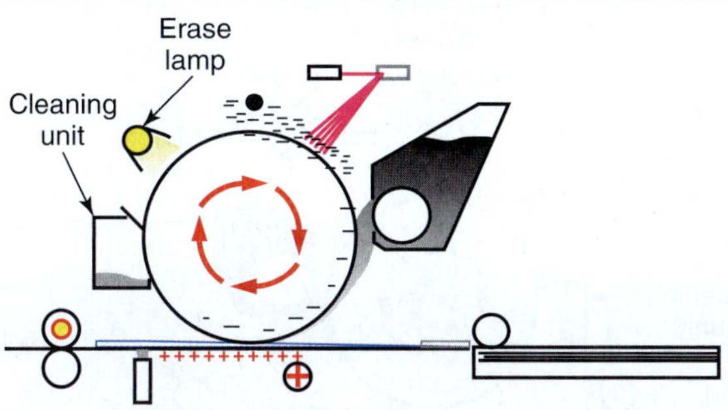

Figure 12-7 After a cleaning unit removes any toner buildup, and an erase lamp removes the charge from the toner, the printer is ready for its next print job.

A high-intensity light is also shone onto the drum to remove any remaining charge from the drum's surface. The drum is now ready to be charged again by the primary corona wire, and the printing process can be repeated. Figure 12-8 shows all the parts together.

Note that in the example of the laser-printing process, the drum illustrated was negatively charged. The same process can occur using opposite polarities. Different manufacturers use different charging levels and polarities to create the same printing process that was shown in our example.

These principles of operation employed in the black-and-white laser printer can also be applied to a color laser printer. A color laser printer uses four separate print engines, one for each of the major colors. The major colors used in a color laser printer are blue, red, yellow, and black. Often, blue is represented by the color cyan, and the red is represented by the color magenta.

> **Tech Tip**
>
> Due to high currents required for the laser printer process, it is *not* recommended to connect a laser printer and computer system to the same UPS.

LED Printer Operation

An **LED printer** uses an array of light-emitting diodes (LEDs) to write the image to the drum. Its operation is very similar to laser printer operation. The main difference between a laser printer and an LED printer is the use of LEDs instead of a laser, which eliminates several moving parts required by the laser-printing process. By reducing the number of parts, the LED printer can claim better reliability because there are fewer mechanical parts to fail. Also, LED printer manufacturers claim that a more compact-size printer can be produced. While it is true that the printer is more reliable mechanically because of fewer moving parts, there is no significant reduction in physical size when comparing a laser printer to an LED printer.

A+ 1101: 3.7

Color Inkjet Printer Operation

An **inkjet printer**, sometimes called a *bubble jet printer*, uses specially designed cartridges that spray a fine mist of ink as they move horizontally in front of a sheet of paper. The inkjet *printhead* is the part that fires the ink onto the paper. The two most common types of inkjet printers use either a *thermoresistor* or a *piezo cell crystal* to produce a force that fires a drop of ink through a nozzle directly onto the paper.

The construction of an inkjet is simple and follows the concept idea that ink must be forced out of the printhead. Figure 12-9 is an exploded view of a single nozzle and its major parts: nozzle, firing chamber, and (in this model) thermoresistor. The ink flows into the firing chamber from the ink cartridge reservoir. An electrical pulse from the computer enters the thermoresistor, and the ink in the firing chamber is instantly heated to over 1,112°F (600°C). The extreme heat expands the ink in

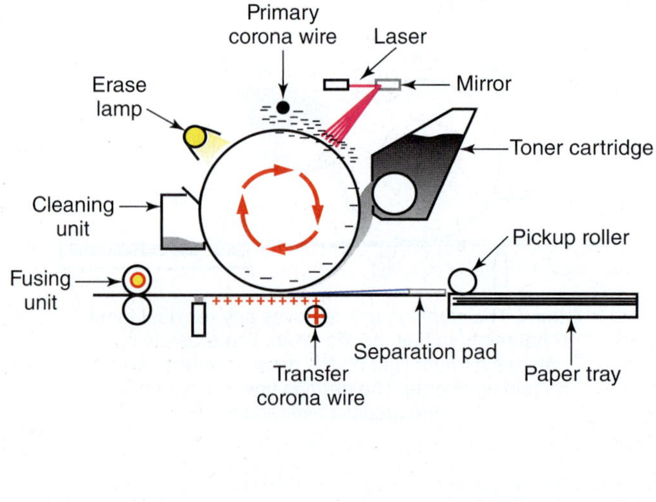

Figure 12-8 In this example, the drum is negatively charged. Some printers may reverse the charges on the drum and paper, but the process stays the same.

Goodheart-Willcox Publisher

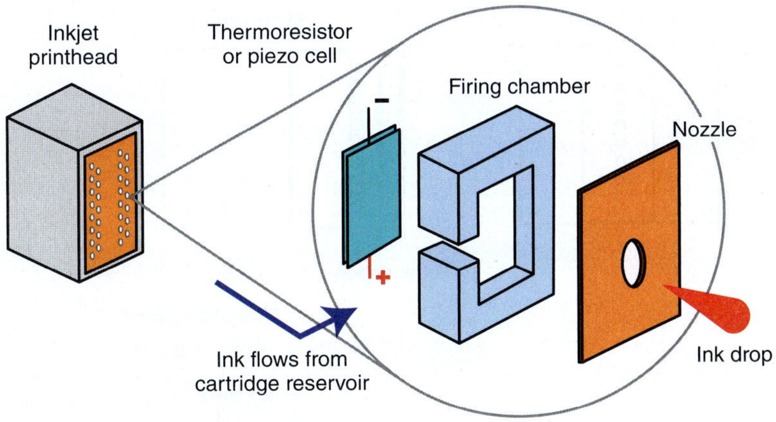

Figure 12-9 In an inkjet printer, ink flows into the firing chamber from the reservoir. Next, the ink is heated, which causes it to expand and fire through the nozzle onto the paper. As the chamber cools, the resulting vacuum draws more ink into the firing chamber.

the chamber, causing it to fire through the nozzle and onto the paper. As the chamber cools, a vacuum is created that draws more ink into the firing chamber from the ink cartridge reservoir, and the process repeats. An inkjet printer can fire its chamber many times a second.

The single ink droplet is quite small. A typical low-cost inkjet printer can produce 720 × 720 dots per square inch (dpi). High-quality inkjet printers can produce a dpi of 1200 × 1200 and higher.

A piezo cell could be used instead of the thermoresistor. A ***piezo cell*** is a crystal that deflects or bends when energized by an electrical pulse. The bending is so rapid, it is often described as vibrating. When a piezo cell is used in place of the thermoresistor, the piezo cell flexes every time an electrical pulse is sent, which causes an ink drop to fire through the nozzle. When the electrical pulse stops, the crystal returns to its original shape, which creates a vacuum in the firing chamber like with the thermoresistor, drawing more ink into the chamber.

A color inkjet printer uses **CMYK**, which is a four-color process consisting of cyan, magenta, yellow, and a key color—most often black. This is a standard combination of colors used in the printing industry as they can be mixed to make other hues such as green, orange, brown, and gray.

Dot Matrix Printer Operation

1101: 3.7 A+

The **dot matrix printer**, sometimes referred to as an ***impact printer***, derives its name from the pattern, or matrix, of very small dots it prints to create text and images. Dot matrix printers were some of the earliest printers. They are now uncommon, and you are unlikely to see many—if any—of these. As a result, the A+ Certification Exams place less emphasis on dot matrix printers.

The dot matrix printhead consists of a line of small metal rods called print pins, Figure 12-10. In appearance, the metal rods look much like a series of small nails. An electrical coil, called a solenoid, controls each print pin. When energized, the solenoid creates a magnetic field. The print pin is constructed with a magnet at one end. When the solenoid is energized, the magnetic end of the pin is attracted to the coil, and the print pin rapidly moves forward, striking an ink ribbon situated between the printhead and paper. Each energized solenoid causes that individual print rod to strike the ribbon, leaving a dot of ink on the paper.

To form a letter, a series of electrical pulses is sent to the printhead. The pulses are coded in a sequence that forms the given letter on the paper as the entire printhead moves horizontally across the paper. The two most common printhead styles are 9-pin and 24-pin.

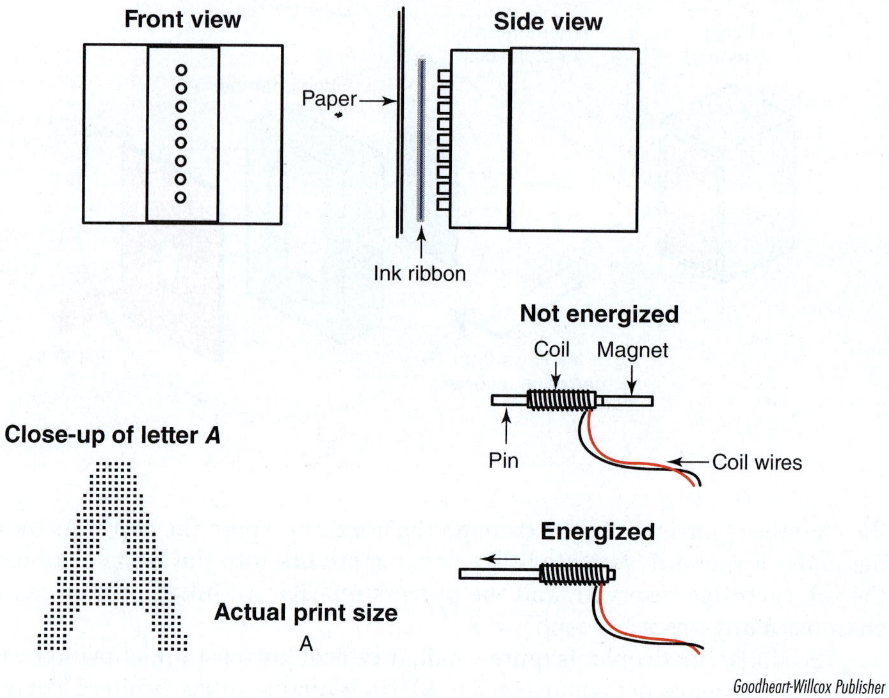

Figure 12-10 Dot matrix printers generate a pattern of dots to create images.

Dot matrix printers require special paper referred to as ***impact paper*** or ***dot matrix paper***. The paper has a series of holes running along the edges, which align to a set of spiked gears at each side of the printer called a ***tractor feed***. When the printer is printing, the spiked gears rotate and advance the paper. Improper alignment of the paper with the spiked gears can cause a paper jam to occur during the print operation.

Printed documents with only partial letters are a sign of a faulty printhead, often caused by one or more pins in the dot matrix printhead not firing properly. Another sign of a faulty or damaged printhead is the appearance of horizontal lines across the document. In this case, a printhead pin is most likely stuck in the striking position, causing the pin to drag across the ribbon and paper. This may require a printhead replacement.

Overall, poor-quality text on the document typically indicates a worn or dry ink ribbon that needs to be replaced. If replacing the ribbon does not correct the problem, the printhead may be damaged or loose.

Dot matrix paper jams are typically caused by a small piece of paper or a foreign object lodged in the gears or rollers. Many times, the bit of paper or foreign object can be removed with a paper clip shaped like a hook. If this fails, you will have to disassemble the dot matrix printer. Always disconnect the power cord before performing any type of physical repairs.

Check the printer manufacturer's website for detailed information about dot matrix disassembly, printer ribbon and printhead replacement, and cleaning and recommended maintenance practices.

A+ 1101: 3.7

Color Thermal Printer Operation

Color thermal printers operate based on the principle of applying color by heating a special ribbon that is coated with a wax-like material. Heat is used to melt the wax, which is then sealed to the surface of the paper by Teflon-coated rollers. See Figure 12-11.

The heating unit consists of an array of small heaters that melt the wax in small dots. The small dots of heated wax represent the data sent from the PC to the printer. The paper must be run through the process four separate times. Each time the paper is run through, a new CMYK color is added to the paper. For the correct print operation to occur, the heating element must remain clean, which is considered routine maintenance for this type of printer.

A unique issue for thermal printers is storing the paper. Since the paper used in thermal printers is heat sensitive, it must be stored in a cool location. This does not require refrigeration, but the temperature cannot be allowed to exceed the specifications for that paper manufacturer.

Color thermal printers are used for high-quality drawings and illustrations. These printers produce high-quality print but at a relatively high cost per sheet, since they use special paper and expensive wax supplies. Many corporations use them for special applications such as reports to the board of directors when color photos and charts are required. They are not used for mass copies, only high quality, and are not commonly found in home use.

Dye-Sublimation Printer Operation

A **dye-sublimation printer** produces near photo-quality printed images by vaporizing inks, which then solidify onto paper. *Sublimation* is a scientific term that refers to the transition of a solid substance into gas. Dye-sublimation printers operate similarly to the color thermal printer process described in the previous section. The difference is that in dye sublimation, the color penetrates the paper, while in thermal print operation, the color is printed to the surface of the paper.

The major parts used in the dye-sublimation process are the drum, transfer roll, and heater, as shown in Figure 12-12. A special paper is mounted directly on the drum, and the transfer roll consists of a long sheet of plastic material coated with CMYK colors. As the drum rotates, the plastic transfer sheet (roll) passes under the drum and across the heater.

The heater consists of thousands of tiny heating elements arranged in a close array, which heat up in patterns representing the data patterns sent from the computer system. The heating elements can heat to 256 different temperature levels, which cause the dye to be transferred at 256 different levels of intensity.

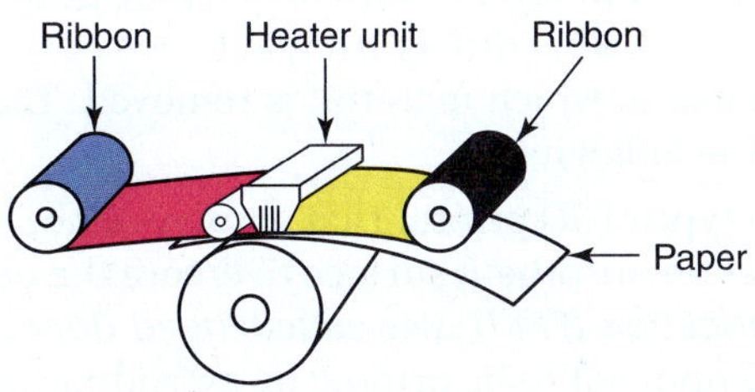

Goodheart-Willcox Publisher

Figure 12-11 Color thermal printers operate by heating colored wax, which seals to the paper.

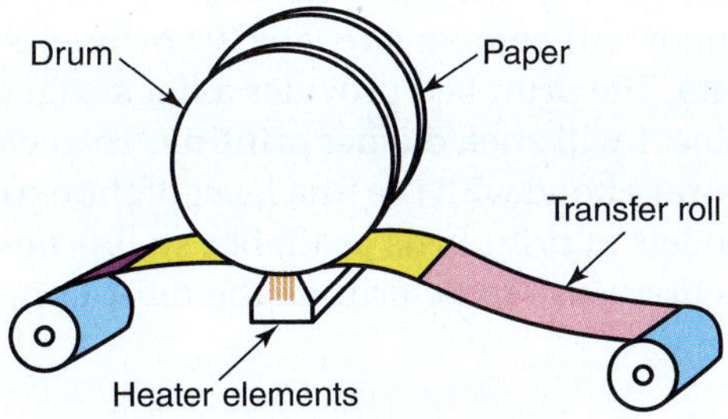

Goodheart-Willcox Publisher

Figure 12-12 A dye-sublimation printer vaporizes inks, which then solidify onto paper. The major parts used in the dye-sublimation process are the drum, transfer roll, and heater.

The drum rotates four times. During each revolution of the drum, a different color passes from the transfer roll into the paper and is absorbed into the paper fibers as opposed to coating the top of the paper. The four colors sublimate to the paper and combine to create over 16 million colors.

Dye-sublimation printers and materials are very expensive. However, the dye-sublimation process provides significantly higher resolution and better color representation than the laser or inkjet processes.

Solid Ink Color Printer Operation

A **solid ink printer** uses solid ink cartridges similar to wax. The printhead consists of four long rows of many individual nozzles, and each row produces one of the four CMYK colors. The four colors are heated and flow into individual reservoirs. As the paper passes by the printheads, the nozzles are fired, releasing a fine mist of color to the paper. One advantage of the solid ink color printer is that it uses ordinary paper for its process. However, printer and ink supplies are expensive when compared to laser and inkjet supplies.

All-in-One Products

In recent years, manufacturers have introduced all-in-one products, especially for home- and small-office use. The all-in-one units are a combination of four common office devices that rely on printing techniques to accomplish their tasks: printer, fax, copier, and scanner. The all-in-one devices are a cost-effective way to purchase office equipment. The downside is that when the all-in-one device fails, typically you cannot use any of the devices.

A+ 1101: 3.7

3D Printers

Three-dimensional (3D) printers manufacture tangible objects by using code from a computer-aided drafting (CAD) file to deposit a plastic filament from a printhead onto a surface and then onto the model itself. The operation is similar to traditional printers; in fact, the first working models were derived from inkjet hardware heavily modified to use resin instead of ink. These printers are becoming far more common.

Technically, the plastic filament used in 3D printers is a stream of a resin that is melted and then deposited in layers, similar to a glue gun feed. This approach is a called an *additive process*. This differs from a device such as a CNC mill, which uses a *subtractive process* in which material is removed. There are many types of 3D printers, including the following:

- *Material jetting* is a type of 3D printer that employs a nozzle with liquid material drawn over an absorbent surface to create the object.
- *Fused filament fabrication (FFM)*, also called *fused deposition modeling (FDM)*, enables a component to be printed by extruding small streams of material which harden, forming layers.
- *Binder jetting* involves the deposition of a binding adhesive substance onto layers of a material, thus building the component one layer at a time.

One of the more important components of a 3D printer is the *print bed*, sometimes called a *build plate*. The print bed provides a flat surface for the bottom layer to which the printed object will stick during printing. To accomplish this task, the print bed forms a temporary bond with the first layer of the extruded filament. There are many types and models of print beds available, so it is best to consult with the printer manufacturer's literature to determine the most appropriate type for your printing tasks.

12.2 Printer Installation and Configuration

1101: 3.6 A+

Printers connect to computers in several different ways, including directly via USB cable or indirectly via Wi-Fi, Internet, Infrared, Bluetooth, or network connection. The most common printer connections used today are USB, RJ-45, and wireless. FireWire is also an option but only with older Apple computer systems. When connected directly to a computer, the printer connection is referred to as a **local printer connection**. When connected by other means than a direct connection to a computer, the connection is referred to as either a **network printer connection** or *shared printer connection*.

Printers can also be connected through web services such as HP Smart and Apple AirPrint. Web printer services are designed for portable devices such as smartphones, tablets, and laptops. The printer must be enabled for web service to use the service, and you must obtain an e-mail address for the printer from the print service provider. After an e-mail address is obtained for the printer, you can then send an e-mail with to the printer over the Internet, along with an attachment to be printed, such as a document or photo.

Google Cloud Print services also provide web-service printing used with HP, Apple, Dell, Epson, Kodak, Samsung, or any print or mobile device capable of accessing cloud storage. You can configure the print service using a Google account. After the printer has been identified, you can send documents and photos stored on your Google cloud storage service to your printer using the Internet.

This may seem like a trivial matter, but unboxing the printer is part of the installation. To unbox the device, open the box from the bottom. Open all the box flaps and then turn the box upside down to slowly slide the printer and its packing material (often Styrofoam) out. To set up the printer, you should place it on a flat surface near its intended operational location. The location is an important consideration, as well. Do not place the printer in a location that will receive direct sunlight, as the plastic housing can be damaged from the sun's UV rays. Additionally, be aware of temperature fluctuations. Ideally, the printer should be placed in a climate-controlled area free from direct sunlight and risk of moisture.

Local Printer Installation

1102: 1.4 A+

The term *local printer* refers to a printer that connects directly to a PC. In this way, the printer is local to that particular computer. Not all printers are local printers, however. For example, a printer can be connected to a PC through a network and shared by many different PCs. This type of connection is covered later.

Most printers are automatically detected and configured, but not *all* printer configurations are simple. Sometimes, the printer configuration must be accomplished manually, so a technician must become familiar with the setup options and properties available for printer systems. Be aware that the users you serve are easily frustrated by inoperable equipment or by new computer equipment that does not perform to expectations. Knowledge can generate confidence in the user and lessen some frustrations during setup or repair.

There are a variety of ways to install a printer. One method is to navigate to **Start>Control Panel>Hardware and Sound>Devices and Printers>Add a printer**. Another method, which is discussed in this section, is to navigate to **Start>Settings>Devices>Printers & scanners>Add a printer or scanner**, as shown in Figure 12-13.

Windows will walk you through the printer installation process regardless of the method you use to start the install. Notice the **Add a printer or scanner** option shown in Figure 12-13. This option takes you through the installation procedure.

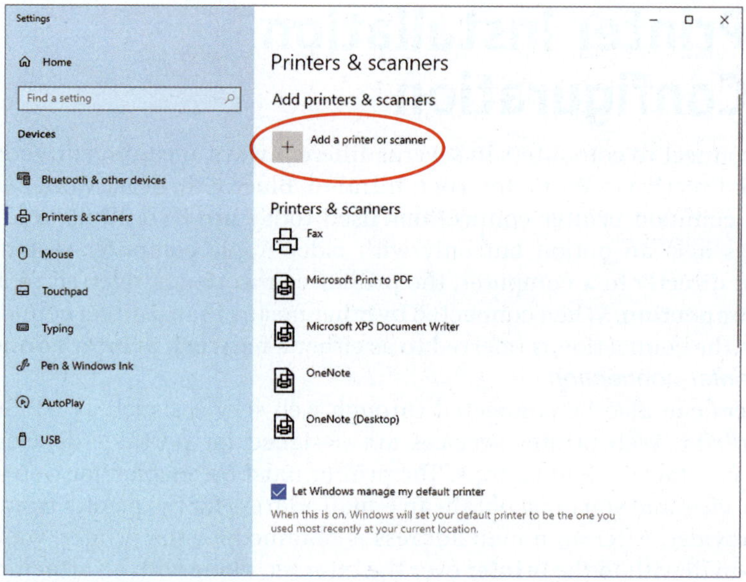

Figure 12-13 A printer can be installed by navigating to the device settings menu.

Goodheart-Willcox Publisher

The same is true if you are installing through Control Panel. When activated, the device settings menu will begin searching for printers and scanners installed on the PC or connected via network access. After selecting the desired device, you can choose to make it the default printer or remove it from the list.

A+ 1101: 3.6

An important configuration setting is the printer tray options and settings. To establish tray settings, navigate to the Devices and Printers menu, right-click your printer, and select **Printing Preferences** from the shortcut menu. From here, you can configure selections such as default paper size and type as well as the primary source of paper. Some printers have multiple paper trays so users can print on different paper types or colors. Often, the default tray stores plain white paper, while other trays house specialty paper such as card stock or different colors.

Selecting a Printer Port

You are unlikely to use COM ports any longer, as most printers connect via USB or wireless. The information on selecting COM ports is not emphasized on the current A+ Certification Exams and is included here simply in case you encounter a very old printer or computer. The number of ports to choose from when manually configuring a printer port can be very confusing. Microsoft maintains backward compatibility with older printers, and as a result, you will still see choices of printer ports listed as COM and LPT. COM is a legacy serial port, and LPT is a legacy parallel port. Some printer manufacturers write their own proprietary software applications for automatically configuring a printer port. Those proprietary ports can show up in the list of available printer ports.

When applicable, there are usually four COM ports identified as COM1, COM2, COM3, and COM4. COM1 and COM3 share the same IRQ assignment, and COM2 and COM4 share the same IRQ assignment. Look at the table in Figure 12-14 to see the assigned IRQ and port memory address for each COM and LPT port. Note, the lowercase *h* in the Port Address column signifies a hexadecimal number.

LPT is a parallel port used to connect to a printer or other device that requires a parallel connection. It, too, has an assigned IRQ and a port memory address. LPT ports are still in use to some extent for printers. Businesses, governmental, and educational institutions often use equipment like printers much longer than home users.

A+ 1101: 3.6

As mentioned, the preferred cable connection for local printers is USB. When USB is used to connect to a printer, the port may be identified as a DOT4 port, which is a virtual port. The DOT4 port provides two-way communication between the printer and the computer, allowing the printer to send messages to the computer indicating errors or functionality messages such as an empty paper tray or low ink or toner levels.

The **Web Services for Devices (WSD)** is a printer-port monitor service developed by Microsoft. It was first introduced in Windows Vista and is still available in Windows 10. The WSD printer port monitor allows printers and computers to discover each other when connected on a home or office network. The printer must be WSD-compliant to allow for communication between the printer and computer(s) on the network.

A+ 1102: 1.3

The **HP network re-discovery port monitor** is a wireless port used to support connections to a wireless printer. When the printer is an all-in-one printer with a fax, a second HP network re-discovery port monitor will appear in the list. Network discovery protocols and applications are covered in much more detail in the chapters concerning networking.

Device Manager can be used to look at available printer devices that are installed. The types of printer devices and connections listed vary according to the type of printer connected to the computer and the way the printer is connected. For example, a wireless connection to a printer may only show as a WSD Print Provider, and there will be no **Ports (COM & LPT)** entry if the computer motherboard does not have these ports available. After the port is selected, the wizard will search for a printer.

Selecting a Printer and Printer Driver

A+ 1101: 3.6

Usually, the wizard will automatically identify the correct printer. If the wizard fails to identify the appropriate printer correctly, you will need to add the printer manually, as shown in Figure 12-15. Windows will then search for all available printers connected and will even download drivers for them when selected. A printer driver contains the code necessary to allow the computer to communicate to the printer and differs from one operating system to another. That is, if you have a Windows computer, be sure to download the printer driver designed specifically for Windows. The correct driver for the correct operating system is essential to ensure proper printing of the desired text or image. Without the correct OS driver, the printer may operate incorrectly or not at all. For example, when you attempt to print without the correct driver, some common actions are a constant ejection or feed of paper, printing a document with no margins, and printing gibberish or unrecognizable symbols.

Windows provides a wide assortment of printer models from which to choose. This way, all the printer drivers at the time of the operating system release are available on the hard drive. However, this is not always the case. If the needed driver were not loaded during installation, the wizard would attempt to locate it automatically from both the computer and online sources. Many times, you must go to the printer manufacturer's website and download the correct printer driver.

Sometimes, the printer you are installing will not be listed. New models of printers are constantly being developed, and the desired driver may not be present. When the model to be installed is not listed, select the option that allows you to install drivers

COM and LPT Assignments

COM Port	IRQ Assignment	Port Address	Comment
COM1	4	3F8h-3FFh	Serial port
COM2	3	2F8h-2FFh	Serial port
COM3	4	3E8h-3EFh	Serial port
COM4	3	2E8h-2EFh	Serial port
LPT1	7	378h-37Fh	Parallel port
LPT2	Any available	278h-27Fh	Parallel port

Goodheart-Willcox Publisher

Figure 12-14 COM and LPT ports have unique addresses.

Figure 12-15 The Add Printer wizard allows users to request help from Windows, enter the name of a shared printer, or add a printer using a TCP/IP address, Bluetooth wireless settings, or through local network means.

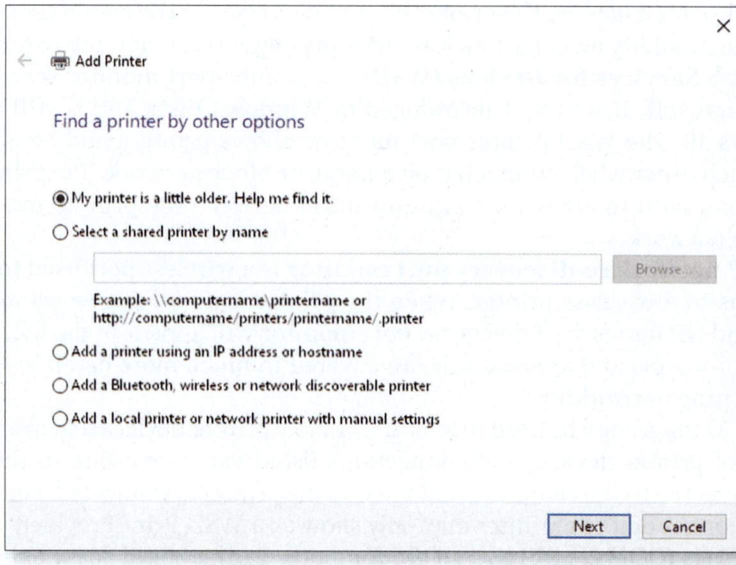

Goodheart-Willcox Publisher

from a disc or USB drive. A CD with drivers should come in the packaging with the printer; though, checking for the latest drivers at the manufacturer's website is always the preferred option. If the drivers included with the printer are on a CD, be sure to change from A:\ to D:\ or to the correct CD/DVD drive letter for your PC. It is more common to go to the printer manufacturer's website and download the appropriate driver. If you are downloading the drivers from a different device, save the drivers to a USB flash drive, and locate that drive when searching for the appropriate driver.

Virtual Printer Installation

A **virtual printer** is a software-based application installed on a computer used to create documents. This provides a type of file conversion or transfer. Virtual printers function similarly to physical printers, but the user does not actually print anything tangible. Instead, the print drivers are established to send output to a separate application, not a physical printer. Four common uses for virtual printers include printing to other files, printing to PDF, printing to XPS, and printing to an image.

Print to File

Print to file is still available for some applications in Windows 10. For example, the Notepad application has an option to print to file, as shown in Figure 12-16. Users select the printer they want to use, in this case **Microsoft Print to PDF**, and select the **Print to file** option. It is far more common for the user to desire to print to a more usable format.

Print to PDF

Print to PDF employs a virtual printer driver that prints to a file coded as PDF rather than sending a byte stream to a physical printer. Notepad's print to PDF option is shown in Figure 12-16. This method is similar to exporting to an alternate format or converting to an alternate format.

Print to XPS

Print to XPS employs a virtual printer driver that prints to a file coded as XPS rather than sending a byte stream to a physical printer. This method is analogous to exporting or converting to an alternate format. XPS is a specification for a page description language and a fixed-document format developed by Microsoft in 2009.

Originally known as the XML Paper Specification, it has transformed into the Open XPS standard with a file extension of **.oexps**, which functions much like PDF.

Print to Image

Print to image is similar to print to file. It is used to take, for example, a PDF file and print it to an image format. This approach can be useful when you transfer your file to another user who does not own your fonts or if you want to control editing of a PDF.

1101: 3.6 A+

Print Server Properties

The **Print server properties** option appears after selecting a printer in the **Devices and Printers** dialog box, Figure 12-17. When selected, the **Print Server Properties** dialog box will open. The dialog box provides access to information about the printer properties as well as a means to change the printer configuration properties. Figure 12-18 shows the dialog box for each tab: **Forms**, **Ports**, **Drivers**, **Security**, and **Advanced**.

A+ Note

To help you prepare for the printer portion of the CompTIA A+ Exams, download a printer manual from a printer manufacturer and familiarize yourself with the setup, basic maintenance, and troubleshooting procedures.

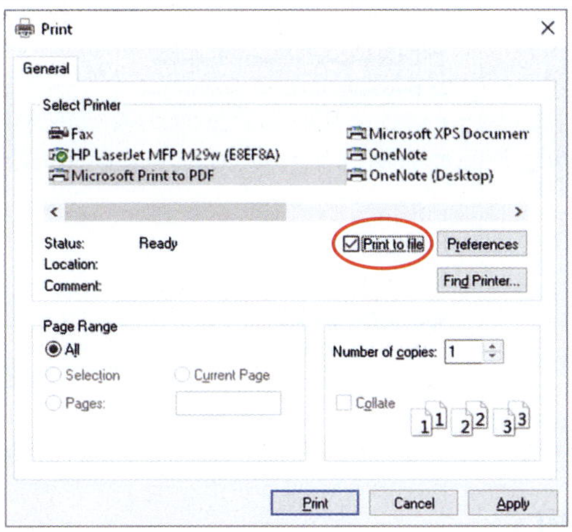

Goodheart-Willcox Publisher

Figure 12-16 Notepad maintains a print to file option.

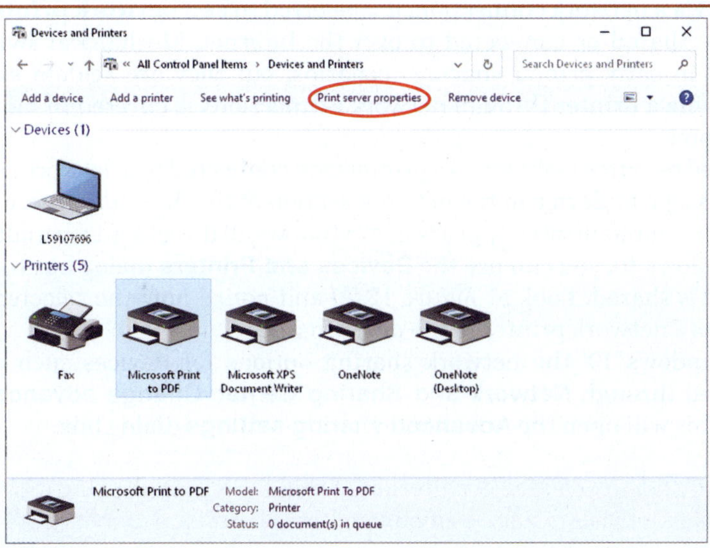

Goodheart-Willcox Publisher

Figure 12-17 Clicking **Print server properties** will open the **Print Server Properties** dialog box, providing access to the most common printer properties, such as paper properties, drivers, port assignment, and security.

Figure 12-18 The tabs in the Print Server Properties dialog box are **Forms**, **Ports**, **Drivers**, **Security**, and **Advanced**.

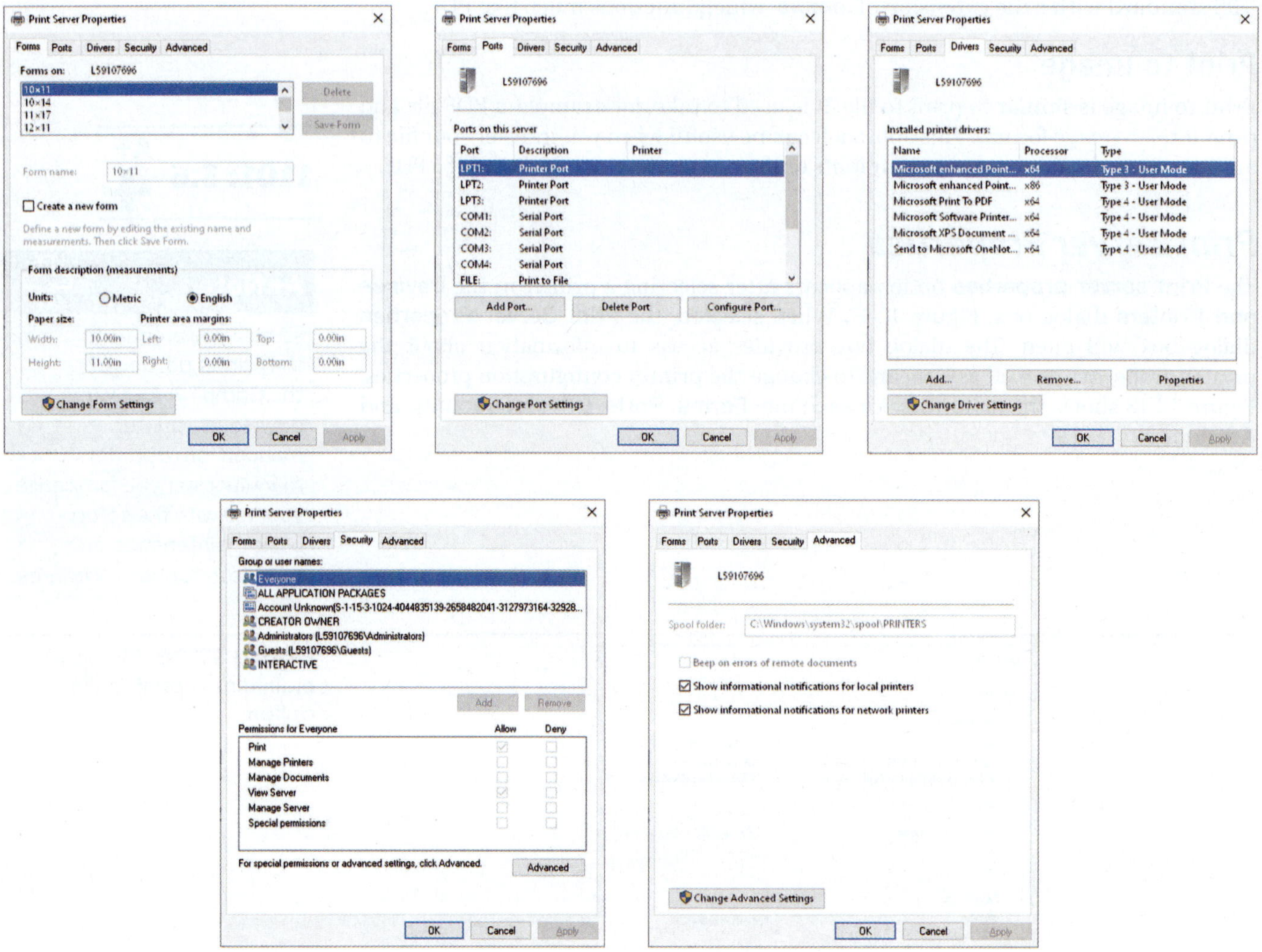

Goodheart-Willcox Publisher

A+ 1101: 3.6
1102: 1.6

Sharing Printers

Printers are commonly shared over wired or wireless networks. When a printer is connected via a network connection, it is referred to as a **network printer**. Printers can also be shared or connected to over the Internet. Mechanical switches were often used in early printer-sharing scenarios, but they are seldom encountered today. Sharing a printer through network connections is covered in more detail in a later chapter.

A shared resource is shown as a printer icon connected to a network cable or simply listed as a print device in the network section of the directory tree. Figure 12-19 shows how a shared printer appears in a Windows 10 directory tree under Network.

In Windows 10, you can use the **Devices and Printers** dialog box to determine if a printer is shared. Look at Figure 12-20 and notice how the selected printer is identified as a network printer in the device name.

For Windows 10, the network sharing options for devices such as printers are accessed through **Network and Sharing Center>Change advanced sharing settings**. This will open the **Advanced sharing settings** dialog box.

Tech Tip

A *shared* printer is a printer connected directly to a computer and then configured as a network share for use by other computers. A network printer is connected independently as part of a network, either wired or wirelessly, and then shared to other computers.

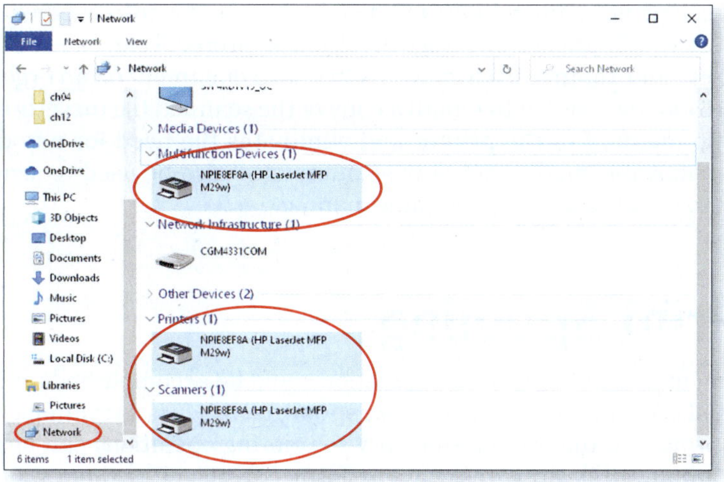

Goodheart-Willcox Publisher

Figure 12-19 Shared printers are listed under the Network portion of the file tree in Windows.

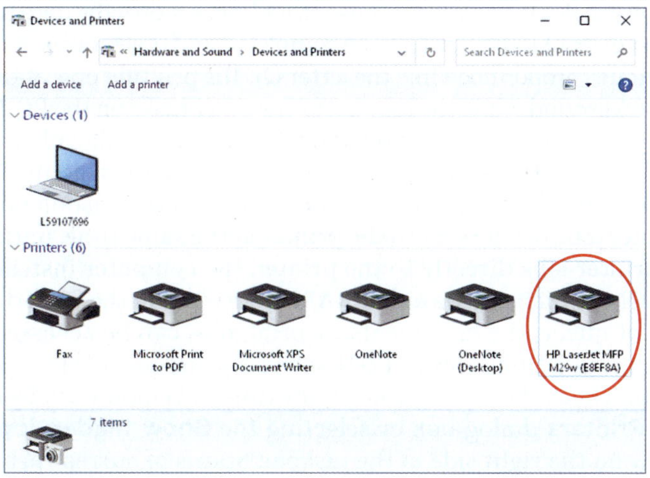

Goodheart-Willcox Publisher

Figure 12-20 Network printers are identified in the **Devices and Printers** menu.

Printer Security

A+ 1101: 3.6

Usually in a small-office/home-office (SOHO) setting, printer security is not essential, but in any large organizational setting, securing the printer is quite important. If the printer is in a publicly accessible area, you want to limit who can print to the printer and be able to track what is printed. A few simple tasks can increase the security of any printer, the first of which is user authentication.

Just as you do with any service on a network, users should authenticate to the printer to use it. This allows you to track what is printed and by whom. In addition to authentication, audit logs provide details as to what was printed, when it was printed, and who printed it. Using audit logs goes beyond simple printer security, as it also allows you to track printer utilization, which can be helpful when developing organizational policies and budgets. For example, if you review the audit logs and determine that one department uses more print resources than another, you can adjust policies accordingly.

Secure printing is another security feature for printers in which users need to enter a PIN at the printer in order to release the print job. In some cases, an RFID badge can be used instead of a PIN for additional security. Similar to audit logs, secure printing is not only an excellent security measure but also a valuable tool for tracking printer utilization and preventing unauthorized personnel from printing.

Securing a printer, much like any other device, can be enhanced with network scanning services. The Server Message Block (SMB) protocol can be used for sharing access to files. For example, if a user needs to scan a document on an organizational printer, SMB can be enabled to e-mail a copy of the scanned file directly to the user. This frees up memory in the printer and eliminates the need for any direct connection or removable media. Network scanning can also be used to send scanned documents to cloud services in the same manner.

A+ **1101: 3.6, 5.6**
1102: 1.4

12.3 Print Spooling

In early computer systems, no other operation could be accomplished until the computer finished printing. Today, printers use **spooling**, which is a technique that stores data to be printed in the printer's memory so printing operations can be completed in the background while other tasks are performed by the PC without waiting for the printer to complete its job. Many input/output (I/O) devices and operations use spooling to store data temporarily, freeing up CPU resources and allowing other activities to be performed on the PC. When a printer uses spooling, it stores the data to be printed in a buffer. This list of print jobs waiting to be completed and their status is also referred to as the **print queue** (pronounced like the letter *Q*). The printing operation can be completed in the background while the user performs other tasks on the PC. Print spooling and print queues are unique to each operating system. If you download the incorrect driver, both of these features will likely malfunction or not run at all. This is another reason why it is so important to select the correct driver upon installation.

Many printer jobs can be sent to the printer at the same time. Rather than sending multiple printer jobs directly to the printer, the computer instead sends them to the print queue, which can be either RAM or an area on the hard drive. With the data in the print queue, the documents, or print jobs, can be accessed and printed by the printer one at a time. Figure 12-21 shows a print queue window with no jobs queued. You can check the print queue at any time in Windows 10 by accessing the **Devices and Printers** dialog box or selecting the **Show hidden icons** button in the system tray on the right side of the taskbar. Status of current print jobs can be indicated as "printing." Other status possibilities are "paused" and "spooling." If the printer is shared by more than one PC, the owner of the job will be displayed.

The same print job may be repeated twice in the queue. It is very common to have many copies of the same file sent to a print queue because of a stalled printing process. When a page fails to print, a novice user will attempt to print the document several times before calling for technical support. One of the first things a technician should do when responding to a print call is to purge all the duplicate print jobs from the queue. Sometimes a printer is locked up because of a document sent by a shared user. By purging a particular user's document, the printing problem may be cleared, and the remaining documents will print as they should. Look at Figure 12-22 to see the options available from the **Printer** menu in the print queue window. You can select **Pause Printing**, **Cancel All Documents**, **Sharing**, and more.

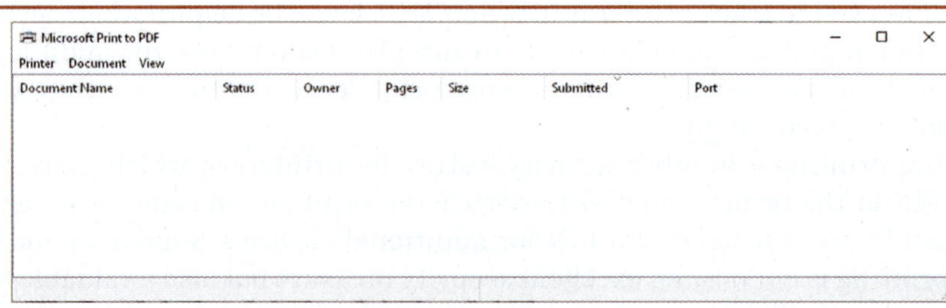

Figure 12-21 The print queue window lists pending print jobs.

Goodheart-Willcox Publisher

12.4 Printer Memory

Legacy printers usually have memory in the form of SIMMs or DIMMs. Modern printers have sufficient memory to meet most printing needs, including printing photo-quality pictures. The amount of memory with which a printer is equipped determines the resolution and size of the subject to be printed. If a printer does not have sufficient memory to print a file, it will generate an error code, which is a common occurrence when printing large, memory-intensive, graphic images. The exact error code will depend on the printer manufacturer and model. One sure sign of insufficient memory is a printer that only prints a portion of an image or document.

Installing more printer memory is a relatively simple task. Consult the printer documentation to determine the recommended type of memory as the best solution for additional memory. Once the printer documentation is consulted about the appropriate memory type to use, the memory installs just as it would to the RAM banks on a motherboard. Review Chapter 6 for information about installing RAM modules. The amount of memory in the printer can usually be verified by a self-test performed at the menu on the printer.

Flash memory ports are available on many printers to support printing directly from the memory module, as shown in Figure 12-23. The flash memory becomes an extension of the printer memory and can be used to store documents and images that require frequent printing. For example, sales brochures, product information, or catalogs can be stored on a memory card and then printed as needed. You should consult the printer specifications to determine the exact type of memory with which the printer is compatible.

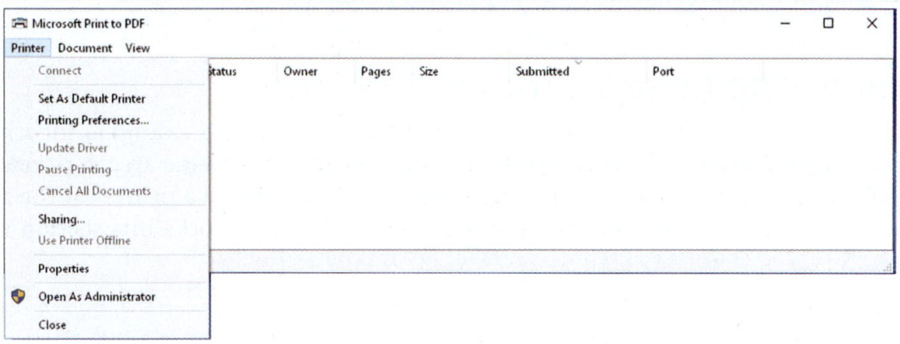

Goodheart-Willcox Publisher

Figure 12-22 The Printer menu of the print queue window provides additional print options.

USB flash memory port

Flash memory card ports

Goodheart-Willcox Publisher

Figure 12-23 Printers can print directly from devices such as USB flash memory and flash memory cards.

A+ 1101: 5.6

12.5 Troubleshooting Printers

Troubleshooting printers is easy if you understand the printing process and know the function of the printer driver. The paper train and the function of printer drivers are similar for all printers. Error codes are designed by printer manufacturers to help you with the troubleshooting process, but they differ from one manufacturer to another.

Interpreting Error Codes and Messages

Error codes produced on some printer LCD displays provide a frequent source of confusion. Some errors generated are straightforward such as Paper Jam or Refill Paper Tray. Other errors are cryptic and require decoding. They simply refer to a number such as 40 ERROR or E22. Some of these errors can be translated by using the owner's manual, but other times, you may need to access the manufacturer's website for more information. Many printer manufacturers also include printer diagnostic software that can determine problems such as paper jams, no paper, low toner/ink, and most other commonly encountered problems.

Some of the codes are not published publicly, as manufacturers feel these repairs involve work beyond the typical user's expertise. For example, a defective fuser that requires a replacement fuser module may simply generate an error code with a statement such as Contact ABC.inc, where "ABC.inc" is the printer manufacturer.

Printer manufacturers also provide diagnostic software applications over the Internet. For example, HP provides diagnostic services for many of its products. These applications can help troubleshoot problems such as paper jams, cartridge jams, ink not printing, and most other commonly encountered problems for printing, scanning, and faxing, as shown in Figure 12-24.

A+ 1101: 3.7

Diagnosing General Printer Problems

Many general printer problems are created by the user. For example, incorrect colors, paper jams, blank areas, printer offline, and other problems are user-created problems. The user may not fully understand how to configure a printer or the fact that a local printer needs the computer to be turned on to work. This section will

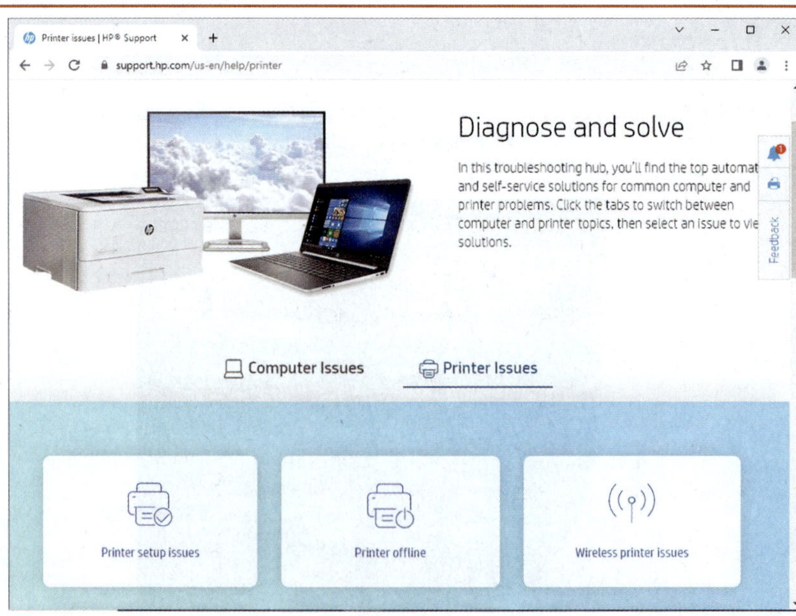

Figure 12-24 HP provides several printer diagnostic software applications for free download.

Goodheart-Willcox Publisher

present some of the most commonly encountered problems usually created by the user. The problems presented here may apply to any printer type.

Incorrect Colors

A+ 1101: 5.6

Printing the incorrect color is a sign that the print cartridges are installed incorrectly. Ink cartridges have a particular order in which they must be installed. Also, be aware that a printer may not correctly match the color that appears on the monitor. Windows provides the **Color Management** dialog box, shown in Figure 12-25, which is accessed through the printer **Properties** dialog box. The color can be adjusted to better match what is being printed to what appears on the monitor or digital photos.

Blank Areas in Printing Job

If blank areas are appearing on the printing job, there is a good chance the wrong paper length has been selected at setup. Check if there is a mismatch in paper length. Also check for debris in the printhead.

Paper Jams

A+ 1101: 5.6

Paper jams occur when a printer pulls one or more sheets through its mechanism, and the paper becomes wedged inside. They are a common problem associated with most printers. There are many causes of paper jams, but with proper care, most jams can be avoided.

Paper quality is an important issue when it comes to paper jams. Low-quality paper produces a lot of paper lint, which accumulates in all printers. Accumulation around sensitive printer parts can cause jams. Also, paper with creases, folded corners, and damaged edges will cause paper jams.

Another issue is moisture. When paper arrives from an outside storage area that is not climate controlled, condensation can be created due to the change in temperature. This can make the paper damp, which is almost sure to jam in a printer. The paper should be stored at the same room temperature and humidity level as the printer for approximately twenty-four hours before use.

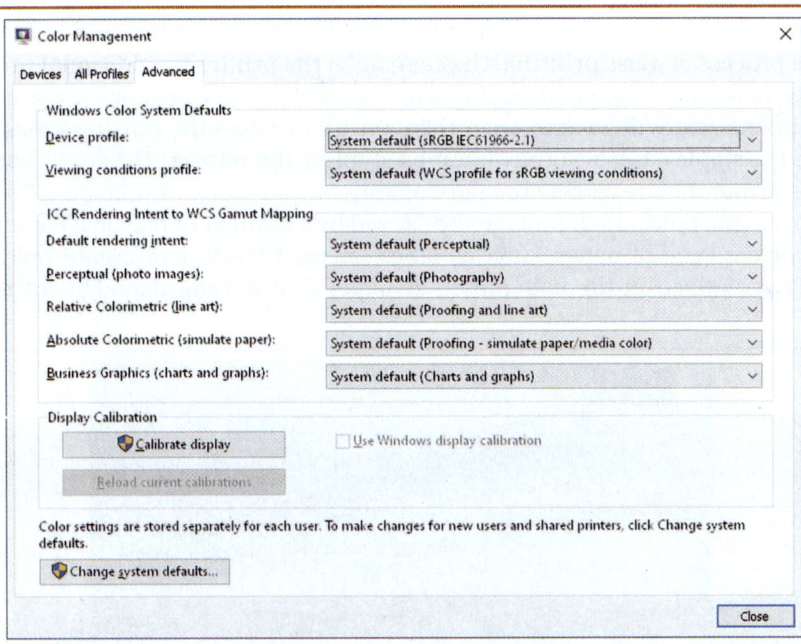

Goodheart-Willcox Publisher

Figure 12-25 The **Color Management** dialog box can be adjusted to better match what is being printed to what appears on the monitor or digital photos.

A+ 1101: 5.6

Another common cause of paper jams is worn parts along the paper train. The **paper train** is the route that paper follows through a printer and consists of several rubber rollers and a paper separator pad. The paper separator pad is designed to allow only one sheet of paper at a time to enter the paper train from the paper tray. As the paper separator pad wears, jams become increasingly more common. In this case, the only remedy is to replace the separator pad. Worn pickup rollers can also cause jams. Sometimes, cleaning the rollers or removing paper lint can solve the problem, but other times, the pickup rollers must be replaced. See Figure 12-26.

The direction of paper can influence the number of jams created in the printer. Most paper is manufactured with a natural curve, and the outside wrapping of a ream of paper will include and arrow to indicate the side of the stack of paper that should be used first in any printer or copy machine. However, not all paper packages are marked with an indicating arrow. If you are experiencing a definite curl to the finished printed page, check for markings on the paper wrapper for the correct positioning of the paper into the paper tray.

The paper you use and place in the feeder can also be an issue. First, lower quality paper is more likely to jam. Secondly, using the incorrect paper size can cause a problem. This is easily resolved by ensuring the paper size is appropriate for both the printer and the print job. You should also confirm that the paper is oriented correctly. Incorrect paper orientation can lead to the print being laid out on the paper differently than you had wished. Staples in the paper can lead to paper jams when run through an automatic feeder, so you should always remove all staples before printing, scanning, or otherwise putting paper through a printer or scanner.

A+ 1101: 5.6

Speckling on Paper

Speckling on printed pages is most often caused by foreign materials in the printer. While there are multiple ways that such foreign materials can be introduced to the printer, the paper feed is the most prominent. Keeping the paper train and the rest of the printer clean is an important preventive maintenance task that can help eliminate this issue. Issues with the toner or ink cartridges could also cause speckling on pages, so it may also be a valuable use of time to check those as well.

A+ 1101: 5.6

Finishing Issues

Many multifunctional printers have finishing options, such as automatic collating, stapling, and hole punching. While these features are convenient and help streamline the process of mass printing, they can open the printer to additional problems. Just like handheld staplers, the stapling mechanism in a printer can jam. When this happens, you will have to open the door that houses the finishing mechanics, remove the staple case, clear any jammed staples, and reinsert the staple case back into the printer before closing the door again.

Jams in the hole punch unit can be caused by a number of reasons. For example, the incorrect type of paper, such as labels or card stock, can create hole punch jams. Paper lodged in the hole punch or paper that did not dislodge entirely can

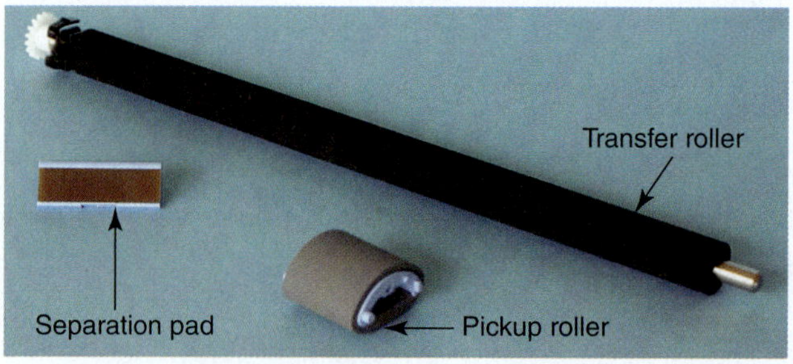

Figure 12-26 Printer maintenance kits for the paper train provide the most common parts that require periodic replacement. Shown are the separation pad, transfer roller, and pickup roller.

Goodheart-Willcox Publisher

also create hole punch jams. Often, hole punch units have a small wheel you can turn with your thumb to manually push paper out of the unit. Many printers will have built-in troubleshooting to help guide an average user through the process of clearing finishing issues, but when in doubt, consult the manufacturer's literature.

Printer Trips the Circuit Breaker

If the circuit breaker trips when the printer is running, it is a good sign that electronic or other parts of the printer are failing. However, you must remember that a laser printer uses heat to fuse the toner to the paper and may draw as much as 15 amps of current while processing a page. If the printer is on the same circuit as another piece of heavy-load equipment, the combined load from the two running at the same time can trip a breaker. A coffeepot, copy machine, toaster oven, and microwave are good examples of equipment that may be found on the same circuit breaker as the printer. The combination of these types of equipment sharing the same breaker as the printer can cause frequent breaker trips. Check carefully, as a circuit can span more than one room. The overloaded equipment may not be near the printer location. Also, note that this issue is most common with laser printers and highly unlikely with inkjets.

Printer Is Offline

A printer can have power but be offline or on standby, which makes it unable to print. An offline printer may sound like too simple or obvious of a problem, but it is encountered frequently. When giving support over a telephone, the technician should first inquire about the power source and whether the printer is offline. Do not be surprised if the person on the other end of the telephone does not exactly know what you mean by "offline."

Cannot Access Local Printer

There are two main reasons that you are unable to connect to a local printer configured as a shared printer. The first reason is you do not have permission to access the printer. When a printer is configured as a shared local printer, the host computer must be configured to allow other users to access the printer. The host computer can configure the local printer to be accessed by everyone or only by specific people or computers. The second reason you may fail to access a local printer remotely is that the host computer is off or in sleep mode, or the printer is off.

Cannot Access Network Printer

The first reason not to be able to access a network printer is that you do not have permission to access the printer. On some networks, printer access is determined by the network administrator. The network administrator selects the persons and computers that can access the network printer. The second reason is the network printer may be turned off or in offline mode. There will be more about network problems as related to devices in a later chapter.

Creased Paper

Creased paper is often the result of a misaligned paper feed. This behavior can be caused by a worn plate or poor alignment when replenishing the paper tray. A good practice to incorporate is to thumb the edge of the paper as though you were flipping through the pages of a book. This helps to separate the paper, so only one sheet is fed through at a time.

Creased paper can also indicate some type of foreign object or debris in the paper train. Most often, when something blocks the train, the printer jams. However, this is not always the case. Be sure to check the path of the paper through the printer to rule out a foreign object.

A+ 1101: 5.6

Paper Not Feeding

A common reason for paper not to feed is that the roller simply cannot grip the paper. Often, changing the paper in the tray or removing some paper will solve the problem. The paper should align with markings in the tray to assist with the pickup of individual pages. Remember, thumbing the edge of the paper can be beneficial to providing separation.

A+ 1101: 5.6

Vertical Lines on a Page

Vertical lines appearing on a page can occur in laser printers when the roller has residue on it. All laser printers and related printers require maintenance, the simplest form of which is cleaning what is readily visible. Some printers provide the user with specific instructions for cleaning wires and other parts of the mechanism. Be wary of using a regular vacuum cleaner—these generally do not have the appropriate filters for fine toner particles. Vertical lines without toner potentially indicate end-of-life for a toner cartridge.

No Image on Printer Display

When an image does not appear on the printer display, the problem could be as simple as not having the power on. If that is not the case, it is also possible the unit has received excessive voltage and the parts no longer work. Power off and on and see if anything changes. It is best to protect your investment in hardware with at least a surge suppressor of quality and, at best, an uninterrupted power supply (UPS) with conditioned power.

A+ 1101: 5.6

Grinding Noise

Grinding noises from a printer can, unfortunately, have many causes. The quickest method is to check if a cover or door was not closed completely. The next thing to check would be to see if there is an obstruction somewhere in the printer. If the noises occur immediately after installing new toner or ink, they could be caused by faulty installation of the cartridge(s). Less likely—and more difficult to diagnose—causes include rollers or gears in the printer needing repair. Depending on the printer, it may be more cost effective to replace rather than repair, as you will likely have to call a specialist to come assess the damage and repair the device.

A+ 1101: 3.7

Diagnosing and Maintaining Inkjet Printers

Inkjet printers are among the most-used home printers. They are simple in design, but there are several commonly encountered problems and some simple maintenance routines with which you should be familiar.

Inkjet Printer Cleaning Guidelines

Inkjet printers operate on the principle of controlling a fine mist of ink to print images on the paper. Because of this printing technique, the mist of ink often collects on the inside and outside of the printer case. To remove ink deposits from the outside of the printer case, you should use a soft cloth and distilled water. If the case does not clean properly with water, you may use a mild detergent diluted in distilled water. It is important to use distilled water because cleaning a printer with water that has severe mineral deposits can make the printer case look worse than before it was cleaned. *Never* clean a printer case with alcohol or any form of strong commercial cleaners, as they can ruin many plastics.

Most printer designs have been engineered to allow for some accumulation of ink inside the printer. In general, you should never attempt to clean the inside of the printer with water, alcohol, or any commercial solvents because they can damage the electrical components inside the printer. The only areas inside the printer that may require cleaning are the print cartridges. To help keep the cartridges clean, consider turning the printer off after the last printing process has completed. When the printer has finished printing, the ink cartridge is returned to "home" position, which is engineered to cover the ink ports to prevent them from drying out. Inkjet ports often dry out because of long periods of nonuse.

A small, fine brush or an antistatic vacuum should be used to remove paper dust and lint. Do *not* use compressed air to remove dust. The compressed air may actually force the dust deeper inside the printing mechanism and cause more harm than good.

Never attempt to lubricate parts inside the inkjet printer. Lubricants can cause an increased buildup of dust and lint inside the printer. Lubricants can also damage electronic components.

These are general guidelines to follow and may vary somewhat when working with specific printers. The best policy is to download a copy of maintenance and cleaning instructions for the exact printer model from the manufacturer's website.

Automated Calibration and Head Alignment

A+ 1101: 3.7

Inkjet printer calibration and head alignment and head cleaning are performed to ensure the best quality printed image possible. In many cases, a user can enter into a maintenance screen from the utility software built into the printer, and when **Align Printer** is selected, the head alignment is performed automatically without user intervention. The alignment consists of the printer printing lines on a test paper and shining a light beam onto the paper. The light is reflected back to a sensor, which records the amount of light and correlates it to the color and line width of the ink line. The printer automatically calculates the physical attributes of the lines on the paper to determine if they are within acceptable tolerances. If the printhead is not correct, the printer will automatically adjust to align it. Printhead alignment is routinely performed after replacing ink cartridges. Figure 12-27 shows an HP Officejet Pro 8600 printhead-alignment test sheet.

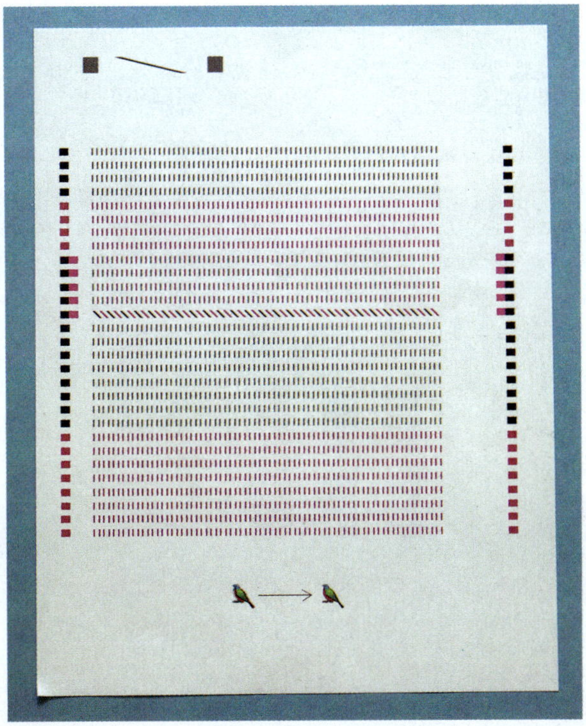

Goodheart-Willcox Publisher

Figure 12-27 Printhead alignment is performed by printing a pattern of lines on paper and then shining a light on the paper. The light is reflected back to a sensor to verify or correct printhead alignment.

Another test performed is print quality diagnostics. Figure 12-28 shows the diagnostic sheet for an HP Officejet Pro 8600. The top of the diagnostic sheet is used to check if the printhead is properly aligned. You would visually check to verify that the lines are straight and that the corners of the box where the lines meet are properly aligned. Any gap or overlapping at the corners indicates a problem with the printhead alignment.

A thin white line appearing across the color bars indicates that there is a problem with the ink cartridges, which likely would need to be cleaned. The following are some other problems associated with the ink cartridges but that may be due to incorrect printer settings:

- The print is smeared
- Color bars are faded
- Color bars appear jagged along the edges

A+ 1101: 5.6

Incorrect Inkjet Printer Settings

If the printer passes the print quality diagnostics and the test patterns appear to be correct, it does not mean that the printer does not have a problem. The quality print test is a self-diagnostic test and does not reflect user configuration settings. For example, a document or image that appears too light or low quality can be caused by user configuration.

The printer configuration settings could be incorrect for the print job. One common error is the use of the wrong type of paper setting. For example, if you are using high-quality, glossy photo paper and the printer is configured for plain copy paper, the ink will most likely smear.

If the printed images appear faded or not sufficiently sharp, then the printer might be configured for a print quality that is too low. Low print quality is often configured to save on ink, but when a later project requiring high-quality printer, such as a brochure or advertisement flyer, the images may appear low quality. The user would need to configure the printer for high quality.

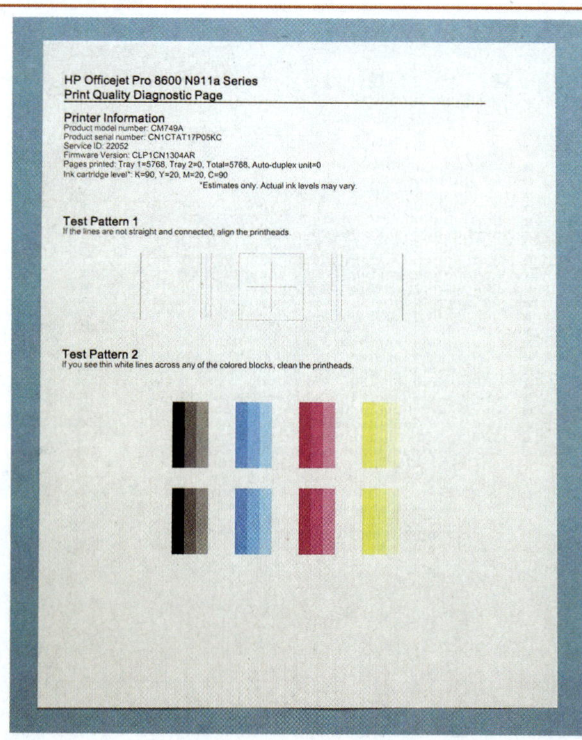

Figure 12-28 The print quality diagnostic sheet is used to determine if the printer needs printhead alignment and to diagnose if there is a problem with the ink cartridges.

Goodheart-Willcox Publisher

A common problem with inkjet printers is the ink cartridges dry out from lack of use over a long period. To correct such a problem, clean the printhead by using the automatic cleaning function. If this fails to correct the dry ink cartridge problem, replace the ink cartridge.

Diagnosing Laser Printer Problems

A+ 1101: 3.7

Laser printers are frequently used in both home and office settings. Understanding the complete printing process of the typical laser printer, as well as the electrophotographic process, will give you a quick insight into the problem. Most printers are equipped with a self-test program as part of a diagnostic routine and running it can eliminate many printer faults. The following covers ten of the most common problems you may encounter with a laser printer. Examine them along with their causes and solutions.

Printing Gibberish

A+ 1101: 5.6

If the printer is printing gibberish or unintelligible symbols, Figure 12-29, but prints fine during the self-test, you probably have an incorrect or corrupted printer driver. An incorrect printer driver can be loaded when a user attempts to print a document burned to a disc from another PC with a different printer installed. Some word-processing packages save the document along with the printer setup to the disc. When the document is loaded on a different PC with a different printer, it can cause the printer to print gibberish or just continually print a series of blank pages. Check **Devices and Printers** to determine if you have printers other than the one you are using. If so, this is most likely the problem.

You may also have a corrupt printer driver and may need to reinstall the printer driver. Even a minor malfunction can corrupt a driver, but reinstalling the printer driver will correct this problem. Reinstalling the driver is accomplished just like the initial installation, using the **Add Printer** wizard. The computer will install the new driver over the old, corrupt driver. You can also visit the manufacturer's website for updated drivers.

Pages Have Light Streaks

If pages are printing light images or have light streaks vertically down the page, Figure 12-30, the printer is low on toner. Remove the toner cartridge, shake it gently from side to side, and then reinstall it. If the quality of the printed pages improves, replace the toner cartridge.

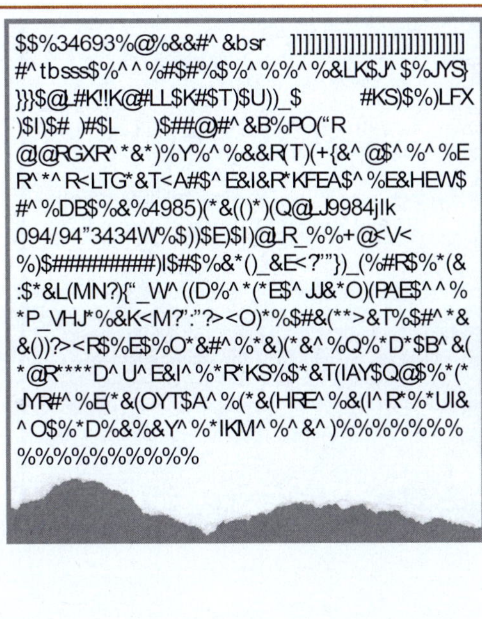

Goodheart-Willcox Publisher

Figure 12-29 If your printed page has gibberish on it, there is likely a problem with your printer driver.

Pages Print Solid Black

When pages print solid black or with a great deal of gray in the areas that should be white, the most likely problem is the toner cartridge is seated improperly, allowing toner to dump on the paper. An example of the results of an improperly seated toner cartridge can be seen in Figure 12-31. It is also possible that the toner cartridge is defective. Fixing an improperly seated toner cartridge is as simple as removing the cartridge and replacing it correctly.

Although less likely, there is also the possibility that the laser may not be working or the mirror may be defective. The primary corona wire could also be at fault, meaning there is no initial charge placed on the drum. Remember that the polarities used depend on the manufacturer and determine if the page prints are totally black or totally white. You must first determine whether the laser on the printer writes the images or writes the background. If any of these parts have gone bad, a qualified technician needs to be contacted.

Figure 12-30 When toner cartridges run low, the printed page will show insufficient toner coverage.

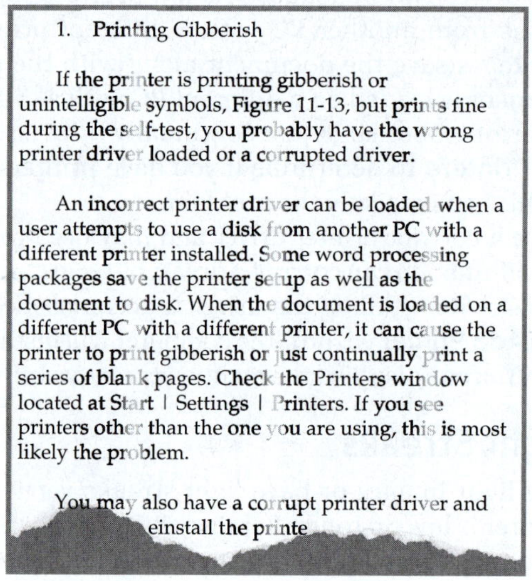

1. Printing Gibberish

If the pr nter is printing gibberish or unintelligibl symbols, Figure 11-13, but prin s fine during the s lf-test, you pro ably have the w ong printer drive loaded or a co rupted driver.

An inco rect printer dri er can be loade when a user attempt to use a disk om another PC with a different pri ter installed. S me word proces ing packages sa e the printer se up as well as th document t disk. When th document is loa ed on a different PC with a differen printer, it can ca use the printer to pr nt gibberish or ust continually rint a series of bla k pages. Check the Printers win ow located at St rt | Settings | rinters. If you s e printers oth r than the one ou are using, thi is most likely the pr blem.

You may also have a co rupt printer driver and einstall the printe

Goodheart-Willcox Publisher

Figure 12-31 If extra toner appears on a page, you should first check if the toner cartridge is seated correctly.

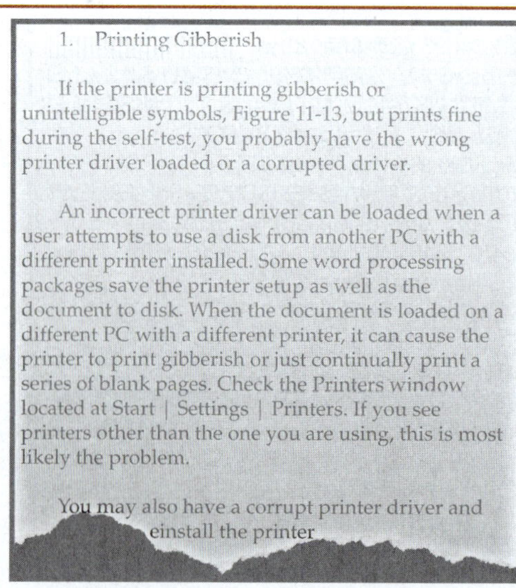

1. Printing Gibberish

If the printer is printing gibberish or unintelligible symbols, Figure 11-13, but prints fine during the self-test, you probably have the wrong printer driver loaded or a corrupted driver.

An incorrect printer driver can be loaded when a user attempts to use a disk from another PC with a different printer installed. Some word processing packages save the printer setup as well as the document to disk. When the document is loaded on a different PC with a different printer, it can cause the printer to print gibberish or just continually print a series of blank pages. Check the Printers window located at Start | Settings | Printers. If you see printers other than the one you are using, this is most likely the problem.

You may also have a corrupt printer driver and einstall the printer

Goodheart-Willcox Publisher

Pages Print Blank

A+ 1101: 5.6

Always check the easy things first. A common error that causes blank pages occurs when the toner cartridge is changed. Often users fail to remove the sealing tape that keeps the toner slot closed during shipping and transfer. If you are getting blank pages, always remove the toner cartridge first to ensure that the sealing tape has been removed.

An incorrect or corrupted driver can also cause blank pages. If only alternate pages or just the first page is blank, it is likely a printer setup problem, and you should check the printer configuration. Try reconfiguring the printer to correct the first page from being blank or alternate pages printing blank.

If all the pages of the print job are blank, the transfer corona may be at fault. Without a charge on the paper, it cannot attract toner from the drum. A qualified technician must be called for this problem.

Poor Print Quality

A+ 1101: 5.6

With poor-quality prints, first check that the toner cartridge is not low on toner or completely empty. Also, check if the printer is configured for economy or draft mode, which is used to conserve toner. This option usually can be accessed in the printer setup window of the operating system and through the printer menu options controlled by the buttons on the printer. Usually, any settings on the printer will override settings created with the operating system interface.

Toner Smears on Paper

A+ 1101: 5.6

As stated earlier, always check the simplest thing first. With toner smears, the easiest thing to check is the wrong type of paper loaded into the printer. Some printers require special paper, and if there are multiple types of printers at a location, there is a chance the wrong type of paper may have been placed into the paper tray.

However, when toner smears across the paper when touched, such as the paper shown in Figure 12-32, it is a good indication that the fusing unit is out. With the fusing unit out, the toner is never melted to the paper.

Printer Acts Completely Dead

If a printer acts dead, first ensure the printer is online. If there is no response, check the printer cables, as they may have become loose. Of course, never forget to check the power cable and to make sure there is power at the outlet. A dead printer can also be a driver problem.

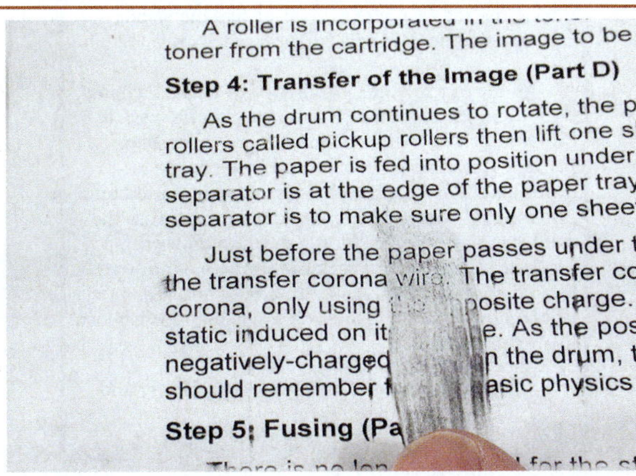

Figure 12-32 If toner is not sealed properly to paper, it smears easily.

Goodheart-Willcox Publisher

Printed Characters Are Fuzzy

With fuzzy printing, check the type of paper loaded into the printer. If the wrong type of paper is used, the toner may scatter outside the character outline.

Constant Dark or White Spots

If you find dark or white spots that appear in the same place on multiple printed sheets, the problem is likely a scratched drum. With a scratch on the drum, it may not be able to hold toner, or it may hold toner on the spot at all times. Replacement drums can be purchased and installed easily for most laser printers.

A+ 1101: 5.6

Ghost Images

A ghost image is a second image that appears on the paper in the background of the image you are trying to print, similar to Figure 12-33. A ghost image is usually a sign that the erase lamp is burned out. When the erase lamp is out, the image of the last print run will remain on the drum and appear in subsequent print jobs.

A+ 1101: 3.6

Diagnosing USB Connection Problems

The USB connection has become the standard cable connection for printers, replacing the parallel cable and earlier serial connections. While USB is easy to install and typically configures automatically, there are several problems commonly associated with this type of connection.

Insufficient or No Electrical Power

It is most important to mention that you should always check for the simplest and easiest solution first when dealing with printer problems. Check if the printer is turned on and online. An LED generally indicates power to a printer. If the LED is lit, the USB port selected for the printer connection may not be providing sufficient electrical power to operate the printer. While the majority of electrical power is supplied to the printer through its own electrical plug, the USB cable also provides a small amount of energy required to run the printer. This problem is easily remedied by installing a powered USB hub capable of supplying the higher electrical power needed by the printer.

Figure 12-33 Ghost images appear when the image from a previous print is not erased from the drum.

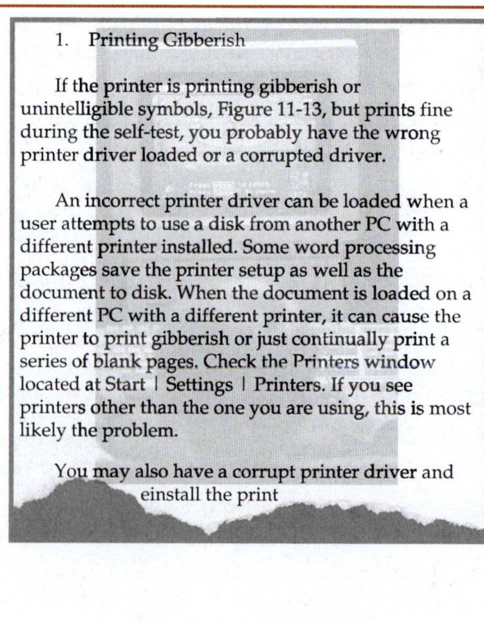

1. Printing Gibberish

If the printer is printing gibberish or unintelligible symbols, Figure 11-13, but prints fine during the self-test, you probably have the wrong printer driver loaded or a corrupted driver.

An incorrect printer driver can be loaded when a user attempts to use a disk from another PC with a different printer installed. Some word processing packages save the printer setup as well as the document to disk. When the document is loaded on a different PC with a different printer, it can cause the printer to print gibberish or just continually print a series of blank pages. Check the Printers window located at Start | Settings | Printers. If you see printers other than the one you are using, this is most likely the problem.

You may also have a corrupt printer driver and einstall the print

Goodheart-Willcox Publisher

Conflicting Devices

1102: 1.9 A+

Theoretically, USB devices are not supposed to conflict, conflicts do arise occasionally and are generally caused by either the BIOS/UEFI setup or the USB device driver. One of the devices may be programmed to take over the bandwidth of the port, causing the other devices to go into a hibernation state or simply lock up.

Microsoft furnishes basic device code to developers to use and modify for their USB devices. Microsoft will also test the software and hardware compatibility for a small charge. If the device passes Microsoft testing, the device is added to the Microsoft Hardware Compatibility List (HCL) for the operating system version for which it was tested. However, some manufacturers develop their own driver software and only refer to the Microsoft guidelines. Either they do not submit their code for testing, or it is tested after the release of the hardware device. If a problem is found, the manufacturer will simply provide a patch at their website.

To troubleshoot a USB device, remove all other USB devices from the port to which the printer is connected. This will help eliminate the possibility of a conflict between the devices connected to the same port.

Check the Device Manager for a problem with the USB port indicated by an exclamation or question mark, both of which indicate that the printer is not properly recognized or configured. The software drivers, BIOS/UEFI, or both may need to be upgraded. Check the printer manufacturer's website for more information.

Toner Spills

1102: 4.5 A+

Toner will be spilled from time to time, especially when replacing toner cartridges. Toner is composed of extremely small particles, usually a combination of carbon and polyester resin. Since the particles are so small and the toner is designed to adhere permanently to paper and similar products, some precautions should be observed.

Small spills should be cleaned up with an approved vacuum cleaner. An approved vacuum cleaner designed for toner spills is made with a dust-tight motor. Normal household vacuum cleaners do not have dust-tight motors and can create static discharge inside the vacuum cleaner housing. A static discharge can cause an explosion of toner particles, especially since one of the main ingredients is carbon. Approved toner vacuums also have a conductive hose designed to prevent static discharge created from the moving parts inside the vacuum.

Caution

Do not user a standard household vacuum cleaner to remove toner spills. Only an approved vacuum expressly approved to clean toner spills should be used.

The approved vacuum typically has a High-Efficiency Particulate Air (HEPA) filter. The HEPA filter can filter out smaller particles than a normal household vacuum cleaner. Attempts to vacuum toner spills with a normal household vacuum will produce a cloud of toner particles that could cause harm if inhaled.

Small toner spills on hard surfaces such as tile can be swept with a broom. Be sure to use a slow sweeping action so as not to create a cloud of toner dust. Never use hot water to wipe or mop a toner spill, as hot water will set the toner and cause a permanent stain. This is especially true for clothing. Always try to remove loose toner from clothing before washing and only use cold water to wash clothing covered with toner.

Spills on a printer case can be removed with a soft dry cloth. Toner can be removed from case areas that are difficult to clean with a cloth by using a small paintbrush. Again, slowly brush the areas as not to create a cloud of toner dust.

For information about any special precautions or dangers associated with toner and other chemical products, you should consult the material safety data sheet (MSDS) for that specific product. By law, all chemical products must have an MSDS available on request to answer all questions about how the product should be handled. This includes safe handling and cleanup. Printer toner is considered safe when handled in the intended manner.

Products associated with technical equipment, such as printers, generate billions of tons of waste, which can be harmful to our environment. To reduce the impact on our environment, most manufacturers such as Xerox and Hewlett-Packard have recycling programs that allow a consumer to recycle toner and ink cartridges as well as other consumables. You can view the manufacturer's website to obtain information about their recycling program.

Tech Tip

Windows Help and Support provides a lot of easy-to-understand step-by-step instructions for most print installation and configuration needs. Be sure to check the Help and Support feature when troubleshooting a printer problem or before performing a printer configuration with which you are unfamiliar.

Windows Printer Troubleshooter

Windows provides a printing troubleshooter through its Help and Support software. The printer troubleshooter, shown in Figure 12-34, helps solve printer problems. The easiest way to launch the printer troubleshooter is to navigate to **Control Panel>Hardware and Sound>Devices and Printers**, right-click on the printer you want to troubleshoot, and select **Troubleshoot** from the shortcut menu. Note, if your Control Panel menu has an icon-based view, you can select **Devices and Printers** directly from the opening page. Alternatively, you can access **Start> Settings>Update & Security>Troubleshoot** and run the general troubleshooting wizard before selecting printer-specific troubleshooting.

Most operating systems, and all Windows operating systems, will have some type of printer troubleshooting tool similar to the one shown in Figure 12-34. The exact sequence of troubleshooting Windows will vary according to the problem and possible solutions. In Windows 10, the user or technician must download the printer troubleshooter software from Microsoft.

The troubleshooter conducts a series of tests such as checking the printer spooler for errors and checking for the latest drivers. The troubleshooter may offer a solution and allow the user to apply the solution automatically. If needed, the troubleshooter may also offer additional resources to help find a solution, such as requesting help through the Remote Assistance feature. Remote Assistance allows you to send an e-mail or instant message to someone, giving them limited control of your computer as a way to let them fix the print problem for you. You can also perform a system recovery, which will allow you to reset your computer system settings to an earlier time, as well as an option for online support and technical assistance from Microsoft. There will be much more about these options later in a later chapter.

12.6 Fonts

A **font** is a design for a set of symbols, usually text and number characters, within a specific typeface. The physical size of a font is described in points and pitch. The height of a letter is measured in **points**. Each point is equal to 1/72 of an inch.

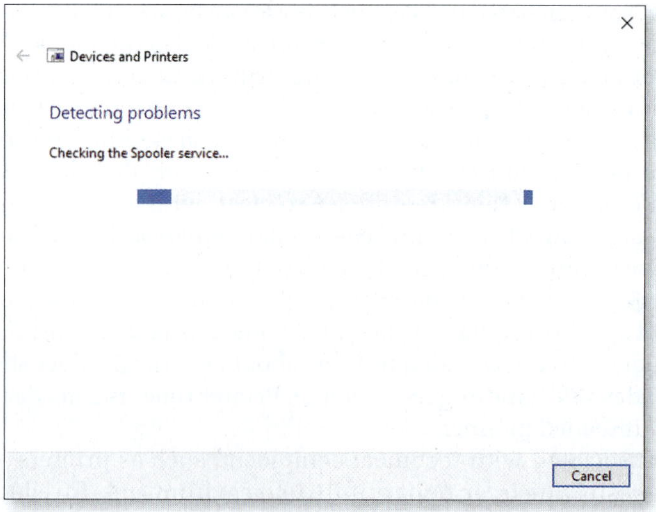

Figure 12-34 Windows provides a troubleshooting wizard specifically for printers. The wizard takes the user through a series of steps that automatically detect the problem, offer solutions, and provide additional help.

Goodheart-Willcox Publisher

The width is measured in **pitch**. A font describes characteristics associated with a symbol such as the size, pitch, and spacing between symbols as well as the subvariants of the main typeface. Look at Figure 12-35.

The two main classifications of fonts are *bitmap* and *vector*. A **bitmap font** uses a pattern of dots to represent each letter. The bitmap images of the text are stored in memory. As you type, the bitmap images are placed on the screen by a process similar to a cut-and-paste process. Each font requires a different bitmap pattern. A bitmap font must also use a separate bitmap for each size of the letter.

A **vector font**, also referred to as an *outline font*, draws the outline of the letter rather than storing a separate bitmap pattern for each font. The angles, turns, and distances are calculated for each character, which makes vector fonts more easily scaled to larger or smaller sizes because the letter is based on an algorithm. Vector fonts tend to look better on high-resolution output devices, while bitmap fonts tend to look better on low-resolution devices.

1101: 3.6 A+

Vector fonts are used with *page description language (PDL)*. Common PDLs are Adobe PostScript (PS), Hewlett-Packard's Printer Control Language (PCL), and Microsoft TrueType, among others. PCL and PostScript tend to be among the most widely used, and while PCL tends to be faster, PostScript results in higher-quality graphics. Additionally, PCL is device dependent, meaning PCL drivers use the printer's hardware to help create printed data, which speeds up the printing process. PostScipt, however, does not rely on hardware, making the output consistent from one device to another. The same is essentially true for TrueType.

While there are differences in the specific implementations, page description languages share some commonalities. For example, a page description language treats everything on a page as a graphic image. The PDL translates the picture on the monitor into a set of printer codes that will exactly duplicate the image seen on the screen. This is often referred to as *what you see is what you get (WYSIWYG)*. Adobe's PDF is also a printer language, though you may be most familiar with PDF as used with Adobe PDF documents.

Figure 12-36 shows all the ways the Microsoft Word program can manipulate a font. The manipulation feature is typical in most word-processing packages. Available fonts can be viewed in Windows by accessing **Start>Control Panel>Appearance and Personalization>Fonts**, as shown in Figure 12-37. In the Font folder, you will find all available, installed fonts, Figure 12-38. You can print a sample of the selected font by right-clicking the folder and selecting **Print** from the shortcut menu.

Sample Fonts

This is a sample of Times New Roman 8 point font.

This is a sample of Times New Roman 12 point font.

This is a sample of Times New Roman 18 point font.

This is a sample of Courier 8 point font.

This is a sample of Courier 12 point font.

This is a sample of Courier 14 point font.

This is a sample of Brush Script 16 point font.

This is a sample of Brush Script 20 point font.

This is a sample of Tahoma 10 point font.

This is a sample of Tahoma 14 point font.

This is a sample of Myriad 10 point font.

This is a sample of Myriad 16 point font.

This is a sample of Myriad 16 point italic font.

This is a sample of Myriad 16 point bold font.

Goodheart-Willcox Publisher

Figure 12-35 A font is a design for a set of symbols, usually text and number characters, within a specific typeface.

Figure 12-36 Windows displays each format type for a font, such as bold, italic, or regular (A) as well as a sample of text and sizing for each format (B).

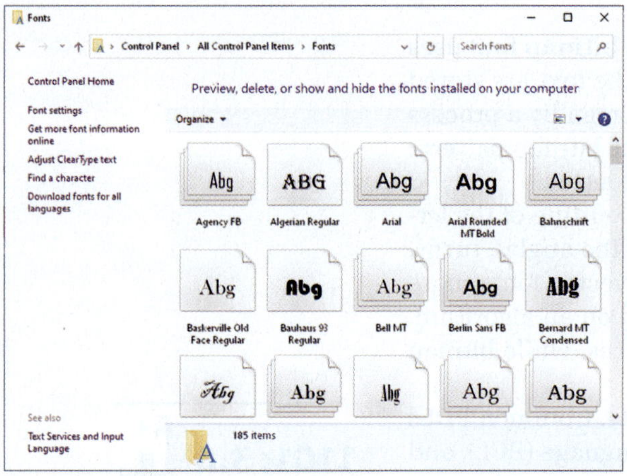

A

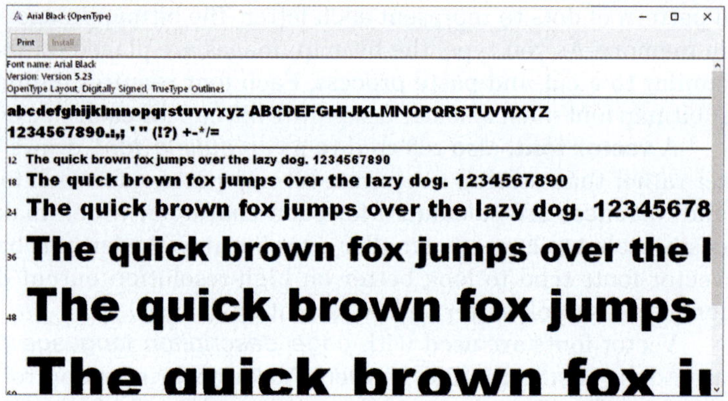

B

Goodheart-Willcox Publisher

Figure 12-37 Fonts can be accessed by navigating to **Start>Control Panel>Appearance and Personalization>Fonts.**

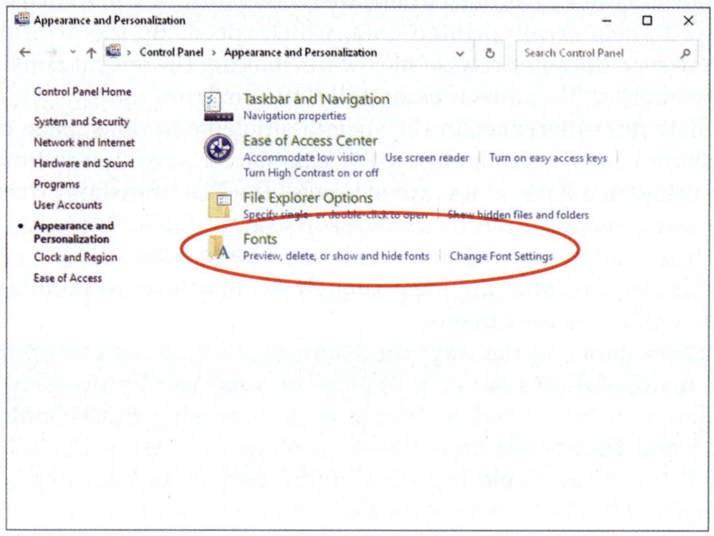

Goodheart-Willcox Publisher

Figure 12-38 All available, installed fonts are shown in the Fonts folder.

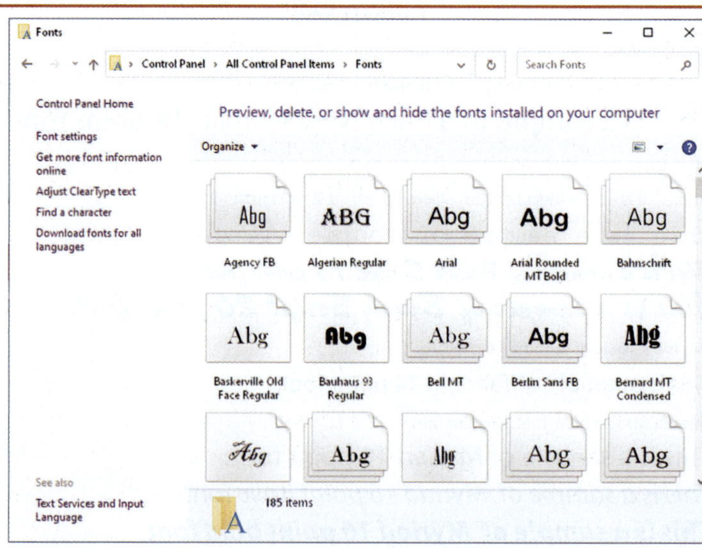

Goodheart-Willcox Publisher

Chapter Summary

12.1 Printer Types

- A printer is an electromechanical device that converts computer data into text or graphic images printed to paper or other presentation media.
- Numerous types of printers are available to install into a computer.
- Laser printing uses a process called the electrophotographic process. The seven laser printing stages are processing, charging the drum, exposing or writing the image, developing the image, transferring the image, fusing the image, and cleaning the drum.
- LED printers use an array of light-emitting diodes to write an image to the drum. The main difference between a laser printer and an LED printer is the use of LEDs instead of a laser, which eliminates several moving parts required by the laser-printing process.
- Inkjet printers use either a thermoresistor or a piezo cell crystal to produce the force needed to spray a fine mist of ink onto paper. Ink flows into the firing chamber from the ink cartridge reservoir. An electrical pulse from the computer enters the thermoresistor, and the ink in the firing chamber is instantly heated. The extreme heat expands the ink in the chamber, causing it to fire through the nozzle and onto the paper. As the chamber cools, a vacuum is created that draws more ink into the firing chamber from the ink cartridge reservoir.
- Dot matrix printers use a printhead consisting of small metal rods which, when affected by the magnetic field of an energized solenoid, strike an ink ribbon and leave a dot of ink on paper.
- Color thermal printers operate on the principle of applying color by heating a special ribbon that is coated with a wax-like material, which is sealed to the surface of the paper by Teflon-coated rollers. Each time the paper is run through, a new color is added to the paper.
- Dye-sublimation printers print images by vaporizing inks, which then solidify onto paper. The process is similar to the color thermal printer process. The difference is that in dye sublimation, the color actually penetrates the paper, while in a thermal print operation, the color is printed to the surface of the paper.
- Solid ink printers use solid ink cartridges similar to wax and a printhead that consists of four long rows of many individual nozzles, each row producing one of the CMYK colors.
- All-in-one products are a combination of printer, fax, copier, and scanner.
- A 3D printer takes a computer-aided drafting (CAD) file and uses that code to deposit a plastic filament from a printhead onto a surface and then onto the model itself. Technically, the plastic filament is a stream of a resin that is melted and then deposited in layers, similar to a glue gun feed.

12.2 Printer Installation and Configuration

- A printer can be connected directly via cable, called a local printer connection, or via network, called a network or shared printer connection.
- Local printer connections require a specific port. This is often a USB port, but COM and LPT ports have been used historically.
- A virtual printer is a software-based application installed on a computer used to create documents. Four common uses for virtual printers include printing to other files, printing to PDF, printing to XPS, and printing to an image.
- A shared printer is typically referred to as a network printer.

12.3 Print Spooling

- Printers use spooling, which is a technique that stores data to be printed so printing operations can be completed in the background while other tasks are performed by the PC without waiting for the printer to complete its job.
- When a printer uses spooling, it stores the data to be printed in a buffer. This list of print jobs waiting to be completed and their status is also referred to as the print queue.
- The print queue is a list of print jobs waiting to be completed. The print queue window can be used to check the status of a print job and to manage the print job.

12.4 Printer Memory

- The amount of memory with which a printer is equipped determines the resolution and size of the subject to be printed. If a printer does not have sufficient memory to print a file, it will generate an error code.
- Before installing more printer memory into a printer, you should first consult the printer documentation to determine what type of memory is recommended.
- Flash memory ports are available on many printers, which support printing directly from the memory module. The flash memory becomes an extension of the printer memory and can be used to store documents and images that require frequent printing.

12.5 Troubleshooting Printers

- Many printer problems are simple and can be easily solved by users or technicians.
- Error codes provide confusion, but they can often be decoded by investigating manufacturer literature or websites.
- Some errors, such as incorrect colors, paper jams, blank areas, and an offline printer are universal and can be resolved easily.
- The paper train and the function of printer drivers are similar for all printers.
- Inkjet printers have unique maintenance, such as cleaning and calibration. They also have specific settings that must be configured and monitored to ensure high-quality prints.
- Diagnosing laser printers often comes down to toner. Common problems include printing gibberish, which often is the result of a bad driver; pages printing with light streaks, solid black, or blank areas, all of which are toner-related issues; poor print quality, which is often the result of an incorrect printer setting; toner smears, which indicates a problem with the fusing unit; offline printers, which result from a loose or missing cable; fuzzy characters, which is often the result of the wrong paper type; and dark spots or ghost images, both of which indicate a problem with the drum.
- USB-connected printers have unique problems such as insufficient or nonexistent electrical power and conflicting devices.
- If and when toner spills, be sure to use the correct type of vacuum to clean it. You should *never* use a standard household vacuum for toner spills.
- Windows provides the Printer troubleshooter feature through its Help and Support software.

12.6 Fonts

- A font is a design for a set of symbols. A font describes the characteristics associated with the symbol.

- A bitmap font uses a pattern of dots to represent each letter. A vector font, also referred to as an *outline font*, draws the outline of the letter rather than storing a separate bitmap pattern for each font.
- The height of a font is measured in points; the width is measured in pitch.

Review Questions

1. Explain the operating principles of a laser printer.
2. Explain the operating principles of an LED printer.
3. Explain the operating principles of an inkjet printer.
4. Explain the operating principles of a dot matrix printer.
5. Explain the operating principles of a color thermal printer.
6. Explain the operation of a dye-sublimation printer.
7. Explain the operation of a solid ink printer.
8. Describe the operation of a 3D printer.
9. List various ways a computer can connect to a printer.
10. Summarize print spooling.
11. What is a print queue and how can one use it to view and manage print jobs?
12. Summarize the process of upgrading printer memory.
13. List commonly encountered general printer problems.
14. What are the two common reasons that you are unable to connect to a local printer configured as a shared printer?
15. A user comes back from a long vacation, and now their inkjet printer is no longer working. What is *most likely* the problem and how do you remedy it?
16. A color laser printer that is shared by other users was working fine yesterday. Today, the printer is producing faded or low-quality images of pictures. What is *most likely* the problem?
17. After a laser printer prints a page of text, the toner smears when touched. What is *most likely* the problem?
18. Differentiate between a bitmap font and a vector font.
19. What unit of measure is used for font height?
20. What unit of measure is used for font width?

Sample A+ Exam Questions

1. What type of printer uses a piezo cell crystal?
   A. Laser
   B. Dot matrix
   C. Dye-sublimation
   D. Inkjet
2. What type of printer uses pins driven by a solenoid striking a ribbon to make dots conforming to letters, symbols, and pictures?
   A. Laser
   B. Dot matrix
   C. Dye-sublimation
   D. Inkjet

3. Which type of printer uses thermoresistors to force the ink from a reservoir?
   A. Laser
   B. Dot matrix
   C. Dye-sublimation
   D. Inkjet
4. Which of the following best describes the term *fusing* in relation to the electrostatic process?
   A. The protective device installed in electrostatic laser printers to prevent electrical overload of the circuits
   B. The transfer of toner to the paper to construct the printed image
   C. The bonding of the toner to the paper
   D. A special module that prevents the voltage from exceeding the 600-volt positive charge
5. Which of the following includes all the correct processes in the correct order for electrostatic printing?
   A. Processing, charging the drum, exposing or writing the image, developing the image, transferring the image, fusing the image, cleaning the drum
   B. Processing, charging the drum, transferring the image, exposing or writing the image, developing the image, fusing the image, cleaning the drum
   C. Processing, cleaning the drum, charging the drum, transferring the image, developing
   the image, charging again, exposing or writing the image, fusing the image
   D. Processing, exposing or writing the image, charging the drum, developing the image, transferring the image, fusing the image, cleaning the drum
6. Which of the following is represented by the acronym LPT?
   A. Local printer transferring-port
   B. Line printer terminal
   C. Local printer terminal
   D. Line port terminal

7. What does the printer term *spooling* mean?
   A. It describes the mechanical device that holds the ribbon in place on a dot matrix printer.
   B. It is a method of connecting a local printer to a network printer group.
   C. It is the method used to store print jobs waiting to be processed in an orderly fashion.
   D. It is a method of determining the amount of rotation or "print spooling" required for blank spacing between lines of text in a document.
8. Which item is required for inkjet printhead alignment?
   A. Compressed air
   B. Flat-tip screwdriver
   C. Toner wrench
   D. Software application
9. A paper comes out of a laser printer, and its printed surface is completely black. What is *most likely* the cause?
   A. The toner cartridge is seated improperly.
   B. The charge is too low on the drum.
   C. The laser is defective.
   D. The fuser is overheating the paper.
10. A laser printer prints a page, and the document smears when touched. What is the *most likely* cause of the image smear?
    A. The primary corona is defective.
    B. The transfer corona is defective.
    C. The toner is damp.
    D. The fuser is defective.

Chapter 13

Laptops and Mobile Devices

Learning Outcomes

13.1 Compare and contrast mobile devices.
13.2 Identify portable PC parts.
13.3 Differentiate among power-management options.
13.4 Compare and contrast mobile operating systems.
13.5 Discuss factors to consider when installing a wireless connection.
13.6 Identify methods for securing mobile devices.
13.7 Describe the process of disassembling a laptop for proper reassembly.
13.8 Discuss methods used to upgrade a laptop.
13.9 Identify common symptoms of poor laptop performance and list preventive maintenance guidelines.

A+ Certification Exam Objectives

The following A+ Certification Exam Objectives are covered in this chapter.

Exam 220-1101

1.0 Mobile Devices

- 1.1 Given a scenario, install and configure laptop hardware and components.
- 1.2 Compare and contrast the display components of mobile devices.
- 1.3 Given a scenario, set up and configure accessories and ports of mobile devices.
- 1.4 Given a scenario, configure basic mobile device network connectivity and application support.

2.0 Networking

- 2.3 Compare and contrast protocols for wireless networking.

3.0 Hardware

- 3.6 Given a scenario, deploy and configure multifunction devices/printers and settings.

5.0 Hardware and Network Troubleshooting

- 5.2 Given a scenario, troubleshoot problems related to motherboards, RAM, CPUs, and power.
- 5.4 Given a scenario, troubleshoot video, projector, and display issues.
- 5.5 Given a scenario, troubleshoot common issues with mobile devices.
- 5.7 Given a scenario, troubleshoot problems with wired and wireless networks.

Exam 220-1102

1.0 Operating Systems

- 1.4 Given a scenario, use the appropriate Microsoft Windows 10 Control Panel utility.
- 1.8 Explain common OS types and their purposes.

2.0 Security

- 2.1 Summarize various security measures and their purposes.
- 2.2 Compare and contrast wireless security protocols and authentication methods.
- 2.5 Given a scenario, manage and configure basic security settings in the Microsoft Windows OS.

- 2.7 Explain common methods for securing mobile and embedded devices.
- 2.9 Given a scenario, configure appropriate security settings on small office/home office (SOHO) wireless and wired networks.

3.0 Software Troubleshooting

- 3.1 Given a scenario, troubleshoot Microsoft Windows OS problems.
- 3.4 Given a scenario, troubleshoot common mobile OS and application issues.
- 3.5 Given a scenario, troubleshoot mobile OS and application security issues.

4.0 Operational Procedures

- 4.4 Given a scenario, use common safety procedures.
- 4.5 Summarize environmental impacts and local environmental controls.

Key Terms

accelerometer
airplane mode
ad hoc network
Android
Apple picking
app store
biometrics
bridge
Chrome OS
company app
encryption
encryption key
geotracking
global positioning system (GPS)
gyroscope
hard reset
infrastructure network
Integrated Circuit Card Identification Number (ICCID)
International Mobile Subscriber Identity (IMSI)
iOS
iPadOS
jailbreaking
multi-touch
passcode lock
remote wipe
rooting
security key
service set identifier (SSID)
smart card
subscriber identity module (SIM)
synchronization
wireless access point (WAP)

Overview

The portable PC is a computer that is designed to go wherever the user needs it. There are a variety of portable PCs on the market, and they go by names such as laptops, notebooks, tablets, and smartphones. All modern portable PCs are battery-powered devices that use some type of flat-panel screen technology to keep weight and power consumption to a minimum. For this chapter, we will consider devices with complex computing abilities, such as laptops, as compact portable desktop devices and consider devices with minimal components, such as tablets and smartphones, as mobile devices. Both laptops and mobile devices have similar technologies, including networking, security, modems, e-mail, and cloud services. While these technologies are covered in detail individually later in this textbook, they will also be briefly discussed here, as this chapter is designed as an introduction and overview to portable devices.

A+ Note

The CompTIA A+ Exams have many questions relating to mobile computing devices. Be prepared to answer questions related to mobile device connectivity, synchronization, remote backup services, and security.

Caution

Most mobile devices and laptops contain toxic elements and should not be disposed of in traditional waste receptacles. Contact local electronics stores or recycling centers regarding where best to dispose of used devices and components.

13.1 Mobile Devices

In simplest terms, a laptop is a mobile PC. However, a distinction can, and should, be made between a laptop and a mobile device. While a laptop is mobile, the phrase *mobile device* is most often used to refer to a computing device smaller than a laptop, such as a smartphone, tablet, or wearable technology. Mobile devices are designed to be lightweight, compact, and Internet-ready wherever you are. There are many unique features associated with mobile devices that make them quite different from their desktop counterparts, such as the use of accelerometer and gyroscope technology.

Laptop and Mobile Device Comparison

To better understand the differences between a mobile device and a laptop, look at Figure 13-1. Laptops have CPUs that can support demanding software applications such as 3D games, drawing programs, and office suites, while the CPUs in tablets and smartphones are RISC processors that are typically soldered permanently into the device circuit board and only capable of running minimal applications. As such, mobile device CPUs are generally not field upgradable or replaceable. Technically, one with extensive electrical engineering training and equipment could upgrade these CPUs, but this is typically not practical.

Modern laptops commonly have a minimum of 500 GB of storage space, though there are certainly laptops available with more, and laptops today mostly use solid-state drives (SSDs). Smartphones typically have much less storage space compared to laptops as they have no traditional disk drive system. Instead, they have flash memory chips embedded into the motherboard, and since the storage space is limited, mobile devices often augment storage space by using flash drives, SD cards, and cloud storage, depending on the device. As a result of their minimal storage space, mobile devices typically have a very simple directory structure.

Most modern laptops are not manufactured with optical storage drives. This is largely due to an emphasis placed on small sizes and low weight, as well as the rise in USB storage and streaming media. However, optical drives are available as external devices or through custom builds. While they are still occasionally included in laptops, they are physically impossible to design as an internal device for tablets and smartphones.

Figure 13-1 There are a number of differences in the capabilities of laptops compared to mobile devices.

Comparison of Laptop and Mobile Device Components

Component	Laptop	Tablet	Smartphone
CPU	High performance	Low performance	Low performance
Hard drive	Magnetic, solid state, or combination	Solid-state storage	Solid-state storage
Storage size	Large; varies by storage type but often exceeds 500 GB	Small	Often same as tablet
Optical read/write device	No, most often; device-dependent	No	No
Standard keyboard	Yes	No; can sometimes be docked to device	No
Repair/replace parts	Yes	No	No
Upgradable	Yes	No or limited	No

Goodheart-Willcox Publisher

All laptops have standard keyboards, while tablets and smartphones do not, due to physical size limitations. In contrast, mobile devices rely on a digital keyboard shown on the display for entering text into a mobile device, though most mobile devices are also equipped with a voice-recognition app for dictation. Look closely at Figure 13-2, which shows the Safari web browser on an iPad. Notice the microphone symbol in both the keyboard and address bar. When the microphone is selected, you can simply talk to the device, and your voice will be converted to text, which is often faster than typing manually. The voice-to-text feature is not always accurate, and a virtual keyboard is still often required to enter the correct text, but voice recognition is improving, and it can be "trained" on most devices.

Figure 13-3 shows a tablet equipped with an optional dock that is designed to work as a keyboard and touch pad for this particular tablet. Similar keyboard docks may include additional features such as USB ports, Secure Digital (SD) card reader(s), and a charging port. The same model tablet is shown in Figure 13-4 without the keyboard. Notice how the screen is oriented in landscape mode in both images. This is an example of the gyroscope working inside the tablet to maintain the same view no matter which way the tablet is turned. If the tablet in Figure 13-4 were turned 90 degrees, the screen would turn with it and reorient into portrait mode.

The size of tablets makes them unable to accommodate ports the way a laptop does. As such, keyboard accessories are used to provide standard-size USB ports

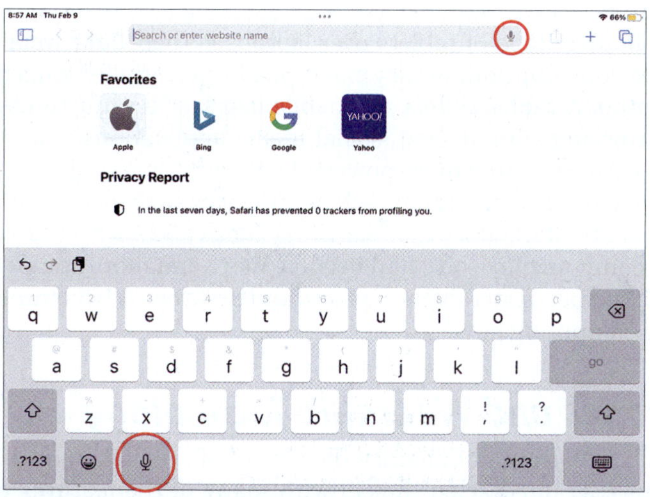

Figure 13-2 A virtual keyboard can be used to enter or dictate text.

Goodheart-Willcox Publisher

Figure 13-3 Some tablets are equipped with an optional keyboard that also serves as a docking station. After the tablet is docked into the keyboard, it resembles a laptop.

Sompetch Khanakornpratip/Shutterstock.com

Figure 13-4 Tablets can be used with or without a docked keyboard.

Pit Stock/Shutterstock.com

as well as a flash drive or memory card ports. Some are also equipped with small, flat rechargeable batteries, which provide additional electrical power for the tablet, though some are rechargeable.

Laptops have many parts that can be easily replaced, such as solid-state drives, batteries, and memory. However, replacing tablet and smartphone parts is more difficult. Typically, mobile devices must be exchanged or sent back to the manufacturer for repair.

The overall advantage of tablets over laptops is their light weight and diminished electrical consumption, so they can typically perform for longer periods compared to a laptop. A tablet is best for mobile users who want to use applications for Internet browsing, e-mail, chat, social media applications, and games, though mobile devices are becoming more powerful with every passing year.

As of this writing, local retailers sell new devices such as iPhone 14 pro with as much as a terabyte of memory and Samsung Galaxy S22 with 512 GB of memory. As electronic components evolve and become more and more compact and powerful, the distinction between tablets, laptops, and desktops is becoming more of form rather than of computing power.

Smartphones and Wearable Technology

Smartphones have been popular since the advent of the first Apple iPhone in 2007. They are essentially hand-sized tablets with many of the features of larger computing devices. Many current smartphones have eight-core processors from the ARM family of devices and can connect to many accessories. Wearable technology, such as smartwatches, is often paired with smartphones. These accessories connect through Bluetooth and offer a variety of functions, including phone and messaging functionality and health monitoring, which can be independent or built into a smartwatch and track pulse rate, heart rate, steps taken, and stairs climbed. Virtual and augmented reality headsets have also grown in popularity and have a wide variety of applications, including gaming, design, manufacturing and training, and medical treatment.

E-Readers

An e-reader, also called an ***e-book***, is a mobile device designed for the storage and use of digital books and periodicals. The best-known examples of e-readers are Amazon's Kindle and Barnes and Noble's Nook, though Apple's iPad also has e-reader capabilities. In the case of the Nook, the hardware resembles Samsung tablets with different trim. In both cases, the software that drives the e-reader is available for just about any other device, including smartphones. Amazon developed the Kindle in the early 2000s and created their own software to run it. Barnes and Noble, on the other hand, chose to base the Nook on the Android operating system. While the Nook utilizes the portable document format (PDF) to present books, the Kindle has three proprietary formats: **.azw**, **.kf8**, and **.kfx**. Sony also has an e-reader format, but the Kindle and the Nook have the largest market penetration—particularly the Kindle with over half the sales of all formats. However, as of this writing, standalone e-reader devices are becoming less popular because their functionality is included in most tablets.

Mobile Device Components

As with any computing device, mobile devices consist of multiple components working together to perform computing actions. It is important to keep in mind that devices such as tablets and smartphones are small computers, so they have many of the same components as a traditional desktop PC. The biggest difference is in functionality, as mobile devices do not need the same degree of computing power as desktop PCs normally do. Common mobile device components include processors, antennas, SIM cards, and touch screens.

Processors

Much like any computer, mobile devices require a central processing unit (CPU). Typically, CPUs in devices such as smartphone will use *System on a chip (SoC) processors*, which integrate many different functions into a single integrated circuit. This normally includes not only a CPU, but also memory and secondary storage. It may also include a graphics processing unit (GPU), Wi-Fi, and other technologies. This is a stark contrast to traditional PCs, which employ motherboards with various circuits attached to them, including a CPU, memory, and secondary storage.

Antennas

Given the obvious need for wireless capabilities in mobile devices, antennas represent a vital part of cellular communications. Antennas are used to transmit and receive electromagnetic (EM) waves and consist of one or several radiating elements through which an electric current circulates. Antennas are typically characterized by directivity, radiation pattern, gain, and efficiency. In some sources, you will see the term *aerial* used for *antenna*.

There are two primary classes of antennas: omnidirectional and directional. As the names suggest, an *omnidirectional* antenna radiates EM in all directions, while *directional* antennas radiate in a particular direction. There are subsets of each of these, which will be explored later in this chapter. However, all antennas can be classified into one of these two families.

The simplest and most widely used type of antenna is the *dipole* antenna, sometimes called a *doublet*. These antennas consist of an electric dipole that has a radiating structure, so the current has only one node at each end. Dipole antennas commonly consist of two conductors oriented end to end and connected by a *feed line*, which is a cable that sends radio signals back and forth between a transmitter and receiver.

SIM Cards

As you may be aware, SIM cards are an important element for smartphones and cellular-enabled tablets and laptops. A **subscriber identity module (SIM)**, also called a *subscriber identification module* is an integrated circuit used to securely authenticate a user's identity for a mobile device. The SIM card stores important information such as the IMSI and ICCID. The **International Mobile Subscriber Identity (IMSI)** is a 15-digit number used by a telecommunications company to identify a SIM on its cellular network. The **Integrated Circuit Card Identification Number (ICCID)** is a unique code 18–22 digits in length that identifies the SIM card's country, home network, and ID number. Think of the two values as the unique identifier for the card. Similarly, each phone has an **International Mobile Station Equipment Identity (IMEI)**, which is a numeric identification number given to a mobile device. The identification numbers associated with SIMs are unique to each card and must be activated by the carrier service before the device can be used. Most modern phones have removable SIMs, which means you could change out the SIM and essentially have a different phone with a different number. This process is explained in detail later in this chapter.

In addition to identification, a SIM card may also contain personal information of the user and data such as contacts, phone numbers, and text messages. When you configure a mobile device with a password or PIN, the password or PIN is also stored on the SIM card.

A+ 1101: 1.2

Screen

Mobile device screens are commonly made from organic LED (OLED) displays, which are constructed from carbon-based materials rather than traditional crystalline structures. For example, the iPhone 14 Pro uses a Super Retina XDR OLED display. However, some phones still use a liquid-crystal display (LCD), such as the Samsung Galaxy A12.

Recall that there are variations of LCD technology. For example, an LED-backlit LCD is a traditional liquid-crystal display that uses light-emitting diodes for backlighting. Another variation of LCD technology is the thin film transistor liquid crystal display (TFT LCD), which uses a thin transistor film to improve image quality.

Tablets and smartphones use touch screen technology for the user interface by reacting or responding to a person's touch or gestures to launch apps or navigate the directory structure. For example, tapping on any of the application icons launches a particular app, and spreading two fingers apart or pinching them together zooms in or out of a given screen. Using two or more fingers to zoom in or out is a form of **multi-touch**, which is the action of touching any surface-sensing device, such as a tablet touch screen or touch pad, with two or more fingers. Finger gestures can also be used to open or close an application, perform scrolling, flip or rotate windows, and more. *TouchFLO* is another term used similarly as multi-touch that was first introduced with the HTC corporation smartphone interface. The objects on the display move according to the direction a finger is moved across the display surface.

Most mobile devices require calibration just as input devices such as pen, stylus, or speech do because each user is unique. The Windows **Pen and Touch** dialog boxes are used to calibrate an input stylus for a tablet, configure pen or stylus gestures, and calibrate gestures and handwriting for individual users.

Accessories

There are a variety of accessories available for portable devices. The most common accessory is a case, which offers protection as well as aesthetic customization. Automobile docking kits are becoming more mainstream, particularly with the rise of ride-sharing apps and smartphones now serving as both GPS navigator and media control center.

A+ 1101: 5.5

Protective Covers

Mobile devices are expensive and easy to damage, which almost requires the use of protective covers or cases. Many cases are built to withstand drops from a certain height without damaging the device, while others are built to make the device waterproof or water resistant. While they do not add any functionality, protective covers and waterproofing are common and encouraged with smartphones and all other mobile devices, which tend to end up in harm's way. Waterproofing is important because liquid damage to a phone can be extensive enough that the phone cannot be repaired. Phones can be dropped into pools, bathtubs, or other bodies of water. If this happens, you should let the phone completely dry before trying to use it. If the phone does not boot, this will require a phone repair specialist company.

Automobile Docking Kit

An *automobile docking kit* is a mobile accessory that attaches to an automobile's windshield or dashboard and cradles the device so it can be viewed while driving without having to take one's eyes off the road. Some kits also come with a charging cable that plugs into the vehicle's auxiliary power port. These are especially useful for people who participate in ride-sharing services, as the dock allows them to use the ride-sharing app or other GPS-enabled apps safely.

Accelerometer and Gyroscope Technology

Accelerometer and gyroscope technology provides a means of input for a mobile device based on changes in physical position. A mobile device equipped with an accelerometer and gyroscope can produce the same effects as a joystick does for a desktop or laptop computer; the device itself becomes an input device.

In electronics terminology, an **accelerometer** is an electromechanical device that measures the force of acceleration. A **gyroscope** is a device that measures vertical and horizontal orientation. Together, these two electronic devices provide data related not only to speed but also to the physical orientation of a device. These two technologies enable the immersion and interactivity for many games. For example, a device with a gyroscope can enable the user to move the device like a steering wheel in a race car game.

Global Positioning System

1101: 1.4 A+
1102: 2.7

The **global positioning system (GPS)** is a satellite-based system developed by the Department of Defense (DoD) and provides positioning, navigation, and timing services. GPS relies on a series of satellites in *geocentric orbit*, which occurs when satellites are set at an altitude that matches the rotation of Earth. The altitude to achieve geocentric orbit is approximately 22,369 miles (36,000 kilometers) from Earth's surface, according to NASA. By matching the rotation of Earth, the satellite is always above the same location on Earth. These satellites are used as reference points to find the location of a GPS-enabled device. A radio wave is transmitted to and from a group of satellites, and the time it takes for the radio wave to travel between the GPS device and three or more satellites is measured. The GPS-enabled device uses the measurements between the device and the three satellites to calculate the exact location of the GPS-enabled device, expressed in longitude and latitude coordinates. The longitude and latitude coordinates are then plotted on a digital map.

Geotracking is the act of tracking the GPS location of one device with another device. For example, you can track the location of a mobile device and display the location on a map in a web browser on a laptop. This option is used to locate friends, children, and even lost mobile devices. As a security precaution, GPS services can be toggled on or off through the device's location settings.

Cloud Services

A+
1102: 2.7

Cloud services are computer services from a remote location on the Internet. Popular uses of cloud services include storage and application software. Cloud storage services augment computer storage by providing a way for mobile devices with limited storage space to store data such as documents, photos, music, and videos that can be accessed from any Internet-connected device. For example, cloud storage through Google, called Drive, is compatible with Android or Apple phones, as well as all desktop and laptop computers. Figure 13-5 shows a screen capture of Google Drive.

One of the benefits of Google Drive is that it automatically synchronizes documents and more between multiple devices. Another great feature is that data on most cloud-storage locations are automatically backed up, meaning if you lose your phone or tablet, a copy of your work still exists in the cloud. When you replace your device, you can still access your data in the cloud.

Limited storage on mobile devices is one of the driving forces supporting cloud services. Cloud services are offered by Google, Microsoft, Apple, and a wide assortment of other laptop, smartphone, and tablet manufacturers, as well as camera companies.

App Distribution

An **app store** is a location that provides software applications for portable devices such as smartphones and tablets. Apple's App Store, Amazon App Store for Android, Microsoft Store, and Google Play for Android are just a few of the many app-distribution services available.

Applications are written for specific operating systems. For example, an Apple app is designed to run only on Apple products, and Android applications are designed to run only on Android products. The same is true for Microsoft apps. Some apps are designed to be universal and will work on any device, and for those that are not, users will often customize their device to remove manufacturer or carrier restrictions to allow it to run other applications. This is called *jailbreaking* the device and will be discussed in more detail later in this chapter.

A+ 1101: 1.3, 1.4, 2.3

Bluetooth Standard

Recall from Chapter 7 that *Bluetooth* refers to a standard developed for short-range radio links between portable computers, mobile phones, and other devices. The standard was created by many of the world's leaders in mobile computing equipment as a royalty-free standard that enables major manufacturers to develop compatible equipment. For example, PCs, tablets, and smartphones using the Bluetooth standard can all communicate with one another via small transmitters

Figure 13-5 Google Drive is a cloud service that automatically synchronizes documents and more among multiple devices through one account.

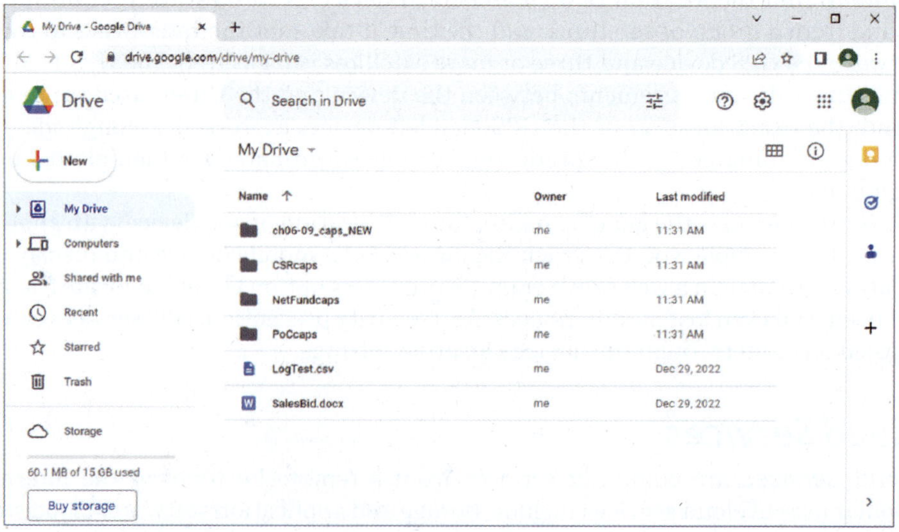

Goodheart-Willcox Publisher

and receivers incorporated into the devices that transmit data and commands on a 2.45-GHz radio band. Bluetooth standards support data transfer speeds as high as 1 Mbps, though the actual speed is closer to 700 kbps to 800 kbps. The Bluetooth classifications are as follows:

- **Class 1**: 100 meters or 300 feet range; used primarily in industry
- **Class 2**: 10 meters or 33 feet range; most common class found in mobile devices
- **Class 3**: 1 meter or 3 feet range

Connecting a Bluetooth device to a computer or mobile device is called *pairing*. In most cases, once the Bluetooth device is turned on, you simply press or hold a button to start pairing mode, and your mobile device will automatically locate or connect to it. In some cases, it may be necessary to enable a setting that makes the Bluetooth device "discoverable." You may also have to enter a security PIN, which is usually only three or four digits in length. Some devices such as mice often connect automatically, while devices such as the headset shown in Figure 13-6 may have more complex connection requirements.

There are some common problems encountered with Bluetooth and wireless devices such as intermittent or no connectivity. If you are experiencing no Bluetooth connection, check if the device has Bluetooth or wireless enabled. This is especially true for mobile devices because, depending on the design, some are easily disabled by accident. Often, you can avoid wireless and Bluetooth interference simply by moving to a new location, sometimes as little as a few feet. Intermittent connections are usually the result of interference or reaching the maximum distance that the connection can maintain. Some Bluetooth devices only have a range of a few feet.

Cloud-Based E-Mail Configurations

The iCloud product is Apple's version of cloud storage, though it includes e-mail as well as storage. When a user signs up for iCloud, they are granted 5 GB of free storage. An Apple user's iCloud storage often consists of e-mail, photos, contacts, messages, notes, and other data from a mobile device and account, though the user can customize what data gets synchronized and stored in their iCloud account. While the first 5 GB are free, upgrading the capacity is not. Currently, Apple offers 50-GB, 200-GB, and 2-TB plans, the costs of which vary and are subject to change, so Apple's website should be consulted before decisions on capacities are made.

Google also provides cloud services in the form of the previously mentioned Drive and, more recently, with the release of Google One. Each user receives a free 15 GB of storage when they create a Google account, and as with iCloud, they may purchase more cloud storage as needed. Much of the storage in a Google account comes from a user's Gmail data, but photos, videos, and other data can be stored as well. Currently,

Chimpinski/Shutterstock.com

Figure 13-6 A Bluetooth headset can be paired to any Bluetooth-enabled mobile device.

Google storage schemes include plans for 100 GB, 1 TB, 2 TB, 10 TB, 20 TB, and 30 TB. As with Apple, the costs of these plans vary and are subject to change.

Microsoft provides cloud services with the e-mail server known as Microsoft Exchange. The primary e-mail client is Outlook, which is available in both local and cloud-based versions and is an integral part of the Microsoft Office suite of products. The local version reflects the history of the e-mail product, and the cloud-based version is similar to—but not quite the same as—the local product.

Despite Yahoo's financial woes, Yahoo E-mail is one of the oldest cloud-based e-mail products still in use today. For users of Gmail and Outlook, the Yahoo e-mail offering may appear antiquated, but it is stable and used by millions.

A+ 1101: 1.4

PRI and PRL Updates

Product Release Instructions (PRI) often include identification numbers, network and country codes, and additional data that allows a cell phone to connect to the correct provider's network. They also provide updates to the operating system, such as additional features or patches. *Preferred Roaming Lists (PRLs)* detail the service providers or frequencies a given carrier prefers a device uses. Since the device needs the most up-to-date version of this data to function, it is important to look for and install updates when available. In most cases, when an update makes a change to the cell phone firmware, the update will occur over the air (radio).

A+ 1101: 1.4

Radio Firmware Updates

As mentioned previously, baseband updates nearly always modify the device's firmware, which is software stored in secure, nonvolatile memory. A firmware update, or *baseband update*, on a device can solve multiple problems when troubleshooting. Often, these updates are sent to devices from the carrier with operating system updates, but sometimes they are pushed to devices separately. Refer to the settings of the device to determine which firmware version is installed and whether a new version is available.

A+ 1101: 1.4

Synchronization

In computing, **synchronization** is the act of matching data between multiple devices. Synchronization is often used in conjunction with cloud storage, though that is not the only option. Synchronizing allows users to view, update, or delete a given file from any of their linked devices. For example, if a journalist were traveling to a foreign country to cover a diplomatic event, they could start the article at work in the office, synchronize their devices, and access it from their phone or tablet while in a hotel, airport, or at the event. Types of data that can be synchronized are shown in Figure 13-7.

A user can synchronize to the cloud if they have a cloud-based account with services such as Dropbox, Google Workspace, Microsoft 365, iCloud, or Microsoft OneDrive, just to name a few. In general, accounts are created and configured by navigating to the website, and selecting the option to create an account. You will need to provide an e-mail address and password to establish an account, and you will have to choose a data cap. Recall that cloud providers often have data cap restrictions, and if you are choosing a higher-capacity plan, you will also have to provide a credit card for payment. The finer details of account creation and setup will vary by provider, but the previously mentioned steps will likely hold true for any cloud provider. Part of the setup includes synchronizing devices and choosing which folders and files to be synchronized. All cloud-based systems assume a connection through either a computer network or cell phone towers; that is, the cloud must be accessible.

Synchronizing to the cloud is only one method, however. A user can also synchronize to a Windows desktop PC using the Windows Sync Center, which is accessed by

Types of Data Users Can Synchronize	
App Type	**Synchronization Location**
Contacts	Synchronized through Microsoft Outlook, Google Gmail, or other e-mail provider
Applications	Browser apps (plug-ins); desktop applications themselves are constrained by license requirements.
E-mail	Cloud-based e-mail syncs automatically. Desktop e-mail must synchronize by downloading and uploading to a mail server.
Pictures	Uploads and downloads through a cloud-based service or manually
Music	Uploads and downloads through a cloud-based service or manually
Videos	Uploads and downloads through a cloud-based service or manually
Calendar	Cloud-based calendars sync transparently. Desktop e-mail must synchronize by downloading and uploading to a server.
Bookmarks	Browser settings
Documents	Uploads and downloads through a cloud-based service or manually
Location data	Controllable at the browser level through privacy setting
Social media data	Synchronized in the cloud
E-books	Uploads and downloads through a cloud-based service or manually
Passwords	If using a cloud-based service, the passwords will synchronize in real time. Otherwise, the tool can refer to a database on a server.

Goodheart-Willcox Publisher

Figurev 13-7
Synchronization is the act of matching data across multiple devices.

navigating to **Start>Control Panel>Sync Center.** This utility allows you to manage offline files, configure new settings, or view current pairings. Alternatively, users can synchronize devices manually using removable storage media or the charging cable for the device. When used for synchronizing, the cable is disconnected from the 120-VAC plug (charger), and the USB end connects to a PC. Once a device is connected to a computer, it will appear in the directory structure in file system, just as a USB flash drive would.

The Sync Center is designed especially for mobile-device data exchange to ensure that the very latest file version is available and not confused with an older file version. The Sync Center only works with files that are configured for sharing in a network environment, even one as small as a home network containing only two devices. Once the desired folder is established as a share, a file can be synchronized using the Sync Center, which enables the latest version of the file to be readily available for use by either device. Apple's iTunes works similarly for synchronizing Apple devices to a PC.

The Sync Center is shown in Figure 13-8. Notice that it allows folders and files to be accessed, viewed, and modified offline. You can synchronize the contents of a folder used by two or more computers or portable devices so that the very latest version is always available for use.

Additionally, users can synchronize devices to an automobile. Most of the time, users will synchronize their cell phones with the Bluetooth capability on their car. Previously discussed requirements such as discoverability apply, and a security PIN are likely required. Note, synchronizing to an automobile will only work for voice-enabled commands, phone calls, and—depending on the vehicle—photos.

Many users take advantage of single sign-on when synchronizing devices. ***Single sign-on (SSO)*** is a form of authentication allowing users to access multiple services or applications with only one set of credentials. This means a user can use

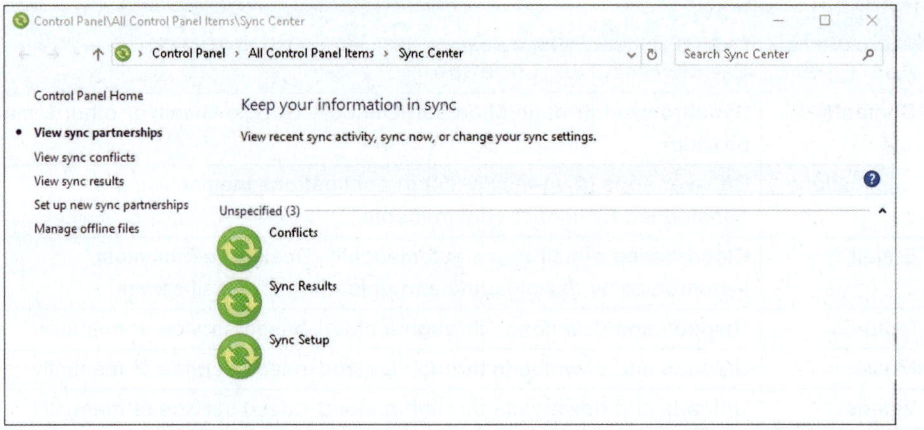

Figure 13-8 Windows Sync Center is designed to ensure the latest versions of files exchanged with mobile devices are available and distinguishable from older versions.

Goodheart-Willcox Publisher

one account, such as a Google account, to log into other cloud-based applications. However, information will now be linked through the Google account and could represent a security risk. The use of multifactor authentication is often advised when using SSO features.

The best way to enable synchronization is to purchase a service that supports this capability. Anybody with a Google account is allotted 15 GB of storage at no cost just for having an account, and additional storage can be purchased if needed. Other approaches include local Wi-Fi synchronization and NFC.

A+ 1101: 1.4

Common Mobile Services

Regardless of the brand of phone you prefer, there are some common services that exist in all mobile phones. Location services is one such common service. Typically, cell phones can be configured to provide cellular location service. The following outlines steps needed to adjust location services for iPhones.

1. Navigate to **Settings**>**Privacy & Security**>**Location Services**.
2. The top menu option is a toggle switch allowing you to turn location services on or off, which functions as a master switch for the entire device. However, iPhone allows you to adjust location services for individual apps. If you want the phone and certain apps to be able to use your location, make sure the switch is toggled **On**.
3. To set the location permissions for a specific app, scroll down until you find the desired app, and tap it to open the app's location settings.
4. Choose the desired location options. As of this writing, the available list of options includes **Never**, which prevents the app from accessing location services information; **Ask Next Time Or When I Share**, which allows you to defer a selection until you use the app or share your location; **While Using The App**, which allows the app to use Location Services only when the app or one of its features is visible on the screen (indicated by a blue location icon in the status bar of the phone); or **Always**, which allows the app to access your location even when running in the background.

To adjust location settings on devices running Android 12 and beyond, the steps are as follows:

1. Swipe down from the top of the screen.
2. Touch and hold **Location**. If you do not see **Location**, tap **Edit** or **Settings**, and drag **Location** into your **Quick Settings** so it is more easily available next time you wish to change this setting.

Another common service is mobile device synchronization. This can include synchronizing with enterprise applications, another computing device, or the cloud. One can synchronize mobile devices with Office 365, Google Workspace, iCloud, and many others. Whatever service is being synchronized, the goal is to have the data across devices and services to be the same, which enables a user to access and work with the same data and a range of devices.

Connecting Directly to a PC

Mobile devices exchange data with full-size PCs for a variety of reasons outside of synchronization, including to exchange information between personal and work devices. For example, employees equipped to work remotely will often have to work on the road or from home. Once the employee comes into the office, they may want to work on a full-size PC. To facilitate data exchange, the mobile PC must be able to communicate with the desktop PC.

The direct connection between a PC and a laptop can be accomplished with a serial or parallel null modem cable (sometimes known as a parallel link interlink cable), USB link cable, crossover network cable, infrared ports (hardly used today), and wireless connection. Null modem cables are still available but seldom encountered because of the lack of serial ports on modern computers, and infrared transmission is hardly used today. The most common methods used to exchange data are USB link cable, wireless, or a small network system using a hub and two network cables. A ***USB link cable*** is a special USB cable with matching connectors on each end and an integrated chip that allows the two devices to exchange data. A regular USB cable extension will not allow the direct exchange of data. Wireless is fine for exchanging small amounts of data, but a USB link cable works better for large volumes of data because wireless often suffers from radio interference, and Bluetooth devices have a very limited data rate.

The best way to exchange large volumes of data is to create a small network using a network hub or switch. Speeds in the range of 1 Gbps to 10 Gbps can be achieved in a small network system. Network systems such as this are presented in later chapters. See Figure 13-9 for a comparison of direct data exchange methods.

Since almost all modern laptops have built-in wireless technology, Windows no longer has a direct connection option. Beginning with Windows Vista, you need to use either an ad hoc wireless connection or a small network connection using wireless or cable media to configure a direct connection. You can still connect two Windows computers using a USB link cable because the USB link cable comes with

Methods for Connecting a Laptop to a PC

Media	Theoretical Data Rate	Comments
Infrared	115 kbps–4 Mbps	Uses a direct line of sight but is immune to radio and magnetic interference
Network cable	10 Mbps–10 Gbps	Excellent for large volumes of data exchange
Parallel null modem	500 kbps–2 Mbps	Rate too low to be used today
Serial null modem	115 kbps	Rate too low to be used today
USB link cable	USB 2.0, 480 Mbps USB 3.0, 4.8 Gbps	Excellent for high volumes of data exchange
Wireless (Bluetooth, Wi-Fi, WiMAX)	700 kbps–300 Gbps	Wireless devices vary greatly because of all the various standards, and possibility of radio interference

Goodheart-Willcox Publisher

Figure 13-9 There is more than one method for creating a direct connection between a laptop and computer.

required support software. Transfer cables, like the USB link cable, are often used to transfer system and user settings between two computers. Look at Figure 13-10 to see the **Set Up a Connection or Network** wizard. The easiest way to launch this wizard is by navigating to **Control Panel>Network and Internet>Network and Sharing Center>Set up a new connection or network.**

13.2 Portable PC Components

A portable PC functions similarly to a full-size PC, though alterations have been made to the design of the portable PC to allow it to be carried easily, used anywhere, and connected quickly to other PCs and networks. To enable this functionality, laptop computers are equipped with some parts that full-size PCs do not have, such as large storage batteries. Laptop computers also have had other common PC components such as the mouse altered significantly, and to keep laptops adaptable like their full-size counterparts, PCMCIA and ExpressCards were developed to enable the addition of new devices to laptops. These extension cards, however, have since been replaced almost entirely by USB connections.

Frames

As you explore the figures in this chapter, you may discern a variety of frames or housings for the various devices. At the low end will be a variety of relatively inexpensive plastics, and at the high end of the plastic material will be ABS—a strong plastic resistant to abrasion and temperature changes. Upscale devices are often made from metal; for example, Apple has explored the use of magnesium and aluminum for housings, and other PC laptop vendors continue to offer robust and expensive housing options.

A+ **1101: 1.1**
1102: 4.4, 4.5

Batteries

Batteries, such as the one shown in Figure 13-11, are a vital part of portable computing. The type of battery is extremely important when selecting a portable PC as it determines the number of hours a PC can be used independently, and it also

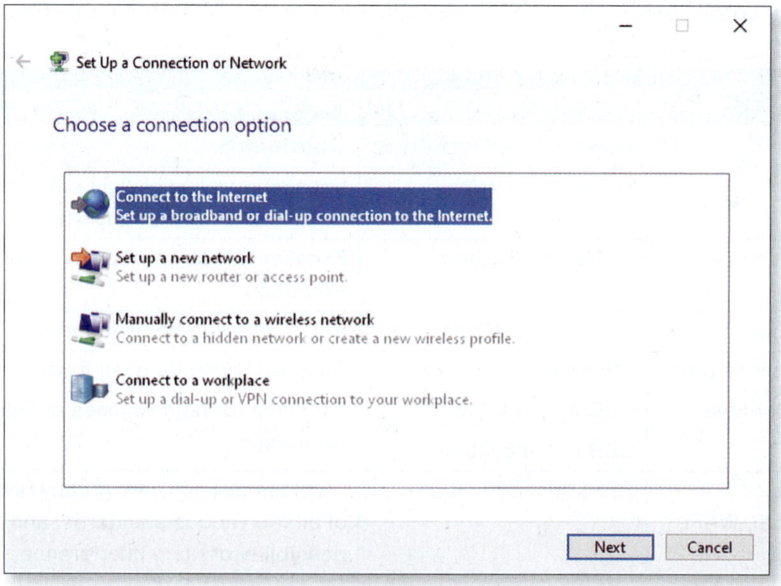

Figure 13-10 The **Windows Set Up a Connection or Network** wizard will assist you in creating an ad hoc (computer-to-computer) network.

Goodheart-Willcox Publisher

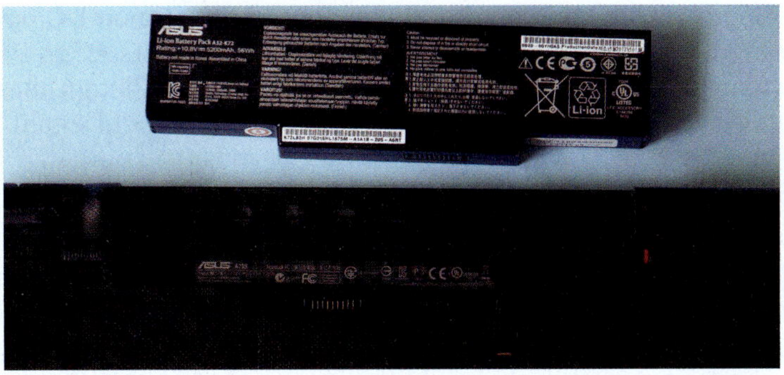

Goodheart-Willcox Publisher

Figure 13-11 Lithium-ion batteries are the most commonly encountered type of battery for portable computers.

greatly affects the weight of the PC. The major types of rechargeable batteries found in use for portable computers and devices are alkaline, nickel cadmium (NiCad), nickel-metal hydride (NiMH), lithium-ion (Li-ion), lithium-ion polymer (Li-poly), and—more recently—lithium-ion phosphate (LFP, Li-IP).

1101: 5.5 A+

Alkaline batteries are commonly found in small devices and are not used much with newer computers or mobile devices. Nickel-cadmium (NiCad) batteries were used for many years, as they are one of the least expensive batteries, but they can take up to 12 hours to recharge fully and are susceptible to ***memory effect***, which means that a battery will not last as long if it is not fully drained before a recharge. For example, if a battery is recharged after only one hour of use, the battery may only last for one hour on subsequent charges. Nickel-metal hydride (NiMH) batteries were an improvement over NiCad batteries since they do not suffer from memory effect and store up to 50 percent more charge time, but they can only be recharged approximately 500 times before they begin to fail. Lithium-ion (Li-ion) batteries have the highest electrical potential of all the batteries discussed thus far. Lithium-ion is lightweight and compact, and Li-ion batteries contain no poisonous metals, making them a popular and safe choice. However, they are more expensive than other battery types. Lithium-ion polymer (Li-poly) batteries are thinner, making them popular for mobile devices, which are designed to be thin and lightweight, but they are unable to support high current and cannot be used to power equipment with significant electrical power.

Most rechargeable batteries are regulated because of the hazardous materials they contain. As a result, the exact method of disposal varies according to governmental authorities such as cities, counties, state, and the federal government. Almost all states have adopted their own set of guidelines that exceed the federal regulations. The following is a list of common battery types and their potential hazards:

- **NiCad batteries**: NiCad batteries contain the toxic metal cadmium.
- **Mercury batteries**: Mercury batteries are toxic.
- **Lithium-ion batteries:** Lithium-ion batteries contain lithium, which is highly reactive with water, though not all lithium-ion batteries are considered a waste hazard.
- **Lead-acid and lead-gel batteries**: These batteries contain the toxic metal lead. You are unlikely to find these in computing devices aside from uninterruptible power supplies.

Caution

Never attempt to incinerate, puncture, crush, physically damage, short circuit, or solder wire leads to a battery.

In most areas, recycling facilities take old batteries and either recycle them or send them to another facility for recycling or disposal. If a battery is rechargeable, it is usually recyclable. Do *not* attempt to disassemble a battery for recycling. It takes a highly skilled and trained individual and special safety equipment to disassemble a battery for recycling.

As a PC technician, you and your company will encounter more than the average number of recyclable batteries. You must adhere to all laws and regulations when disposing of batteries. The regulations vary according to the number of batteries accumulated over a set period.

Because portable computers, especially laptops, operate on DC power from a battery, they will have an external power source that converts AC to DC. All these devices have an input port for power, usually a DC jack, though many modern devices use the USB 3.1 or "C" type connector for both power and signal.

Extra Battery Packs and Battery Chargers

While some laptops have batteries that can only be replaced at the factory, others have readily available battery compartments for quick battery replacement with a battery pack. Some laptops will accept an external battery pack, particularly if a port or port replicator supports it. New laptops may even be able to charge through a USB port, similar to a mobile device. In this case, an external battery pack or portable battery charger can be used to extend the life of your battery even further.

A+ 1101: 1.3

Docking Station

A **docking station** is an electronic cradle that provides power for a laptop, allowing users to turn the laptop into a full-size PC when portability is not necessary. Once the laptop slides into the docking station and snaps into place, it can operate from the power provided by the docking station rather than from a battery or a battery charger. Some docking stations contain slots for expansion devices and bays for additional storage devices. Many times, the docking station automatically connects the laptop to the company network or the Internet. By connecting to the docking station, you can also connect a full-size keyboard, mouse, or other less portable equipment to your laptop easily. It should be noted that some laptop docks operate more like a hub in the sense that they are standalone devices that plug into a laptop via USB cable.

Normally, a portable computer needs to have the desired configuration identified while docking or undocking. For example, a laptop is equipped with an LCD screen, but a docking station may use a larger screen as a display. When the laptop is connected to the docking station, the video must be configured for the larger display. When the laptop is removed from the docking station, it must be reconfigured for the LCD screen. Beginning with Windows 7, the Windows operating system will automatically configure laptop video when docked, though it is still advisable to view the display settings and adjust as needed.

Keyboard

The keyboard is one of the biggest advantages of a laptop over a mobile device. Laptops are built with full-size or compact keyboards, depending on the size of the device. Full-size keyboards resemble those found with desktop PCs, though they may not include the number pad found on the far-right of desktop keyboards. Compact keyboards omit the number pad entirely and typically have keys with more than one function, some of which include

- volume controls;
- brightness controls;
- network connections; and
- various vendor-selected options.

Powerful laptops may also have dedicated media controls such as forward, stop, rewind, eject, and more. Laptops will often have keyboard backlighting for work in dark areas, controllable through a function key or the Windows Control Panel.

Screens

Laptop screens are typically LED or LCD technology, and their orientation can be controlled in Windows 10 using the sequence [Ctrl][Alt][Arrow] until the desired orientation occurs. Windows 10 and other versions of Windows can also change orientation through the display menu. Also, note that many modern laptops and Chromebooks have screens that can be physically rotated nearly 360 degrees, allowing them to operate as tablets when necessary.

Multiple Screens

Mobile devices are small by nature and, as a result, a user can have difficulty viewing the contents of the display. Assuming the laptop's graphics can support it, most laptops also support a second monitor. In Figure 13-12, you can see the options to duplicate or extend the monitor through a projector, which functions as a second monitor.

The shortcut key combination to access the projector options is [Windows key] [P]. After using the key combination, a side-panel will pop up on the screen, similar to that shown in Figure 13-12. Alternatively, the Windows **Display** menu provides options for configuring multiple devices, as shown in Figure 13-13A. If multiple displays are connected to the laptop, you can select the **Detect** button to find them, though in most cases, the operating system will automatically detect the second monitor. Another option is to open the **Advanced display settings** menu shown in Figure 13-13B, which allows you to adjust each display individually.

Once you have made sure that your video card can support a second monitor, follow these steps to add the additional monitor:

1. Turn off your computer and monitor.
2. Connect the second monitor to the unused video port.
3. Plug the second monitor into an electrical power source and turn it on.
4. Turn on your original monitor and computer.

In most cases, Windows will automatically detect a second monitor. You may be prompted to install driver software for the monitor. If you cannot connect to a projector or second display, perform the following troubleshooting steps:

- Make sure the monitor or projector is turned on and plugged into the correct video port on your computer.

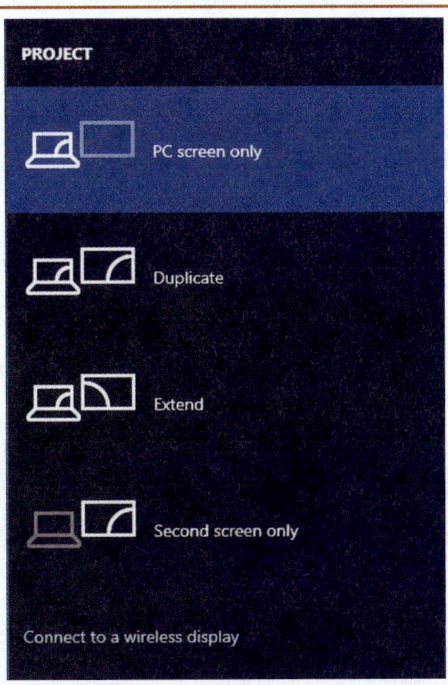

Goodheart-Willcox Publisher

Figure 13-12 Laptops and mobile devices are designed to duplicate or extend the display or connect the device to a projector.

Figure 13-13 The Windows **Display** menu (A) offers an option to automatically detect multiple displays, and the **Advanced display settings** menu (B) provides the user with options for customizing each display.

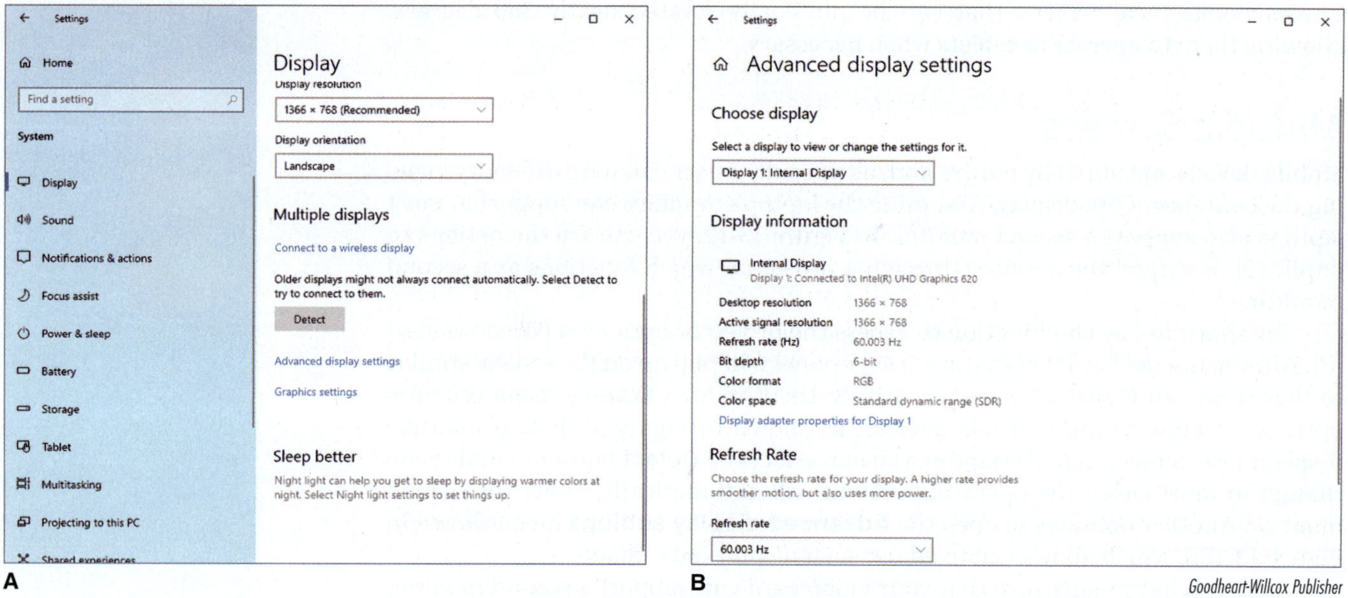

Goodheart-Willcox Publisher

- Make sure you have selected the correct video input port on the second monitor or projector. Many display devices such as televisions have options for multiple inputs and must be selected through a remote control or buttons located on the display device.
- As always, check the manual for the monitor or projector. You can download the manual from the manufacturer's website.

A+ 1101: 1.3

Port Replicator

A **port replicator** is an external device for a computer that provides additional ports to be used by a computer system. The most common computer systems to use a port replicator are laptop computers and other portable devices, which typically have a limited number of available ports due to their compact design. For the same reason, it is often difficult or impossible to add additional ports by using expansion cards, so adding a PCI card is not a practical solution. A port replicator solves the problem of adding additional ports via USB 3.1 (type C) port.

A port replicator allows for the addition of devices such as a printer, camera, joystick, external optical drive, monitor, extra hard drive, external modem, scanner, keyboard, mouse, or any other digital device used by a full-size PC. In many ways, a port replicator serves the same function as a docking station. The use of a port replicator is not limited to just small digital devices; you can also use a port replicator to add additional ports that are not usually found on a typical computer, such as SCSI ports. It is also important to note that a USB hub designed to add additional USB ports could also be classified as a port replicator.

Portable Motherboards

Portable PC motherboards do not follow a standard form factor, as seen in Figure 13-14. Laptop form factors are often proprietary, and to help keep the PCs small, most portable PCs incorporate the processor directly into the motherboard. To reduce heat in the portable PC, the processor is often purposely set to run at a lower speed than it is capable of if installed in a full-size PC. Portable PCs leave little room for cooling because of the compact design. They incorporate large, flat heat sinks inside the case, but there is not sufficient room for a full-size cooling fan. Slowing down the processor extends battery life as well.

Touch Pads

Laptops are manufactured with touch pads, as shown in Figure 13-15. Also referred to as *track pads*, touch pads are a standard feature for most laptop computers that operate on the same principles as a touch screen and provide a minimalistic and effective alternative to using a mouse. Touch pads can be toggled on and off by navigating to **Start>Settings>Devices>Touchpad**. A user might wish to disable the touch pad when using a mouse if the touch pad is extremely sensitive. For example, if one is using a wireless USB mouse, they may find that they accidentally brush against the touch pad while typing on the laptop keyboard. Since some touch pads are also capable of reading multi-touch gestures, this can result in unexpected selection or zooming. Disabling the touch pad avoids this potential issue entirely.

PCMCIA Cards

While PCMCIA cards have largely been replaced by USB devices, you might still encounter these in older laptops. However, the CompTIA A+ Exams will likely not ask about PCMCIA cards. The Personal Computer Memory Card International

Goodheart-Willcox Publisher

Figure 13-14 Laptops have the same internal components as full-size PCs. However, the layout of the laptop is very different to keep the size and weight down.

Aleksandr Finch/Shutterstock.com

Figure 13-15 A touch pad is an input device that serves the same function as a mouse.

Association (PCMCIA) designed a set of standards for adding memory and expanding a portable PC using devices resembling thick credit cards. The resulting ***PCMCIA cards***, such as the one shown in Figure 13-16, were designed to add memory or functionality to a portable PC. PCMCIA cards were often referred to as simply a ***PCM*** or ***PC card*** and installed in a PCMCIA slot on the side of the portable PC. These slots are used in place of expansion slots as the way to install additional devices. As with USB connections, many PCMCIA cards are hot-swappable. All PCMCIA cards have the same rectangular shape (85.6 mm by 54 mm), but they vary in thickness because their thickness classifies the card type. There are three classifications of cards:

- **Type I** is 3.3 mm thick and is used primarily to add memory to a laptop.
- **Type II** is 5.0 mm thick and is usually used to add modems and network cards to the portable PC. The cards are equipped with either RJ-11 or RJ-45 connectors.
- **Type III** is 10.5 mm thick and is designed to support hard drives or external CD, DVD, or tape drives.

There is a selection of slots to go with the cards. A Type I slot can hold one Type I card. Type II slots can hold one Type II card or two Type I cards. Type III slots can hold one Type III card or one Type I card and one Type II card. All of the smaller cards fit into larger slots on their own. Type IV cards are in development, but they have not been ratified by the PCMCIA consortium at this time. Type IV cards are expected to be 16 mm thick and will be used for large-capacity hard drives.

ExpressCards such as the one shown in Figure 13-17 were the next evolution of PCMCIA cards as the choice for laptop computers before USB dominated this market and could be used as modems, analog and digital television tuners, wireless network cards, exterior SATA connections, and expansion to the PCIe bus for connecting other devices. The card is available in two widths: 34 mm and 54 mm, as shown in Figure 13-18, and the choice of width is based on the type of device the card incorporates. ExpressCards are designed to connect internally to the USB 2.0 bus, USB 3.0 bus, or the PCIe bus. When using the USB 2.0 bus, the data rate for the ExpressCard is 480 Mbps, and the data rate for USB 3.0 is approximately 5 Gbps.

Figure 13-16 PCMCIA cards were originally designed to add functionality to laptops. The card shown here provides a laptop with an Ethernet port for wired network connectivity.

Claudio Divizia/Shutterstock.com

Figure 13-17 ExpressCards can be used as modems, analog and digital television tuners, wireless network cards, exterior SATA connections, and expansion to the PCIe bus for connecting other devices.

Goodheart-Willcox Publisher

Wireless Devices

Most laptops come with a wireless device incorporated into the motherboard or as an add-on, though the exact type of wireless technology varies. When the wireless device is not already incorporated into a laptop, a PCMCIA card, ExpressCard, or USB device is used to provide wireless network support. The wireless connection can be turned on or off either using Control Panel or from the system tray in the Notification Area of the taskbar in the lower right-hand corner of the screen.

Special Function Keys

The keyboards of portable PCs typically have function keys that are activated by pressing the [Fn] key in combination with other function keys identified in blue, Figure 13-19. The [Fn] key in Figure 13-19A is positioned on the left side of the keyboard, and the function keys in Figure 13-19B are positioned on the right side of the keyboard. Other special function keys are located along the top or along the right side of the keyboard.

Many times, a new laptop user will inadvertently press a combination of keys that causes unexpected results while typing on the keyboard. They may accidentally turn off the sound, put the laptop in sleep mode, change the brightness of the display, or toggle their Internet connection, among other actions. At times, the user may

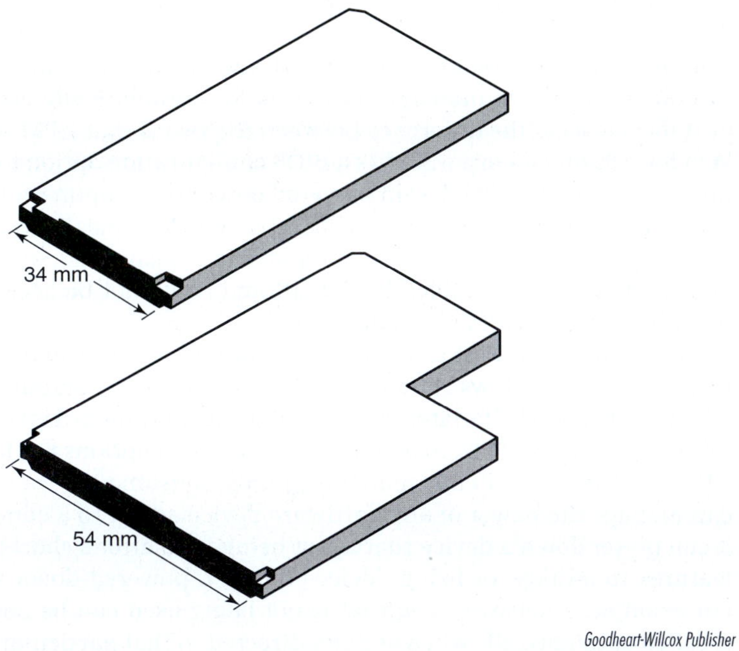

Figure 13-18 ExpressCards come in two widths: 34 mm and 54 mm.

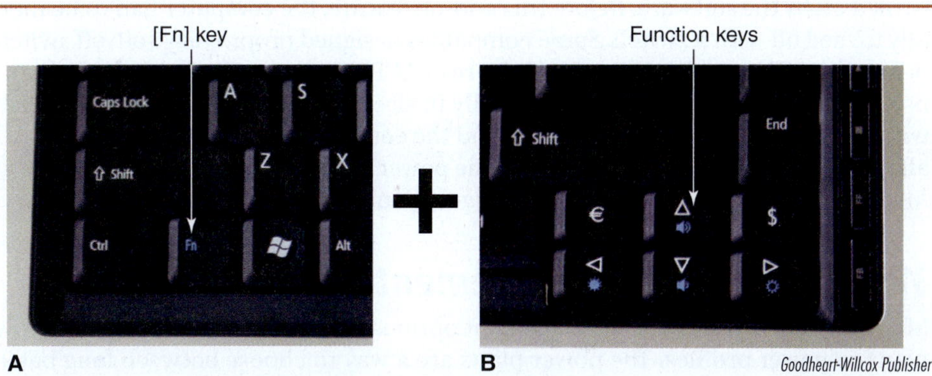

Figure 13-19 To access special laptop functions, simultaneously press the [Fn] key (A) and the desired function key (B).

make the same mistake several times, causing them to think something is wrong with the laptop and call tech support to resolve the problem. If misdiagnosed, the laptop may be unnecessarily packaged and sent to a repair depot.

In addition to special function keys, many laptops have physical switches that control functionality such as wireless access, Internet access, sound, and more. The switches are often placed along the top of the keyboard or along the outside edge of the laptop. The problem with physical switches along the outside edge of laptop computers is that they can be switched off accidentally, for example, while being placed into a bag. The accidental moving of the switch to an off position can confuse the user and cause them to think they have a problem with the laptop operating system or some component such as the wireless card.

A+ 1102: 1.4

13.3 Power Management

Power management is an important aspect of mobile computing, and the incorrect configuration of power-management settings can reduce the battery power and length of charge considerably. Through proper power management, a user can reduce the amount of power used by the display, CPU, and hard drive, which are the three major components that consume power.

Tech Tip

Power management is not limited to portable devices. Desktop systems also have power-management configuration options to conserve electrical energy.

APM and ACPI

Automatic Power Management (APM) and Advanced Configuration and Power Interface (ACPI) are industry standards for automatically configuring power on portable devices. The difference between the two is that APM was first available in Windows 95 and incorporated as a BIOS configuration option to conserve electrical power. The simple APM design powered down the computer after a predetermined amount of inactivity and also included a switch, typically located at the front of the computer case, that put the computer in a suspended, or sleeping, state when activated. APM was enabled by default and could not be accessed directly by the operating system. APM is no longer used.

ACPI replaced APM as a natural evolution in power management. It was first introduced in Windows NT and Windows 98 operating systems and is still used in Windows 10 and 11. The latest revision of the ACPI standard is version 6.5, which was released in August 2022. ACPI has more advanced options not found in the original APM. ACPI is not limited to managing power consumed by the display and CPU and can manage the power of any hardware device added to a computer. For example, it can power down a device that is not being used after a short period and includes features to awaken or bring devices out of a powered-down state when needed. For example, a network card that is not being used can be powered down but be recalled automatically when activity directed to that particular card is detected.

ACPI also provides a feature referred to as ***soft-off*** that allows the computer to be turned off by the software. Before this add-on feature, the computer had to be manually turned off with a switch. Some companies designed proprietary soft-off switches before the ACPI standard. Another feature of ACPI is support for a switch that can be used to place the computer automatically in sleep mode. All the features associated with ACPI are controlled by the BIOS, and the configuration is stored in CMOS. ACPI allows the operating system to control the power configuration features directly, and Microsoft has incorporated energy configuration features in all their products.

A+ 1102: 1.4

Windows Power-Management Options

Microsoft Windows power-management options are based on preconfigured power plans or power profiles. The power plans are a way to choose between long battery life and computer performance and are located in **Control Panel>Hardware and Sound>Power Options**. Notice in Figure 13-20 that there are three power plans available in Windows: **Balanced**, **High performance**, and **Power saver**. The **Balanced** power plan equally emphasizes battery conservation and system performance. **High performance** sacrifices battery life but allows for top computer performance and is often required for intense activities such as viewing movies, playing graphic-intense computer games, and editing photos. The **Power saver** plan slows the performance of the CPU and lowers the backlighting of the LCD display, both of which save considerable electrical energy. Additionally, Windows allows users to create custom power plans by selecting **Create a power plan**.

Notice in Figure 13-21 that you can select how the laptop will react when the power button or the sleep button is pressed or when the laptop lid is closed. The settings for these features are located in **Control Panel>Hardware and Sound>Power Options>Choose what the power buttons do**. The power-button options are **Do nothing**, **Sleep**, **Hibernate**, **Shut down**, or **Turn off the display**. Notice that each selection is correlated to when the laptop is supplied battery or AC power. The sleep button has the same options, only without **Shut down**. The lid-closure options do not include **Turn off the display**, as that happens automatically. The **Do nothing**,

A+ Note

Be sure to know the differences among power options. The CompTIA A+ Exams typically include a question regarding the differences between sleep and hibernation.

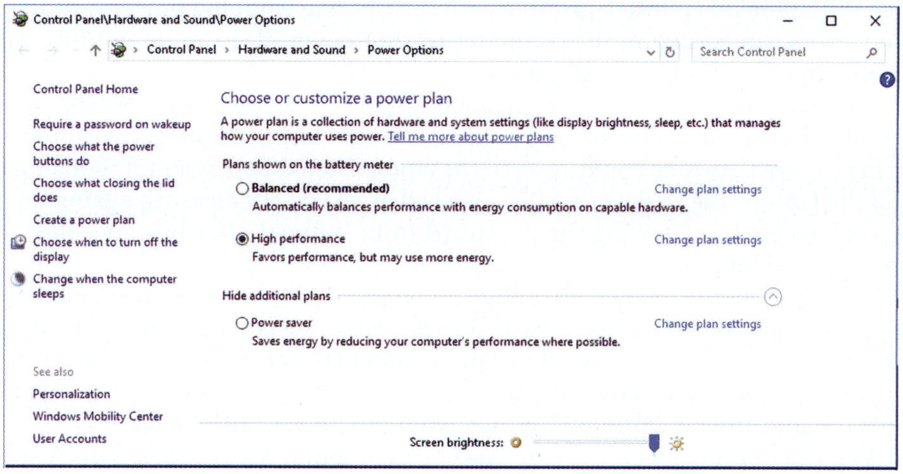

Goodheart-Willcox Publisher

Figure 13-20 Windows features three power-management options: **Balanced**, **High performance**, and **Power saver**.

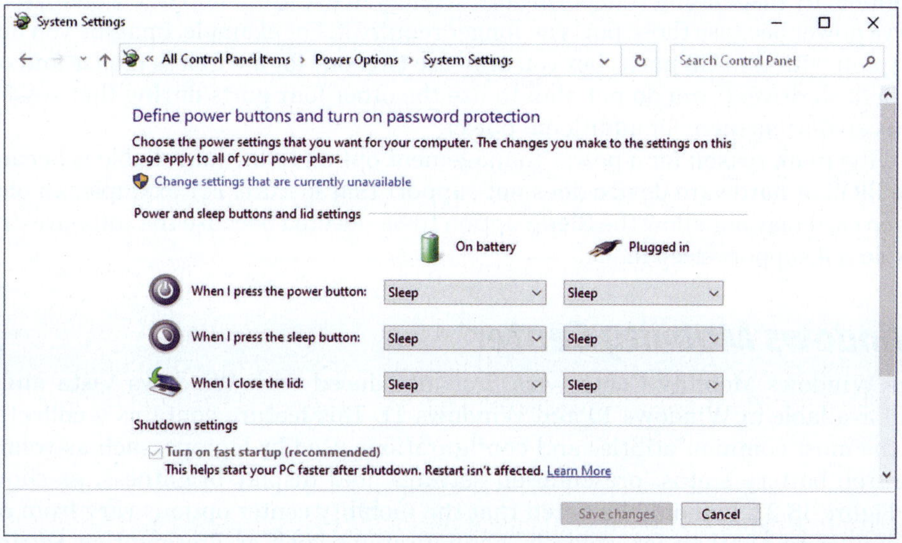

Goodheart-Willcox Publisher

Figure 13-21 Windows lets users customize power options for the power and sleep buttons, as well as lid closure.

Shut down, and **Turn off the display** options are straightforward and should need no further explanation, but **Sleep** and **Hibernate** do require some explanation, as there is often confusion between the two.

The **Sleep** option saves all documents and folders that are in use when the sleep command is invoked. When the computer is awakened, the same open files automatically reappear on the desktop. **Sleep** causes little drain on laptop battery, similar to a *standby mode*. Some computers have a hybrid sleep feature that saves working files to both RAM and the hard drive while sleeping to maintain a fast recovery when awakened as well as protection against data loss due to lost power or battery failure. Hybrid sleep requires BIOS that supports this feature.

The **Hibernate** option uses less battery life than **Sleep**, saves open files and current work to the hard drive, and reopens the files and current work when the PC is awakened. The main difference between sleep mode and hibernate mode is where the open files and current work are saved. **Sleep** saves the files and current work in RAM, and **Hibernate** saves the files and current work to the hard drive. The computer takes longer to restart from **Hibernate** than from **Sleep** because **Sleep** stores the files in RAM. However, open files and work can be lost if a laptop placed in **Sleep** loses power.

A+ 1102: 1.4

Similarly, the **Choose what closing the lid does** option is also found in **Control Panel>Hardware and Sound>Power Options** and allows you to decide what occurs when the laptop lid is closed. Just like with the **Choose what the power buttons do** menu, users can configure the computer to shut down, sleep, or do nothing when powered by either battery or AC power.

Another Windows power-management feature is *password protection*, which is provided as an option for scenarios such as when closing the lid of the laptop and leaving the area. Anyone could awaken the laptop from **Sleep** by simply opening the lid of the laptop. The password option is used as a security measure against unauthorized access by requiring the password to be entered after bringing the computer out of **Sleep**.

A+ 1102: 1.4

Fast Startup, also called Fast Boot, is another Windows feature enabled by default on most newer laptops. Fast Startup works by changing how the system shuts down. Rather than close all programs and files, the system hibernates those files, allowing for a much faster startup. To enable or disable this feature, navigate to **Control Panel>Power Options>Choose what the power buttons do.**

A+ 1102: 1.4

A creative option for conserving power can be found with the Selective Suspend option, which allows the system to conserve power by putting specific USB ports into suspend mode. This is found in **Control Panel>Hardware and Sound>Power Options.** By suspending USB ports not currently in use, the computer is able to conserve power because those ports no longer require it. For example, imagine you have a laptop with six USB ports, but you only use two: one for a wireless mouse and one for a flash drive. If you do not plan to use the other four ports during that session, you can disable them for additional power.

The main reason for a power-management option to be unavailable is because the BIOS or hardware device does not support that feature. For example, an older video card may not allow the **Sleep** option to be selected because the software drivers do not support sleep mode.

Windows Mobility Center

The Windows Mobility Center was first introduced with Windows Vista and is still available in Windows 10 and Windows 11. This feature contains a collection of the most common utilities and configurations used by laptops, such as volume control, battery status, presentation settings, and display brightness, as shown in Figure 13-22. It should be noted that the mobility center options vary from one computer to another; for example, configurations such as Presentation Settings will not appear unless the computer has previously been configured for a projector. Additionally, computer hardware manufacturers often modify the Windows Mobility Center to incorporate their own special mobile service. See Figure 13-23 for a description of each feature.

13.4 Mobile Operating Systems

A+ 1102: 1.8

Laptops use standard operating systems just like desktops, but smaller mobile devices such as tablets and smartphones require special operating systems that are compact and accommodate minimal software applications referred to as apps. Mobile operating systems are more compact than traditional operating systems because mobile devices have limited hardware abilities. A desktop PC or laptop has much better performance in comparison with a mobile device. Desktops and laptops can have very powerful CPUs, large amounts of memory, large hard drive storage, and powerful graphics processors, but mobile devices have much more conservative hardware and are designed to consume as little electrical power as possible while still maintaining some decent performance.

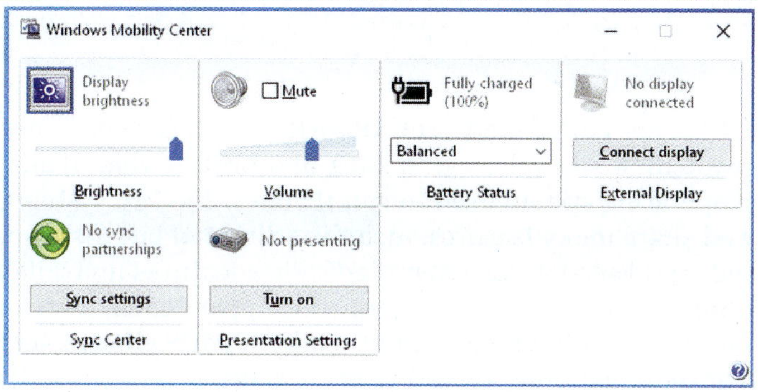

Goodheart-Willcox Publisher

Figure 13-22 The Windows Mobility Center contains a collection of the most common utilities and configurations used by laptops.

Windows Mobility Center Features	
Feature	**Description**
Battery Status	Allows you to modify the battery usage by selecting a different power plan for the laptop
Brightness	Controls the brightness of the LCD monitor
External Display	Used to set up a second or third display automatically; an external display is often connected to a laptop PC via a cable or docking station.
Presentation Settings	Allows you to preconfigure presentation settings, such as the volume or which projector to use if more than one projector is typically connected; the projector can be automatically detected through a wizard, or you can enter the URL or a UNC address of the projector. After the presentation settings are configured, you can simply access the present configuration and start your presentation immediately without a further configuration.
Sync Center	Maintains the latest version of a file or collection of files that are commonly transferred between the laptop and another device
Volume	Allows you to adjust the portable laptop speaker volume
Wireless Network	Turns wireless network adapter on or off and displays status of wireless network connection; will not display if disabled

Goodheart-Willcox Publisher

Figure 13-23 Common Windows Mobility Center features include Battery Status, Brightness, External Display, Presentation Settings, Sync Center, Volume, and Wireless Network.

All mobile operating systems, as well as those for the desktop, will have end-of-life (EOL) issues at some point. In some cases, the hardware no longer supports newer software, which is not uncommon with cell phones and tablets. For example, Microsoft regularly ends support for old operating systems, such as Windows 7, Windows 8, and Windows 8.1. Even older Chromebooks may have issues updating to the latest Chrome OS, although good-quality five-year-old hardware can still support the current Chrome OS.

Compatibility concerns occur between different versions of the operating system. For example, Android 9 broke some apps. Also, Windows RT was never designed to be identical to the Intel-based Windows product for laptops and desktops. There are many operating systems designed for mobile devices, but the four dominant mobile operating systems are iOS, iPadOS, Android, and Chrome OS.

A+ 1102: 1.8

iOS

All smartphones created by Apple run **iOS**, which is Apple's proprietary smartphone operating system. Apple only allows iOS to be used on its smartphones, and if iOS is used on other manufacturer's products, it cannot be customized. This is in sharp contrast to Android, which allows manufacturers to modify the Android operating system code.

A+ 1102: 1.8

iPadOS

Apple-branded tablets, called iPads, run **iPadOS**, which is Apple's proprietary tablet operating system. It was released in 2019, and prior to that, iPads operated on iOS, the same operating system used to run iPhones. The two systems are remarkably similar and share many features, including Siri, AirPlay, AirDrop, geolocation services, iCloud, and Face ID. However, iPadOS has features unavailable to iPhone users. For example, iPadOS interfaces with the Apple Pencil, a stylus that is not made to be compatible with iPhones. Additionally, iPadOS allows users to open and run two apps at the same time, as well as open multiple sessions in the Safari web browser app.

A+ 1102: 1.8

Android

Android is a mobile operating system owned by Google that is derived from the Linux open-source operating system. *Open source* means that the programming source code is not secret and is freely available for viewing so that anyone can modify the code. The Android operating system was originally developed by a company called Android Inc., which was bought by Google. Android differs from iOS in that different hardware manufacturers can customize Android to meet their individual needs and developers can customize Android for their particular device. For example, the Android operating system on a Samsung tablet does not exactly match the Android operating system installed on an ASUS tablet, which can lead to compatibility issues.

A+ 1102: 1.8

Chrome OS

Chrome OS is a Linux-derived operating system merged with Google's flagship web browser, also called Chrome. The result is a lightweight operating system that provides basic functionality. Powerful Chromebooks, such as the Google Pixelbook, also make it easy to access a version of Linux, a choice the user can make and implement in roughly ten minutes. A unique selling point of Chrome OS is the provision for antimalware protection by Google. Hence, except for firmware-based issues such as Specter and Meltdown, Chromebooks are virtually immune to malware contamination.

13.5 Wireless Connections

1101: 1.2 A+

A wireless connection is commonly used to connect a laptop or mobile device to a full-size PC or to join a small network using radio waves. A much more detailed description of wireless networking is covered later in this textbook. This section only covers terminology related to wireless data transfer. When installing a wireless connection, be sure to consider the type of connection, potential interference, and adherence to IEEE wireless standards.

Ad Hoc Network

1101: 3.6 A+

An **ad hoc network** is a network formed between two or more wireless devices, such as a workstation and a notebook, as shown in Figure 13-24. Fittingly, the name *ad hoc* is a Latin expression that translates to *for this purpose*. You can think of an ad hoc network connection as a direct cable connection that uses radio waves as the connection medium rather than cable. Ad hoc connections are not normally permanent and are primarily used for transferring data.

Wireless Infrastructure Network

1101: 3.6 A+

Another classification of wireless connection is called an infrastructure network. An **infrastructure network** differs from an ad hoc network in that it contains a **wireless access point (WAP)**, which is a device that supports communication between wireless devices and a hard-wired network system, as shown in Figure 13-25. A wireless access point is often used as a **bridge**, which is a device used to connect two dissimilar networks. In the example shown, the wireless access point is bridging the connection between the hard-wired network and the wireless network.

Radio Waves

Radio waves are used to deliver or exchange information throughout the world. To prevent radio waves from interfering with each other, the FCC regulates radio frequencies by assigning specific frequencies to various types of equipment. For example, remote-controlled toy cars typically function at 27 MHz and 40 MHz. When you tune your car radio, you are actually selecting a radio frequency. When you select a radio

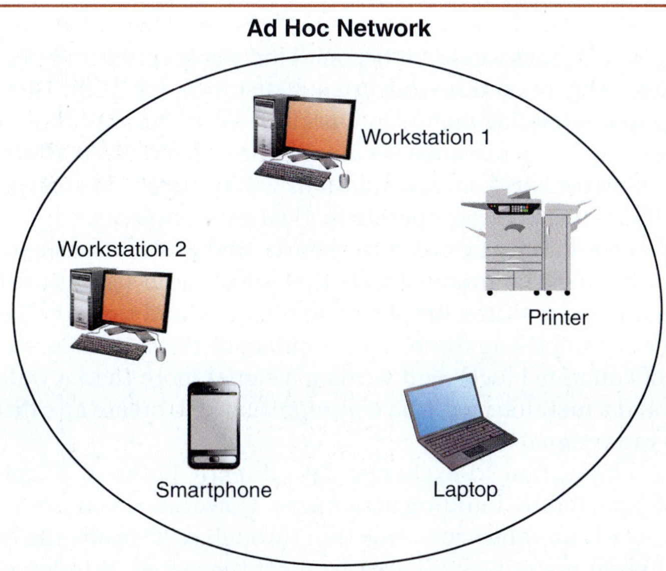

Goodheart-Willcox Publisher; (workstations and laptop) romvo/Shutterstock.com; (printer) VectorShow/Shutterstock.com; (smartphone) Tetiana Yurchenko/Shutterstock.com

Figure 13-24 Some devices are connected together by radio waves in an ad hoc network, which can consist of 2 to 64 wireless devices.

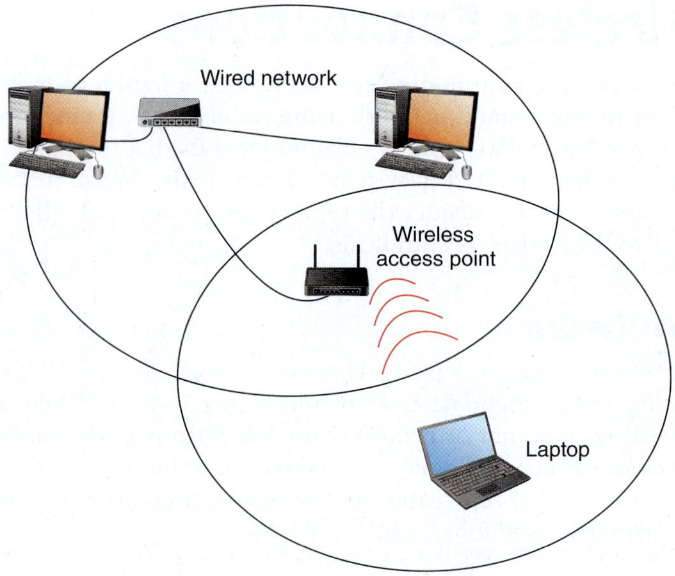

Figure 13-25 A wireless access point acts as a bridge between the wireless device and the wired network system.

Goodheart-Willcox Publisher; (workstations and laptop) romvo/Shutterstock.com; (hub and router) Vadim Ermak/Shutterstock.com

station such as 104.5 FM, you are tuning the radio receiver to a transmitted carrier wave of 104.5 MHz. The carrier wave is a set frequency, which is used to carry the information from the transmitter to the receiver.

Radio Signal Interference

Radio signal interference is a radio wave transmission that corrupts or distorts a desired radio wave signal. Some common sources of wireless computer communication devices are wireless telephones, medical equipment, microwave ovens, cell phones, and other devices and appliances containing electrical motors. While all electronic equipment generates some interference, these specific devices share the same radio wave frequencies that wireless network cards use, approximately 2.48 GHz.

Another major factor that affects wireless communication is the distance between the source and destination. As the distance between the source and destination increases, throughput decreases. This is because the greater the distance of the transmitted radio signal, the weaker the signal becomes. For example, a wireless connection rated at 300 Mbps may actually only be 100 Mbps or as low as 1 Mbps or less. As the signal becomes weaker, it becomes more susceptible to radio interference.

On average, the maximum advertised distance for IEEE 802.11b wireless devices is approximately 250 meters indoors and 450 meters outdoors, though there is no definitive maximum distance because of the variables that affect radio waves. Realistic distances for wireless transmissions will be much shorter than advertised because wireless systems rarely operate in ideal environments.

Objects placed directly between the source and destinations can also weaken a radio signal. The most common objects that affect radio signals are building partitions, file cabinets, furniture, fireplaces, appliances, and similar objects. The density and material comprising these objects influence the signal. For example, a wall constructed of concrete blocks will weaken a signal more than a wall constructed of sheetrock, and a metallic partition commonly used to create an office cubicle will likely block a radio signal entirely.

A wireless connection to exchange data directly between a laptop and a PC should not be affected by building structures. However, if you are using a laptop on a patio to access an Internet connection through a PC inside the home, the distance and building materials will greatly affect the signal. Windows and wireless device manufacturers have utilities that allow you to monitor the wireless network.

Figure 13-26 shows the strength of the wireless signal displayed as a bar graph. The speed of the data is also displayed as 585.0 Mbps.

Mobile Phone Connectivity

In addition to Wi-Fi and cellular, there are other methods for mobile phones to connect to resources. Near Field Communication (NFC) is a common method. This involves being very close, usually a few millimeters from the device to which one is connecting. The most obvious example of NFC is Apple Pay, Samsung Pay, and other tap-to-pay features at many retail outlets. Rather than putting a credit card in a chip reader, one simply gets the card very close to the payment device, and the payment is authorized via NFC. This has its own unique security concerns, however. On one hand, not having to insert a card eliminates the risk of a skimmer having been placed over the chip reader. On the other hand, if NFC works just by being close to the receiver, anyone with a receiver could theoretically harvest data if they got close enough to you.

A+ 1102: 3.4

If NFC fails to function on your device, the device likely needs to be unlocked. If the device is already unlocked, confirm NFC is enabled in the device settings, and try holding the device a different way so the antenna makes better contact. If that fails, try removing the case on the device and restarting the phone. If all troubleshooting seems to fail, contact the manufacturer or service provider for further help.

A+ 1102: 3.4

Bluetooth is another common form of mobile phone connectivity. In addition to its use in synchronizing devices, Bluetooth is also the main technology used in Apple's AirDrop feature, which allows you to send files to another Apple device in close proximity. AirDrop also uses Wi-Fi to find and transfer files between devices on the same network, including iPhones, iPads, and Macintosh computers. For mobile devices, this setting can be toggled on or off by navigating to **Settings**>**General**>**AirDrop**.

A+ 1102: 3.4

In the event AirDrop fails to function properly, the first thing to check is to ensure that it is enabled by navigating to the AirDrop settings and confirm that either **Contacts Only** or **Everyone** is selected. **Contacts Only** is the suggested option; otherwise, anyone with an Apple device close in proximity can send data to your device. You should then toggle your Wi-Fi and Bluetooth options to re-establish a connection, confirm the device is unlocked, and ensure the two devices are close enough for AirDrop to work. If all that fails, you can perform a hard reset or contact Apple support.

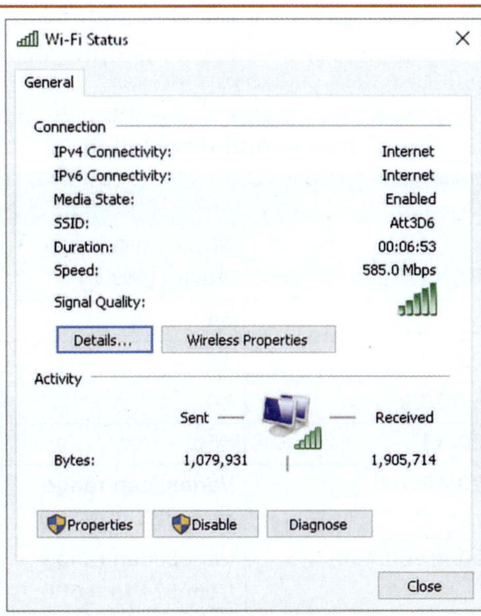

Goodheart-Willcox Publisher

Figure 13-26 The Wi-Fi Status dialog box displays the strength of the signal.

A+ 1101: 2.3. 3.6

Wireless Standards

The IEEE organization developed and released several wireless communication standards so equipment designed by different manufacturers can communicate with each other. The wireless standards 802.11, 802.11a, 802.11b, 802.11g, and 802.11n recommend characteristics and specifications for wireless networking, including frequencies, maximum bandwidth, and communication procedures.

The original 802.11 standard was first developed to standardize wireless devices that would transmit data at 1 Mbps and 2 Mbps. The frequency, or radio band, assigned to 802.11 by the FCC is 2.48 GHz. It was a very short time before 802.11 had to be modified to provide for higher data rates and was soon followed by 802.11a and 802.11b. Although both standards were released at the same time, 802.11b became the de facto standard for small-office and home wireless devices.

Figure 13-27 summarizes the most useful and common standards since the turn of the century. For reference, *modulation* is the act of changing a signal so it can transmit data. Within the modulation column, *DSSS* stands for direct sequence, spread spectrum and is designed to reduce interference; *OFDM* is orthogonal frequency-division multiplexing and is used for encoding; and *MIMO* is multiple input, multiple output, used to multiply capacity by signal switching. There will be more about modulation in a later chapter.

An 802.11n device can support wireless connections at both 2.4 GHz and 5 GHz. In general, wireless technologies are classified as 2.4 GHz and 5 GHz, but the actual frequency ranges are rarely used in product identification. The standard provides for 14 channels, spaced 5 MHz apart for the 2.4 GHz band, but in North America, only 11 of these channels are available.

The 802.11 standard is constantly being upgraded and enhanced. For example, 802.11ac was an improvement to 802.11n and includes wider channels (80 or 160 MHz). The IEEE 802.11af standard allows wireless communication in the TV whitespace spectrum, and IEEE 802.11ai adds faster linkup times to the 802.11 standard. These are just a few examples of enhancements to the 802.11 standard.

For home use, the Z-Wave protocol exists, designed for a "mesh" approach to networking and allowing appliances to communicate with one another. The stated physical range is 100 meters, although this is contingent on interference and signal quality.

ANT+ (Adaptive Network Topology Plus) is a wireless protocol often used with sensor data such as for medical equipment and exercise applications. It operates at 2.4 GHz and is similar in concept to Bluetooth Low Energy. Since it is primarily used in sensors, it has built-in power consumption modalities and can be configured to stay in low power/sleep mode until called for communication, before resuming

Figure 13-27 IEEE 802.11 standards vary drastically in speed, range, and modulation.

802.11 Standards

Standard	Year Developed	Frequency (GHz)	Bandwidth (MHz)	Maximum Data Rate (Mbps)	Modulation Type
802.11a	1999	5.0	5/10/20	54	OFDM
802.11b	1999	2.4	22	11	DSSS
802.11g	2003	2.4	5/10/20	54	OFDM
802.11n	2009	2.4, 5.0	20/40	450	MIMO
802.11ac (Wi-Fi 5)	2013	5.0	20/40/160	Varies; can range from 433 to 1,300	MIMO/OFDM
802.11ax (Wi-Fi 6)	2019	2.4, 5.0, 6.0	20/40/80/160	Varies; can range from 574 to 9,600	MIMO/OFDM

Goodheart-Willcox Publisher

sleep mode once communication is completed. Each ANT channel has one or more transmitting nodes and one or more receiving nodes. It should be noted that the channels are bi-directional, meaning any channel can send or receive.

ZigBee is a standard developed by a consortium of electronic manufacturers for mainly residential applications of wireless devices as related to appliances and security. Despite being represented by a trade name, it is based on the 802.15.4 standard. The term *ZigBee* is used similar to the way the term *Wi-Fi* is used.

13.6 Security

Security is a high priority at all times, especially when dealing with laptops and mobile devices that may contain important company information such as customer lists, contract information, proposed business ventures, and other sensitive communication. Information for connecting to the company network may also be contained on the hard drive. As such, techniques used to secure these devices, such as encryption, file system security, and network security must be applied, among other options.

Encryption

A+ 1102: 2.9

Encryption is the act of encoding data in such a way that it cannot be converted back to meaningful words without a key. Encryption works based on the details of the **encryption key**, which is a mathematical formula for substituting values in strings of data. For example, a text-based code could be developed based on the number four, meaning data in a file would be stored with every letter changed to one that is four places further in the alphabet, as shown in Figure 13-28. The message is rewritten in code and then stored, and you would need the key in order to decode the message. This is an overly simplified example; true encryption codes are significantly more complex.

BitLocker and BitLocker To Go

A+ 1102: 2.7

Microsoft BitLocker and BitLocker To Go are Windows encryption features that allow the user to encrypt the entire hard drive, including the operating system. BitLocker was introduced in Windows Vista, and BitLocker To Go was introduced in Windows 7. Both encryption features are still available in Windows 10 and 11. The main difference between BitLocker and BitLocker To Go is that BitLocker To Go is designed to be used with removable storage media such as a flash drive or a portable hard drive.

Sample messge:

THIS IS THE TIME FOR ALL GOOD MEN...

Change the position of all letters by four positions in the alphabet.

A B C D E F G H I J K L M N O P Q R S T U V W X Y Z
E F G H I J K L M N O P Q R S T U V W X Y Z A B C D

Coded message:

XLMW MW XLI XMQI JSV EPP KSSH QIR...

Goodheart-Willcox Publisher

Figure 13-28 Encryption can be as simple as changing letter position in the alphabet.

Tech Tip

A FAT system can be set up with similar file restrictions used for NTFS when running the NT operating system. However, the file restrictions are lost when the files are transferred to another directory or operating system.

NTFS vs. FAT

NTFS is designed with many improvements over FAT16, FAT32, or exFAT. A typical security system using FAT16 or FAT32 allows for only two types of file access when shared: full access and read-only. These options are set when a file or directory is shared. NTFS4.0 and NTFS5.0 allow more choices when file and directory security are set up, and many more options to choose from when a file share is created. These options are referred to as *permissions*.

For example, a Windows system using FAT16, FAT32, or exFAT can only set file access options to full access, read-only, or no access. With full access capabilities, another user can do anything to the file that the file originator can do, such as deleting, copying, and creating a new file. When the NTFS system is used, access to the shared file can be controlled through more precise options, including read-only, modify, read and execute, write, and list files. The people who have the right to modify or delete the file can be tightly controlled.

The strongest security feature for NTFS is its file encryption capabilities, which FAT does not allow. This means that a low-level disk-editing utility can be used to access the contents of a hard drive formatted with FAT. NTFS system files, on the other hand, are protected.

Figure 13-29 shows a text file that was created and saved to the hard drive of a FAT system and viewed through the Norton Disk Editor program, which is used to inspect the disk storage system and reveal the contents of the clusters, byte by byte. In Figure 13-29, you can see the contents of a file located at cluster 291,629. The Norton Disk Editor reveals the contents as ASCII code on the right side of the screen and as hexadecimal codes on the left side.

Notice the hexadecimal number 73 in the center field of hexadecimal numbers. The number 73 is equal to the ASCII character code for the letter *s*. If you count the hexadecimal position locations, you can see that the hexadecimal code 73 occurs at the fourth, seventh, and eleventh position in the line of hexadecimal characters, all of which correspond to the location of the ASCII text for the letter *s* on the right. With NTFS, you could not view the file system this way because of the encryption capabilities built into the system. The files created by the user can be saved as encrypted files that would have no meaning to the person opening them in Norton Disk Editor.

Another feature of NTFS that makes it more suitable than FAT or exFAT for laptops is its use of smaller cluster sizes when formatting the drive. Portable systems generally have less storage space available than full-size PCs because of their physically smaller storage drives. The smaller NTFS cluster sizes result in less wasted space on a hard drive, making it the preferred storage file system for portable PCs.

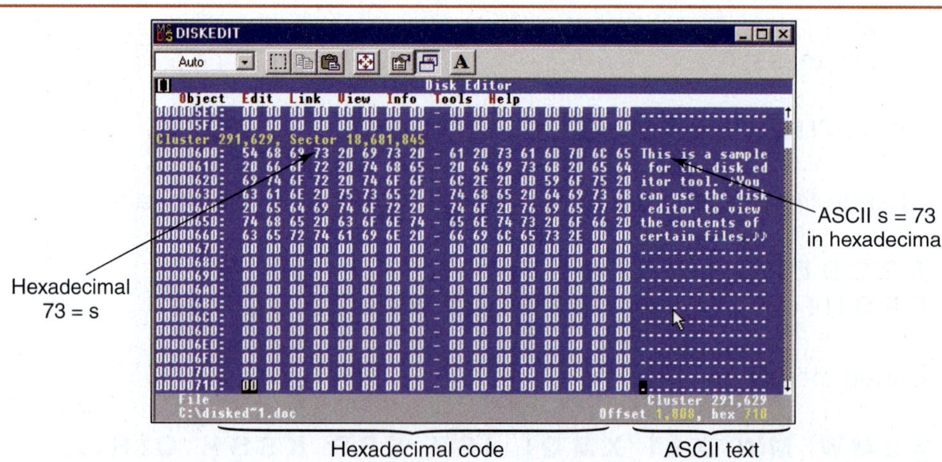

Figure 13-29 An unencrypted text file viewed through a disk editor often shows ASCII code, which can be read or translated.

Goodheart-Willcox Publisher

Smart Cards

1102: 2.1 A+

A **smart card** is identical in size and feel to a credit card and stores information on a chip located within the body of the card. These chips can hold a variety of information and can be used commercially for retail or vending operation. With portable computers, they also work well for security. A smart card configuration can be used to allow you to access a laptop or full-sized PC, and without the card, the computer cannot be accessed. The smart card works in conjunction with a smart card reader, which connects to the PC via USB or PCMCIA card slot. The smart card is supported by all the latest Microsoft operating systems and by many other operating systems.

Wireless Configuration for Mobile Devices

Mobile devices use wireless technology to access the Internet and networks. In Figure 13-30, you can see the **Settings** window of an Android tablet with options for Wi-Fi and Bluetooth access. You would identify the wireless network by the SSID and then enter the security key to gain access to the secure network. Many locations do not use secure access, so there is no need for a security key. For most mobile devices, Bluetooth can be toggled on and off by simply clicking on the Bluetooth logo. For Windows, Bluetooth is accessible through **Settings**>**Devices**>**Bluetooth & other devices.**

Wireless Network Security and Encryption Types

1102: 2.2, 2.9 A+

There are currently three major types of wireless network security: Wired Equivalent Privacy (WEP), Wi-Fi Protected Access (WPA, WPA2, and WPA3), and 802.1x. Wired Equivalent Privacy (WEP) is an old network security method and not recommended because it can be cracked easily. While not recommended, WEP is still available because some old devices only have WEP encryption. WEP requires you to set up a **security key**, which encrypts the information that one computer sends to another computer across the network. When you manually configure a wireless network connection to a secured network, you must supply the security key, which is also known as a *passphrase*, *password*, or *passcode*. Security keys are not utilized in unsecured networks.

There are several variations of Wi-Fi Protected Access such as WPA-Personal, WPA2-Personal, WPA-Enterprise, WPA2-Enterprise, and WPA3. WPA requires a user to provide a security key and is less secure than WPA2. With WPA-Personal and WPA2-Personal arrangements, each user is given the same passphrase. WPA-Enterprise and WPA2-Enterprise are designed to be used with an 802.1x authentication server, which distributes different keys to each user. 802.1x is typically used to

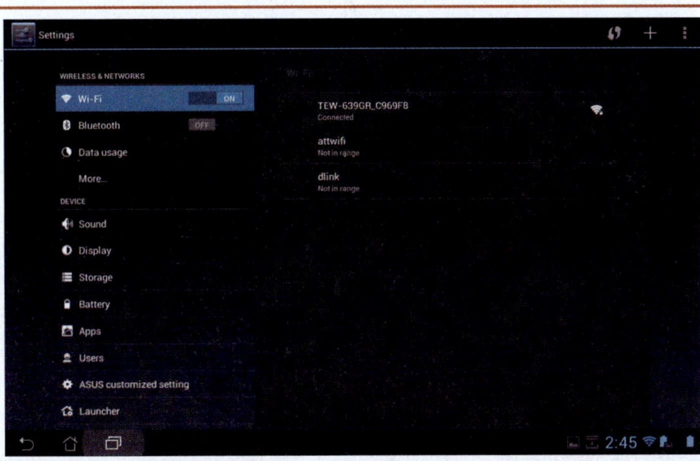

Goodheart-Willcox Publisher

Figure 13-30 The Android Settings window has options for Wi-Fi and Bluetooth configurations.

connect to a workplace network that contains a network server, which authenticates a user security key. 802.1x can work with WPA, WPA2, or WEP keys.

WPA3 is currently the latest and most secure option for wireless access. If available, WPA3 should be implemented, and under no circumstances should you still be using WEP or WPA. WPA3 encrypts all traffic from individual machines to the wireless access point and requires attackers to interact with your Wi-Fi for every password guess they make, making it much harder and time-consuming to crack passwords. WPA3 also makes connecting to a wireless access point much simpler for authorized users with its Wi-Fi Easy Connect feature, which allows you to connect a device by merely scanning a QR code on your phone.

A+ 1102: 2.2

Figure 13-31 shows the dialog box used when manually connecting to a wireless network. The network name is the broadcasted name of the wireless access point and is also known as the **service set identifier (SSID)**. When the wireless access point is secured, each device connecting to it must match the security type, encryption type, and security key. Some of the possible security types are WEP, WPA2-Personal, WPA-Personal, WPA-Enterprise, 802.1x, and WPA3. Recall that WPA3 should be used when possible, as it is the latest and most secure type. After selecting the security type, you would next select the type of encryption, commonly one of AES or TKIP.

The last bit of information is the security key, which is a set of numbers and case-sensitive letters that must be the same for all devices. The exact number of characters and the range of letters vary according to the encryption type being used, as shown in Figure 13-32.

Look again at Figure 13-32 to see the rules associated with particular types of encryption and correlated security keys. The dialog box allows you to hover the mouse pointer over the textbox to see the rules. Also, if you enter a security key incorrectly, a message box will appear telling you what the rule is for a specific type of security key.

Some wireless access points are configured not to broadcast their name or SSID. In the case of such a configuration, you would need to provide the name or SSID of the wireless access point to connect to it.

Securing Mobile Devices

Mobile devices can be expensive and often contain the user's personal or business data. As such, they should always be secured immediately after purchasing. Mobile devices can be secured in many different ways. The exact method used is determined by the type of device, the operating system used, and the service provider.

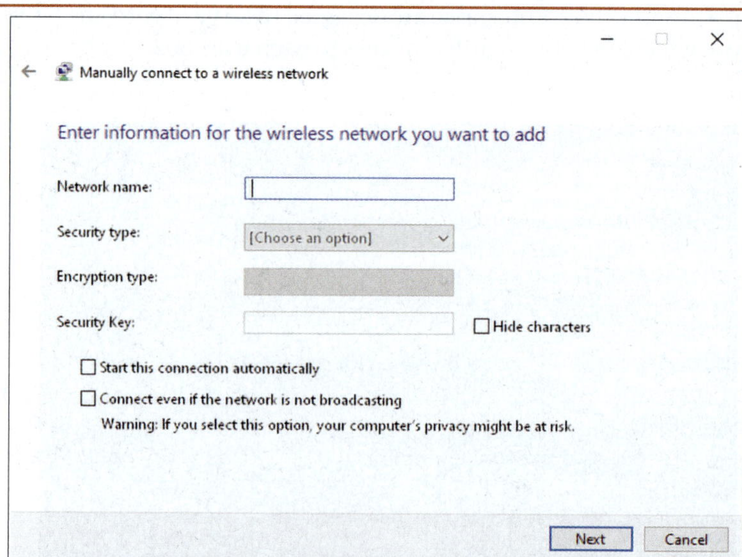

Figure 13-31 The Windows **Manually connect to a wireless network** dialog box allows users to connect to hidden connections by entering the SSID, security type, and password.

Goodheart-Willcox Publisher

Figure 13-32 WEP and WPA3-Personal security types have different rules for passwords.

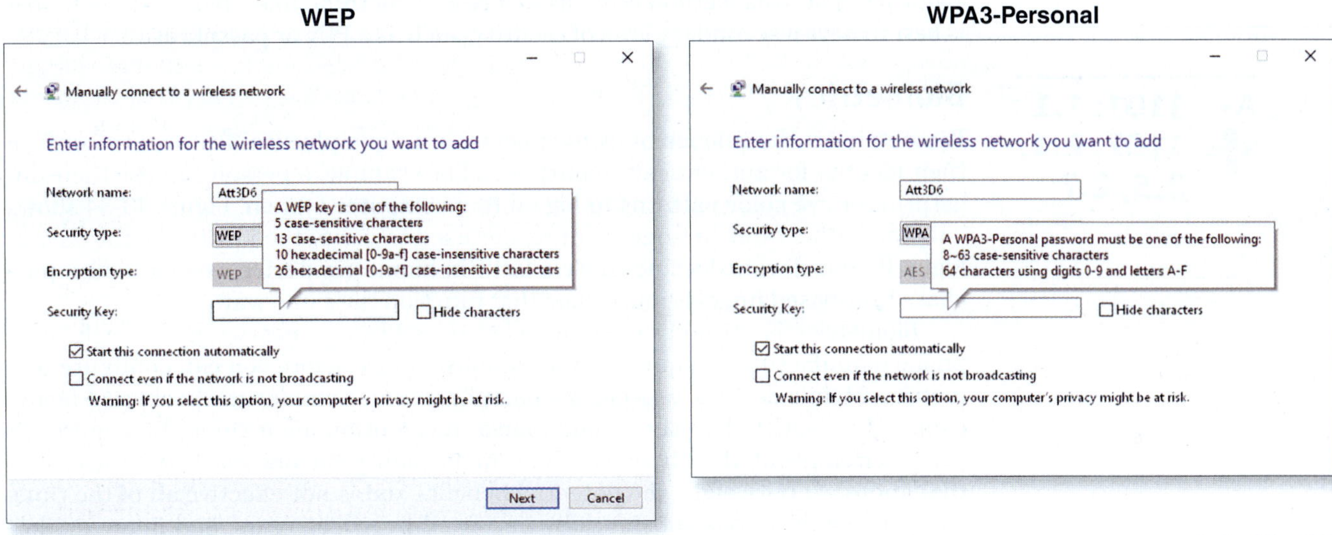

Goodheart-Willcox Publisher

A+ 1101: 1.4

Regardless of the method used to secure a device, the best approach is to employ *multifactor authentication*, which is a combination of two or more authentication techniques and requires the use of more than one factor to gain access to a device. In multifactor authentication, authentication methods are grouped into three categories.

- Type I authentication is *something you know*, such as a password or PIN.
- Type II authentication is *something you have*, such as a swipe card or key.
- Type III authentication is *something you are*, which is biometric authentication such as facial recognition or fingerprint reading.

Similar to multifactor authentication is *two-factor authentication*, also known as *dual-factor authentication* or *strong authentication*, which is the use of two different methods from two different categories. For example, using both a PIN and retinal scan employs a Type-I factor (PIN) and a Type-III factor (biometrics).

Passcode Locks

A+ 1102: 2.5, 2.7

A **passcode lock**, sometimes called a *personal identification number* or *PIN*, is typically a set of numbers used as a password. The numbers must be entered in the correct sequence to access the device. Another method that is similar to a password is a picture password. When using a picture password, the user can select an image and three gestures related to the picture to use as a key to unlock the device. The term *gesture* is used because the user can tap three locations or slide his or her finger to three different locations on the picture. Figure 13-33 shows Windows PC settings for configuring security through facial recognition, PIN, password, picture password, dynamic locks, and general privacy settings.

Patterns

A+ 1102: 2.7

Patterns, also called *swipe locks*, have become common for Android phones in recent years. A pattern lock involves the user creating a pattern of connected dots on the home screen to log in. As of this writing, Apple iPhones do not employ pattern-based authentication, though there are third-party apps that can be used to add similar functionality. Patterns are considered Type-I authentication just like passwords and PINs.

Patterns work on a touch screen device and uses a variety of user-defined "swipes" to unlock the device. The downside of this approach occurs if the screen of the phone is not wiped clean. When a device is locked with a darkened screen, other people will be able to see smudges left on the touch screen, often showing the user's swipe pattern. This method is not as secure as something like a biometric lock, so it is best to have a secondary level of security, such as a PIN or passphrase.

A+ 1101: 1.1
1102: 2.1, 2.5, 2.7

Biometrics

Biometrics is the science of using a person's unique physical features to confirm their identity for authentication purposes. For example, a person can use their fingerprint or eye color patterns to log on to a computer system. Figure 13-34 shows a laptop with a built-in fingerprint reader used to verify the identity of the user at login. If your device does not have a built-in biometric device, you can often purchase USB-based fingerprint readers that function the same way.

Biometrics is strongly recommended over PINs or passwords, though most phone manufacturers require you to establish a PIN before you can configure biometrics. Mobile devices, especially smartphones, may employ the backward-facing camera to identify the user through facial-recognition algorithms. This approach can be circumvented with an extremely high-quality silicone mask, but the cost of that approach outweighs the potential benefits and is not effective all of the time. Facial recognition has substantially improved in recent years, and many models

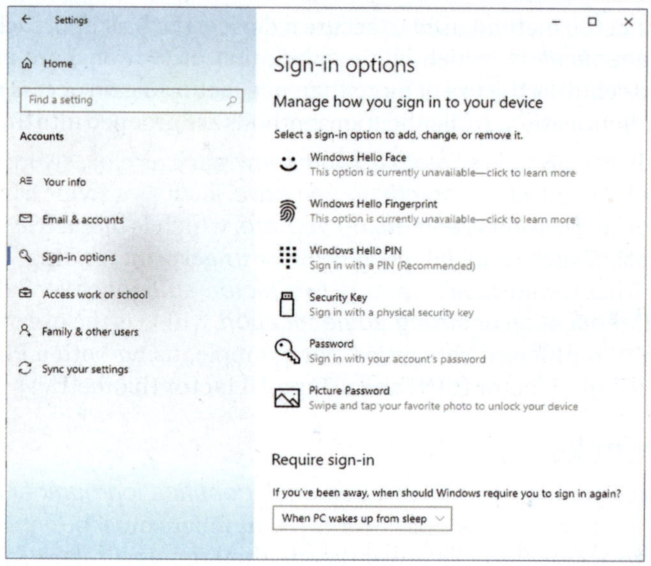

Figure 13-33 Windows provides multiple methods for applying or enhancing security.

Goodheart-Willcox Publisher

Figure 13-34 Some laptops often come equipped with fingerprint readers to verify users' identities.

Martin Gregor/Shutterstock.com

even have means to detect if the face is live, as opposed to a photograph. Unlocking by fingerprint is also a viable means of protecting a device.

Device Access Failure

1102: 2.7 A+

Devices are typically configured to limit the number of attempts to access the device. For example, if a person fails to enter the PIN for an Android device correctly, the person will have to wait a set period before the device will allow access to be reattempted. Continued failure will cause a permanent denial of access until the device is sent back to the factory to be restored.

Some devices provide an option to perform a **hard reset**, which returns the device to its original condition and removes all user data, passwords, and apps. The hard reset typically requires the user to perform some sort of button combination while booting the device. For example, the user must hold down the sleep/wake and home button until the device reboots. Devices sent back to the factory for reset result in complete data loss. Some systems allow the user to reset the device by performing synchronization with a PC or a cloud service.

Jailbreaking and Rooting

1102: 3.5 A+

The boot process used for mobile devices is designed to prevent users from having complete control over the device. The device owner can change many device configurations but does not have unlimited abilities by default. For example, the owner of an Apple product cannot install applications that are not specifically designed for the Apple device. Many users bypass these restrictions through **jailbreaking**, which is the process of overcoming the operating system's user limitations. After jailbreaking, the user can modify the operating system and applications.

The term **rooting** describes the process of taking complete control of an Android device without limitations. Rooting provides the user with unlimited configuration abilities to the mobile device. The word *rooting* is associated with the Linux operating system, which is the operating system from which the Android was derived or modeled after. Linux has a security system based on a hierarchy of users, and the user who controls the entire system is referred to as the *root user* or *superuser*. Other users are simply referred to as *users* and are considered limited because they do not have the same privileges as the root user. The most powerful user of the Linux operating system can control the root, hence the term *rooting*.

Apple Picking

Apple picking is the act of stealing a user's mobile device while they are using it. The word *apple* is used in the term because of Apple devices being stolen in this manner. The thief simply runs by a person and snatches the device out of the person's hand during operation. This can often be avoided simply by being aware of one's surroundings or by using a case that has some kind of handle or tether built into it.

Security Policy

A mobile device security policy consists of apps that call for the user to follow specific procedures such as using a password to access the device. The security policy can also mandate password complexity requirements, such as a minimum of eight characters and inclusion of at least one letter, number, and special character. Some security policies are encapsulated into company apps.

Company Apps

1102: 2.7 A+

A **company app** is an application that ensures and enforces security policies on a mobile device. The app may be designed to allow the company to disable the SD card, encrypt internal storage, and remotely delete all mobile device content and settings, thus rendering it useless to a thief. Some synchronization services such as Google Sync allow an individual user to reset their mobile device remotely, and many mobile devices have some sort of **remote wipe**, which is an application that allows the user to wipe all user information, data, and settings if the device is stolen.

Settings Menu

Apple, Android, and Windows mobile devices all have a menu item called **Settings** that is used to configure the device. In this regard, the **Settings** option is similar to the Windows Control Panel. Typical options under **Settings** include theming options, e-mail accounts, Internet sharing, lock screen, Wi-Fi, Bluetooth, location, brightness, and speech. The exact step-by-step procedure varies by device and is outlined by the manufacturer.

Airplane Mode

Every mobile device capable of supporting wireless communication is required to have an **airplane mode**, which disables wireless services so the device cannot send or receive telephone calls or text messages. Airplane mode disconnects cellular, Wi-Fi, Bluetooth, GPS, and location services, but most devices allow users to re-enable Wi-Fi and Bluetooth while in airplane mode. When in airplane mode, many functions are supported that do not require connection services, such as games and music. Beginning with Windows 8, airplane mode can be toggled on and off through the touch screen, tablet-type block menu. Alternatively, users can use the [Windows][X] keyboard combination to open the Windows Mobility Center and turn it on or off that way. Depending on which version of iOS is used, this is often accomplished on mobile Apple devices by using the **Control Center** or in **Settings**, as shown in Figure 13-35.

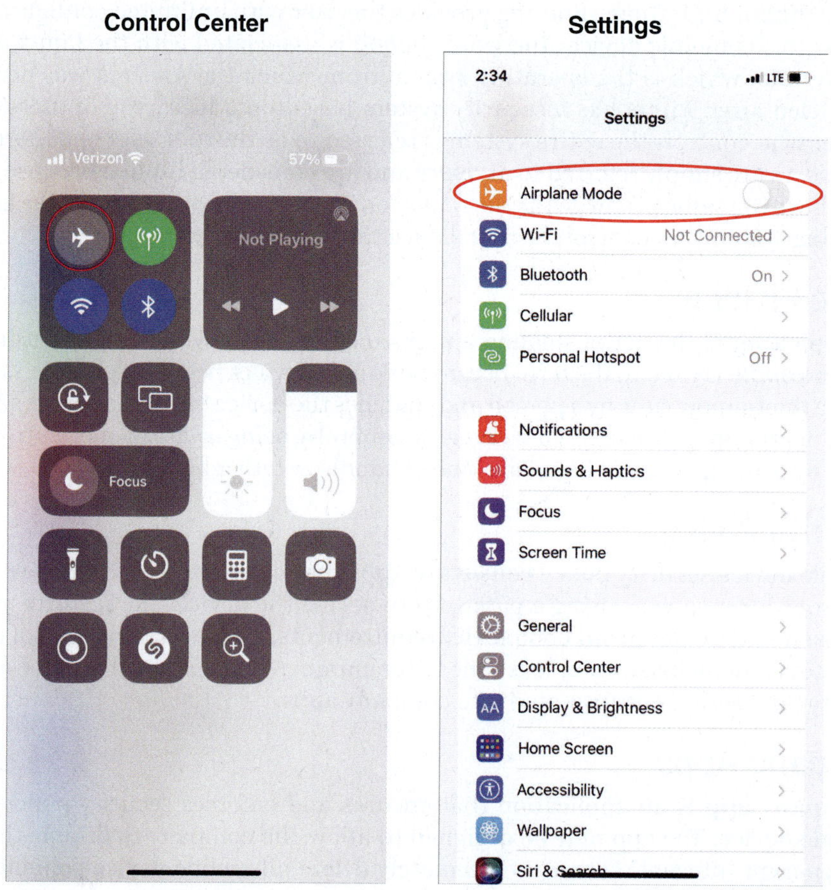

Goodheart-Willcox Publisher

Figure 13-35 Airplane Mode can be accessed on Apple mobile devices through the **Command Center** or **Settings**.

Physical Locks

1101: 1.1 A+
1102: 2.1

Not all security is related to encryption and passwords. There is also a physical aspect of security, which may entail locking a device. Cable locks are available that physically secure your computer to a fixed object such as a table, desk, or even part of the building. There are many different variations of physical security lock systems that utilize either a combination lock or a key. In many cases, the cable lock is typically a flexible steel cable coated with a protective plastic cover that inserts into a security lock slot that is built into many laptops and portable devices. Not all devices have a lock slot, so an attachment point must be made another way such as a steel lock attached with epoxy. Some locks also incorporate an alarm that goes off when the cable is cut, or the lock is removed without the combination. There are also alarms that can be incorporated into the computer in which the alarm sounds when the device is removed from a designated area.

MDM and MAM

A+ 1101: 1.4

Mobile device management (MDM) and *mobile application management (MAM)* are two important aspects of mobile device security. MDM and MAM are similar in the sense that both are part of a broader topic called *enterprise mobility management (EMM)*, which enables companies to have control over what occurs on company-owned mobile devices. However, their focuses differ. MDM focuses on topics such as device policies, segregating corporate data, and wiping or locking lost devices, while MAM focuses on managing and securing apps. For example, one MAM policy may be that specific corporate applications, such as company e-mail or instant messaging, be installed on the device at all times.

Security Concerns

A+ 1102: 3.5

The previous subsections addressed methods for securing mobile devices. This section will explore security threats. Malicious applications are always a concern, particularly for Android devices. One might download an app that contains a virus or spyware. Apple devices can only install apps from the Apple Store, but Android devices can install any Android Package (APK) file, meaning an Android user can download an APK from a website and install it on the phone. This freedom leads to an increased chance for malicious, bootleg, or spoofed applications. *Application spoofing* is an attack in which a malicious application presents itself with the visual appearance of a valid app with the goal of tricking the user into believing they are using the genuine app while actually sending data to the attacker.

Another Android-specific concern is developer mode, which allows a user to access system functions. As the name suggests, this mode is meant for developers to test their apps. It is also used in phone forensics. However, leaving a phone on developer mode makes that phone vulnerable to a wide range of attacks.

1101: 5.5 A+
1102: 3.5

Usually, malware tries not to be discovered, so if you do have a malicious app on a device, it may not be obvious. A common symptom of a malware infection on a mobile device is high network traffic. An increase in network traffic can indicate malware is either harvesting data—for example, spyware—or communicating with a command-and-control server. This can also lead to a data-usage limit notification from your carrier if you do not have unlimited data. Sluggish response time is another symptom of malware because the malware is consuming system resources. More obvious signs include fake security warnings and a high number of ads. If you identify any of these symptoms, malware could be the culprit.

Mobile Device Troubleshooting

Later in this chapter, there is a section that is devoted to troubleshooting and preventive maintenance, but that is focused primarily on laptops. While there is a fair

A+ 1101: 5.2
1102: 3.1, 3.4

amount of overlap between the two, this section is focused primarily on mobile phones and tablets. There are many issues that can go wrong with a phone, so you should be prepared to work with common troubleshooting scenarios.

If the problem is an app, then the easiest first step is to update the app. The problems you are facing may have already been addressed already in an update from the vendor. If updating the app does not work, then a common next step is to uninstall, then reinstall, the app. This is often reserved for issues that result in the app failing to update or continually closing or crashing.

A+ 1102: 3.1

Another issue is *time drift*, also called *clock drift*. This occurs when the clock on the device is not running in sync with a reference clock, often an atomic clock. Usually, the time drift is quite minor and not noticeable for a long time. However, if you are experiencing noticeable time drift, this is likely an operating system issue and you should check with the vendor for a patch.

A+ 1102: 3.4

A more common problem occurs when the screen does not auto rotate when you turn the phone. This can occur due to a flaw in a third-party app or a problem with a gyroscopic sensor. Often, simply rebooting the phone will correct the issue. The most likely scenario, however, is a system setting in connection to screen rotation. To check screen rotation settings on an Android phone, navigate to **Settings**>**Display**>**Auto-rotate screen**. With iPhone, you can access it via Control Center by swiping down from the top-right corner of the screen. The screen rotation lock setting is a small icon that resembles a lock with an arrow around it, as shown in Figure 13-36. The screen rotation lock is toggled on when it appears white in the Control Center, and it will prevent the screen from orienting when the phone is turned. Simply tap the icon to toggle it off.

Tech Tip

If you have an iPhone with a Home button (iPhone models prior to iPhone X as well as the iPhone SE), you will have to swipe up from the bottom of the screen to open Control Center.

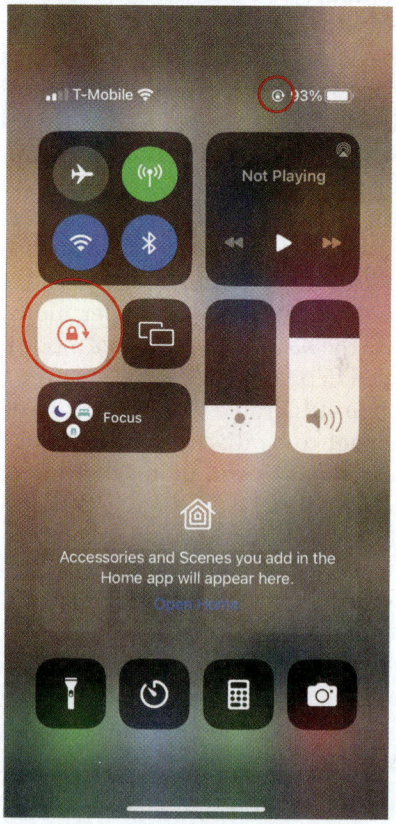

Figure 13-36 The screen rotation lock in iOS is easily found in Control Center. When engaged, the screen will not orient to match a rotated phone.

Goodheart-Willcox Publisher

Another, less common, problem is the phone randomly rebooting. For either iPhone or Android, one step to take is to ensure the operating system is updated. Often, system updates are pushed to devices via notification, but you can perform this action manually by navigating to the Settings menu on the device and checking for available updates.

1102: 2.7, 3.4 A+

If you have recently installed a new app, that could also be the source of the problem. Try updating or uninstalling and reinstalling the app. If none of these steps correct the problem, you may wish to factory reset your phone. This is a rather drastic step as it removes all apps, contacts, and personal data, but it can sometimes be the only solution to some problems. Factory reset in iPhone is found in **Settings>General>Transfer or Reset Phone.** For Android the path is **Settings>Backup and Reset.**

13.7 Disassembling Process for Proper Reassembly

This section details a general disassembly process for laptops. Before attempting to disassemble any laptop, always consult the manufacturer's website for the correct sequence and procedures. These steps are not intended for use on mobile devices such as smartphones or tablets, and it is not advisable to disassemble devices such as those. In those cases, it is better to seek help from a service provider or manufacturer.

A+ Note

Be sure you are familiar with the disassembly of a laptop computer. Download a copy of the laptop repair manual and study the procedure for at least two different types of laptops. This will prove to be a valuable aid if you are planning to take the CompTIA A+ Exams.

Laptops can be very difficult to disassemble, and doing so incorrectly can result in damage. Always use a system to keep track of the location of any screws removed while disassembling the device. Some laptops have over 24 screws that must be removed to replace a critical part. A digital camera and a small multi-bin storage container can be helpful during disassembly. The screw threads are usually—but not always—the same, and the length of screws can also vary.

Do *not* attempt an upgrade such as installing a better optical drive without first checking the manufacturer's website. At the website, you can find information about upgrade requirements such as hardware requirements and upgrading firmware.

Some laptop manufacturers offer special training and certification for their products. After training, your place of business or employment can become an authorized repair location.

While individuals likely have their own methods for disassembling a given device, CompTIA's recommended methodology includes documenting and labeling cable and screw locations, organizing parts, using the manufacturer resources as a guide, and ensuring the use of the appropriate hand tools.

Document and Label Cable and Screw Locations

Labeling can save you time during reassembly. Always label both the connector and the connection at the same time using an electronic label maker or masking tape. Color coding helps when you have the materials to support this approach. Screw locations are important because a device will sometimes have screws of different sizes, depths, pitches, and heads.

Organize Parts

When you attempt to reassemble the device, having the parts organized will save you time and potentially help you avoid a mistake. One of the best ways to organize parts is to use a multi-bin storage container, but small plastic bags or paper cups can be used to organize all like parts together while keeping them separate from dissimilar parts. That is, all motherboard screws should be together in one location, and screws to hold the hard drive should be together in a separate location. The method used does not matter so long as the parts remain organized, and you apply it consistently.

Refer to Manufacturer Resources

Manufacturers typically produce PDFs that reference disassembly or reassembly. Download the manufacturer documentation whenever feasible, specifically files that supply part names, part numbers, and directions for which parts go to which location in the device.

Use Appropriate Hand Tools

Many times, the screws you remove from a mobile device are extremely small, so you will want to have a tool kit with fine screwdrivers or replaceable bits to drive the screws. Using a power tool can cause over-torque on the screws, particularly when a screw is cross-threaded, leading to damage to the device.

13.8 Upgrading the Laptop

Despite their size and difficulty in disassembly, laptops can be upgraded easily, especially memory and hard drive upgrades. Some of the internal parts for laptops are smaller and more delicate than their full-size PC counterparts, so handle all parts with care, and be sure to ground yourself. The CPU upgrade is usually not an option because of the design, and upgrading a CPU is a very difficult task, even for an experienced electronics technician.

By now, you are aware that most computer repairs are required because of software or operator error. Third-party downloads and add-ons can cause a system lockup or crash. Most repair techniques related to software or operator error that are used for a full-size PC work equally as well on portables.

A+ 1101: 1.1

Upgrading Memory

Adding or replacing memory is a very common laptop upgrade. The memory modules for laptops are accessed through panels under the laptop. Laptops use SO-DIMM, which you should recall represents *small outline* memory modules. Installing SO-DIMM is not difficult, but you should consult the manufacturer's documentation before performing the memory replacement or upgrade. The following list provides the general steps for replacing or upgrading SO-DIMM memory in a laptop:

1. Before performing any hardware replacement or upgrade, remove the laptop battery and unplug the power cord or adapter.
2. Remove the retaining screws that hold the memory access panel in place.
3. Depending on the laptop model, you will have to either gently pull the retaining clips from each end of the memory module or rotate the memory module to a 30- to 45-degree angle to remove. You should consult the manufacturer's information about this procedure before attempting to remove and replace the memory.
4. Align the new memory-module key notch to ensure the correct direction and alignment of the module into the memory socket.
5. Gently press the memory module into the socket until it is seated evenly and snugly.
6. Replace the memory-module access panel and retaining screws.

7. Replace the power cord and battery.
8. Power on the computer and check the **System** dialog box to see that the new RAM is properly identified by size. If not, you may need to reseat the memory module. Be sure to remove the battery and the power cord. Most of the time, a memory upgrade or replacement failure is caused by improperly seating the memory in the socket.

Replacing an Internal Hard Drive

1101: A+
1.1, 3.3

The hard disk drive can be accessed either under an access port on the bottom of the laptop or through a sliding tray in the side of the laptop. See Figure 13-37. When installed in the side, such as what is demonstrated in Figure 13-37A, the hard drive typically has at least one screw to keep the hard drive in place. When it is located on the bottom of the laptop, it may have several screws, as shown in Figure 13-37B. Replacing the physical hard drive is an easy task, but you must use a form factor designed for laptop computers. Desktop computer hard drives are much too large to fit inside a laptop.

Replacing the Battery

Before performing any repairs on a laptop computer, you should first remove the battery and disconnect any AC source of power. Some areas of the motherboard are still energized by battery power or by AC through the power adapter even when the laptop is turned off. Working inside a laptop with a battery or the AC adapter still plugged into an AC source could cause a short circuit and damage the motherboard or other components.

Figure 13-38 shows two common ways batteries are mounted in a laptop configuration. In some models, the battery slides out of the side of the laptop, Figure 13-38A. In other models, the battery is removed from the bottom of the laptop, Figure 13-38B. For both configurations, a latch is used to secure the battery in place.

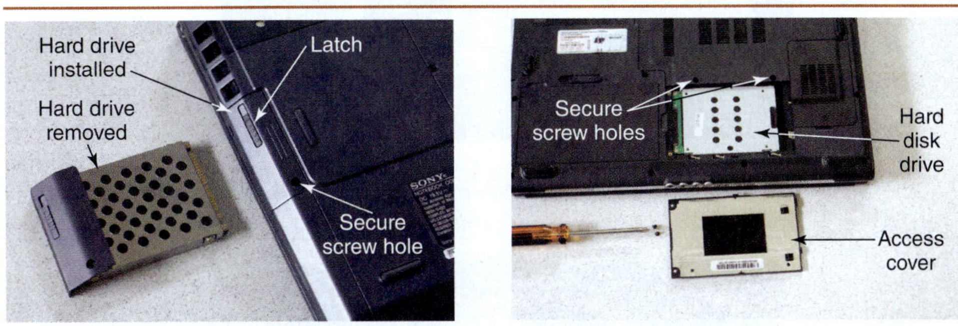

Goodheart-Willcox Publisher

Figure 13-37 Most laptop hard drives are removed using a sliding tray in a side access panel of the device (A). However, some are removed from the bottom of the device (B).

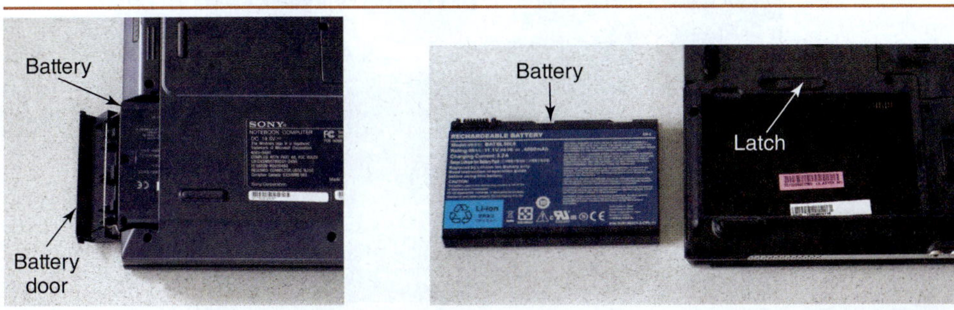

Goodheart-Willcox Publisher

Figure 13-38 Some laptop batteries fit inside the back of the laptop and are held in place by a spring latch (A). Others are held in place by a latch on the underside of the device (B).

A+ 1101: 1.1, 1.2

Replacing a Wireless Card

Almost all laptops have a wireless card installed inside the case. Older laptops use wireless devices connected through the exterior of the case via a USB port, PCMCIA slot, or ExpressCard slot.

Figure 13-39 shows a wireless network card installed inside an Acer laptop originally designed for Windows Vista. Despite the age of the device in the photo, the process has not changed substantially and is generally transferrable to new devices. Notice that the wireless card is held in place by a bracket and includes two wires, one black and one white, which run from the card through the inside of the case into the LCD display housing where the antenna is installed. A common error by new technicians is forgetting to reconnect the wires running from the card to the antenna.

Replacing the CPU

Replacing a laptop CPU is not an easy task, and you should never attempt to do so without first studying the manufacturer's manual for that particular model. The replacement of the CPU often requires a tedious disassembly of the cooling fan and heat sink and may involve the removal of other parts. Looking at Figure 13-40,

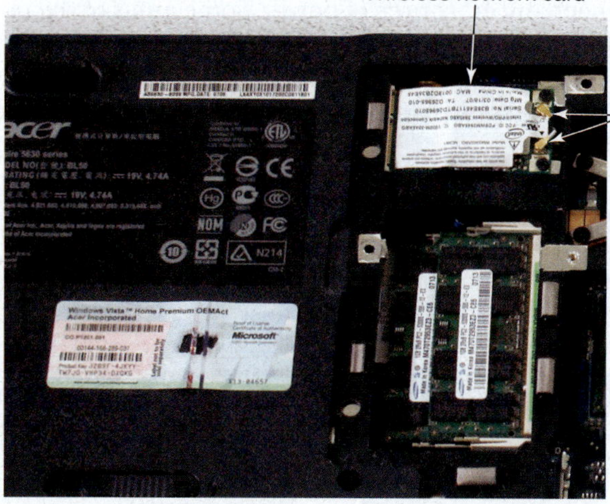

Figure 13-39 A wireless network card installed inside a laptop PC. Notice the black and white wires that connect the network card to the antenna.

Goodheart-Willcox Publisher

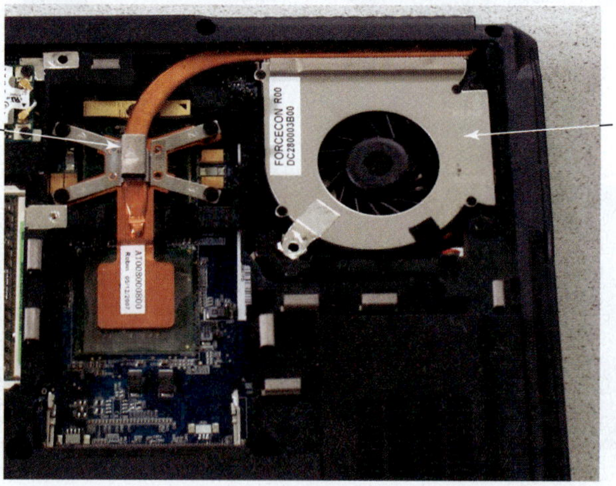

Figure 13-40 To replace a laptop CPU, the heat sink—and possibly the cooling fan—need to be removed before anything else.

Goodheart-Willcox Publisher

you can see that the CPU is covered by the heat sink assembly and may also require the removal of the cooling fan before removing the heat sink.

Replacing the SIM Card

Recall that all cellular-enabled devices have ***subscriber identity module (SIM) cards***, which are integrated circuits used to securely authenticate a user's identity for a mobile device. Turn your attention to Figure 13-41 to see what a SIM card looks like. Figure 13-41A shows a SIM card, which is built into additional plastic roughly the size of a credit card and surrounded by perforations for easy removal. Figure 13-41B shows how the chip is installed into a smartphone. Mobile devices are rarely upgraded or repaired in the field and typically need to be returned to the manufacturer for repair or replacement, though replacing a SIM card has become an increasingly common task.

Removing a SIM card is an easy operation. The SIM card is usually located either under the battery or in the side of the device, depending on the manufacturer. For example, iPhones include an access tray in the side of the device that can be accessed by inserting a SIM ejection tool or paper clip into the SIM card ejection port. Look at Figure 13-42 to see the steps for removing a SIM card from a mobile device. First, locate the ejection port and insert either a straightened paper clip or SIM tool into the port to eject the SIM tray. The existing SIM card can then be removed from the SIM tray, where the new card is installed before the tray is reinserted into the device. You should follow electrostatic discharge (ESD) rules while handling a SIM card.

Tech Tip

The SIM card is a serviceable item. It can be replaced if damaged or corrupted, but some SIM cards are programmed to work only with a specific service provider or set of specific devices.

Figure 13-41 A SIM contains the personal information of the user and data such as an address book, phone numbers, and text messages. When first received from a provider, the SIM is part of a larger card, roughly the size of a credit card (A) and is perforated so it can be removed easily. Once removed, it is inserted into a tray that loads into a device (B).

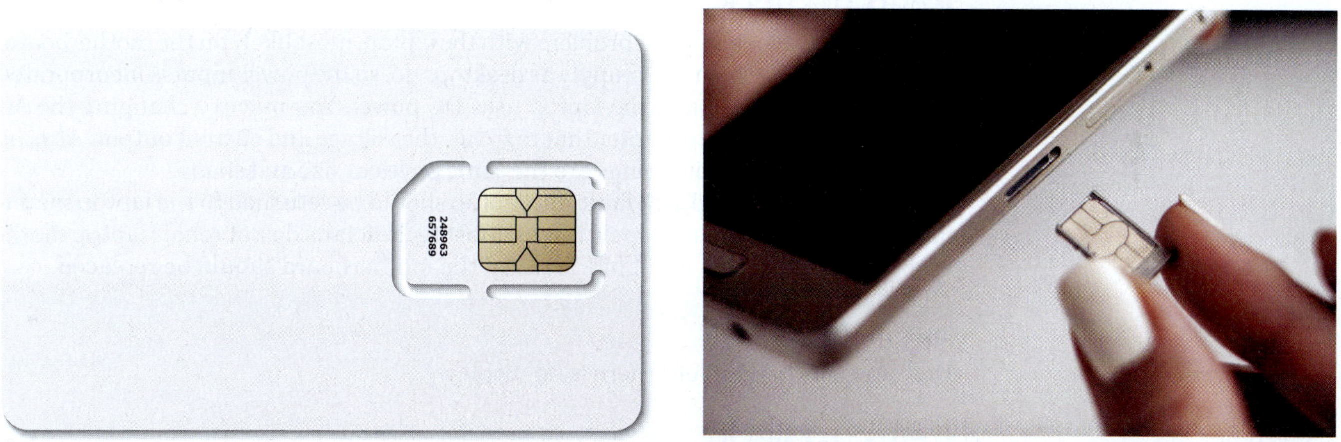

A B *Goodheart-Willcox Publisher; (A) RealVector/Shutterstock.com; (B) Mikhail Artamonov/Shutterstock.com*

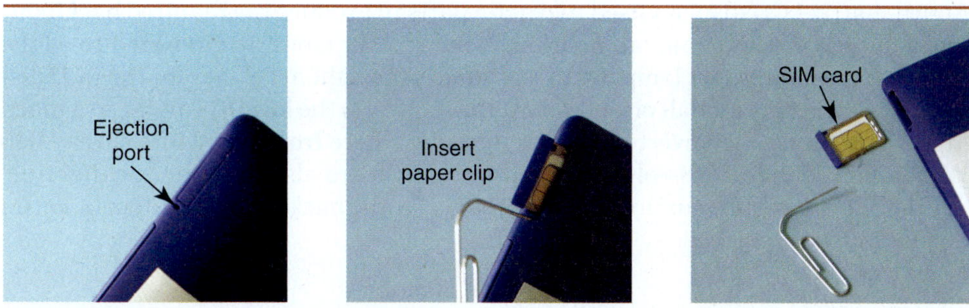

Goodheart-Willcox Publisher

Figure 13-42 A SIM card can be removed from most devices using a straightened paper clip.

13.9 Troubleshooting and Preventive Maintenance

Through a combination of troubleshooting and preventive maintenance, a laptop or mobile device can last a long time and provide exceptional functionality to a user. In this section, you will be introduced to some common symptoms as well as items to check for troubleshooting those symptoms. You will also learn about basic preventive maintenance that applies to laptops, tablets, and smartphones. Following these procedures can help extend the life of your devices.

A+ 1101: 5.5

Troubleshooting

There are some very common laptop troubleshooting practices with which you should be familiar. This section is brief and intended only as an introduction. For more in-depth troubleshooting, review the troubleshooting chapter that appears later in this textbook. Before looking at specific symptoms below, you should be familiar with some general guidelines. Given the small size of mobile devices, it is frequently the case that a damaged part cannot be repaired or replaced. For example, physically damaged ports on a phone or laptop usually cannot be repaired or replaced, and if they can, the work is typically performed by a team or company that specializes in mobile device repair. Other physical damage, such as a cracked screen, usually can be replaced.

Symptom 1:

No power LED, or other LEDs are lit when the laptop is plugged into AC power source

Items to check:

This indicates a major power problem with the laptop, most likely on the motherboard. Laptops do not have a power supply as desktops do, so the power input is incorporated into the motherboard and the laptop uses DC power. You may try changing the AC adapter first, but use an adapter that matches the voltage and current output. Also, be aware that not all adapter plugs are the same physical size and shape.

If the motherboard *is* at fault, the laptop should be returned to the laptop manufacturer for motherboard repair issues. Most technicians do not repair laptop motherboards. If the laptop is out of warranty, the motherboard should be replaced.

Symptom 2:

Device seems to boot, but there is no display

Items to check:

When the laptop boots and the display appears black, gray, very dim, or discolored, it is a symptom that the backlight is defective, or the LCD inverter has failed. Active-matrix LCD displays used two main parts to produce the required backlighting: a fluorescent lamp and an inverter. A fluorescent lamp, also referred to as the cold cathode fluorescent lamp (CCFL), produces the light necessary for the LCD display. The inverter is a small circuit board that converts the low DC voltage to a much higher AC voltage. An inverter may produce anywhere from 500 VAC to over 1,000 VAC from a 12-volt to 18-volt laptop battery. LEDs are also used for backlighting, but they do not require an inverter. In either case, the backlighting system or entire display must be replaced.

Symptom 3:

Slow laptop, and too many pop-ups

Items to check:

The laptop may be infected with spyware. Install and run a reputable antispyware program. Additionally, it may help to close any unnecessary programs and stop unneeded programs from launching on startup.

Symptom 4:

1102: 3.1 A+

Laptop freezes and will not respond, even to the power button

Items to check:

Unplug the power cord and remove the battery from the laptop. Replace the battery and power cord, and the laptop should reboot and respond normally. If not, the laptop may be defective.

When a system appears to be frozen, it may be so active it cannot accept more input. A rational response is to wait and see if the system spontaneously recovers. If not, the next response will be to perform what is called a *Power-on Reset (POR)*. A POR occurs when the system is crashed using the vendor-recommended method. On laptops, this means holding in the power button until the system shuts down.

Symptom 5:

Laptop boots slower and slower over time

Items to check:

Typically, this symptom suggests too many programs and downloads have been installed on the computer. The programs are all loaded into RAM at startup, thus slowing the boot time and overall computer performance. Remove unnecessary programs from the laptop. You can also stop many programs from loading during startup by running the System Configuration Utility (**msconfig.exe**) and selecting which programs to load at startup. Using the System Configuration Utility is covered in a later chapter. Also, before the NTFS file system and frequent background defragmentation, the fragmented state of the hard drive could slow the system down.

Symptom 6:

1102: 3.1 A+

A blue screen and error message appears during the boot process

Items to check:

This symptom is typical of a major problem. The easiest way to remedy this problem is to reinstall the Windows operating system completely. Be aware that a complete reinstall may cause you to lose all data and files stored on the laptop.

Symptom 7:

1101: 5.5 A+
1102: 3.5

Device acts strangely

Items to check:

When the laptop "acts strangely" and unpredictable results occur when certain programs or certain actions are taken, it is a good sign that the laptop has a virus or malware. The computer may randomly stop running, automatically shut down, or take you to a website you did not intend to launch. All these symptoms are usually a good indicator that a virus has infected the computer. Install and run an antivirus program. This applies to all mobile devices, not just laptops.

Symptom 8:

Incorrect characters appear on the screen

Items to check:

A very common client complaint is that the laptop prints characters on the screen when the number keys are pressed. Again, this is very common, especially for new users. The most likely cause is that a function key or function key combination has been pressed, setting the default state of the keys to characters rather than numbers. Also, be aware that laptop keyboards often have more special function keys than a traditional full-size keyboard. This causes many other problems for users who are not familiar with that particular keyboard or who have recently changed from a desktop system to a laptop.

A+ 1101: 5.5

Symptom 9:

Battery is not charging, or the battery life is extremely short

Items to check:

Sometimes the obvious is overlooked. Make sure there is electrical power (120 VAC) at the outlet where the laptop is plugged in for power. Next, check for loose connections. Many times, a cable appears to be plugged in but is not actually making good electrical contact. Simply disconnect and reconnect all plugs.

Extremely short battery life means the device is running at full brightness, or the battery is dying. Other issues that can reduce battery life include disk-intensive applications, searching for a Bluetooth connection, searching for wireless connectivity, or a bad charger.

If you are seeing normal charging activity with excessive battery consumption or power drain, check your usage with a battery analysis app. Android and iOS both have this capability built in, or you can download an app designed to perform this function. On laptops, you may be using a mechanical device like a hard drive or supporting external powered devices through the various ports, all of which consume power. Disconnect peripheral devices and measure the battery level to rule out external consumption.

A+ 1101: 5.5

Symptom 10:

Mouse cursor moves on its own

Items to check:

This condition, often referred to as a *ghost cursor* or *cursor drift*, is generally associated with a wireless mouse and is usually the result of the mouse being too far from the radio receiver, the batteries becoming weak, or a combination of both. Change the batteries in the mouse and move the receiver closer to the mouse. Some wireless receivers plug directly into a USB port on a computer that may be too far from the mouse. Others have cords that can plug into the USB port on one end and house a wireless receiver on the other end, which allows the receiver to be placed closer to the mouse. The same is true for a wireless keyboard.

A+ 1101: 5.4

Symptom 11:

Display is on, but dim

Items to check:

A dim display can be the product of several causes. First, check or change the display settings to ensure the brightness setting is at an expected level. Next, verify that the laptop has not gone into battery saver mode. Finally, test the battery or power to the laptop and make any necessary adjustments based on the results of those tests. The laptop may be suffering from insufficient voltage.

Symptom 12:

Keys on the keyboard stick when pressed

Items to check:

On a laptop, sticking keys can be caused by spilled liquids that did not disable the motherboard but did leave a residue. If the unit can be dismantled, the keys can be cleaned. Note that using liquids to clean the keyboard should not be tried first and certainly not when power is applied from either an AC source or the batteries.

Symptom 13:

Intermittent wireless or no wireless connectivity

1101: 5.5 A+
1102: 3.4, 3.5

Items to check:

Intermittent wireless involves both the receiver and transmitter. If the router is not in an ideal location, the quality of the signal will vary, even if the receiving device is not moved. This problem can often be solved by moving the router up and out of the way of obstacles, particularly those with metal contents. The receiving device has an antenna, so moving the receiving device may also solve the problem. Also, the user can change channels or bands to see if that makes a difference in wireless performance. Most of these actions also apply to no wireless connectivity. Additionally, check for a dead router or one that has been turned off, and verify that you have the login password for network access.

If your signal drops or weakens periodically, check your position in the room relative to the position of the router to which you are connected. Often, people will install their routers too low, which causes the signal to have to go around obstacles. Position the router or routers higher in the room and recheck signal strength. It is convenient to have a smartphone app for this. You may also check the power to the routers, which may have seen an interruption.

Symptom 14:

[Num lock] indicator lights

Items to check:

The most common issue when these lights are on inappropriately occurs when a device driver becomes corrupted. However, first ensure that [Num Lock] is activated or deactivated appropriately. There may be a function key used for this. If the problem persists, consider rolling back or uninstalling the driver. To uninstall a device driver, navigate to Device Manager and expand the **Keyboard** selection. Right-click on the keyboard and select **Properties** from the shortcut menu. Select the **Driver** tab and choose **Uninstall**. Reboot the system and allow the drivers to install automatically or navigate to the vendor website and install them manually.

Symptom 15:

No Bluetooth connectivity

1101: 5.5 A+
1102: 3.4

Items to check:

The obvious first step is to ensure that Bluetooth is enabled on the mobile device, followed by verifying the same thing for the accessory device. Both systems may require that the devices be "discoverable."

Symptom 16:

Cannot display to external monitor

Items to check:

Verify that the external monitor is attached via the appropriate cable: USB, HDMI, and Type C. After, select how you want the desktop to display. The keyboard combination [Windows][P] activates projection settings you can use to adjust how the system is displayed. If you have an external monitor, the PC should detect it automatically. If no monitors are visible, navigate to the **Display** settings menu and select **Detect**. Next, navigate to the multiple displays options and define what your desktop displays across both screens.

A+ 1101: 5.5

Symptom 17:

Touch screen is nonresponsive or inaccurate

Items to check:

A touch screen can become non responsive if the user has a covering on their fingers. The simplest immediate action is to power down the device and power it back on. If the touch screen is broken, the electrical connectivity may be compromised; this situation requires the replacement of the touch screen. Users with touch-enabled phones or tablets may have insurance that pays for repair.

To correct inaccurate touch screen response, you can try to calibrate the screen. If that does not work, power down the device and clean the screen with a cloth intended for electronic screens or eyeglasses. After you have finished cleaning the screen, power the device back on to see if the problem was corrected. Next, check your fingers to ensure there are no chemicals or coatings that should reduce the ability of the touch screen to detect the presence of your fingers. Finally, check the manufacturer's troubleshooting guide for other steps.

A+ 1101: 5.2
1102: 3.4

Symptom 18:

Apps are not loading

Items to check:

The word "app" is used to describe lightweight software designed specifically for a mobile device. Microsoft extended the use of the term starting with Windows 8 operating system, using it to refer to applications, typefaces, and lightweight applications used for Windows including Windows 10 and 11. If the app is obsolete, the operating system may refuse to load or execute it. Check that the app is compatible with the operating system and is up to date. In some cases, antimalware software will issue a false positive and prevent the software from loading.

A+ 1101: 5.7
1102: 3.1

Symptom 19:

Slow performance or data speeds

Items to check:

Slow performance can be caused by the presence of active malware. A good first step would involve a scan with antimalware. If the mobile device is a laptop computer with a mechanical hard drive, the drive may need defragmentation with the **Defragment and Optimize Drives** utility, readily available from the menu system. For slow data speeds, check to see if you activated the metered-line capability in the operating system, especially any version of Windows. On cell phones and tablets, verify whether you are connecting through the cell phone towers or Wi-Fi.

Symptom 20:

Unable to decrypt e-mail

Items to check:

If you are unable to decrypt e-mail, verify that your service supports encryption and decryption as some services do not support this capability. Run your antimalware program to see if malware has encrypted your e-mail and check S/MIME, which provides another layer of security for e-mail sent to and from an Exchange account. With Windows 10, S/MIME allows you to encrypt outgoing messages and attachments so that only the expected recipient can read them. Users can also digitally sign a message, which allows the recipients to verify the sender's identity, thereby reducing the probability of tampering.

Symptom 21:

A+ 1101: 5.5

Device is overheating

Items to check:

Overheating can have several causes, the most common of which occurs when the laptop fan ceases to function. The solution to this problem is the replacement of the fan, assuming it does not spin after a reboot. Also, systems with plastic cases do not transfer heat as well as those with metal cases. The user should make sure the vents on the device are open and that the device is not placed on a lap or a cloth surface that doesn't allow for heat transfer. In some cases, you may want to purchase or recommend an auxiliary fan device called a "chill pad." Make sure the chill pad has external power since deriving power from the laptop is unlikely to lower the temperature.

Symptom 22:

No sound from speakers

Items to check:

If you are using external speakers, confirm they are connected. Next, ensure the speakers are unmuted by clicking the speaker icon in the system tray. If you still have no sound, verify which speakers are being controlled from the same icon, which will likely be listed at the top of the pop-up menu when you choose the speaker icon. If you still have a problem, examine the status of the speaker drivers.

Symptom 23:

GPS is not functioning

Items to check:

Smartphones, tablets, Chromebooks, and laptops are commonly equipped with an internal GPS. If the GPS appears to be nonfunctional, verify that your system has GPS and it is enabled. Look in the device settings for **Location** settings. Finally, consider the weather and location. It is possible that the satellites are unable to find the device due to blockage.

Symptom 24:

A+ 1101: 5.5

Battery is swollen

Items to check:

Any swollen battery should be considered dangerous. Removal of such a battery should be performed by someone who has the proper protective gear. A shorted battery can catch fire, but a swollen battery can explode. Direct removal is not recommended without proper training for this issue.

Symptom 25:

Screen lockout

Items to check:

Users can become locked out of their devices if they try the wrong password too many times or if the security software enabled on the device determines the device has most likely been stolen and locks out the user as a result. In the case of the security software, most systems allow for a remote override from a computer. In the case of too many passwords, the user may have to POR the device and try again. The worst case would involve wiping the device remotely and starting over again, assuming the device permits a factory reset like this. Review the manufacturer's documentation to avoid making the situation worse.

In some cases, company equipment may be configured to only allow access during certain times or in certain locations. Consult with your employer to determine if there is any geofencing or time-specific limitations on your device. If so, ensure you comply with the appropriate parameters before attempting to log in.

Symptom 26:

Unintended Wi-Fi connection or Bluetooth pairing

Items to check:

Devices should be configured in a way that requires approval before connecting to a network, especially an unknown network. It is also advisable to use a virtual private network (VPN), which will assure some level of privacy, even if you inadvertently connect with an unfamiliar network. If the network connection is unknown or unsecured, disconnect from the network and select the option to have the device "forget" the connection. For accidental Bluetooth pairings, make sure the pairing mode is turned off on your hardware. As with an unintended Wi-Fi connection, you should configure the device so you must approve a connection request.

A+ 1102: 3.4

Symptom 27:

Operating system fails to update

Items to check:

The first thing to check in the event an OS fails to update is the Internet connection. Updates are pushed out automatically, but the device will not be able to download and install them without being connected to the Internet. If the connection is good, run the update troubleshooting utility on the device. In Windows, this is called Windows Update Troubleshooter and can be located by navigating to **Start**>**Settings**>**Update & Security**>**Troubleshoot**>**Additional troubleshooters**>**Windows Update**>**Run the troubleshooter**. In the event the troubleshooter fails to find an issue, run the System File Checker (SFC), and if all else fails, restore Windows from a backup.

A+ 1102: 3.5

Symptom 28:

Leaked personal files/data

Items to check:

Encrypting files will help stop the leaking of personal files or data. Files should always be encrypted if the operating system supports it. In the case of Windows, you can purchase applications that provide high levels of encryption. For cell phones and tablets, you will need to check with your vendor to see what level of encryption comes with your version of the operating system. For example, some vendors supply an app that routinely implements VPN and encrypts all communication for a nominal monthly fee.

Symptom 29:

Data transmission over the limit

A+ 1102: 3.5

Items to check:

With Windows, you want to configure your network as a metered connection. With cell phones and tablets, this capability is often lacking, requiring a conversation with the vendor about your usage. Some versions of Android and iOS have the same kind of meter checking as Windows. You may also be able to configure the delivery of notifications if you are approaching a preset level of usage, depending on your carrier and vendor.

Symptom 30:

Unauthorized account access, location tracking, or camera/microphone activation

Items to check:

You want to check the router, the PC, and the connected devices to verify that you are using strong passwords and that your system is secure. All of these should be rebooted at some interval; for example, the router can be powered off and on monthly, the cell phone weekly, and similar routines.

In the event of unauthorized location tracking, turn off all location services and run an antimalware scan. Good antimalware will notify you if your location is being tracked. If using a browser, you can set a notification for the same purpose. Also, note that browsers on PCs will notify you by default.

If a camera or microphone is activated or accessed illicitly, turn off all access to the services and run an antimalware scan. High-quality antimalware software will notify you of microphone and camera activation, particularly if you did not activate through a set of keystrokes or mouse events.

Symptom 31:

High resource utilization

Items to check:

When a system's resources are being used heavily, the first step is to open Task Manager and check CPU and disk usage statistics using a detailed view. If you are reviewing your system shortly after you have booted the PC, you may see the antimalware program consuming significant resources, which is usually normal to ensure the integrity of the system before use. If you see high resource utilization after about 10 minutes of wait time, use the same method to identify the application that is responsible, and if necessary, close the application by selecting it and choosing **End Task**. You may need to reboot the system to eliminate the problem completely. Insufficient RAM can also cause resource issues.

A+ 1102: 4.5

Laptop Preventive Maintenance

Preventive maintenance of laptops and portable devices is always outlined in the user manual that comes with the device. Preventive maintenance is common for all such devices, but the most common preventive maintenance tips are as follows:

- Never store a portable device or laptop in direct sunlight, as it can harm the plastic case, causing it to yellow and make the plastic brittle, which can cause the case to break easily when dropped.
- Never leave a portable device in a car because extreme heat can damage the components, such as the motherboard capacitors. Extreme cold can cause condensation problems when taking the portable device from a very cold car into a hot and humid environment, causing water to condense inside the case and damage motherboard components.
- Never use harsh chemicals to clean the case, especially the screen area.
- Do not spray liquids directly on the screen area as they can drip down and enter the display at the display edge and damage the inverter or other components. When you must use a spray, spray the liquid directly on a soft cloth, and then use the lightly damp (not wet) cloth to wipe the screen.
- Clean the keyboard with compressed air or a small paintbrush. Never use liquid or sprays directly on the keyboard. The keyboard is mounted over the motherboard, and any liquid that seeps through the keyboard will wet the motherboard components and cause a short circuit.

Chapter Summary

13.1 Mobile Devices

- Laptops contain many modules that can be easily upgraded; mobile devices such as tablets and smartphones do not.
- All laptops have standard keyboards, while tablets and smartphones do not because of their physical size limitations. Tablets and smartphones generally use an on-screen keyboard simulator.
- The overall advantage of tablets over laptops is they are lightweight and use less electrical energy.
- Smartphones and wearable technology have become popular and offer a wide variety of functionality.
- E-readers are portable devices designed for the storage and use of digital books and periodicals.
- Common mobile device components include processors, antennas, SIM cards, and touch screens.
- Many mobile devices include GPS, accelerometers, and gyroscope technology.
- Due to the smaller size of portable devices, cloud storage may be a necessity.
- Mobile devices can be synchronized to ensure uniformity across all devices, and they can be connected directly to a computer for file transfer.

13.2 Portable PC Components

- Laptop computers are equipped with some parts that full-size PCs do not have, such as a battery, touch pad, and ports for PCMCIA cards and ExpressCards.
- The major types of rechargeable batteries found in use for portable computers and devices are alkaline, nickel cadmium (NiCad), nickel-metal hydride (NiMH), lithium-ion (Li-ion), and lithium-ion polymer (Li-poly).
- Additional parts found on most portable PCs include frames and plastics, docking stations, built-in screen, possible additional screens, extra battery pack, protective covers or cases, automobile docking kits, port replicators, wireless devices, and function keys.

13.3 Power Management

- Portable computers and mobile devices rely on energy management software to lengthen the life of the batteries.
- Automatic Power Management (APM) and Advanced Configuration and Power Interface (ACPI) are industry standards for automatically configuring power on portable devices.
- The power-management configuration reduces the amount of power used by the three major power consumption devices: display, CPU, and hard drive.
- There are three power plans available in Windows: **Balanced**, **High performance**, and **Power saver**.
- Additional power-management options include **Choose what the power buttons do**, **Choose what closing the lid does**, password protection, Fast Startup, and Selective Suspend.
- The Windows Mobility Center contains a collection of the most common utilities and configurations used by laptops such as Volume, Battery Status, and Wireless Network.

13.4 Mobile Operating Systems

- Mobile devices such as tablets and smartphones require special operating systems such as iOS, which is used on Apple devices; Android, which is derived from Linux and owned by Google; Windows CE, which is a compact version of Windows for limited-hardware devices; and Chrome OS, which is a Linux-based OS, merged with Google's proprietary browser.

13.5 Wireless Connections

- When a wireless network is formed between two or more wireless devices, such as a workstation and a notebook, it is called an ad hoc network.
- An infrastructure network differs from an ad hoc network in that it contains a wireless access point (WAP).
- To prevent radio waves from interfering with each other, radio frequencies are regulated by the FCC.
- Radio signal interference is a radio wave transmission that corrupts a desired radio wave signal. Some common sources of wireless computer communication devices are wireless telephones, medical equipment, microwave ovens, and cell phones.
- IEEE 802.11n transmits at 2.4 GHz and 5 GHz and is backward compatible with 802.11a, 802.11b, and 802.11g.
- Additional standards include 802.11ac, 802.11af, 802.11ai, Z-Wave, ANT+, and ZigBee.

13.6 Security

- Some of the ways to secure a mobile device are encryption, passcode locks, security policies, company apps, and physical locks.
- The file system used in a device determines specific levels of security within the device. For example, NTFS allows for granular permissions that FAT does not.
- Additional security measures include facial-recognition or biometric locks, swipe locks, device-access failure protocols, preventing jailbreaking and rooting, and security policies.

13.7 Disassembling Process for Proper Reassembly

- Always consult the manufacturer's website for the correct sequence and procedures.
- A digital camera and a small multi-bin storage container can be used to keep track of the location of any screws removed while disassembling a laptop.
- The CompTIA-recommended methodology for disassembling a laptop includes documenting and labeling cable and screw locations, organizing parts, using the manufacturer resources as a guide, and ensuring the use of the appropriate hand tools.

13.8 Upgrading the Laptop

- Upgrades such as installing more memory and replacing the hard drive, battery, and wireless card can be performed on a laptop.
- Replacement of the CPU is not an easy task.
- Removing a SIM card is an easy operation.

13.9 Troubleshooting and Preventive Maintenance

- Some very common laptop troubleshooting practices can help you evaluate and repair a faulty laptop.

- Some common preventive maintenance tips are never to store a portable device or laptop in direct sunlight, never use harsh chemicals to clean the case, and do not spray liquids directly on the screen area.

Review Questions

1. Compare and contrast common mobile devices.
2. Differentiate between PRI and PRL updates.
3. List ways a user can synchronize a mobile device.
4. List common portable PC parts.
5. Which battery is the preferred choice for portable PCs?
6. List five devices that can be connected through a port replicator.
7. List and describe power-management options in Windows.
8. List features of Windows Mobility Center.
9. Differentiate between sleep, hibernate, and hybrid sleep modes.
10. Compare and contrast mobile operating systems.
11. Discuss factors to consider when installing a wireless connection.
12. Differentiate between an ad hoc network and an infrastructure network.
13. Identify methods for securing mobile devices.
14. Differentiate among wireless network security and encryption types.
15. Describe the process of disassembling a laptop for proper reassembly.
16. What should you do before attempting to disassemble any laptop or mobile device?
17. Discuss methods used to upgrade a laptop.
18. Why is the CPU often not an upgradable component in a laptop?
19. Identify common symptoms of poor laptop performance.
20. List preventive maintenance guidelines.

Sample A+ Exam Questions

1. Which term is used to describe bypassing the security on an iOS, thus allowing an unauthorized app to be installed?
   A. Jailbreaking
   B. Hijacking
   C. Rooting
   D. Drafting
2. Which type of memory is most commonly used for laptop computer RAM?
   A. SIMM
   B. SO-DIMM
   C. EPROM
   D. DIMM
3. What two pieces of information are required to connect to a secure wireless access point? Select two.
   A. MAC address
   B. SSID
   C. Security key
   D. Authorization code

4. Which is the best example of battery memory effect?
   A. A battery supplies the same level of voltage when connected to various types of laptop computers because it remembers the voltage level required the last time it was used.
   B. A battery loses its charge after the amount of time lapse of its last usage, even if the battery is designed to last longer.
   C. A battery is designed to remember the total length of the warranty and will cease supplying voltage after the expiration date.
   D. A battery remembers the orientation of the connection polarity after being removed from the case for reinstallation at a later date.
5. Which type of battery would you *most likely* find in a new laptop computer?
   A. Lithium-ion
   B. Alkaline
   C. NiCad
   D. Nickel-metal hydride
6. Under which Windows 10 Control Panel option would you *most likely* find the option to configure a second display monitor?
   A. System and Security
   B. Ease of Access
   C. Programs
   D. Appearance and Personalization
7. Which statement is true for the proper disposal of a laptop battery?
   A. It must be disposed of by incineration to protect the environment.
   B. You must follow local, state, and federal guidelines.
   C. Any container that is lined in plastic can be used.
   D. Lithium-ion batteries do not need to be disposed of because they can be recharged indefinitely.

8. Which situation best describes an ad hoc network?
   A. An Ethernet network with two wireless access points: one for WAN and the other for LAN service
   B. A notebook PC connected to a full-size PC transferring files by radio signal
   C. A group of computers using radio waves to communicate through a centralized access point on a 1000BaseT network
   D. A network consisting of several access points each using a different frequency
9. What is the maximum data transfer described by the IEEE 802.11b standard?
   A. 2 Mbps
   B. 5 GHz
   C. 11 Mbps
   D. 54 GHz
10. Which form of wireless security requires an authentication server?
   A. WEP
   B. WPA
   C. 802.1x
   D. BitLocker

Chapter 14

Modems and Transceivers

Learning Outcomes

14.1 Recall the characteristics of the public telephone system.
14.2 Summarize the function of a telephone modem.
14.3 Describe the operation of a digital subscriber line.
14.4 Provide advantages and disadvantages of cable-based Internet.
14.5 List characteristics of satellite Internet.
14.6 Explain the basic operation of a multiplexer and demultiplexer in T-carrier lines.
14.7 Identify characteristics of mobile broadband.
14.8 Summarize the process of installing and configuring a residential Internet connection.
14.9 List common troubleshooting practices to diagnose modem problems.

A+ Certification Exam Objectives

The following A+ Certification Exam Objectives are covered in this chapter.

Exam 220-1101

1.0 Mobile Devices

- 1.3 Given a scenario, set up and configure accessories and ports of mobile devices.
- 1.4 Given a scenario, configure basic mobile-device network connectivity and application support.

2.0 Networking

- 2.2 Compare and contrast common networking hardware.
- 2.7 Compare and contrast Internet connection types, network types, and their features.

Key Terms

bandwidth
cable modem
Code Division Multiple Access (CDMA)
Data Over Cable Service Interface Specification (DOCSIS)
digital subscriber line (DSL)
DSL modem
Global System for Mobile Communications (GSM)
Long Term Evolution (LTE)
mobile broadband
mobile hotspot
modem
multiple input multiple output (MIMO)
multiplexer
router
T-carrier line
tethering
Universal Mobile Telecommunications System (UMTS)
USB modem
WiMAX

Overview

One of the basic functions of the modern PC is communication with other computers, usually through Internet access. In this chapter, you will learn about the modem, modem installation, and communication software setup. Some of the material covered here will be seen again in the chapters discussing the basics of networking.

Modems allow you the freedom to browse the Internet, connect with others through e-mail and social networking, send pictures around the world, take part in conference calls, and participate in many other communication activities. While the modern modem is a plug-and-play device, there is still much to learn about modems and modem-related issues.

A+ Note

A variety of questions related to modems of all types may appear on the CompTIA A+ Certification Exams. While modems are less common than before, many locations have only telephone service rather than high-speed Internet service. You should practice configuring a telephone modem to familiarize yourself with the terminology associated with the device. In addition, you should look at the latest troubleshooting information located on Internet service provider websites.

Tech Tip

The public telephone system is often referred to as POTS, which is an acronym for *plain-old telephone system*.

A+ Note

For the CompTIA A+ Exams, you should know the difference between an RJ-11 and an RJ-14 telephone connection. An RJ-11 connector has two contacts for two wires, whereas an RJ-14 connector has four contacts for four wires.

14.1 Public Telephone System

To understand the complete communication model, you must first understand the public telephone system, which has been serving the public for over 100 years. As the technology associated with the telephone system evolved, it has retained its own backward compatibility to existing equipment. The original telephone system was designed to transmit voice as an analog signal across the country and world and only had to accommodate the frequency spectrum of sound associated with voice communication, which operated between 200 Hz and 4,000 Hz. This frequency spectrum is more than adequate for carrying voice, but it is not adequate for high-speed modem connections that demand higher bandwidth, which is a primary reason people switch to cable television carriers for Internet access. The cables used for cable television can carry much higher frequencies than the simple twisted-pair telephone cable, and the larger bandwidth allows for much more information to be transported in less time.

Bandwidth refers to the range or limit of frequency that a cable or device is designed to carry. For example, a cable with a bandwidth of 4 kbps is designed to carry a maximum frequency of 4 kbps. It should be noted that *bandwidth* is also used to describe a portion of the frequency spectrum. For example, television channels use a bandwidth of 6 MHz for each channel, meaning each channel has a frequency range of 6 MHz.

Telephone technology has made tremendous advances over the years, but issues with backward compatibility have made it difficult to implement all the latest technologies. The main bottleneck of the entire telephone system is the last few hundred feet of connection that serve each building, especially in private homes. Most of the public telephone network system (PTNS) is constructed of high-speed fiber-optic cables, microwave transmitters and receivers, digital equipment, and computerized telephone control units. While all these major parts of the telephone network system are composed of cables and media that have high data transfer rates, the last few hundred feet of twisted pair from the main system to the individual connection point severely limit the speed of data transmission.

Tech Tip

A modem is sometimes referred to as a *transceiver*, which is an electronic device that not only transmits, but also receives, data.

14.2 Telephone Modems

Telephone modems, or *dial-up modems*, are far less common than they once were, but they do still exist—especially in rural areas. In fact, a number of companies such as NetZero and Juno provide dial-up Internet access even as late as 2022. A **modem** is an electronic device that converts a digital signal into an analog signal, and then transmits a signal across telephone lines. Another modem on the receiving end converts the analog signal back to a digital signal. The term *modem* is a combination of two words—*modulator* and *demodulator*—and is derived from the field of electronics. A modem can be integrated into a motherboard installed in the form of an adapter card or connected outside the computer case as a peripheral device.

As shown in Figure 14-1, a modem converts a digital signal from a computer system to an analog signal that can be carried over telephone lines. When the analog signal reaches the destination PC, the modem converts the analog signal back to a

Figure 14-1 Modems convert digital signals to analog to transmit over phone lines, and then they convert them back to digital to be read by computers.

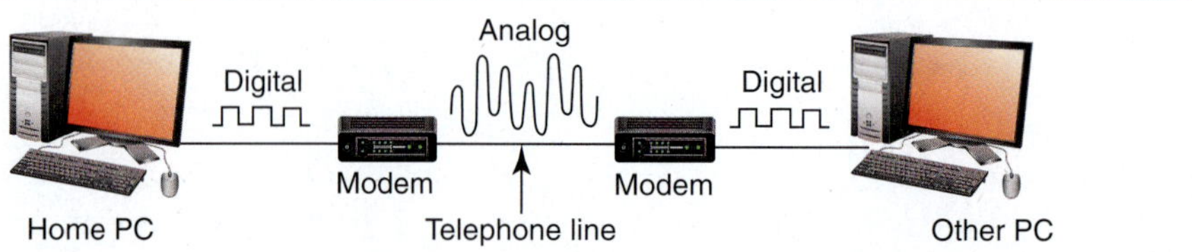

Goodheart-Willcox Publisher; (workstation icons) romvo/Shutterstock.com; (modem icons) Vadim Ermak/Shutterstock.com

digital signal. The latest CompTIA A+ Exams do not test for knowledge about dial-up modems, but it is possible to still encounter them in the field. As such, the following information is provided for your familiarity.

Modem Connections and Processes

Modems perform several steps to make and maintain connections between computers. The act of connecting to another computer using a modem is often referred to as ***modem negotiation***. The entire operation of the modem is a combination of coordinating the operating system software, modem controller chip, and ***universal asynchronous receiver-transmitter (UART) chip***, which is the main chip of the modem. The entire process seems complicated, but it appears transparent to the typical user. The user simply clicks an icon and connects. Often, these steps can be observed on an exterior modem with lights or LEDs. The process of modem negotiation is a series of signals and commands, which includes the following:

- Data Terminal Ready (DTR)
- Data Set Ready (DSR)
- Transmit Data (TD)
- Receive Data (RD)
- Carrier Detect (CD)
- Request to Send (RTS)
- Clear to Send (CTS)

A software program commands a modem with a ***Data Terminal Ready (DTR)*** signal, which tells the modem that the user wants to make a connection to another location. If the modem is ready, it sends a ***Data Set Ready (DSR)*** signal back to the software. Both signals must be present before any data can be transmitted. Next, the PC sends a ***Transmit Data (TD)*** signal to the modem, which commands the modem to dial a particular phone number. The remote modem replies with a ***Receive Data (RD)*** signal and proceeds to open a connection on the phone line. A series of electrical pulses flows from the modem through the telephone line, which mimics dialing a number. When the remote modem receives the signal, it responds to the originating modem and now uses a ***Carrier Detect (CD)*** signal to let the originating PC know that a carrier signal has been received from the modem.

There are many different modem styles and software systems, so the two modems now communicate back and forth trying to establish a common ground for exchanging data. The communication includes such matters as the transmission speed, number of start and stop bits, type of parity that will be used, and the resolution of half-duplex and full-duplex. Data speed, or ***baud rate***, must be the same for both modems. The absolute base speed is 300 baud, but it will normally be above 1,200 baud. Data is sent across telephone lines by a modem in packets. A single bit is used to mark the beginning of a packet, and either one or two bits are used to mark the end of the packet, as shown in Figure 14-2.

The type of parity must also be agreed between the two modems. ***Parity*** is a way to check the accuracy of the data packet being sent. There are three options: no parity, odd parity, and even parity. When the number of bits inside the data packet is added up, it will equal an odd or an even number. The systems agree to send an

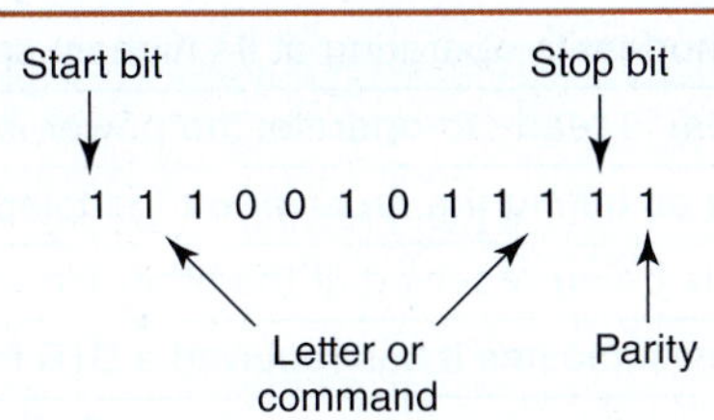

Goodheart-Willcox Publisher

Figure 14-2 In a typical modem data packet, a start bit, stop bit, and parity bit surround the data.

additional bit that represents either an odd number or an even number. A zero can represent either odd or even parity, and the same is true for a one. The receiving system adds the bits in the data and compares that number to the parity bit to check for errors.

The last item to resolve is the half- and full-duplex condition. The two communicating systems must agree which system will be responsible for half-duplex transmission and which will be responsible for full-duplex transmission. The terminal responsible for full-duplex is responsible for displaying data on the screen for both PCs. If this condition does not agree, either no system will display the data on the screen, or both systems will display data on the screen, meaning data will display twice on each screen.

After all the responsibilities have been negotiated between systems, messages can begin to be transmitted. The modem sends a *Request to Send (RTS)* signal asking if the other modem is ready to receive data, and it replies with a *Clear to Send (CTS)* signal. The two computers can send data back and forth in continuous operation, even simultaneously.

Many of these commands and activities can be monitored when using a modem connected outside the PC unit. External modems have lights that indicate different stages of activities. Figure 14-3 is a list of typical light abbreviations and their meanings.

A+ 1101: 2.7

14.3 Digital Subscriber Lines

A **digital subscriber line (DSL)** provides high-speed Internet access over telephone lines and has become one of the most popular methods for connecting to the Internet. There are many different variations of DSL available, such as ADSL, HDSL, VHDSL, and SDSL. This textbook uses the acronym DSL to represent the technology generally and will not address any particular type of DSL.

DSL can provide a constant connection to the Internet, and it can be used to send and receive both voice and data over the same line. Regular telephone lines are designed to carry low-frequency voice communication in a range of 0 kHz to 4 kHz, but DSL telephone lines are designed to carry much higher frequencies at 25 kHz to 1 MHz, and these higher frequencies can be used for high-speed Internet access. DSL is not available in all areas, and it is more expensive than legacy dial-up services.

The maximum distance DSL can span is limited by the high frequencies it uses. The typical maximum distance for DSL ranges from 1,000 feet to 18,000 feet, measured from the DSL modem to the telephone central office. The exact limit depends on the type of DSL used and any special equipment, such as loading coils, or media, such as fiber-optic cable, that might exist on the telephone line.

Figure 14-3 The outside of a modem will often denote status with LEDs marked with abbreviations.

Modem Abbreviations

Abbreviation	Meaning
AA (Auto Answer)	Ready to accept incoming calls automatically.
CD (Carrier Detect)	The modem has detected a carrier signal.
HS (High Speed)	The modem is operating at its highest speed.
MR (Modem Ready)	Modem is ready to operate; the power is on.
OH (Off Hook)	Same as taking the receiver off the telephone hook.
SD (Send Data)	Data is being received at the other modem.
TR (Terminal Ready)	Modem indicates it has received a DTR from the software package.

Goodheart-Willcox Publisher

A *loading coil* is used to amplify analog voice signals, but it will not amplify a DSL signal. In fact, a loading coil reduces or blocks the higher-frequency DSL signal. Media might also change between the subscriber location and the central office. For example, the copper-conductor cabling may change to fiber-optic cabling at some point, which will prevent the application of DSL, as DSL technology is applied only to copper wiring, not fiber-optic.

The actual physical attributes of the copper core in the cable comprise another factor that determines the maximum distance DSL can be applied. The copper-core length, diameter, and number of twists per foot in the cable pairs affect the actual distance and throughput of the DSL service. The diameter of the cable is expressed in a measurement referred to as AWG, which stands for *American Wire Gage*. The three common diameters are (from largest to smallest) 22, 24, and 26 AWG. The smaller the diameter of the cable, the shorter the distance the cable can span, and the greater the number of twists in the cable, the lower the frequency it can carry. The most significant factor affecting DSL performance is the overall cable length.

DSL Types

There are many types of DSL systems, and they all vary in upstream and downstream bandwidths, as shown in Figure 14-4. The term *upstream* is used for the data flow direction from the customer to the carrier, and the term *downstream* is used to describe the data flow direction from the carrier or provider's site to the customer.

ADSL is the original DSL service and is commonly used by Internet service providers for residential services. ADSL2+ is an improved version of the original ADSL with greater service distances and higher data rates. VDSL is a high-speed, short-distance DSL service typically used for short runs from the home or office to a higher-speed fiber-optic cable service.

SDSL and HDSL are both symmetric services, meaning the upstream and downstream data rates match. Services that start with the letter *A* are asymmetric, meaning the upstream and downstream data rates do not match. SDSL is a basic service, while HDSL is a high-speed data rate form of DSL.

RADSL stands for *Rate Adaptive DSL*, meaning the connection is shared and the actual connection speed (or data transfer rate) will vary depending on the number of persons using the service. When more people are using the service, the actual connection speed drops in increments. For more information on the various DSL technologies, visit your local service provider's website.

Tech Tip

When comparing information about xDSL from other sources, you will see that data rates and maximum distances will vary greatly. This is because some sources only reflect its company's technologies. A major factor is the electrical characteristics of the copper wire.

DSL Variations			
DSL Type	**Upstream**	**Downstream**	**Maximum Distance (ft.)**
ADSL	800 kbps	1.5 Mbps–8 Mbps	12,000–18,000
ADSL2+	2 Mbps	24 Mbps	5,000
HDSL	1.544 Mbps	1.544 Mbps	15,000
SDSL	1.544 Mbps	1.544 Mbps	10,000
VDSL	1.5 Mbps–2.3 Mbps	13 Mbps–52 Mbps	1,000–4,500
VDSL2	1 Mbps–16 Mbps	30 Mbps	4,000
VDSL2+	2 Mbps	24 Mbps	5,000
RADSL	1 Mbps	7 Mbps	1,000–18,000
G.lite ADSL	192 kbps–2.3 Mbps	192 kbps–2.3 Mbps	14,000

Goodheart-Willcox Publisher

Figure 14-4 DSL types vary in upstream bandwidth, downstream bandwidth, and maximum distances.

A+ 1101: 2.2

DSL Modem and Cables

A **DSL modem** enables high-speed Internet access over existing phone lines. A typical DSL modem is shown in Figure 14-5 as well as its power adapter, telephone cable, and Ethernet cable. The power adapter converts the standard 120 VAC to the 12 VDC needed to power the modem, the telephone cable connects the DSL modem to the telephone wall jack using RJ-11 connectors, and the Ethernet cable is a standard Cat 5 or Cat 5e cable used to connect the back of the DSL modem to the network adapter card installed in the PC, as illustrated in Figure 14-6. Some DSL modems bypass a network adapter by using a USB cable to connect to the PC's USB port.

An additional device called a *filter* may be required if there is other equipment such as telephones or fax machines connected to the same telephone line used for Internet access. Fax machines and telephones can be plugged into the same DSL line as the PC, but they must do so through a filter to prevent low-frequency signals to and from these devices from interfering with or corrupting the high-frequency signals used for the Internet connection. A filter is never installed in the line between the DSL modem and the PC because it will block the high-frequency signals used by the Internet connection.

DSL is a point-to-point connection, meaning it will provide a steady bandwidth and will not fluctuate like other broadband connections. For example, cable television access used for Internet connections is shared by other connections in the local neighborhood and varies according to how many other people are accessing the Internet using the shared cable.

Both cable Internet access and DSL can be used to support multiple devices such as other computers or gaming consoles. A device called a *router* or *gateway* is installed after the modem to distribute additional connections using cable or wireless radio signals. In some cases, the modem can be a combination of router and modem.

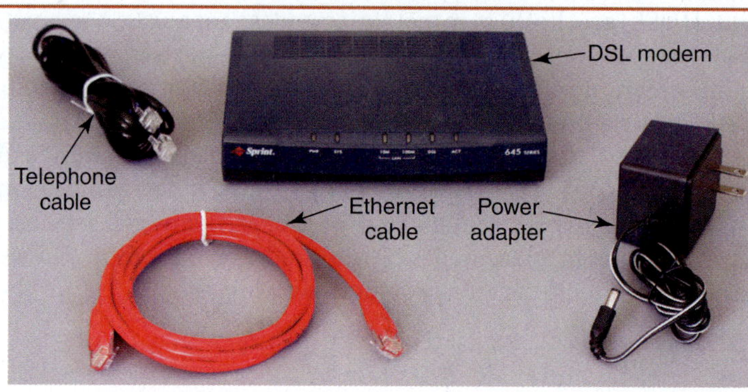

Figure 14-5 Typical DSL components include a modem, power adapter, Ethernet cable, and telephone cable.

Goodheart-Willcox Publisher

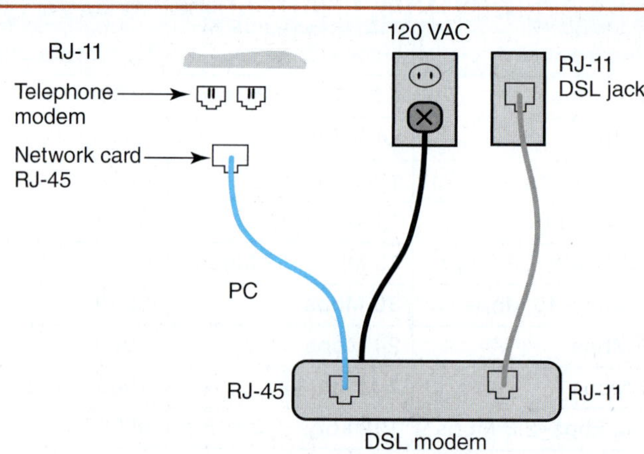

Figure 14-6 The DSL modem is connected between the DSL telephone line and the network card on the PC.

Goodheart-Willcox Publisher

14.4 Cable

1101: 2.7 A+

Cable Internet service provides high-speed Internet access using lines designed for cable television and a cable modem to provide a continuous connection to the Internet without having to dial in. One of the biggest benefits of cable Internet is the continuous connectivity; provided you have the proper equipment, you have an Internet connection ready whenever you are. The connection does not time out from lack of use, and you have your own IP address, so the provider does not need to revoke it to make it available to other users.

Today, most home- and small-business Internet connections are provided via cable modem. However, you may still occasionally encounter older connections such as DSL. Both DSL and cable provide much more bandwidth than legacy 56k telephone modems, but one drawback of cable is that its Internet bandwidth varies greatly depending on the number of users accessing the Internet through the shared connection. Thus, as more people access and use data-intense services, such as video and audio downloading, your data speeds will decrease. In some cases, you can expect speeds as high as 50 Mbps or higher, but this speed varies based on a variety of factors. Another drawback of cable Internet service is there is often only one choice of cable service provider per neighborhood. Therefore, if you are unhappy with your service provider, your options are limited.

Cable Media

1101: 2.7 A+

There are two major types of cable television media used for access: coaxial cable and fiber-optic cable, as illustrated in Figure 14-7. Coaxial cable consists of a solid copper conductor surrounded by thick insulating material. An outer conductor is made of braided copper or a foil jacket surrounding the insulating material. An insulating jacket, used to provide physical protection to the cable assembly, covers the entire assembly, and coaxial cable connectors are crimped onto the ends. Coaxial cable is easily spliced or extended and has a maximum data transfer speed of 350 MHz. Originally, a conventional telephone line was used to establish the connection to the Internet, and coaxial cable was used to download from the Internet. Today, coaxial cable is a two-way data transmission system and does not require a separate telephone line to establish the connection.

Fiber-optic cable consists of a glass or plastic core, both of which are quite small in cross-sectional area and very flexible. Fiber-optic cable transmits light rather than an electrical signal through the core and has many advantages over coaxial or any type of copper-core cable. It is lightweight, resistive to corrosion and water, and immune to electrical interference, and it also provides excellent security because it is almost impossible to tap into fiber-optic cabling. One big advantage of fiber-optic cable is that it is immune to lightning strikes. When lightning strikes traditional copper-core cable, a high current can run through the cable and damage

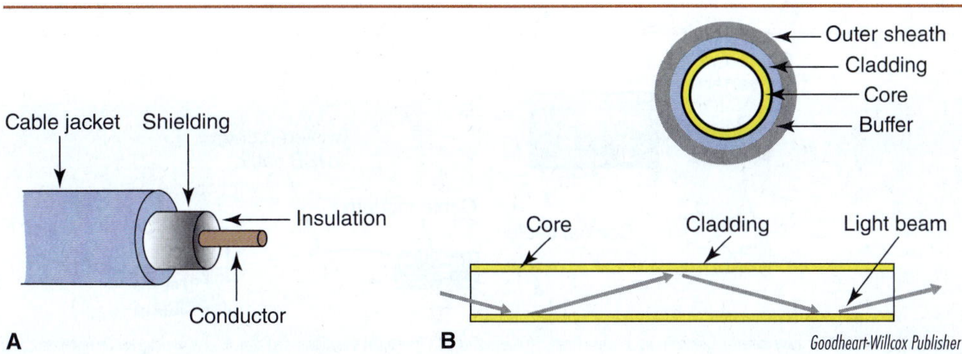

Figure 14-7 Coaxial cable (A) has a center conductor surrounded by layers of insulation. Fiber-optic cable (B) has several outer layers that protect and reflect the light transmitted through the core.

sensitive electronic equipment, including computers. Fiber-optic cable can also be run for longer lengths with less signal loss than conventional copper-core cables. The downside of fiber-optic cable is the price, as it is expensive to install, and special equipment is required for splicing the cable.

Fiber-optic cable through the television company is usually divided into different channels, each using a 6-MHz channel to transmit separate television channels or networks, such as ABC, CBS, or NBC. The same principle is used for Internet connections; two channels, each 6 MHz, are provided to transmit data to and from the Internet.

Currently, there is no single standard for cable modem specifications, and instead, you must check with the local cable ISP to see what type or brand of cable modem you will need. One standard that has been established for cable modems is the **Data Over Cable Service Interface Specification (DOCSIS)**, which is a standard that enforces compatibility among cable modems. Any DOCSIS cable modem can communicate with any other DOCSIS cable modem.

A+ 1101: 2.2

Cable Modem

Similar to a DSL modem, a **cable modem** is a transceiver that allows existing cable television coaxial cable to be used for Internet access, as shown in Figure 14-8. Remember, the same cable provides both television and Internet access, so a splitter should be installed to divide the connections between your modem and your television. In this configuration, the coaxial cable can supply a television signal to the television and provide Internet access for the PC silumtaneously. The cable television coaxial cable connects to the cable modem from the splitter, and an Ethernet or USB cable is used between the cable modem and the PC. More than one PC can use the cable Internet connection if a router or gateway is installed, though the router may be part of the modem.

eMTA Modem

An *Embedded Multimedia Terminal Adapter (eMTA) modem* combines the functionality of a DOCSIS cable modem and a phone adapter in one device, allowing a service provider to provide both Internet access and telephone service to a customer using one device and cable. The eMTA modem is usually provided by the service provider, but it can be purchased to avoid rental fees. The only requirement is that the eMTA modem must be compatible with the service provider requirements. As with dial-up Internet, eMTA is far less common today than it once was.

A+ 1101: 2.7

14.5 Satellite

Satellite systems can be used for Internet access and are ideal for remote or rural locations when a home or office is located a great deal away from city services.

Figure 14-8 The cable modem is installed between a splitter and the PC. The splitter separates the cable television signal from the Internet signal.

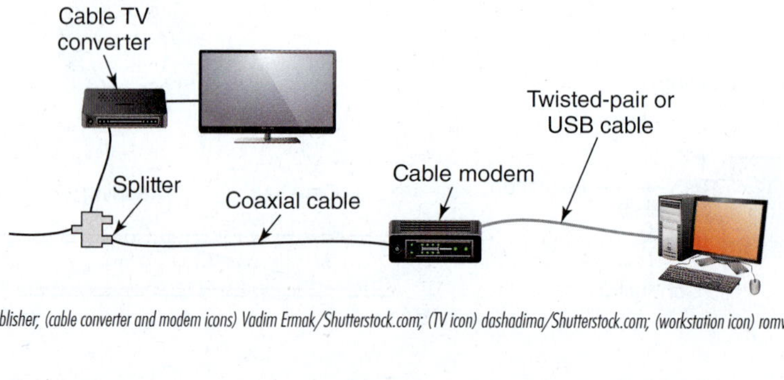

Goodheart-Willcox Publisher; (cable converter and modem icons) Vadim Ermak/Shutterstock.com; (TV icon) dashadima/Shutterstock.com; (workstation icon) romvo/Shutterstock.com

Satellite Internet service typically costs more to set up than other residential forms of service because you typically must either rent the satellite equipment or buy it for several hundred dollars. Of all the Internet-connection models discussed, satellite is among the fastest-growing connections. For example, as of this writing, it is estimated that there are roughly 43 million people using satellite Internet globally, which is expected to grow to 110 million by 2029 through advancements such as SpaceX's Starlink satellites.

Typically, satellites providing Internet access use the Ku band and can perform downloads at up to 506 Mbit/second and uploads up to 14 Mbit/second, though rates will vary. The Ku Band is a portion of the electromagnetic spectrum in the 12- to 18-GHz range, which is in the microwave region of the electromagnetic spectrum. Satellite-based access provides a constant connection to the Internet in similar fashion to xDSL and cable systems, but they function as line-of-sight systems, which means they must have an unobstructed direct view to the source. Trees and buildings can obstruct the satellite receiver from the source. A satellite system is also susceptible to weather conditions, such as heavy rainstorms.

14.6 T-Carrier Lines

A **T-carrier line** is an Internet connection designed to carry voice and data over four wires. T-carrier lines were first introduced in 1993 by AT&T and can carry data at a much higher rate than traditional phone lines. Businesses, governmental organizations, and educational institutions are the primary customers who lease T-carrier lines. An important part of the T-carrier line system is the use of a multiplexer and a demultiplexer. A **multiplexer** is a special electronic device that controls the flow of data and voice over a T-carrier line. Think of it as a funnel that combines lower-frequency lines together to take advantage of the higher-frequency transmission rates of the T-carrier. Look at Figure 14-9 to view a multiplexer and T-carrier.

As you can see in the illustration, several low-speed lines are tied into the multiplexer. As data is transmitted through the multiplexer, it is reorganized into smaller packages called *data packets* and sent through the T-carrier in an organized manner. The data packets then travel at the maximum speed of the T-carrier until they reach the opposite end of the T-carrier, where a demultiplexer reverses the process by rearranging the packets back into their original structures and releasing them to lines with lower data rates. The levels of T-carrier lines are identified as follows:

- T-1: 1.544 Mbps or 24 voice channels
- T-2: 6.312 Mbps or 96 voice channels
- T-3: 44.736 Mbps or 672 voice channels
- T-4: 274.176 Mbps or 4,032 voice channels

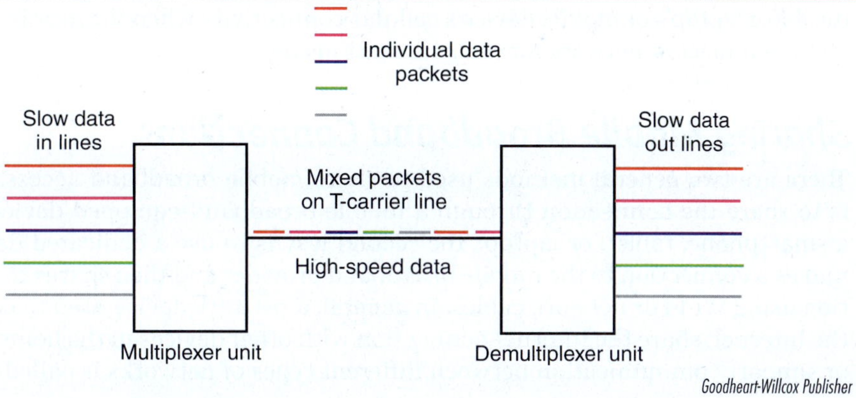

Figure 14-9 A multiplexer organizes slower-speed data and voice signals into a series of high-speed data packets. The packets are converted back to a lower speed at a demultiplexer unit.

An additional label, called a *fractional T-1*, is a T-1 line that is only partially issued to a customer. Think of a fractional T-1 line as a line shared among different parties who, individually, do not require full T-1 line capacity.

A+ 1101: 2.7

14.7 Mobile Broadband

Tech Tip

There are several different definitions of broadband speed. For example, the FCC's definition of high-speed access is at least 25 Mbps downstream and 3 Mbps upstream. The IEEE defines broadband as having instantaneous bandwidths greater than 1 MHz and supporting data rates greater than 1.5 Mbps.

Mobile broadband is a wireless Internet connection based on mobile phone technology. *Broadband* is an electronics term and classification of a communication with a bandwidth in excess of 256 kbps. When you see the term *broadband* used in the context of mobile devices, it is referencing any form of wireless communication that supports data rates at or above 256 kbps. In many cases, a USB modem can be used as a mobile broadband modem to connect a device that does not have built-in broadband capabilities technology. A **USB modem** is a tiny mobile broadband device that plugs into any laptop with a USB port and allows the laptop to connect to the Internet using a mobile broadband service. Some companies refer to their USB modems as *laptop sticks* or *data cards*. Some USB modems can also be used as storage devices similar to a USB flash memory device and will often include installation manuals, software applications, and required drivers. Many devices, such as laptops and tablets, now come with built-in cellular capabilities in addition to Wi-Fi, making USB modems less common.

Cellular Connections through Mobile Broadband Tower

Although the majority of laptop computers and mobile devices have wireless connectivity methods such as built-in 802.11 cards, laptops and mobile devices may also have another form of wireless connectivity capability, such as *cellular connectivity*. This feature allows individuals who are not in range of a wireless Internet connection to connect to the Internet through a cellular tower. However, data rates may apply when connecting a laptop or mobile device to a cellular tower for Internet usage, and it is important that users understand and comply with their data plans and agreements. Therefore, it is beneficial for technicians and users to be aware that cellular connectivity options can be turned on and off similarly to how an 802.11 or Bluetooth connectivity option can be turned on and off.

If an individual's laptop or mobile device has cellular connection capabilities, the laptop or mobile device will have a physical control button, a combination of hotkeys, or a software utility that allows manual control for the connection to turn on or off. The advisement of this capability can diminish the use of cellular data of an individual's cellular data plan. Furthermore, as of this writing, 802.11 connections are still of preference to a user when it is available in comparison to cellular tower connections. Therefore, technicians should try to encourage their users to disable a laptop's or mobile device's cellular connectivity when the user is within an 802.11-connected network for their Internet needs.

Sharing Mobile Broadband Connections

There are two general methods used to share mobile broadband access. The first is to share the connection through a mobile broadband-equipped device such as a smartphone, tablet, or laptop. The second way is to use a dedicated device that makes a connection to the mobile broadband provider and then shares the connection using Wi-Fi or network cables. In general, a network device used to connect to the Internet, share the Internet connection with other devices in the home or office, or support communication between different types of networks is called a **router**.

A mobile broadband router is used to connect wirelessly to a cell service and is often called other names by the service provider such as *jetpack* or *wireless pocket router*. There will be more information about routers in a later chapter.

Tethering

1101: 1.3, 1.4 A+

Tethering refers to the sharing of one device's Internet connection with another connected device that does not have an Internet connection. Mobile broadband services are provided by communication companies such as Verizon Wireless, T-Mobile, and AT&T, and a single device can be configured to share access to mobile broadband services. For example, a smartphone can share its mobile broadband service with other devices such as computers or tablets by creating and sharing a local Internet connection point.

Look at the Figure 14-10 to see the Internet sharing configuration on a Windows 10 computer. To get to this location, use the [Windows][X] key combination and choose **Network Connections**. From the menu, select either Wi-Fi or Ethernet, whichever has an Internet connection, and then select **Change adapter options** from the Advanced network settings portion of the menu, which will open the **Network Connections** dialog box. Right-click on your active Internet connection and select **Properties** from the shortcut menu. Then, select the **Sharing** tab and ensure the **Internet Connection Sharing** check box is selected. In some cases, you will need the broadcast name (SSID) and password to connect to the Internet share. The password is also referred to as a *security key*, *passphrase*, or *passcode*.

Another way of sharing an Internet connection is with a dedicated device that is especially designed to connect to the Internet wireless broadband service and then distribute the connection to other devices. For example, you can use a tablet or smartphone to host an Internet connection, as demonstrated in Figure 14-11. In this example, an iPhone is configured as a Wi-Fi connection point for devices without cellular capabilities. When configured in this way, the iPhone is considered a *personal hotspot*, similar to standalone mobile hotspot devices.

Mobile Hotspots

1101: 1.3, 1.4 A+

A **mobile hotspot**, such as the one shown in Figure 14-12, is a portable wireless router that allows multiple devices to share a common Internet connection. The mobile hotspot connects to a mobile broadband service and shares the connection with other devices using Wi-Fi. Some mobile hotspots have mobile broadband capability

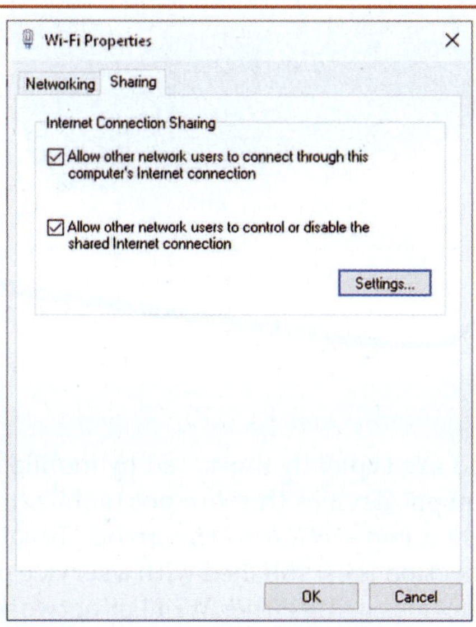

Goodheart-Willcox Publisher

Figure 14-10 *Tethering* refers to devices sharing an Internet connection through a mobile broadband device.

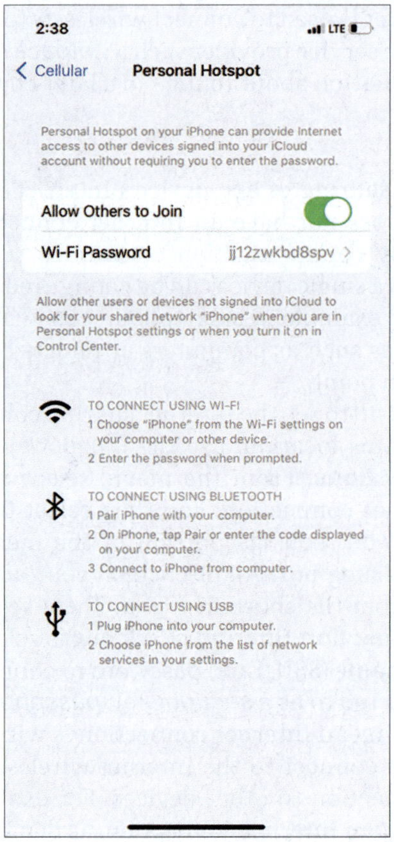

Figure 14-11 Most tablets and smartphones have configuration options for tethering or creating mobile Wi-Fi hotspots.

Goodheart-Willcox Publisher

Figure 14-12 A mobile hotspot allows multiple devices to share a common Internet connection.

Virrage Images/Shutterstock.com

built into the device and are typically marketed by mobile broadband service providers. Other mobile hotspot devices that are not mobile broadband-enabled use a USB modem to establish a connection to the mobile broadband service provider. After a broadband connection is established with a service provider, the connection can be shared to other devices using either Wi-Fi or network cable connections.

3G and 4G

1101: 1.4 A+

When used in respect to mobile broadband systems, the acronyms *3G* and *4G* represent the third generation and fourth generation of broadband technology, respectively. There have been multiple generations of mobile wireless technology, starting with the first mobile wireless communication device: the walkie-talkie. A radical change in the development of portable wireless communication that requires all new electronic concepts and parts is referred to as a *generation*, and in most cases, one generation is not compatible with devices from previous generations, meaning you cannot upgrade a device from one generation to be compatible with devices in the next generation.

3G and *4G* are neither technical terms nor specifications. Instead, they refer to a full set of various standards and electronic technologies. The terms *3G* and *4G* are used in advertisement and marketing of broadband wireless portable devices. In fact, when used in advertisement and marketing, 3G or 4G may be based on entirely different sets of mobile radio communication standards, depending on the service provider. In general, with respect to devices and services classified as 3G and 4G, 4G is far superior compared to 3G. You can download or upload significantly more data with 4G as compared to 3G. As of this writing, neither 3G nor 4G is the most up-to-date generation, as 5G began rolling out in 2019.

5G

1101: 1.4 A+

The 3G and 4G standards were widely recognized among mobile users, but the need for mobile and cellular data transmissions is always increasing. Furthermore, to adhere to private and business practices, mobile and cellular data transmission speeds need to increase. Thus, 5G capabilities are in the process of being implemented into our mobile and cellular networks, beginning with widespread rollouts that started in 2019.

One of the reasons for 5G was increased data rates. As a result, 5G can achieve download speeds of up to 10 GB/s. The 3rd Generation Partnership Project (3GPP) defines cellular standards and considers any system using 5G NR software as 5G. There is a wide range of implementations for 5G, including low-band, mid-band, or high-band, with speeds of 24 GHz to 54 GHz. There are three primary areas of application for 5G:

- *Enhanced Mobile Broadband (eMBB)* is for general mobile services and is what most people use when they use 5G.
- *Ultra-Reliable Low-Latency Communications (URLLC)* is for use with mission-critical applications.
- *Massive Machine-Type Communications (mMTC)* is used for IoT devices.

Broadband Data Rates

Data rates vary greatly among broadband service providers, technologies, and generations. In general, each generation is significantly faster than its predecessor, but data rates are affected by many factors. At best, the actual data rates are much lower than advertised data rates. For example, you will see data rates as high as 100 Mbps downlink and 50 Mbps uplink for 4G LTE wireless. In actuality, the average data rates are 5 Mbps to 12 Mbps downlink and 2 Mbps to 5 Mbps uplink. The variance between advertised and actual speed stems from radio interference, distance from the service provider, and the number of users accessing the service at the same time. The newer 5G can theoretically reach data speeds as high as 10 Gbps.

Radio interference can be a real problem for broadband data because so many devices rely on radio technology, that the air is full of signals generated from many different sources. Additionally, the farther the mobile device is from the service provider, the lower the data rate because the radio signal becomes weaker over distance, thus causing a loss of data generally in direct proportion to the distance.

Lastly, the total number of users sharing the same frequency can cause a fluctuating data rate. Since the frequency is a shared medium, there is a direct correlation between the number of users sharing the frequency and individual user's download and upload data rates. Another factor that affects data rates is location, which is directly related to the data rate factors mentioned before. A mobile device might work great in one city but seem to operate sluggishly in another city. This is because of all the factors previously mentioned.

Figure 14-13 shows approximate data rates recommended for use of different services. The table contains suggested or recommended data rates for good performance. You can still obtain some of these services with lower data rates, but the performance will be poor. Verizon Wireless advertises the following data rates, which are based on an independent third-party test:

- 5G: 50 Mbps to 1 Gbps, depending on the RF channel, load on the base station, and other factors
- 4G Long Term Evolution (LTE): download speeds of 5 Mbps to 12 Mbps and upload speeds of 2 Mbps to 5 Mbps
- 3G Evolution Data Optimized (EVDO): download speeds of 600 kbps to 1.4 Mbps and upload speeds of 500 kbps to 800 kbps

Metered Bandwidth Consumption

Most mobile broadband service providers charge users by the amount of bandwidth they consume. For example, a mobile broadband service provider may sell a service plan based on consuming 2 GB of bandwidth per month at $40.00 per month, but an additional 1 GB may cost an additional $15.00. In other words, it is like an electric bill: the more you consume, the more it will cost you. Since most plans charge for additional usage, many wireless mobile devices have some type of metering so you can view your total consumption. Some devices will also send you a text message, push notification, or e-mail to let you know when you are getting close to exceeding your total bandwidth allocation.

Assigned Frequencies

Wi-Fi has definite assigned frequencies—for example, 2.4 GHz and 5 GHz—depending on which standard is applied, such as 802.11a, 802.11b, 802.11g, and 802.11n. There is no one assigned radio frequency for mobile communication, so several assigned frequencies can be used by service providers. Some commonly encountered frequencies are 700 MHz, 800 MHz, 850 MHz, 900 MHz, 1,700 MHz, 1,800 MHz, 1,900 MHz, and 2,100 MHz. Additionally, there are many dual-, tri-, and quad-band devices, which means they work on two, three, and four bands, respectively.

Figure 14-13 Data rates affect a device's ability to perform certain functions.

Recommended Broadband Data Rates by Application

Application	Description	Data Rate
Multimedia messaging	A combination of text and image messaging	8 kbps–64 kbps
Video telephony	Telephone with a live video feed	64 kbps–384 kbps
General web browsing	Web-page viewing from a simple static web page to a dynamic web page with animation	32 kbps–1 Mbps
Video and audio streaming	Viewing both video and audio media, such as television or movies, with modest resolution	32 kbps–2 Mbps
High-definition video streaming	Viewing both video and audio media, such as television or movies, with excellent resolution	4 Mbps and higher

Goodheart-Willcox Publisher

Cellular configuration options for most mobile devices include Global mode; LTE and CDMA; and LTE, GSM, or UMTS. It can be very confusing because cell phone and mobile broadband technology is global and applies to many different standards and electronics technologies. When accessing mobile broadband services, you may need to match the technology to the device before you can obtain service. For example, you may need to configure the device for LTE and CDMA mode before the device will access the mobile broadband service. The following sections describe the most common operational modes to help you better understand the specifications of mobile broadband equipment and services.

Global System for Mobile Communications

A+ 1101: 1.4

Global System for Mobile Communications (GSM) was originally an analog wireless communication system used for voice communications or wireless telephones that evolved into a wireless digital communication system for transmitting mobile voice and data. The European Telecommunications Standards Institute (ETSI) developed the standards for the second generation (2G), which became the de facto standard all over the world. These standards are maintained by the GSM Association—a group of cellular network operators and associated companies.

Universal Mobile Telecommunications System

Universal Mobile Telecommunications System (UMTS) is a 3G standard developed by the 3rd Generation Partnership Project (3GPP). UMTS is a component of the International Telecommunication Union (ITU) set of communication standards. UMTS also incorporates the electronics technology of CDMA.

Code Division Multiple Access

A+ 1101: 1.4

Code Division Multiple Access (CDMA) is an electronic technique used to encode digital information when using radio as a medium. CDMA greatly increases the amount of data and number of users that can be carried on a single radio channel. Major carriers Sprint and Verizon Wireless mainly use CDMA technology, while AT&T and T-Mobile use GSM technology, though all these carriers also support 3G networks.

Long Term Evolution

Long Term Evolution (LTE) is an evolution of the GSM and UMTS standards. LTE is considered 4G and has high advertised data rates, but as mentioned earlier, the advertised rates vary greatly from the actual data rates. LTE has been widely used for streaming music, videos, and high definition, but 5G is quickly replacing 4G/LTE in most areas.

WiMAX

WiMAX is a wireless technology similar to Wi-Fi but has a much greater range as well as a controllable radio broadcast direction. Wi-Fi is limited to a few hundred feet at best, but WiMAX can be used at distances of 30 miles for fixed stations and 3 to 10 miles for mobile stations. The data rates for WiMAX are approximately 46 Mbps for downlink and 7 Mbps for uplink but may vary according to interference, distance, location, number of users, and other factors. Some factors that affect the distance and throughput are terrain, weather, and large buildings. A Wi-Fi broadcast signal is typically omnidirectional, meaning it broadcasts in a 360-degree radius from the transmitter. However, a WiMAX broadcast signal can be shaped to transmit in omni, sector, or point-to-point, based on the type of antenna selected, as shown in Figure 14-14.

- *Omni* means the radio wave is broadcast in all directions (360 degrees).
- *Sector* refers to a portion of the 360-degree broadcast, such as 60, 90, or 120 degrees.

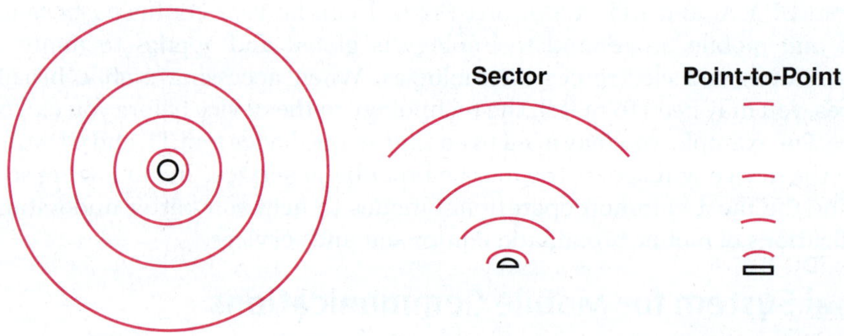

Goodheart-Willcox Publisher

Figure 14-14 WiMax broadcast signals are shaped depending on the style antenna used.

- *Point-to-point* means the radio wave is broadcast in a narrow beam or direct line of sight.

The assigned frequencies for WiMax range from 2 GHz to 66 GHz, though the most commonly applied frequencies are 3.5 MHz, 5 MHz, 7 MHz, 8.75 MHz, and 10 MHz. It should also be noted that other frequencies may be assigned by the FCC in the future.

Multiple Input Multiple Output

Multiple input multiple output (MIMO) is a wireless technology that uses two or more streams of data transmission to increase the data throughput and range of a wireless network. You can think of it as a device that uses two or more parallel channels to communicate, thus doubling the data rate. When a device has multiple antennas, it is usually a MIMO device. While two or more antennas is a sign of MIMO technology, be aware not all devices have visible antennas. Many devices hide the antennas inside the case of the device for aesthetic reasons. There will be additional information about MIMO in a later chapter.

Comparing Connection Types

As you have seen in the preceding sections, there are numerous ways to connect to the Internet. Each has advantages and disadvantages. Figure 14-15 lists the pros and cons of some of the most widely used connection types and those you are most likely to encounter.

14.8 Setting Up a Residential Internet Connection

A residential Internet connection can be set up easily. The term *residential* is used to differentiate from a network system, which is significantly different, and the requirements for a large network are covered later in this textbook. Most of the residential setup is done using a setup wizard program, but there may be times when even the setup wizard needs information from you.

Most ISPs provide software to assist you in automatically connecting with their services. Running the software starts a wizard that helps you set up your connection to the Internet, and in many cases, the PC has setup software for several ISPs preloaded onto the desktop. These ISPs can be added quickly by clicking the

Figure 14-15 Every Internet connection type has a unique set of advantages and disadvantages.

Pros and Cons of Connection Types			
Connection Type	**Bandwidth**	**Pros**	**Cons**
Modem (56.6)	56 Kbit/s downstream; 33.6 Kbit/s upstream	Inexpensive, uses existing telephone lines.	Low bandwidth
Cable (DOCSIS 3.0)	1,215 Mbit/s downstream; 216 Mbit/s upstream	Uses existing cable television systems	Requires cable television access
Cable (DOCSIS 4.0)	10 Gbit/s downstream; 6 Gbit/s upstream	Uses existing cable television systems	Requires cable television access
Fiber Optic (GPON)	2,488 Mbit/s downstream; 1,244 Mbit/s upstream	Very reliable	Expensive to install
Fiber Optic (NG-PON2)	40 Gbit/s downstream; 10 Gbit/s upstream	Very fast and very reliable	Expensive to install
Wireless (802.11 ad)	7.14–7.2 Gbit/s downstream; 7.14–7.2 Gbit/s upstream	Inexpensive, good bandwidth, wireless	Short range
Wireless (802.33 ax, Wi-Fi 6)	11 Gbit/s downstream; 11 Gbit/s upstream	Inexpensive, good bandwidth, wireless	Short range
Wired (Cat 6)	1 Gbit/s downstream; 1 Gbit/s upstream	Inexpensive, long range	Possible issues with cabling
Wired (Cat 7)	10 GB/s downstream; 10 GB/s upstream	Inexpensive, long range	Possible issues with cabling

Goodheart-Willcox Publisher

associated icon on the display, and this work is often performed automatically. At times, you may be required to do some manual configuration, especially in a business environment or in a PC with a security system such as a firewall.

For a typical home PC, you will need to enter the telephone number of the ISP, your user ID such as JonesB, and a password issued by the ISP. Other items that you may need to enter are the name of the e-mail server accessed at the ISP location and type of e-mail protocol being used, such as POP3. These last two items are usually provided by the ISP. You may also need to select the type of protocol used to transmit data to the ISP over the telephone line, such as PPP or SLIP. Typically, PPP is used.

When you are setting up your Internet connection, you may be required to input a choice of protocol. The standard protocol used for the Internet is TCP/IP, which stands for Transmission Control Protocol/Internet Protocol.

An *IP address* will be assigned to the modem, which serves as an identification for an Internet-connected device. All devices connected to the Internet, as well as all websites, have IP addresses. The Internet communicates using the IP address to identify a website or device as opposed to using the site name seen in a web browser, such as www.g-w.com. Software converts the IP address into the name of the site you are trying to reach.

Since you are connecting to the Internet and expect other websites and people to respond to you, your PC also will have an IP address. If you use a dial-up ISP, the IP address you use may not be permanent, and a new address will be issued each time you access the Internet through your ISP. This allows the ISP to have a smaller number of IP addresses and distribute them to users as they need them. The phone number dialed as you access the Internet is just the phone number of the ISP used by your PC, not your IP address. There will be much more about TCP/IP and Internet device identification later in the textbook.

Wireless Access

Whether one is using cable modem, DSL, WiMAX, or some other connection, one will need some provider on the other end of the connection to be able to access the Internet. The term *Internet Service Provider* refers to any services providing clients access to the internet. There are different types of ISPs. For example,

- *hosting ISPs* provide web hosting and storage, e-mail or cloud services; and
- *transit ISPs* provide upstream access to smaller ISPs.

A+ 1101: 2.7

The term *Wireless Internet Service Provider (WISP)* refers to an ISP that provides Internet access via wireless technology. This is usually at specific frequencies including 900 MHz, 2.4 GHz, 4.9 GHz, 5 GHz, 24 GHz, and 60 GHz, though there are additional frequency bands that have been allocated in the United States by the Federal Communications Commission.

Ookla Speed Test

A good, free utility to test the actual speed of the Internet media is the Ookla Speed Test, shown in Figure 14-16. The utility tests the transfer of data packets for both upstream and downstream connections and then displays the result on the webpage. During the speed test, the user's computer sends a message to the Ookla server, which responds to the message. The round-trip time is measured in milliseconds and performed multiple times with the lowest value representing the final test score. It does this to test both the download and upload speeds of the user's Internet connection. There are dozens of free speed tests, including the web-based Ookla and Google tests, as well as Microsoft's app-based Network Speed Test.

14.9 Troubleshooting Modems

Troubleshooting procedures are very similar for all Internet devices. Most commonly, the modem in question requires some form of reset such as a *power cycle*, which is the process of shutting down a device, disconnecting it from power, waiting, then reconnecting the power and rebooting the device. The following troubleshooting information should be considered as a general guide, and you should always visit the service provider's website for detailed troubleshooting information.

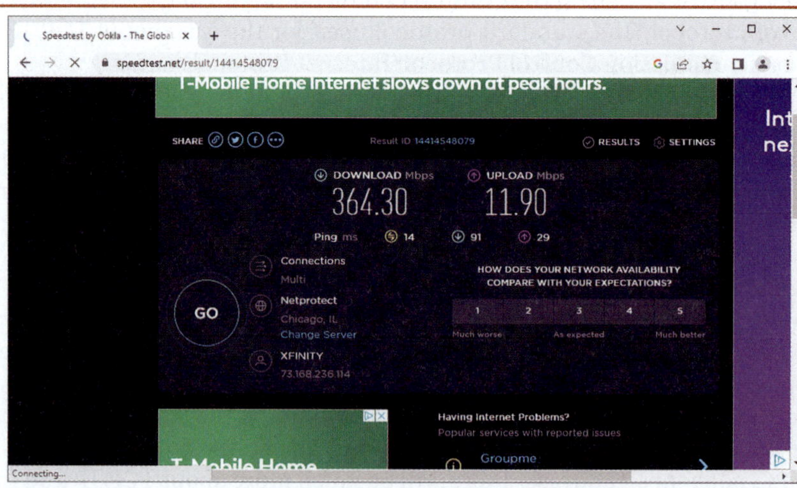

Figure 14-16 The Ookla Speed Test website is an excellent utility to determine the speed of your Internet connection.

Goodheart-Willcox Publisher

Telephone Modem Troubleshooting

Use the following suggestions when troubleshooting a telephone modem:

- Always check the modem cables and connections first. People tend not to check cabling unless told to do so, but you should *not* waste valuable time until you check the most obvious and common problem. A modem connection can be easily disturbed by vacuum cleaners, plugging in other equipment, or moving furniture.
- Check the telephone cable and telephone line. Faulty wiring along the telephone cable can be the cause. Try plugging in a standard telephone.
- Try dialing a local or test telephone number. Use the computer's Phone Dialer to call the phone number of a phone on a neighboring desk. If the modem is operational and installed correctly, the phone should ring.
- Check the call-waiting function on the modem or dialer setup.
- Check if there is a time-out feature being used for the modem. Some modems cut off after a set period of inactivity.
- Check with the phone company if any lines are out. Look for communication vehicles in the area of the company or residence with a modem problem. If you are called to a business for a modem problem and you see a communication vehicle sitting beside a ditch on your way there, it may save you a lot of frustration troubleshooting the modem if you stop and ask a few questions.
- If the modem is connecting but you are receiving or transmitting gibberish, then you probably have a software issue. Check the manufacturer's website for recent upgrades and patches.
- Always assume that someone has already attempted to correct the problem before you were called. You may have to correct several problems before you detect the original one.

DSL Modem Troubleshooting

Use the following suggestions when troubleshooting a DSL modem:

- Check the status lights on the DSL modem.
- Check the cable connections at the DSL modem, computer, and the telephone wall jack.
- Reboot the computer.
- Reboot the DSL modem by disconnecting the power to the DSL modem, waiting for 30 seconds or more, and then reconnecting the power to the DSL modem.
- Call your service provider for further assistance.

Cable Modem Troubleshooting

If the cable modem has a reset button, press and hold it for five seconds before releasing. If it does not have a reset button, try power cycling it. The following steps can be used to power cycle your modem:

1. Shut down your computer.
2. Unplug the cable modem from the electrical outlet.
3. Leave the cable modem unplugged for at least 10 seconds.
4. Plug the cable modem back into the electrical outlet, wait at least 30 seconds or more, and restart your computer.
5. Check your cable service provider for possible outage.

eMTA Modem Troubleshooting

Resetting an eMTA modem is similar to resetting a cable modem but with one distinct difference. The eMTA modem typically has a reset button not found on cable modems. To reset the eMTA mode, press the reset button on the back of the eMTA with a pen or other pointed, nonmetallic object. Keep the button pressed until the lights in the front of the device go off and then release the reset button. The unit will reset itself, but it could take up to five minutes. If the reset does not correct the problem, you should call the service provider.

Mobile Broadband Modem Troubleshooting

Troubleshooting a mobile broadband modem is easy in contrast to troubleshooting a telephone modem. If it is a USB device, remove it from the USB port, then wait a few minutes, and reinsert it. If it is a hotspot device, disconnect it from the electrical power, wait a few minutes, and then plug it back into the outlet. Since mobile wireless broadband is actually a form of network, other methods of testing the connection are explained in the networking section of the textbook. Some devices have troubleshooting software applications that will guide you through some tests. Additionally, service providers have troubleshooting steps and frequently asked questions (FAQs) listed at their websites, typically under a support web page.

Wireless Hotspot Troubleshooting

Use the following steps when troubleshooting a wireless hotspot:

1. Verify that you are in your service provider coverage area.
2. Power the unit off for 30 seconds and then turn it back on.
3. Check if the SIM is inserted properly.
4. Verify device status and signal strength as displayed by the device LEDs.
5. Check if "work offline" mode has been enabled.
6. Open **Windows Network and Sharing Center** and disable the Wi-Fi connection; then, reconnect to the Wi-Fi hotspot network.

Chapter Summary

14.1 Public Telephone System

- The public telephone system has been serving the public for over 100 years.
- The voice frequency spectrum for the telephone industry operated between 200 Hz and 4,000 Hz. This frequency spectrum is more than adequate for carrying voice, but it is not adequate for high-speed modem connections.
- Bandwidth refers to the range or limit of frequency that a cable or device is designed to carry.
- The public telephone network system (PTNS) is constructed of high-speed fiber-optic cables, microwave transmitters and receivers, digital equipment, and computerized telephone control units.

14.2 Telephone Modems

- The term *modem* is a contraction of two words: *modulator* and *demodulator.*
- Modems perform several steps to make and maintain connections between computers. The act of connecting to another computer using a modem is often referred to as *modem negotiation.* The process of modem negotiation is a series of signals and commands, which includes Data Terminal Ready (DTR), Data Set Ready (DSR), Transmit Data (TD), Receive Data (RD), Carrier Detect (CD), Request to Send (RTS), and Clear to Send (CTS).

14.3 Digital Subscriber Lines

- A digital subscriber line (DSL) provides high-speed Internet access over telephone lines and has become one of the most popular methods for connecting to the Internet.
- DSL can provide a constant connection to the Internet, and it can be used to send and receive both voice and data over the same line.
- The maximum distance DSL can span is limited by the high frequencies it uses. The typical maximum distance for DSL ranges from 1,000 feet to 18,000 feet, measured from the DSL modem to the telephone central office.
- There are many types of DSL, including ADSL, ADSL2+, VDSL2, VDSL2+, SDSL, HDSL, and RADSL.
- A typical DSL modem has a power adapter that converts the standard 120 VAC to the 12 VDC needed to power the modem. A telephone cable connects the DSL modem to the telephone wall jack using RJ-11 connectors. An Ethernet cable—a standard Cat 5 or Cat 5e cable—connects the DSL modem to the network adapter card installed in the PC.
- An additional device called a filter may be required to prevent lower-frequency signals to and from the devices on the same line from interfering with or corrupting the higher-frequency signals used for the Internet connection.
- DSL is a point-to-point connection.

14.4 Cable

- Cable Internet service provides high-speed Internet access over lines designed for cable television and a cable modem to provide continuous connection to the Internet without having to dial in.
- There are two major types of cable television media used for access: coaxial cable and fiber-optic cable.

- A cable modem is similar to a DSL modem. It is installed between a splitter and the PC. The cable splitter divides the signal between a modem and a television. In this configuration, the coaxial cable can supply a television signal to the television as well as provide Internet access for the PC. The cable television coaxial cable connects to the cable modem from the splitter. An Ethernet cable or USB cable is used between the cable modem and the PC.
- Embedded Multimedia Terminal Adapter (eMTA) combines the functionality of a DOCSIS cable modem and a phone adapter in one device, allowing a service provider to provide both Internet access and telephone service to a customer using one device and cable.
- As with dial-up internet, eMTA is far less common today than it once was.

14.5 Satellite

- Satellites are line-of-sight systems that can be used to provide a constant connection to the Internet.
- The data rates for satellites vary greatly.
- Trees and buildings can obstruct the satellite receiver from the source, and satellite systems are also susceptible to weather conditions.

14.6 T-Carrier Lines

- A T-carrier line is an Internet connection designed to carry voice and data over four wires.
- A multiplexer organizes slower-speed data and voice signals into a series of higher speed data packets.
- A demultiplexer converts the packets back to a lower speed.
- There are five levels of T-carrier lines: T-1, T-2, T-3, T-4, and fractional T-1.

14.7 Mobile Broadband

- Mobile wireless broadband is a term used to describe wireless Internet connections based on mobile phone technology.
- Broadband is an electronics term and is a classification of a communication with a bandwidth in excess of 256 kbps.
- A USB modem is a tiny mobile broadband device that plugs into any laptop with a USB port and allows the laptop to connect to the Internet using a mobile broadband service.
- Tethering refers to the sharing of one device's Internet connection with another connected device that does not have an Internet connection.
- A mobile hotspot is a portable wireless router that allows multiple devices to share a common Internet connection.
- The acronyms 3G and 4G represent third generation (3G) and fourth generation (4G) when used in respect to mobile broadband systems.
- 5G capabilities are in the process of being implemented into our mobile and cellular networks, beginning with widespread rollouts that started in 2019. 5G can achieve download speeds of up to 10 GB/s.
- There are three primary areas for 5G application: Enhanced Mobile Broadband (eMBB), Ultra-Reliable Low-Latency Communications (URLLC), and Massive Machine-Type Communications (mMTC).
- Cellular configuration options for most mobile devices include Global mode; LTE and CDMA; and LTE, GSM, or UMTS.
- WiMAX is a wireless technology similar to Wi-Fi but has a much greater range as well as a controllable radio broadcast direction.

- Multiple input multiple output (MIMO) is a wireless technology that uses two or more streams of data transmission to increase the data throughput and range of a wireless network

14.8 Setting Up a Residential Internet Connection

- Most ISPs provide a disc with a wizard program to assist you in setting up a residential Internet connection.
- An *IP address* will be assigned to the modem, which serves as an identification for an Internet-connected device. All devices connected to the Internet, as well as all websites have IP addresses. The Internet communicates using the IP address to identify a website or device as opposed to using the site name seen in a web browser. Software converts the IP address into the name of the site you are trying to reach.
- Actual Internet connection speeds can be determined by running the Ookla Speed Test utility.

14.9 Troubleshooting Modems

- Troubleshooting procedures for Internet service devices are very similar for all devices in that the modem in question requires some form of reset.
- In general, always check your connections first; then escalate.
- Each Internet connection type has unique troubleshooting steps.

Review Questions

1. Recall the characteristics of the public telephone system.
2. What is the main factor that limits the speed of data transfer over the residential telephone system?
3. Summarize the function of a telephone modem.
4. Summarize the process of installing a telephone modem.
5. What are the characteristics of Integrated Services Digital Network (ISDN)?
6. How many channels does a standard ISDN line have, and which channel is used to carry control signals?
7. Describe the operation of a digital subscriber line (DSL).
8. What is the difference between DSL connections and other broadband connections?
9. Provide advantages and disadvantages of cable-based Internet.
10. Give five advantages that fiber-optic cable provides over coaxial cable and typical telephone wiring.
11. List characteristics of satellite Internet.
12. Explain the basic operation of a multiplexer and demultiplexer in T-carrier lines.
13. How is data reorganized as it is transmitted through a multiplexer?
14. Identify characteristics of mobile broadband.
15. What configuration term describes connecting a mobile wireless device such as a smartphone to another device?
16. List and describe three primary areas of application for 5G.
17. Summarize the process of installing and configuring a residential Internet connection.
18. How does the Ookla Speed Test website test a connection speed?
19. List common troubleshooting practices to diagnose modem problems.
20. What is a power cycle?

Sample A+ Exam Questions

1. Which statement best describes the operation of a modem?
   A. A device that converts digital signals from the PC bus system to analog signals that are transmitted across telephone lines
   B. A device that transmits digital signals across telephone lines
   C. A device that converts analog signals from a USB port to digital signals that are transmitted across telephone systems
   D. A device that sends digital signals across various network systems until a digital signal reaches a predetermined PC connection
2. Which of the following has the slowest data transfer rate?
   A. ISDN TA
   B. DSL modem
   C. Cable modem
   D. Dial-up modem
3. Which is an example of tethering?
   A. Using a USB cable to connect two PC desktops together
   B. Sharing a mobile telephone Internet connection with a tablet
   C. Connecting two or more devices to the same UPS
   D. Following a person closely as they enter a secure area
4. What should you do first when you lose a cable modem connection?
   A. Shut the modem down, wait 10 or more seconds, and then restart the modem.
   B. Select a recent system restore point on the first computer that connects to the cable modem.
   C. Go to the outside of the building and disconnect the cable modem cable. Wait two minutes and then reconnect the cable modem.
   D. Replace the cable modem with a known good cable modem.
5. What factors affect the data rate of 3G and 4G services? Select all that apply.
   A. Radio interference
   B. Distance from the service provider
   C. Number of users accessing the service at the same time
   D. Which software application you are using
6. Which connection type is typically found in a residential telephone jack outlet?
   A. RJ-45
   B. RJ-11
   C. BNC
   D. AT-45
7. Which connection type is typically found between a PC and a DSL modem?
   A. RJ-45
   B. RJ-11
   C. BNC
   D. AT-45

8. What would *most likely* affect the bandwidth of a cable Internet connection?
   A. The amplitude of the signal modulation
   B. The number of subscribers sharing the cable line
   C. The distance from the cable modem to the cable provider
   D. Changes in media between the subscriber location and the central office
9. What is the maximum bandwidth using an ISDN line?
   A. 56 kbps
   B. 1.54 Gbps
   C. 128 kbps
   D. 256 kbps
10. What transfer speed is a T-1 line capable of reaching?
   A. 56 kbps
   B. 1.54 kbps
   C. 1.544 Mbps
   D. 2.56 Mbps

Chapter 15

Physical Security and Authentication

Learning Outcomes

15.1 Summarize steps that can be taken to physically secure a workstation.

15.2 Recall methods used to authenticate users and secure individual workstations.

15.3 Discuss the importance of user security education.

A+ Certification Exam Objectives

The following A+ Certification Exam Objectives are covered in this chapter.

Exam 220-1101

1.0 Mobile Devices

- 1.1 Given a scenario, install and configure laptop hardware and components.
- 1.4 Given a scenario, configure basic mobile-device network connectivity and application support.

3.0 Hardware

- 3.4 Given a scenario, install and configure motherboards, central processing units (CPUs), and add-on cards.

Exam 220-1102

1.0 Operating Systems

- 1.1 Identify basic features of Microsoft Windows editions.
- 1.3 Given a scenario, use features and tools of the Microsoft Windows 10 operating system.
- 1.4 Given a scenario, use the appropriate Microsoft Windows 10 Control Panel utility.
- 1.5 Given a scenario, use the appropriate Windows settings.
- 1.7 Given a scenario, apply application installation and configuration concepts.

2.0 Security

- 2.1 Summarize various security measures and their purposes.
- 2.2 Compare and contrast wireless security protocols and authentication methods.
- 2.3 Given a scenario, detect, remove, and prevent malware using the appropriate tools and methods.
- 2.4 Explain common social-engineering attacks, threats, and vulnerabilities.
- 2.5 Given a scenario, manage and configure basic security settings in the Microsoft Windows OS.
- 2.6 Given a scenario, configure a workstation to meet best practices for security.

- 2.7 Explain common methods for securing mobile and embedded devices.
- 2.8 Given a scenario, use common data destruction and disposal methods.
- 2.9 Given a scenario, configure appropriate security settings on small office/home office (SOHO) wireless and wired networks.
- 2.10 Given a scenario, install and configure browsers and relevant security settings.

Key Terms

authentication
dumpster diving
hard disk drive (HDD) password
mantrap
multifactor authentication
power-on password
principle of least privilege (POLP)
privacy filter
radio-frequency identification (RFID)
rainbow table
sanitation
shoulder surfing
social engineering
tailgating
Trusted Platform Module (TPM)
virtual smart card

Overview

This chapter focuses on physical security practices and authenticating users. Computer system security is a vast and detailed subject that cannot be completely covered in a single chapter. Rather, the topic of computer security can fill an entire textbook. This chapter presents an overview of the most common physical security elements required to adequately secure a computer system, authenticate users, and help prepare you for the A+ Certification Exams.

A+ Note

The topic of security has been a major focus of A+ Certification for some time now. It is essential that you be familiar with common security and authentication practices as outlined in this chapter.

A+ 1102: 2.1

15.1 Physical Security

Physical security is the practice of protecting a computer system by securing the computer itself as well as the computer's physical area. First and most importantly, you need to secure the physical location by controlling access to the computer system and data storage areas. If one can physically access a device, it is much easier to break into the device than it would be to break in remotely. Furthermore, if one can physically access a device, there are many options for tampering with the device or simply stealing it, making physical security quite important.

A+ 1102: 2.1, 2.4

As simple as it sounds, you should always lock doors that access the computer and data-storage areas for both personal and large, corporate systems. However, even a locked door can be compromised through actions such as **tailgating**, which occurs when an unauthorized person closely follows an authorized person into a secure area and bypasses the "gate" system. Tailgating can be prevented in high-security areas using a **mantrap**, which is a physical configuration that allows access to exactly one person at a time. A mantrap can be as simple as a turnstile or an *access control vestibule*, which is two sets of doors with a short distance between them. Often, the second set of doors is either on a time delay or some other type of security access feature, such as security guards, biometrics (for example, fingerprint pads), PIN entry, radio-frequency identification (RFID), or proximity cards, all of which are covered later in this section. *Magnetometers*, commonly known as *metal detectors*, can also be employed to enhance entry security.

Electronic methods allow for a digital *entry control roster*, which is similar to a guest list for an exclusive event. If someone is not on the list, they do not get in. A security guard can check names from the list, but having an electronic database with digital means of verification allows for speedy determination of who entered and departed the area under observation.

A+ 1102: 2.1

Securing the Physical Area

The simplest way to secure the physical area of computers or areas containing sensitive data is a common door lock that requires a physical key to gain access. When the lock controls access to the server room, the lock is called a *server lock*. Electronic door lock systems can be used to provide additional security measures as compared to traditional door locks. For example, an electronic door lock system can be equipped with a radio-frequency identification (RFID) system and a push-button system for entering a PIN. Obviously, the more sensitive the data or area being secured, the more advanced the lock you may wish to consider using.

When securing the physical area, it is important to consider the ease with which a person can navigate a building and its surrounding campus. An environment lacking in security can lead to devices being stolen, and then an intruder has unlimited time to work on cracking the system and collecting data. Often, deterrents such as fencing and well-placed lighting—particularly motion-activated lighting—can prove to be a hindrance to thieves or malicious actors. Of course, the precise placement and parameters of deterrents depends entirely on the security needs and building in question.

While fencing and lighting may be useful against unwanted foot traffic, they are not be as protective against vehicles as measures such as bollards. *Bollards* are large, heavy items such as stone planters or metal posts used as barriers in front of buildings or along sidewalks. You have likely seen these in the form of metal poles outside retail stores or governmental buildings to prevent a vehicle from crashing into the building. In some cases, bollards can retract into the ground, such as at the entryway of parking lots, to allow authorized vehicles to enter while keeping unauthorized vehicles out. Effective use of bollards can mitigate vehicle traffic and can help deter actions such as terrorism or robberies.

In addition to securing the outside of a building and the area surrounding computers and servers, an administrator can also secure individual computers and even ports. For example, establishing USB permissions can prevent unauthorized use of USB storage devices and USB locks can be used to prevent unauthorized usage of the USB ports in a computer. USB locks often insert or snap into the desired USB port before being secured and provide the ability to

A+ 1101: 3.4

- restrict organizational data from being copied or transferred to the end-user;
- secure laptops and portable devices when moving the devices;
- secure console panels in a data center that cannot be otherwise disabled;
- protect an organization from malware due to an infected USB device; and
- protect an organization from breaches.

RFID scanners are used in a variety of secure locations, including warehouses, college dorms, and high schools. Many different types of identification badges and key fobs are designed to interact with RFID security systems, and each badge or key fob is unique, allowing them to be assigned to a specific user. Both device types produce exclusive radio signal patterns that activate an electronic lock when a user passes their assigned badge or key fob by the reader. The system can also be programmed to require each user to wave the badge or fob past the reader and enter a PIN into the keypad. The combination of PIN and RFID is an example of *multifactor authentication*, which will be discussed in detail later in this chapter.

Another example of physical security can be a device purchased from a third party, such as Absolute Home and Office. Absolute is a tracking and recovery system that allows the user to lock, locate, and delete files from devices remotely. When a laptop is stolen, the user contacts the police and software company, and the next time the device is connected to the Internet, it is monitored and located by the software company. Absolute was modeled after the LoJack vehicle-recovery system, which uses RFID to recover stolen vehicles.

Many hardware devices can be adopted for user authentication. Some of the different hardware authentication systems use specially designed badges or tokens referred to as *key fob*, *RFID badge*, *RSA token*, and similar names.

Tech Tip

The term *fob* is believed to be based on a word that describes an object other than keys placed on a key ring. Before the digital era, these were often weighted items used to balance a vest and pocket watch.

Radio-Frequency Identification

A+ 1102: 1.7, 2.1

Radio-frequency identification (RFID) is an electronic system that uses radio waves to identify objects or people. A good example of an RFID system is an inventory system for a business or organization. RFID can be incorporated into a hardware device for authentication of personnel. An RFID system consists of an RFID transponder and an RFID reader. The transponder is also referred to as an *RFID tag*, an *RFID badge*, or a *key fob*. Turn your attention to Figure 15-1 to see examples of

Figure 15-1 Radio-frequency identification (RFID) is an electronic system that uses radio waves to identify objects and is often used for tasks such as securing parking lots (A), controlling access to secure rooms (B), and activating mantrap turnstiles (C).

A koonsiri boonnak/Shutterstock.com B Teerasan Phutthigorn/Shutterstock.com C Teerasan Phutthigorn/Shutterstock.com

RFID readers in various applications. There are two major classifications of RFID transponders:

- *Active RFID transponders* use batteries to produce radio wave power.
- *Passive RFID transponders* use the radio wave power received from the reader.

Figure 15-2 illustrates the main parts of a passive RFID system.

An RFID reader consists of an electronic circuit board containing a processor, antenna, and other electronic components. A transponder consists of an antenna and integrated chip, and, depending on the type, it may also have a battery for power. Each transponder is encoded with a unique series of numbers and assigned to a specific person; hence, a unique numeric code represents each person. The RFID reader contains all the electronic components necessary for transmitting and receiving radio waves as well as decoding radio waves from transponders.

The abilities of RFID readers vary by different models and manufacturers. In general, RFID readers can be programmed to respond in a variety of ways, such as sounding an alarm for an unauthorized transponder or opening an electronic door lock for an authorized one. An RFID reader can also be programmed to store information or transmit information to a computer system, which then records the reader's activity. A complete list of personnel who have entered a facility or area can be recorded and stored in a database, most commonly with a time stamp and location of the entry point. The database can be reviewed later to pinpoint the possible source of a security breach. RFID readers can also be programmed to allow only certain transponders to access the area on specific days and at specific times.

The electronic theory of RFID system operation is simple, as shown in Figure 15-3. The RFID reader constantly emits short radio wave pulses. When the transponder is brought into proximity of the RFID reader, the pulsing radio waves emitted from the RFID reader antenna cross over the transponder antenna, creating electrical energy in the transponder antenna and energizing the transponder's integrated chip. When the RFID reader radio wave pulses subside, the transponder's integrated chip transmits a short radio wave pulse to the RFID reader representing a unique sequence of binary numbers. If the transponder's unique code matches a preprogrammed code, the person using the transponder is admitted to the area. If not, the person is denied access.

An active transponder would likely be used to monitor personnel movement inside a facility. The movement of a person could be tracked simply by being in proximity to the reader, and the person would not need to swipe the transponder close to a reader. However, passive transponders have much shorter ranges when compared to active transponders.

A+ 1102: 2.1

Similar to transponders, companies may employ the use of hardware or software tokens. The functionality of hardware tokens varies greatly among devices. Tokens can use RFID technology, biometric data, USB, or Bluetooth in their functionality. Some have to be connected to the computer interface, and others generate a single-use passkey. Hardware tokens come in several forms. For example,

Figure 15-2 A passive RFID transponder uses the radio-wave power received from the reader.

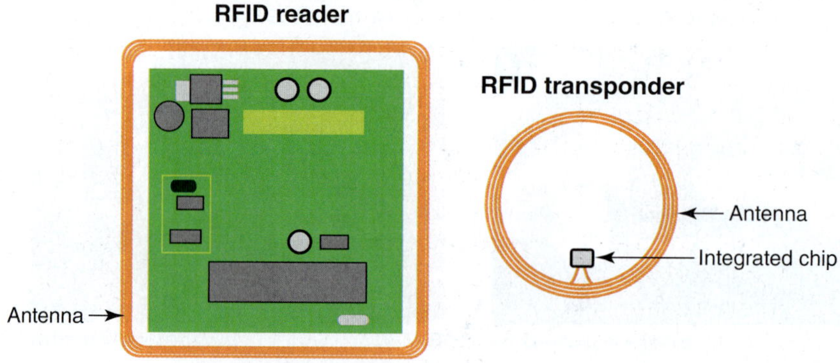

Goodheart-Willcox Publisher

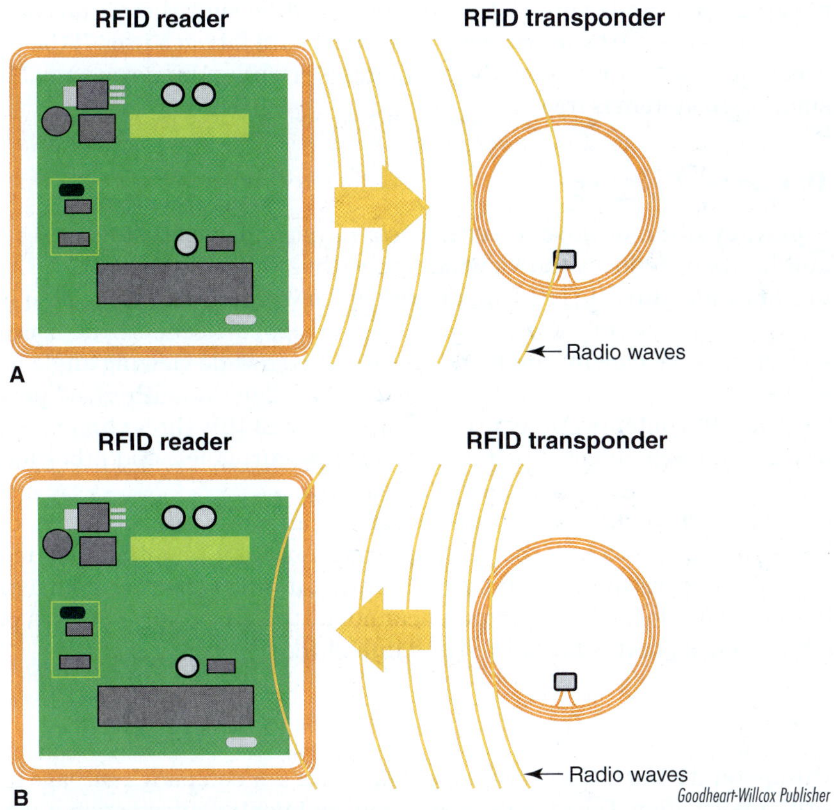

Figure 15-3 When a transponder is brought into the proximity of an RFID reader's radio waves, the integrated chip on the transponder is activated (A). The integrated chip transmits a short radio wave that represents a series of binary numbers (B).

connected tokens must be physically connected to the computer when authenticating, while disconnected tokens, also called *external hardware tokens*, are usually a type of keychain with an on-screen display that shows a passcode or something similar. The choice of hardware tokens depends on both security needs and budget, and the configuration of hardware tokens is specific to the model used.

As the name implies, software tokens run on software and are often used as a form of two-factor authentication and are normally disconnected tokens. For example, authentication apps for smartphones generate a single-use passcode or token to be used in addition to login credentials.

Smart Cards and Virtual Smart Cards

A+ 1102: 2.1

Smart cards are often used as hardware-connected tokens in conjunction with a PIN or password. In this arrangement, the card is inserted into a reader or scanned, and then the user enters a PIN to gain access to the computer system. Windows 8 was the first Microsoft operating system to introduce a virtual smart card application, but the technology still applies to Windows 10 and 11 as well as Windows Server 2016 and 2019. Similar to smart cards are Common Access Cards (CACs), which are used by the US military. These cards serve the same purpose as smart cards in that they are manufactured with integrated chips used for authentication, but they also serve as identification cards.

A **virtual smart card** is a simulated card created by a combination of software and integrated circuits instead of a physical card. If there are multiple users for a single computer, each user can have his or her own virtual smart card. Virtual smart cards use a *Trusted Platform Module (TPM)*, which is an integrated chip discussed later in this chapter. Chances are, if the computer uses UEFI firmware, it has a TPM incorporated into the motherboard.

Virtual smart cards have two advantages over physical smart cards. First, virtual smart cards are more convenient than physical smart cards because they are always present and cannot be lost or misplaced. Second, there is no cost of purchasing a physical smart card reader and a smart card for each user. If the motherboard is equipped with a TPM and the computer is running Windows 10 or 11, the virtual smart card system is free.

A+ 1101: 1.1

Privacy Filters

A **privacy filter**, or *privacy screen*, is a physical device that attaches to a display and limits or reduces the viewing angle, thus reducing the risk of shoulder surfing. **Shoulder surfing** is the unauthorized viewing of a display to gain information. Computer and mobile device screens are designed to enable the user to have the widest-possible viewing angle. While providing a wide viewing angle is convenient for the user, it poses a security risk because it allows unauthorized persons also to view screen contents. Many users do not think of this threat and use their mobile devices in public places such as coffee shops, airplanes, and other locations that make shoulder surfing quite easy and effective.

On most Windows computers, users can press the keyboard combination [Windows key][L] to lock the desktop to help prevent unauthorized access when a user is not operating the computer. However, it is less effective than a privacy filter because when locked, the computer cannot be used to perform tasks. A privacy filter offers security both when locked and unlocked.

A+ 1102: 2.4

Dumpster Diving

Dumpster diving is the act of inspecting a user's or company's garbage to locate sensitive information. Documents containing confidential information must be secured properly, such as in locked areas or file cabinets equipped with locks, and when a document is no longer needed, it should be destroyed and not simply thrown into the trash. For example, medical records contain patient information that often includes home addresses, phone numbers, credit card numbers, insurance data, and other sensitive information concerning the patient. These documents contain information that can be used for identity theft, so they should be destroyed when no longer needed.

Documents should be shredded with a cross-cut shredder and, if possible, burned. Even in this modern age of digital systems, many security breaches occur from improperly stored and improperly disposed of paper documents. There are service companies that specialize in the destruction of documents and can be contracted if an organization handles a significant amount of sensitive data.

A+ 1102: 2.8

Disposal of Computer Equipment

Computer equipment is often replaced or updated, which leads to the disposal of the original, obsolete equipment. For example, all the PCs in a company or department could be updated with new PC models, and all the old PCs could be donated to a charity or auctioned off to members of the public. The old computer systems could contain user identity information such as Social Security numbers, addresses, and more. Sensitive material is not just limited to personal information. Think of all the data collected by banks, medical offices, credit card companies, police departments, personnel departments, education facilities, and department stores. Computer equipment also may contain company secrets related to manufacturing and design.

The data-storage system of any device being discarded should be completely wiped clean or made secure by destroying the media. The procedure for erasing data is often based on company policies and preference of individual users. Removal of data from a storage media such as a hard drive is referred to as **sanitation**. One way to erase data from a hard drive and allow it to be used again without risk is to perform a low-level format, which completely erases data stored on a hard drive by writing a series of binary zeros across the entire drive, no matter which operating system created the directory and file structure. Low-level format utilities are available through hard drive manufacturers or third-party software companies.

In contrast, the Windows **Quick Format** option does not completely erase the data. Instead, the **Quick Format** option only erases file names and leaves the data in the file, which can be recovered by third-party tools. The **Quick Format** is intended for actions such as an operating system refresh.

Low-level formatting can take a long time, especially for large storage systems. Faster methods of destroying data that do not take a great deal of time are drilling a hole through the storage media, degaussing the media, and physically destroying the media using a hammer. Drilling a hole through a hard drive will shatter the discs, rendering the drive unusable. *Degaussing* the drive is a matter of bringing a very strong electromagnetic tool in proximity to the hard drive, which will erase all data on the hard drive. When you use a degaussing tool, you will *not* be able to reuse the hard drive. This method will only work successfully with a magnetic hard disk drive and will not work on a solid-state drive (SSD), so physical destruction is the surest approach to reducing the risk with an SSD. Methods of destruction include

A+ 1102: 2.8

- shredders;
- drills and hammers for hard drives and circuit boards;
- overwriting of memory (zeros, ones, and random values), called a *drive wipe*; and
- incineration of paper material.

Additionally, a company or user can opt to have a third party destroy the hardware and issue a certificate of destruction. This verifies that the device has been destroyed and data cannot be recovered.

Physical Drive Encryption

A+ 1102: 2.6

Encryption is a method of coding data so it cannot be converted back to meaningful words without a key. In terms of securing a computer system, encryption is often the last line of defense. Imagine a situation in which a person bypasses all physical security measures and accesses a computer system containing sensitive data, such as Social Security numbers. Without encryption, that data could easily be compromised. Systems of encryption vary in their levels of complexity; however, the generally accepted rule is that the more heavily something is encrypted, the safer it is. While the encryption itself is digital, it is a means of securing physical devices that can be easily removed and inserted into a pocket or bag, such as hard drives and flash drives. Examples of encryption that are relatively easy and inexpensive to implement include Trusted Platform Module (TPM) and BitLocker. Both file encryption and drive encryption are types of *data-at-rest encryption*, meaning the data is stored and not in transit. This contrasts from e-mail encryption, which is a form of *data-in-transit encryption.*

Trusted Platform Module

A+ 1101: 3.4

The **Trusted Platform Module (TPM)** is an integrated chip incorporated into motherboards that can create and store cryptographic keys. The keys protect information such as file contents, passwords, and PINs. The TPM standard was developed by the Trusted Computing Group (TCG) organization, and its properties are specified in the ISO/IEC 11889 standard. TPM is at the very heart of Windows BitLocker Drive Encryption and virtual smart card system security. As of this writing, the current iteration of TPM is 2.0, which is a system requirement for Windows 11.

The TPM is also used as part of a security system that checks a computer for changes during the boot sequence that could compromise the system. For example, the TPM stores an encrypted description of the condition of the computer system relating to the BIOS configuration and any changes to the startup programs and files. However, for this to function properly, the BIOS of the computer must support

TPM or USB devices at startup. Normally, a drive with BitLocker enabled checks the computer TPM for the PIN or key during the boot operation automatically. If no security concern or problem has been detected, the computer continues its normal boot sequence. However, if a change to the computer startup files or BIOS has been detected, the TPM requires a special recovery key to unlock the encrypted system. The recovery key is created when the BitLocker feature is first enabled on the computer. The security check made by the BitLocker feature and TPM goes unnoticed by the user unless prompted for the recovery key when a security problem is detected. BitLocker will be discussed in detail in a later section.

TPM helps ensure that only designated hardware is attached to the machine and provides support for encryption. TPMs consist of a specialized processor chip that is dedicated to cryptographic functions, which often involves generating and storing cryptographic keys.

A+ 1101: 3.4

Hardware Security Module

A *hardware security module (HSM)* is a physical device that manages digital keys and signatures and performs encryption/decryption tasks. There are two general types of HSMs: plug-in cards and embedded modules, which are often built as part of other hardware such as smart cards or appliances. Federal Information Processing (FIPS) standard 140 lists cryptographic modules as one of the requirements for certain levels of FIPS security, and they have become a central piece for ensuring data security. They can function at either the workstation or server level and secure a wide range of data, including banking information, mobile and online payments, cryptocurrencies, medical devices, and digital documentation, among others. HSMs usually have technology to prevent tampering with the device itself to prevent would-be attackers from removing or disabling it.

A+ 1101: 3.4
1102: 2.1, 2.5

BitLocker Drive Encryption

BitLocker Drive Encryption, shown in Figure 15-4, is a Microsoft feature that allows the user to encrypt an entire hard drive. BitLocker stores the encryption key in the TPM, and when a TPM is not incorporated into the motherboard, BitLocker can store the encryption key on a flash drive. Beginning with Windows 10, BitLocker supports both 128-bit and 256-bit XTS-AES keys. What makes BitLocker unique as compared to NTFS file encryption is BitLocker encrypts the entire drive, not just directory files. Additionally, BitLocker protects the data against theft. For example, if someone

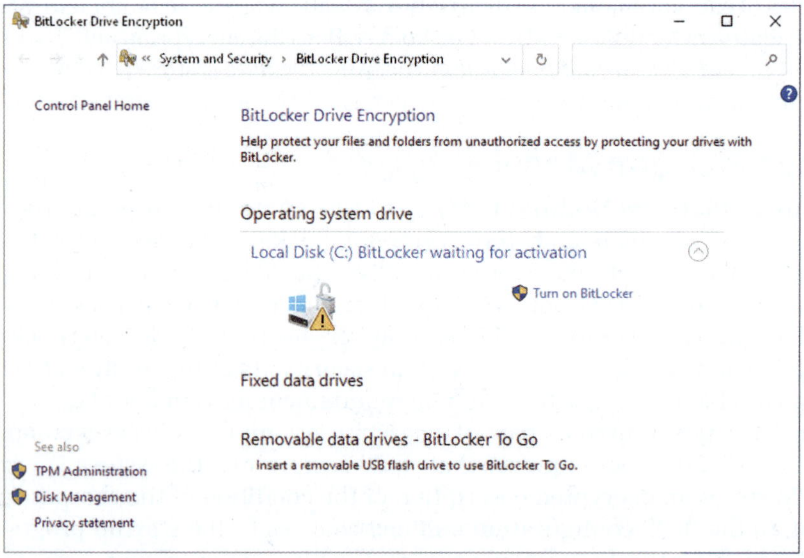

Figure 15-4 Windows BitLocker Drive Encryption encrypts the contents of an entire hard drive. BitLocker To Go can encrypt removable data drives.

Goodheart-Willcox Publisher

removes a hard drive protected by BitLocker and then attempts to access the drive, that person will be prompted for a PIN or encryption key, and the drive contents will remain inaccessible unless the PIN or key is entered correctly. This is also true when an unauthorized person attempts to access the BitLocker-secured drive from across a network system. BitLocker was first included in Windows 7 Ultimate and Enterprise editions and remains available in Windows 10 and Windows 11 Professional editions. BitLocker is not available for Windows Home editions.

Also introduced in Windows 7, BitLocker To Go is a version of BitLocker designed for the encryption of portable storage devices, such as external USB hard drives or USB flash drives. Files on a USB drive can be encrypted and then the drive removed, taken to another computer, and opened with the PIN. Like BitLocker, BitLocker To Go is not available for Windows Home editions.

15.2 Authentication and Workstation Security

1102: 2.2 A+

Authentication is the process of verifying a user's identity. Authentication is at the very heart of computer security and can be software-or user-based. Examples of software-based authentication include Remote Authentication Dial-in User Service (RADIUS), which performs the function of server authentication, and Terminal Access Controller Access Control System (TACACS). TACACS is quite dated, but variations of it such as TACACS+ and XTACACS are widely used. In terms of user-based authentication, the most common form is the user account password.

Passwords

1102: 2.5, 2.6 A+

Passwords are a controversial topic, with some people even claiming passwords to be "dead." However, as of 2023, passwords are still widely used, though it is always best to use a password with a secondary form of authentication such as biometrics or a keycard. Most sources recommend passwords that are complex and composed of a random mixture of letters (both uppercase and lowercase), numbers, and symbols. The symbols that can be used as part of the password depend on the operating system. There may be also a minimum and maximum length for the password. Passwords should not be names or words found in a dictionary, as these are considered weak passwords. By contrast, strong passwords are those created using combinations of words and other symbols that a reasonable person would not be able to guess. As shown in Figure 15-5, the security of a password can be improved

Password Examples

Complex	Simple
Night$tar1	Star
Brend^01	Brenda
Dog$uper5	BigDog
Pa$$word_1	Password
Acce$$005	Access
Mountain_Blue3	Bluemountain
Rock{123}Surf	RockSurf
[h^rle$_01	Charles

Goodheart-Willcox Publisher

Figure 15-5 A complex password combines numbers, letters, and special symbols in a way that has no meaning to a typical person. Common names, words, and phrases make for poor passwords.

by substituting symbols for letters, such as the dollar symbol ($) for *S*, the caret symbol (^) for *A*, or the open bracket symbol ([) symbol for *C*.

The problem with secure passwords—ones that are seemingly random—is that they are quite difficult to remember. A passphrase is often easier to remember. A **passphrase** is a short phrase that is not easily guessed, relevant specifically to you, memorable, and able to be made complex. For example, if soccer is one of your hobbies, do not use any passphrase connected to soccer that might be guessable. Instead, use something that is contrary to your own personality. In this instance, a good passphrase would be *ILoveBasketball* since no one is likely to guess that, and you can then replace letters with numbers or symbols, turning it into *!Lov3B@$k3tb@ll*. You now have a 15-character passphrase with numbers, letters, and special characters. Additionally, it is contrary to your personality, which makes it unlikely to be guessed, but it is also very easy to remember.

A+ Note

The A+ Certification Exams often have test items regarding password protection. A good rule of thumb is to select the answer that provides for the most secure password.

A+ 1102: 2.10

Rainbow Tables

Windows and many other systems store passwords as hashes, and many people have an interest in breaking hashes. *Hashing* is the process of transforming a password or text string into new values. Cryptographic hashes are not reversible, which is why many systems use them to store passwords. However, a simple technique called a rainbow table has been developed to try and extract passwords from lists of hashed passwords. A **rainbow table** is a password-cracking method that uses a precomputed table of password hashes to search for a given hash, which yields the plaintext used to produce the hash.

Obviously, rainbow tables get very large very fast. Assuming passwords must be limited to keyboard characters, that leaves 52 letters (26 uppercase and 26 lowercase), 10 digits, and roughly 10 symbols, or about 72 characters total. As you can imagine, even a six-character password has a very large number of possible combinations. This means there is a limit to how large a rainbow table can be, and this is why longer passwords and passphrases are more secure than shorter passwords.

Since the development of rainbow tables, there have been methods designed to thwart such attacks. The most common is *salting*, which adds random bits to password hashes to further secure encryption. Essentially, random bits, called a *salt*, is intermixed with the message that is to be hashed. For example, assume your password is *pass001*, which translates to 01110000 01100001 01110011 01110011 00110000 00110000 00110001 in binary. A salt algorithm adds bits somewhere within the binary code, such as an extra eight bits at the end or sets of four bits spaced throughout. The value is then hashed and stored. All this is transparent to the end user, who is unaware that salting is occurring. Should an attacker using a rainbow table uncover this hash, they should end up receiving the incorrect password due to the extra bits added throughout the binary string.

A+ 1102: 2.4

Protecting Your Password

Even a secure password can be jeopardized by telling someone your password or creating a password that is easy to guess. The following suggestions can help you protect your password:

- Never let anyone watch you enter your password.
- Never reveal your password to anyone or transmit a password in an e-mail.
- Never reveal your password to a supervisor or system administrator.
- Hint features are not recommended, but if you have to use one, do not use an obvious hint, such as My dog's name.
- Do not use the "remember password" feature found in programs such as Outlook, Facebook, or other websites.
- Do not allow your browsers to store passwords (in most cases, you must deliberately turn off this feature).

- Never write down a password.
- Do not give your password to someone temporarily.
- Do not give your password to a PC technician.
- Change passwords often, at least every four to six months, and do not reuse passwords when changing.
- Passwords should contain numbers, special characters, and a mix of both uppercase and lowercase letters. This helps to prevent or reduce the likelihood of a *brute force attack*, which is when a person repeatedly tries various usernames and passwords until a combination works.
- Never use words found in any dictionary as a password. This helps prevent *dictionary attacks*, which is a type of brute force attack that relies on a long list of commonly used words and phrases, called a *dictionary list*, that a person uses to try to crack a password.

System Configuration Passwords

A+ 1101: 3.4
1102: 2.6

The operating system typically prompts for a username and password at login, which is the last step in a successful system boot. However, there can be other passwords configured for a computer. For example, the BIOS/UEFI can be configured with a password to restrict access to BIOS/UEFI configuration changes. The user must present a password before changes can be made.

Another type is the **power-on password**, also known as the *computer user password* or *boot password*, which is a BIOS/UEFI password entered during the POST before the operating system is loaded. This prevents booting from external devices, such as flash drives or external hard drives.

Similar to a BIOS/UEFI user password is a third type of hardware password known as the HDD password. The **hard disk drive (HDD) password**, also known as the *drive lock password* or *hard disk drive lock password*, is a type of password that requests a login password from the user. Comparable to BitLocker, the HDD password is unique to the hard drive, not the computer. It is intended as additional protection in the event a hard drive is stolen and prevents unauthorized access to the data stored on the hard drive.

Screen Saver Password

A+ 1102: 2.6

Ideally, a user should log off from the computer system when away from the computer. However, many people forget to do so. To account for this, Microsoft has an option that allows a computer to be protected when a user steps away from it. The screen saver program has an option that, when enabled, requires the user to log on to the computer using a password, as shown in Figure 15-6. The exact amount of time required to force a user logon screen varies. Similarly, the computer can be set to lock after an established amount of time, requiring a password to unlock it.

Biometrics

A+ 1102: 2.1, 2.7

Recall from Chapter 13 that *biometrics* is the science of using a person's unique physical features to confirm their identity for authentication purposes. Common biometric devices are fingerprint scanners, palm scanners, and retinal eye scanners. Figure 15-7 shows a biometric fingerprint reader that can be installed on any computer with a USB port. Once installed, the device creates a virtual hard drive partition that only gives access to the user who configured the fingerprint scanner. A fingerprint device, when used in conjunction with a user password, is an example of multifactor authentication.

Multifactor Authentication

A+ 1102: 2.1, 2.2, 2.5

Multifactor authentication is a combination of two or more authentication techniques and makes unauthorized access much more difficult. Authentication

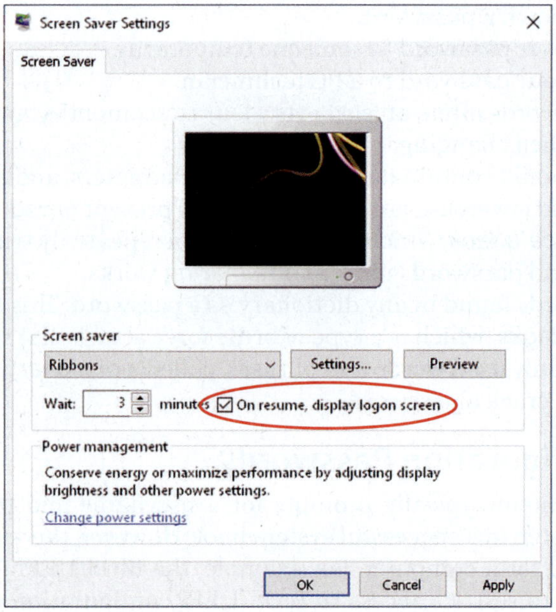

Figure 15-6 Screen savers can be configured to require a user to log on using a password after the computer has been unattended for a period.

Goodheart-Willcox Publisher

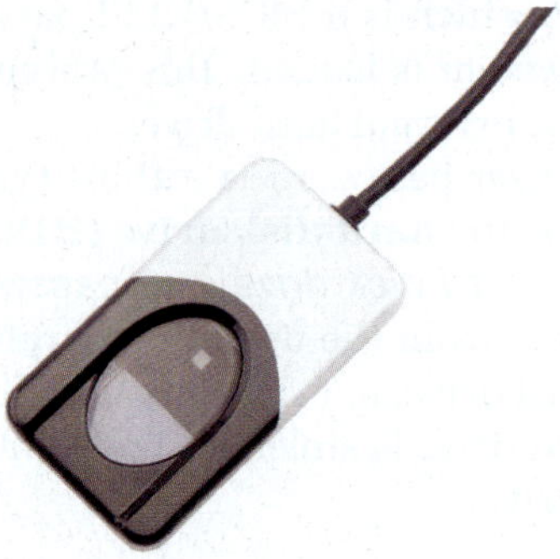

Figure 15-7 USB biometric fingerprint readers can be added to an existing computer system using any available USB port.

dailin/Shutterstock.com

techniques are divided into three categories: something you know, something you have, and something you are.

- **Something you know:** password, PIN, or pattern
- **Something you have:** smart card, key fob, or ID card with a magnetic strip
- **Something you are:** biometric identifier such as fingerprint, retinal eye scan, voice recognition, or facial recognition

The exact methods of authentication required depend on the desired level of security for protecting the computer system and storage data. You would expect the common home user to need no more than password protection, but systems within organizations like a bank, investment company, or governmental buildings would certainly require much more than a simple password.

A+ 1101: 1.4

A+ 1102: 2.1

Currently, many social media and governmental platforms provide *two-step authentication*, which involves signing into an account and verifying the action on a separate device linked to the same account. This requires a person to have access to more than one device. Examples of organizations that allow two-step authentication include Google, Facebook, Twitter, the Social Security Administration, and many more.

A common way to accomplish multifactor authentication is via short message service (SMS) message. When a user attempted to log on to a system, a code is messaged to the user, which they enter along with their password. These codes are usually used one time, and they expire in a short period of time. This can also be accomplished with a voice call; however, SMS messaging is more convenient and thus more common.

User Accounts

1102: 1.3, 1.4, 1.5, 2.5, 2.6 A+

Of all the methods to achieve authentication, none is used more often than the user account. The user account, which consists of a username and password, is assigned during the installation of the computer operating system or after a user purchases a computer. When a user purchases a computer, the user account is created the first time the user boots the new computer. A network administrator can also create a user account, the process of which is covered in detail later in the textbook. A user account created and stored on a computer is referred to as the *local user account.* A user account created for a network is referred to as a *domain user account* or *network account.*

User accounts determine a user's privilege and permission set, which are two different aspects of computer security. By Microsoft definition, permissions apply to objects, while privileges apply to user accounts. In other words, the term *permission* applies to a user's ability to access an object such as a file and *privilege* applies to a user's ability to make changes to the computer configuration or install a software program. The term *rights* is also used to describe user permissions and privileges such as the right to access a specific file or folder.

Tech Tip

The three terms *permissions*, *privileges*, and *rights* are often used interchangeably, even though they have subtle differences in their meanings.

The username and password are controlled under the local computer **User Accounts** dialog box. In Windows 10, it is accessed through **Control Panel>User Accounts>Credential Manager.** Figure 15-8 shows the **User Accounts** category, which allows you to change the account type, manage account credentials, and remove user accounts.

User accounts are created in the **User Accounts** dialog box, which appears in Figure 15-9. In Windows 10, the user can create an account at **Control Panel>User Accounts>User Accounts>Manage Accounts.** The User Account Control (UAC) feature is incorporated into the user account and determines which permissions or privileges are assigned to the user. The UAC assigns permissions to the user account, and those permissions determine what the user can do to the computer system, such as install a software program.

Microsoft operating systems come with a set of built-in user account assignments that vary somewhat according to the operating system version. Beginning with Windows Vista, the three account assignments have been administrator, standard, and guest. Features and restrictions for those account assignments are as follows:

1102: 2.5 A+

- **Administrator**: Administrators can create, change, or delete a user account; install programs and access all files; and make system-wide changes. While performing system changes, the administrator may be required to provide the administrator password.

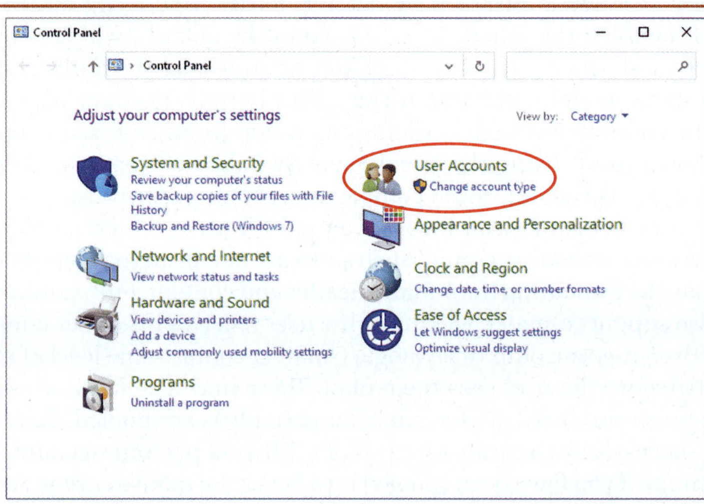

Goodheart-Willcox Publisher

Figure 15-8 Username and password settings and options are controlled in the Windows 10 **Control Panel>User Accounts** menu.

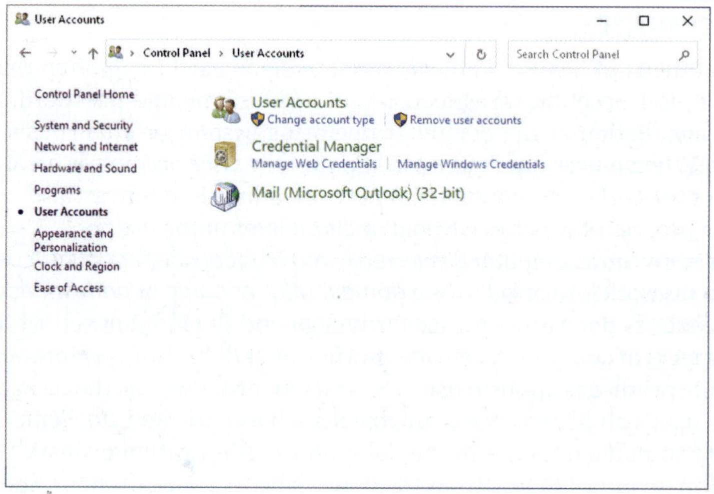

Figure 15-9 The **User Accounts** menu is used to create, delete, or modify user accounts on the local computer.

Goodheart-Willcox Publisher

- **Standard:** This account is designated for everyday use and not as powerful as the administrator account. If you want to make configuration changes that affect other users of the computer, such as installing software or changing security settings, you may need to provide the administrator password.
- **Guest:** This account allows the user to perform basic functions such as checking e-mail and using the Internet. Guest accounts are typically used as temporary accounts, and they cannot make any changes to the system configuration or install new software or hardware. The guest account is disabled by default, but it can be enabled through the **User Account Control** dialog box.

When you create an administrator, standard, or guest account in Windows, you can choose two ways to sign in: local account or Microsoft account. With a local account, you sign in with a username (with or without a password), and you can access files, settings, and apps on just your local PC. With a Microsoft account, you sign in with an e-mail address as your username, and you are given access to not only your favorite apps and unique settings and preferences on any PC, but also to Microsoft cloud services. This enables you to access your Microsoft cloud from any PC on any network.

Tech Tip

Regardless of the operating system, always create at least two user accounts with administrative privileges. If you only have one account with administrative privileges and that account becomes corrupted, you may not be able to access the computer system and thus lose access to all computer files and directories.

Two common security recommendations concerning user accounts in all Windows versions are changing the default usernames and ensuring the guest account is disabled. The concept of changing default usernames generally refers to the built-in administrator account. Beginning with Windows Vista, the built-in administrator account is disabled by default. Earlier operating systems, such as Windows XP, enabled the administrator account by default, which is now considered a security risk since anyone would likely assume that the built-in administrator account name is *Administrator*. If the administrator account also has a weak password, the computer system could be easily compromised. You can restore the administrator account using the Local Security Policy editor, provided you use a password that meets the minimum complexity rule for passwords.

A+ 1102: 2.4

Another user account issue involves e-mail filtering, which employs software designed to remove offending e-mail. Such software can be in the form of a filter used to remove spam by evaluating the e-mail's header and content. Full-suite antimalware programs also support e-mail checking. If the user receives his or her e-mail through a Microsoft Exchange account or a Google Gmail account, some level of malware filtering occurs before the user sees the e-mail. There may also be times when e-mail appears to come from a known user, but it has actually been spoofed. *Spoofing* occurs when a user successfully commits a forgery of a different person's account. The easiest way to determine if you have been spoofed is to hover the mouse cursor over the sender's information address to see if more accurate address details appear on the screen.

Principle of Least Privilege

1102: 2.1 A+

Principle of least privilege (POLP) is a security concept that states a user should only have enough privileges to complete their work tasks. In other words, not all users need to have full administrative privileges. This principle is the cornerstone of security and while simple, POLP alone can dramatically improve security. While POLP is not a common practice for home use, it is not only designed for the workplace. If a user account is compromised while the user is performing routine tasks and the user has been assigned full administrative privileges, then the entire computer system is vulnerable because the unauthorized person is equal to the administrator. Microsoft, as well as security experts, recommends that all users, including the system administrator, use a standard or limited user account when performing day-to-day tasks on a computer.

Local Security Policy Management

1102: 1.4, 1.5, 1.7 A+

The **Local Security Policy** editor is a feature that allows a computer user with administrator privileges to modify the default security configuration of a computer. The system security configuration is described as a policy, and the **Local Security Policy** sets the parameters of user permissions. Establishing permissions allows or limits the performance of certain tasks such as installing software. This helps maintain both device and network security as well as limits the impact of potential security breaches.

Permissions can be configured to make computer system features more secure than their default settings. For example, user passwords can be enforced to be more secure using a Password Policy. In Figure 15-10, the **Local Security Policy** editor has the security settings for **Password Policy** expanded, showing the security settings that can be configured for the user password to enhance security. The settings related to password security are **Enforce password history**, **Maximum password age**, **Minimum password age**, **Minimum password length**, **Password must meet complexity requirements**, and **Store passwords using reversible encryption**. These security options are not enabled by default but can be enabled through the **Local Security Policy** editor to force all users to follow enhanced security password best practices.

The **Local Security Policy** editor also allows you to change the default name of the built-in administrator or guest account. To access the **Local Security Policy** editor, enter secpol.msc into the **Search** box. The **secpol.msc** file is a Microsoft

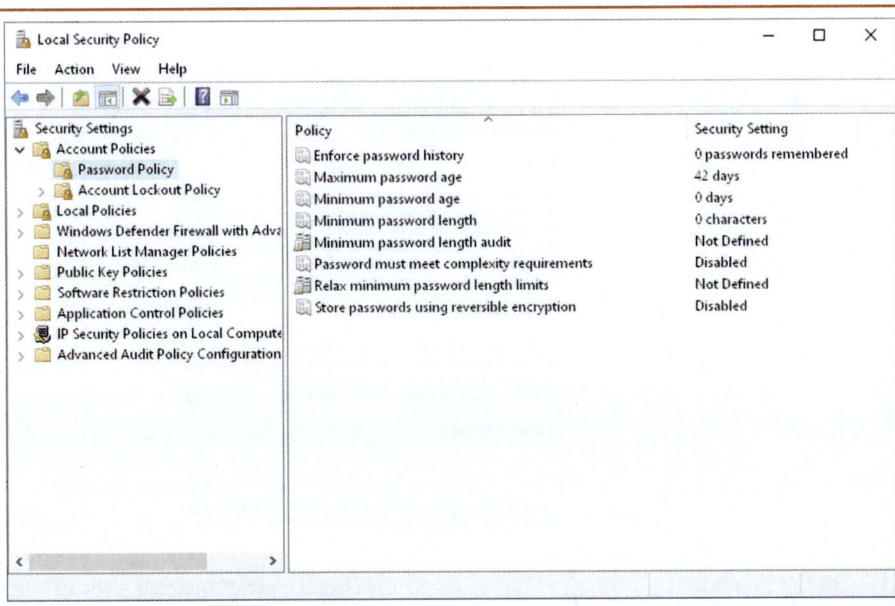

Goodheart-Willcox Publisher

Figure 15-10 The Windows **Local Security Policy** dialog box allows the system administrator to change the default security settings of the computer system.

Management Console snap-in application and is only available for Windows editions such as Professional, Ultimate, and Enterprise. It is *not* available in Home editions.

Figure 15-11 shows the **Security Options** section of the **Local Security Policy** editor. The first policy listed relates to the Administrator account status. Figure 15-12 shows the dialog box presented for restoring the Administrator account as well as an explanation concerning enabling and disabling the Administrator account.

The **Local Security Policy** editor provides a vast array of options to increase or decrease computer system security, such as security features concerning network

Figure 15-11 The **Local Security Policy** editor allows you to change default security configurations, including **Security Options**.

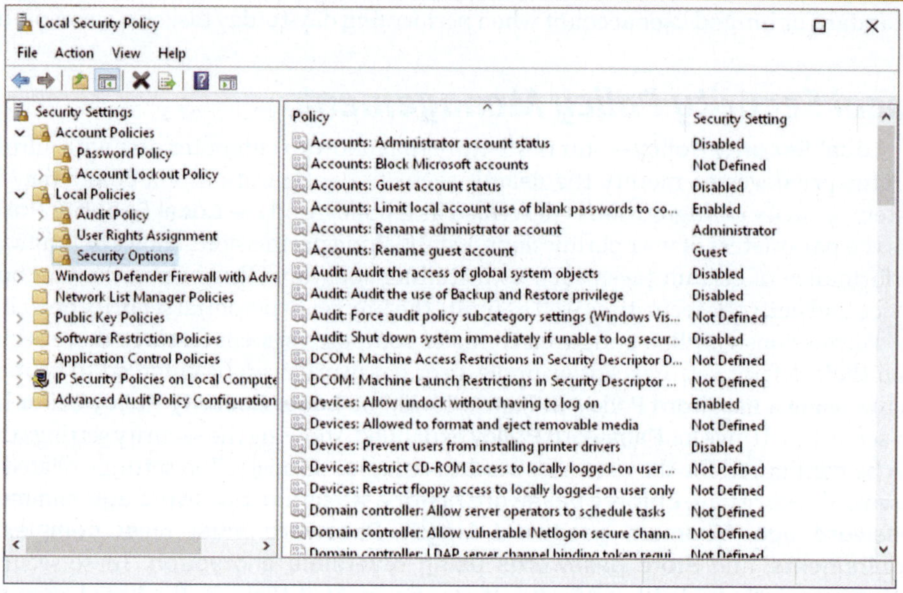

Goodheart-Willcox Publisher

Figure 15-12 Beginning with Windows Vista, the built-in administrator account is disabled by default (A) and cannot be enabled unless a user has privileges equal to those found in an administrator account (B).

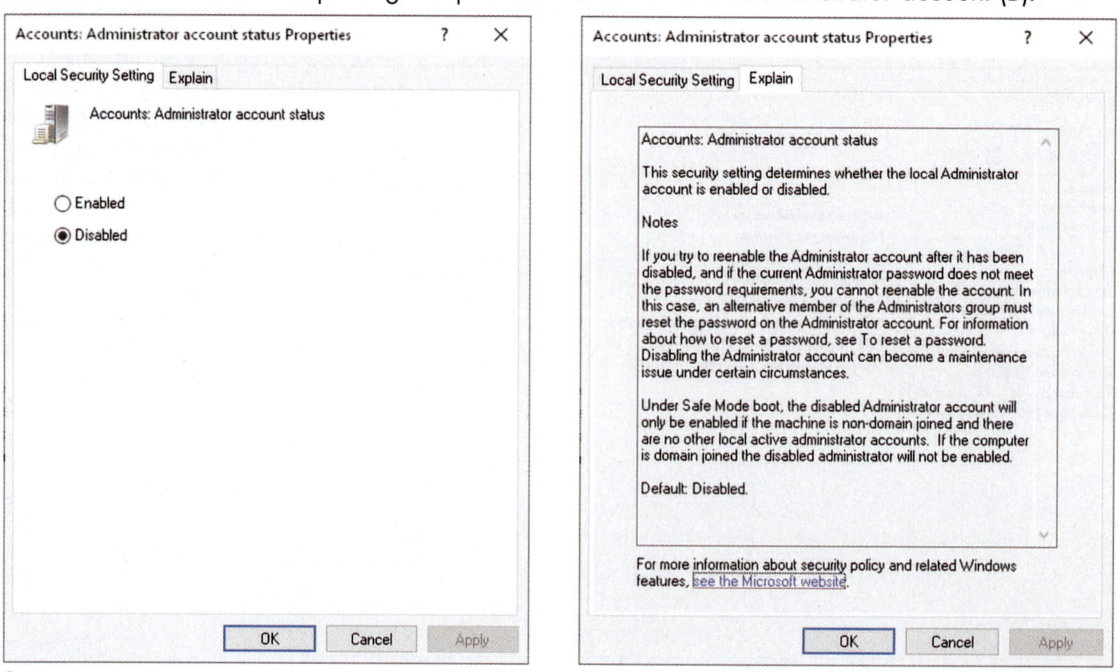

A B

Goodheart-Willcox Publisher

access, software restrictions, hardware device restrictions, and more. To see an example of just how restrictive some of the policies are, look at the expanded **User Rights Assignment** section in Figure 15-13 and take note of the **Back up files and directories** option. Any user can be restricted from making copies of any file or directory on the computer system, and it is common to configure computers to restrict users from making copies of sensitive computer information. Figure 15-14 shows the dialog boxes presented when the **Back up files and directories** option is selected.

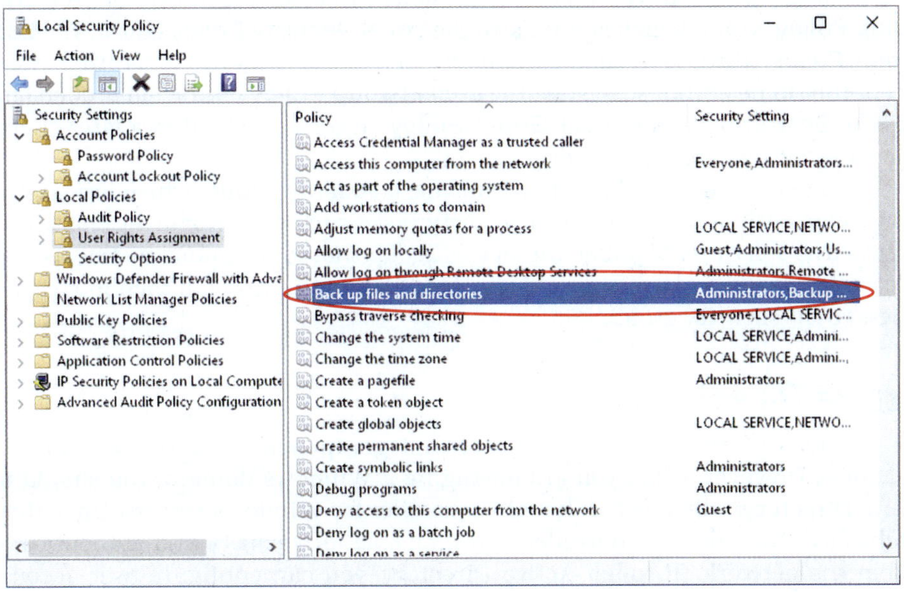

Figure 15-13 The **Local Security Policy** editor provides a policy to restrict the ability to copy files or directories to other media, such as USB-attached storage devices.

Goodheart-Willcox Publisher

Figure 15-14 When a security option is selected, the **Local Security Policy** editor will display dialog boxes that allow modification (A) or explanation (B).

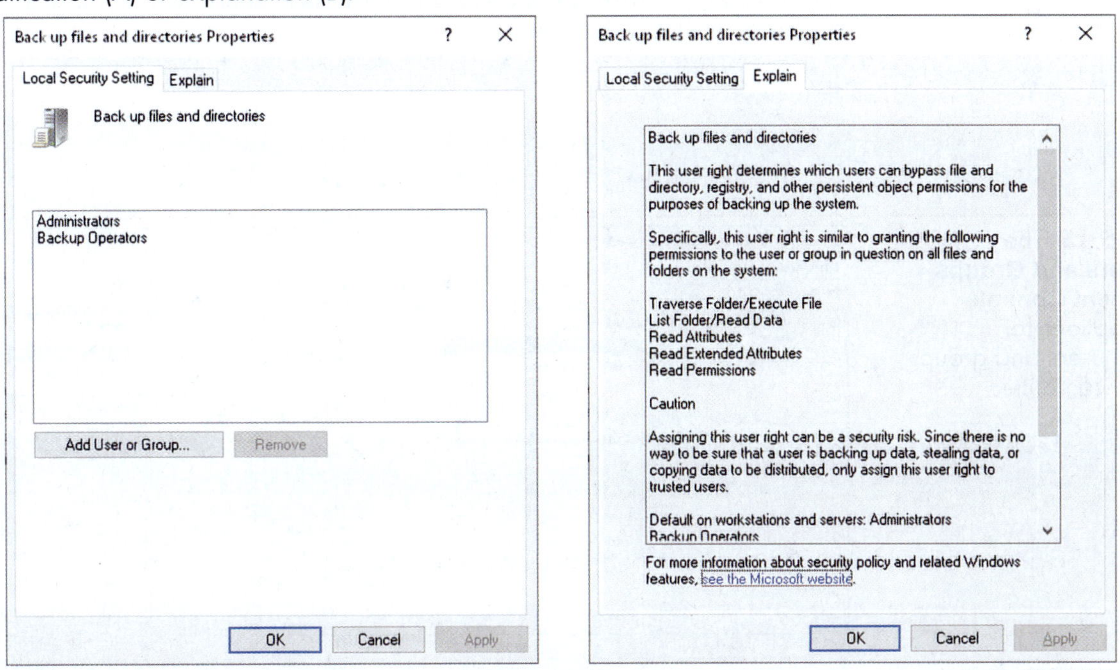

A **B**

Goodheart-Willcox Publisher

A+ 1102: 1.3

Users can launch the **Local Users and Groups Management Console** by entering lusrmgr in the Windows search and selecting **lusrmgr.msc** from the results list. In some cases, you may have to launch PowerShell or Command Prompt and enter lusrmgr.msc to open the Local Users and Groups Management Console. Once opened, you should see a screen similar to that shown in Figure 15-15. From here, you can manage users and groups on the local machine, which is a fundamental aspect of security.

A+ 1102: 1.1, 1.3, 2.1

Local Group Policy Management

Users have a set of permissions by default that allows them to perform certain functions on a computer. The assigned permissions can be changed through the **Local Group Policy** editor, which is similar to the **Local Security Policy** editor. The **Local Group Policy** editor is available in all editions of the Windows operating system except the Home editions. To start the **Local Group Policy** editor, enter gpedit.msc into the **Search** box. The **Local Group Policy** editor is covered in a later chapter when presenting network security.

A+ 1102: 2.1

Local and domain groups should include a *security group*, which is a group of individuals authorized to perform security tasks such as configuring the firewall or antivirus software. Membership in this group should be guided by the principle of least privileges, and users should only be added to this group if their job requires access to the security group.

A+ 1102: 2.1

Active Directory

The previous sections about local user and group policies apply to individual machines. However, when you are managing a Windows domain, you should use Active Directory, which is the domain controller for Windows servers. Once this is established, the domain controller is responsible for security and authentication within the network. Through Active Directory, you can configure user accounts and group policies in a manner much like the previously described local configurations; the main difference is that with Active Directory, these accounts and policies will apply to an entire domain rather than a single workstation. Active Directory can also provide Active Directory Certificate Services, which allows you to have your own on-premises public key infrastructure. There will be more about Active Directory in a later chapter.

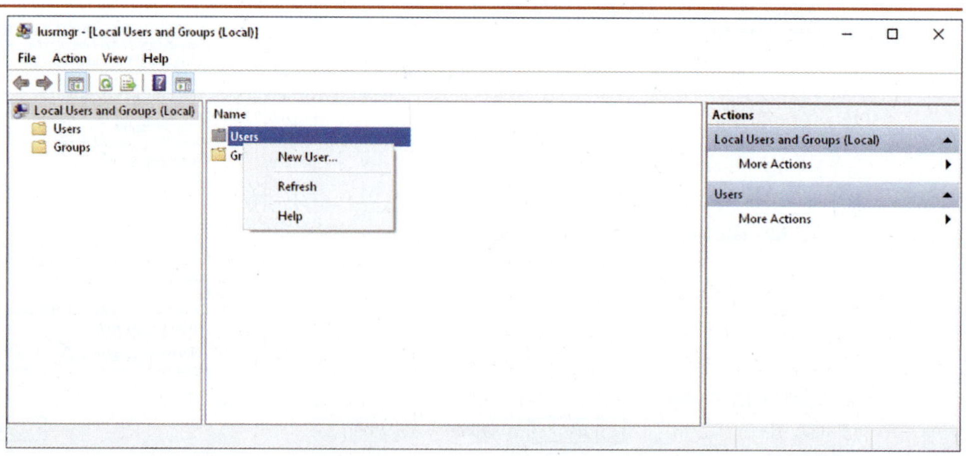

Figure 15-15 The **Local Users and Groups Management Console** provides options for managing users and groups on a local computer.

Goodheart-Willcox Publisher

Specific Security Policies

1102: 1.7 A+

Whether configuring local or domain security policies, there are specific items that must be addressed. An important configuration is to ensure standard users cannot install new applications. Nothing should be installed on any device without having been vetted and approved, as the installation of unauthorized software can frequently lead to viruses, Trojan horses, and spyware infecting machines. When reviewing applications, you should consider the impact the software will have to the device and its operation as well as the impact on the network and the business. Not having appropriate application policies will usually have a significant adverse effect on operations and the business as a whole.

There also should be specific policies for dealing with suspected malware. The first step should be *quarantining*, which is the process of isolating a device suspected of being infected. This means disconnecting it from the network and using software to detect and remove the malware. Additionally, since the computer became infected with malware, the existing precautions should be reviewed, and additional tools added if necessary.

Some websites, such as Virus Total and McAfee, offer services in which you can upload a file that is suspected of being infected with malware, and the website will scan it with multiple antivirus tools. Some of these websites also allow you to enter a URL and check a website for malware. Each of these sites can aid in identifying malware and may also provide instructions for removing the malware in question. Once the malware is removed, one should investigate to find out how it got on the system. This can be from improper application installation, download of an infected attachment, or clicking on an infected link, among others. Understanding how a system was infected can aid in improving your security and preventing future malware outbreaks.

Kerberos

1102: 2.2 A+

Kerberos is the most widely used authentication protocol today. It was invented at MIT and derives its name from the mythical three-headed dog that was reputed to guard the gates of Hades in Greek mythology. The system is rather complex, and the full details are not necessary for A+ Certification. However, a brief overview is warranted as you may have to use it.

When a user logs in, the authentication server verifies the user's identity and then contacts the ticket-granting server—often the same machine as the authentication server. The ticket-granting server then sends an encrypted ticket to the user's machine that identifies the user as being logged in. Later, when the user needs to access a resource on the network, the user's machine uses that ticket to gain access to the target machine. There is a great deal of verification for the tickets, and these tickets expire in a relatively short time.

Digital Certificates

1102: 2.10 A+

Digital certificates serve many roles, such as confirming that the holder of the certificate is who they claim to be and providing users with the public key of that certificate. The international standard for certificates is X.509: the most common type of digital certificate. Basic items in an X.509 certificate include the following, though there can be additional, optional information as well:

- **Version**: This is the version of X.509 with which the certificate complies.
- **Certificate holder's public key**: This is the primary method of receiving a public key from the certificate holder's X.509 certificate.
- **Serial number**: This is a unique identifier for this certificate.

- **Certificate holder's distinguished name**: This is often a domain name or e-mail address associated with a certificate.
- **Certificate's validity period**: This is the length of time during which the certificate is valid—often one year.
- **Unique name of certificate issuer**: This is the certificate authority that issued this certificate.
- **Digital signature of issuer**: This field and the next are used to verify the certificate.
- **Signature algorithm identifier**: This identifies the digital signature algorithm used.

To best understand how digital certificates are used, consider the following hypothetical scenario. You open your preferred web browser and navigate to your bank's website. You will need to do two things: verify this is truly the website of your bank, and retrieve the bank's public key. Once you have accomplished both, your browser will retrieve the digital certificate of the bank website, examine the listed certificate issuer on the certificate, and confirm that the CA is one trusted by the browser. If so, your browser communicates with that CA to get that its public key, which the browser uses to verify the CA signature on the certificate. If the certificate is fake, the digital signature will not be recognized. This means a certificate not only provides you with the certificate holder's public key, but also gives you a method of verifying that entity with a trusted third party. An untrusted certificate poses a serious security risk because that means the web server could not be authenticated. In general, websites with invalid certificates should be avoided.

A+ 1102: 1.3

Microsoft has built a certificate manager into all versions of Windows beginning with Windows 2000. You can launch the certificate manager either by searching for certmgr or by using the **Run** window to launch **certmgr.msc**. As shown in Figure 15-16, the certificate manager stores the digital certificates of the various certificate authorities that Windows trusts, which allows Windows to quickly verify any certificate that purports to be from such a certificate authority.

Wireless Authentication and Security

Due to the nature of its functionality, wireless communication requires stringent security and authentication. The first protocol for wireless security and authentication was Wired Equivalent Privacy (WEP), invented in 1997. WEP is no longer secure

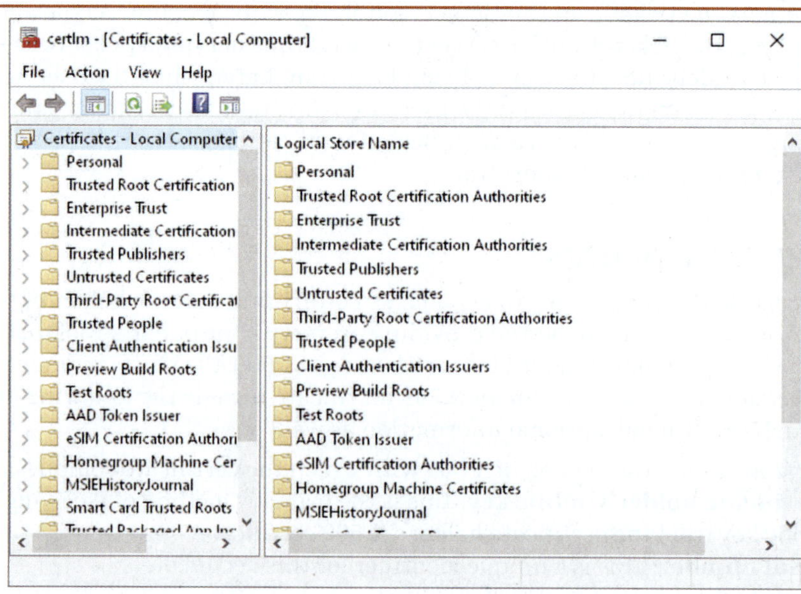

Figure 15-16 The Windows certificate manager stores the digital certificates from various trusted certificate authorities, which allows for quick verification.

Goodheart-Willcox Publisher

and should not be used any longer. WPA (Wi-Fi Protected Access) and its successors, WPA2 and WPA3, have been used for many years. You will likely see either WPA2 or WPA3 the most in the field, and these are far more likely to appear on the A+ Certification Exams than the previously mentioned authentication methods.

WPA used Temporal Key Integrity Protocol, which encrypted each packet with a separate key. WPA2 uses a four-way handshake to authenticate two points and establish ***robust security network associations (RSNAs)***, which are associations between a client and access point that provide protection against security threats. Initial authentication is provided with either a pre-shared key (PSK) or using the Extensible Authentication Protocol (EAP). WPA3 was announced in January 2018 and replaced the PSK used in WPA2 with a process called ***Simultaneous Authentication of Equals (SAE)***, which is a password authentication method that also establishes key exchange. SAE is a variation of the Dragonfly Key Exchange protocol that was defined in RFC 7664.

Workstation and SOHO Security

Individual and small-office/home-office (SOHO) workstations are two places where security is sometimes inadequately addressed. Even in the case of a workstation on a network wherein all the network infrastructure (i.e., routers, switches, servers, etc.) is secure, a security gap on an individual workstation can undermine the entire network.

In the case of an individual workstation, there are fundamental steps that must always be taken. The first is to ensure the system is updated with all required patches to better protect against malware. For example, the WannaCry virus of 2017 only affected unpatched Windows computers. If a computer was patched, WannaCry had no effect. The next issue for workstations is to have appropriate security policies in place. The specifics of policies will vary from organization to organization, but many policies follow common sense as well as the principle of least privilege. However, policies are only effective if used universally throughout an organization. Each individual workstation should also have its own appropriately configured antimalware software and firewall.

A+ 1102: 2.9

For SOHO devices, one must ensure that workstation security is applied to all connected workstations. The next step is to ensure the security of routers, switches, and wireless access points. For a SOHO arrangement, there is typically one router or wireless access point, and it was usually purchased at a commercial electronics store and self-configured. All commercial routers/WAP have a relatively simple web interface from which one can configure firewall settings and IP filtering. From the administrative interface, you can also check to see that the router's software is updated. This is often overlooked in the SOHO environment but can render a router vulnerable if not completed. Many commercial routers and WAPs have additional features such as the ability to filter traffic and establish a guest Wi-Fi, as well as other general security and useability features.

15.3 User Security Education

A+ 1102: 2.3

One of the best methods of securing computer systems and data is user education. Sometimes, user education is considered part of ***data loss prevention (DLP)***, which refers to strategies that ensure users do not transmit sensitive or company-critical information outside of the network. Users often represent the weakest link in a company's security chain, and you should never assume that a user understands security concepts. Users need not understand how to configure the **Local Security Policy** editor and **Local Group Policy** editor or how to allow a specific program to pass data through a firewall, and the average user should *not* be able to access these capabilities. However, users *do* need to understand how to create a complex password and why it is important as well as the dangers of opening certain e-mail attachments, even if they come from a legitimate sender. They also need to understand why they must follow company security policy, such as never giving their passwords to anyone, including the computer technician. Security involves educating users about how social engineering can be used to compromise the computer system.

A+ 1102: 2.6

All companies need to conduct security education on a regular basis, and all new employees should be trained in security and company policies regarding security standards before they begin working with the computer system. Even the most secure hardware and software system can be accessed or compromised because of a user not following or understanding effective user security. For example, users should be educated about potential security issues when using out-of-office methods of storage, such as flash drives, SD cards, and other media. The most advanced security systems can be rendered useless if users are not educated in how to use the computer systems safely. In short, it is always best to ensure users follow *all* policies and best practices to maintain security and protection of critical hardware.

A+ 1102: 2.4

Social Engineering

Social engineering is the act of manipulating people to get them to divulge confidential information about a computer system. Social engineering can come in the form of a phone call, e-mail, or even direct in-person contact. For example, a person could call, e-mail, or show up in person and present themself as a company technician working on a network problem or investigating a network security breach. The impostor then requests a user's account name and password to inspect the local computer system. If the user account information is given to the impostor, the entire system can be compromised. This is called *impersonation*. A proficient social engineer will use actual names of people at the firm, particularly if this individual knows the person is on vacation or otherwise indisposed and unavailable for verification. The only real protection from social engineering is through user security education as previously described.

Chapter Summary

15.1 Physical Security

- Security practices for securing the physical area of the computer and data storage areas include locking access doors, implementing a mantrap, and incorporating biometrics, a PIN key entry system, radio-frequency identification (RFID), or proximity cards.
- Security policies should provide details about how best to dispose of sensitive data and equipment and prevent actions such as dumpster diving.
- Digital security measures include incorporating encryptions through TPMs and software such as BitLocker.

15.2 Authentication and Workstation Security

- The best security practices include enforcing complex passwords, using multifactor authentication, and implementing the principle of least privilege.
- Passwords alone are rarely enough to prevent unauthorized access.
- Establishing Local Security Policies and Local Group Policies is another way an administrator can provide security on a computer.
- Individual and small-office/home-office (SOHO) workstations are two places where security is sometimes inadequately addressed.
- In the case of an individual workstation, the first is to ensure the system is updated with all required patches to better protect them against malware. The next issue for workstations is to have appropriate security policies in place.
- For SOHO devices, one must ensure that workstation security is applied to all connected workstations. The next step is to ensure the security of routers, switches, and wireless access points. All commercial routers/WAP have a relatively simple web interface from which one can configure firewall settings and IP filtering. From the administrative interface, you can also check to see that the router's software is updated. This is often overlooked in the SOHO environment but can render a router vulnerable if not completed.

15.3 User Security Education

- One of the best methods of securing computer systems and data is to educate users.
- Social engineering is the act of manipulating people to get them to divulge confidential information about a computer system. The only real protection against this is through user security education.

Review Questions

1. Summarize steps that can be taken to physically secure a workstation.
2. How can tailgating be prevented?
3. Differentiate between active and passive RFID transponders.
4. How is a smart card used?
5. What two advantages does a virtual smart card have over a physical smart card?
6. List four ways data can be destroyed on a hard drive before disposal.
7. What is a Trusted Platform Module?
8. List methods used to authenticate users.
9. What are the characteristics of a complex password?

10. How does salting a hash thwart attacks such as rainbow tables?
11. List the three multifactor authentication techniques.
12. What is the difference between local and domain user accounts?
13. Differentiate between privileges, permissions, and rights.
14. List and describe three account types in Windows.
15. Summarize the principle of least privilege.
16. What is the Local Security Policy?
17. List steps for securing individual and SOHO workstations.
18. Discuss the importance of user security education.
19. How often should security education be conducted for employees in a company?
20. Provide an example of social engineering.

Sample A+ Exam Questions

1. Which of the following functions has a storage location for cryptographic keys?
   A. Front-side bus
   B. Back-side bus
   C. Trusted Platform Module
   D. BitLocker
2. Which of the following is the *best* password to use to prevent possible compromise or intrusion?
   A. Secret
   B. Big$tar_5
   C. President Roosevelt
   D. Password
3. What AES keys bit-types are supported by BitLocker in Windows 10? Select all that apply.
   A. 128-bit
   B. 256-bit
   C. 384-bit
   D. 512-bit
4. Which of the following is *not* an example of software-based authentication?
   A. TACACS
   B. RADIUS
   C. SecureDNS
   D. TPM

5. Which management tool is used to change default user permissions?
   A. User Account Control
   B. Local Security Policy
   C. BitLocker
   D. Windows Defender
6. Which type of password is prompted for during the POST?
   A. HDD password
   B. Screen saver password
   C. Power-on password
   D. System configuration password
7. Which of the following describes a lookup table used to reverse hash a password?
   A. Salt table
   B. Hash table
   C. Rainbow table
   D. UEFI table
8. How often should passwords be changed?
   A. Every day
   B. At least every 4–6 months
   C. At least once every year
   D. At least every 1–3 years
9. Which formatting should be used to erase a hard drive?
   A. Quick format
   B. Low-level format
   C. Refresh format
   D. Degauss format
10. Which of the following most effectively prevents tailgating?
    A. Privacy filter
    B. Sanitation
    C. USB lock
    D. Mantrap

Chapter 16

Security Applications and Malware

Learning Outcomes

16.1 List common Microsoft security applications.
16.2 List and describe categories of malware.
16.3 List and describe common threats other than malware.
16.4 Summarize the purpose of a firewall.

A+ Certification Exam Objectives

The following A+ Certification Exam Objectives are covered in this chapter.

Exam 220-1101

2.0 Networking

- 2.1 Compare and contrast Transmission Control Protocol (TCP) and User Datagram Protocol (UDP) ports, protocols, and their purposes.
- 2.2 Compare and contrast common networking hardware.

3.0 Hardware

- 3.4 Given a scenario, install and configure motherboards, central processing units (CPUs), and add-on cards.

Exam 220-1102

1.0 Operating Systems

- 1.4 Given a scenario, use the appropriate Microsoft Windows 10 Control Panel utility.
- 1.5 Given a scenario, use the appropriate Windows settings.
- 1.6 Given a scenario, configure Microsoft Windows networking features on a client/desktop.
- 1.9 Given a scenario, perform OS installations and upgrades in a diverse OS environment.

2.0 Security

- 2.1 Summarize various security measures and their purposes.
- 2.3 Given a scenario, detect, remove, and prevent malware using the appropriate tools and methods.
- 2.4 Explain common social-engineering attacks, threats, and vulnerabilities.
- 2.5 Given a scenario, manage and configure basic security settings in the Microsoft Windows OS.
- 2.7 Explain common methods for securing mobile and embedded devices.
- 2.9 Given a scenario, configure appropriate security settings on small office/home office (SOHO) wireless and wired networks.
- 2.10 Given a scenario, install and configure browsers and relevant security settings.

3.0 Software Troubleshooting

- 3.2 Given a scenario, troubleshoot and resolve PC security issues.
- 3.3 Given a scenario, use best practice procedures for malware removal.

Key Terms

adware
backdoor virus
boot sector virus
botnet
browser hijacker
cookie
data miner
denial-of-service (DoS)
firewall
grayware
hoax
logic bomb
macro virus
malicious software
man-in-the-middle (MITM) attack
MBR virus
Measured Boot
password virus
pharming
phishing
polymorphic virus
port number
ransomware
rootkit
service
spam
spyware
stealth virus
Trojan horse
Trusted Boot
virus
virus signature
worm
zero-day attack

Overview

Security is both physical and digital. Physical security refers to securing the computer using physical means, such as physical locks and security devices. In relation to security, the term *digital* refers to controlling security through software applications, such as antimalware, antispyware, and a firewall; authentication; and user privileges and permissions. This chapter will guide you through commonly encountered digital security tools, features, and applications. Additionally, you will learn about different types of malware as well as malware prevention and removal.

A+ Note

As you now should know, the topic of security is a major focus of A+ Certification. A vital part of the exams is the ability to identify malware types when presented with a brief description. You must also be familiar with Microsoft security applications as outlined in this chapter. Practice with all the security utilities so you are familiar with the various configuration options for each when it comes time to take your certification exams.

> **A+ Note**
>
> CompTIA often uses the term *digital security* in the A+ Certification Exam Objectives to include all aspects of security that are not considered physical. Digital security encompasses software applications or programs designed to secure access to a computer system and data.

16.1 Microsoft Security Applications

Security has been a primary concern for computer users over the years. As a result, Microsoft has developed many different software applications used for computer security. Many of the tools come preinstalled, while others can be downloaded from the Microsoft website. Enabling Windows Update is the best way to keep the computer system patched with the very latest version of the free tools.

Windows Security

> **A+ Note**
>
> Pay close attention to window and interface names when taking the A+ Exams. A tricky question could use some combination of Action Center, Windows Security Center, and Windows Security in the multiple-choice options. Windows Security Center would be correct for a question concerning an operating system feature before Windows 7, and Action Center would be the correct response for a question related to Windows 7 and Windows 8. However, this menu was renamed Windows Security in Windows 10 and has the same name in Windows 11.

The Windows Security Center monitors security features such as the status of the firewall, virus or malware protection, automatic updates, and other security configuration options related to operating system applications. It was first introduced in Windows XP Service Pack 2 (SP2) and remained very similar in Windows Vista.

In Windows 10 and 11, Microsoft renamed this menu to **Windows Security**, and the security overview can be accessed by using the [Windows][X] keyboard combination, then selecting **Settings**>**Update & Security**>**Windows Security.** The operating system performs numerous self-checks and recommends action to the user when action is required. Clicking on any of the options shown in Figure 16-1A will take the user to a more detailed screen; for example, the firewall selection reports on the

Figure 16-1 The **Windows Security** menu (A) offers a centralized location for monitoring the status and configuration of the firewall, automatic updates, virus protection, and more. From this menu, you can also launch the **Security at a glance** menu (B) for additional details about the security and health of a device.

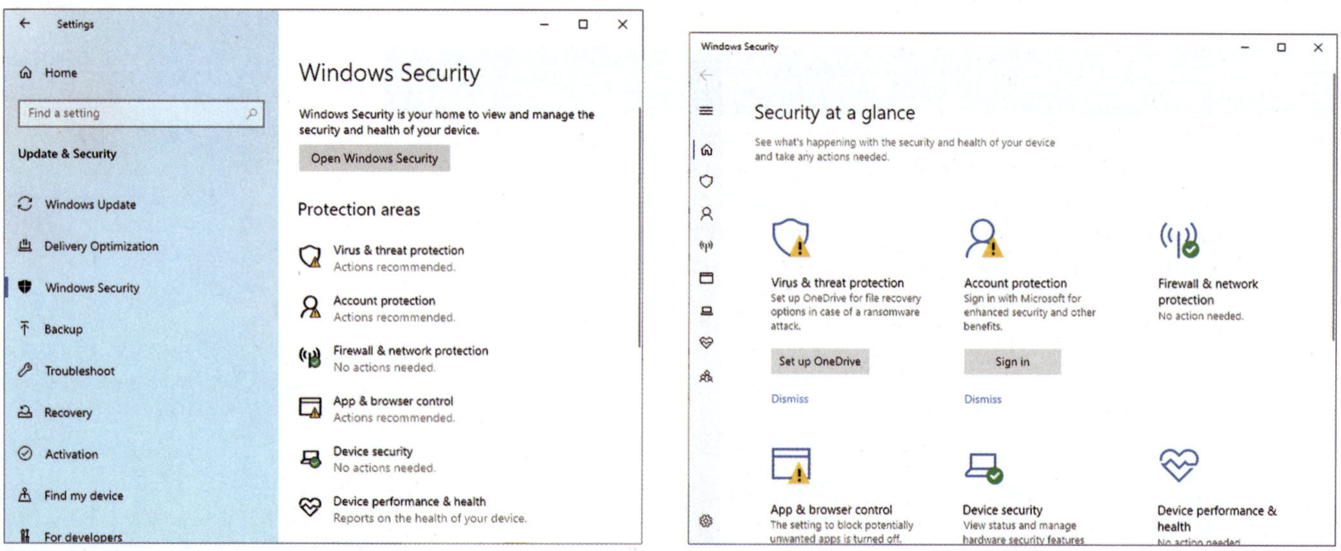

A B

Goodheart-Willcox Publisher

domain network, the private network, and the public network. There are a number of options including virus protection, device security, and firewall configuration, among others. More importantly, this Microsoft app tells you if one of these features requires some attention. Selecting the **Open Windows Security** button launches the Security at a glance, shown in Figure 16-1B, which provides additional details about the protection areas listed in the Windows Security menu.

Beginning with Windows 10, Windows added a new feature called Controlled Folder Access, which allows you to designate folders in such a way that any change to that folder will require your approval. To enable this feature, navigate to **Windows Security** and select **Virus & threat protection.** Scroll down to the Ransomware protection portion of this window, as shown in Figure 16-2, and toggle the Controlled folder access button. Should your computer become infected with ransomware, the system will notify you and require your permission when that malware attempts to encrypt files or folders. This is a simple, effective way to combat ransomware.

Tech Tip

The Windows Controlled Folder Access feature requires the creation and configuration of a Microsoft OneDrive account. Additionally, the presence of a third-party antivirus program such as McAfee or Norton may disable Windows Defender and prevent Ransomware protection from appearing in your menu.

User Account Control

1102: 2.5 A+

Since Windows XP, Microsoft has been working to improve user access security. One improvement that Microsoft developed was the User Account Control (UAC), which was first introduced in Windows Vista and has continued to be a vital part of all Windows operating systems.

The original Windows Vista version of the UAC annoyed users. Each time a change to the computer configuration was made, the user was prompted for the administrator password. As a result, Windows Vista was not a popular operating system, and at that time, many computer manufacturers offered to substitute Windows XP operating system in place of Windows Vista.

Because of the public criticism of Windows Vista, Microsoft designed the next operating system to be less restrictive by default. Thus, Windows 7 did not have nearly as many security-enabled prompts as Windows Vista had. Instead, it introduced a slider that allows the user to fine-tune the security level of the user account.

The **User Account Control Settings** dialog box is used to control how the operating system will notify you of potentially harmful programs attempting to make changes to your computer system. Figure 16-3 shows the User Account Control set to default.

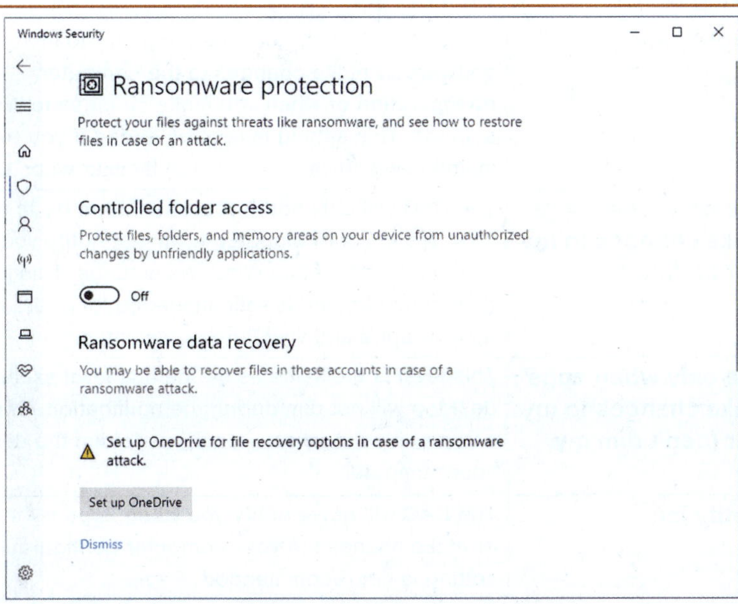

Goodheart-Willcox Publisher

Figure 16-2 The Controlled Folder Access feature allows you to secure your files and folders against ransomware attacks.

The **User Account Control Settings** dialog box has four setting adjustments: **Always notify me, Notify me only when apps try to make changes to my computer (default), Notify me only when apps try to make changes to my computer (don't dim my desktop)**, and **Never notify me.** Figure 16-4 describes each setting.

The **Notify me only when apps try to make changes to my computer (default)** and **Notify me only when apps try to make changes to my computer (don't dim my desktop)** settings are the same, except the latter of the two will not dim the desktop during notifications. Some computers have a long delay when they dim the screen at the default setting, so Microsoft created the same security setting with an option that will not dim the screen when the notification appears. The **Never notify**

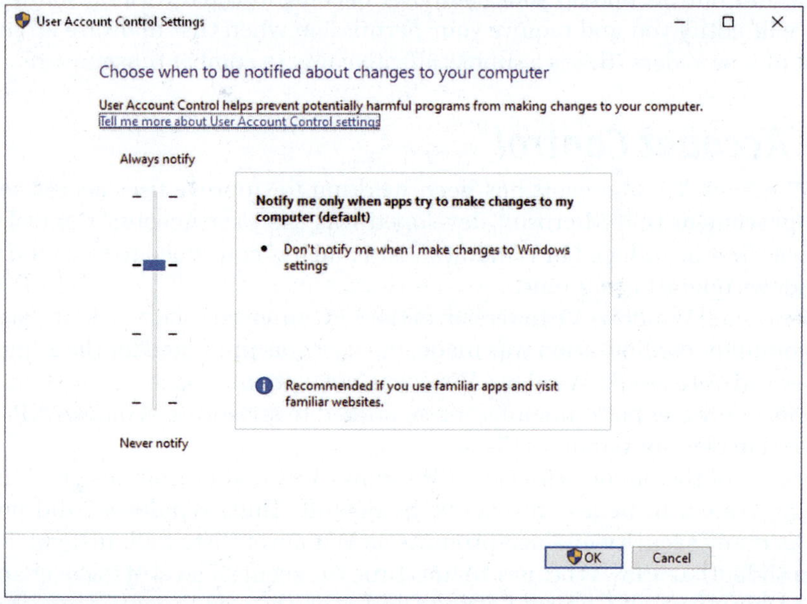

Goodheart-Willcox Publisher

Figure 16-3 The **User Account Control Settings** dialog box is used to control how the operating system will notify you of potentially harmful programs attempting to make changes to the computer system.

Figure 16-4 The **User Account Control Settings** dialog box has four setting adjustments.

Decoding UAC Settings

UAC Setting	Description
Always notify me	The UAC will notify you when apps try to install software or make changes to the computer configuration or when you make changes to Windows settings. This setting is recommended if you routinely install new software and visit unfamiliar websites.
Notify me only when apps try to make changes to my computer (default)	The UAC will only notify you when apps try to make changes to your computer. It will not notify you when you make changes to Windows settings. This is the default setting and is recommended for users who run familiar apps and visit familiar websites.
Notify me only when apps try to make changes to my computer (don't dim my desktop)	This level is the same as the default level except the desktop will not dim during the notification. Choose this setting only if it takes a long time to dim the desktop on your computer.
Never notify me	The UAC will never notify you when apps try to install or make changes to your computer configuration. This setting is not recommended.

Goodheart-Willcox Publisher

me setting is selected when users do not ever want the security warning messages to appear on their screen and is not recommended because it defeats the purpose of having the User Account Control in the first place.

New to Windows 10 is the Dynamic Lock setting, found in **Start>Settings> Accounts>Sign-in options**. Once you have opened the **Sign-in options** menu, scroll down until you see Dynamic lock, as shown in Figure 16-5. From here, you can have Windows automatically unlock your computer when a paired device (such as your phone) is within a certain range. This same menu also allows you to change the sign in options to include things such as Windows Hello Fingerprint, provided you have the hardware for fingerprint reading.

Parental Controls and Family Options

A+ 1102: 2.9

Windows Vista introduced the Parental Controls feature. In Windows 8, it was renamed Family Safety, and in Windows 10, it was renamed again to Family Options. This feature monitors and limits a user's computer and network activity. Look at Figure 16-6 to see the Windows 10 **Family Options** dialog box.

Windows 10 and 11 Family Options gives the option to set screen-time limits; block certain apps, websites, and games; and other features that were present in previous versions of Windows. However, it also added the ability to receive weekly activity reports of online activity and has an option called Check the health and safety of your family's devices that takes the user to the Microsoft website and displays all known devices. From there, the user can select from options to control Windows 10, Xbox gaming consoles, and Android phones. These additional options include family settings, screen-time limits, content filtering, and e-mail notification of Microsoft Store purchases.

Trusted Boot and Measured Boot Security

Trusted Boot and Measured Boot are security features that were initially integrated into Windows 8. They have also been included in subsequent Windows operating systems. While these security features at first appear very much the same, the differences are apparent when directly related to required hardware. For example,

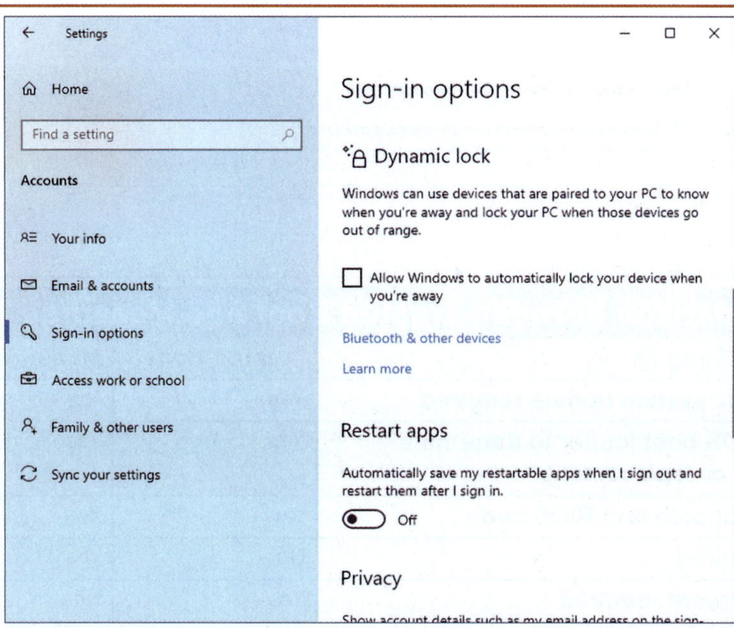

Goodheart-Willcox Publisher

Figure 16-5 The **Dynamic lock** setting enables the computer to lock or unlock automatically when a paired device exits or enters a specific range of the computer.

Trusted Boot requires UEFI firmware. Measured Boot does not, but it can be implemented on a system that utilizes UEFI firmware. Also, Measured Boot is designed to work with a Trusted Platform Module (TPM). The table shown in Figure 16-7 compares Trusted Boot and Measured Boot.

A+ 1101: 3.4

Tech Tip

Secure Boot is an open-source security application, not a Microsoft proprietary application.

Trusted Boot

Trusted Boot is a Windows feature that checks the integrity of the operating system during the boot process and only allows digitally signed software to boot and run on the computer. It is designed to prevent malware from hijacking the boot operation and taking over the computer. The boot period of the startup process is a vulnerable time for computers because the antivirus software and software firewall are generally not active. Trusted Boot, a Microsoft term, is also referred to as *Secure Boot* and *UEFI Secure Boot*. Rather than BIOS, Trusted Boot requires UEFI firmware.

If Microsoft does not approve a software application, it will not be installed on a computer that uses Trusted Boot. This type of security is common to other operating systems and devices such as Android and Apple devices. If you want to install a third-party application on a device using the Trusted Boot feature, you would first need to bypass security features on the device, thus becoming the overall system

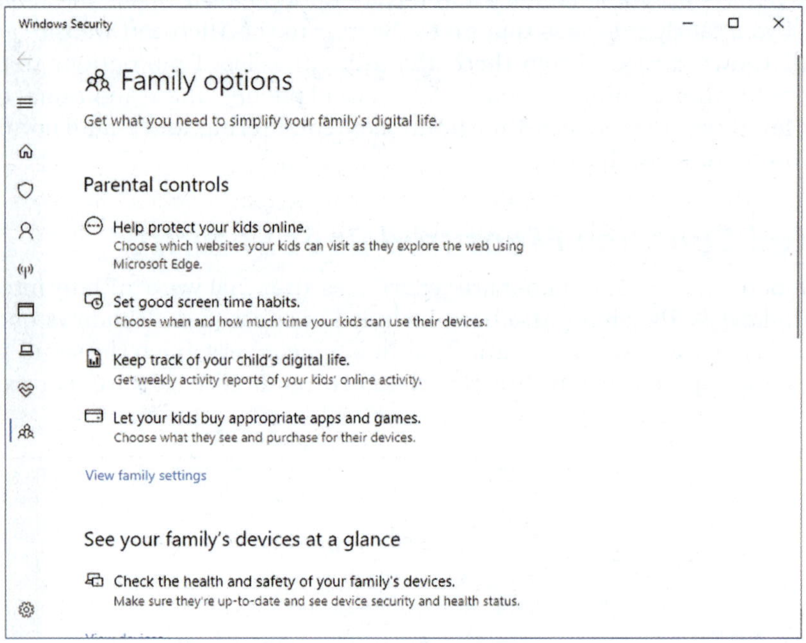

Goodheart-Willcox Publisher

Figure 16-6 The Windows **Family Options** menu is used to limit and monitor user account activity on a computer or network.

Figure 16-7 Trusted Boot is a Windows security feature that checks the integrity of the operating system during the boot process and only allows digitally signed software to boot and run on the computer. Measured Boot works with a TPM to verify the successful launch of the operating system and then stores the information in the TPM.

Comparison between Trusted Boot and Measured Boot

Security Feature	Trusted Boot	Measured Boot
Automatic system update required	Yes	No
Inspect OS boot loader to determine changes or replacement	Yes	Yes
Scan boot path and BIOS code	No	Yes
TPM required	No	Yes
UEFI firmware required	Yes	No

Goodheart-Willcox Publisher

administrator. After bypassing the Trusted Boot feature, you can then install unauthorized software applications. This approach is a classic example of the way users compromise security features soon after they appear.

Measured Boot

Measured Boot works with the Trusted Platform Module (TPM) to verify the successful launch of the operating system and store the information in the TPM. This information is then used to validate computer integrity, which is required before remote services, such as cloud computing, are enabled. Remote services access the information stored in the TPM, verify that the computer contains no malware, and ensure it is safe to allow the computer or device to join the cloud service or the network.

The Measured Boot feature is required for cloud computing and other types of remote services. It ensures the computer has up-to-date antimalware software installed, the antimalware initializes properly, and the computer is virus free. Measured Boot is used to limit the spread of malware across the Internet to servers, which is essential for cloud computers and remote server access.

The Measured Boot feature provides antimalware software with trusted logging of all boot components that start before the antimalware software. The antimalware software then uses this log to determine if any components are compromised by malware. The antimalware application on the client machine can then send the log to a remote server for further evaluation. The remote server may initiate countermeasures either by working with software already on the client system or through external means.

Trusted Boot and Measured Boot go unnoticed by users, but they both ensure the operating system is not infected with malware. The only time a user may become aware of these features is when access to a remote website or cloud service is denied due to the lack of a security feature. For example, a user may attempt to connect to a cloud service and be denied because the computer does not have up-to-date antimalware software or operating system security patches installed. To learn more about Trusted Boot and Measured Boot, conduct an online search using the phrase Microsoft Trusted Boot Measured Boot.

Microsoft Security Tools

Originally, operating systems did not incorporate any security software applications. Rather, security software applications had to be installed separately. Beginning with Windows XP, Microsoft has incorporated several different security tools into its operating systems or has provided these tools as add-in programs. You can still install additional security tools, which is recommended and a common practice.

There are several Microsoft security tools available for Windows operating systems. For the most part, these tools do not provide the same level of protection that commercial antimalware software programs provide. These tools are provided by Microsoft so the computer has minimal protection, rather than no protection at all.

Microsoft has many security software applications integrated into the operating system or available for download. Many have overlapping features making them quite confusing to distinguish. Explore the Microsoft web page dedicated to security. Simply enter the search terms Microsoft Security into a web browser and look for results that link you to the Microsoft website.

A+ Note

Even though the CompTIA A+ Certification is advertised to be vendor-neutral, it is still oriented to Microsoft Windows. Therefore, you should be familiar with all the various Windows security features.

Microsoft Malicious Software Removal Tool

1102: 2.3, 2.7 A+

All versions of Windows from Windows XP to Windows 10 include the Microsoft Malicious Software Removal Tool (MSRT). If for any reason it is not on your computer, you can download it from the Microsoft website. Even if you know the name and location of the malware file, attempts to delete it will not remove the file in its entirety, and most malware is designed to re-infect the computer unless all parts of the malware are removed. If not removed completely, the malware can remain in RAM and re-infect the computer periodically even after the original file has been removed. The MSRT is designed to completely remove malicious software from your computer.

The Microsoft Malicious Software Removal Tool is updated every month by default if the computer has automatic updates enabled. There is also an option to download and install a copy of the tool manually. Running the Malicious Software Removal Tool automatic update in Windows 10 is an easy process:

1. Select **Start**>**Settings**>**Update & security**>**Windows Update.** If you want to check for updates manually, select **Check for updates.**
2. Select **Advanced options.** From the **Choose how updates are installed** drop-down menu, select **Automatic (recommended).**

To run the Malicious Software Removal Tool, perform the following steps:

1. Open the **Run** dialog box by using the [Windows][R] keyboard combination.
2. Enter MRT and click **OK.** If the **User Account Control** dialog box appears, select **Yes.**
3. Respond to the dialog boxes.

It is important to emphasize that the MSRT does not *replace* an antimalware product. It is strictly a post-infection removal tool, meaning MSRT does not prevent the installation of malware; it only removes known versions of malware. You should always install an up-to-date antimalware product designed to work with the version and edition of your operating system. Commercial antimalware software tools are designed to not only remove existing malware but also detect potentially dangerous malware *before* it infects a computer.

Windows Security

Windows Security is included in all versions of Windows starting with Windows XP. It was originally named Windows Defender and was designed to protect the PC against spyware, but it has since evolved into a number of security-specific offerings,

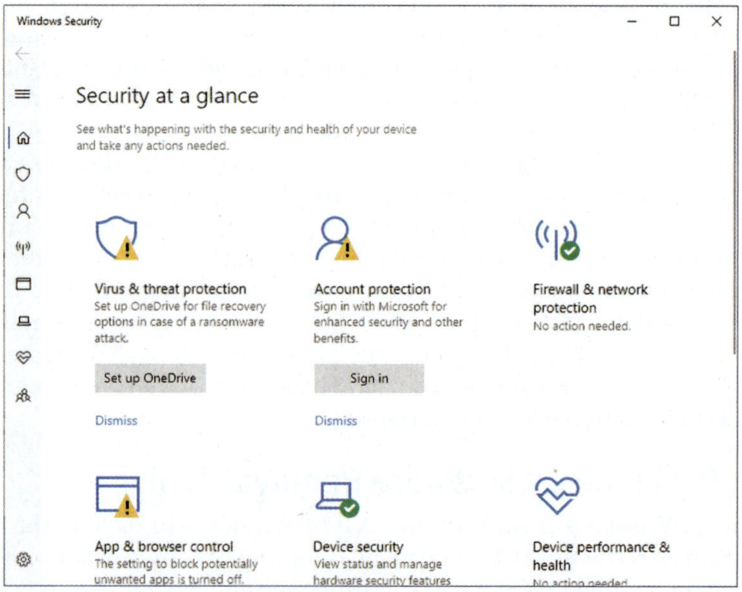

Figure 16-8 Windows Defender has gone through several iterations and evolutions to become Windows Security, which now includes features such as malware removal, family options, and control of apps and browsers.

Goodheart-Willcox Publisher

as shown in Figure 16-8. For example, beginning with Windows 8, Windows Security—then titled Windows Defender—was an enhanced version of its predecessor that began offering malware protection in addition to spyware protection.

Windows Defender is activated by default, but users can activate or deactivate it as needed. Windows Defender can be launched by conducting a search for Windows Security or Defender and selecting the **Windows Security** app. Within that app are options such as Windows Firewall and Windows Defender settings, the latter of which are found under the Virus & threat protection heading, as shown in Figure 16-9.

Windows Defender Offline

1102: 2.5 A+

Windows Defender Offline (WDO) is one of Microsoft's most powerful malware scanners and is part of the standard installation in Windows 10. It is a standalone software application and runs independently of the operating system. As part of your technician tool kit, you should download a copy and save it to a USB flash drive so you can use it to check a client's computer for suspected malware infection.

SmartScreen

SmartScreen is an additional safety feature first incorporated into Windows 8 and still present in Windows 10 and 11. It is designed to protect the computer system from new malware that antimalware software has most likely not detected. SmartScreen was originally designed for Internet Explorer but was improved for Windows 10 so it could function with both Microsoft Edge and Microsoft Store apps.

SmartScreen checks an application when it is downloaded from the Internet and warns the user based on the reputation of the source. If the source of the app is known to distribute malware intentionally or accidentally, a warning message will be displayed on the screen. Figure 16-10 shows the SmartScreen configuration in Windows 10, which can be accessed through **Start>Settings>Update & Security>Windows Security>App & browser control>Reputation-based protection settings.**

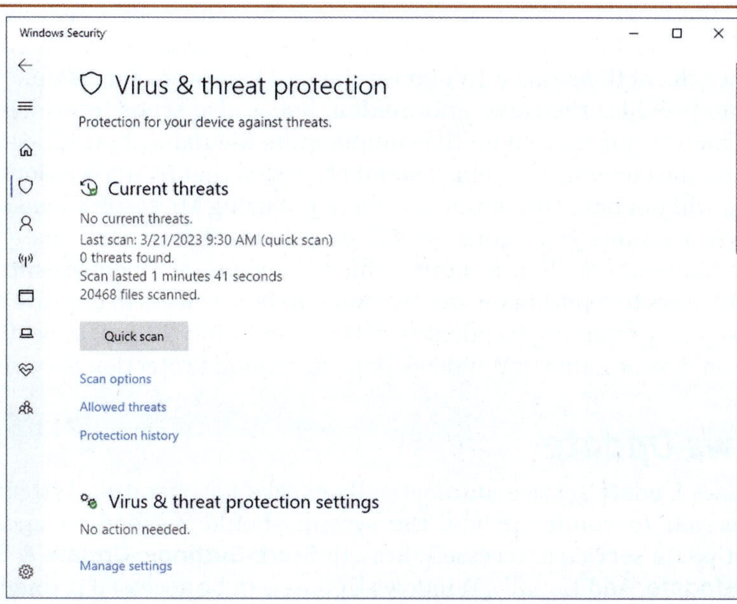

Goodheart-Willcox Publisher

Figure 16-9 Windows Defender provides a variety of settings, including firewall options and virus protection.

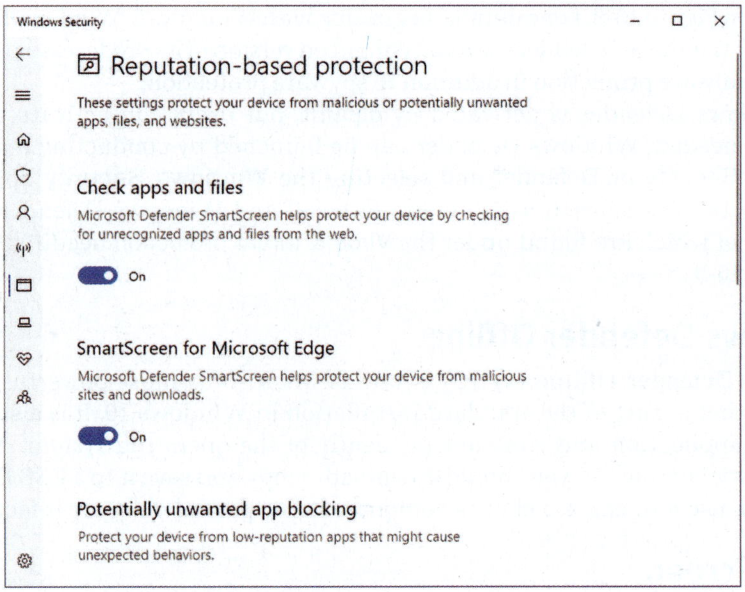

Figure 16-10 SmartScreen can be configured to warn or block a download from a malicious site.

Goodheart-Willcox Publisher

Microsoft Safety Scanner

Microsoft Safety Scanner checks the computer system for all forms of malware. It is not installed by default, but it is free to download and run on any Microsoft operating system. The Microsoft Safety Scanner is a standalone program that only runs when activated by the user, meaning it does not provide constant protection by running in the background of the operating system. The Microsoft Safety Scanner is compatible with other malware scanners and can coexist on a system that has an active malware scanner already installed, but it has a limited lifespan and must be downloaded again after approximately 10 days. Safety Scanner aids in removing malicious software from PCs running a variety of operating systems, including Windows 10, Windows 11, Windows Server 2016, and Windows Server 2019.

Tech Tip

Microsoft also uses the acronym *MAP* to represent the Microsoft Assessment and Planning Toolkit.

Microsoft Active Protection Service

Microsoft Active Protection Service (MAPS) automatically reports malware to Microsoft. There are two levels of membership: basic and advanced. Basic membership sends information to Microsoft about the malware, where it came from, and whether the actions taken to remove the malware were successful. Advanced membership provides the same information, but it also sends information about where the malware is located on the computer, its file name, how it operates, and its impact on the computer system. It should be noted that MAPS is a cloud security tool, so you will not have this option if you are not using Microsoft Cloud services.

MAPS is a voluntary program, so you can choose not to participate. It is also part of the Microsoft SpyNet program, which is a volunteer membership program designed for users to report malware. The point of the service is to improve Microsoft protection while protecting the identity of the user. In July 2016, Microsoft changed the service endpoint name to Windows Defender Cloud Protection Services.

A+ 1102: 1.5, 1.9, 2.4

Windows Update

The Windows Update service automatically checks for operating system updates and allows you to configure how the system should respond to updates. The Windows Update service is accessed through **Start**>**Settings**>**Update & Security**>**Windows Update**. Additionally, Windows Update can be accessed through **Control Panel** or by conducting a search using the entry update or check for updates.

After the Windows Update service is selected, a dialog box similar to that in Figure 16-11 will appear. The **Windows Update** dialog box provides information about the status of the computer updates as well as several related options. You can configure a time and day of the week to check for updates automatically, or you can manually check for updates at any time by selecting the **Check for updates** option. You have the option to select all updates or only important updates to install. When updates are not installed, they are saved as hidden updates that can be installed later, if desired. Traditionally, Windows Update has provided the following options for handling updates:

- **Install updates automatically (recommended)**
- **Download updates but let me choose whether to install them**
- **Check for updates but let me choose whether to download and install them**
- **Never check for updates (not recommended)**

Microsoft changed the location of these options in Windows 10. To locate the update options, select the **Advanced options** link in the **Windows Update** dialog box. It is worth noting that with the release of Windows 10, users are no longer able to choose not to update. Instead, users can only delay an update for up to 35 days.

Microsoft recommends the automatic download and installation of all updates. Many network administrators do not choose to download and install updates automatically for two main reasons. First, downloading and installing updates while performing other tasks can significantly degrade computer performance and make the computer appear sluggish. Second, there are times when a particular update can adversely affect a software application or a hardware device not on the Microsoft approved list. A network administrator often tests updates before installing them on a network of computers to ensure compatibility with all network computer hardware and software applications.

Windows Event Viewer

Computer activity can be monitored with the Windows Event Viewer, which records activity related to security events such as failed login attempts, which can indicate an instance of attempted unauthorized computer access. Look at the Event Viewer

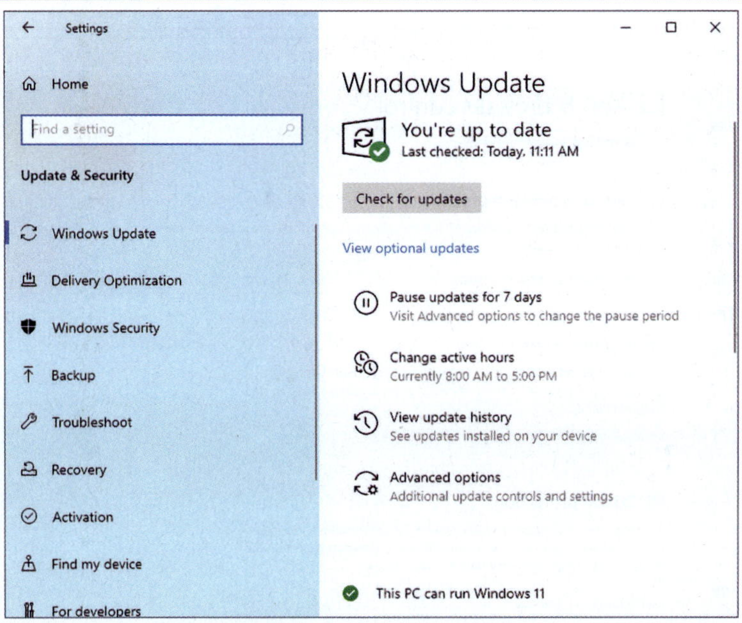

Goodheart-Willcox Publisher

Figure 16-11 Windows Update provides information about the current status of the computer updates, as well as several related options.

in Figure 16-12. The Event Viewer has indicated a series of events or login attempts from a computer named L59107696. It also lists the time it occurred and an event ID, which can be used to find more information about the cause of this type of failure. You can double-click the event and a window will appear, providing more information. Event Viewer is covered in detail in a later chapter.

Microsoft App and Browser Control

The Microsoft **App & Browser control**, shown in Figure 16-13 allows you to use a variety of protection measures for application and Internet security. For example, the Isolated Browsing option puts Microsoft Edge in a sandbox wherein items in that sandbox cannot access the operating system. This provides a safe method of browsing the Internet. Reputation-based protection allows you to block various apps

Figure 16-12 Windows Event Viewer records activity related to security events.

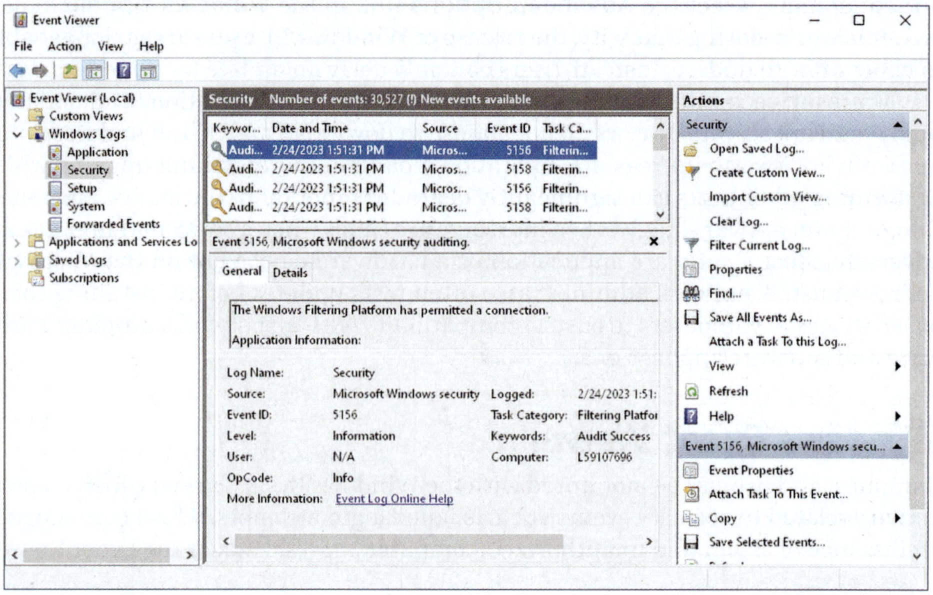

Goodheart-Willcox Publisher

Figure 16-13 Microsoft's **App & browser control** menu provides app protection and online security options in one location.

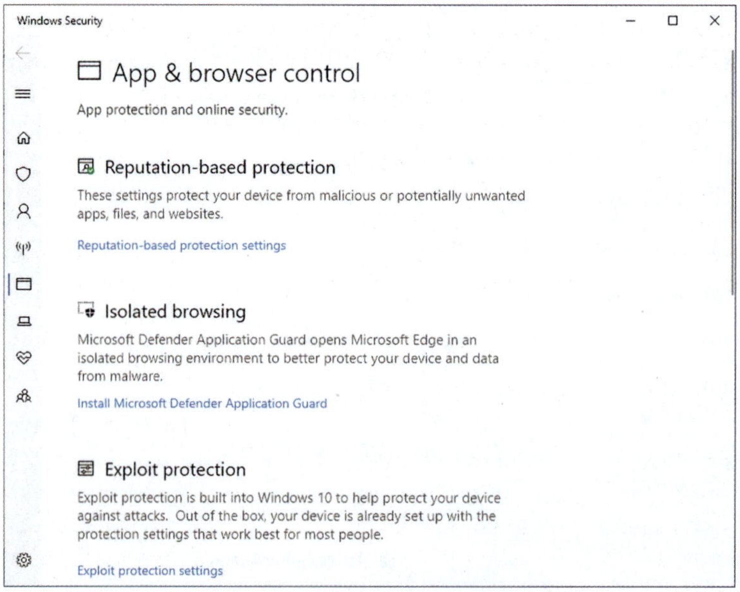

Goodheart-Willcox Publisher

and includes the previously described SmartScreen. The Exploit protection option includes a number of technologies for protecting your computer, including address space layout randomization (ASLR), which randomly arranges memory to prevent attacks that exploit memory.

Browser Selection and Installation

A+ 1102: 2.10

Web browsers might not seem like a security issue, but they can be, as there are a range of browsers on the market, and each has its strengths and weaknesses. Browsers are often installed by default in operating systems; for example, Safari is the default browser for macOS, and Microsoft Edge is the default browser for Windows. However, there are a variety of third-party browsers you may wish to install. This section lists popular options along with their advantages and disadvantages.

While it may not be as well known as some of the other browsers in this section, Mozilla Firefox is quite popular. It is open source, giving its users full access and even allowing users to view and modify the source code if they desire. One of the reasons for Firefox's popularity, and also one of its greatest strengths, is the wide number of available add-ons. Among the free add-ons are tools that notify you if a website is trying to extract personal information, block certain threats, check your privacy settings, and more.

Google Chrome obviously is preferred by various Google services, which is one reason it is quite popular. Chrome offers a number of built-in tools, including the Google Translate, which can translate 52 languages as of this writing. Additionally, if you are using Google on multiple devices, you can synchronize bookmarks, settings, and history across all devices.

The Opera web browser is somewhat less widely known, but it advertises as the fastest browser. This is due in part to its limited feature set, though it does support build in pop-up blocking as well as tabbed browsing. You can also configure the browser to delete all private data with the click of a button. It should be noted that all modern browsers provide some mechanism for deleting private data on exit.

The real issue is the location from which you download a browser. For security purposes, you should only download from the actual vendor site, as it is certainly conceivable for malware to be masquerading as a browser. For example, if you wish to download Firefox, you should only do so from Mozilla's official website.

Password Managers

A+ 1102: 2.10

Users often have difficulty remembering all their passwords, which can lead to users writing them down—a serious breach of security. Often, password managers can be used to securely store all the users' passwords. A *password manager* is a software application that stores user passwords, enabling the use of long, complex passwords without the user having to remember all of them. There are a number of password managers on the market, but you should carefully research which one is right for you. Reputable online sources such as CNET, PCMag, and Forbes often publish their own lists of products they consider to be the best. These lists include excellent information and resources for determining which password manager is best for your need.

16.2 Malicious Software

A+ 1102: 2.3

Malicious software, also called *malware,* is software written for the express purpose of modifying a computer's configuration or causing damage to a computer system. There are many different categories of malicious software, such as a virus, worm, rootkit, and more. In this section, basic information relating to all forms of malicious software is presented.

A+ 1102: 2.3

A **virus** is software that self-replicates. Normally, a virus will also have some malicious activity or payload, its self-replication is key. For example, the original ILOVEYOU virus of 2000 had no malicious payload, though later variants did cause some damage to files. The original iteration simply copied an e-mail saying "I Love You" to everyone in your address book, and the excess traffic was sufficient to disrupt networks.

A virus typically has three phases: infection, replication, and execution.

- *Infection* occurs when the virus arrives from a source, such as a portable USB drive, e-mail, or network connection to a computer.
- *Replication* occurs when the virus duplicates itself to other programs, files, drives, or other computers on a network. If a virus continually replicates itself, it can easily use all available disk space.
- *Execution* can take many forms. Some malware is harmless and just annoying. For example, the well-known Melissa virus infected Microsoft Word files and then replicated itself across the network by sending an e-mail to the first 50 names on the user's contact list. Others can be very destructive by performing such actions as erasing files and locking up hardware.

A+ 1102: 2.5

Viruses are said to have *signatures*. A **virus signature**, also called a *virus definition*, is a combination of characteristics that includes such things as its length, file name(s) used, mode of infection or replication, the areas of the system that are attacked, the type of software programs that are attacked, and the name or length of the file attachment. A virus signature describes a particular virus. These signatures are what most antimalware software programs use to catch viruses on your computer, which is why it is important to keep the signature database current. Microsoft security tools, and all antimalware software, must have updated virus signatures or definitions to allow protection against new threats. Ensure that all security software such as antivirus or Intrusion Detection System has updated definitions. Many antimalware programs also employ exploratory approaches to intercept malware before it can do any harm.

Malicious software causes a tremendous amount of destruction and aggravation. Sooner or later, you *will* encounter a virus or worm. You must have the appropriate knowledge and experience to deal with these threats. Understanding different classifications of malware may be one of the most important topics you will learn.

Malware Classifications

Most malicious programs (malware) that infect computers are referred to as viruses. In fact, the term *computer virus* has taken on a very broad definition with the public. However, the software companies that develop antimalware software programs have developed a variety of classifications, which vary somewhat from company to company. In addition to viruses, there are other malicious programs, each with unique features. Common classifications of computer infections include worm, Trojan horse, logic bomb, macro, password, backdoor, and hoax, though there are many others. While some classes will seem similar, there are sufficient variations in their style to allow a classification system to be used. Note, there are many instances of malware composed of the features of multiple classifications, making classification somewhat difficult.

Worm

While many viruses attach themselves to other programs to slip into your computer, worms operate on their own. A **worm** is a destructive program that contaminates files on the infected computer and spreads to other computers without prompting from the user. A worm is essentially a more virulent version of a virus. Its ability to spread to other computers is what makes it different from a virus.

It is important to note that worms are self-replicating. Once infection takes place, the worm replicates or transmits itself to other computers without user intervention. A classic example of its reproduction is through an e-mail application. When a worm is sent as a file attachment, it replicates itself by using the list of contacts in the user's e-mail database, and the recipients of the e-mail inadvertently infect the people on their lists. The infection rate is exponential, as demonstrated in Figure 16-14. The previously referenced Melissa virus was a worm.

Trojan Horse

A+ 1102: 2.3

The Trojan horse classification is named after the Trojan horse from the associated legend. As the story goes, the Greeks left a huge wooden horse for the city of Troy. Presumed to be a gift symbolizing the end of the Trojan War, the horse was taken inside the walls of the city. However, the horse was hollow and filled with Greek soldiers, and when night came, the Greek soldiers climbed out of the horse, attacked the guards, and opened the gates to the city, allowing additional Greek soldiers to enter and defeat the city of Troy. The virus acts very much like the Trojan horse in the legend.

The **Trojan horse** class of malware appears as a desirable download, but when the file is opened, the malware activates. A Trojan horse can have a harmless outward appearance, often advertising itself as a utility to assist with computer operation. Since the Trojan horse is disguised, users may not realize that they have infected their computer. Some cause immediate damage, while others wait until a later date. After a time, unusual operations or glitches appear in the computer. For example, the hard drive may be erased or overwritten, leaving no space for other files to be saved. There are too many possible symptoms of Trojan horses to list them all, but you can expect many unusual operations on the computer and may not recognize the problem until damage occurs.

On any Windows system, you can often open Task Manager and see which processes are consuming time. This action will perhaps enable you to identify a Trojan horse. However, it is far better to have aggressive prohibition by a reputable antimalware program.

Boot Sector Virus

A+ 1102: 2.3

As its name implies, a **boot sector virus** is a type of virus that infects the boot sector of the drive. Such viruses can be difficult for antivirus software to find because most antivirus software runs within the operating system, not in the boot sector.

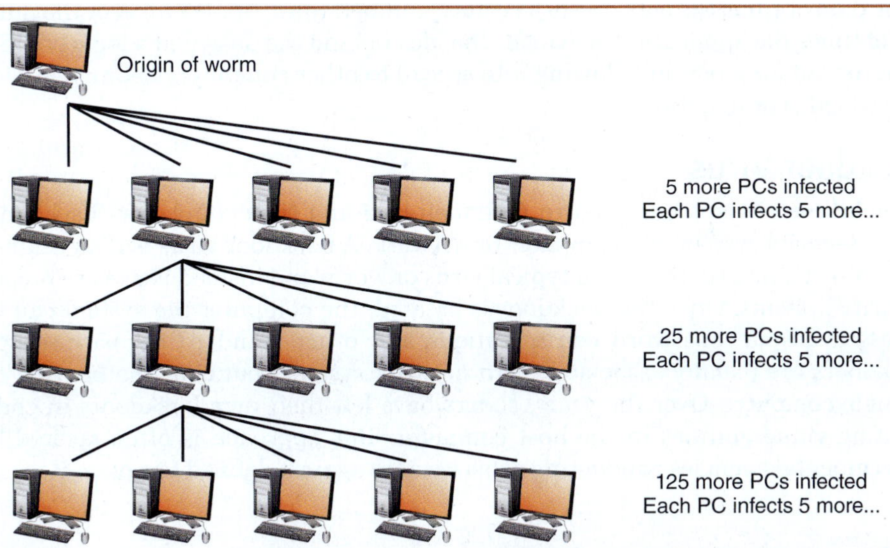

Goodheart-Willcox Publisher; (workstation icons) romvo/Shutterstock.com

Figure 16-14 A worm is a destructive program that contaminates files on the infected computer and spreads to other computers without prompting from the user.

Removing such a virus may require formatting the drive. Symptoms of infection include slowed operation, disappearing or encrypted files, lack of boot activity, blue screen errors, or the inability of the OS to load.

Macro Virus

A **macro virus** is a virus created using a macro programming language and is attached to documents that use the language. It is named after the macro software-programming tool. A standard macro program is designed to assist a computer user by converting repetitive tasks into one simple key code or name. Macros can record a set of user keystrokes and then save the set of keystrokes under a file name. When needed, the set of keystrokes can be easily loaded at any time. For example, a set of keystrokes used to create a template that will be used repeatedly can easily be created using the macro feature in Microsoft Word. A typical letter heading including a company's name, address, phone number, and the contact person is an example. When loaded, the macro automatically recreates the keystrokes, producing the desired information.

This same method is used to create some virus programs. They are often distributed as e-mail attachments, and once a computer is infected, the virus attaches itself to any new file created with the infected software application. Macro viruses are very common and estimated to account for 75 percent of all viruses. Some macro viruses can be as simple as running what appears to be a nonsense string in a Windows batch file but is, in fact, a carefully chosen string of bits designed to launch an attack.

Tech Tip

One point of interest is the **fdisk/mbr** command used to repair the MBR. Certain known virus programs move the location of the MBR, so applying the **fdisk/mbr** command will not remedy the problem. In fact, it will most likely do more damage when the command reconstructs the MBR with a damaged file and saves the damaged file as the backup copy.

MBR Virus

An **MBR virus** attacks the master boot record (MBR) of a hard drive and is considered extremely destructive. When activated, the virus plants hexadecimal codes in the master boot record, rendering it useless and resulting in hard disk failure. Damage is usually limited only to the master boot record, which can be rebuilt if backups have been made. Many antimalware programs perform MBR backups as part of their installation and require a CD, DVD, or flash drive to save necessary records for rebuilding the system.

Logic Bomb

A **logic bomb** is a destructive program that is slipped into an application and remains dormant until some event takes place. The event could be the arrival of some date or time; the entering of a certain number, word, or file name; or the number of times the application is loaded. The idea behind the design of a logic bomb is for it to wait for a period, allowing it to spread to other computers before releasing its payload of destruction.

Backdoor Virus

A **backdoor virus** is designed to go undetected and leave a hole, or "backdoor," in the security system of a computer or network. A backdoor virus is not designed to be directly destructive like a typical virus or worm and instead is used to breach security systems. Once the backdoor is created, the computer file system can be accessed despite password configurations and other standard security setups. Backdoors are usually associated with network systems but can also be used on a single computer. Over the years, coders have left their own backdoors in code, creating vulnerabilities in the host computer. This approach is often favored by governmental agencies conducting cyberwarfare against defined targets.

Password Virus

1102: 2.3 A+

A **password virus** is designed to breach security and steal passwords. The passwords are stolen and redirected to another location— possibly a separate system on the Internet—so the attacker can access them later. Often, the system housing the stolen passwords is not even aware that it is being used to hold stolen material.

A password virus is closely associated with a backdoor virus, and they may be used in combination. Both types are designed for illegally accessing networks, though either can be used to access a single computer when it is connected to the Internet.

1102: 2.3 A+

Similar to a password virus, a *keylogger* is malware that, after being installed on a computer, keeps track of all keys pressed by the user. In many ways, it is an expansion of a password virus. A keylogger records the keystrokes in a file, which can later be retrieved and used to learn the user login name, password, and other confidential information. Keylogger programs are often distributed through Trojans attached to an e-mail. Both keylogging and password viruses render the use of long and complex passwords unimportant; despite this, the user should still use these kinds of passwords and employ antimalware that detects keylogging and password capture.

Multipartite Virus

Multipartite viruses attack the computer in multiple ways. For example, the virus may infect the boot sector of the hard disk as well as one or more files. Multipartite viruses are considered more damaging than traditional viruses due to their multipronged attack methods. These types of viruses also tend to be fast-acting, which also makes them more concerning than traditional malware.

Stealth Virus

A **stealth virus** hides from normal detection by incorporating itself into part of a known, and usually required, program for the computer. The signature of a stealth virus is difficult to acquire unless the original computer system has an antimalware program installed when new. When the antimalware program is installed on a clean computer, the program monitors changes in all files, especially those susceptible to a stealth virus. A good rule of thumb is that if an important file unexpectedly changes in length, it is often a sign that it may have been infected with a stealth virus.

For example, the Melissa virus installed itself in the formatting code of Microsoft Word files. However, Word does not use markup and instead has traditionally stored formatting code in the terminus of the file. Knowledgeable users could examine a known infected file with a programmer's editor and see the malware.

A *sparse infector virus* is a type of stealth virus that attempts to elude detection by only performing its malicious activities sporadically. With a sparse infector virus, the user will see symptoms for a short period, then no symptoms for a time. In some cases, the sparse infector targets a specific program but only executes every tenth or twentieth time the target program opens. In other examples, a sparse infector may have a burst of activity and then lie dormant for a period of time. There are a number of variations on the theme, but the basic principle is the same: reduce the frequency of attack and thus reduce the chances for detection.

Polymorphic Virus

A **polymorphic virus** changes as it evolves to resist detection. It can randomly change its program length and the location or type of file it chooses to infect, and by constantly changing its profile, it can go undetected by antimalware programs that compare the signature or profile of the known virus. A rare type of polymorphic virus, called a *metamorphic virus*, is a special case in which the virus completely rewrites itself periodically. The most modern and dangerous viruses use both polymorphic and stealth characteristics to protect themselves. The best antimalware programs use estimation and statistics to attempt detection of this type of behavior.

Hoaxes

Not actually a virus, a **hoax** is a false message spread about a real or unreal virus. These messages could be classified as pranks, but while hoaxes do not directly damage the computer or destroy files, they are not harmless either.

A hoax is considered harmful because it can cause losses. While the damage is not usually directed to the computer or data system files, money is lost in the form of labor costs or through the loss of production time. If a hoax warns of a virus, such as a logic bomb that will activate at 12:00 on June 5, people who believe the hoax will stop working and use antimalware software to clean their computer before resuming work. It may take some time before they find out the message was not real, and no real virus exists. If this message spreads through a large corporation, thousands of computers could be shut down. Another trick used by hoaxes is to pick the name of a legitimate file used by a computer's operating system, claim that it is a virus, and warn users to delete the file. The best way to prevent against being fooled by a hoax is to visit one of the websites of an antimalware software manufacturer, which usually have pages dedicated to discussing common hoaxes.

A+ 1102: 2.3

Rootkit

A **rootkit** consists of a collection of software programs that installs on a computer and allows an intruder to take administrative control. What makes a rootkit so difficult to detect and remove is that it boots and runs before the operating system does, meaning it takes over the computer before the operating system can. It is like having two operating systems installed on the computer running simultaneously.

Rootkits are difficult to remove and often require a manual, step-by-step removal procedure. At times, the only way to eliminate a rootkit is to perform a complete low-level format of the hard drive. You may even need to flash the system BIOS or firmware.

There are four rootkit classifications, based on the location in which it resides:

- A *firmware rootkit* replaces or overwrites the computer firmware. This type of rootkit exists during the computer system POST.
- A *boot rootkit* replaces the operating system bootloader file, which is used to start or load the operating system.
- A *kernel rootkit* replaces some or all of the entire operating system kernel.
- A *driver rootkit* replaces a legitimate, trusted driver file used to support hardware.

Earlier in this chapter, security measures such as Trusted Boot and Measured Boot were introduced. These measures are incorporated into the computer system and are mainly designed to detect malware such as a rootkit. Computers equipped with UEFI and a Trusted Platform Module (TPM) are the best at detecting and preventing rootkits.

A+ 1102: 2.4

Botnet

A **botnet**, or *robot network*, is a collection of infected computers controlled by a source computer to send spam simultaneously to millions of computers connected to the Internet. This type of arrangement can also be used to create a **denial-of-service (DoS)**, which is an attack in which a network server or web server is flooded with false requests to the point that it cannot fulfill legitimate requests, causing the requests to time out. A web server would appear to the requester as being out of service, and in the practical sense, it is. A specific type of DoS is a *distributed denial-of-service (DdoS)* attack, which is a DoS that originates from more than one attacking the computer.

Grayware

The exact definition of grayware depends on which antimalware manufacturer website you visit. In general, **grayware** refers to a collection of malware that is not regarded as very dangerous, but rather more of a nuisance. Examples of grayware include pop-up ads, adware, joke programs, spyware, and data-mining software. While grayware is not as damaging as something like a Trojan, MBR virus, or worm, it *does* slow computer performance because it often uses the Internet connection to send information back to the originator or collection point.

To help combat grayware, some browsers have taken precautions against targeted ads and adware. For example, as of version 71, the Google Chrome browser will deny the appearance of advertising if the ads do not meet certain standards. Additionally, most browsers can block advertising and most pop-ups through settings or add-in software.

Adware

A+ 1102: 2.10

Adware is designed to support advertisements such as pop-ups and may also gather information about the user. It most commonly infects computers through free downloads, such as screensavers, free-trial software programs, and file-sharing programs. Adware is not overtly destructive as many malware programs are, but it can cause computer performance to suffer. Adware programs often send data to the originating source to keep track of a user's Internet habits. Computer performance suffers because while the user is trying to use the Internet and search the web, the adware program may keep sending information to the source, thus reducing bandwidth. Adware typically uses pop-up browser windows to display ads, and while the use of a pop-up blocker will prevent the ads from displaying, it will *not* prevent adware from getting on your machine. Many browsers now have built in pop-up blockers that can be activated in the browser settings or privacy settings, depending on the browser being used.

The right to use adware on the computer is typically stated in an end-user license agreement (EULA), which most users never read. When a user agrees to an EULA during software installation, they often grant permission to let the company spy on the computer or to gather information about the user and their browsing habits. It is important to note that this is completely legal, and many antimalware programs do not remove adware. Rather, you should install an additional program designed specifically for removing adware and spyware. Windows Defender also combats adware and spyware, as do many other competent antimalware programs.

Spyware

A+ 1102: 2.3

Spyware is designed to track a user's habits such as their web-browsing tendencies. Spyware is often included as part of a free, downloadable software package. Although sometimes classified as grayware, some spyware may be malicious. The main difference between spyware and adware is that spyware is considered malicious or illegal because the user has not given consent to install the program on his or her computer. Spyware and adware can be used to generate pop-ups on a computer as the user surfs the Internet. Some forms of spyware may monitor the user's keystrokes and read cookie contents stored on the computer.

Data Miner

A **data miner** gathers information about a user's web-browsing habits, which is then used for marketing purposes. Essentially, *data miner* is another name for spyware, and data-mining programs are classified as spyware by most antimalware organizations. As such, they are also considered a form of grayware. Data mining programs are often embedded into downloaded software, especially free applications or trial versions of software. It is usually legal because when the software or trial version is downloaded, the user agreement often states that the software will be using a data miner to gather information about the use of the product and the user's browsing activities. When users agree to the terms, they permit the company to mine data from their computer or, simply put, to be spied on.

Spam

Spam is unsolicited junk e-mail or newsletters and is responsible for drastically reducing the bandwidth of the Internet. Millions of pieces of spam are circulating the Internet at any given moment. Spam is illegal in most countries, but it is difficult to stop when coming from a country that does not have laws against it. Also, spam is often distributed by taking over a computer and using the computer as a source of spam e-mail. For example, a malicious software package can be downloaded and installed on an unsuspecting user's computer. The computer is under the control of a hacker and is used for other purposes, such as forwarding e-mail spam. Computers that have been taken control of and used for purposes such as sending spam are called *zombies*.

A+ 1102: 2.3

Ransomware

Ransomware is a type of malware that seizes control of your computer and demands payment to unlock it. Often, payment must be made using *cryptocurrency*, which is digital currency that is very difficult to trace. Ransomware encrypts all files on the computer, which makes them unusable. If the ransom is paid, the criminals may unlock the computer by decrypting the files, though there is no guarantee that they will. *Always* report a ransomware attack to law enforcement officials.

A recent example of ransomware is the Mindware malware, which became a substantial threat in 2022. Attacks with this ransomware were first noted in March and April 2022. Among other targets, Mindware was used against nonprofit mental-health providers. In addition to ransomware, the malware steals data. For example, data from victims in the financial and manufacturing industries that was stolen by Mindware was later posted to the Internet. Each Mindware payload is configured for a particular target, which is rather unusual in the ransomware arena. Once the target is infected, the payload drops a hardcoded ransomware note demanding payment and discouraging attempts to circumvent the ransomware.

A+ 1102: 2.3

Cryptominers

Cryptominers are malware that infect your machine so the malware can use your machine's resources to mine cryptocurrency such as bitcoin. Often, the only damage to the infected computer is resource exhaustion, which can seriously degrade the computer's overall performance. Removal of cryptominers is accomplished in the same way as removing any other malware: using antivirus software or manually removing the files and all corresponding registry entries (if it is a Windows computer).

Browser Hijackers

A **browser hijacker** is a program that changes the configuration of a browser, such as replacing the default home page to one that was not intentionally installed by the user. Other times, they may install unwanted icons or modify the toolbar to take users to a website they did not intend to connect to or view. Some forms of browser hijackers are identified as adware by some antimalware software packages, and in most cases, competent antimalware programs should detect this change and block it. However, it is up to the user to ensure the antimalware settings incorporate this blocking.

Phishing

1102: 2.3, 2.4 A+

Phishing (pronounced *fishing*) is an e-mail used to impersonate a legitimate company, person, or institution, thus fooling the user into believing the e-mail is from a trusted source. The phishing e-mail requests information from the user, such as their username, password, account number, Social Security number, or some combination of personal information, which is then used for illegal actions. A very common phishing scam is to send millions of e-mails that look like legitimate e-mails from a widely used company such as eBay requesting that the user confirm personal information, such as the username, password, and account number. If the user responds to the bogus e-mail, their account is compromised by the criminal. Phishing is also considered a form of social engineering, but the user can mitigate this situation by never responding directly to these e-mails. From an organizational standpoint, anti-phishing training, such as online modules requiring employees to determine whether an example e-mail is or is not phishing, can go a long way in preventing phishing attacks.

1102: 2.3 A+

There are many variations of phishing. For example, *spear phishing* is a related term that refers to highly targeted phishing campaigns directed at a specific user, often through e-mail. When the target is particularly valuable, such as a company's Chief Information Security Officer, this practice is called *whaling*. When voice or Voice over IP (VoIP) is used instead of e-mail, it is called *vishing*. A common feature of vishing attacks is a spoofed caller ID that makes the caller appear more legitimate; these attacks are significantly more successful when launched against senior citizens or individuals who are not technologically savvy. Another variation is called *smishing*, which is when a user is tricked into downloading malware or providing confidential information via text message. The name comes from a combination of *short messaging service (SMS)* and *phishing*. Often, a user receives a text message with a link to verify a device, and when the user opens it, malicious software is downloaded to the device.

Pharming

Pharming, also known as *DNS cache poisoning* or simply *DNS poisoning*, is a deceptive practice based on poisoning a Domain Name Service (DNS) server with an incorrect IP address for a website. DNS servers are located all over the Internet at different levels. For example, each Internet service provider (ISP) is responsible for running a DNS server at its location. All websites have a domain name (the name of the website, usually) and an IP address, and when you request a web page, such as www.google.com, your request is sent to the local ISP, where their DNS server matches the domain name to the domain name's IP address, such as 8.8.8.8. The IP address is then used to find and connect to the requested website.

Pharming takes place when the requested domain name is realigned with a different IP address. When this happens, any request through the DNS server is redirected to the counterfeit website. For example, you request to connect to a company selling computers and are unknowingly redirected to a replica of the real site. When you find the computer you want, you attempt to purchase the computer by providing your name, address, credit card information, and more. In reality, the fake website collected all the information needed to use your credit card anywhere in the world. In this way, pharming is a very sophisticated method of identity theft.

The pharming strategy takes place on a remote computer so traditional antimalware, antispam, and other malware protection programs cannot prevent it. Pharming can only be prevented at the DNS server by ensuring the DNS server is using protection mechanisms.

Cookies

A **cookie** is a small text file used to send information about a user to a server. Cookies were originally designed to assist users in finding topics or information on a server. For example, if a user browses a website and purchases a fishing pole, a cookie is generated and stored on the user's computer. The next time the user visits that particular website, information is displayed related to fishing poles, such as wading boots, fishing lures, and any related fishing merchandise that might be on sale. The cookie and the text information stored within it identify the special interest of the user. Most cookies are from legitimate websites and will not harm your computer. Some advertisers place them onto your computer for research and selling purposes. However, if a hacker gains access to your cookies, you are at risk because they can be used to steal any information stored or saved from a website. Cookies also can be used to target you for a scam based on your Internet history. Modern browsers can be set to remove cookies automatically on exit, or the user can manually execute a cleanup procedure from within the browser or using special tools.

A+ 1102: 2.10

Private browsing modes can often save time when it comes to clearing cookies. When using private browsing mode, a temporary session is created that is isolated from the browser's primary session and data. No browsing history is saved in private browsing mode, and the cookies and web cache are automatically cleared when the session ends.

A+ 1102: 2.10

One countermeasure against malicious cookies is to clear browsing data. Regardless of what browser you use, all major browsers give you the ability to clear all browser data, and the browser can be configured to clear data automatically each time the browser is closed. For example, Firefox users can open the menu from the upper-right corner of the browser and select **Settings>Privacy and Security**. From there, you can set to clear browsing data, clear cache, and turn on private browsing, all of which help mitigate threats from cookies. The process is similar in Microsoft Edge; open the browser menu from the upper-right corner of the screen and select **Settings>Privacy, search, and services**, which has settings for clearing browsing data, clearing cache, and opening private browser, among other security-related configurations. The process with Chrome is almost identical to that of Firefox; open the browser menu and navigate to **Settings>Privacy and Security**.

A+ 1102: 2.4

Man-in-the-Middle (MITM)

A **man-in-the-middle (MITM) attack**, sometimes referred to as an *on-path attack*, is an interception of a transmission over a network. When this occurs, the person intercepting the transmission obtains, reads, and places the transmission back en route to its original destination. An MITM attack is not necessarily a virus or malware; rather, it is a serious network security breach. Attacks such as these can often be avoided by using strict access permissions or by proximity-based filtering methods, such as geofencing. *Geofencing* is the process of creating a virtual boundary around a physical location. It is commonly used with global positioning systems (GPS) but can also be used with regard to secure facilities. The most exotic form of geofencing involves running the data transmission lines through a pipe pressured with a gas with sensors that can detect a physical breach.

Buffer Overflow

A *buffer-overflow attack*, also called a *buffer-overrun* attack, occurs when someone tries to put more data into a buffer than it was designed to hold. Any program that communicates with the Internet or a private network must take in some data, which is stored, at least temporarily, in a space in memory called a *buffer*. Assuming the programmer who wrote the application was careful, data too large to fit into a buffer is either simply truncated or outright rejected. Given the number of applications that might be running on a target system and the number of buffers in each application, the chances of having at least one buffer that was not written properly are significant enough to cause any prudent person some concern.

Someone who is moderately skilled in programming can write a program that purposefully writes more into the buffer than it can hold. For example, if the buffer can hold 1,024 bytes of data and you try to fill it with 2,048 bytes, the computer simply loads the extra 1,024 bytes into memory. If that extra data is actually a malicious program, then it has just been loaded into memory and is now running on the target system. Alternatively, perhaps the perpetrator simply wants to flood the target machine's memory, thus overwriting other items that are currently in memory and causing them to crash. Either way, the buffer overflow is a very serious attack.

Fortunately, buffer-overflow attacks are a bit harder to execute than DoS attacks or simple Microsoft Outlook script viruses. To create a buffer-overflow attack, you must have a good working knowledge of some programming language (C or C++ is often chosen) and understand the target operating system or application well enough to know whether it has a buffer overflow weakness and how that weakness might be exploited.

It must be noted that modern operating systems and web servers are not generally susceptible to common buffer-overflow attacks. Windows 95 was quite susceptible, but it has been many years since a Windows operating system was as susceptible as Windows 95. Certainly Windows 10 or 11 cannot be compromised with this type of attack, but the same cannot necessarily be said for all the custom applications developed to run on various systems. It is always possible that an Internet-enabled application, including but not limited to web applications, might be susceptible to this kind of attack.

Essentially, this vulnerability exists only if programmers fail to program correctly. If all programs truncate extra data, then a buffer overflow cannot be executed on that system. However, if the program does not check the boundaries of variables and arrays and allows excess data to be loaded, then that system is vulnerable to a buffer overflow.

Creation of Viruses

A basic understanding of how viruses are created may make you better able to detect a virus. Viruses are created in several ways using many different programming tools. For example, one common way viruses are created is through macros. As discussed in the previous section about macro viruses, a macro is a short program written to save keystrokes. Macros are written in macro language programs, such as Visual Basic for Applications (VBA) or similar programming tools and are developed to help users. However, the same techniques used to save you time can also be applied for destructive purposes.

Programming software such as Visual Basic, C++, and ActiveX are commonly used tools to develop viruses and worms. Even the simple macro editor that comes with Microsoft Word can be used. Some websites will even sell password, backdoor, and worm programs, though they are advertised "for educational use only."

Most virus and worm paths can be tracked and often traced back to the source, especially when delivered by e-mail. The properties of an e-mail message can be revealed to expose the real e-mail address, e-mail server name, and originating IP address, as shown in Figure 16-15. Once the TCP/IP address is known, a trace can begin, and an ISP can revoke access to any user who violates privacy or harasses another computer site. Remember, accessing another person's computer without express permission and distributing a virus is a crime.

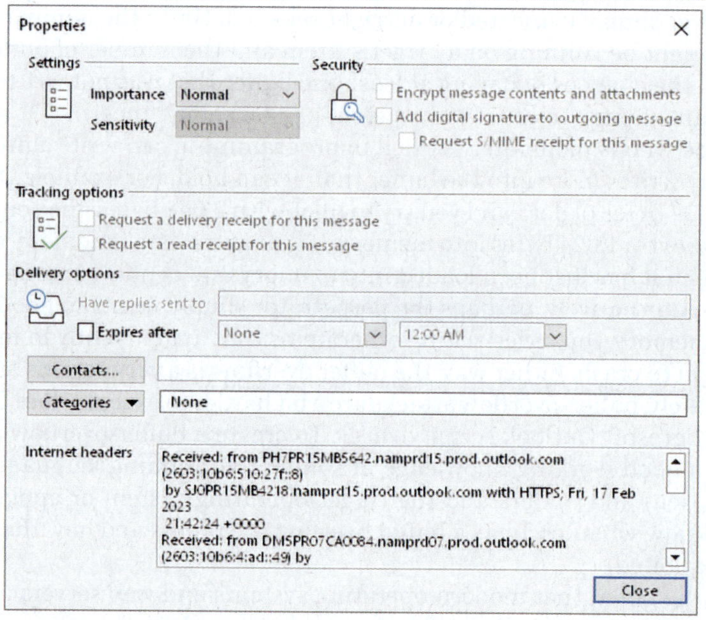

Figure 16-15 The source information of an e-mail can be revealed in Microsoft Outlook by opening the message and selecting **File>Properties**.

Goodheart-Willcox Publisher

A+ **1102: 2.3, 2.4, 2.7, 2.10**

Malware Prevention

Keeping a computer free of viruses can be a difficult task. Most malware can be prevented, but with new malware appearing all the time, it is difficult to prevent them all. Worms make use of existing program security flaws. For worms, there is no other protection than to avoid all contact on networks and the Internet, and for most people, this is not an option.

Most malware infections can be prevented by following some simple practices. Additional practices will help keep damage to a minimum if you are infected. The following suggestions will help keep your computers and networks safe:

- Always use a firewall to protect your computer from Internet access.
- Always install an antimalware program to combat malware.
- Never open unsolicited e-mails or e-mail attachments.
- Follow security protocols and maintain a compliant system; those without such protocols are considered *non-compliant systems.*
- Remain wary of e-mail, even when it comes from a known sender.
- Only download software from a trusted source, such as the Microsoft Store, and avoid downloading anything from an untrusted source.
- Whenever feasible, always rescan downloaded software with a custom scan using installed antimalware.
- Use e-mail filters.
- Never reveal your password to anyone or transmit a password in an e-mail.
- Never respond to any e-mail that requests your password, account numbers, Social Security number, or any other information that could put you at risk.
- Always have a *required* password.
- Do not accept file attachments on e-mails from unknown sources. It is true that you can still get a virus from a known source, but this usually only happens when friendly sources do not know they are spreading a virus. However, your chances are lessened by accepting attachments from only known sources. Regular acceptance of file attachments from completely unknown sources will almost surely cause a problem sooner or later.
- Never load a file from media that you have not checked first with up-to-date antimalware software. The number of infections that have occurred by simply exchanging discs or flash drives (especially games) is enormous.

Tech Tip

A virus or worm designed to crack an e-mail list is specific to a particular e-mail software package. Since each e-mail system has a unique program design, malware must be designed especially for that e-mail software package. This means other e-mail software packages cannot be cracked by the same virus or worm.

- Before giving a file to anyone, check the storage media using an antimalware program.
- Encrypt your important files. Encrypted files are essentially useless to another user without the encryption key. Even if you have files stolen, minimal damage is done.
- Always perform regular daily backups of important files. Not all malware can be stopped before doing damage to a computer system. Performing regular backups is your best insurance against a malware disaster.

If you have any doubts about taking the time to protect yourself or taking the time to back up your files, consider the following questions regarding your options if a virus destroys your files:

- Do you have the discs or media to reload everything, from operating system to leisure programs?
- How much time would it take to reconstruct everything on your computer?
- How many of the items on your computer are one of a kind?
- Are there important documents on your hard drive, such as term papers, legal papers, financial data, or income tax forms? If so, do you have any hard copies of this information?
- What happens if you are responsible for a corporation? What would the corporation lose if the computer were wiped clean?

After thinking about the individual or corporate losses, it is easy to see the benefits of protecting your computer and backing up important files.

Tech Tip

Cloud service providers run antimalware to protect user data. Cloud storage is an excellent choice for backing up critical files.

A+ 1102: 2.4

Unprotected systems—those without antivirus or firewall configurations—pose a massive vulnerability to not only data but also an entire network. This is the equivalent to having every door on a bank locked except for one. Once an unprotected system is breached, any device connected to it can be at risk, as well as the data stored on it. Equally vulnerable are end-of-life operating systems, which can pose a significant threat in terms of malware. Normally, operating systems that reach the end of their life are no longer protected by the developer. For example, Windows 7 is no longer supported by Microsoft, so no new security patches are being developed and released. As a result, if you have a computer that is still running Windows 7, any existing vulnerability will remain because Microsoft is no longer creating patches for it.

Malware Removal

A+ 1102: 2.3

While preventing the arrival of a virus or worm is ideal, there is a good chance that, at some point, you will encounter an infected computer. Remember that a virus or worm is simply a program designed to annoy, amuse, or destroy. You eliminate a virus that has never been run as you would any unwanted program: you delete it by placing it in the **Recycle Bin** and then emptying the **Recycle Bin**. This approach works if you know with certainty that the virus has not been activated. To be safe, it makes sense to read and apply the steps presented in the following section.

Once a virus has been activated, it can be a much more complicated task to remove it. The removal of some viruses and worms is as easy as locating and erasing the file containing the virus, and in most cases, removal often involves removing various files, installing a software patch, and adjusting registry settings. Most antimalware manufacturers provide a small downloadable program that does many of these tasks automatically. When a widespread virus is first discovered and publicized, your first move should be to go to the website of your antimalware provider, check its alert bulletins for a description and remedy, and update the antimalware database on the client side.

A+ 1102: 2.4

The first step in virus removal is identification. Just because a computer is acting strangely does not mean it has contracted a virus. Any number of things can produce the same effects of known viruses. Check your antimalware manufacturer website for information about the particular virus characteristics. The website will give you a complete description of the virus and its effects, including its symptoms, size, and general location; how it spreads; and what areas of the computer system it affects. Most viruses and worms have hidden, system, or read-only file attributes set to help protect it. This is especially helpful for *zero-day vulnerabilities*, which are previously unknown vulnerabilities that have existed since software was released. These often go undiscovered until malware is created to exploit them or until a system is patched. A **zero-day attack** is one that exploits a previously unknown vulnerability before it can be patched. The name stems from the first day in the count of days after a vulnerability is discovered.

The next step is removal. Usually, antimalware manufacturers provide a removal tool, which is an executable program you download and run. Often, this is contained in the graphical font-end of the software. The executable program does all the complicated steps for you behind the scenes by removing all the infected files and, if need be, correcting any altered registry settings. If there is no removal tool available, you can usually find step-by-step instructions on the Internet, but be sure you are visiting a trusted, reputable website for this information. If your antimalware tool does not do so, you must manually delete *all* infected files and, if registry changes are needed, you must open the registry program and make the alterations as specified. You must be *extremely* careful when altering the registry. If you make even so much as a typographical error in your registry alteration, trouble may ensue. To avoid these types of problems, most modern antimalware software does all of this for you.

Tech Tip

When an antimalware program identifies a virus or malware item but fails to remove it successfully, try running the computer in Safe Mode and then start the antimalware program.

A virus may make additional copies of itself so that it can re-infect your computer if the original virus file is erased. For example, it can attach itself automatically to any drive when files are saved to that drive. This means that if the bug has not been detected and you save a file to a flash drive, CD/DVD, or a network hard drive, the virus also saves a copy of itself to the same media. When media such as a flash drive or CD/DVD is used to load a file to a hard drive or to RAM, the virus tags along, loading itself as well. Many viruses spread this way. As part of eliminating a virus, all removable media must be scanned as it is the only way to ensure the complete removal of the virus. A suitable sequence for malware removal might go as follows:

A+ 1102: 3.3

1. Identify and research malware symptoms.
2. Quarantine the infected systems.
3. Disable System Restore (in Windows).
4. Remediate the infected systems.
   A. Update the antimalware software.
   B. Scan and use removal techniques (Safe Mode, pre-installation environment).
5. Schedule scans and run updates.
6. Enable System Restore and create a restore point (in Windows).
7. Educate the end user.

A+ 1102: 3.3

Other methods of malware removal involve using Windows recovery mode. Recovery mode offers several options, including the ability to reset the PC to before an app was installed. This is especially useful if you suspect a downloaded app is actually a Trojan horse. Recovery mode also offers the ability to restore the computer to a specific recovery point.

There are a few ways to access recovery mode. The most common method is to open the **Start** menu and press and hold the [Shift] key while you select the power button from the **Start** menu. This action will launch the screen shown in Figure 16-16, which offers a number of recovery options.

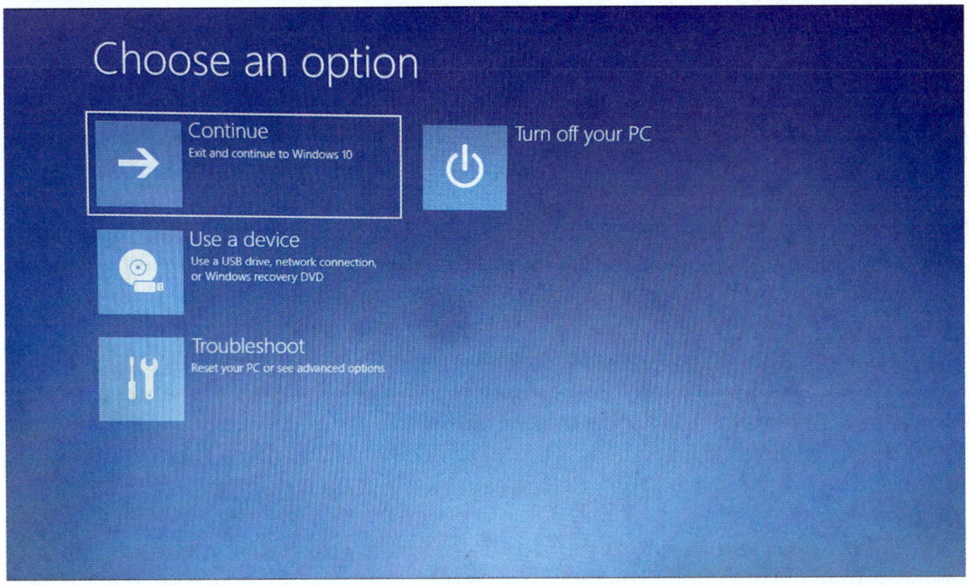

Goodheart-Willcox Publisher

Figure 16-16 Recovery mode offers several options to repair a PC, including reset the PC to a time before a problem was encountered.

Legal Aspects

Legal punishment for the creation and distribution of a virus is severe, and individuals can be held liable for the cost of financial losses suffered by any corporation harmed by the virus. The FBI National Computer Crime Squad (NCCS) has classified computer crimes into certain categories. These categories include the following:

- Intrusions of the public phone system, including cell phone providers or carriers
- Major computer network intrusions
- Network integrity violations
- Privacy violations
- Industrial espionage
- Pirated software
- Other crimes committed by using a computer

In addition to the federal crime statutes, most states have their own criminal statutes comparable to the federal statutes, and computer crimes are not taken lightly. An example of harsh consequences can be seen in the cases of several young students who have used computer systems to break these laws. The outcome is usually simple. While the students serve no time for their mistakes, their entire computer systems have been confiscated, and they may be banned from using a computer for five years or more.

You may be wondering why there are laws dealing with intrusion into the public telephone system. The public telephone system provides a medium for a tremendous amount of Internet use. Many hackers have attempted to gain, or have successfully gained, access to telephone company records, allowing them to use other people's identifications when accessing the Internet for illegal purposes. Illegal access to the public telephone system carries severe penalties.

The last classification, "other crimes committed using a computer," is a catchall. If a computer crime is not specifically listed, then the act of any criminal nature committed using a computer will fall under this statute. This law is important because people who are determined to do damage or illegally use computer systems invent new crimes on a continual basis.

Mistaken Identification

Often, a problem occurs on a computer and the computer software automatically assumes it to be a virus. Some technicians automatically assume that many difficult-to-solve problems are caused by a virus, but the result of some user errors often appear similar to problems caused by a virus. A classic problem occurs when a user accidentally hits a key combination that has devastating effects. For example, when the [Ctrl][A] key combination is used in Microsoft Word, the entire document is highlighted, and the very next keystroke will replace all the text in the document, making it seem as though the entire manuscript disappeared, with the user unaware that they are the cause of the problem. In this scenario, it would be easy to assume that a virus has attacked the computer system.

Another problematic key combination is [Ctrl][Alt][Arrow]. Depending on the direction of the arrow used, this combination will cause the display of a monitor to rotate in 90-degree increments. If a user accidentally enters this combination, it would be easy to assume that a virus caused the screen to flip, when it was actually just a simple mistake.

A follow-up phenomenon is the repeat of the keystroke error. Once a mistake is made, human nature allows that person to repeat the same mistake. Since the technician will probably never view the error in progress and will only get a verbal description of the situation, it may be difficult to diagnose the problem. A frantic description of time lost on a document does not make for easy computer diagnosis, so the assumption is that it must be a virus. A few simple steps can help if the user has not tried to repair the error first. The key combination [Ctrl][Z] can save a tremendous amount of time if the user has not typed too many additional keystrokes before you arrive. In addition, many applications have a setting for saving as often as every minute. For example, documents created in the cloud are often saved every few seconds.

Users often assume a virus has attacked their computers as things go wrong, but there are many different reasons that a computer can exhibit unusual actions. Possibilities include power glitches, magnets too close to the computer or monitor, network glitches, and more. A strong magnetic field can completely erase computer disks. If this happens, it will probably be reported as a virus.

A+ 1102: 3.2

It is important to remember that not every issue encountered by a user will be related to or caused by malware. Sometimes, an issue could be on the vendor-side of software. Other times, it could be an outage that is entirely out of the user's control. Figure 16-17 lists common symptoms encountered and possible resolutions for them.

16.3 Threats beyond Malware

While malware represents a significant threat to computer systems, there are many other threat types that can be equally detrimental. For example, uneducated users pose a significant threat because they may open compromised files or attachments or fall victim to phishing or social engineering attacks. In general, two significant threat types beyond malware are insider threats and web-based attacks.

A+ 1102: 2.4

Insider Threat

An *insider threat* is not a specific attack; rather, it is a generalized term to describe any threat that originates from someone who is a part of the network. These threats are particularly harmful because the threat actor already has some level of access to the network. Effective countermeasures for insider threats start with the concept of least privilege, meaning no employee should have any more access privileges than absolutely required by their job. Monitoring the software installed on network computers and analyzing network traffic can also help to counter insider threats.

Common PC Symptoms and Resolutions	
Symptom	**Possible Cure(s)**
Random or frequent pop-ups	Use a browser setting or extension to block
Browser-related symptoms, such as redirections	Adjust browser settings; run antimalware software
Security alerts	Ensure alerts are turned on
Slow performance	Check Task Manager to see what processes are running; adjust disk access; add additional RAM
Internet connectivity issues	Consult ISP for outages; reboot router and modem; verify firewall is operational and permitting online access
PC lockup	Reboot to Safe Mode to see if the problem goes away; remove problematic applications
OS update failure	Consult OS website regarding vendor-side failures; restart PC
Rogue antivirus	Uninstall and reinstall software
Spam	Use e-mail filters
Unexpected changes to system or personal files (including altered, renamed, or missing/disappearing files)	Run antimalware; consult OS website for bugs; conduct frequent backups
File permission changes	Run antimalware
Hijacked e-mail	Never click through an e-mail link; hover mouse over address to avoid spoofing; monitor, block, and ignore
Certificate warnings, such as invalid certificate (trusted root CA)	Avoid website as certificates are there to protect users
System or application log errors	Schedule regular log checks; look for anomalies
False alerts regarding antivirus protection	Likely a scam, run antimalware software to be sure
Unwanted notifications within the OS	Adjust OS settings to minimize or prevent unnecessary notifications

Goodheart-Willcox Publisher

Figure 16-17 Some common symptoms are easily resolved without the use of antimalware programs.

Web Attacks

Web-based attacks are just as much an issue as malware and can devastate a network if successful. A common web-based attack is an ***injection attack***, which is the insertion of malicious code into a web application to exploit vulnerabilities or modify software commands. Preventing injection attacks such as SQL injections and cross-site scripting normally involves either the administrator of the web server or the programmers that develop the website.

SQL Script Injection

1102: 2.4 A+

An ***SQL script injection*** is a code-injection technique that involves a threat actor passing Structured Query Language (SQL) commands to a web application and getting the website to execute them. SQL injections are among the most popular types of attack on websites and are often performed to side-step the login authentication or access an underlying database. In recent years, more websites have taken steps to mitigate the dangers of these attacks, but unfortunately, many websites are still susceptible.

A+ 1102: 2.4

Cross-Site Scripting

Cross-site scripting (XSS) is an attack method in which an attacker injects client-side scripts into web pages viewed by other users. The key is that the attacker enters scripts into an area with which other users interact so when users go to that part of the site, the attacker's script is executed instead of the intended website functionality. For example, imagine retail websites that allow users to review products. Rather than creating a review, an attacker might enter JavaScript code that redirects the user to a phishing website. When another user views that "review," the script executes and takes the user to the new site. Again, such attacks can be prevented by simply filtering all user input.

A+ 1101: 2.1, 2.2

A+ 1102: 1.4, 1.5, 1.6, 2.3, 2.5, 2.7

16.4 Firewall

No chapter concerning computer security would be complete without covering the firewall. A **firewall** is a hardware device or software application that protects the computer from unauthorized access or malware delivered through a network or Internet connection. This section will provide you with a short introduction to firewalls, but more information is provided in later chapters.

To fully understand the digital mechanics of how a firewall operates, you need detailed knowledge about protecting a network system by blocking access to specific ports or by filtering IP addresses, packet contents, services, and protocols. The details of these topics require you to understand the basics of network and Internet address systems and network protocols. For now, firewalls will be introduced in general terms rather than detailed technical specifics of how a firewall works based on packet contents and Internet addresses.

A+ 1102: 2.5

Windows operating systems include a firewall that protects the computer from unauthorized access from a person or some types of malware, as shown in Figure 16-18. To enable or disable the Windows Firewall, navigate to **Start>Control Panel>System and Security>Windows Defender Firewall.** If a computer is never connected to a network system and the Internet, there would be no need for a firewall, but since many programs rely on an Internet connection, a firewall is an essential requirement for safe computing. For example, many programs check for

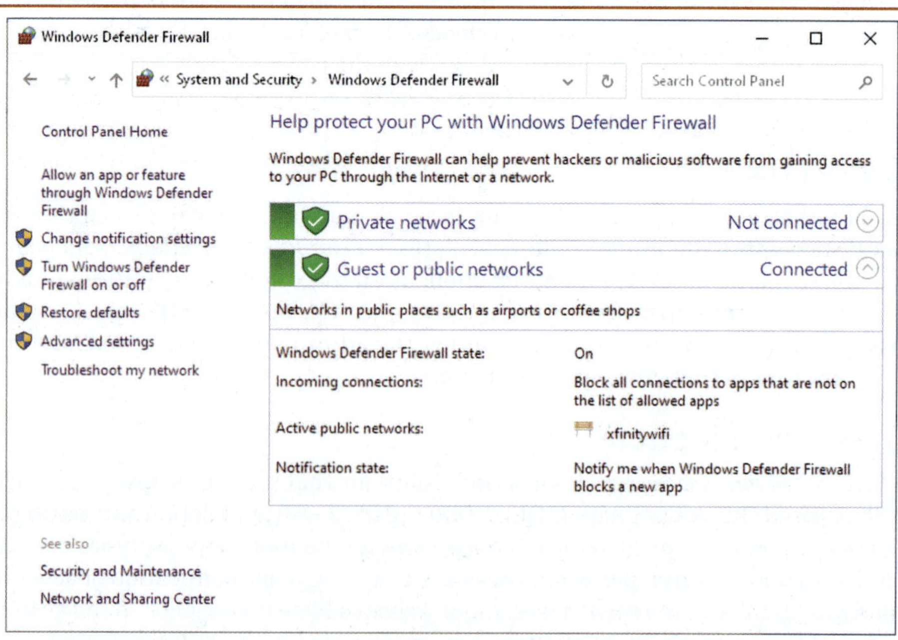

Goodheart-Willcox Publisher

Figure 16-18 The Windows Defender Firewall protects computers from unauthorized access and some malware types.

system updates or require an Internet connection to perform normal duties such as checking e-mail, engaging in social media, or playing an online multiplayer game. There is a constant flow of information in the form of data blocks called *packets* to and from the computer. Each packet contains a port number in addition to the data.

For additional firewall settings and options, users can select **Advanced settings** from the left side of the **Windows Defender Firewall** window to open the **Windows Firewall with Advanced Security** window. From this window, users can change inbound and outbound rules for individual programs by right-clicking on the desired program and selecting **Properties** from the shortcut menu. Once the program's properties window is open, users can customize the protocol or port number used and establish exceptions for the program, among other options.

A **port number** is a logical address, ranging from 0 to 65,535, used by all software applications on a network system to identify the software application or service. The software application is identified by a port number so the packet can be delivered to the intended software application.

The flow of packets to and from a computer on a network requires each packet contain a port number; hence, the flow of data can be controlled by blocking specific port numbers or ports. The term *port* is used when referring to a specific destination. Most port numbers or ports are blocked by default, but some remain open to allow special software applications—called services—to function. A **service** is a software application that performs specific network functions, such as assigning network addresses or supporting remote access to the computer desktop.

There are times when you may need to block or unblock a specific port. For example, a firewall is set up to block all nonessential ports, but a user may need certain ports open for an online game. Assume an online game requires the use of TCP ports 5,222 and 5,795–5,847. These ports can be opened by entering their numbers in the firewall service properties dialog box, which allows data to pass through the firewall so two computers can communicate freely during a gaming session.

Notice in Figure 16-18 that the Windows 10 Firewall has two broad categories of default configuration: **Private networks** and **Guest or public networks**. Private networks are those that support Internet access in homes or, sometimes, small business offices. Guest or public networks are Internet access locations such as airports, coffee shops, or other similar public locations. Public networks are the most vulnerable to attacks and as such, have the most restrictive default configuration, which blocks all port access except for vital ports. Private networks are less restrictive because they typically do not connect directly to the Internet and usually have some sort of security device, such as a router or a firewall that provides protection to the computers and network system. When using a public location, the computer user has no control over the Internet access being provided. Thus, there is no insurance that the connection is protected by a security device, nor is there any guarantee as to how strict the security configuration settings are.

Most modern antimalware also provides a firewall for the operating system. Generally, the antimalware installation process will disable the Windows Firewall briefly and install its own firewall. However, it is wise to verify the status of the firewall, both through the antimalware interface and through the operating system.

There are numerous types of firewalls, and each type has multiple variations. However, most firewalls can be categorized as either packet filtering or stateful packet inspection. *Basic packet filtering* is the simplest form of firewall and involves inspecting packets and checking to see if each packet meets the firewall rules. For example, it is common for a packet-filtering firewall to consider three questions:

- Is this packet using a protocol that the firewall allows?
- Is this packet destined for a port that the firewall allows?
- Is the packet coming from an IP address that the firewall has not blocked?

These are three very basic rules, and some packet-filtering firewalls check additional rules. However, packet-filtering firewalls do not check the preceding packets from that same source. Essentially, each packet is treated as a singular event, without reference to the preceding conversation, making packet-filtering firewalls quite susceptible to some DoS attacks, such as SYN floods.

A ***stateful packet-inspection (SPI) firewall*** examines each packet and permits or denies access based on not only the examination of the current packet, but also data derived from previous packets in the conversation. The firewall is therefore aware of the context in which a specific packet was sent, making it far less susceptible to ping floods, SYN floods, and spoofing. For example, if a firewall detects that the current packet is an ICMP packet and a stream of several thousand packets has been continuously coming from the same source IP, the firewall will see that this is clearly a DoS attack, and it will block the packets.

A stateful packet-inspection firewall can also look at the actual contents of a packet, which allows for some very advanced filtering capabilities. Most high-end firewalls use the stateful packet-inspection method; when possible, this is the recommended type of firewall.

Chapter Summary

16.1 Microsoft Security Applications

- Windows Security provides an overview of the firewall, virus protection, updates, and other security configuration options.
- The User Account Control (UAC) can be customized to prompt users for administrative passwords when configuring vital parts of the operating system or computer.
- Parental Controls and Family Options allow users to filter websites, set screen-time limitations, restrict app functionality, and receive weekly activity reports. These tools can be used in the home with children or in the workplace with employees.
- Microsoft antimalware security tools include Microsoft Malicious Software Removal Tool, Microsoft Defender Offline, SmartScreen, Microsoft Safety Scanner, Microsoft Active Protection Service, Windows Update, and Windows Event Viewer.

16.2 Malicious Software

- Common classifications of malware are worm, Trojan horse, macro, MBR, logic bomb, backdoor virus, password virus, multipartite virus, keylogger, stealth virus, polymorphic virus, hoax, rootkit, botnet, grayware, spam, adware, spyware, ransomware, data miner, browser hijacking, phishing, pharming, cookies, man-in-the-middle attacks, and buffer-overflow attacks.
- Most virus and worm paths can be tracked.
- In most cases, malware removal often involves removing various files, installing a software patch, and adjusting registry settings.
- Legal punishment for the creation and distribution of a virus is severe.
- Many times, a problem occurs on a computer and the computer software automatically assumes it to be a virus. However, users make errors when using their computers, and the results can often appear similar to problems caused by a virus.

16.3 Threats beyond Malware

- An *insider threat* is not a specific attack; rather, it is a generalized term to describe any threat that originates from someone who is a part of the network. These threats are particularly harmful due to the fact that the threat actor already has some level of access to the network.
- A common web-based attack is an *injection attack*, which is the insertion of malicious code into a web application to exploit vulnerabilities or modify software commands.
- An *SQL script injection* is a code-injection technique that involves a threat actor passing Structured Query Language (SQL) commands to a web application and getting the website to execute them.
- A *cross-site scripting (XSS)* attack is an attack method in which an attacker injects client-side scripts into web pages viewed by other users.

16.4 Firewall

- A firewall is a hardware device or software application that protects the computer from unauthorized access or malware delivered through a network or Internet connection.

- Windows operating systems include a firewall that protects the computer from unauthorized access from a person or some types of malware.
- Most modern antimalware also provides a firewall for the operating system.

Review Questions

1. List common Microsoft security applications.
2. What is the most common way to eliminate or disable annoying messages that appear when a standard user attempts to make changes in the computer configuration?
3. Differentiate between Trusted Boot and Measured Boot.
4. What Microsoft application allows you to monitor security events such as unsuccessful login attempts?
5. List categories of malware.
6. Summarize the three major stages of a computer virus.
7. How is a worm different from a virus?
8. What is a Trojan horse virus?
9. How does a macro virus infect a computer?
10. What happens when an MBR virus is activated?
11. What two technologies incorporated into a computer system offer the best protection against rootkits?
12. What is a botnet?
13. What is grayware?
14. List and describe three types of malware that can be referred to as grayware.
15. What is the difference between adware and spyware?
16. What steps can you take to prevent malware infections?
17. List and describe common threats other than malware.
18. Describe the purpose of a firewall.
19. What is the difference between the Windows Firewall configuration categories?
20. Differentiate between a packet-filtering firewall and a stateful packet-inspection firewall.

Sample A+ Exam Questions

1. Which is the *least likely* way to contract a virus?
   A. Loading a game program on a computer from a flash drive given to you by a trusted friend
   B. Downloading a file from a reputable Internet site
   C. Connecting to another computer on a corporate network
   D. Loading a new operating system from a DVD taken directly from a sealed shrink-wrapped box
2. Which of the following methods is typically used to spread worms?
   A. E-mail attachments
   B. Exchanged flash drive contents
   C. The system BIOS whenever two computers connect on the Internet
   D. Exclusively by text editor programs

3. Which application would you run to enhance password security in Windows 7, 8, 8.1, and 10?
   A. **msconfig.sys**
   B. **secpol.msc**
   C. **ipconfig**
   D. **sysconfig**
4. Which accounts are disabled by default in Windows 10? Select all that apply.
   A. Administrator
   B. Standard
   C. Guest
   D. Limited
5. The characteristics that describe the uniqueness of a virus are referred to as a ______.
   A. signature
   B. reputation
   C. payload
   D. morphic synopsis
6. Which malware type changes the DNS server address of a legitimate website and replaces the IP address with a bogus website?
   A. Phishing
   B. Zombie
   C. Trojan horse
   D. Pharming
7. Which management tool is designed to prevent unauthorized access to a computer through an Internet connection?
   A. Windows Defender
   B. BitLocker
   C. Windows Firewall
   D. Local Security Policy
8. Which technique or software program is based on poisoning the DNS database of a DNS server?
   A. Rootkit
   B. Phishing
   C. Pharming
   D. Data mining
9. Which version of Windows introduced Action Center?
   A. Windows XP
   B. Windows 7
   C. Windows 8.1
   D. Windows 10
10. Which of the following does TPM need to function?
   A. UEFI firmware
   B. BitLocker
   C. BIOS
   D. Antivirus software

Chapter 17

PC Troubleshooting

Learning Outcomes

17.1 Identify common-sense practices when troubleshooting a PC.
17.2 List the most likely causes of boot failure at each boot stage.
17.3 Recognize common problems or failures and identify their causes.
17.4 Compare Windows diagnostic utilities.
17.5 Recall the Windows boot sequence.
17.6 Describe preventive computer maintenance.
17.7 List the CompTIA A+ troubleshooting steps.

A+ Certification Exam Objectives

The following A+ Certification Exam Objectives are covered in this chapter.

Exam 220-1101

5.0 Hardware and Network Troubleshooting

- 5.1 Given a scenario, use the best practice methodology to resolve problems.
- 5.2 Given a scenario, troubleshoot problems related to motherboards, RAM, CPUs, and power.
- 5.3 Given a scenario, troubleshoot and diagnose problems with storage devices and RAID arrays.
- 5.4 Given a scenario, troubleshoot video, projector, and display issues.
- 5.5 Given a scenario, troubleshoot common issues with mobile devices.

Exam 220-1102

1.0 Operating Systems

- 1.2 Given a scenario, use the appropriate Microsoft command line tool.
- 1.3 Given a scenario, use features and tools of the Microsoft Windows 10 operating system.
- 1.4 Given a scenario, use the appropriate Microsoft Windows 10 Control Panel utility.

3.0 Software Troubleshooting

- 3.1 Given a scenario, troubleshoot common Windows OS problems.

4.0 Operational Procedures

- 4.3 Given a scenario, implement workstation backup and recovery methods.
- 4.5 Summarize environmental impacts and local environmental controls.

Key Terms

archive bit
blue screen error
differential backup
hive
incremental backup
Microsoft Dynamic Link Library (DLL)
POST card
registry key
startup problem
system image

Overview

Troubleshooting a PC requires a combination of a technician's knowledge, intuition, and experience. Microsoft Windows operating systems include many diagnostic tools as standard programs, and there are many diagnostic tools available from third-party vendors that can assist in the troubleshooting process. Third-party vendor programs range from freeware and shareware to systems costing several thousands of dollars, with the more expensive programs including a diagnostic board that plugs into the PC's expansion slots.

Most problems can be diagnosed without expensive diagnostic tools, but the value of these tools is their ability to save time and money when trying to identify problems that may be caused by two or more components. For example, it can be difficult to determine if a problem is caused by a troublesome CPU or a bad motherboard. When this situation arises, a simple solution is to substitute a known or good CPU for the suspect CPU. However, this substitution alone can be very expensive.

A+ Note

The A+ Certification places a great deal of weight on knowing the basics of troubleshooting. You need to become familiar with the limitations and purpose of various diagnostic tools, and the best way to become familiar with troubleshooting tools is by using them.

17.1 Common-Sense Practices

When troubleshooting and repairing PCs, remember that "time is money." This means you should always strive to take the quickest, most efficient path first. Adhering to the following common-sense practices can help tremendously:

- Determine the major area at fault
- Determine what action occurred just prior to failure or problem
- Proceed carefully
- Write down settings before you change them
- Think the problem through

Determining the Major Fault Area

The first step is to try to determine what major area is the most likely source of the fault. There are four major fault areas to be considered:

- Hardware failure
- Software failure
- User-generated problems
- Internet and network connection failure

User-generated problems tend to be the most common error or problem encountered. Some users like to tinker with Control Panel, and others will try to solve their problems alone. In some cases, this is probably fine, but most users are unlikely to possess the appropriate technical knowledge, and users with little technical knowledge can be the most dangerous. They often attempt to fix a problem before calling the technician, so it is vital that technicians understand that a user's permissions can either be augmented or diminished via the User Account Settings in Control Panel and apply the principle of least privilege. Nevertheless, technicians will experience issues with a personal computer, regardless of the administrative and safety practices they implement on their machines.

When this happens, you may be faced with more than one problem. First, the original problem likely still exists, and then there may be additional problems created by the user. Repairing computers in a school setting can be the most frustrating, as some students love to experiment with the settings on a school's computer before trying the activity on their home computer. Nevertheless, technicians can observe and troubleshoot these issues more efficiently and effectively than a user will when implementing fixes in their personal computers.

Figure 17-1 illustrates the Control Panel from the Windows 10 operating system, and its functionality and features. There are three different views for Control Panel: **Large icons**, **Small icons**, and **Category**, which is shown in Figure 17-1. From Control Panel, a technician can determine if all drivers are installed and up to date, observe the computer's firewall, verify software that is installed, document whether remote access has been granted for external computers inside and outside of the user's network, obtain service logs, and confirm the machine is working to its fullest capability with its hardware. Technicians can also determine the current and recent functionality of the machine for their documentation purposes.

By default, a user's network settings update automatically when their personal computer is powered on, and a network is detected via its network adapter. However, if a network requires the personal computer to input the network information manually, technicians may do so via the Control Panel. Nevertheless, it is rare that networks do not allow automatic configuration and most networks broadcast their network updates to the connected computers automatically.

It is also a good practice to begin by considering what reasonably could have caused the problem. For example, if a solid-state drive will not boot, likely causes include operating system failure and drive corruption. By contrast, network connectivity is highly unlikely to be related to the issue.

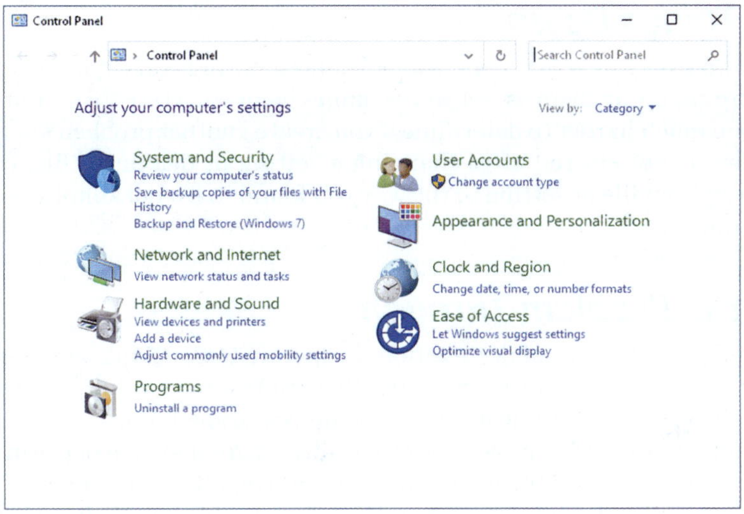

Goodheart-Willcox Publisher

Figure 17-1 Control Panel houses several functional utilities and features in one location.

What Happened Last?

1102: 3.1 A+

It is critical to determine from the computer user what the last action on the computer was prior to the problem occurring or before computer failure. Often, the last action taken by the user can lead the technician directly to the problem. For example, the installation of new hardware or software can possibly lead to operational malfunctions, as can a recent download from the Internet. Ask the user as many questions as possible because obtaining as much information as possible can save valuable time later. It is also important to verify requirements before installing new hardware or software. If the system does not have all the requirements, you can experience a wide range of problems. All commercial software lists the specific requirements for installation. For example, the following represents the minimum requirements for Windows:

- 1 GHz or faster processor with two or more cores
- 4 GB of RAM
- 64 GB of storage
- UEFI Secure Boot
- Trusted Platform Module 2.0
- Graphics Card with Direct X 12 or later with WDDM 2.0 driver

Suppose you install Windows 11 on a computer that meets all the requirements except the graphics card. You will likely experience a wide range of display problems that will be difficult to diagnose.

Tech Tip

Some problems can be intermittent and related to a loose hardware connection or excessive heat. For example, partially blocked airflow could cause heat to build slowly inside a computer and the memory modules to overheat. Once the memory module has overheated, the system locks up. Always be aware of "what happened last" when troubleshooting a computer.

Proceed Carefully

Take your time when diagnosing problems; rushing through a diagnosis or operating in a hurry will likely lead to sloppy work, create new problems, or cause you to overlook something important. In contrast, proceed in a methodical yet constant pace. Customers will not appreciate a technician who is standing around talking, socializing, or any other activity that appears to be a nonproductive use of time, because they are typically paying a premium price for service and losing the use of their computers while they are inoperable. Do not waste the customer's time or money, or they will likely call someone else next time there is a problem.

Write Things Down

Do not rely on your memory alone while troubleshooting. Take note of current settings before changing them as well as file names before deleting them. You can make the problem much harder to determine if you create another problem along the way. If a problem is not cleared after changing a setting or deleting a file, you should return the system file or setting to the way you found it. Do not simply move on and try something else.

Think the Problem Through

Do not try operations out of desperation. Desperate technicians will often run the same test twice knowing the results from the first test were valid. These are acts of desperation, and they occur when a technician is stumped. While it might seem an odd recommendation for a professional, it is often a good idea to perform an online search for the specific problem you are encountering. It is quite likely that others have encountered a similar problem and may have published their resolution, saving you a significant amount of time in the long run.

When you run out of tests, *stop and think* about the situation. It can be helpful to create two lists: one listing items you know are *not* the problem and other listing potential issues that could still exist. Then, check the website of the manufacturer of the PC, BIOS, and operating system for corrections that have been posted for the exact symptoms you are encountering. Many times, a problem is discovered that affects a particular setup or combination of hardware and software programs and solutions are posted. Again, if you are experiencing this issue, it is likely someone else also has.

Do not hesitate to contact the manufacturer of the hardware or software in question by e-mail with a description of the problem. Most questions will be answered in 24 to 48 hours at no cost for the service. You can get much faster replies by calling, but that service is seldom free.

Your fellow technicians are another important source of information. As you progress in the PC repair world, you will make many friends, and it is a standard practice to share information with a colleague who may have encountered a similar problem. A peer may have a quick and easy answer to a problem that you have not encountered before. Other times, simply discussing the problem with a peer can be quite helpful, as explaining the problem forces you to summarize the situation and describe it in logical terms. Just the act of verbalizing the problem may allow you to solve it. Never be embarrassed to ask for help.

17.2 Troubleshooting by Boot Stage

There is no one foolproof method to troubleshooting. There are too many variables that can cause a computer to fail, but there are recommended procedures that can be used to help you organize your approach to solving a computer problem. The causes of failure discussed are not all-inclusive and should be interpreted as a guide to solving a computer-related problem or complete system failure.

When troubleshooting computer problems, the first thing you must do is isolate the problem to determine whether it is a hardware, software, or user-generated problem. This is easier said than done, but the best way to go about this is to determine at what stage of computer operation the problem is occurring. The three general stages of computer operation are

- the POST;
- the loading of operating system files and initialization of hardware; and
- the loading of startup programs and running of applications and services after logon.

First Stage

A+ 1102: 3.1

If the problem occurs during POST, it is most likely a hardware failure since no operating system software or application software has been loaded at this stage. The POST may fail to complete if a damaged hardware device fails POST or its own diagnostic routine. For example, a modem that has been damaged during a thunderstorm may cause the computer to lock up during or immediately after the POST.

If you just built the computer system and it fails to boot successfully the first time during POST, you may have improperly installed the RAM, CPU, or CPU cooling device. A high-speed CPU with an improperly installed cooling fan or heat sink may generate excessive heat in seconds, causing the computer to freeze while performing the POST. Improperly seated RAM may also cause the computer to fail during POST, but the computer will typically issue a beep code indicating a problem with the RAM. Go back, reinstall these devices, remove all devices not required for system operation, and reboot the system. If the problem continues to persist, you can either substitute parts to determine which hardware device is causing the failure or use a third-party utility that uses a POST card to diagnose the problem.

Firmware POST Codes

A+ 1101: 5.2

The firmware (BIOS or UEFI) produces specific error codes, known as *beep codes* or *POST codes*, which can be used diagnostically. POST codes are not universal and can vary significantly depending on the manufacturer of the computer, motherboard, or firmware. A beep code is used to indicate failures before the video system is initialized when there is no display on which to print screen messages. After the video is enabled, a message will appear on the screen during or immediately after the POST indicating the problem by either an alphanumeric code or short message.

Some computers indicate a successful POST with a single beep while others do not, and some BIOS/UEFI firmware allow the single beep to be disabled because it annoys some users. To identify a problem via beep code, you must consult the computer, motherboard, or firmware manufacturer. For example, a series of short and long beeps on a Dell computer indicates a problem that does not necessarily match the same series of beeps on an ASUS computer. One thing you can be sure of is if you hear a series of beeps, it is an indication of a major hardware failure.

POST Cards

A **POST card** is an expansion card that plugs into a motherboard and displays error codes generated during a computer's power-on self-test (POST). These cards are extremely helpful in troubleshooting computers that do not start up. POST cards include some type of digital readout, as shown in Figure 17-2, that displays hexadecimal digits that correspond to startup errors, much like diagnostic trouble codes

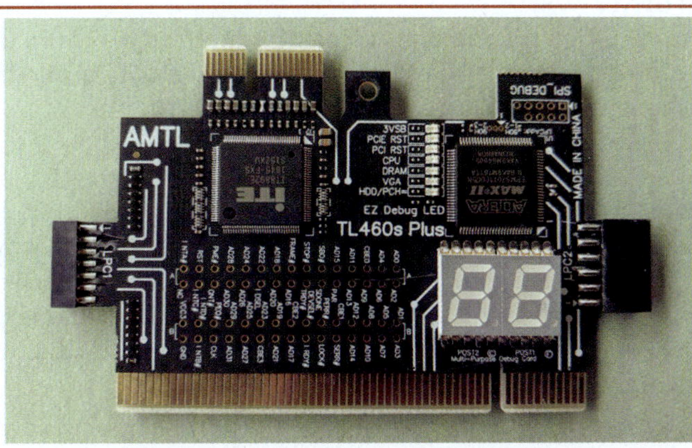

Markus Kuhn/Public Domain

Figure 17-2 A POST card is an expansion card that plugs into a motherboard and displays error codes generated during a computer's power-on self-test (POST).

(engine codes) in automobiles. A very popular third-party utility suite used by repair centers is PC-Doctor Service Center Kits, which has historically been used by Dell Computers to perform computer diagnostics in the service department.

The POST card is inserted into any PCI slot and used to diagnose errors during POST caused by hardware failure such as the CPU, RAM, or the motherboard. A POST error code is displayed on the LEDs, and the technician can then match the code to the diagnostic chart in the user manual. Without a POST card, a technician would have to rely on beep codes or substitute the CPU, RAM, and motherboard with a known good component, which can be time-consuming and expensive. The technician also runs the risk of damaging a part during the substitution process.

As motherboards have improved, the need for POST cards has lessened, but they still have a valuable place in a PC technician's tool kit. Be aware that every manufacturer is different, so the problem associated with a given code for one motherboard may not be the same issue on a different motherboard. Additionally, ensure that the POST card is compatible with the motherboard before using it. For example, not all motherboards broadcast their POST codes to the PCI slots. In these cases, you will have to rely on the beeps.

For more information on problems that can occur during the POST stage, see the following chapter sections: Typical Startup Problems, Hard Drive Failures, Additional Mechanical Problems, and Boot Sequences.

A+ 1101: 5.3
1102: 3.1

Second Stage

If the problem occurs during the second stage—operating system loading and initialization—the problem is most likely related to a corrupt operating system file or a driver. Many computer systems display the results of the POST as it occurs, so you can often identify when stage two starts simply by observing the screen display. For example, you will see the RAM check verified and the hard disk drive and other devices that are present identified on the screen, and soon after the POST turns the loading of the operating system to the bootstrap program, you will see a progress bar appear on the screen. When you see the progress bar, you know that the second stage has begun, and the operating system has successfully loaded the system kernel. The operating system then initializes the hardware devices.

A+ 1102: 3.1

Failure during the second stage is usually the result of a corrupt system file such as ntldr or failure to properly detect and initialize a piece of hardware. It can also be caused by a corrupt hardware driver. The fastest way to repair a system failure that occurs during the loading and initialization of the operating system is by reinstalling required system files. Simply insert the installation CD/DVD and then reboot the computer. When the installation CD/DVD boots, follow the screen prompts. If your computer does not have an optical drive, you should be able to download the necessary files to a USB flash drive and boot from it the same way as you would boot from an optical drive.

For more information on problems caused by hard drive failure that can occur during the second stage, see the Hard Drive Failures section. Detailed troubleshooting methods for this stage are covered in a later chapter.

Third Stage

System logon marks the end of the second stage. Keep in mind that not all operating systems require a logon, so the third stage truly begins when the desktop first appears. During the third stage, startup programs, services, and applications are loaded. The most common problems that can occur during this time are usually due to corrupt or incompatible drivers and files.

File Corruption

1101: 5.3 A+

Files can be corrupted in various ways, such as by virus attacks and hardware failures. For example, an intermittent RAM failure can also corrupt files if the file contents are transferred or copied during the time of RAM failure. File corruption can occur when data is stored in an area of the hard drive that has a bad sector; all data saved to the bad sector is lost, thus corrupting the contents of the complete file. Files can also be corrupted by an unexpected power outage or shutting down the computer system while installing updates.

Overwritten DLL File

Certain files, such as a DLL file, can cause a system failure when inappropriately applied in a software program or when they become corrupt. A **Microsoft Dynamic Link Library (DLL)** file is an executable file that can be called and run by Microsoft software applications or by third-party software programs. Rather than write code from scratch each time a new software application is written, programmers can simply call a DLL from within the program they have written and run the needed function automatically. One DLL can be used by more than one software program at the same time, and by reusing the same code contained in the DLL, a programmer saves time and uses less memory and disk space. The term *dynamic* is used because the file can be loaded, run, and then unloaded from computer memory when no longer needed.

One of the major software problems in the past occurred when a user loaded a software application from a disc that contained the necessary DLL files to run a software application. All too often, the DLL file on the software disc overwrote the existing DLL residing on the computer, and if the overwritten file were newer than the file on the disc, an error would occur when the user started an application other than the one just loaded. A classic example is when a user loaded an old version of a software game on a computer that had other games requiring a similar DLL file. While the older game ran perfectly, one or more of the other games ran incorrectly or not at all.

DLL files usually have a **.dll** file extension, for example **mon.dll**, though the DLL will sometimes have an **.exe** file extension. Look at Figure 17-3 to see the search results for files with the **.dll** extension. There are over 62,000 files that have a **.dll** extension on this particular computer. As you can see, there are thousands of possible DLL files that can be used as part of multiple software applications and hardware drivers.

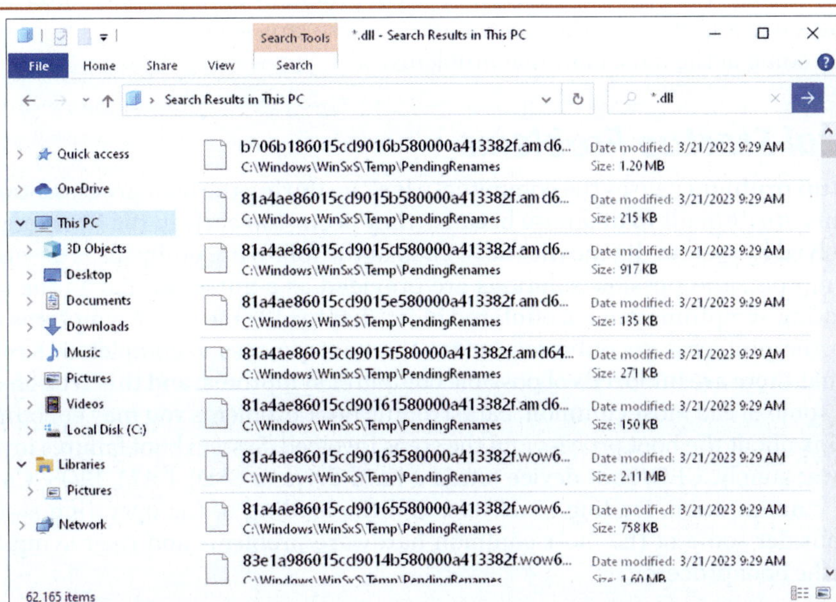

Goodheart-Willcox Publisher

Figure 17-3 DLL files are called by software applications to perform common tasks.

A+ 1101: 5.2
1102: 3.1

Tech Tip

A malicious software program can attack a computer at any time, not just after the system logon. For example, if the MBR is corrupted by a virus, the computer will fail before switching from text mode to graphic mode.

Blue Screen Error

During the third stage of booting, the system may experience a blue screen error commonly referred to as the *Blue Screen of Death (BSoD)*. A **blue screen error** is a blue screen that appears with an error code and then freezes the system. Microsoft also refers to blue screen errors as *fatal errors*, *stop errors*, and *stop error messages* because the system is not recoverable at the time of the error and must be restarted before you can attempt to remedy the problem. Some of the most common causes for blue screen errors include

- defective hardware;
- corrupt files on the hard drive;
- system BIOS settings that are beyond the capabilities of the hardware;
- third-party software containing bad code; and
- bad code in the Windows operating system.

The error codes displayed on the blue screen can be quite cryptic. You should copy the error code and use it as a reference when searching Microsoft's Support website.

The most appropriate utility for diagnosing a problem after the logon is the System Configuration Utility (**msconfig.exe**). This and other utilities for diagnosing problems during this stage are covered in the Windows Diagnostic Utilities section, as well as in a later chapter. You may also check out Microsoft TechNet for detailed information and articles.

Tech Tip

When troubleshooting a PC, always attempt the simplest tests first before moving on to the more complex and labor-intensive tests.

17.3 Commonly Encountered Problems

While every computer system is unique, they all have similar components, which all have similar lifespans. For example, many system failures stem from startup, mechanical failures, and intermittent issues. This section presents an overview of commonly encountered problems categorized by problem type. In general, four common problem types include

- startup problems;
- hard drive failure;
- mechanical problems; and
- system and intermittent device failure.

Remember that these are not the only types of problems one may encounter while working on computers in the field. Rather, these are generalized categories to describe some of the most common problems.

Typical Startup Problems

A **startup problem** causes the computer to lock up during the boot process. Startup problems are difficult to diagnose because they occur too early in the PC operation to be solved by system diagnostic tools. Each of the following problems is described as a symptom, and possible solutions are provided as a guide, similar to the troubleshooting symptoms you encountered in in Chapter 13. The list of symptoms centers on the problems encountered before the boot process is completed. Keep in mind that there are hundreds of possible computer symptoms, and this section only details some of the most common, catastrophic boot problems you may encounter.

Think about the boot process and the steps involved. System boot failures involve the power supply, CPU, boot device (often a hard drive or SSD), RAM, BIOS, CMOS, system configuration, loading of drivers, and the loading of the operating system. Now consider some of the most common hardware problems and their symptoms during the boot process.

When reading the list that follows, assume that there is one hard drive labeled C: and a disc drive labeled D:. Note that these are recommended procedures, not absolute procedures. Also, be aware that viruses can imitate some of the described symptoms, so you should always check for the presence of a virus on the hard drive.

1101: 5.2, 5.3 A+

Symptom 1:

There is no power light, no fan running, and no sound of boot operation. It appears that the PC is completely dead.

Items to check:

Before you open the case, make sure the PC is plugged in. Next, check the power from the wall outlet, power strip, or both to ensure there is power to the unit. If you have power, then the likely problem is the computer's power supply. Open the case and test the power supply outputs. Replacing the power supply is generally more cost-effective than fixing a broken one.

Most computers include indicator lights to identify activity such as hard drive activity, the presence of power, or data transfer activity. These lights can help troubleshoot basic issues. For example, a red LED indicator light indicates a substantial problem, a yellow light indicates a warning, and a green light indicates everything is running normally. There are also LED lights associated with network interface cards, for which a solid green or yellow light indicates proper functionality, while a blinking light indicates actual network activity.

1101: 5.2, 5.3 A+
1102: 3.1

Symptom 2:

The power light (LED) is on, the fan is running, but there is no activity. The system appears dead.

Items to check:

Check the power supply for a power good signal. The power good signal is sent to the BIOS system to signal that the power supply is on and ready.

If the power supply passes the power test, try reseating the RAM and the CPU. The CPU or RAM may not be making a good electrical connection in their sockets. Try reseating the RAM first because it is significantly faster and easier than reseating the CPU. Both components operate on very low voltages, so even a slight oxidation buildup on one of the device pins operating at 3.3 volts or less is sufficient to render the CPU or RAM dead. Cleaning the oxidation will bring it back.

If you perform all the listed operations and the system still fails to activate, you may have defective components. If you have RAM modules or a CPU that is known to be good, you can use those to eliminate defective parts as a possibility. In that event, you may have a defective motherboard.

1101: 5.2, 5.4 A+
1102: 3.1

Symptom 3:

The system tries to boot, and you hear two or more beeps, and then nothing (no video). The fan is running, and there is a power light.

Items to check:

Make sure the monitor is plugged in correctly, both to the PC and the power source. There are a number of different cables used with video, so it is also important to ensure you are using the correct cable. HDMI is quickly becoming the most widely used, but many monitors still connect via SVGA, DisplayPort, or other connection type. The first thing to look for is any frays or wearing in the cable. If you see any degradation along the cable jacket or connectors, replace the cable. If the cable appears to be in working order, test its functionality by plugging it into a monitor that is known to be in working condition. If the video still fails, you can operate with the knowledge that the cable is likely bad and needs to be replaced. If the cable appears to be working, check the monitor source. Many modern monitors allow for multiple sources, so you might simply have the monitor set to the incorrect data source.

In the event the cable and monitor are found to be functional, the next logical step is to check and reseat the video card; then do the same to the RAM. If those actions do not help, try to decode the beep error code by consulting the manufacturer literature. Newer manuals often come as a PDF file on disc as opposed to the traditional paper booklet. If there is no manual, look up the BIOS chip manufacturer on the Internet. First, copy all information from the BIOS chip or motherboard and then consult the manufacturer's website.

In some cases, a technician can access information from the Event Viewer Log regarding when a monitor has been turned off or the display of an image was interrupted. The Event Viewer will advise when the monitor experiences errors, along with potential warning indicators as to what actions need to be taken to resolve the error. However, monitor access must be available to obtain information regarding the Event Viewer Log.

A+ 1102: 3.1

Symptom 4:

A setup error is indicated on the screen.

Items to check:

This is probably a CMOS setup problem. Access the BIOS setup utility by using the key combination indicated on the screen. If no key combinations are given, try those with which you are familiar, such as those listed in Figure 3-43 from Chapter 3. You can also look up the keystroke combination for accessing the BIOS at the BIOS manufacturer's website.

A+ 1101: 5.2

Normally, CMOS settings do not change. However, the settings sometimes change when you install a new hard drive that is automatically detected. Also, if the battery used to hold the CMOS data is going bad, you could lose the settings. The date and time not matching the true date and time is a good indication that your battery is going bad.

Be sure to write down the existing CMOS settings before making any changes. This is extremely important if you are going to try something like the **Return to default settings** option. When that option is selected, many settings will change instantly, and you will not be able to tell which settings have changed or what they changed from. Check the manufacturer's website for the correct CMOS settings for your particular model of PC. Having baseline CMOS settings on hand can save you a tremendous amount of time. Sometimes people get curious and go into the setup utility to see what it looks like. They also make changes either intentionally or accidentally. If you know what the settings *should* be, it is much faster to restore them.

A+ 1101: 5.3

Symptom 5:

The PC powers on, but there is no drive activity.

Items to check:

Check the system CMOS settings, and make sure the correct drive is identified. The drive and the number of cylinders, heads, and sectors should be identified in the setup utility, and the hard drive manufacturer and hard drive model number will often flash on the screen when the BIOS detects it during the boot process. If the drive is not detected during the boot, the screen will flash something similar to *No hard disk drive*.

You should also check the connections between both the power supply and the hard drive and the motherboard and the hard drive to ensure they are tight. If all that checks out, boot the system with a recovery disc or the operating system installation disc, and see if you can access the hard drive from the command prompt.

Symptom 6:

A+ 1101: 5.3

The computer attempts to boot to the wrong device.

Items to check:

This can be caused by several issues. The device boot order is controlled by the BIOS/UEFI setup configuration, and an inexperienced user may have changed the boot order while trying to install a program from disc and never returned the boot order to the correct sequence. Another possible reason is the computer had an external storage device, such as a hard disk drive attached to a USB port, and was configured to boot from this device. The device has been removed and now the computer is looking for the device during a normal boot. Inspect the setup utility configuration and correct as necessary.

Symptom 7:

The computer continually reboots on failure.

Items to check:

Some computers can be configured to reboot on a detected error. However, this may cause the system to continuously reboot, so you will have to disable this option to stop the continuous reboots and diagnose the cause of the failure. Windows also provides an option in the **Startup and Recovery** dialog box that can configure the way the computer reacts when encountering an error. The **Startup and Recovery** dialog box is accessed through **Control Panel**>**System and Security**>**System**>**Advanced system settings**>**Settings**. The option to restart the computer automatically is the default setting in Windows. Figure 17-4 shows the **Automatically restart** option enabled.

Symptom 8:

1101: 5.2 A+
1102: 3.1

The system crashes or reboots for no apparent reason.

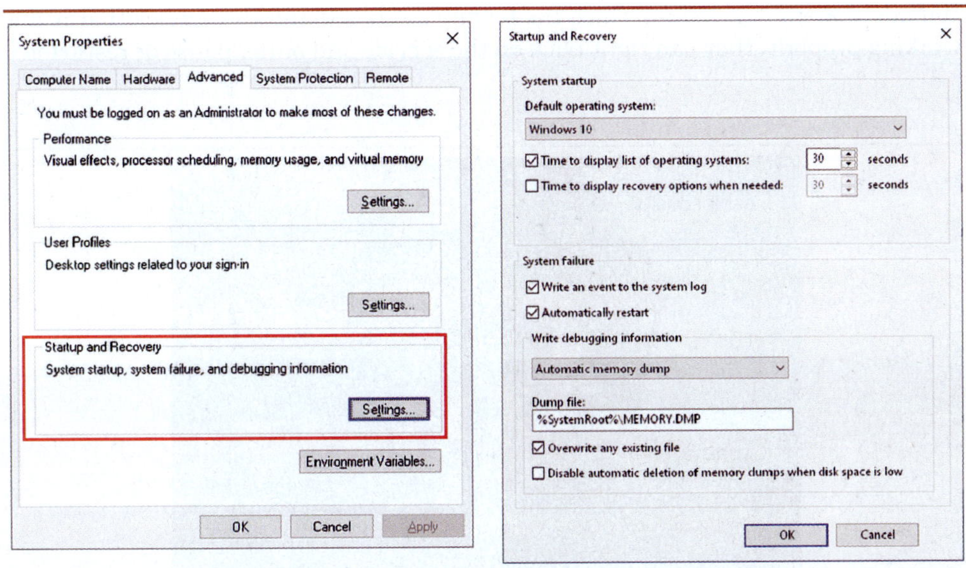

Goodheart-Willcox Publisher

Figure 17-4 The **Startup and Recovery** dialog box is set by default to reboot continuously when a system error is encountered.

Items to check:

Check the power supply and cables to ensure they are all tightly connected. Check for excessive heat on the CPU and memory chips, and make sure all DIMMs are seated properly. Additionally, try reseating the CPU. Finally, check the BIOS/UEFI configuration to verify the correct amount of RAM.

A+ 1101: 5.2

Symptom 9:

A burning smell or smoke is coming from the computer.

Items to check:

This is most likely the result of a defective power supply. While not required, a power supply suspected of severe electrical damage can be easily removed from the computer to be opened and inspected. Severe electrical damage is very easy to identify, as shown by the power supply in Figure 17-5, which exhibits the following signs of severe damage caused by a failed capacitor:

- An imperfection in the side of the capacitor that appears like a dent or bulge.
- A smoke stain on the clear plastic insulation cover that protects the electrical parts from the metallic cover.
- A deposit of ash from the electrical fire created by the defective capacitor.

You do not have to be an electrical engineer to tell this power supply is bad.

If the power supply hardware appears okay, the motherboard is most likely defective or there is a problem with the hard drive. Swapping the hard drive with one you know is working should show where the problem lies. If the hard drive is causing the problem, check for a virus or a corrupt operating system. Always think about the last thing that occurred on the PC before the problem developed. Hard drive failures will be discussed in detail in a later section.

A+ 1102: 3.1

Symptom 10:

The computer fails to start services.

Items to check:

When a technician experiences a service that will not run, they can use the Windows Services utility for their troubleshooting strategies. The Windows Services utility displays all the properties and information about the services that run on the Windows operating system. Once the technician has found the service that is not working properly, they can right-click on the service and either pause or restart it.

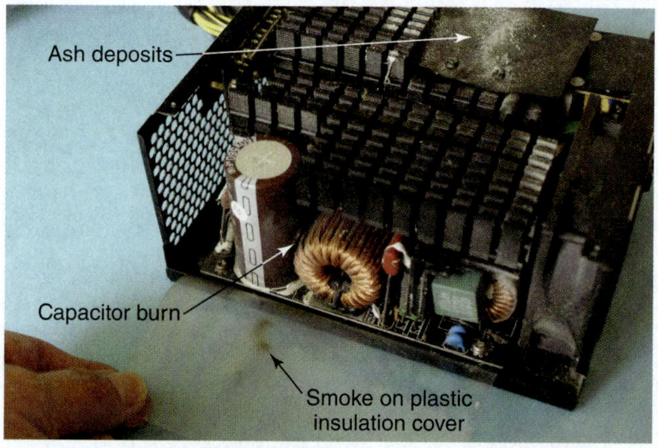

Figure 17-5 Typically, a suspected damaged power supply can be verified by a visual inspection.

Goodheart-Willcox Publisher

Symptom 11:

The user's profile loads slowly.

1102: 3.1 A+

Items to check:

Depending on the content of a user's profile, a user may experience an ample amount of time for their account to load as they are logging in to their personal computer. Technicians confronted by this issue should first delete any unneeded documents and programs that are on the user's computer and conduct a virus scan to search for any malicious software that might be causing the profile to deem faulty via the user's perception. However, if problems with a user's account persist, it is recommended that a new profile be generated for the user, or an attempt made to rebuild their profile via Safe Mode to eliminate any malicious or unneeded data and programs.

When a technician boots a Windows operating system into Safe Mode, the Windows operating system only runs the minimal number of resources necessary to allow the operating system to function. Furthermore, a technician can decide what programs will or will not operate and in what order the boot sectors and drives will operate. Therefore, technicians can rebuild or modify a user's profile with minimal interference and operating system resources.

Symptom 12:

The computer generates a low memory warning.

1102: 3.1 A+

Items to check:

One of the first things to check on a Windows 10 or 11 computer is the virtual memory. The easiest way to do this is to conduct a search using the keyword System and select the **System** option from the list of results. From there, select **Advanced system settings** to open the System Properties dialog box; then select **Settings** from the Performance section of the **Advanced** tab. This will open the Performance Options dialog box, from which you should select the **Advanced** tab, as shown in Figure 17-6.

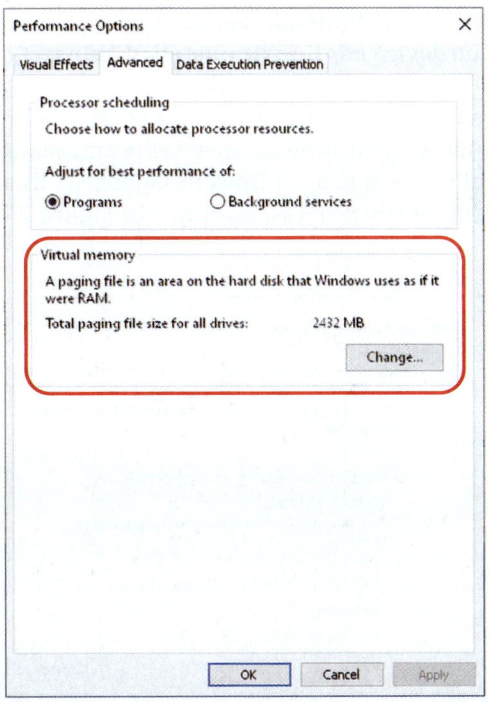

Goodheart-Willcox Publisher

Figure 17-6 Virtual memory should account for one-and-one-half times the size of your physical memory.

From this screen, you can not only change the Virtual Memory, but you can also adjust programs and services for best performance. Virtual memory should normally be one-and-one-half times the size of your physical memory. Workstations should generally be optimized for program performance, whereas servers should be optimized for background services.

It may also simply be that you have unnecessary programs running, so examining your startup programs and services may lead to you being able to remove some unneeded services, freeing up more RAM for other programs. If nothing else corrects the problem, you may run the Windows Memory Diagnostics Tool. You can access this tool by searching for memory and selecting **Windows Memory Diagnostics** from the list of results. This will launch a dialog box from which you can restart the computer to check for problems or defer the diagnostics until the next time the computer is booted, as shown in Figure 17-7.

A third solution is to simply add more resources. If your system is notifying you of low RAM, adding more RAM is a viable solution to this problem, but it is best to first ensure that more RAM is needed. By performing the previously discussed troubleshooting steps, you should be able to confirm the amount of RAM needed and present in the computer. If adjusting the virtual memory and Windows Memory Diagnostics do not alleviate the problem, then adding resources is the next logical step.

A+ 1102: 3.1

Symptom 13:

The computer generates a USB controller resource warning.

Items to check:

When plugging in a USB device, one might see an alert such as USB controller resource warning or perhaps Not Enough USB Controller resources, both of which relate to an issue common to USB 3.0 ports called *endpoint limitation*. In general, a system can manage up to 16 USB-in and 16 USB-out devices, even though addressing allows for up to 127 devices. One way to attempt to solve this is to reinstall the USB host controllers via Device Manager. Launch Device Manager by conducting a search for devmgmt and select **Device Manager** from the list of results. Once in Device Manager, extend the Universal Serial Bus controllers category, right-click the USB 3.0 controller, and select **Uninstall device** from the shortcut menu, as shown in Figure 17-8. Once the device has been uninstalled, reinsert the device to reinstall the controller.

You can also attempt to run the device diagnostic tool in Windows 10 or 11. Open command prompt with administrator-level permissions and execute the following command syntax: msdt.exe -id DeviceDiagnostic. This command launches the Windows device diagnostic process, as shown in Figure 17-9.

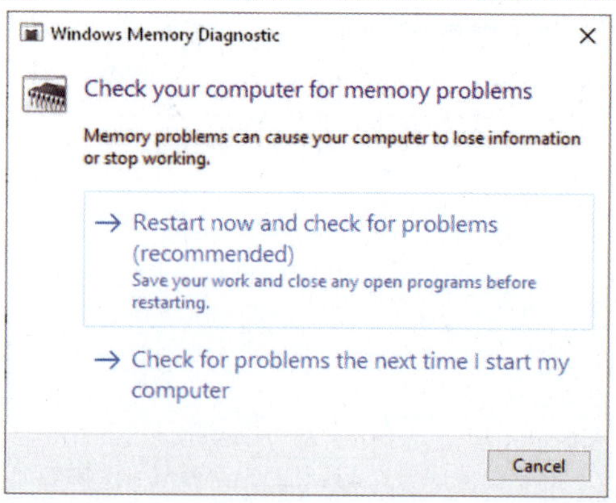

Goodheart-Willcox Publisher

Figure 17-7 The Windows Memory Diagnostic Tool can help determine why a computer is generating low memory warnings.

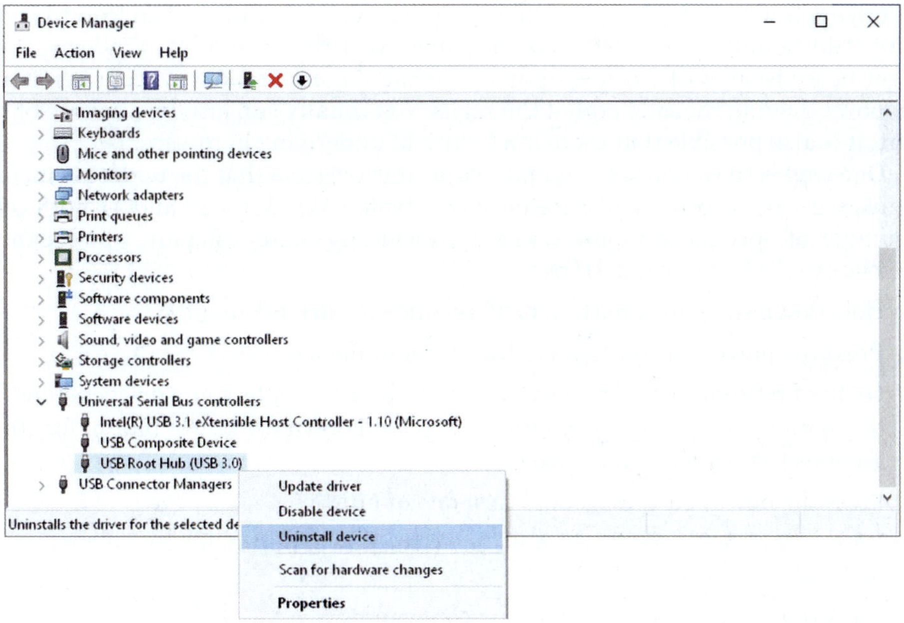

Goodheart-Willcox Publisher

Figure 17-8 Uninstalling and reinstalling the USB 3.0 controller may help solve USB controller issues.

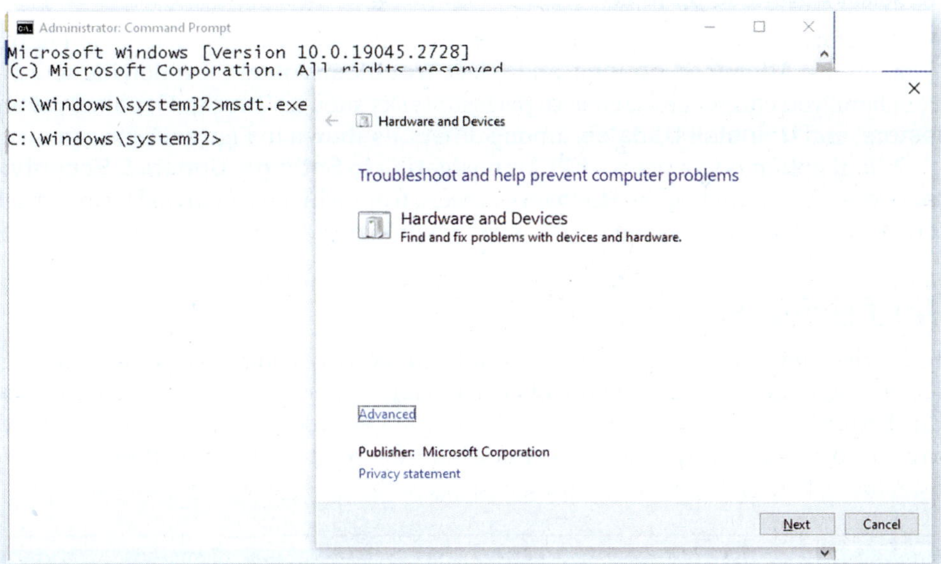

Goodheart-Willcox Publisher

Figure 17-9 The Hardware and Devices troubleshooter can be launched with the command syntax msdt.exe -id DeviceDiagnostic.

If neither of these solutions alleviates the problem, a more drastic option is to go into the UEFI settings and disable the XHCI mode option. This has the effect of downgrading USB 3.0 ports to USB 2.0. As stated, this is a rather drastic measure and should only be used as a last resort.

Symptom 14:

The system seems unstable.

A+ 1102: 3.1

Items to check:

This is a broad symptom that includes any indicators that the operating system is itself unstable, including system crashes, the system hanging, and services failing to start, among many others. System instability can be caused by a number of underlying issues. For example, using a beta version of Windows can lead to instability. Additionally, if you have recently upgraded the version of Windows, there might be an issue with hardware drivers being incompatible with your version of Windows. Having recently edited the registry manually can also be a source of the issue. It is also possible that there is a failure in underlying hardware.

A+ 1102: 3.1

One step is to remove recent updates, as it is possible that the update is incompatible with some other software on your system. Windows 10 and 11 both offer a number of options to repair Windows, including System Repair, which can be launched with the following steps:

1. Hold down the power button for 10 seconds to turn off your device.
2. Press the power button again to turn on your device.
3. On the first sign that Windows has started (for example, some devices show the manufacturer's logo when restarting) hold down the power button for 10 seconds to turn off your device.
4. Press the power button again to turn on your device.
5. When Windows starts again, hold down the power button for 10 seconds to turn off your device.
6. Press the power button again to turn on your device.
7. This time, allow your device to fully start up.
8. Select **Advanced options.**

If performed correctly, you should see a screen similar to that shown in Figure 17-10. Choose **Advanced options**, and select **Troubleshoot** on the following screen. From here, you can reach screens to perform tasks such as **Startup Repair**, **System Restore**, and **Uninstall Updates**, among others, as shown in Figure 17-11.

A final option is to reset your PC by navigating to **Settings**>**Update & Security**>**Recovery.** This launches the **Recovery** screen, from which you can perform a reset or take other troubleshooting steps, as shown in Figure 17-12.

Hard Drive Failures

Hard drives fail more often than one would think. Any component that combines electrical and mechanical components will fail after a period of time, and hard drives can also fail because of software issues. As an example, a corrupt MBR can cause hard drives to become unresponsive. It is important for you to determine if more than a

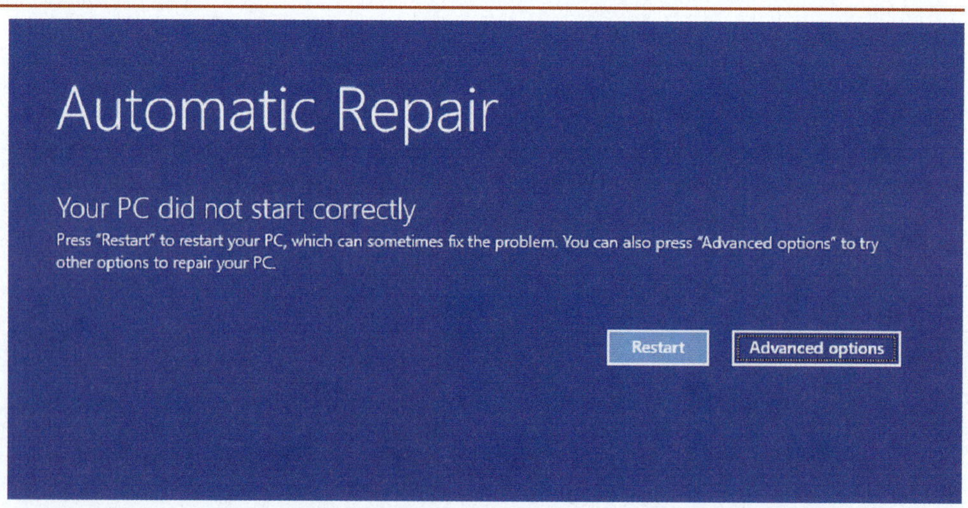

Goodheart-Willcox Publisher

Figure 17-10 Performing several hard resets of your device will launch the Windows Automatic Repair option.

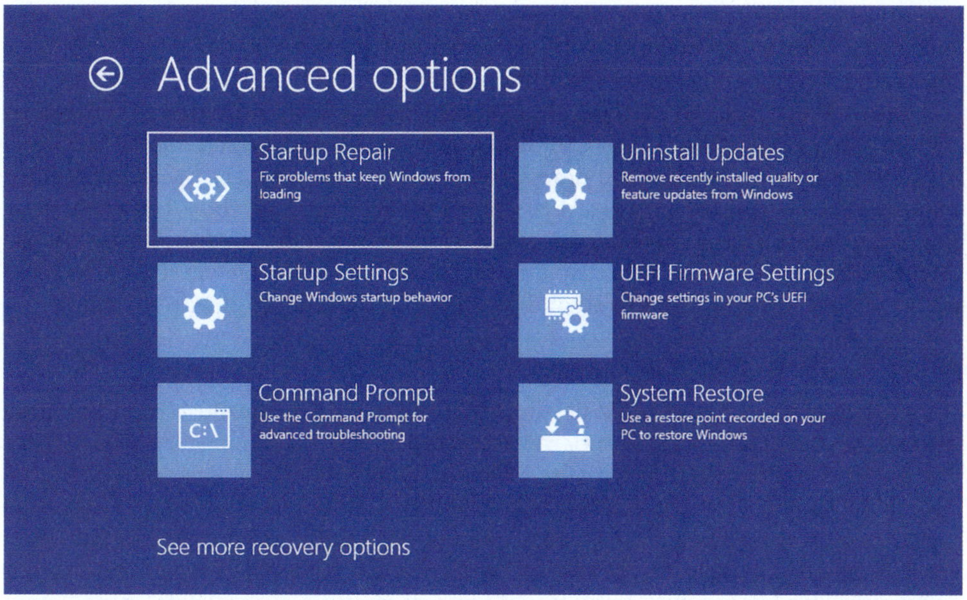

Goodheart-Willcox Publisher

Figure 17-11 The Windows Advanced boot options include actions such as **Startup Repair**, **System Restore**, and **Uninstall Updates**, among others.

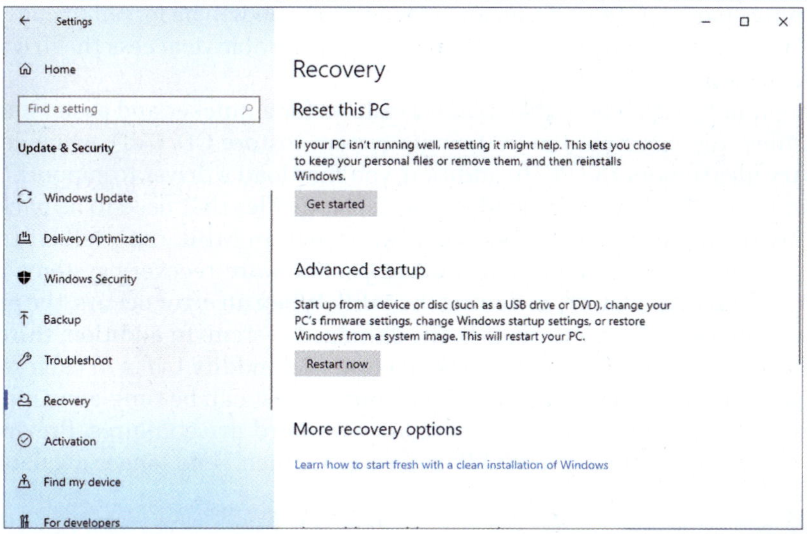

Goodheart-Willcox Publisher

Figure 17-12 The Windows Recovery menu allows you to perform a system reset or launch other troubleshooting measures.

hard drive is bad, but it is equally important that you also determine *why* it is bad. A bad hard drive or a corrupt MBR will generate a screen message, such as

- invalid partition table;
- error loading operating system; or
- missing operating system.

If any of these error messages appear, you likely have a hard drive problem. To check, try booting the system from a bootable CD/DVD or USB drive. If the system boots normally, you can confirm a hard drive problem.

Mechanical Hard Drive Failure

While solid-state drives are far more common today than the older platter-based hard drives, both are still mechanical and, as you are aware, mechanical parts wear out. A sure sign of an upcoming mechanical hard drive failure is an unusual sound coming from inside the computer when it is being accessed (a read or write operation is being performed), such as a high-pitched whining or clanking. Strange sounds coming from the hard drive are mechanical in origin and likely cannot be repaired, making replacement the only solution.

The only guaranteed method of fully recovering from a hard drive failure is by regularly backing up data. You can always reinstall a collection of software when replacing a hard drive, but the data will be lost unless a recent backup has been made. Users should be instructed to back up data regularly, but it is even more important when a hard drive begins making strange sounds. Data should be backed up immediately, and a technician should be called to prepare for the crash. The technician should have parts on hand and be prepared to replace the hard drive.

MBR Failure and Recovery

Hard drives can also fail because of corrupted files and data. The most important area of the hard drive is the master boot record (MBR), and if it is damaged, the hard drive will not support the booting process. However, you will still be able to boot from a bootable USB or CD/DVD. Once you boot from the USB or CD/DVD, try to look at the hard drive by entering the **dir C:** command at the command prompt, as shown in Figure 17-13. If you can view the files on the hard drive, then you can perform a repair and may be able to remedy the situation. As a precaution, back up all data immediately.

You will not be able to back up the files in every situation, but if you can see files on the hard drive, you should be able to back up important data to some kind of data storage media. Generally, on an older system, you will be forced to copy files to a disc. However, on some newer systems, you may be able to access the drive via an existing network connection.

A computer with a bootable CD/DVD allows for a quicker and easier backup of system files. You can boot the PC using a system restore CD/DVD, which loads all necessary files to boot the PC. In addition, you may load a driver to support the CD/DVD, and once the drivers are loaded, you can copy files that need to be backed up.

Many third-party software systems can repair an MBR, especially if the software is installed before the problem develops. Software recovery systems make a copy of all vital information, including the MBR. When an error occurs, the recovery software can use the copy to recover the damaged system. In addition, third-party software systems can be used to inspect, copy, and modify bytes in each sector of the hard drive. This is a very powerful tool, but using it can be time-consuming.

Windows has built-in utilities to assist with hard drive failures. Previous versions of Windows included the **fsidk** command, which is no longer available as of

```
C:\Windows\system32\cmd.exe
Microsoft Windows [Version 10.0.19045.2673]
(c) Microsoft Corporation. All rights reserved.

C:\Users\GW>dir C:
 Volume in drive C is Local Disk
 Volume Serial Number is 189F-F845

 Directory of C:\Users\GW

01/31/2023  08:24 AM    <DIR>          .
01/31/2023  08:24 AM    <DIR>          ..
01/31/2023  08:24 AM    <DIR>          .ms-ad
02/04/2022  03:05 PM    <DIR>          3D Objects
12/07/2022  08:46 AM    <DIR>          Classnotes
02/04/2022  03:05 PM    <DIR>          Contacts
02/07/2023  02:56 PM    <DIR>          Desktop
02/06/2023  03:08 PM    <DIR>          Documents
01/27/2023  01:54 PM    <DIR>          Downloads
02/04/2022  03:05 PM    <DIR>          Favorites
02/04/2022  03:05 PM    <DIR>          Links
02/04/2022  03:05 PM    <DIR>          Music
02/04/2022  03:07 PM    <DIR>          OneDrive
02/04/2022  03:07 PM    <DIR>          Pictures
02/04/2022  03:05 PM    <DIR>          Saved Games
02/04/2022  03:06 PM    <DIR>          Searches
10/26/2022  09:52 AM    <DIR>          Videos
               0 File(s)              0 bytes
              17 Dir(s)  196,650,336,256 bytes free

C:\Users\GW>
```

Goodheart-Willcox Publisher

Figure 17-13 Users can examine the hard drive through the command prompt. If files are shown, you should be able to repair the drive and save the data.

the release of Windows 7 and **bootrec.exe**, which was removed in Windows 8. For Windows 10 and 11, you should use the **diskpart** command interpreter, which helps manage the drives installed on a computer. When the **diskpart** command is issued at the command prompt, you launch the diskpart prompt, which allows you to issue other **diskpart** commands, such as those shown in Figure 17-14. In Figure 17-15, you can see DiskPart being used to display details about the disk.

A GUID partition has a protected backup of the partition located on the hard drive and automatically rebuilds the GUID partition table on failure. Also, the Windows operating system has an option to create an image of the entire disk, including the GUID partition table, which can be used to recover the entire computer system.

Read and Write Failure

1101: 5.2, 5.3 A+
1102: 3.1

Although there are multiple methods for repairing a hard drive, there is still a possibility that a hard drive may become faulty during its functionality before, during, or after its repair. If the read-write head becomes damaged or impaired, users and

DiskPart Commands	
Command	**Function**
clean	Removes all formatting from the active disk
create	Creates a new partition
delete	Removes an existing partition
detail	Displays detailed information about the selected disk/partition/volume
exit	Exits the diskpart command interpreter
filesystems	Displays information about the file system of the currently selected volume
format	Formats a disk or volume
help	Displays all available commands
repair	Repairs RAID 5 volumes
select	Allows you to select a disk, partition, or volume

Goodheart-Willcox Publisher

Figure 17-14 DiskPart is a command-line interpreter used to manage Windows disks and partitions.

```
C:\Windows\system32\diskpart.exe

DISKPART> select disk 0

Disk 0 is now the selected disk.

DISKPART> detail disk

CT250MX500SSD1
Disk ID: {1B6E239F-762A-49E3-A51C-B99AE46573DA}
Type   : RAID
Status : Online
Path   : 0
Target : 0
LUN ID : 0
Location Path : PCIROOT(0)#PCI(1700)#RAID(P00T00L00)
Current Read-only State : No
Read-only  : No
Boot Disk  : Yes
Pagefile Disk  : Yes
Hibernation File Disk  : No
Crashdump Disk  : Yes
Clustered Disk  : No

  Volume ###  Ltr  Label        Fs     Type        Size     Status     Info
  ----------  ---  -----------  -----  ----------  -------  ---------  --------
  Volume 0     C   Local Disk   NTFS   Partition    232 GB  Healthy    Boot
  Volume 1         SYSTEM       FAT32  Partition    260 MB  Healthy    System
  Volume 2                      NTFS   Partition    509 MB  Healthy    Hidden

DISKPART>
```

Goodheart-Willcox Publisher

Figure 17-15 The **detail disk** command reveals information about a disk, including the disk ID, disk type, status, path, target, LUN ID, location, and its status as a boot disk, among other facts.

technicians may not be able to retrieve data from the hard drive. Even if the technician *is* able to retrieve data, they will not likely be able to make modifications to it. Lastly, damage to the platters or read-write head of a hard drive may cause the functionality of the hard drive to perform more slowly, along with a noticeable amount of noise, such as grinding or clicking, when the hard drive is not performing to its utmost functionality. To further investigate whether a hard drive is faulty, a technician can utilize a machine's S.M.A.R.T. error screenings.

A+ 1101: 5.3

RAID and S.M.A.R.T. Error Detections

As of the writing of this chapter, the majority of hard drive implementation for a server is utilized via cloud-based technologies; however, technicians may encounter server hard drives such as a *Redundant Array of Independent Disks (RAID).* RAID implementation can be recognized as a form of hardware and software for its hard drive disk management. The Disk Management tool of a Windows server can be configured to use RAID 0 or RAID 2. For a technician to observe and repair errors via a RAID's functionality, a technician may observe and repair any errors that may have occurred through what is called S.M.A.R.T. Error Detections.

The S.M.A.R.T. Error Detection Tool can be found in Control Panel in both standard Windows and Windows Server. When a technician uses this tool, they can discover when a drive produced an error, was not functioning properly, or if a drive needs to be replaced. Furthermore, the S.M.A.R.T. Error Detection Tool may provide fixes for technicians such as the hard drive needing to be reformatted or if the disk needs to have miscellaneous data removed to utilize the necessary hard drive space needed for present and future files and data.

Disk Management

While the prior-mentioned criteria were based on hardware, other precautions may be taken to adhere to the health of a hard drive. One precaution a technician can utilize is using the Disk Management tool, which can be found easily via a Windows search. From this tool, a technician can defragment, partition, add arrays, and control the amount of storage space allotted to a user. Although this implementation is still in practice, it is important for technicians to understand that hard drive utilization is diminishing for both personal computers and servers, and that data is being stored via cloud-based technologies.

Additional Mechanical Problems

A number of other mechanical faults can cause problems in PCs. Boards, cards, and cables can go bad, but these occurrences are not all that common. You will find that, along with hard drive failure, most other mechanical problems arise from two areas: improper hardware upgrades and accumulation of dust in the system.

Problems after Hardware Upgrades

Many possible system failures can occur after a hardware upgrade. The first thing to check when a system fails to boot is the power and cable connections. While working inside the case, cables are often pulled loose, so look for any free-hanging cables. Take caution when reconnecting the cable so as not to damage any pins, and make sure you connect it to the correct location. There are multiple examples of technicians reconnecting cables to the wrong connection point or reconnecting a cable upside and bending a pin in the process. Additionally, cables can be pinched when systems are reassembled, so ensure cables are tucked away before reassembling the case.

Another major problem occurs when mixing different generation technologies together inside the same PC. When a PC has been upgraded several times, problems do arise. For example, an older BIOS chip may not be able to recognize a new memory module or see the new hard drive that has been installed. Check the system resources for conflicts using Device Manager or the Microsoft System Information utility.

Dust Accumulation

A+ 1102: 4.5

The accumulation of dust inside a PC is typical, and the type of environment in which the PC operates, as well as its age, determines how much dust has accumulated. Large amounts of dust can cause heating problems by blocking air filters and by collecting on processor heat sink fins and fan components, preventing the proper dissipation of heat. The dust acts like an insulator and holds the heat to the CPU rather than allowing the cooling fans to dissipate it. Dust can also clog air filters and render a fan inoperable.

Remove dust carefully using a can of compressed air or a special vacuum cleaner designed for PC cleaning. Standard vacuum cleaners generate a tremendous amount of static electricity, which is very dangerous to computer chips, so you should only use vacuum cleaners made specifically for electronic equipment.

System and Intermittent Device Failure

The chapter has provided you with excellent troubleshooting tactics by providing information of what criteria and data is needed for a personal computer to boot and access its operating system. However, other symptoms may cause a personal computer to lock up, overheat, cause loud disruptive noises, and other intermittent device failures. When a technician understands that these issues may arise, it also augments their troubleshooting abilities.

System Lockups

Regardless of a personal computer model and its operating system, a technician should always assume that eventually, a user will experience what is called a lockup. *Lockups* are primarily discovered when an operating system cannot be modified and users perceive that the screen has frozen, since they do not see their mouse moving or their applications functioning. In reality, what has happened is that either the RAM has been overutilized or the CPU has been overclocked. Although users are resistant toward the troubleshooting tactics to fix this issue, normally powering the machine off and advising the user not to run as many applications is the best solution to fix a system lockup.

Intermittent Device Failures

Personal computers may experience intermittent device failures, and it is important that a technician understands the warning signs of these failures. Although each model of a personal computer may be vastly different, it should have a serial number or service tag located on the console portion of the machine for a technician to obtain parts and warranty information. Once these numbers are obtained, it is recommended that a technician either call the vendor's customer service line or access its website to ascertain the most common device failures their machines are experiencing. Once this information is obtained, it is still vital that a technician take other precautions than only the common device failures advised by the vendor of the machine.

A+ 1101: 5.2, 5.3

A computer will often overheat if it becomes too dusty, has been operating for an ample amount of time, or has a faulty cooling fan. Furthermore, when a machine tends to overheat or internal hardware components of the machine become faulty, it will make an ample amount of noise, such as grinding or clicking. Should a technician experience this, they will need to remove the case of the personal computer and troubleshoot the origin of the problem. Should a technician not be able to find the cause of the faulty hardware, they will then need to either access the system's

BIOS or boot into Windows Safe Mode to obtain the proper error logs and codes to determine which piece(s) of hardware is faulty. Nevertheless, if a technician is not able to repair the hardware needed to make a personal machine functional, they will need to adhere to data recovery techniques.

A+ 1101: 5.5

Mobile Device Issues

If a user is experiencing a mobile device that is not loading applications or is not functioning properly, the first troubleshooting precaution for a technician to take is to make sure the mobile device is not overheating. This is a common factor among mobile device failures, and technicians should always check to see if the battery appears to be swollen if the mobile device feels warm. If the battery appears to be excessively swollen, it is vital that the technician take the mobile device to a cooler area and not attempt to work on the phone until it has cooled down and the battery swelling decreases. Once the mobile device is safe to troubleshoot, technicians may adhere to their troubleshooting implementation.

Other common mobile device errors that users experience include when their mobile devices freeze, or they have forgotten their credentials to log into their devices. If a user's mobile device becomes frozen, the technician will be forced to shut the device down manually, which unfortunately means that any data that was being used at the time will be lost. Furthermore, when a user forgets their login credentials for their mobile device, technicians will have to format the mobile device to its factory state if there is not a second method of entry into the device, such as administrative access via a Google account through an Android device.

Another troubleshooting technique is obtaining application log error files. Assuming the user synchronizes their data to a Windows PC, the technician can find crash reports by locating those reports on the PC, often in the C:\Users\<USERNAME>\AppData\ folder. However, be advised that this information provides details regarding how or why a phone failed when it was running a certain application or applications, not detailed hardware information.

A common hardware issue for mobile devices is a broken screen. Minor cracks are often purely cosmetic, and the device can continue operating in its current state. However, substantial breaking presents a safety issue and should be replaced. These types of screens are generally not field replaceable and often have to be sent back to the manufacturer for repairs. As a result, cases and screen protectors are highly recommended.

17.4 Windows Diagnostic Utilities

Most Microsoft operating systems incorporate the same troubleshooting utilities. You need to become familiar with these utilities to save time when troubleshooting a system problem. Common diagnostic utilities native to Windows include DirectX Diagnostic Tool; System File Checker; Registry Editor; Event Viewer; Problem Steps Recorder; Remote Assistance; Problem Reports and Solutions; Performance, Resource, and Reliability Monitors; Memory Diagnostics Tool; and Component Services.

DirectX Diagnostic Tool

DirectX is a software development tool used for multimedia applications that allows programmers to access many Windows built-in features, but a poorly written program using DirectX can cause severe system hangs or crashes. The DirectX Diagnostic Tool (**dxdiag.exe**) looks at every DirectX program file on the computer, as shown in Figure 17-16. You can look for non-Microsoft-approved program labels here. If a file is Microsoft approved, you should not have a problem. That cannot be said for other programmers' tools.

DirectX program files are abundant and used for game development and all types of multimedia programs. The DirectX Diagnostic Tool is incorporated into all Windows operating systems but has become much more sophisticated.

System File Checker

1102: 1.2, 3.1 A+

The System File Checker (**sfc.exe**) can be run to check for corrupt, changed, or missing files from Windows-based applications and restore system files. You can launch the System File Checker by entering sfc/scannow at the command prompt, but the command prompt must be run as an administrator. This is accomplished easiest by using the [Windows][X] keyboard combination and selecting **Command Prompt (Admin).** The **sfc/scannow** command scans all protected system files and replaces incorrect versions with correct versions, as shown in Figure 17-17. System

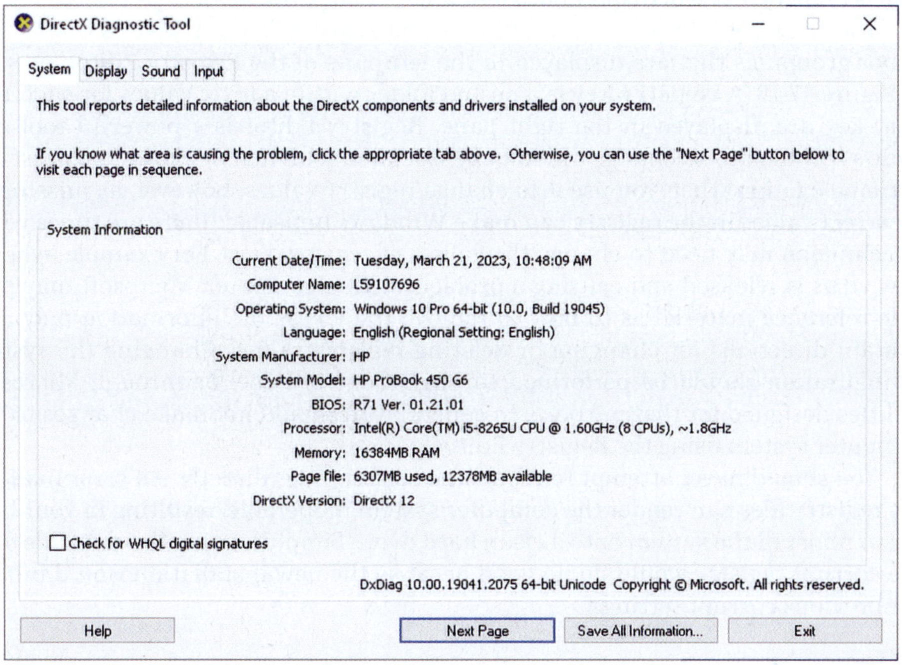

Goodheart-Willcox Publisher

Figure 17-16 The DirectX Diagnostic Tool checks for problems with DirectX files.

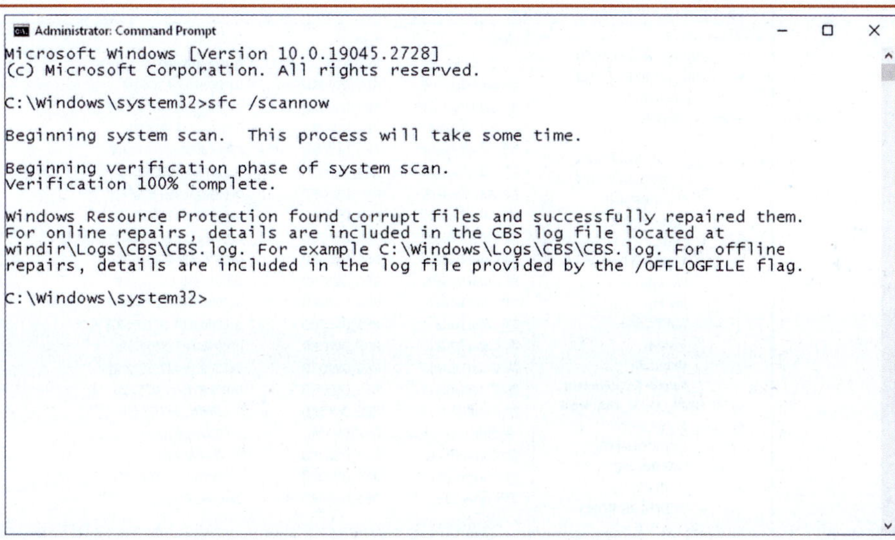

Goodheart-Willcox Publisher

Figure 17-17 System File Checker (**sfc.exe**) can be used to check the integrity of system files.

File Checker is also incorporated into the **Advanced Boot Options** menu. When **Repair Your Computer** is selected, the System File Checker is run automatically, and some Windows machines also run the System File Checker after a system failure is detected.

Tech Tip

Microsoft Register Server (**regsvr32.exe**) is a command-line tool used for adding or removing DLLs and ActiveX controls to or from the system registry. Using Microsoft Register Server will avoid generating system error messages.

Registry Editor

Registry Editor is a Microsoft software tool used to view and modify the system registry files. There are several versions of the tool available depending on the operating system installed and whether you are running a 32-bit or 64-bit operating system. The executable file for 32-bit Windows operating systems is **regedit.exe** and **regedt32.exe**, though running **regedt32.exe** will simply run the **regedit.exe** executable file. The default 64-bit version of Registry Editor is launched using **regedit.exe** and is included with 64-bit versions of Windows. When the 64-bit version is launched, it will display both 64-bit keys and 32-bit keys.

The Registry Editor consists of hives and registry keys. A **hive** is one of five major groupings that are displayed in the left pane of the Registry Editor, as seen in Figure 17-18. A **registry key** is a nested folder within a hive. Values for each registry key are displayed in the right pane. Registry Editor is a powerful tool and allows technicians to change the values associated with registry keys. You must use extreme caution when you use it to change registry values, however, as missing or incorrect values in the registry can make Windows unusable. There are times when a technician may need to change the values of registry keys. For example, when a new virus is released and causing a problem with a computer, Microsoft may provide reference material as to how to remove the virus. The information may also contain directions for changing or deleting registry values. Changing the system configuration should be performed through Control Panel or through Microsoft utilities designed for that purpose. In general, you should not make changes to the computer system using the Registry Editor.

You should never attempt to repair the registry files directly. An error made in the registry files can render the computer system inoperable, resulting in your having to reinstall the system onto a clean hard drive. Simply loading the software over the corrupt registry would do no good because the new installation would inherit the previous corrupt settings.

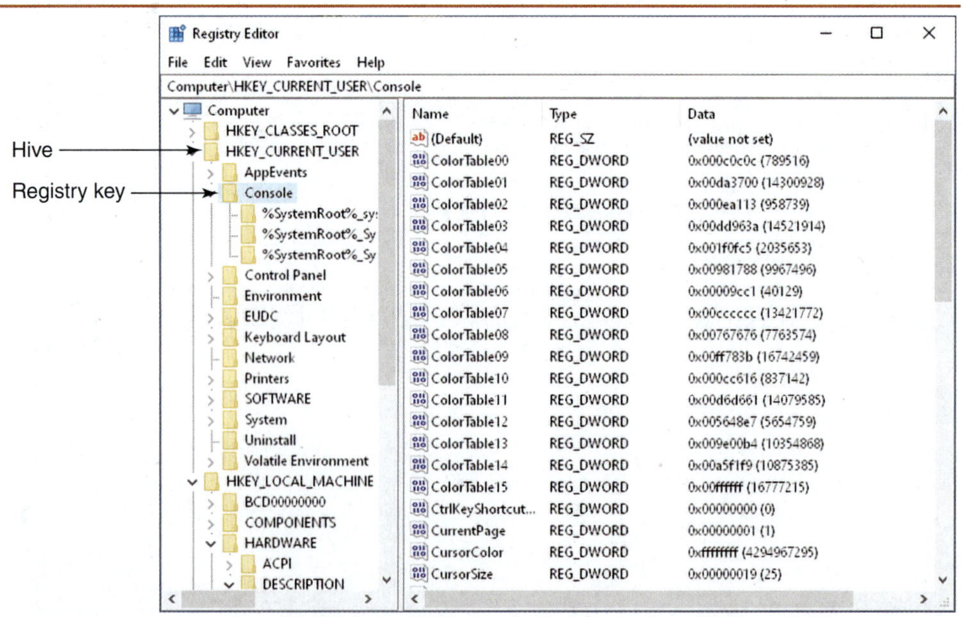

Goodheart-Willcox Publisher

Figure 17-18 Registry Editor is a Microsoft software tool that is used to view and modify the system registry files.

Event Viewer

A+ 1102: 1.3

Event Viewer, shown in Figure 17-19, is a centralized depository of various logs relating to system setup and configuration, applications, security, and more. These logs are categorized by event types, including

- *Error*, indicated by a red circle with an exclamation point;
- *Warning*, indicated by a yellow triangle with an exclamation point;
- *Information*, indicated by a white circle with a blue I; and
- *Audit success*, indicated by a key icon.

Each log can be viewed in chronological order or by categories such as event and user. Since the log files in Event Viewer retain a history of events that have occurred on the PC, they are a valuable troubleshooting tool. For example, users typically do not want to reveal information about installed software such as games, especially if gaming software is against company policy. Using Event Viewer, a technician can quickly view a list of software changes and obtain objective data that can be used to identify possible causes of system problems.

Specific types of events can be selected from the list of Windows logs located in the left pane of Event Viewer, and individual events (located in the middle pane of Event Viewer) can be opened to reveal details about the event, as shown in Figure 17-20. Notice that more information about the event can be accessed through the **Event Log Online Help** option. To find more about the extensive capabilities of the Event Viewer, use Windows Help and Support.

There can be many different log files on a computer system, not just the ones discussed in this section. Software and hardware manufacturers write their own log file collection programs to assist them (and you) in determining problems that may have occurred during the installation of their hardware or software package. The log files can be used to relay information to technical support personnel by e-mail or telephone. Sometimes these files can be accessed remotely by technical support personnel.

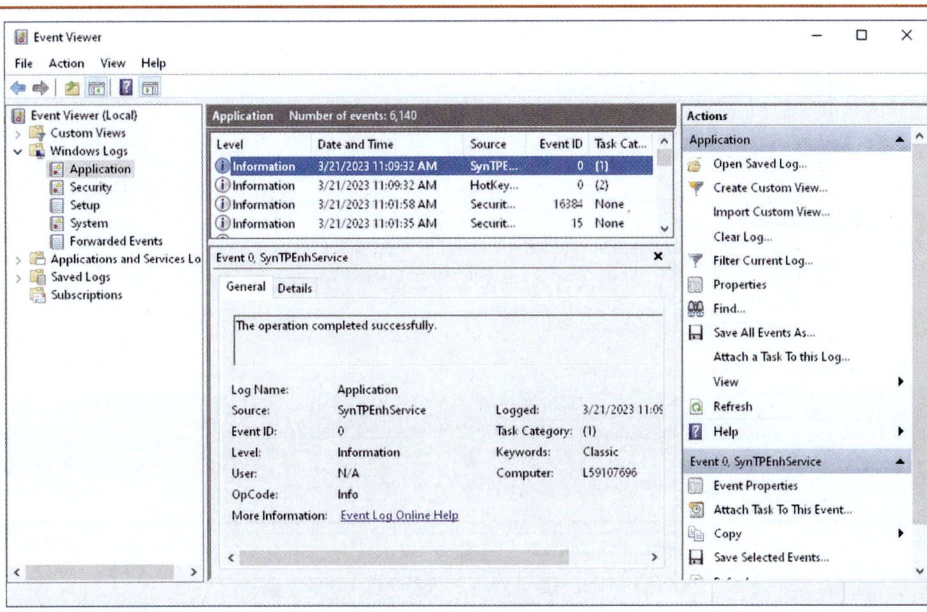

Goodheart-Willcox Publisher

Figure 17-19 Event Viewer collects information about events that happen relating to the computer system, and it stores a description of the event in a log.

Problem Steps Recorder

Problem Steps Recorder is a screen capture tool to record a problem as it is occurring. A series of screen captures are generated while the utility is running, and once the recording is stopped, comments can be added, and the entire recording session can be saved as a zipped (compressed) file in the MIME HTML (MHTML) format. The file can then be sent by e-mail to a technician or help desk for viewing. The technician can see exactly what problem occurred on the computer. The recorder is launched by entering psr into the **Search** box located off the **Start** menu in Windows 10 or Windows 11 and then selecting **Steps Recorder** from the results.

The Problem Steps Recorder is a very simple and intuitive tool. As you can see in Figure 17-21, it has controls for recording, pausing, or stopping the recording. Saving and naming the file is accomplished similarly to any other program. It should be noted that not all types of problems can be recorded, but most involving software applications can, especially ones that generate cryptic error messages that users cannot interpret.

Remote Assistance

Remote Assistance was first introduced with Windows XP and continues to be a part of all Windows operating systems. It allows a user to invite another user to access their computer and assist in repair. The user needing help sends an e-mail invitation to another person, such as a technical support person, and technical support can then repair the system while chatting with the user.

Remote Assistance should not be confused with Remote Desktop, which allows a user to connect directly to their computer from another location. For example, a user could connect to the office computer from a home computer and have complete control over the office computer just as if they were sitting at its keyboard. Remote Assistance is a temporary connection, and a person must be present at both locations.

Figure 17-22 shows the Remote Assistance and Remote Desktop options listed in the **System Properties** dialog box. Remote Desktop can only be initiated from a computer running Windows Professional and Ultimate editions, but any version

Figure 17-20 Detailed information about an event is shown in the **Event Properties** dialog box, which is accessed by double-clicking the event.

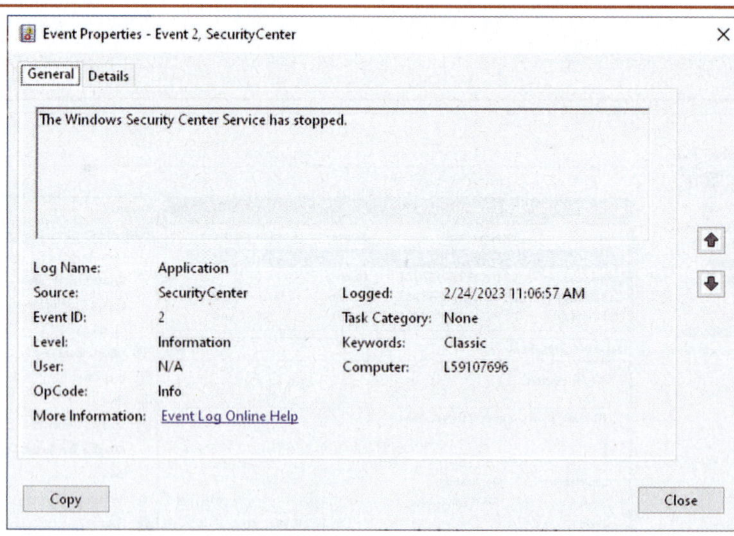

Goodheart-Willcox Publisher

Figure 17-21 The Problem Steps Recorder tool creates a series of screen captures while recording computer problems.

Goodheart-Willcox Publisher

of Windows can return the connection to the computer that starts the Remote Desktop connection. For example, you can start a Remote Desktop connection session from any location running Windows Professional and then access the Windows Professional computer system from another computer running Windows Home Basic. There are no such restrictions for Remote Assistance.

Windows Security and Maintenance

As shown in Figure 17-23, Windows 10 features a utility called Security and Maintenance, which identifies problems as they occur on the system and can be used to automatically find solutions. Problems are automatically reported to

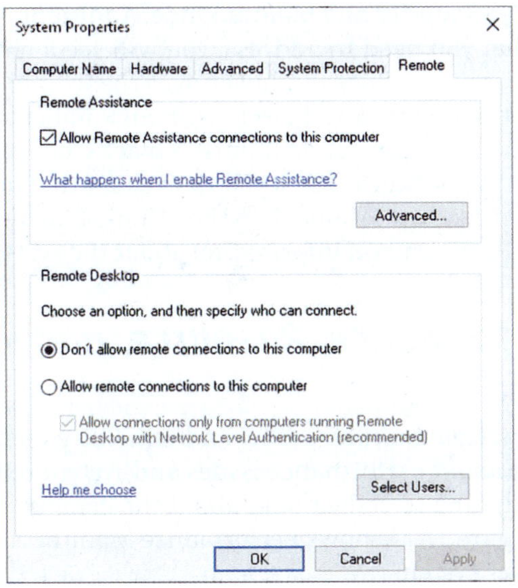

Goodheart-Willcox Publisher

Figure 17-22 Two remote access programs are available in Windows: Remote Assistance and Remote Desktop.

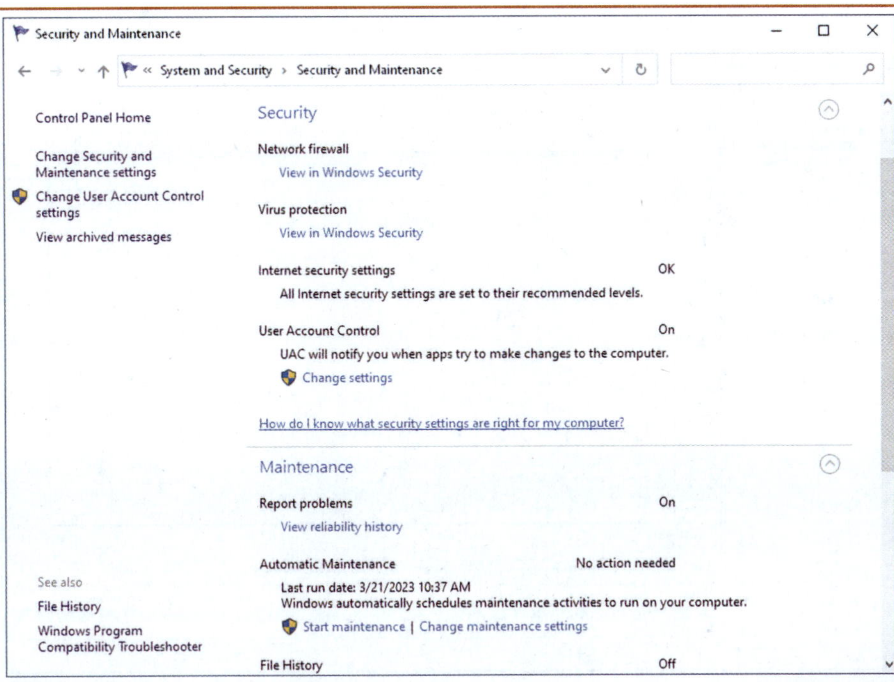

Goodheart-Willcox Publisher

Figure 17-23 The **Security and Maintenance** menu in Windows provides an easy way to assess the security and functionality of a computer.

Microsoft via the Internet, and if a solution is known, it is sent to the computer. A complete history of all problems and solutions can be archived for future use and diagnostics, which is a significant improvement over previous versions of error-reporting utilities. Security and Maintenance is the successor to Problem Reports and Solutions utility introduced in Windows Vista and the Action Center that existed in Windows 7 and Windows 8.

You can use Security and Maintenance to review important notifications about security and maintenance settings that need your attention, obtain information about specific system settings, and perform recommended maintenance tasks. You can also find helpful links to troubleshooters and other tools that can help fix problems. Note, you must be connected to the Internet to check for solutions to the problems shown in this utility.

A+ Note

Be sure you familiarize yourself with all the various diagnostic tools available in the Windows operating systems. Open the Microsoft System Configuration Utility (**msconfig.exe**) and select the **Tools** tab to see a list of some of the most common diagnostic tools.

Security and Maintenance is accessed by selecting **Start**>**Control Panel**>**System and Security**>**Security and Maintenance.** Additionally, if a problem occurs on your computer that you need to address, you will see a notification in the notification area of the taskbar. When you hover over the icon in the taskbar, you will see all the recent notifications. A red circle with an *x* indicates a message about a serious problem, such as an application failure. A black clock means there is a scheduled task running in the background. A yellow exclamation point represents informational issues, which are less serious than those indicated by a red circle with an *x*. A blue *i* is used to indicate general information about the system and is not serious.

A+ 1102: 1.3

Windows Performance, Resource, and Reliability Monitors

Windows includes performance, resource, and reliability monitors, which provide detailed information about performance issues and system reliability. Performance Monitor can be configured to collect data about the computer system and specific hardware devices. Figure 17-24 shows Performance Monitor running and collecting data about a computer system.

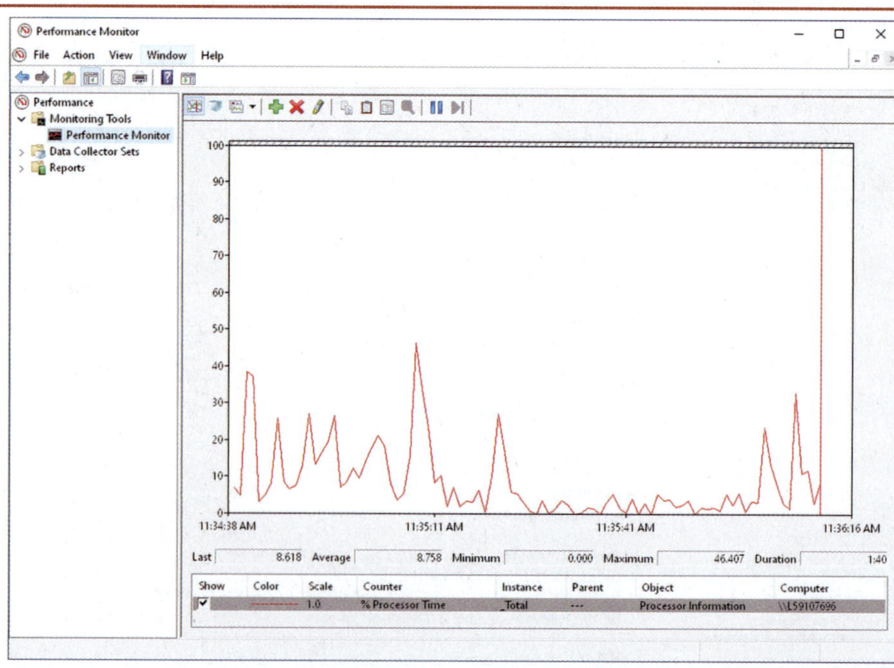

Figure 17-24 Performance Monitor examines how programs affect the computer's performance.

Goodheart-Willcox Publisher

Resource Monitor allows you to observe the effects of specific programs and services on computer hardware and resources. In Figure 17-25, Resource Monitor displays charts of system performance as it relates to the CPU, disk drive, network connection, and memory. You can select services and programs to monitor by clicking the box next to the service or program.

A+ 1101: 5.2

Both Performance Monitor and Resource Monitor can be very useful in determining the reason behind problems such as sluggish performance. Identifying the process(es) consuming the most resources can help you to find the root cause for the sluggish performance. For example, you may need to add more resources, such as RAM, to your device to run a particular process, or you may need to shut down unneeded processes to free additional resources. Either way, Performance Monitor and Resource Monitor can help you make that determination.

Reliability Monitor observes and records computer events that affect computer stability. It produces a historical graph appearing as a linear calendar of recorded events and indicates the seriousness of the events using icons such as a red *x* for severe events, a yellow triangle with an exclamation point for warnings, and a blue *i* for information. The effect on computer stability is displayed in graphic form on a scale from one to ten, with ten being the most severe. See Figure 17-26. This tool is similar to Event Viewer but, as you can see, much more compact and easier to interpret. Reviewing the reliability history will help locate the origin of computer problems. Reliability Monitor is another great addition to the technician's assortment of troubleshooting tools.

As of the release of Windows 7, Reliability Monitor is no longer listed as a separate tool and is instead shown as a chart listing reliability issues. The Reliability Monitor history is accessed through **Start>Control Panel>System and Security>Security and Maintenance>View reliability history**, as shown in Figure 17-27.

Windows Memory Diagnostics Tool

A+ 1102: 1.4

Memory problems can be difficult to identify because they can occur intermittently. For example, if a computer slowly overheats after an extended period of time, RAM could stop working or cause software program errors. Often, a technician may completely reinstall the operating system only to have a random error reoccur.

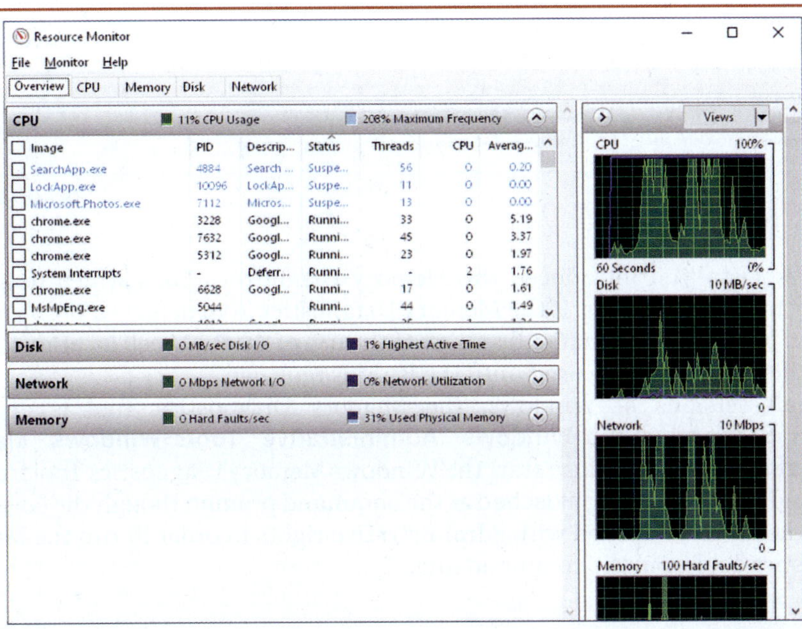

Goodheart-Willcox Publisher

Figure 17-25 Resource Monitor allows you to view the performance of computer systems and resources, such as the CPU, memory, disk, and network system.

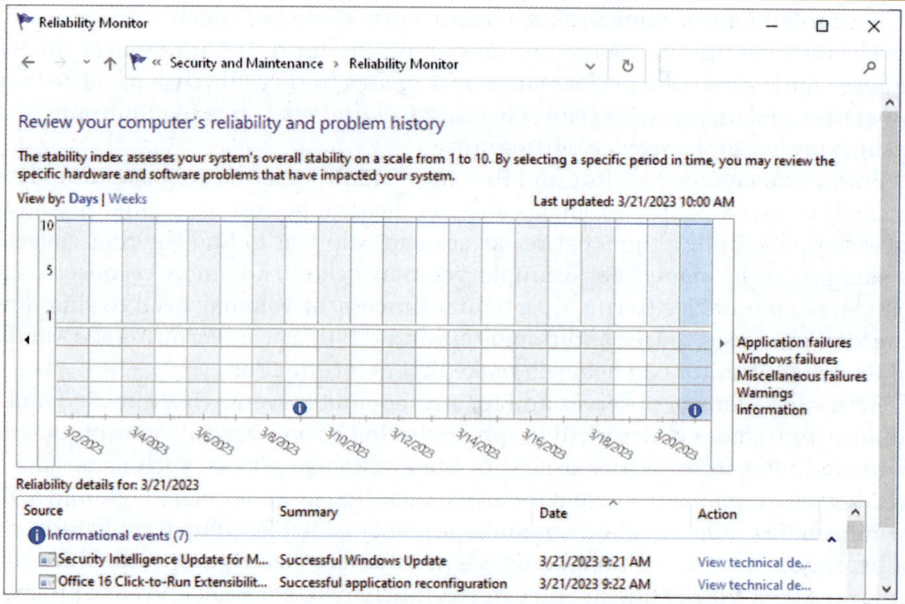

Goodheart-Willcox Publisher

Figure 17-26 Reliability Monitor shows the history of all problems that have occurred on the computer.

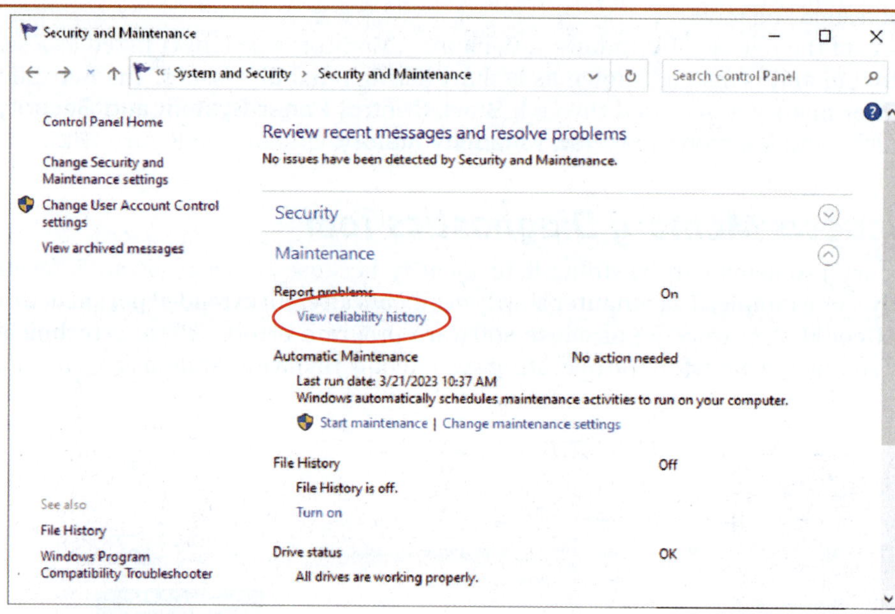

Goodheart-Willcox Publisher

Figure 17-27 The Reliability Monitor is accessed through the Security and Maintenance window.

Windows Vista first introduced the Memory Diagnostics Tool, which diagnoses memory module problems. If the Memory Diagnostics Tool detects a problem with a section of RAM, it automatically restricts the use of the RAM cell locations, which allows the computer to be used until the RAM is replaced.

In all versions of Windows, the Memory Diagnostics Tool is accessed through **Start>All Apps>Windows Administrative Tools>Windows Memory Diagnostic Tool**. You can also start the Windows Memory Diagnostics Tool from the command line by entering mdsched at the command prompt, though the command prompt needs to be opened with administrative rights in order to run the Memory Diagnostics Tool from the command line.

Figure 17-28 shows the **Windows Memory Diagnostics Tool** dialog box. Notice that the test can be performed immediately or scheduled to run the next time the computer is started. The **Windows Memory Diagnostics Tool** in progress looks similar to that in Figure 17-29. Notice that the status of the memory diagnostics appears on the screen in text mode, not graphic mode. The progress of the tests is presented as a bar graph and as a numerical percentage. Any problems identified are also presented on the screen.

Component Services

A+ 1102: 1.4

The Component Services utility contains a Component Object Model (COM) that provides a suite of low-level drivers and interfaces that are needed to communicate and operate certain aspects of a personal computer. With the COM, certain software will not be able to be functional on a personal computer. Although it is suggested that a technician not make modifications to COM settings since they are installed when software installation is complete and seldom need to be configured, technicians are able to view or make modifications to COM settings, as shown in Figure 17-30.

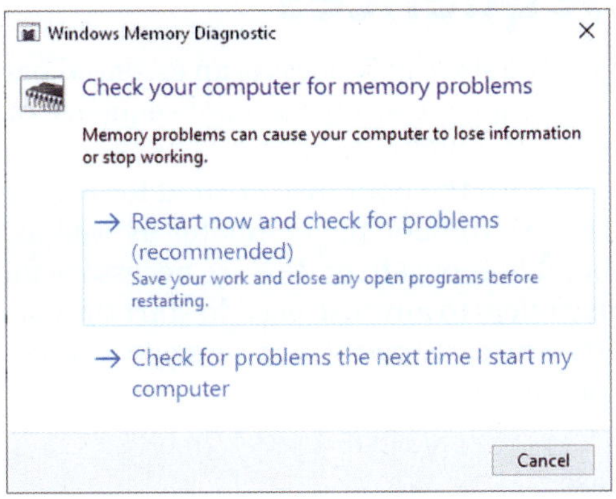

Goodheart-Willcox Publisher

Figure 17-28 The Windows Memory Diagnostics Tool was first introduced in Windows Vista.

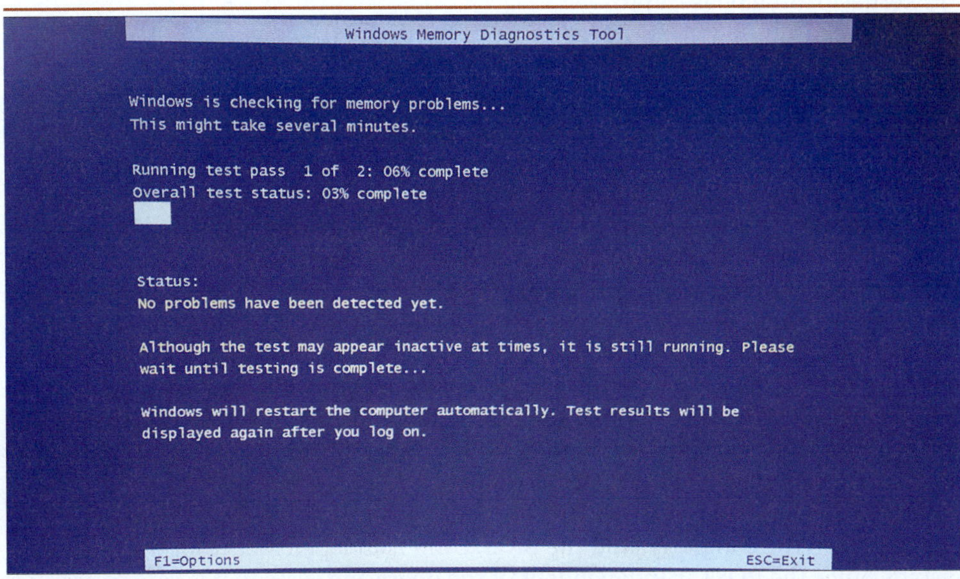

Goodheart-Willcox Publisher

Figure 17-29 The Windows Memory Diagnostics Tool diagnoses memory module problems.

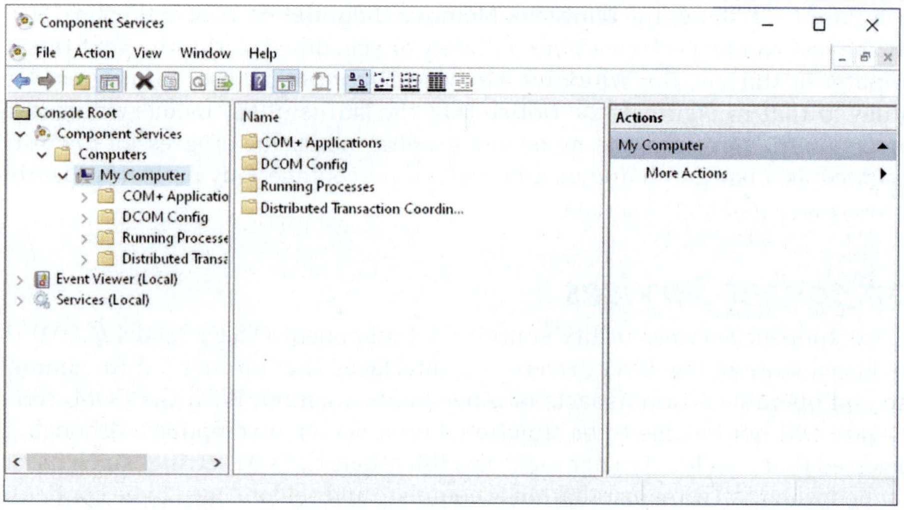

Figure 17-30 Component Services provides a suite of drivers needed to communicate with certain aspects of the computer.

Goodheart-Willcox Publisher

17.5 Boot Sequences

A good understanding of the startup process is an essential part of troubleshooting. Therefore, it is imperative that you study the boot sequence of all standard operating systems and compare the differences. One way to accomplish this is to study the programs associated with the boot disc created for each system. The boot disc contains the files necessary to boot the computer as well as some of the various enhancement files. Not all files on a boot disc are necessary for booting the system. Note, the term *boot disc* refers to any disc used to start the computer system. This is synonymous with *startup disc*, *recovery disc*, or *system repair disc*. The six phases of the Windows boot process are

- POST;
- initial startup phase;
- Windows Boot Manager phase;
- Windows Boot Loader phase;
- kernel loading phase; and
- logon phase.

Power-On Self-Test (POST)

As you now know, when a computer has power first applied to the motherboard by pressing the power switch, the BIOS or UEFI will start the boot process with a quick check of hardware components to verify that all hardware devices listed in the firmware configuration database (CMOS) are present and appear to be in working order. The firmware configuration settings are typically automatically detected or manually modified when the computer is first assembled and started the very first time. The BIOS/UEFI has a default configuration that will start most computers without a problem, but not always. Some BIOS/UEFI configurations require technician modification. The hard drive is automatically detected and configured by the BIOS/UEFI and typically does not need to be modified by the technician because all configuration data is then stored in the CMOS memory.

All systems today use either BIOS or UEFI as the first computer software routine to run on the computer, and the BIOS/UEFI is independent from the operating system. Since the POST is independent of the operating system, it is safe to assume that there is a hardware problem if the computer fails during the POST, or the POST generates an error message or series of beeps. You can research the error message or beep codes at the BIOS or motherboard manufacturer website or conduct an online search using the contents of the error message as the key terms. The following is a partial list of the system hardware checked during the POST:

- CPU system clock
- CPU registers
- Keyboard controller
- Video controller
- RAM
- Disk controllers
- Motherboard bus
- Adapter card ROM

When POST is complete, some adapters such as video cards or hard drives may conduct their own firmware diagnostics routine, which is independent from BIOS diagnostics.

The United Extensible Firmware Interface (UEFI) is a new approach to the BIOS system. The original BIOS program was first developed in the late 1970s, and before that, each computer manufacturer had to have a matching operating system designed especially for that computer. After the BIOS was developed, you could run a variety of operating systems on the same computer. The BIOS was responsible for linking the communication between the operating system and the PC hardware.

Extensible Firmware Interface (EFI) was first introduced by Intel, but now a large group of computer hardware manufacturers is involved with creating a set of standards of design for EFI. The group organization is the United EFI (UEFI), thus EFI is now referred to as UEFI. It can be installed to work directly with the BIOS or as a replacement for the BIOS. UEFI is required on computers to use a GUID Partition Table (GPT). The transition from BIOS to UEFI has been, and will continue to be gradual, not abrupt.

There are extreme differences when comparing BIOS systems to UEFI-based systems. The BIOS is limited in size—typically less than 1 MB of ROM—and it uses 16-bit drivers. UEFI, on the other hand, is not limited in size and can load 32-bit and 64-bit drivers before the operating system is loaded. UEFI can also load and run applications during the POST without the loading of an operating system. For example, a diagnostic utility or disaster recovery tool, or even a virus scanning program, can be run before the operating system is loaded.

BIOS is not governed by any collective organization, and there is no one set of standards controlling the design of BIOS code. The United EFI (UEFI) organization has designed the EFI to be vendor-neutral, so no one operating system or BIOS manufacturer can control the firmware coding. All source code is open and shared so all software and hardware designers have full access to the EFI coding.

Initial Startup Phase

For the initial startup phase in a BIOS-based system, the POST completes and then looks for the boot device where the MBR is stored. The BIOS configuration determines the order for the computer system to locate the next boot device. The boot device could be the hard drive, optical drive, or USB flash drive. The exact order can be changed in the BIOS setup utility and stored in the CMOS memory. In general, the computer uses the hard drive as the boot device, but exceptions exist such as when a boot disc is used to start the computer or when an installation CD/DVD is used to install or recover an operating system. After identifying the location of the MBR, the BIOS loads the MBR or ntldr file into RAM or the Windows Boot Manager (bootmgr), depending on the operating system installed.

Keep in mind, you cannot use a nonbootable CD, DVD, or flash drive to start the computer. When nonbootable media is encountered during the boot sequence, an error message will appear on the screen. Some possible errors include the following:

- Non-system disc
- Missing Ntloader (ntldr)
- Hard disk errors

In a UEFI system, a GUID Partition Table (GPT) is used instead of an MBR to locate partitions on a physical disk. This table overcomes the partition limitations imposed by the MBR. Before GPT, Microsoft operating system partitioning was based on the limitations of the MBR. Partitions could consist of four primary partitions or three primary partitions plus one extended partition subdivided into logical partitions. This is an archaic partitioning system, which evolved from the DOS file system and had a maximum number of 128 partitions that could be supported by the Microsoft MBR. Since the GPT partitioning system does not have the same limitations of MBR-based partitions, you can have an almost unlimited number of partitions using GPT. UEFI does not require a GPT and can be used with a partition system based on MBR. Additionally, UEFI can use a disk system that contains both GPT and MBR partitions.

Windows Boot Sequence

Starting with Windows Vista, ntldr has been replaced by the Windows Boot Manager (bootmgr) and Windows Boot Loader (**winload.exe**). Ntdetect is incorporated into the kernel. Windows now also uses Boot Configuration Data (BCD) in place of the **boot.ini** file. This section begins with the Boot Manager phase.

Boot Manager Phase

The Windows Boot Manager (bootmgr) is used to select which operating system to load when more than one operating system is present on a computer. If more than one operating system is installed on a computer, a screen similar to the one in Figure 17-31 will appear. The Windows Boot Manager screen does not appear if only one operating system is installed on a computer, though it still runs even if it does not appear on the display. The default for the boot manager is 30 seconds, but the delay is reduced to approximately two seconds when only one operating system is present. It is during this two-second interval that the [F8] key can be pressed to interrupt the boot process causing the **Advanced Boot Options** menu to appear. As stated previously, the process was changed from simply pressing [F8] to pressing

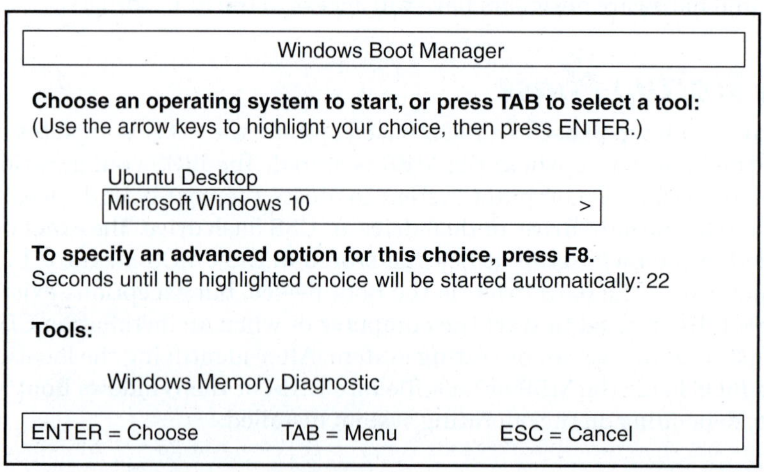

Goodheart-Willcox Publisher

Figure 17-31 The Windows Boot Manager menu will appear by default if there are multiple operating systems on the computer.

[Shift][F8], but this key combination often does not work because the system simply boots too fast to interrupt the system. Instead, you can modify startup in the **Advanced startup** menu accessed through **PC settings** as presented earlier in the chapter. Once the appropriate boot device is selected, the Windows Boot Manager passes control to the Windows Boot Loader.

Boot Loader Phase

In this phase, the Windows Boot Loader first loads the kernel (**ntoskrnl.exe**) into RAM but does not yet execute it. The Windows Boot Loader file is determined by the type of firmware used: BIOS or UEFI. A BIOS-based system uses **winload.exe**, and a UEFI-based system uses **winload.efi**. Next, the hardware abstraction layer file (**hal.dll**) is loaded into RAM as well as the system registry hive. Certain key services are started to support various device drivers that are required during the boot process. Lastly, the kernel (**ntoskrnl.exe**) is executed and takes over operation of the computer system.

Kernel Loading Phase

After the kernel (**ntoskrnl.exe**) is executed, it and the hardware abstraction layer (**hal.dll**) work together to communicate with software applications, drivers, and hardware. Additionally, driver files that do not require user security clearance are typically loaded. For example, the driver and services required to minimally run the printer are loaded at this time.

The kernel and hardware abstraction layer work together to process information stored in the registry, which is required to complete the boot process. The kernel also creates a new registry key, which contains information about the drivers and devices loaded so far and through the rest of the boot operation. This information is used for the **Last Known Good Configuration** boot option when troubleshooting the system or attempting to recover from a system failure. The kernel then loads the Session Manager (**smss.exe**) and the boot process switches from text mode to graphic mode, indicated by a progress bar appearing at the bottom of the screen. The Session Manager continues to run in the background until the computer is shut down.

The Session Manager starts and runs an abbreviated version of chkdsk to determine if the system volumes and partitions are in working order. The Session Manager is also responsible for loading the page file or virtual memory. The page file supplements the amount of RAM installed on the computer.

Microsoft does not allow third-party software applications to access hardware and certain operating system files directly. However, when access is needed by third-party software applications, the Session Manager manages the activities. If the startup process fails here, you will see a blue screen error. Recall that a blue screen error is a full-screen text message describing the error on a plain, blue background. There will be a cryptic error code that can be used to conduct a search at the Microsoft website to find the most likely cause. Microsoft has a very extensive collection of troubleshooting information at its TechNet website.

Logon Phase

The logon phase is the last phase in the startup process during which the Windows logon file (**winlogon.exe**) is executed, and the Windows **Logon** dialog box appears. A user typically enters their logon name and password to proceed to the operating system desktop.

After a successful logon, the Local Security Authority (LSA) file (**lsass.exe**) loads and runs, followed by the service subsystem file, **services.exe**. The exact services loaded and started are determined by the computer's configuration and the user's credentials. Only the services the user is allowed to access will start. If there is only one default user and the computer is not connected to a network with a server, the user can access and run all services for the computer. However, if a user has a limited account, they will only be able to run services allocated by the system administrator.

Startup programs are loaded and run at this point. Any problems such as the computer locking up or the desktop taking a long time to appear are associated with the startup files and services. If a user installs many programs over a period of time, the appearance of the desktop after completing logon will take more time.

After a successful logon, the boot process is considered a success. The registry is updated and will become the registry reference for the "Last Known Good Configuration." A failure of the system after logon is usually a sign of a failed service or a software startup application. One of the best utilities for analyzing failures after logon is the Microsoft System Configuration Utility (**msconfig.exe**). Services and software applications that might be causing the problem can be selected and isolated from startup with this utility.

17.6 Preventive Maintenance

Performing routine maintenance on the PC can help prevent future problems and improve system performance. Some of the most common but often overlooked routine maintenance items are listed in this section. To help ensure regular maintenance is performed, many of the items can be scheduled to perform automatically.

A+ 1102: 4.3

System Backups

Backups should be performed as part of routine system maintenance. You may not be able to repair a failed computer system, but you can at least restore critical data after installing a clean copy of the operating system. If the system has been configured to perform automatic backups, check to ensure the backups are being performed, as the automatic backup configuration may have been turned off or corrupted. Most backup programs keep a backup log, which is accessible through the program's main menu and can be used to verify that the backup job has run at the scheduled time and that the backup was successful. You should occasionally verify that the data could be read and restored from the backup tape.

If you have installed a patch, however, you should verify that you could still restore data. Microsoft has many problems with their DLL files, which are used in the restoration process and could develop a problem after a system patch is installed. Remember, a system backup is the best data protection against viruses, malware, or other disasters. Antimalware software does not protect files or restore them; only a system backup can do that.

Aside from a full backup, which backs up all data regardless of whether it was updated, there are two commonly accepted methods of backing up files: *incremental* and *differential*. The difference between the two is determined by the **archive bit**, which is a single bit within a file that indicates whether that file has been backed up. This issue is important on large data systems where backups are performed daily to ensure against data loss.

A+ 1102: 4.3

A *synthetic backup*, often called a *synthetic full backup*, begins with the previous full and incremental backups created over a period of time and combines them into a synthesized full backup. This has the effect of creating a full backup, without the time-consuming process normally associated with a full backup.

An **incremental backup** is an operation that only backs up files that have changed since the last backup. An incremental backup requires a disc or tape for each daily backup, and in this instance the archive bit is reset. To reconstruct an entire collection of data, a copy of the last full data backup plus each incremental backup in sequence must be used, as shown in Figure 17-32. When performing a **differential backup**, *all* data changes since the last full backup are copied. Only one disc or tape is needed to perform the differential backup because it copies all changes in data since the last full backup was performed. To restore the data, you need only the last full backup and the last differential backup. With a differential backup, the archive bit is *not* reset.

The reason for selecting an incremental or differential backup is based on the amount of time and disc or tape space required for each type of backup. Since the incremental backup only copies changes from the last incremental backup, there is less to copy. This results in a shorter time period required to perform the backup. A differential backup copies all data changes since the last full backup. This can require a significant amount of storage space and time if there is a great number of days between full backups. These differences may seem insignificant at first, but when you are talking about the large volumes of data that some corporations generate, you can be talking about significant periods of time and backup storage space.

System Image

Windows includes a utility for creating a **system image**, which is an exact replica of a hard drive partition, including all personal and operating system files. The system image can be used to repair a computer system to an exact copy the day the system image was created. The main difference between making a system backup and creating a system image is the selection of files and folders. A system backup allows you to choose which files and folders to back up, but a system image does not allow you to choose which files and folders to copy.

Figure 17-33 shows the options available to create a system image, create a system repair disc, and automatically back up the computer. A system repair disc contains a collection of system recovery files and produces a system recovery menu. The exact look and collection of files is determined by the operating system for which it is created.

You should make a system image immediately after the initial configuration of a new computer system. You should also periodically create a new system image after making major changes to a computer system such as the installation of a new software application. A system image is vital to computer system recovery after a major system failure.

System backups can be performed on a routine basis such as once a week at a particular time. The backup should be located at another location such as a network drive.

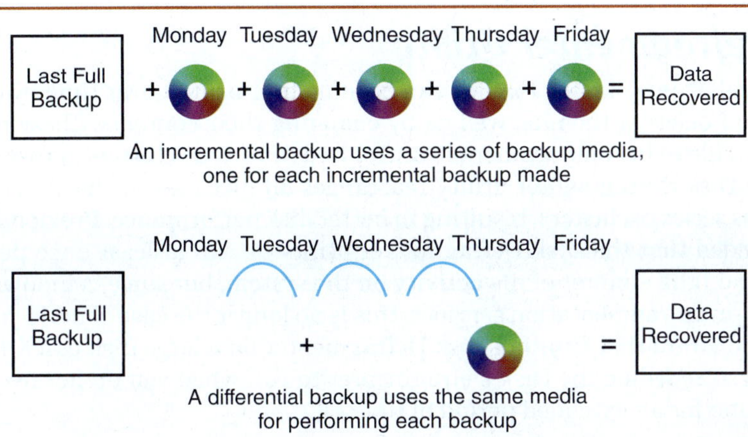

Goodheart-Willcox Publisher

Figure 17-32 The incremental method requires the complete set of discs or tapes plus the last full backup to restore the system data. The differential method requires only the last differential backup made plus the last full backup to restore the system.

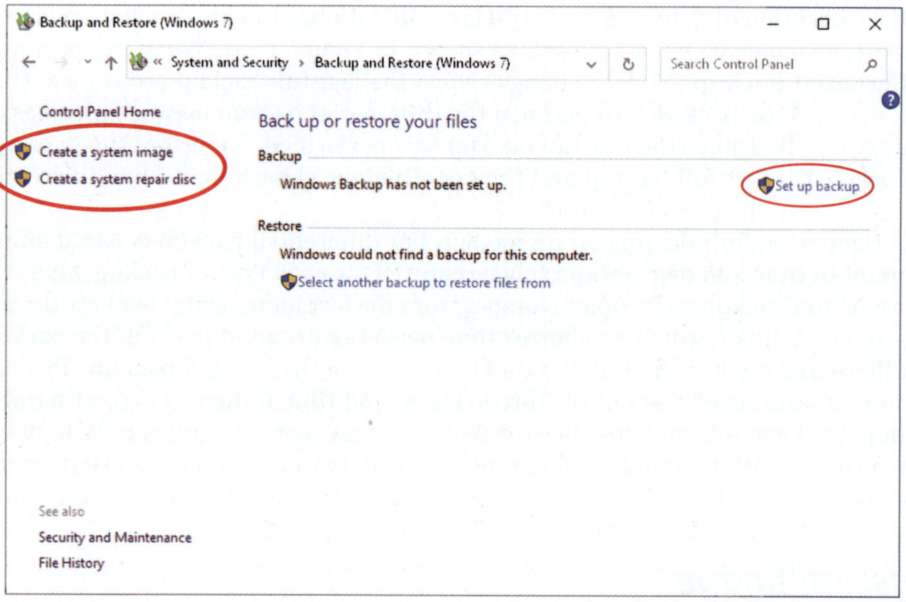

Goodheart-Willcox Publisher

Figure 17-33 A system image and a system backup are two of the best options for protection from malware that damage or destroy system files and folders. A system repair disc can be created and used to start a computer that fails to complete the boot sequence.

A+ 1102: 1.3

Disk Cleanup Utility

The Disk Cleanup utility can be used to regain hard drive space consumed by such items as temporary files, files sitting in the Recycle Bin, unused Windows components, unneeded installed programs, and old restore points created by System Restore. Some of the temporary files that Disk Cleanup allows you to remove are downloaded program files, temporary Internet files, and offline files. The Disk Cleanup utility performs the functions of other Windows programs, such as Recycle Bin and Add or Remove Programs. From this one utility, the Recycle Bin can be emptied, saving you the extra steps of accessing Recycle Bin and clicking **Empty Recycle Bin**. Windows components and installed programs can be uninstalled, rather than accessing Add or Remove Programs.

The Disk Cleanup utility can be used to remove all but the most recent restore points created by System Restore, which automatically backs up system information. This information can be used to restore a computer to a previously operational state. Depending on factors such as how much hard drive space is available, how much hard drive space is allocated to System Restore, and the amount of activity on the hard drive, System Restore can save one to three weeks of system information in restore points.

Disk Defragmenter Utility

As you recall from Chapter 10, files can become fragmented over time by opening, closing, and deleting them as well as by changing their contents. These activities can cause a file to become segmented and stored in various clusters across the hard drive. The Disk Defragmenter utility rearranges all files on your hard drive into a continuous series of clusters, resulting in better disk performance. Previously, it was recommended that the Disk Defragmenter utility be run at least once per month depending on the amount of file activity on the system, but since Windows 10 provides built-in defragmentation services, this is no longer the case. Should you desire to do so, be aware that running Disk Defragmenter on a large disk can take a very long time, so schedule the Disk Defragmenter to run when you do not need to use the computer for an extended period of time.

Chkdsk

1102: 1.2 A+

Windows systems use chkdsk to inspect the hard drive and correct errors in the file structure, such as bad sectors, lost clusters, cross-linked files, and directory errors. Some computer problems can be solved, and performance improved, by making sure that the hard drive has no errors.

Figure 17-34 shows the **chkdsk** command and its results. Two common switches used with the chkdsk command are the **/F** switch and the **/R** switch.

- The **/F** switch is used to fix errors automatically as they are located during the disk inspection.
- The **/R** switch is used to locate bad sectors on the disk and recover readable information.

Chkdsk can also be accessed through the hard drive **Properties** dialog box as shown in Figure 17-35. Notice the option for error-checking and the **Check** button. To access the **Properties** dialog box for a hard drive, right-click the drive that you

A+ Note

ScanDisk is an earlier version of a disk-checking program similar to chkdsk. You may see ScanDisk as a distraction answer on the A+ Certification Exam.

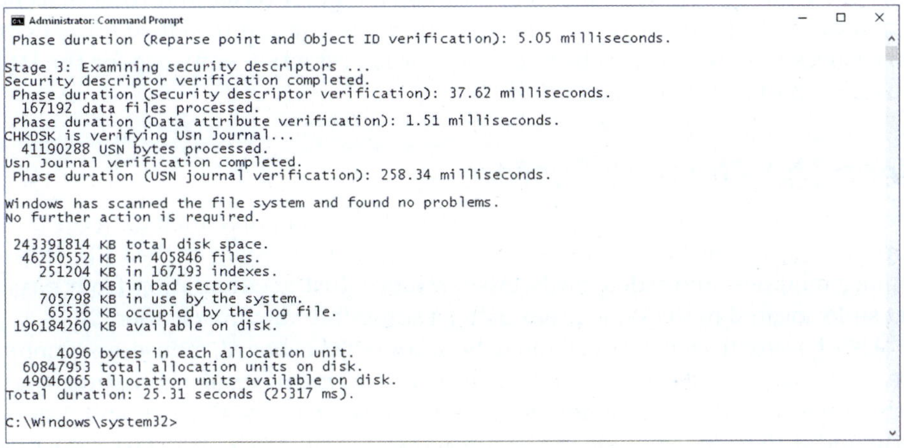

```
Administrator: Command Prompt
 Phase duration (Reparse point and Object ID verification): 5.05 milliseconds.

Stage 3: Examining security descriptors ...
Security descriptor verification completed.
 Phase duration (Security descriptor verification): 37.62 milliseconds.
  167192 data files processed.
 Phase duration (Data attribute verification): 1.51 milliseconds.
CHKDSK is verifying Usn Journal...
  41190288 USN bytes processed.
Usn Journal verification completed.
 Phase duration (USN journal verification): 258.34 milliseconds.

Windows has scanned the file system and found no problems.
No further action is required.

 243391814 KB total disk space.
  46250552 KB in 405846 files.
    251204 KB in 167193 indexes.
         0 KB in bad sectors.
    705798 KB in use by the system.
     65536 KB occupied by the log file.
 196184260 KB available on disk.

      4096 bytes in each allocation unit.
  60847953 total allocation units on disk.
  49046065 allocation units available on disk.
Total duration: 25.31 seconds (25317 ms).

C:\Windows\system32>
```

Goodheart-Willcox Publisher

Figure 17-34 The **chkdsk** command is used to check the hard drive for disk errors.

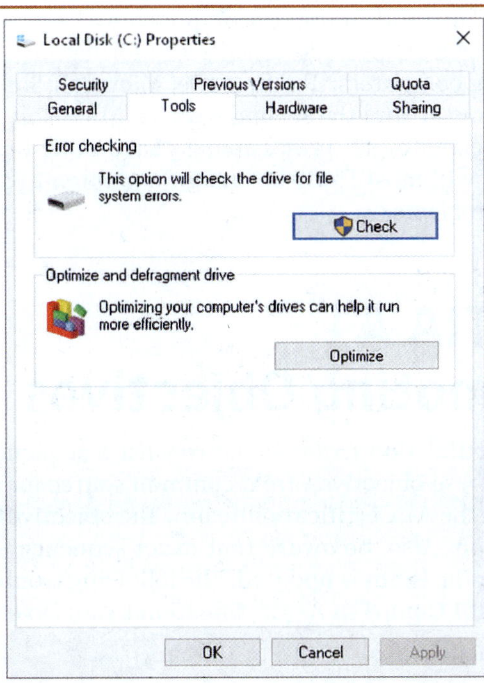

Goodheart-Willcox Publisher

Figure 17-35 The hard drive **Properties** dialog box has an option for checking the disk for errors and correcting them, if necessary.

want to check, click **Properties**, and then click the **Tools** tab. Under **Error-checking**, click **Check now**. If you select to repair disk errors automatically and the disk is in use, you will be prompted to reschedule the disk check for the next time you restart the computer.

Install Patches

Check for the latest software patches for your operating system. Patches should be installed on a regular basis, especially as a matter of security. Many operating system security problems are discovered after the release of an operating system. Checking for and installing patches on a regular basis will keep the security level high on the computer system. Some patches can have adverse effects on your computer system, so be sure to back up your system files before installing a patch.

Virus Protection Updates

Virus protection software requires updates on a regular basis, and your virus protection can fail to protect your system if it does not contain the latest virus definitions. Check the company website of your virus protection software for the latest virus information and updates.

Clean the Physical System

Routinely check and clean the cooling system on the computer, including the power supply fan(s) and the fans located on critical components such as the CPU, chipset, memory modules, and video cards. Also, remove dust accumulation from passive heat sinks located in the same areas using a static-free vacuum cleaner.

Also, be sure to remove dust and debris from the keyboard, mouse, and monitor screen. Do not use chemicals when cleaning the plastic parts of a computer system or the screen area. First, attempt to clean the plastic parts with a dry, soft, lint-free cloth, and if that does not clean the area, try a damp cloth. As a last resort, you may use a mild cleaning solution, but keep water away from electronic components inside the computer and computer vents, and avoid the use of any harsh chemicals for cleaning the computer and computer components.

Two Microsoft websites provide extensive information that will be valuable when troubleshooting computers. The first site, Microsoft Support, is designed for the average computer user, and the second website, Microsoft TechNet, is designed for advanced technicians or IT professionals. Save both links in your Internet browser because you will most likely be using them often to assist you in troubleshooting computer problems.

A+ 1101: 5.1

17.7 CompTIA A+ Troubleshooting Objectives

The CompTIA A+ Certification Exam Objectives list a sequence of actions related to troubleshooting. These objectives are a common source for at least one troubleshooting question on the A+ Certification Exam. The objectives are ambiguous and need some explanation. Also, be aware that exact sequence and objective phrasing may change when the exam is updated. The following troubleshooting steps are taken from the 220-1101 CompTIA A+ Certification Exam Objectives in Domain 5:

1. Identify the problem.
2. Establish a theory of probable cause (question the obvious).

3. Test the theory to determine cause.
4. Establish a plan of action to resolve the problem and implement the solution.
5. Verify full system functionality and, if applicable, implement preventive measures.
6. Document findings, actions, and outcomes.

To better prepare you for any questions that may appear on the exam related to these objectives, each step has been expanded and a more detailed explanation given.

Identify the Problem

A+ 1101: 5.1

The first step to the troubleshooting process is to identify the problem correctly. You must gather information from the user. The following are typical questions that you should ask as a technician:

- What is the computer doing or not doing?
- When did the problem first occur?
- Did you recently install a software application?
- Can you demonstrate the problem for me?

Do not be surprised if a user is not totally truthful with you. A user will most likely not tell you they attempted to do something against company policy or something they knew was wrong. For example, if the last thing a user did before the problem began was attempt to install a game or a software application, the user may fear losing their job and lie to hide that fact from you.

While not listed as a separate step, you should perform a backup (if possible) before you begin attempting to correct the problem or making any changes to the computer system. After backing up the system, look in Event Viewer, which may prove to be a better source of information than the user regarding what changes have occurred. For example, if the user attempted to install a software package, it will be listed in one of the event logs or the reliability history as an informational event. If the customer has caused the problem, do not make the customer feel uncomfortable about it. Simply tell them, "This type of problem happens all the time," and then go on to repair the system.

Also, always get a customer's permission before performing major corrections to the computer system such as replacing a motherboard or reinstalling the operating system, which could wipe out all previous software packages that the customer installed. Furthermore, this maintains transparency in your work while allowing you to converse with the user more in-depth about the issue.

As mentioned previously, a user may feel embarrassed or frightened to admit to the technician that they may have caused an issue to their device. However, it is vital that information regarding the environmental and infrastructural changes that may have occurred is obtained. In other words, something environmental may have caused the machine to become faulty, or perhaps the user allowed another coworker to use their machine to complete some of their work. While it may sound mundane, this information and criteria will help a technician derive and establish a theory of probable cause.

Establish a Theory of Probable Cause

A+ 1101: 5.1

Once you have gathered sufficient information from the user about the problem and backed up the system files, you can form your theory about the probable cause. Recall the information presented earlier in the chapter about the three stages of system operation—hardware failure, software failure, and user-generated problems—to determine when the problem occurs. If necessary, conduct external or additional internal research based on the symptoms presented to help you establish a theory of probable cause. Nevertheless, also be sure to consider your organization's policies before implementing any changes regarding your theory.

If your theory and probable cause can be implemented according to your organization's polices, you may then determine if the cause was internal or external. If the cause was internal, you may need permissions from other administrators to investigate your theory further. An example of this would be files that are transmitted via the Human Resources office. In order to test this theory, you may need to have someone from the Human Resources office present with you, since there will be confidential information about members of the organization.

A+ 1101: 5.1

Test the Theory to Determine Cause

Test your theory with corrective actions related to what you believe is the cause of the problem. If your theory proves irrelevant to the issue with which you are confronted, you will need to determine if another theory needs to be generated or if the issue needs to be escalated to another means of action or technician with more experience. Once you establish another theory of probable cause, take corrective actions again. Repeat the sequence of establishing a theory and performing corrective action until the problem is solved. If you encounter a problem that you feel too inexperienced to fix, do not hesitate to escalate the issue to a technician with more experience than you have. It is better to ask for help than to make the problem worse.

A+ 1101: 5.1

Establish a Plan of Action

Establishing a plan of action to resolve the problem and implementing the solution relates to more than just repairing the computer; you need to ensure that the problem will not occur again. The plan of action may be as simple as replacing the power supply. In the last step, you tested the possibility that the power supply was defective and changed out the original power supply for one that is in known working order. The change fixed the problem, so you can now notify the customer that a new power supply is needed and provide a price quote for repair. If the customer gives permission, you can go order the replacement and repair the computer. Since components can differ significantly from one manufacturer to another, *always* refer to a vendor's instructions for guidance. This can save time if you get confused or become unsure of how to proceed. It can also help identify any unique actions that must be taken for a given component.

To prevent a reoccurrence of the problem, you can ask if the customer has surge protection or a UPS unit. The installation of a surge protector or UPS can help prevent losing a power supply in the future due to power surges. You also need to establish the fact that a power supply can still fail due to wear and tear or old age.

A+ 1101: 5.1

Verify Full System Functionality and Implement Preventive Measures

To verify full system functionality, you should not only check the system yourself, but also have the customer test the computer system. You need to establish that the computer is truly fixed to the customer's satisfaction.

A+ 1102: 3.1

In the example from the previous section with the damaged power supply, implementing preventive measures can be any number of procedures ranging from installing a UPS unit for surge protection to customer education. The education for the customer should be as simple as possible and not condescending in nature. You should *never* make customers feel uneducated about something they did if they are the cause of the problem. For example, if a computer failed because of a recent driver update, show the client how to "roll back" the driver, which will go a long way in winning a customer's confidence in you. It is not all about making money from customer repairs. The customer who brought a computer in for repair will most likely not attempt a repair, even if it is as simple as rolling back the driver. The customer will respect the fact that you are willing to show how to make the repair, and it will also make the customer confident that you are not out to inflate the repair bill. A good customer relationship is the most valuable asset that a computer repair business can have.

Document Findings, Actions, and Outcomes

A+ 1101: 5.1

Documentation of the findings, actions, and outcomes is standard practice in the computer-repair industry, largely so another technician can see what has been done to the system. For example, if the original technician does not come in because of illness and another technician takes over the repair or provides a status report to the customer, the documentation will prove vital. Clients are not going to be happy when they call about the computer repair and the response is, "I do not know. The person working on it is not here." Documentation also proves valuable when computers return for the same problem, which happens frequently. The existing documentation should have details about the problem, how it was fixed, and next steps should the problem reoccur.

Troubleshooting becomes much easier with experience. There will be times when you can immediately identify the source of a problem, though it will not be as easy other times. This is especially true with an intermittent problem. Do not hesitate to ask for help from other technicians or from sources such as the manufacturer website and the Internet in general, but always consider the source of information. There is a lot of bad information about computer repair on the Internet, especially in chat rooms or discussion groups, and many times, the solutions you find from questionable sources will cause more problems rather than fix the system. With time, dedication, and study, you will become an excellent technician.

Chapter Summary

17.1 Common-Sense Practices

- When troubleshooting, determine the major area at fault, determine what action occurred just prior to failure or problem, write down settings before you change them, go slowly, and think the problem through.

17.2 Troubleshooting by Boot Stage

- When troubleshooting computer problems, the first thing you must do is isolate the problem. The best way to go about this is to decide when the problem is occurring. In other words, at what stage of computer operation is the problem occurring?
- The three stages of computer operation are the POST, the loading and initialization of the required operating system files, and after the logon when services and application software are loaded and running.
- If the problem occurs during POST, it is most likely a hardware failure. A beep code is used to indicate failures before the video system is initialized, when there is no display on which to print screen messages.
- If the problem occurs during the second stage—operating system loading and initialization—the problem is most likely related to a corrupt operating system file or a driver.
- During the third stage, startup programs, services, and applications are loaded. The most common problems that can occur during the third stage are usually due to corrupt or incompatible drivers and files.

17.3 Commonly Encountered Problems

- A startup problem causes the computer to lock up during the boot process. These problems occur too early in the PC operation to be solved by system diagnostic tools.
- Common startup problems involve the power supply, CPU, hard drive (boot device), RAM, BIOS, CMOS, system configuration, loading of drivers, and the loading of the operating system.
- Hard drives have a high failure rate because mechanical systems have a higher failure rate than electronic systems.
- Hard drives can also fail because of corrupted files and data.
- If the read-write head becomes damaged or impaired, users and technicians may not be able to retrieve data from the hard drive.
- The S.M.A.R.T. Error Detection Tool can be used to discover when a drive produced an error, was not functioning properly, or if a drive needs to be replaced. Furthermore, the S.M.A.R.T. Error Detection Tool may provide fixes for technicians such as the hard drive needing to be reformatted or if the disk needs to have miscellaneous data removed to utilize the necessary hard drive space needed for present and future files and data.
- Besides hard drive failure, most other computer mechanical problems arise from two areas: improper hardware upgrades and accumulation of dust in the system.
- Many possible system failures can occur after a hardware upgrade. The first thing to check when a system fails to boot is the power and cable connections.
- Large amounts of dust can cause heating problems by blocking air filters and by collecting on processor heat sink fans and fan components, preventing the proper dissipation of heat.
- Other symptoms may cause a personal computer to lock up, overheat, cause loud disruptive noises, and other intermittent device failures. When a technician understands that these issues may arise, it also augments their troubleshooting abilities.

- System lockups are primarily discovered when an operating system cannot be modified and users perceive that the screen has frozen, since they do not see their mouse moving or their applications functioning.
- Although each model of a personal computer may be vastly different, it should have a serial number or service tag located on the console portion of the machine for a technician to obtain parts information along with the machine's warranty information.
- Should a technician not be able to find the cause of the faulty hardware, he or she will then need to either access the system's BIOS or boot into Windows Safe Mode to obtain the proper error logs and codes to determine which piece(s) of hardware are faulty.

17.4 Windows Diagnostic Utilities

- Some of the diagnostic utilities included in Windows are the DirectX Diagnostic Tool, System File Checker, Registry Editor, Event Viewer, Problem Steps Recorder, Widows Security and Maintenance, Performance Monitor, Resource Monitor, Reliability Monitory, Windows Memory Diagnostics Tool, and Component Services.
- DirectX is a software development tool used for multimedia applications that allows programmers to access many Windows built-in features, but a poorly written program using DirectX can cause severe system hangs or crashes.
- The System File Checker (**sfc.exe**) can be run to check for corrupt, changed, or missing files from Windows-based applications and restore system files.
- Registry Editor is a Microsoft software tool used to view and modify the system registry files. You should never attempt to repair the registry files directly. An error made in the registry files can render the computer system inoperable, resulting in your having to reinstall the system onto a clean hard drive.
- Event Viewer is a centralized depository of various logs relating to system setup and configuration, applications, security, and more. Logs are categorized by event type, including Error, Warning, Information, and Audit success.
- Problem Steps Recorder is a screen capture tool to record a problem as it is occurring.
- Remote Assistance allows a user to invite another user to access their computer and assist in repair.
- Windows Security and Maintenance identifies problems as they occur on the system and can be used to find solutions automatically.
- Performance Monitor can be configured to collect data about the computer system and specific hardware devices. Resource Monitor allows you to observe the effects of specific programs and services on computer hardware and resources. Reliability Monitor observes and records computer events that affect computer stability.
- Windows Memory Diagnostics Tool diagnoses memory module problems, and when problems are detected, it automatically restricts the use of the RAM cell locations, allowing the computer to be used until the RAM is replaced.
- The Component Services utility contains a Component Object Model (COM) that provides a suite of low-level drivers and interfaces that are needed to communicate and operate certain aspects of a personal computer.

17.5 Boot Sequences

- The major boot sequence phases for Windows are POST, initial startup, Windows Boot Manager, Windows Boot Loader, kernel loading, and logon.

17.6 Preventive Maintenance

- Performing regularly scheduled maintenance can prevent future problems and improve system performance.
- System backups should be performed regularly as part of routine maintenance.

- A system image is an exact replica of a hard drive partition, including all personal and operating system files. The system image can be used to repair a computer system to an exact copy the day the system image was created.
- The Disk Cleanup utility can be used to regain hard drive space such as that consumed by temporary files, files sitting in the Recycle Bin, unused Windows components, unneeded installed programs, and restore points created by System Restore.
- The Disk Defragmenter utility rearranges all files on your hard drive into a continuous series of clusters, resulting in better performance.
- Chkdsk is used to inspect the hard drive and correct errors in the file structure, such as bad sectors, lost clusters, cross-linked files, and directory errors.
- Staying up to date on patches, virus updates, and regular cleaning of the device can also help prevent issues.

17.7 CompTIA A+ Troubleshooting Objectives

- The A+ Certification Exam troubleshooting steps are identify the problem; establish a theory of probable cause; test the theory to determine cause; establish a plan of action to resolve the problem; verify full system functionality; and document findings, actions, and outcomes.

Review Questions

1. Identify five common-sense practices you should follow when troubleshooting a computer.
2. List four major fault areas to consider when troubleshooting a computer.
3. What are the three major stages of computer operation?
4. List the most likely causes of boot failure at each boot stage.
5. What are the most common causes for blue screen errors?
6. What is the most likely cause when you have a computer with no power lights and an inoperable fan?
7. Diagnose a computer that attempts to boot to the wrong device.
8. What actions should be taken if a user's profile is slow to load?
9. List three screen messages that may appear due to a bad hard drive or corrupt MBR.
10. What command can be used in Windows to recover an MBR?
11. What two areas of mechanical problems can arise other than hard drive failure?
12. What are potential causes of system lockups or intermittent device failures?
13. List and describe four Windows diagnostic utilities.
14. Which four hardware resources are monitored by the Resource Monitor?
15. Recall the Windows boot sequence.
16. How has the current Windows boot process changed since the release of Windows Vista?
17. Describe eight preventive maintenance tasks.
18. What is the difference between an incremental backup and a differential backup?
19. List the CompTIA A+ troubleshooting steps.
20. At what point should a technician escalate the problem?

Sample A+ Exam Questions

1. Which of the following is *not* checked during the POST?
   A. CPU system clock
   B. RAM
   C. Drivers
   D. Video controller

2. Which of the following typically causes a failure during the POST?
   A. Corrupt operating system boot files
   B. A printer driver
   C. A critical hardware device
   D. A software application
3. Which two files are required to load the Windows operating system for versions after Vista? Select two.
   A. **ntldr**
   B. **bootmgr**
   C. **autoexec.bat**
   D. **ntoskrnl.exe**
4. What is the name of the kernel in Windows versions after Vista?
   A. **ntldr**
   B. **ntoskrnl.exe**
   C. **ntdetect.com**
   D. **service.exe**
5. Which command is used to detect and automatically fix errors on a Windows 10 hard drive?
   A. **chkdsk/f**
   B. **fmbr**
   C. **scandisk**
   D. **msconfig32**
6. Which utility scans for corrupt, changed, or missing files from Windows-based applications?
   A. **regedit.exe**
   B. **msconfig.exe**
   C. **bootrec.exe**
   D. **sfc.exe**
7. How do you access the Backup and Restore feature in Windows?
   A. **Start>All Programs>System Restore**
   B. **Start>Control Panel>System and Security>Backup and Restore**
   C. Right-click **Computer**, select **Properties** from the shortcut menu, and then select the **System Restore** tab
   D. **Start>All Programs>Accessibility>System Restore**
8. Which command can be run to view and manually edit the system registry in Windows?
   A. **msconfig**
   B. **sysconfig**
   C. **regediting**
   D. **regedt32**
9. Which command can be issued to open the Microsoft System Configuration Utility?
   A. **sfc**
   B. **sysconfig**
   C. **msconfig**
   D. **regedit**
10. What would be used to diagnose a problem that occurs during the POST phase of the system boot operation?
    A. A POST card
    B. A multimeter
    C. System Configuration Utility
    D. A DOS disk

Chapter 18

Data Recovery

Learning Outcomes

18.1 Provide examples of troubleshooting methods and utilities used to recover from a system startup failure.

18.2 Summarize concepts associated with data recovery.

18.3 Differentiate among backup types.

A+ Certification Exam Objectives

The following A+ Certification Exam Objectives are covered in this chapter.

Exam 220-1101

3.0 Hardware

- 3.4 Given a scenario, install and configure motherboards, central processing units (CPUs), and add-on cards.

5.0 Hardware and Network Troubleshooting

- 5.3 Given a scenario, troubleshoot and diagnose problems with storage drives and RAID arrays.

Exam 220-1102

1.0 Operating Systems

- 1.3 Given a scenario, use features and tools of the Microsoft Windows 10 operating system.
- 1.4 Given a scenario, use the appropriate Microsoft Windows Control Panel utility.
- 1.9 Given a scenario, perform OS installations and upgrades in a diverse OS environment.

3.0 Software Troubleshooting

- 3.1 Given a scenario, troubleshoot Microsoft Windows OS problems.

4.0 Operational Procedures

- 4.3 Given a scenario, implement workstation backup and recovery methods.

Key Terms

3-2-1 rule
clean install
clean room
Computer Management
grandfather-father-son
Recovery Console
restore points
system upgrade

Overview

In the event of computer failure or data loss, the ability to recover data is vital. Obviously, the best method for mitigation of data loss is regular backup of files. However, even files that have been backed up must be recovered and implemented in the event of disaster. Fortunately, many operating systems provide built-in utilities to help technicians recover data. In a way, this chapter serves as a companion or extension to the previous chapter. While the previous chapter discussed troubleshooting computers, this chapter presents information about recovering from a system startup failure, data recovery, and backup types.

A+ Note

There may be times when all security measures fail or uncontrollable events such as inclement or disastrous weather cause a system to crash. When this happens, you will have to know how to recover a system. The CompTIA A+ Exams place emphasis on being able to recover a system, and the information presented in this chapter will help you understand options for recovering from startup failure and recovering data.

18.1 Recovering from System Startup Failure

Recovering from a system startup failure requires advanced skills, including knowledge of applicable utilities. Many of the utilities described in this section should *not* be used by an inexperienced user because they can cause additional problems if not used correctly. To become an effective, experienced technician, you should practice using these utilities in a lab setting or virtual machine before attempting to use them on a customer's PC. You can also download extensive information about each of the utilities from the Microsoft Support website.

A+ 1101: 3.4

Advanced Boot Options

Aside from the normal mode a PC boots into by default, there are several different modes used for troubleshooting into which you can force a PC to boot. These modes are useful if your computer has any of the following symptoms:

- system stalls for an unusually long period of time
- printer problems (as a last resort only)
- video display problems
- computer shuts down or locks up for no apparent reason
- intermittent error conditions

In Windows 10 and 11, there are several ways to access the boot options menu. The first is to hold down the [Shift] key as you restart the computer. You can also navigate to **Start**>**Settings**>**Update & Security**, which will launch the **Update & Security** screen. From there, you can select **Recovery**, as shown in Figure 18-1. Once in the **Recovery** menu, you can select **Restart now** under the Advanced startup section, as shown in Figure 18-2.

A third method used to access the advanced startup window is from the command prompt. When the command prompt is launched with administrative privileges, executing the command **shutdown /r /o** will result in a restart with the Advanced Boot Options shown.

Whichever method you use, you will reach the **Choose an option** screen shown in Figure 18-3. As you can see in the figure, options for recovery include using a device to launch Windows Recovery or the proprietary troubleshooter, which provides the opportunity to reboot in Safe Mode.

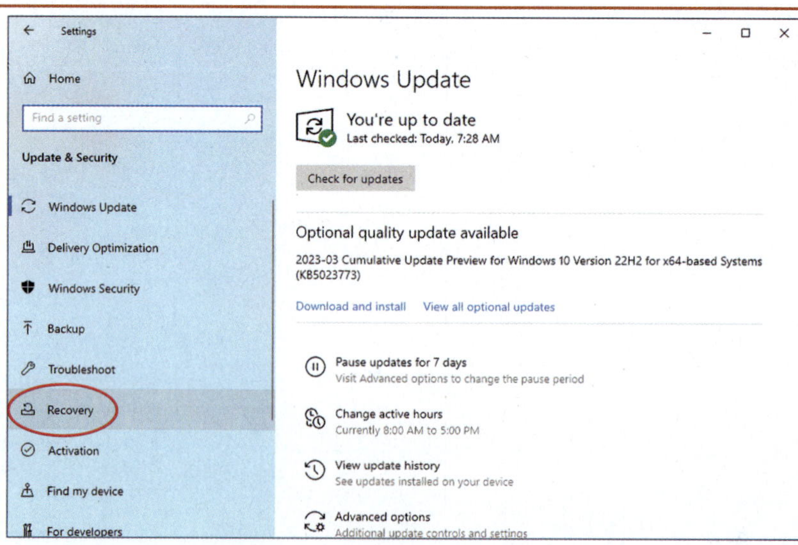

Figure 18-1 The **Recovery** option in the Windows **Update & Security** menu launches a variety of recovery options.

Goodheart-Willcox Publisher

Recall that Safe Mode is a bootup option that disables Windows device drivers and starts the display in VGA mode. Safe Mode will start automatically if Windows detects a system startup failure, but you can also launch Safe Mode through System Configuration. Use the [Windows][R] keyboard combination to launch the **Run** dialog box and enter msconfig before clicking the **OK** button. Once the System Configuration menu opens, select the **Boot** tab and click into the **Safe boot** checkbox, as shown in Figure 18-4. Then click **Apply** and **OK**. Notice in the figure that there are multiple startup options under the **Safe boot** checkbox. The following is a description of each startup mode.

- **Minimal**: This option starts Safe Mode with the absolute minimal number of drivers and services while still providing the standard Windows GUI.
- **Alternate Shell**: This option starts Safe Mode with a command prompt instead of the Windows GUI. Using the **Alternate Shell** option requires knowledge of advanced text commands and the ability to navigate the operating system without a mouse.

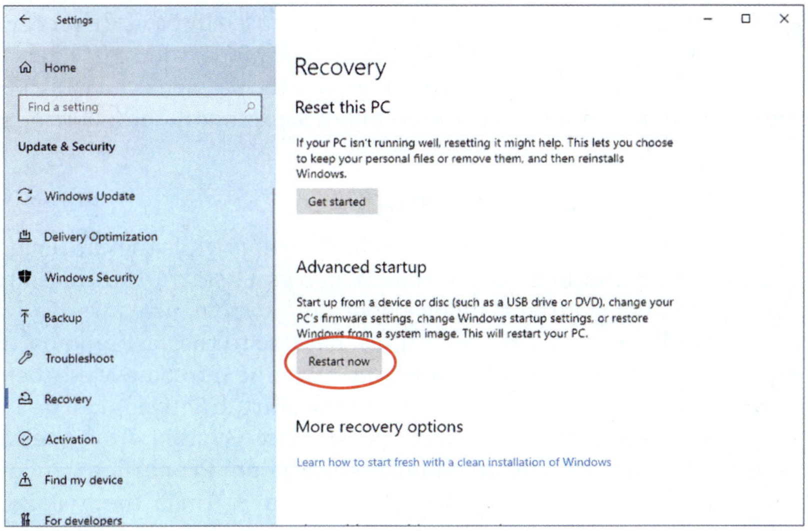

Goodheart-Willcox Publisher

Figure 18-2 The **Restart now** button can be selected to restart the PC with the goal of booting into a different mode or from a different drive.

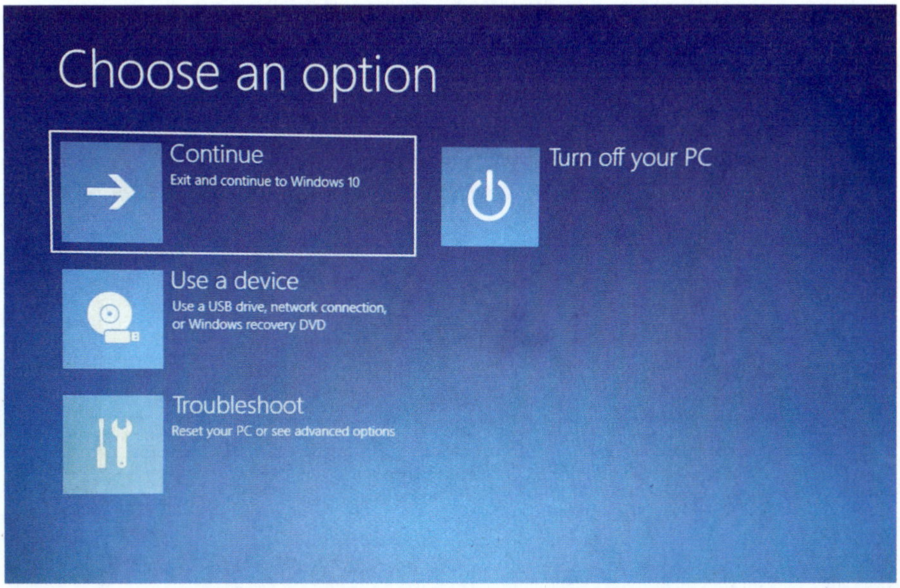

Goodheart-Willcox Publisher

Figure 18-3 Advanced restart provides an administrator with recovery options, including using a device to launch a recovery drive and troubleshooting the PC.

- **Active Directory Repair**: This option starts Safe Mode with access to machine-specific information, such as hardware models. If the Active Directory were corrupted from an unsuccessful hardware installation, Safe Mode can be used to restore system stability by repairing corrupted data or adding new data to the directory.
- **Network**: This option starts Safe Mode with the necessary services and drivers for networking as well as the standard Windows GUI.

In addition to choosing one of these safe boot options, you can also choose **No GUI Boot**, which boots with just a command window; **Boot log**, which creates a log of all information from the boot process (this document can be very useful for troubleshooting); **Base video**, which loads the drivers for VGA graphics instead of those for a video card; and **OS boot information**, which shows each driver name as they are loaded during the boot process.

Safe Mode allows you to establish a probable cause of the computer problem. The absence of presence of a problem in Safe Mode can help you determine whether the issue is with basic system resources or with something else, such as a specific application or driver. For example, if the problem no longer exists while the computer is running in Safe Mode, the problem is most likely not caused by basic drivers or system files. If the computer problem still exists while in Safe Mode, you most likely need to perform a system refresh, and if that does not resolve the problem, you will likely need to perform a system reset. There will be more about Safe Mode in the following section.

Windows 10 Startup Settings

Windows 10 allows users to modify their Startup Settings while they are logged onto their machine, and it should be noted that Windows 11 startup settings are quite similar. In prior versions of the Windows operating system, users were advised to boot into Safe Mode to modify these settings, but due to the vast amount of hardware upgrades, it is often difficult to boot the machine into Safe Mode before the Windows 10 operating system boots. Therefore, the Startup Settings can be accessed by selecting **Start**>**Control Panel**>**System and Security**>**System**>**Advanced system settings.** This will open the **Advanced** tab of the **System Properties** window.

Once a user has entered into the Advanced System Settings, they will be able to choose performance options that allow only certain programs to load during boot. Users can also select to disallow loading any programs that are nonessential for the operating system to function. Furthermore, performance options are recommended for the user, such as **Best Performance and Best Appearance**, which are

Figure 18-4 Users can manually enter Safe Mode by navigating to **System Configuration**.

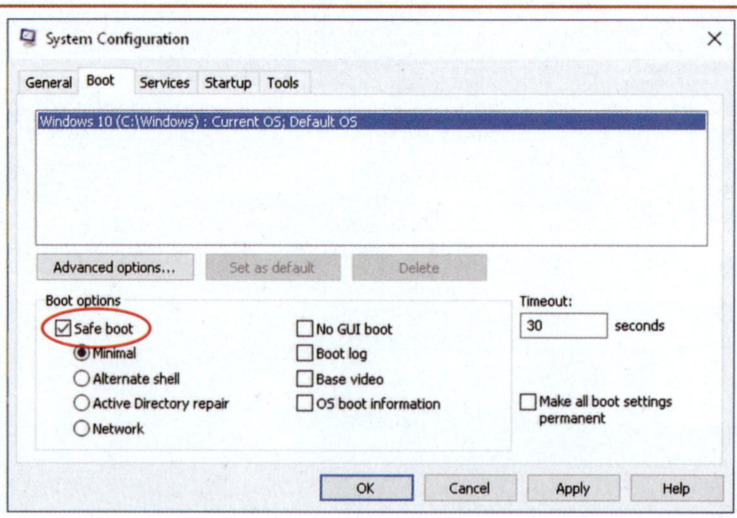

Goodheart-Willcox Publisher

startup templates generated by the Windows 10 operating system assessing the personal computer's hardware and user's behaviors with software while interacting with the Windows 10 operating system. However, if a user wants additional options, they may use the **msconfig** utility, as previously described.

Recall that holding the [Shift] key while selecting **Restart** can reboot the operating system into Safe Mode. Once the machine restarts, the user will be prompted with the following selections:

- **Enable debugging**: starts Windows in an advanced troubleshooting mode and is intended for IT professionals with some programming experience
- **Enable boot logging**: creates a file called **ntbtlog.txt**, which lists all the drivers that are installed during startup, which is useful in identifying any drivers that did not load
- **Enable low-resolution video**: resets the video to a low-resolution configuration setting
- **Enable Safe Mode**: starts Windows with a minimal set of drivers and services
- **Enable Safe Mode with Networking**: starts Windows with a minimal set of drivers and services, though networking is enabled in the event you want to access other computers on the network
- **Enable Safe Mode with Command Prompt**: starts Windows with a minimal set of drivers and services and provides a command prompt
- **Disable driver signature enforcement**: allows drivers without Microsoft-approved signatures to be installed
- **Disable early launch antimalware protection**: prevents the loading of an antimalware protection driver, which can also allow malware to be installed
- **Disable automatic restart after failure**: prevents Windows from automatically restarting when a failure is detected, as the automatic restart option can cause a computer system to reboot continuously

System Restore

1102: 3.1 A+

System Restore, shown in Figure 18-5, is a feature available in all Windows operating systems and can be used to restore a system to a previously working state. The actual look of the dialog boxes can vary according to which operating system you

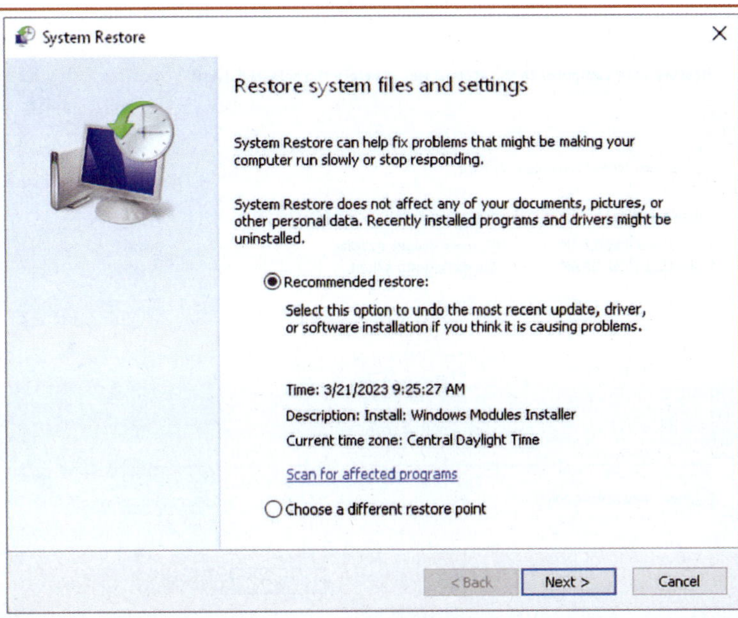

Goodheart-Willcox Publisher

Figure 18-5 System Restore is used to revert a system to a previously known working state.

are using, but the main system restore principles and characteristics are the same. **Restore points** are backups of system settings and configurations used to correct a computer problem.

System restore points can be created manually, but most of the time they are created automatically when changes to the system settings and configurations are made, such as when new drivers, programs, or hardware components are installed. Anything that significantly changes the operating system configuration is recorded as a system restore point, but system restore points are not affected by changes in stored data such as documents, pictures, and videos. As a safe practice, Microsoft recommends manually creating a restore point when changing configurations, such as when adding hardware or installing software. If something happens to the system that results in improper operation, the System Restore feature can be used to return the system to its previous state. In Windows 10, you can access System Restore either by conducting a search using the term system restore or by navigating to **Control Panel>System and Security>System>System protection>System Restore.** Figure 18-6 shows the way Windows 10 displays the system restore points as well as information such as the date and time it was created, a description, and the type of restore point it is.

A+ 1102: 1.9

In some cases, System Restore may be too severe of a correction for a problem. For example, if a problem developed after installing a new or updated driver, it can be beneficial to first use the **Roll Back Driver** option instead of System Restore. This option can be located by navigating to **Start>Settings>Devices>Printers & scanners** (or **Connected devices**)>**Device manager.** Alternatively, you can use the [Windows][X] keyboard combination and select **Device Manager** from the list of options. Once **Device Manager** is opened, double-click the device for the driver you recently installed; then select the **Driver** tab. From there, select the **Roll Back Driver** option. If this does not solve the issue, then System Restore should be used to revert the system to a previously known functional state.

A+ 1102: 4.3

Recovery Console

The **Recovery Console** is a last-resort recovery utility available in Windows often used when a problem is so severe, a technician cannot access the Safe Mode startup option. Recovery Console is also referred to as *command console* and *repair console*, as it is not a GUI utility; rather, it is a command-line interface utility with commands

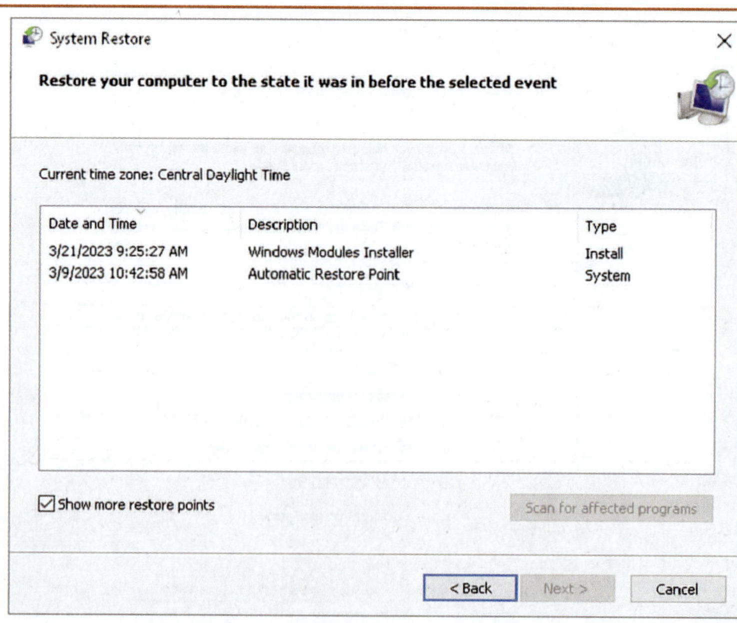

Figure 18-6 Restore points provide a method to restore a computer to the way the system was operating at a previous date.

Goodheart-Willcox Publisher

issued at the Recovery Console command prompt, which sets Recovery Console apart from some of the other recovery utilities discussed in this chapter. The commands are very similar to the old DOS-style commands issued at the DOS prompt. You are probably familiar with many of the commands, but there are some new ones. The chart in Figure 18-7 is a partial listing of the many commands available in Recovery Console.

Recovery Console looks very much like the Windows command-line interface, but it is not the same. For example, Recovery Console is not installed by default, and unless the computer system has been previously configured to run Recovery Console from the hard drive, you must use the installation CD to start the Recovery Console. To do this, insert the installation CD into a bootable CD-ROM drive. You may need to configure the BIOS settings to allow the CD-ROM drive to be the first device in the boot sequence.

When the PC boots to the installation program, press the [R] key to repair the system and the [C] key to enter Recovery Console. Pressing the [R] key will command the Recovery Console to perform an automatic recovery of the system much like the **Last Known Good Configuration** option. Pressing the [C] key displays the Recovery Console command prompt, from which you can issue commands or copy missing files to the operating system directory. The Recovery Console should only be used by technicians with advanced troubleshooting experience. Beginning with the

Recovery Console Commands

Command	Description
attrib	Clears or sets file attributes
bootcfg	Used to recover multiboot system failures and to reconfigure the boot.ini file
cd or **chdir**	Changes directory or folder location
chkdsk	Checks for and may repair bad disk sectors, and checks the surface of the disk
copy	Copies a file
del or **delete**	Deletes a file
dir	Displays the contents of a directory
disable	Disables a service or driver
diskpart	Manages the partitions on a disk
enable	Enables a service or file
exit	Closes the Recovery Console
expand	Extracts a compressed file known as a cabinet (.cab) file
fixboot	Writes a new boot sector on a partition
fixmbr	Repairs the master boot record
format	Formats a partition, volume, or logical drive
help	Displays a list of Recovery Console commands
listsvc	Lists all available services and drivers
logon	Lists all Windows 2000 and XP systems and lets you log on to one particular system
md or **mkdir**	Creates a directory or folder
rd or **rmdir**	Removes a directory or folder
ren or **rename**	Renames a file

Goodheart-Willcox Publisher

Figure 18-7 Recovery Console utilizes a number of text-based commands.

release of Windows Vista, Microsoft redesigned the Recovery Console into a much more sophisticated utility called the Windows Recovery Environment, which is discussed in the following section.

A+ 1102: 1.4, 4.3

Windows Recovery Environment

The Windows Recovery Environment (WinRE) is a vast improvement over earlier startup repair utilities developed by Microsoft for their operating systems. Historically, it was launched by booting to the Windows installation DVD, but since newer versions of Windows may not come with a disc, the user is instead prompted to create a recovery disc when the computer is first started, which becomes the recovery disc used to start the Windows Recovery Environment (WinRE). The recovery disc takes you directly to WinRE, where you will be prompted by a dialog box to select the keyboard layout and regional preferences, such as language. The next screen presents an option to perform a system repair.

Toward the lower left-hand side of the dialog box, you will see an option to **Repair your computer.** The letter *R* is underlined, which represents the fact that you can simply press the letter [R] key to start the repair process. This feature is a standard option in repair scenarios because the mouse might not be working, and you may only have use of the keyboard.

The first dialog box to appear requests that you identify the drive or partition to repair. The second dialog box to appear prompts you to select the type of repair. The options include

- **Startup Repair**, which searches for and replaces corrupt or missing system files;
- **System Restore**, which provides access to the System Restore utility from which you can restore the system to a point in time that the system was working;
- **Windows Complete PC Restore**, which makes an image of the hard drive including files such as the MBR, which normally cannot be accessed or copied without the use of third-party tools;
- **Windows Memory Diagnostics Tool**, which loads the Windows Memory Diagnostics Tool; and
- **Command Prompt**, which provides access to the command prompt from which you can use command line utilities to repair the system.

It should be noted that the **Windows Complete PC Restore** option is only available in Windows Business, Ultimate, and Enterprise editions, not Home versions. It is also the most complete restoration option because it replaces the entire collection of operating system files as well as all data. You can even restore the complete system to a brand-new computer if the original computer cannot be recovered.

Some computer manufacturers preinstall System Recovery Options. To access System Recovery Options in a preinstalled system, press [F8] during the boot process and then select **Repair Your Computer** from the **Advanced Boot Options** menu.

WinRE will launch automatically if a boot failure is detected. When the computer starts, the Windows boot loader stores a binary code indicating the boot process has started, which is normally cleared before the Windows logon screen is displayed. However, if the boot fails, the binary code is not cleared. The next time the computer starts, the binary code is detected, and the operating system assumes that a boot failure occurred on the previous startup attempt. This action causes the boot loader to launch WinRE instead of the operating system.

A+ 1102: 1.9

Windows Recovery Partition

Recovery partitions help restore a computer system back to its original condition and have been used by OEMs for many years as separate hard drive partitions that contain all the files necessary to reinstall the operating system. Some are designed simply to format the C: partition and reinstall the operating system, thus deleting all valuable user files such as documents and photos, and others are designed to reinstall the operating system without formatting the partition, thus saving valuable user files. However, these types of partitions may fail to repair the computer system because of a hidden virus contained in one of the user files.

Microsoft first incorporated a recovery partition feature called Refresh your PC in Windows 8. To check if a recovery partition has been created for the computer, access the command prompt with administrator privileges and enter recimg/showcurrent. The status of the refresh image will be displayed on the screen.

To create a refresh image, first create a folder for the recovery partition by entering mkdir C:\RefreshImage at the command prompt. Then, create the refresh image by entering recimg -CreateImage C:\RefreshImage. You may notice that the default drive selected for the image is C:, but you could use another partition or even a flash drive for the location of the refresh image.

You can also create a recovery partition or drive by entering recovery into the Windows **Search** box. Notice that when recovery is entered in the **Search** box, several recovery options are listed, as shown in Figure 18-8. Select **Create a recovery drive.** This option will create a set of recovery files, which can be stored on an external drive, a CD/DVD disc, or a USB flash drive.

Microsoft System Configuration Utility

1102: 1.3, 1.4 A+

With the Microsoft System Configuration Utility (**msconfig.exe**), also referred to as *msconfig* or *System Configuration*, you can perform a diagnostic startup or select specific services and applications not to load. System Configuration is used to eliminate items that can cause a problem during the startup of the computer system and after user logon. Using the process of elimination, you can determine which service or application is causing the problem. This is one of the most common and useful troubleshooting utilities provided by Microsoft as part of the operating system.

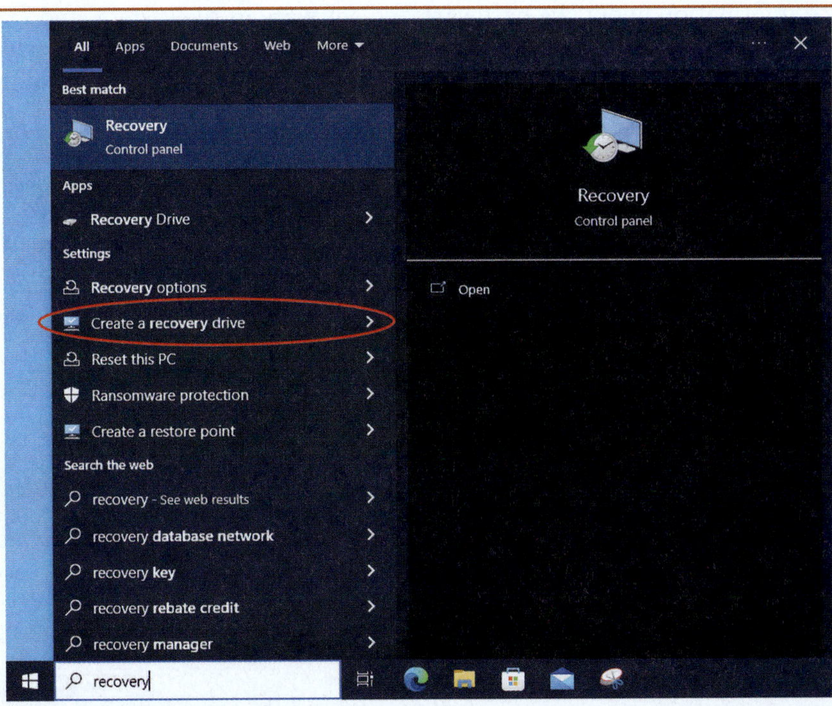

Goodheart-Willcox Publisher

Figure 18-8 Windows provides many options for recovering the computer system after a system failure, but it is important to create a recovery drive *before* a failure occurs.

Figure 18-9 shows the Windows 10 version of System Configuration. This utility is very similar in most versions of Windows, particularly the **General**, **Boot**, **Services**, **Startup**, and **Tools** tabs, though the exact look of the utility may change after installing service packs.

When you suspect the source of the computer problem to be directly related to a startup program or service, System Configuration is your best choice to isolate the suspect program or service. Users could select the **Startup** tab to view programs that begin running when a computer is first turned on until the release of Windows 8, at which time, the **Startup** tab only provided a link to Task Manager, which is where the list of startup programs is now shown. Using this list, you can disable one or more of the suspect startup programs and services and then restart the computer. Once you discover the program or service causing the problem, you can take corrective action, such as uninstalling the program or service.

Computer problems that appear after the user logon are usually related directly to a startup program or service, so disabling all services and startup programs will quickly confirm if one of the many services or programs is causing the problem. If disabling all services and startup programs clears the problem, you can re-enable programs and services one by one or in a group until you isolate the offending program or service. You can also use the information displayed in Event Viewer to coordinate which service or program to disable. Also, notice the **Hide all Microsoft services** option in Figure 18-10. Most of the time, Microsoft services will not be the cause of a computer problem. The cause of the problem is more likely a third-party software application service. You can quickly eliminate all the Microsoft services at once by selecting this option.

Other tools available for troubleshooting are located under the **Tools** tab, Figure 18-11, from which you can launch tools such as Windows Troubleshooting, Computer Management, System Information, and Event Viewer. It is important to understand, however, that the exact listing of tools depends on which operating system you are using.

Microsoft System Information

As shown in Figure 18-12, Microsoft System Information (**msinfo32.exe**) displays detailed information about the hardware and software in the system, and expanding the directory in the left pane of the interface displays additional information. All Windows versions can run System Information through the **msinfo32** command,

Figure 18-9 System Configuration is a handy tool for solving PC problems that occur after system logon.

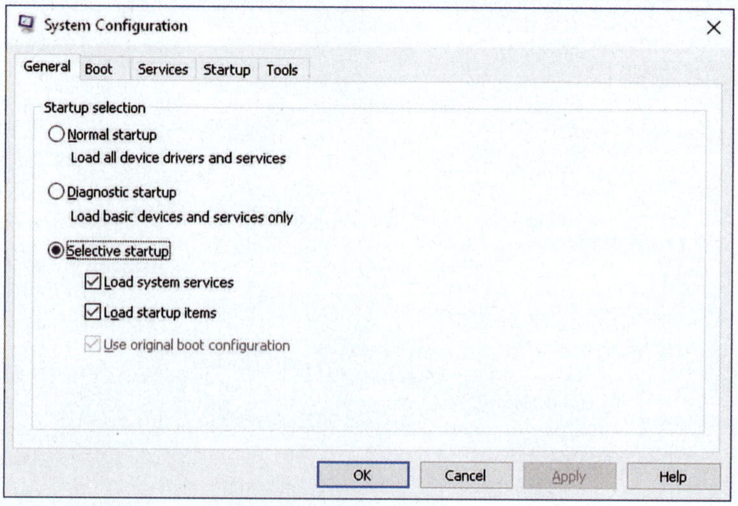

Goodheart-Willcox Publisher

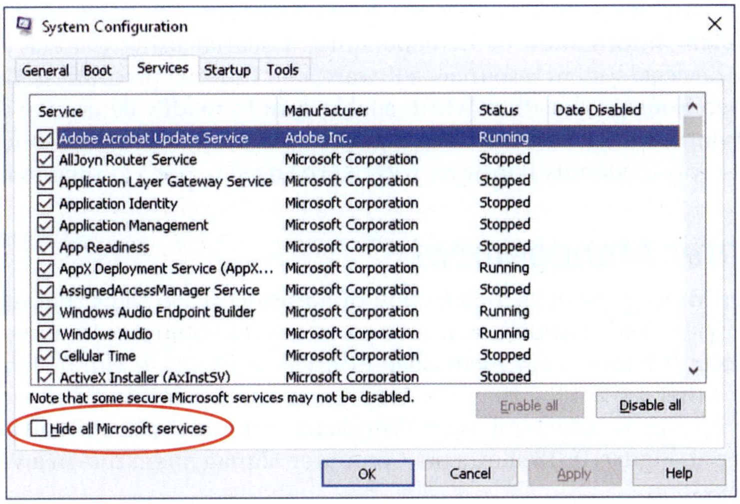

Goodheart-Willcox Publisher

Figure 18-10 The **Hide all Microsoft services** option is a quick way to hide all Microsoft services running on the computer.

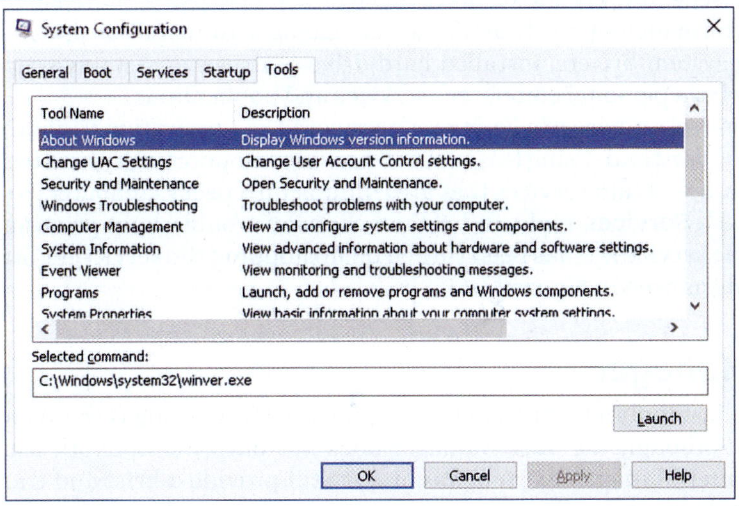

Goodheart-Willcox Publisher

Figure 18-11 The **Tools** tab within System Configuration can be used as a centralized location for launching other troubleshooting tools.

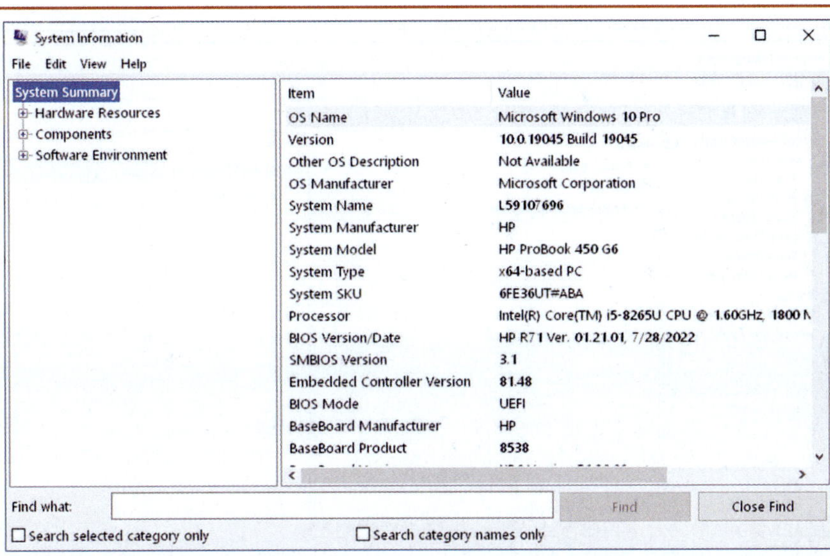

Goodheart-Willcox Publisher

Figure 18-12 System Information contains a collection of information about the computer hardware, components, and software environment.

but it can also be launched through **Start>All apps>Windows Administrative Tools>System Information** or by conducting a search using the entry msinfo32. Hardware devices, system resources, software, and Internet program settings can all be displayed from this location, which enables you to readily determine conflicts in system resources and locate most startup problems. Microsoft System Information is also a great way to identify hardware without the need to open a computer case.

A+ 1102: 1.4

Computer Management

Computer Management is a collection of administrative tools that allows technicians to view information about a user's personal computer in a manner more detailed than the previously mentioned utilities and tools. It can be found on any Windows either by conducting a search using the entry computer management or by navigating to **Start>All apps>Windows Administrative Tools>Computer Management**. Figure 18-13 shows the Computer Management tool in a Windows 10 operating system.

As seen in the screen capture, the Computer Management tool can provide detailed information to a technician, including tasks a personal computer runs on a consistent schedule, events that have taken or will take place, shared folders among users, performance of hardware, a device manager to install or update Windows operating system drivers, installed hard drive or drives and storage capacity, and the control of a personal computer's services and applications.

The control and use of a computer's services and applications is vital for a technician to understand. Using this tool will provide an opportunity for a technician to start and stop certain services that are running on a user's computer. For example, a computer's **Services** tool can help a technician troubleshoot printing errors by starting the service if it has been turned off or stopping the service for further troubleshooting as seen in Figure 18-14.

A+ 1102: 1.3, 3.1

Task Manager

One of the last tools a technician may use for troubleshooting is the Windows Task Manager. Although the Task Manager does not have the in-depth features that the Computer Management tool has, it can still provide a brief and transactional method to diagnose hardware or memory issues along with ending a program that is currently running. Figure 18-15 provides insight into the types of information

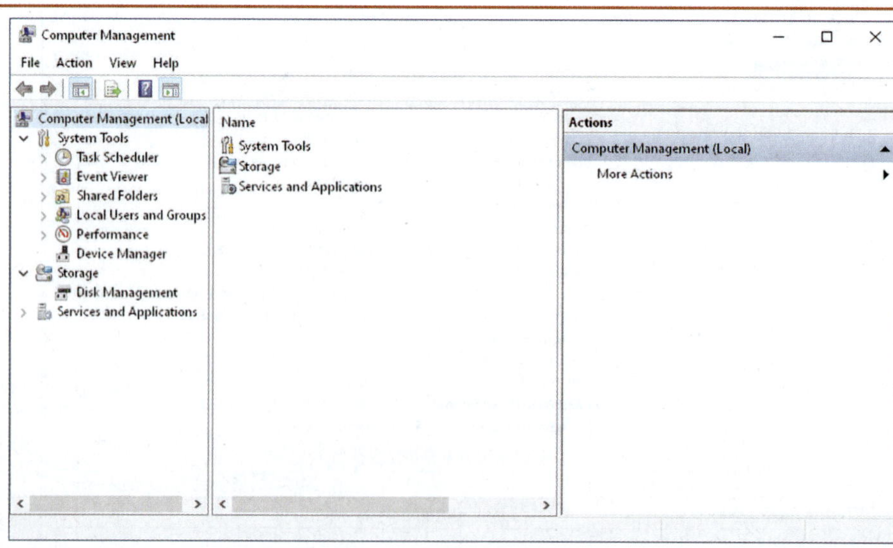

Figure 18-13 The Computer Management tool allows technicians to view elaborated information about a computer.

Goodheart-Willcox Publisher

Windows Task Manager allows a technician to utilize for troubleshooting via the Windows 10 operating system.

The Task Manager tool can be accessed on any Windows operating system by simultaneously pressing [Ctrl][Alt][Delete] and then selecting the **Task Manager** option from the Security Options screen. Alternatively, a user can use the keyboard combination [Ctrl][Alt][Esc] to bypass the Security Options screen and open Task Manager directly. Once Task Manager is accessed, a technician may choose from the tabs in the upper-left part of the tool to diagnose where the user's issue may be generated. However, as mentioned before, the Task Manager provides only general information and does not elaborate on services.

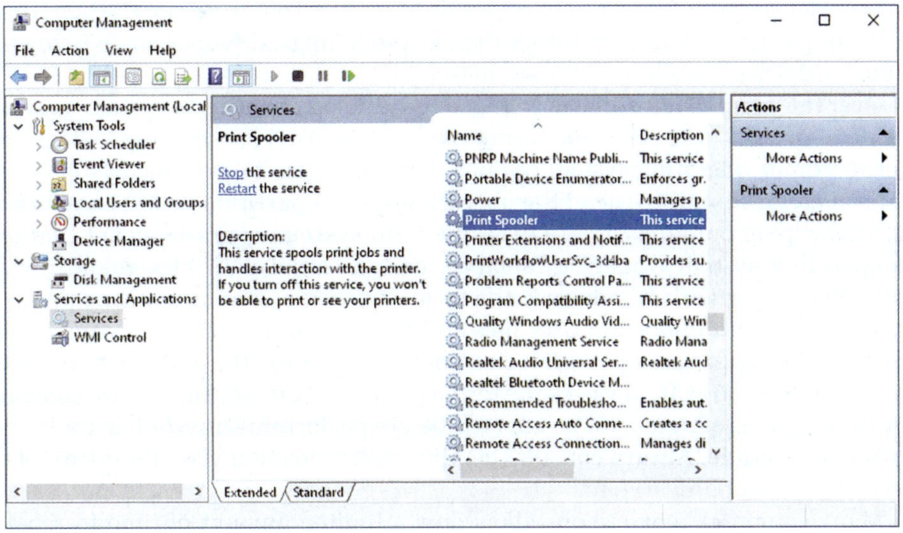

Figure 18-14 Using the Computer Management tool provides an opportunity for a technician to start or stop certain services running on a computer.

Goodheart-Willcox Publisher

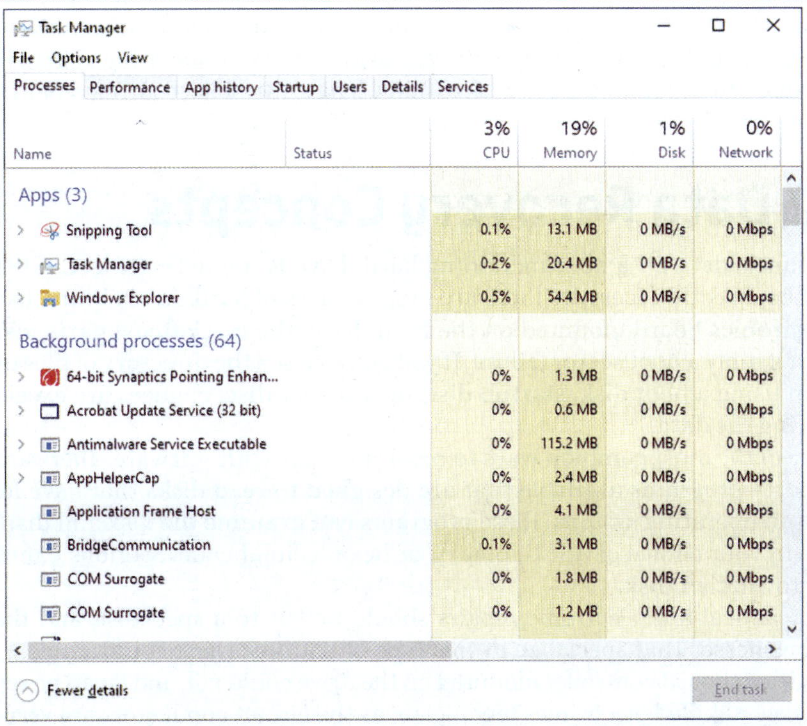

Figure 18-15 Although the Task Manager does not have the in-depth features that the Computer Management tool has, it can still provide a method to diagnose hardware or memory issues, along with ending a program that is currently running.

Goodheart-Willcox Publisher

If a technician is presented with a program that is not functioning, they can end the program via the **End Task** feature of the Task Manager, which is located in the **Processes** tab. However, if a technician wants to restart or repair a service, they may do so in the **Services** tab of the Task Manager by right-clicking and selecting **Restart** on the service they want to restart or repair.

A+ 1101: 5.3
1102: 3.1

Reinstall the Operating System

Reinstalling an operating system is the very last resort to recovering from a system startup failure, but if you cannot repair the system using the utilities provided, you will likely need to use this option. When reinstalling the operating system, first try to perform a system upgrade or a system refresh rather than a clean install or a system reset, as these allow you to retain the data files that reside on the hard drive. Performing a new installation rather than a system upgrade wipes out existing files on the hard drive, thus losing *all* data files.

Over the years, Microsoft has changed terminology relating to system upgrades and clean installs, and the same terminology is not used consistently by technical information or operating system options. Early Microsoft operating systems used the term **clean install** to mean the operating system partition would be reformatted, thus wiping out all user data files. The term **system upgrade** meant that only the operating system would be replaced, and personal data files would remain intact. Beginning with Windows 7, the term *upgrade* sometimes means performing a backup of all important user files and then formatting the operating system partition, thus wiping the partition clean before installing the upgrade of the operating system. Microsoft now uses the terms *reset* and *refresh*, but be sure you know how the user files are going to be affected before performing a system install, reset, refresh, or upgrade. Always consult the Microsoft website if you are unsure of the effect on the computer system.

Many computer repair shops allow only a limited amount of time to repair a computer system before the computer is wiped clean and a new copy of the operating system is installed, because repair to computer systems can be labor-intensive, often resulting in a large bill for the customer. The customer may not want to pay hundreds of dollars to repair a computer and may prefer that the technician simply wipe the system clean and reinstall the operating system or a newer operating system instead. Many times, this will be less expensive than a lengthy troubleshooting repair.

18.2 Data Recovery Concepts

Many times, data on a nonfunctioning hard drive is not actually lost, although it cannot be directly accessed. There are many causes of hard drive failure, including the electronics board mounted on the hard drive, the mechanical parts inside the drive, or simply a boot sector failure. If you can still see the directory of files on drive C: when using a boot disk, startup disc, or recovery disc, chances are excellent for recovering the data.

One of the most common ways to recover data is with software. There are many third-party programs available that are designed to read disks that have failed to boot to an operating system. These programs can examine the disk and display the sectors in your choice of ASCII, binary, or hexadecimal code. Sections can then be copied to another disk.

Mechanical and electronic repairs should be left to a specialist, and there are many businesses that specialize in this type of data recovery. For example, an electronic circuit board controller mounted on the drive could fail, and it can be replaced, but it takes a skilled electronics technician, as the circuit conductors are very fragile and easily broken. Hard drive platters can also be removed and installed on other drives, but again, it takes special tools, training, and a **clean room**, which is an environment where dust and foreign particles have been eliminated completely.

The creation of disaster recovery plans is a preparation every technician needs to make. It is also important that technicians understand which files take precedence over others and which applications are more critical than others. One common misconception is that organizations may deem all data and applications to be critical, but the most important factor of this theory is conducting a plan detailing the files and applications that need to be restored for the organization to experience the least amount of downtime. Furthermore, this same theory applies to the accounts on the active directory, and it is vital that technicians have a backup administrative account in case there has been a deactivation of all active directory administrative accounts. Lastly, it is a must that these methods of backup and restoration plans are tested to make sure they are effective and efficient.

A+ 1102: 4.3

One of the testing methods that needs to take place is how quickly and effectively data and production can be restored based on cloud storage backups in comparison to local storage backups. Technicians need to understand that cloud storage backups are easily accessible but do not guarantee the most effective method of backup implementation since the data is not within the technician's physical accessibility range. Although local storage backups must be rendered to the majority of the members of an organization, a locked external hard drive with all of the organization's data will grant a technician the quickest method of data and productivity retrieval. However, if the local storage option becomes damaged or stolen, a technician will not have a means of data and productivity retrieval. Therefore, it is recommended to utilize both forms of storage backups.

18.3 Backups

The topic of backups has been discussed periodically throughout this chapter, but the details of how to back up data have not been explored. This section is designed to provide further insight into the concept of backing up data in an effective, efficient manner. While many variations of backups exist, there are three basic backup types:

- **Full**: all changes
- **Differential**: all changes since last full backup
- **Incremental**: all changes since last backup of any type

A+ 1102: 4.3

There is no single best backup approach, and each backup strategy should be considered on an individual basis to determine the best approach for a given situation. You will need to examine your own organization and determine which type of backup is best for your situation. One way to understand the difference is to contemplate a scenario. Imagine a scenario in which you perform a full backup at 2:00 a.m. every morning. However, you have concerns about a server crash before the next full backup, so you opt to perform an additional backup every two hours. The specific type of backup you select will determine the efficiency of performing those frequent backups and the time needed to restore. Consider each of the following backup types and what would occur if the system were to crash at 10:05 a.m.

Full Backup:

Following the two-hour rule established in the previous paragraph, you perform full backups every two hours between 2:00 a.m. and 10:00 a.m. before the system crashes. To restore data in this scenario, you only need to restore the last full backup, which was performed at 10:00 a.m., making restoration incredibly simple. However, running a full backup every two hours is very time-consuming and resource-intensive, and it will have a significant negative impact on your server's performance.

Differential Backup:

In this scenario, you perform differential backups every two hours. To restore the data after the system crash, you will need to restore the last full backup, which was performed at 2:00 a.m., as well as the most recent differential backup, which was performed at 10:00 a.m. This is slightly more complex than the full backup strategy, and each differential backup is going to be larger than the previous one each time the backup is performed. As a result, they will become more time-consuming and resource-intensive.

Incremental Backup:

In a third scenario, you decide to perform incremental backups every two hours. To restore the data after the system crash, you need to restore the last full backup, which was performed at 2:00 a.m., as well as each incremental backup completed thereafter. Additionally, they must be restored in order. This type of restoration is much more complex, but each incremental backup is small and does not take much time or consume many resources.

A+ 1102: 4.3

Grandfather-Father-Son

Grandfather-father-son (GFS) is a backup rotation scheme consisting of three or more backup cycles, such as daily, weekly, and monthly. The generational labels in this scheme's name are used to designate time periods and dates back to when tapes were used and reused as the primary backup medium. For example, you might have seven tapes, one for each day of the week, as well as an additional tape for each week, and a third tape for each month. When you get to the end of the week and make the weekly backup, then you can begin reusing the daily tapes, and when you get to the end of a month and make the monthly backup, you can then begin reusing the weekly tapes. In this backup scheme, the *grandfather* is the tape covering the longest time-span, which is the monthly backup in this case. The *father* is the weekly backup, and the *son* is the daily backup. When implementing GFS, you can use any desired time period, such as hourly, daily, and weekly, but keep in mind the toll taken on the system to perform these backups.

A+ 1102: 4.3

3-2-1 Backups

There are two approaches to storing backup media: off-site or on-site. *On-site storage* is more convenient since it is in the same building as most users, but if there is a major physical disaster such as a fire, you can lose all backup media. *Off-site storage*, while less convenient, is often safer because the backups are isolated from the network. This had led to the **3-2-1 rule**, which states you should have three copies of your data using two different media types, with one copy being off-site. The three copies of the data often consist of one in production and two backups—one on-site and one off-site. This provides the best of both worlds; you have the convenience of having on on-site backup, with the security of also having an offsite backup.

Chapter Summary

18.1 Recovering from System Startup Failure

- Windows can be started in several different modes by pressing [Shift] before the Windows logo appears. Other options include navigating to **Start>Settings>Update & Security>Recovery>Restart now** and executing the command **shutdown /r /o.**
- A variety of modes exist within Safe Mode, including Minimal, Alternate Shell, Active Directory, Repair, and Network.
- Windows 10 Startup Settings can be accessed by selecting **Start>Control Panel>System and Security>System>Advanced system settings.**
- Utilities such as System Restore, Recovery Console, Windows Recovery Environment, Recovery Partition, System Configuration, System Information, Computer Management, and Task Manager can help with data recovery.
- When all recovery options fail, reinstalling the operating system should fix the issue.

18.2 Data Recovery Concepts

- Software is the most common method for recovering data from a failed hard drive.

18.3 Backups

- A full backup stores all changes. A differential backup stores all changes since the last full backup. An incremental backup stores all changes since the last backup of any kind.
- Grandfather-father-son (GFS) is a backup rotation scheme consisting of three or more backup cycles, such as daily, weekly, and monthly.
- The 3-2-1 rule states you should have three copies of your data using two different media types, with one copy being off-site.

Review Questions

1. List examples of troubleshooting methods and utilities used to recover from a system startup failure.
2. What is the navigation path for accessing the Advanced Boot Options menu in Windows 10?
3. What command syntax results in a restart with the Advanced Boot Options shown?
4. Summarize how Safe Mode can help establish a probable cause for the computer problem.
5. How does Safe Mode differ from a normal boot process?
6. List troubleshooting options available to a user after they have rebooted Windows 10 in Safe Mode.
7. Which Safe Mode option prevents Windows from automatically restarting when a failure is detected?
8. Which file contains boot log entries?
9. Which utility allows a technician to restore a system to a previously working state?
10. What is a *restore point*?

11. What sets Recovery Console apart from some of the other recovery utilities discussed in this chapter?
12. How do you start the Windows Recovery Environment?
13. What are the five Windows Recovery Environment options?
14. List the tabs found in System Configuration.
15. List three ways to launch Microsoft System Information.
16. What is the most common way for recovering data, and how do they function?
17. Summarize the importance of a disaster recovery plan.
18. Differentiate among backup types.
19. Summarize the grandfather-father-son backup scheme.
20. What is the 3-2-1 rule?

Sample A+ Exam Questions

1. How do you access Safe Mode in Windows while the system is booting?
   A. Press the [Del] key.
   B. Press the [F8] key.
   C. Press [Ctrl][Alt][Del].
   D. Hold down the [Windows] key.
2. Which boot option creates the file labeled **ntbtlog.txt**?
   A. **Last Known Good Configuration**
   B. **Enable boot logging**
   C. **Debugging Mode**
   D. **Directory Services Restore Mode**
3. Which boot option would you use to start the computer in troubleshooting mode?
   A. **Last Known Good Configuration**
   B. **Safe Mode with Networking**
   C. **Safe Mode with Command Prompt Only**
   D. **Debugging Mode**
4. Which is the recommended way to back up the system registry files in Windows?
   A. Insert the Windows installation CD into the CD drive. Reboot the computer and then select **Backup registry** from the menu.
   B. The Windows registry is backed up each time the operating system is started.
   C. Open **Control Panel** and then double-click the **Registry Backup and Restore** icon.
   D. Create a restore point.
5. Which Recovery Environment would you use to search for and replace corrupt or missing system files?
   A. **System Restore**
   B. **Complete PC Restore**
   C. **Memory Diagnostics Tool**
   D. **Startup Repair**

6. Which command syntax displays the status of a recovery partition?
   A. mkdir C:\RefreshImage
   B. recim /showcurrent
   C. recimg –CreateImage C:\RefreshImage
   D. mkdir C:\Recover
7. What is the purpose of the Computer Management tool?
   A. Allows technicians to view elaborated information about a user's personal computer
   B. Displays detailed networking data
   C. Enables or disables Administrator Mode
   D. Creates system image
8. Which of these will *not* enable recovery from a startup failure?
   A. Task Manager
   B. Recovery Console
   C. Event Viewer
   D. **msconfig.exe**
9. Which reinstallation option requires a full reformat of the OS partition?
   A. System reset
   B. System upgrade
   C. System refresh
   D. System restore
10. Prior to reinstalling an OS, what should a technician attempt to retain data on the hard drive?
   A. System upgrade
   B. System reset
   C. Reformat
   D. Disk replacement

Chapter 19

Introduction to Networking

Learning Outcomes

19.1 Recall the benefits of a network.
19.2 Compare and contrast the client/server and peer-to-peer administrative models.
19.3 Differentiate among network classifications and topologies.
19.4 Differentiate among network equipment, network resources, and the function of each.
19.5 Summarize the installation and features of a network interface card.
19.6 List the layers of the OSI model.
19.7 Identify important elements of network security.
19.8 List common IEEE 802 standards.

A+ Certification Exam Objectives

The following A+ Certification Exam Objectives are covered in this chapter.

Exam 220-1101

2.0 Networking

- 2.2 Compare and contrast common network hardware.
- 2.4 Summarize services provided by networked hosts.
- 2.5 Given a scenario, install and configure a basic wired/wireless SOHO network.
- 2.7 Compare and contrast Internet connection types, network types, and their features.

3.0 Hardware

- 3.4 Given a scenario, install and configure motherboards, central processing units (CPUs), and add-on cards.
- 3.6 Given a scenario, deploy and configure multifunction devices/printers and settings.

Exam 220-1102

1.0 Operating Systems

- 1.6 Given a scenario, configure Microsoft Windows networking features on a client/desktop.

2.0 Security

- 2.4 Explain common social-engineering attacks, threats, and vulnerabilities.
- 2.9 Given a scenario, configure appropriate security settings on small office/home office (SOHO) wireless and wired networks.

4.0 Operational Procedures

- 4.1 Given a scenario, implement best practices associated with documentation and support systems information management.

Key Terms

active hub
adapter teaming
bus topology
campus area network (CAN)
client
client/server network
collision domain
dedicated server
defense in depth
diskless workstation
global area network (GAN)
hub
hybrid topology
local area network (LAN)
media access code (MAC) address
mesh topology
metropolitan area network (MAN)
network
network interface card (NIC)
network operating system (NOS)
node
Open Systems Interconnection (OSI) model
passive hub
peer-to-peer network
personal area network (PAN)
ring topology
segment
server
spatial multiplexing (SM)
star topology
storage area network (SAN)
switching hub
topology
wake-on LAN (WOL)
wide area network (WAN)
wireless mesh network (WMN)
wireless range extender
wireless router
wireless topology

Overview

Technical support of multiple computers in a home or office requires special skills. All technicians will encounter some form of a network when troubleshooting a computer system, so you must have a basic understanding of the principles and operation of networked computers. Additionally, CompTIA has increased the percentage of questions related to networking on the A+ Certification exams in recent years. While computer networking is a vast topic that normally necessitates its own course of study, this chapter—as well as the following four chapters—introduces you to the basic knowledge required to successfully network and support a small group of computers and related equipment.

A+ Note

Be sure you can identify the layers of the OSI model and identify the various network topologies. You should also be familiar with network protocols and network cable media.

19.1 Network Benefits

A computer **network** consists of two or more computers connected together to share data, hardware, programs, and resources, as well as communicate via e-mail and video conferencing. A basic example of a server-based network is shown in Figure 19-1. In the illustration, there are several computers connected to a **server**, which is essentially a computing device that provides a service. Examples of common servers include HTTP for web pages, FTP for file transfer, and e-mail for sending and receiving messages, though there are many other services. Normally, servers have more resources—such as RAM and processing power—than workstations, because they are expected to receive much more traffic. However, any computer device that responds to requests for some service is technically a server.

There are numerous benefits to the creation of a network, including

- shared resources;
- shared data;
- system management;
- productivity;
- cost efficiency; and
- security.

A+ 1102: 1.6

Shared Resources

Networks provide an economical solution for sharing hardware such as printers. Look again at Figure 19-1, in which a printer is connected to one of the computers. When connected as a network device, the printer can be accessed by any of the computers connected to the network due to the server message block (SMB) protocol, which is used for file and printer sharing. Through this arrangement, all the computers on the network share a common printer instead of each workstation having its own.

Shared Data

The main reason for installing a network system is to share data simultaneously among a large group of users. For example, a retail company likely has sales, supply, distribution, and accounting departments. If the company did not have a network, daily operation would depend on written or verbal communication between these departments, and the various departments would have to work closely and carefully to organize complex tasks, such as ordering inventory for projected seasonal sales trends or reducing sales discounts to slow-paying customers.

Figure 19-1 A simple client/server network consists of workstations, called *clients*, and other devices, called *nodes*, connected to a file server.

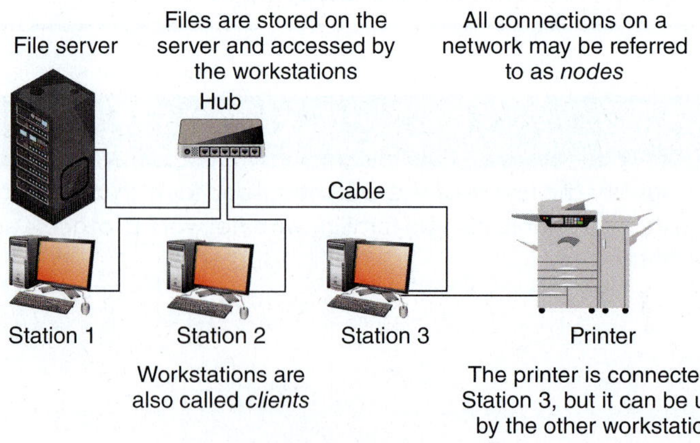

Goodheart-Willcox Publisher; (workstation icons) romvo/Shutterstock.com; (server icon) fullvector/Shutterstock.com; (hub icon) Vadim Ermak/Shutterstock.com; (printer icon) Vector Show/Shutterstock.com

Before computer networks, this system required a large quantity of paperwork, such as customer order forms, inventory forms, and customer invoices. The completion of these forms consumed personnel time, and the exchange of information could take days or even weeks, depending on the size of the company. A network system alleviates the lag time required to match customer orders to warehouse inventory and distribution, and the sales department has immediate, often real-time, access to the warehouse and distribution system of the company. Customer orders are processed instantly, and since a running tally is kept electronically for each item in the inventory, there is no need to do a physical inventory of the warehouse.

As soon as the sales force enters an order, the products can be pulled from the warehouse, sent to distribution, and put in the mail or loaded on a delivery truck. The invoice can be generated at the same time and automatically mailed to the customer. If the inventory levels drop below predetermined limits, the items are automatically reordered or manufactured to replenish the inventory. Additionally, customer information is added to a customer database, which can be used for catalog distribution. This speed can only be achieved with a network in which the inventory, billing, and distribution information is stored on a file server and shared by all who require it.

Computer System Management

A network can make managing many computers much easier. For example, distribution of new software or upgrades can be handled quicker using a network than with individual computers. Consider a large corporate network composed of hundreds or even thousands of computers. If the word-processing application used by the company's personnel is installed in one central location and accessed by all users, it is relatively easy to upgrade or swap with a new software package. In contrast, loading software onto hundreds of computers can be very time-consuming.

Productivity

A folder of information, such as a client list containing telephone numbers, addresses, and e-mail addresses, can be shared easily and instantly by users on a network. A business's inventory can be constantly updated as orders are placed. Additionally, shipping can be automated.

Cost-Effective

Network systems can be expensive to implement, but they can actually save money when compared to the cost of individual computers needed to accomplish the same scope of work. Savings are realized through the sharing of expensive equipment and reduced labor costs.

Security

Security is a major issue in the IT world, and a network enhances security by limiting data access to authorized personnel only. Network operating system (NOS) software can determine who can read, copy, or erase the contents of a file, and the network can also keep a log of all files accessed, who accessed them, and from which workstation they were accessed. Additionally, the network administrator can configure settings such as the hours and days of the week a user is authorized to use the network, locations from which users can access the network, the appearance of a workstation display, and the programs and information the user can access.

19.2 Network Administrative Models

There are two main network administrative models: client/server and peer-to-peer. The type of administrative model chosen is usually dependent on characteristics of the network, such as size, number of users, and security needs. In the following section, both models will be compared. In either model, devices connected to the network are often referred to as **nodes**. Nodes are typically connected by a **hub**, which provides a quick and easy method of connecting equipment via cables.

Client/Server

A **client/server network** is a network model in which the network is made up of computers that are designated as either clients or servers. A **client** is an individual PC or workstation that accesses a server's resources and shared files. Recall that a *server* is a computing device used to provide a service. A typical client/server network is represented in Figure 19-1.

The client/server model provides a method for *centralized administration* of the network, meaning a network administrator controls the operation of the file server, which controls workstation access to the files located on the server. The network operating system software located on the file server also controls how each workstation interacts with other workstations, printers, and any devices connected to the network.

Clients

Clients are computers connected to a client/server network that access network resources controlled by the server. The term *client* is also used to define the software program that runs on a computer and accesses the resources on the network. For example, an e-mail client sends and receives e-mail stored on the network mail server. Clients are cross-platform. For example, you can connect a client running a Microsoft Windows operating system to a server running Unix or Linux.

Servers

A server is similar to a standard PC in design. In fact, early versions of servers were simply PCs designated as servers. Today, many small networks still use a typical PC for the network server, but for large network systems, the server is often an enhanced, more powerful PC. It may contain two, four, or more CPUs and 10 times the amount of RAM normally found on a typical PC to enable faster information processing when connected to many workstations. The server is usually equipped with several hard drives and may also have a duplicate set of hard drives used for backing up the data saved on the first set of hard drives. Backup systems for servers will be covered in greater depth later in the textbook.

A network system may consist of one or more **dedicated servers**, which are servers with special functions. Examples of dedicated servers include

- *file servers*, which are used to store data files that can be accessed by individual workstations;
- *print servers*, which coordinate printing activities between PCs and network printers;
- *administrative servers*, which may be used to administer network security and activities; and
- *database servers*, which contain data files and software programs that locate and extract data from a database.

Peer-to-Peer

A **peer-to-peer network** is a network model in which all the connected PCs connected are considered equal, or peers, as illustrated in Figure 19-2. Devices on a peer-to-peer network are also connected together by a hub. This model is usually used on small networks of fewer than 25 workstations, which are typically standard PCs.

Peer-to-peer networks rely on *decentralized administration*, so each workstation has equal administrative powers over the network. This means a workstation must grant permission to the other workstations before they can access its files or use its hardware. In many cases, a peer-to-peer network is inexpensive to install and simple to administer as long as it remains small, though it can be quite difficult to manage this type of network. For example, if all the workstations had to access a database of company customers, each user would have to be aware of the file location as well as any other needed files or software. Unlike the client/server model, a peer-to-peer network requires no costly network-specific software. In fact, you can build a simple peer-to-peer network using only Windows 95 or later and minimal hardware.

Tech Tip

Approximately 45 percent of all networks used in the world are composed of fewer than 25 computers. This number does *not* include home networks.

19.3 Network Classifications and Topologies

Networks are classified not only by their administrative model, but also the size and complexity of the system. Additionally, every network has a specific topology, which describes its arrangement and organization. It is important to note that there is no correlation between these two factors, and while some topologies work better in certain classifications, there is no standard mandate. Any network classification can operate under any topology as long as it fulfills the needs of the organization while remaining cost-effective to operate.

Classifications

A+ 1101: 2.7

Networks are classified into eight major categories: local area network (LAN), metropolitan area network (MAN), wide area network (WAN), campus area network (CAN), personal area network (PAN), global area network (GAN), wireless mesh network (WMN), and storage area network (SAN). These classifications are based on the physical size, management, and use of a telecommunication system such as the telephone network.

A **local area network (LAN)** is a small network of computers contained in a relatively small area, such as an office building, and operates under a single management. An example of a LAN is a computer network in a small-business office.

A **metropolitan area network (MAN)** is a group of two or more interconnected LANs operating under a single management. An example of a MAN is a city's network system that connects its streetlights, traffic lights, and parking meters. Each element (streetlights, traffic lights, and parking meters) may have its own LAN, but the interconnection of these LANs comprises a MAN.

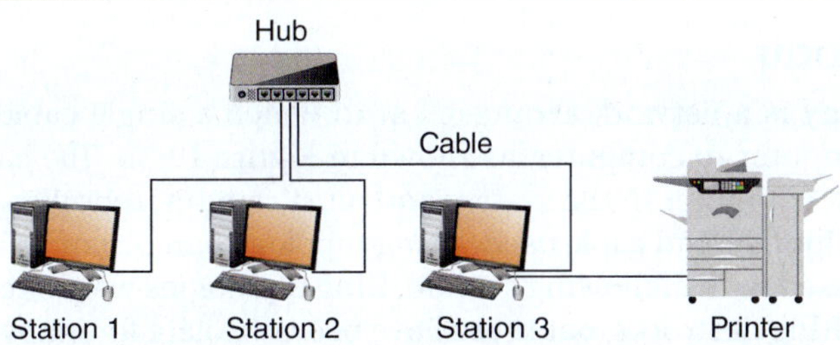

Goodheart-Willcox Publisher; (workstation icons) romvo/Shutterstock.com; (hub) Vadim Ermak/Shutterstock.com; (printer icon) Vector Show/Shutterstock.com

Figure 19-2 A peer-to-peer network consists of devices connected together by a hub, with all devices considered equal, or *peers*.

Tech Tip

A subclassification of a wide area network is *wireless WAN (WWAN)*, which is based on cellular phone technology. Cellular phone access media can be used as part of a network system.

Tech Tip

Wireless PAN is described in the IEEE 802.15 standard.

A **wide area network (WAN)** is typically a large number of computers spread over a large area and under the control of a centrally located administrator. The biggest difference between a WAN and a MAN is that WANs are not limited to one metropolitan area. A WAN is usually composed of a group of LANs interconnected through a telecommunication network, which enables communication over a large area. A good example of a WAN is a governmental network that spans multiple states.

A **campus area network (CAN)** is a network that spans a limited geographic area. You can think of CANs as somewhere between a LAN and WAN. There is not an exact size that differentiates among LANs, CANs, and WANs, but a campus area network is usually located in one geographic location spanning multiple buildings. The name stems from a college campus which typifies the previous description.

A **personal area network (PAN)**, sometimes called a *piconet*, is a short-range network that connects devices such as a PC, smartphone, tablet, camera, and printer. PAN connections are typically wireless and based on Bluetooth, 802.11, or IrDA standards.

A **global area network (GAN)** is a WAN spread over a geographical area spanning multiple countries or continents. The Internet is the best example of a GAN, as it exists in nearly every country in the world.

A **wireless mesh network (WMN)** is a network system composed of wireless networking devices and base stations organized in a way so all nodes can continuously communicate with all adjacent nodes. The nodes provide the quickest and safest routes through dynamic routing. This type of organization is called a *mesh topology*. Network topologies will be discussed in the following section. A good example of a WMN are devices linked through the Google Home application. Smart devices such as Chromecast, personal assistants, and smartphones are all able to directly connect to one another wirelessly.

A **storage area network (SAN)** is an isolated network built entirely to handle data storage. Rather than a single server, one might have several servers and network storage devices, which all appear as a single storage device to the user. The precursor to SANs was *direct attached storage (DAS)*, which is simply a storage device attached to one's network. Thes eventually evolved into a completely separate network used for storage.

A+ 1102: 4.1

Topologies

A **topology** is the physical arrangement of hardware and cabling in a network. Three major topologies include *bus*, *ring*, and *star*, all of which are illustrated in Figure 19-3. Making a diagram of the network model is helpful in ensuring the model chosen is the best fit for the area in which the network will be installed.

Bus Topology

Tech Tip

In a bus topology, the single conductor that connects two or more devices is often referred to as the *trunk* or *backbone*. While the bus topology is no longer a valid local area network type, it is still used to connect separate networks.

A **bus topology** is a network arrangement in which a single conductor connects to all the computers, as illustrated in Figure 19-3A. A bus topology uses less cable than the other cabled topologies and requires a 50-ohm terminating resistor at each end of the cable to absorb the transmitted signals when they reach the end of the bus. Without the terminating resistors, some of the transmitted signals would be reflected back through the cables, distorting the data.

Ring Topology

A **ring topology** is a network arrangement in which a single cable runs continuously from computer to computer, as shown in Figure 19-3B. The cable begins and ends at the first computer in the system and must remain unbroken. Depending on the type of equipment and cable used, a ring topology can resemble a star topology, which is discussed in the following section. Ring topologies were once common and used in Token Ring networks, but those have been obsolete for many years.

Star Topology

A **star topology** is a network arrangement in which cables run from each computer to a single point, forming a star, Figure 19-3C. At the center of the star is usually a hub or switch, which provides a common electrical connection to all the computers in the network.

Hubs are classified as either passive or active. A **passive hub** simply acts as a connection point in the topology, and transmitted digital signals from one computer are passed to all devices and networks connected to the hub. An **active hub** has a source of power connected to it and regenerates the signals it receives. An active hub can be used to extend the range of a signal transmission, which is something a passive hub cannot do.

A **switching hub** reduces excessive data transmissions on a network by segmenting a network, which can reduce the number of frames transmitted over the entire network. This will only reduce the traffic if there is a significant number of transmissions between computers on the same network segment. Examine Figure 19-4, and imagine Station 3 is attempting to communicate with Station 1. The switching hub will not allow the data frame to be transmitted through the hub to other parts of the network. Instead, the hub directs the frame directly to Station 1.

Tech Tip

Hubs can also be referred to as an *Ethernet hub*, *active hub*, *network hub*, *repeater hub*, or *multiport repeater*.

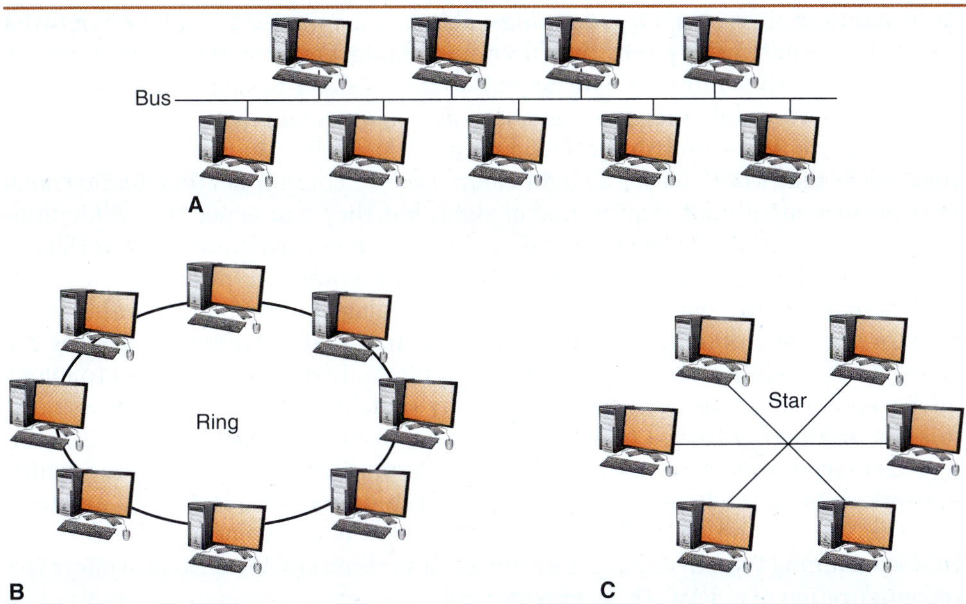

Goodheart-Willcox Publisher; (workstation icons) romvo/Shutterstock.com

Figure 19-3 In a bus topology (A), all workstations are connected by a single conductor called a backbone. In a ring topology (B), all workstations are connected in series, forming a closed loop. In a star topology (C), all workstations are connected to a center point, such as a hub or switch.

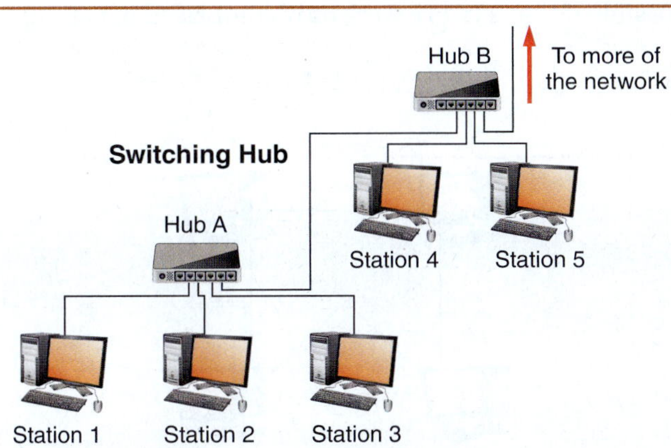

Goodheart-Willcox Publisher; (workstation icons) romvo/Shutterstock.com; (hub icons) Vadim Ermak/Shutterstock.com

Figure 19-4 Switching, or intelligent, hubs are used to segment the network, reducing unnecessary data traffic.

Hybrid Topology

A **hybrid topology** is simply a mixture of star, bus, and ring topologies. Imagine a scenario where an organization has multiple departments. Each department may be arranged in a topology best suited for its needs, but all departments connect to the organization's central network. For example, sales may be a bus topology, distribution may be a ring topology, and operations may be a star topology, and when all these departments are networked together in the organization's main network, the result is a hybrid topology. Hybrid topologies are very common and often use wireless and cellular technology.

Mesh Topology

A **mesh topology** is a network system in which each node connects directly to every other node on the network, as shown in Figure 19-5. This is the most reliable network topology but also the most expensive because of the increased cost of cabling and equipment. A mesh is only practical when cost is not a barrier, and the network mission is critical. For example, a network consisting of multiple servers may use a mesh topology to ensure the reliability of the servers.

A+ 1101: 2.7

Wireless Topology

As its name implies, a **wireless topology**, also called a *wireless local area network (WLAN)*, is a network system that uses no cabling between the computers and instead uses either infrared light or radio transmission to communicate among devices. Unfortunately, infrared transmissions require an unobstructed line of sight between devices to establish connections, meaning nothing can be placed between the devices that would block the light beam used for communication. Radio transmission systems do not require line of sight, but they can experience difficulties caused by the building structure and other interference generated by a variety of electrical equipment, such as radios, motors, welders, and microwaves.

There are many reasons to use wireless topologies. One reason is the versatility of the connection. In the modern world, many unconventional devices are enabled for wireless connection, including vehicles. Installing a wireless topology allows an administrator to connect company vehicles to the network via a transmission originating from a building antenna or even a satellite. Wireless technology also enables faster, less-expensive installation. Consider a scenario in which network cabling connects two buildings separated by a wide metropolitan street or river. Connecting those buildings with cable could be more expensive and time-consuming than installing transmitters and receivers. Wireless also offers fast reconfiguration of a network, as moving cables to rearrange computers may not be as easy. Finally, wireless offers a much wider coverage area than wired connections. Consider how frequently you connect your smartphone to a Wi-Fi network. This would not be possible if the network were only comprised of cabling.

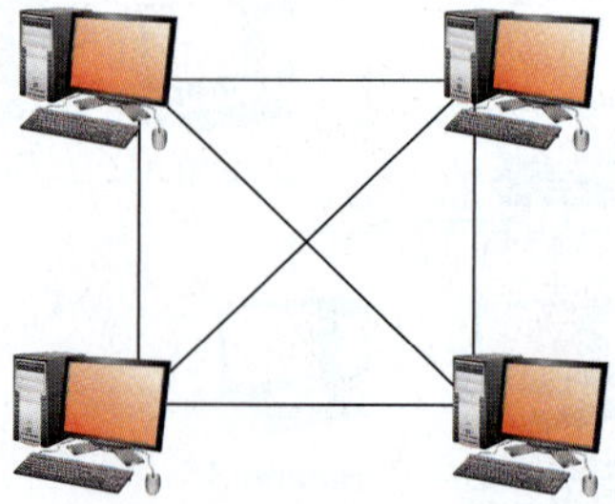

Figure 19-5 A mesh topology connects each node to every other node on the network.

Goodheart-Willcox Publisher; (workstation icons) romvo/Shutterstock.com

Segments

Segmenting a network is the separation of certain portions of network traffic to increase performance, security, or reliability. The term **segment** refers to a physical or logical portion of a network. In the physical sense, a segment is a section of cable between two network devices, such as the backbone or drop cables in a bus topology, the cables between nodes and hubs, or the cables between hubs in a star topology. In a logical sense, a segment is a portion of a network that shares a collision domain. A **collision domain**, sometimes referred to as a *contention domain*, is a section of a network where data collisions occur.

Figure 19-6 illustrates how a network can be subdivided into three smaller sections using switches, with each switch creating a network segment or section. A bridge, switch, or router can be used to separate network devices into segments. Switches and routers are discussed in detail later in this chapter, and bridges are discussed in a later chapter.

Network performance for individual users is increased by segmenting a large network, because reducing the size of a network through segmenting increases the available bandwidth for each segment. For example, if a network has 100 users with equal access to a 1,000-Mbps network system, all 100 users would share the same 1,000-Mbps maximum available bandwidth (roughly 10 Mbps per user). By segmenting the network into two or more logical segments, the available bandwidth is theoretically increased to 1,000 Mbps for each segment, thus increasing the available bandwidth for users. The original 1,000-Mbps network provided approximately 10 Mbps of availability for each of the 100 users, but by dividing the network into two segments, the original 100 users now are divided into two groups of 50 users. This results in each segment having an available bandwidth of 1,000 Mbps and each user having an available bandwidth of 20 Mbps—an increase of 100 percent.

Segmenting a network also serves as a basic security measure for large networks by separating the network into common workgroups, and this separation (both physical and logical) makes it harder for an unauthorized person to gain access to sections of a computer system. For example, a school network can be segmented into student, teacher, and administration workgroups. Imagine a scenario in which a threat actor wanted to harvest data from the school's network. They would have to determine which segment housed the desired data and bypass security measures for not only the network, but also the targeted segment.

Tech Tip

As applied to networking, the definition of the term *segment* has changed over time and depends on the context and the source of technical information. When applied to IP addresses, MAC addresses, physical cabling, and wireless networking, *segment* can have a contrasting definition for each application. When you "segment" a network, you "divide" it according to the context of the material being presented.

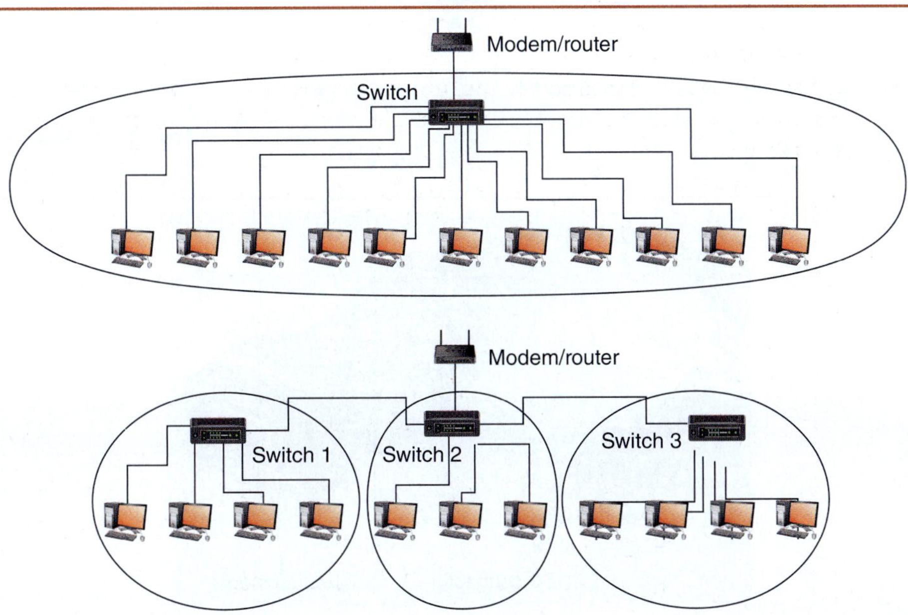

Figure 19-6 Networks are often segmented to increase performance, security, and reliability.

Goodheart-Willcox Publisher; (workstation icons) romvo/Shutterstock.com; (modem/router and switch icons) Vadim Ermak/Shutterstock.com

Segmenting a network can also improve reliability. Dividing a large computer system into many smaller systems by segmentation helps ensure at least part of the network will be up and running, even if a switch or router fails.

19.4 Network Equipment and Resources

A variety of devices and resources are used to create networks. The most common network devices used in a home or small-office network are network interface cards, powerline network devices, hubs, switches, routers, wireless routers, wireless adapter cards, wireless range extenders, diskless workstations, thin clients, network operating systems (NOS), and DNS.

Network Interface Cards

A **network interface card (NIC)**, also called a *network adapter card* and *Ethernet card*, connects media, usually twisted-pair cabling, to individual network devices such as workstations, file servers, and printers. Network adapter cards come in a variety of designs. For example, the adapter in Figure 19-7 is designed to be installed into a motherboard expansion slot. Network adapters integrated into the motherboard can fail and are not typically repairable, but a network adapter card can be installed into a motherboard slot to replace the existing integrated network adapter. Another replacement alternative is a USB-to-Ethernet adapter, such as the one shown in Figure 19-8, which plugs into any available USB port and provides an Ethernet RJ-45 connection.

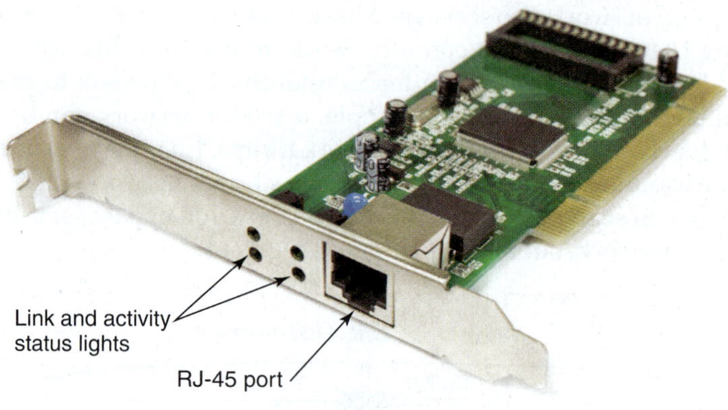

Figure 19-7 Network adapter cards are often designed to fit into a motherboard expansion slot.

Pakpoom Phuymmee/Shutterstock.com

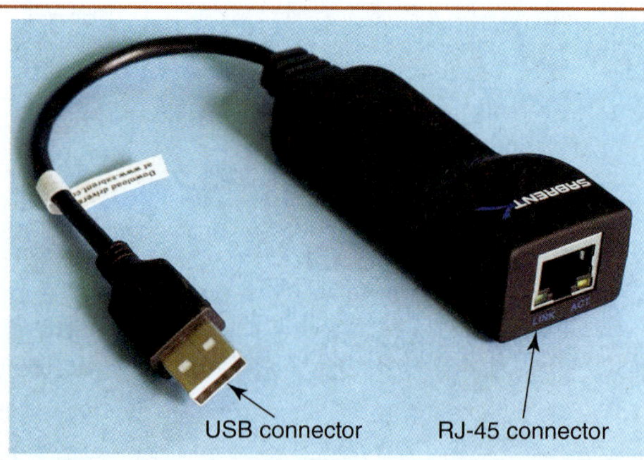

Figure 19-8 USB network adapters are designed to connect to any available USB port.

Goodheart-Willcox Publisher

Network adapters are installed to not only replace a failed integrated network adapter, but also upgrade an existing system. For example, a legacy computer may have a network adapter rated for 100 Mbps. To upgrade the computer for higher network performance, an adapter rated for 1,000 Mbps can be installed via motherboard slot or USB port, or a wireless network adapter can be installed. However, simply upgrading a computer network adapter may not increase network performance if the maximum ratings of the other devices, such as the router or cable modem, are less than that of the network adapter. Network performance is limited to the slowest network device.

Most personal computers have an onboard NIC installed that only produces transmission speeds of 100 MB. There is also the possibility that organizations may have servers with NICs that only operate at 100 MB, but this may also be a rarity. Nevertheless, if a server is supporting methods of file sharing and roles such as e-mail implementation, it is vital that the server have a gigabit NIC installed along with network cabling and infrastructure that supports at least 1-Gb transmissions. Without these server NICs and network infrastructures, users will experience latency in their file transmissions and e-mail communication.

As discussed previously, each network adapter card has a unique **media access code (MAC) address**, which is a hexadecimal number programmed into the card's chip. The address is composed of twelve digits divided into two equal sections. The first six digits identify the card's manufacturer, and the second six-digit sequence is a unique identifier assigned by the manufacturer for every card produced. Two network adapter cards cannot have the same MAC address on the same network, because the network uses the MAC address to identify the different nodes on the network. If two cards match, the network cannot communicate properly with either card. You can think of a MAC address much like telephone numbers in a telephone system. If two people had the same telephone number, each one might receive calls that were intended for the other.

A typical PC has both a physical address assigned through the network adapter card and a logical address assigned by the technician when the NIC is installed. The MAC address is often referred to as the *physical address* because it is physically burned into the card. Names used to identify computers or network nodes are referred to as the *logical address*. For example, a computer may have a physical address of 0020AF012AB3 and a logical address such as Station 12.

The MAC address is also referred to as the *data link control (DLC) identifier*. In the IEEE 802 standard, the Data Link layer of the OSI model is subdivided into the logical link control (LLC) and the media access control (MAC) sublayers. The MAC sublayer communicates directly with the network, while the LLC sublayer uses a protocol such as Address Resolution Protocol (ARP), which is part of the TCP/IP protocol suite. ARP resolves MAC addresses to computer names, such as Station 1. Using the computer name Station 1 is more convenient than trying to remember the hexadecimal code number for the node.

Powerline Network Devices

Powerline network devices, such as those shown in Figure 19-9, are designed to extend a network by using the existing 120-volt electrical wiring system. These devices are particularly useful for providing a hard-wired Ethernet connection where a wireless connection would otherwise be required. Extending an existing network using powerline network technology requires two powerline network devices, each equipped with an RJ-45 Ethernet port and a standard 120-volt plug. The RJ-45 Ethernet ports are used to connect to network equipment such as a router, computer, or other network device, and network packets are carried over the 120-volt powerline. Some powerline devices are designed to be used as a hub, typically providing four RJ-45 Ethernet ports at one of the devices.

Advertised data rates of powerline devices are as high as 500 Mbps, but this is rare in practice. The very nature of the 120-volt power cable design does not allow it to support advertised speeds. In reality, the actual speed is much lower, and network communication may not work at all for long runs of cable. The actual length of an electrical cable run can be deceiving because the cables are hidden in the walls. Also, be aware that some electrical distribution systems, especially in commercial buildings, use transformers to step down the voltage to the 120-volt level. A transformer will not support the high frequencies associated with network transmissions.

It is important to note that powerline devices typically only function if they are plugged in on the same circuit. For example, assume a client runs a business out of their home. Their modem and router are on the first floor, and they want a hard-wired connection in their office on the second floor. In most cases, a powerline device is not a solution because the two rooms are likely on separate circuits. If they move their modem and router to the office, the powerline devices will then present a viable option.

A+ 1101: 2.2

Hubs

A *hub* is a device that connects network equipment together quickly and easily. The hub represented in Figure 19-10 has eight RJ-45 ports for quick connection of twisted-pair cable. True hubs are rare today, largely because their functionality has been built into other devices. A hub does nothing to direct traffic; instead, all packets coming in one port are simply sent to all other ports. Realistically, if you go to an electronics store and ask for a hub, you will most likely be handed a switch.

A+ 1101: 2.2

Switches

A *switch* is a networking device equipped with more sophisticated electronic components than a simple hub. You can think of switches as intelligent hubs. While hubs broadcast all incoming packets to all its RJ-45 ports—as well as additional devices

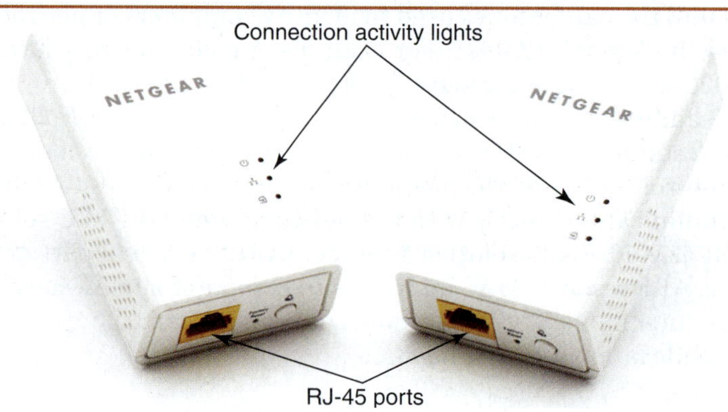

Ackab Photography/Shutterstock.com

Figure 19-9 Powerline network devices extend a network over existing 120-volt power wiring.

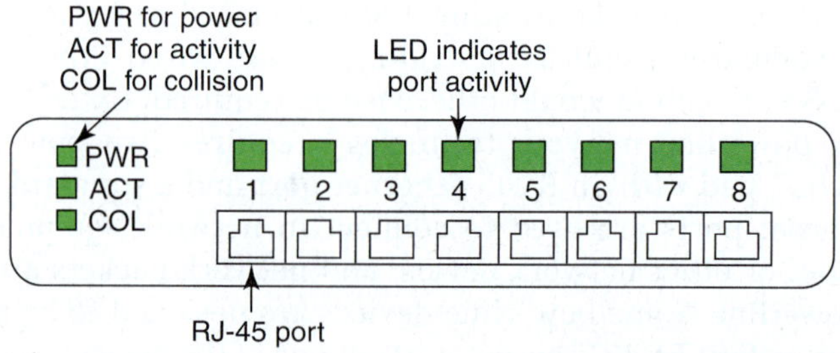

Goodheart-Willcox Publisher

Figure 19-10 The RJ-45 ports on a hub allow twisted-pair cabling to be connected. Various LEDs make the current status visible at a glance.

in a cascading hub arrangement—switches only forward packets to the intended recipient. As stated earlier, each network device has an assigned MAC address, and the electronic design of a switch allows it to match each MAC address with a corresponding port, thus only forwarding the packet to the intended device. As a result, overall network traffic is greatly reduced. Switches were once considered very expensive, but today, they are competitively priced with hubs, resulting in switches being used in place of hubs. In fact, hubs are seldom encountered in small networks.

Some switches are referred to as ***smart switches*** or ***managed switches***, as these switches have more capabilities than ordinary switches, including many of the same capabilities as routers. By contrast, switches can also be categorized as unmanaged. An ***unmanaged switch*** allows Ethernet devices to communicate with each other on the network. They are less costly than managed switches, but they also have fewer features. For example, unmanaged switches are shipped with factory-configured settings that cannot be changed by the end user.

Routers

1101: 2.2 A+

Recall from Chapter 14 that a ***router*** is a network device used to connect to the Internet, share the Internet connection with other devices in the home or office, or support communication between different types of networks. Commonly found in homes and small offices, routers are more electronically sophisticated than switches and can be configured to perform many more tasks than switches. For example, specific router ports can be designated to function in a particular way.

A+ Note

For the A+ Exams, stick to the simplest definition of hub, switch, and router.

Home and small-business routers commonly incorporate a wireless access point, thus making the router the central device for both the wired and wireless portions of the network. Additionally, some cable modems have built-in routing capabilities, meaning only one device is needed for wired and wireless connectivity. Most home routers are limited to only four RJ-45 ports, but the total number of ports can be increased by connecting a hub or switch to one of the router ports. You should avoid adding additional routers, because they could cause network conflicts. For example, routers have the capability to issue IP addresses to local area network devices by default. Using two routers in a network could cause problems with issuing IP addresses. There will be more about switches and routers in a later chapter.

Wireless Routers

1101: 2.2 A+

A **wireless router**, such as the one shown in Figure 19-11, is a combination of a wireless access point, switch, and router and is commonly used in homes and small offices as centralized distribution points for wireless and wired connections to

Goodheart-Willcox Publisher

Figure 19-11 A wireless router is a combination of a wireless access point, switch, and router.

Tech Tip

The exact name of a device will vary depending on the manufacturer and intended purpose of the device.

computers and mobile devices. Some wireless routers also incorporate a cable modem, and others allow users to adjust the radio power levels, potentially reducing both interference and range while potentially saving electrical costs to power the device.

Figure 19-12 shows the connections on the back of a wireless router. The RJ-45 port labeled "Internet" connects directly to a DSL or cable modem, enabling Internet access. The USB port can also be used to connect to a DSL or cable modem. The reset button is used to restore the router to its original factory settings. For example, if the router security password (passphrase or security key) is forgotten, the reset button can be used to erase the existing security password and return it to the factory default. Users often forget their security password, and the reset button is the only way to regain access. The reset button is recessed below the case surface and can only be pressed by inserting a paper clip or other pointed object into the hole, which prevents it from being accidentally pressed. To reset the router, the button is held for a short period of time, usually for about 10 seconds.

You should always configure a wireless router with a security encryption key to prevent unauthorized access, especially in an environment such as apartments or other closely spaced housing. Without security, anyone can easily access an unsecured wireless router and gain access to your network, and once someone gains access to your network, they can also use your Internet connection. The effects of accessing the Internet through your or your client's router can have devastating results. For example, additional charges could be billed to the owner if the total bandwidth is exceeded, or the unauthorized user could download copy-protected materials such as games. To the Internet provider, it appears that the owner of the router has downloaded the copyrighted materials, not an unauthorized user.

A+ 1102: 2.9

WPS

Wi-Fi Protected Setup (WPS) is a standard developed by the Wi-Fi Alliance and intended to make it easy to configure secure access to a wireless router. Many wireless routers or other devices are WPS-compliant, meaning it is likely built with a preprogrammed WPS Personal Identification Number (PIN) consisting of a series of numbers, letters, or a combination of both. There are three common configuration methods for using the WPS feature: manual configuration, the WPS push-button method, and the software wizard method.

Tech Tip

WPS is *not* a security feature; rather, it is a feature that makes it easier to configure security features for wireless network devices.

Another option is to configure the security manually, which requires the network name (SSID), selecting the encryption, and entering the passphrase. WPA3 is the newest encryption protocol for wireless and should be used whenever possible. There will be more about wireless encryption in a later chapter.

Another option to configure the secure connection to a wireless router is by pressing a WPS button on the router and the client device. In most instances, you simply press a WPS button physically located on the router (if equipped) and then you have a period of approximately two minutes in which to press the WPS button on the client device. The client device might have a physical WPS button or software

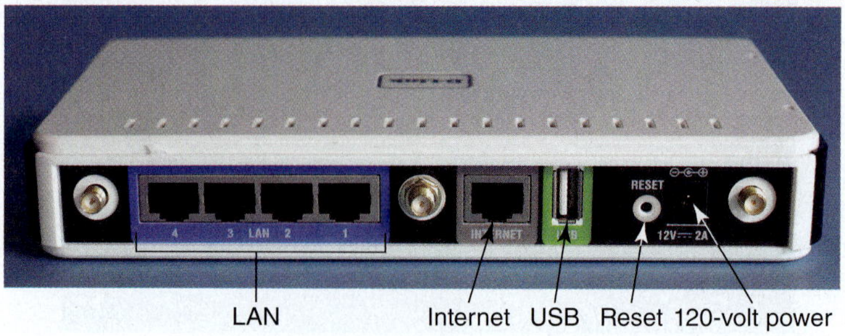

Figure 19-12 Wireless routers provide connections to wireless and Ethernet devices.

Goodheart-Willcox Publisher

application that generates the WPS connection negotiation with the router. You may also be presented with an option to copy the setup configuration to a USB flash drive and then use the flash drive to configure other devices without the need to use a WPS push button or wizard.

When using the software wizard method to connect a device to a wireless router, you may be prompted to enter a WPS PIN. The PIN is *not* the security key or passphrase; rather, it simply makes it easy to configure a secure connection between the router and a network device. The WPS PIN may be requested during the automatic configuration process or entered into the software wizard or on the client device, depending on the manufacturer. Figure 19-13 shows a WPS PIN located on a sticker on the bottom of the router.

There are many advantages to using the WPS feature. For example, WPS automatically configures the network connection to the wireless router or wireless access point without needing to know the SSID or the security key (passphrase). Additionally, the security key (passphrase) is randomly generated and complex, making it more difficult for an unauthorized user to guess. Finally, WPS has been supported in all Windows operating systems since Windows Vista. There are also disadvantages to WPS, though. For example, each wireless device must be WPS-compliant to take advantage of the feature. Noncompliant devices can still be connected to the network, but they must be configured manually. Manual configuration can be difficult because the security key (passphrase) often consists of a long series of random letters and numbers, making it difficult to remember and often resulting in typing errors.

MIMO

Recall from Chapter 14 that *multiple input multiple output (MIMO)* is a wireless technology that uses two or more streams of data transmission to increase the data throughput and range of the wireless network. Two or more streams of data transmitted in the same frequency channel is referred to as **spatial multiplexing (SM)**. MIMO was introduced with the 802.11n standard and continues in the more recent 802.11 ax (also called Wi-Fi 6). The 802.11 ax standard uses *multiuser MIMO (MU-MIMO)* and operates at 2.4/5 GHz similarly to 802.11n, but it can also function at 6 GHz. Additionally, 802.11 ax can provide bandwidth from 2 Gbps to 10 Gbps. Compare that to the older 802.11 ac, which reached a maximum bandwidth of 1.3 Gbps and the even older 802.11n, which reached a maximum of 300 Mbps. Though not released as of this writing, 802.11 be (Wi-Fi 7) is scheduled to be released in 2024 and will likely increase speeds even more.

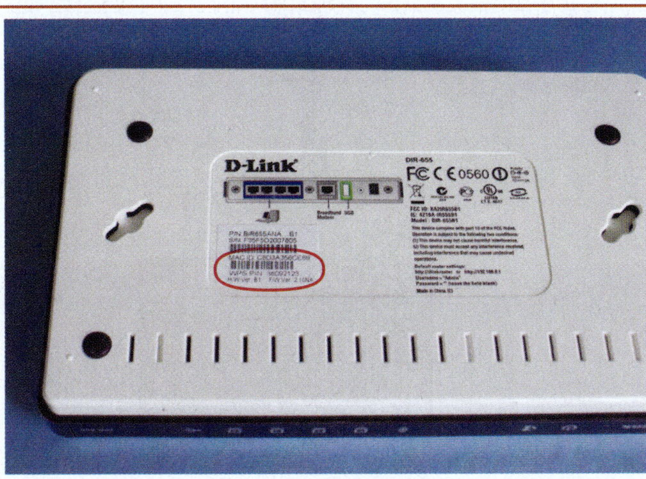

Goodheart-Willcox Publisher

Figure 19-13 The MAC ID and WPS PIN are often located on the bottom of a wireless router.

Wireless Adapter Cards

A *wireless adapter card* is an expansion card that enables wireless communication in a device that otherwise would not be wireless-enabled. There are many wireless network adapter designs available from which to choose. The wireless network adapter in Figure 19-14 is equipped with an antenna and designed to be installed inside a desktop computer in an available motherboard expansion slot. The disadvantage of this wireless design is the antenna is located on the back side of the desktop computer, which may affect the wireless range. Look at the diagram in Figure 19-15, which shows a PC with a wireless adapter card installed with an antenna in the back of the computer case. Since the placement of the antenna is at the back of the case, the wall, monitor, or case itself may block the radio signals, thus reducing the overall range of the network adapter. Some wireless cards of this type have replacement antennas that consist of a flexible coaxial cable with an antenna that replaces the shorter original antenna and can be placed on the desk or wall.

There are also many different USB wireless network adapters from which to choose. Figure 19-16 shows a mini- and a micro-USB wireless network adapter. These styles can fit into any available USB port on the computer. In the figure, a full-size network adapter card is placed beside the two USB wireless adapters for the purpose of scale. As you can see, the USB connectors are quite small in overall dimensions.

Figure 19-14 Some wireless adapter cards are designed to be installed inside a desktop computer in an available motherboard expansion slot.

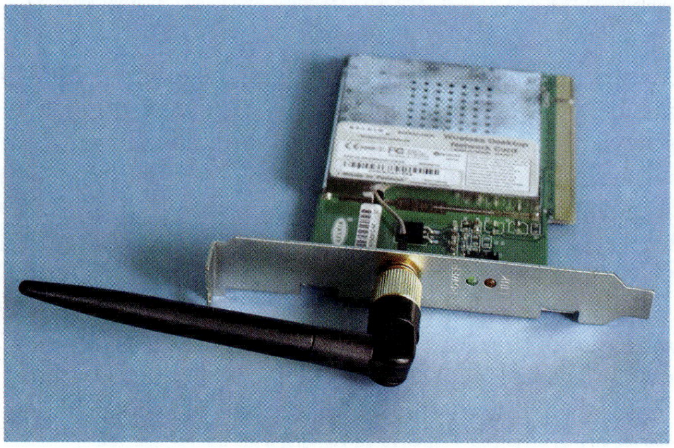

Goodheart-Willcox Publisher

Figure 19-15 The placement of a wireless network adapter can greatly affect the overall range of the wireless adapter.

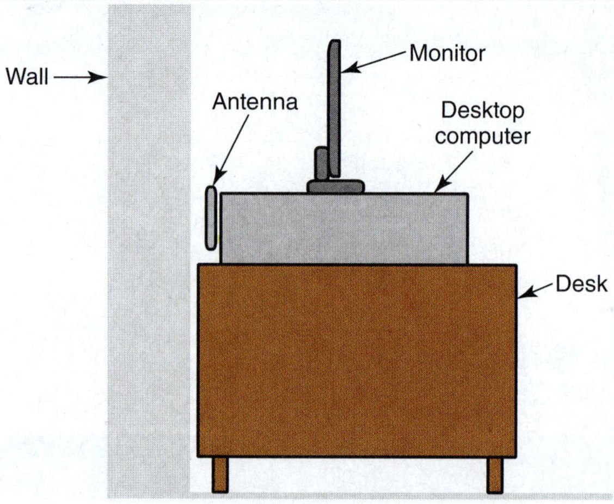

Goodheart-Willcox Publisher

A USB wireless network adapter, such as the one shown in Figure 19-17, is often equipped with a much longer antenna than normal wireless network adapters. The increased antenna size directly affects the overall range of the wireless adapter. Some adapters have the added advantage of a long USB cable extension that allows the adapter location to be easily changed without moving the computer. A slight change in wireless antenna or device location can greatly affect the range of the wireless adapter. In many cases, the wireless drivers must be installed first before connecting the adapter, which is also true for other wireless devices, such as wireless access points and wireless routers.

The IEEE 802.11 standards do not express distances for wireless adapter cards. The actual distance is a direct reflection of the output power of the wireless adapter expressed in watts. Distances are subject to many factors such as physical objects and sources of radio interference. Examples of physical objects include building walls, partitions, metal storage cabinets, and metal buildings. Some common sources of radio interference are microwave ovens, electric welding machines, cordless phones, electrical power lines, radio transmitters, portable radio equipment, baby monitors, wireless surveillance equipment such as cameras, and garage door openers.

Goodheart-Willcox Publisher

Figure 19-16 There are many different USB wireless network adapters from which to choose.

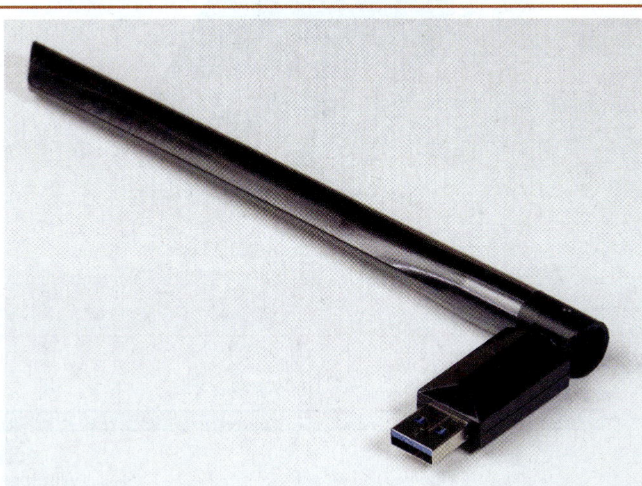

MMXeon/Shutterstock.com

Figure 19-17 USB wireless adapters often have longer antennas than normal wireless adapters, which often results in a larger range for the adapter.

A+ Note

The A+ Certification Exams have many questions requiring knowledge about wireless networking, both ad hoc and infrastructure. Be sure to memorize the data rates and assigned frequency for each of the IEEE wireless standards.

Wireless Range Extenders

A **wireless range extender**, sometimes called a *wireless repeater*, extends the range of a wireless network by receiving the wireless signal and rebroadcasting it. The range extender in Figure 19-18 also provides an RJ-45 port to provide a way to configure the range extender directly from a computer. This particular wireless range extender also uses a WPS button to connect with the main wireless router.

Wireless range extenders are affected by building materials and placement just as wireless routers and the devices connecting to them are. Building materials such as metal, concrete, and some types of glass adversely affect radio signals, as does the placement of wireless devices in relationship to each other and the angle of a wall separating the devices. Look at Figure 19-19 to see how placement can greatly affect the wireless signal strength when penetrating a wall at an angle of only a few degrees. When two devices such as a router and mobile device are at an angle that closely matches the length of the wall, the overall distance through the wall material is greatly increased. This is the same effect as attempting to penetrate a wall several feet thick and results in significant degradation of the wireless signal.

Electrical devices such as appliances, ceiling fans, 2.4-GHz cordless phones, microwave ovens, and similar devices generate electrical interference that can also degrade the wireless device range. Try to keep wireless devices at least three feet from all electrical appliances.

Diskless Workstations

A **diskless workstation** is a computer that runs without a hard disk drive. Some have small-capacity hard drives, but they are used solely as cache rather than data storage. A diskless workstation relies on the file server's hard drive for application software and data storage. As you know from previous study, the hard drive contains

Figure 19-18 Wireless range extenders receive the original wireless signal and rebroadcast it to extend the range of the original signal.

MMXeon/Shutterstock.com

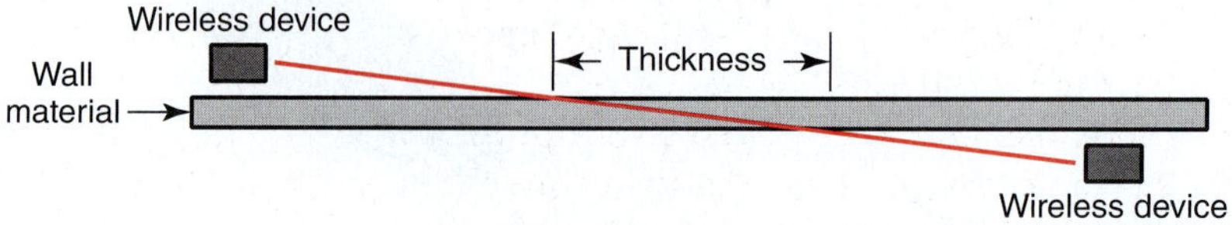

Figure 19-19 A wireless signal can be greatly degraded by the angle of transmission through a wall.

Goodheart-Willcox Publisher

the bootstrap program needed to boot the workstation, but a diskless workstation is booted from the interaction of the NIC and the file server. The NIC is equipped with a BIOS ROM chip, which contains the boot code needed to boot the workstation and connect to the network file server.

There are significant advantages to diskless workstations. For example, diskless workstations provide extremely good security, because without a disk system for employees to use, there is no way for data files to be electronically duplicated at the workstation. In addition, diskless systems eliminate the possibility of acquiring viruses from portable storage media, such as flash drives and optical discs.

Another consideration is the overall cost of installation. Eliminating the cost of hard drives and optical drives results in substantial savings, especially when installing several hundred or thousands of PCs in an enterprise system. Diskless workstations are also substantially easier for administration; since all workstations are dependent on the file server for their application software, thousands of diskless workstations can be upgraded at the same time, resulting in a tremendous savings in labor costs of installing software on individual computers. The only real disadvantage is that when the network is down, all workstations are affected.

Thin Client

Recall from Chapter 2 that a *thin client* is a computer that has minimal hardware resources and relies on cloud services for software. In a sense, thin clients are similar to diskless workstations, but unlike diskless workstations, thin clients cannot process their own environments. Instead, a typical thin client relies on other computer equipment such as network servers or the cloud as a resource for running software applications and processing data. For example, a computer intended for use by a bank employee who simply services customer accounts does not require top-of-the-line hardware such as a large hard disk storage system, very fast processor, high-performance video card, or any other hardware associated with high-performance computer systems. Since the bank employee will most likely only need to access information stored on a network server and record transactions, a thin client is perfect. Thin clients that rely on cloud resources are also referred to as *cloud computers* or *cloud clients*.

Thin clients reduce the cost of equipment and software since software applications run from the cloud or from a server save overall cost. Rather than installing multiple copies of a software application on each computer, a single software application can be accessed through cloud services or from an application server.

In the context of discussing the term *thin client* to describe a minimal hardware system, a standard-size computer system is often referred to as a *thick client*, which is often used to run desktop applications not serviced by an application server or cloud. Be sure that the client meets the minimum requirements for your selected NOS before installing it onto the network, and if necessary, upgrade the workstation to fulfill the minimum specifications.

Network Operating Systems (NOS)

A **network operating system (NOS)** provides communication between computers, printers, and other intelligent hardware on the network. The most common network operating systems today are Linux Server (many different versions), Windows Server (many different versions), and macOS Server. A network need not consist of a single brand of hardware or software, however. For example, a network may consist of Linux Servers, Windows Servers, and client operating systems, such as Windows, macOS, SUSE Linux, and Kali Linux.

The NOS is also composed of software programs that provide security, user identity, remote access, and sharing for printers and other devices. Without the NOS, a network would be a useless collection of parts.

After completing your studies for computer service and repair, you might consider specializing in a specific server operating system such as Microsoft Server or Linux Server, as mastering a server operating system will greatly enhance your technical credentials.

A+ 1101: 2.4, 2.6

DNS

Domain Name Service (DNS) translates human-friendly names into IP addresses. For example, the domain name https://www.g-w.com/ is easy for humans to remember and use, but to reach that website, your computer needs that URL translated into an IP address such as 162.252.106.220. The process works by your computer contacting a DNS server and looking for a record that matches the domain name being searched.

DNS records come in various types, such as the following:

- *A records* are the most common and map a domain name to an IPv4 address.
- *AAAA records* operate in the exact same way as A records, except they point to an IPv6 address.
- *CNAME records* are very commonly used to link a subdomain to a domain's A or AAAA record.
- *Name Server (NS) records* point to other domain name servers.
- *MX records* point to e-mail servers.
- *Text (TXT) records* let the owner of a domain store text values in the DNS.
- *Pointer (PTR) records* provide a domain name for reverse lookup. This is essentially the opposite of an A record, as it provides the domain name linked to an IP address instead of the IP address for a domain.
- *SRV records* enable storage of IP addresses and port assignments for specific services.

In recent years, more and more has been tied to domain names. For example, *Domain Keys Identified Mail (DKIM)* is a security measure meant to mitigate e-mail forgeries. DKIM allows the receiver to check that an e-mail claiming to have come from a specific domain was indeed authorized by the owner of that domain. This is accomplished using a digital signature on each outgoing e-mail.

Sender Policy Framework (SPF) is a similar e-mail authentication method that detects forged senders via the e-mail envelope. *Domain-based Message Authentication, Reporting and Conformance (DMARC)* is yet another e-mail authentication protocol meant to prevent a domain from being used in various scams such as phishing and business e-mail compromise.

A+ 1101: 3.4

19.5 Network Interface Card Installation and Features

When selecting a network interface card that inserts into a motherboard expansion slot, compatibility cannot be stressed enough. Be sure to choose a card that matches the motherboard slot type. Speed is also an important consideration. You will want to get the most value, so look for a card that not only fits your motherboard, but also matches the speed of the network.

Antistatic precautions must be taken when handling a NIC, just as with any static-sensitive device. Firmly push the NIC into the appropriate expansion slot and boot the computer after it is installed. Assuming you are using Windows 7 or later, the operating system should automatically detect the new hardware, assign system resources, and install the proper driver, but if the operating system does *not* detect the card automatically, you will have to install the drivers manually. Device manufacturer websites provide complete instructions for installing a particular network adapter, and some devices also come with a CD/DVD that contains detailed instructions.

When installing a relatively new device as compared to the computer system, you may encounter a problem with the computer's ability to detect the device. In most cases, you must install a driver before physically installing a new device into an older computer system. Network adapters differ greatly physically but most have similar configuration options, such as Wake-on-LAN and adapter teaming.

> **A+ Note**
>
> The CompTIA A+ Certification Exams often ask questions about full-duplex and half-duplex modes of operation, as well as the Wake-on LAN feature. Be mindful of this while studying for the exams.

Wake-on-LAN

Wake-on-LAN (WOL), also referred to as *Remote Wake-Up (RWU)*, is a network adapter feature that allows the adapter to wake the computer from sleep or hibernation or power on a computer when network activity is detected. This feature is often disabled for security purposes and enabled for remote network administration by network system administrators. For the computer to be completely WOL-capable, the network adapter, operating system, and the computer BIOS/UEFI must support the feature. For Windows, the Wake-on-LAN is enabled by default in desktop computers but disabled in laptops, and the wake-up message sent to the network adapter is referred to as a *magic packet* by Microsoft and Intel, as shown in Figure 19-20.

Adapter Teaming

Another NIC feature is **adapter teaming**, which allows two or more network adapters to share the network load and ensure network reliability. The number of packets is divided between the two or more network adapters, which increases network performance and improved reliability. If one network adapter fails, another is still working.

Network Adapter Speed and Operation Mode

1101: 3.6 A+

Network adapter speed and mode of operation are typically detected and configured automatically. Most network adapters can support many different network speeds such as 10, 100, and 1,000 Mbps, but the network adapter automatically detects other devices' speed capabilities and adjusts the speed of the adapter accordingly. Network adapters also automatically configure the mode of operation, as shown

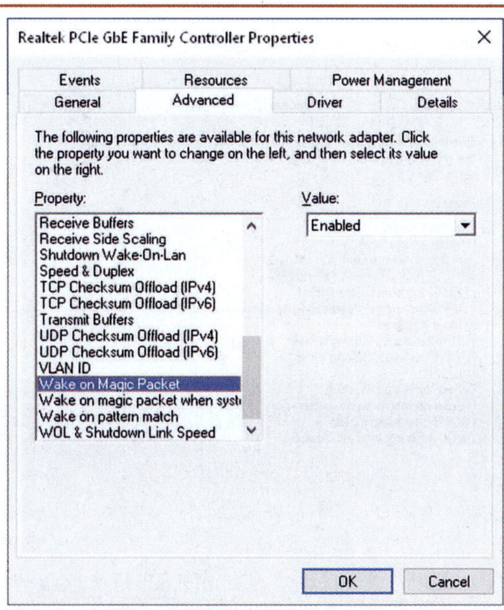

Goodheart-Willcox Publisher

Figure 19-20 Wake-on-LAN is a network adapter feature that allows the adapter to wake the computer from sleep or hibernation when network activity is detected.

in Figure 19-21. There are two modes of operation: half-duplex and full-duplex. A network adapter configured for ***half-duplex*** can send or receive network packets, but not simultaneously. When configured for ***full-duplex***, the network adapter can send and receive packets simultaneously.

Many other options are available for most network adapters. Only the most common options were introduced here. To learn more about network adapter configuration options, visit a network adapter manufacturer website such as Intel.

A+ Note

The A+ Certification Exams will require some knowledge of the OSI model.

19.6 OSI Model

The **Open Systems Interconnection (OSI) model** is a seven-layer model used to describe how hardware and software should work together to form a network communication system. The OSI model was a joint effort of international members to standardize network communication systems and consists of the following layers:

- Layer 1—Physical
- Layer 2—Data Link
- Layer 3—Network
- Layer 4—Transport
- Layer 5—Session
- Layer 6—Presentation
- Layer 7—Application

Physical Layer

The Physical layer is the most basic layer of the model. It consists of the physical elements of a network, such as cable and adapter cards. The structure of this layer determines how electrical signals are carried between the devices on a network.

Data Link Layer

The Data Link layer describes the network's level of operation at which the raw data is packaged for transfer from one network card to another. It packages binary numbers (1s and 0s) into frames or packets for transmission between nodes.

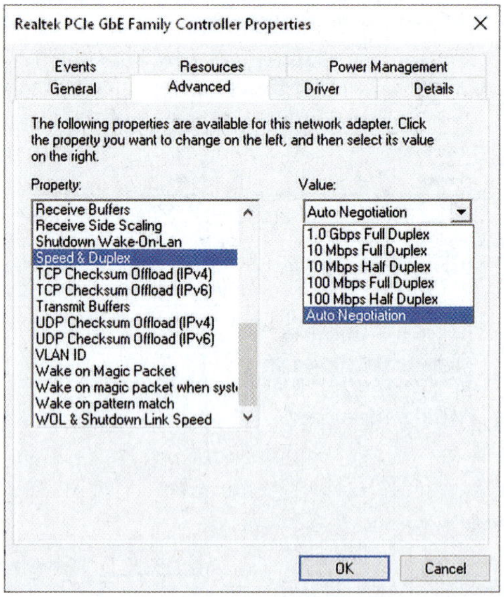

Figure 19-21 The speed of a network adapter is automatically negotiated by the network adapter itself, as well as full-duplex or half-duplex operational modes.

Goodheart-Willcox Publisher

Network Layer

The Network layer is responsible for routing packets of data from one network card to another. Routing provides a means of preventing or limiting congestion on large networks while prioritizing the transmission of data. As data is transmitted from one computer to another, several different routes may be used. If the equipment senses too much traffic along one cable section, the data can be transmitted along a different route to avoid the congestion.

Transport Layer

The Transport layer's main responsibility is to ensure the data received from a transmission is reliable. It sequences the packets of data and reassembles them in their correct order. The individual data packets that comprise a single file or message may arrive by different routes when transmitted over many miles, and they may not arrive in the same sequence in which they were transmitted, requiring reassembly into the correct order. This reassembly is especially important in the transmission of graphic images.

Session Layer

The Session layer is the layer at which a connection is established between two different computers. This layer also provides system security based on computer and username recognition and resolves compatibility problems between dissimilar systems, such as a PC and a Macintosh or a mainframe. Sometimes, the Session and Transport layers are combined into one layer.

Presentation Layer

The Presentation layer ensures character code recognition by converting the character codes from the originating computer to another form that can be recognized by the receiving computer. For example, most PCs use the American Standard Code for Information Interchange (ASCII), but mainframe computers widely use the Extended Binary Coded Decimal Interchange Code (EBCDIC). The Presentation layer is responsible for converting ASCII into EBCDIC when data packets are sent from a standard PC to a mainframe computer.

Application Layer

The Application layer manages network processes such as file transfer, mail service, and file-server database access. When you hear the term *application*, you likely think of application software, such as word-processing, spreadsheets, or graphic-design programs. These are not the same applications referred to by this layer. Think of the Application layer as a network browser. In the OSI model, the Application layer strictly applies to network applications designed as a communication interface for the user.

The OSI model clearly demonstrates the complexity of transmitting data from one computer to another. Therefore, it should be used as a model for a well-designed protocol. However, not all software companies follow the strict guidelines of the OSI model, and many systems were already in place long before the model was developed and adopted. Additionally, some protocol systems combine two or more layers into a single unit. It is important to remember that the OSI model is simply a guide for future protocol development.

Network Devices Defined by the OSI Model

Network devices are often defined by the part of the OSI model with which they align. For example, the best definitions of the three most commonly encountered network devices—router, switch, and hub—are based on how they deliver network data to a destination or device based on MAC address or IPv4 and IPv6 assigned addresses. Figure 19-22 lists the layer to which a standard hub, switch, and router belong. Keep in mind that the definition of specific devices gets clouded as more capabilities are added and then advertised by manufacturers, such as the difference between a smart switch and a managed switch.

A+ 1102: 2.9

19.7 Network Security

Keeping a network secure becomes more important with each passing year, because the number of cyberattacks increases annually, as does the cost associated with the damage caused by those attacks. While there are a variety of technological means for mitigating the threat of cyberattacks, it is important not to forget the basics, such as not using default usernames and passwords. All devices come with a default username and password, and changing those defaults should be part of the configuration process for every new device. Additionally, disabling unused ports and services is another basic security measure that should be part of that process. Any service or port is a possible attack vector, so if you do not use a given service or port, disabling it closes that attack vector. Eliminating guest access on any system, unless it is truly needed, will also close another possible attack vector. Another fundamental security measure is to keep systems updated. This includes updating the firmware of network devices such as routers and switches.

Most operating systems and network devices come with some type of built-in firewall that allows you to filter traffic. There are many types of filtering performed by these firewalls, such as IP filtering, which allows you to filter access by IP address. However, you can also configure a firewall to filter based on domain names, specific software, MAC address, and other unique identifiers. One strategic method is to conduct research on cyberthreat websites to stay up to date on the latest threats and configure your firewall to block those signatures. Firewalls should be implemented throughout a network, not just at the network perimeter. This helps establish a concept known as **defense in depth**, which is the presence of multiple, redundant levels of protection in case one of the security measures fails. Imagine a scenario in which an attacker breaches your network perimeter. Without defense in depth, the rest of your network is open to them. By implementing security measures at every switch or router—as well as on all computers—you make it much more difficult for an attacker to steal data or cause damage to a network.

Similar to the concept of changing default usernames and password, you should also change a wireless router's default SSID and password. However, you should not use a name that makes your network easily identifiable. For example, assume you were hired by an accounting organization called Smith CPA. Renaming the SSID to

Figure 19-22 Network devices are defined by the OSI layer at which they operate.

Network Equipment by OSI Layer

Device	OSI Layer	Description
Hub	Layer 1	Simply provides network connections
Switch	Layer 2	Directs packet destination based on MAC address
Router	Layer 3	Directs packet destination based on IPv4 and IPv6 addresses

Goodheart-Willcox Publisher

SmithCPA makes it easier for anyone wishing to target the organization to find the right network. You can also set most wireless access points not to broadcast the SSID, and while this will not stop a skilled attacker from finding the SSID, it will at least keep some attackers from targeting your Wi-Fi.

Related to changing or hiding your SSID is the topic of an *evil twin*, which is a wireless access point established by an attacker with the same SSID as your actual wireless access point. This can lead users to mistakenly connect to the fake access point rather than the real one. Once this occurs, the attacker has a relatively easy time extracting data from the users' network traffic.

A+ 1102: 2.4

Physical security is an important aspect of cybersecurity that should not be ignored. This involves secure placement of devices, starting with wireless access points being placed close to the center of an organization so their coverage does not extend any farther outside of your office area than necessary. This also involves placing servers in secure rooms and physically securing network devices such as routers and switches.

Another security measure that is often ignored in small office and home networks is a *virtual local access network (VLAN)*, which allows you to configure ports on your switch or router as though they were a separate network. This helps facilitate defense in depth and can be especially useful if different portions of your network require different levels of security. Consider a small office with a 12-port switch. One could create a VLAN with four of the ports and make that VLAN more secure than the other eight. These ports then become an ideal place to connect sensitive machines such as a database and file servers. The other eight ports could have normal levels of security.

19.8 IEEE 802 Standards

The Institute of Electrical and Electronic Engineers (IEEE, pronounced *I triple E*) is a professional organization that continually develops standards for the networking and communication industry. The organization consists of scientists, students, commercial vendors, and other interested professionals within the industry. The IEEE's network standards are identified with an 802 prefix, of which several are listed as follows:

- IEEE 802.1: Bridging and network management
- IEEE 802.2: Logical Link Control and Media Access Control
- IEEE 802.3: Ethernet (CSMA/CD)
- IEEE 802.4: Token Bus (disbanded)
- IEEE 802.5: MAC layer for Token Ring (inactive)
- IEEE 802.6: Metropolitan Area Networks (disbanded)
- IEEE 802.7: Broadband LAN using coaxial cable (disbanded)
- IEEE 802.8: Fiber-optic token-passing network (disbanded)
- IEEE 802.9: Integrated voice and data (disbanded)
- IEEE 802.10: Interoperable LAN security (disbanded)
- IEEE 802.11: Wireless LAN and mesh (Wi-Fi certification)
- IEEE 802.12: Demand priority (disbanded)
- IEEE 802.13: Not used
- IEEE 802.14: Cable modems (disbanded)
- IEEE 802.15: Wireless PAN
- IEEE 802.16: Wireless Broadband (WiMAX certification)
- IEEE 802.16e: Mobile Broadband
- IEEE 802.17: Resilient Packet Ring
- IEEE 802.18: Radio Regulatory Technical Advisory Group
- IEEE 802.19: Wireless Coexistence Technical Advisory Group

- IEEE 802.20: Mobile Broadband Wireless Access
- IEEE 802.21: Media Independent Handoff
- IEEE 802.22: Wireless Regional Area Network

Many of the standards are inactive or disbanded because there is no longer any need for them, or another organization or entity has assumed responsibility for the standard. For example, Token Ring is no longer a viable choice of network media and is no longer in need of an up-to-date set of standards, so it is now inactive.

The specifications outlined in the IEEE 802 standards are not to be thought of as laws; rather, they are a set of recommended practices designed to ensure the quality of a network system. However, if a contract to install a network system refers to the IEEE 802 standards, they should be thought of as law. For example, if a new network is required to meet the IEEE 802 standards and problems arise because the standards were not followed, the installation contractor or designer of the network system can be held liable. The IEEE 802 standards will be referred to constantly throughout your studies of network systems. The most up-to-date information on the IEEE 802 standards can be obtained at the IEEE Standards Association website.

Chapter Summary

19.1 Network Benefits

- A computer network consists of two or more computers connected together to share data and resources.
- The benefits of using a network are shared resources, shared data, system management, productivity, cost efficiency, and security.

19.2 Network Administrative Models

- There are two main network administrative models: client/server and peer-to-peer. The client/server model is centrally administered and made up of computers that are either clients, individual PCs, or workstations that access a server's resources and files, or servers.
- The peer-to-peer model is not centrally administered, and all PCs connected together are equals.

19.3 Network Classifications and Topologies

- A local area network (LAN) is a small network of computers contained in a relatively small area.
- A metropolitan area network (MAN) is a group of two or more interconnected LANs operating under a single management.
- A wide area network (WAN) is typically a large number of computers spread over a large area and under the control of a centrally located administrator.
- A campus area network (CAN) is a network that spans a limited geographic area.
- A personal area network (PAN), also called a *piconet*, is a short-range network, wired or wireless, that connects devices such as a PC, cell phone, tablet, camera, and printer.
- A global area network (GAN) is a WAN spread over a geographical area that covers multiple countries or continents, such as the Internet.
- A wireless mesh network (WMN) is a network system composed of wireless networking devices organized so that all devices can communicate directly with each other.
- A storage area network (SAN) is an isolated network built entirely to handle data storage. Rather than a single server, one might have several servers and network storage devices, which all appear as a single storage device to the user.
- *Topology* refers to the physical arrangement of hardware and cabling in a network system.
- A bus topology is a network arrangement in which a single conductor connects to all the computers.
- A ring topology is a network arrangement in which a single cable runs continuously from computer to computer.
- A star topology is a network arrangement in which cables run from each computer to a single point, forming a star.
- A hybrid topology is simply a mixture of star, bus, and ring topologies.
- A mesh topology is a network system in which each node connects directly to every other node on the network.
- As its name implies, a wireless topology is a network system that uses no cabling between the computers and instead uses either infrared light or radio transmission to communicate between devices.

- Segmenting a network is the separation of certain portions of network traffic to increase performance, security, or reliability. The term *segment* refers to a physical or logical portion of a network.

19.4 Network Equipment and Resources

- A network interface card (NIC) connects media, usually twisted pair, to individual network devices such as workstations, file servers, and printers.
- Powerline network devices are designed to extend a network by using the existing 120-volt electrical wiring system.
- A hub is a device that connects network equipment together quickly and easily.
- A switch is equipped with more sophisticated electronic components than a simple hub.
- A router supports communication between different types of networks.
- A wireless router is a combination of a wireless access point, switch, and router.
- A diskless workstation relies on the file server's hard drive for application software and data storage.
- There are some very strong advantages to diskless workstations, including security and cost of installation.
- A thin client is a computer that has minimal hardware resources and typically relies on other computer equipment for running software applications and processing data.
- Thin clients reduce the cost of equipment and software.
- The most common network operating systems are Linux Server, Windows Server, and macOS Server.
- The NOS is also composed of software programs that provide security, user identity, remote access, and sharing for printers and other devices.
- Domain Name Service (DNS) translates human-friendly names into IP addresses.
- DNS records come in various types, including A records, AAAA records, CNAME records, NS records, MX records, TXT records, PTR records, and SRV records.

19.5 Network Interface Card Installation and Features

- When installing a typical network interface card, take proper antistatic precautions and firmly push the adapter into the appropriate expansion slot in the motherboard.
- *Wake-on-LAN (WOL)*, also referred to as *Remote Wake-Up (RWU)*, is a network adapter feature that allows the adapter to wake the computer from sleep or hibernation or power on a computer when network activity is detected.
- Another NIC feature is *adapter teaming*, which allows two or more network adapters to share the network load and ensure network reliability.
- A network adapter configured for *half-duplex* can send or receive network packets, but not simultaneously. When configured for *full-duplex*, the network adapter can send and receive packets simultaneously.

19.6 OSI Model

- The Open Systems Interconnection (OSI) model is a seven-layer model used to describe how hardware and software should work together to form a network communication system.
- The OSI model layers are Physical, Data Link, Network, Transport, Session, Presentation, and Application.

- The Physical layer is the most basic layer of the model. It consists of the physical elements of a network, such as cable and adapter cards.
- The Data Link layer describes the network's level of operation at which the raw data is packaged for transfer from one network card to another.
- The Network layer is responsible for routing packets of data from one network card to another.
- The Transport layer's main responsibility is to ensure the data received from a transmission is reliable.
- The Session layer is the layer at which a connection is established between two different computers.
- The Presentation layer ensures character code recognition by converting the character codes from the originating computer to another form that can be recognized by the receiving computer.
- The Application layer manages network processes such as file transfer, mail service, and file-server database access.

19.7 Network Security

- Keeping a network secure becomes more important with each passing year, as the number of cyberattacks increases annually, as does the cost associated with the damage caused by those attacks.
- While there are a variety of technological means for mitigating the threat of cyberattacks, it is important not to forget the basics, such as not using default usernames and passwords.
- Disabling unused ports and services is another basic security measure that should be performed upon initial configuration.
- Another fundamental security measure is to keep systems updated.
- Firewalls should be implemented throughout a network, not just at the network perimeter. This helps establish defense in depth.
- Similar to the concept of changing default usernames and password, you should also change a wireless router's default SSID and password.
- Disabling the broadcast of an SSID can help prevent an evil twin, which is a wireless access point established by an attacker with the same SSID as your actual wireless access point.
- Physical security is an important aspect of cybersecurity that should not be ignored. This involves secure placement of devices, starting with wireless access points being placed close to the center of an organization so their coverage does not extend any farther outside of your office area than necessary.
- Another security measure that is often ignored in small office and home networks is a *virtual local access network (VLAN)*, which allows you to configure ports on your switch or router as though they were a separate network.

19.8 IEEE 802 Standards

- The IEEE 802 standards ensure the quality of a network system.

Review Questions

1. Recall the benefits of a network.
2. How does a large network server differ from a typical PC?
3. Name three types of dedicated servers.
4. Compare and contrast the client/server and peer-to-peer administrative models.

5. Which network classification best matches an arrangement of six computers connected together in a classroom without the presence of a server?
6. Which network classification best matches an arrangement in which a computer connects to a powerful computer in another building?
7. Differentiate among network classifications.
8. Which network classification best describes the Internet?
9. Differentiate among common network topologies.
10. Differentiate among network equipment and their functions.
11. What are the three most common network operating systems?
12. What is WPS?
13. Summarize the installation and features of a network interface card.
14. What is the difference between half-duplex and full-duplex operation?
15. List the layers of the OSI model from layer 1 to layer 7.
16. Summarize the function of DNS.
17. Identify important elements of network security.
18. Define defense in depth.
19. List common current IEEE 802 standards.
20. Which IEEE standard describes wireless local area networks?

Sample A+ Exam Questions

1. Which of the following statements best defines a peer-to-peer network?
   A. A group of computers in which each has control of its own resources
   B. A group of computers controlled by one central computer
   C. A group of computers in which one is designated the control unit and the rest are defined as peers
   D. A group of computers in which each computer can remove any other computer from the group
2. A network limited to one floor of an office building would *most likely* be classified as a _____.
   A. LAN
   B. MAN
   C. WAN
   D. CAN
3. Which layer of the OSI model is concerned with network cables and connectors?
   A. Application
   B. Session
   C. Transport
   D. Physical
4. Which layer of the OSI model is concerned with establishing a connection between two different computers?
   A. Application
   B. Session
   C. Transport
   D. Physical

5. What feature allows for automatic security configuration between two wireless devices?
   A. WPA
   B. WEP
   C. WPS
   D. Adapter teaming
6. Which layer of the OSI model is concerned with routing packets of data from one network card to another across a large network?
   A. Application
   B. Session
   C. Network
   D. Physical
7. Which of the following best represents a network card MAC address?
   A. 123.202.16.24
   B. 1673452
   C. 00 A1 23 12 C2 F1
   D. CF12D
8. At which layer of the OSI model would a web browser be located?
   A. Presentation
   B. Application
   C. Session
   D. Network
9. Which of the following devices reduces excessive data transmissions on a network?
   A. Router
   B. Access point
   C. Switching hub
   D. Workstation
10. Which organization established the 802 standards?
   A. EIA
   B. ANSI
   C. CompTIA
   D. IEEE

Chapter 20

Network Communication, Media, and Tools

Learning Outcomes

20.1 Explain the communication process between networks.
20.2 Identify network media.
20.3 Identify the proper cable or network tool for a given task.

A+ Certification Exam Objectives

The following A+ Certification Exam Objectives are covered in this chapter.

Exam 220-1101

2.0 Networking

- 2.1 Compare and Contrast Transmission Control Protocol (TCP) and User Datagram Protocol (UDP) ports, protocols, and their purposes.
- 2.2 Compare and contrast common networking hardware.
- 2.3 Compare and contrast protocols for wireless networking.
- 2.4 Summarize services provided by networked hosts.
- 2.7 Compare and contrast Internet connection types, network types, and their features.
- 2.8 Given a scenario, use appropriate networking tools.

3.0 Hardware

- 3.1 Explain basic cable types and their connectors, features, and purposes.

Exam 220-1102

2.0 Security

- 2.7 Explain common methods for securing mobile and embedded devices.
- 2.9 Given a scenario, configure appropriate security settings on small office/home office (SOHO) wireless and wired networks.

Key Terms

Automatic Medium Dependent Interface Crossover (Auto-MDIX)
backoff interval
cable crimper
cable tester
cable tracer
Carrier Sense Multiple Access with Collision Avoidance (CSMA/CA)
Carrier Sense Multiple Access with Collision Detection (CSMA/CD)
coaxial cable
cross talk
Ethernet network
fail-over
fiber-optic cable
insulation displacement connector (IDC)
load balancing
loopback plug
network media
Optical Network Terminal (ONT)
packet
Power over Ethernet (PoE)
protocol suite
punch down tool
rollover cable
sequence number
sinkhole attack
tone generator
Transmission Control Protocol/Internet Protocol (TCP/IP)
twisted-pair cable

Overview

Networking is a large component of the A+ Exams and in the daily tasks of an IT technician. To install, troubleshoot, upgrade, or repair a network, one must first understand networking media and all the associated topics. This chapter presents an overview of network communication, media, and tools. Heavy emphasis is placed on communication protocols, such as TCP, IP, LLDP, and UDP; copper-core cabling, such as Ethernet and coaxial; fiber-optic cabling; and cable tools, such as crimpers, punch down tools, and testing equipment.

A+ Note

Be sure you can identify the layers of the OSI model as well as the various network topologies. You also should be familiar with network protocols and network cable media.

20.1 How Networks Communicate

For two or more computers to communicate, they must use the same system of identification and data transfer. Data is divided into **packets**—also called *frames*—which are small units of data into which larger amounts are divided for passage through a network. Like an envelope going through the mail system, each packet contains the address of the sender and the intended recipient. When all the packets have arrived at their destination, they are reassembled to form a complete message or file.

How Data Is Packaged

Data is sent across a network in the form of digital pulses, or rapidly changing levels of voltages. For data to be sent across a network from one node to another, a common data-packaging scheme must be used. The sequence and length of the information is the key to coding and decoding the data frames.

The digital pulses represent binary and hexadecimal codes, which, in turn, represent the data being transmitted. Different network operating systems use different encoding schemes for transmitting data. In a typical data frame, the first six bytes represent the MAC address of the destination network interface card (NIC), and the second six bytes represent the MAC address of the NIC transmitting the data. Additional blocks of encoded data may contain information such as the length of the packet being sent, a sequence number for the packet, and an error-checking code. Error checking is incorporated into the packet to ensure the data was not corrupted during transmission. A data frame has a maximum length, usually approximately 1,500 bytes.

A data packet's **sequence number** ensures data will be reassembled in the exact order in which it was transmitted. Some network systems, such as the Internet, are very complex, so the various packets of information that comprise a message may not be routed through the same path and may not arrive at their destination in the same order in which they were sent. Without a sequence number, the packets arriving at different times would be garbled when reassembled, resulting in diminished quality or data loss. The amount of time it takes information to arrive at its destination is influenced by the

- length of route taken;
- type of media and equipment used to route the data; and
- amount of data traffic on that particular route.

A+ 1101: 2.3

The packaging and transmission of data is dependent upon networking regulations. These can include regulations that have the force of law, such as those from the Federal Communications Commission (FCC), as well as nongovernmental regulations such as IEEE and ISO. IEEE networking standards all fall under the 801 category, to which you have already seen references in this textbook. There are many other IEEE networking standards, such as Ethernet standard 802.3 and body area networks standard 802.15.6. When setting up a new network, it is important to be familiar with regulations, including those of voluntary groups such as IEEE.

A+ 1101: 2.1

Protocols

For computers to communicate with each other, they must use the same *protocol*, which is a set of rules for formatting the data stream transmission between two computers or devices. Protocols are also used for describing how to transmit data, usually across a network. The protocol determines the size of the data packets transmitted between two computers. It also compresses the information to allow for faster transmission rates, verifies that the information transmitted is complete, and reassembles the information packets when they are received. Protocols also usually have some error-checking capabilities. Common protocols include the following:

- TCP/IP (Transmission Control Protocol/Internet Protocol)
- SMB (Server Message Block)

- CIFS (Common Internet File System)
- LDAP (Lightweight Directory Access Protocol)
- SNMP (Simple Network Management Protocol)
- LLDP (Link Layer Discovery Protocol)
- DHCP (Dynamic Host Configuration Protocol)
- DNS (Domain Name System)
- UPnP (Universal Plug-and-Play)
- SSDP (Simple Service Discovery Protocol)
- NetBEUI (NetBIOS Extended User Interface)
- FIP
- ATM
- FTP (File Transfer Protocol)
- SFTP (Secure File Transfer Protocol)
- Telnet (Teletype Network Protocol)
- SSH (Secure Shell)
- POP3 (Post Office Protocol version 3)
- HTTP (Hypertext Transfer Protocol)
- S-HTTP (Secure Hypertext Transfer Protocol)
- IMAP (Internet Message Access Protocol)
- RDP (Remote Desktop Protocol)
- SMTP (Simple Mail Transfer Protocol)
- AFP (AppleTalk Filing Protocol)
- VoIP (Voice over IP)

Every program or protocol that runs on a computer and waits for another computer to connect to it uses a designated port to wait for a connection. While waiting for the connection, the port is referred to as a *listening port*, and each protocol has a designated listening port. Figure 20-1 shows listening ports for common protocols.

Listening Ports of Common Protocols

Protocol	Listening Port
FTP	21
SSH	22
Telnet	23
SMTP	25
DNS	53
HTTP	80
POP3	110
IMAP	143
HTTPS	443
RDP	3386
NetBIOS/NetBT	137–139
SMB/CIFS	445
SLP	427
AFP	548
DHCP	67/68
LDAP	389
SNMP	161/162

Goodheart-Willcox Publisher

Figure 20-1 Every program or protocol that runs on a computer and waits for another computer to connect to it uses a designated port to wait for a connection.

A+ 1101: 2.1

The terms *protocol* and *service* can cause confusion. Often, both the protocol and service are identified by the same acronym, such as DHCP or DNS, but protocols and services are not the same. A protocol and service are directly related in that both are typically required for the computer system to function properly, but services are typically small programs that act on the information contained in the protocol. Required services are programs, also known as *processes*, which usually start automatically and run continuously in the background.

When information is exchanged between two services, the information is assembled in a standard format identified by the protocol standard. You can think of this relationship similarly to how a web browser and web page content are distributed. In this comparison, the web browser can be considered a service in the sense that the actual code that creates the individual web page conforms to a protocol standard. The web browser provides the service, and the content is assembled in a specific manner as defined by the protocol.

Protocol Suites

A **protocol suite** is a combination of individual protocols, each designed for a specific purpose. TCP/IP is an example of a protocol suite and is identified by two of the protocols in the suite: Transmission Control Protocol (TCP) and Internet Protocol (IP). Some protocols within a suite guarantee delivery of a data packet, while others do not. For example, if a command is issued from one computer on a local network to another on the same local network, delivery is almost guaranteed. No method of checking for delivery is completely necessary. However, if one computer sends a message to another across the country, a method needs to be used to verify delivery.

As technology progresses, newer protocols must be added to existing suites. For example, when transmitting a collection of data such as a large document, there is no requirement that the individual packets representing the entire document arrive at the destination in proper sequence or with extraordinary speed, because the document can be reassembled at the destination in a reasonable amount of time. However, when transferring data such as sound or video, the data must be received in proper sequence in a short period of time. For example, imagine a telephone conversation over a VoIP (Voice over IP) connection. The conversation is divided into packets just like any other form of data, and if those packets are received out of order, the conversation would sound garbled.

TCP/IP

A+ 1101: 2.2

Originally developed for Unix communication over the Internet, **Transmission Control Protocol/Internet Protocol (TCP/IP)** is the standard default Internet protocol. TCP/IP is a protocol suite that combines Transmission Control Protocol (TCP) and Internet Protocol (IP). TCP is designed to guarantee delivery of all packets, and IP simply delivers packets and assumes they are received. Originally, TCP/IP was the default protocol installed in a Windows operating system environment, but today, there are two default TCP/IP protocols: IP version 4 (IPv4) and IP version 6 (IPv6). Both protocols are enabled by default and run simultaneously, though each version uses a unique set of numbers to identify network devices. IPv6 is designed to solve many of the problems associated with IPv4, such as mobile networking and automatic network device configuration.

IPv4

Internet Protocol version 4, also known as *TCP/IPv4* or simply *IPv4*, has been a standard network protocol for many years. The main design of the IPv4 protocol is the identification of the source and destination computers in the form of 32-bit addresses. The IPv4 address is one way a network device is identified and is written as sets of four decimal numbers in the range of 0 to 255 separated by a period, such as 192.168.0.23.

IPv6

Internet Protocol version 6, also known as *TCP/IPv6* or simply *IPv6*, was designed to replace TCP/IPv4. TCP/IPv6 was first introduced in Windows XP but was not enabled by default until Windows Vista. Now, both IPv4 and IPv6 are enabled by default for all Windows operating systems. There will be more about IPv4 and IPv6 in a later chapter, which will present differences between the two in much more detail.

Tech Tip

There are hundreds of protocols in use, which can be very confusing because they appear to perform similar functions. IPv4 and IPv6 serve as a classic example of two protocols that seem to perform the same function but have many technical differences between them.

SMB

Server Message Block (SMB) is a protocol that is designed to provide shared access to services on a network. This includes files, printers, and similar resources. Microsoft has a version of SMB that is called *Common Internet File System (CIFS)*, which attempted to standardize a universal protocol for sharing files over the Internet. Today, CIFS is considered a dialect of SMB.

LDAP

Lightweight Directory Access Protocol (LDAP) is an industry standard for maintaining a distributed directory of services over an IP network. LDAP has sometimes been described as the "phone book" for your network because it enables you to find servers, workstations, printers, services, and other connected devices. LDAP is standardized via IETF standards.

SNMP

As its name suggests, *Simple Network Management Protocol (SNMP)* is used to manage a network. The SNMP Protocol has two sides: the agent and the management stations.

- A *managed device* is a network node that implements an SNMP interface to allow unidirectional (read-only) or bidirectional access to node-specific information.
- An *agent* is a network-management software module that resides on a managed device. An agent has local knowledge of management information and translates that information to or from an SNMP specific form.

The agent sends data about itself to the management station, which collects data from all the agents on the network. It should be noted that the protocol is not identical on each side; the agent sends alerts called traps and answers requests that were sent by the management station. The management station catches and decodes the traps, and it also requests specific information from the agent.

LLDP

The *Link Layer Discovery Protocol (LLDP)* is a vendor-neutral protocol standard described by the Institute of Electrical and Electronic Engineers (IEEE) that allows network devices to advertise and exchange information such as their MAC address and network function. Examples of network functions include client, switch, router, and wireless access point. The requirement of vendor neutrality ensures that any device that implements LLDP will be able to exchange information with any other device, even if different companies manufactured the two devices.

It took a long time for the committee to agree to a universal set of standards to determine the final design of LLDP, and during this time, many vendors developed their own proprietary version that closely matched the final vendor-neutral standard. Each major company wanted to be the first to implement the improved features associated with LLDP.

There are several proprietary versions of LLDP protocols. The most common discovery protocols are the Cisco Discovery Protocol (CDP), Cabletron Discovery Protocol (CDP), and Nortel Discovery Protocol (NDP). The Cisco Discovery Protocol (CDP) is used for CISCO network devices. Cabletron Discovery Protocol (CDP) is designed by Enterasys Networks and is used for some Ethernet switches. NDP is used for Nortel telephone networks. Microsoft developed the Link-Layer Topology Discovery protocols.

Microsoft Link-Layer Topology Discovery Protocols

The Microsoft version of the Link Layer Discovery Protocol (LLDP) is identified by two protocols in the **Properties** dialog box for a network connection: Link-Layer Topology Discovery Mapper I/O Driver and Link-Layer Topology Discovery Responder. These two protocols work together to discover other network devices and exchange information. The information exchanged allows network devices on the local area network to discover each other and automatically make some network configurations. For example, a Windows computer using LLTD can automatically configure itself to join an existing local area network. It can automatically discover the local area network router and will automatically create an Internet connection unless the router has security measures enabled.

With the release of Windows 8, Microsoft added two more protocols to the **Properties** dialog box for a network connection: Microsoft LLDP Protocol Driver and Microsoft Network Adapter Multiplexor Protocol. These properties were retained in Windows 10, as shown in Figure 20-2. Neither of these protocols are enabled by default, and in most cases, you will not need to enable either of them.

Microsoft LLDP Protocol Driver

The *Microsoft LLDP Protocol Driver* supports the exchange of information to the Microsoft data center network system. The Microsoft data center is a server that acts as a centralized data storage system.

Microsoft Network Adapter Multiplexor Protocol

The *Microsoft Network Adapter Multiplexor Protocol (MNAMP)* provides both load balancing and fail-over support. **Load balancing** is a process that occurs when a computer has multiple network adapters installed and balances or divides the

Figure 20-2 Windows 10 includes LLTD Mapper I/O Driver and LLDP Responder, which were introduced in Windows 8.

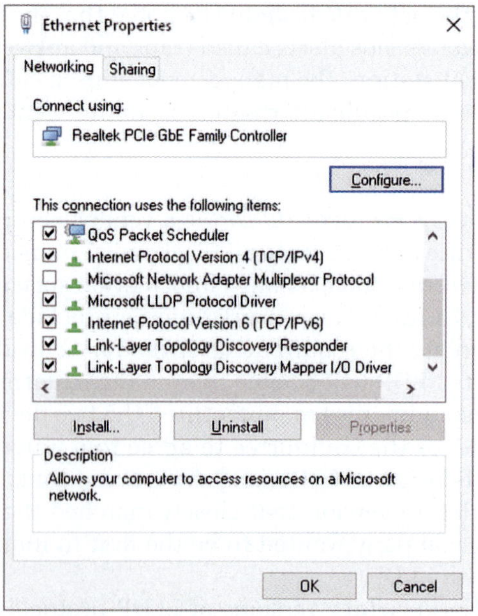

Goodheart-Willcox Publisher

exchange of packets among the multiple network adapters. The term **fail-over** is used by Microsoft to describe the process that occurs when one system fails, and another system takes over. When used with network adapters, fail-over means that when one network adapter card fails, another installed network adapter will take over the responsibilities of the failed adapter.

DHCP

A+ 1101: 2.4

Dynamic Host Configuration Protocol (DHCP) is an important protocol that enables a network server to assign IP addresses automatically when a machine connects to the network. Shared devices such as servers and printers are often configured with *static IP addresses*, meaning their addresses are set manually and do not change. Without DHCP, addresses would have to be assigned manually, which is not only time-consuming, but can also result in duplicate addresses. There will be much more about DHCP in a later chapter.

DNS

A+ 1101: 2.4

Recall from Chapter 19 that *Domain Name Service (DNS)* translates human-friendly names into IP addresses. Users communicate on networks such as the Internet using domain names, which would not be entirely possible without DNS. When you enter a website's domain name into a web browser, that name is converted to an IP address before communication begins.

UPnP

A+ 1102: 2.9

Similar to LLDP, *Universal Plug-and-Play (UPnP)* is a suite made up of protocols that exchange information with other devices such as printers, cameras, phones, web cameras, and similar devices. It allows these devices to connect to an existing computer, tablet, or network device with almost no effort by the user. The UPnP specification was developed by the UPnP Forum, which consists of hundreds of device manufacturers with the goal of enabling their devices to exchange information in a network with minimal user intervention.

SSDP

The *Simple Service Discovery Protocol (SSDP)* is another network protocol used for discovery of network services and device information. SSDP works in conjunction with the UPnP protocol and is intended for use in home- or small-office networks to detect Networked Home Entertainment Devices (NHED). SSDP was jointly developed by Microsoft and Hewlett-Packard.

NetBEUI

NetBEUI is an enhanced version of *NetBIOS*, which is software that provides basic services for the transfer of data between nodes, enabling a computer to communicate with many other computers. IBM and Microsoft jointly developed the NetBIOS Enhanced User Interface (NetBEUI) protocol for use in small network systems of 100 or fewer computers. The ideal small computer network system for NetBEUI consists of 25 or fewer computers, because if more than 25 computers are installed on a network using the NetBEUI protocol, the system starts to slow down significantly because of user activity.

NetBEUI is now obsolete as a network protocol and is no longer supported by Microsoft as of the release of Windows Vista. However, you can still see configuration options for NetBIOS in the **Advanced TCP/IP Settings** dialog box in all Windows versions, as shown in Figure 20-3.

Figure 20-3 Even though NetBIOS is basically obsolete, you can still find configuration options for it under the network adapter Advanced TCP/IP Settings dialog box.

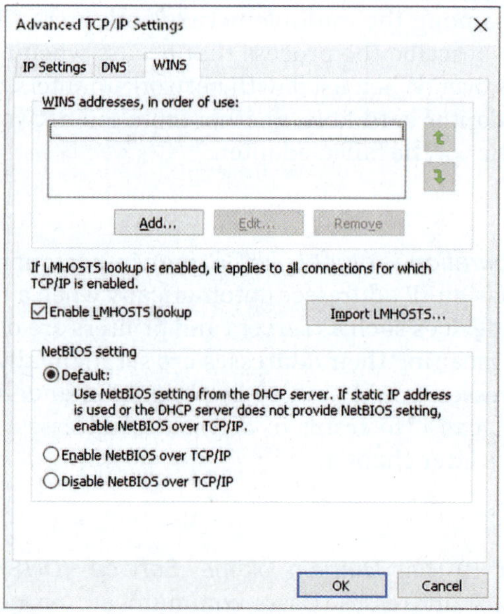

Goodheart-Willcox Publisher

FIP

Fast Infrared Protocol (FIP) is used for transmitting data from laptop computers to desktop PCs without the use of cables. This protocol governs the transmission of data by infrared light.

ATM

Asynchronous Transfer Mode (ATM) is a protocol used for simultaneously transmitting data, voice, and video over the same line. It rearranges the packets in such a way that the quality of the voice or video is not degraded when transmitted. Data is broken into packets containing 53 bytes each and communicates between any two nodes in the system at rates ranging from 1.5 Mbps to 622 Mbps.

FTP

File Transfer Protocol (FTP) is a protocol used for transferring computer files between a server and a client on a network or across the Internet. FTP is most often used to upload and download files. Using FTP, credentials are transmitted in clear-text. Many variations of FTP exist, such as secure FTP (sFTP), which is used to encrypt transmissions. Another FTP variation is Trivial File Transfer Protocol (TFTP), which uses UDP rather than TCP.

Telnet

Telnet is a protocol that provides bidirectional communication for remote devices such as a router or computer. It is part of a suite of protocols inside TCP/IP. It can be used to connect dissimilar systems or to program remote routers. Since Telnet is not encrypted, it is recommended that you only use it within a VPN.

SSH

Secure Shell (SSH) is an open-source secure communication protocol that operates similarly to Telnet, except all traffic is encrypted. As such, it is preferred over Telnet. SSH can be used on any operating system that supports TCP/IP, and while Microsoft does not directly support SSH due to its own security mechanisms, third-party software can be installed to provide SSH support.

POP3

Post Office Protocol version 3 (POP3) is an e-mail protocol that allows e-mail clients to connect and retrieve messages on the mail server and store the e-mail on the e-mail client. Messages are not stored on the mail server permanently. There will be more information about POP3 in a later chapter.

HTTP

Hypertext Transfer Protocol (HTTP) is likely the protocol you use the most, as it allows you to visit web pages. HTTP was developed by Tim Berners-Lee at CERN in 1989 and operates at the Application layer of the OSI Model. HTTP has been updated many times since its inception and functions using a client-server model that depends on a request-response protocol in which browsers issue a request, and a web server responds. A popular variant of HTTP is *S-HTTP (Secure Hypertext Transfer Protocol)*, which uses Transport Layer Security (TLS) to secure HTTP communication and is identified in a URL as https://.

IMAP

Internet Message Access Protocol (IMAP) is another e-mail protocol used by e-mail clients using a TCP/IP connection to connect and retrieve messages on the mail server. The messages are then stored on the e-mail client. There will be additional information about IMAP in a later chapter.

RDP

Remote Desktop Protocol (RDP) is a protocol developed by Microsoft for connecting two computers over a network. The protocol transmits across TCP/IP connections and provides security by encrypting packets. RDP operates by default on port 3389, which must be opened in a computer's firewall.

SMTP

Simple Mail Transfer Protocol (SMTP) is a protocol used for sending e-mail messages among mail servers and essentially functions as the opposite of POP3 and IMAP. Where those protocols are used to receive and download messages, SMTP is used to send and upload. However, all three protocols work together. There will be more information about SMTP in a later chapter.

AFP

Apple Filing Protocol (AFP) is a proprietary protocol from Apple used on macOS to access system files from non-Apple networks. It relies on TCP/IP ports 548 and 427 for communication. Older versions relied on AppleTalk for communication. As such, it was originally named AppleTalk Filing Protocol.

VoIP

Voice over IP (VoIP) is a protocol suite that supports voice communication over an existing network system. Originally, networks were designed to exchange text-based information, which does not require high-speed network systems. As network systems evolved, network media and equipment were designed to meet the requirements for high-resolution images, movies, and music. With the increase in network bandwidth, it became possible to move telephone communication to existing networks, rather than to keep two separate lines—one for networking and one for telephone conversations.

Telephone companies first combined telephone and network media before making VoIP available for residential users. Today, telephone and television services are combined with Internet access and provided by networks designed by service providers.

The big problem for ISPs was providing telephone conversations in real time. Text, movie, and television downloading does not require real-time packet transfers, but delays cannot be tolerated when exchanging network packets containing voice messages. A movie or television show can be downloaded over a long period of time and then played back, but a telephone conversation must exchange voice messages instantly without a delay between network packets.

VoIP was first introduced as an alternative telephone system for overseas calls because it was approximately half the cost of a traditional telephone connection. Later, it became very cost-effective to use as an everyday service, especially when combined by a service provider with other services, such as television and movies.

To accomplish real-time voice packet exchange, a new set of telephone protocols had to be developed to ensure quality of service. The protocol developed was aptly named *Quality of Service (QoS)* and assigns a higher priority to packets that contain time-sensitive information, such as voice.

Figure 20-4 shows a typical Windows network connection **Properties** dialog box. Notice that the QoS Packet Scheduler has been installed by default. The IPv4 and IPv6 protocols combine with QoS Packet Scheduler to provide telephone service through a computer for users with an Internet connection. To learn more about VoIP, visit the governmental Federal Communications Commission VoIP website.

Client for Microsoft Networks

The Client for Microsoft Networks is installed by default and is used to access resources on a Microsoft LAN. In the early days of networking, there were several different network operating systems, such as Novell NetWare and Apple AppleTalk. To communicate with these network systems and access resources, you needed to install a network client designed for the corresponding network. A NetWare client was required for Novell NetWare, and an AppleTalk client was required for Apple networks. Today, everything is compatible with Client for Microsoft Networks.

Ethernet

An **Ethernet network** is a computer network that communicates by broadcasting information to all the computers on the network. This is similar to a room full of

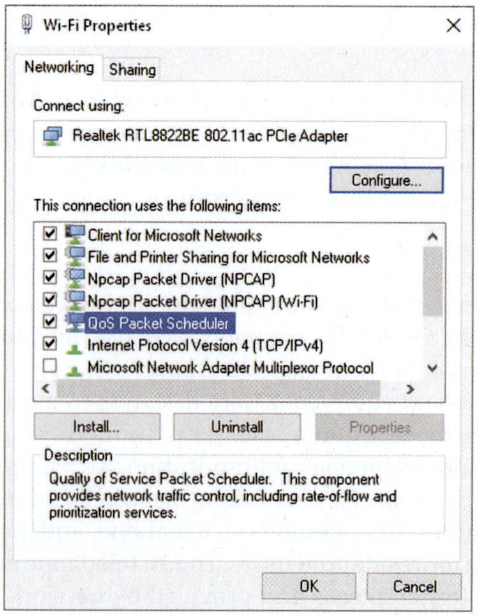

Goodheart-Willcox Publisher

Figure 20-4 The **Properties** dialog box for a local wireless connection displays the protocols and services for which a network adapter is configured. Notice that the QoS Packet Scheduler has been installed.

people talking and one person yelling, "Bob, do you hear me?" Everyone in the room hears Bob's name being called, but only Bob will reply if he is in the room.

In an Ethernet system, each computer on the network is given a unique name, which can be almost anything you desire, such as Station1, Accounting3, or even WildBill. Each computer in the system also has a unique six-byte hexadecimal address programmed into the network card inside the computer, such as C0 0B 08 1A 2D 2F. No other computer on the network has the same number. See Figure 20-5 for an example of a MAC address affixed to a network interface card. Using the hexadecimal number system to communicate would be difficult for humans. Therefore, a database automatically corresponds the unique number of the network card to the unique name given to the computer.

A typical session on an Ethernet network occurs similarly to the following scenario. Using the network, Bob wants to use Station 1 to send a message to Sue at Station 4. When Bob sends the message to Sue, he actually sends the message to all computers on the network, but only Sue's computer accepts the message, as illustrated in Figure 20-6.

Bob's computer transmits the first six bytes of data—the address of the target computer—followed by six additional bytes detailing Bob's computer's address. Then, the message data is sent, followed by the frame check sequence. When Sue's computer receives the transmission, it recognizes its own address in the first six bytes of data and accepts the packet. When the data packet is accepted, the next six bytes, which identify the sending PC, are decoded and stored for a return message. Next, the actual message is decoded, and the transmission is checked for errors.

Tech Tip

The act of sending a message or command to all nodes on the network is referred to as *broadcasting*. Sending a message or command to more than one node, but not to all nodes, is called *multicasting*.

Tech Tip

The term *Ethernet* is used to identify the type of network system communication and identifies a specific type of network protocol.

Goodheart-Willcox Publisher

Figure 20-5 All networked devices have a unique six-byte hexadecimal address programmed into the network interface card.

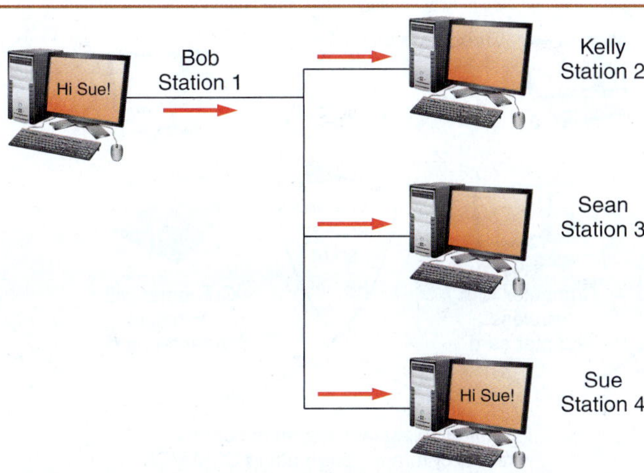

Goodheart-Willcox Publisher; (workstation icon) romvo/Shutterstock.com

Figure 20-6 A typical session on an Ethernet network includes one user sending a message to another. That message is actually sent to all computers on the network, but only the intended recipient's computer accepted the message.

If there are no errors detected, a return message is transmitted to Bob's PC to verify receipt of the message. If Bob's PC does not receive the return message, it will continue to retransmit the data packets until the return message is received.

CSMA/CD

One inherent problem with Ethernet communication is the collision of data being transmitted across the network. When two data packets collide on the network, they both become corrupted and cannot be delivered. Ethernet networks use a protocol called **Carrier Sense Multiple Access with Collision Detection (CSMA/CD)**, which is a media access method used to control and ensure the delivery of data.

The operation can be summarized with the following scenario. A workstation listens for data traffic on the network before transmitting data. When the network is silent, the workstation transmits data to another workstation. However, another station may choose the same lull in activity to transmit data, and if the data packets from the two stations collide on the network, each station waits for a random period of time, known as the **backoff interval**, before trying to retransmit the data. Since a typical network transmits thousands of data packets in one second, the backoff interval is normally a very small fraction of a second. Typically, collisions do not noticeably affect the performance of a properly installed network. However, a poorly designed network may operate very slowly due to excessive collisions.

CSMA/CA

Wireless communication uses another type of network access called **Carrier Sense Multiple Access with Collision Avoidance (CSMA/CA)**, which is a media access method that works much like CSMA/CD but tries to avoid, rather than detect, collisions. There are times when wireless networks cannot detect collisions, so the Ethernet method cannot be used as a media access method.

The major security concern with CSMA access methods is the possibility of a malicious node modifying the sequence number, making a sinkhole attack possible. A **sinkhole attack** occurs when a compromised node on the network attacks the network by advertising a fake update of the routing table.

A+ 1101: 2.2

Look at Figure 20-7. In the drawing, a wireless access point and two computers with wireless adapter cards are connected to a cabled network. The limited range of the wireless network cards does not allow the two computers to communicate directly with each other, so they can only communicate with the wireless access point, which controls all communication. To prevent both computers from

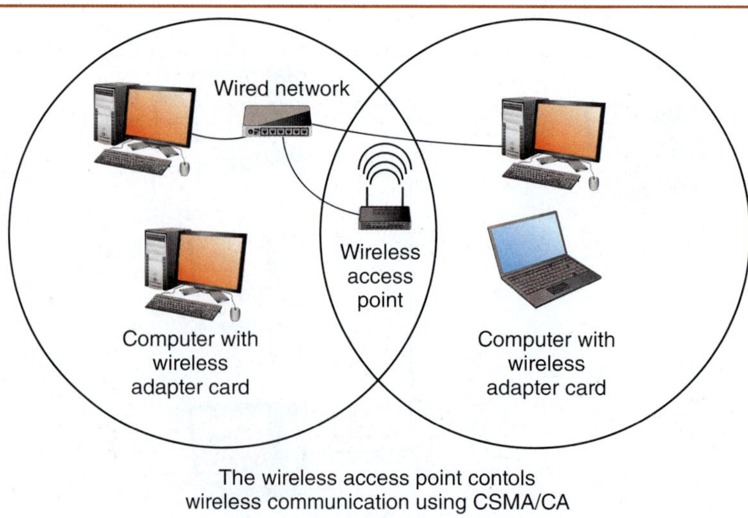

Figure 20-7 Wireless systems use collision avoidance to control communication.

Goodheart-Willcox Publisher; (workstation and laptop icons) romvo/Shutterstock.com; (WAP and hub icons) Vadim Ermak/Shutterstock.com

communicating with the wireless access point at the same time, causing collisions, each computer must first ask permission by sending a very small packet requesting permission to transmit before sending larger packets to the wireless access point. If the wireless access point is not busy communicating with the other computer on the wireless network, it responds by giving permission for communication.

When a wireless network uses a wireless access point to control communication, the wireless network is referred to as an *infrastructure design*. The wireless access point creates a communication bridge between the cable network and the wireless network.

20.2 Network Media

A+ 1101: 3.1

Network media is the means by which an electronic signal is transmitted. An electronic signal can be transmitted via cable-based or wireless media through a variety of network devices such as modems and routers. Generally, there are three types of cable-based media from which to choose: coaxial, twisted pair, and fiber-optic. There are also two types of wireless media: infrared and radio transmission. The radio transmission media breaks down into several different media types described in what is known as *standards*.

Digital Subscriber Line

Recall from Chapter 14 that *digital subscriber line (DSL)* is a technology that provides high-speed Internet access over telephone lines. There are several types of DSL, including High Data Rate Digital Subscriber Line (HDSL/HDSL2), which was the first DSL technology to use a higher-frequency spectrum of copper, twisted-pair cables. Most DSL today is Asymmetric Digital Subscriber Line (ADSL), for which the volume of data flow is greater in one direction than the other.

Cable Modem

Recall from Chapter 14 that a *cable modem* is a transceiver that allows existing cable television coaxial cable to be used for Internet access. Cable modems provide bidirectional data on hybrid fiber-coaxial cable (HFC) and coaxial cable and are standardized with IEEE 802.14. *Data Over Cable Service Interface Specification (DOCSIS)* is the standard for high-bandwidth data transfer over existing cable television networks.

Coaxial Cable

A+ 1101: 3.1

Coaxial cable, or *coax*, is a network cable consisting of a core conductor surrounded by an insulator, which is covered with a shield of either a solid foil or a braided wire layer to protect the cable core from stray electromagnetic interference, as illustrated in Figure 20-8. Coaxial cable is difficult to work with and relatively expensive when compared to other wiring media.

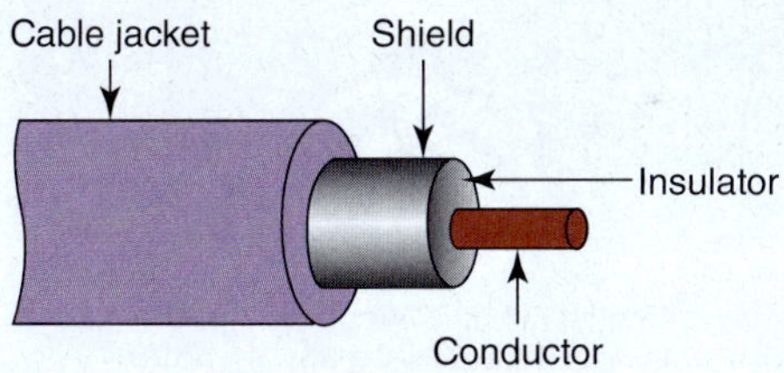

Goodheart-Willcox Publisher

Figure 20-8 A typical coaxial cable consists of a core conductor surrounded by an insulator, shield, and cable jacket.

Tech Tip

The term *coaxial cable* describes any cable that shares the same physical cable characteristics.

Tech Tip

The ANSI/TIA/EIA-570 Residential Telecommunications Cabling Standard specifies RG-6 coaxial cable for multimedia systems installed in homes.

Coaxial cable uses two main types of connectors: BNC and F-type. BNC is not threaded and simply makes a connection by pushing onto the connection post and then twisting to the right. F-type coaxial cable connectors have threads and make a much better connection, as shown in Figure 20-9. Coaxial cable is classified by its electrical characteristics and best application for its use.

Coaxial cable was designed to be used as media for radio systems, hence the acronym *RG*, which represents *Radio Guide*. The acronym *RG* is still used to classify the various types of coaxial cable. Commonly encountered types of coaxial cable are RG-6, RG-8, and RG-59.

RG-6

RG-6 is similar in design to RG-59, but there are sufficient differences that make RG-6 better suited for high-frequency systems such as cable TV (CATV) and satellite. RG-59 was originally used for CATV and satellite systems, but as more data throughput, more channels, and higher frequencies became standard, RG-6 became the replacement for RG-59.

RG-8

RG-8, also called *RG-8/U* or *thicknet*, coaxial cable is thicker when compared to RG-6, with a 2.17-mm core compared to the 1.0-mm core of RG-6. RG-8 also tends to have thicker insulation, which makes it suitable for outdoor environments, such as satellite dish connections. RG-8 has a 50-ohm resistance and is primarily used for amateur radio transmission signals. A thinner version named RG-8/X has similar characteristics to RG-8/U with a diameter similar to RG-59.

RG-59

RG-59 is still used for some low-frequency applications such as audio systems. It does not work well in applications involving gigahertz or higher frequencies, but it does work well for lower frequencies such as video and audio distribution inside a building or home. The following summarizes the applications for RG-59 and RG-6:

- RG-59 is used in analog video systems.
- RG-6 is used for digital video systems and supports higher frequencies than RG-59.

Figure 20-9 Coaxial cable uses two main types of connectors: BNC (unthreaded) and F-type (threaded).

Goodheart-Willcox Publisher

Twisted-Pair Cable

1101: 3.1 A+

Twisted-pair cable, also called *Ethernet cable*, consists of four pairs of conductors twisted around each other. It has been available for many years and was first used to carry voice transmissions by telephone companies, and today, twisted pair is the most common choice for network wiring. The two broad classifications of twisted pair are *shielded twisted pair (STP)* and *unshielded twisted pair (UTP)*. The difference between the two is that STP has a foil shield surrounding the conductors, which greatly reduces the effects of radio signal interference from other electrical sources in a similar manner that coaxial cable shielding helps shield the coaxial core conductor. Some specific types of STP, notably some Cat 5e versions, are rated so they can be buried underground. These types of cable often have *direct burial* or *DB* stamped on the side of the cable or included in the cable name. As its name implies, unshielded twisted pair does not have such a shield.

Tech Tip

Not all Cat 5 cable can reach the Cat 5e standard, but much of it can. The real difference is in the amount of cross talk permitted for Cat 5e compared to Cat 5. The difference is only slight.

While duplex Ethernet connections use all four pairs of conductors, common Ethernet networks use only two of the pairs in the cable. In a typical standard Ethernet installation, the extra two pairs can be thought of as spares; however, when only two pairs are used for the network, the remaining two pairs are often used for telephone communication.

The twists in the pairs are necessary to eliminate cross talk between the conductors. **Cross talk** is the imposition of a signal on one pair of conductors by another pair of conductors that run parallel to it. Twisting each pair inside the cable greatly reduces the effect of cross talk because when twisted, the two pairs are no longer parallel to each other.

Wire sizes range from #18 AWG to #26 AWG, with #24 AWG used most often. Recall that AWG stands for *American Wire Gauge*, a standard method for sizing wire. The categories or classifications of twisted-pair cable that follow are based on the physical design of the cable. The chart in Figure 20-10 summarizes the maximum frequency and maximum speed of the most used twisted-pair cable types.

Category 1

Category 1 cable consists of two twisted pairs. While this design was sufficient for electrical signals representing voice transmission, it is entirely inadequate for computer networks.

Category 2

Category 2 cable consists of four twisted pairs. This design was used in some early applications that were limited to 4 Mbps, but like its predecessor, it is not acceptable for today's networking systems, which run at a minimum of 10 Mbps.

Maximum Frequency and Speed by Cable Type

Category	Maximum Frequency	Maximum Speed
Cat 3	16 MHz	16 Mbps
Cat 4	20 MHz	20 Mbps
Cat 5	100 MHz	100 Mbps
Cat 5e	100 MHz	1,000 Mbps/1 Gbps
Cat 6	250 MHz	1,000 Mbps/1 Gbps
Cat 6a	500 MHz	10 Gbps
Cat 7	600 MHz	10 Gbps
Cat 8	1,600–2,000 MHz	40 Gbps

Goodheart-Willcox Publisher

Figure 20-10 Twisted-pair cable types are categorized by frequency and bandwidth ratings.

Category 3

Category 3 cable consists of four twisted pairs with three twists per foot. This can be found on legacy networks usually rated at 10 Mbps and 16 Mbps and in many legacy telephone installations.

Category 4

Category 4 cable consists of four twisted pairs. This cable handles 20 Mbps and is only a slight improvement over Cat 3 cable because it reduces cross talk and signal loss.

A+ 1101: 3.1

Category 5

Category 5 cable consists of four twisted pairs and offers a transmission speed of 100 Mbps. It is found commonly in 10BaseT and 100BaseT installations, which are IEEE network cable classifications that will be discussed later in this chapter.

A+ 1101: 3.1

Category 5e

Category 5e is an enhanced version of the Cat 5 standard that provides a little less signal loss. It is designed for Fast Ethernet and Gigabit Ethernet transmissions, which are also IEEE network cable classifications. The Cat 5e standard is not a new generation or advancement in cable technology; rather, it is an addendum to the existing standard to expand the qualities of existing Cat 5 cable.

A+ 1101: 3.1

Category 6

Category 6 cable supports frequencies as high as 250 MHz and data throughput of 1 Gbps. The high data throughput is achieved by using all four twisted pairs of wiring. See Figure 20-11 to see a physical comparison of Cat 5e and Cat 6 cable. Cat 6a is a new classification that operates at 500 MHz, reduces crosstalk, and can be used for 10 Gbps applications, but the maximum distance is reduced to 55 meters.

Category 7

Category 7 is not on the CompTIA A+ Certification Exams, but you may encounter it in the field. Category 7 cable provides data transmission speeds as high as 600 MHz and uses a different construction technique to achieve the higher transmission speeds. Cat 7 is constructed of four pairs of twisted conductors with a protective foil or a conductive braid surrounding each pair. In addition to the individual pair

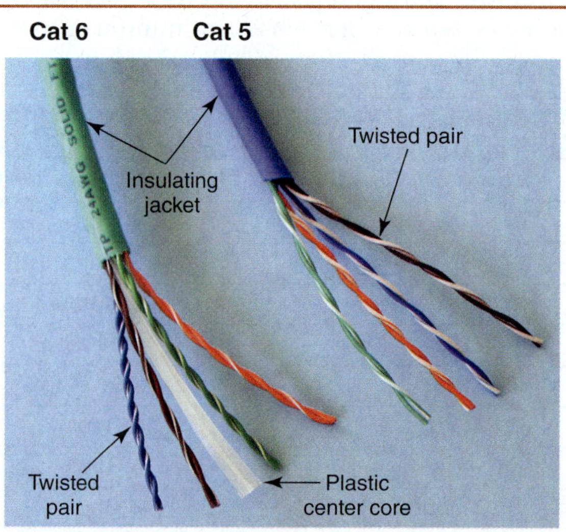

Figure 20-11 Cat 6 can support a much higher data rate than Cat 5 because of the physical design of the cable. Cat 6 has a plastic spacer separating the conductor pairs.

Goodheart-Willcox Publisher

shields, there is an overall protective foil or conductive braid surrounding the complete assembly. See Figure 20-12.

Category 8

Category 8 is also absent from the CompTIA A+ Certification Exams, but it represents the newest IEEE standard for copper Ethernet cable. Cat 8 includes shielding as part of the cable jacket, which results in a substantial increase in speed. Additionally, cable pairs are wrapped in foil to eliminate crosstalk without sacrificing data speed. Cat 8 provides data transmission speeds up to 2,000 MHz and a maximum speed of 40 Gbps.

Ethernet Twisted-Pair Wiring Standards

A+ 1101: 3.1

The two standard wiring configurations for Ethernet twisted-pair cable are 568A and 568B. There is no real electrical difference between the two standards, only the arrangement of the conductors in the pin areas. Compare the two standard arrangements for the 568A and 568B connectors in Figure 20-13.

Ethernet twisted-pair cables have two common classifications of assembly: straight-through and crossover. A straight-through cable is used to connect a computer with a hub, and a crossover cable is used to connect a computer with another

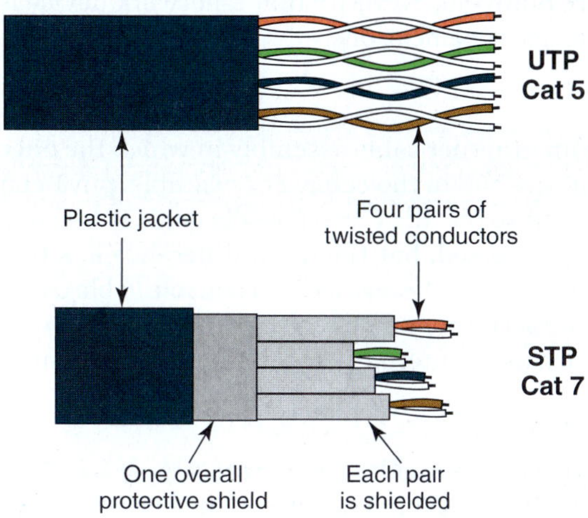

Goodheart-Willcox Publisher

Figure 20-12 Category 5 cable is constructed of four pairs of twisted conductors. Category 7 has a shield over each conductive pair and an overall shield between the plastic jacket and the individual pair shielding.

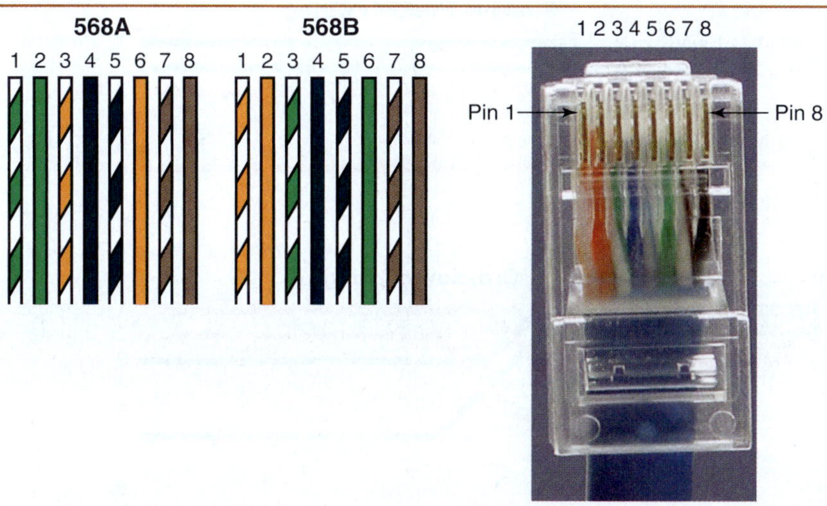

Goodheart-Willcox Publisher

Figure 20-13 The only difference between the 568A and 568B wiring standard is the arrangement of the conductors as identified by jacket color.

computer. The straight-through cable is constructed with each numbered pin connecting to the matching numbered pin on the opposite end of the cable, as shown in Figure 20-14. Notice that in the straight-through wire map, pin 1 connects to pin 1, pin 2 connects to pin 2, and so on. However, in the crossover wire map, pins 1 and 2 cross to pins 3 and 6, respectively.

When a two-workstation Ethernet network is configured, a crossover cable must be used for the network cards to communicate. A crossover cable has two pairs (four individual conductors) that are cross-connected, which allows a transmit signal from one computer to be sent to the receive pins of a network card on the other computer. This enables the computers to communicate without a hub. Crossover cables are only needed when connecting computers directly, not when a hub is used, because the circuitry at each access port crosses the connection internally. Additionally, network devices and Ethernet adapters that incorporate the Auto-MDIX feature do not require the use of a crossover cable.

Auto-MDIX

Automatic Medium-Dependent Interface Crossover (Auto-MDIX) is an electronic chip technology incorporated into the IEEE 1000BaseT (802.3ab) gigabit Ethernet standard for network devices such as switches and network adapters. The Auto-MDIX device automatically reassigns the pin functions so a crossover cable is no longer required for communication. Not all devices are Auto-MDIX compliant, especially if they are quite old. To verify that a network device is Auto-MDIX compliant, look at the device specifications.

Rollover Cable

A **rollover cable** is an Ethernet cable assembly in which the pin order is completely reversed on the opposite end of the cable. For example, pin 1 connects to pin 8, pin 2 connects to pin 7, and so on. The Cisco console cable is wired like a rollover cable. The pin numbers are reversed, but the main difference is a rollover cable uses an RJ-45 connector on each end, whereas a Cisco console cable uses an RJ-45 connector on one end and a DB-9 serial connector on the other. Rollover cables connect a PC to a network device, such as a router, which can then be programmed by the PC.

A+ 1101: 2.2

Power over Ethernet (PoE)

Power over Ethernet (PoE) provides a means to supply small amounts of electrical power (typically 13 watts at 48 volts) to network devices such as a camera, IP phone,

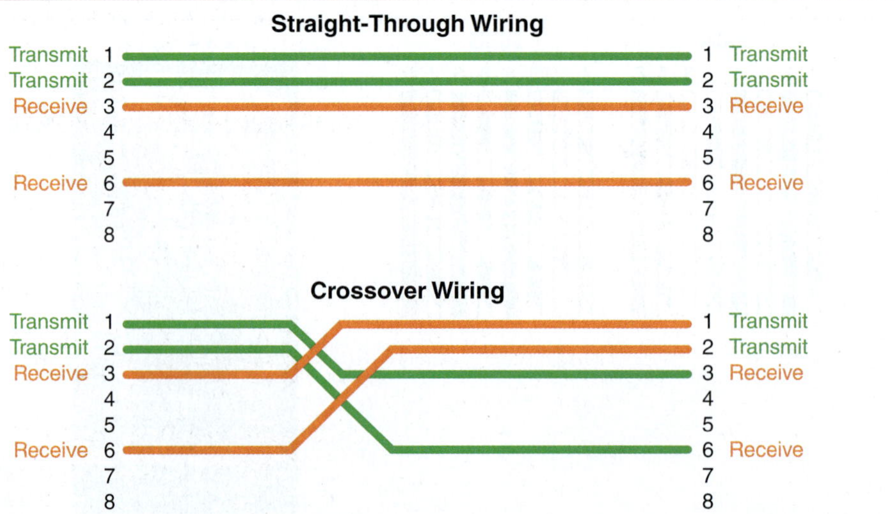

Goodheart-Willcox Publisher

Figure 20-14 A crossover cable switches the position of cable pair 1 and 2 with cable pair 3 and 6.

wireless access point, or speakers, via Ethernet connection. The cable used for PoE must be rated as Cat 5 or better. Two of the four cable pairs are used for network communication and one pair is used to supply the electrical power. The advantages of PoE include the following:

- Time and cost savings of not having to incur the expense of electrical power cabling for the device
- Flexibility to place devices such as IP cameras and wireless access points wherever they are most needed
- Ability to protect network equipment from overload
- Ability to be backed up by a UPS
- Scalability due to simple installation and distribution
- Ability to add PoE capability to non-PoE devices with *injectors*

Another more electronically sophisticated method is used for gigabit networks in which all cable pairs are used to carry network communication. Electrical power is supplied using two of the existing cable pairs that provide network communication. To learn more about the electronic aspect of PoE, visit the Power over Ethernet website.

A common PoE application is for providing building and area security when electrical power is not readily available. Using PoE is very cost-effective compared to installing electrical circuits to power devices such as cameras.

Another common application involves the incorporation of PoE switches into the network. *PoE switches* have built-in Ethernet injection, meaning the PoE switch is able to detect PoE-compatible network devices and enable power for those devices automatically.

Fiber-Optic Cable

1101: 2.7, 3.1 A+

Fiber-optic cable, often referred to as *fiber*, contains a glass or plastic center used to carry light, as shown in Figure 20-15. The electronic signals transmitted from the computer are converted to a signal consisting of a fluctuating beam of light, carried to the destination, and converted back to an electrical signal. The use of fiber-optics has many advantages over conventional copper wire systems, including increased security, greater resistance to corrosion, immunity to lightning strikes, longer transmission distances per segment, and decreased weight. Its biggest disadvantages are greater expense and the increased difficulty of field installations. Due to its increased security and speed, fiber-optic cable is ideal for network backbones.

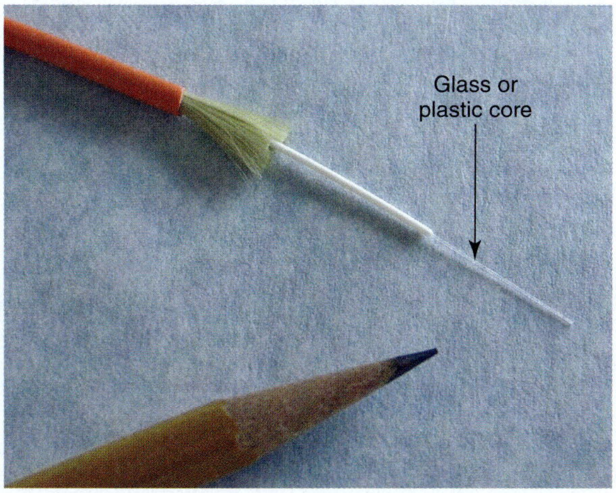

Goodheart-Willcox Publisher

Figure 20-15 Fiber-optic cable contains a glass or plastic core, which is used as a conduit for light.

The broad classifications of fiber-optic cable based on the diameter of the core are multimode and single-mode. In general, multimode fiber-optic cable has a larger core diameter than single-mode fiber-optic cable. The core diameter has a direct relationship to the distance the cable can carry light signals. The larger the core diameter, the greater the signal loss, or ***attenuation***. Single-mode fiber-optic cable has a much smaller core diameter than multimode cable, resulting in single-mode fiber-optic cable being able to carry light signals farther than multimode fiber-optic cable.

Fiber-optic core dimensions are measured in micrometers (μm), or millionths of a meter. The size of a fiber-optic cable is expressed in two numerical values separated by a slash. For example, a fiber-optic cable identified as 62.5/125 indicates that the core diameter is equal to 62.5 micrometers and the overall core and cladding diameter is 125 micrometers. Typical multimode core dimensions are 50/125, 62.5/125, and 100/140, though 100/140 is an older technology and is not encountered very often. A typical single-mode core is 8.3/125.

A+ 1101: 3.1

There are many different fiber-optic cable connectors in use, but the five most common connector styles are Straight Tip (ST), Subscriber Connector (SC), Fiber Channel (FC), Lucent Connector (LC), and Mechanical Transfer Registered Jack (MT-RJ). Figure 20-16 illustrates the general shape of each type of connector. Be sure you can identify fiber-optic connector types, as this is frequently tested on the CompTIA A+ Certification Exams.

The ST connector must be pushed directly in and then twisted to the right to lock in place. Similarly, the SC connector pushes directly in and snaps into place. Both connectors offer a quick way to connect and disconnect a fiber-optic cable. The FC style is designed with screw threads and offers superior connection strength when compared to the other connectors in Figure 20-16.

The LC style of connector has a smaller form factor when compared to SC, ST, and FC styles. LC is designed for a single cable but can be modified to form an LC duplex connector to accommodate two cables. The pair of LC connectors are held together using a clip and thus form a duplex connection.

The MT-RJ style connector is similar to the shape of a copper-cable RJ connector but is unique in that it incorporates two fiber cables into one assembly without the use of a clip. The MT-RJ has a small form factor and is considered a duplex connector like the LC duplex. To learn more about network cables and connectors visit the Black Box Network Services website.

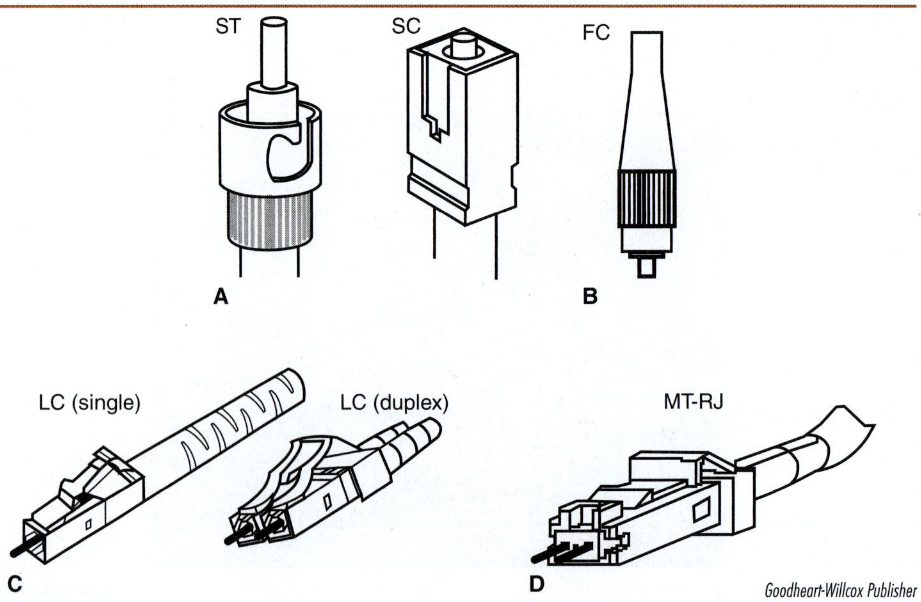

Figure 20-16 Five common fiber-optic cable connectors are ST, SC (A), FC (B), LC single and duplex (C), and MT-RJ (D).

Often used in fiber-optic applications, an **optical network terminal (ONT)** is a device that converts analog fiber-optic signals from the fiber-optic cable into digital signals. This process makes it so devices like a router can understand fiber-optic signals. If you have fiber optics to the premises, then an ONT is required to convert the fiber-optic signal so your router can understand and route the traffic. ONTs are considered *customer-premises equipment (CPE)*, meaning they are kept at the customer's location rather than the service provider's location. Usually the ONT is connected to your gateway router, though some Internet service providers package the ONT with a router in the same box.

A+ 1101: 2.2

Wireless

A+ 1101: 2.2

Wireless media for local area networks are based on the IEEE 802.11 standard. The two common wireless modes are ad hoc and infrastructure. Recall from Chapter 13 that *ad hoc* refers to a peer-to-peer configuration in which all wireless devices can connect directly to each other, such as a wireless laptop connecting to a PC that has an installed wireless device, and *infrastructure* refers to a network in which a wireless access point (WAP) is used to control the flow of data between each wireless device in the network. A wireless access point is also used to provide a connection to and from a wireless network to a wired network system. The wireless media is assigned specific radio frequencies as listed in Figure 20-17.

Be aware that some wireless network card manufacturers exceed the standard data rate set by the IEEE organization. However, 802.11ac is the most commonly used current wireless standard, though the exact data rate varies quite a bit.

A+ 1101: 2.2

IEEE Specifications by Wireless Standard

IEEE Standard	Radio Frequency	Frequency Range	Maximum Data Rate	Approximate Range	Comments
802.11a	5 GHz	5.15 GHz–5.825 GHz	54 Mbps	50 m	Obsolete
802.11b	2.4 GHz	2.4 GHz–2.4832 GHz	11 Mbps	100 m	N/A
802.11g	2.41 GHz	2.4 GHz–2.4835 GHz	54 Mbps	50 m	Compatible with 802.11b
802.11n	2.4 GHz or 5 GHz	2.4 GHz–2.4835 GHz or 5.15 GHz–5.825 GHz	300 Mbps	200 m	Compatible with 802.11a, 802.11b, and 802.11g
802.11ac	5 GHz	5.15 GHz–5.825 GHz	1.3 Gbps	60 m	Compatible with 802.11a, 802.11b, 802.11g, and 802.11n
802.11ax	2.4 GHz, 5 GHz, or 6 GHz	1 GHz–7.125 GHz	574 Mbps–9.6 Gbps	Up to 240 m	Compatible with 802.11a, 802.11b, 802.11g, and 802.11n

Goodheart-Willcox Publisher

Figure 20-17 Wireless media is assigned to certain frequencies based on the IEEE standard that applies to it.

A+ 1101: 2.2

Software-Defined Networking

Software-defined networking (SDN) is an approach to networking that uses software-based controllers or application programming interfaces (APIs) to communicate with underlying hardware infrastructure and direct traffic on a network. The use of a virtual machine to host various operating systems is a widespread implementation of SDN, though it can be accomplished on many levels. In some implementations, the entire network—all devices, all services, etc.—are virtualized. SDN offers a number of advantages over traditional network management. For example, with all devices being controlled via software, management can be accomplished from a single console. It also allows for increased flexibility and ease of making changes.

A+ 1101: 3.1

Plenum and PVC

Not all cables are approved for installation in a commercial building in the area referred to as the *plenum*, which is the space above a ceiling or raised floor and is designed to carry return air in a closed air-conditioning system. Cables installed in the plenum space are required to be *plenum-rated*, meaning if the cable burns, it will not give off harmful gases. The protective jackets and insulators of many cables are constructed from polyvinyl chloride (PVC), which produces deadly gases when burned. Thus, any cable that contains PVC cannot be installed in any building plenum area.

IEEE Network Cable Classifications

The Institute of Electrical and Electronic Engineers (IEEE) classifies network cables according to their abilities and physical descriptions. Network cables are classified with a short description that summarizes how a cable can be used. Take the 100BaseT classification as an example. The "100" represents the speed of transmission—in this case, 100 megabits per second. Note that the speed is rated in bits, not bytes. The "Base" refers to *baseband*, meaning data travels across the network one message at a time rather than in multiple simultaneous messages. When the last character or characters are letters, they provide specific information about the cable used. For example, when the last letter is a *T*, the name denotes twisted pair with a maximum distance of 100 meters. An *F* represents fiber-optic cable. The table in Figure 20-18 lists the specifications of some common cables.

A+ 1102: 2.7

Internet of Things (IoT)

The *Internet of Things (IoT)* refers to the incorporation of embedded technology into nontraditional devices for communication over a network. In today's world, IoT is

Figure 20-18 IEEE classifies network cables according to their abilities and physical descriptions.

IEEE Network Cable Classifications

Category	Classification	Data Rate	Minimum Segment Length	Maximum Segment Length	Cable Type
10 Mbps	10BaseT	10 Mbps	0.5 m	100 m	Cat 3, 4, and 5
Fast Ethernet	100BaseT4	100 Mbps	0.6 m	100 m	Cat 3, 4, and 5
Fast Ethernet	100BaseTX	100 Mbps	0.6 m	100 m	Cat 5
Gigabit Ethernet	1000BaseT	1,000 Mbps	0.6 m	100 m	Cat 5e
10 Gigabit Ethernet	10GBaseT	10 Gbps	0.6 m	55 m	Cat 6
10 Gigabit Ethernet	10GBaseT	10 Gbps	0.6 m	100 m	Cat 6a

Goodheart-Willcox Publisher

everywhere. For example, smart thermostats, automated vehicles with Wi-Fi connectivity, smartwatches, and intelligent personal assistant services all fall under the IoT umbrella. There are many variations of IoT including Internet of Medical Things or Internet of Military Things (IoMT), Industrial Internet of Things (IIoT), and Ocean of Things (OoT), which is a defense-led project using floating sensors to monitor naval traffic. In general, there are four basic groups or types of IoT components:

- **Things**: various devices, including sensors, which can be independent or part of some other device
- **Network**: network used for IoT to connect the various components
- **Computer Backend**: systems that provide computing power to process data and, in some cases, execute command and control functions
- **Interface**: applications for user interaction, often via application programming interface

There are a number of commercially available *IoT platforms*, which are software programs that provide a variety of functions that are required by IoT systems. This functionality will often include provisioning and management of endpoints, protocol communication and conversion, data processing, and even data analytics. Common IoT cloud platforms include AWS IoT, Google Cloud IoT, Microsoft Azure IoT Suite, GE Predix, Cisco IoT cloud, Oracle IoT platform, and Intel IoT.

Regardless of the application, IoT can use a wide range of protocols. Wi-Fi and 5G are commonly used, as is Zigbee, which specifically supports mesh networks of low-power devices. RuBee is another networking protocol sometimes used with IoT that operates on low bandwidth but is not impeded by obstacles such as water or steel, making it ideal for some environments. Similarly, Z-Wave also supports low-powered mesh networks and is frequently used with IoT devices. Message Queue Telemetry Transport (MQTT), a messaging protocol, is mostly used for remote monitoring in IoT and connects devices and networks with applications and middleware. Its primary task is to acquire data from many devices and transport it to the IT infrastructure.

While Linux and Android are sometimes used as IoT operating systems, there are a number of operating systems used specifically for IoT. *Real-Time Operating System (RTOS)* and *Contiki* are often used for IoT devices. The Contiki operating system was specifically developed for systems that have low power and limited memory, as it is not resource-intensive. It is often used for street lighting, radiation monitoring, and smart cities. *TinyOS* is an open-source operating system often used in wireless sensors. The programming language used with TinyOS is nesC, a variation of C.

20.3 Networking Tools

There are a variety of networking tools with which you need to be familiar. Not all tools are made the same, and the exact construction can vary quite a bit between different manufacturers. Some important tools include cable crimpers, cable cutters, cable strippers, punch down tools, cable tracers, tone generators, loopback plugs, Wi-Fi analyzers, and network taps.

Cable Crimper

1101: 2.8 A+

A **cable crimper** is a tool designed to crimp (squeeze) an RJ-45 connector onto the end of a twisted-pair cable, thus making the electrical connections between each of the eight conductors and the connector, Figure 20-19. The individual RJ-45 connector pins align with each conductor of the twisted-pair cable, Figure 20-20. The crimper presses the pins through the insulation and into direct contact with the copper core of each wire, Figure 20-21. A standard crimper usually incorporates a cable stripper and a cable cutter.

Figure 20-19 A cable crimper is designed to crimp an RJ-45 cable connector onto the end of a twisted-pair cable.

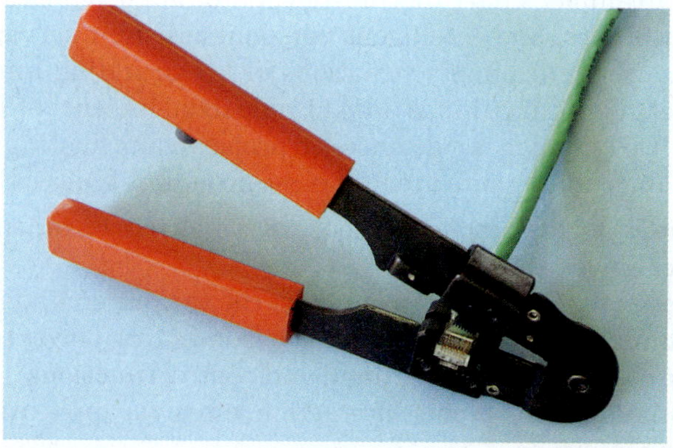

Goodheart-Willcox Publisher

Figure 20-20 The top view of an RJ-45 connector shows the individual connector pins that align with the individual wires.

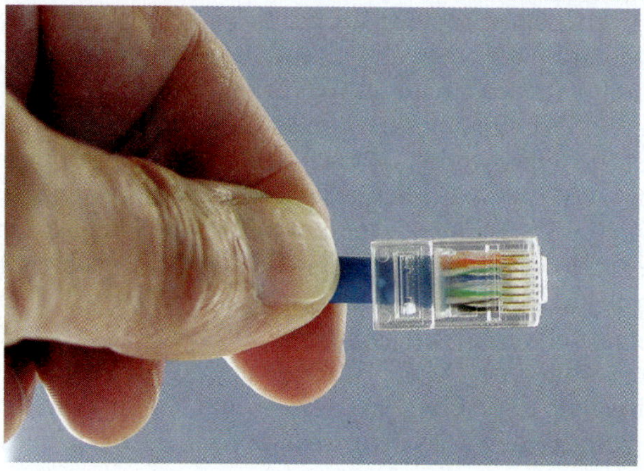

Goodheart-Willcox Publisher

Figure 20-21 The RJ-45 connector pins are pressed through the cable insulation and into direct contact with the individual wires.

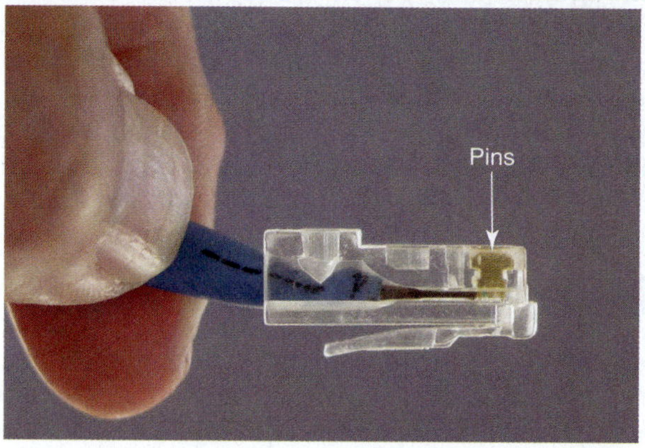

Goodheart-Willcox Publisher

A+ 1101: 2.8

Cable Cutter and Cable Stripper

Figure 20-22 shows two more tools commonly associated with cables, a cable cutter and cable stripper. A cable cutter can cut through a variety of cable types to a desired length, including twisted-pair and coaxial cable. The cable stripper shown in Figure 20-22 is designed to remove the outer jacket from a cable to expose the individual conductors within. The overall cable jacket is first removed using a cable stripper, but there is no need to remove the insulation from the individual wires.

Punch Down Tool

1101: 2.2, 2.8, 3.1 A+

A **punch down tool** is a networking tool used for inserting twisted-pair conductors into a slotted post called an insulation displacement connector (IDC). An **insulation displacement connector (IDC)** is an electrical connector that connects to the conductor of an insulated cable by a method that forces a sharpened blade through the insulation. This means there is no need to strip the individual pairs of any insulation as the insertion results in the connector being *cold-welded* to the conductor. IDCs are found on patch panels and punch down blocks. See Figure 20-23 for an example of both a punch down tool and an IDC. A punch down tool is also used for inserting wires into RJ-45 *keystone modules*, which snap into a keystone wall plate, allowing RJ-45 cables to be terminated at wall outlets.

The punch down tool is an *impact tool* because it has an internal spring-loaded mechanism that snaps the wire into place in the IDC. The spring mechanism ensures that the required pressure is reached for inserting the wire. The tool not only inserts the wire into the slot, but it also trims excess conductor. The tip of the tool is referred to as a *blade* and comes in two standard sizes: 66 and 110. These numbers represent punch down block types.

Cable Tracer and Tone Generator

1101: 2.8 A+

A cable tracer and tone generator work in tandem to allow a technician to trace the exact location of cable runs inside walls, ceilings, or under floors to identify unmarked cables. The **tone generator** attaches to one end of a cable and transmits an analog or digital signal through the cable, and the **cable tracer** receives the signal transmitted through a cable and produces a tone if it is near the cable. When a cable fault is encountered, the signal ends or changes pitch.

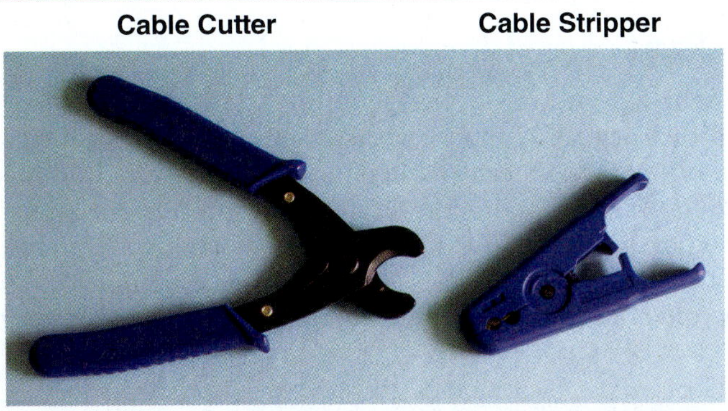

Goodheart-Willcox Publisher

Figure 20-22 Cable cutters and cable strippers are commonly associated with twisted-pair cabling.

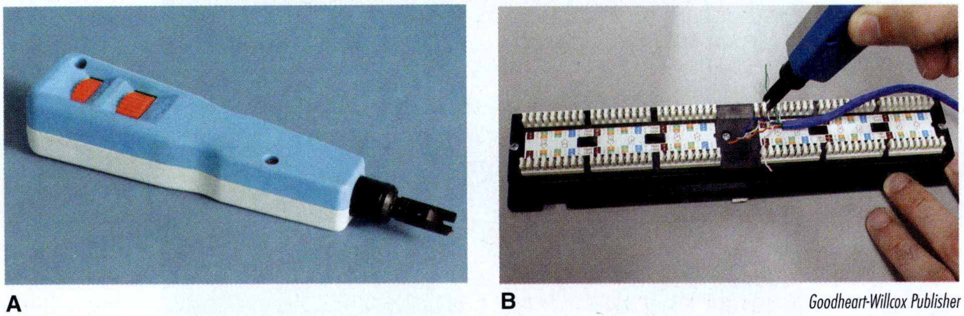

Goodheart-Willcox Publisher

Figure 20-23 A punch down tool inserts twisted-pair conductors into a special termination block called an IDC. The tip of the punch down tool inserts the wire into the connector and trims off excess wire (A). The punch down tool inserts the insulated individual conductors into IDCs on patch panels and punch down blocks (B).

A+ 1101: 2.8

Cable Tester

A **cable tester** is a tool used to assess newly made and existing network cables. The complete cable tester consists of two devices: master and remote. The master is a battery-equipped device that transmits a signal on each cable wire, and the remote receives the signals. A light flashes for each cable wire, indicating it is properly wired, as shown in Figure 20-24. Some testers are equipped with BNC connections as well as RJ-45 and RJ-11 ports so they can test twisted-pair and coaxial cable as well as telephone cable.

A+ 1101: 2.8

Loopback Plug

A **loopback plug** is used to assess an Ethernet network card by simulating a network. The plug or cable is inserted into the RJ-45 port on the network adapter and completes the electrical circuit between the *transmit* and *receive* pins. The **ping 127.0.0.1** command is then issued at the command prompt, and you observe the link and activity lights on the network adapter. A normal network card periodically sends out network packets to probe the network for other devices, thus generating network activity.

A+ 1101: 2.8

Wi-Fi Analyzer

A *Wi-Fi analyzer* is a software-based tool that detects Wi-Fi networks, calculates signal strength, and assists in identifying potential risks or threats. Hardware-based analyzers are also available, but a software-based tool can be loaded into most systems, including mobile devices. A good example of such software is a network analyzer smartphone app. These apps are made to identify interference and help you optimize placement of your routers, repeaters, antennas, and other essential wireless networking components.

A+ 1101: 2.8

Network Tap

A *network tap* is an external device that monitors traffic on a network. Taps are often dedicated hardware devices with four ports: two network ports and two monitoring ports. The network ports connect to two nodes at each end of the cable being monitored collect traffic from each direction, and the monitoring ports copy this traffic to an attached monitoring device. The incorporation of a network tap enables administrators to view traffic on the network easier, prevent network downtime by redirecting the traffic flow, and obtain copies of traffic in the event of an attack or inside threat.

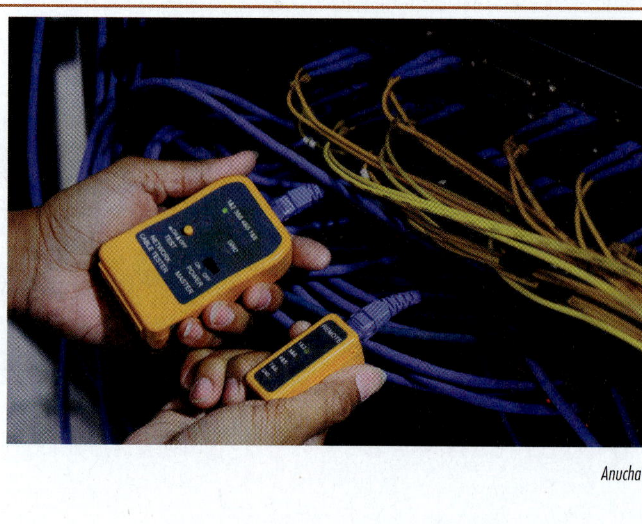

Figure 20-24 A cable tester is used to check the wiring assembly of a newly created network cable.

Anucha Cheechang/Shutterstock.com

Chapter Summary

20.1 How Networks Communicate

- Data is divided into smaller units called packets or frames. A packet is a small unit of data into which larger amounts are divided for passage through a network. Like an envelope going through the mail system, each packet contains the address of the sender and the intended recipient. When all the packets have arrived at their destination, they are reassembled to form a complete message or file.
- Data transmitted on a network is broken down into packets or frames, which contain the address of the PC sending the data, the address of the intended recipient, an error-checking program, and a sequence number.
- In a typical data frame, the first six bytes represent the *network interface card (NIC)* to which the data is being sent. The second six bytes represent the NIC that is transmitting the data.
- Attached to each packet of data is a sequence number. The sequence number ensures the data will be reassembled in the exact order they were transmitted.

20.2 Network Media

- Coaxial cable consists of a core conductor surrounded by an insulator.
- Coaxial cable is difficult to work with and relatively expensive when compared to some of the other wiring media and uses two main types of connectors: BNC and F-type.
- Twisted-pair cable has been available for many years and was first used to carry voice transmissions by telephone companies. Today, twisted pair is the most common choice for network wiring.
- The two standard wiring configurations for Ethernet twisted-pair cable are 568A and 568B.
- Fiber-optic cable contains a glass or plastic center used to carry light.
- Software-defined networking (SDN) is an approach to networking that uses software-based controllers or application programming interfaces (APIs) to communicate with underlying hardware infrastructure and direct traffic on a network.
- Wireless media for local area networks are based on the IEEE 802.11 standard.
- The IEEE classifies network cable according to abilities and physical descriptions.
- The *Internet of Things (IoT)* refers to the incorporation of embedded technology into nontraditional devices for communication over a network.

20.3 Networking Tools

- A cable crimper is a tool designed to crimp an RJ-45 connector onto the end of a twisted-pair cable.
- A cable cutter can cut through a variety of cable types such as twisted-pair and coaxial cable. A cable stripper is designed to remove the outer jacket from a cable.
- A punch down tool is used for inserting twisted-pair conductors into a slotted post called an insulation displacement connector (IDC).
- A cable tracer and tone generator both allow a technician to trace the exact location of cable runs inside walls, ceilings, or under floors to identify unmarked cables.
- A cable tester is used to test newly made and existing network cables.

- A loopback plug is used to test an Ethernet network card.
- A network tap is an external device that monitors traffic on a network.

Review Questions

1. Explain the communication process between networks.
2. What does a typical frame of data contain?
3. What three things affect the time it takes for data to arrive at its destination?
4. Which protocol is designed to allow network devices to advertise and exchange information?
5. Which protocol is associated with transferring data using infrared light?
6. What is the purpose of the QoS protocol?
7. List and describe three types of network cable.
8. Where would you *most likely* encounter RG-6, RG-8, and RG-59 coaxial cable?
9. What are the two broad classifications of twisted pair?
10. What is the purpose of the foil shield in STP cable?
11. In twisted-pair cable, what is the purpose of twisting conductors into pairs?
12. Which network media is likely to be the most secure from eavesdropping devices?
13. What are the major advantages of fiber-optic cable systems?
14. What are the major disadvantages of fiber-optic cable systems?
15. What technology replaces the need for a crossover cable?
16. You want to install a remote web camera outside a business for security purposes but there is no available electrical power at the outside location. What feature or specification would you look for concerning the camera?
17. Summarize the function of a cable crimper, cable cutter, and cable stripper.
18. What is the purpose of a punch down tool?
19. What is the purpose of a loopback plug?
20. Describe the function of a cable tracer and tone generator.

Sample A+ Exam Questions

1. Which category of twisted-pair cable contains a plastic spacer?
   A. Category 4
   B. Category 5
   C. Category 5e
   D. Category 6
2. What protocol is used for transmitting data from laptop computers to desktop PCs without the use of cables?
   A. FIP
   B. NetBIOS
   C. SIP
   D. NetBEUI
3. Which protocol combines the function of a computer network with the telephone system?
   A. RDP
   B. VoIP
   C. TCP/IP
   D. ATM

4. _____ provides transmission speeds as high as 600 MHz and employs a protective or conductive braid around each pair.
   A. Category 5
   B. Category 5e
   C. Category 6
   D. Category 7
5. What is the name of the network adapter feature or specification that enables a network administrator to turn on a computer remotely?
   A. QoS
   B. Wake-on-LAN
   C. VoIP
   D. RDP
6. Which cable type is the most susceptible to radio interference?
   A. UTP
   B. STP
   C. Fiber-optic
   D. RG-6
7. What feature allows for automatic security configuration between two wireless devices?
   A. WPA
   B. WEP
   C. WPS
   D. Adapter teaming
8. The unintentional transfer of data between individual wires inside a network cable, such as Cat 5e, is called _____.
   A. impedance
   B. attenuation
   C. cross talk
   D. broadcast storm
9. Cat 5e provides less signal _____ than Cat 5 cable.
   A. strength
   B. loss
   C. quality
   D. cost
10. Identify the following connector:
   A. SC
   B. ST
   C. RJ-45
   D. BNC

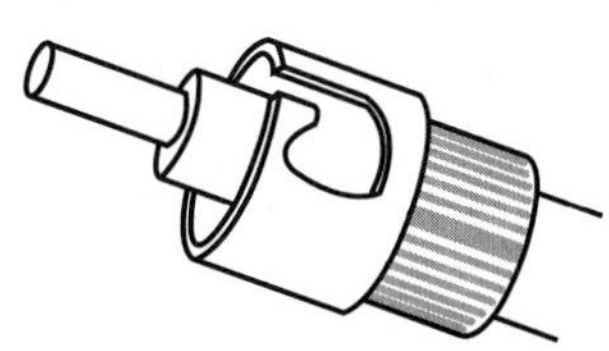

Chapter 21

Managing Networks

Learning Outcomes

21.1 Discuss considerations made during network administration.
21.2 Differentiate among permission types.
21.3 Identify roles used to organize networks.
21.4 Compare and contrast server roles.
21.5 Identify features of Windows Server.
21.6 Recall the general procedure used for unattended installations.
21.7 Identify the most common RAID levels and their characteristics.
21.8 Summarize methods used to troubleshoot basic network issues.

A+ Certification Exam Objectives

The following A+ Certification Exam Objectives are covered in this chapter.

Exam 220-1101

1.0 Mobile Devices

- 1.4 Given a scenario, configure basic mobile-device network connectivity and application support.

2.0 Networking

- 2.4 Summarize the services provided by networked hosts.
- 2.6 Compare and contrast common network configuration concepts.

3.0 Hardware

- 3.3 Given a scenario, select and install storage devices.
- 3.6 Given as scenario, deploy and configure multifunction devices/printers and settings.

5.0 Hardware and Network Troubleshooting

- 5.7 Given a scenario, troubleshoot problems with wired and wireless networks.

Exam 220-1102

1.0 Operating Systems

- 1.1 Identify basic features of Microsoft Windows editions.
- 1.2 Given a scenario, use the appropriate Microsoft command line tool.
- 1.4 Given a scenario, use the appropriate Microsoft Windows 10 Control Panel utility.
- 1.6 Given a scenario, configure Microsoft Windows networking on a client/desktop.
- 1.8 Explain common OS types and their purposes.

2.0 Security

- 2.1 Summarize various security measures and their purposes.
- 2.2 Compare and contrast wireless security protocols and authentication methods.

- 2.5 Given a scenario, manage and configure basic security settings in the Microsoft Windows OS.
- 2.6 Given a scenario, configure a workstation to meet best practices for security.
- 2.7 Explain common methods for securing mobile and embedded devices.

3.0 Software Troubleshooting

- 3.2 Given a scenario, troubleshoot common personal computer (PC) security issues.

Key Terms

Access Control List (ACL)
administrative shares
answer file
deployment image
domain
domain user account
fault tolerance
group
intrusion detection system (IDS)
intrusion prevention system (IPS)
local user account
network administration
network administrator
redundant array of independent disks (RAID)
Security Accounts Manager (SAM)
Security Identifier (SID)
share
unattended installation
user
Windows Automated Installation Kit (WAIK)

Overview

This chapter provides an overview of the fundamentals of network administration, the central focus of which is network security and coordination of shared resources on the network. It is important to have a basic understanding of network operations when troubleshooting PCs that are connected to a network, because you must be able to determine if the problem is PC- or network-related. This chapter is not intended to prepare you for the Network+ Certification Exam, but it will help you begin the process of achieving such additional certification if you desire.

Network administration in the corporate world is a vast subject requiring years of study and experience, and it can take years to achieve competency in a single networking software package. However, home and small-business networks are becoming more popular every day, particularly with the rise in remote work in a post-pandemic world, so it is imperative that you have a basic understanding of both peer-to-peer and centralized networks.

This chapter also introduces the basic concepts of Windows Server. A complete understanding of Windows Server administration would take a complete course of study. This introduction serves as an overview of the important elements needed as a PC technician.

A+ Note

The CompTIA A+ Certification Exams will evaluate your basic knowledge of network administration. You should be prepared to answer questions about system logon and security controls, the mechanics of logging on, and configuring a peer-to-peer share. Also, be prepared to identify differences between share permissions and security (NTFS) permissions.

21.1 Network Administration

Network administration is the use of network software packages to manage network system operations. The central focus of network administration is network security and the coordination of shared resources on the network. Peer-to-peer (P2P) networks are common, especially in home and small-business offices, and can be easily set up and administered to allow users to share files, printers, hardware, and Internet connections. You can establish a peer-to-peer network using any Windows PC operating system, though Windows operating systems typically limit the number of concurrent connections from 10 to 20 users, depending on the OS edition. Larger networking systems require a client/server operating system. Network administration relies on considerations such as whether the administration will follow a peer-to-peer or centralized model, as well as how sharing should be implemented.

Peer-to-Peer Administration

Administrative functions in a peer-to-peer network are not highly organized and are best described as *decentralized*. Recall that in a decentralized administrative system, no one person controls the network. Instead, all users have equal rights on the network, and each user usually controls access to their own files and hardware.

To create a peer-to-peer network, all that is required is an operating system that supports peer-to-peer networking and a network adapter card for each PC participating in the network. Creating a peer-to-peer network with Windows is very easy. In fact, Microsoft has continued to make peer-to-peer networking easier with each new edition of an operating system.

A+ 1102: 1.1, 1.6

Peer-to-peer is also referred to as a *workgroup network*. Computer membership configuration to a workgroup or domain is selected when the Windows operating system is first installed, though the computer is likely configured to a workgroup by default. A **domain** is an organized collection of all groups and users on the network. You can view the name of the workgroup or domain by opening the **System** dialog box. In Figure 21-1, you can see how the name of the domain appears.

A+ 1101: 2.4 1102: 1.6

Centralized Administration

The client/server network model, also called a *centralized network model* or *domain network model*, is based on administration of the network being controlled by a

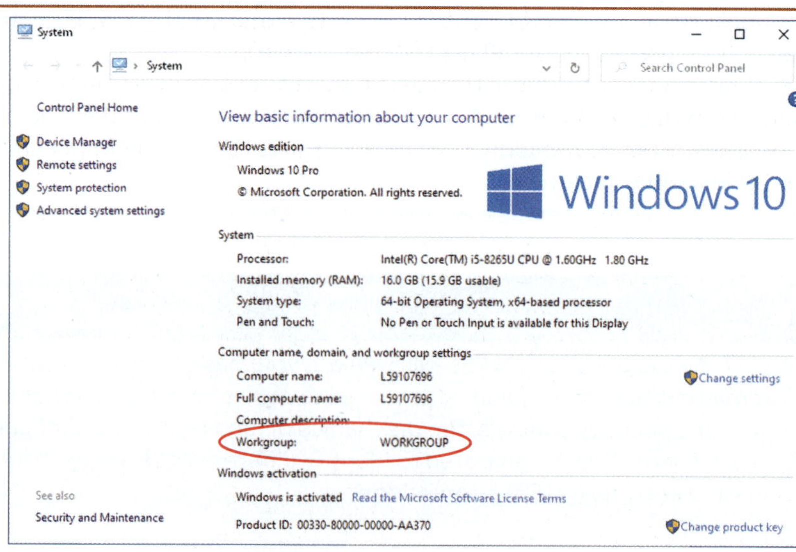

Figure 21-1 The name of the workgroup or domain to which a computer belongs can be viewed in the **System** dialog box.

Goodheart-Willcox Publisher

centralized server and administrator. This type of network typically has a server that controls the user authentication and is most often found in businesses or companies with many different network users sharing many different resources, including legacy systems such as older operating systems, embedded systems such as appliances or thermostats, and supervisory control and data acquisition (SCADA) systems such as those seen in a power plant. In Windows, this is accomplished via the Active Directory service.

All files pertaining to users, groups, and computers connected to the client/server network are contained in the file server. A network may be composed of many file servers sharing the burden of the network system. In the early Windows NT networks, one file server was known as the primary domain controller and the others were called backup domain controllers. The ***primary domain controller (PDC)*** kept the master record of all user accounts, and the ***backup domain controllers (BDCs)*** kept backup copies of the user accounts. This redundancy helped to protect against losing information about the users if the PDC failed or crashed. In today's systems, all servers can be configured with equal responsibilities and no longer require the *primary* and *backup* notations. In fact, the terms *primary domain controller* and *backup domain controller* have become legacy terms, and newer network operating systems technologies do not require a primary domain controller or a backup domain controller, except when the network incorporates legacy network systems. In modern networks, you simply see the term *domain controller*, which implies a primary domain controller.

Centralized administration relies on the use of a network operating system (NOS). The most commonly encountered network operating systems used for managing large networks are Windows, Unix, Novell, and Linux. Each of these systems will be briefly introduced in the following sections.

Tech Tip

You may seem the term *platform* used when describing network operating systems. In this context, *platform* and *operating system* are synonymous.

Microsoft Windows Server

1102: 1.6, 2.1 **A+**

Microsoft has provided a wide variety of Windows Server operating systems since 1993 when it first introduced Windows NT Server, which was the first server operating system that featured a GUI. Prior to Windows NT, server operating systems only used a command-line interface. Like the early Novell platforms, users had to enter commands at a prompt when configuring the server, such as adding or configuring user accounts. As you can imagine, when Microsoft introduced the GUI, the Windows Server operating system gained in popularity. Some other network operating systems, such as Novell, were slow to embrace the GUI and consequently lost dominance in the server operating system market. Today, Microsoft provides more server operating systems than any other company.

Tech Tip

Active Directory is typically taught as an entire course, and Microsoft has a certification specifically for Active Directory design and configuration.

The next significant development Microsoft made to the operating system was Active Directory, which is still part of the Microsoft Server operating systems. Windows 2000 Server was the first server operating system designed on Active Directory technology, which removed many restrictions imposed by the Windows NT domain file-structure limitations. Active Directory technology is based on the Lightweight Directory Access Protocol (LDAP).

Early network systems were limited in size compared to today's large network systems, and the size constraints made it difficult to configure file servers for multiple servers present in a network system. With the implementation of Active Directory, a user or group member can simply log on once and have complete access to resources across the entire system. This is a significant improvement over the earlier Windows NT Server operating systems, which required user authentication for each individual domain, as well as trust relationships established between network domains.

Unix

Unix is the oldest of the four server operating systems. It was written in the C programming language and was mainly intended for use on minicomputers. One of the things that made it so popular was that it was not specific to one type of computer.

In the early days of computers, operating systems were written specifically for certain computer types, and you could only use an operating system on a specific brand and model of computer. Today, you can run most software across the boundaries of different manufacturers with relatively few restrictions.

Unix was adopted by IBM and became the standard operating system for its RISC-based systems and is still used on many mainframe computers and enterprise servers. The original Unix operating system required a mainframe computer to meet the operating system hardware requirements, as early PC models did not have sufficient hardware to support Unix. Today, many variations of Unix exist, such as the numerous Linux versions that are designed to run on PCs, which now have more computing power than the early mainframe computers.

Novell NetWare/SUSE

Novell NetWare was developed by Novell and was a popular network operating system in the 1980s and 1990s. The early versions of NetWare were complex to use because they were only equipped with a command-line interface. Later versions incorporated a graphical user interface (GUI), and you could simply point and click to access their features. In 2004, Novell acquired SUSE Linux and offered the SUSE Linux Enterprise server as an alternative to NetWare. Today, Novell no longer exists as the original Novell NetWare Company. In 2011, Novell was acquired by The Attachment Group, which was itself acquired by Micro Focus International in 2014. Novell products and services are now integrated within Micro Focus products and divisions. However, SUSE Linux is still widely available, especially in open-source platforms.

A+ 1102: 1.8

Linux

Linux is one of the latest network operating systems to be fully developed, and there are many different Linux operating systems available due to its source code being freely available to the public. Its open-source code makes Linux popular, as well as a relatively inexpensive price compared to other network operating systems.

Most software companies guard their source code and only release sufficient information about it to allow third-party developers to write software that enhances the product. By having the complete listing of source code for the Linux operating system, programmers can write any feature they desire into the networking software. Anyone with reasonable programming skills can use the open-source code to build a network operating system of their own specifications. Even though major software companies now build networking software packages based on Linux, the pricing remains very reasonable.

However, complete access to source code does have a price, such as security. Providing users access to the source code inherently also provides access to every interested hacker in the world. To abide by the Linux software copyright regulations, if you use the Linux source code to develop your software system, you must allow access to any modifications to the code when you market it. This means that in terms of security, everyone has a road map to your system's operations when the source code is freely distributed.

Linux is used as the programmable operating system for many electronic products, such as digital recorders, television and media systems, and telephones. To enhance security, many network models incorporate a Linux server and a server of another network operating system. For example, the front-end server (the part that allows users to access the network) uses a standard high-security package such as those provided by Unix or Windows Server. To cut operating costs, a Linux system is used as a mail server or web server.

Sharing

A+ 1101: 3.6

One of the hallmarks of a network is the ability to share files and resources. However, there are many ways to implement sharing, depending on the type of network you are administering. One of the most straightforward methods is to incorporate a file server that can be accessed by anyone who needs to do so. This type of server will be discussed in more detail later in this chapter. Without a dedicated file server, a resource must be created as a share for other people to access it.

A **share** is an object that is distributed across the network, such as a file, hard drive, optical drive, printer, and scanner, among others. Sharing has changed quite a bit from the early days of computing and can vary according to which operating system you are using. As Windows operating systems have evolved, Microsoft introduced new sharing techniques such as Simple File Sharing in Windows XP, the Public Folders feature in Windows Vista, and HomeGroup and Libraries in Windows 7. All Windows operating systems also use advanced (classic) file sharing, in which a user configures a folder as a shared resource and selects who can access the folder and with what permissions. The basic concepts of advanced sharing continue today for all Windows operating systems. Each major operating system sharing method is explored in the following sections.

Network and Sharing Center

A+ 1102: 1.4

A+ Note

The A+ Exams usually have several questions about shares, permissions, and user accounts.

The Network and Sharing Center is a centralized location in Windows that provides links to many related networking tools and wizards and displays the current network status, as shown in Figure 21-2. From the Network and Sharing Center, you can view the status and name of a network connection, access and change the network adapter configuration and sharing settings, add and configure new network connections, and more. Notice the **Change advanced sharing settings** link in the left pane, which takes you to the **Advanced sharing settings** dialog box and allows you to configure the sharing settings. The **Advanced sharing settings** dialog box is covered later in this chapter.

The Network and Sharing Center is available through **Start**>**Settings**>**Network and Internet**>**Network and Sharing Center** in Windows 10. Alternatively, a user can navigate to Control Panel and select **Network and Internet**>**Network and Sharing Center**. When a user or technician is in the Network and Sharing Center, they will be able to see the location and name of each network connection.

Although the primary use of the Network and Sharing Center is for connectivity to networks, it may also be used for file, folder, password, and printer sharing,

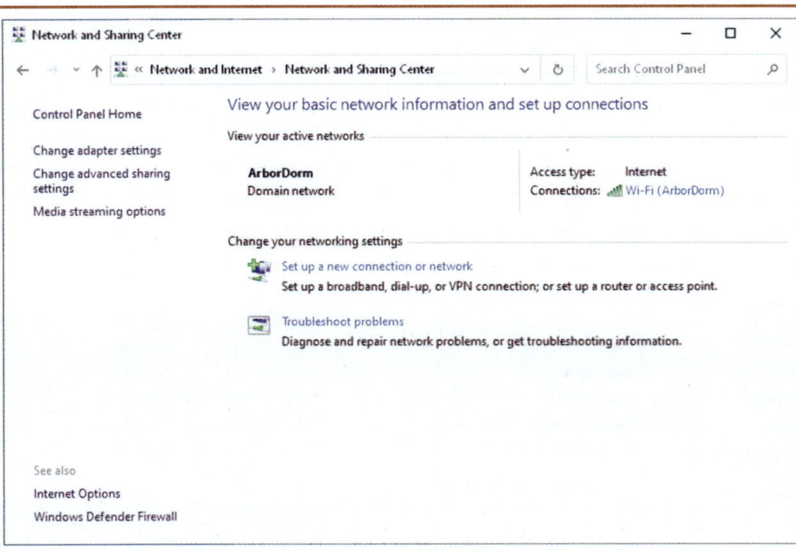

Goodheart-Willcox Publisher

Figure 21-2 The Network and Sharing Center provides a centralized location to view the current status of the local area network and provides links to many related network configuration tools and wizards.

as well as media streaming. Thus, it is vital that technicians advise users to be cautious regarding with whom they share their devices and data. Furthermore, it is also vital that technicians disable sharing permissions for confidential data or devices.

Simple File Sharing

Windows XP introduced the Simple File Sharing feature, which designates the **Shared Documents** folder as a shared resource, and any file placed in the Shared Documents folder is automatically shared with other users. This feature is enabled by default but can be easily disabled in most versions of Windows. While Windows XP is obsolete and unlikely to be encountered in today's workforce, the concept of a singular location for shared material is utilized in current Windows operating systems as well.

Tech Tip

Users who do not have permission to access a shared folder will not be able to see the folder. Prior to Windows Vista, it was possible to view a shared folder even when you did not have permission to access the folder.

Public Folders

Windows 10 uses a feature similar to Simple File Sharing called Public Folders to enable sharing. When the Public Folders feature is enabled, the **Public** folder located under C:\Users\ is configured as a share, as shown in Figure 21-3. Notice the two-person icon shown on the bottom of the window; this represents a shared folder in Windows.

By default, the **Public** folder includes **Public Desktop**, **Public Documents**, **Public Downloads**, **Public Music**, **Public Pictures**, and **Public Videos**, as shown in Figure 21-4. The **Public** folder and its subfolders are created by default, but sharing is not enabled. Once the Public Folder feature is enabled, its contents and subfolders can be shared with other users of the same computer or with anyone on the local area network.

The sharing of other folders can be simplified by enabling the Sharing Wizard through the **File Explorer Options** dialog box. Once opened, select the **View** tab and

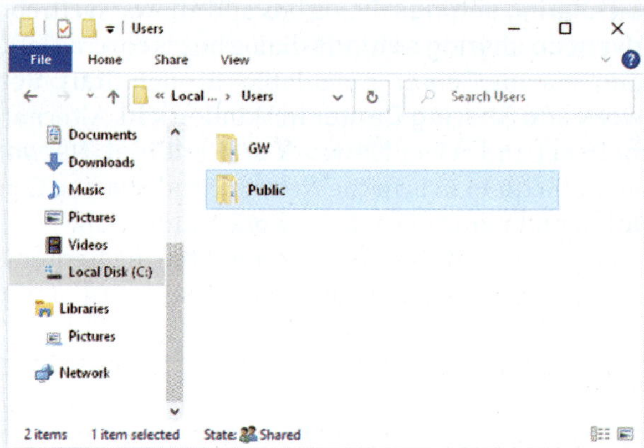

Figure 21-3 The **Public** folder is designed to be a central location for shared files.

Goodheart-Willcox Publisher

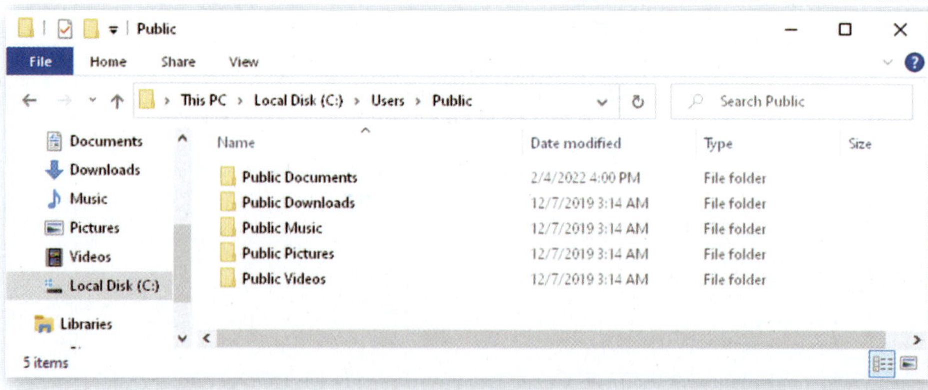

Figure 21-4 There are several default folders created within the **Public** folder.

Goodheart-Willcox Publisher

ensure the **Use Sharing Wizard (Recommended)** option is checked within the Advanced settings: portion of the dialog box, as demonstrated in Figure 21-5. These options can be located by opening Windows Explorer and navigating to **View**>**Options**>**Change folder and search options**, or by conducting a search for Folder Options and selecting **File Explorer Options**. The Sharing Wizard is activated when a user right-clicks a file or directory to be shared and selects **Share with**. The wizard then guides a user through setting up the share, such as selecting the users with whom to share the file or directory and selecting the permission to assign them.

Tech Tip

The name of the Folder Options menu may vary depending on the method used to access it. If a user navigates to **View>Options>Change folder and search options**, the menu will be titled **Folder Options**. However, if a user opens this menu via search, it will be titled **File Explorer Options**. Despite having different names, these two menus are identical, and changes made to one automatically updates the other.

Libraries

Windows 10 and 11 includes Libraries by default, but they are not enabled. To enable Libraries, open Explorer and select **View**>**Navigation pane**>**Show libraries**. The **Library** folders and files will then display as a single collection on the computer, but they are actually located on other computers.

There are four default libraries (**Documents**, **Music**, **Pictures**, and **Videos**), but additional libraries can be created. For example, a collection of a specific type of document, such as work documents, can be added to the library. The user can then move between a desktop computer and a laptop or tablet and have virtual access to the collection of work documents created on the original computer.

The user has complete access to these files. All that is required is that the user create a user account on each computer with the same account name and password. The Library then identifies the user's files on all computers in which the user has an account and it puts them together as a virtual collection on each computer.

Previously, the Windows HomeGroup feature enabled easy sharing among devices within the same group. HomeGroup was removed from Windows 10, as of Version 1803, but you can still share folders by right-clicking on the folder or file, selecting **Properties**, and selecting the **Sharing** tab.

Tech Tip

It is very important that you set passwords for shares, especially if that same workstation will be connecting to the Internet.

Password-Protected Sharing

Users can establish password-protected sharing by navigating to **Control Panel**>-**Network and Internet**>**Network and Sharing Center**>**Change advanced sharing settings**. In Figure 21-6, notice the options to enable and disable password-protected sharing: **Turn on password protected sharing** and **Turn off password protected**

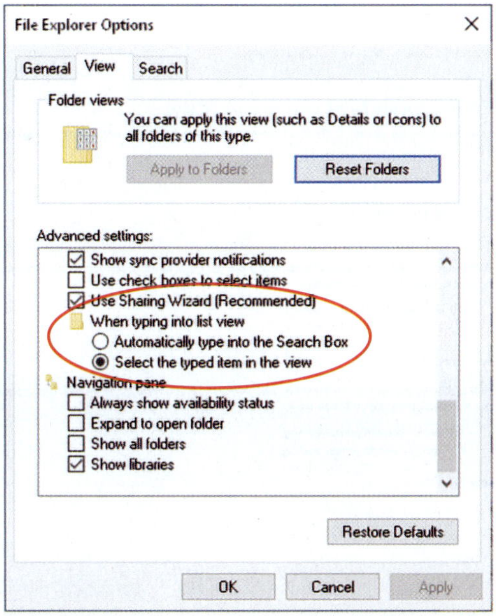

Goodheart-Willcox Publisher

Figure 21-5 To enable or disable the Sharing Wizard, navigate to Windows Explorer and select **View>Options>Change folder and search options** or conduct a search for Folder Options.

sharing. When password-protected sharing is enabled, users on other computers will not be able to access shared folders on that computer, including the **Public** folder(s). To access the shared folder from a different computer, the user must have a local user account on the computer with the shared resource. To provide access to a shared resource, you must either configure each computer with the same user account name and password or enable password-protected sharing. Remember, when you disable password-protected sharing, everyone on the network can access the shared resource and no user account or password is required.

A+ 1102: 1.6

Network Discovery

Notice the **Network discovery** option in Figure 21-7. Network Discovery makes setting up and configuring a network easy as it automatically detects and configures a

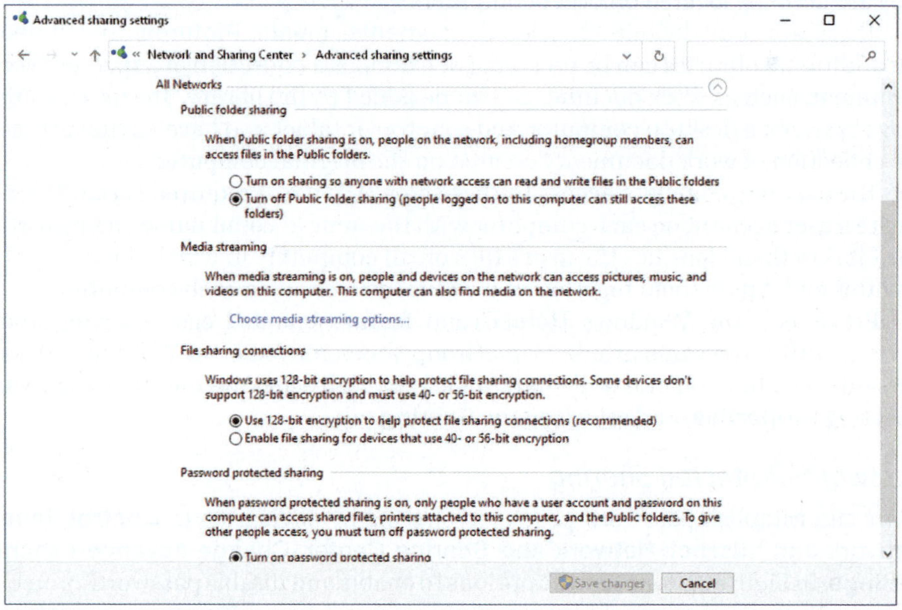

Figure 21-6 The All Networks profile has an option for password-protected sharing.

Goodheart-Willcox Publisher

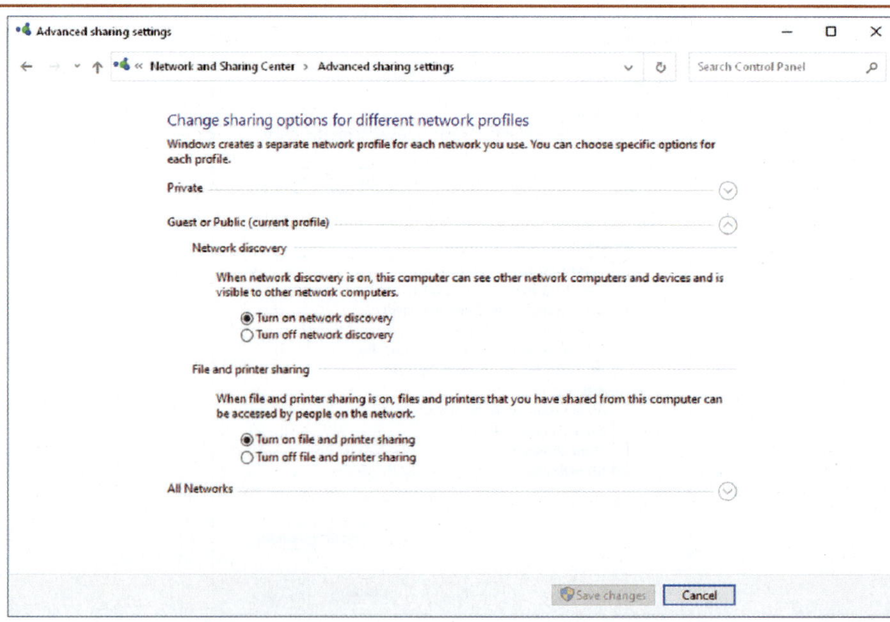

Figure 21-7 Network Discovery makes setting up and configuring a network easy, as it automatically detects and configures a network and sets up a share and Internet connection.

Goodheart-Willcox Publisher

network and sets up a share and Internet connection. This feature was introduced in Windows Vista and continues to be supported by Windows. It is directly related to the network location chosen when connecting to a wired network, a wireless network, or remotely across the Internet to a work location. Windows 10 and 11 allow for one of three network location types:

- **Public**: This is the default setting for new installation and represents an untrusted network connection. This option is appropriate for networks in public places, such as airports and hotels.
- **Private**: This option is appropriate for a home network and must be adequately protected with a router or any appropriate defense control.
- **Domain**: This option is appropriate for a computer used to connect to a company network.

Changing the network location is simple in Windows 10 and can be accomplished by navigating to **Start>Settings>Network & Internet.** Select the **Properties** button for the network you want to change, choose the desired options from the Network profile portion of the connection properties, and then close the screen to save the settings. This same process also works for wired network connections.

Advanced File Sharing

All Windows operating systems can use the Advanced File Sharing options, which provide more detailed options that are not used in Simple File Sharing. These options, however, are not intended for the novice user.

When a folder is made private, only the owner of the folder has access to it; not even the system administrator can access the folder. When the folder is configured as a share on the network, everyone has access to the shared folder contents, which they can read but not edit. When the option to allow network users to change files is selected, all network users can access and change the folder contents.

To set up advanced sharing in Windows 10, select the desired file, and then select the **Share** tab followed by **Advanced security.** This will open the **Advanced Security Settings** dialog box for the specific file, as shown in Figure 21-8. From there, you can edit permissions, modify sharing options, and view both auditing properties and effective access. Permissions can also be accessed by right-clicking the file and selecting **Properties** from the shortcut menu. Next, open the **Security** tab in the file properties dialog box and select **Edit.** This will open the permissions dialog box.

Figure 21-8 The Advanced Security Settings dialog box in Windows 10 allows users to edit permissions, modify sharing options, and view auditing properties and effective access.

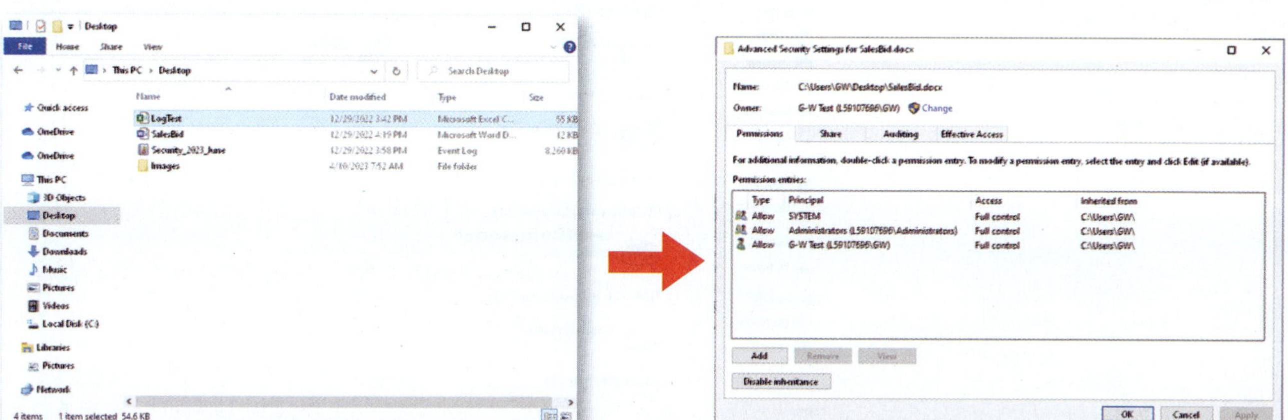

Goodheart-Willcox Publisher

Moving and Copying Folders and Files

There is often confusion about the actions and permissions that take place when either moving or copying folders and files. When a file is moved or copied from one location of a hard drive or server to another location on the same hard drive or server, Windows will adhere to the original file permissions, provided the content is being moved or copied to the same volume. However, if a file or folder is moved or copied to a different volume or storage medium, the permissions could be lost, and the content will be assigned the same permissions that are assigned to the destination where it is being moved, regardless of the file formatting or drive.

A+ 1102: 2.5

File Attributes

File attributes are settings that are associated with a computer's or server's files that grant or deny users access to the files. Furthermore, file attributes contain metadata with each file that contains information of who has generated, modified, or obtained files on a computer or server. In other words, the file attributes determine who is able or unable to access or modify files, along with a documented history of the file's behaviors on a computer or server.

Accessing a Shared Resource

Shared resources are accessed by first opening Windows Explorer and expanding the **Network** folder located in the left pane. This will expose all the network locations, such as other computers, external drives, network storage, and devices.

Figure 21-9 shows the **Network** folder expanded and a list of computers, media devices, multifunction devices, network infrastructure devices, and other devices. The other devices can be almost anything that is accessible through the network, such as remote cameras and television interface devices.

To access the shared resource, you simply navigate to the network device through Windows Explorer and then double-click the device icon. You can also right-click the device and select **Open** from the shortcut menu. You will then be presented with a **Windows Security** dialog box prompting you for a user account name and password for the remote location, Figure 21-10. Notice that there is a **Remember my credentials** option, which is used to save your logon name and password (credentials). When checked, the next time you access the share, you will

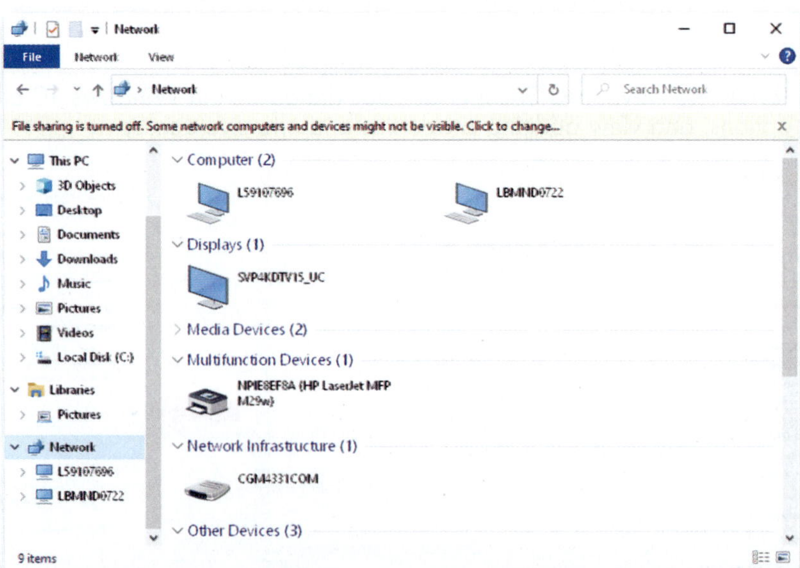

Figure 21-9 When the Network folder is expanded in Explorer, all devices connected to the network are shown.

Goodheart-Willcox Publisher

not need to supply a user account name and password. When you access a network share and do not check the **Remember my credentials** option, you can still access the network resource for several hours without the need to enter your username and password. The user account name and password control access to the network device, and improper credentials will result in an access failure. Additionally, failure can occur from a bad cable or the device being offline. A network connection failure usually generates a message box similar to the one in Figure 21-11.

Network share access in a network domain does not require individual user accounts for each network resource. The user account credentials are activated when you log on to the domain.

Administrative Shares vs. Local Shares

Although administrative shares were more common in operating systems such as Windows XP, they can still be utilized in Windows 10 and 11. **Administrative shares** are hidden shares on a Windows machine that have a dollar sign ($) at the end of the shared path. An example of this would be accessing a user's local C: drive from another machine. For example, assume a user's machine was named Gary in the network's domain. A network administrator or technician with administrative rights would be able to go to an address bar, enter \\Gary\C$, and access all the files and folders that were saved locally. However, other users can only retrieve local shares if a user on a local machine grants another user rights to view or modify the file(s) on the machine.

Local shares are often implemented more with users in a workgroup and not in a domain. Users can grant access to other users via their file or folder **Properties** box by either granting everyone access or by inserting only the user to whom they want to give access.

21.2 Permissions

With regard to networking, *permissions* define the degree of access granted to an individual user or group of users to a specific object or file. Administrators can

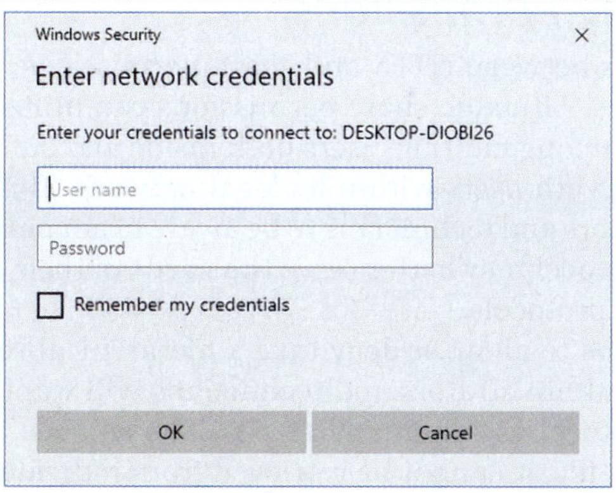

Goodheart-Willcox Publisher

Figure 21-10 When accessing a shared resource, you will be presented with a **Windows Security** dialog box prompting you for a user account name and password for the remote location.

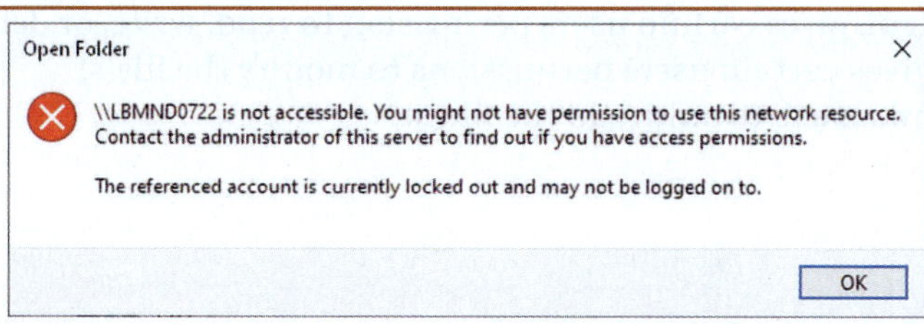

Goodheart-Willcox Publisher

Figure 21-11 A message box similar to this one typically appears after a failed logon attempt to a network resource.

maintain network security and prevent duplication or accidental deletion of files by implementing the principle of least privilege. At all times, network users should only have access to the data and resources needed to perform their necessary job functions. This can be achieved through share permissions, security permissions, allow or deny permissions, and permission propagation.

A+ 1102: 2.5

Share Permissions and Security Permissions

Shared folders have a combination of two different types of permissions used by Windows: share permissions and security permissions (also known as *NTFS permissions*). Share permissions apply to users who access a resource over the network and do not apply if a user logs on to the computer locally. Security permissions can only be applied to resources that are located on a volume or partition that is formatted with the NTFS file system. When a resource has a FAT partition, share permissions are limited to Full Control, Change, and Read. NTFS partitions, however, support a much wider range of permissions, including options such as Full Control, Modify, Read & execute, List folder content, and Read, among others.

Tech Tip

When you share a folder, the Everyone group is given the Read permission by default.

A+ 1102: 2.1

When a user logs on to a computer, they are assigned a unique **Security Identifier (SID)**, which is an identification code used to determine the assigned permissions for that user. Every user, group, and computer has a unique SID assigned and stored in an ACL database. In an Active Directory domain controlled by a Windows server, an **Access Control List (ACL)** is a database is used to match a user SID to the resource and then allow or deny access to it.

During a local computer logon, the user logs on using the local user account in the **Security Accounts Manager (SAM)**, which is a registry file used to maintain the user account database on a computer. A local logon grants access only to that computer's resources. Local user and group SAM membership are used to manage access to local resources. After a successful logon, a user is issued a security token that contains security information based on the SID. The contents of the security token are compared to the SAM or ACL, which determines if the user has the correct permissions to access a shared resource.

Allow vs. Deny Permissions

There are differences between NTFS and share permissions, and both serve their own unique purposes. Although share permissions can utilize FAT and FAT32 file systems for sharing among multiple users both inside and outside a network, NTFS is only able to share with users within its local network. Thus, it is important for network administrators and technicians to be aware of not only each characteristic, but also why one protocol may better serve the needs of their users in a network in comparison to other protocols.

NTFS permissions to allow or deny take a hierarchical role in their network's structure. Network administrators and technicians will want to use the deny permissions in this protocol as minimally as possible, as once a deny permission is placed on a folder or file, it cannot be retrieved from individuals who are lower in the hierarchy or not within the user's Active Directory group. Therefore, it is a better practice for users to implement one of the following allow permission controls:

- **Full Control**: gives certain users permission to read, write, or delete the file(s)
- **Change**: gives certain users permissions to modify the file(s)
- **Read**: allows users to only read the file(s)

Permission Propagation

1102: 2.5 A+

There are two types of objects: child objects and parent objects. A *child object* is essentially created from a previously existing object, such as a domain or group, which then becomes a *parent object*. Often, child objects have *inherited permissions*, which are permissions assigned by a Windows operating system or server from a parent object. When a Windows operating system or server passes permissions from parent objects to child objects, network administrators and technicians are adhering to *permission propagation*. Remember that permissions can be set to any folder, file, or policy, but changes can emerge at any time on a per-object basis or inherited from a parent object via Active Control Lists from the NTFS permissions of Windows. Whereas network administrators and technicians want to adhere to a stable method of file and folder permissions, be aware that as organizations change the permissions of their files and folders, the organization of those permissions will change as well. Therefore, permissions such as inherited permissions are well documented and updated in an organization's information technology policy.

21.3 Network Organization

Each major software vendor uses its own terminology to describe its network organization. They are all similar, and terminologies can be transferred easily from one system to another without losing their intended meanings. The terminology used in this chapter is primarily based on the Microsoft network systems, as concentrating on one system in generic fashion will be less confusing than explaining different systems in one unit.

Centralized networks are organized administratively into sections or roles. These sections are called *domains*, *groups*, and *users*. Recall that a *domain* is an organized collection of all groups and users on the network. A **group** is a collection of users organized together by similarities in their job tasks. A **user** is an individual who may use the network system resources. Additional roles include the system administrator and specific user groups, such as local user, power user, and domain user.

Domains

1102: 2.1 A+

The entire network organization is usually referred to as a domain. For example, ABC Inc. may be a domain, and the entire organization is one unique network system. Inside the domain are groups of users with related tasks, such as the personnel in the accounting or sales departments, and each of these groups is composed of individual users, such as John Doe in accounting and Jane Doe in sales. Remember, the word *domain* has two meanings. One refers to the definition provided in this section, and the other refers to Internet locations, such as .com or .org. Be sure to use the word correctly in all cases.

Groups

The next level in the network organization is the group. Groups are composed of workers who share common responsibilities and can be thought of as a set. For example, the payroll, marketing, research, design, and administrative departments of an organization could easily form five distinct groups of network users. The workers within the group usually require similar system resources (files, software, printers, etc.) to perform their jobs.

A+ 1102: 2.5

Users

A user is an individual who uses the network system. Each user is assigned an account, which includes all available information about them. The account contains such information as the user's password, username, restrictions, and the group(s) to which they belong, which is stored on the file server. Each user must have an account before they can use the network system, and once an account is created, the user can receive access to any area of the network by the system administrator. The user usually belongs to one or more groups, but group membership is not required.

Local User Account

The **local user account** is the primary account configured on the workstation that controls access to resources on that specific workstation. A PC can have multiple local user accounts, one assigned to each user of that workstation. Local user accounts are created in the **User Accounts** dialog box, which is accessed through **Control Panel>User Accounts>User Accounts.**

For added security in a peer-to-peer network, a user account should be established for each user on a given computer, as well as all computers that individual plans to use. Local user account characteristics include

- association with a peer-to-peer, or a workgroup-based, network;
- ability to access resources at the local computer;
- authentication through the computer at which the account is created; and
- maintenance performed by the computer on which the account is created.

A+ 1102: 2.5

Legacy systems such as Windows XP and Windows 7 utilized local accounts exclusively. However, on newer systems such as Windows 10 and Windows 11, users may be prompted to use a Microsoft account instead. The difference between the two is that a local account works only on an assigned workstation; that is, a user cannot log in to a neighboring computer using their local account. A Microsoft account, formerly known as a Microsoft Live ID, provides a user access to all Microsoft services regardless of workstation and enables the ability to synchronize files across all devices connected to this account. While Microsoft accounts are far more convenient, local accounts technically provide more security as they only work on one computer. Additionally, users can be locked out of their Microsoft account after a number of failed login attempts, which means they are also locked out of all other devices.

A+ 1102: 2.5

Local Power Users

Although it is recommended that network administrators and technicians be the only individuals who have administrative rights to install, uninstall, or make modifications to a personal computer, there may be occasions where users may need more rights than those assigned to a standard user. These occasions typically occur when a user needs to be able to modify files or grant permission to other users in the network to read or modify files. There are two methods by which users can be granted these permissions: local machine and Active Directory.

If a user creates a folder or file on their local machine or maps a drive that is connected to the local machine, they can right-click the file or folder and then select who has the right to read, write, or modify the folder or files. This action can be taken by right-clicking on the user's name in the Active Directory and selecting the necessary administrative rights.

A+ 1102: 2.5

Domain User Account

When the computer is configured as part of a domain, the user is configured with a **domain user account**, which provides access to network domain resources as well as resources on the workstation. Domain security is configured to control access at the domain level, which means configuring user access for multiple computer and network resources. The software system used by Microsoft to control access to the network system at the domain level is called *Active Directory Domain Services (AD DS)* or simply *Active Directory*.

When a user account is part of a network administrative security database, the user of that account can

- authenticate through the domain server;
- access resources anywhere in the network domain; and
- log on through any computer in the domain.

The domain user account is created on the network server, but it can be created at the server or remotely from a workstation. Even when the domain user account is created from the workstation, the domain user account is created and controlled by the domain server, not the workstation. The domain user account controls access to network resources and access to the workstation and is an example of a single sign-on user account. The user can then access resources throughout the network without the need to supply a password again.

Administrative vs. Standard User

1102: 2.5 A+

Two account types that a network administrator and technician need to be aware of when working in the Active Directory are administrative accounts and standard user accounts. *Administrative accounts* allow a user to have access to most of the network's resources, including files and settings of local machines, along with the ability to install, uninstall, or update software on the machines in their network. However, *standard users* are limited to the use of the local machine and are only able to generate, obtain, and modify documents that are on their local machine or shared to them from other users via their domain controller.

System Administrator

The **network administrator**, also called the *system administrator*, is a person (or persons) with the highest security rating on the network. System administrators are more important in client/server models than they are in peer-to-peer models because they are responsible for delegating authority all the way down to the user level. The other users on the network can exercise only the authority granted to them by the network administrator.

Network administrators and technicians need to be aware that they will be presented with a mixture of current and legacy network servers, equipment, and devices. Therefore, they may encounter a single machine offering multiple services, such as one computer functioning as both a print and web server. However, this is not always the best practice, and with the requirements of today's networking standards, it is possible that this type of implementation will not be possible. Although some devices, such as routers, have built-in services such as DHCP embedded into the device's firmware, it is still the responsibility of the network administrators and technicians to observe, document, modify, and replace equipment as needed to adhere to their network's needs.

Delegating Administrators

The network administrator controls all aspects of the network. However, in a large organization with thousands of users spread all over the country, it would be difficult, if not impossible, for one person to perform all the duties associated with running a network. For this reason, the network administrator usually grants limited administrative powers to a middle-management level of administrators who take care of routine duties, such as adding or deleting users from the network; setting up printers, files, and programs to be shared; and performing routine data backup.

Network logon involves identifying the user by name and password. The username identifies the individual, and the password verifies their identity. The network administrator issues the username and initial password as well as a prompt for the user to change their logon password following the first successful logon. This is the typical password administrative scenario used.

Choosing Usernames

One typical format for a username is a combination of the user's first and last names, such as the user's last name followed by the underscore symbol and ending in the first letter of user's first name or the first letter of the user's first name followed by their last name. For example, this textbook author's username would likely be Easttom_C or CEasttom. There are many different naming styles, but once a naming style is chosen, it should remain consistent as new user accounts are added to the network. Inconsistent naming styles can easily lead to confusion. Newer versions of Windows also allow users to use their e-mail address as a logon name.

Creating Passwords

Passwords should be complex, meaning they should consist of numbers, uppercase and lowercase letters, and special symbols. Despite their complexity, they should remain easy to remember for the user. Review Chapter 15 for information about complex passwords and password security.

A+ 1102: 1.2

Administrative Commands

While one can perform a great deal of administrative tasks via the GUI or Control Panel in Windows, the Windows command line provides a number of utilities for administrating Windows. Commonly used administrative commands include **net use**, **gpupdate**, **gpresult**, **diskpart**, and **winver**.

A+ 1102: 1.6

The **net use** command displays information about the current mapped drives and devices that are connected to a Windows Server or Windows personal computer. A *mapped drive* is a shortcut to a shared folder or location on a remote computer or server. Mapping drives makes it easier to access shared storage areas over a network.

The **net use** command is available via the command prompt in most versions of Windows. In addition to the basic **net use** command, switches, such as \\computername\sharename, will also display the shared items for each individual machine that shares a printer with other computers in a room but not the entire network. This information can be valuable to a network administrator when diagnosing sharing problems or when trying to pinpoint a device on a network.

The **gpupdate** command allows you to update policies in a Windows network. As with most commands, there are a number of flags to be used with this command. Common flags or switches include

- /target:, which defines a user or computer policy setting to be updated;
- /force, which reapplies all policy settings; and
- /boot, which causes the computer to reboot after the group policy settings are applied.

The **gpresult** command displays the Resultant Set of Policy (RSoP) for a remote computer or user. This command has a number of flags, including

- /s, which specifics the name or IP address of the remote computer;
- /u, which allows you to use the credentials of a particular user to execute this command;
- /user, which specifies a remote user whose RSoP data will be displayed; and
- /r, which displays RSoP summary data.

The **diskpart** command allows you to manage disk partitions. Once you execute the **diskpart** command, you will notice the command prompt change to DISKPART>. From here, you can execute various commands for disk partitions. Administrators often start with the **list disk** command, which lists all the partitions on the computer. There are many commands specific to **DiskPart**, including **create partition primary**, which enables a user to create a primary partition. Review Chapter 10 for additional information about **DiskPart**.

The **winver** command has only one purpose: displaying a window showing the Windows version. The window will also reference the build number for that version of Windows.

Default Users and Groups

1102: 2.1, 2.5 A+

Server operating systems typically have a set of default users and groups composed of the most common users and groups required in most server systems, such as Administrator, User, and Guest accounts, Print Operators, Backup Operators, DHCP Administrators, and Domain Administrators groups. Default users and groups save time when setting up a server.

The exact title of a user or group account will vary according to the operating system used. Each group can have a specific set of permissions, which dictates what the members of the group can do, access, or modify. Users are simply added to each group and the users are restricted to the permissions of the group.

Additional users and groups can be added to meet the needs of the environment. For example, in a school setting, a group named Teachers and another group named Students can be established on the server. A user named Teacher and another user named Student can be added to their respective user lists, and students can log on using the username Student, but the student would be restricted according to the permissions set in the Students group. The same scenario can be applied to the teachers. Each teacher can log on using the username Teacher and would be restricted according to the permissions set in the Teachers group.

Assigning Resources at the Group Level

If a company has several hundred or thousands of employees, the amount of time required to set up individual shares for each employee would be unreasonable. Although access to system resources can be granted to individual users, network administrators can save a great deal of time by assigning resources to groups rather than users. In this case, each group can be allowed access to the normal software programs, files, and hardware required by that group. When it is necessary to add new users to the network, it is much quicker and simpler to assign a new individual to an existing group than it is to authorize each individual to use specific network resources.

As you have learned, networks are organized by domains, users, and groups, which are often created to mimic the different divisions or departments in the corporate structure. Although all these departments are part of the same company and may have many common needs, they each will likely have special needs based on their different job requirements. For example, all departments will need some sort of word-processing package, but only a few would need access to the accounting software or payroll database. Each group's needs and security requirements must be determined individually. Even when resources are assigned at the group level, each employee must still have an account.

A+ 1101: 1.4
1102: 2.1

MDM Policies

Mobile Device Management (MDM) policies are implemented in networks to determine which devices can access the network's resources. Since some organizations are faced with their members using their own devices such as mobile phones and tablets, organizations need to implement a policy where information is encrypted among the devices in the network.

MaaS360 is the most common implementation of MDM and was designed by IBM to provide network administrators and technicians the ability to have control over the mobile devices connected to their network. Furthermore, the MDM portion of the MaaS360 automatically acts and immediately notifies the network administrator or technicians when a user does not adhere to the policy. In other words, if a user violates the MDM policies, their mobile device will lose access to the network, and the information technology department will receive notification of the breach of policy. However, action will not have to be taken via the information technology department, as the user will be removed from the network automatically.

Recall from Chapter 13 that, like MDM, *mobile application management (MAM)* is a part of *enterprise mobility management (EMM)*, which enables companies to have control over what occurs on company-owned mobile devices. MAM primarily focuses on managing and security company apps, such as company-created applications or company communication applications.

21.4 Server Roles

Network operating systems such as Windows Server allow network administrators to control and modify their servers via *server roles*. In other words, server roles allow the features of what would be perceived as multiple servers, such as a web server and file server, to be placed on a single server and utilized as a server role. At the beginning of server implementation, network administrators would experience multiple servers since the source code of the server was broad but vital to the server's use; now, network administrators are utilizing Windows Server's Features on Demand to increase functionality of their server roles and diminish the payload of their networks.

What this means is that they only use the roles needed for their networks, and by doing so, they are not allowing a broader source code for roles they are not using. In turn, this increases security measures of their network and data. Thus, there are certain roles that have more functionality than others, but the network administrator can now choose which roles to implement in their server functionalities.

A+ 1101: 2.4

While there are multiple server roles from which a network administrator may choose, this chapter provides you with the most common server roles implemented in Windows-based networks. However, be advised that these roles will be defined for their intended purposes and, if not tended to carefully by a network administrator, may leave server and network vulnerabilities open to individuals who may be seeking default server role settings. Therefore, always generate roles carefully, and practice ethical documentation when implementing any of the mentioned server roles of this chapter along with monitoring of the **Syslog** to observe the modifications you make to your network's infrastructure and prevent downtime of your servers.

A+ 1102: 2.1

Since every computer in a given network relies on at least one type of server, it is crucial that servers remain as secure as possible. This includes not only digital security measures that require administrator-level credentials to access or operate them, but also physical security measures to alert staff to possible malicious activity. Some physical security measures often implemented in server rooms include video surveillance, alarm systems, and motion sensors that are configured to alert security staff to anyone's presence in the server room. When security staff receives the alert, they can tap into the video feed and determine if the person in the server room is authorized or not.

Web Server

A *web server* is a device with software and hardware that processes HTTP requests. Microsoft's default web server is called Internet Information Services (IIS). Network administrators may want to consider the web server role as one of the first roles they implement onto their server, as it allows users that are connected to its domain controller access to the Internet. Furthermore, when a web server is implemented, users can access web-based applications and transfer files from various applications. Most importantly, it provides users with a connection to Port 80, which utilizes an HTTP connection. Without access to Port 80, users are not able to connect to various websites and resources.

File Server

1101: 2.4 A+
1102: 1.6

A *file server* is a device that controls access to files and is one of the primary reasons servers exist. Without it, users connected to a Domain Controller would not be able to save or back up their data centrally to a secure device in their network and would be forced to save locally to their own personal computer. The file server also allows members in a network to share their data in a secure fashion.

With the use of NTFS volumes and security, an author of a file is able to determine who is able or unable to read or modify the files. Furthermore, features such as Encrypting File System (EFS) allow users connected to the server to encrypt their data via the NTFS-formatted volumes on their server. In turn, this can also implement Distributed File System (DFS), which allows a hierarchal file system for all data on a server and can limit who can or cannot obtain certain files. Therefore, without the file server role, data may become disorganized, and the security would be left to the creators of the data.

Print Server

1101: 2.4 A+

A *print server* is a device that connects networked computers to printers. With the use of the print server, network administrators can have a centralized location where all printers, drivers, and IP addresses are stored. Imagine having to manually install the printer software, its driver(s), and its form of connection (such as via an IP address) on every machine in a network and for every user of each machine. This would create network administrators and technicians a significant amount of work. By utilizing the print server and its features, network administrators and technicians can save themselves a tremendous amount of time along with a significant workload.

The previously mentioned time and workload can be diminished by using print server characteristics such as Windows Management Instrumentation (WMI), which can manage all the printers on a network remotely. Furthermore, this feature also allows network administrators to determine who can or cannot access certain printers and when. Most importantly, utilizing the print server and its features allows easier forms of troubleshooting when users are experiencing printing errors.

DHCP Server

1101: 2.4, 2.6 A+

The *Dynamic Host Configuration Protocol (DHCP) Server* is a network server that assigns IP addresses and gateways to clients and is almost a necessity for network administrators and technicians. Without the utilization of a DHCP server, IT employees and technicians would be required to utilize static IP addressing, in which an IP address is manually assigned to every device that requires Internet or network connectivity. However, a DHCP server allows *dynamic IP addressing*, which means IP addresses of devices in a network are assigned automatically once the device is a part of the DHCP server's network.

A DHCP server can assign IP addresses dynamically due to having a predetermined IP address range termed as a *scope*, which is generated via the DHCP server by allocating the TCP/IP configuration. The TCP/IP configuration allocates the dynamic IP addresses based on the network's subnet mask information, the IP address of its default gateway, and the IP address of the Domain Name System (DNS). Nevertheless, the DHCP server can also have static IP addresses on certain devices. For example, network administrators and technicians should assign reserved static IP addresses on essential networking devices, such as wireless access points and network printers.

A+ 1101: 2.4, 2.6

DNS Server

Domain Name System (DNS), also termed as a *DNS server*, is not a true server role but rather a service that translates IP addresses and domain names based on database entries. However, since DNS has become a crucial role in server implementation, it has been termed as a DNS server in regular IT vocabulary. Regardless of how this role is termed, it is vital that network administrators and technicians incorporate it into their networks for easier communication for their users.

DNS creates a hierarchal database that links names to devices and services, and without this database, users would be forced to know every IP address for the devices or services to which they wanted to connect. Therefore, the DNS can be compared to a large telephone book, only the DNS removes the need to look for the number associated with the name of the device or service.

Imagine if users had to know the address of every website they needed to access. It is likely that users would find it frustrating and difficult to have to input an IP address on an Internet browser address bar every time they needed to access a website. Thus, the DNS is not only a useful role to implement onto your network's servers, but it is almost deemed a necessity by today's standards and practices.

A+ 1101: 2.4

Proxy Server

Although firewalls and other security measures exist on a user's local machine, a *proxy server* role can be utilized to function as an additional firewall or web filter. In other words, this role helps direct network traffic to its proper location and protects the network's internal users from accessing malicious or harmful data that can be transmitted from an external source that presents itself as a legitimate internal resource of the organization. While there are other security measures that need to be implemented, the proxy role is a valuable tool to utilize.

A+ 1101: 2.4

Mail Server

A *mail server* is a device that enables the transmission of e-mail messages. It is an essential role that is needed for almost any organization of which a network administrator or technician will be a member. Without the implementation of this role, members of an organization would have to utilize an external source for their e-mail implementation, since they would be otherwise unable to send or receive e-mail from their organizational or domain name e-mail extension. Thus, the mail server role must exist if users in an organization want to utilize their organizational or domain name e-mail extensions and to organize how their e-mail is stored in an e-mail program such as Microsoft Outlook.

A mail server stores e-mail messages and their corresponding data, processes requests from a client, and receives and stores incoming e-mails from an external source, such as another network. While this process may seem self-explanatory, multiple protocols are being utilized when a mail server is used. These protocols, including Simple Mail Transfer Protocol (SMTP), Internet Message Access Protocol

(IMAP), and Post Office Protocol (POP), are based off TCP/IP and installed once the server role is added to a network's server.

SMTP is an Application-layer protocol used for the routing and transferring of e-mail among various hosts via the Internet. IMAP is protocol that works with e-mail that remains on a mail server for users to access across multiple devices, such as a personal computer or mobile phone. The key to this protocol is if a user sends an e-mail message via their computer, the message will appear in the "Sent Folder" of the user's e-mail account. POP is another Application-layer protocol that allows users to retrieve the e-mail from their mail server. Although POP was more used in servers such as Windows Server 2003, it can still be utilized today. Nevertheless, in today's current standards, users are more adherent to other protocols that allow users to always have access to their e-mail and across multiple platforms.

Hijacked E-Mail

Users should be made aware of many personal computer security issues, including the possibility of their e-mail being hijacked. The most common hijacking e-mail methods are spam, phishing, and malware.

Spam refers to unsolicited e-mail messages that appear to be from legitimate sources. However, these e-mails are usually phishing attempts where the user is asked to reply with confidential information, such as their banking account information. Furthermore, once opened, these e-mails can then release forms of malware to a user's personal computer and hijack their e-mail programs.

If malware infects a user's machine, it will be able to send e-mails from their e-mail address, meaning that e-mail account will send messages to other users that are linked to the user's contacts and addresses from recent e-mails that have either been received or sent via the e-mail address and program. This may also cause the user's e-mail account to generate automated replies to e-mail that has been received. Nevertheless, if this type of e-mail behavior has been detected, a network administrator or technician should change the password of the infected user's e-mail account and either remove all miscellaneous software from their machine or replace the user's personal computer. Antimalware and antispyware utilities should also be run.

E-Mail Decryption Errors

If a user claims they cannot decrypt e-mail on a personal computer or mobile device, the first advisement you should give is the notion that e-mail encryption relies on public and private keys. In other words, you should advise the user that if they replaced a device or obtained a new e-mail address, the new device might not be set up to adhere to a prior decryption process, and the private key on the new device may not use a previously stored key. However, it is recommended that a user with this issue notify other users they are e-mailing that the encryption standards are being updated on their new device.

Endpoint Management Server

Any device that connects or requires access to a network is considered an *endpoint*. An *endpoint management server* inspects endpoints and verifies that they adhere to the network policies before they can access the network. Furthermore, the endpoint management server can provide network updates to the endpoints connected to it.

Authentication Server

1101: 2.4 A+

An *authentication server* stores and confirms the usernames and passwords of users from the network's Active Directory to facilitate authentication to the network. Without this server role, users would not have certain permissions or access to certain files and folders of their network. For example, without an authentication server, a user may have access to all files and folders, and every user may be able to see every file that is saved and modified in the network. This presents vulnerabilities as well as the potential for sensitive data to be seen or used by unauthorized personnel. For example, network administrators and technicians may not want all users to see the data of those from the accounting or human resources department of their organization, and without the use of authentication, this could be a reality for organizations.

Authentication servers are often programmed to implement *authentication, authorization, and accounting (AAA)*, also known as the *triple-A framework*, which is used to control and track user access across a computer network. Within this framework, *authentication* refers to the verification of a person's identity, *authorization* refers to what assets or resources they should be able to access, and *accounting*, sometimes called *auditing*, monitors or logs user activity. Protocols such as RADIUS and TACACS+ are often incorporated to provide this type of functionality.

A+ 1102: 2.2

RADIUS

Remote Authentication Dial-In Service (RADIUS) is a wireless server that uses the 802.1X protocol, which incorporates authentication that communicates between a user's device and the wireless access point(s) to which it is connected. Therefore, to use this protocol, a network administrator must configure a RADIUS server that supports 802.1X. This practice is only suggested when network administrators and technicians want to authenticate their wireless users without needing to encrypt their data that is being transmitted.

A+ 1102: 2.2

TACACS

Terminal Access Controller Access Control System (TACACS) is an authentication protocol that uses a person's username and password via their network credentials on the Active Directory to determine whether access can be granted on the network. TACACS is common among Unix networks and platforms but can be implemented via Windows networks. It is important to note that TACACS is an outdated system and protocol and has been replaced by protocols such as *TACACS+*, which relies on forms of TCP/IP and is more reliable than the access control methods of TACACS.

UTM

Unified Threat Management (UTM) is a hardware appliance that provides network security features similar to those provided by network devices such as a router and firewall. Its primary purpose is to protect a network from malicious traffic, and since a UTM provides a network with security, network administrators and technicians will have less overhead to adhere to in their networking activities. The UTM is to be implemented and connected between the network and its primary Internet connection point.

A+ 1102: 1.8

21.5 Windows Server

The following paragraphs illustrate differences between a simple peer-to-peer network and a more sophisticated network system. This is not an in-depth study of Windows Server 2019 or 2022. Rather, this is intended to introduce you to some of the capabilities and features of a network operating system. A complete study of any Windows Server system would require a complete textbook of its own.

Windows Server operating systems parallel the look of the current Windows style and features of the Windows PC operating systems of the same era. Both Windows Server 2019 and even 2022 look similar to the Windows 10 or 11 desktop and **Start** screen. Figure 21-12 shows the Windows 2022 desktop and **Start** screen.

Figure 21-12 The Windows Server desktop (A) and Start screen (B) are visually similar to those in the Windows 10 operating system.

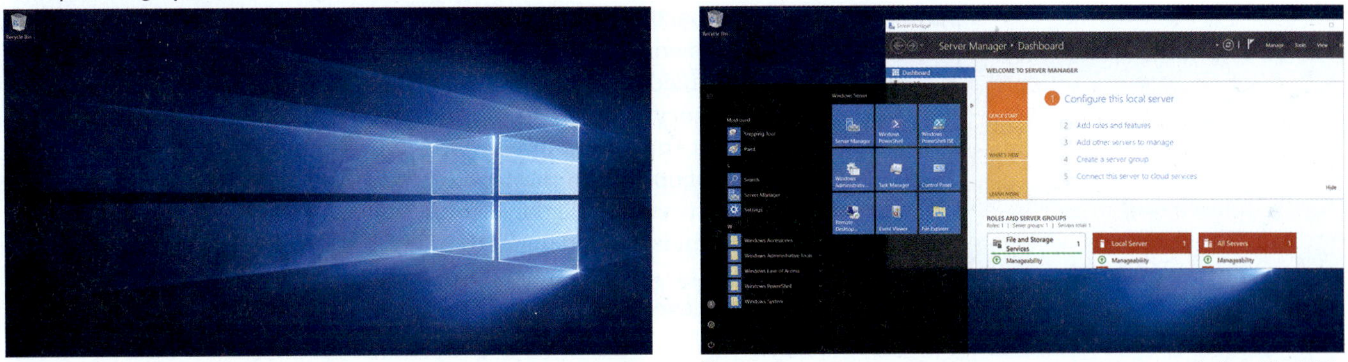

A B

Goodheart-Willcox Publisher

User Management

The Active Directory Users and Computers management utility is used to enter or examine information about users, groups, domains, and other objects in the Active Directory structure, as shown in Figure 21-13. Notice in the figure that the right pane contains a listing of the names and descriptions of the network's built-in users and groups.

From the **Active Directory Users and Computers** window, you can add or delete users and groups. Microsoft is famous for providing software wizards to assist users with their tasks, and Microsoft Server is no exception. Microsoft provides several wizards, such as the New Object wizard shown in Figure 21-14, to assist the network administrator. This wizard helps add users to the network in a systematic way, ensuring that no important security features are inadvertently left out.

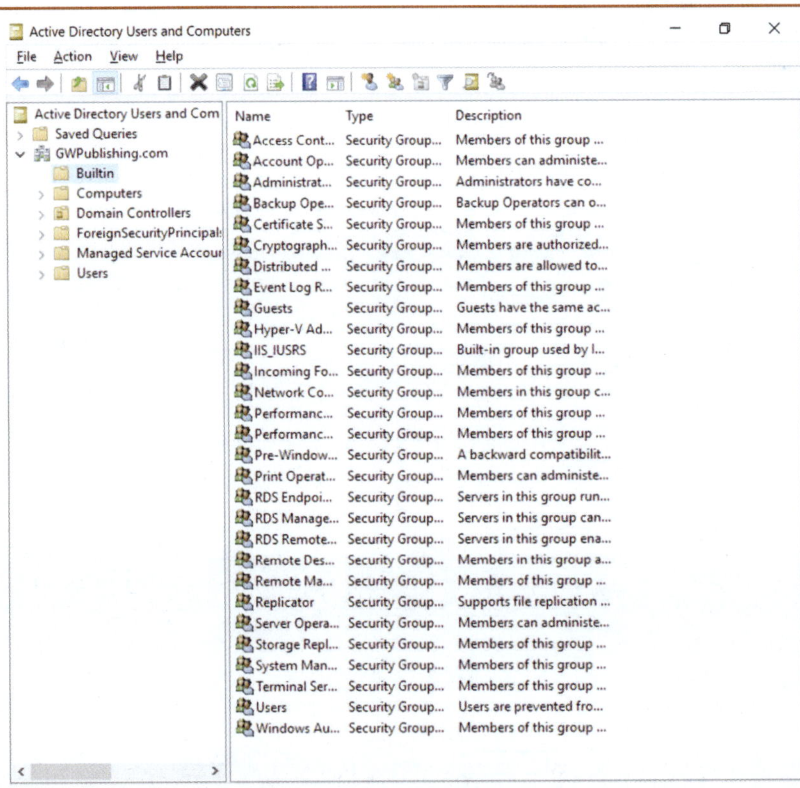

Figure 21-13 Information about Active Directory objects is displayed in the **Active Directory Users and Computers** window.

Goodheart-Willcox Publisher

After a domain user is created, the user account will have a **Properties** dialog box, such as the one shown in Figure 21-15. Important information about a user is displayed in the user **Properties** dialog box, which can also be used to configure user properties, such as password security and group memberships.

The deletion of an account via a network's Active Directory is a simple process. Once the Active Directory is open, an administrative user may right-click on the user account and select the **Delete** option. Be advised that an account may also be disabled from this set of options. If the account only needs to be locked, it is advised that an administrative user disable the account instead of deleting it, because if the Active Directory account is deleted instead of disabled, it may be difficult to retrieve the account's data in the event it must be reinstated. The administrator can also reset a password in the event a user loses it.

Figure 21-14 When adding users to the network system in Windows Server 2016, new users are created using the New Object wizard. The first dialog box (A) appears during the creation of a new user. Password settings for the new user are entered next (B), and settings are verified in the final window (C).

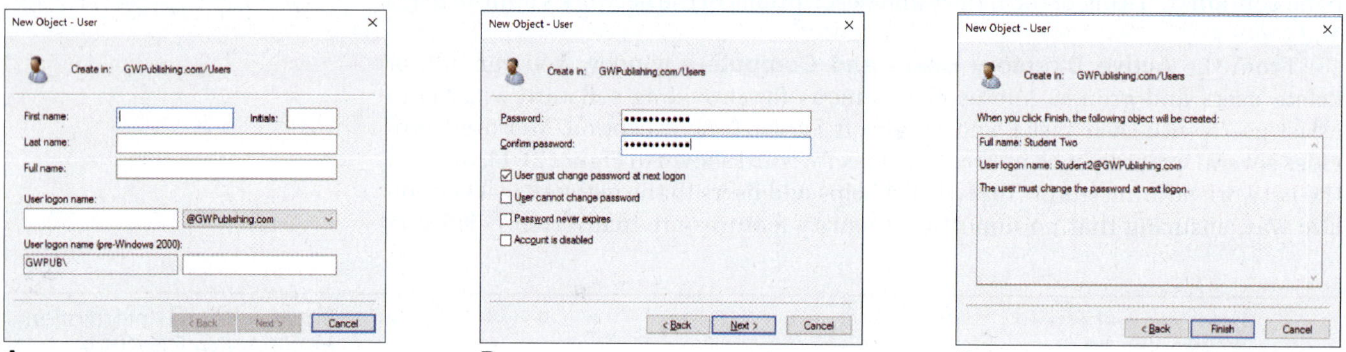

A B C

Goodheart-Willcox Publisher

Figure 21-15 Everything that needs to be known about a user can be viewed through the user's **Properties** dialog box.

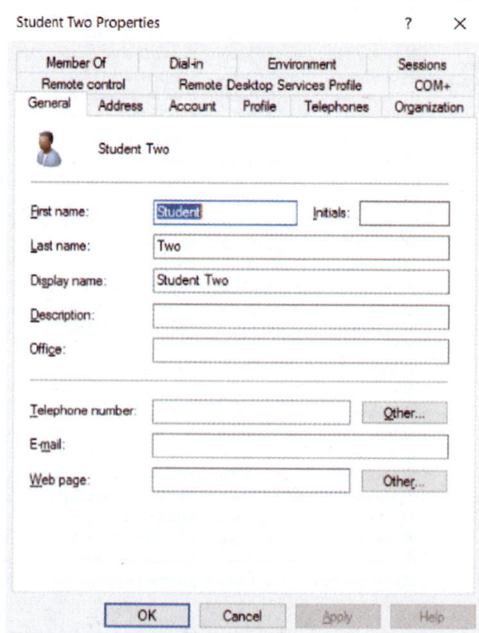

Goodheart-Willcox Publisher

Data Sources

A+ 1102: 1.4

The ability to observe and modify the Open Database Connectivity (ODBC) data sources can be accomplished via the Data Source Administrator. If a network administrator or technician is given access to these Data Sources, they will be able to manage a database and its drivers, as well as test its connection(s) to databases in the network(s). This tool can be accessed via the Control Panel or Windows Administrative Tools.

Security Options

Many standard security options are incorporated into Windows Server. These features include password, account lockout, and time policies. The security features associated with the user account are set to a minimum level of security, but when needed, a network administrator can alter the default settings.

Password Policy

A+ 1102: 2.6

Windows Server creates a default password policy that sets the standards for domain user access, though these default settings can be altered by the administrator. Figure 21-16 shows the Windows Server **Create Password Settings** dialog box, which allows an administrator to alter the password policy for all domain users.

The domain password policy contrasts with the password policy used to access the server locally. The **Local Security Policy** dialog box is used to configure local computer access or, in this case, the server. In short, the Local Security Policy sets the configuration of security features for password access to the computer (server), and the Active Directory Domain Services (AD DS) password policy configures the security settings for access to the network domain. Figure 21-17 shows the **Group Policy Editor** dialog box, which looks similar to the **Local Security Policy** dialog box in the Windows operating system.

Notice that selecting **Password Policy** from the left pane of the **Local Security Policy** dialog box reveals six password policy features on the right. The following security features are listed:

- Enforce password history
- Maximum password age
- Minimum password age
- Minimum password length
- Password must meet complexity requirements
- Store passwords using reversible encryption

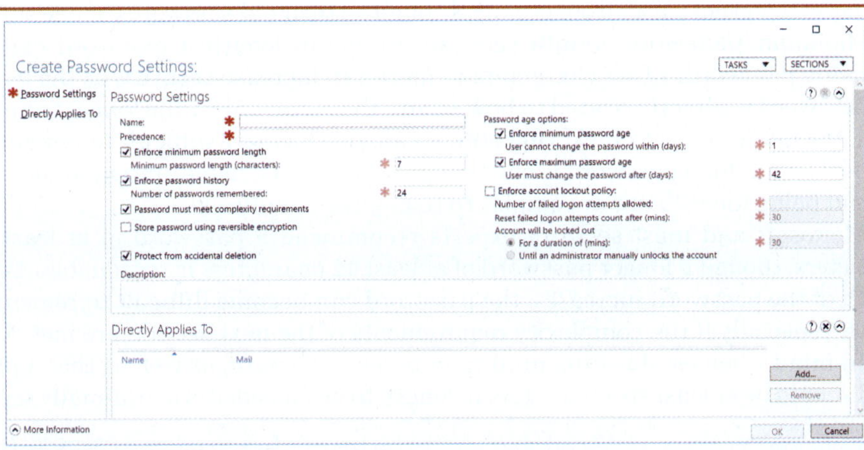

Goodheart-Willcox Publisher

Figure 21-16 Windows Server can be configured to enforce password policies that directly affect all domain user passwords.

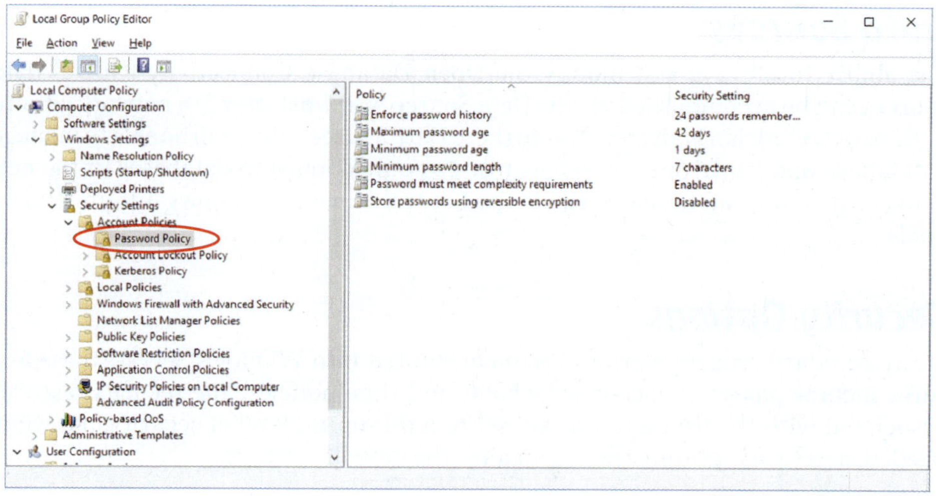

Figure 21-17 A password security policy can be configured for access to the server in similar fashion to the password policy used on a simple computer system.

Goodheart-Willcox Publisher

Enforce password history determines how long old passwords are remembered by the system. Password controls can be set to require a user to use a different password every time they change passwords. A value can be entered that determines how many times the user must change passwords before being allowed to repeat an old password. If this were not set, the user could simply rotate between two passwords, weakening system security.

Maximum password age is the maximum number of days a password can be used before it must be changed. Passwords should be changed frequently, but not so frequently that it becomes a bother to the user. The recommended password age is 30 to 90 days, but the permitted range is from 0 to 999 days.

The **Minimum password age** is the number of days old a password must be before it can be changed. **Minimum password age** is a required feature when using the password history policy. Values range from 0 to 998 and must be set at a value less than maximum. If there were no minimum password age and a value were set in **Enforce password history** that determined a user must change a password seven times before being allowed to reuse an old password, a user could change their password to meet the maximum password requirement and then immediately change the password back to the original. For example, if a user's original password were MyPassword_1, the user could create a series of passwords based on the last digit, such as MyPassword_2, MyPassword_3, and so on. When the password series reached the value set in **Enforce password history**, the user once more could use the original password, MyPassword_1. Setting the minimum password age feature to as little as one day will prevent a user from cycling through all their old passwords at one sitting.

Minimum password length sets the minimum length a password can be. Enforcing passwords of six characters or more can increase security, as the length of a password is directly related to how secure the password is. The longer the password, the harder it is to crack. However, it can also be more difficult to remember. An ideal length for a password is one that provides a reasonable amount of security without being too difficult or complex to remember or enter.

Microsoft and most security experts recommend a password of at least six characters, though a longer password of at least 12 characters is reasonable. As the length of the password increases, the password can become difficult to remember or use, especially if the complexity requirements of the next section are met. Keep this in mind when establishing minimum password length, as well as that a password should be at least six characters in length to be considered a minimally secure password.

The **Password must meet complexity requirements** options prevents a user from choosing a password that is easily compromised by cracking tools such as dictionaries. Complex passwords require a minimum length and the use of an assortment of letters, numbers, and special symbols in the password because this makes the password extremely difficult to compromise.

Store passwords using reversible encryption hides the user password by encrypting the characters so they cannot be seen by unauthorized probes of the security database.

Account Lockout Policy

1102: 2.1, 2.6, 2.7 A+

The **Account Lockout Policy** dialog box accessed through **Default Controller Security Settings>Account Policies** allows the system administrator to select a lockout duration for a set number of failed logon attempts. For example, if a person tries and fails to log on to a network three consecutive times, the system locks the user out for a period of time, which can range from 0 to 99,999 minutes. The idea is to cause a reasonable delay between login failures to prevent a brute force attack by an unauthorized person. Even a delay of a few minutes will ward off most attacks.

Time Policy

1102: 2.6 A+

The time (days and hours) a user may access the network can be easily controlled through **Logon Hours** dialog box, as shown in Figure 21-18. In the figure, logon hours are configured so the user can only access the network system from 6:00 a.m. to 8:00 p.m. Monday through Friday, so users are denied access to the network any other day or time they attempt to log on. This security feature prevents someone from accessing the network with a stolen username and password during off hours. One option of this feature forces users off the system when their time expires, while another option allows them to continue (or finish) working in their current program or document but does not allow them to open any new files or services.

Monitoring the System

In addition to monitoring the users on the network, the system can monitor itself, record events in the system log, and alert the system administrator to potential problems. Various features available in Windows Server allow the network administrator to observe and track system performance. The features are discussed in the following sections.

Event Viewer

The Event Viewer in Windows Server displays recorded events that occur on the server. Notice in Figure 21-19 that the Windows Server Event Viewer has the same look and feel as the Windows PC version of Event Viewer. It also serves the same function. Events that are directly related to security, applications, the operating

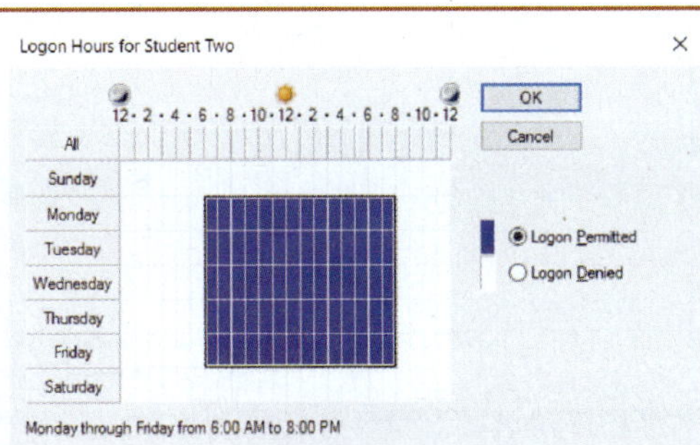

Goodheart-Willcox Publisher

Figure 21-18 A user's access to the network can be limited to certain hours in a day or days of the week.

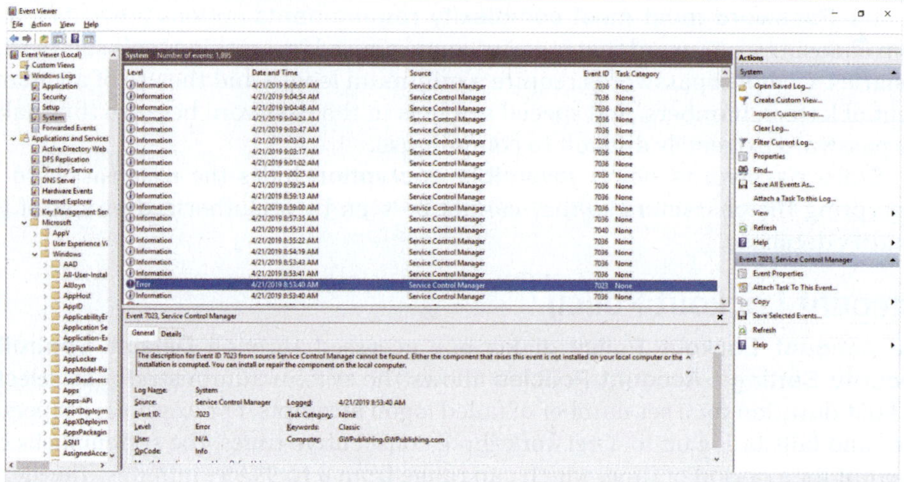

Figure 21-19 The Event Viewer in Windows Server has the same look and serves the same function as the personal computer version of Event Viewer.

Goodheart-Willcox Publisher

system, and more are recorded and can be viewed later. Event Viewer is a handy tool to use when analyzing system failures and security breaches.

Performance Monitor

The administrator can use the Performance Monitor utility to monitor the performance of some of the computer system components. The main difference between the Performance Monitor for Windows Server when compared to the Windows PC version is the server version provides options to diagnose Active Directory performance issues. In Figure 21-20, the Performance Monitor displays the CPU activity, expressed as a percentage from 0 to 100. The administrator can use this tool to diagnose various network problems, such as network congestion or failing hardware.

You will find many of the same tools in the server version of Windows as compared to the PC version. By learning to use the Windows PC version of tools and utilities, you will have already gained a valuable insight into the Windows Server.

Intrusion Detection and Prevention

An **intrusion detection system (IDS)** is a system that monitors network traffic for suspicious activity or breaches and alerts a system administrator when such activities are found. It can be configured to monitor an entire network or individual

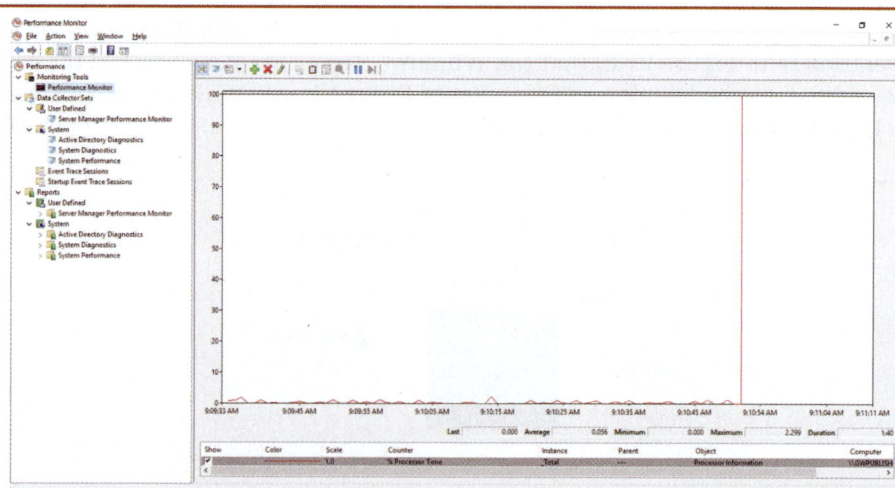

Figure 21-20 The Windows Server Performance Monitor can be used to analyze not only the server hardware performance but also Active Directory problems.

Goodheart-Willcox Publisher

computers on a network. When suspicious activity occurs, the IDS will activate a signal for the network administrators and technicians. IDS will only send a signal to the network administrators and technicians; it is *not* capable of blocking any malicious traffic or activity.

An **intrusion prevention system (IPS)** is similar to IDS as it monitors a network or certain devices for malicious traffic or activity, but it also blocks the connection where malicious traffic or activity is being generated. The concept of IPS is derived from the theory of IDS, and although it is perceived to be a more valuable option for network security, network administrators and technicians may still prefer to use IDS in their networking implementations.

Login Scripts

1102: 2.1 A+

Login scripts are used to assign actions and tasks that are central to a user's Active Directory account, the local machine(s) they have logged into, the mapped drives the user is to have access to, printers the user will have access to, and their user logs in the network's domain. These login scripts can be generated in forms such as batch or VBScript. When an Active Directory user logs into a personal computer or device on their network, the login script will obtain the previously mentioned user criteria, after the user has entered their username and password. The login script will also identify to network administrators any users who have logged in to each device on their network along with the day(s) and time(s) when they logged in to each device.

Permissions

A network security system maintains a database of security information on all network users. The exact terminology used to describe the individual features varies according to the network operating system software used. The database stores information such as the group(s) the user belongs to and their access rights to files and drives. The administrator can alter, copy, delete, or simply read the contents of a profile. There are many aspects to the individual user profile. In Figure 21-21, you can see that each share has a **Properties** dialog box that controls who has permission to access the network share. This dialog box can be used to add or remove users and change the individual user permissions.

In the **Advanced Security Settings for Network Share Students** dialog box shown in Figure 21-22, you can see part of the default restrictions assigned to users

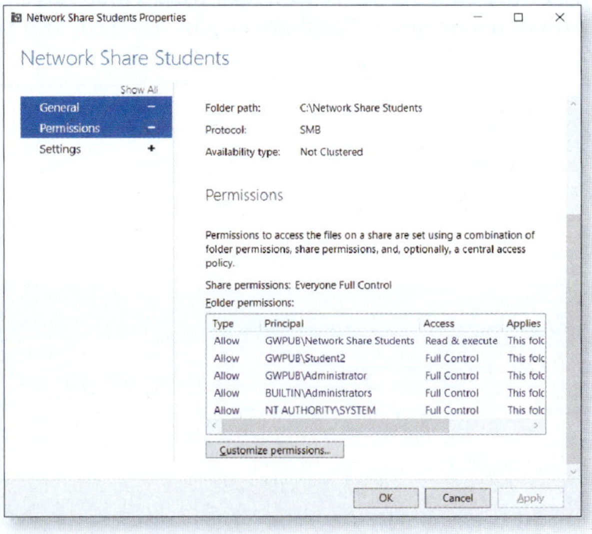

Goodheart-Willcox Publisher

Figure 21-21 The server provides a centralized location to manage network share permissions.

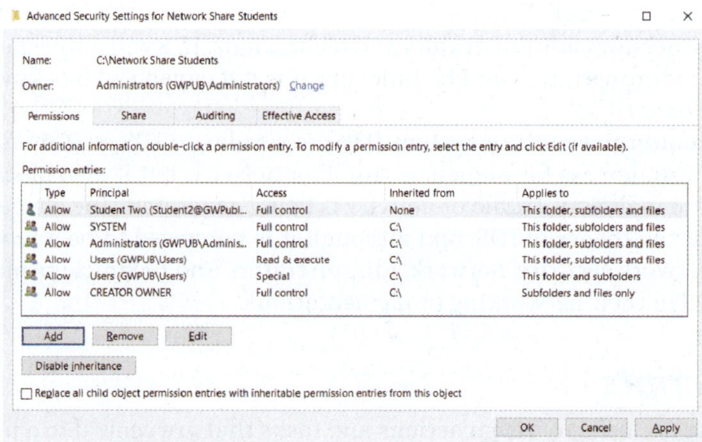

Figure 21-22 Each share has an **Advanced Security Settings** dialog box, which is used to configure who has permission to access the net share, add clients, and more.

Goodheart-Willcox Publisher

accessing the shared network folder called Network Share Students. This network share has been created to allow students to store files and folders on the network. It was created by the network administrator, who has full control over the share. Notice that Users has been assigned limited permissions only to read and execute files stored in the share. As you can see, the network administrator can place strong limits on a user to ensure a secure network environment. The administrator can limit a user's access so the user may only run the programs and access the files authorized by the network administrator.

Access to shares can also be controlled by the **Permission Entry for Users** dialog box. As shown in Figure 21-23, the share permissions are very similar to the ones encountered in peer-to-peer Simple File Sharing.

Permissions can be assigned to individual users or groups. Look at Figure 21-24. When permission is assigned to a group, all members of that group inherit that permission. It is common in network domains to assign a specific set of permissions to a group as related to a resource rather than assigning permissions for each individual. If a group of people share the same resource on a network, it is easier to assign individuals to a group and then assign permissions to each group. For example, a **Homework** folder, **Tests** folder, and **Assignment** folder could be created in a school setting. The collection of folders could be placed in another folder called **Student Resources**. The network administrator could then create a group called Students, which would be assigned the Read permission for the **Student Resources** folder. All folders inside the **Student Resources** folder would also have the Read permission. Another group of users called Teachers can be created, and teachers could be

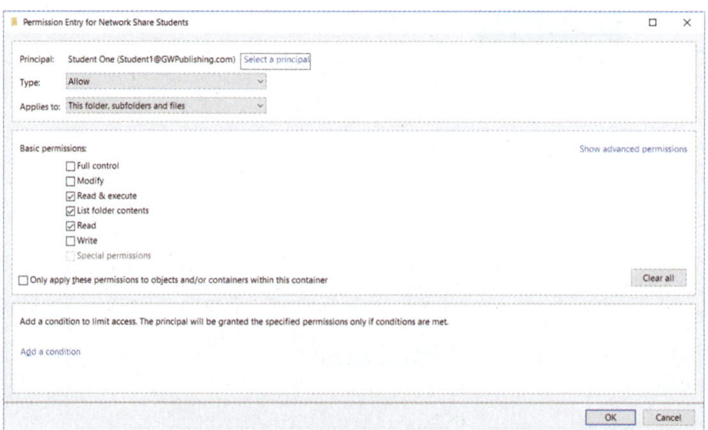

Figure 21-23 Basic user permissions are similar to the ones encountered in peer-to-peer Simple File Sharing.

Goodheart-Willcox Publisher

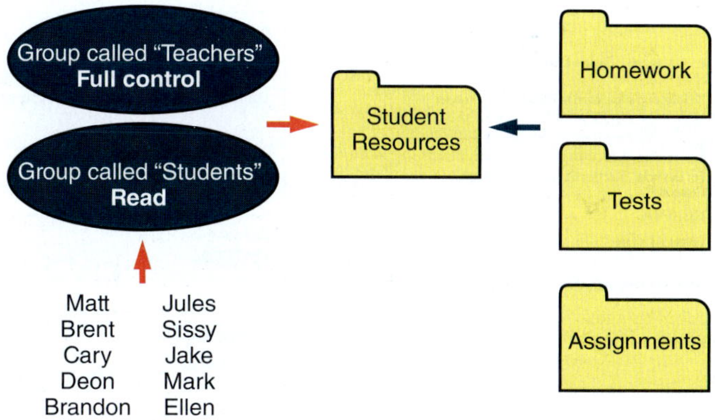

Goodheart-Willcox Publisher

Figure 21-24 Assigning users to groups and then assigning permission to each group is the most efficient way to manage large numbers of users on a domain network.

assigned to the Teacher group. The Teacher group could then be given full control, so all teachers assigned to the Teacher group would have full control over the whole collection of student resources. Assigning group permissions is the most efficient way to manage large numbers of users and large numbers of resources.

Folder Redirection

1102: 2.1, 3.2 A+

Often, users may become frustrated by an inability to access folders from local machines, such as the **Documents** folder or a folder on their desktops or network drive. Administrators and technicians can avoid this frustration by implementing folder redirection, which is accomplished by linking their folders such as the **Documents** folder to the folder on their Active Directory account or via Group Policy Manager. Implementing folder redirection can be considered a shortcut to the users' **Documents** folders on their local machines, similar to their **Home** folders on their network's server. This also provides a means of data restoration if a user's local machine fails or needs to be replaced.

Joining a Windows Server Domain

Computer membership configuration to a workgroup or domain is first selected when the Windows operating system is first installed. The default configuration for the Windows operating system is as a member of a workgroup. Domain membership can be created during the operating installation process, but it is not typically configured for home computer use.

The membership configuration can be changed at any time after the operating system has been installed by opening the **System Properties** dialog box and selecting the **Change** button. The **Computer Name/Domain Changes** dialog box will open, allowing you to rename or change the computer domain or workgroup membership, as shown in Figure 21-25.

Home editions of Windows versions typically do not provide the option to join a network domain and instead, users are limited to a workgroup. Users can only join a domain in Windows 10 if the PC is running Windows 10 Pro or Enterprise editions.

A+ Note

For the A+ Exams, you do not need an expert's level of knowledge about the unattended installation tools and methods mentioned in this chapter. The unattended installation questions on the A+ Exams are targeted at a general knowledge level. In contrast, Microsoft requires expert-level knowledge of unattended installation procedures for the Microsoft Windows operating system certifications.

21.6 **Network Unattended Installation**

When working with small networks, a technician is often required to install new operating systems or perform upgrades. For a very small network system, it is acceptable to perform manual installation at each computer, but as the size of the network grows, this becomes a time-consuming task. A better method of deployment is

Figure 21-25 Changing membership from a workgroup to a domain is accomplished through the **System Properties** and **Computer Name/Domain Changes** dialog boxes.

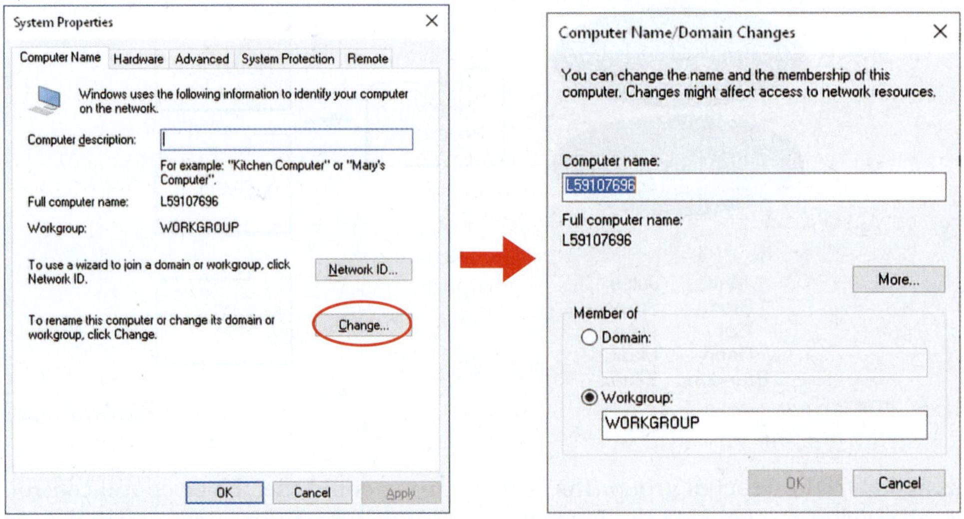

Goodheart-Willcox Publisher

performing an **unattended installation**, which is a fully automated installation of a new operating system or upgrade of an existing operating system. Microsoft refers to the operation of massive installation as *deployments* and provides a complete set of tools designed for installing multiple copies of the operating system and application software onto multiple computers.

This section will familiarize you with the unattended installation process. To further enhance your knowledge and become an in-depth expert in mass deployments, please visit the Microsoft TechNet website, where there is extensive material written about performing unattended installations and remote network installations.

Look at Figure 21-26 to see the three computer designations discussed in the unattended installation process. In an unattended installation, there is a technician computer, reference computer, and target or destination computers. The *target* or *destination computers* either contain no operating system or contain operating systems that will be upgraded.

Figure 21-26 Massive deployment machines are identified as the technician computer, reference computer, and target or destination computer(s).

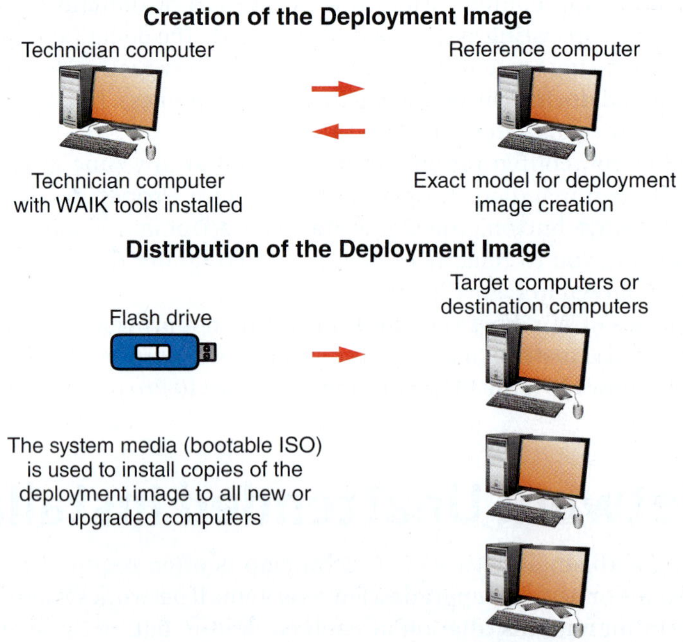

Goodheart-Willcox Publisher; (workstation icons) romvo/Shutterstock.com

Reference Computer

A *reference computer* is a model computer representing what a typical desktop used in the organization should look like. Microsoft also refers to the reference computer as the *master computer* in some of its documentation. The reference computer has the operating system installed as well as software applications, such as Microsoft Office, and any required hardware drivers that might be needed that are not contained on a typical Windows installation DVD. The reference computer is used to create a **deployment image**, which is an exact copy of all the files contained on the hard disk drive of the reference computer.

Technician Computer and WAIK

The *technician computer* contains all the various software tools used to configure the deployment image. The *Windows Automated Installation Kit (WAIK)* is installed on the technician computer. In some system configurations, there is no need for a keyboard or monitor located at the reference computer, though a device known as a keyboard-video-mouse (KVM) switch can be used.

Performing an Unattended Installation

The general steps for creating and performing an unattended installation are as follows:

1. Download and install the Windows Automated Installation Kit (WAIK) on the technician computer.
2. Create a reference computer (master computer) containing the operating system and software applications.
3. Create an answer file.
4. At the technician computer, run the System Preparation Tool (**Sysprep**) to prepare and create a deployment image of the reference computer.
5. Create a bootable Windows system media (bootable ISO) such as a CD, DVD, or USB flash drive, or copy the image to a network location to be used for distribution of the image.
6. Distribute the system media. At the destination computer, insert the distribution media and then press [Ctrl][Alt][Del] to boot the computer and start the unattended installation process.

While the list of key steps makes the distribution process sound simple, it is not. The successful distribution of the operating system using an unattended file takes many hours of preparation, but it is far less time-consuming than manually installing the operating system and software on each computer individually.

Installing the Windows Automated Installation Kit

The **Windows Automated Installation Kit (WAIK)** is a collection of tools and software applications used to make an exact copy of all content located on a computer hard disk drive and deploy that copy to other workstations. Becoming an expert in the use of the WAIK takes many hours of training, study, and practice. Microsoft provides hundreds of pages of documentation concerning the Windows automated deployment strategy and deployment techniques.

Creating a Reference Computer

The *reference computer* is the model of what all the computers in the network should look like when the distribution of the operating system is finished. It contains the operating system and other software, such as Microsoft Office and hardware drivers.

It is advisable, but not required, that the reference computer has the same hardware components as the destination computers. If the corporation requires a variety of computers, several reference computers can be created. For example, computer hardware and software requirements used for accounting and sales departments can vary greatly when compared to the distribution department. A reference computer should be created for each department so all users within a department have identical workstations.

Creating an Answer File

The answer file is what truly makes an automated installation process possible. The **answer file** is a text-based document used in conjunction with the Sysprep tool to configure the unattended destination computer. It is created by using the Windows System Image Manager (Windows SIM) tool and contains all the answers to questions that are normally encountered during an operating system installation procedure, as well as a series of commands that perform such activities as preparing the partition when required. The answer file can automatically supply information for the configuration, such as the name of the computer, time zone, language, network domain, and other configuration information, which makes the installation possible without human interaction, thus the term *unattended installation.*

The answer file can also be configured to make the user answer specific questions during the first time the computer boots, such as when a new owner of a computer first boots their brand-new computer. Some typical new owner questions that may require user intervention are regarding the username and password, language, and time zone. The answer file can be simple or complex, depending on the environment where the computer will be located and the need for any additional driver software applications. Microsoft provides samples of answer files to make the creation of the file less complicated.

Running Sysprep and Creating a Deployment Image

When the operating system is first installed on the reference computer, a user account is created, and the computer is given a name. Also, a product key is generated as well as other security features, such as Security Identifiers (SIDs) and product ID that make the computer unique. Before copies of the reference computer can be distributed to multiple computers, all unique information must be removed. The Sysprep tool (**sysprep.exe**) removes all system identification and security features associated with an individual user account and computer, thus creating a deployment image. The deployment image contains all the files associated with the reference computer, except the unique configuration information is removed. You can think of the reference computer as a generic computer with an operating system and other software applications and drivers but no user account, computer name, product key, or security identifier.

Creating Bootable Windows System Media

The deployment image can be burned to a disc or copied to a USB flash drive or external storage drive and then used for distribution to computers. The deployment image can also be stored on a network share and used for distribution across the network to new or upgraded computers. When used for installation to new computers with no existing operating system, the Windows Preinstallation Environment (WinPE) is used to start the installation process from the new computer. WinPE is a minimal Windows operating system similar to the legacy DOS boot disk. It can boot and run a computer but does not provide a GUI and only responds to text-based commands. WinPE is required to start the blank destination computer when performing an unattended installation from a network share and contains a set of generic drivers that supports most commonly used hardware devices.

Distributing the System Media

It is possible to deploy multiple copies of the distribution media and start the installation process at multiple locations. At each destination computer, insert the distribution media and then press [Ctrl][Alt][Del] to boot the computer and start the unattended installation process. In most cases, you will not need to be at the computer locations while performing the installation. You can return after a period of time to retrieve the distribution media and verify the installation was successful.

Tech Tip

Before performing the actual distribution of the system media, you should first run a test to verify the system media will install properly and confirm that the finished destination computer will perform as desired.

21.7 Fault Tolerance via RAID Systems

A+ 1101: 3.3

Fault tolerance is a system's ability to recover after some sort of disaster. Disasters present themselves in a variety of ways, including a failed hard drive, crashed operating system, or simple user error. Networks can recover from these types of disasters through a variety of fault tolerance methods. However, the two most common methods of fault tolerance are RAID systems and tape backups. In this section, we will explore common RAID configurations used with Microsoft servers.

A **redundant array of independent disks (RAID)**, also called a *redundant array of inexpensive disks*, is a system of several hard drive units arranged in such a way as to ensure recovery after a system disaster or to ensure data integrity during normal operation. There are four forms of RAID associated with Microsoft servers: level 0, level 1, level 5, and level 10. Figure 21-27 illustrates the first three forms.

Level 0

RAID level 0 is also called *striped without parity.* A *striped set* is two or more areas across two or more disks to which data is written or from which data is read. The main purpose of a striped set is to speed up the data read/write process. Data is recorded more quickly when written simultaneously to multiple disks, and when data is recorded in a striped set, it is equally divided, with equal portions of the data written to each hard disk drive.

A striped set spreads the data across two drives or volumes, and data is written alternately to each drive or volume in 64-kB blocks of data. When two separate hard drive controllers are used, one for each drive, the read and write times are faster than those of a single drive. The disadvantage to this RAID arrangement is that there is no data protection. If one of the drives fails, all data on that drive is lost. To prevent the loss of data, the arrangement for data storage must use *parity*, which you should recall is a technique used to ensure data is correct. See Figure 21-27A.

Level 1

RAID level 1, or *disk mirroring*, requires two hard drives. One drive keeps an exact copy of all data on the other drive. This way if one drive fails, all its data can be retrieved from its duplicate. See Figure 21-27B.

Level 5

RAID level 5 can use between 3 and 32 hard drives of equal partition size to form what is called a *striped set with parity.* Parity is used to reconstruct data lost on either of the two hard drives used to store data. For example, data is duplicated on two hard drives and the third is used to store the parity of the two. Parity is staggered across all drives when a minimum of three are used. See Figure 21-27C.

Remember from previous chapters that parity is the sum of two bytes of data added together, and the two bytes will be either odd or even. By reversing the

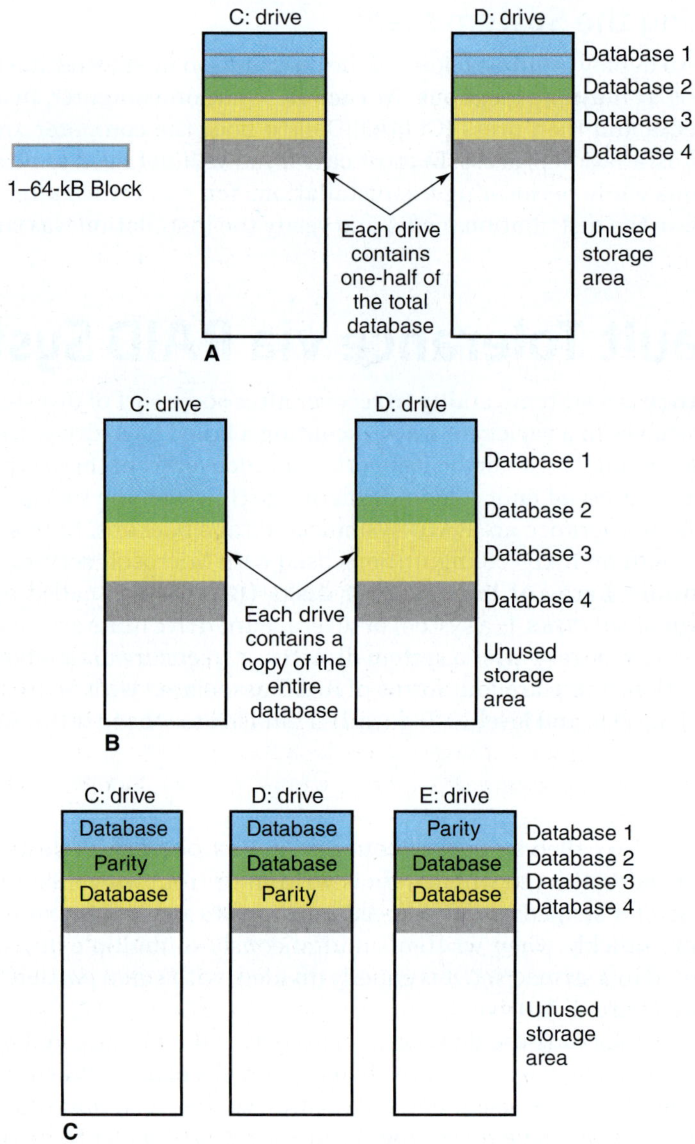

Figure 21-27 Three forms of RAID used on a Microsoft server are RAID 0 (A), which offers no data protection; RAID 1 (B), which uses at least two volumes to duplicate data; and RAID 5 (C), which is a striped set with parity to reconstruct lost data.

Goodheart-Willcox Publisher

operation, the missing data can be reconstructed using the value stored in the parity section. It is important to remember that while RAID can be useful in terms of providing recovery, none of the techniques discussed is infallible, meaning data can still be destroyed or lost. Regular backups are the only way to guarantee fault tolerance.

Level 10

As its name suggests, RAID level 10, also referred to as *RAID 1+0*, is a combination of RAID 0 and RAID 1. RAID 10 is a combination of mirroring and striping and provides the redundancy of two hard drives in a mirror configuration with the speed of a striped set of disks. RAID 10 provides the fastest storage data rate with an added redundancy feature but at a higher cost than the other RAID levels.

Storage Spaces and Storage Pools

Similar to RAID systems, Microsoft introduced two storage technologies known as Storage Spaces and Storage Pools. *Storage Spaces* are virtual disks created from the free space in a *Storage Pool*, which is a collection of physical disks acting as one large storage device or configured to represent multiple storage units.

Storage Spaces provide three storage layouts similar to RAID types and can be configured as a Simple (RAID 0), Mirror (RAID 1), or Parity (RAID 5). The minimum number of disks required for each type of Storage Pool matches the same requirements of RAID.

Storage Spaces that provide protection, such as mirror and parity, automatically rebuild themselves after failure. When the failed hard drive is replaced, the server rebuilds the Storage Pool using the data in the remaining disks.

21.8 Basic Network Troubleshooting

A+ 1101: 5.7

Several issues can occur with any type of network regardless of size, purpose, or network operating system. For example, *jitter* is a variation in the signal pulses of the network. This is particularly an issue for streaming video and Voice over IP. One way to address jitter is by configuring routers appropriately so real-time communications have priority. You can also simply increase bandwidth. Either option addresses jitter, as well as poor VoIP quality. One can also implement jitter buffers (sometimes called *de-jitter buffers*), which are used to mitigate jitter issues.

Network latency refers to the amount of time it takes data to travel from one endpoint to another and is usually measured in some fraction of a second. There will always be some delay, such as processing delays due to the time it takes a processor to process the packet. There can also be transmissions delay due to the time needed to transmit data across the network media. *High latency* is loosely defined as latency that causes an unacceptable degradation of network performance and must be addressed quickly. If the delay is temporary, then it is likely due to improper packet prioritization, or a sudden and temporary spike in bandwidth used. The best solution to long-term latency is to upgrade media or equipment to provide more bandwidth.

Related to latency is simply having slow network speeds. There are a variety of reasons network speeds can be slow, including latency and external interference, among others. In the case of external interference, you likely have some source of electromagnetic radiation interfering with your network. This will usually require some coordination with outside parties to address. Slow network speeds can also be due to poor packet prioritization, spikes in user utilization of certain services (such as streaming video), or many other causes. If the slow network speed is consistent and sustained, the best way to address it is to increase bandwidth.

Port flapping, sometimes called *link flapping*, causes router or switch ports to fluctuate between up and down, which can seriously degrade network performance. Port flapping can be caused by poor or improper configuration of routers and switches, as well as by problems in the media. One way to assess whether port flapping is the cause of a network issue is to simply try a different port. If using the new port fixes the problem, then port flapping is the likely culprit.

Intermittent wireless connectivity issues are often related to a problem with the external Internet connection. They can also be due to an issue with the wireless access point itself. The key to troubleshooting wireless issues is to identify what conditions have changed since the connectivity issues began and troubleshoot based on the changes made in that time period.

Chapter Summary

21.1 Network Administration

- *Peer-to-peer (P2P) networks*, also called *workgroup networks*, are common, especially in homes and small-business offices and can be easily set up and administered to allow users to share files, printers, hardware, and Internet connections.
- The client/server network model, also called a *centralized network model* or *domain network model,* is based on administration of the network being controlled by a centralized server and administrator.
- The most commonly encountered network operating systems used for managing large networks are Unix, Linux, and Windows.
- A share is an object that is distributed across the network, such as files, hard drives, optical drives, printers, and scanners, among others.
- The theory behind the Simple File Sharing feature in Windows XP paved the way for file sharing features in later operating systems, such as the Libraries feature in Windows 10 and 11, and the Public Folders feature.
- When password-protected sharing is enabled, users on other computers will not be able to access shared folders on that computer, including the **Public** folder(s). To access the shared folder from a different computer, the user must have a local user account on the computer with the shared resource.
- Network Discovery makes setting up and configuring a network easy as it automatically detects and configures a network and sets up a share and Internet connection.
- *File attributes* are settings that are associated with a computer's or server's files that grant or deny users access to the files.
- Shared resources are accessed by first opening Windows Explorer and expanding the **Network** folder located in the left pane.
- Administrative shares are hidden shares on a Windows machine that have a dollar sign ($) at the end of the shared path.

21.2 Permissions

- Shared folders have a combination of two different types of permissions used by Windows: share permissions and security permissions (also known as *NTFS permissions*). Share permissions apply to users who access the resource over the network and do not apply if a user logs on to the computer locally. Security permissions can only be applied to resources that are located on a volume or partition that is formatted with the NTFS file system.
- When a resource has a FAT partition, share permissions are limited to Full Control, Change, and Read. NTFS partitions, however, support a much wider range of permissions, including options such as Full Control, Modify, Read & execute, List folder content, and Read, among others.
- In Active Directory, there are two types of objects: child objects and parent objects. A *child object* is essentially created from a previously existing object, such as a domain or group, which then becomes a *parent object.* Often, child objects have *inherited permissions*, which are permissions assigned by a Windows operating system or server from a parent object.

21.3 Network Organization

- Centralized networks are organized administratively into sections. These sections are called *domains*, *groups*, and *users.*
- The network administrator, also called the *system administrator*, is a person (or persons) with the highest security rating on the network.
- Although access to system resources can be granted to individual users, network administrators can save a great deal of time by assigning resources to groups rather than users.
- When the computer is configured as part of a domain, the user is configured with a domain user account, which provides access to network domain resources as well as resources on the workstation.
- *Mobile Device Management (MDM)* policies are implemented in networks to determine which devices can access the network's resources.

21.4 Server Roles

- Network operating systems allow network administrators to control and modify their servers via server roles, such as web server, file server, print server, DHCP server, DNS server, proxy server, mail server, endpoint management server, and authentication server.
- Unified Threat Management (UTM) is a hardware appliance that provides network security features similar to those provided by network devices such as a router and firewall.

21.5 Windows Server

- Windows Server operating systems parallel the look of the current Windows style and features of the Windows PC operating systems of the same era. For example, Windows Server 2019 desktop and **Start** screen looked very similar to the Windows 10 desktop and Start screen, so it stands to reason that Windows Server 2019 looks similar to the Windows 10 desktop and **Start** screen.
- The Active Directory Users and Computers management utility is used to enter or examine information about users, groups, domains, and other objects in the Active Directory structure.
- Many standard security features are incorporated into Windows Server. These include password, account lockout, and time policies.
- Windows Server provides various features, such as Event Viewer and Performance Monitor, that allow the network administrator to observe and track system performance.
- An *intrusion detection system (IDS)* is a system that monitors network traffic for suspicious activity or breaches and alerts a system administrator when such activities are found.
- An *intrusion prevention system (IPS)* is similar to IDS as it monitors a network or certain devices for malicious traffic or activity, but it also blocks the connection where malicious traffic or activity is being generated.
- Login scripts are used to assign actions and tasks that are central to a user's Active Directory account, the local machine(s) they have logged into, the mapped drives the user is to have access to, printers the user will have access to, and their user logs in the network's domain. These login scripts can be generated in forms such as batch or VBScript.

- Each share has a **Properties** dialog box that controls who has permission to access the network share. This dialog box can be used to add or remove users and change the individual user permissions.

21.6 Network Unattended Installation

- An unattended installation is a fully automated installation of a new operating system or upgrade of an existing operating system.
- Windows Automated Installation Kit (WAIK) is a collection of tools that support the Windows deployment process.
- A reference computer, or *master computer*, is a model computer representing what a typical desktop used in the organization should look like. It is used to create a deployment image, which is an exact copy of all the files contained on the hard disk drive of the reference computer.
- The destination computer is the machine where the unattended installation will take place.
- The technician computer contains all the various software tools used to configure the deployment image.
- The answer file is a text-based document that is used in conjunction with the Sysprep tool to configure the unattended destination computer.

21.7 Fault Tolerance via RAID Systems

- Fault tolerance is a system's ability to recover after some sort of disaster.
- A redundant array of independent disks (RAID), also called a *redundant array of inexpensive disks*, is a system of several hard drive units arranged in such a way as to ensure recovery after a system disaster or to ensure data integrity during normal operation.
- RAID is a way to ensure data integrity and fault tolerance through multiple drive volumes.
- RAID level 0 is called striped without parity.
- RAID level 1, or disk mirroring, requires two hard drives.
- RAID level 5 can use from 3 to 32 hard drives of equal partition size to form what is called a striped set with parity.
- RAID 10, or RAID 1+0, is a combination of RAID 0 and RAID 1.
- Storage Spaces are virtual disks created from the free space in a Storage Pool. Storage Pools are collections of physical disks that function as one large storage device.

21.8 Basic Network Troubleshooting

- *Jitter* is a variation in the signal pulses of the network. This is particularly an issue for streaming video and Voice over IP. One way to address jitter is by configuring routers appropriately so real-time communications have priority. You can also simply increase bandwidth. One can also implement jitter buffers (sometimes called *de-jitter buffers*), which are used to mitigate jitter issues.
- *Network latency* refers to how long it takes data to travel from one endpoint to another and is usually measured in some fraction of a second. *High latency* is loosely defined as latency that causes an unacceptable degradation of network performance and must be addressed quickly. The best solution to long-term latency is to upgrade media or equipment to provide more bandwidth.

- There are a variety of reasons network speeds can be slow, including latency and external interference, among others. Slow network speeds can also be due to poor packet prioritization, spikes in user utilization of certain services (such as streaming video), or many other causes. If the slow network speed is consistent and sustained, the best way to address it is to increase bandwidth.
- *Port flapping*, sometimes called *link flapping*, causes the router or switch ports to fluctuate between up and down, which can seriously degrade network performance. Port flapping can be caused by poor or improper configuration of routers and switches, as well as by problems in the media. One way to assess whether port flapping is the cause of a network issue is to simply try a different port. If using the new port fixes the problem, then port flapping is the likely culprit.
- Intermittent wireless connectivity issues are often related to a problem with the external Internet connection. They can also be due to an issue with the wireless access point itself.

Review Questions

1. Discuss considerations made during network administration.
2. Who controls the access to shares on a peer-to-peer network?
3. List the most commonly encountered network operating systems used for managing large networks.
4. List the various techniques used to share resources across a network.
5. Differentiate between share and security permissions.
6. List and describe three allow permission sets.
7. Identify roles used to organize networks.
8. How do MDM policies help maintain security on a network?
9. Compare and contrast server roles.
10. What is the difference between RADIUS and TACACS?
11. Identify features of Windows Server.
12. What is the name of the utility in Windows Server that allows an administrator to enter or examine information about users, groups, domains, and other objects in the Active Directory structure?
13. List and describe three security options of Windows Server.
14. Summarize the function of a login script.
15. Recall the general procedure used for unattended installations.
16. List and describe the three computer designations in an unattended installation process.
17. Identify the most common RAID levels and their characteristics.
18. What is the difference between Microsoft Storage Pools and Microsoft Storage Spaces?
19. Summarize methods used to troubleshoot issues with jitter, latency, and slow transfer speeds on a network.
20. Summarize methods used to troubleshoot port flapping and intermittent wireless connectivity in a network.

Sample A+ Exam Questions

1. Which of the following is the best password to use to prevent possible compromise or intrusion?
   A. secret
   B. Big$tar_5
   C. President Roosevelt
   D. Password
2. Which is *not* a typical Windows share permission?
   A. Read
   B. Full control
   C. Partial
   D. Change
3. What does a user need to access a network system? Select all that apply.
   A. Username
   B. Password
   C. Group membership
   D. A security clearance
4. Who determines a user's rights on a client/server network?
   A. Each computer user determines the user rights for their own workstation.
   B. Users set their own individual rights based on their total system knowledge.
   C. The network administrator sets individual rights on the network system.
   D. All users automatically have full rights to use the entire network when they are issued an account on the network.
5. Where are user accounts set up in a Windows Server network?
   A. Active Directory Users and Computers
   B. Performance Monitor
   C. Event Viewer
   D. User Share Setup

6. Where is a user password changed in a Windows network system?
   A. In the **Active Directory Users and Computers** dialog box
   B. In the **Account Policy** dialog box
   C. At the user's workstation under the **Change Password** icon in **Control Panel**
   D. A user password can never be changed once it is issued
7. Which program can be used to monitor user activity on a computer system?
   A. Event Viewer
   B. Net Monitor
   C. Performance Monitor
   D. Net Movement
8. Which program would you select to check the total amount of activity through the CPU?
   A. Net Monitor
   B. Performance Monitor
   C. CPU Monitor
   D. CPU Pole Watch
9. Which term refers to a collection of Windows users who have similar tasks and are consequently assigned the same user rights?
   A. Group
   B. Covey
   C. Pod
   D. Corporate entity
10. Which of the following best describes the entire business network in a centralized network with user logon controlled by the server?
    A. Corporate entity
    B. Select pod
    C. Domain
    D. Group

Chapter 22

Network Operation and Connectivity

Learning Outcomes

22.1 Summarize characteristics of TCP/IP addressing.
22.2 List and identify networking equipment.
22.3 Differentiate among common diagnostic utilities associated with networks.
22.4 Summarize Internet navigation.
22.5 Differentiate among e-mail protocols.
22.6 List common Internet protocols and their characteristics.
22.7 Detail cloud service characteristics, infrastructure, and implementation models.
22.8 Troubleshoot common network connectivity issues.

A+ Certification Exam Objectives

The following A+ Certification Exam Objectives are covered in this chapter.

Exam 220-1101

1.0 Mobile Devices

- 1.4 Given a scenario, configure basic mobile device network connectivity and application support.

2.0 Networking

- 2.1 Compare and contrast Transmission Control Protocol (TCP) and User Datagram Protocol (UDP) ports, protocols, and their purposes.
- 2.2 Compare and contrast common networking hardware.
- 2.5 Given a scenario, install and configure a basic wired/wireless SOHO network.
- 2.6 Compare and contrast common network configuration concepts.

4.0 Virtualization and Cloud Computing

- 4.1 Summarize cloud computing concepts.
- 4.2 Summarize aspects of client-side virtualization.

5.0 Hardware and Network Troubleshooting

- 5.7 Given a scenario, troubleshoot problems with wired and wireless network networks.

Exam 220-1102

1.0 Operating Systems

- 1.2 Given a scenario, use the appropriate Microsoft command-line tool.
- 1.6 Given a scenario, configure Microsoft Windows networking features on a client/desktop.

2.0 Security

- 2.1 Summarize various security measures and their purposes.
- 2.9 Given a scenario, configure security settings on a small-office/home-office (SOHO) wireless and wired networks.

3.0 Software Troubleshooting

- 3.4 Given a scenario, troubleshoot common mobile OS and application issues.

4.0 Operational Procedures

- 4.9 Given a scenario, use remote access technologies.

Key Terms

Address Resolution Protocol (ARP)
Anything as a Service (XaaS)
Automatic Private IP Addressing (APIPA)
brouter
circuit switching
client-side virtualization
community cloud
Domain Name Service (DNS)
dynamic addressing
Dynamic Host Configuration Protocol (DHCP)
File Transfer Protocol (FTP)
gateway
hybrid cloud
Hypertext Markup Language (HTML)
Hypertext Transfer Protocol (HTTP)
hypervisor
Infrastructure as a Service (IaaS)
Internet Control Message Protocol Version 6 (ICMPv6)
Internet Corporation for Assigned Names and Numbers (ICANN)
Internet Protocol (IP) address
IPSec
octet
packet switching
ping
Platform as a Service (PaaS)
private cloud
proxy server
public cloud
repeater
Secure Shell (SSH)
Secure Sockets Layer (SSL)
Software as a Service (SaaS)
static IP addressing
subdomain
subnet mask
switch
Telnet
time to live (TTL)
Uniform Resource Locator (URL)
Windows Internet Naming Service (WINS)

Overview

Many corporations include thousands of computers in their network systems, which often stretch across multiple cities or states, and understanding how connected devices communicate can be a difficult task. It may seem like all the traffic would slow the network to a snail's pace, since there are packets of information being sent everywhere.

In this chapter, the basic concepts of network operation and communication are introduced along with the technologies that make networks possible. The types of equipment, protocols, and techniques are examined, as is how data is delivered over the Internet. You will learn how e-mail gets to its destination and how your web browser locates a particular web page in the Internet's endless tangle of cables, routers, and computers. Some of the subjects in this section are vast enough to fill textbooks of their own. The purpose of this chapter is to help you gain a basic understanding of network operation and explain some of the technical terminology associated with it.

A+ Note

The A+ Certification Exams require knowledge of the basic operation of network systems. In recent years, CompTIA has greatly expanded the network portion of the exam objectives, so be sure you can distinguish between DNS, WINS, and DHCP services, as you will likely encounter one or more questions directly related to these topics. You will most likely be asked several questions related to common network protocols and port address assignments, and you may also be asked to identify an example of an IP address and a subnet mask.

22.1 TCP/IP Addressing

The TCP/IP protocol suite is the secret to communicating over networks and the Internet. It was designed for the Internet and is the dominant protocol suite for data exchange on a typical LAN, MAN, or WAN. *TCP/IP addressing*, also referred to as *IP addressing*, is a method of identification used to identify every node or host on a network. The terms *host* and *node* are used interchangeably to identify individual PCs, printers, and network equipment that may require an address.

Tech Tip

ICANN, under the supervision of the Department of Commerce, has assumed the name and responsibilities of InterNIC. Currently, InterNIC is a website that provides services and information about Internet-assigned names and numbers.

ICANN

Internet Corporation for Assigned Names and Numbers (ICANN) is a nonprofit organization that monitors the use of domain names, IP addresses, and related protocols. The Internet uses TCP/IP to route data packets all over the world, and every network device has an Internet Protocol (IP) address assigned to it. An **Internet Protocol (IP) address** is a numeric identifier that uniquely identifies a device on a network. IP addresses can be assigned manually or automatically, but no two can be the same. All IP addresses are regulated and assigned through ICANN.

ICANN operates under the direction of the Department of Commerce and is responsible for regulating the Internet, overseeing the issue of domain names, and assigning IP addresses to them. A user does not directly contact ICANN for an IP address or domain name. Instead, the user places an application through a *registrar*, which is a private-sector company to which users apply for an IP address or domain name. The registrar is regulated by ICANN, which allocates IP addresses much like the way the government issues telephone area codes to long distance carriers and telephone companies. IP addresses must be similarly regulated or there would be chaos in the computer world. While ICANN is the ultimate source of IP addresses, many people obtain addresses through third parties that also provide web hosting and domain registration, including companies such as GoDaddy, Wix, Amazon Web Services, and HostGator, among others.

A+ 1101: 2.5
1102: 1.6

IP Addresses

An IP address is assigned to nodes on a network for the purpose of identification. The terms *host* and *node* represent network equipment that requires IP addresses for communication, such as computers, servers, network printers, routers, and gateways. The IPv4 address was originally designed for Internet access and communication between Internet-connected devices. Networks did not always access the Internet; originally, very few computers accessed the Internet, and IP addresses were not required. Instead, local area networks used a MAC address to identify a host. Today, it is rare that a computer does not access the Internet is rare, so all computers are now automatically configured to use two types of IP addresses: IPv4 and IPv6.

IPv4 was introduced in 1981 and has been used to identify computers in large networks. With the rapid expansion of the Internet in the 1990s, there were too many computers and network devices requiring IP addresses, so the IPv6 address standard was introduced to provide a larger pool of IP addresses to accommodate the increasing number of computers. An IPv5 was under development, but it was abandoned and was never accepted as an alternative to IPv4.

An IPv4 address consists of four sets of decimal numbers in the range of 0 to 255, and each set of decimal numbers is derived from an **octet**, which is an eight-bit binary number. The IPv4 format is known as dotted decimal notation and appears as x.x.x.x where the *x* represents decimal numbers in the appropriate range, for example 183.24.202.17.

An IPv6 address consists of eight groups of hexadecimal numbers with each set in the range of 0000 to FFFF. The IPv6 format is x:x:x:x:x:x:x:x where the *x* represents hexadecimal numbers in the appropriate range, for example fe80:c21d:bc23:acf4:578:34da:f0b2:dc56. Look at Figure 22-1 to see an IPv4 and IPv6 address assigned to the same network adapter in Windows 10. Also, notice the MAC address is listed for the network card, which is noted as a Physical Address.

Notice that each set of decimal numbers in the IPv4 address is separated by a period, but each set of hexadecimal numbers in the IPv6 address is separated by a colon. A double colon is used in an IPv6 address as an abbreviated form of an all-zero entry. For example, the IPv6 address 2601:248:4100:2b40:0:0:e43b can be written as 2601:248:4100:2b40::e43b. A series of zeros can be replaced by a single set of double colons, but you can only replace one string of zeros, not two.

Early operating systems used only the IPv4 address and the MAC address. Windows XP was the first operating system that would allow you to assign an IPv6 address to a network adapter, but it was not configured by default. Windows Vista was the first operating system to assign both an IPv4 and IPv6 address to a computer by default.

Advantages of IPv6

1101: 2.5, 2.6 A+
1102: 2.9

IPv6 provides many advantages and improvements when compared to the limitations of IPv4. The main improvements of IPv6 over IPv4 include a much larger pool of Internet and network addresses, reduced broadcast traffic, better security, improved quality of service, and support for network discovery.

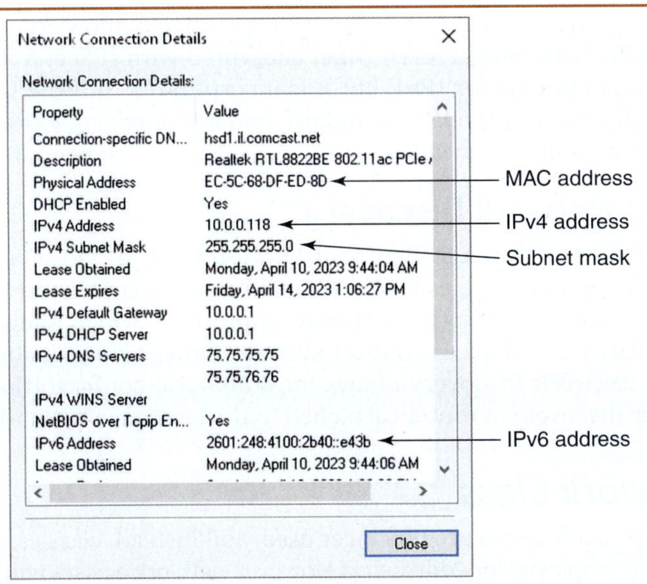

Goodheart-Willcox Publisher

Figure 22-1 By default, Windows assigns IPv4 and IPv6 addresses to a network card.

Tech Tip

IPv4 provides 4,294,967,296 possible addresses, while IPv6 provides 340,282,366, 920,938,463,463,374,607, 431,768,211,456 possible IP addresses.

Larger Pool of IPv6 Addresses

The main reason IPv6 was implemented was to increase the number of available Internet addresses. An IPv4 address is equal to 32 bits or approximately 4,000,000,000 addresses, but IPv6 uses 128-bit addresses, which is approximately equal to 340,000,000,000,000,000,000,000,000,000,000,000,000 possible addresses. As you can see, the possible number of unique addresses seems inexhaustible, though the same thing was thought about IPv4 when it was initially developed.

Reduced Broadcast Traffic

IPv4 utilizes the Address Resolution Protocol (ARP) to resolve IPv4 addresses to MAC addresses, and a unique MAC address is assigned to each network adapter card. IPv6, however, uses the Neighbor Discovery (ND) protocol, which is carried inside a series of Internet Control Message Protocol (ICMP) packets on the local area network. ND will eventually replace ARP broadcasts, resulting in reduced network traffic on LANs. Much of a network's traffic is caused by a constant repetition of ARP requests generated on a network system by various software applications, which constantly verify the presence of other devices. At this time, the implementation of both IPv6 and IPv4 by default does not result in totally reduced LAN traffic.

Improved Security

IPv6 incorporates IPSec to provide better security than IPv4. **IPSec** is a collection of protocols that encrypt and authenticate each packet that uses an IP address over the Internet. The reason IPv6 has improved security is that IPSec is mandatory for use with IPv6 and only optional for IPv4.

Better Quality of Service

Quality of service (QoS) refers to a protocol's ability to deliver certain packets in a timely fashion. For example, a long text document can have delays between packets because the delays do not affect the content of the text document, but packets that contain live video or audio must not have delays between them because a long delay between packets can result in a choppy conversation with parts of speech missing. IPv4 *does* have a QoS feature, but the delivery of packets is slowed when using a security protocol such as IPSec. The IPv6 standard significantly improves quality of service and does not let IPSec cause long delays between packets, thus ensuring a better quality of service.

IPv6 has a feature built into the header called the *flow label field*, which contains information that identifies the packet as special and allows routers to stream the content of the IPv6 packet, even when encrypted with IPSec. Additionally, the IPSec standard is optional for IPv4, but it is incorporated into the IPv6 standard. IPSec was developed after the IPv4 standard, and it is supported as an add-on feature, thus creating more overhead.

Support for Network Discovery

The **Internet Control Message Protocol Version 6 (ICMPv6)** is a protocol and service for exchanging messages between neighboring network nodes on the same link. This is the basis of the Network Discovery protocol, which allows a computer system to identify other devices connected to the same section (subnet) of a local area network. Network Discovery allows for automatic configuration of network devices and the discovery of routers attached to the local area network.

IPv4 Network Class

Classes of network addresses are no longer used, and instead, classless inter-domain routing (CIDR) is employed for addressing. However, network classes will be briefly discussed in this section for historical purposes. CIDR will be discussed in a later section.

IPv4 networks were originally divided into three classifications: Class A, Class B, and Class C. Large networks were assigned a Class A classification, and a *Class A network* could support up to 16 million hosts on 127 networks. Medium-sized networks were assigned Class B status, and a *Class B network* supported up to 65,000 hosts on 16,000 networks. Small networks were assigned a Class C classification, and a *Class C network* supported 254 hosts on 2,000,000 networks.

A+ 1101: 2.5

IPv4 addresses can also be categorized as private or public. *Private IP addresses* are those used for internal devices that do not connect to the Internet. Conversely, *public IP addresses* are assigned to Internet-facing devices and must be unique from all other Internet devices. Private addresses only need to be unique on the network they are on. For example, you might have a workstation with the private IP address of 10.10.10.3, which cannot be duplicated in that network, but other networks might use it. There are three ranges of IP addresses set aside as private IP addresses:

- 192.168.0.0–192.168.255.255 (65,536 IP addresses)
- 172.16.0.0–172.31.255.255 (1,048,576 IP addresses)
- 10.0.0.0–10.255.255.255 (16,777,216 IP addresses)

Remember, the above-listed addresses can only be used as private, internal network addresses, not as public IP addresses.

IPv4 Subnet Mask

A+ 1101: 2.6 1102: 1.6

An organizational network may be divided into several smaller networks known as *subnets*. A **subnet mask** is a 32-bit number, usually in dotted decimal notation, used to determine the subnet to which a particular IP address refers. At first glance, a subnet mask may appear identical to an IP address, but it is easily distinguishable from an IP address because it begins with one or more octets of 255, which is impossible for an IP address. The subnet mask can be used to identify the class of network but is really intended to allow the network address to be broken down into smaller subnetworks.

The octets of a subnet mask correspond to octets in the IP address, but the actual numbers found in a subnet mask depend on the class of the network and the number of subnetworks into which it is divided. The subnet mask is combined with the IP address using the bitwise "AND" operation, and the resulting address is the subnet address. The details of the bitwise "AND" operation are beyond the scope of this textbook; for now, just remember that the subnet mask is used to identify any subnetworks at a network address. IPv6 does not require a subnet mask, nor is there a need for one, because IPv6 incorporates a subnet mask function as part of the assigned address.

The rise in classless inter-domain routing (CIDR) has enabled network administrators to effectively cease usage of IP classes and subnets. With CIDR, you simply write out the IP address followed by a forward slash and an integer indicating the number of bits used for both the network and node portions of that IP address. For example, in the past when addresses were limited to three classes, you might have an IP address of 28.23.14.01 with a subnet mask of 255.0.0.0. In this arrangement, the first number (28) is used for the network, and the rest for the node. However, while humans are comfortable seeing base-10 numbers, the computer actually sees the address in base-2, meaning 28 is actually 0001100. Classes A, B, and C only allowed three options, but CIDR allows you to "mask" any number of bits for the network. Using CIDR, you could have IP address of 28.23.14.01/8, indicating the first eight bits are for the network and the rest for the node. Or you might choose 28.23.14.01/5, indicating only the first five bits are for the network and the rest for the node. Put simply, CIDR offers far more flexibility.

Similar to a subnet is a Virtual Local Area Network (VLAN). *Virtual Local Area Networks (VLANs)* broadcast their domains in a Layer-2 technology, such as a virtual bridge via a network switch, and provide smaller, more private networks. In other words, organizational departments, such as an accounting or human resources department, can have a private portion of the network where only employees within those departments can communicate and transfer data with other devices and users in the department.

A+ 1102: 2.9

Related to subnetting is ***screened subnetting***, which refers to the use of a firewall to create an isolated perimeter network or separate the internal network from the Internet. This is particularly useful to improve security in small-office/home-office (SOHO) environments. A screened subnet essentially creates a subnet that serves as a logical network to itself, which provides a location for an administrator to put public-facing devices without exposing their entire network. In this sense, they are quite similar to a demilitarized zone (DMZ), which will be discussed in a later chapter.

A+ 1102: 1.2

Running Ipconfig

Information about the computer's IPv4 and IPv6 addresses, MAC address, and network adapter can be obtained by running the **ipconfig** command from the command prompt. Figure 22-2 shows the results of running **ipconfig** from the Windows 10 command prompt. Adding the **/all** switch to the **ipconfig** command reveals even more detailed information about the network adapter, as shown in Figure 22-3. Additional data includes detailed information concerning the DHCP configuration, DHCP and DNS server-assigned IP addresses, NetBIOS over TCP/IP, and more.

A+ 1101: 2.1, 2.5, 2.6

A+ 1102: 1.6, 2.9

DHCP

Originally, computers on a network needed to have their IP addresses assigned manually as part of the process to get a PC ready to communicate on a network and over the Internet. The manual assignment of IP addresses is referred to as **static IP addressing**. This is a time-consuming operation if hundreds or thousands of hosts are on a network, and it requires a log of computer names, locations, MAC addresses, and the assigned IP addresses to be recorded. Moreover, since having two devices with the same IP addresses causes communication conflicts and erratic behavior, technicians had to be certain that each address was unique at the time it was assigned.

Most network systems are now configured using **Dynamic Host Configuration Protocol (DHCP)**, which automatically assigns IP addresses to hosts. The act of automatically assigning IP addresses is known as **dynamic addressing**. DHCP was

Figure 22-2 The **ipconfig** command is used to gather information about a network adapter, such as its assigned IPv4 address and subnet mask, as well as the IPv6 address, MAC address, and default gateway.

```
C:\Windows\system32\cmd.exe

C:\Users\GW>ipconfig

Windows IP Configuration

Ethernet adapter Ethernet:

   Media State . . . . . . . . . . . : Media disconnected
   Connection-specific DNS Suffix  . : gwp.com

Wireless LAN adapter Local Area Connection* 1:

   Media State . . . . . . . . . . . : Media disconnected
   Connection-specific DNS Suffix  . :

Wireless LAN adapter Local Area Connection* 2:

   Media State . . . . . . . . . . . : Media disconnected
   Connection-specific DNS Suffix  . :

Wireless LAN adapter Wi-Fi:

   Connection-specific DNS Suffix  . : hsd1.il.comcast.net
   IPv6 Address. . . . . . . . . . . : 2601:248:4100:2b40::e43b
   IPv6 Address. . . . . . . . . . . : 2601:248:4100:2b40:cee8:ac98:166f:4392
   Temporary IPv6 Address. . . . . . : 2601:248:4100:2b40:102f:5373:903b:2f9f
   Link-local IPv6 Address . . . . . : fe80::ea18:af14:8f46:1ce2%4
   IPv4 Address. . . . . . . . . . . : 10.0.0.118
   Subnet Mask . . . . . . . . . . . : 255.255.255.0
   Default Gateway . . . . . . . . . : fe80::3e82:c0ff:fed9:9ec5%4
                                       10.0.0.1

Ethernet adapter Bluetooth Network Connection:

   Media State . . . . . . . . . . . : Media disconnected
   Connection-specific DNS Suffix  . :

C:\Users\GW>
```

Goodheart-Willcox Publisher

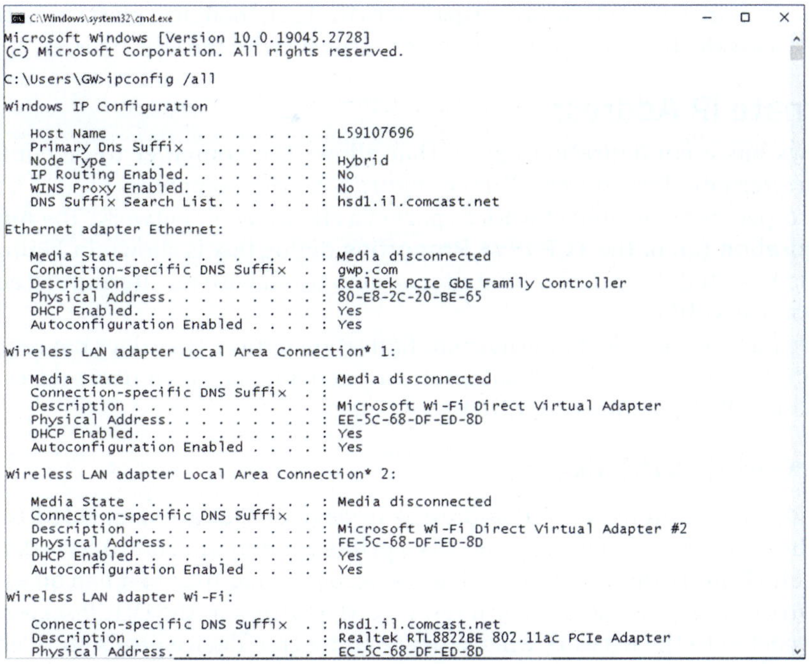

```
C:\Windows\system32\cmd.exe
Microsoft Windows [Version 10.0.19045.2728]
(c) Microsoft Corporation. All rights reserved.

C:\Users\GW>ipconfig /all

Windows IP Configuration

   Host Name . . . . . . . . . . . . : L59107696
   Primary Dns Suffix  . . . . . . . :
   Node Type . . . . . . . . . . . . : Hybrid
   IP Routing Enabled. . . . . . . . : No
   WINS Proxy Enabled. . . . . . . . : No
   DNS Suffix Search List. . . . . . : hsd1.il.comcast.net

Ethernet adapter Ethernet:

   Media State . . . . . . . . . . . : Media disconnected
   Connection-specific DNS Suffix  . : gwp.com
   Description . . . . . . . . . . . : Realtek PCIe GbE Family Controller
   Physical Address. . . . . . . . . : 80-E8-2C-20-BE-65
   DHCP Enabled. . . . . . . . . . . : Yes
   Autoconfiguration Enabled . . . . : Yes

Wireless LAN adapter Local Area Connection* 1:

   Media State . . . . . . . . . . . : Media disconnected
   Connection-specific DNS Suffix  . :
   Description . . . . . . . . . . . : Microsoft Wi-Fi Direct Virtual Adapter
   Physical Address. . . . . . . . . : EE-5C-68-DF-ED-8D
   DHCP Enabled. . . . . . . . . . . : Yes
   Autoconfiguration Enabled . . . . : Yes

Wireless LAN adapter Local Area Connection* 2:

   Media State . . . . . . . . . . . : Media disconnected
   Connection-specific DNS Suffix  . :
   Description . . . . . . . . . . . : Microsoft Wi-Fi Direct Virtual Adapter #2
   Physical Address. . . . . . . . . : FE-5C-68-DF-ED-8D
   DHCP Enabled. . . . . . . . . . . : Yes
   Autoconfiguration Enabled . . . . : Yes

Wireless LAN adapter Wi-Fi:

   Connection-specific DNS Suffix  . : hsd1.il.comcast.net
   Description . . . . . . . . . . . : Realtek RTL8822BE 802.11ac PCIe Adapter
   Physical Address. . . . . . . . . : EC-5C-68-DF-ED-8D
```

Goodheart-Willcox Publisher

Figure 22-3 Using the **/all** switch with the **ipconfig** command reveals additional information about a network adapter's assignments in greater detail.

written to replace static IP addressing and can be provided by a router or dedicated server. It functions based on a *pool*, or list, of IP addresses. Each host is assigned an address from the pool as it logs on to the network, but the IP address issued to each host is temporary. The address is released after a period of time and may be reissued to another host later.

Every address assigned by DHCP has a time limit called a *lease*, and at the end of the lease, the IP address is reclaimed and can be re-assigned. When a DHCP server leases an IP address to a client, it records the MAC address of that client, and the pool of available IP addresses is reduced by one until the lease is expired or the client relinquishes the IP address.

Users can still assign static IPv4 and IPv6 addresses to network adapters, and static addressing is often used for network devices such as servers, routers, and printers. This ensures that the same IPv4 or IPv6 address will be used for the device.

A DHCP assignment does not guarantee the same IPv4 or IPv6 address will be assigned to a device every time an address is issued, which can cause communication problems, especially for devices that host web pages. A computer uses a cache to store web-page names resolved to IP addresses. As such, a web-page hosting device, such as a web server, requires a static IP address because a computer will cache the web-page server address. If the web server constantly changes its assigned IPv4 or IPv6 address because it is configured for DHCP, then the computer seeking the web page will display an error and will not be able to connect to the destination based on the older IP address.

A+ Note

Make sure you know the difference between the information produced by the **ipconfig** and **ipconfig / all** commands.

A+ 1101: 2.6

Automatic Private IP Address

A+ 1101: 2.5

Automatic Private IP Addressing (APIPA) is a Windows feature that allows a computer to issue an IP address to itself when a DHCP server is unavailable. A computer requires an IP address to communicate, even on a local area network, and when an IPv4 DHCP address cannot be issued to the computer, the computer automatically issues an Automatic Private IP Address to itself, so it can communicate with other computers and equipment on the local area network. The APIPA range is from 169.254.0.1 to 169.254.255.254.

When the DHCP problem is resolved, the computer drops the Automatic Private IP Address, and the DHCP server automatically issues a new IP address to the computer.

These actions are automatic and transparent to the user, though in most cases, the user cannot access the Internet until the problem is solved with the DHCP server.

Alternate IP Address

Windows has a configuration option that allows the computer to be configured with an alternate IPv4 address. This configuration is for computers used at home on a peer-to-peer network and at work as part of a client/server network. The **Alternate Configuration** tab of the **TCP/IPv4 Properties** dialog box is shown in Figure 22-4. It should be noted that when a computer is configured with an alternate IP address, it cannot use APIPA.

IPv6 has no equivalent alternate configuration option. IPv6 does not require an alternate IP address because it automatically generates its own IPv6 address similarly to how IPv4 generates an APIPA.

A+ 1101: 2.6
1102: 2.9

Reserved IP Addresses

Although DHCP can provide IP addresses to devices that are connected to a network, there are certain devices—such as a printer or domain controller—that must have their IP addresses reserved so devices needed to connect to it can do so at any time. Furthermore, if a device has a reserved IP address in the DHCP server and is not connected to the network when a newly connected device needs an IP address, the DHCP server knows that it cannot issue a reserved IP address.

Link-Local IPv6 Address

Unlike IPv4, which only assigns one address, a network adapter can have multiple IPv6 addresses. Microsoft uses the term *link-local* in reference to the IPv6 address assigned to support communication on the local area network, meaning it serves the same function as IPv4 Automatic Private IP Addresses. IPv6 link-local addresses are automatically assigned with FE80 as the first hexadecimal identifier and are required for the Network Discovery feature. Without a link-local IPv6 address, Network Discovery will not function. This is why Microsoft operating systems automatically configure link-local address with the prefix FE80 for network devices. An example of a link-local IPv6 address can be seen in Figure 22-2 under the Wireless LAN adapter Wi-Fi section of the **ipconfig** results.

Figure 22-4 The **Alternate Configuration** tab of the **Internet Protocol Version 4 (TCP/IPv4) Properties** dialog box allows a computer to be configured with a static IPv4 address.

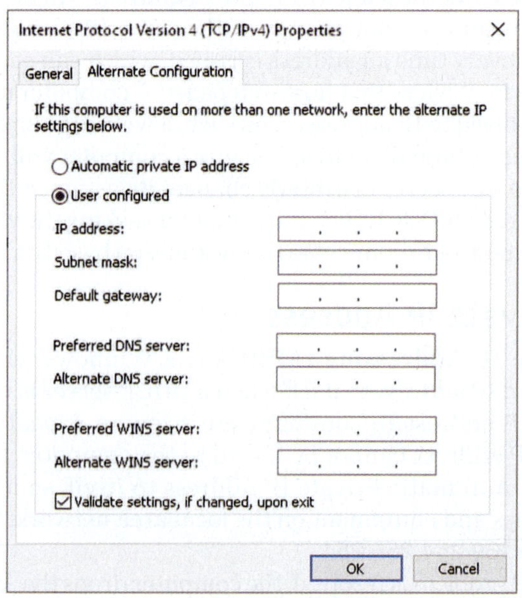

Goodheart-Willcox Publisher

WINS

The **Windows Internet Naming Service (WINS)** is a software service that resolves a computer name, such as Station1, to the equivalent IP address on the network. DHCP servers assign IP addresses to hosts from a pool of IP addresses, though a host may have a new IP address each time it logs on to the local network. To correlate a computer name to its current IP address, WINS works closely with the DHCP server.

As of the release of Windows 2000, WINS is not required but remains a configuration option for the network adapter. Today's operating systems rely on DNS rather than WINS to resolve computer names to IP addresses.

DNS

1101: 2.1, 2.6 A+
1102: 1.6

The **Domain Name Service (DNS)** is a service that translates domain names to IP addresses. DNS is used across the Internet, assisting computers in identifying and talking to each other. It translates domain names to IP addresses similarly to how WINS translates computer names. DNS is also used in smaller network systems to match computer and network services to IP addresses. Domain names are easier to remember than actual IP addresses, and when a user inputs a human-friendly name, the DNS service resolves the name to a computer or device.

When a domain name is entered, the DNS service searches its database for the matching IP address and connects the user to that address. Web addresses are entered into a browser or search engine, then passed and copied throughout the Internet by routers. Once a domain is located, the Internet service provider's server retains a copy of the domain name and corresponding assigned IP address in a database. When a DNS query is made from a corporate domain, a copy of the domain name used in the query is saved on the corporation domain server as well.

Another copy of the resolved DNS query is saved on the computer that initiated the search, and the copy is referred to as the *DNS cache*. The DNS resolver cache contains a list of recent domain queries saved on the local computer, and when a query is made, the computer first looks in the DNS cache before conducting the query on the ISP and the Internet to see if a record has been saved.

Figure 22-5 shows the results of issuing the **ipconfig/displaydns** command, which displays the content of the DNS cache, also called *client-side DNS*. The host computer name is client.wns.windows.com, which also functions as a domain name. The operating system automatically appends the computer or other local area network devices with a domain name so the assigned IP address can be resolved to the user-friendly computer or network device name by the DNS service. Additional commands directly related to DNS are listed in Figure 22-6.

A+ Note

There is usually at least one question asked about DHCP and DNS. Often, WINS is used as a distractor. Be sure to know the difference between DHCP, DNS, and WINS.

Tech Tip

In relation to DNS, the term *query* describes the act of conducting a DNS search to resolve a domain name to an IP address.

22.2 Network Equipment

Any network requires equipment to direct traffic and manage a tremendous amount of packet traffic. To accomplish this, special equipment must be used to route data to and from hosts across the network. Certain pieces of equipment are used in a network environment when all the hosts are using the same protocol to communicate, and other types of equipment are used when a mixture of protocols is used. For example, protocols designed for satellite transmission and telephone systems do not directly match the Ethernet and TCP/IP suite of protocols, so these protocols need to be translated to other protocol formats.

In Figure 22-7, you can see a variety of media and devices that support communication between people and places. There is also a mixture of different networking protocols, such as Ethernet, Bluetooth, and Frame Relay. These separate technologies work together, even though the data packets created by each system differ.

```
C:\Windows\system32\cmd.exe
C:\Users\GW>ipconfig/displaydns

Windows IP Configuration

    client.wns.windows.com
    ----------------------------------------
    Record Name . . . . . : client.wns.windows.com
    Record Type . . . . . : 5
    Time To Live  . . . . : 108
    Data Length . . . . . : 8
    Section . . . . . . . : Answer
    CNAME Record  . . . . : wns.notify.trafficmanager.net

    Record Name . . . . . : wns.notify.trafficmanager.net
    Record Type . . . . . : 1
    Time To Live  . . . . : 108
    Data Length . . . . . : 4
    Section . . . . . . . : Answer
    A (Host) Record . . . : 20.25.241.18

    ctldl.windowsupdate.com
    ----------------------------------------
    Record Name . . . . . : ctldl.windowsupdate.com
    Record Type . . . . . : 5
    Time To Live  . . . . : 117
    Data Length . . . . . : 8
    Section . . . . . . . : Answer
    CNAME Record  . . . . : wu-bg-shim.trafficmanager.net

    Record Name . . . . . : wu-bg-shim.trafficmanager.net
    Record Type . . . . . : 5
    Time To Live  . . . . : 117
    Data Length . . . . . : 8
    Section . . . . . . . : Answer
    CNAME Record  . . . . : cds.d2s7q6s2.hwcdn.net

    Record Name . . . . . : cds.d2s7q6s2.hwcdn.net
    Record Type . . . . . : 1
    Time To Live  . . . . : 117
    Data Length . . . . . : 4
    Section . . . . . . . : Answer
    A (Host) Record . . . : 209.197.3.8
```

Figure 22-5 The DNS cache is displayed through the **ipconfig/displaydns** command.

Goodheart-Willcox Publisher

Figure 22-6 There are multiple commands associated with DNS that can be issued in the command prompt.

DNS-Related Commands	
Ipconfig Command	**Description**
ipconfig /displaydns	Displays the contents of the DNS client resolver cache
ipconfig /dnsflush	Flushes and resets the contents of the DNS resolver cache This command is used for troubleshooting when the DNS cache is suspect. The DNS resolver cache is emptied, forcing the computer to use the next available Internet DNS server to resolve the DNS query.

Goodheart-Willcox Publisher

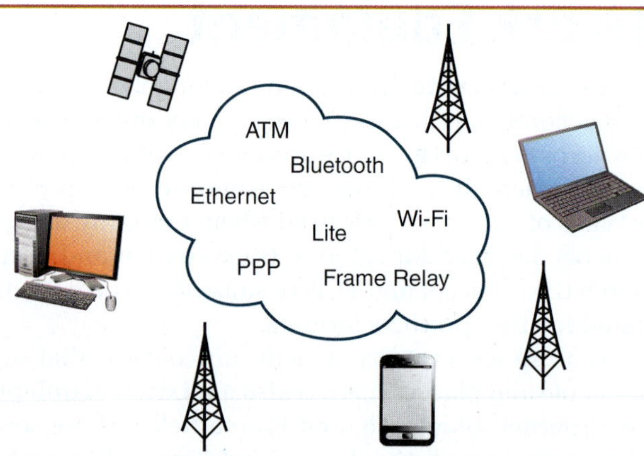

Figure 22-7 The wide array of networking media and technologies are complex and require a wide variety of specialized equipment.

Goodheart-Willcox Publisher; (workstation and laptop icons) romvo/Shutterstock.com; (smartphone icon) Tetiana Yurchenko/Shutterstock.com

For the many different protocols to communicate with each other, special hardware and software must be used. This section covers the major types of equipment and briefly explains the function of each in a network environment.

Repeater

A **repeater** is a piece of equipment that regenerates a weak digital signal. Network cable standards recommend a maximum cable length to prevent the loss of data signals, and beyond those lengths, a repeater must be installed. For example, the maximum recommended length for a typical Ethernet cable (Cat 5 and Cat 6) is 100 meters. If you needed a cable to run for more than 100 meters, you would need to incorporate a repeater in your network design. As a digital signal travels farther from its source, it degrades, eventually becoming unintelligible. At great distances, a network adapter cannot distinguish between the 0s and 1s transmitted through the cable. A repeater receives the degraded digital signal, reshapes it to its original form, and retransmits it over the cable, as shown in Figure 22-8. A repeater is often incorporated into other devices such as switches and routers to send data across many miles.

A+ Note

A *repeater* is often referred to as an *amplifier*. Technically speaking, an amplifier increases the original signal strength rather than reshaping the signal to its original form. On the A+ Certification Exams, the only correct answer may equate a repeater with an amplifier. In this case, choose the answer that implies that a repeater works like an amplifier.

Bridge

A *bridge* is a piece of equipment that joins two dissimilar network segments. For example, a bridge may connect an Ethernet twisted-pair cable network to a satellite or fiber-optic network. The bridge simply passes packets from one system to the other regardless of the protocol and maintains a list of MAC addresses that are connected to it so it can provide filtering services. For example, if two network segments are connected by a bridge, the bridge can be programmed to pass only data packets that match the MAC addresses of hosts on the other side of the bridge, as illustrated in Figure 22-9. By filtering out packets to unrecognized addresses, data traffic is minimized.

Router

A *router* connects networks together and controls the flow of exchanged data packets. The term *routing* means moving a packet of data from a source to a destination. A router performs much more complex tasks than a bridge by not only connecting hosts together on a network, but also determining the best route to use. The router calculates the "cost" of a number of different routes and uses the least expensive method based on the use of leased lines and equipment, the time to transmit, and the distance. Additionally, routers add information to the data frame surrounding the data packet to expand the identification of the packet's origin, its destination, and its route.

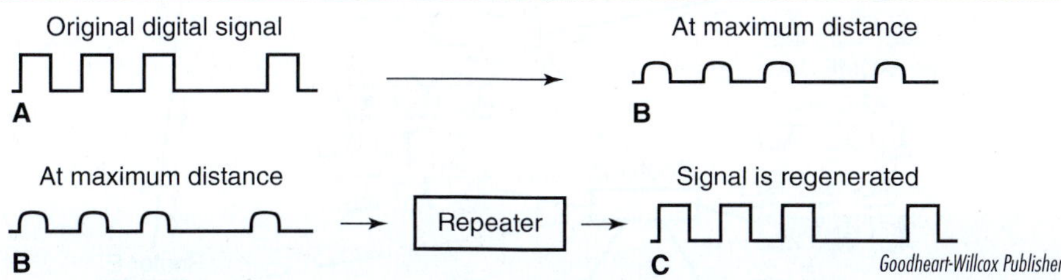

Figure 22-8 In a digital signal transmission (A), the only values in the signal are 1s and 0s. As the signal approaches its maximum transmission distance (B), the "shoulders" of the signal slump, creating graduated values (analog) in the transmission. Also, note the crests of the signal are no longer at maximum height. The repeater (C) restores the signal to its original strength and shape.

In Figure 22-10, you can see that the function of the router is to determine the least "expensive" route from one host to another. In networking, the term ***expensive*** refers to the cost of routing data through a network system. Distances between the source and destination in a network system are measured by routers. Each pass of data through a router is referred to as a ***hop***, and the more hops required to meet a destination, the more expensive the route.

Routers are available in two styles: static and dynamic. A ***static router*** is programmed with a database of IP addresses, subnet masks, and network IDs and does not broadcast information on a constant basis. A ***dynamic router*** communicates with other routers on the network and constantly exchanges data about each other's location and database tables. See Figure 22-11 for a quick comparison of bridging and routing.

A+ 1102: 2.9

Security of the router is also of paramount importance. Typically, large organizations have dedicated technical staff that address router security, but small-office/home-office (SOHO) networks sometimes do not pay adequate attention to router security. One fundamental issue is ensuring your router is not using any default passwords, which should be changed immediately. Another issue is updating the router; just like any other device you use, your router needs to be updated from time to time to ensure the newest security definitions and updates are in place.

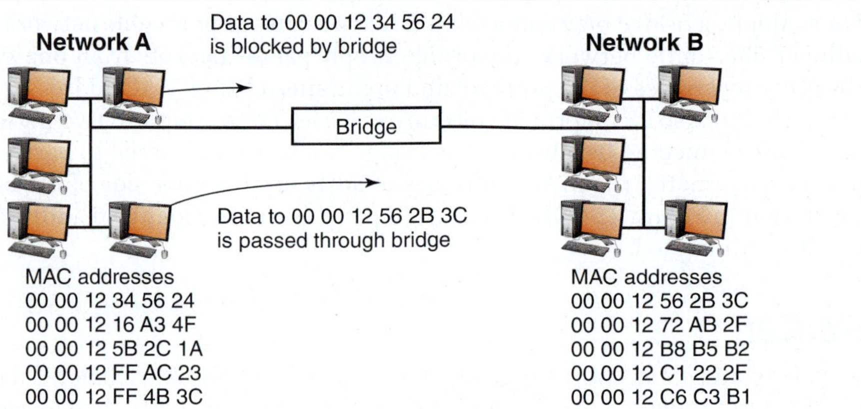

Goodheart-Willcox Publisher; (workstation icon) romvo/Shutterstock.com

Figure 22-9 A bridge limits the number of hosts affected by data broadcasts. The bridge passes or blocks data based on the MAC address in the destination address in the packet header. If a large network were constructed without bridge techniques, the constant broadcast of data packets would slow the entire network.

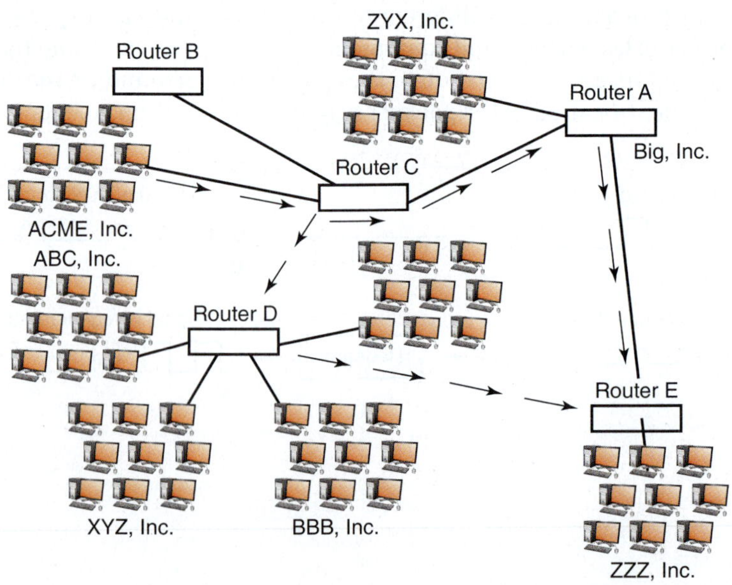

Goodheart-Willcox Publisher; (workstation icon) romvo/Shutterstock.com

Figure 22-10 Routers send data traffic across the entire world. They also select the least expensive route to use. As shown, several routes could be chosen to send a data packet from ACME, Inc. to ZZZ, Inc.

Bridging vs. Routing	
Bridge	**Router**
Forwards broadcast traffic	Blocks broadcast traffic
Uses MAC addresses	Uses IP addresses
Does not add to packet information	Adds to packet information
Forwards packets to unknown addresses	Blocks packets to unknown addresses

Goodheart-Willcox Publisher

Figure 22-11 Bridges and routers serve a similar purpose, but they operate in vastly different ways.

Brouter

A **brouter** is a combination bridge and router and applies the best characteristics of both systems. A bridge can pass network data packets that contain MAC addresses but not IP addresses. Conversely, a router forwards packets based on IP address rather than MAC address. Brouters, therefore, provide both actions.

Switch

A **switch** filters data packets and forwards them between network segments. Switches are usually intelligent hubs, meaning they can determine on which side of the switch a packet's destination is located.

There are two types of switching communication used for computer networks: packet switching and circuit switching. **Packet switching** divides data into packets, which can take a variety of routes to get to their destination, while **circuit switching** makes a permanent connection for the duration of the transmission, with data transmitted in a steady stream. For example, when you make a connection with a modem, a circuit switch is closed to keep the modem in constant connection. On the network, the packet-switching method is used rather than a permanent connection for the duration of the browsing session.

Gateway

1101: 2.5 A+
1102: 1.6

A **gateway** is a networking device that translates information between two networks that use different protocols to communicate. Think of a gateway as a language translator because it translates commands and data from one protocol to another or from one format to another. For example, H.323 is a telephone protocol used to support VoIP over traditional telephone equipment, but it must be converted when it connects to a standard Ethernet TCP/IP network system. In this instance, a gateway may be required to translate protocols for Voice over IP (VoIP).

A gateway may be a dedicated piece of hardware or a software package loaded onto a server or a router. It is important to understand that a network server can provide more than one service. For example, a computer can simultaneously serve as a gateway, proxy server, firewall, and file server. The exact name used for the server is relative to the network service being discussed.

Proxy Server

1101: 2.5 A+
1102: 1.6

A **proxy server** is a computer server that hides all the PCs in a network from direct connection with PCs outside of it. This provides better security than if each PC had direct access to outside the network. The server acts as a go-between for distant sites and the users by relaying the requested information for the client, leaving the client anonymous to the outside network. Users outside of the network from locations across the Internet cannot communicate directly with the computers located behind the proxy server. The function of the proxy server is often incorporated into network devices such as routers and various modem types.

Additionally, proxy servers make accessing the web more efficient for network clients by caching frequently requested web pages. By caching the frequently accessed web information, the process of accessing distant web pages is expedited.

A+ 1101: 2.2

Firewall

The term *firewall* refers to a barrier that prevents direct contact between computers outside the organization and computers inside the organization. All data communication to and from an organization is routed through the proxy server, and the firewall software decides whether to forward the data. A firewall can be either a dedicated piece of network equipment or a software package. For example, Windows Firewall is a software package, but some network devices, such as routers or wireless access points, are also referred to as a firewall because they can also limit port connections.

One way a firewall determines whether to block or pass a network connection is by the assigned port number of the packet, which identifies the program or service that can utilize the information or command contained inside the network packet. For example, a packet with an assigned port number of 80 is to be sent to a web-browsing program or service and then opened by the appropriate web browser. Port numbers are assigned according to three ranges:

- system ports (0–1,023)
- user ports (1,024–49,151)
- private ports (49,152–65,535)

System ports, also known as *well-known ports*, are assigned by the Internet Assigned Numbers Authority (IANA) and cannot be used except for their intended purpose. *User ports*, also known as *registered ports*, are assigned by the IANA for use by software companies, such as Microsoft or Cisco Systems. The private company requests the reservation of the port number for use with one of its software programs, and the IANA assigns the port number to the company software service. *Private ports*, also known as *dynamic ports*, are not assigned by the IANA. Anyone can write a software application to use this range of port numbers, and you will often encounter port numbers in this range for supporting online gaming communication and management. Network system managers select which ports to block to prevent unauthorized use of the Internet connection. Figure 22-12 lists some of the most common port number assignments used.

A+ Note

The table shown in Figure 22-12 contains the most common port numbers that are used in questions for the CompTIA A+ Exam. Always check the CompTIA website for the very latest complete set of port numbers.

Figure 22-12 Common port numbers are often associated with a widely used protocol or service.

A+ 1101: 2.1

Common Port Numbers

Port Number	Protocol or Service
21	FTP
23	Telnet
25	SMTP
53	DNS
67/68	DHCP
80	HTTP
110	POP3
137/139	NetBIOS/NetBIOS over TCP/IP (NetBT)
143	IMAP
161/162	SNMP
389	LDAP
443	HTTPS
3,389	RDP

Goodheart-Willcox Publisher

In Figure 22-13, you can see some of the many-assigned port numbers viewed through **Windows Firewall with Advanced Security** in Windows 10. Notice the list of services or programs, assigned port numbers, and status, such as *enabled*.

Double-clicking a particular service or program listed in **Windows Firewall with Advanced Security** produces a dialog box similar to the one in Figure 22-14, which shows the DNS properties for this particular computer. As you can see, it is used to enable and allow connection for this service. The DNS port number assigned is 53, and

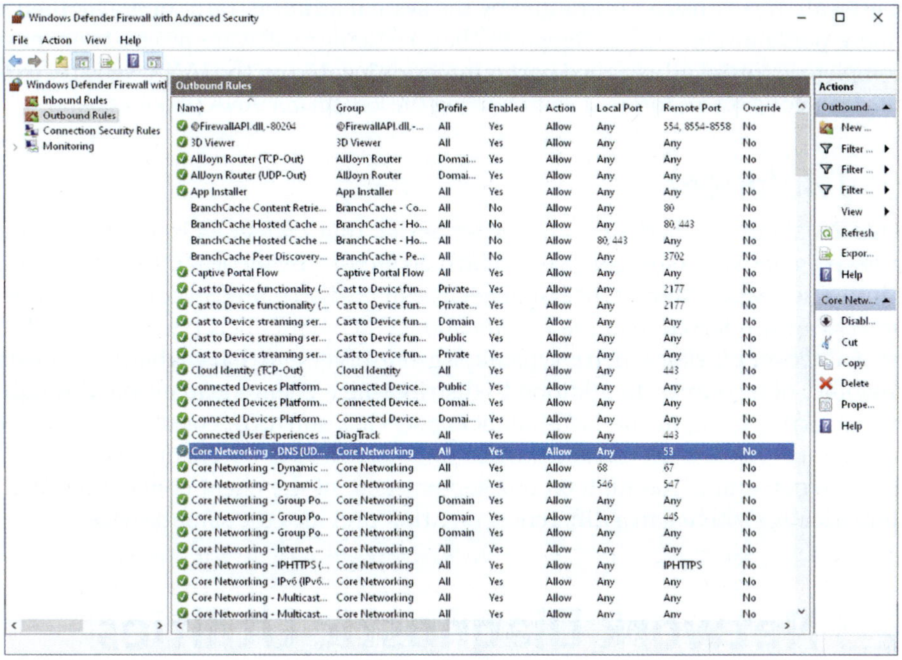

Goodheart-Willcox Publisher

Figure 22-13 Port numbers of software programs and services can be viewed through **Windows Defender Firewall with Advanced Security**.

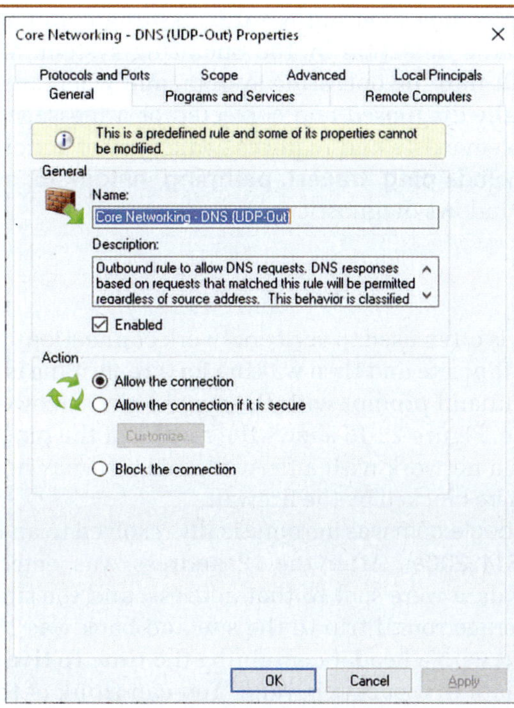

Goodheart-Willcox Publisher

Figure 22-14 In **Windows Defender Firewall with Advanced Security**, the **Properties** dialog box for a service or program provides options related to the port number, such as **Allow the connection**, **Allow the connection if secure**, and **Block the connection**.

only port number 53 can be used for the DNS service because the DNS service is what is known as a *core network service* and cannot be changed or reassigned. The Microsoft operating system prevents the changing of core port numbers, while other network port assignments for programs such as games are easily reassigned or disabled.

The default settings of Windows Firewall typically do not need to be reconfigured, though there will be times when you will be prompted to allow the assignment of a particular port number from the dynamic port range, such as when you install a particular software program. The message usually does not request a particular port number; rather, it asks permission to allow the program to communicate through the firewall. If permission is granted by the system administrator or equal, then one or more port numbers are assigned to that particular software program or service. A complete listing of all assigned port numbers is located on the IANA website. To find it, you can conduct an Internet search using the key terms IANA port numbers.

A+ 1102: 1.2

Load Balancer

A *load balancer* is a network or Internet device that transmits requests to various servers on a network based on pre-established factors. By incorporating load balancers into a network system, processing needs can be distributed over multiple servers, a process aptly referred to as *load balancing*. Load balancing is typically included as part of a *failover cluster*, which is typically a group of servers that enable near-constant availability of resources. In addition to distributing a client's load evenly through all servers participating in the load-balancing service, software constantly checks the performance of each server and makes decisions based on client/server demand. When the demand is too high on one server, some of the client connections can be automatically switched to a different server that provides the same service.

22.3 Network Diagnostic Utilities

Standard utility programs, such as **ping** and **tracert**, are very handy when troubleshooting networked PCs. In most cases, troubleshooting the network will be a combination of running troubleshooting wizards, issuing commands at a command prompt, and automatic detection by the operating system. Many network diagnostics are now built into the operating system, and when an error is detected, it is either automatically diagnosed and corrected or a message appears informing the user that a problem exists and requires some type of action. Some of the most common utilities include **ping**, **tracert**, **pathping**, **nslookup**, **netstat**, **nbtstat**, net services, **arp**, and Windows diagnostic tools.

A+ 1102: 1.2

Ping

Ping is a utility that is often used to verify network connections to websites by sending a packet to a distant site and then waiting for a reply. Ping is executed as a command from the command prompt with the syntax ping followed by an IP address or URL. For example, Figure 22-15 shows the results of the **ping google.com** command. If you are on a network with a firewall, this test may not work because the **ping** command may be blocked by the firewall.

When pinged, google.com was automatically resolved to an IPv6 address, listed as 2607:f8b0:4004:814::200e:. After the IP address was determined, four packets with 32 bytes of data were sent to that address, and the site echoed back with four replies. The average round trip to the site and back was 16 milliseconds. The ping packets are sent with a header containing the **time to live (TTL)**, which is the length of time the data in a packet is valid. You can think of the TTL setting as a self-destruct countdown because it tells the network to disregard the packet after the set time. If the destination did not exist, the ping would circulate the Internet forever, and the Internet would soon become burdened with millions of ping packets. The TTL feature limits the maximum time that the ping packet can circulate the Internet looking for the destination.

A number of switches can be used with the **ping** command. The additional switches for the **ping** command can be viewed with the command syntax ping /help or ping.

Pinging the network card is a quick way of confirming the card is responding to TCP/IP transmissions and is referred to as a *loopback test*. The IPv6 loopback address is the reserved IP address of the network interface card and is used to confirm an IP address is configured for the network interface card and the network interface card is functioning normally. The loopback address for IPv4 is 127.0.0.1, and the loopback address for IPv6 is 0:0:0:0:0:0:0:1 or ::1. Note that the double colon eliminates fields containing only zeros. An example of double colons is also shown in the IPv6 address in Figure 22-15.

To perform a loopback test for the IPv4 protocol, enter ping 127.0.0.1 at the command prompt. The same command for IPv6 is ping ::1 or ping localhost. The ::1 represents the IPv6 localhost address. To specify IPv4 for the localhost ping, you must use the **ping -4 localhost** command, as shown in Figure 22-16.

Tracert

1102: 1.2 A+

The **tracert** (*trace route*) utility is more advanced than the ping utility. Like **ping**, it sends a packet out and waits for a reply, but in addition to the information that **ping**

```
C:\Windows\system32\cmd.exe
Microsoft Windows [Version 10.0.19045.2728]
(c) Microsoft Corporation. All rights reserved.

C:\Users\GW>ping google.com

Pinging google.com [2607:f8b0:4009:809::200e] with 32 bytes of data:
Reply from 2607:f8b0:4009:809::200e: time=15ms
Reply from 2607:f8b0:4009:809::200e: time=18ms
Reply from 2607:f8b0:4009:809::200e: time=16ms
Reply from 2607:f8b0:4009:809::200e: time=16ms

Ping statistics for 2607:f8b0:4009:809::200e:
    Packets: Sent = 4, Received = 4, Lost = 0 (0% loss),
Approximate round trip times in milli-seconds:
    Minimum = 15ms, Maximum = 18ms, Average = 16ms

C:\Users\GW>
```

Goodheart-Willcox Publisher

Figure 22-15 The **ping** utility is often used to verify network connectivity.

```
C:\Windows\system32\cmd.exe
Microsoft Windows [Version 10.0.19045.2728]
(c) Microsoft Corporation. All rights reserved.

C:\Users\GW>ping -4 localhost

Pinging L59107696 [127.0.0.1] with 32 bytes of data:
Reply from 127.0.0.1: bytes=32 time<1ms TTL=128
Reply from 127.0.0.1: bytes=32 time<1ms TTL=128
Reply from 127.0.0.1: bytes=32 time<1ms TTL=128
Reply from 127.0.0.1: bytes=32 time<1ms TTL=128

Ping statistics for 127.0.0.1:
    Packets: Sent = 4, Received = 4, Lost = 0 (0% loss),
Approximate round trip times in milli-seconds:
    Minimum = 0ms, Maximum = 0ms, Average = 0ms

C:\Users\GW>
```

Goodheart-Willcox Publisher

Figure 22-16 When issuing the **ping -4 localhost** command in Windows, the localhost is identified with the IPv4 localhost address.

provides, the **tracert** command also displays information about the route that was taken to the destination, as shown in Figure 22-17. As with the **ping** command, this test may not work on a network, depending on how the firewall is configured.

In Figure 22-17, the **tracert** command reveals the actual route taken by the data packet. Among the information provided is the IPv6 addresses of the various routers and service providers along the packet's route, as well as the time it takes each packet to reach its destination. This feature is extremely useful in locating bottlenecks along the route.

Many third-party software developers offer utilities that further enhance the function of **tracert**. For example, NeoTrace is a commercial product developed and distributed by McAfee that functions as a powerful diagnostic and investigation tool. The program traces the route to any destination over the Internet and returns information about the hosts on the route taken, including registered details of each host along the route, such as address, telephone number, e-mail address, and IP address. The information can be displayed as a detailed listing similar to a spreadsheet and as a graphical display in which the route is displayed on a map.

A+ 1102: 1.2

Pathping

The **pathping** utility is an enhanced combination of the **ping** and **tracert** utilities. When issued from the command prompt, it performs in a similar fashion to **tracert**, but with additional information such as delivery statistics, as shown in Figure 22-18.

After pinging the path to the destination and displaying the results similarly to **tracert**, **pathping** continues to ping the destination with additional test packets. After 125 seconds, the additional information is displayed, indicating the percentage of additional test packets that reached the destination. This test is much more thorough than **tracert** because it tests the connectivity to the final destination over a longer period of time, which can reveal intermittent connectivity issues that would otherwise not be revealed by a simple **ping** or a **tracert**. **Pathping** is also used to detect intermittent connection problems or bottlenecks in the traffic flow, which is the main advantage the **pathping** utility has over the **tracert** utility.

A+ 1102: 1.2

Nslookup

The **nslookup** utility is used to diagnose Domain Name Service (DNS) server problems. There are two basic ways to execute the **nslookup** utility. The first method involves testing connectivity to a specific domain or server, in which case, you can use either the IP address or the URL of the domain being tested. The second method does not include a target domain. When a domain is not included in the command syntax, **nslookup**

Figure 22-17 The **tracert** utility is used to obtain information about the route that was taken from one network location to another.

```
C:\Windows\system32\cmd.exe
Microsoft Windows [Version 10.0.19045.2728]
(c) Microsoft Corporation. All rights reserved.

C:\Users\GW>tracert google.com

Tracing route to google.com [2607:f8b0:4009:807::200e]
over a maximum of 30 hops:

  1     4 ms     3 ms     3 ms  2601:248:4100:2b40:3e82:c0ff:fed9:9ec5
  2     *      326 ms    12 ms  2001:558:4040:95::1
  3    15 ms    14 ms    12 ms  2001:558:302:1000::1
  4    14 ms    12 ms    13 ms  2001:558:300:21a2::1
  5     *        *        *     Request timed out.
  6     *        *        *     Request timed out.
  7     *        *        *     Request timed out.
  8    20 ms    21 ms    15 ms  2001:559::11ba
  9    16 ms    16 ms    14 ms  2607:f8b0:831c::1
 10    15 ms    15 ms     *     2001:4860:0:1::5676
 11    16 ms    16 ms    16 ms  2001:4860:0:1::191f
 12    25 ms    24 ms    17 ms  ord08s13-in-x0e.1e100.net [2607:f8b0:4009:807::200e]

Trace complete.

C:\Users\GW>
```

Goodheart-Willcox Publisher

queries the nearest DNS server and displays the information contained in its DNS database for the corresponding IP address. Figure 22-19 shows the **nslookup** utility resolving the IP address 8.8.8.8. Notice that Google is matched to the IP address.

Netstat

A+ 1102: 1.2

The **netstat** (network statistics) utility displays network connections and is often used to diagnose network connection and traffic problems. Figure 22-20 shows the results of the **netstat** command issued without a switch. The results show the active TCP connections by address, though you can also see which computers have a current connection established in the local area network. Figure 22-21 lists the common **netstat** command switches.

Nbtstat

The **nbtstat** command is used for troubleshooting NetBIOS name resolution problems. Microsoft originally used NetBIOS names for network computers and devices, and the NetBIOS naming convention used a maximum of 15 characters for a name. The name was assigned to each device on the network, and a two-letter code identified the type of device, such as a computer, server, or workgroup.

```
C:\Windows\system32\cmd.exe

C:\Users\GW>pathping google.com

Tracing route to google.com [2607:f8b0:4009:817::200e]
over a maximum of 30 hops:
  0  L59107696.hsd1.il.comcast.net [2601:248:4100:2b40:11e2:d7cc:95c8:231c]

  1  2601:248:4100:2b40:3e82:c0ff:fed9:9ec5
  2  2001:558:4040:95::1
  3  2001:558:302:1000::1
  4  2001:558:300:21a2::1
  5  2001:558:300:1e::1
  6     *        *        *
Computing statistics for 125 seconds...
            Source to Here   This Node/Link
Hop  RTT    Lost/Sent = Pct  Lost/Sent = Pct  Address
  0                                           L59107696.hsd1.il.comcast.net
 [2601:248:4100:2b40:11e2:d7cc:95c8:231c]
                                0/ 100 =  0%   |
  1    6ms     0/ 100 =  0%     0/ 100 =  0%  2601:248:4100:2b40:3e82:c0ff:
fed9:9ec5
                                0/ 100 =  0%   |
  2   ---    100/ 100 =100%   100/ 100 =100%  2001:558:4040:95::1
                                0/ 100 =  0%   |
  3   14ms     0/ 100 =  0%     0/ 100 =  0%  2001:558:302:1000::1
                                0/ 100 =  0%   |
  4   14ms     1/ 100 =  1%     1/ 100 =  1%  2001:558:300:21a2::1
                                0/ 100 =  0%   |
  5   21ms     0/ 100 =  0%     0/ 100 =  0%  2001:558:300:1e::1

Trace complete.

C:\Users\GW>
```

Goodheart-Willcox Publisher

Figure 22-18 The **pathping** utility is an enhanced combination of the **ping** and **tracert** utilities.

```
C:\Windows\system32\cmd.exe
Microsoft Windows [Version 10.0.19045.2846]
(c) Microsoft Corporation. All rights reserved.

C:\Users\GW>nslookup 8.8.8.8
Server:   cdns01.comcast.net
Address:  2001:558:feed::1

Name:     dns.google
Address:  8.8.8.8


C:\Users\GW>
```

Goodheart-Willcox Publisher

Figure 22-19 The **nslookup** command is used to diagnose DNS server problems.

Network adapters configured for NetBIOS over TCP/IP resolved NetBIOS names through network mechanisms, such as WINS broadcasts and DNS server queries. Beginning with Windows Vista, NetBIOS is not required for computers, but the commands related to NetBIOS, such as **nbtstat**, are still valid on later Windows operating systems. Some of the more common switches used for **nbtstat** are listed in Figure 22-22.

Figure 22-23 shows the results of the **nbtstat -n** command, and Figure 22-24 shows the results of the **nbtstat -r** command. Notice the results are NetBIOS names resolved by using broadcasts on the local area network. It is important to note that the last operating system to depend on NetBIOS was Windows XP. Therefore, any operating system later than Windows XP will produce limited results when issuing the **nbtstat** command.

Figure 22-20 The **netstat** command is used to display detailed information about network connections, statistics, and routing table information.

```
C:\Windows\system32\cmd.exe
Microsoft Windows [Version 10.0.19045.2846]
(c) Microsoft Corporation. All rights reserved.

C:\Users\GW>netstat

Active Connections

  Proto  Local Address          Foreign Address        State
  TCP    10.0.0.118:2869        10.0.0.1:47660         TIME_WAIT
  TCP    10.0.0.118:49696       52.159.127.243:https   ESTABLISHED
  TCP    10.0.0.118:49771       10.0.0.1:49153         TIME_WAIT
  TCP    10.0.0.118:49778       10.0.0.1:49153         TIME_WAIT
  TCP    10.0.0.118:49779       10.0.0.1:49153         TIME_WAIT
  TCP    10.0.0.118:49786       10.0.0.1:49153         TIME_WAIT
  TCP    10.0.0.118:49790       10.0.0.1:49152         TIME_WAIT
  TCP    10.0.0.118:49793       10.0.0.1:49153         TIME_WAIT
  TCP    10.0.0.118:49794       10.0.0.1:49153         TIME_WAIT
  TCP    [::1]:49772            L59107696:wsd          TIME_WAIT
  TCP    [::1]:49787            L59107696:wsd          TIME_WAIT
  TCP    [2601:248:4100:2b40:5989:967c:ebbd:440f]:49754  [2001:4de0:ac10:
:1:1:19]:http  TIME_WAIT
  TCP    [2601:248:4100:2b40:5989:967c:ebbd:440f]:49755  [2001:4de0:ac10:
:1:1:19]:http  TIME_WAIT
  TCP    [2601:248:4100:2b40:5989:967c:ebbd:440f]:49761  [2001:4de0:ac10:
:1:1:19]:http  TIME_WAIT
  TCP    [2601:248:4100:2b40:5989:967c:ebbd:440f]:49763  [2001:4de0:ac10:
:1:1:19]:http  TIME_WAIT
```

Goodheart-Willcox Publisher

Figure 22-21 There are a number of switches that can be used with the **netstat** command.

Common netstat Flags	
Netstat Command	**Description**
netstat -a	Displays all connections and "listening" ports
netstat -r	Displays routing tables
netstat -e	Displays Ethernet statistics
netstat -s	Displays statistics by protocol
netstat -n	Displays IP addresses and port numbers in numerical order

Goodheart-Willcox Publisher

Figure 22-22 Similar to the **netstat** command, a number of switches can be used with the **nbtstat** command.

Common nbtstat Flags	
Nbtstat Command	**Description**
nbtstat -c	Displays the contents of the NetBIOS name cache
nbtstat -n	Displays names of all devices registered through broadcasts by NetBIOS applications
nbtstat -r	Displays NetBIOS names resolved by using broadcasts on the local area network
nbtstat -s	Displays the current network NetBIOS sessions and the status of each

Goodheart-Willcox Publisher

Hostname

A+ 1102: 1.2

The **hostname** command is another utility commonly used in network management. As shown in Figure 22-25, this command displays the computer name. This command also exists in Linux and performs the same function.

```
C:\Windows\system32\cmd.exe
Microsoft Windows [Version 10.0.19045.2846]
(c) Microsoft Corporation. All rights reserved.

C:\Users\GW>nbtstat -n

Ethernet:
Node IpAddress: [0.0.0.0] Scope Id: []

    No names in cache

Bluetooth Network Connection:
Node IpAddress: [0.0.0.0] Scope Id: []

    No names in cache

Wi-Fi:
Node IpAddress: [10.0.0.118] Scope Id: []

                NetBIOS Local Name Table

       Name               Type         Status
    ---------------------------------------------
    L59107696      <00>  UNIQUE      Registered
    WORKGROUP      <00>  GROUP       Registered
    L59107696      <20>  UNIQUE      Registered

Local Area Connection* 1:
Node IpAddress: [0.0.0.0] Scope Id: []

    No names in cache

Local Area Connection* 2:
Node IpAddress: [0.0.0.0] Scope Id: []

    No names in cache

C:\Users\GW>
```

Goodheart-Willcox Publisher

Figure 22-23 The **nbtstat -n** command provides a list of NetBIOS name assignments for the local computer and the workgroups to which they belong.

```
C:\Windows\system32\cmd.exe
Microsoft Windows [Version 10.0.19045.2846]
(c) Microsoft Corporation. All rights reserved.

C:\Users\GW>nbtstat -r

    NetBIOS Names Resolution and Registration Statistics
    ----------------------------------------------------

    Resolved By Broadcast     = 0
    Resolved By Name Server   = 0

    Registered By Broadcast   = 3
    Registered By Name Server = 0

C:\Users\GW>
```

Goodheart-Willcox Publisher

Figure 22-24 The **nbtstat -r** command lists the computer names on the LAN resolved by broadcast.

```
C:\Windows\system32\cmd.exe
Microsoft Windows [Version 10.0.19045.2846]
(c) Microsoft Corporation. All rights reserved.

C:\Users\GW>hostname
L59107696

C:\Users\GW>
```

Goodheart-Willcox Publisher

Figure 22-25 The **hostname** utility displays the name of the computer from which the command is launched.

Net Services

Net services are a set of two- or three-word commands that can display and manage local user accounts, shared folders, and start or stop services. For example, **net view** displays a list of computers that are members of the local area network or domain, as shown in Figure 22-26.

Some of the more common net services commands are listed in Figure 22-27, but this is just a few of the many net services commands available. To learn more about Microsoft net services commands, visit the Microsoft TechNet website.

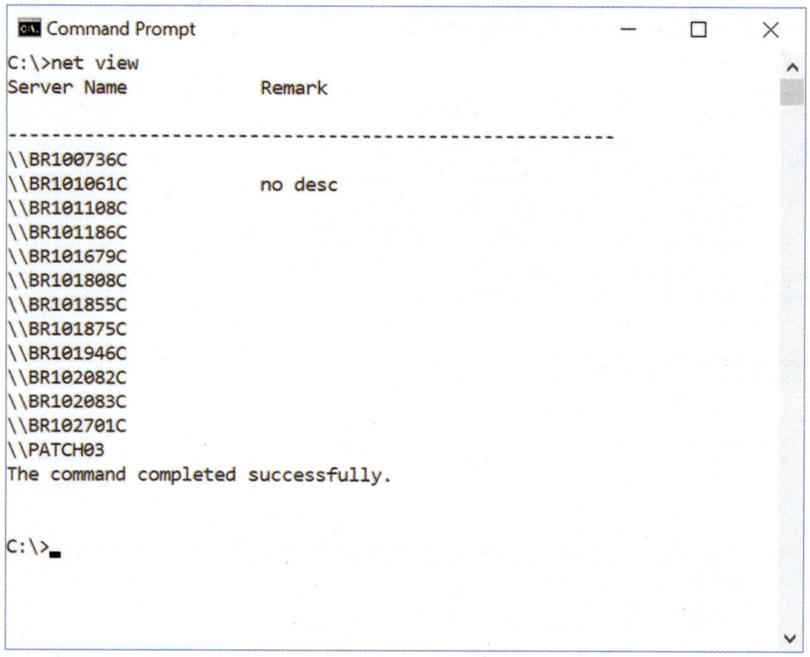

Figure 22-26 The **net view** command displays a list of local computers connected on a LAN.

Goodheart-Willcox Publisher

Figure 22-27 There are many net services commands that can be issued in the command prompt.

Common Net Service Commands	
Net Services Command	**Description**
net view	Displays computers connected to the local area network
net share	Displays information about local shares
net user	Displays information about the local device users
net accounts	Displays information related to the local user account, such as password configuration options
net groups	Displays information related to local computer groups
net stop	Stops a network service
net start	Starts a network service
net print	Manages print jobs
net statistics workstation	Displays workstation network statistics
net statistics server	Displays server network statistics

Goodheart-Willcox Publisher

ARP

Address Resolution Protocol (ARP) is used to resolve IPv4 addresses to physical addresses. The ARP cache holds a list of IPv4 addresses correlated to MAC addresses. There is also a command called **arp**, which displays the contents of the ARP cache, as seen in Figure 22-28. IPv4 relies on the ARP cache to locate other devices on the local area network, as IPv4 must convert IPv4 addresses to MAC addresses to communicate on the local area network. The ARP command can also be used to verify that the IPv4 protocol is properly identifying devices by MAC address. IPv6 does not use ARP to resolve MAC addresses to IP addresses and instead communicates directly with other local area network devices without the need to identify the MAC address.

Windows Diagnostics

Windows 10 and 11 provide several built-in network utilities. For example, you can get a visual representation of your network connectivity by navigating to **Start**>**Settings**>**Network & Internet**>**Status**. If the laptop icon connects to the globe icon without any interruption, as shown in Figure 22-29A, you know you are connected to the Internet. However, if there is no connection, as shown in Figure 22-29B, you

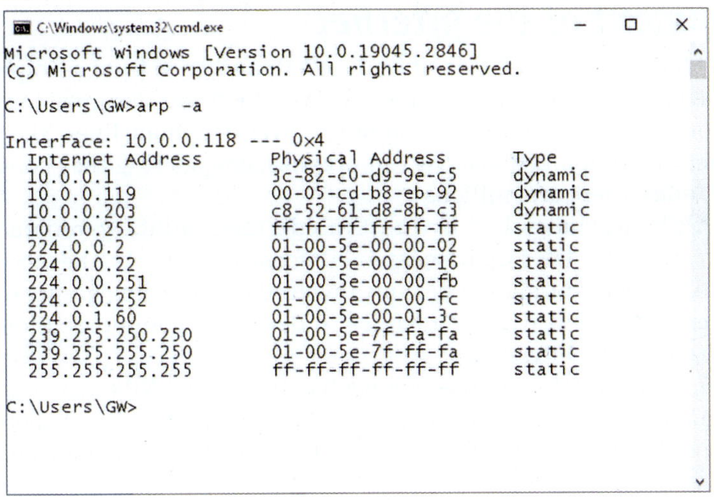

Goodheart-Willcox Publisher

Figure 22-28 Address Resolution Protocol (ARP) is used to resolve IPv4 addresses to physical addresses.

Figure 22-29 A steady Internet connection is identified by an uninterrupted path from the computer icon to the globe icon in the Status window (A), but a lack of connectivity is identified by no path to the globe as well as text informing the user of no Internet connection (B).

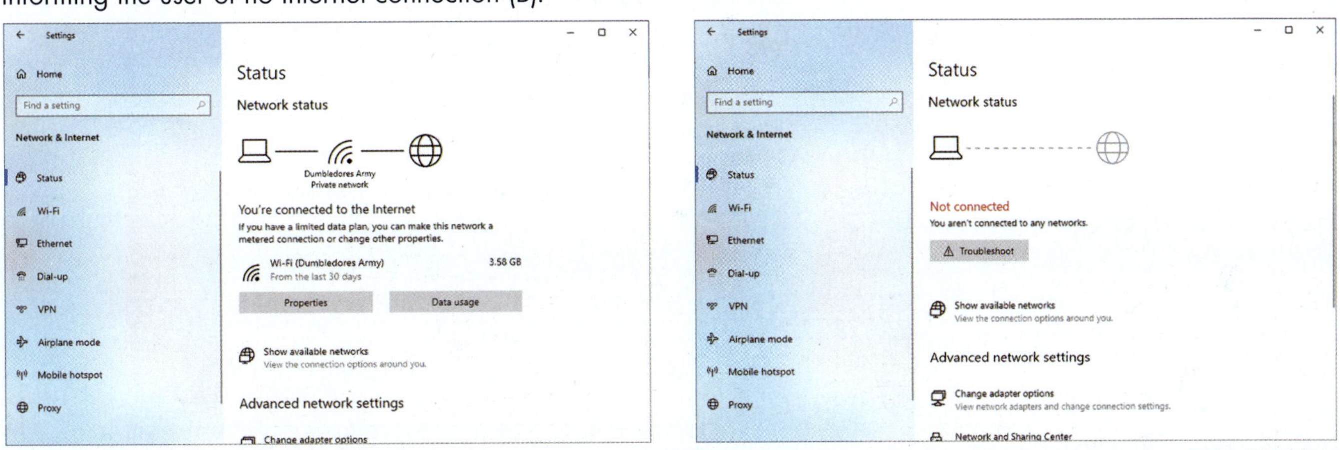

A B

Goodheart-Willcox Publisher

are not connected to the Internet, which is confirmed by text reading Not connected. Windows also provides other network troubleshooting tools or wizards. Looking again at Figure 22-29B, you can see a **Troubleshoot** button. The Windows network troubleshooter is available in all versions of Windows and produces a list of network adapters to diagnose, as shown in Figure 22-30.

The diagnostic wizards for the Windows operating system incorporate a series of diagnostic programs similar to the ones run from the command prompt. The wizard interprets the results and then displays a message on the screen related to the diagnosed problem. If a problem is detected, you will be given likely solutions to try. As operating systems evolve, they incorporate more automatic network connection–problem detection systems and also automatically correct problems.

22.4 Internet Navigation

No discussion about networks would be complete without a discussion of the Internet. This section will give you a brief historical background of the Internet and its development, and it will make you aware of how complex the Internet really is.

Development of the Internet

The Internet has been in existence since the 1960s and grew from a simple project of the Advanced Research Project Agency (ARPA), which was designed to test the feasibility of communication between computers over telephone lines. The first experiments were very simple but also very impressive, considering they contained only four hosts. Today, there are millions.

Later, ARPA was absorbed by the United States military, renamed DARPA, and operated by the US Department of Defense (DOD). As the network grew, the National Science Foundation became involved by awarding grants to many different universities and private companies to develop a communication model for what is now called the Internet.

In 1985, some of the centers connected by the DARPA network's 56-kbps backbone included Cornell University, the National Center for Supercomputing Application at the University of Illinois, the Pittsburgh Supercomputing Center in

Figure 22-30 Windows provides troubleshooting utilities to help diagnose network connection problems.

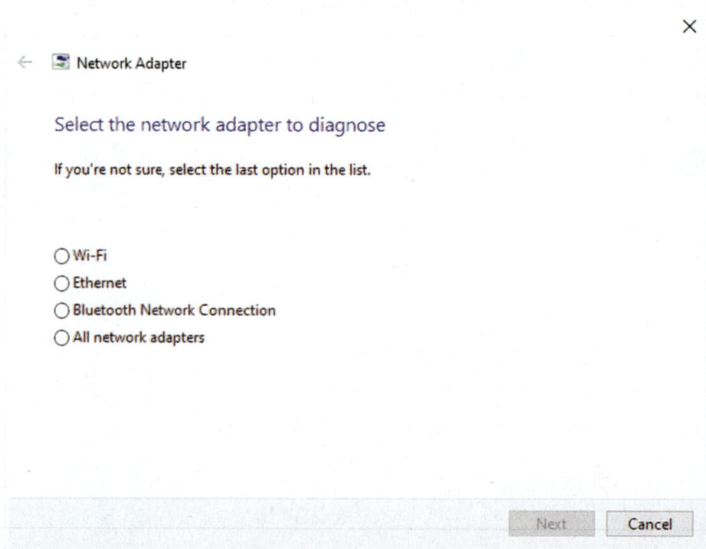

Goodheart-Willcox Publisher

Pittsburgh, the University of California in San Diego, and Princeton University in New Jersey. This backbone is viewed by many people as the true beginning of what was to become the Internet. Over the next several years, many more universities, private companies, and research centers connected to the line. Within three years, the increased traffic forced the original 56-kbps backbone to be replaced with a T-1 line that could carry 1.544 Mbps. The new line connected six diverse regional networks in the United States, including the National Center of Atmospheric Research in Colorado, the original computer centers previously listed, and the Merit site at the University of Michigan.

In 1990, Merit, IBM, and MCI started a nonprofit organization called Advanced Network and Services, Inc. (ANS). The backbone was expanded to 16 major sites connected by a T-3 line, which could carry 43 Mbps. A T-3 line consists of 672 lines, each with a capability to carry 64 kbps.

By 1993, the National Science Foundation designed a series of Network Access Points (NAPs) for private companies to connect to the backbone. Private companies could develop their own networks and then tie directly into the backbone, but only at a NAP. Originally, four locations were designated to serve as access to the backbone. These locations were San Francisco, Chicago, New York (actually in Pennsauken, New Jersey), and Washington, DC, but more locations were added as demand grew.

Merit was chosen to maintain a database of information about the Internet and act as the arbitrator for disputes. The Internet then came into full power, based on the original ARPA backbone project. Private communication companies constructed their own backbones as well. Some companies constructed MANs in large metropolitan areas to allow businesses to have access to high-speed backbone systems spanning the US.

Growth has continued at an astounding rate. The Internet consists of fiber-optic and copper-core cables, wireless devices, infrared devices, satellites, and millions of miles of old telephone lines. The Internet grows so fast and diversely, that there is no real map of all the lines and connections in existence. Individual companies have information regarding connection and traffic lines, but they only have what is limited to their direct control. There are over 4,500 companies making changes to the Internet daily, making it impossible to create an up-to-date and all-inclusive map of the Internet.

The diversity arises from the Internet's practice of sending data along the shortest route between two points. Most Internet providers have agreements allowing access to each other's backbones and parts of their individually constructed networks, which enables wider access to the Internet. For example, one customer may use Company A as their Internet provider, and another customer may use Company B, which is located across the street from Company A. If it were not for mutually beneficial agreements established between the two companies, the data sent between those two customers might very well be routed hundreds or even thousands of miles to a national backbone before making a return trip to the other provider's lines.

There are thousands of agreements in place between providers to lease line access from one another, which shortens data routes considerably. This is one of the main reasons there are so many routers used on the Internet. The routers are constantly updated to find the least expensive route between two points on the Internet. In short, the Internet is a network of interconnected networks, forming a huge spiderweb of communication circuits.

URLs and Domain Names

Uniform Resource Locators (URLs) are the global addresses for websites all over the Internet. The first part of a URL identifies the protocol used and the second part identifies the domain name. Many people confuse URLs and domain names because they appear so similar, but a domain name is an alphanumeric name that identifies one or more IP addresses and is combined with the protocol type to form the URL. For example, consider the URL https://www.g-w.com/contact/contact. Each element within this URL specifies something unique, as shown in Figure 22-31. In this example, the domain is g-w.com, and the resource, contact, is a web-based form accessed using the S-HTTP protocol. A URL that begins with ftp:// uses the File Transfer Protocol to access the web page. There will be more about FTP later in this chapter.

The Domain Name System (DNS), as mentioned earlier, is a system used to identify domain names of sites on the Internet and resolve them to their IP addresses. When you enter a URL in your web browser, a query is sent to a local resolver consisting of a database of domain names and matching IP addresses. The query requests the resolver for a matching IP address for the domain name that you entered. The resolver transmits the requested IP address to your computer, and you are then seamlessly connected to the requested site. If the resolver's database does not contain the requested IP address, it forwards the query to the next resolver in the network. This continues until the IP address is located and you are connected to the requested site, or until all the resolvers are searched without success, resulting in an error message.

From the Internet's inception until 1995, InterNIC issued domain names and matching IP addresses. Then, the InterNIC commercialized the system, turning it over to the private sector. Today, InterNIC retains control of the system, but it has delegated the responsibility of dealing with the public to the not-for-profit organization known as *Internet Corporation for Assigned Names and Numbers (ICANN)*. In turn, ICANN oversees the day-to-day operations associated with issuing domain names to private-sector companies. However, you can access a list of authorized domain-name registration companies from the InterNIC site. Domain name suffixes, such as .com or .gov, are assigned according to the domain's function. Figure 22-32 lists some common suffixes found in domain names. The top portion of the table lists common domain suffixes and the types of organizations that use them, and the rest of the table contains some of the latest domain suffixes and the types of organizations that use them.

Subdomains

A **subdomain** is a division of a group of networks. Subdomains create a third level to a website and function similarly to folders in a file system by offering another way to organize a website. For example, https://www.google.com is the regular URL without a subdomain. In https://news.google.com, news is the subdomain for the google.com website. The website is organized as follows: .com represents the first-level domain, google represents the second-level domain, and news represents the third-level domain. The ability to create subdomains is determined by the company hosting the website. Web-hosting companies vary on this issue, but most allow subdomains. Some web-hosting companies provide free website hosting, which typically provides the user with a subdomain.

Subdomains allow you to create shorter URL addresses, which are often easier to remember and can be used to point to a file location deeply embedded into a website. For example, the URL http://downloads.XYZcorp.com may serve as a type of shortcut to a full web address of http://www.XYZcorp.com/products/updates/downloads.

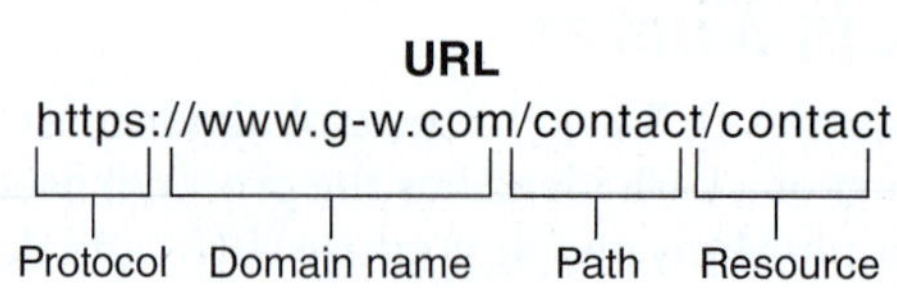

Figure 22-31 The structure of a URL consists of a protocol, domain name, and, if necessary, path and resource.

Goodheart-Willcox Publisher

Common Domain Name Suffixes	
Domain	**Type of Organization**
.com	Commercial business
.edu	Educational
.gov	Government
.mil	Military
.net	Host or gateway
.org	Organizations (usually, but not necessarily, nonprofit)
.aero	Global aviation authority
.arts	Art and cluture
.asia	Pan-Asia and Asian Pacific region
.biz	Restricted to business
.info	Information services
.jobs	Human resources management community
.mobi	Mobile products
.museum	Museums and related areas
.name	Individual personal names
.nom	Individuals
.pro	Reserved for licensed professionals
.rec	Recreational and entertainment
.store	Merchants
.travel	Travel industry
.web	Web activities

Goodheart-Willcox Publisher

Figure 22-32 Domain names and suffixes are assigned according to a domain's function.

Subdomains can be password-protected and be accessed by designated company employees or affiliate companies. They can also be used to create departments within the organization such as Finance, Engineering, blog or forum, help, and FAQs.

22.5 E-Mail Communication

E-mail allows users to send messages anywhere in the world and has become one of the most popular uses of the Internet. Originally, e-mail was little more than a system to exchange ASCII text files, but it has grown to become a complete communication system, allowing for not only text-based messages but also attached files, such as reports, spreadsheets, database information, photos, illustrations, animations, and sound. There are numerous e-mail software packages available. The e-mail software packages encapsulate the available Internet e-mail protocols and greatly enhance the user interface.

Setting up an E-Mail Account

You must have certain information to establish an e-mail account, such as your username and password and the name and type of mail server being used for both incoming and outgoing messages. A protocol is required to communicate with a mail server that is hosting the e-mail software and the Internet connection. Common e-mail protocols include Post Office Protocol 3 (POP3), Internet Message Access

Tech Tip

Some e-mail services provide an e-mail storage option for their POP3 servers, but this is not generally the case.

Protocol (IMAP), Hypertext Markup Language (HTML), and Simple Mail Transport Protocol (SMTP). In many cases, your Internet service provider (ISP) provides your username, password, and e-mail server name.

A mail server usually stores all e-mail communication until the user retrieves it. In a strict network environment, e-mails can be delivered directly to individual PCs. Once you log in to your ISP, you can open your e-mail account, which is stored on the server, and access your personal e-mail. E-mail protocols vary according to the way they manage e-mail messages and interact with the e-mail server.

A+ 1101: 1.4, 2.1

POP3

Post Office Protocol 3 (POP3) is a common e-mail protocol used to download incoming e-mails from an e-mail server. POP3 mail servers hold e-mail messages until a user checks their e-mail, at which time, the e-mail message and any attachments are downloaded to the computer. When the e-mail transfer is complete, the original e-mail is deleted from the POP3 mail server.

A+ 1101: 2.1

SMTP

Simple Mail Transfer Protocol (SMTP) is an e-mail protocol used to upload and transfer outgoing e-mail messages between e-mail servers. SMTP servers send e-mail to the Internet and transfer e-mail between mail servers. For home-user applications, the SMTP mail server is located at the ISP, though for business applications, the SMTP mail server may be either at the ISP or on the organization's network. SMTP servers manage outgoing e-mail and are used in conjunction with a POP3 or IMAP incoming mail server.

A+ 1101: 1.4, 2.1

IMAP

Internet Message Access Protocol (IMAP) is an e-mail protocol used to access e-mail from a server. IMAP mail servers allow you to view e-mail message content without the need to download the e-mail, enabling users to preview, delete, and organize messages while they are still on the mail server. In addition, copies are stored on the server until you choose to delete them. If you have several computers or networking devices that can access an e-mail account, each device will see the same e-mail content. By comparison, when using POP3 with several different devices, e-mail will be downloaded to each device, and you will need to read and delete the e-mail from each device as needed. IMAP is most common for business e-mail accounts, though it should be noted that IMAP has been gradually supplanting POP3 in general.

Webmail

Webmail, also referred to as *HTML e-mail*, is an e-mail service—often free of charge—based on using a web browser to access e-mail, such as Gmail, Outlook.com, or Yahoo! Mail. When you configure webmail, you do not need to supply the outgoing or incoming mail server or select an e-mail type. You simply choose an available e-mail address for your account and select an available user account name and password. The downside of webmail is that it is usually inundated with commercial advertisements, and webmail service providers have been suspected of collecting user information and selling it to marketing services.

A+ 1101: 1.4

Port and SSL Settings

When a network administrator or technician is configuring a mobile device or personal computer to their organization's e-mail, it is important that they have records of their network's port and Secure Sockets Layer (SSL) settings. The mail provider can determine the port and SSL settings when the port numbers are available and not used, but there are also default ports that are assigned by SSL such as POP3S 995 and IMAPS 993. The ports generated via the SSL settings keep information encrypted between the user and the receiver of e-mail messages and data. Without the ports that are generated via SSL, e-mail messages and data risk the possibility of being intercepted during the transmission of the messages. It should be noted that while most sources state SSL, SSL was supplanted by Transport Layer Security (TLS) in 1999.

E-mail security is critical and usually begins with implementing SSL/TLS. As has been discussed, SMTP, POP3, and IMAP all have encrypted versions, which should be utilized whenever possible. In addition to encrypted e-mail, good password management, and multifactor authentication (MFA) are also recommended.

1102: 2.1 A+

Spam Gateway

1102: 1.2 A+

A *spam gateway*, sometimes referred to as an *antispam gateway*, is a software-based virtual device that is logically arranged behind a firewall to prevent spam e-mail from reaching its destination. This not only improves productivity, as employees have fewer nonessential e-mail messages to read, but also helps eliminate many phishing threats.

Sending an E-Mail

To send an e-mail, you must enter the unique address of the recipient, such as JoeSmith@email.com. Two or more users can have the same alpha name on the same network, but they are usually given a numeric extension to maintain the uniqueness of the address, such as JoeSmith012@email.com. A message is then entered into the message space and the **Send** button is clicked, sending the e-mail to its destination. The menus provide the user with many common computing options, including the ability to delete and save messages. However, several options are unique to e-mail, such as reply, reply to all, resend, forward, and file attachment.

Off-Site E-Mail Applications

As an e-mail server continues to obtain more messages and data, its functionality may experience diminished qualities such as speed. Although users of an organization could simply delete their e-mail messages, network administrators and technicians are discovering that users in an organization tend not to delete any of their received e-mails. However, offsite e-mail applications such as the archive option in Microsoft Outlook or Mozilla Thunderbird allow users to save their e-mails in a program instead of placing multiple e-mails and corresponding data on an e-mail server.

MIME and S/MIME

1101: 1.4 A+

When a nontext file is attached to an e-mail message, it must be converted to a form that can be understood by text-oriented e-mail protocols. The *Multipurpose Internet Mail Extensions (MIME)* standard is the specification for formatting nontext files, such as graphics, audio, and video, for transmission over the Internet. A newer version of MIME is S/MIME, in which the *S* stands for *secure*. S/MIME allows the sent message to be encrypted and signed with a digital signature or certificate. Methods used to ensure S/MIME security are discussed in the following section.

> **A+ Note**
> The A+ Exams typically have several questions about e-mail protocols. Remember, SMTP sends e-mail to a mail server. POP3 and IMAP download e-mail from the mail server.

Digital Signatures and Encryption/Decryption Keys

Three components are required to digitally sign and encrypt a message: a public key, a private key, and the appropriate encoding software. To obtain a public and private key, you must first apply for a digital ID from a third-party software vendor by using e-mail, and then the certifying authority verifies your identity.

Your digital ID provides you with two digital keys. The first key is a private key, which you keep entirely to yourself and is used to sign your e-mail and encrypt messages. The receiving party will be warned if a signed message has been tampered with. The private key also verifies your identity to the recipient. The other key is a public key, which you distribute to people with whom you want to communicate. The public key allows others to decode messages encoded with your private key and allows them to encode messages that can only be decoded by your private key.

When you digitally sign an e-mail, software compresses the message contents to a few lines of text known as a ***message digest***, which is then encoded using the sender's private key. The resulting data is the sender's ***digital signature***, which is added to the end of the message.

The receiver can decode both the signature and the message using the sender's public key. When the message is decoded, it results in the same data used to create the message digest and, by extension, the signature. If the receiver compresses the message, and the resulting message digest does not match the message digest extracted from the key, the recipient knows that the message has been altered.

22.6 Internet Protocols

Hundreds of protocols have been developed over the years. Protocols began as simple programs that carried out commands and transported plain ASCII text files, but they have evolved into much more sophisticated programs. In the strictest sense, protocols are software programs that establish a set of rules to enable two entities to communicate. As protocols evolve, they take on the appearance of application software and are, therefore, classified as such. As technology evolves, there will always be new protocols, usually built on top of the older protocols to maintain backward compatibility between systems.

Protocols are assembled into packages of data containing addresses and data or commands and are designed to either encapsulate or be encapsulated by other protocols. When you connect to a distant web page, several protocols work together to complete the transaction. A request for an Internet web page requires several different protocols, such as Ethernet, IP (IPv4 or IPv6), TCP, and HTTP, and each protocol has a distinct responsibility for the successful download of a single page of HTML code.

Ethernet contains the MAC addresses of the source and destination devices and also encapsulates IPv4 or IPv6, which contains the source and destination IPv4 or IPv6 addresses. IP encapsulates TCP, which contains the port addresses of the source and destination, and TCP also encapsulates HTTP, which contains the HTML data. See Figure 22-33 for a summary of what each protocol contains.

Ethernet

Ethernet is both a protocol and a networking standard. The Ethernet protocol is designed to encapsulate other protocols and carry them to and from devices located on an Ethernet network based on the MAC addresses of the source and destination devices. The Ethernet standard describes the network system as related to media and function.

Figure 22-33 A request for an Internet web page requires several different protocols, including Ethernet, IPv4 or IPv6, TCP, and HTTP.

Protocol Functions of a Web Page Request

Protocol	Contains
Ethernet	MAC address of the source and destination devices
IP	IPv4 or IPv6 address of the source and destination devices
TCP	Port addresses of the source and destination devices, also encapsulates HTTP
HTTP	HTML code data for the browser to interpret the web page

Goodheart-Willcox Publisher

IP

The Internet Protocol (IP) communicates across the Internet and contains the destination and source IP addresses. It also routes packets containing other protocols across the Internet through a series of routers. Currently, there are two IP protocols used: IPv4 and IPv6.

TCP and UDP

A+ 1101: 2.1

Transmission Control Protocol (TCP) and User Datagram Protocol (UDP) are two of the main protocols associated with the TCP/IP protocol suite. TCP is described as a *connection-oriented* protocol, and UDP is described as a *connectionless* protocol. In other words, TCP establishes a connection between two network devices and maintains that connection until the purpose of the connection is completed, while UDP does *not* establish a connection with the destination device. For example, connecting to an Internet server and downloading the content from the server using TCP requires the computer and server to establish and maintain a connection until all the content has been downloaded. After several packets are downloaded, a TCP packet is sent to the source to confirm that the connection is still established, and if a packet does not return to the source device, the process to establish a connection will restart. By comparison, TCP generates a lot more network traffic because it must establish and maintain the connection between the two devices.

UDP does not establish a connection and simply sends a command or data to the destination assuming it will be delivered. UDP also does not guarantee delivery of the packet, which might seem like a terrible way to send information, but it is used for applications in which speed is more essential than ensuring packet delivery. For example, when sending time-sensitive material, such as live streaming music or video, using UDP is more efficient than TCP because UDP sends the packets of data directly to the destination and does not check if they arrived intact. The additional packets used by TCP would cause latency between the two devices and create small breaks in live music or live video. Both TCP and UDP use port numbers to determine the destination of the packet.

HTTP

A+ 1101: 2.1

Hypertext Transfer Protocol (HTTP) is a standard protocol used to transport web page content across the Internet. Often confused with HTTP, **Hypertext Markup Language (HTML)** is a programming language used to create web pages. Simply put, HTTP delivers web page content written in HTML code. Turn your attention to Figure 22-34. Figure 22-34A is a screen capture that shows what HTML code looks like. This

Figure 22-34 Web browsers interpret HTML code (A) and display the desired page (B).

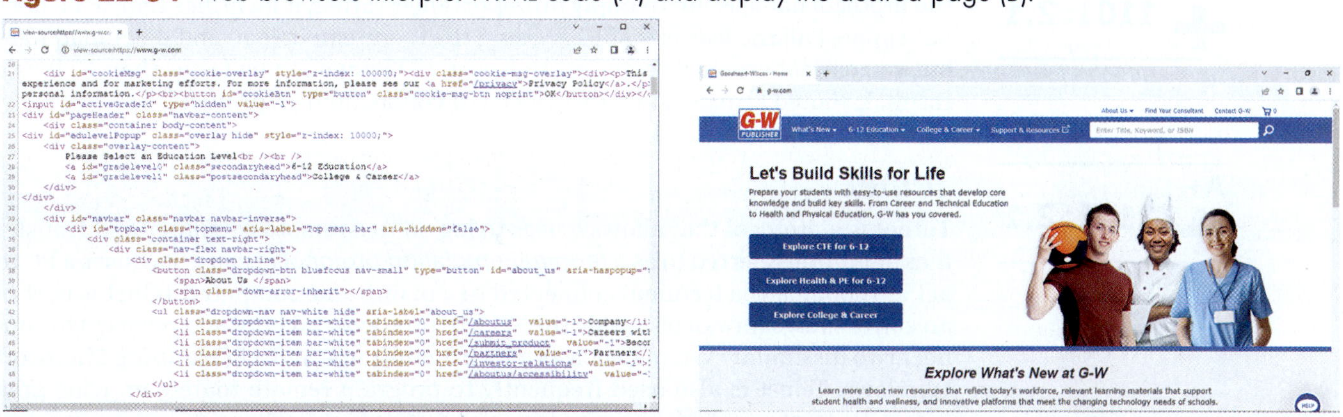

A B

Goodheart-Willcox Publisher

code does not appear to the user unless viewed intentionally. A web browser interprets the HTML code and then displays whatever is written in the code. Figure 22-34B shows the interpretation of the HTML code displayed on the browser.

A+ 1101: 2.1

HTTPS

HTTPS is a combination of HTTP and Secure Sockets Layer (SSL) protocols. **Secure Sockets Layer (SSL)** is a protocol developed by Netscape Navigator to make HTTP-based online transactions secure. While HTTP is fine for browsing the Internet, it does not provide a secure connection for exchanging sensitive information such as credit card numbers. HTTP was never intended to be used for transmitting secure information such as transactions involving personal identification and money.

The combination of HTTP and SSL provides a secure connection to a website using encryption. When used, the website URL location will be HTTPS://, with the *S* representing *secure*, and indicates that you are connected to the distant web page using a secure connection provided by the SSL protocol. Additionally, some websites may include a lock icon or display the URL in a different color to show that the web page is secure. SSL can be used with any protocol in the TCP/IP suite, not just with HTTP.

A+ 1101: 2.1 1102: 4.9

SSH

Secure Shell (SSH), also known as *Secure Socket Shell*, is a protocol that provides secure access to a remote computer. The connection between both computers is encrypted and authenticated using digital signatures, a password, or both. The main difference between SSL and SSH is that SSL does not require a username and password to log in, while SSH typically does. You will encounter SSH in applications such as a remote administrative logon for a secure server or network device. SSH uses port 22, and SSL uses port 443.

A+ 1101: 2.1

FTP

File Transfer Protocol (FTP) is a protocol used for transmitting files across the Internet. FTP is commonly used to upload and download files between a computer and a web-hosting server. Two variations of FTP add security features: FTPS and SFTP. FTP over SSL (FTPS) is a combination of FTP with SSL or TLS encryption, and Secure FTP (SFTP) is based on Secure Shell (SSH) technology. The two protocols appear to be the same and are often confused with each other, but they are two different security schemes. In many cases, you will need a username and password to access an organization's FTP website, but a special FTP, called *anonymous FTP*, allows users to access files for downloading without using a secret password and identity.

A+ 1101: 2.1

Related to FTP is *Trivial File Transfer Protocol (tFTP)*. The inclusion of *trivial* in the protocol name is not to imply unimportance; rather, it identifies that tFTP does not support all the features of FTP. Using tFTP, one can upload and download files, but you cannot create directories. However, tFTP tends to be faster than FTP as a result. It should also be noted that tFTP is a connectionless protocol.

A+ 1101: 2.1

Telnet

Telnet is a protocol that allows a user to log on to a remote computer and transfer files. It is often referred to as a *terminal emulation protocol* because it causes a PC to act as though it is a terminal connected to a mainframe computer. Telnet is part of an entire suite of protocols inside the TCP/IP protocol and is most often used to connect two dissimilar systems, such as a Unix mainframe and a PC running Microsoft Windows. Telnet is also used frequently to program remote routers on wide area networks and to control other computer operations remotely.

SNMP

A+ 1101: 2.1

Simple Network Management Protocol (SNMP) is a protocol that configures and collects information about network devices, such as servers, printers, switches, and routers. SNMP is also a standard as defined by the Internet Engineering Task Force (IETF). Because the SNMP packets have a design standard, different companies can create software packages based on SNMP to create tools that monitor devices and can make configuration changes when necessary.

CIFS

A+ 1101: 2.1

Common Internet File System (CIFS) is a network file-sharing protocol developed for early Microsoft operating systems. Microsoft developed CIFS as an open-source standard and then submitted the standard to the Internet Engineering Task Force (IETF) so anyone could use it royalty-free. CIFS was designed as a file-sharing protocol that utilizes HTTP to support sharing files across the Internet, but it can also support printing across the network.

SMB

A+ 1101: 2.1

Server Message Block (SMB) is a network file-sharing protocol that supports file sharing for client/server applications. The term *server* is not limited to what is commonly known as a dedicated network device, and when there is no server such as in a workgroup configuration, any computer configured to share files can act in a server role. In the context of the SMB protocol, a server is any device that provides services, such as a shared file.

SMB is considered a dialect of CIFS and has been used by Microsoft for many years with many design revisions. There have been three major revisions of SMB since Windows 2000 and Windows XP; SMB 3.0 is used for Windows 10 and Windows Server as the main protocol used to support file sharing.

22.7 Cloud Services

A+ 1101: 4.1

Cloud computing is becoming a popular alternative to configuring a small-office/home-office (SOHO) network manually. Cloud services allow you to share a pool of resources such as storage, application software, and specialized services, including instant messaging, e-mail, and database support. The term *cloud* is synonymous with the Internet symbol used in network drawings, which represent the remote location of the service on the Internet location rather than the individual user's computer.

In a SOHO configuration, each computer has entire software applications, such as Microsoft Word, installed on it, and each computer on the network has complete access and control over the use and configuration of the software application. The user can also store files on the computer as related to the software application. For example, a computer user might have Microsoft Word installed on the computer and store all generated data, such as douments, on the same computer.

In a cloud-computing setting, however, the user installs a very small software application that allows the user to access the larger software application in the cloud service location. In this scenario, the user computer is essentially functioning as a *thin client* because it depends on the software application at the remote location to do most of the work. The user has the option to store the document on the Internet cloud location or on his or her computer.

The cloud service can be provided free of charge or as a paid service. Free options generally provide fewer services and have less storage space as compared to paid services. There are many cloud service providers, such as Google, Apple, Microsoft, Android, Amazon, VMware, and IBM, among others.

Cloud Service Characteristics

The five characteristics of cloud service that have been identified by the National Institute of Standards and Technology (NIST) are on-demand self-service, broad network access, resource pooling, rapid elasticity, and measured service. These common characteristics are used to identify cloud services as compared to traditional on-site network systems. The National Institute of Standards and Technology (NIST) defines *cloud computing* as "a model for enabling convenient, on-demand network access to a shared pool of configurable computing resources (e.g., networks, servers, storage, applications, and services) that can be rapidly provisioned and released with minimal management effort or service provider interaction."

A+ 1101: 4.1

High Availability

One of the most obvious characteristics of cloud services is high availability. Since the data storage for a cloud service is distributed to different geographical areas, it is unlikely for the service to be offline, even in the event of a major natural disaster in one region. This remains one of the major advantages of cloud computing, as well as one of the original reasons for implementing cloud services.

On-Demand Self-Service

The cloud service is readily accessible and requires no real expertise or on-site technical support personnel as in a traditional network model. A network technician is not required to set up the cloud service, making it a self-service oriented system.

Broad Network Access

By its nature, the cloud can be accessed from almost anywhere through a variety of devices, such as workstations, laptops, smartphones, and tablets. Cloud services are also accessed by *thin client software*, which is a minimal software application that does not require a hardware device designed with a large amount of RAM or a high-speed CPU.

Organizations are increasingly reliant on the ability for mobile devices and laptop computers to have services that allow application streaming to be delivered without the need for application installation from the user. This use of application streaming allows users to access their organization's applications and data via a web address or a centralized software application that has been installed on the user's mobile device or laptop personal computer. The user navigates to it via web browser and provides their credentials for access. Similarly, the centralized software application directs the user to the organization's applications, as this software is primarily installed via a network administrator or technician of the organization.

Resource Pooling

The real strength of cloud service is resource pooling and sharing. Computer resources such as documents, pictures, videos, and other types of files can be shared easily with other members of the cloud service. In addition to sharing resources, the cloud provider typically offers software applications appropriate for the type of cloud membership. For example, word-processing, database, e-mail, and digital photo software applications may be provided as a service. The cloud member need not install the software application on their device but rather connect to the cloud host as a thin client and use the software application on the remote server.

For example, a word-processing application need not be installed on the cloud member's computer or portable device because the software is installed on the cloud-hosting server. Instead, the cloud member has a relatively small software application installed on his or her personal device, which supports communication with the cloud host provider's software application. The advantage of the software application being installed on the cloud server is that the software application will be available no matter which device the user decides to use. The cloud member can run the software application from their desktop, tablet, or smartphone. Another advantage is that the cloud provider is responsible for updating the software application, making backups, and providing the necessary technical support.

When software applications are provided through cloud services, it is often referred to as *virtualization.* The software appears to the user as though it is installed entirely on the user's PC or portable device, but the software application is actually installed on the cloud server.

Network Controller

Cloud-based network controllers are becoming more common as networks and data implementation increase in networking and disaster recovery endeavors. Cloud-based networking can be defined as a third-party provider that provides storage and disaster recovery implementation via Internet-based technologies and resources. Since the implementation of cloud-based networking and cloud-based networking controllers is becoming more acceptable and reliable, network administrators and technicians can expect this trend to continue to augment in its popularity among organizations. Furthermore, cloud-based network controllers enable network management, such as an organization's Active Directory and domain, to be accessed from anywhere, provided the user has a broadband connection and login credentials from the organization.

Virtual Network Interface Card

A virtual network interface card, also termed as a *virtual NIC* or *VNIC*, is a piece of software that transmits the MAC address of the physical network interface card (NIC) to obtain access to an organization's virtual network. Once a user attempts to access an organization's network, this software then communicates with the virtual network(s) to determine if the mobile device or personal computer is granted or denied access to the network(s) and its data. The primary uses of virtual NICs are to obtain access to VPN and VMware to have access from remote locations.

Rapid Elasticity

1101: 4.1 A+

Cloud services can be rapidly expanded or contracted as needed. For example, when more server disk space is required for the storage of additional documents or images, the additional space can be added instantly. In a traditional on-site network model, a technician would have to allocate more space or even add additional hardware, such as additional disk drives for storage.

Measured Service

1101: 4.1 A+
1102: 1.6

With the utilization of cloud computing and its services gaining more acceptance among organizations, cloud-computing companies are implementing measured, or metered, services to bill their clients instead of having flat fees. Similar to utility companies that bill you for the quantity of service you use each month, cloud-computing companies are billing organizations based on the amount of storage they use along with the amount of overhead needed to support their remote networking needs. Although this may be perceived as a paradigm shift to some organizations, this provides a billing procedure where the client is only billed for the amount they use rather than having a flat fee each billing quarter and can be more cost-friendly to organizations.

Cloud Infrastructure

Cloud infrastructure allows users to access a network cloud service. There are four major cloud infrastructure, or deployment, models identified by NIST: private cloud, community cloud, public cloud, and hybrid cloud. Any combination of the first three infrastructure models is considered a hybrid cloud. The main differences among the cloud infrastructure models center around who may become a member of or access the cloud structure and who is responsible for maintaining the cloud service.

A+ 1101: 4.1

Private Cloud

A **private cloud** is an infrastructure model typically designed for exclusive use by a single group. A private cloud is operated exclusively for a given organization, but the service may be provided by a third-party vendor. A private cloud does *not* require the infrastructure or support to be exclusive to the private party; only access to the private cloud is exclusive.

A+ 1101: 4.1

Community Cloud

A **community cloud** is a shared infrastructure of users who share a common interest or concern. You can think of Facebook, Twitter, or similar services as a community cloud. A community cloud can also be shared by several different organizations that support a common interest, such as a collection of individual schools or businesses that operate under different authorities. For example, the Department of Defense (DOD) might set up a cloud service to provide and exchange information exclusively to a group of private defense contractors that are all involved in building a new aircraft for the DoD.

A+ 1101: 4.1

Public Cloud

A **public cloud** is an infrastructure open to the general public and may be used by individuals, business organizations, or educational organizations. The main difference between a private cloud and a public cloud is a public cloud is typically hosted by a cloud service provider, which determines membership, and a private cloud is built exclusively for a private entity and provides services only for that entity. A private cloud can be hosted either by the private entity network server or from a cloud service provider. When the private cloud is provided by a cloud-host service provider, the cloud access is controlled by the private entity.

A+ 1101: 4.1

Hybrid Cloud

A **hybrid cloud** is simply a combination of two or more of the other cloud infrastructures. The implementation of a hybrid cloud structure allows organizations more flexibility while also providing greater data-deployment options.

Service Models

The main purpose of a cloud is to provide services to its clients, and there are four classifications of service models: Software as a Service (SaaS), Platform as a Service (PaaS), Infrastructure as a Service (IaaS), and Anything as a Service (XaaS). The services are typically designed to run on minimal computer devices, such as smartphones, tablets, laptops, and desktop computers.

A+ 1101: 4.1

Software as a Service

Software as a Service (SaaS) is a cloud service model that provides software applications to a user either through a web browser or thin client software application. For example, web-based e-mail can be provided as a cloud service; all that is needed to use cloud-based e-mail is a compatible web browser. Another example is running software such as a Microsoft Office application from the cloud. Microsoft Office applications are quite large, and many cannot be installed on portable devices that have minimal processing power, storage space, and RAM. By accessing the Microsoft Office application through a cloud software service, a thin client user can connect to the cloud server hosting the Microsoft Office application and use it as though it were installed on their device. This is also an example of how virtualization is accomplished. The software application appears to the consumer as though it is installed on their device even though they are using the cloud provider's software applications.

Platform as a Service

A+ 1101: 4.1

Platform as a Service (PaaS), also called *Service Platform* by some cloud providers, is a cloud service model that supports programming software by enabling the consumer to deploy original applications onto the cloud using programming languages. In computer science, the term *platform* generally refers to a computer operating system, but in the context of cloud service, it refers to the computer programming language and environment. For example, the Google App Engine is an example of PaaS that allows users to develop software applications for Google using programming languages such as Python, Java, and PHP. In addition to the cloud hosting the consumer programming language, the PaaS cloud can also host libraries of programs and tools used in the creation and distribution of the complete software package, such as a game. This is a great way to host everything used by a large group of programmers working on the same project. The programmers can have access to the very latest version of all programs and program libraries and tools. The consumer does not need to manage the cloud server(s), storage, and operating system, but they do have control over who has access to the project and its parts.

Another example of PaaS is when a database software application such as SQL Server is hosted by a cloud service provider and used by a consumer. The SQL Server software can be programmed into many different database configurations and is not considered a general-consumer software application. An *SQL Server* is a technically challenging programmable database application.

Infrastructure as a Service

A+ 1101: 4.1

Infrastructure as a Service (IaaS) is a cloud service model that provides storage and basic networking functions, which are used by the consumer. The consumer decides what software and applications to use and does not need to worry about typical network support. The cloud provider provides all the necessary network support functions required by the consumer.

You can think of IaaS as a basic type of service that provides the hardware required to operate a cloud, while the consumer is responsible for what will be installed and distributed on it. For example, a cloud provider might provide an IaaS to a game developer. In this application, the game developer writes and distributes games without needing to manage the cloud infrastructure, such as servers, storage, or networking. Instead, the developer simply installs games and controls the distribution of the game to users by controlling who can access the games. Additionally, the developer is responsible for updating the game software.

Anything as a Service

Anything as a Service (XaaS) is a hybrid of the first three types of services (SaaS, PaaS, and IaaS) designed to meet a variety of needs. XaaS can be thought of as an "anything you want to do" type of service. XaaS is not an official NIST service standard, but the term and acronym are used by many providers. In time, it could become a de facto term used to describe hybrid cloud services. The largest cloud service providers will design a cloud service to meet anyone's needs, thus the "anything as a service" designation.

Microsoft Cloud Services

Microsoft offers several versions of cloud services at this time, such as Microsoft 365 and Microsoft Azure. Like other cloud providers, some services are free, while others are not, with fees varying based on the desired services and number of users. For example, the cost of the service can be based on the number of users, based on the number of unique e-mail accounts.

Microsoft 365

Microsoft 365 is a subscription-based SaaS cloud service that provides storage space for files and photos and access to Microsoft software such as Word, Excel, OneNote, PowerPoint, Publisher, Access, e-mail service, calendar sharing, PC-to-PC calling, and videoconferencing. Large groups of consumers, such as educational institutions, small businesses, and midsize-to-large enterprises, find the Microsoft 365 service quite useful, especially since Microsoft provides the support services. This reduces or eliminates the need for a large network support group of technicians, as well as having to purchase costly software packages. This is not to say that individuals could not purchase the Microsoft 365 service, because they can. While individuals can purchase a subscription to Microsoft 365, they likely would not use all the available features and would instead prefer one of the smaller free services.

Microsoft 365 has several different plans with different combinations of software applications and services. You can select the plan based on your needs or your company's needs. For example, the needs of a corporation would be much different from a home user's needs, and the corporate Microsoft 365 package has all the common software applications as required in a corporate environment, such as company e-mail, voice mail, and other server applications. One such optional service is called Windows SharePoint Services, which is designed for creating a public or private website to share information and documents and support collaboration between employees.

Microsoft Azure

Microsoft Azure is Microsoft's complete cloud service offering all variations of cloud service. Azure provides media services such as content streaming with content protection, website hosting, database services, and storage space for backups. You can also build, deploy, and manage applications across a worldwide network. Visit the Microsoft Azure website to learn more.

AWS

Amazon Web Services (AWS) is Amazon's cloud offering. Amazon offers an array of cloud-based services, including storage, networking, content delivery, machine learning, and Internet of Things (IoT). AWS offers a wide range of price points to accommodate different budgets.

A+ 1102: 4.9

Other Cloud-Computing Tools

In a world that provides technological options to accommodate remote work, it is important that technicians understand the third-party tools their users will utilize for screen and file sharing, including services such as Zoom, Skype, Microsoft Teams, Adobe Connect, and Cisco WebEx. Technicians should encourage users to use complex passwords for the user accounts of these third-party tools, and users should be given only the minimal permissions needed to conduct job tasks using the third-party tools. This is performed to practice and implement heightened security measures, especially since remote connectivity is a feature of these tools. Nevertheless, users may have errors when attending third-party online meetings.

One of the most common issues users experience when attending an online meeting is the screen not displaying the material that is being presented. When this issue arises, it is normally due to users neglecting the updates and plugins needed for the program to operate effectively. Therefore, technicians should train their users to run these programs, as they will prompt users on their personal computers or mobile devices that they need to either update their software or install plugins for the software to be operational.

Synchronization Applications

A+ 1101: 4.1

As cloud computing becomes more favored among organizations, network administrators and technicians will encounter a need to provide synchronization options for applications and data. What this means is they will need to provide their users with the ability to work from multiple locations while still being able to retrieve their applications and data. Among the most common tools used to provide the synchronization of applications are Microsoft OneDrive, Dropbox, or even a web-based tool such as Sync. Nevertheless, network administrators and technicians can provide services such as a virtual private network (VPN) or remote software to access their organization's applications and software, but information technology professionals are utilizing the prior-mentioned tools due to their reliability and ease of use for end-users.

Virtual Desktop Infrastructure

A+ 1101: 4.1

Virtual Desktop Infrastructure (VDI) is becoming a common way of implementing desktops. VDI functions by enabling users to store their entire desktop, including the operating system, applications, and files, in the cloud. This allows the employee to log in to any workstation and have the same desktop environment and experience to which they are accustomed. Should a workstation breakdown, then the employee merely needs to move to another workstation and log in as normal. The employee will see the same desktop, have the same applications, and be able to access the same files, which allows work to continue uninterrupted.

A+ 1102: 4.9

Whether one uses virtual desktops or not, desktop management software is important. In fact, it might be more important when not using VDI. *Desktop management software* refers to a comprehensive tool that runs the management and security of workstations within an organization. This relieves technicians and administrators from the burden of ensuring all workstations in the enterprise—including laptops and other devices—are updated and secured while simultaneously facilitating a consistent security approach, which is critical.

Client-Side Virtualization

A+ 1101: 4.2

Client-side virtualization is a software application used to create multiple operating system environments on the host machine. Client-side virtualization is closely related to cloud services. When fully implemented, a client device such as a PC, laptop, tablet, or smartphone accesses software applications, storage, and services on a remote server. There are many client-side virtualization providers, such as VMware, Microsoft Hyper-V, and Citrix XenClient.

In Figure 22-35, you can see the Microsoft Hyper-V client and management tools, which were first introduced in Windows 8. Hyper-V is not installed by default but can be installed through the **Windows Features** dialog box accessed through **Control Panel>Programs> Programs and Features>Turn Windows features on or off.** The firmware installed on the device must support virtualization, otherwise you will notice a message informing you that Hyper-V cannot be installed. Depending on the computer, you may also see a message stating that the processor does not

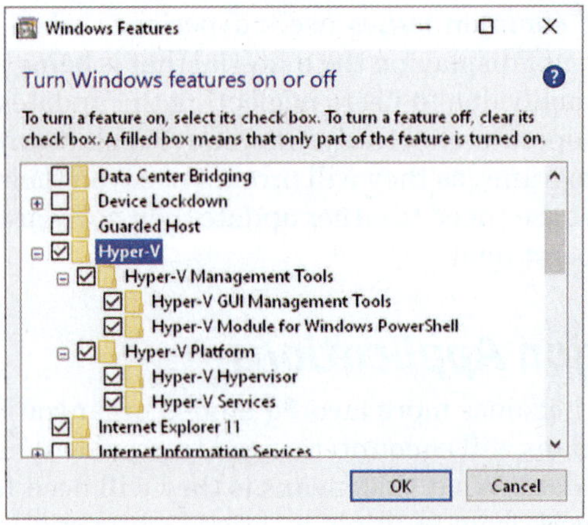

Figure 22-35 The Microsoft Hyper-V client is included in Windows 10 but is not installed by default.

Goodheart-Willcox Publisher

have Second Level Address Translation (SLAT) capabilities. ***Second Level Address Translation*** is the technical term used by Intel and AMD for hypervisor capabilities. In other words, older CPU technology cannot support virtualization.

The client requires a CPU and firmware (BIOS/UEFI) that supports virtualization, as well as a hypervisor. **Hypervisor**, also referred to as a ***virtual machine monitor***, is the technical term used to identify the software that creates the virtual machine on a client device.

Some Linux-based devices implement client-side virtualization called ***Kernel-based Virtual Machines (KVMs)***, which are machines with virtualization software installed directly on the hardware rather than inside a host machine operating system. A KVM client is an example of a ***bare metal device***, which is a device that does not have a standard operating system installed.

Virtualized applications require excellent network bandwidth to operate correctly. Because the virtualized machine requires a constant exchange of data and commands with the remote service, performance is sluggish without ample bandwidth.

Emulator

An ***emulator*** is a software application that acts as an interface between the user and a software application. Put simply, an emulator is two layers of software applications, and you can think of it as a software application designed to run another software application. One such example is Linux WINE, which is an emulator designed to make the Linux user interface look and feel like a Windows user interface.

Emulators often suffer from poor performance due to running two software applications to obtain the same results of running a single software application. As a result, emulation applications consume more system resources because they are actually running two different software applications at the same time.

A+ 1101: 4.2

Virtual Machines

The purpose of virtual machines and virtualization is to reduce the amount of overhead to which network administrators and technicians need to adhere regarding network and user data storage. Furthermore, virtual machines allow for lower hardware requirements than most personal computers that are built to join domain controllers, so this also reduces the cost to organizations that utilize virtual machines. Lastly, when a virtual machine is connected to a high-speed Internet medium, it can access its network resources from both inside and outside of their organization's network.

If a network is running a Windows-based network along with machines that are running a Windows operating system, then resource needs will be minimal.

As mentioned previously, an emulator must be used when using two different platforms such as a Linux-based network running virtual machines that are running a Windows operating system. In this arrangement, the Linux-based machines portray themselves to be of a Windows platform, which requires emulation. Thus, there will be more resources needed from the server that hosts the virtualization and the virtual client from which that the user is obtaining the software access and implementation, such as their personal computer that has been configured as a virtual client.

The security requirements for a network's virtual topology vary depending on the existing topology, such as whether the virtual machines can be used outside of the organization's network and how often the virtual network and its machines are updated. Nevertheless, it is vital that network administrators and technicians are aware that virtual machines are not protected by a virtual host's antivirus software, as most physical servers and domain controls are often isolated from the host. Therefore, it is important that network administrators and technicians understand their virtual network's user agreement carefully to understand when they should adhere to installations of protection packages and other protection software, as this concept varies among all virtualization vendors.

The network requirements for virtual networks are based on the amount of bandwidth consumed by the host. Therefore, it is important for network administrators and technicians to understand that a Virtual Machine Manager, also termed as a *virtual machine monitor* or *hypervisor*, is not capable of exceeding more bandwidth than the host is able to support. An example of exceeding this bandwidth is establishing your host for file sharing, and then multiple users downloading files from it, causing high network traffic. Once the high network traffic exceeds the bandwidth of the network, the computer or device experiences delays in their downloads or may even experience a disconnection in their virtual network session.

Client-side virtual machines provide several advantages. One is that it functions as a *sandbox*, which is a virtual machine used to run software or applications in an isolated testing environment. For example, assume you have a workstation with a virtual machine installed. If you have a file that you think might be malware, you can place the file in your virtual machine, and it can be analyzed with very little danger to your network.

Another advantage to client-side virtual machines is that they can be used for testing programs. For example, consider a programmer writing a program for Windows. They may wish to test the application to ensure it works the same on Windows 10 and Windows 11. However, the programmer may only have Windows 10 installed on their PC. By running Windows 11 in a virtual machine, they can test the program to ensure it runs in Windows 11 without having to restart their device or risk the program causing a problem to their Windows 10 installation.

Virtual machines are also commonly used for application virtualization, particularly cross-platform applications. For example, one might have a macOS computer with a Windows virtual machine to allow the execution of Windows programs. In a similar scenario, one can run legacy applications in virtual environments. For example, an employee might have a Windows 10 PC but wants to use an application from an old Windows 7 device. Since Windows 7 is no longer supported and is considered a security risk, they could run the application in a virtual Windows 7 environment without compromising their device or putting the network at risk.

22.8 Network Troubleshooting

As a technician, you may be responsible for small networks commonly found in homes and small business offices. When troubleshooting equipment that is part of a large enterprise network, you must know where your responsibility for the repair of a PC ends, and the responsibility of the network administrator begins.

When troubleshooting a network, remember the basics of networking. To create a network you need media, a properly configured adapter card, and software support for the network. Most networking problems are simple problems, such as loose connections. Always start small with your troubleshooting, meaning when there are network system problems, check the connections first.

To verify that the local network is working correctly, open the **Network** folder, which should provide a quick analysis of the local area network status. From this folder, you can see the number of network devices currently identified as part of the local area network. If the network connection or adapter had failed, no devices would appear in the **Network** folder.

The next step is to ping the adapter card to verify that it is communicating with the TCP/IP protocol. The command syntax for IPv4 is either ping 127.0.0.1 or ping ::1, and the syntax for IPv6 is ping localhost. Finally, try to connect to a known URL using the **ping** command. If the modem is not connecting to the Internet service provider, you will not get any results.

Keep in mind that adapter settings can be accidentally changed, especially while exploring the dialog boxes during network setup. If you are accessing the network via some type of modem, you will have to check the modem setup. For more information about modems, review Chapter 14.

Problems can also result from malware programs. The malware program could change the configuration of the network adapter in an effort to force the computer to an unwanted website. Keeping antimalware software up to date and scheduling regular scans can be an effective measure against this, however.

Another common problem associated with a network is difficulty logging in. Often, the user is incorrectly entering their username and password or is attempting to use an expired password. As a technician, you will have your own username and password and will be capable of easily determining if the network is accessible.

Wireless network adapters are often configured to connect automatically to the strongest wireless signal available, which can result in an unintended wireless connection and a change in assigned IP address. Check the assigned IPv4 address to see if it is in the APIPA range starting with 169.254, which would indicate a problem with the DHCP server. Most home networks are configured with a router that serves as a DHCP server and automatically issues an IPv4 address. When an APIPA address is assigned, it is best to reset the router.

Most of the problems you will be expected to resolve as a PC technician are simple in nature. More complex issues may require the assistance of the network administrator. With experience, you will soon be able to determine when you need to consult the network administrator or the Internet service provider.

A+ 1102: 4.9

Remote Troubleshooting

Many modern organizations are geographically distributed, including employees working from home. This requires an approach to network troubleshooting that allows for remote troubleshooting. The general approach called *remote monitoring and management (RMM)*, focuses on remotely monitoring workstations and network connections. It also allows the support team to remotely manage system updates and troubleshooting. Microsoft Remote Assistance (MSRA) is Microsoft's answer to remote support and can be launched by executing msra.exe from the **Run** menu. When launched, the Windows Remote Assistance screen will appear, similar to what is shown in Figure 22-36.

Remote support is sometimes coupled with remote video conferencing. There are a number of tools available for video conferencing including Zoom, Microsoft Teams, and GoToMeeting. These tools can be used to facilitate remote troubleshooting.

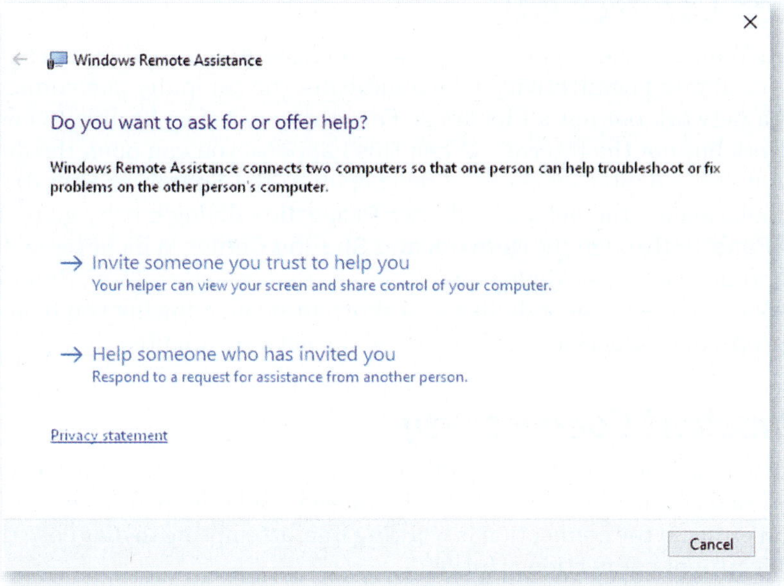

Goodheart-Willcox Publisher

Figure 22-36 Windows Remote Assistance allows Windows users to request or provide help remotely.

SSID Not Found

A *Service Set Identifier (SSID)* is the name for a wireless network. Although personal computers and mobile devices have network settings that will automatically search for an SSID, some network administrators and technicians will not allow the SSID to be broadcasted and instead require the user to manually enter the name of the SSID to join their network. However, users may claim that the SSID cannot be found. If this issue is presented to a network administrator or technician, they should verify that the name of the SSID is inserted correctly and the network controller(s) that supplies power to the SSID is powered on and connected to the network.

No Wireless via Mobile Devices

A+ 1102: 3.4

When troubleshooting a mobile device that does not have wireless connectivity or has intermittent wireless connectivity, the technician should first determine that Wi-Fi settings of the mobile device are on and in discovery mode, confirm Wi-Fi discovery is an option, and verify that the wireless access points are powered on. If all these settings are correctly configured and the wireless network is operational for another mobile device that is known to be functional, the technician should then verify whether airplane mode is enabled on the problematic mobile device and deactivate it if needed. If the mobile device still does not operate after adhering to these troubleshooting techniques, there is a possibility that there are other hardware failures beyond the 802.11 card in the device that causes it to not allow wireless network transmitting.

Mobile devices can be paired to each other via Bluetooth when each mobile device is in discovery mode, and once paired, they can communicate and transmit data. However, these devices may not be able to pair with each other or transmit data if either device does not have its Bluetooth communications enabled. Thus, technicians should be aware that the first troubleshooting step they should take is to make sure Bluetooth is enabled on both devices.

A+ 1101: 5.7

Tech Tip

The most common way to solve most network-connection problems is by either resetting the local area network router or restarting the computer.

Limited Connectivity

Microsoft Windows will sometimes present a message stating that a network connection has limited connectivity, which indicates the computer can connect to the local area network but not all its areas. For example, it may be able to connect to the network but not the Internet. When this happens, you can open the dialog box for the network adapter by entering ncpa.cpl into the **Search** or **Run** dialog box. You can also access the network adapter **Properties** dialog box by going through **Control Panel** or through the **Network and Sharing Center.** Whichever method you use will produce the same dialog box similar to that in Figure 22-37. Right-clicking a network connection icon will display a shortcut menu allowing you to access the status, properties, or perform a diagnosis of the network adapter.

A+ 1101: 5.7

Intermittent Connectivity

Intermittent connectivity can be difficult to diagnose because of its inconsistent nature. A bad connection can only be diagnosed while the poor or no connection condition exists. If the connection is working fine, attempting to diagnose the cause of an intermittent connection is futile.

Diagnosing an intermittent connection requires analysis and experience. You are making educated guesses as to the cause if the signal is working at the time of troubleshooting. It is important to ask questions such as the following:

- When does the connection seem to go out?
- How long has this condition existed?
- Is the connection slow or completely out?

Asking questions can provide enough information for a possible solution. For example, imagine a scenario in which a connection seems to go out every day at 9:00 a.m., which is the time most employees take an office break. It is possible employees are using the microwaves in the break area to heat snacks, resulting in wireless connection interference. This scenario is not to imply that all wireless interruptions are caused by microwave ovens; rather, it serves as an example to help you understand the need to consider seemingly unrelated issues. You must ask questions and gather information to come to a possible solution.

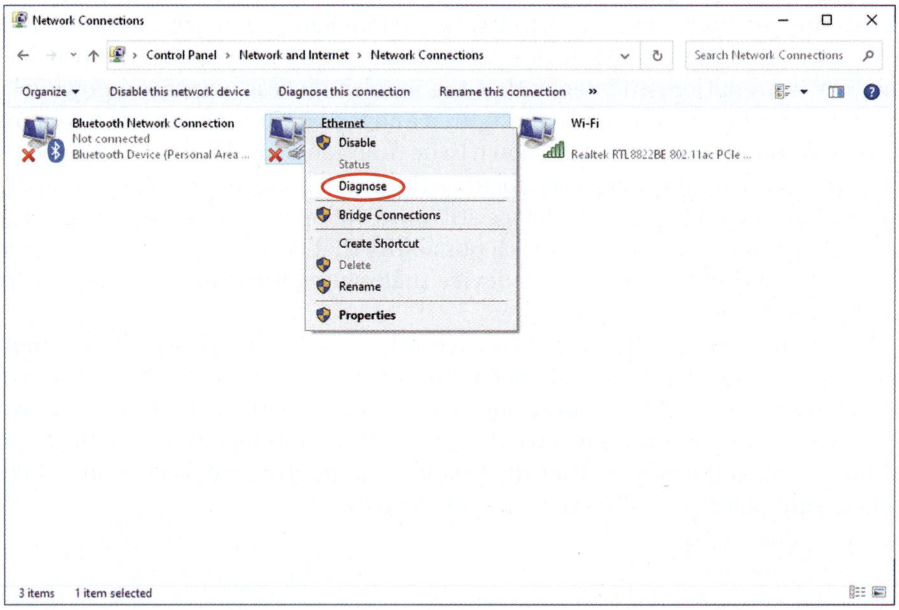

Figure 22-37 The network adapter status and properties can be used to run diagnostics when troubleshooting connectivity issues.

Goodheart-Willcox Publisher

When experiencing intermittent connectivity or no Internet connectivity at all, you should also check with the Internet service provider. The ISP may be servicing its network.

Slow Transfer Speeds

A+ 1101: 5.7

Slow transfer speeds can occur for several different reasons. First, the network could be congested because too many users are downloading or uploading content at the same time. This can be true for not only a local area network, but also Internet access. For example, when too many users using a shared Internet connection are simultaneously downloading from the Internet, the available bandwidth for each user is reduced.

Transfer speeds may seem slow for a variety of other reasons, including a program such as antimalware running in the background and consuming a significant amount of bandwidth or a computer automatically downloading updates. A commonly encountered reason for slow speeds is a computer being used for the first time following a long period of shutdown. When a computer has been shut down for a long time, it will usually connect to the Internet automatically to search for updates for all software applications and look for new drivers. All this background activity affects the overall transfer speed of the computer system because computer resources such as the Internet connection are shared.

IP Conflict

An *IP conflict* occurs when the same IP address is assigned to more than one network device. This is seldom encountered today except for network devices that are configured with a static IP address. Legacy network systems allowed for the same IP address to be statically configured for more than one device, but when the same IP address is configured twice, only one of the devices can successfully connect to the network. The second device will fail to connect to the network, and a message box will inform the user that there is a conflict with the assigned IP address. Today, a message will appear when you configure a duplicate IP address, resulting in your inability to complete the configuration. However, the message will only appear if the device that has a duplicate IP address is online. If the device with a duplicate IP address is offline, the message will not appear, but a problem will arise after that device attempts to connect. This is why DHCP servers are often used to assign addresses dynamically, resulting in a steep decline of duplicate IP addresses.

Low RF Signal

A low RF signal for a wireless device is usually caused by either distance or position. As the distance between wireless devices increases, the connection loses signal strength. To fix the problem, you must move the devices closer together or install a wireless range extender, which will increase signal strength between the devices. You may also opt to install a more powerful wireless device, such as a wireless USB adapter equipped with a longer antenna, as this will allow it to broadcast farther and receive low RF signals better.

Low RF signals can also be caused by radio interference from many different sources. Sometimes it can be remedied by simply repositioning the RF receiver a few feet or even a few inches. Many times, the antenna orientation also makes a big difference in signal strength. The wireless adapter signal strength is indicated in the wireless adapter **Properties** dialog box.

Chapter Summary

22.1 TCP/IP Addressing

- The TCP/IP protocol suite is the secret to communicating over WANs and the Internet.
- IPv4 uses four sets of decimal numbers in the range of 0 to 255.
- IPv6 uses eight sets of hexadecimal numbers in the range of 0000 to FFFF.
- The main improvements of IPv6 over IPv4 are a much larger pool of Internet and network addresses, reduced broadcast traffic, better security, and improved quality of service.
- An organizational network may be divided into several smaller networks known as ***subnets***. A subnet mask is a 32-bit number used to determine the subnet to which a particular IP address refers.
- Similar to a subnet is a Virtual Local Area Network (VLAN). ***Virtual Local Area Networks (VLANs)*** broadcast their domains in a Layer-2 technology, such as a virtual bridge via a network switch and provide smaller, more private networks.
- Information about the computer's IPv4 and IPv6 addresses, MAC address, and network adapter can be obtained by running the **ipconfig** command from the command prompt.
- Most network systems are now configured using Dynamic Host Configuration Protocol (DHCP), which automatically assigns IP addresses to hosts.
- Automatic Private IP Addressing (APIPA) is a Windows feature that allows a computer to issue an IP address to itself when a DHCP server is unavailable. The APIPA range is from 169.254.0.1 to 169.254.255.254.

22.2 Network Equipment

- A typical network must manage a tremendous amount of packet traffic. To accomplish this, special equipment must be used to route data to and from hosts.
- Navigation across networks is enabled by network devices, such as repeaters, bridges, routers, brouters, switches, gateways, proxy servers, and firewalls.

22.3 Network Diagnostic Utilities

- Common network diagnostic utilities include **ping**, **tracert**, **pathping**, **nslookup**, **netstat**, **nbtstat**, net services (such as **net view**), and **arp**.
- Windows includes built-in diagnostic utilities, such as visual cues in the Network and Sharing Center, and the Windows Troubleshooter.

22.4 Internet Navigation

- The Internet is a collection of networks that are all interconnected by fiber-optic and copper-core cables, wireless devices, infrared devices, satellites, and millions of miles of old telephone lines.
- Uniform Resource Locators (URLs) are the global addresses for websites all over the Internet.
- The Domain Name System (DNS) is a system used to identify domain names of sites on the Internet and resolve them to their IP addresses. When you enter a URL in your web browser, a query is sent to a local resolver, a database of domain names and matching IP addresses. The query requests a matching IP address for the domain name that you entered.

- A subdomain is a division of a group of networks. Subdomains create a third level to a website and function similarly to folders in a file system by offering another way to organize a website.

22.5 E-Mail Communication

- Three common e-mail protocols are POP3, SMTP, and IMAP.
- Webmail is an e-mail service based on using a web browser to access e-mail and is often free.
- When a nontext file is attached to an e-mail message, it must be converted to a form that can be understood by text-oriented e-mail protocols.
- MIME is used for graphics, audio, and video; S/MIME is a secure version of MIME.

22.6 Internet Protocols

- The Ethernet protocol is designed to encapsulate other protocols and carry them to and from devices located on an Ethernet network based on the MAC addresses of the source and destination devices.
- The Internet Protocol (IP) communicates across the Internet and contains the destination and source IP addresses. It also routes packets containing other protocols across the Internet through a series of routers.
- Transmission Control Protocol (TCP) and User Datagram Protocol (UDP) are two of the main protocols associated with the TCP/IP protocol suite.
- Hypertext Transfer Protocol (HTTP) is a standard protocol used to transport web page content across the Internet. HTTPS is a combination of HTTP and Secure Sockets Layer (SSL) protocols.
- Secure Shell (SSH), also known as *Secure Socket Shell*, is a protocol that provides secure access to a remote computer.
- File Transfer Protocol (FTP) is a protocol used for transmitting files across the Internet.
- Telnet is a protocol that allows a user to log on to a remote computer and download or upload files.
- Simple Network Management Protocol (SNMP) is a protocol that configures and collects information about network devices, such as servers, printers, switches, and routers.
- Common Internet File System (CIFS) is a network file-sharing protocol developed for early Microsoft operating systems.
- Server Message Block (SMB) is a network file-sharing protocol that supports file sharing for client/server applications.

22.7 Cloud Services

- The five characteristics of cloud service that have been identified by the National Institute of Standards and Technology (NIST) are on-demand self-service, broad network access, resource pooling, rapid elasticity, and measured service.
- Cloud infrastructure can be deployed as a private, community, public, or hybrid cloud.
- Four classifications of cloud service to consumers are Software as a Service (SaaS), Platform as a Service (PaaS), Infrastructure as a Service (IaaS), and Anything as a Service (XaaS).
- Microsoft offers several versions of cloud services, such as Microsoft 365 and Microsoft Azure.

22.8 Network Troubleshooting

- Remember the basics of networks when troubleshooting network problems.
- To quickly verify that the local network is working correctly, open the **Network** folder. The **Network** folder in Windows Explorer provides a quick analysis of the local area network status.
- The next step is to ping the adapter card to verify that it is communicating with the TCP/IP protocol.

Review Questions

1. Summarize characteristics of TCP/IP addressing.
2. What is the difference between an IPv4 and IPv6 address?
3. List advantages of IPv6 compared to IPv4.
4. What is a *subnet mask*?
5. What does the **ipconfig** command reveal about a PC connected to a network?
6. List and describe networking equipment.
7. Differentiate among common diagnostic utilities associated with networks.
8. What command is used as the loopback check for IPv6?
9. List and describe five net services commands.
10. Explain Internet navigation.
11. What is the difference between a domain name and a URL?
12. Differentiate among e-mail protocols.
13. What three components are required to digitally sign and encode an e-mail message?
14. List common Internet protocols and their characteristics.
15. Differentiate between TCP and UDP.
16. What is the difference between HTML and HTTP?
17. What are the five characteristics of cloud service that have been identified by NIST?
18. List and describe four cloud infrastructure models.
19. What are the four classifications of cloud service to consumers?
20. List three factors that could affect network transfer speeds.

Sample A+ Exam Questions

1. Which is an example of a typical IP address?
   A. 168.23.145.25
   B. 10 2D C4 56 DE FF
   C. JohnH@netcom.org
   D. 255.255.255.000
2. What command issued at the command prompt allows you to inspect the IP address on a Windows system?
   A. **winipconfig**
   B. **winipcfg**
   C. **ipconfig**
   D. **configip**

3. Which of the following services automatically issues an IP address to a PC when it boots?
   A. WINS
   B. DHCP
   C. IPSETUP
   D. DNS
4. Which of the following services is responsible for resolving domain names to IP addresses?
   A. WINS
   B. DHCP
   C. IPSETUP
   D. DNS
5. Which of the following equipment is used primarily to extend the length of a network cable run?
   A. Repeater
   B. Hub
   C. Gateway
   D. Router
6. What command can be used as a quick test to see if a network card is functioning properly with IPv4?
   A. **ping 127.0.0.1**
   B. **tracert 128.10.10.285**
   C. **cardTest**
   D. **NICset**
7. Which of the following is an example of a URL?
   A. JoeB@AcmeNet.Gov
   B. www.g-w.com
   C. 127.34.002.145
   D. BlakeManufacturing@setpoint.com
8. Which command would you use to check cable connectivity between a workstation named Station12 and a file server named Ntserver? (Note that the command is being issued from Station12.)
   A. **ping station12 via ntserver**
   B. **ping ntserver**
   C. **ping ntserver/station12**
   D. **ping station12/ntserver**
9. Which of the following best reflects a characteristic of an IPv4 address?
   A. Four octets
   B. A set of 24 binary numbers separated by three colons
   C. A group of 24 hexadecimal numbers
   D. Four three-digit decimal numbers ranging from 000 to 999
10. Which is an example of a Class C subnet mask?
   A. 255.255.000.255
   B. 255.255.000.000
   C. 000.255.255.255
   D. 255.255.255.000

Chapter 23

Small-Office/Home-Office (SOHO) Networking

Learning Outcomes

23.1 List factors that should be considered when designing a SOHO network.
23.2 Explain the process of establishing a SOHO network connection in Windows.
23.3 Identify and troubleshoot common problems that can occur in a new SOHO network installation.
23.4 Summarize the process of connecting to a remote computer via Remote Desktop.

A+ Certification Exam Objectives

The following A+ Certification Exam Objectives are covered in this chapter.

Exam 220-1101

1.0 Mobile Devices

- 1.4 Given a scenario, configure basic mobile device network connectivity and application support.

2.0 Networking

- 2.2 Compare and contrast common networking hardware.
- 2.5 Given a scenario, install and configure a basic wired/wireless SOHO network.
- 2.6 Compare and contrast common network configuration concepts.

3.0 Hardware

- 3.6 Given a scenario, deploy and configure multifunction devices/printers and settings.

4.0 Virtualization and Cloud Computing

- 4.1 Summarize cloud computing concepts.

5.0 Hardware and Network Troubleshooting

- 5.7 Given a scenario, troubleshoot problems with wired and wireless network.

Exam 220-1102

1.0 Operating Systems

- 1.4 Given a scenario, use the appropriate Microsoft Windows 10 Control Panel utility.
- 1.6 Given a scenario, configure Microsoft Windows networking features on a client/desktop.

2.0 Security

- 2.2 Compare and contrast wireless security protocols and authentication methods.
- 2.4 Explain common social-engineering attacks, threats, and vulnerabilities.
- 2.5 Given a scenario, manage and configure basic security settings in the Microsoft Windows OS.
- 2.6 Given a scenario, configure a workstation to meet best practices for security.

- 2.7 Explain common methods for securing mobile and embedded devices.
- 2.9 Given a scenario, configure appropriate security measures on small office/home office (SOHO) wireless and wired networks.

3.0 Software Troubleshooting

- 3.2 Given a scenario, troubleshoot common personal computer (PC) security issues.

4.0 Operational Procedures

- 4.9 Given a scenario, use remote access technologies.

Key Terms

demilitarized zone (DMZ)
fully qualified domain name (FQDN)
Home Phoneline Networking Alliance (HomePNA) technology
HomePNA adapter
network-attached storage (NAS)
packet sniffer
port forwarding
port triggering
powerline communications (PLC)
single port forwarding
small-office/home-office (SOHO) network
virtual private network (VPN)
Zero Configuration Networking

Overview

Installing a network in a home or small office is one of the most common tasks for a computer technician. This chapter helps prepare you for the installation, configuration, and support of a small-office/home-office (SOHO) network by applying many of the concepts presented earlier in the textbook. You will learn how to use common Windows network wizards to configure a SOHO network and how to troubleshoot common problems that can occur. You will also learn about the many factors that determine SOHO network design and look at many of the features available on a typical network router, such as DHCP, port forwarding, port triggering, and MAC filtering.

Most of the technologies presented in this chapter have already been covered in detail in earlier chapters. This chapter works to bring together the information already learned and apply it to creating a small-business or home network.

A+ Note

CompTIA has increased the percentage of questions pertaining to networking on the A+ Certification Exams, largely due to the growing number of small-office/home-office (SOHO) networks. You need to be familiar with all aspects of SOHO networking, and it is vital that you possess some hands-on experience setting up a small network system with shared Internet access using a variety of media and equipment. You should also be familiar with setting up routers and some form of virtualization. Be prepared to answer several questions directly related to SOHO router configuration, such as MAC filtering and port forwarding.

23.1 Designing the SOHO Network

A **small-office/home-office (SOHO) network** is a simple peer-to-peer LAN used to share resources and data in a home- or small-office environment. Although any computer hardware connected to the SOHO network can be shared, printers and Internet-access devices are shared more often than other devices.

As a computer technician, you may be called on to design and configure a SOHO network. There are several factors to consider in its design. These factors include the

- type of media that will be used to connect the PCs together;
- methods of hosting file sharing services for the SOHO network;
- way the networked PCs will access the Internet;
- level of administration that will be used to secure resources and data; and
- methods of security that will be used to protect the network from intruders and secure individual workstations.

The following sections examine each of these factors as they introduce the configurations and technologies commonly used in a SOHO network.

SOHO Media

The four common choices of networking media for SOHO networks are copper cable (Cat 5e and Cat 6), wireless, existing home telephone lines, and existing power lines. The choice is based on cost, building construction, and user or installer preference. For example, copper cable is inexpensive, but the building structure may prove difficult for installing the cables, especially in buildings with open spaces, high ceilings, and concrete floors. Wireless technology is easy to install, but it has some security issues. Existing telephone lines are economical and convenient but may not be suitable for an office environment. Using existing power lines is inexpensive but undesirable to many people who do not like the idea of connecting the network to 120 volts of AC power.

There are many variables to consider when determining the type of network media to use. The following sections explore each of these variables and introduce the implementation of a mixed network environment and using a prewired home system.

A+ 1101: 3.6

Copper Cable

Copper cable has been the primary choice of network technicians for many years. However, the main objection to using copper cable is that it is often difficult to run through walls. To overcome this difficulty, copper cable can be used in one room and another form of network media can be used in a different room. This type of network configuration is known as a hybrid, or mixed, network environment and is discussed later in this chapter.

A+ 1102: 2.9

Wireless

Wireless is a popular choice of SOHO media because it is quickly installed, and the location of the networked PCs can be changed easily. It is the ideal solution for a building in which it is difficult to run cable. However, be aware that when using a wireless NIC to access the network, the default settings allow the network to be compromised by an intruder. The default setup configuration uses a default SSID and no data encryption. However, it is easy to change the SSID and configure all packets to be encrypted, and doing so increases network security, as demonstrated in Figure 23-1.

When you use wireless media for a SOHO network, you should configure and encrypt the wireless network so only designated persons can access the network through a wireless access point. There are two common encryption types associated with wireless network adapters: Advanced Encryption Standard (AES) and Temporal Key Integrity Protocol (TKIP). The encryption types also have several security types used to secure data, such as WPA-Personal, WPA2-Personal, WPA3-Personal,

Figure 23-1 The **Wireless Network Properties** dialog box provides options for configuring the wireless security type and encryption type.

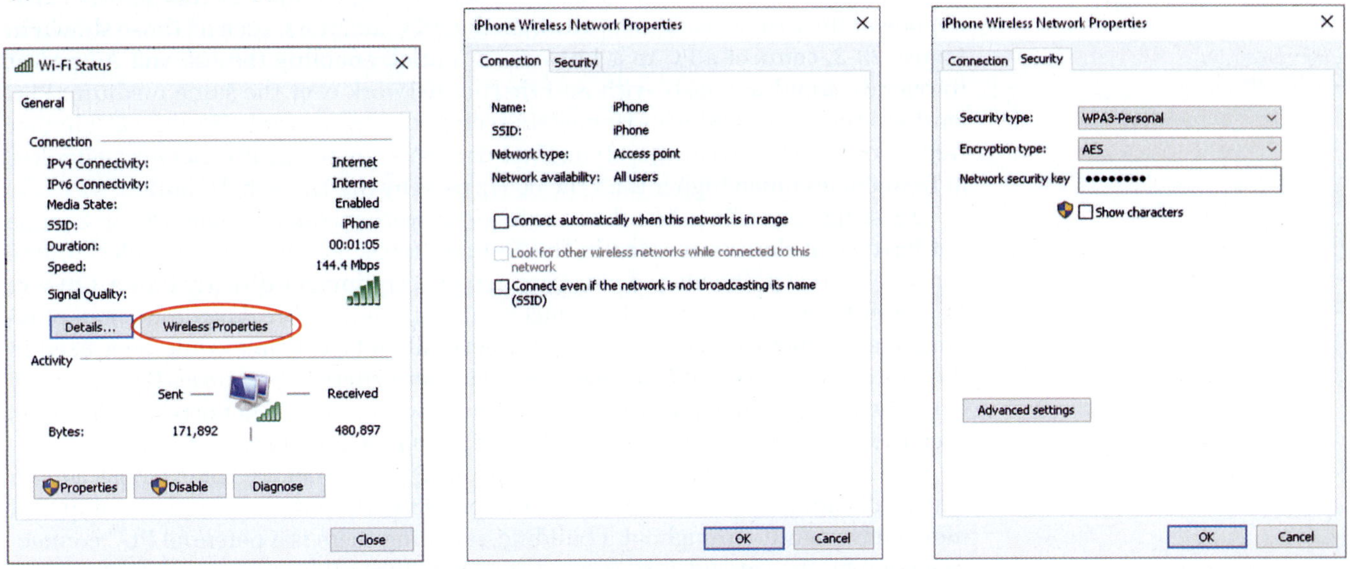

Goodheart-Willcox Publisher

WPA-Enterprise, and 802.1x. There will be more about wireless security in a later section. For additional information about these encryption and security types, review Chapter 13, which covers basic wireless security features for mobile devices.

Another task to consider when configuring a wireless network is selecting the channels for your WLAN. A *channel* is a specific frequency within the frequency band, and in North America, the 2.4-GHz frequency Wi-Fi uses channels 1 through 11. Channels can be manually configured to avoid interference, but most networks are configured to permit the device to scan for the channel that has the fewest devices on it. Ensuring that channels on which your wireless access points are operating do not overlap can prevent congestion of wireless traffic.

1102: 2.9 A+

Existing Phone Lines

Home Phoneline Networking Alliance (HomePNA) technology allows existing home telephone lines to be used as network media. Any telephone jack can be used as a connection point for the network system, meaning network cables and a hub are not required for making the connections. All that is needed is a **HomePNA adapter**, which is a networking device that allows every telephone jack in a building to be part of the network. Some HomePNA adapters include two RJ-11 ports, with one used to connect to the telephone jack and the other used to connect to a telephone or cascade to another HomePNA device, as illustrated in Figure 23-2. Cascading HomePNA adapters is useful when there is an inadequate number of telephone jacks for each PC.

Using existing telephone lines as network media does not interfere with telephone calls. Typical voice and sound data transmitted on a residential telephone system are of relatively low frequencies, usually between 0 Hz and 4 kHz. The HomePNA adapter uses a frequency higher than 4 kHz to transmit data across the existing telephone line, so the two frequencies do not interfere with each other.

While HomePNA technology is a practical solution for homes and for some businesses, it is not recommended for commercial buildings. Most corporate offices use a private branch exchange (PBX) as the centralized point of the telephone system, and since the telephone lines for a typical PBX system run directly from each telephone jack to the PBX, a complete network circuit cannot be established. The telephone lines in a home, however, typically run in a daisy-chain fashion from one telephone jack to the next, making a complete loop throughout the house.

Existing Power Lines

Powerline communications (PLC) is a networking technology that allows existing power lines to be used as network media. PLC adapters, such as those shown in Figure 23-3, connect a PC to a 120-volt AC outlet, enabling the 120-volt AC power to operate simultaneously with an Ethernet network over the same medium. PLC works in the same fashion as HomePNA technology by transmitting data at a higher frequency than the existing system. Data transmission on the PLC network operates at frequencies much higher than the 60 Hz used by the 120-volt AC outlet.

Existing power lines have been used as network media for some time in Europe but have been slowly accepted in the United States, largely due to peoples' innate fear of electricity. The idea of plugging network equipment directly into a 120-volt AC outlet leaves users somewhat concerned, but it is no more dangerous than plugging in any other electrical device. All electrical and electronic equipment used in the United States is tested for safety by the Underwriters Laboratories (UL), and any equipment designed to plug directly into the power outlet of a home is safe. After all, even the PC plugs directly into the 120-volt AC outlet, and it is safe to use.

PLC has a number of advantages over HomePNA technology. For example, a room is typically limited to one telephone jack or possibly two, but power outlets are spaced more conveniently throughout a building, meaning there is a potential PLC connection point for the network just about anywhere in the building. It is important to note, however, that for PLC technology to function to the best of its ability, the devices being connected through the power lines should be on the same circuit.

Mixed Network Environment

It is increasingly common to have a mixed network environment, such as a home- or small-office network with copper-core cable in one room and wireless technology in

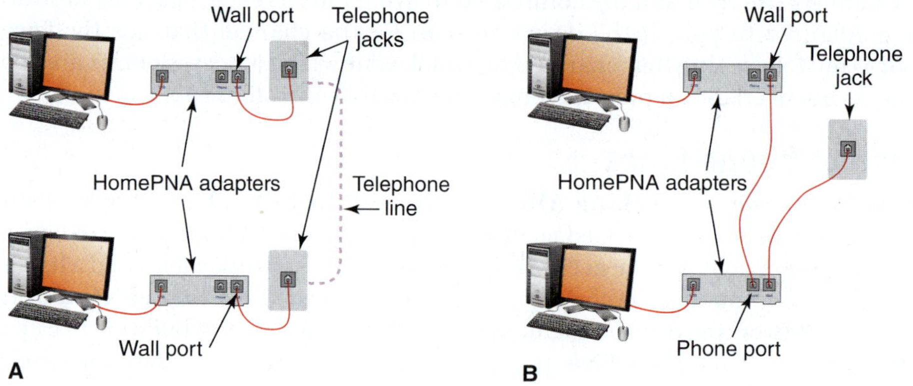

Goodheart-Willcox Publisher; (workstation icons) romvo/Shutterstock.com

Figure 23-2 PCs connect directly to separate telephone jacks through HomePNA adapters (A). In this arrangement, telephone jacks must share the same telephone line. PCs can also connect to the same telephone jack through cascading HomePNA adapters (B).

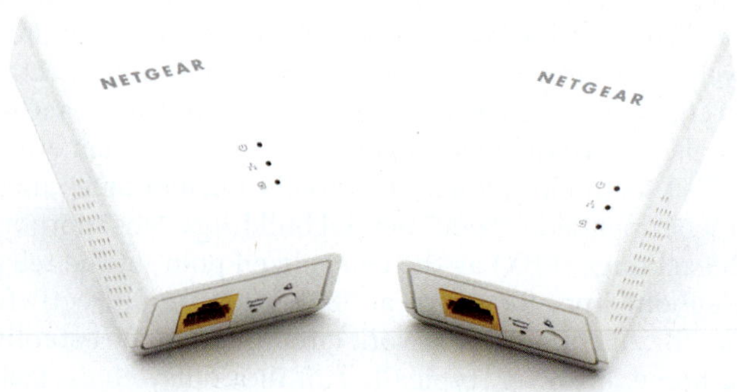

Ackab Photography/Shutterstock.com

Figure 23-3 These PLC adapters plug directly into AC outlets. Some PLC adapters have separate power cables.

others. When converting from one network medium to another, a network bridge is required. Recall from Chapter 22 that a *bridge* connects dissimilar network media while making no decisions about packet contents, destination, or filtering. Bridges use MAC addresses to communicate, which allows all packets to pass through, no matter which protocol is used.

Connecting a wireless network to another type of network always requires a wireless bridge referred to as a *wireless access point*, which is shown in Figure 23-4. When a router is used to combine different media and provide an Internet connection, it is sometimes referred to as a *gateway router* or *gateway*. The exact terminology used can vary between vendors.

Home Prewired Systems

New homes are often prewired for all types of low-voltage communication systems, such as telephone, audio, television, and computer network systems. Communication equipment suppliers manufacture cabinets to make telephone, television, sound, and computer network system installation simple and convenient. These cabinets often provide a common connection point for each home communication system and are designed to configure network cables together quickly.

Data Transfer Rates

1102: 2.9 A+

A comparison of data transfer rates is helpful for selecting the best media for the network. The table in Figure 23-5 compares commonly used media in a SOHO network. As indicated in the table, copper cable has the only predictable data rate,

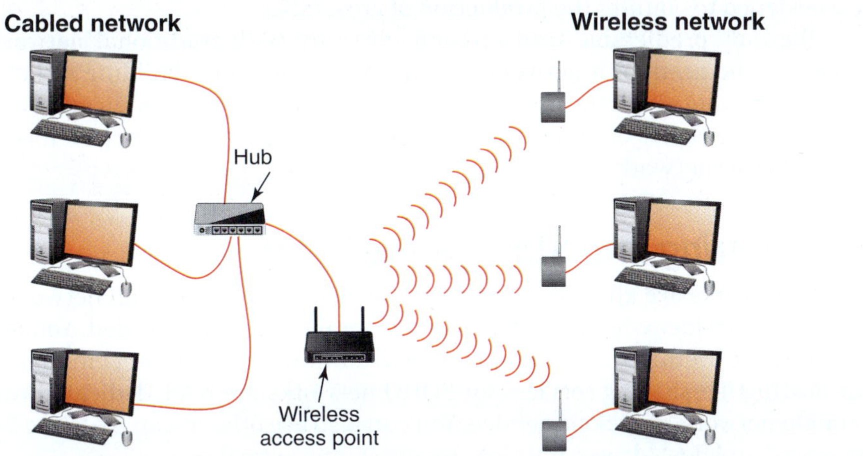

Goodheart-Willcox Publisher; (workstation icons) romvo/Shutterstock.com; (hub and WAP icons) Vadim Ermak/Shutterstock.com

Figure 23-4 Wireless access point functions as a bridge connecting a cabled network to a wireless network.

Data Rates of Common SOHO Media

Media	Maximum Data Rate	Remarks
Copper cable	10 Mbps or 100 Mbps	Predictable data rates
Wireless (802.11a, b, g, n, and ac)	100 Mbps or higher	Data rate is drastically affected by distance, building materials, and interference; rates below 10 Mbps are not uncommon
Existing power lines (PLC)	No standard	Advertised as 75 Mbps, but in reality is 4 Mbps–10 Mbps
Existing phone lines (HomePNA)	No standard	Advertised as high as 32 Mbps, but in reality is 4 Mbps–10 Mbps

Goodheart-Willcox Publisher

Figure 23-5 Data rates vary among common SOHO network media.

Tech Tip

In terms of data rates, Cat 6 Ethernet cable and wireless are the two best choices for performance, but cable is more secure than wireless.

as data throughputs vary greatly for wireless, existing power lines, and existing telephone lines. Often, vendors emphasize the maximum achievable throughput for these media, but this is not the normal throughput. Actual throughput varies because of environmental conditions. For example, a wireless network may advertise a throughput of at least 100 Mbps but can only achieve it if the wireless network devices are close in proximity, free from radio interference, and have no barriers or partitions between them. The farther apart the transmitter and receiver, the lower the throughput rate drops. The transmission rate also drops if wireless devices must transmit through walls, especially if the walls are constructed of a dense material such as concrete.

PLC technology has a limited throughput because power line conductors are not designed for data transmission. Also, power line conductors may be connected to sources of interference such as electric motors. Since interference on the power line corrupts packets, the packets must be retransmitted, thus reducing the actual system throughput.

Using existing telephone lines is unpredictable because older-generation lines were not designed to carry high frequencies. The length of the telephone cable also reduces throughput. Cable signal losses known as *attenuation* increase directly with cable length. As cable length increases, the digital signal strength deteriorates, which results in corrupt data packets that must be retransmitted. The loss of data packets and the need to retransmit each lost packet causes the loss of effective bandwidth. At some point, the cable will reach a length where all data packets are corrupt.

Another factor to consider when determining cable length is crosstalk. Older-style telephone cable was not designed with twisted pairs and is much more likely to produce crosstalk, even on a very short length of cable. The twists in the cable pairs are designed to counter the production of crosstalk.

The only predictable transmission rates are with traditional network cable. However, the need for a network medium that overcomes building structure limitations may outweigh the disadvantages of the lower and unpredictable rates. It is, therefore, the choice of the network user or installer regarding the best media to use for the SOHO network.

File Sharing and Storage Methods

Small networks are all about sharing, and when planning a small network system, you must consider which file sharing and storage method is needed. You must also consider the overall cost for equipment and administration. Four common methods for hosting file-sharing services for SOHO networks are NAS, dedicated computer, domain network, and cloud service. You can also use other means to share files such as e-mail and flash drives, but they are often impractical.

Network-Attached Storage

Ideal for a small-office or home-office network, **network-attached storage (NAS)** is a form of data storage that provides a means of centralized file sharing with little administrative overhead. The NAS can be configured to provide a backup service for all local network PCs, and some NAS manufacturers also provide cloud backup services. A common implementation of NAS is to arrange it as a RAID configuration to provide data protection.

The equipment cost of NAS can be somewhat expensive compared to using a spare computer as a shared access storage unit but less expensive than server-based sharing. In addition, the actual cost of the NAS unit is increased by the number of hard disk drives required for storage or RAID configuration. NAS units typically support a limited number of users, approximately 25 simultaneous connections, which is likely much less than the total number of connections supported by a server but more than adequate for a small business office or home use.

Dedicated Computer

You can create a dedicated file-storage and file-sharing device from a surplus computer workstation. This can be a cost-effective option, especially if using a workstation that has been replaced by a newer model. You can add additional hard disk drives to increase the amount of storage space and even configure the hard disk drives into a RAID. However, configuring a centralized dedicated computer requires specialized skills, such as those learned in this course.

While a single computer is less expensive than using a server or NAS, it can only support a limited number of simultaneous client connections. For example, both Windows 10 and Windows 11 support up to 20 connections, and while this number may seem limited in terms of an enterprise network, it should be more than adequate for a home or small business.

Domain Network

Creating a domain network using a server provides the best way to meet the needs of the client in a network environment. You can create a network with an unlimited number of clients and have complete detailed control of all users. The big disadvantage of a domain network is that it requires specialized skills to administer, and these skills can require two or more years of schooling and experience. Also, if the network is to be available 24/7, you need a staff of at least four technicians with administrator-level skills to oversee the domain network. The cost of employees to maintain a network with 24/7 availability as well as the cost of special equipment and software to create a domain network can be very expensive.

Cloud Services

The cloud is quickly becoming the main choice for file sharing, file backup, and remote access. Many cloud services are provided for free and are easily configured, but the service is only free for a limited storage size and the number of clients accessing it. Once either limit is exceeded, you must pay for the cloud service. While the cost may increase for the cloud service, it will not be nearly as expensive as a domain network system. The cloud service does not require specialized training to configure compared to a domain network; nor does it require many support technicians because support personnel and special equipment are provided by the cloud service. The cost of the technical support personnel and special equipment is shared by all cloud service customers, thus reducing the cost of creating and maintaining a single SOHO network. This reduced cost and lack of need for multiple technicians comprise the two main advantages of cloud services over a domain network. Cloud services also enable users to access shared both internal and external resources.

The disadvantage to cloud services is that you do not have complete anonymity. Someone else always has physical access to your storage and some control over your network system. The one exception is if you create your own cloud service using your own domain network. Review Figure 23-6 for a quick comparison of NAS, cloud, domain, and dedicated computer.

Cloud services are particularly important to SOHO networks because they can significantly expand the services supported by the network. Typically, a SOHO network will not have dedicated IT staff, but cloud services allow the SOHO to support all the same services as a major corporate network. One can use *Software as a Service (SaaS)* to utilize software hosted in a cloud, which allows you to quickly deploy software and not be burdened with maintaining it. *Platform as a Service (PaaS)* allows you to perform a similar function as SaaS, only with entire operating systems. For example, if you have a Windows-based SOHO but have a specific need to provide Linux, PaaS can provide that to you via a cloud. One can even go as far as to use *Infrastructure as a Service (IaaS)*, in which a substantial part of the network infrastructure is provided via the cloud.

Figure 23-6 Each networking storage method has unique advantages and disadvantages.

Advantages and Disadvantages of File Storage and Sharing Methods		
Method	**Advantages**	**Disadvantages**
NAS	Easy to administer Centralized storage Remote access	Equipment cost Limited number of clients
Dedicated computer	Similar to a domain network Less expensive than a domain network	Requires regular administration Requires specialized skills Limited number of clients
Cloud	Easy to administer Cost-effective Unlimited number of clients Remote access	Does not have complete anonymity
Domain	Maximum control and security Maximum customization Centralized administration Unlimited number of clients Remote access	Can be expensive Requires specialized skill set

Goodheart-Willcox Publisher

A+ 1101: 4.1

Virtual Desktop Infrastructure (VDI) is another popular cloud offering in which a user's entire desktop, including the operating system, applications, files, etc., is hosted in a cloud. The user simply logs in to the cloud service from any computer and has instant access to their entire desktop. VDI is often supported in enterprise networks with on-premises servers, but a cloud solution is more practical for SOHO networks, as the cloud provider will manage most of—if not all—the support.

Related to cloud services is software-defined networking (SDN), which uses software and application programming interfaces to control the underlying network hardware and makes network management much simpler. Simplified network management is often critical for a SOHO network.

Regular Backups

Closely related to file sharing and storage is the concept of regularly backing up data. Backups are the best method of preventing the loss of shared data. Antimalware may not prevent data loss, and equipment failures happen—often unexpectedly. Additionally, damage to stored data can result from disasters, such as a fire, flood, or even a disgruntled employee. The very best protection from natural disasters is a backup location far away from the network site. Often, cloud services perform automatic backups, which is one of the primary advantages of utilizing the cloud to share and store data.

A+ 1102: 2.9

Internet Access

Several typical Internet-access configurations can be used in SOHO networks. The exact configuration depends on the building's environment and the type of Internet-access device selected, but the most common choices of Internet-access devices in a SOHO network are the DSL modem, cable modem, and wireless hotspots. This section covers various network configurations that use a DSL or cable modem to access the Internet.

Internet Shared Access

When using a modem as the primary Internet-access device, the configuration varies depending on the number of PCs that are networked. A two-PC network may be connected directly from PC to PC without the use of a hub. Figure 23-7 shows a two-PC network that uses a modem to connect to the Internet. In this configuration, the two PCs are connected directly from one NIC to another with a crossover cable, which is the simplest way of connecting PCs together in a SOHO network. When the computers are configured with network cards that utilize the Auto-MDIX feature, no crossover cable is required, as all modern Ethernet network cables are Auto-MDIX compliant.

Notice in Figure 23-7 that the PC with two network adapters is designated as the *host* because it provides the Internet connection for both PCs. A PC that accesses the Internet through the host is called a *client*.

For the host to provide Internet access, Internet Connection Sharing (ICS) must be established. ICS is Microsoft's simple application of the network address translation (NAT) standard, which was developed by the Internet Engineering Task Force (IETF) and is described in detail in RFC 1631. NAT was specifically designed as a standard for sharing a single Internet connection and providing a type of firewall protection. NAT can support more clients than ICS and is more versatile than ICS. Additionally, it was designed for IPv4 and is not required for IPv6. The host in a typical ICS configuration may be assigned the IP address 192.168.000.001, and the clients may be assigned IP addresses in sequence starting at 192.168.000.002. In general, the term *host* describes any computer that provides a service, and the term *client* describes a computer that uses a service provided by the host. In the example of an ICS system, the host provides Internet access to the client computers.

Tech Tip

Different router manufacturers may use a wide variety of default IP address assignments for the router such as 192.168.0.1, 192.168.100.1, and 192.168.1.1. However, they all start with the first two octets of 192.168.

Another SOHO Internet access arrangement is that in Figure 23-8. Notice that the three PCs are connected using a switch or hub, which is a typical Ethernet cable arrangement. Again, note that the PC connected to the Internet is the host, while the other two are considered clients. When a client sends a request to access the Internet, the host automatically connects to the Internet service provider (ISP); however, the host must be turned on for the clients to access the Internet.

Figure 23-9 shows a typical SOHO Internet access arrangement when a router with wireless access capabilities is used. The router acts as both a wireless access point and the main connection point for the Ethernet network cables. In this arrangement, the router is the host, providing Internet access to all the devices in

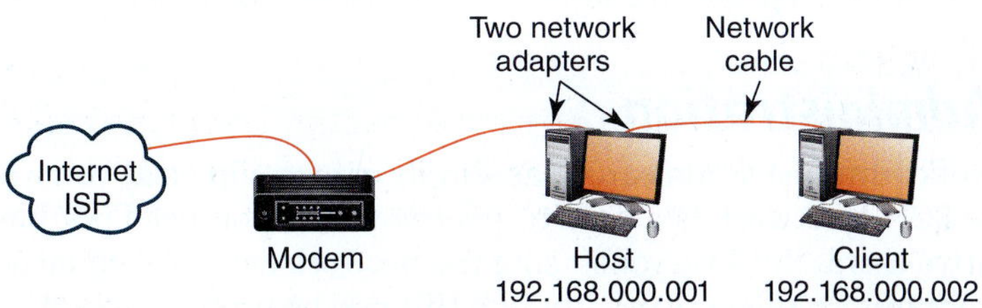

Goodheart-Willcox Publisher; (workstation icons) romvo/Shutterstock.com; (modem icon) Vadim Ermak/Shutterstock.com

Figure 23-7 A two-PC network may be connected directly from PC to PC without the use of a hub.

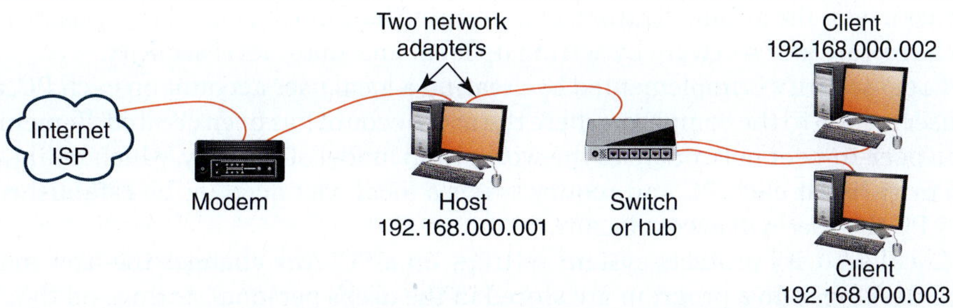

Goodheart-Willcox Publisher; (workstation icons) romvo/Shutterstock.com; (modem and hub icons) Vadim Ermak/Shutterstock.com

Figure 23-8 In a typical Ethernet cable arrangement, multiple PCs are connected using a switch or hub.

Figure 23-9 Routers can provide a common connection point for Ethernet network cables and serve as a wireless access point.

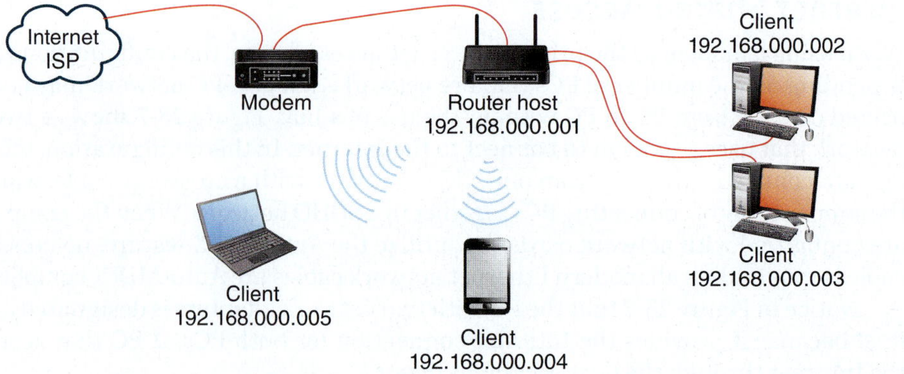

Goodheart-Willcox Publisher; (workstation and laptop icons) romvo/Shutterstock.com; (modem and router icons) Vadim Ermak/Shutterstock.com; (smartphone icon) Tetiana Yurchenko/Shutterstock.com

Tech Tip

A router is a complete small computer system. It contains a CPU, memory, and software.

the local area network. Some network devices provide the combined function of a DSL modem and router, as well as both Ethernet network ports and wireless access, thus eliminating the need for multiple devices.

A+ 1101: 1.4

Mobile Hotspot and Tethering

A mobile hotspot provides a direct connection to an ISP through mobile broadband service. The hotspot can provide wireless Internet connections, provided it has cellular service. For a SOHO network or business applications that must have 24/7 Internet access, a mobile hotspot can be installed as a backup option for Internet access. For example, when using a cable modem for Internet access, you could use a mobile hotspot as a backup system; that way, if the cable modem goes down, you can switch to a mobile hotspot to maintain the Internet access until the modem is back online.

Similar to a mobile hotspot is the concept of device tethering. Recall from Chapter 14 that *tethering* is the sharing of a device's Internet connection with other connected devices that do not have an Internet connection. It is also referred to as *phone-as-modem (PAM)*. Tethering and hotspots offer very similar convenience, but they function differently. Telecommunication providers often supply hotspots to allow users to connect as an alternative to logging into a LAN. Conversely, tethering involves connecting one device with the capability of Wi-Fi Internet to another device that is unable to connect wirelessly. Devices can be connected through a wireless LAN (Wi-Fi), a physical connection, or through Bluetooth.

SOHO Administration

SOHO network administration can be as simple or as complex as you wish to make it. Since the SOHO network is a peer-to-peer network, you need not have any real administrative hierarchy. Everyone using the network can have equal access to all files and programs on the network, though this can be problematic. With everyone having equal access, anyone can change the properties of any PC in the network. A better scenario is to have a single administrator with limited authority delegated to other users. The administrator can determine how much control other users have over hardware and software by setting up local and share-level security.

Local security is implemented by creating a local user account on each PC, and the user logs on to the computer where the user account has been created. Remember that a peer-to-peer network uses the workgroup model of security, which maintains a security list at each PC and requires that a local user account be established at every PC the user will access locally.

Local security protects system settings on a PC. Any changes the user makes to the desktop or to a program are stored in the user's personal settings on that PC. These changes do not affect other local users.

Share-level security protects resources accessed from across the network by either requiring a password to access the share or limiting its access. For example, network users may only have read access to files on another PC, or they may not be able to access the files at all unless they know the password.

Even in a home network, local and share-level security should be implemented to avoid disastrous situations. To reinforce how important security is, consider a typical home network in which no security has been implemented as an example.

Consider the following scenario, in a home network consisting of two PCs, two parents use one of the PCs and two children use the other. Each PC has been set up with a single user account, and a color printer is attached to the parents' PC but shared to allow the children to print to it from their computer. Drive C: on the parents' computer is also shared and allows full access to all files. Both parents use their PC for work-related activities as well as personal finances. The children use their PC for school assignments and use the color printer to print their school assignments and graphics they find on the Internet. They also use their PC for computer games. The children are constantly downloading sample gaming software and exchanging software games with their friends. The children often need to use the PC at the same time, and when this happens, one of them uses the parents' PC.

As you are probably sensing, this casual setup can cause severe problems. With everyone using the same local user account, anyone can change it. For instance, the children could delete important files on their parents' PC. They could even delete important files from across the network if share-level security has not been configured on the parents' local hard drive. Also, one of the children can download a game on their parents' PC and then change the PC's default settings to optimize the game. Alternatively, by simply installing the computer game, a DLL file or some other file can possibly be overwritten, which can lock up, or crash, the PC.

SOHO Security

PCs in a SOHO network are vulnerable to attacks from outside the LAN if the LAN is connected to the Internet. The Internet is public media, and users from anywhere in the world can access a networked PC through the Internet connection or intercept a PC's message content. There are several ways to establish security to protect the SOHO network from intruders and protect data as it travels across the Internet. Two common security implementations that should be configured for the SOHO network are a firewall and a virtual private network (VPN).

Firewall

1101: 2.2 A+
1102: 1.6, 2.5

In Chapter 22, you learned that a firewall protects a LAN by blocking access to specific ports or by filtering packets by IP addresses, contents, services, and protocols. For example, a firewall can filter out echo requests, which stops a site that is being probed with the **ping** command from displaying its IP address via echo.

A firewall can be configured to block all nonessential ports and modified to allow needed ports. For example, a person may desire to participate in an online game that requires the use of TCP ports 2,346, 2,347, and 2,348. These ports can be opened by entering these numbers in the firewall service properties dialog box, which will allow data to pass through the firewall so two computers can communicate freely during a gaming session.

Tech Tip

As with other equipment, services, and protocols in the computing industry, the terminology surrounding allow lists and deny lists is changing. Historically, these were referred to as *whitelists* and *blacklists*, respectively.

Firewalls can be configured with an allow list or a deny list. An *allow list* is a policy in which Internet connections from all websites included on the list are accepted. If a website is not on the allow list, it is not permitted access. A *deny list* is a policy in which Internet connections from all websites included on the list are not accepted, and any website not on the deny list is permitted access.

The firewall must be configured to allow file and printer sharing. Windows automatically configures the correct port numbers in the firewall when you first establish a file or printer share. However, if you are not using a Windows-based firewall, you could encounter problems related to blocked ports.

Windows Firewall, the standard firewall that comes with Windows operating systems is actually an *Internet Connection Firewall (ICF)*, which is software that can be configured to keep unauthorized users from accessing the network. Windows Firewall automatically controls the opening of ports to support Microsoft software applications and does not adversely affect the network. Each computer should have the Windows Firewall enabled. Many third-party utilities can also be used to increase SOHO security. Using the Network Setup Wizard to install an ICF is covered later in this chapter.

A+ 1102: 2.5

Another type of firewall is a *web application firewall (WAF)*, which is primarily used to protect and security web applications. WAFs function through filtering and monitoring HTTP traffic between the Internet and web applications. These types of firewalls are particularly useful for preventing cross-site scripting and other injection-based attacks.

A firewall is automatically configured according to the type of network location you select when establishing the network. The firewall settings, or *profiles*, are automatically configured for different network locations such as Domain, Private, and Public during the network configuration. For example, when configuring a new network connection, you are prompted for the type of location you are configuring. When you select the new network location, such as Home, Work, or Public, the firewall configuration is automatically configured to match.

A+ 1101: 2.6
1102: 4.9

Virtual Private Network (VPN)

A **virtual private network (VPN)** is a security configuration that creates a private tunnel between the source and destination PCs and encrypts packet contents within that tunnel to ensure data sent across the Internet is not intercepted, read, or modified. As the term *tunnel* implies, all messages are exchanged privately as though their travel across the public space of the Internet were encapsulated in a secure tunnel that no one else can see into or access, as illustrated in Figure 23-10. A VPN should be created to ensure security when communicating across the Internet through an ISP, but a VPN can also be created if you are permanently connected to the Internet via a cable or DSL modem.

Since data is normally encoded in plain ASCII text, the content of a typical packet is completely viewable through a **packet sniffer**, which is a utility that captures packets on a network and displays their contents. When a VPN connection

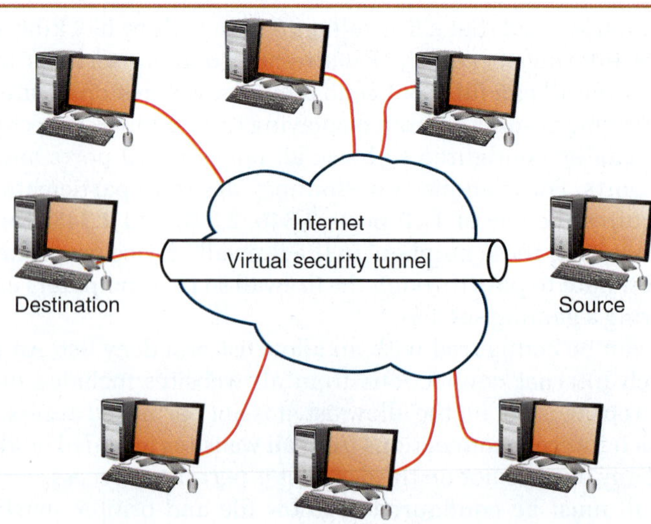

Figure 23-10 A virtual private network (VPN) creates a private tunnel between the destination and source PCs. The data flowing between the PCs cannot be interpreted by other computers on the Internet.

Goodheart-Willcox Publisher; (workstation icons) romvo/Shutterstock.com is made, all the contents of the packet are encrypted except for the destination address, which remains readable so it can travel across a series of Internet routers to reach its destination. The VPN is transparent to users at the destination and the source.

The two main security connection protocols associated with a VPN connection are Point-to-Point Tunneling Protocol (PPTP) and Layer 2 Tunneling Protocol (L2TP). These protocols also incorporate other protocols, such as IPSec, IKE, and CHAP, to enhance their security features further.

Be aware that some ISPs do not allow VPN connections through their systems and will filter out protocols associated with VPNs. Check with your ISP to determine if you can use a VPN.

Modern operating systems and sophisticated firewalls have eliminated most configuration problems, so firewalls are automatically configured to permit VPN connections, at least for the most part. Figure 23-11 shows the VPN wizard in Windows 10, which allows you to configure a VPN connection between two computers. The VPN wizard is accessible by navigating to **Start>Settings>Network & Internet>VPN>Add a VPN connection**. In many cases, the most likely problem associated with a VPN is an incorrect destination address, which must be either a fully qualified domain name (FQDN) or an IP address.

Wireless Router Security

Wireless networks are much more of a security risk than a wired network because access to wired networks is not readily available due to the nature of the network medium. Cables are typically inside the building structure, which means an unauthorized person would need to be inside the building to gain access. However, a wireless network can be accessed from outside the building. Apartment buildings, hotels, and some commercial buildings may have a variety of separate areas, such as individual units, special rooms, and private office areas, which results in easy access to one or more wireless network systems. However, some common security best practices can help secure the wireless network system, such as encrypting data, changing default names, enabling MAC filtering, and disabling the SSID broadcast.

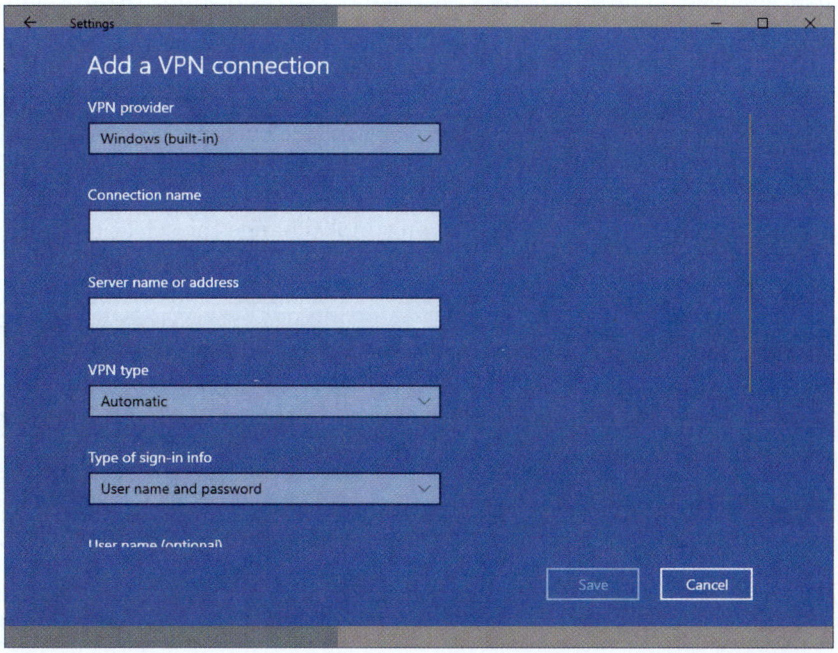

Goodheart-Willcox Publisher

Figure 23-11 Windows provides a simple VPN wizard that automatically configures a VPN connection between two computers.

A+ 1102: 2.2

Encryption Types

The methods for securing Wi-Fi have evolved over the years. Initially, there was Wired Equivalent Privacy (WEP), but WEP has since been supplanted by Wi-Fi Protected Access (WPA), WPA2, and, most recently, WPA3. WEP uses the stream cipher RC4 to secure the data and a CRC-32 checksum for error checking. Standard WEP (known as WEP-40) uses a 40-bit key with a 24-bit initialization vector (IV) to effectively form 64-bit encryption, and 128-bit WEP uses a 104-bit key with a 24-bit IV.

Because RC4 is a stream cipher, the same traffic key must never be used twice. The purpose of an initialization vector, which is transmitted as plain text, is to prevent any repetition, but a 24-bit IV is not long enough to ensure this on a busy network. The way its IV is used also opens WEP to a related key attack. For a 24-bit IV, there is a 50 percent chance the same IV will repeat after 5,000 packets.

WPA uses Temporal Key Integrity Protocol (TKIP), which is a 128-bit per-packet key, meaning that it dynamically generates a new key for each packet. WPA2 is based on the IEEE 802.11i standard and provides the Advanced Encryption Standard (AES) using the Counter Mode-Cipher Block Chaining (CBC)-Message Authentication Code (MAC) Protocol (CCMP). This provides data confidentiality, data origin authentication, and data integrity for wireless frames.

WPA3 requires attackers to interact with your Wi-Fi for every password guess they make, making it much harder and time-consuming to crack. With WPA3's "Wi-Fi Easy Connect," however, you can connect a device by merely scanning a QR code on your phone. One of the important new security features is that with WPA3, even open networks will encrypt your individual traffic. As such, WPA3 should be employed as your default encryption type whenever possible. If it is not available, use WPA2.

A+ 1102: 2.6, 2.9

Change Default Names

Wireless access points and routers are configured with default device names, as well as default administrator names and passwords. As a result, an unauthorized person could simply view available networks with a wireless device and identify wireless routers using a default assigned name. After identifying the default router name, they can conduct an online search to find the default administrator name and password to gain control of the wireless router. To prevent unauthorized access to the router, the default name of the router, administrator name, and password should be changed. Figure 23-12 lists the default SSID and administrator name and password for some major brands of routers.

Enable MAC Filtering

One of the best ways to secure a wireless network is by applying MAC filtering to the wireless network router. MAC filtering is a router configuration that accepts or rejects connections based on device MAC addresses. To enable MAC filtering in the gateway device shown in Figure 23-13, you simply change the selection in the MAC

Figure 23-12 Default names, passwords, and IP addresses vary from one router brand to another.

Default Credentials by Router Brand

Router Brand	SSID	Administrator Name	Administrator Password	IP address
Linksys	linksys	admin	admin	192.168.1.1
D-Link	dlink	admin	admin	192.168.1.1
Netgear	NETGEAR	admin	password 1234	192.168.0.1
Cisco	Cisco	Cisco	Cisco	192.168.0.1

Goodheart-Willcox Publisher

Filtering Mode drop-down menu to **Allow** and manually input the MAC addresses you want to allow or use the list of Auto-Learned Wi-Fi Devices. Conversely, you could also set the MAC Filtering Mode to **Deny** and create a deny list. To reveal a computer's MAC address, simply run the **ipconfig /all** command at the command prompt and look for the physical address entry.

Disable SSID Broadcast

1102: 2.9 A+

Basic wireless security measures call for disabling the wireless router SSID broadcast, as shown in Figure 23-14. When disabled, the wireless router will not appear to

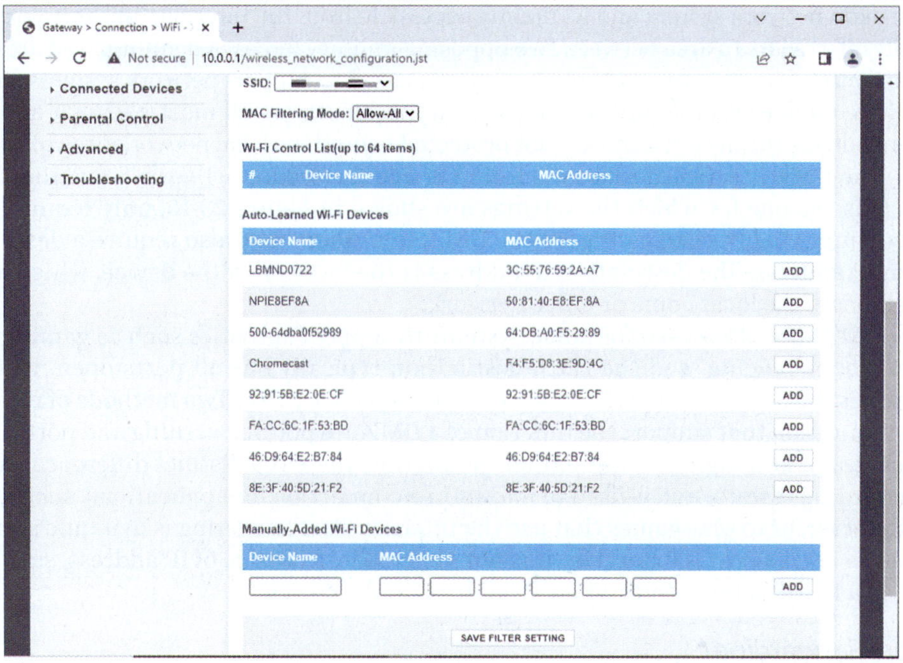

Goodheart-Willcox Publisher

Figure 23-13 A router can be configured to accept or reject device connections based on device MAC addresses.

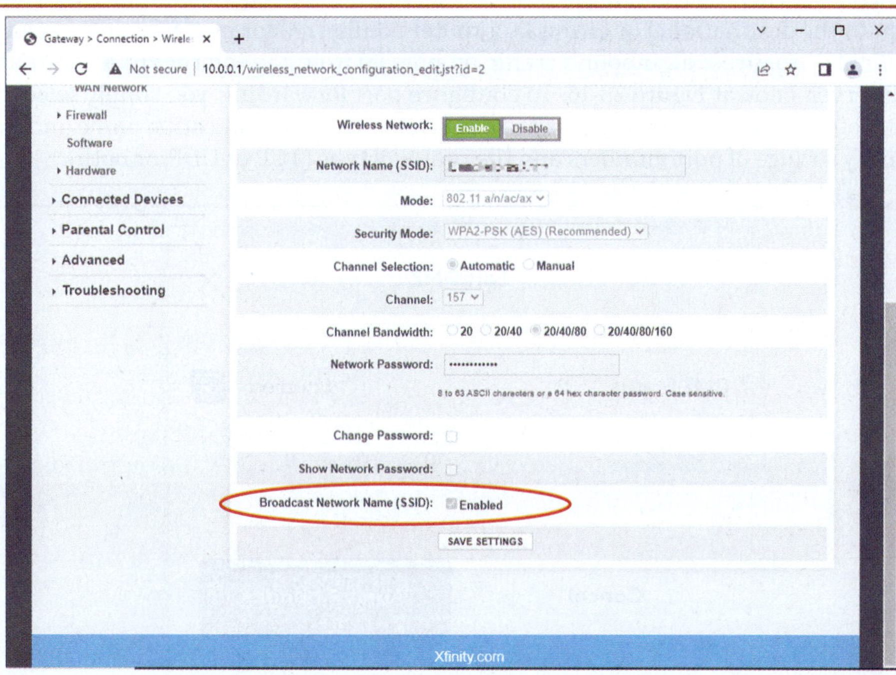

Goodheart-Willcox Publisher

Figure 23-14 Most wireless routers have an option to disable the SSID broadcast.

users looking for a wireless connection. Stopping the broadcast will not completely secure the router, but it will prevent most unauthorized persons from discovering its presence. While this security measure is effective for preventing an average user from discovering the existence of a wireless router, it will not prevent the discovery of the wireless router from a trained technician using a protocol analyzer or some other sophisticated software application.

Demilitarized Zone (DMZ)

Network security often involves configuring a **demilitarized zone (DMZ)**, which refers to an area of a network system that is intentionally created to be less secure than the main network system and is directly accessible from the Internet. This term originally referred to an area between two opposing military forces. A demilitarized area is less secure than a secure, occupied area and is used to support network systems such as web, mail, FTP, and VoIP servers. These types of servers all must allow for access from outside the network and are not protected behind the local network firewall.

The DMZ is exposed to access from outside the secure network. Some routers, such as the one for which the settings are shown in Figure 23-15, only require an incoming IP address to configure the DMZ, but others may also require a destination IP address. The destination IP address is the location of the device, which is a member of the local home or office network.

DMZs are often used for home systems to support activities such as gaming or video conferencing, and the DMZ destination typically has all ports open, which exposes the destination to the Internet and is a security risk. Two methods of router configuration that support the function of a DMZ are port forwarding and port triggering, and although they are similar in function, there is a distinct difference. Port forwarding is static and is used to maintain a connection for applications, such as a web server, or to play games that use the Internet. Port triggering is dynamic and is used to open a port temporarily. It is not affected by a change of IP address, such as when a DHCP server issues a new IP address to the device.

A+ 1102: 2.9

Port Forwarding

Port forwarding, also referred to as *port mapping*, is a router configuration set to forward packets to a destination computer or server by allowing specific ports to remain open to the destination. For example, a router configured for port forwarding can be configured to direct all inbound traffic on port 80 from the Internet to a designated web server. Look at Figure 23-16. To configure port forwarding, you simply select the connected device for which to forward a port as well as the application name and then identify a range of port numbers and the protocol type (TCP or UDP, or both).

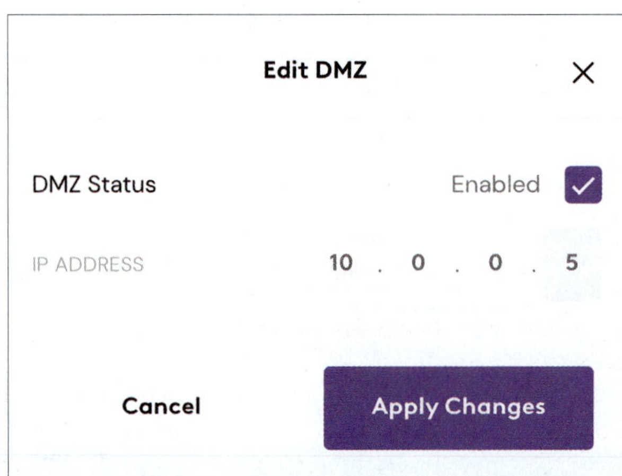

Figure 23-15 Most routers provide a configuration option for creating a home-network DMZ.

Goodheart-Willcox Publisher

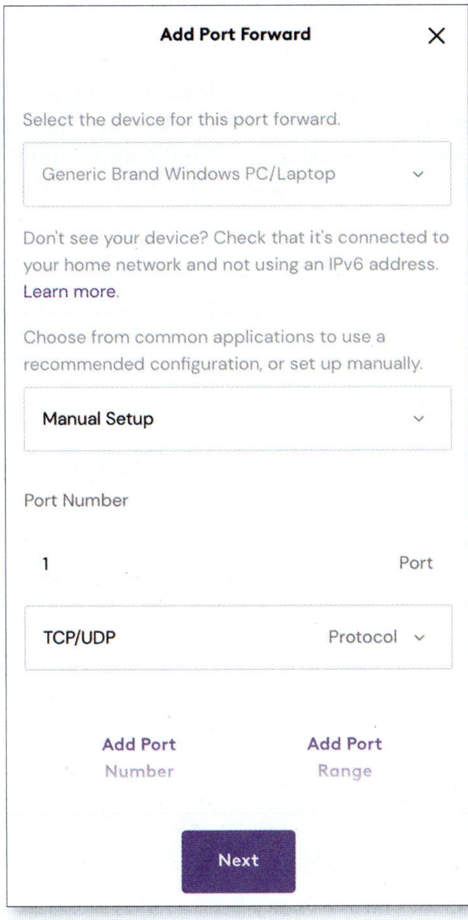

Goodheart-Willcox Publisher

Figure 23-16 Port forwarding allows a range of port numbers to be opened in the firewall for a particular computer or network device.

Port Triggering

Port triggering is a router configuration that monitors outbound traffic by port number. When data passes from the outgoing port, the designated inbound port automatically opens. For example, a router can be configured to detect outbound traffic on port 3300 and then automatically open port 3100 on a designated IP address for inbound traffic in response. After the connection is terminated, the port is closed. The router remembers the IP address of the computer that sent the outgoing data on a particular port. The outgoing data triggers the opening of an inbound port. The incoming data is then sent to the computer identified by the outgoing IP address.

Port triggering is dynamic and does not require a static IP address, as shown in Figure 23-17. Only the software application and the ports need to be identified. You can also specify a range of ports that can trigger the opening of the matching forwarded port.

Single Port Forwarding

1102: 2.9 A+

Single port forwarding is a router configuration that works in similar fashion as port forwarding but only a single designated IP address is identified instead of all IP addresses in the local area network. When single port forwarding is configured, one particular computer or server is designated by IP address.

Routers can control the opening and closing of specified ports and direct the inbound and outbound traffic to and from a single IP address or range of IP addresses. Port forwarding and port triggering provide much more security than the creation of a DMZ, which opens all ports to the Internet.

A+ 1101: 2.5, 2.6
1102: 2.9

DHCP Configuration

SOHO routers provide an option for DHCP services, which means the router will automatically issue IP addresses to the network devices. In Figure 23-18, the router setup software has an option for enabling the DHCP service. The default settings for this particular router are assigned IP address 10.0.0.1 and subnet mask 255.255.255.0. The router can issue 252 IP addresses in a range from 10.0.0.2 to 10.0.0.253.

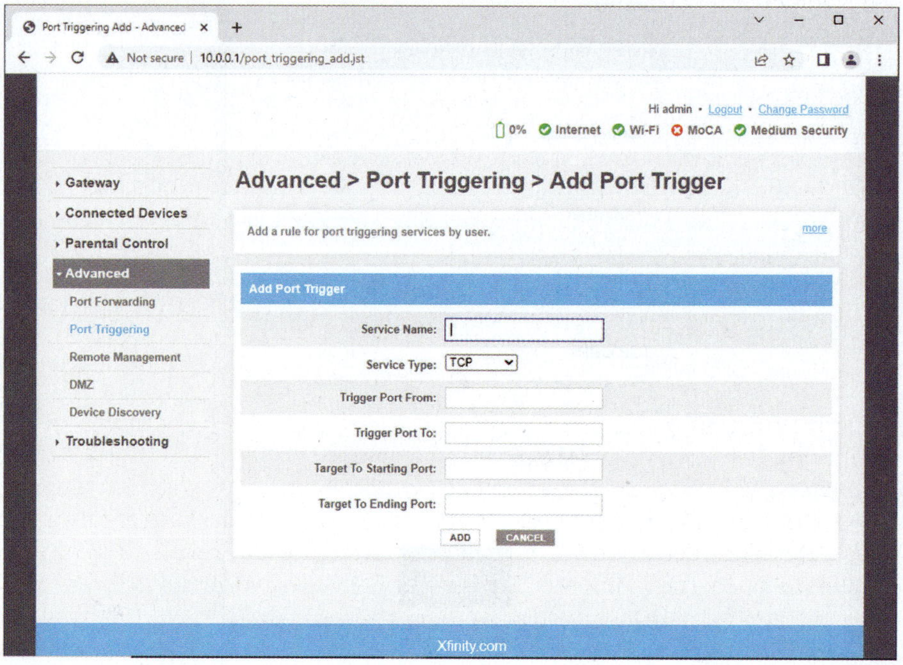

Figure 23-17 Port triggering is the temporary port opening of an inbound port, which occurs only after data is sent through a particular outbound port.

Goodheart-Willcox Publisher

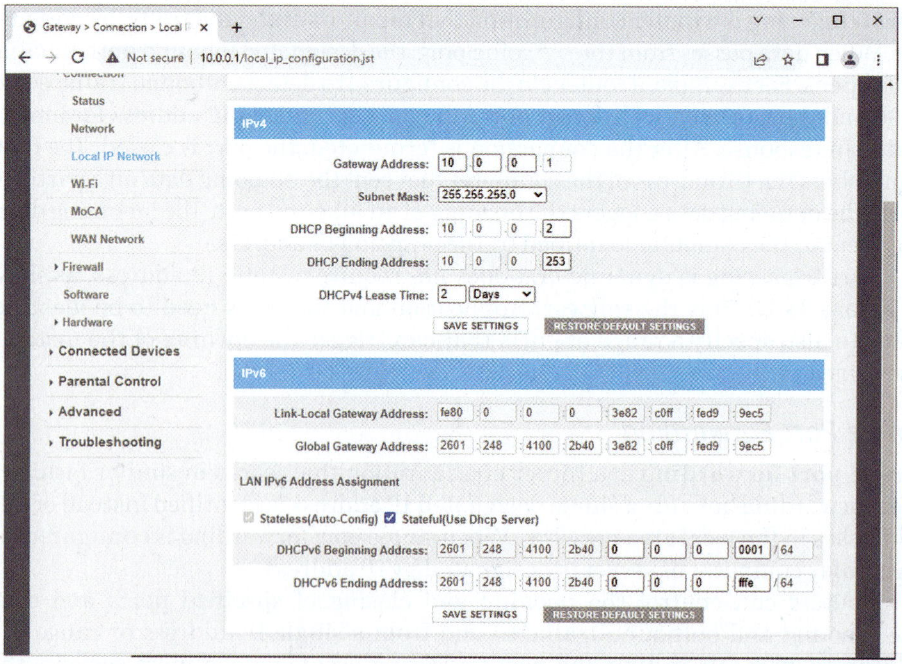

Figure 23-18 Routers have the capability to issue IP addresses to local network devices automatically.

Goodheart-Willcox Publisher

Most routers can also issue reserved or static IP addresses to specific network devices. For example, some devices, such as printers and network storage, may require static IP addresses, and the router can reserve an IP address for each of these devices. Figure 23-19 shows the option to use a reserved DHCP assignment. The router identifies all existing network devices and their IP and MAC addresses. All you do is select the device and enter the desired IP address.

Proxy Server

Recall from previous chapters that a ***proxy server*** is a computer server that hides all the PCs in a LAN from direct connection with PCs outside of the LAN and serves as an intermediary between the Internet and a network of client computers. The most common proxy server is a web server proxy, which stores web-page content frequently accessed by network users. For example, if a company has employees who must access company content at a remote site, the proxy server can store content that is frequently accessed by the users, which is the same principle as a web-page cache. This way, the content can be accessed much faster from the proxy server, and there is no need to access the remote site. The web page appears to be accessed faster than when actually downloading the remote location content. A proxy server can also improve security by applying a filter that prevents specific ports from being used.

Using Policies to Harden Security

1102: 2.4, 2.7 A+

Considering the rise in mobile technology and telecommuting becoming the norm for corporate networks, companies must be prepared to develop procedures and revise policies to incorporate these devices appropriately and safely. For employees who work out of offices, they likely conduct business on a smartphone, laptop, or tablet. Therefore, decisions must be made whether these devices will be owned by the company or by the employee. A policy in which employee-owned devices are used to conduct business is called ***bring your own device (BYOD)***, and companies must ensure these devices are managed in accordance with company policies and procedures. Regardless of whether the device is company-owned or BYOD, there are

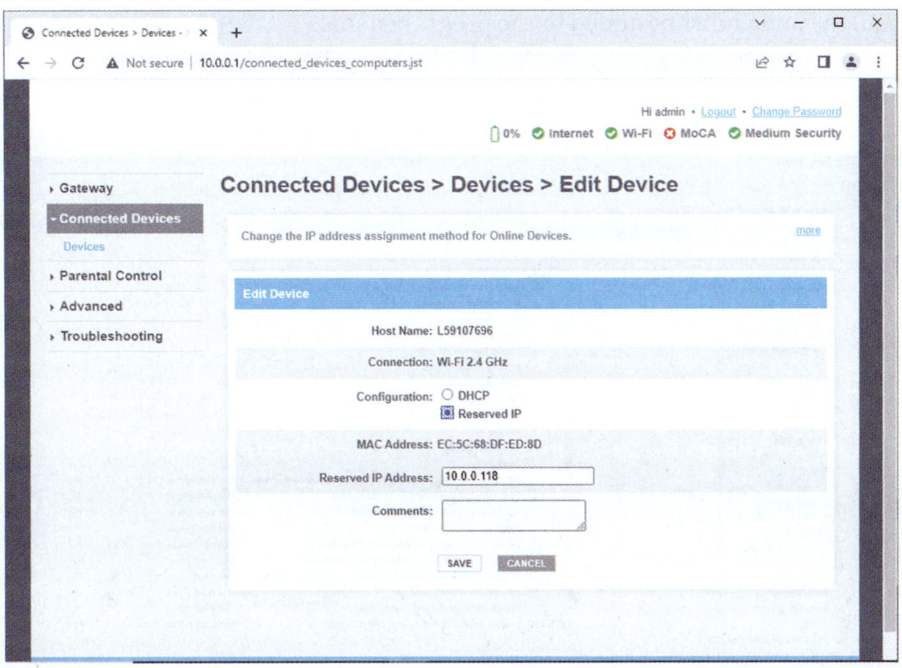

Goodheart-Willcox Publisher

Figure 23-19 Specific IP addresses can be reserved, which means a device such as a printer or a web camera is given a static IP address assignment.

> **Tech Tip**
>
> The Local Security Policy Editor is a subset of the Local Group Policy Editor and is not available in Windows Home editions.

certain security requirements that must be completed before the device can access a network, including encryption, firewall, antimalware, and VPN configurations, as well as profile security requirements that detail how devices are to be used. This ensures all devices meet baseline requirements. The Local Security Policy Editor (**secpol.msc**) and Local Group Policy Editor (**gpedit.msc**) can be used to increase the security of computers in the SOHO network.

The Local Security Policy Editor is run on each computer within a workgroup. When computers are part of a workgroup, each computer has its own local group policy, but when a computer is a member of a domain controlled by a server, the Local Group Policy Editor is run and configured at the server. The policy is applied from the server to all computer users typically by group membership.

In Figure 23-20, you can see the wide array of security policies available for configuration. Under **Windows Components**, there is a long list of Windows features that can be restricted through policies.

Online browsing and navigation always has the potential to cause serious security problems for a network, but the network administrator can set policies to restrict the downloading of files that contain ActiveX controls, prevent bypassing smart screen filter warnings, control the Internet Settings configuration, and more. A system administrator should add restrictions to the computer system but not to the extent of hampering the user's ability to complete assigned tasks. When a particular problem arises, such as visits to unsafe websites, the administrator can configure a policy to raise the minimum level of the Internet Settings configuration of the default browser, thus eliminating the problem.

In a domain network, policies are controlled through the domain server, so it is not necessary to configure each workstation individually. When network domain users complain that a Windows feature is missing from their workstation, it is usually the result of a group policy configuration restricting the use of some feature. Windows components such as Instant Messaging, Game Explorer, Remote Desktop Services, and Microsoft Edge configuration options are commonly disabled through the Local Group Policy Editor.

To open the Local Group Policy Editor, enter gpedit.msc in the **Search** or **Run** dialog box. The **.msc** extension must be added to the program name. To open the Local Security Policy Editor, enter secpol.msc in the **Search** or **Run** dialog box. Again, the **.msc** must be added to the program name.

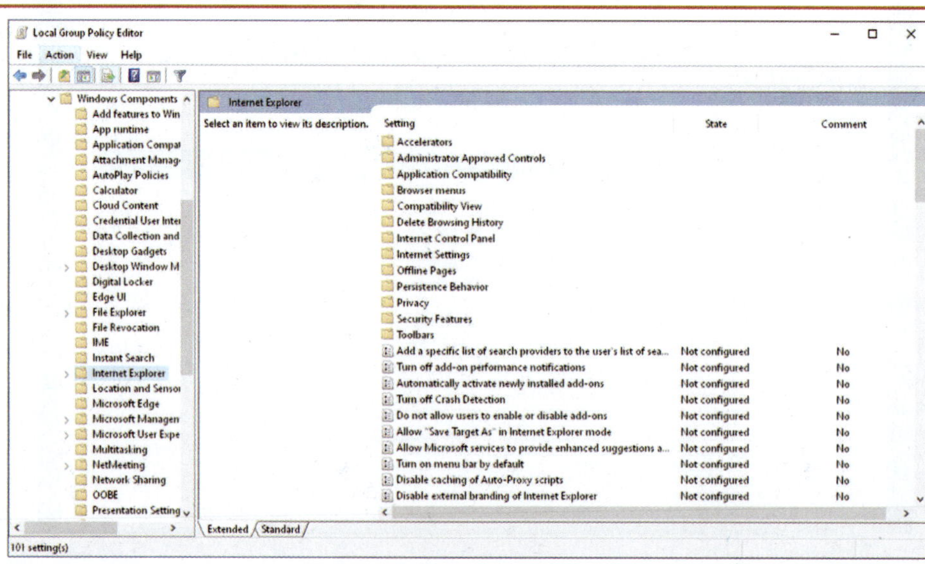

Figure 23-20 The Local Group Policy Editor can harden the security of workstations on the network.

Goodheart-Willcox Publisher

23.2 Configuring the SOHO Network with Windows

In an ideal scenario, all PCs in a SOHO network would use the latest operating system, as this provides for the easiest installation. Unfortunately, this is not always the case, and many SOHO networks are constructed with various operating systems and equipment. Incorporating legacy computer systems with modern ones can be challenging, but it can be accomplished if carefully thought out.

When setting up a SOHO network in a mixed operating system environment, use the PC with the latest or most up-to-date operating system as the host or the computer that will share other resources, such as a printer. Typically, the latest operating system will have the technology available to support older operating systems. It will also have a wizard that assists in configuring the network.

Network and Sharing Center

A+ **1102: 1.4**

The Network and Sharing Center displays all aspects concerning the local area network in one centralized location. This feature allows you to view the local area network, configure sharing options, and control the Network Discovery feature. The Network and Sharing Center is accessed through **Control Panel>Network and Internet>Network and Sharing Center**.

View the Network Adapter Card Status

To view the status of a network connection in Windows, select the **Change adapter settings** link and double-click the connection you wish to view. Review Figure 23-21 to see the Windows 10 **Ethernet Status** dialog box. Selecting the **Details** button in the **Ethernet Status** dialog box reveals additional details about the connection, including the IPv4 address, IPv6 address, physical or MAC address, and DNS suffix. You should already be familiar with these details from the previous chapter.

By right-clicking on a connection and selecting **Properties** from the shortcut menu, you can view the **Ethernet Properties** dialog box, shown in Figure 23-22. Notice the Link-Layer Topology Discovery Mapper I/O Driver and Link-Layer Topology Discovery Responder listed under the This connection uses the following items section.

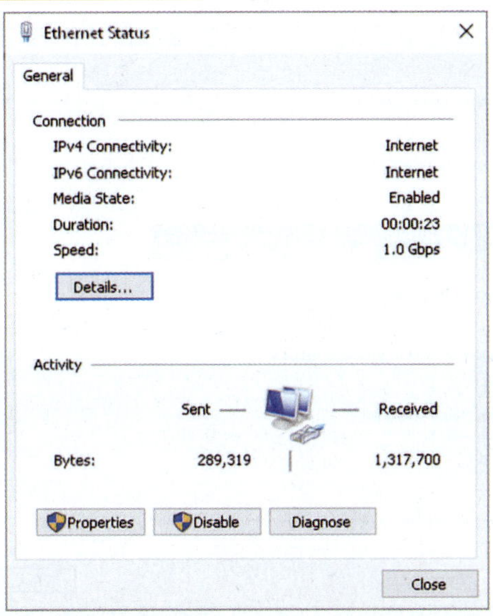

Goodheart-Willcox Publisher

Figure 23-21 The Windows **Ethernet Status** dialog box reveals information about the computer's local area connection.

A+ 1102: 1.6

Tech Tip

Generally, you cannot join a domain in *any* Windows Home edition.

Configure a New Network Connection

All versions of the Network and Sharing Center have an option for configuring a new network connection. To access this option, select **Control Panel>Network and Internet>Network and Sharing Center>Set up a new connection or network**, which launches a dialog box that prompts you to select a particular type of network configuration choice. You can connect to the Internet, set up a new network, manually connect to a wireless network, or connect to a workplace via dial-up or VPN connection, as shown in Figure 23-23.

After selecting the desired network configuration type, a series of dialog boxes will appear, prompting you to make configuration choices. After the first network configuration is complete, it becomes even easier to add additional computers to the local area network. The Windows discovery protocols work with UPnP to automatically detect network devices, such as routers, and configure the connection. Joining a network domain that is controlled by a server is more complicated and requires a user account to be created for the domain network, as discussed in Chapter 21.

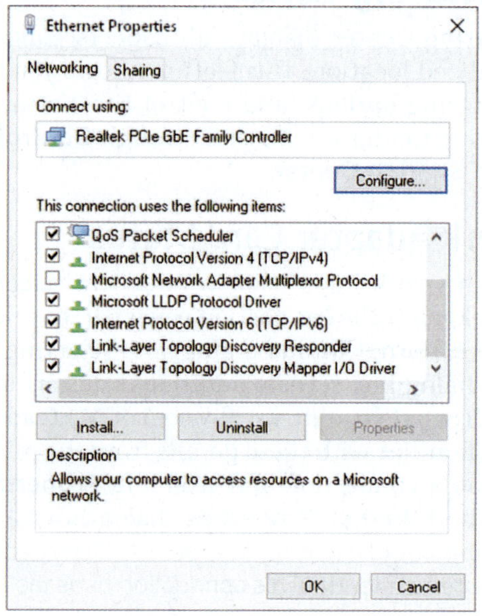

Figure 23-22 The Windows **Ethernet Properties** dialog box reveals information such as the protocols being used by the connection.

Goodheart-Willcox Publisher

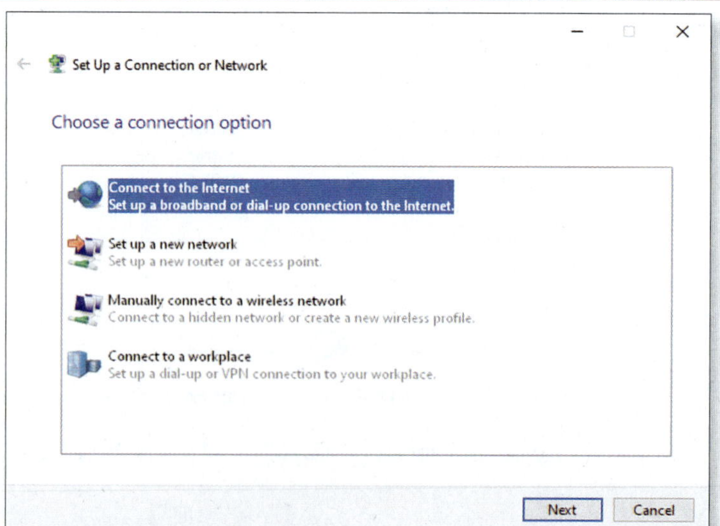

Figure 23-23 The **Set Up a Connection or Network** menu allows users to connect to the Internet, set up a new network, manually connect to a wireless network, or connect to a workplace.

Goodheart-Willcox Publisher

Share a Printer in Windows

1101: 3.6
1102: 1.6

Configuring a printer share in a Windows SOHO environment is very similar to configuring a file or folder share. The exact method of configuring a printer share will be determined by the number of clients with which you wish to share the printer and the amount of control you wish to have over the printer. However, the two basic ways of installing a shared printer are to attach a printer to a PC and then share access through the PC or connect the printer to the network as a standalone printer. A third, less common, option is to incorporate a USB Printer Auto-Sharing switch, which allows a printer to be shared between two or more computers without the need for network configuration.

Sharing a printer that is connected to a PC has one major problem: the computer must be on for other clients to use the printer. This can also be an advantage if you wish to limit access to the printer.

A network printer provides access to all users on the network and does not require a single dedicated PC. The network printer can be configured with password access to prevent unauthorized access.

In Figure 23-24, you can see what a typical set of permissions for a printer share looks like. The printer share permissions are quite different from shared folder permissions and are designed to match the function of a network shared printer. Other network devices have share permissions similar to folder share permissions.

When configuring a network printer as a share, you must provide some information for the configuration. A default name will be listed, but you can change it to a name that identifies the printer location. This is helpful if there are many people sharing access to the printer and the printer is in another room. For example, you may want to identify the printer as Art Department LaserJet1200, as this name identifies the department where the printer is located and the type of printer it is. You could also include the room number or the building number for a large network system.

If you select the **Sharing** tab of the printer **Properties** dialog box, you will see the **Render print jobs on client computers** option, shown in Figure 23-25. Selecting this option directs print job processing to the client computer and not the computer to which the printer is connected directly. The advantage to this is the computer/server connected directly to the printer will not be inundated with print requests from other computers.

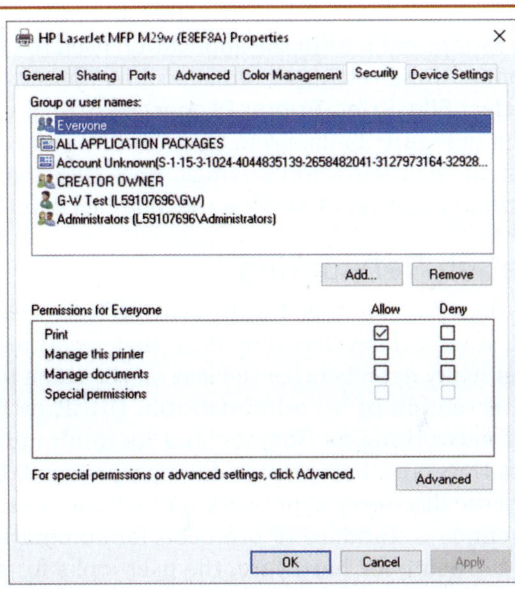

Goodheart-Willcox Publisher

Figure 23-24 Shared devices, such as printers, have a special set of share permissions that can be assigned to users.

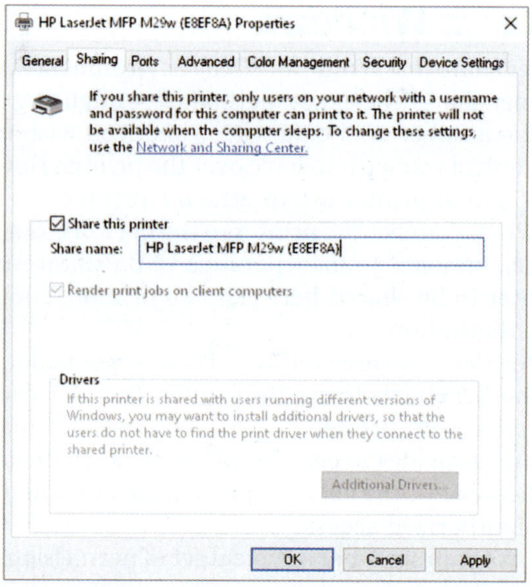

Figure 23-25 The **Sharing** tab provides options to deliver drivers to computers running different operating systems.

Goodheart-Willcox Publisher

Offline printing is supported, which means that the client computer can send a print job to the printer computer/server even when not connected. When the connection is reestablished, the print job will automatically be spooled to the printer and then print.

In Figure 23-25, notice the option to install additional drivers. When a printer is configured as a local printer and shared to the network, the installed print driver matches the local computer. If a computer accesses the shared printer and does not have the exact same driver as the local printer, then a driver error will likely occur. For example, if the local computer connected to the printer has a 64-bit Windows 10 operating system, the driver for the printer will be a 64-bit version, but if the shared printer is accessed by a 32-bit version of Windows, the printer job will fail because the Windows operating system is 32-bit, and the printer driver is 64-bit. Selecting the **Additional Drivers** option will install additional drivers, making the network printer compatible with other versions of operating systems.

Sharing a printer via a SOHO network allows for the establishment and configuration of printer settings that control orientation and quality of prints. These settings can also be configured within the application used to create the document to be printed. To update these settings from a local computer, open the document to be printed, and select **File>Print>Printer Properties**, which will display a screen similar to that shown in Figure 23-26. From this window, you can select the appropriate tabs to adjust the configuration settings. Note that the available tabs and appearance of the window can vary based on the installed printer.

Zero Configuration Networking

Printers can also be shared using **Zero Configuration Networking**, also known as *Zeroconf*, which is a standard developed by IEEE that recommends how to design a device that automatically detects other devices on the same network or a nearby segment without intervention by an administrator, DHCP, or DNS. Apple devices refer to this type of networking as *Bonjour*, and its minimum requirements are IPv4/IPv6, multicast DNS, and line printer daemon protocol. Both Zeroconf and Bonjour allow automatic discovery of network services, devices, and computers on networks. Zeroconf employs standard IP protocols for automatic discovery of each other, so instead of browsing for hardware, the user looks for services specific to the needed task. For example, if a user wanted to print notes from a meeting, they

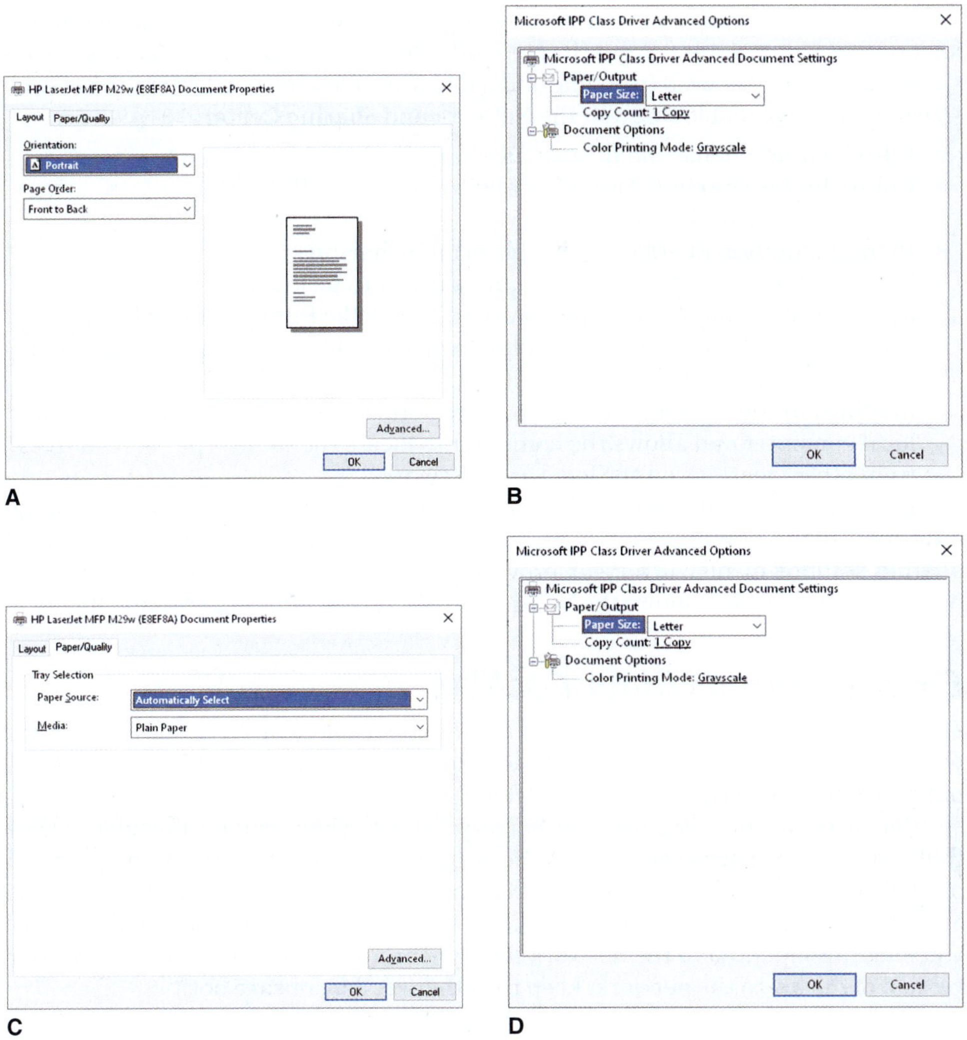

Goodheart-Willcox Publisher

Figure 23-26 Printer settings can be adjusted locally from the application generating the print job or for the entire network. From this menu, users can adjust the layout (A), advanced document layout settings (B), paper/quality (C), and advanced paper settings (D).

could generate a list of available printers, select one, and use it without having to configure anything.

AirPrint

Similar to Bonjour, AirPrint is an Apple-specific feature built into most macOS and iOS devices that allows for Wi-Fi printing either to shared or AirPrint-compatible printers. What is unique to AirPrint is that it does not require printer-specific drivers. When AirPrint was first developed, it was intended for mobile devices to be able to print to a networked printer, but in 2012, AirPrint started being included in macOS desktop platforms, which allowed users to print to computers networking via Ethernet.

Share Files and Folders in Windows

Sharing in Windows has been made very simple through the introduction of the Public Folders feature, which was first introduced in Windows Vista and has been maintained in every Windows release since. The Libraries features are also used in Windows 10, but they must be enabled by opening Explorer and selecting **View>Navigation Pane>Show libraries**. For detailed information on Public Folders and Libraries, see Chapter 21.

Tech Tip

All users need a network location to share information with each other, and all users need a network location that is private for their own personal storage that is accessible only by that user.

Again, the Network and Sharing Center provides an easy way to manage shared folders, files, and printers. From the **Network and Sharing Center**, select the corresponding feature you wish to enable or disable. The following is a description of each sharing option available through the Network and Sharing Center:

- **File sharing**: Enable and disable file sharing
- **Public folder sharing**: Automatically configure the **Public** folder for sharing on the network or disable it
- **Printer sharing**: Enable and disable printer sharing
- **Password protected sharing**: Requires a user to have a local user account on the local computer and a password to access the **Public** folder, files, and printer attached to the local computer; when disabled, all users have access to shared files, **Public** folder, and printer
- **Media sharing**: Provides access to shared music, pictures, and videos on the local computer and allows the computer to locate the same types of resources from other locations on the local area network

In Windows, file and printer sharing can be managed by selecting the **Change advanced sharing settings** option in the Network and Sharing Center. The **Advanced sharing settings** menu will appear, providing options to turn printer and file sharing on and off. Figure 23-27 shows the Windows 10 **Advanced sharing settings** menu.

Enable Shared Folder Caching

The caching feature for shared folders makes it possible to access shared contents when the share is unavailable or offline. The caching feature is also referred to as *offline sharing* and is not enabled by default.

The share-caching feature can be very helpful when using a portable device that is frequently disconnected from the network system. It allows you to work with cached files in a similar manner as when you are connected through the network, and when you reconnect to the network, the file is synchronized so that any changes you make are updated to the network file. Synchronization allows you to save your version of the file to the network, keep the other version, or save both.

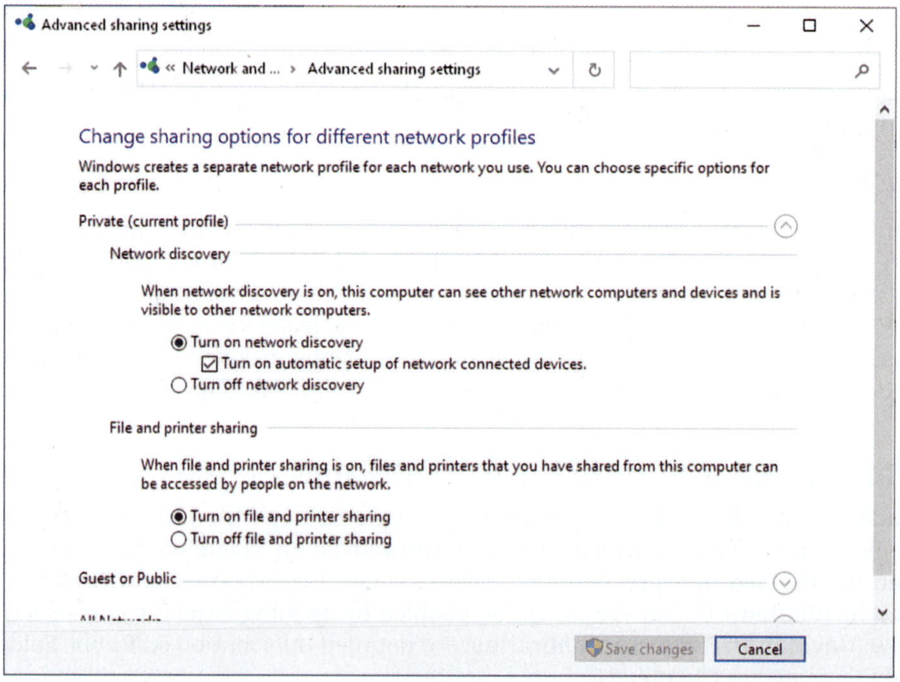

Goodheart-Willcox Publisher

Figure 23-27 The Windows Network and Sharing Center **Advanced sharing settings** menu allows you to enable and disable file and printer sharing.

Share caching is easy to configure. You simply open the shared folder's **Properties** dialog box, select the **Sharing** tab, and then select the **Advanced Sharing** button. The **Advanced Sharing** dialog box appears, which allows you to select the **Caching** button, as shown in Figure 23-28. The **Offline Settings** dialog box will appear with options to choose which files will be available for offline caching.

Enable Disk Quotas

Disk quotas are an important configuration option for shared storage space. Users tend to use much more space on shared media than on local storage and often save anything whether it is important or not. It does not take long to use up an entire disk when multiple users are storing information, pictures, videos, music, and more. To prevent one or more users from using too much disk space, each user can be assigned a maximum amount of space, which is referred to as a *disk quota*. The default setting is **Do not limit disk usage**, but when enabled, administrators can limit a user's disk space, and set a warning to be issued to the user when they are close to exceeding the allocated disk space. Notice in Figure 23-29 the disk space is limited to 100 GB and the warning is set to alert the user at 75 GB.

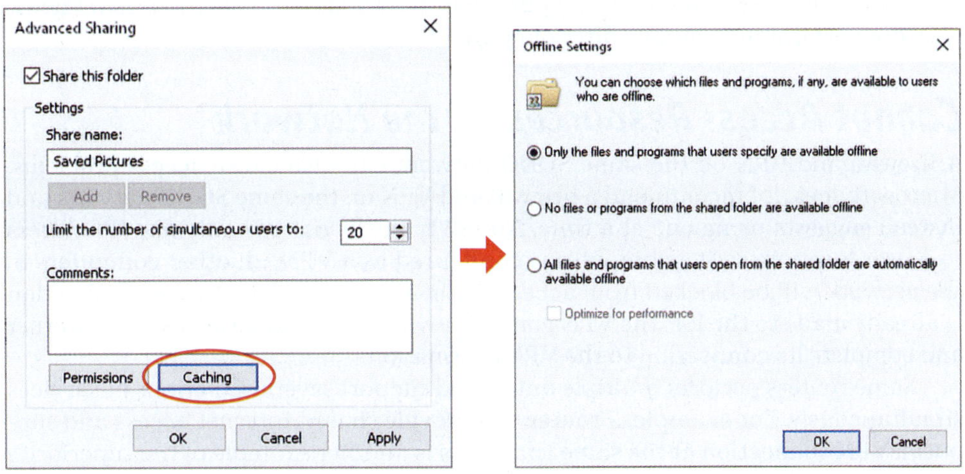

Goodheart-Willcox Publisher

Figure 23-28 The caching feature for shared folders makes it possible to access shared content when the network share is not available.

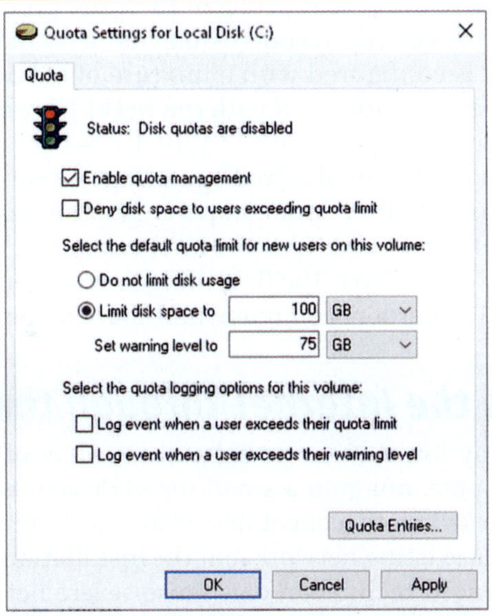

Goodheart-Willcox Publisher

Figure 23-29 Disk quotas allow you to limit the amount of disk storage space a network user can utilize.

23.3 Troubleshooting the SOHO Network

Once you have installed and configured your SOHO network, you may find that you cannot access certain resources or that access is slow. This section covers the most common problems that can occur with a new SOHO network installation. These problems involve sluggish Internet access, inability to access network resources, inability to access the Internet through the ICS host, incompatible hardware or software, and a message stating the network path was not found, among other issues.

Internet Access Is Sluggish

The shared Internet connection can be extremely slow or sluggish if someone on the network is downloading large files or streaming media. Files containing graphics or sound clips are excessively large when compared to text files, and since the bandwidth of the local network is shared by everyone connected to the network, large file transfers can reduce the network response time for everyone. This problem can be eliminated by blocking the ports associated with the large file transfers. For example, iTunes music sharing uses TCP port 3689. If excessive use of iTunes is reducing network performance, simply filter out port 3689.

A+ 1102: 3.2

Cannot Access Resources on the Network

A firewall and VPN on the same SOHO network can also cause access problems. Microsoft does *not* recommend a firewall and VPN on the same SOHO network and instead suggests using one at a time. An ISP typically assigns only one IP address to a user location, so if a computer is configured as a VPN, all other computers in the network will be blocked from accessing the Internet. If the Internet connection is already made to the ISP, the VPN computer will not be able to access the Internet and complete its connection to the VPN destination.

Some routers perform multiple duties and support several functions or services simultaneously. For example, a router can provide shared Internet access and support a VPN connection at the same time. This is another example of the superiority of a router used in a small network system. Otherwise, you will need to separate the computer using the VPN from the rest of the network.

Setting up a PC with a different protocol than the other PCs on the network prevents that PC from accessing resources on the network. This can often happen when the network is configured with a mixture of old and new computers, as the older computers may be configured with the NetBEUI protocol by default while the newer computers are configured with TCP/IP. There may also be a conflict in the names of computers in a network of mixed operating systems. NetBIOS only allows 15 characters in the name, but modern computer systems assign additional names to computers that conform to the NetBIOS 15-character rule to enable backward compatibility with legacy systems. The first thing to check on a new network is the correct spelling of the workgroup, computer, and share name.

Cannot Access the Internet through the ICS Host

You should not use any form of server software on any of the local workgroup workstations. For example, imagine a small network system that is growing and will eventually need to switch to a client/server model. A combination file and web server is installed in the existing network, but the installation of the server and web server by an inexperienced technician can cause severe network communication problems. A server is typically configured as a DHCP server or DNS server, which will interfere with the ICS host on the network. Remember, the ICS wizard automatically configures IP addresses, so if the server is configured for DHCP or DNS, it will also attempt to issue IP addresses and cause intermittent access problems or even complete failure of the ICS feature.

Incompatible Hardware or Software

Tech Tip

Not all devices absent from a HCL will cause problems. Many function perfectly.

Incompatibility can be a real problem, so it is important to check the hardware compatibility list before setting up a SOHO network. If a device that is not on the hardware compatibility list (HCL) is installed and is incompatible, any number of unexpected occurrences might happen. The device may try to constantly broadcast, or simply communicate in only one direction. It might respond to text-based commands such as **ping** and **tracert** but not communicate at a higher level. If a network is composed of mixed computers (computers with various types of hardware and operating systems), some of the computers may support communication with the legacy device and some will not. Anything might happen when using devices that have not been thoroughly tested.

Network Path Not Found Message

1102: 3.2 A+

Tech Tip

Port numbers 137, 138, 139, and 445 must be open in the firewall to access a shared folder.

Receiving the error message "Network path not found" is common. Typically, it can be caused by one of several reasons, including

- an incorrectly keyed network path;
- a nonexistent network connection or location; or
- incorrect permissions to access the desired location.

When making a new network connection, it is common to enter the network location incorrectly or leave out the proper punctuation. You can ping the network location to verify that you have correctly typed the network path and that all network media and devices are working properly. Verifying the network location with the **ping** command will rule out the first three reasons listed.

Another common reason for generating a "network path not found" error message is that the user does not have permission to access the network location share or device. Network share or location permission can be easily verified through the network administrator.

Other Network Problems

1101: 5.7 A+

Slow network speed is a common problem that can be caused by increased traffic on a network or outdated networking equipment. The key to troubleshooting this issue is to compare current speeds to previous speeds and determine what has changed. In addition to a consistent drop in network speed, there are other related issues that can degrade network performance, such as jitter. If you are experiencing jitter, the **tracert** command can identify what segment of the network is causing it. Similarly, latency can cause slow network speed. Again, identifying the specific part of your network that is causing the delay is critical to troubleshooting.

There can also be network issues related to the network hardware itself. For example, port flapping can be caused by physical cabling, network issues, or a failure of the device itself. Port flapping occurs when one or more of a switch's ports toggles between the status of up and down.

23.4 Remote Desktop

1102: 3.2 A+

Originally known as Microsoft Terminal Services Client (MSTSC), *Remote Desktop* is a useful feature that allows a user to access and take control of one computer from

Tech Tip

The Remote Desktop feature is an example of a VPN application. To use the Remote Desktop feature, TCP port 3389 must be open in the firewall.

another. The computer from which you are connecting is referred to as the *client*, and the computer to which you are remotely connecting is referred to as the *host*. For example, you could access your work computer (host) from your home computer (client) and perform tasks just as though you were sitting at your work computer. Once remote connection is made, the user can open documents and modify them as though they were sitting at the actual location of the remote computer; this includes accessing all their programs, files, and network resources at work from their home computer.

Accessing a remote computer using the Remote Desktop Connection program is easy; you simply enter the name of the remote computer and the name of the user account configured on the remote computer, as shown in Figure 23-30. You will be prompted for the user account password when the connection is being established.

The computer name is your choice for a connection on the local network, but to connect to a computer using the Internet, you must supply a **fully qualified domain name (FQDN)**, which is a combination of the host (computer) name, the domain name, and all the higher-level domains. For example, the fully qualified domain name of a computer named WindowsOffice located at www.g-w.com would be www.WindowsOffice.g-w.com or WindowsOffice.g-w.com. The www is optional. You can also use the remote computer IP address in place of the computer name. After the first time a Remote Desktop connection is established, the logon dialog box will be much simpler, as only the user password needs to be entered. Figure 23-31 shows a Remote Desktop logon dialog box after a previous connection has been established.

A+ 1102: 4.9

Remote Assistance

Remote Desktop and VNC should not be confused with Microsoft Remote Assistance (MSRA), which provides access to a computer by sending an invitation to another person to help with a computer problem. For example, a user can send a request for remote assistance to another user by sending the user an e-mail with a Remote Assistance attachment, and the person receiving the e-mail with the Remote Assistance request attachment can access the sender's computer. The difference between Remote Desktop and Remote Assistance is that for Remote Assistance, the user must be present at the computer being accessed, but for Remote Desktop the user is not present at the computer being accessed. Another difference is that when using Remote Assistance, the person requesting assistance can limit access to the computer and disconnect the Remote Assistance connection at any time.

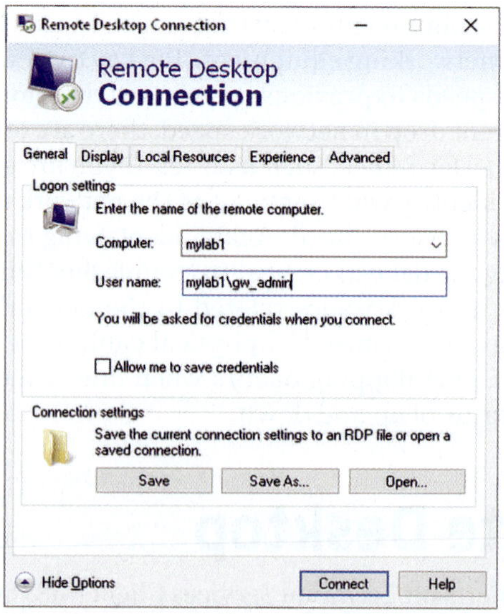

Goodheart-Willcox Publisher

Figure 23-30 To establish a Remote Desktop connection, you must enter the computer name and the username. You will be prompted for the account password when connecting to the remote computer.

Remote Assistance is popular with corporate technical support teams. To enable this feature, enter remote assistance in the Windows **Search** box and select **Invite someone to connect to your PC and help you, or offer to help someone else**. This will open the Windows Remote Assistance screen, as shown in Figure 23-32.

Other Remote Access Programs

1102: 4.9 A+

Windows Remote Desktop is not the only form of remote access. The Telnet protocol is commonly used to connect remotely to a system and works on port 23. There is a Telnet client and server included in Windows 10 and 11, but it must be added via **Programs and Features**. It should be noted, however, that Telnet is not encrypted and should only be used within a virtual private network (VPN). An alternative to Telnet is Secure Shell (SSH), which is encrypted by default and works on port 22. Many Linux distributions come with an SSH client. There are many free SSH clients for Windows available for download, the most popular option being PuTTY. Conduct an online search using the search phrase putty remote access for more information There are, of course, third-party tools for remote access. This includes video-conferencing software such as Zoom, Microsoft Teams, and GoToMeeting, all of which also include screen-sharing software.

Goodheart-Willcox Publisher

Figure 23-31 After the initial Remote Desktop connection is established, the logon dialog box will be presented with the user account name and the computer name already completed.

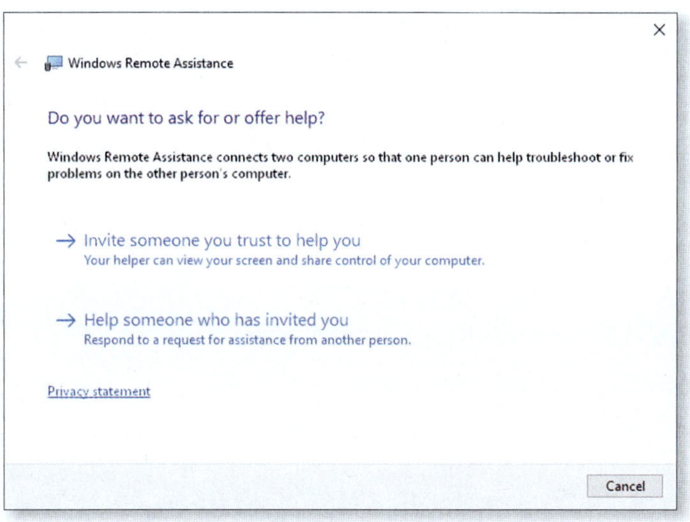

Goodheart-Willcox Publisher

Figure 23-32 Windows Remote Assistance allows a remote person to take control of your computer to troubleshoot a problem.

A+ 1102: 4.9

Virtual Network Computers (VNC) is a method that lets one use a graphical desktop remotely. Unlike Remote Desktop, VNC is platform independent, meaning it can be used on devices running software other than Windows. However, these connections will often be executed over a VPN for security reasons. The VNC process consists of a server that provides a virtual desktop, and the VNC client that accesses and uses the virtual desktop. The communication is managed with the Remote Framebuffer (RFB) protocol, which is specifically for remote access to a GUI.

A+ 1102: 4.9

Related to remote access is *remote monitoring and management (RMM)*, which is any software application that allows someone to remotely monitor activity on a computer and manage actions like software updates and system settings. This technology is widely used in corporate networks to ensure compliance with corporate policies. Many companies use desktop management software to ensure consistent and compliant desktops throughout the corporate network.

File transfers via FTP are not truly remote access because the user does not have control of a remote machine. However, it *does* allow one to upload and download files. Windows IIS includes an FTP server that can be enabled, and there are numerous open-source file transfer clients. One of the most used is FileZilla, which has versions for Windows, macOS, and Linux. For more information about FileZilla, conduct an online search using the keyword filezilla.

Chapter Summary

23.1 Designing the SOHO Network

- The small-office/home-office (SOHO) network is a simple peer-to-peer LAN used to share resources and data in a home- or small-office environment.
- Some of the factors to consider when designing a SOHO network are the type of media that will be used to connect the PCs together, the way the networked PCs will access the Internet, and the level of administration that will be used to secure resources and data.
- Typical media used in a SOHO network are copper cable, wireless, existing phone lines, and existing power lines.
- It is not uncommon to have a mixed network environment.
- Four common methods of hosting file-sharing services for SOHO are NAS, dedicated computer, domain network, and cloud service.
- Other storage methods such as e-mail and flash drives can be used, but they are not practical methods.
- Closely related to file sharing and storage is the concept of regularly backing up data. Backups are the best method of preventing the loss of shared data.
- Common choices of Internet-access devices in a SOHO network are the DSL modem, cable modem, and wireless hotspots.
- The exact configuration depends on the building's environment and the type of Internet-access device selected.
- SOHO network administration can be as simple or as complex as you wish to make it.
- The best scenario for SOHO administration is having a single administrator with limited authority delegated to other users and setting up local and share-level security.
- Local security is implemented by creating a local user account on each PC.
- Share-level security protects resources accessed from across the network by requiring a password to access the share or by limiting its access.
- Common security implementations that can be configured for the SOHO network are a firewall or a virtual private network (VPN).
- Some ways to secure a wireless router are changing the default SSID, login name, and password; disabling the SSID broadcast; configuring encryption; and enabling MAC filtering.
- In network security application, the DMZ is an area of a network system that is intentionally created to be less secure than the main network system and is directly accessible from the Internet.
- SOHO routers provide an option for DHCP services, which means the router will automatically issue IP addresses to the network devices.
- A proxy server serves as an intermediary between the Internet and a network client computer. The most common proxy server is a web server proxy, which stores web-page content that is frequently accessed by network users.

23.2 Configuring the SOHO Network with Windows

- Windows includes the Network and Sharing Center, which displays in one centralized location all aspects concerning the local area network.

- When setting up a SOHO network in a mixed operating system environment, use the PC with the latest or most up-to-date operating system as the host or as the computer that will share other resources, such as a printer.
- Configuring a printer share in a Windows SOHO environment is very similar to configuring a file or folder share.
- The caching feature for shared folders makes it possible to access shared contents when the share is not available or the shared device location is offline.
- To prevent one or more users from using too much disk storage space, each user can be assigned a maximum amount of storage space, which is referred to as a disk quota.

23.3 Troubleshooting the SOHO Network

- The shared Internet connection can be extremely slow or sluggish if someone on the network is downloading large files or streaming media. This problem can be eliminated by blocking the ports associated with the large file transfers.
- A firewall and VPN on the same SOHO network can also cause access problems. Microsoft does not recommend a firewall and VPN on the same SOHO network and instead suggests using one at a time.
- Setting up a PC with a different protocol than the other PCs on the network prevents that PC from accessing resources on the network.
- You should not use any form of server software on any of the local workgroup workstations.
- Incompatibility can be a real problem, so it is important to check the hardware compatibility list before setting up a SOHO network. If a device that is not on the hardware compatibility list (HCL) is installed and is incompatible, any number of unexpected occurrences might happen.
- Receiving the error message "Network path not found" is common. Typically, it can be caused by one of several reasons, including an incorrectly keyed network path, a nonexistent network connection or location, or incorrect permissions to access the location.
- Slow network speed is a common problem that can be caused by increased traffic on a network or outdated networking equipment. The key to troubleshooting this issue is to compare current speeds to previous speeds and determine what has changed. In addition to a consistent drop in network speed, there are other related issues that can degrade network performance, such as jitter. If you are experiencing jitter, the **tracert** command can identify what segment of the network is causing it. Similarly, latency can cause slow network speed. Again, identifying the specific part of your network that is causing the delay is critical to troubleshooting. There can also be network issues related to the network hardware itself. For example, port flapping can be caused by physical cabling, network issues, or a failure of the device itself.

23.4 Remote Desktop

- Using Windows Remote Desktop, you can access your work computer from your home computer and perform tasks just as though you were sitting at your work computer.
- The computer from which you are connecting is referred to as the *client*, and the computer to which you are remotely connecting is referred to as the *host*.
- To use the Remote Desktop feature, TCP port 3389 must be open in the firewall.

- Windows Remote Desktop is not the only form of remote access. The Telnet protocol is commonly used to connect remotely to a system and works on port 23. It should be noted, however, that Telnet is not encrypted and should only be used within a virtual private network (VPN). An alternative to Telnet is Secure Shell (SSH), which is encrypted by default and works on port 22.
- Third-party tools such as Zoom, Microsoft Teams, and GoToMeeting, can also be used for remote access and screen sharing.
- Related to remote access is *remote monitoring and management (RMM)*, which is any software application that allows someone to remotely monitor activity on a computer and manage actions like software updates and system settings.
- File transfers via FTP are not truly remote access because the user does not have control of a remote machine.
- Related to Remote Desktop is Microsoft Remote Assistance (MSRA), which allows a remote person, someone you trust, to take control of your computer to troubleshoot a problem.

Review Questions

1. List factors that should be taken into consideration when designing a SOHO network.
2. Explain some of the limitations associated with each of the SOHO network media.
3. Differentiate among file sharing and storage methods in a SOHO network.
4. Compare and contrast Internet access methods.
5. List and describe two security levels employed in SOHO administration
6. List different methods of security employed in SOHO administration
7. Describe two instances of when a VPN should be created.
8. What is the difference between port forwarding and single port forwarding?
9. Explain the process of establishing a SOHO network connection in Windows.
10. Summarize Zero Configuration networking.
11. Why might a shared printer require different drivers?
12. List sharing options found through the Network and Sharing Center.
13. What is the purpose of a disk quota?
14. Identify common problems that can occur in a new SOHO network installation.
15. What might cause a network to perform sluggishly, and how can it be eliminated?
16. What two devices installed on the same network can cause problems with accessing resources?
17. List three common reasons for a network path to not be found.
18. Summarize the process for troubleshooting slow network speed.
19. Summarize the process of connecting to a remote computer via Remote Desktop.
20. Differentiate between Remote Desktop and Remote Assistance.

Sample A+ Exam Questions

1. Which technology would provide the best protection against unauthorized access from the Internet?
   A. Standard V92 modem
   B. Firewall
   C. A good Internet access password for modem access
   D. Antivirus program
2. Phil has been mistakenly assigned to two different user groups: Teacher and Student. The Teacher group has full control over the folder named Grades. The Student group has only read permissions. How will this affect Phil when he tries to access the Grades folder?
   A. Phil will not be able to access the Grades folder.
   B. Phil will be able to read the contents of the Grades folder.
   C. Phil will have full control over the Grades folder.
   D. Phil's user account will be automatically locked out until the share permission conflict is resolved.
3. What is the typical IPv4 address assigned to an ICS host?
   A. 123.145.000.001
   B. 192.168.000.1
   C. 127.000.000.1
   D. 255.255.255.255
4. A small SOHO network has been set up in a local insurance company, which consists of four Windows 10 Professional workstations. Jim has successfully created a local user account on Workstation_1 for his own use. All workstations belong to the same workgroup. Jim is unsuccessful at logging on to the other workstations. What is *most likely* the problem?
   A. Jim does not have a local user account set up on Workstation_2 through Workstation_4.
   B. The network cabling has been disconnected from Workstation_2 through Workstation_4.
   C. Share-level security must be configured on Workstation_2 through Workstation_4.
   D. A user on a peer-to-peer network may not log on to more than one PC at a time.
5. Carlos is working late at the office. The office consists of eight computers configured as a peer-to-peer network. The office manager's computer is an ICS host and has a telephone modem installed to access the ISP. The system was installed two months ago and has worked well. Everyone has shut down their computer and has gone home except for

Carlos. Carlos attempts to access his e-mail before leaving but finds he cannot access the Internet. What is *most likely* the problem?

A. The IP address supplied to the ICS host by the ISP has changed.
B. The connection cannot be established because the ICS host has been shut down.
C. The Internet Connection Firewall is configured to prevent Carlos from accessing Internet port 110.
D. The ISP does not provide telephone support after 6 p.m.

6. Which technology allows existing power lines to be used as network media?
A. VPN
B. PLC
C. ICS
D. HomePNA

7. A(n) _____ ensures that data sent across the Internet are not intercepted, read, or tampered with.
A. PLC
B. firewall
C. ICS
D. VPN

8. Which of the following describes a router that is used to combine different media and to provide an Internet connection?
A. Bridge
B. Access
C. Internet
D. Gateway

9. Which wireless router feature will prevent unauthorized access to the router?
A. Disabling the SSID broadcast
B. Configuring the router for 802.11n frequency
C. MAC filtering
D. Port forwarding

10. Which option is used to secure a workstation by preventing clients from accessing specific Windows features?
A. BitLocker
B. Local Group Policy Editor
C. Firewall
D. Port filtering

Chapter 24

Customer Support, Communication, and Professionalism

Learning Outcomes

24.1 Differentiate among organizational models for customer support.
24.2 Identify types of documentation that ensure best practices for customer and employee support.
24.3 List best practices for change management.
24.4 Describe important employability skills.
24.5 Identify key steps related to managing an incident involving prohibited content or activity.

A+ Certification Exam Objectives

The following A+ Certification Exam Objectives are covered in this chapter.

Exam 220-1102

2.0 Security

- 2.6 Given a scenario, configure a workstation to meet best practices for security.

4.0 Operational Procedures

- 4.1 Given a scenario, implement best practices associated with documentation and support systems information management.
- 4.2 Given a scenario, implement basic change-management best practices.
- 4.6 Explain importance of prohibited content/activity and privacy, licensing, and policy concepts.
- 4.7 Given a scenario, use proper communication techniques and professionalism.

Key Terms

call center
chain of custody
change management
customer support
depot technician
emoticons
help desk
live support
personally identifiable information (PII)
professionalism
protected health information (PHI)
small business service counter
teamwork

Overview

This chapter covers the basic skills necessary to function in a customer- or client-related environment. While you will not have to meet and work with customers or clients daily, you will likely have to do so with some regularity as a technician. You probably assume you already know how to interact with people, but there are specific skills required to keep customers and clients happy of which you may not be aware.

In this chapter, you will be introduced to specific support scenarios and learn about the forms of conduct that have been accepted as industry standards. You may be the most skilled technician in your organization, but if you do not deal with people professionally and courteously, you will most likely lose your job or be banned from meeting with customers and clients. You will also never be raised to a position of leadership or management, and other career options may become limited. The importance of learning the skills in this chapter cannot be emphasized enough. Reading, understanding, and being able to put into practice the skills covered in this chapter may determine your future in a computer-related career.

A+ Note

The CompTIA A+ Exams contain questions related to proper communication and professionalism. You will most likely encounter questions related to customer relations, such as communicating clearly with the customer, listening to the customer, and conveying a positive attitude to the customer.

24.1 Customer Support

Simply put, **customer support** is the delivery of customer assistance, training, and services. This section provides an overview of customer support, giving you the big picture of how organizational models work together to resolve customer and client computer problems. You will learn how different levels of support can be distributed across these models and will be made aware of the level of customer interaction typical of each model.

Customer Support Organization Models

There are several standard organizational models for customer support. Some of these models include a help desk, call center, small business, service counter, depot technician, corporate enterprise support, and ticketing systems. The exact model of your company and how you fit within that model depends on the

- number of people requiring support;
- product being supported; and
- customer location (local or global).

Some organizations operate as a combination of several models working together as a team. For example, a help desk service may be outsourced to a foreign country, and this help desk may work closely with an organization in the United States that performs the physical work. In the following sections, several of the most common support organization models are presented.

Help Desk

A **help desk** is a central point of contact that provides technical support to clients, including in-house employees or customers. Contact is often initiated by an online ticketing system, though telephone and e-mail can also be used. Examples of organizations that typically provide help desk support are Internet service providers (ISPs), hardware and software manufacturers, corporate businesses, and educational and governmental institutions.

The help desk is the first level of support used to resolve common computer hardware and software problems. In most instances, a service request and repair ticket are generated from the first moment of contact with a client. The help desk can be a single, dedicated location or part of a larger organization such as a call center, as shown in Figure 24-1.

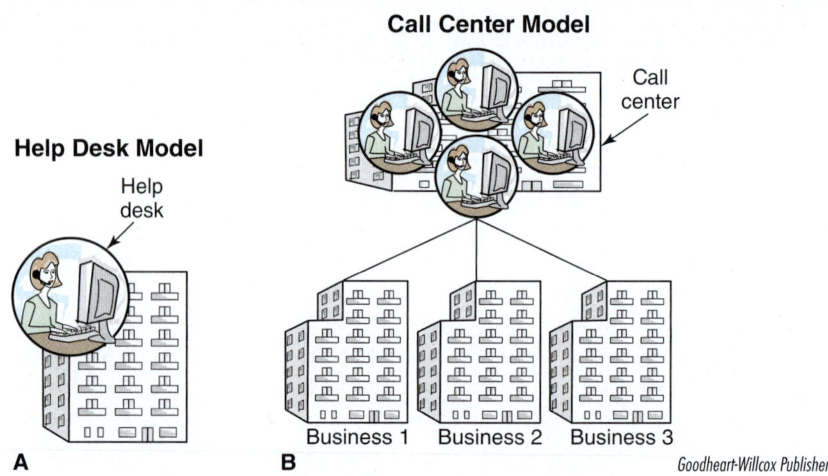

Figure 24-1 In the help desk model (A), the help desk is part of the company. In the call center model (B), the help desk is part of a call center, which provides support for many different businesses.

Call Center

A **call center** is typically a large collection of support personnel located in a common facility equipped with telephones and computer network support. Call centers can be located anywhere in the world, and many call centers provide support for more than one company or product. Employees in a call center do not necessarily have the technical skills required for repairing computer-related problems and are instead more likely trained to read prepared scripts correlated to the most common general problems. If they cannot adequately fix the problem, the support request is forwarded to the next level of a repair technician, who is usually located at the company that manufactures the equipment or writes the software. For example, a large company such as Cisco could outsource its first level of support to a call center, and if the call center cannot immediately resolve the problem, the support request is forwarded to the next level of support, which may be a technician located at Cisco who is trained to handle more difficult problems requiring intervention by a person with much more expertise.

Small Business Service Counter

A **small business service counter** is an independent company that specializes in light maintenance and repair. Small businesses are said to be the backbone of the American economy, as over half of all American employment opportunities are in small businesses. You will very likely start your career in a small-business environment; you may even start your own small business. In a small-business environment, you will meet customers face-to-face regularly, so good customer relation skills are a key factor in your success.

The customer may be at the counter to make a purchase, request assistance in a purchase, or solicit technical support for an item purchased at the vendor location. In a small-business environment, a service technician will most likely fulfill multiple roles for the employer, such as being responsible for selling computer hardware, software, and related materials or for technical support and answering customer questions in person, by telephone, or through e-mail. A technician may also be dispatched to a customer location to install or troubleshoot computer equipment or provide training.

Depot Technician

A **depot technician** is a technician who performs repair work usually covered by warranty. The technician receives the hardware item after the client has contacted customer support through a call center or help desk, or if the first contact does not immediately resolve the problem. Once the equipment arrives at the depot, it is assigned to a technician for inspection and repair or replacement. A depot technician has very limited customer contact or no customer contact at all.

Corporate Enterprise Support

In a large, corporate environment, technical support services can be composed of many people working as a team. Typically, an employee contacts a help desk, and the help desk technician generates a repair or incident ticket, such as the example shown in Figure 24-2. If the help desk technician fails to assist the fellow employee in making the necessary adjustments to the item, the ticket is then assigned to a technician who will report to the employee's location.

At the employee's location, the technician will either repair or replace the equipment in question. This model is found where there are enough computers and related equipment to justify the cost of a full-time staff dedicated to this function.

Figure 24-2 A repair ticket summarizes the customer's problem or concern and lists actions taken and parts used.

Repair Ticket

Job Request Number: ____________

Contact Information

Name: ______________________ Initial contact date: ____________

Department: ______________________ Phone number: ____________

Equipment Information

Brand: __________ Model: __________ SN: __________

Equipment description (CPU, amount of RAM, etc.): ______________________

____

Operating system (if applicable): ______________________

Problem description: ______________________

____

____

____

Repair Information

Service date: __________ Service technician: __________

Diagnosis: ______________________

____

____

____

Actions taken: ______________________

____

____

____

____

____

____

Parts used:

____

____

____

____

Date repair completed: __________

Contact signature: ______________________ Date: __________

Technician signature: ______________________ Date: __________

Goodheart-Willcox Publisher

A+ 1102: 4.1

Ticket System

Regardless of the specifics of the support environment, it is important to have a system for tracking all support requests. This process is usually called a ticket system. Requests for support are submitted as tickets, which can be paper based or via software such as a web form. Every ticket must include specific information about the customer and the issue. In many cases, tickets include the following:

- **User information**: Includes contact information for the user reporting the problem
- **Device information**: Explicit details of the device, such as type, model, model number, and serial number

- **Description of problem(s)**: Specific, detailed description of the problem
- **Category**: Used to organize tickets based on area of attention needed, such as network connectivity, hardware failure, or software issue
- **Severity**: Used to prioritize tickets based on how severe the problem is; can be as simple as mild, moderate, and high, or much more detailed
- **Escalation level(s)**: Documents the layers of technical support needed to resolve the problem
- **Clear, concise written communication**: All communication must be as clear and understandable as possible; acronyms, slang, and jargon should be avoided whenever possible
- **Progress notes**: Notes items such as escalation levels, as well as status updates and name of technician(s) assigned to the problem
- **Problem resolution**: Details how the problem was resolved to assist future technical support personnel in resolving similar problems

Ticketing systems all function in a similar manner, but they also have unique features. This section was designed to provide a general description of ticket systems, and it is important to note that the system and the information needed on a ticket can be modified and expanded to fit an organization's needs.

Support Software

There are many software packages designed to keep track of service requests and the results, which is typically how service is organized and tracked. For example, when a customer or client first contacts the help desk with a service request, the call is logged and information such as the date, time, and a description of the problem is recorded. Often, this information is entered into a form or software that generates a repair ticket.

The help desk technician may resolve the problem immediately or dispatch a technician to the client's location. A copy of the repair ticket is distributed to the client and the technician who will report to the physical location of the problem.

Once the problem is resolved, the technician completes the ticket by adding the procedure used to resolve the problem. Any hardware or software that needs to be provided or has been provided to remedy the problem is also listed. A follow-up of the incident can be reviewed at the end of the day to ensure all problems have been resolved.

Levels of Support

There are typically three levels of support within an organization, as listed in Figure 24-3. Level-one support is the initial technical support contact. This is typically made with technical support from a help desk, website, or call center. Most problems can be corrected at this level.

Level-two support occurs when a problem is elevated to a person with more experience or expertise than the first person possesses. While level-one support manages most problems, the person at level one typically answers general technical support questions from cue cards or a software program that has answers available for the most common customer problems and questions. Level-two support,

Common Support Levels	
Support Level	**Description**
One	Help desk, website, or call center
Two	Supervisor over the level-one response team
Three	Supervisor (level two) working with third-party support from a larger company

Goodheart-Willcox Publisher

Figure 24-3 There are typically three general levels of support through which a problem can flow.

however, provides more individualized solutions for problems that are more unique or less commonly encountered. For example, a new software application that has just been released to the public conflicts with another software application, and the problem is so new that there is little to no information available. The level-two support technician works closely with the customer to solve the problem. For example, the technician may need to view how the problem arose on the customer's computer or recreate the problem before being able to find a procedure to correct it.

Level-three support is typically provided outside the immediate technical support location. For example, a third-party company, such as Microsoft or IBM, provides level-three support when a problem cannot be solved locally by the first two levels of support. This is often a combined effort to solve a customer problem and is coordinated by the original level-two support member. Level-three support may involve software programmers and engineers, and consumers are generally never involved with level-three support personnel.

Most level-one technical support is free, at least for a limited time. The highest level of support is typically not free and is set up on a cost-per-incident basis or through a service contract. It may also be based on a specific number of incidents or minutes of **live support**, which is real-time support that allows a customer or client to talk directly to support personnel for technical assistance instead of using an FAQ list or web page.

Outsourcing

Customer support is often outsourced to a specialized technical-support company that may reside in the United States or be located overseas. The main reason for outsourcing is often the cost of the support service, of which the primary cost is employee wages. It is often less expensive for a company to use a call center located in a foreign country because the wages may be far less than if the same service were provided locally.

A software or hardware company may find it more cost-effective to outsource level-one support and instead opt to provide level-two support locally. This enables all common or routine problems encountered by customers or clients to be answered by the outsourcing service, while level-two technicians are reserved for local issues at the company's location or authorized service centers scattered across the United States and around the world.

For example, the ABC Laptop manufacturer has all client and customer support requests directed to an 800 number or chat-based support on their website. The first level of support is outsourced and provided by the XYZ Corporation located in Mumbai, India, which is authorized to represent the ABC Laptop manufacturer in the United States. The XYZ Corporation manages all routine calls, provides help to customers, and covers basic problems by talking customers through the process of verifying that

- power LEDs are lit;
- all cables are connected; and
- memory has been reset.

They may also talk the customer through the procedures for using a support CD to reinstall an operating system and other basic tasks. If the problem cannot be resolved, the outsource support company forwards the problem to the ABC Laptop manufacturer, where more sophisticated troubleshooting diagnostics or the actual physical replacement of hardware items can be performed. The customer is given an address for mailing in the laptop or a pickup ticket for FedEx, UPS, or similar service so the laptop can be delivered to the ABC Laptop manufacturer for diagnostics and repair.

Frequently Asked Questions (FAQs)

Most businesses have a Frequently Asked Questions (FAQs) section posted on their websites that is designed to answer the most commonly asked customer questions and inquiries. FAQs comprise a valuable tool that can help save many hours of customer support, especially if the company or business does not have technical staff available 24 hours a day. Large companies typically have a very extensive FAQ section on their websites, as shown in Figure 24-4.

Microsoft also provides information for common customer questions. Notice in the Microsoft Support page in Figure 24-5 that many Microsoft products are listed, and a search bar is available for obtaining support for a specific issue. This site is designed for general users with minimal technical expertise. Microsoft provides both written and video demonstrations for many of the most common Microsoft customer questions.

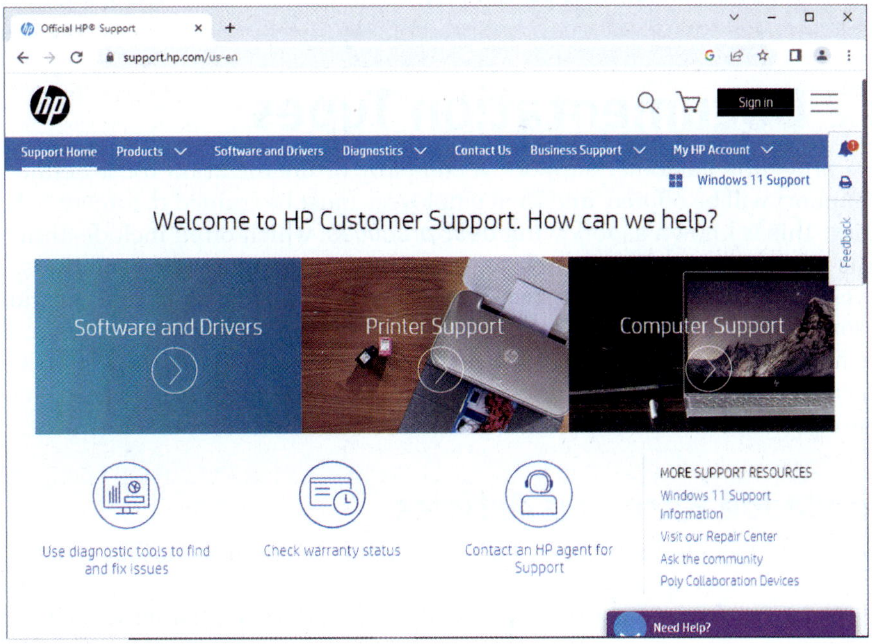

Goodheart-Willcox Publisher

Figure 24-4 HP provides a knowledge base that functions as an FAQ web page to allow users to search for solutions to the most commonly asked questions.

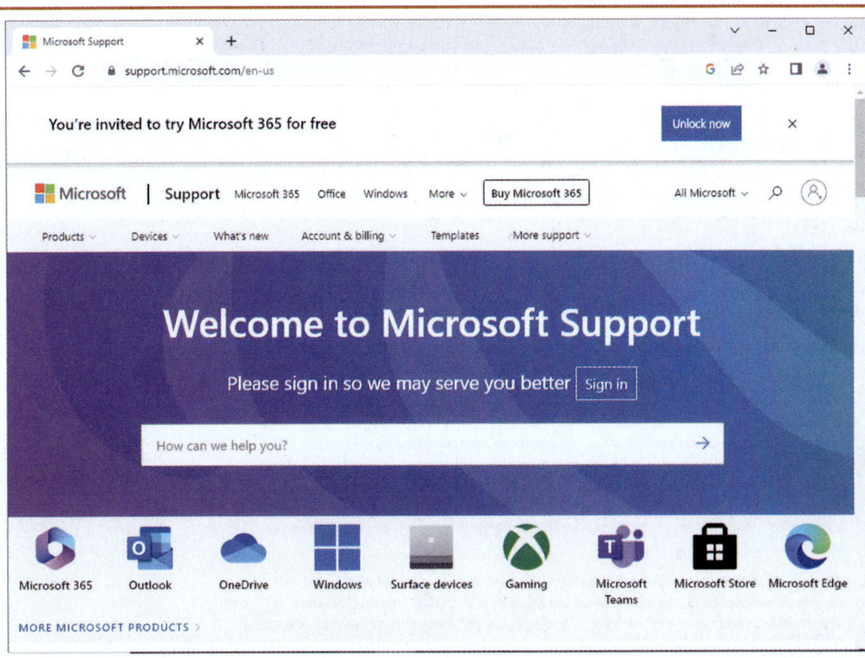

Goodheart-Willcox Publisher

Figure 24-5 Microsoft provides extensive technical support for all its products, with information addressing the most common customer questions.

You can also find the information to most common technical support questions by simply conducting an online search using terms such as Microsoft Tech Support followed by the product or issue, such as wireless networks. You then look for search results with a link directed to a Microsoft Support or TechNet site, which will take you to a Microsoft support article about your issue. Figure 24-6 shows one such article located using the search parameters described previously.

Companies save thousands of dollars in the workforce by posting answers to the most commonly asked customer questions while simultaneously satisfying customer needs all around the globe by providing customer support 24 hours a day. It is interesting to note that many companies provide the very same information that could be found on the Microsoft Support website, though some companies have personalized information for their customers.

24.2 Documentation Types

Before providing customer support, a company or organization must define how that support will be offered, and then employees must be trained to adhere to those policies. This is known as following ***best practices***, which often include anticipating the needs or concerns of employees and customers and posting solutions. This ensures someone looking for answers will be able to find them in one centralized location without having to call for support. Examples of such documentation, aside from the previously mentioned FAQ web pages, include knowledge base information and articles, incident documentation, regulatory and compliance policies, acceptable use policies, standard operating procedures, and inventory management.

A+ 1102: 4.1

Knowledge Base and Articles

A ***knowledge base*** is a repository for tech support or troubleshooting articles and can be effective for capturing counterproductive events, machine failures, and software issues. Organizations utilize knowledge bases in two different ways: the first

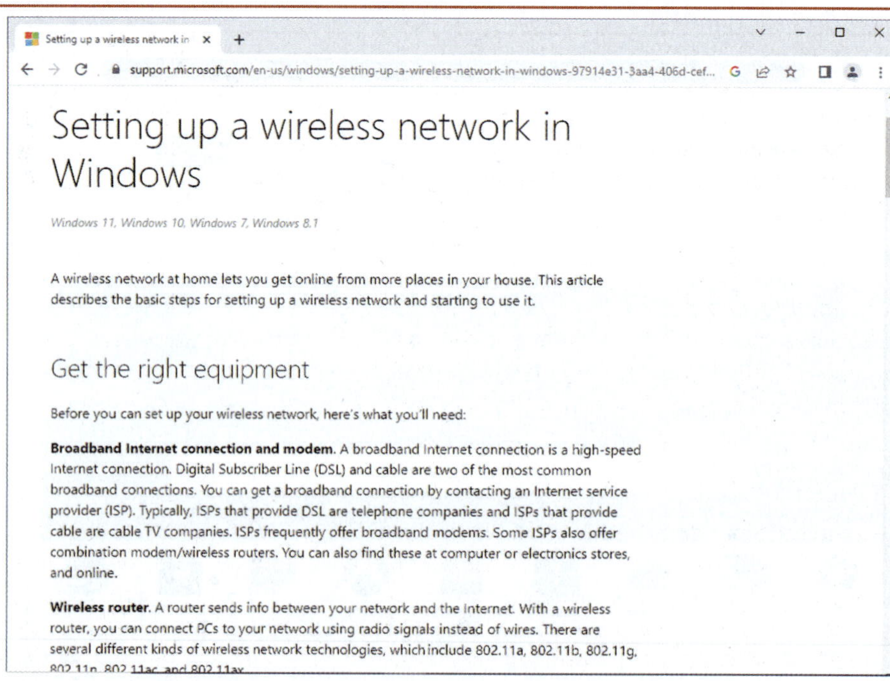

Figure 24-6 Microsoft provides written and video-based technical support for common customer questions.

Goodheart-Willcox Publisher

is for external users who are troubleshooting an issue, and the second is for internal employees. Articles for external users are normally written either by a company employee or a certified expert and are designed for those interested in self-service. In many cases, the steps outlined in knowledge base articles are the same steps used in level-one support. For internal users, a knowledge base contains articles relevant to company or organizational processes and are often referred to as *job aids*. These articles may be formatted according to the *Failure Mode and Effects Analysis (FMEA)* format, which is a structure that identifies and addresses potential problems and the effects of those problems before the problem occurs.

Incident Documentation

1102: 4.1 A+

Incident documentation is a means for recording undesirable events, actions taken, and the results of those actions. As a computer problem-solver, you may ask to see any incident documentation related to the problem for which you were hired. If you are lucky, you will find detailed descriptions and steps taken regarding the problem. Often, it is best not to expect detailed documentation, but to be receptive to it whenever you receive it.

Regulatory and Compliance Policy

1102: 4.1, 4.6 A+

Part of the regulatory and compliance policy for any mid-level to large business is covered by the Sarbanes-Oxley Act, which has stringent requirements primarily for accounting but also for other business functions. Also, the company itself may have requirements for hardware cycles as well as a document retention policy, which permits the destruction of specific classes of documents, but only after a well-defined time has passed. Data retention is an important aspect of regulatory compliance. In some cases, laws require that documents be kept for a specific period of time. For example, electronic records in publicly traded companies must be kept for five years. Even if there is not a legal or regulatory requirement to maintain records, there needs to be an organizational policy regarding documentation and records retention.

1102: 4.1 A+

A *splash screen* is a graphical element or page on a website or in software that displays information, advertisements, or provides entertainment while the desired page is loading. Alternatively, it can serve as an introduction page on a website. Splash screens can also be quite helpful in regulatory compliance. For example, a splash screen can remind users of specific policies when a computer starts or when an intranet page loads. You might have the same splash screen message all the time, or you might rotate through specific messages.

Acceptable Use Policy

1102: 4.1 A+

An *acceptable use policy (AUP)*, sometimes called a *usage agreement*, is a set of guidelines used and defined most often by the administrator of a network or service. This type of policy controls how the network or service may be used. It also sets directions regarding usage within the limits of the documented policy.

Standard Operating Procedures

1102: 4.1 A+

All organizations should have a document outlining *standard operating procedures (SOP)*, which details step-by-step instructions for performing certain actions or following processes. For example, imagine your company hired a new technician who is set to start working in a week. Part of the SOP document should identify a *new-user setup checklist* to identify what is needed to onboard the new employee, including technological equipment, ID cards, employee handbook, and anything else that is needed for new network users and employees. Similarly, the SOP document should also include an *end-user termination checklist*, which outlines how to recover company assets and track when users leave the system. Ideally, an SOP document should also contain steps for performing custom installation of software packages. For example, when software is installed, it generally installs with third-party applications such as web browsers or unneeded software referred to as *bloatware*. Instead of installing all this, an SOP document should outline the exact elements to be installed to save time, storage space, and possibly prevent issues later.

A+ 1102: 4.1

Inventory Management

Traditionally, a business has two kinds of hardware inventory: *capital inventory* for depreciable items with multiyear lives, and *expenses inventory* for consumable items. Expenses inventory is sometimes referred to as *M and O inventory* because the supplies are often related to maintenance and operations.

Capital inventory, such as a desktop or laptop computer, usually receives a difficult-to-remove asset tag with a bar code used for inventory. Because this inventory is part of the taxable base for the company, it must be accounted for during its lifetime and formally disposed of with appropriate documentation when it will no longer be used.

Consumable inventory may also have bar coding to speed up the maintenance of inventory activities, such as cycle counting. With asset tags or bar codes, you as a technician must let the client know when you are performing an activity that removes the tags or significantly affects the definition of what the machine is and its purpose or usage.

Asset management is an important element of inventory management. *Asset management* is a systematic approach to tracking equipment and supplies used to run an organization and involves taking several steps to document the assets in your organization, including the following:

- **Inventory lists**: Detailed inventory of all assets, including serial numbers, locations, and other pertinent details
- **Database System**: Refers to an electronic collection of asset records as opposed to a paper-based system
- **Asset tags and IDs**: Refers to bar codes or other identifier that is difficult to remove and used to track a product's life cycle
- **Procurement life cycle**: Documents how assets are procured, including the process of procurement, life cycle of assets, how assets are retired, and how often this cycle repeats
- **Warranty and licensing**: Tracks warranty information, such as length of time and hardware or services covered, and licensing rights for software
- **Assigned users**: Tracks the user(s) assigned to each asset

It can be surprising how many organizations lose track of assets. However, with proper asset control processes, this issue can be mitigated easily.

24.3 Change Management Best Practices

Change management refers to business or organizational guidance that prepares, equips, and supports internal employees to adopt or incorporate changes. Just as with documentation for customers, there are specific activities that constitute best practices for change management. These activities include documenting business processes, stating the purpose of the change, outlining the scope of the change, performing risk analysis, planning for change, allowing end-user acceptance, creating and maintaining a change board, drafting a backout plan, and documenting the changes once they take place. When considering and implementing changes, remember to be patient and open-minded, as people generally do not respond to change well.

Documented Business Processes

1102: 4.2 A+

An effective way to document business processes is to look at existing standards that require such documentation. For example, ISO-9000 and Sarbanes-Oxley specify the kinds of documentation required to meet those standards, the structures for which are freely available or, sometimes, purchasable for a modest fee. For computer-oriented documentation, you can use Military-Standard-498, the IEEE standards, or standards from other countries in which you will be doing business.

While not entirely essential, it can be helpful to include diagrams within documentation as a means of illustrating before and after states. This not only provides context as to why certain work was performed, but also ensures correct reassembly in the event any component of a network system had to be removed for repair.

1102: 4.2 A+

Change management includes an initial request form wherein the requested change is detailed along with the rationale for the change. Once the change has been approved, the date and time for the change to be initiated must also be documented. Any systems that might be affected by the change, even minimally affected, should be documented and, perhaps most importantly, a risk analysis that details any risks associated with the change should be conducted to assign a risk level to the proposed change.

Purpose of the Change

1102: 4.2 A+

Stating the purpose of the change is necessary for both employees and customers. Imagine being a regular customer for a business that provides IT support. If that company suddenly changed how service calls were received, estimated, or executed, you would likely be upset, or at least confused. Now imagine being the employee who now must change the way the work is performed and answer questions from customers regarding those changes. By stating the purpose of the change clearly, as well as providing a brief outline for how the change is to be implemented, the company provides transparency to interested parties.

Scope of the Change

1102: 4.2 A+

The word *scope* denotes the boundaries of a change, and its purpose is to provide some level of control to avoid the spread or growth of change ideas. Additionally, the statement of scope specifies how the change is to be measured, generally with paired indicators to keep the results honest. For example, revenue, or income, is often paired with a standard gross margin (a statement of profit) to determine the profitability of a company and how much profit is being made. In software development, lines of code are often paired against the number of defects per line of code.

Risk Analysis

1102: 4.2 A+

A *risk analysis*, sometimes called a *risk assessment*, is the identification of potential issues that could impact a business or organization negatively. There are typically six steps in conducting risk analysis: identify hazards, decide who or what could be harmed, evaluate risk and decide how to control, record and implement findings, review analysis, and update if necessary. In many cases, risk is categorized according to a risk level using a risk matrix, which organizes risks into defined impact levels. For example, an organization may categorize risk according to the following levels of impact to a system:

- **Catastrophic**: Refers to changes that stop or severely hinder an organization's functionality
- **Major**: Refers to changes that have a major negative impact on an organization or its revenue
- **Significant**: Refers to changes that cause a loss of productivity or significant financial burden
- **Minimal**: Refers to changes that create minor inconveniences for employees or may require additional changes to be made
- **None**: Refers to changes that have little to no impact on an organization

A+ 1102: 4.2

Plan for Change

Once the change, scope, and risk factors have been assessed, the change-management team should create a plan to enhance their ability to track progress. The plan should have regular milestones that allow the team to calculate the current state and make in-progress adjustments to align with the reality of the project. This approach suggests the team should have a documented process that defines the steps they must take to realign their plan. These regular milestones are both reviews and anticipations, looking both backward and forward. When drafting a plan, it should include the previously discussed elements as well as the *project lead*, which is the responsible staff member overseeing the change, as well as guidelines for evaluating the change in a sandbox environment, if needed. Sandbox testing is usually only implemented if new software is being installed. By testing in a sandbox environment, technicians can run the software without putting their computers or the network at risk.

A+ 1102: 4.2

End-User Acceptance

End-user acceptance is sometimes called *customer buy-in* and is similar to the transparency discussed previously. Consider the same scenario that was presented in the Purpose of the Change section; the change would be counterproductive if it causes resistance from either the employees involved or the downstream stakeholders such as customers and suppliers. Convincing end-users to accept changes may be the most difficult part of change management.

A+ 1102: 4.2

Change Board

A *change board* is typically a team of appointed individuals who have the responsibility for approval or rejection of changes. In most cases, all changes must receive approval from the change board before any process begins. Approaches that are more formal use terminologies such as *configuration management*, which includes the concepts of configuration identification, control, status and accounting, and auditing. Small changes typically do not require this level of formality, although formalizing the process is unlikely to yield negative results. Regardless of the perceived size of the change, all changes should be documented.

A+ 1102: 4.2

Backout Plan

A *backout plan*, also called a *rollback plan*, is a plan or process that restores a given situation to its original or earlier state in the event of undesired results. Each milestone review should incorporate an *escape point*, which occurs when measurements indicate you are not achieving the results defined in the documented plan. Once an escape point is activated, the team will execute a backout plan designed to minimize the negative consequences of the project.

Document Changes

Every change should be documented. With computer software, this can be accomplished using version-control tools. Hardware changes call for changes in drawings and material control systems, and organizational changes should follow a known standard, such as ISO-9000. Undocumented change opens the door to out-of-control modifications, about which the organization may not be aware.

24.4 Employability Skills

Employers often look for a particular set of skills or traits when seeking new employees. In general, skills needed to perform job functions can be learned or enhanced through training, but soft skills cannot. ***Soft skills*** are the skills used to communicate and work well with others and are considered essential ***employability skills***, which are skills that help an individual find a job, perform well in the workplace, and gain success in a job or career. These types of skills are not specific to one career and are transferable to any type of position. Examples of desirable employability skills include

- communication skills;
- body language;
- attitude;
- cultural sensitivity;
- punctuality;
- attentiveness;
- listening skills;
- telephone skills;
- writing skills;
- professionalism; and
- teamwork.

A+ Note

On the CompTIA A+ Exams, there may be questions related to communication skills. Generally, the best answer to the question is one that serves as an example of "good manners."

1102: 4.7 A+

Communication Skills

Communication skills are vital to support roles and are often the area in which computer technicians will most likely have the greatest room for improvement. Communication with a customer is not limited to an actual conversation; it includes other forms, such as body language and attitude. Although some communication skills are unspoken, they present a clear message to customers about your level of willingness and concern for fixing their problems.

The secret to a successful business is repeat customers, and the secret to having repeat customers is customer satisfaction. Customers are satisfied when you are helpful, courteous, and express genuine sincerity when dealing with their problems and complaints. This may sound like a simple task, but one slip of your tongue while you are frustrated could mean the difference between success and failure in customer relations.

When communicating with customers and clients, always speak clearly and concisely and avoid using technical jargon or acronyms. You may think using such language makes you sound smarter or more knowledgeable, but it can actually break down the confidence of the customer by making them feel less knowledgeable. The customer or client should feel comfortable while engaged in a conversation with you. If using industry terminology is unavoidable, try to explain what the terms mean or rephrase the explanation in a way anyone would understand.

Always begin your conversation with a warm greeting. For example, "Good morning, what can I do to be of service to you?" While engaged in conversation with customers or clients, use positive words to establish a can-do attitude, and use reinforcing statements such as, "We should have this fixed in no time," or "This is a very common problem. Many people have trouble at first." Do whatever you can to build the customers' self-esteem and confidence in both you and your company. The following are some good and bad examples of statements used when communicating with a customer or client:

Good examples:

- "Yes, we can fix that."
- "No problem, we can handle that."
- "Yes, we fix that type of problem all the time."
- "If you have any more problems, please do not hesitate to call."
- "You are no bother. This is what I am here for."

Bad examples:

- "I hope we can help you."
- "I have never fixed that type of problem before."
- "I do not know, but I'll try."
- "I will be busy later, so we should get this finished now."

Body Language

Body language is nonverbal messaging sent through gestures, facial expressions, and posture. It can say more than the spoken word and reveal your true feelings. For example, as an employee, you may say, "How may I help you?" However, if you continue to work on a computer and avoid eye contact with the customer, you are sending a nonverbal message of, "I am very busy right now and do not have time for your problem." If you greet a person with a smile or handshake, you warmly say nonverbally, "I am open to your problem." On the other hand, if you greet the customer with arms folded across your chest and a scowl on your face, you are sending a completely different message. The following are key points to keep in mind about body language:

- Smile
- Maintain eye contact with the customer while discussing the issue
- Face the customer squarely
- Never look away from the customer or stare off at a distant point while conversing
- Do not fold your arms across your chest or take a defensive posture

By maintaining eye contact with the customer while discussing their problem, you tell that customer you are truly interested in helping them.

Fizkes/Shutterstock.com

When discussing a customer's problem, face them directly and squarely. Do not turn away or engage in other activities when you should be talking to the customer; they will appreciate your undivided attention. If another task presents itself and cannot be ignored, politely excuse yourself and arrange for the new task to be completed at the next available opportunity. For example, imagine you are working at a help desk and talking to a customer. You are the only technician in the office, and the phone begins to ring. It is appropriate for you to apologize to the customer and excuse yourself to answer the phone, but you should either put the new customer on hold or ask if you can return the call before returning to the customer who was there first. Then, return the call at your next opportunity.

Attitude

1102: 4.7 A+

Attitude is easily perceived by a customer but very hard to define in objective terms, though every person knows a good or bad attitude when they experience it. For this chapter, the best definition of ***attitude*** is a subjective judgment of character made by a customer based on the perception of how a technician presents themself and meets customers' needs. It is critical to your success to always maintain a positive attitude while working with people. Without it, you may not have a job. It does not take long to earn a reputation for your attitude—good or bad.

Show the customer that their problem is your main concern by asking probing questions such as, "How long have you had this problem?" Take care not to come across as judgmental or indicate that the customer may have caused the problem, even if they did. Instead, use training techniques and suggestions to help the customer avoid the problem in the future.

A customer or fellow worker will feel you are not interested if you do not give them your full attention. For example, when working on a project, always stop your work to talk to a customer, which gives the customer a feeling of importance, shows that you care about their problem, and earns their confidence. It will also keep you from making an error on your project because you are distracted.

Cultural Sensitivity

1102: 4.7 A+

Cultural sensitivity is the knowledge, awareness, and acceptance of other people's culture and cultural identities. There is never a good reason to antagonize a customer, and using the correct cultural language is an easy way to avoid a problem. Whenever possible, try to use gender-neutral language by referring to an issue as "the customer's problem" or "their problem," instead of "his problem" or "her problem." Similarly, use appropriate professional titles, whenever applicable, and if working with a customer or vendor in a different country, use their preferred titles. If you are meeting with a religious client or clergy member, you should prepare by researching the appropriate titles and references.

Cultural awareness is an understanding of the differences and similarities between one's culture and the culture of another person or group. It is important to learn how a person's culture influences how they live each day and the life decisions they make. ***Cultural intelligence***, often abbreviated as ***CQ***, is the ability to adapt to unfamiliar cultural situations, ***not*** a measure of the intellectual capability of a person or the intelligence of those in a particular culture. An individual with high cultural intelligence is aware of values, beliefs, and attitudes of those from a different culture and can change their own personal behaviors to better match. Since the ability to change personal behaviors requires cultural awareness, the link between cultural awareness and cultural intelligence is inherent.

Cultural competency is the acknowledgment of cultural differences and the ability to adapt one's communication style to send and receive messages successfully despite those differences. Think of cultural competency as a two-step process.

The first step requires a person to be aware of cultural barriers, which is the development of cultural awareness. The second step requires taking necessary precautions to overcome those barriers, which is the application of cultural intelligence. Striving for cultural competence in any given situation will surely help you navigate potential communication or cultural barriers you may encounter on the job.

A+ 1102: 4.7

Punctuality

Put simply, *punctuality* is being on time, and being punctual can set you apart as a concerned professional. As the adage states, "If you are on time, you are already late." Early arrival provides extra time to account for traffic mishaps and gives you an opportunity for a final check of appearance, tool kit, and attitude. However, unexpected events are a part of life, and there will be times when you are unable to hold an appointment. In these instances, be sure to contact the customer as soon as possible and inform them that you are running late. *Never* wait until the time of appointment to reach out to the customer.

A+ 1102: 4.7

Attentiveness

Being *attentive* simply means giving someone else your undivided attention. Distractions are a part of life, but professionals do not allow distractions to interrupt their work, especially in the presence of a client or customer. Conducting personal business during work can quickly tarnish your professional demeanor and reputation. While on the job, you should avoid taking personal calls, reading or sending text messages, viewing social media, talking to other people while interacting with customers, and other personal interruptions. In the event of an emergency or if a phone call must be answered, ask the customer if it is okay for you to accept the call and always apologize for the inconvenience. If you must research something on a mobile device, apologize to the customer again and explain that you must conduct some research.

A+ 1102: 4.7

Listening Skills

Listening skills are the most important trait listed by employers in surveys conducted to identify the skills most desired in customer support. Nearly all employers agree that employees who work with clients and customers must have excellent listening skills, which seems like such a simple task. So how is it possible not all people have good listening skills? Many people tend to think ahead of the customer and miss important details as a result. Avoiding this habit will keep your customers from feeling inadequate. The following is a list of guidelines to put into practice:

- Always maintain eye contact while listening.
- Avoid distractions while listening, and do not try to perform other tasks while the customer or client is talking to you. Focus on the speaker.
- Never eat or drink while talking with a customer.
- Always allow customers or clients to complete their sentences. Do not cut them off or interrupt them by trying to anticipate what they are going to say.
- Restate the problem to the customer or client. This will ensure that you understand the issue or problem.

Consult the International Listening Association website, which is dedicated to listening skills. The website provides many interesting facts, such as only seven percent of the meaning in a conversation is transmitted by actual words.

Telephone Skills

Telephone etiquette is using good manners when speaking on the telephone. Many of the same skills used in face-to-face communication also apply to telephone support. Always speak clearly and concisely and avoid trade jargon, slang, acronyms, or sophisticated technical terminology. Customers are not typically sophisticated computer users and are frequently intimidated by your conversation. Always use language that anyone can understand, no matter their technical background. Customers will not be impressed by your usage of technical terms, and if you want to impress a customer, use terms that express your sincere desire to help with their problem.

Never engage in other activities while talking to the customer or client. A person can always tell when someone is not focused on their conversation. If the customer feels you are not fully engaged with the conversion, they will get the sense that you are not truly concerned with their problem. This will lead to them getting upset or frustrated.

Always avoid using speakerphone, as this only confirms that you are not paying attention to the caller. If you must be "hands-free," use a headset or wireless Bluetooth device; this way, the customer will feel that they are the focus of your conversation. Unless it is necessary to use the computer or remotely access the customer's computer, keep your hands off the keyboard. Customers can hear that you are using the keyboard and may conclude that it does not have to do with their problem.

It may sound foolish, but smiling while on the phone with a customer can help put the customer at ease and reassure them that you are interested in helping. A person on the other end of the telephone conversation can perceive when a person is happy on the telephone, which is interpreted as a feeling that the support person is pleased to hear from the customer and wants to help.

Writing Skills

Writing skills reflect a person's ability to use good manners and proper grammar when communicating in written form. Writing is a part of all customer support and technician duties. As a customer support representative, you will either write by hand on repair tickets or enter specifics about a repair into a software program. Content typically consists of a description of the problem and the repair procedure used to fix it. Often, your writing and documentation of this information becomes valuable company information for problems encountered in the future.

Smiling while on the telephone can help you convey that you are pleased to hear from the customer and want to help.

Trzykropy/Shutterstock.com

When creating written communication, always use formal language based on standard English usage, which follows the accepted rules for spelling, grammar, and punctuation. All word-processing packages and software programs that require written responses have spelling- and grammar-checking software; use it to your advantage. When writing, avoid long sentences by limiting them to 15 to 20 words.

Always be polite in your correspondence, and *never* use sarcasm, as the customer or client may very well misinterpret your intent. Sarcasm is based on familiar personalities, and you are not familiar with all who might read your correspondence.

Another function of customer support may involve writing training manuals or a set of procedures for a company. Often, part of a contract for installing computer equipment and software involves training the customers on how to use the equipment. Many times, technical support personnel must write training packages to support the customer, and you may very well find yourself responsible for part of the written package.

E-Mail

In addition to general writing requirements, you will likely have to respond to customer and client e-mails, either through your e-mail client or the help desk software package. In fact, much of your day may be consumed by responding to e-mails from customers and clients. When writing e-mails to customers and clients, avoid computer jargon, acronyms, and abbreviations, just as you would when speaking with a customer or when writing customer-facing materials. Communicating in writing with other technicians is not the same as communicating in writing with customers and clients. While it might be perfectly acceptable to use an acronym or abbreviation on a customer repair ticket, you should avoid acronyms and abbreviations when communicating with customers.

Automatic Responses

Using an automatic e-mail response can show customers or clients that you care about them and their problems. Automatic responses are programs provided by e-mail service providers that create an automatic response to a received e-mail. The response gives the illusion that someone has just read the e-mail sent by the customer or client and will be answering the request very soon. This allows for an immediate reply regardless of working hours. An automatic response can also be used to notify customers that you are out of the office for a brief time.

Internet Acronyms and Emoticons

Internet acronyms are very popular with all forms of electronic communication, but they should never be used in customer support communication. These acronyms save keystrokes, but their usage comes across as informal, and customers will likely question your professionalism if you include them. You may receive Internet acronyms or emoticons from customers, but you should never respond in these terms.

You should also avoid using **emoticons**, which are pictorial representations of faces or emotions made from keyboard symbols. The word is a combination of the words *emotion* and *icon*. Digital versions of emoticons are called *emojis* by various companies and users and are most often used to express emotions in e-mails, letters, and text messaging.

If you have trouble communicating with customers via e-mail, practice regularly in a business format. Try sending a few e-mails every day to friends and relatives using the principles previously discussed to sharpen your skills and receive feedback. The following is a list of key points you should always remember when communicating through e-mail with customers and clients:

- Check your e-mail regularly.
- Keep e-mails concise.

- Do not use emoticons or emojis.
- Limit the size of file attachments.
- *Never* use all capital letters in an e-mail to emphasize a word or phrase. If you must emphasize a word or phrase, use italics or an asterisk, for example, **this is very important**. Do not use bold or underline, as this can be misinterpreted as a link.
- Never send sensitive or inappropriate information in e-mail.
- Do not send personal greetings, jokes, or other materials that are not appropriate for the work environment.

> **A+ Note**
>
> There will often be one or two questions related to professionalism on the CompTIA A+ Exams. While one might think that the subject of professional dress would be obvious, some students always seem to try to justify their inappropriate dress as suitable for working on computers. Remember that you are not simply working on a computer; you are representing your employer.

Professionalism

Professionalism is the act of exhibiting appropriate character, judgment, and behavior by a person who is trained to perform a job. It is a businesslike characteristic reflected in a person's attitude and dress as well as an organization's décor and general atmosphere. This section explores various aspects of professionalism in an employee and work environment.

Professional Image

1102: 4.7 A+

Businesses and their employees are often judged by a customer's first impression of them. For example, if a technician looks professional, the customer feels confident in the technician, but if the technician looks sloppy, dirty, unkempt, or bizarre, the customer or client might have less confidence about the technician. Dressing professionally means dressing appropriately, and in the work environment, there are two distinct types of acceptable dress: formal business and business casual. In general, formal business attire usually means a suit with a skirt or pantsuit with sensibly heeled shoes for women and a collared shirt and tie with dress pants and leather shoes for men. However, as a computer technician, business casual is typically appropriate. Business casual generally means a polo or collared shirt (often with no tie), dress or casual slacks, leather shoes, and, in rare cases, tennis shoes.

Many businesses provide shirts for their support staff, which implies a particular dress code. When working in customer support, a polo-style shirt is most appropriate, but be aware that some companies require more formal attire when dealing with customers and clients at their locations. In general, you should match the attire of the given environment, and if in doubt, ask a manager about the dress code.

Unisex dress refers to the same attire for everyone and is typically the best and safest choice. As a computer technician, you will likely be crawling on the floor or reaching behind desks. As such, employees should never wear clothing that is too revealing if they must work in this environment. The following are some tips that should become a part of your professional image:

- Dress professionally. Clean, neat dress pants and a shirt with a collar are much more appropriate than a T-shirt with a slogan, especially if the T-shirt has a controversial slogan or image printed on it.
- Hair should be neat and clean. Hair with spikes or wild colors might be trendy, but it may be considered unprofessional in the workplace.
- Speak to customers as a professional. Never use profane or inappropriate language or terms, even to emphasize certain points.
- Do not eat, drink, or use tobacco products while interacting with a customer.

Many students feel that if they have exceptional technical skills, they will never be fired. Nothing could be further from the truth. More employees have lost their jobs because of their unprofessional manner than from technical incompetence. Most employers will tolerate employers having average technical skills but will not accept employees who conduct themselves in an unprofessional manner, as it reflects poorly on the company. When employers contact other professionals for hiring recommendations, they typically request someone who can work well with people rather than request the "smartest" or most technically skilled person. The most important thing to the employer is an employee's image and personality. Employers rarely, if ever, call a second time if an unprofessional person comes in for an interview. Remember, the required skills for the job can often be taught or trained, but in most cases, professionalism cannot.

A+ 1102: 2.6, 4.7

Customers' Confidential Materials

Computers are used by a wide range of people and contain a wide assortment of information. Customer devices may contain confidential information, such as bank account numbers and balances, private e-mails or correspondence, customer client lists, Social Security numbers, medical information, and business information.

Customers and clients expect privacy, and violating their privacy is a breach of trust that will cause, at a minimum, the loss of future business. It will likely damage your business reputation and may also result in legal action. For example, patient medical records are considered confidential and are protected by federal and state laws. The same is true for intellectual properties such as inventions, formulas, and some forms of business data such as customers' personal and financial information. Releasing this information via e-mail, text message, or any other form of communication to unauthorized persons or without cause will almost certainly result in legal action.

Some businesses require computer support personnel to sign a nondisclosure agreement (NDA) before working on business computers or before being hired as an employee. The agreement provides for the legal protection of proprietary information such as customer lists, trade secrets, financial information, business strategies, and intellectual property. Violating the agreement can result in job loss and financial punishment. In short, a computer technician has no reason to be viewing customer or client personal information except if requested by the customer or client, such as during data recovery.

A+ 1102: 4.6

There are specific types of regulated data for which policies must be in place. The first of these is **personally identifiable information (PII)**, which is any data that can identify a person, including a Social Security number, credit card information, or address. Personally identifiable information also includes personal government-issued information such as driver's license numbers and passport details. The next type of data that is heavily regulated is payment card data. The *Payment Card Industry Data Security Standard (PCI DSS)* is a regulation that details how businesses or organizations are to manage credit-card transactions and information. For companies that do business overseas, adherence to the *European Parliament and Council's General Data Protection Regulation (GDPR)* must be ensured, which is similar to the regulations regarding PII data. Lastly, companies must have policies in place to manage **protected health information (PHI)**, which is a person's demographic information, medical history, testing results, mental health information, and other healthcare information. Information that falls into one or more of these regulated data types must be managed securely and discreetly and adhere to the chain of custody rules, which will be presented later in this chapter.

Work Environment

The image of the working environment is also critical and often a direct result of the employees' efforts to maintain a professional image. The work environment must represent a professional atmosphere. If the work environment is to be visited by customers and other employees, it should be maintained so as not to be offensive to others. For example, you may enjoy a particular style of music while you are working; however, it may not be the choice of many customers. The customer should not be offended by loud music of any generation. In general, it is best to entirely avoid music in the work environment where customers may be present, except for soft, neutral background music.

Also, be aware that listening to music through earphones is offensive to many people. You should be concentrating on the customer or client. This applies when working at a client's workstation and in the corporate environment as a whole. The following are some tips to help you maintain a professional environment in your workplace:

- Keep your location and workstation clean and well organized.
- Never keep food containers, cups, and general trash on counters or work areas.
- Do not play music that is not in the mainstream, and do not play any music at high volumes.
- The workplace is not a social club; do not visit with friends around the store or workspace.
- Do not display inappropriate posters, pictures, or signs. You may think they are fun or entertaining, but not all customers share your view.

Managing Difficult Situations

A+ 1102: 4.7

When a client is angry and upset, they will vent emotions toward the person who represents the company or problem. Dealing with difficult people requires patience and composure, and it is important not to take complaints personally. Never react to a difficult customer, but rather listen and respond with empathy. ***Empathy*** is the ability to understand another person's feelings and their situation. You will encounter many situations that warrant a statement like, "I can understand how this problem is frustrating you." You should always show empathy and never dismiss a customer's problem, even if it seems trivial to you.

A coworker or customer might normally be very pleasant and fun to be around until a situation causes that person to be very angry. While in an angry state, the person may say things that they normally would never say to another person. Arguing with an upset person will only make things worse.

Your job is to defuse the situation by letting the customer vent frustrations, so use a calm and assuring voice when responding to the customer. Allow the customer to talk and explain the issue; then, at an opportune time, simply say, "Let me see what I can do to resolve this problem." When you start to work on the problem or tell the customer what you are planning to do, ensure it is all right with the customer.

If the customer continues to vent, find out what will make the customer happy. For example, a customer may have brought their computer to the shop several times for the same problem. It may or may not be the same problem, but that is the customer's perception. Find out what will make the customer happy by asking for a description of their ideal solution.

The customer may want their bill adjusted or to have costs waived for the present repair. If you are not authorized to waive the costs, simply say, "I will see what we can do for you," and then check with your supervisor. If a person is upset, it will only become worse if the person thinks that they are not being taken seriously.

Is the Customer Always Right?

A+ 1102: 4.7

There is a saying in business: "The customer is always right." This is true most of the time, but there are situations when this sentiment does not apply, such as if a customer or client asks you to do something unethical or illegal. For example, a customer may request you write a receipt for more value than the actual cost of the repair, or a customer may ask you to violate some copyright law. Under no circumstances should you do something that violates a law, ethical practices, or company guidelines or policy.

Another situation that can arise is a customer using inappropriate language, raising their voice, or threatening you. In many cases, you are unlikely to be able to solve this customer's problem, and you should never have to fear for your life or bodily harm. If the customer threatens you, politely ask the person to leave, and if the customer will not, call the police or security. This also applies if a client or customer is intoxicated or becomes abusive. An intoxicated or violent customer is not only a threat to you and the business, but also to any other people present.

A+ 1102: 4.7

Follow-Up

A follow-up helps to build a good relationship with the customer or client and should be performed after you have had a break in contact with them. For example, after a customer's problem has been fixed, follow up a few days after completing the repair to see if the customer is satisfied and all went well. This technique improves service and builds a client's trust. Customers and clients love the fact that someone is checking whether the problem was handled in a timely fashion and if they were dealt with professionally.

A+ 1102: 4.7

Your Word

One of the most important assets you have is your word, and it costs you nothing. Your word or promise can make or break your client relationship, so it is imperative that you be a person of your word and let it be part of your reputation. Suppose you tell a customer you will contact them with a repair estimate within 24 hours, but you run into a problem with a vendor. The vendor does not respond to your inquiry, so in turn, you do not have the customer's estimate ready. If you told the customer you would call the next morning, do so, even if it is to say you do not have the estimate yet. It is important that you be a person of your word.

Similarly, you should strive to keep any promises made to a client or customer. If you say you will arrive in the morning, be there. The client may have rearranged their schedule to accommodate you. If you have a problem, call ahead, and always apologize. However, it is important not to make a habit of this type of behavior. Regularly missing or rescheduling appointments can lead to customers thinking you are unreliable, which you do not want to become your business signature.

A+ 1102: 4.7

Contracts

If a company is large, it may be necessary to create a written document or contract to be sure everyone has the same expectations. The contract should contain a description of the work to be performed, the estimated or actual cost, the estimate of completion time, and other terms on which the two parties agree. By having a customer signature before work, you always protect yourself against a misinterpretation of expectations. A client or customer should never receive less than they agreed to. At times, they may receive more, but never less.

Teamwork

Teamwork is the cooperative efforts by individual team members to achieve a goal. In this case, the team goal of customer support is customer satisfaction. When you work as part of a team, you place the common goal of the team above your own goals, such as recognition and promotion. Teamwork is an essential component of a successful business.

As a team member, you must be willing to help other team members and share your expertise and knowledge with others. For example, a customer calls and asks about the status of their computer. If the person assigned to repair the computer is out of work that day, you should check the job ticket to review the status of the repair to help the customer, even if it is not your assigned repair. Make a note of the customer call and record your actions. For example, you might write a note on the ticket such as, "Customer called and asked status update about repair and was informed that the computer is awaiting parts and should be ready in a day or two." Then, sign the note.

When working as a member of a team, you should be willing to share your knowledge with other team members. Knowledge is not just limited to technical issues. It also covers company procedures or any other bit of knowledge that might help another team member perform their duties.

Job Protection

A common, yet unattractive, trait in the business world occurs when a person will not share their knowledge with another team member. The concept is referred to as *job protection* and often happens when one person is the only person who knows how to perform specific tasks and is not willing to share this information or train another person. The person thinks they are secure in their position with the company if they are the only person who knows how to perform that task.

In reality, this type of person is jeopardizing their position with the company, as the company management or owner will not like the fact that an employee is not willing to share knowledge for the good of the company. If the person is unwilling to share knowledge or to help other team members, they will most likely find themself looking for other employment. Remember that working as a team requires supporting other team members, especially by sharing knowledge and reinforcing good work. If you are not willing to function as a team member, then you will likely not be a member of the team for very long.

Helping Team Members

You must be willing to do more than only what you have been assigned. For example, a collection of repair tickets might be divided among team members, each of whom is assigned four tickets. If you finish your repairs before anyone else, you should not assume that you are done for that day; instead, ask your coworkers if they need help with their work.

Employers do not like to see employees who are doing just enough to get by or wasting company time and prefer to see employees going beyond their assigned duties. When you finish your assigned tasks, you should immediately inform your supervisor and volunteer to help other team members with their assigned duties. This will not only impress your employer, but also be appreciated by fellow team members. Remember, the *company* goal is to repair all the customers' computers, not just the ones assigned to you that day.

24.5 Managing Prohibited Content or Activity

When a technician services or repairs a computer or is maintaining a network system, they may encounter prohibited content or activity. In these instances, it is the technician's responsibility to report illegal activity and content to their immediate supervisor, and in some cases, directly to law enforcement.

Prohibited content and activity can be any one of numerous activities and content, including anything illegal, malicious, harassing, invasive of personal privacy, libelous, pornographic, offensive, and infringing on copyright. Keep in mind this is not an exhaustive list. A good rule of thumb is to report anything you think could be prohibited or illegal content.

It is not just data or the network system at risk of being compromised. Organizations can be held responsible for the actions of their employees or members of the organization. For example, if harassing e-mails are discovered and no action is taken, the victim may choose to retain an attorney and file a lawsuit claiming they were forced to work in a hostile work environment. If the company has not taken any corrective actions, it can be held legally responsible for the actions of the employee creating and distributing the harassing e-mails.

Tech Tip

When you use your employer's equipment, such as computers and the network system, you no longer have the right to privacy as you do when using your computer at home. Employers have the right to monitor employee activities on the company computer as well as the network system.

Any person engaged in a prohibited activity or dealing in prohibited content can be issued a written reprimand for the offense, fired by their employer, or prosecuted for criminal activity in some cases. The following is a list of common prohibited activities and content. However, this is not a complete list of all prohibited activities and content.

- Engaging in illegal activities
- Distributing spam
- Soliciting or distributing personal information
- Collecting information from a minor
- Engaging in harmful, malicious, or harassing activity
- Discriminating against, bullying, or humiliating other people
- Accessing a person's computer or area of a network without authorization
- Interfering with or interrupting a network service
- Intentionally uploading viruses or other malicious programs

Companies, schools, and governmental agencies often include a long sample list in their company conduct or policy books. Additionally, most organizations have policy and procedure books that detail how a security incident is to be managed and provide examples of forms that must be completed for any incident that occurs. The procedure for handling incidents can be broken down into three general steps:

1. Identify precisely what happened when an unauthorized activity or prohibited material was discovered.
2. Write a complete detailed description of the incident and the procedures you followed.
3. Document the chronological order of the handling of evidence from the time it is first discovered until it reaches trial or conclusion.

A security event form can be used for the first—and possibly the second—step of the procedure. See Figure 24-7 for an example security event form. If additional information must be documented and the security event form does not provide enough space, additional written documentation can be added to the form.

A routine incident typically does not require much detailed information. For example, when malware attacks a computer or network system, a simple remedy may be provided by one of the many antivirus vendors. The malware is removed, and normal operation is restored. In contrast, an incident involving theft or breach of security causing the loss of sensitive data may require much more detailed information than a routine incident, and in this case, you should provide as much detail as possible in the documentation. Normally, additional pages may be required to record all pertinent facts concerning the incident.

If the incident results in legal action by law enforcement, you may need to recall important facts about the incident later, and it is not unusual for a technician to be called in for a legal deposition or to testify at a date one to two years after the incident has occurred. Memories fade, and the only way to be accurate and detailed about the incident is to record as much detail as possible when the incident first occurs. For this reason, it is always best to follow all policies and security best practices as completely as possible.

Once law enforcement becomes involved in an event, they take over the responsibility for managing the evidence or chain of custody. They will most likely collect the original incident report, so you should make a copy for your records.

Experience is the best teacher for determining whether an incident is considered routine or serious. This is why, as a new technician, you should rely on your supervisor's judgment about how to proceed after the initial report is created. Large companies and organizations have policies established as to how to manage most security incidents. Be sure to review your company's security policy publications, so you know how to respond to an incident.

Computer Security Event Form

Person who reported incident:

Name ________________ Title ____________________ Department ___________

Phone ________________ E-mail __________________

Location of incident: Building _________________ Room __________________

Time incident was reported: Date __________________ Time _________________

	Virus/Malware		Social Engineering		User Account Compromised
	Hoax		System Misuse		Network Intrusion
	Theft/Loss		Physical Security Violation		Other

Virus/Malware: Describe virus/malware in general terms and the impact on the system.

Technical or Physical Vulnerability: Describe the nature and effect of the incident in general terms.

Equipment Lost or Stolen: Provide details of data or equipment lost or stolen.

Host/Network Information

IP Address	Host Name	MAC Address

Suspected Source of Intrusion or Unauthorized Activity

Source IP Address	Resolved IP Host Name	Application used to verify

Goodheart-Willcox Publisher

Figure 24-7 A security event form can be used for reporting prohibited content or activity.

First Response/Incident Response

1102: 4.6 A+

The first response is to identify what happened when an unauthorized activity or prohibited material was discovered. A security incident could entail discovering phishing e-mail, malware, unauthorized access to a user account, removal of data, or any activity considered to be an unauthorized use of organizational equipment. Many organizations routinely run software applications that detect security problems and breaches, but organizations can also monitor employee activities on a network or workstation and generate reports containing the date, time, and type of activity. For example, there are software applications that monitor user Internet activity and record the locations visited, the amount of time at the location, and even the type of transaction conducted at a location, such as a purchase or e-mail and chat room activity. It is normal for an organization to have employees, students, or other users of the computer system sign agreements describing permissible network and workstation conduct. After the incident is properly identified or classified, the incident must be documented.

A+ Note

The CompTIA A+ Exams require knowledge of how to respond to a security incident. Questions may require knowledge of the chain of custody, how to respond to an incident, and what constitutes an incident.

Identify the Issue

Sometimes, identifying the issue can be the most difficult part of problem-solving, particularly when you are dealing with an emergency. Human tendency is to use what we already know to label the problem. Unfortunately, our labels are often wrong. If the situation is not an emergency, take the time to verify that your assumptions are correct, and then use the most appropriate nomenclature for the problem.

A+ 1102: 4.6

Report through Proper Channels

If you are part of an enterprise, make sure you communicate the situation to the proper individuals. Make sure you document what you are doing, especially if e-mail is available. Use of paper or electronic documentation provides an audit trail for subsequent investigation and post-intervention analyses. Often, this means informing not only your manager, but also law enforcement if the incident violates any laws.

A+ 1102: 4.6

Preserve Data and Devices

Any time you deal with a problem or opportunity, assume that chain of custody is important. Document every handoff and keep the evidence protected from modification or inadvertent damage. All hardware items and printouts should be labeled and dated by each person handling them. This often means making a copy of a hard drive to preserve its data integrity and redundancy.

A+ 1102: 4.6

Documentation

You should write a complete, detailed description of the incident, including what procedures were followed. Review your organization's established policies and procedures for reporting an incident and complete any necessary forms. This may include completing a security event form like the one shown in Figure 24-7 to record information directly related to the event. The collection of all security events can be reviewed later and serve as the basis for making decisions affecting security, such as a change in established policies and procedures.

A+ 1102: 4.6

Chain of Custody

A **chain of custody** is a method of preserving, tracking, and ensuring the integrity of evidence. You cannot simply collect evidence and leave it on your desk or in some other unsecured area where anyone can tamper with or take it. A chain of custody includes documentation of the chronological order of the handling of evidence from the time it is first discovered until it reaches trial or a conclusion. The chain of custody ensures that the evidence is unchanged and as close as possible to its original condition when it was first discovered and secured. A chain of custody form, such as the example shown in Figure 24-8, tracks the evidence by listing every person who took possession of it; it also details the time and date it was taken and the method used to store it securely.

Evidence can appear in many forms. For example, the evidence of a security breach may be simply a copy of the event captured by a software application, such as Microsoft Event Viewer or by a commercial product. In the case of a software application, a copy can be made to a flash drive or disc, which is then sealed in a labeled evidence bag and secured in a locked file drawer or cabinet to which only you have access. Another example is the unauthorized use of a company cell phone or tablet. The device can be confiscated and secured until it is needed as evidence of the incident.

Computer Evidence Chain of Custody

To be completed by initial collector

Evidence collected by (name): ____________________

Date/time collected: ____________________

Description of evidence: ____________________

____

Collection method (operating system, utility, commands, etc.):

____

____

Where is evidence originally stored? ____________________

How is evidence originally secured? ____________________

Collector signature: ____________________

Evidence copy history:

Date	Copied By	Copy Method	Disposition of original and all copies

Transfer History:

Date	Released by (print name, sign)	Received by (Print name, sign)	How is evidence secured?

Goodheart-Willcox Publisher

Figure 24-8 A computer evidence chain of custody form should be used whenever unethical, illegal, or prohibited content or activity is discovered on a device.

Security Training

It is important that *all* members of an organization, not just the security team and technicians, be trained in responding to a security incident. All members of the organization must be made aware of what is considered unacceptable activity when using the organization's devices and network. The most common response from members of an organization when questioned about an unauthorized activity is, "I did not know that I was not allowed to do that," or simply "I did not know."

Chapter Summary

24.1 Customer Support

- There are several standard organization models for customer support. Some of these models are a help desk, call center, small business service counter, depot technician, and corporate enterprise support.
- A help desk or call center is usually the first contact point for service and can belong to a single company or be part of a call center; a call center typically provides support for more than one company or product.
- A depot technician is one who performs repair work usually covered by warranty.
- Level-one support is the initial technical support contact. Most problems can be corrected at this level.
- Level-two support is when the problem is elevated to a person with more experience or expertise than the first contact person.
- Level-three support is typically provided outside the immediate technical support location.
- Customer support is often outsourced to a specialized technical-support company that may reside in the United States or be located overseas. A software or hardware company may find it more cost-effective to outsource level-one support and opt to provide level-two support on a local basis.
- Most businesses have a Frequently Asked Questions (FAQs) section posted on their websites that is designed to answer the most commonly asked customer questions and inquiries.

24.2 Documentation Types

- A *knowledge base* is a repository for tech support or troubleshooting articles and can be effective for capturing counterproductive events, machine failures, and software issues.
- Articles for external users are normally written either by a company employee or a certified expert and are designed for those interested in self-service. In many cases, the steps outlined in knowledge base articles are the same steps used in level-one support.
- For internal users, a knowledge base contains articles relevant to company or organizational processes and are often referred to as *job aids*.
- The *Failure Mode and Effects Analysis (FMEA)* format is a structure that identifies and addresses potential problems and the effects of those problems before the problem occurs.
- Incident documentation is a means for recording undesirable events, actions taken, and the results of those actions.
- Part of the regulatory and compliance policy for any mid-level to large business is covered by the Sarbanes-Oxley Act, which has stringent requirements primarily for accounting but also for other business functions.
- An *acceptable use policy (AUP)*, sometimes called a *usage agreement*, is a set of guidelines used and defined most often by the administrator of a network or service.
- Traditionally, a business has two kinds of hardware inventory: *capital inventory* for depreciable items with multiyear life, and *expenses inventory* for consumable items.

24.3 Change Management Best Practices

- Change management refers to guidance from a business or organization that prepares, equips, and supports internal employees to adopt or incorporate changes.
- Best practices for change management include documenting business processes, stating the purpose of the change, outlining the scope of the change, performing risk analysis, planning for change, allowing end-user acceptance, creating and maintaining a change board, drafting a backout plan, and documenting the changes once they take place.
- The word *scope* denotes the boundaries of a change, and its purpose is to provide some level of control to avoid the spread or growth of change ideas.
- A *risk analysis*, sometimes called a *risk assessment*, is the identification of potential issues that could impact a business or organization negatively.

24.4 Employability Skills

- *Employability skills* are skills that help an individual find a job, perform well in the workplace, and gain success in a job or career. These types of skills are not specific to one career and are transferable to any type of position.
- Effective communication skills include various aspects of communication, both verbal and nonverbal.
- When communicating with customers and clients, always speak clearly and concisely and avoid using technical jargon or acronyms.
- Begin with a warm greeting, use positive words, and do whatever you can to build the customer's self-esteem and confidence in both you and your company.
- Body language and mannerisms can say more than the spoken word and reveal your true feelings.
- Attitude is a subjective judgment of character made by the customer based on the perception of how the technician presents themself and meets the customers' needs. Every person knows a good attitude or a bad attitude when they experience it.
- Whenever possible, try to use gender-neutral language. Similarly, use appropriate professional titles, whenever applicable, and if working with a customer or vendor in a different county, use the titles preferred in their country.
- *Cultural awareness* is an understanding of the differences and similarities between one's culture and the culture of another person or group.
- *Cultural competency* is the acknowledgment of cultural differences and the ability to adapt one's communication style to send and receive messages successfully despite those differences.
- Punctuality can set you apart as a concerned professional.
- *Listening skills* are the most important trait listed by employers in surveys conducted to identify the skills most desired in customer support.
- Many of the same skills used in face-to-face communication also apply to telephone support.
- When creating written communication, always use formal language based on standard English usage, which follows the accepted rules for spelling, grammar, and punctuation.
- In addition to general writing requirements, you will likely have to respond to customer and client e-mails, either through your e-mail client or the help desk software package.

- Professionalism concerning a person is identified in a person's attitude and dress; in the work environment, it is identified in its décor and general atmosphere.
- Teamwork is the cooperative efforts by individual team members to achieve a goal.

24.5 Managing Prohibited Content or Activity

- The key steps for managing a prohibited activity or content incident are to precisely identify what happened when the unauthorized activity or prohibitive material was discovered, write a complete detailed description of the incident and the procedures you followed, and document the chronological order of the handling of evidence.

Review Questions

1. Differentiate among organization models for customer support.
2. List and describe three levels of support within a given organization.
3. Why might an organization outsource its customer service?
4. How can FAQs help supplement customer support?
5. Identify types of documentation that ensure best practices for customer and employee support.
6. What is a *knowledge base*?
7. What is an acceptable use policy?
8. What is the difference between capital inventory and expenses inventory?
9. What is *change management*?
10. List best practices for change management.
11. In terms of change management, what is the *scope* of a change?
12. Which part of change management is likely to be the most difficult?
13. Describe important employability skills.
14. Describe appropriate verbal communication with customers and clients.
15. What are the key points of body language you should use?
16. Differentiate between cultural awareness, cultural intelligence, and cultural competency.
17. Identify key steps for managing an incident involving prohibited content or activities.
18. Give at least five examples of prohibited activity or content, as related to computer use.
19. Define *chain of custody* and explain its importance in handling prohibited content or activities.
20. Within an organization, who should be training for responding to a security incident?

Sample A+ Exam Questions

1. Which is an example of level-one support?
   A. A software engineer at Microsoft
   B. A hardware engineer at Apple
   C. The FAQ section of a customer support website
   D. A live conversation with a level-one supervisor
2. It is 9:00 a.m. and you are repairing a customer's computer that must be ready by 3:00 p.m. because it was promised to the customer. The phone suddenly rings, and you answer to find that it is a new customer calling about a problem with their computer. Which is the best way to deal with customer support on the telephone?
   A. Do nothing except focus on the new customer and their problem. You should write down key points during the conversation, starting with their name.
   B. You should continue to work on computer repairs while listening to the customer. This is the most efficient use of time, and your supervisor will be pleased.
   C. Have the customer call back later after another employee comes into the shop.
   D. Tell the customer you are in the middle of an important repair and that you will return their call later in the day. Take down the customer's name and telephone number.
3. Which is the most expensive element of customer service?
   A. Employee wages
   B. Support software
   C. Support hardware
   D. Technical support articles and website access
4. The company you work for performs computer system repairs in addition to selling new computers and hardware. A repair ticket is completed at the time of repair, and the status of the repair is recorded on the ticket. Some notes recorded on the ticket describe when the repair was completed or when parts were ordered for the repair. A customer dropped off their computer at your company computer shop three days ago, and the repair technician is not currently available. You answer the phone and find the customer is calling to find out the status of the repair of their computer. What is the most appropriate response to their inquiry?
   A. Tell them their computer is being worked on, but the technician is not in today and will call them back as soon as possible.
   B. Tell them to hold for a minute while you check the status of the repair ticket.
   C. Tell them you are not the one that has been assigned to their repair and to call back later.
   D. Tell them to come by the shop and pick up the computer. The computer is most likely repaired, but if not, you can have it repaired before they get there.

5. Which of the following statements best describes the likely attitude of a customer support technician who is frowning or scowling while on the phone with a customer?
   A. It's really good to hear from you!
   B. How can I help you?
   C. I don't have time for your problem.
   D. I'm open to your problem.
6. When is it proper to use all uppercase letters in an e-mail?
   A. When emphasizing an important point
   B. When making a list of steps in sequential order
   C. When listing parts in an e-mail
   D. A message in all uppercase is never appropriate for an e-mail.
7. An irate customer calls and complains about how they brought their computer home to find it has the same problem it had before they brought it in for repair. What is the first thing you should do?
   A. Smile so that the customer will sense your willingness to help them.
   B. Let the customer finish speaking and venting their anger.
   C. Interrupt them by asking what it will take to make them satisfied.
   D. Hang up and hope they will call back when they are in a better mood.

8. A customer brings into the shop a computer exhibiting a problem you have never encountered before. Which of the following responses would be most appropriate?
   A. Yes, we can fix that.
   B. Yes, we fix that type of problem all the time.
   C. I've never fixed that type of problem before.
   D. I don't know if I can fix it, but I'll try.
9. You need to explain the cause of a boot failure to a customer. Which of the following explanations would build the customer's confidence in your company?
   A. A virus corrupted the MBR.
   B. A virus corrupted the master boot record.
   C. A virus corrupted the boot sector, which stores partition information.
   D. A virus corrupted an area of the hard drive that is required for startup.
10. A customer uses profane language because you will not write a receipt for more value than the actual cost of the repair. You can tell that the customer is intoxicated. What is the first thing you should do?
   A. Write the receipt for the amount they specify.
   B. Politely ask them to leave.
   C. Call the police.
   D. Respond with empathy.

Chapter 25

CompTIA A+ Certification Exams Preparation

Learning Outcomes

25.1 Summarize the characteristics, requirements, and format of the CompTIA A+ Certification Exams.
25.2 Identify strategies for preparing for the CompTIA A+ Certification Exams.
25.3 Evaluate your readiness for taking the CompTIA 220-1101 Exam.
25.4 Evaluate your readiness for taking the CompTIA 220-1102 Exam.

Key Terms

CompTIA A+ Certification Exam
examination objective

Overview

If you are reading this chapter, you are probably near the completion of your course. By now, you have gained foundational knowledge of computer service and repair and acquired many skills by performing the lab activities found in the *Computer Service and Repair Lab Manual.* You have certainly reached a milestone in your education in computer service and repair, and your next step, should you decide to make computer service and repair a career, is to become certified. Certification proves to a potential employer that you have the knowledge and skills needed to perform the typical job duties and tasks of a PC service technician.

A+ Note

Always check the CompTIA website for the latest news concerning the A+ Certification Exams, as the requirements for both Exams change frequently. Typically, CompTIA reviews the exams at least once a year, and minor changes are made to the objectives. Major changes to the examination objectives occur approximately every three years or following the release of the latest Windows operating system. The testing format also changes from time to time. While every attempt is made to provide you with the latest information in this textbook, changes do occur after the release of the textbook; your best source of exam information is the official CompTIA website at https://www.comptia.org.

25.1 A+ Certification Exams

The **CompTIA A+ Certification Exam** is an introductory computer-repair certification consisting of two tests: CompTIA A+ 220-1101 and the CompTIA A+ 220-1102. The CompTIA A+ 220-1101 Exam measures the fundamentals of computer technology, and the CompTIA A+ 220-1102 Exam measures the skills related to more advanced topics in computer technology. You must pass both exams to receive the CompTIA A+ Certification, which is valid for three years. You can keep your certification current either through the CompTIA Continuing Education Program, or by retaking the exams at the three-year boundary.

The two CompTIA A+ Certification Exams measure a candidate's competency equivalent to an entry-level IT professional with the approximate knowledge of at least 12 months of experience in the lab or field. Knowledge required to pass the exams is based on the ability to assemble components according to customer requirements; install, configure, and maintain devices, PCs, and software for end-users; understand the basics of networking and security; and properly and safely diagnose, resolve, and document common hardware and software issues while applying troubleshooting skills. Successful candidates will also provide appropriate customer support and understand the basics of virtualization, desktop imaging, and deployment.

CompTIA's website is the principal source for the **examination objectives**, which outline the required skills and knowledge needed to pass the exams. The objectives are derived from industry surveys that determine the actual job requirements of PC service technicians and categorized according to *domains*, or topic areas. The CompTIA A+ Certification Exam Objectives are *not* a comprehensive listing of all exam content and are instead meant to be used as a guide to the general test content; there can be material on the test not included in the exam objectives. Figure 25-1 lists the domains measured by each exam and the extent to which each domain is represented.

A+ Note

Always check the CompTIA website for the very latest information on the CompTIA A+ Certification Exam Objectives.

Content on the CompTIA A+ Exams is constantly being reviewed and updated, and the exams can change from the list of original objectives. The CompTIA organization always includes a disclaimer as part of the exam objectives, which says that the exam objectives are subject to change without notice. This means that you should always check the CompTIA website for the very latest test objectives before taking the exam.

CompTIA A+ Percentage of Examinations by Domain

Test	Domain	Percentage of Examination
220-1101	1.0 Mobile Devices	15%
220-1101	2.0 Networking	20%
220-1101	3.0 Hardware	25%
220-1101	4.0 Virtualization and Cloud Computing	11%
220-1101	5.0 Hardware and Network Troubleshooting	29%
220-1102	1.0 Operating Systems	31%
220-1102	2.0 Security	25%
220-1102	3.0 Software Troubleshooting	22%
220-1102	4.0 Operational Procedures	22%

Goodheart-Willcox Publisher

Figure 25-1 Each test has a different set of domain objectives, and each domain constitutes a certain percentage of the exam.

CompTIA A+ 220-1101 Exam

CompTIA A+ 220-1101 focuses mostly on hardware, devices, and hardware- and network-based troubleshooting. The only domain that is not hardware-centric is virtualization and cloud computing, which has fewer questions than any other domain in this exam. Any student who has paid attention to the instructor and has performed the required lab activities, thus meeting the expected level of experience, should not have much trouble passing the CompTIA A+ 220-1101 Exam.

If you have covered all test objectives, you should do fine on the exam, but many students do not cover all test objectives. In fact, many only cover the areas they find appealing or important but do not cover other objectives they think are uninteresting. For example, many students can often explain the principles of overclocking a system in greater depth than is required on the exam but do not understand printers well enough to pass the printer portion of the exam. You need to study *all* test objectives, which can be accomplished easily by building a study plan based on the objectives.

The biggest difference between this iteration of the exam and the previous 1000-series is the expansion of attention given to mobile devices, including configuration for 5G networks as well as apps used on these networks. Synchronization across devices is also being given more weight. Additional topics recently added to the 220-1101 Exam include Cat 6a cable, DDR4 RAM, and 3D printers. Students unfamiliar with these concepts may have difficulty in these portions of the exam.

CompTIA A+ 220-1102 Exam

CompTIA A+ 220-1102 covers operating systems, security, mobile devices, and troubleshooting. These domains require a more in-depth knowledge of computer systems than those for the CompTIA A+ 220-1101 Exam. The CompTIA A+ 220-1102 Exam covers a lot of material and requires some hands-on experience, making it the more difficult of the two exams. Many questions, but not all, are in scenario format, requiring you to think and apply knowledge and make decisions based on the given situation. Always read the questions carefully.

The first domain of the CompTIA A+ 220-1102 Exam is *Operating Systems*, which can prove to be quite difficult, especially when you are required to differentiate among operating system features. You will need a good understanding of the configuration options and features of all Windows operating systems for the last ten years, as this exam covers all the commonly encountered editions of Windows operating systems. Be aware that when a new Windows operating system is released, it takes CompTIA approximately one year before adding additional questions for the newest operating system. For example, while Windows 11 is not explicitly listed in the current 220-1102 objectives, it will likely be added over the next year or so—certainly before the next major revision of the exam objectives.

Some areas of the exam can be quite difficult and require memorization. For example, questions appear on the test requiring you to identify correctly which operating system edition can be upgraded to another operating system edition. Another difficult area is correctly matching operating system features to the correct operating system and edition.

There are usually questions about command prompt that require you to match a correct command and switch to the desired result. For example, you may be asked to identify a specific command and switch combination that is used to automatically inspect a hard disk drive and repair errors. The *Operating System* domain is quite extensive and accounts for 31 percent of the exam objectives.

Security and troubleshooting questions will also prove to be difficult. Many of the troubleshooting questions will most likely occur in a scenario-type question. These questions will require you to make an analysis based on given facts or characteristics of the problem.

You may encounter questions that have two possible correct answers, but CompTIA only wants you to choose one. When there are two correct answers, you will need to pick the one that is *most* correct or the most reasonable. For example, you could be asked about the best way to protect a computer from malware. Among the possible answers, you may be presented with options such as installing antivirus software or performing regular backups. However, one of these answers is more correct than the other, and if you are unable to identify which one, you may need to consider studying more. Additionally, pay attention to the question's wording, in this case, the term *protect*. The *Software Troubleshooting* domain represents 22 percent of the exam objectives.

Certification and Exam Requirements

CompTIA recommends that a test candidate have at least 12 months of hands-on lab or work experience. This is a recommendation, not a requirement; in fact, there are no prerequisites, and anyone is eligible to take an A+ Certification Exam. However, work experience alone does not ensure that a candidate will pass the exams. Formal training provides the best opportunity for passing. Some candidates pass the exams by using self-study techniques, but your best preparation for passing the exams is a combination of structured classroom-related experiences and hands-on lab activities that reinforce classroom training and textbook studies.

When you feel you are ready to take an A+ Certification Exam, you must make an appointment to test at a registered testing center. When reporting to the testing center, you must show two proofs of identification; one is typically a photo ID and the other is a document with your signature, such as a credit card. Credible examples of photo IDs are state driver's licenses and US passports. Always check the requirements for identification before reporting to the testing center.

After proving your identity, you will be assigned a workstation in the testing area at which you will take your exam. You will not be allowed to bring any reference material into the testing area. You are provided with scrap paper on which you may want to do a quick "brain dump" of any material you think you may have problems remembering during the exam. You must turn this paper over to the proctor before you leave the testing center.

Exam questions are not *weighted*, or scored, equally. This means that exam questions are worth different point values. It is impossible to determine the exact weight of a question because CompTIA does not reveal it, though the weight of one question compared to another is often rather obvious. A question that asks you to identify a component likely carries less weight than a question that asks you to apply analytical thinking. For example, a question that asks which component on a motherboard is responsible for processing instructions likely carries less weight than a question that asks you to identify the order of the Windows 10 boot process.

The usual number of questions for each exam is 90 but can vary because CompTIA sometimes adds additional questions that do not count toward the score. The additional exam questions are *field-test questions*, meaning CompTIA is testing how effective they are as potential certification questions, and you are helping CompTIA develop new exam questions by answering them. Field testing ensures each question has been clearly written and the correct answer is clearly indicated in the list of answers. If an experimental exam question is too difficult to understand or does not have a clear, correct answer, it is evident to CompTIA by a higher-than-average number of incorrect responses to the question, and these questions are rewritten and tested again before becoming a valid exam question.

Each exam has a time limit of 90 minutes. The passing score for the CompTIA A+ 220-1101 Exam is 675 (on a scale of 100–900). For the CompTIA A+ 220-1102 Exam, it is 700 (on a scale of 100–900). However, because each question is weighted, it is difficult to translate these passing scores into percentages.

Question Format

All questions are presented by computer and fall into one of two formats: multiple-choice and performance-based. A vast majority of questions on the CompTIA A+ Exams are in multiple-choice format, and most will have four answers to choose from, but there may be questions that require you to choose more than one answer from more than four choices. For example, you may be asked to choose the three best answers from a list of six possible options.

You will likely encounter performance-based questions that ask you to complete a task rather than select the correct answer as in a multiple-choice question. An example of a performance-based question for a CompTIA A+ Exam is to enter the command to check the assigned IP address of a computer. Another example is to arrange the given list in the correct order for installing an additional PATA drive, such as the following list:

- power off the computer
- format the PATA drive
- power on the computer
- install the drive
- partition the drive

The CompTIA website provides sample questions to help you determine if you are ready to take the test. The sample is also provided to help you know what to expect during the test. The CompTIA website also provides a link to more information about performance-based questions and provides a sample of what you might encounter.

25.2 Exam Preparation

To prepare for an A+ Certification Exam successfully, you must design an exam preparation strategy. A few possible strategies are presented. Using them will increase your chances of obtaining an A+ Certification on your first attempt.

General Study Tips

Some questions are simple memorization, which require using common memorization techniques, such as flash cards. For example, you may need to know the requirements to install Windows 10 or the function of common ports such as SMTP 25 and POP2 110. Memorization is the best method for mastering this type of information, but the process of memorizing can be rather tedious, so it is recommended you perform any memorization study in short intervals.

Other questions require understanding of some underlying concept. For example, Chapter 3 discusses motherboards, a topic that does not rely on memorization so much as understanding the role of motherboards and major components. One way to study for these types of questions is to find a study partner and practice teaching this concept or topic to each other. If you can successfully teach a topic to another person, you likely have mastered that topic.

It is also important to read the text differently than you might read a novel. When you read a chapter, you may read through once casually, but then make a second pass through, perhaps highlighting concepts that are either new to you or that you believe might require some additional study time for you. Pay particular attention to terms that are defined, as well as tables, as these can summarize information for you. You may even give a third pass through to some chapters that you find particularly difficult.

Establish a Study Schedule

Establishing a realistic study schedule is an important step in preparing for these exams. Use a calendar and plan dates and times for study, allocating enough time each day based on your typical study habits. You can also ask your instructor for input about how many hours of additional study you might need before taking the exam. Having a planned schedule for study allows you to set times for other activities, such as movies, dates, family plans, and leisure. If you have a set study schedule, you will most likely think twice about those other activities to schedule your study time around them.

Reading a text repeatedly is an ineffective study technique, though spaced repetition may be effective, especially for knowledge-oriented questions. *Spaced repetition* is a learning technique that employs an increased amount of time between subsequent reviews of the content being studied. It works by creating flash cards of the content you need to learn, such as vocabulary, commands, troubleshooting techniques, or other content related to the A+ Certification Exams. Those flash cards are stored in one of three boxes. As you learn the material, you move flash cards you have mastered to the second box, keeping the unlearned cards in the first box. During the next study session, flash cards mastered in the second box move to the third box, and flash cards forgotten from the second box move back to the first. The process repeats, each time with unknown or forgotten content moving back to the first box and learned material advancing to the next box. This system can be made from 3×5 index cards and tissue or shoe boxes or with software.

Another technique supported by research is to create your own test questions and randomize the questions and answers before taking your self-created quizzes. Grade it honestly and repeat as needed. This reinforces memorization of the material, but it will also serve as a study guide since you are creating the quizzes.

Get Hands-On Experience

Hands-on experience provides you with many of the required skills tested on the A+ Certification Exams, especially when you consider that some questions are performance-based. You should spend as much time as possible practicing many of the skills that are tested. For example, you should practice setting up and formatting partitions on a hard drive, rather than just reading and memorizing procedures. For many of the skills tested, there is no substitute for hands-on experience, and the corresponding *Computer Service and Repair Lab Manual* will provide you with many of those skills. It is highly recommended you practice performing the lab activities and review the questions at the end of each lab, as many of the lab review questions are designed to prepare you for an A+ Certification Exam. Begin your review at the beginning of the lab manual; often, students forget the basics that were covered early in the course.

Read a Variety of Computer-Related Material

It is helpful to read a variety of computer-related material. Sometimes, reading the same topic in a different book or manual can illuminate the information in a new way or can commit it better to memory.

Textbook Material

Review the textbook material covered in the course. Just as it was suggested for the lab activities, start your review at the beginning of the textbook to help reinforce concepts and terms you may have forgotten. Review all tests, end-of-chapter Review Questions, Sample A+ Exam Questions, chapter tests or quizzes, and classroom handouts.

Instructional Web Pages and Websites

There are hundreds of web pages available to assist you in learning more about computer technology. Seeing the same material presented in a different format by a different writer can be extremely helpful, especially when learning difficult concepts. For example, if you have difficulty learning the differences in RAID types, you could search the Internet using the keywords RAID or RAID types. You will find many sources about RAID, including short tutorials. A few websites you may find useful are iFixIt Computer Repair, Computer Hope, and The Fundamentals of Networking by IBM. You can also find useful information regarding specific technologies such as Bluetooth, solid-state drives, and many other topics on other websites such as computer forums and Wikipedia, but you should also consider fact-checking the information gleaned from these sites.

Create a Study Guide

A great technique to use in preparing for the A+ Certification Exams and reviewing for the course is to make your own study guide. Teacher handouts are convenient, but they are seldom studied in-depth by the average student. There are also many study guides on the Internet, but some contain material that is no longer required for the exam or is not included in the examination objectives. To increase your retention of the subject matter, it is recommended that you make your own study guide. One suggested method of creating a study guide is to list the examination objectives on a sheet of paper, leaving ample space in which to write your own notes between the content items.

A better way to copy the examination objectives is to use a word processor, again leaving an ample amount of space between the content items listed, as shown in Figure 25-2. When studying, write in by hand the information you have collected about each objective and content item. Using this method will not only give you a set of notes matching the exact exam objectives, but also will serve as an excellent study tool and provide you with a systematic solution to studying for this exam.

When completing your study guide, be aware that many content items are listed under more than one objective. When you see a content item that is listed more than once, look for keywords in the related objective that identify the desired information for that content item. For example, if *USB port* is listed under more than one objective, one occurrence may be under an objective that is concerned with the USB port's identification and characteristics and the other occurrence may be concerned with troubleshooting. Write your notes about the content item according to the specifics of each objective. You may also reorganize the material so the main item in your study guide is USB port and subordinate items are port identification, port characteristics, and troubleshooting.

If creating your own study guide is not a viable option, consider reviewing the practice activities and referential information found in the corresponding *Computer Service and Repair Study Guide*. The activities in the study guide correlate to the material covered in this textbook and are designed to help prepare you for the CompTIA A+ Certification Exams. The study guide also contains a CompTIA Reference Guide that explores each exam objective individually.

Join or Form a Study Group

A group formed of individuals who are serious about preparing for the A+ Certification Exams can be an excellent way to prepare. One word of caution, though, is to make sure the study group functions as a study group and not as a social group. A group of friends gathered for study can quickly get off track and spend a lot of time discussing sports, movies, and other topics. It is critical that the

My Study Guide

1.1 Given a scenario, install and configure laptop hardware and components.

Hardware/device replacement

Battery

Keyboard/keys

Random access memory (RAM)

Hard disk drive (HDD)/solid-state drive (SSD) migration

HDD/SSD replacement

Wireless cards

Physical privacy and security components

Biometrics

Goodheart-Willcox Publisher

Figure 25-2 Creating a study guide provides you with a set of notes matching the exam objectives and serves as an excellent study tool.

study group remains focused on the task at hand: exam preparation. The following guidelines can help ensure the group stays on topic:

- Stay on task.
- Set a regular schedule of dates, times, and duration. (Every day is best, but not always possible.)
- Write practice exam questions for each other.
- Share resources such as sample exams or websites that support your studies.

A study group can make exam preparation fun and provide you with the additional motivation you need to study. The members of the study group help keep one another on task. For example, you may plan to study every night for the next two weeks for three hours each night. However, when it comes to executing the plan, you may easily find a reason not to study. When two or more of you plan to study together, each member feels more obligated to meet at the established time.

The study group can also share some of the burden of exam preparation. Each member of the study group can take a particular area covered on the exam and write a set of questions for the other members. When you meet at your regularly

> **A+ Note**
>
> The CompTIA A+ Exams often include questions about items not specifically listed in the exam objectives. For example, there may be a question about the OSI model as related to networking. The objectives serve the purpose of a general guide and are not all-inclusive of the exam parameters. Be prepared for possible topics not precisely identified by the objective outline.

scheduled time, you can exchange the questions as well as resources that you have found helpful in your personal studies, such as sample exams or websites.

Take Practice Exams

Practice exams are an excellent way to determine your test readiness and to identify weak areas. For example, by taking practice exams, you may discover that you do not know the printing process as well as you thought. Practice exams are an important ingredient to your exam preparation strategy, and you can use the results to design the content for your review sessions. After taking a practice exam, identify the topics in which you feel you need more help, and then review materials covering those topics.

There are numerous websites offering free online or downloadable practice exams. While many are quite reputable, some are rather questionable. There are hundreds of sample exams located throughout the Internet, but these exams provide only a sampling of a full test bank. Some have been found to be flawed or misleading, and others are intentionally designed to have the student fail. The marketing idea is to show the student how little they know about the subject so they might be lured into purchasing the full test bank of questions. You may take the free sample exams because they still have many good questions, but do not consider them a true measure of your ability to pass the exam.

Many students want a perfect score on their A+ Certification Exam and constantly take practice exams and achieve a score less than 100 percent. Because of this, they never feel prepared for an A+ Certification Exam. While scoring a 100 percent on a practice exam is a worthy goal, it is unrealistic for many, if not most, students. To determine if you are prepared to take an A+ Certification Exam, consider a passing score of 80 percent on a practice exam as a good indication.

A common-sense practice exam approach increases what educators call automaticity. *Automaticity* means you have become more fluent with test questions. Automaticity also improves your guessing skills.

Schedule a Test Date

Scheduling a test date is an excellent component to add to the established study schedule. As soon as you think you know the amount of preparation you will need, set a time and date for the exam. Do not wait until you know the material in its entirety. Chances are, you will most likely never feel you know the material totally. Procrastinating when setting a test date will quickly put you out of date with the material you have studied. Set a date to give yourself a deadline for preparation.

25.3 Sample CompTIA A+ 220-1101 Exam

The following is a practice exam intended to simulate the type and depth of questions commonly encountered on the CompTIA A+ 220-1101 Exam. Always check the CompTIA website for the very latest list of detailed objectives. The objective contents can change at any time.

1. What is the maximum data rate for 802.11ax? (1101: Domain 2)
   A. Gbps
   B. 9.6 Gbps
   C. 450 Mbps
   D. 54 Mbps

2. Which log contains a list of all drivers that are loaded during system startup? (1101: Domain 5)
   A. **repair.txt**
   B. **details.txt**
   C. **ntblog.txt**
   D. **startup.txt**
3. Which printer connection type requires direct line of sight to transfer information from a mobile device to a printer successfully? (1101: Domain 1)
   A. Infrared
   B. 802.11x
   C. Bluetooth
   D. Wi-Fi
4. A computer is not connecting to the Internet but is connecting to local network shares. You inspect the computer-assigned IP address and see that it is 169.254.10.1. What is *most likely* the problem? (1101: Domain 4)
   A. The WINS server is down.
   B. The DHCP server has failed.
   C. The network card is defective.
   D. The network cable has become disconnected from the PC.
5. A user complains that when he uses his laptop, the Internet connection is slow or intermittent. What is *most likely* the cause? (1101: Domain 5)
   A. The wrong type of encryption is configured for the wireless access point.
   B. The laptop is configured for IPv6, not IPv4.
   C. The laptop is too far from the wireless access point.
   D. The wireless network card is incorrectly configured.
6. Which network system provides the most secure connection between two computers across the Internet? (1101: Domain 4)
   A. 802.11g
   B. VPN
   C. 801.11a
   D. Workgroup membership
7. Which are the two major types of ISDN services available? (1101: Domain 2)
   A. BRI and PRI
   B. Static and dynamic
   C. Fixed cost and variable
   D. DSL and cable
8. Which of the following virtual programs is open-source and free to install? (1101: Domain 4)
   A. Parallel Desktop
   B. Oracle VirtualBox
   C. VMware Player
   D. VMware Fusion
9. Which type of CPU would *most likely* be installed on a tablet device manufactured in 2018? (1101: Domain 1)
   A. Core
   B. Phenom II
   C. ARM
   D. Core i3

10. Which item is required for inkjet head alignment? (1101: Domain 5)
    A. Compressed air
    B. Software application
    C. Flat-tip screwdriver
    D. Toner wrench
11. Which IPv4 address is an example of an APIPA address? (1101: Domain 2)
    A. 169.254.12.43
    B. 192.168.10.100
    C. Fe80:2bc3:3c3b:4212:4f23%12
    D. 10.10.10.1
12. Which two port types are used to connect to an internal HDD? (Select two.) (1101: Domain 3)
    A. PATA
    B. USB
    C. FireWire
    D. PATA
13. After a PC has completed the boot process, you notice that the time and date are incorrect. What is *most likely* the cause? (1101: Domain 5)
    A. The HDD is about to fail.
    B. The system is overheating because of excessive dust accumulation in the heat sink cooling fins.
    C. System updates have not been configured automatically.
    D. The CMOS battery has failed.
14. Which troubleshooting tool is used to diagnose start-up errors? (1101: Domain 5)
    A. Oscilloscope
    B. Tone generator
    C. POST card
    D. Multimeter
15. Which of the following is *not* a NIST characteristic of cloud service? (1101: Domain 4)
    A. Broad network access
    B. Immunity to downtime
    C. Resource pooling
    D. Rapid elasticity
16. Which cable type provides no protection from EMI? (1101: Domain 3)
    A. STP
    B. UTP
    C. Fiber
    D. RG-6
17. According to the troubleshooting steps outlined by CompTIA, what is the first thing you should do when troubleshooting a computer on a service call? (1101: Domain 5)
    A. Run a credit check on the customer to be sure they can pay for the service.
    B. Ask the customer probing questions to pin down what exactly the problem is.
    C. Test the 120-volt power outlet to ensure a proper voltage level.
    D. Check if the computer is still under warranty.

18. What is the purpose of CPU cache? (1101: Domain 3)
    A. Creating the digital clock signal used by the CPU
    B. Synchronizing IRQ signals with other motherboard components
    C. Storing data temporarily
    D. Storing BIOS setup configuration data
19. Which port number is associated with DNS? (1101: Domain 2)
    A. 21
    B. 80
    C. 3389
    D. 53
20. Which standard provides the lowest bandwidth? (1101: Domain 1)
    A. IEEE 802.11b
    B. Bluetooth
    C. IEEE 802.11n
    D. IEEE 802.11g
21. After you have selected to restart the computer, which key or key combination would you press during the boot process to access the **Advanced Boot Options** menu for Windows 10? (1101: Domain 5)
    A. [Ctrl][Z]
    B. [F4]
    C. [F8]
    D. [Shift]
22. Which tool would you select to make a network cable connection to a 110 termination block? (1101: Domain 5)
    A. Standard wire crimper
    B. Wire stripper
    C. Punch down tool
    D. Flat-tip screwdriver
23. Which step of the laser printer process uses laser light to write images on the laser printer drum? (1101: Domain 3)
    A. Developing
    B. Exposing
    C. Processing
    D. Fusing
24. Which protocol is used to map all local network addresses to one single Internet address? (1101: Domain 2)
    A. DMA
    B. NAT
    C. UDP
    D. TCP
25. Which of the following closed ports would prevent a Remote Desktop connection? (1101: Domain 4)
    A. 137
    B. 445
    C. 3389
    D. 2247
26. Which port number is assigned to POP3 incoming mail? (1101: Domain 2)
    A. 80
    B. 110
    C. 21
    D. 443

27. Which of the following would *most likely* cause a BSOD error? (1101: Domain 5)
   A. Improperly seated RAM module
   B. Misconfigured modem
   C. Faulty or failed CPU fan
   D. Loose connection to a SATA drive
28. What is the purpose of a KVM switch? (1101: Domain 3)
   A. To increase the bandwidth of an Internet connection
   B. To allow more than one user to share two or more desktop computers
   C. To increase security for a home office
   D. To reduce the number of computer station input and output devices
29. Which is an example of an IPv6 address? (1101: Domain 2)
   A. 192.168.1.01
   B. Fe80::2bc3:3c3b:4212:4f23
   C. AF 2B 12 C2 3t4 D1
   D. 10100011011101
30. A computer program is no longer responding. Which keyboard combination can be used to access Task Manager? (1101: Domain 5)
   A. [Ctrl][F8]
   B. [Ctrl][Shift][Del]
   C. [Ctrl][Alt][Del]
   D. [Alt][F8]
31. Which laser printer part is *most likely* the cause of a printer suddenly printing blank paper? (1101: Domain 3)
   A. Low toner
   B. Defective fuser
   C. Tripped electrical breaker
   D. Defective transfer corona wire
32. A home office uses a centralized network switch to connect all computers and printers using UTP cable. Which network topology would this physical arrangement most closely match? (1101: Domain 2)
   A. Bus
   B. Mesh
   C. Star
   D. Ring
33. What is the loopback address associated with IPv4? (1101: Domain 5)
   A. 192.168.0.1
   B. 10.0.0.1
   C. 255.255.255.255
   D. 127.0.0.1
34. Which of the following refers to matching data on a mobile device to a laptop or desktop? (1101: Domain 1)
   A. Synchronization
   B. Tethering
   C. Matching
   D. Clouding
35. Which command would you use to identify a computer MAC address? (1101: Domain 2)
   A. **ipconfig**
   B. **msconfig**
   C. **ping**
   D. **tracert**

36. Which of the following summarizes the differences between platter-based drives and solid-state drives? Select all that apply. (1101: Domain 1)
    A. Solid-state drives have no moving parts
    B. Solid-state drives work similarly to flash drives
    C. Solid-state drives have longer lifespans
    D. Solid-states drives are less susceptible to magnetic interference
37. You want to install the very latest printer drivers for a customer's printer. Where would you locate the latest drivers? (1101: Domain 3)
    A. At the Microsoft Support website
    B. On the DVD that accompanied the printer when purchased
    C. On the latest version of the Windows operating system installation DVD
    D. On the printer manufacturer's website
38. Which selection is *not* a Windows 10 System Recovery option? (1101: Domain 5)
    A. Startup Repair
    B. Registry Editor
    C. System Restore
    D. Windows Memory Diagnostics
39. How do you upgrade the BIOS? (1101: Domain 3)
    A. Download the BIOS upgrade from the BIOS manufacturer and then flash the BIOS.
    B. Remove the CMOS chip and replace it with the newest version from the manufacturer.
    C. The BIOS is automatically upgraded each time you install the latest Windows service pack.
    D. BIOS cannot be upgraded. You must replace the motherboard.
40. Which subnet mask is associated with a Class B network? (1101: Domain 2)
    A. 255.255.255.000
    B. 255.255.000.000
    C. 000.000.000.255
    D. 255.000.000.00
41. How do you access **System Restore** in Windows 10? (1101: Domain 5)
    A. Right-click **Computer**, select **Properties** from the shortcut menu, and then select the **System Restore** tab
    B. **Start**>**All Programs**>**System Restore**
    C. **Control Panel**>**System and Security**>**System**>**System protection**>**System Restore**
    D. **Start**>**All Programs**>**Accessibility**>**System Restore**
42. Which of the following is *not* an advantage of IPv6 over IPv4? (1101: Domain 3)
    A. Larger pool of addresses
    B. Better security and quality of service
    C. Faster transfer rates
    D. Support for Network Discovery
43. Which would be the most common maintenance task for an impact printer? (1101: Domain 3)
    A. Replacing the toner cartridge
    B. Replacing the pickup rollers
    C. Replacing the impact head
    D. Replacing the ribbon cartridge

44. Which Device Manager symbol is used to indicate a disabled device driver? (1101: Domain 5)
    A. The device will not appear in the list of devices when it is disabled.
    B. Red X
    C. Yellow triangle
    D. Red stop sign
45. What is the data rate per second for a USB 3.0 port? (1101: Domain 3)
    A. 1 GB
    B. 3 GB
    C. 5 GB
    D. 2 GB
46. When used in reference to a virtual machine, to what does *sandboxing* refer? (1101: Domain 4)
    A. The invasion of malware on a process
    B. A consistent slowdown in performance
    C. Any permitted process
    D. A safe environment, isolated from other parts of the system
47. A user is unable to log into the LAN, but other users are not experiencing the same problem. You can log in as the user from a remote station, but you are unable to log in at the user's computer. Which of the following is *most likely* the cause of the problem? (1101: Domain 5)
    A. User does not have rights to access LAN
    B. Incorrect password
    C. Bad network cable
    D. DHCP is down
48. You have a printer configured to share with other devices in your home-office network. The printer was working fine yesterday but today you cannot print. What is *most likely* the cause of the problem? (1101: Domain 3)
    A. The printer is out of toner.
    B. The printer is no longer shared.
    C. The printer is offline.
    D. The printer driver is corrupt.
49. What does the acronym DNS represent? (1101: Domain 2)
    A. Dominant Network System
    B. Domain Network Services
    C. Domain Network System
    D. Domain Name System
50. A laser printer produces copies that easily smear when touched. What laser printer component is *most likely* causing the problem? (1101: Domain 3)
    A. Laser
    B. Fuser
    C. Drum
    D. Transfer corona
51. A laptop computer has a very dim display. Which component would you replace first? (1101: Domain 1)
    A. Display wiring harness
    B. LCD inverter
    C. Video adapter card
    D. Laptop battery

52. What is the last step of the troubleshooting process? (1101: Domain 5)
    A. Establish a plan of action to resolve future problems.
    B. Verify full system functionality.
    C. Confirm theory and solutions.
    D. Document findings, actions, and outcomes.
53. Which of the following is *not* a cloud-based service? (1101: Domain 4)
    A. Google TensorFlow
    B. Microsoft Azure
    C. Amazon Web Services
    D. Oracle Cloud
54. Which option in the **Advanced Boot Options** menu will start the computer with minimal drivers? (1101: Domain 5)
    A. System Image Recovery
    B. Safe Mode
    C. Last Known Good Configuration
    D. Disable Driver Signature Enforcement
55. You hear a clicking noise during the boot process and periodically while using the computer. What is *most likely* the cause of the clicking noise? (1101: Domain 5)
    A. RAM
    B. CPU
    C. HDD
    D. CMOS
56. Which service model is cloud-based? (1101: Domain 4)
    A. Server as a Service
    B. Software as a Service
    C. Router as a Service
    D. Sandbox as a Service
57. A user has recently installed a new printer driver and now the printer will not print at all. Which is the best method to recover from this issue without the possibility of changing other drivers or system file updates? (1101: Domain 5)
    A. Perform a System Restore from any recent restore point.
    B. Open Device Manager, select the printer, and then select Roll Back Driver option.
    C. Perform a clean system install and then install the latest service pack.
    D. Power off and disconnect the printer, and then power the printer back on and follow the screen prompts to install a new driver.
58. When using a multimeter to measure voltage, how close should the measurement be to the expected voltage? (1101: Domain 5)
    A. Within 40 percent
    B. Within 20 percent
    C. Within 10 percent
    D. Within 50 percent
59. Which operating system is used by Apple mobile devices? (1101: Domain 1)
    A. iOS
    B. Android
    C. Windows CE
    D. macOS

60. Which type of motherboard interface would you use for an SLI graphics card configuration? (1101: Domain 5)
    A. PCI
    B. PCIe
    C. ISA
    D. AGP
61. What is the name of the technology that only lets specific wireless devices connect to a wireless access point? (1101: Domain 2)
    A. MAC filtering
    B. Dynamic addressing
    C. Channel selection
    D. Port forwarding
62. Which tool can be used to measure ohms? (1101: Domain 5)
    A. ODM
    B. Toner probe
    C. Loopback plug
    D. Multimeter
63. What type of HDD is used internally on a modern laptop computer? (1101: Domain 1)
    A. 3.5 PATA
    B. 2.5 SATA
    C. 3.5 SATA
    D. 2.5 PATA
64. Which set of voltage levels are associated with a standard ATX power supply? (1101: Domain 3)
    A. 3.3, 12, 24
    B. 3.3, 5, 12
    C. 6, 12, 18
    D. 3.3, 6.6, 18.8
65. Which type of battery is most commonly found in laptop computers? (1101: Domain 1)
    A. NiMH
    B. Li-ion
    C. NiCad
    D. Lead acid
66. Which are the two most common methods of connecting an all-in-one printer to a computer? (Select two.) (1101: Domain 3)
    A. RS-232
    B. USB cable
    C. Serial cable
    D. RF Wireless
67. What term is used to describe the temporary storage of a file before it is sent to a printer? (1101: Domain 3)
    A. Spooling
    B. Imaging
    C. Share
    D. Writing

68. You have been tasked with running a length of cable over 95 meters (approximately 311 feet). The cable needs to support speeds up to 10 Gbps. Which cable should you use? (1101: Domain 2)
    A. Cat 5
    B. Cat 5e
    C. Cat 6
    D. Cat 6a
69. Which operating systems have their source codes made readily available for customization? (Select two.) (1101: Domain 1)
    A. iOS
    B. Microsoft
    C. Android
    D. Linux
70. What two pieces of information require identification by the user when connecting to a secure wireless device? (Select two.) (1101: Domain 2)
    A. MAC
    B. SSID
    C. Passcode
    D. IP address
71. Where is the TPM located on a computer system? (1101: Domain 3)
    A. In the hard disk drive
    B. Virtually located in RAM
    C. On the network adapter
    D. On the motherboard
72. What is true about the network connection based on the screen capture of the network adapter details? (1101: Domain 2)

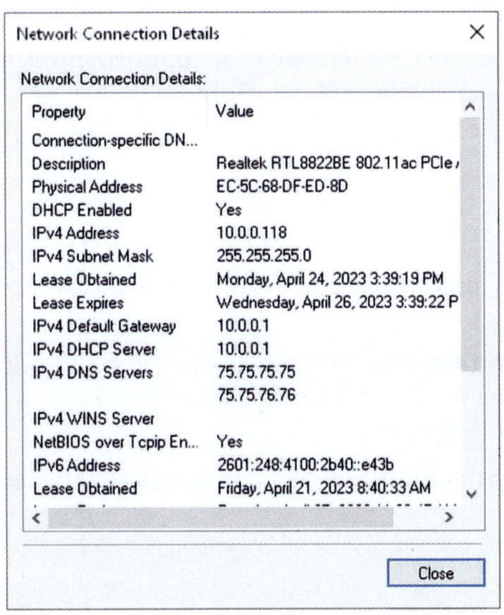

Goodheart-Willcox Publisher

    A. The network is connected using a 100BaseT connection.
    B. The computer is connected to the network using a public IPv4 address.
    C. The computer cannot establish a connection with the DNS server.
    D. The computer is connected to the network using a private IPv4 address.

73. Which of the following is a symptom of a failed capacitor in a power supply? Select all that apply. (1101: Domain 5)
    A. Smoke stains on the insulation cover
    B. Swollen or bulging capacitor
    C. Computer continually reboots
    D. Incorrect system date or time
74. Which type of memory module is used for laptop computer RAM? (1101: Domain 1)
    A. SIMM 168-pin
    B. SODIMM 204-pin DDR4
    C. DIMM 240-pin DDR4
    D. SIMM 72-pin
75. Which protocol is designed to support network file sharing? (1101: Domain 2)
    A. SNMP
    B. SSH
    C. SMB
    D. SFTP
76. What type of connector is in the following image? (1101: Domain 3)
    A. RJ-45
    B. DB-232
    C. STP
    D. F-type

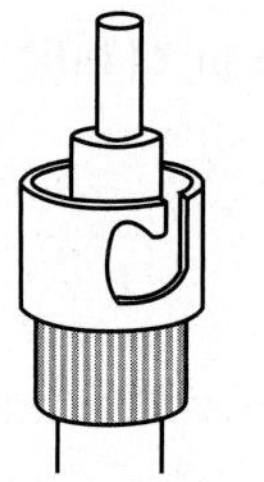

Goodheart-Willcox Publisher

77. What is the name of the CPU feature that supports multiple paths for data processing through each core? (1101: Domain 3)
    A. Hyperthreading
    B. Throttling
    C. Flash Flow
    D. Flash Bus
78. Where in Control Panel would you disable a hardware device? (1101: Domain 5)
    A. Device Manager
    B. Devices and Printers
    C. Power Options
    D. Administrative Tools
79. Which of the following multimeter readouts shows the least resistance? (1101: Domain 5)
    A. 20
    B. 100
    C. Infinity
    D. 0
80. Which of the following best describes the storage location for a file used with cloud-based computing? (1101: Domain 4)
    A. Redundancy-based file system
    B. Designated single server
    C. Designated pair of servers
    D. Linux-based system

81. What are the two power options associated with shutting down a Windows 10 laptop? (1101: Domain 1)
    A. Standby and Suspend
    B. Snooze and Nap
    C. Sleep and Hibernate
    D. Restart and Sleep
82. Which two devices are commonly connected to the southbridge? (Select two.) (1101: Domain 3)
    A. DIMM
    B. Mouse
    C. Video card
    D. Keyboard
83. A client reports that his computer date and time on the taskbar is always incorrect every time he boots his computer. What is *most likely* causing the problem? (1101: Domain 3)
    A. The BIOS battery is bad.
    B. The OS has a corrupt driver file.
    C. The CPU is going bad.
    D. The power supply connection is loose.
84. Which application would *most likely* need QoS to function properly? (1101: Domain 2)
    A. Telephone modem
    B. E-mail
    C. Instant Messaging
    D. VoIP
85. Which of the following best summarizes the CompTIA troubleshooting process? (1101: Domain 5)
    A. Identify the problem, establish a theory of probable cause, test the theory to determine the cause, establish a plan of action to resolve the problem, verify system functionality and implement preventive measures, document findings and outcomes
    B. Identify the problem, establish a plan of action to resolve the problem, establish a theory of probable cause, test the theory to determine the cause, document findings and outcomes
    C. Establish a theory of probable cause, test the theory to determine the cause, establish a plan of action to resolve the problem, document findings and outcomes
    D. Establish a plan to resolve the problem, establish a theory of probable cause, test the theory to determine the cause, verify full system functionality, document findings and outcomes
86. Which type of address must be manually configured? (1101: Domain 2)
    A. Dynamic
    B. DHCP
    C. APIPA
    D. Static
87. Which cloud infrastructure model is open for general use by anyone? (1101: Domain 4)
    A. Hybrid
    B. Private
    C. Public
    D. Community

88. What task must be performed first after physically adding a new additional hard disk drive to a Windows 10 computer? (1101: Domain 3)
    A. The hard disk drive must be formatted.
    B. The hard disk drive must be erased.
    C. The hard disk drive must be assigned a drive letter.
    D. The hard disk drive must be initiated.
89. Which type of connection is most commonly used to synchronize a smartphone with a desktop PC? (Select two.) (1101: Domain 1)
    A. Wi-Fi
    B. RS-232
    C. SATA
    D. USB
90. Where would you configure an additional monitor for a laptop computer running Windows 10? (1101: Domain 1)
    A. Device Manager
    B. Display
    C. Administrative Tools
    D. Windows Mobility Center

25.4 Sample CompTIA A+ 220-1102 Exam

The following practice exam is intended to simulate the type and depth of questions commonly encountered on the CompTIA A+ 220-1102 Exam. The structure of the 220-1102 Exam is like the 220-1101 Exam except that it is more difficult. Always check the CompTIA website for the very latest list of objectives. The objective contents can change at any time.

1. Which Linux command operates as a screen-oriented text editor? (1102: Domain 1)
    A. **dd**
    B. **apt-get**
    C. **vi**
    D. **su/sudo**
2. What is multifactor authentication? (1102: Domain 2)
    A. When two or more encryption keys are used to access a resource
    B. When two or more security measures are used, such as something you know and something you have
    C. When two persons are required to enter a facility
    D. When an encryption cypher key is run two or more times during the encryption process
3. Which encryption type provides the least security? (1102: Domain 2)
    A. WPA2
    B. AES
    C. WEP
    D. WPA

4. Which is the quickest way to remove or counter a rootkit? (1102: Domain 2)
   A. Scan the system registry and then restore the default settings.
   B. Start the computer system in Safe Mode and then run a good antivirus program.
   C. Install and then run a good antispam tool.
   D. Perform a clean installation of the operating system.
5. Which of the following allows a user to log into a device virtually? (1102: Domain 4)
   A. Telnet
   B. CSMA/CA
   C. SSH
   D. CSMA/CD
6. What is the purpose of an MSDS? (1102: Domain 4)
   A. It protects hardware items from electrical shock.
   B. It provides instructions about how to handle specific materials.
   C. It protects technicians from electrical shock.
   D. It provides information about the proper technique to install computer components.
7. A user installed an updated hardware driver for her computer and now the computer boots to a blue screen and freezes. Which method would you use to repair the computer? (1102: Domain 3)
   A. Reinstall the operating system using the installation DVD.
   B. Start the computer in Safe Mode and then go to the command prompt and enter bootrec/fixboot.
   C. Start the computer in Safe Mode and then roll back the device driver.
   D. Remove the offending hardware device and then reboot the computer.
8. Which is the best method to prevent unauthorized access to a wireless router from an unauthorized portable computer? (1102: Domain 2)
   A. Configure a MAC filter.
   B. Place the wireless router inside a secure closet.
   C. Change the SSID.
   D. Use only 802.11n devices.
9. What is the maximum amount of RAM recognized by the Windows 7 64-bit operating system? (1102: Domain 1)
   A. 16 GB
   B. 32 GB
   C. 1 TB
   D. 128 GB
10. Which Microsoft Windows tool is used to create a disk image? (1102: Domain 1)
    A. Robocopy
    B. Backup and Restore
    C. Msconfig
    D. Computer Management
11. Which command is used to access the local group policy editor for Windows 10? (1102: Domain 4)
    A. **poledit.exe**
    B. **local.msc**
    C. **gpedit.msc**
    D. **grplocal.exe**

12. Which Windows feature allows a user to encrypt an entire HDD? (1102: Domain 2)
    A. BitLocker
    B. Windows Firewall
    C. Rainbow Table
    D. Disk Defragmenter
13. Which of the following describes a PowerShell script file? (1102: Domain 4)
    A. **.ps1**
    B. **.pps**
    C. **.vbs**
    D. **.py**
14. Imagine a scenario in which you replaced a storage device in a Windows PC. You attempt to use the Windows installation media to install Windows on the new drive, but you are presented with an error informing you that Windows cannot be installed to the hard disk. Which of the following represents the *most likely* problem? (1102: Domain 1)
    A. The new disk requires formatting and partitioning.
    B. The new disk is Dynamic.
    C. You are attempting to install the wrong Windows version.
    D. The drive is not connected correctly.
15. Which Windows 10 application is designed to protect a PC against spyware? (1102: Domain 2)
    A. Firewall
    B. Defender
    C. BitLocker
    D. Msconfig
16. Which Windows file system(s) can use EFS? (1102: Domain 1)
    A. FAT32
    B. NTFS
    C. FAT16
    D. Any Microsoft Windows compatible file system can use EFS.
17. Which type of installation requires the **sysprep** tool? (1102: Domain 1)
    A. Unattended installation
    B. Clean install
    C. System upgrade
    D. System migration
18. Which is an example of a biometric security system? (1102: Domain 2)
    A. RFID chip
    B. Fingerprint scanner
    C. Photo ID worker badge
    D. PIN card
19. What would you do to restrict access to a specific folder to only a few select persons working in an office? (1102: Domain 2)
    A. Place the folder in a hidden directory and only tell specific people the location.
    B. Place the folder in a BitLocker drive and provide only specific people with the password.
    C. Encrypt the folder and then place a copy in each person's Document folder.
    D. Set folder permissions to allow only specific persons to access the folder.

20. What is the maximum amount of RAM recognized by 32-bit Windows operating systems? (1102: Domain 1)
    A. 16 GB
    B. 1 TB
    C. 1 GB
    D. 4 GB
21. Which power setting saves your work to the hard drive and takes the longest period to wake? (1102: Domain 1)
    A. Sleep
    B. Hibernation
    C. Suspend
    D. Pause
22. Which of the following best describes a computer under the control of a hacker? (1102: Domain 2)
    A. Phish
    B. Pharm
    C. Bot
    D. Zombie
23. Which utility would you use to prevent a specific software application from loading at startup? (1102: Domain 1)
    A. **sysconfig**
    B. **chkdsk**
    C. **msconfig**
    D. **system32**
24. Which security practice is designed to protect sensitive data stored on a mobile device that is missing or has been stolen? (1102: Domain 2)
    A. Remote wipe
    B. System reset
    C. Pairing
    D. SSL configuration
25. Which of the following is the best method of removing the dust from a computer? (1102: Domain 4)
    A. Any vacuum cleaner to remove the dust
    B. A combination of compressed air and a static cloth
    C. A combination of compressed air and ESD vacuum
    D. A combination of an ESD cloth and isopropyl alcohol
26. What is the best protection from electrical surges? (1102: Domain 4)
    A. Electrostatic wrist straps
    B. ESD mats
    C. Oscilloscope
    D. UPS
27. Which editions of Windows 10 support BitLocker? (Select all that apply.) (1102: Domain 2)
    A. Windows 10 Ultimate
    B. Windows 10 Home
    C. Windows 10 Enterprise
    D. Windows 10 Professional

28. Which computer component normally contains firmware required to start the computer boot operation? (1102: Domain 3)
    A. RAM
    B. BIOS
    C. Hard disk drive
    D. CPU
29. A Windows 10 computer fails to complete startup to the system logon. You suspect that one or more system files are corrupt. You can access the command prompt from the **Advanced Boot Options** menu. Which course of action would you choose to repair or replace system startup files? (1102: Domain 3)
    A. Run **msconfig/repair**
    B. Run **system32/repair**
    C. Run **fdisk/mbr**
    D. Run **sfc/scannow**
30. Which tab in the **Internet Options** dialog box do you use to change the default home page address for Microsoft Edge? (1102: Domain 1)
    A. Privacy
    B. General
    C. Security
    D. Connections
31. Which of the following demonstrates good communication skills? (1102: Domain 4)
    A. Offering a variety of repair or replacement options
    B. Locking of all personal material located on a hard drive
    C. Using as much technical jargon as possible when speaking
    D. Interrupting the customer's issues with possible solutions
32. What two security considerations should be made when configuring a device? (1102: Domain 1)
    A. Impact to the device and impact to the usability
    B. Impact to the device and impact to the network
    C. Impact to the user and impact to the device
    D. Impact to the usability and impact to the network
33. Which PC computer component tests hardware devices and loads the boot loader program? (1102: Domain 1)
    A. Hard disk drive
    B. RAM
    C. Operating system
    D. BIOS
34. Which of the following best describes the outcome of executing the **gpedit.msc** command in the command prompt window? (1102: Domain 1)
    A. You are redirected to a help screen
    B. Group Policy Editor opens
    C. You receive an error message telling you the command is unrecognizable
    D. Command prompt requests an administrator password
35. Which command would you use from the Windows 10 Recovery Environment to rewrite the boot code for the MBR? (1102: Domain 3)
    A. **fdisk/boot**
    B. **mbr/repair**
    C. **bootrec.exe/fixboot**
    D. **fdisk/mbr**

36. Which of the following locks a computer and demands payment to unlock it? (1102: Domain 2)
    A. Dialer
    B. Zombie
    C. Browser hijacker
    D. Ransomware
37. Which command launches the **System Configuration** dialog box? (1102: Domain 1)
    A. **system32**
    B. **msconfig**
    C. **regedit**
    D. **sfc**
38. Which of the following would provide the best method of recovery assuming an organization can only lose data for up to 24 hours before work is impacted? (1102: Domain 3)
    A. Nightly backups
    B. Weekly patch updates
    C. Monthly disk maintenance
    D. Random antivirus updates
39. A computer on a Windows domain has been identified as not having the most current policy. Which of the following tools would a technician run on the local machine to rectify this? (1102: Domain 3)
    A. **gpresult**
    B. **gpupdate**
    C. **msconfig**
    D. **ipconfig**
40. Which is the best practice to prevent phishing in the corporate environment? (1102: Domain 2)
    A. Educate the user
    B. Installing a good antivirus program
    C. Disable the autorun feature for the disc drive system
    D. Set the Internet browser security setting to high
41. What should you do before replacing a computer electronic component or device? (Select two.) (1102: Domain 4)
    A. Disconnect the electrical power.
    B. Follow the recommended ESD procedures.
    C. Wipe all hand tools with alcohol to ensure all contaminants and oily residue are removed.
    D. Review the BIOS setup configuration.
42. Which of the following is *not* an example of physical security? (1102: Domain 2)
    A. Mantrap
    B. Entry control roster
    C. USB locks
    D. Group policy
43. Which command-line tool will verify a network connection through several routers across the Internet and provide the time required for each hop? (1102: Domain 3)
    A. **nslookup**
    B. **net view**
    C. **ping**
    D. **tracert**

44. What is another term for *pharming*? (1102: Domain 2)
    A. DoS attack
    B. DNS poisoning
    C. Data mining
    D. Spear phishing
45. A computer system fails to complete the POST. What is *most likely* the source of the problem? (1102: Domain 3)
    A. A hardware device has had a catastrophic failure.
    B. One or more software applications installed on the HDD are corrupted.
    C. One or more of the operating system essential files are corrupted.
    D. The administrator user account has been compromised.
46. Which input launches a Remote Desktop connect when entered into the **Search** box? (1102: Domain 1)
    A. services
    B. remote
    C. mstsc
    D. regedit
47. Which is the correct order for installation of a multiple-boot system using the Windows 10 and Windows 11 operating systems? The hard disk drive has been prepared with two partitions. The first partition is primary partition C, and the second partition is D. (1102: Domain 1)
    A. Install Windows 10 on the primary partition C and then perform a clean installation of Windows 11 on C.
    B. Install Windows 10 on primary partition C and then install Windows 11 on partition D.
    C. Install Windows 11 on the primary partition C and then install Windows 10 on the second partition D.
    D. Install Windows 10 on the second partition D and then install Windows 11 on the primary partition C.
48. What is the default disk format option used for Windows 10? (1102: Domain 1)
    A. NTFS
    B. EFS
    C. FAT16
    D. FAT32
49. Which is the correct file structure path by default for the **My Documents** folder for a user named Student1? Assume the operating system is Windows 10. (1102: Domain 1)
    A. C:\Windows\My Documents\Student1
    B. This PC\Student1\My Documents
    C. C:\AllUsers\Student1\Library\My Documents
    D. This PC\Documents
50. You are checking a customer's Windows computer. Each time you boot the computer, you see a message on the display immediately following the POST. The message states, "Invalid partition table." Which hardware device is *most likely* the cause of the problem? (1102: Domain 3)
    A. CMOS
    B. CMOS battery
    C. HDD
    D. RAM

51. Which element of Control Panel enables faster results when conducting searches via Windows Explorer? (1102: Domain 1)
    A. File History
    B. Indexing Options
    C. File Explorer Options
    D. Administrative Tools
52. Which command line tool will check and verify the integrity of system files and replace them if necessary? (1102: Domain 3)
    A. **sfc**
    B. **fixboot**
    C. **bootrec**
    D. **fxmbr**
53. How does a logic bomb operate? (1102: Domain 2)
    A. A logic bomb leaves a backdoor in the security system of a network.
    B. A logic bomb attacks the MBR.
    C. A logic bomb steals passwords and operates as a keylogger.
    D. A logic bomb is a dormant program that does not inflict damage until a desired event takes place.
54. Which file types are changed when performing a system restore? (Select all that apply.) (1102: Domain 1)
    A. Register settings
    B. Programs
    C. E-mail contents
    D. System files
55. Which Windows application would you use to see if there have been attempts by unauthorized person(s) to access a computer? (1102: Domain 1)
    A. Internet Explorer
    B. **msconfig**
    C. Event Viewer
    D. Device Manager
56. Which is the recommended minimal length of a secure password? (1102: Domain 2)
    A. 16 characters
    B. 24 characters
    C. 4 characters
    D. 8 characters
57. A computer is approximately five months old. The user says that the computer ran fine at first but over time it is responding slower and slower, and it takes much longer for the computer to boot. What procedure would you try first? (1102: Domain 3)
    A. Run **msconfig** and then remove all unnecessary programs.
    B. Check the BIOS configuration and verify all hardware devices, especially the HDD, have been correctly detected.
    C. Check the amount of RAM and add or replace it if necessary.
    D. Make sure the antivirus program is installed, enabled, and working.
58. Which of the following ensures that every user's access is restricted only to what is needed for their job? (1102: Domain 2)
    A. Entry control roster
    B. Directory permissions
    C. Principle of least privilege
    D. End-user education

59. Which command line tool is used to inspect and create a partition in Windows 10 or later? (1102: Domain 3)
    A. **fdisk**
    B. **diskpart**
    C. **msinfo32**
    D. **format**
60. What Windows operating system feature is used to augment system RAM? (1102: Domain 1)
    A. DMA
    B. Page file
    C. EFS
    D. XP Mode
61. Which is the proper fire extinguisher type for electrical fires? (1102: Domain 4)
    A. Class A
    B. Class D
    C. Class B
    D. Class C
62. Which is the proper way to dispose of an LED monitor? (1102: Domain 4)
    A. Dispose of the monitor at a recycling facility.
    B. Pack the monitor inside a cardboard box and return it to the manufacturer.
    C. Place the monitor inside a metal dumpster and then shatter the screen with a metal hammer while wearing eye protection.
    D. Seal the monitor inside a 55-gallon metal drum and then place it by roadside for regular garbage pickup service.
63. Which of the following refers to the tracking and documentation of computer evidence? (1102: Domain 4)
    A. Evidence status
    B. Chain of custody
    C. Modus operandi
    D. Evidence buffering
64. A month ago, a technician installed a new application on a Windows workstation. Recently, a user opened a help ticket reporting that the workstation is intermittently crashing. The user is unsure if the crashing started before or after the application was installed. Which of the following is the best tool for the technician to use to determine if the crashes are caused by the application? (1102: Domain 3)
    A. Performance Monitor
    B. Component Services
    C. Application Monitor
    D. Event Viewer
65. Which Linux command displays a directory of files? (1102: Domain 1)
    A. **yum**
    B. **chown**
    C. **chown**
    D. **ls**
66. What is the primary function of the DXDIAG tool? (1102: Domain 1)
    A. Detect network connection problems
    B. Check the system registry for errors
    C. Check multimedia features
    D. Check partition fragmentation

67. Which command issued from the Windows 10 command prompt will check the HDD and automatically repair most errors? (1102: Domain 3)
    A. **chkdsk/F**
    B. **scandsk/F**
    C. **chkdsk/R**
    D. **regedit/F**
68. Which of the following is required to be at the computer machine to start the operating system installation? (1102: Domain 1)
    A. Microsoft Office
    B. Optical drive
    C. PXE
    D. Microsoft Edge
69. A user receives an e-mail stating that there has been an attempt to access her bank account and she needs to reset her password using the link provided in the e-mail. Which type of security threat does this exemplify? (1102: Domain 2)
    A. Phishing
    B. Man-in-the-middle
    C. DDoS
    D. Ransomware
70. What is the difference between an integer and a string? (1102: Domain 4)
    A. An integer cannot be a string, but a string can be an integer.
    B. An integer holds a specific numeric value; a string holds a range of characters.
    C. An integer is a command; a string is a what-if scenario.
    D. An integer is higher than a string in the script hierarchy.
71. Which command would you issue from the command prompt to view system information? (1102: Domain 1)
    A. **sysconfig**
    B. **msconfig**
    C. **system**
    D. **msinfo32**
72. How do you access the Windows Recovery Environment (WinRE) in Windows 10? (1102: Domain 3)
    A. **Start**>**Settings**>**Update & Security**>**Recovery**>**Advanced Startup**>**Restart now**
    B. Press [Ctrl][Alt][Del] during the POST
    C. Press [F6] during the boot process
    D. Enter WinRE.msc at the command prompt
73. Which Linux utility searches plain-text data sets for lines that match an expression? (1102: Domain 1)
    A. **chown**
    B. **chmod**
    C. **cd**
    D. **grep**
74. Which of the following is *not* a sure approach to wiping data? (1102: Domain 2)
    A. Degaussing
    B. Quick Format
    C. Shredding
    D. Drilling a hole through the hard drive

75. When is a user prompted for a power-on password? (1102: Domain 2)
    A. After the OS loads
    B. Before the POST
    C. During the POST
    D. After the POST
76. Which file type refers to a script file programmed for bash? (1102: Domain 4)
    A. **.vbs**
    B. **.sh**
    C. **.js**
    D. **.bat**
77. Which protocol or standard is designed to allow a user to connect a wireless device to a secure wireless device without the need to enter a passphrase or key? The device typically uses a push button. (1102: Domain 2)
    A. Dynamic addressing
    B. WPS
    C. FTP
    D. MAC filter
78. What organization is responsible for developing worker safety guidelines? (1102: Domain 4)
    A. OSHA
    B. FCC
    C. IEEE
    D. Microsoft
79. Which type of document would contain information about the safe handling of a particular toner cartridge? (1102: Domain 4)
    A. Original order form
    B. Shipping packing slip
    C. Invoice
    D. MSDS
80. What should you do when dealing with customers? (1102: Domain 4)
    A. Talk using technical terms when discussing the computer problem so that the customer is impressed with your knowledge.
    B. Explain procedures to a customer in a stern manner so that they clearly understand the importance of your work.
    C. Avoid using technical jargon when discussing computer problems with the customer.
    D. Always avoid direct eye contact with the customer while explaining the repair procedure.
81. Which of the following describes the best solution for a customer who loses power (and data) during summer thunderstorms? (1102: Domain 4)
    A. Explain to him that power loss caused by thunderstorms is unavoidable.
    B. Advise him to upgrade his grounding system.
    C. Advise him to install a UPS to provide constant power to the computer.
    D. Advise him to turn his computer off before a thunderstorm and do not use it for thirty minutes after the storm ends.
82. Which command would you issue from the command prompt to view the computer's assigned IP address? (1102: Domain 3)
    A. **ping**
    B. **net**
    C. **ipconfig**
    D. **tracert**

83. Which command syntax would you enter at the command prompt to recover the Windows 10 bootmgr? (1102: Domain 3)
    A. bootrec/now
    B. bootrec/fixboot
    C. fixboot/all
    D. fixboot
84. Which is the correct path to **Windows Update** in Windows 10? (1102: Domain 1)
    A. **Start**>**Settings**>**Windows Update**
    B. Right-click **Computer** and then select **Updates** from the shortcut menu.
    C. Right-click **Computer** and then select **Manage** from the shortcut menu.
    D. [Windows][X]>**Control Panel**>**Update & Security**
85. Which of the following describes a legal contract between a software user and the company that developed the software? (1102: Domain 4)
    A. PNG
    B. WFH
    C. DRM
    D. EULA
86. You are troubleshooting a computer problem. The symptoms are three short beeps followed by two long beeps and no apparent video. What would be your next course of action? (1102: Domain 3)
    A. Consult the video card manual.
    B. Open **System Configuration** and then disable all startup programs.
    C. Search the motherboard firmware website using the key terms "three short beeps two long beeps."
    D. Search the Microsoft TechNet website using the key terms "three short beeps two long beeps no video."
87. During the boot process, you hear multiple beeps coming from the computer. After the POST is complete, the display is blank. Where would you look to decipher the beep codes? (1102: Domain 3)
    A. The motherboard manufacturer website.
    B. Microsoft TechNet website.
    C. The HDD manufacturer website.
    D. The display manufacturer website.
88. What is the first step in removing malware? (1102: Domain 3)
    A. Enable System Restore and create a restore point.
    B. Identify and research malware symptoms.
    C. Quarantine the infected systems.
    D. Educate the end user.
89. Which of the following is true regarding humidity? (1102: Domain 4)
    A. High humidity is characterized by dry air.
    B. A lack of moisture in the air will cause corrosion and component failure.
    C. Computers in environments with low humidity are more susceptible to ESD.
    D. The ideal humidity is between 10 and 25 percent.
90. Which file type refers to a script file in DOS, OS/2, and Windows? (1102: Domain 4)
    A. **.ps1**
    B. **.bat**
    C. **.py**
    D. **.vbs**

A+ Note

Never give up if you fail the exam. Instead, study the areas you feel you lack knowledge in, and register to take the exam again.

Chapter Summary

25.1 A+ Certification Exams

- The examination objectives are categorized according to domains and are based on industry surveys that correlate exam content to actual job requirements.
- CompTIA recommends that a test candidate have at least 12 months of work experience. This is not a requirement.
- When reporting to the testing center, you must typically show two proofs of identification. Always check the requirements for identification before reporting to the testing center.
- The A+ Certification Exams consist of multiple-choice and performance-based questions.

25.2 Exam Preparation

- To ensure success on the A+ Certification Exams, establish a realistic study schedule and stick to it.
- Hands-on experience provides you with many of the required skills that are tested for on the A+ Certification Exams.
- Additional study resources include installation manuals, Readme files, and instructional web pages and websites.
- Creating your own study guide will improve your overall retention of the subject matter.
- Studying with a group of individuals who are serious about preparing for the A+ Certification Exams can be an excellent way to prepare.
- Taking practice exams helps evaluate your weak areas.

25.3 Sample CompTIA A+ 220-1101 Exam

- There are 90 total questions on the 220-1101 Exam. To pass, you must score 675 on a scale of 100–900.
- Approximately 54 percent of the exam will be dedicated to questions about both hardware and troubleshooting hardware and networks. Another 20 percent is dedicated to networking. Mobile devices, virtualization, and cloud computing factor approximately 26 percent.

25.4 Sample CompTIA A+ 220-1102 Exam

- There are 90 total questions on the 220-1102 Exam. To pass, you must score 700 on a scale of 100–900.
- Approximately 31 percent of the exam is dedicated to coverage of operating systems. Troubleshooting software accounts for 22 percent of the exam, and security accounts for another 25 percent. Operational procedures has the fewest questions of all the domains and accounts for 22 percent of the exam.

Review Questions

1. Summarize the characteristics, requirements, and format of the CompTIA A+ Certification Exams.
2. In terms of scoring the exam, what is meant by *weighted*?
3. Which are the largest domains in the CompTIA A+ 220-1101 Exam?
4. Which is the largest domain in the CompTIA A+ 220-1102 Exam?
5. What is a *field-test question*?
6. List strategies for preparing for the CompTIA A+ Certification exams.
7. Summarize the concept of *spaced repetition.*
8. What is the benefit of hands-on experience in preparing for the A+ Exams?
9. What are some general guidelines to follow when working with a study group?
10. Why is it important to set a test date as soon as you think you know the amount of preparation you will need?

Chapter 26

Employment and Advanced Education

Learning Outcomes

26.1 Identify areas in which IT professionals can work as well as sources of career information.

26.2 Summarize the importance of a job interview, as well as the appropriate preparation and attire for an interview.

26.3 Describe qualities employers seek in their employees.

Key Terms

cyberbullying
digital citizenship
digital footprint
problem-solving
soft skills

Overview

This chapter discusses methods used to gain employment and advance in your future career. Since the world of technology is constantly advancing, new ideas become realities, and careers in the computer technology field require continuing education. To keep up with the rapid changes in technology, you must form an action plan that includes strategies for keeping up to date with the changes in technology and using that newfound knowledge to create career advancement opportunities.

Employment issues are also discussed in this chapter. Although you may already be employed in a computer repair or related job, this chapter can help you better define your career goals.

A+ Note

The CompTIA A+ Certification is the first step in a long, productive IT career. While obtaining A+ Certification certainly makes you more marketable as a potential job candidate, remember that A+ is an entry-level certification, meaning there are many others you can obtain to build a specialty. For example, obtaining Network+ and Server+ can make you more marketable as a candidate for a network technician position. Regardless of the specialty you choose to pursue, commit yourself to lifelong learning. Information technology, and computing in general, is an ever-changing field, meaning you will have to learn and relearn as you grow in your career.

26.1 Career Opportunities

By successfully reaching this point in the textbook, you have probably decided whether to pursue a career working with computers. If you have the interest, desire, and ability, you can find a very rewarding career in the computer technology field. By completing this course, you have attained the first level of expertise, and you may even elect to go on for additional training in a more advanced field of computer technology. Being a computer technician is only one broad area in a field rich in choices, and some of the many other fields from which you can choose are shown in Figure 26-1.

Because the tools of the trade are constantly changing, a computer technician must continually learn new software, operating systems, and hardware. You can expand your knowledge to make yourself even more valuable as a computer technician or just to satisfy your own curiosity, and there are no limits to your education in the field of computer technology. In fact, if you stop learning, the technology will soon pass you by. It would only take a few years before you would feel as obsolete as some of the equipment on which you may work. Some possible career positions are listed in Figure 26-2.

There are many outstanding career opportunities for those who earn a computer science or related degree that you may be considering. Some college-level training programs offer specialized degrees in a diverse selection of areas, and others award credit based on technical certifications or work experience.

If you are interested in science and math in high school, you would probably enjoy studying computer science at a four-year college, as mathematics is a large part of computer-related college education. If you do not like mathematics and still want a rewarding career, you may choose to pursue an alternative educational path. For example, people who become software developers who have an engineering background are often called software engineers.

Employment Areas of Computer Technology

• computer engineering	• help-desk support	• system analyst
• computer programming	• network administration	• technical sales
• digital electronics	• network design, installation, and support	• web support

Goodheart-Willcox Publisher

Figure 26-1 *Computer technician* is just one broad area in a career field rich with choices.

Potential Careers in Computer Technology

• analyst	• Internet systems administrator	• programmer
• application developer	• IT consultant	• systems engineer
• chief information officer	• network engineer	• technical writer
• customer service representative	• network hardware specialist	• telecommunications data specialist
• database specialist	• network security specialist	• training specialist
• data communications engineer	• network support specialist	• VoIP engineer
• entry-level help-desk operator	• PC installer	• web developer
• industrial control engineer	• PC support professional	• webmaster

Goodheart-Willcox Publisher

Figure 26-2 There are many possible positions in an information technology career.

One alternative path you may consider is the training offered in the armed forces. The various branches of the military offer many specialized areas of study in the computer technology field. The opportunities for education are very good in the military services, and valuable work experiences are gained along the way, especially in the growing field of cybersecurity.

Another alternative educational path might be the completion of a special technical program offered at a local school, college, or technical center. These programs typically consist of advanced courses leading to globally recognized certifications. For example, Microsoft, Cisco, and many other companies offer certification examinations in many advanced fields of study, such as Microsoft's role-based certifications, which include Enterprise Administrator Expert, Azure Administrator Associate, and Azure AI Engineer Associate, among others. Preparing for certifications such as these can take a significant amount of time and experience or classroom or online training, but obtaining role-based certifications can prove to be a valuable addition to your résumé.

Each person must ask themself several questions before going further into the computer arena. For example, the fact that you are studying computers is a good indicator of interest in this area, but you must ask yourself if you have enjoyed the time you spent during this course of study. Additionally, you should ask yourself if you have enjoyed other computer courses and how well you performed in those courses. Give serious thought to the questions before responding, as your answers may provide you with the insight you need to choose a rewarding career.

Careers in the Information Technology Industry

As noted, there is a wide variety of career options in the information technology (IT) industry. Moreover, since computers, communication, and information systems play a major role in our daily lives, career opportunities for those with IT degrees and certifications exist virtually everywhere. Think of all the things that depend on computer systems today, including the linkage of our communication systems to computer networks and movie studios' use of advanced computer graphics software to create special effects that were impossible before the advent of the computer. Law enforcement, the military, and other governmental units depend on computers and interconnected technologies to communicate and perform their roles effectively.

Additional industries growing more reliant on computers include manufacturing, business, architecture, banking, and medicine. The manufacturing industry uses computer-controlled robots and automated assembly lines. In the business world, computers tie a company's sales department to its accounting and shipping departments for seamless transactions. Architects and engineers use computers to not only design structures, but also get a realistic first-person view of the design as they take a virtual stroll through its corridors. The entire banking industry relies on computers to track money exchanges, post records of interest and earnings, and compile mortgage statistics. In medicine, surgeons can now perform computer-assisted surgeries, patient medical records are all computerized, and medical prosthetics can now be manufactured through three-dimensional (3D) printing, as shown in Figure 26-3. The push toward integrating technology in nearly every industry allows for diverse opportunities for those in IT fields.

Computer technology and the need for those with related skills are positively correlated, meaning as computer technology integrates into every aspect of our world, the need for highly trained and skilled technicians grows. With the development of each new application for the computer, skilled technicians must be trained to maintain and service it, and with the ever-increasing utilization of technology in every aspect of life, the need for people with computer technology training will only continue to grow rapidly.

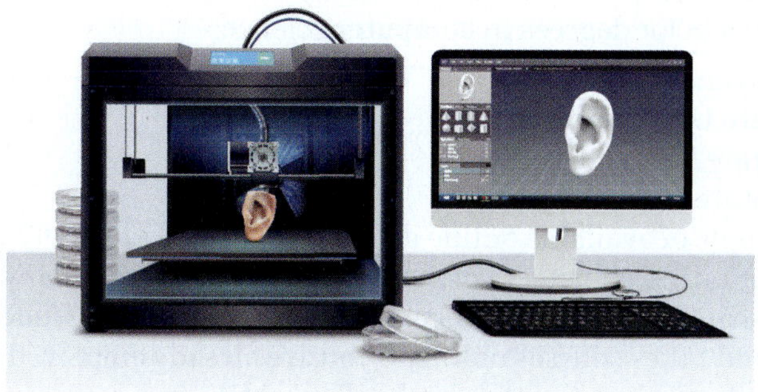

Macrovector/Shutterstock.com

Figure 26-3 The ability to manufacture prosthetics through 3D printing is just one example of the widespread incorporation of IT in medicine.

Career Information Sources

The *Occupational Outlook Handbook* is published by the United States Department of Labor and the Bureau of Statistics and offers information on careers in many industries. Most high school, community college, university, and public libraries have copies of this book, though it can also be viewed online at www.bls.gov/ooh. School guidance counselors, local labor markets, and job-placement offices are other outstanding sources of career information and can help you find information on careers, colleges, and other programs that offer training in areas in which you are interested. Those working within these resources are typically well informed and ready to help in your search for jobs or training. Many colleges offer job information and placement services, as well.

Finding a job can be a time-consuming and difficult task. Start by talking to your parents, neighbors, teachers, and guidance counselors, as they may know of job openings that have not been advertised. City, county, and state employment services may also provide useful job leads. Private employment agencies might also provide leads, but they often charge a fee for job placement.

The Internet also contains a great amount of career and training information and has become the first step in any career search. Many private company websites list employment opportunities, which often state the required skills, preferred educational levels, and a brief job description with a list of duties. Online job boards, such as Monster.com, Indeed, LinkedIn, and ZipRecruiter are also a valuable source of information for your employment search. Many of these websites allow you to create a profile and keep a résumé on file so employers can conduct their own search and reach out to you directly if you fit their need.

Education

The educational requirements for jobs in the information technology industry vary, though it is a safe assumption that most—if not all—will require a minimum of a high school diploma. Some high school graduates enter the industry directly and receive specialized education in employer-sponsored training programs, though most of these workers do not stop at this point. Instead, they continue to study to keep abreast of all the changes and new technologies that develop in the industry. As discussed, specialized training can also be found in colleges, technical schools, or the military.

While one can work in computer repair without any particular degree, you will likely find that many positions require specific credentials. Many state and private universities offer engineering and computer science degrees, and advanced degrees are becoming more commonplace as a means of moving ahead. Fortunately, distance learning education is now quite common, particularly for working adults. The educational website edX has information regarding affordable degrees, including both bachelor- and master-level diplomas. For example, the following universities all offer online bachelor degrees in computer science:

- Auburn University
- Arizona State University
- Colorado State University
- Louisiana State University

This is just a sample of available online degrees, and there are many others. A simple online search for online computer science degree will find you many more.

Distance learning courses are becoming commonplace. A student simply signs up from home and takes courses online. If you are already employed in a technology field and do not have time to attend school regularly, home study may be best for you. Many educational websites offer such programs, but there are many other sources as well. Unfortunately, this type of study takes tremendous self-discipline, and many people do not have the motivation needed to stick with this type of schooling. Another drawback is the lack of hands-on activities, which are essential to be successful in technical areas of study. Without hands-on application, simple memorization of facts is useless.

Tech Tip

Always vet the online degree program and institution before enrolling. Some schools may not be accredited, and degrees from these types of schools are often less marketable during a job search.

Advanced Certification

Certification is one way to advance your knowledge and career in the information technology industry. Often, people who work in the field of computer technology have minimal certification and most likely work under the supervision of another person who already has the certification. As a result, the employee must study at night for certification exams while working during the day in a related job, and this arrangement can limit their career advancement. As an IT professional, you will be learning for the rest of your life because the knowledge base of the computer industry is ever-expanding. Part of what you know now may very well be obsolete within years, and if you do not learn another thing from this point forward, your skills will soon be meager. Combining certification(s) with work experience is the best way to prove your abilities to a potential employer, but it is also a good way to advance within a company and gain job security.

Obtaining your A+ Certification should be only the beginning for you, and you should immediately consider advancing toward another area of certification. The Network+ Certification is a good place to continue and will serve as a springboard to other advanced certificates.

You may choose not to pursue another certification, and this decision is acceptable if you keep your skills current. Subscribe to and read professional journals in your area of work. Take as many courses as you can, such as digital electronics, to enhance your computer repair skills, and keep your existing certification(s) up to date by renewing them when needed.

After you enter the workforce in an entry-level position, you will want to consider further developing your technical skills. If you feel you have a future with your company, you should match the certification route to the company's needs. For example, if the company's network system is based on Microsoft, you should pursue the Microsoft line of certificates. If the company uses a system such as Unix or Linux, you should seek certification in one of these areas.

The time required to earn any certification depends on the individual's abilities. Some people can complete certification within a year; others lack the necessary aptitude and will never earn their certification. A good rule of thumb is to possess at least two years' experience and one year of study before attempting some of the more advanced certifications. Options for certification include additional CompTIA areas as well as Microsoft, Cisco, and other certifications.

CompTIA Certifications

The CompTIA organization offers certification by examination in many areas. Receiving an A+ Certification from CompTIA is just the beginning, however, as CompTIA offers advanced certificates that you may elect to pursue, such as Network+, Server+, Linux+, Cloud Essentials+, and Cloud+, among others. Many of the CompTIA certifications have similar domain objectives. When you earn one certificate, such as A+ Certification, you will have also learned many of the skills tested on for other certificates. The CompTIA certifications discussed in this section are limited to what a CompTIA A+ certified student might consider. Visit the CompTIA website for more detailed information about the various certifications.

Network+

The Network+ Certification assesses knowledge of small and large network systems. The ideal candidate should have 9 to 12 months of networking experience, but experience alone will not prepare you for the examination. You need to prepare for the test by taking an instructor-led course, a distance-learning course, or a self-study program. The test is vendor-neutral, meaning it is not based solely on a proprietary hardware or software system by one manufacturer such as D-Link, Intel, AMD, ASUS, Cisco Systems, and Microsoft. Instead, the examination tests knowledge of universal concepts of network systems.

Although you need to know the basics of network administration to pass the Network+ Certification Exam, the knowledge is only intended as a foundation before going on to network administration certification. The Network+ Certification is recommended before pursuing many advanced certificates.

Server+

The Server+ Certification is designed to assess a person's knowledge about network server hardware and software. The candidate is tested on installation, configuration, and diagnosis of network server hardware and network operating systems. The examination requires an in-depth knowledge of protocols, backup system standards, and system security.

Linux+

The Linux+ Certification assesses a candidate's knowledge of installing, configuring, and troubleshooting the Linux operating system for a single PC and network server. The Linux operating system is much like the operating systems you have studied thus far, though there are enough significant differences to warrant a separate certification. Two proprietary Linux certifications are Red Hat and SUSE, but there is also a vendor-neutral Linux certificate provided through the Linux Professional Institute (LPI), which is like the CompTIA Linux+ Certification. In fact, CompTIA has historically referred to its Linux+ exam as "powered by LPI." Before attempting to obtain Linux+ Certification, candidates may choose to have their exam results forwarded to the Linux Professional Institute, thereby earning them LPIC-1 (Junior Level Linux) Certification if they achieve Linux+ Certification.

Cloud Essentials+

Cloud services have expanded rapidly in the last few years, and as a result, the industry needs people with skills that support cloud services. The Cloud Essentials+ Certification measures basic knowledge related to cloud services. It is designed mainly for both IT and nontechnical professionals such as cloud-service sales representatives. This certification does not require any depth of technical knowledge related to cloud implementation and technical support, though CompTIA recommends that a Cloud Essentials+ candidate have at least six months of experience working for a company that represents cloud services or related IT services.

Cloud+

The Cloud+ Certification measures skills related to the implementation and support of cloud services and cloud infrastructure. This certification requires much more in-depth knowledge of cloud services than the Cloud Essentials+ Certification. For example, a Cloud+ candidate should be familiar with cloud server configuration, network storage, and virtualization technologies. CompTIA recommends 24 to 36 months of work experience in a related IT field, such as networking, network storage, or data center administration. Many cloud service providers also offer certification for their proprietary products, including Cisco Systems, Amazon, HP, IBM, and Microsoft. Many of the other proprietary cloud certifications require passing multiple tests to obtain certification for a company.

Security+

The Security+ Certification measures a candidate's mastery of general security concepts. Areas covered include communication, infrastructure, cryptography, and organizational security. CompTIA recommends candidates have at least two years' experience in networking, excellent grasp and knowledge of TCP/IP, some experience in related network security, and Network+ Certification. While these are recommended, they are not required before taking the exam.

This certification has rapidly become recognized internationally as an excellent verification of basic security principles and application, and the CompTIA Security+ Certification may be used to award credit toward other certifications offered by companies such as Microsoft and Symantec. You should consider the Security+ Certification if you plan to stay in information technology as a career.

Microsoft Certifications

Microsoft has had numerous certifications over time. In recent years, Microsoft has restructured the way a candidate can achieve individual certification. Typically, after successfully passing the CompTIA A+ Exams, many go on to obtain a Microsoft certification, usually by mastering or specializing in a specific area of computing or Microsoft systems. For example, Microsoft offers specialized certifications such as Azure support as well as product-specific certification through their Microsoft Office Specialist (MOS) certification, which is associated with the Microsoft Office application products.

Microsoft formerly offered certification categories such as Microsoft Technology Associate (MTA), Microsoft Certified Solutions Associate (MCSA), Microsoft Certified Solutions Expert (MCSE), and Microsoft Office Specialist (MOS), but these have by and large been replaced by topic certifications. Some that might be useful in computer repair include the following:

- Microsoft Certified: Azure Support Engineer for Connectivity Specialty
- Microsoft Certified: Information Protection Administrator Associate
- Microsoft 365 Certified: Teams Administrator Associate
- Microsoft 365 Certified: Fundamentals
- Microsoft Certified: Identity and Access Administrator Associate

Cisco Training and Certifications

Cisco Systems provides training opportunities at high schools and colleges all over the United States at training sites referred to as a *Cisco Networking Academies*. These academies emphasize network design, implementation, and troubleshooting using Cisco products, which are widely used for network communication. The academy courses are designed as a combination of lecture, textbook, online learning, and hands-on laboratory activities.

Two entry-level certifications offered through the Cisco Networking Academies are Cisco Certified Technician (CCT) and Cisco Certified Entry Networking Technician (CCENT), though some other common certifications include Cisco Certified Network Associate (CCNA), Cisco Certified Network Professional (CCNP), and Cisco Certified Internetwork Expert (CCIE). Cisco also offers many specialized certificates in areas of security, wireless network systems, and IT essentials.

Cisco has restructured its certifications in recent years and divided the areas of certification into career areas. As of this writing, the areas include the following:

- Networking, Network Design, and Security
- Voice and Collaboration Solutions
- Data Center and Storage Networking
- Service Provider

The certification process is then arranged in a hierarchy starting at Entry and progressing to Architect. The five levels of expertise, in order of difficulty, are

- Entry;
- Associate;
- Professional;
- Expert; and
- Architect.

The certificates are obtained by passing specific Cisco examinations. You can learn more about the certifications offered and locate the Cisco Networking Academy nearest you by visiting the Cisco Systems website.

Other Certifications

Many other companies such as 3Com, Corel, Juniper, Nortel Networks, Red Hat Linux, and Oracle have certification programs. Check their websites for in-depth information about the exams. There you will find exam outlines, study materials, schools, available training, and prerequisites.

Entrepreneurs

Entrepreneurs own and operate their own businesses. According to the Small Business and Entrepreneurship (SBE) Council, small businesses with fewer than 500 employees comprise over 99 percent of all businesses in the United States and provide nearly half of the jobs in America. Entrepreneurs usually start with an idea for filling a void in the marketplace, perhaps where a new product or service is needed. Typically, a business plan is produced before a group or individual decides to open a private business, and business plans are often vital to the success of the business. If the entrepreneur is seeking financial support, such as a business loan, then a business plan is always required, and it must outline goals for the business, an action plan, and a timetable for meeting those goals.

In addition to a sound business plan, a successful entrepreneur possesses a good knowledge of their business, industry, service, and product, all of which are used to make smart business decisions. Successful entrepreneurs also have sound management skills that allow them to successfully manage money, time, and employees. Management of each of these is critical to success, and poor management in any of these areas can lead to certain failure.

Entrepreneurial skills, or the ability to think and move creatively and wisely, are also very important for a successful entrepreneur, as these skills allow the business owner to control the business and move it in the right direction. Entrepreneurial opportunities are vast in the IT industry, and tremendous growth in the market has triggered a similar growth in the demand for computer services. These highly demanded services include computer maintenance and repair, training, and Internet services.

Consulting is yet another growing business in the information technology industry. *Consultants* work for clients on special or individual projects, depending on the work needed. Clients pay consultants for their expertise, and when the job is completed, consultants are free to move on to a new job.

26.2 Job Interviews

The three most important factors that determine your ability to land a job are your work history, technical expertise, and the job interview. A work history tells the employer a lot about you as a future employee, even if the job experiences are unrelated to the job for which you are applying. You may just be entering the IT profession, but a positive recommendation from a past employer can make the difference. A recommendation from a former employer shows that you have been a valuable and dependable employee. A person with no work history is a gamble in most employers' eyes; they want to see a track record.

Prior technical experience can prove to be a real asset, whether it is from past jobs or formal training. Other applicants may have no technical employment history or training. They may have simple, informal experience helping friends with their home computer and now believe they can handle a similar professional job. This is where your training and work history puts you ahead of others.

The job interview is the major factor in determining if an applicant gets the job, as it gives the employer a chance to evaluate the applicant through a series of questions. The way a question is answered is often more important than the answer itself. For example, if an employer asks, "What would you do if you could not fix a computer problem?" The way you answer the question may tell the employer about your character, confidence, and ability to work with others. The employer is looking for certain traits in the individual they are interviewing, including honesty, confidence, dependability, and the ability to work well as a team member.

Employers may not ask the same questions of all applicants and will not usually be direct about the qualities they are seeking. Instead, the employer may ask questions to probe for the character and job-related qualities they want. For example, an employer may ask you to describe a time you had a problem with a fellow employee and how it was resolved. The answer to this question can tell an experienced interviewer a lot about the character of the applicant. Once you have secured an interview, it is important to be prepared for it. The following section outlines preparation tips for a successful interview.

Preparation for the Interview

An interview is perhaps the most critical stage in a job search and a process that you can control to a great extent. A good interview can convince an employer to overlook a lack of experience or education, but a poor interview can cause even the most qualified candidate to be passed over. The following are a few tips to help you prepare for your interview:

- *Never* fabricate anything on your résumé or in your interview.
- Research prospective employer's positions. This lets the employer know you are truly interested in the company and that you have the personal initiative to conduct research.
- Review your qualifications for the job to ensure they match those desired by the employer. Do not waste the employer's time or your own with a mismatch.
- Prepare to answer broad questions about yourself. It is wise to practice interviewing with someone who has knowledge about job interviews.

- A quality résumé can make a favorable impression on an employer. Use high-quality paper and a cover sheet. Make sure you have a hard copy the employer may keep as well as a digital copy.
- Plan to arrive 15 minutes before the scheduled time of your interview. Showing up late is unacceptable. Locate the building in advance and determine how much time it will take to get there. Conduct a practice run the day before so you will know exactly how to get to the interview and the length of time it will take you to arrive, taking traffic into consideration.
- Prepare a backup transportation plan in case you have difficulty with your vehicle.

Personal Appearance

The first impression you make on an employer is critical. People are summarily judged on their outward appearance. If you look and act professionally, you will make a favorable impression on your interviewer and future coworkers.

While some IT jobs allow a casual appearance, most employers require more professional attire since many technicians and administrators often interact with professionals within the company. A neat, clean, and appearance shows that you take pride in yourself and in your work. Even if the job is a backroom position, always dress appropriately for the interview. Blue jeans and a T-shirt are never appropriate.

Regardless of the job conditions, you should always dress up rather than down for an interview, meaning dress for a formal business setting. In general, you should dress in a way that reflects the working environment. Dressing more conservatively is not likely to be a disadvantage to you, but you want to show that you understand what is appropriate in the workplace.

Personal grooming is equally as important as attire. Refrain from wearing perfume or cologne, and style your hair in a professional manner. Fingernails should be clean, and all tattoos should be covered. Similarly, all visible piercings should be downplayed. Finally, avoid chewing gum, eating, or drinking during the interview, as this can come across as rude or unprofessional behavior.

The Interview

Once the interview begins, your responses to questions are actively evaluated. The interviewer is trying to determine your work ethic, attitude, intelligence, and competency based on your answers and body language. In general, answer all questions to the best of your ability, and if you do not have an answer, simply say so. Do not try to make up an answer; rather, express your willingness to learn any new topics with which you may not be familiar. Admit your limitations, and you will find the interviewer will most likely respect your honesty.

Speak slowly and concisely using proper English. Avoid slang, and *never* use foul language, even in a joking manner. Similarly, use good manners, and remember to treat everyone you encounter with courtesy. Say "please" and thank you" when necessary, and never assume you have the job until it has been offered to you.

Your body language conveys a great deal about your personality. You want to convey a sense of confidence, but also cooperation and enthusiasm. This can be achieved through smiling, sitting up straight, and maintaining eye contact with the interviewer. Slumping or looking away as you talk can convey a lack of confidence, which could result in a negative experience for both you and the interviewer.

You will almost certainly be given an opportunity to ask questions about the position and the organization. It is advisable that you prepare some questions, as this makes you look better prepared, but limit your questions to conditions you do not understand. Avoid asking about salary unless it was not listed in the job posting, uncovered by your research, or discussed by your prospective employer during the interview. Often, salary can be discussed or negotiated in a second interview or during the subsequent pre-employment process.

The interview has not ended when you start asking questions. In fact, your questions can reveal even more to the employer. For example, asking how many breaks you will get during a day will send an undesirable message to the employer. It is not required that you ask questions, especially if the interview has been thorough, but do not hesitate if you believe there is pertinent information that you must know. Remember, there will be additional time to make any clarifications or salary negotiations after you are offered the job. After the interview has concluded, it is customary to follow-up with a thank-you message, which can be in the form of a written letter, thank-you card, or e-mail. Thanking the interviewer for their consideration and time shows an eagerness to work for that company and helps keep your name in the interviewer's mind while they evaluate candidates.

Employer Testing

Employer testing is very common today as part of the job interview process. An employer can tell a lot about your technical knowledge and communication skills through a test, especially if handwritten answers are required. In these instances, write neatly when taking tests, as poor penmanship can make a bad impression on a prospective employer. When completing your test, you should

- be sure you understand all written test directions, and if you are unclear about anything, confirm it with your interviewer before you begin the test;
- read each question carefully;
- write legibly and clearly; and
- budget your time wisely by not dwelling on one question.

Information to Bring to an Interview

Important documentation required at an interview includes your Social Security and driver's license numbers as well as a copy of your résumé, which should feature a complete chronological list of your education and training. List all your past employment in sequence, and do not leave blank dates. If you stopped your employment to go to school, note the dates. This ensures your potential employer does not think you are trying to leave out an employer who may not give you a good reference. List the reasons for any breaks in your employment history. You may also consider bringing a copy of your completed job application, which should be legible.

You may wish to include copies of training and award certificates, transcripts, and letters of reference with your résumé. Typically, these will be verified anyway if listed on your résumé, but including copies with your résumé may speed up the verification procedure.

References

Providing references, typically three to four, for a job is customary, and the quality of your references can mean a great deal to the employer. Some good sources for references include teachers, past employers, supervisors, and fellow employees. Friends, family, and clergy are not considered good references. Get permission from each person before using them as a reference, and provide a name, address, telephone number, and occupation for each. Also, note if the person was a past supervisor.

26.3 Keeping a Job

Obtaining a job is only part of finding gainful employment. The other, and at times more difficult, part is keeping the job. Remember, as an employee, you represent the company during your normal working hours or when on official company business. When hiring applicants, and especially when promoting employees, employers look for specific characteristics outside of skills, and most employers look for the same qualities, specifically digital citizenship and various soft skills.

Digital Citizenship

Perhaps more important to information technology than any other industry, **digital citizenship** is the standard of appropriate behavior when using technology. Good digital citizenship focuses on using technology positively, rather than using it for negative or illegal purposes. It is necessary to learn to communicate effectively, ethically, and appropriately within a digital society.

Information posted online never really goes away; instead, it leaves a **digital footprint**, which is a data record of all an individual's online activities. Even if something is deleted from the Internet, it remains in a person's digital footprint. Always consider what a potential employer would think of something before posting it online.

Cyberbullying is the use of electronic technology to harass or threaten a person. This includes social media, text messages, or e-mails. Cyberbullying is not only unethical; in many cases, it can be prosecuted as a criminal act. While not necessarily criminal, certain unethical actions, such as flaming, trolling, and spamming, violate *netiquette*, or online etiquette. *Flaming*, also called *roasting*, is purposefully insulting someone, often using profane or offensive language. Similarly, *trolling* is the act of intentionally inciting an argument or sowing discord in online comments, message boards, or forums. *Spamming* is the sending of unwanted mass e-mails or intentionally flooding an individual's social media site or e-mail inbox with unwanted messages.

Soft Skills

Recall from Chapter 24 that **soft skills** are skills used to communicate and work well with others. Contrast these from *hard skills*, which are the essential, critical skills needed to perform required work-related tasks. Soft skills may also be referred to as *employability skills*, *people skills*, or *interpersonal skills*. These are the skills for which virtually every employer looks. Examples of essential soft skills in the workplace include professionalism, communication, punctuality, teamwork, and problem-solving skills.

Professionalism

Professionalism is the act of exhibiting appropriate character, judgment, and behavior by a person who is trained to perform a job. Put simply, it is a person's conduct while at work or representing their employer. A professional employee arrives to work on time each day, productively performs job tasks, dresses appropriately for their job, takes responsibility for their behavior, and is a good communicator. Professionals also possess integrity, honesty, and a positive attitude. For more about professionalism, review Chapter 24.

Communication

Communication skills can be verbal or nonverbal. *Verbal communication* is speaking words to communicate and allowing information to be shared, requests to be made, direction to be given, and persuasion to be applied when action is needed. *Nonverbal communication* is any action, behavior, or attitude that sends a message, including body language, eye contact, touch, personal space, and paralanguage, which is the attitude projected with a tone or pitch of a person's voice.

Nonverbal communication also covers written communication. You can demonstrate good written communication skills by avoiding slang and using standard English. *Standard English* is language usage that follows the accepted rules for spelling, grammar, and punctuation. Even in the IT industry, you will encounter the need for professional writing, whether it is a work order, incident report, or e-mail to a client or supervisor. Sending correspondence that is littered with spelling errors or grammatical mistakes will make you and, by extension, your employer, look bad. It is essential to be able to communicate verbally, in writing, and to be aware of your nonverbal communication. For more about communication skills, review Chapter 24.

Punctuality

Punctuality is being on time and is essential while at work. If you are scheduled to work at 8:00 a.m., then you should be in your designated workspace at that time. Parking your car or entering the building at that time technically constitutes a late arrival. Being constantly late or not showing up for a scheduled shift is inconsiderate and not tolerated in a professional workplace; it can also lead to volatile working relationships with your coworkers. If you know you are going to be late or miss work entirely, it is expected that you notify your employer with enough time to make alternative plans.

Teamwork

Teamwork is the cooperative efforts by individual team members to achieve a goal. Being a good team player is an essential soft skill for career success. Members of a team ideally take pride in their work, share responsibilities and decision-making, and develop a sense of accomplishment when a project is completed. This only happens when the team members work together and focus on their assigned tasks. Showing you are a team player involves collaboration and compromising skills. For more about teamwork, review Chapter 24.

Problem-Solving

Problem-solving is the process of choosing a course of action after evaluating available information and weighing the costs, benefits, and consequences of alternative actions. It involves critical thinking and the ability to use prior knowledge, new data, and good judgment to solve problems. Applying a systematic problem-solving process is a necessary job skill. The steps of this process are shown in Figure 26-4.

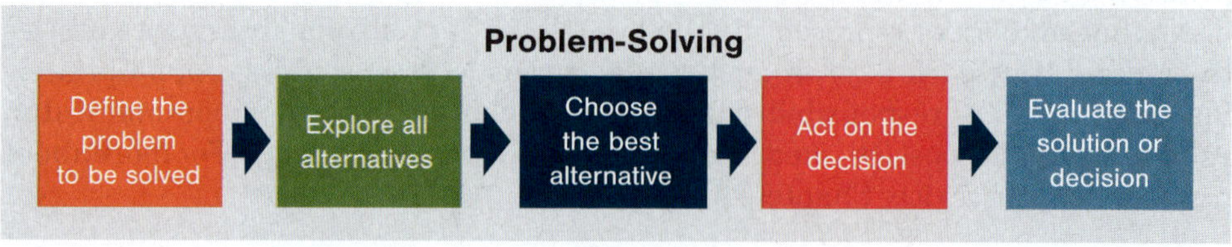

Goodheart-Willcox Publisher

Figure 26-4 Problem-solving is the process of choosing a course of action after evaluating available information and weighing the costs, benefits, and consequences of alternative actions.

Chapter Summary

26.1 Career Opportunities

- An information technology (IT) position requires continuing education; a recognized certification is a way of proving your expertise in a computer technology specialty.
- Because the tools of the trade are constantly changing, a computer technician must continually learn new software, operating systems, and hardware. Expanding your knowledge to make yourself even more valuable as a computer technician or just to satisfy your own curiosity, and there are no limits to your education in the field of computer technology.
- There are many outstanding career opportunities for those who earn a computer science or related degree that you may be considering.
- There are a wide variety of career options in the information technology (IT) industry. Moreover, since computers, communication, and information systems play a major role in our daily lives, career opportunities for those with IT degrees and certifications exist virtually everywhere.
- Industries in which IT professionals can work include communications, entertainment, law enforcement, the military, government, manufacturing, business, banking, and medicine, among others. There are also opportunities for entrepreneurship, small-business ownership, and consultation.
- The *Occupational Outlook Handbook* is published by the United States Department of Labor and the Bureau of Statistics and offers information on careers in many industries.
- Finding a job can be a time-consuming and difficult task. Start by talking to your parents, neighbors, teachers, and guidance counselors, as they may know of job openings that have not been advertised.
- City, county, and state employment services may also provide useful job leads. Private employment agencies might also provide leads, but they often charge a fee for job placement.
- The Internet also contains a great amount of career and training information and has become the first step in any career search. Many private company sites list employment opportunities, which often state the required skills, preferred educational levels, and a brief job description with a list of duties. Online job boards, such as Monster.com, Indeed, LinkedIn, and ZipRecruiter are also a valuable source of information for your employment search.

26.2 Job Interviews

- The job interview is the major factor in determining if an applicant gets the job, as it gives the employer a chance to evaluate the applicant through a series of questions.
- Conduct research on a prospective employer's positions, review your qualifications for the job to ensure they match those desired by the employer, prepare to answer broad questions about yourself, review and revise your résumé so it makes a favorable impression, and plan your route in advance so you can arrive early.
- The first impression you make on an employer is critical. People are summarily judged on their outward appearance. If you look and act professionally, you will make a favorable impression on your interviewer and future coworkers.

- While some IT jobs allow a casual appearance, most employers require a more professional appearance since many technicians and administrators often interact with professionals within the company. A neat, clean, and professional appearance shows that you take pride in yourself and in your work. Regardless of the job conditions, you should always dress up rather than down for an interview, meaning dress for a formal business setting. In general, you should dress in a way that reflects the working environment. Personal grooming is equally as important as attire. Finally, avoid chewing gum, eating, or drinking during the interview, as this can come across as rude or unprofessional behavior.
- If tested by the prospective employer, be sure you understand instructions for the examination.

26.3 Keeping a Job

- *Digital citizenship* is the standard of appropriate behavior when using technology.
- *Soft skills*, also called *employability skills*, *people skills*, or *interpersonal skills*, are skills used to communicate and work well with others.
- Examples of essential soft skills in the workplace include professionalism, communication, punctuality, teamwork, and problem-solving skills.

Review Questions

1. Identify areas in which an information technology professional can work.
2. Identify sources of career information.
3. Describe the importance of certification in the IT industry.
4. List CompTIA certifications aside from A+.
5. Describe characteristics of a successful entrepreneur.
6. Discuss the importance of a job interview.
7. Identify common traits employers look for in job candidates.
8. List important interview preparation strategies.
9. How should you be dressed for the interview?
10. What is an interviewer trying to determine based on your answers and body language?
11. Describe appropriate behavior for a job interview.
12. What items should you take to a job interview?
13. Describe qualities employers seek in their employees.
14. What are *soft skills*?
15. List soft skills valued by most employers.

CompTIA A+ Exam Correlation

The following lists the CompTIA A+ Exam Objectives for Exams 220-1101 and 220-1102 and the chapter and heading at which the objectives are covered within the *Computer Service and Repair* sixth edition textbook.

Exam **220-1101 (Core 1)**

1.0 Mobile Devices

1.1 Given a scenario, install and configure laptop hardware and components.

Hardware/device replacement
- Battery .... Chapter 13
- Keyboard/keys .... Chapter 7, Keyboard Connectors
- Random access memory (RAM) .... Chapter 6, Installing RAM Modules; Chapter 13, Upgrading Memory
- Hard disk drive (HDD)/solid-state drive (SSD) migration .... Chapter 13, Replacing an Internal Hard Drive; Chapter 10, Solid-State Drives
- HDD/SSD replacement .... Chapter 10, PATA Drive Installation, SATA Drive Installation, Solid-State Drives
- Wireless cards .... Chapter 13, Replacing a Wireless Card

Physical privacy and security components .... Chapter 15, Privacy Filters; Chapter 13, Physical Locks
- Biometrics .... Chapter 13, Biometrics
- Near-field scanner features .... Chapter 7, Near-Field Communication (NFC)

1.2 Compare and contrast the display components of mobile devices.

Types .... Chapter 8, Types of Video Displays

Liquid-crystal display (LCD) .... Chapter 8, Liquid-Crystal Displays
- In-plane switching (IPS) .... Chapter 8, Active-Matrix Display
- Twist nematic (TN) .... Chapter 8, Active-Matrix Display
- Vertical alignment (VA) .... Chapter 8, Active-Matrix Display
- Organic light-emitting diode (OLED) .... Chapter 8, Organic LED Displays

Mobile display components .... Chapter 13, Screen

Wi-Fi antenna connector/placement .... Chapter 13, Replacing a Wireless Card, Wireless Connections

Camera/webcam .... Chapter 7, Scanners and Digital Cameras

Microphone .... Chapter 9, Microphone

Touch screen/digitizer .... Chapter 7, Digitizer Pad, Touch Screens

Inverter .... Chapter 8, Backlighting

1.3 Given a scenario, set up and configure accessories and ports of mobile devices.

Connection methods
- Universal Serial Bus (USB)/USB-C/micro-USB/mini-USB .... Chapter 1, USB
- Lightning .... Chapter 1, Lightning
- Serial interfaces .... Chapter 1 DB, Serial and Parallel Data Transfer
- Near-field communication (NFC) .... Chapter 7, Near-Field Communication (NFC)

Bluetooth .... Chapter 7, Bluetooth; Chapter 13, Bluetooth Standard
Hotspot .... Chapter 14, Tethering, Mobile Hotspots
Touch pens .... Chapter 7, Digitizer Pad, Tablet and Smartphone Hardware and Accessories
Headsets .... Chapter 9, Virtual Reality, Augmented Reality, and Audio Headsets
Speakers .... Chapter 9, Speakers
Webcam .... Chapter 7, Scanners and Digital Cameras
Docking station .... Chapter 13, Docking Station
Port replicator .... Chapter 13, Port Replicator
Trackpad/drawing pad .... Chapter 7, Digitizer Pad

1.4 Given a scenario, configure basic mobile-device network connectivity and application support.

Wireless/cellular data network (enable/disable)
2G/3G/4G/5G .... Chapter 14, 3G and 4G, 5G, Global System for Mobile Communications
Hotspot .... Chapter 14, Mobile Hotspot, Tethering; Chapter 23, Mobile Hotspots and Tethering
Global System for Mobile Communications (GSM) vs. code division multiple access (CDMA) .... Chapter 14, Global System for Mobile Communications, Code Division Multiple Access
Preferred Roaming List (PRL) updates .... Chapter 13, PRI and PRL Updates, Radio Firmware Updates
Bluetooth
Enable Bluetooth .... Chapter 13, Bluetooth Standard
Enable pairing .... Chapter 13, Bluetooth Standard
Find a device for pairing .... Chapter 13, Bluetooth Standard
Enter the appropriate PIN code .... Chapter 13, Bluetooth Standard
Test connectivity .... Chapter 13, Bluetooth Standard
Location services
Global Positioning System (GPS) services .... Chapter 13, Global Positioning System
Cellular location services .... Chapter 13, Common Mobile Services
Mobile device management (MDM)/mobile application management (MAM) .... Chapter 13, MDM and MAM; Chapter 21, MDM Policies
Corporate e-mail configuration .... Chapter 22, POP3, IMAP, Port and SSL Settings, MIME and S/MIME
Two-factor authentication .... Chapter 13, Securing Mobile Devices; Chapter 15, Multifactor Authentication
Corporate applications .... Chapter 13, MDM and MAM; Chapter 21, MDM Policies
Mobile device synchronization .... Chapter 13, Synchronization
Account setup .... Chapter 13, Synchronization
Microsoft 365 .... Chapter 13, Synchronization
Google Workspace .... Chapter 13, Synchronization
iCloud .... Chapter 13, Synchronization
Data to synchronize
Mail .... Chapter 2, Sync Your Settings; Chapter 13, Figure 13-7
Photos .... Chapter 2, Sync Your Settings; Chapter 13, Figure 13-7
Calendar .... Chapter 2, Sync Your Settings; Chapter 13, Figure 13-7
Contacts .... Chapter 2, Sync Your Settings; Chapter 13, Figure 13-7
Recognizing data caps .... Chapter 13, Synchronization

2.0 Networking

2.1 Compare and contrast Transmission Control Protocol (TCP) and User Datagram Protocol (UDP) ports, protocols, and their purposes.

Ports and Protocols .... Chapter 16, Firewall; Chapter 20, Protocols, Figure 20-1
20/21–File Transfer Protocol (FTP) .... Chapter 22, FTP, Figure 22-12
22–Secure Shell (SSH) .... Chapter 22, SSH
23–Telnet .... Chapter 22, Telnet, Figure 22-12

- 25–Simple Mail Transfer Protocol (SMTP) ... Chapter 22, SMTP, Figure 22-12
- 53–Domain Name System (DNS) ... Chapter 22, DNS, Figure 22-12
- 67/68–Dynamic Host Configuration Protocol (DHCP) ... Chapter 22, DHCP, Figure 22-12
- 80–Hypertext Transfer Protocol (HTTP) ... Chapter 22, HTTP, Figure 22-12
- 110–Post Office Protocol 3 (POP3) ... Chapter 22, POP3, Figure 22-12
- 137/139–Network Basic Input/Output System (NetBIOS)/NetBIOS over TCP/IP (NetBT) ... Chapter 22, Figure 22-12
- 143–Internet Mail Access Protocol (IMAP) ... Chapter 22, IMAP, Figure 22-12
- 161/162–Simple Network Management Protocol (SNMP) ... Chapter 22, SNMP, Figure 22-12
- 389–Lightweight Directory Access Protocol (LDAP) ... Chapter 22, Figure 22-12
- 443–Hypertext Transfer Protocol Secure (HTTPS) ... Chapter 22, HTTPS, Figure 22-12
- 445–Server Message Block (SMB)/Common Internet File System (CIFS) ... Chapter 22, SMB, CIFS
- 3389–Remote Desktop Protocol (RDP) ... Chapter 22, Figure 22-12

TCP vs. UDP ... Chapter 20, TCP/IP; Chapter 22, TCP and UDP

- Connectionless ... Chapter 22, TCP and UDP
  - DHCP ... Chapter 22, DHCP, Figure 22-12
  - Trivial File Transfer Protocols (TFTP) ... Chapter 22, FTP
- Connection-oriented ... Chapter 22, TCP and UDP
  - HTTPS ... Chapter 22, HTTPS, Figure 22-12
  - SSH ... Chapter 22, SSH

2.2 Compare and contrast common networking hardware.

- Routers ... Chapter 19, Routers
- Switches ... Chapter 19, Switches
  - Managed ... Chapter 19, Switches
  - Unmanaged ... Chapter 19, Switches
- Access points ... Chapter 19, Routers, Wireless Routers, Figure 19-11; Chapter 20, Wireless, Figure 20-7
- Patch panel ... Chapter 20, Punch Down Tool, Figure 20-23
- Firewall ... Chapter 16, Firewall; Chapter 22, Firewall; Chapter 23, Firewall
- Power over Ethernet (PoE) ... Chapter 20, Power over Ethernet (PoE)
  - Injectors ... Chapter 20, Power over Ethernet (PoE)
  - Switch ... Chapter 20, Power over Ethernet (PoE)
- Hub ... Chapter 19, Hubs
- Cable modem ... Chapter 14, Cable Modem
- Digital subscriber line (DSL) ... Chapter 14, DSL Modem and Cables
- Optical network terminal (ONT) ... Chapter 20, Fiber-Optic Cable
- Network interface card (NIC) ... Chapter 19, Network Interface Cards
- Software-defined networking ... Chapter 20, Software-Defined Networking

2.3 Compare and contrast protocols for wireless networking.

- Frequencies
  - 2.4 GHz ... Chapter 13, Wireless Standards
  - 5 GHz ... Chapter 13, Wireless Standards
- Channels
  - Regulations ... Chapter 20, How Data Is Packaged
  - 2.4 GHz vs. 5 GHz ... Chapter 13, Wireless Standards
- Bluetooth ... Chapter 7, Bluetooth; Chapter 13, Bluetooth Standard
- 802.11 ... Chapter 13, Wireless Standards
  - a ... Chapter 13, Wireless Standards
  - b ... Chapter 13, Wireless Standards
  - g ... Chapter 13, Wireless Standards
  - n ... Chapter 13, Wireless Standards
  - ac (Wi-Fi 5) ... Chapter 13, Wireless Standards
  - ax (Wi-Fi 6) ... Chapter 13, Wireless Standards

2.4 Summarize services provided by networked hosts.

Server roles
- DNS .... Chapter 19, DNS; Chapter 20, DNS; Chapter 21, DNS Server
- DHCP .... Chapter 20, DHCP; Chapter 21, DHCP Server
- Fileshare .... Chapter 21, File Server
- Print servers .... Chapter 21, Print Server
- Mail servers .... Chapter 21, Mail Server
- Syslog .... Chapter 21, Server Roles
- Web servers .... Chapter 21, Web Server (IIS)
- Authentication, authorization, and accounting (AAA) .... Chapter 21, Authentication Server

Internet appliances
- Spam gateways .... Chapter 22, Spam Gateway
- Unified Threat Management (UTM) .... Chapter 21, UTM
- Load balancers .... Chapter 22, Load Balancer
- Proxy servers .... Chapter 21, Proxy Server; Chapter 22, Proxy Server

Legacy/embedded systems .... Chapter 21, Centralized Administration
- Supervisory control and data acquisition (SCADA) .... Chapter 21, Centralized Administration

Internet of Things (IoT) devices .... Chapter 20, Internet of Things (IoT)

2.5 Given a scenario, install and configure a basic wired/wireless SOHO network.

Internet Protocol (IP) addressing .... Chapter 22, IP Addresses
- IPv4 .... Chapter 22, IP Addresses
  - Private addresses .... Chapter 22, IPv4 Network Class
  - Public addresses .... Chapter 22, IPv4 Network Class
- IPv6 .... Chapter 22, Advantages of IPv6
- Automatic Private IP Addressing (APIPA) .... Chapter 22, Automatic Private IP Address
- Static .... Chapter 22, DHCP
- Dynamic .... Chapter 22, DHCP; Chapter 23, DHCP Configuration
- Gateway .... Chapter 22, Gateway

2.6 Compare and contrast common network configuration concepts.

DNS Chapter 22, DNS, Figure 22-12; Chapter 21, DNS Server
- Address .... Chapter 19, DNS
  - A .... Chapter 19, DNS
  - AAAA .... Chapter 19, DNS
- Mail exchanger (MX) .... Chapter 19, DNS
- Text (TXT) .... Chapter 19, DNS
  - Spam management .... Chapter 19, DNS
    - (i) DomainKeys Identified Mail (DKIM) .... Chapter 19, DNS
    - (ii) Sender Policy Framework (SPF) .... Chapter 19, DNS
    - (iii) Domain-based Message Authentication, Reporting, and Conformance (DMARC) .... Chapter 19, DNS

DHCP .... Chapter 22, DHCP
- Leases .... Chapter 22, DHCP
- Reservations .... Chapter 22, Reserved IP Addresses, Advantages of IPv6; Chapter 23, DHCP Configuration
- Scope .... Chapter 21, DHCP Server

Virtual LAN (VLAN) .... Chapter 22, IPv4 Subnet Mask

Virtual Private Network (VPN) .... Chapter 23, Virtual Private Network (VPN)

2.7 Compare and contrast Internet connection types, network types, and their features.

Internet connection types
- Satellite .... Chapter 14, Satellite
- Fiber .... Chapter 14, Cable Media; Chapter 20, Fiber-Optic Cable

- Cable ... Chapter 14, Cable
- DSL ... Chapter 14, Digital Subscriber Lines
- Cellular ... Chapter 14, Mobile Broadband, Cellular Connections through Mobile Broadband Tower
- Wireless Internet Service Provider (WISP) ... Chapter 14, Wireless Access

Network types ... Chapter 19, Classifications

- Local area network (LAN) ... Chapter 19, Classifications
- Wide area network (WAN) ... Chapter 19, Classifications
- Personal area network (PAN) ... Chapter 19, Classifications
- Metropolitan area network (MAN) ... Chapter 19, Classifications
- Storage area network (SAN) ... Chapter 19, Classifications
- Wireless local area network (WLAN) ... Chapter 19, Wireless Topology

2.8 Given a scenario, use appropriate networking tools.

Crimper ... Chapter 20, Cable Crimper, Figure 20-19
Cable stripper ... Chapter 20, Cable Cutter and Cable Stripper, Figure 20-22
WiFi analyzer ... Chapter 20, Wi-Fi Analyzer
Toner probe ... Chapter 20, Cable Tracer and Tone Generator
Punch down tool ... Chapter 20, Punch Down Tool
Cable tester ... Chapter 20, Cable Tester, Figure 20-24
Loopback plug ... Chapter 20, Loopback Plug
Network tap ... Chapter 20, Network Tap

3.0 Hardware

3.1 Explain basic cable types and their connectors, features, and purposes.

Network cables ... Chapter 20, Network Media Copper; Chapter 20, Twisted-Pair Cable

- Cat 5 ... Chapter 20, Category 5
- Cat 5e ... Chapter 20, Category 5e
- Cat 6 ... Chapter 20, Category 6
- Cat 6a ... Chapter 20, Category 6
- Coaxial ... Chapter 20, Coaxial Cable
- Shielded twisted pair ... Chapter 20, Twisted-Pair Cable
    - (i) Direct burial ... Chapter 20, Twisted-Pair Cable
- Unshielded twisted pair ... Chapter 20, Twisted-Pair Cable
- Plenum ... Chapter 20, Plenum and PVC
- Optical
    - Fiber ... Chapter 20, Fiber-Optic Cable
- T568A/T568B ... Chapter 20, Ethernet Twisted-Pair Wiring Standards

Peripheral cables

- USB 2.0 ... Chapter 3, USB Cables and Connectors
- USB 3.0 ... Chapter 1, USB; Chapter 3, USB Cables and Connectors, Upgrading to and Adding Extra USB 3.0 Ports
- Serial ... Chapter 1, Serial and Parallel Data Transfer
- Thunderbolt ... Chapter 1, Thunderbolt

Video cables

- High-Definition Multimedia Interface (HDMI) ... Chapter 1, VGA, DVI, and HDMI; Chapter 8, HDMI
- DisplayPort ... Chapter 8, Television and Computers
- Digital Visual Interface (DVI) ... Chapter 1, VGA, DVI, and HDMI; Chapter 8, Television and Computers, Figure 8-22, Figure 8-23, Figure 8-24
- Video Graphics Array (VGA) ... Chapter 1, VGA, DVI, and HDMI; Chapter 8, Display Resolution, VGA vs. Digital Signals

3.2 Given a scenario, install the appropriate RAM.

3.3 Given a scenario, select and install storage devices.

Form factors
M.2 ... Chapter 10, M.2 Drives
mSATA ... SATA 2.5 and Beyond
Drive configurations
Redundant Array of Independent (or Inexpensive) Disks (RAID) 0, 1, 5, 10 ... Chapter 21, Fault Tolerance via RAID Systems
Removable storage
Flash drives ... Chapter 6, Flash Memory Devices
Memory cards ... Chapter 6, Flash Memory Cards
Optical drives ... Chapter 11, Disc Drive Interface, CD, CD-R, CD-RW, DVD, DVD-R, DVD-RW HD DVD and Blu-ray Disc

3.4 Given a scenario, install and configure motherboards, central processing units (CPUs), and add-on cards.

Motherboard form factor ... Chapter 3, Form Factors
Advanced Technology eXtended (ATX) ... Chapter 3, ATX
Information Technology eXtended (ITX) ... Chapter 3, Mini-ITX
Motherboard connector types
Peripheral Component Interconnect (PCI) ... Chapter 3, PCI, MiniPCI and MiniPCIe
PCI Express (PCIe) ... Chapter 3, PCI Express, MiniPCI and MiniPCIe
Power connectors ... Chapter 5, Other Power Connectors
SATA ... Chapter 3, External SATA, SATA Drive Installation
eSATA ... Chapter 1, External SATA; Chapter 3, External SATA; Chapter 10, eSATA Drive Installation
Headers ... Chapter 3, Identifying Motherboard Components
M.2 ... Chapter 10, M.2 Drives
Motherboard compatibility ... Chapter 4, Processor Manufacturers and Evolution, Processor Sockets
CPU sockets ... Chapter 4, Processor Sockets
Advanced Micro Devices, Inc. (AMD) ... Chapter 4, AMD, AMD, Processor Evolution, Processor Sockets
Intel ... Chapter 4, Intel, Intel, Processor Evolution, Processor Sockets
Server ... Chapter 4, Opteron, Virtualization, Multicore and Multi-Socket CPUs, Processor Sockets
Multisocket ... Chapter 4, Multicore and Multi-Socket CPUs
Desktop ... Chapter 4, Installing a Processor
Mobile ... Chapter 4, Intel, Core i9, Ryzen
Basic Input/Output System (BIOS)/ Unified Extensible Firmware Interface (UEFI) settings ... Chapter 2, BIOS, UEFI; Chapter 3, Upgrading the BIOS
Boot options ... Chapter 18, Advanced Boot Options
USB permissions ... Chapter 15, Securing the Physical Area
Trusted Platform Module (TPM) security features ... Chapter 15, Trusted Platform Module
Fan considerations ... Chapter 4, Heat Sink and Fan Assembly
Secure Boot ... Chapter 16, Trusted Boot and Measured Boot Security
Boot password ... Chapter 15, System Configuration Password
Encryption ... Chapter 13, BitLocker and BitLocker To Go; Chapter 15, BitLocker Drive Encryption
TPM ... Chapter 15, Trusted Platform Module
Hardware security module (HSM) ... Chapter 15, Hardware Security Module
CPU architecture
X64/x86 ... Chapter 4, 32-Bit and 64-Bit Technology
Advanced RISC Machine (ARM) ... Chapter 4, Intel
Single-core ... Chapter 4, Enhancing CPU Operation, Multicore Processors
Multicore ... Chapter 4, Multicore Processors
Multithreading ... Chapter 4, Simultaneous Threading
Virtualization support ... Chapter 4, Virtualization
Expansion cards
Sound card ... Chapter 9, Sound Cards, Installing a Sound Card

Video card ....Chapter 1, VGA, DVI, and HDMI; Chapter 8, Video Adapter Cards, Installing a Video Adapter Card
Capture card ....Chapter 8, Video Adapter Cards; Chapter 9, Audio Capture Cards
NIC .... Chapter 19, Network Interface Card Installation and Features
Cooling..........Chapter 4, Cooling the Processor
Fans.......... Chapter 4, Heat Sink and Fan Assembly
Heat sink .... Chapter 4, Heat Sink and Fan Assembly
Thermal paste/pads ....Chapter 4, Cooling the Processor
Liquid..........Chapter 4, Cooling the Processor, Figure 4-29

3.5 Given a scenario, install or replace the appropriate power supply.

Input 110–120 VAC vs. 220–240 VAC.......... Chapter 5, Input and Output Voltage Levels
Output 3.3V vs. 5V vs. 12V .... Chapter 5, Input and Output Voltage Levels
20-pin to 24-pin motherboard adapter ....Chapter 5, Main Power Connectors
Redundant power supply .... Chapter 5, Redundant Power Supplies
Modular power supply.......... Chapter 5, Modular Power Supply
Wattage rating ....Chapter 5, Power

3.6 Given a scenario, deploy and configure multifunction devices/printers and settings.

Properly unboxing a device—setup location considerations .... Chapter 12, Printer Installation and Configuration
Use appropriate drivers for a given OS..........Chapter 12, Step 1. Processing
Printer Control Language (PCL) vs. PostScript .... Chapter 12, Fonts
Device connectivity
USB ....Chapter 12, Printer Installation and Configuration, Selecting a Printer Port, Diagnosing USB Connection Problems
Ethernet.......... Chapter 23, Copper Cable
Wireless.......... Chapter 7, Bluetooth; Chapter 12, Printer Installation and Configuration, Sharing Printers; Chapter 13, Ad-Hoc Network, Wireless Infrastructure Network, Wireless Standards
Public/shared devices
Printer share .... Chapter 12, Sharing Printers; Chapter 21, Sharing; Chapter 23, Share a Printer in Windows
Print server ....Chapter 12, Print Server Properties
Configuration settings..........Chapter 12, Printer Installation and Configuration, Selecting a Printer and Printer Driver; Chapter 23, Share a Printer in Windows
Duplex .... Chapter 12, Printer Types; Chapter 19, Network Adapter Speed and Operation Mode
Orientation.......... Chapter 23, Share a Printer in Windows
Tray settings .... Chapter 12, Local Printer Installation
Quality.......... Chapter 23, Share a Printer in Windows
Security ....Chapter 12, Printer Security
User authentication ....Chapter 12, Printer Security
Badging..........Chapter 12, Printer Security
Audit logs ....Chapter 12, Printer Security
Secure prints..........Chapter 12, Printer Security
Network scan services ....Chapter 12, Printer Security
E-mail..........Chapter 12, Printer Security
SMB..........Chapter 12, Printer Security
Cloud services..........Chapter 12, Printer Security
Automatic document feeder (ADF)/flatbed scanner .... Chapter 7, Scanners and Digital Cameras; Chapter 12, Printer Types

3.7 Given a scenario, install and replace printer consumables.

Laser ....Chapter 12, Laser Printer Operation
Imaging drum, fuser assembly, transfer belt, transfer roller, pickup rollers, separation pads, duplexing assembly..........Chapter 12, Laser Printer Operation

4.0 Virtualization and Cloud Computing

4.1 Summarize cloud computing concepts.

4.2 Summarize aspects of client-side virtualization.

Resource requirements .... Chapter 22, Client-Side Virtualization
Security requirements .... Chapter 22, Virtual Machines

5.0 Hardware and Network Troubleshooting

5.1 Given a scenario, use the best practice methodology to resolve problems.

Always consider corporate policies, procedures, and impacts before implementing changes .... Chapter 17, Establish a Theory of Probable Cause
1. Identify the problem .... Chapter 17, Identify the Problem
   Gather information from the user, identify user changes, and, if applicable, perform backups before making changes .... Chapter 17, Identify the Problem
   Inquire regarding environmental or infrastructure changes .... Chapter 17, Identify the Problem
2. Establish a theory of probable cause (question the obvious) .... Chapter 17, Establish a Theory of Probable Cause
   If necessary, conduct external or internal research based on symptoms .... Chapter 17, Establish a Theory of Probable Cause
3. Test the theory to determine cause .... Chapter 17, Test the Theory to Determine Cause
   Once the theory is confirmed, determine the next steps to resolve problem .... Chapter 17, Test the Theory to Determine Cause
   If theory is not confirmed re-establish new theory or escalate .... Chapter 17, Test the Theory to Determine Cause
4. Establish a plan of action to resolve the problem and implement the solution .... Chapter 17, Establish a Plan of Action
   Refer to the vendor's instructions for guidance .... Chapter 17, Establish a Plan of Action
5. Verify full system functionality and, if applicable, implement preventive measures .... Chapter 17, Verify Full System Functionality and Implement Preventive Measures
6. Document findings, actions, and outcomes .... Chapter 17, Document Findings, Actions, and Outcomes

5.2 Given a scenario, troubleshoot problems related to motherboards, RAM, CPUs, and power.

Common symptoms
- Power-on self-test (POST) beeps .... Chapter 17, Firmware POST Codes
- Proprietary crash screens (blue screen of death [BSOD]/pinwheel) .... Chapter 17, Blue Screen Error
- Black screen .... Chapter 17, Symptom 3
- No power .... Chapter 17, Symptom 1, Symptom 2
- Sluggish performance .... Chapter 17, Windows Performance, Resource, and Reliability Monitors
- Overheating .... Chapter 17, Intermittent Device Failures
- Burning smell .... Chapter 17, Symptom 9
- Intermittent shutdown .... Chapter 17, Symptom 8
- Application crashes .... Chapter 13, Mobile Device Troubleshooting, Symptom 18
- Grinding noise .... Chapter 17, Intermittent Device Failures
- Capacitor swelling .... Chapter 17, Symptom 9
- Inaccurate system date/time .... Chapter 17, Symptom 4

5.3 Given a scenario, troubleshoot and diagnose problems with storage drives and RAID arrays.

Common symptoms
- Light-emitting diode (LED) status indicators .... Chapter 17, Symptom 1
- Grinding noises .... Chapter 17, Intermittent Device Failures, Read and Write Failure
- Clicking sounds .... Chapter 10, Loud Clicking Noise; Chapter 17, Read and Write Failure
- Bootable device not found .... Chapter 17, Second Stage, Symptom 2, Symptom 5, Symptom 6; Chapter 18, Reinstall the Operating System
- Data loss/corruption .... Chapter 10, ReFS; Chapter 17, Second Stage, File Corruption
- RAID failure .... Chapter 10, RAID Not Found, RAID Stops Working

Self-monitoring, Analysis, and Reporting
Technology (S.M.A.R.T.) failure............ Chapter 10, S.M.A.R.T. Errors, RAID and S.M.A.R.T. Error Detections
Extended read/write times .... Chapter 10, Slow Performance
Input/output operations per second (IOPS).. Chapter 10, Performance Measures
Missing drives in OS .... Chapter 17, Symptom 5, Symptom 6

5.4 Given a scenario, troubleshoot video, projector, and display issues.

Common symptoms
Incorrect data source .... Chapter 17, Symptom 3
Physical cabling issues .... Chapter 17, Symptom 3
Burned-out bulb .... Chapter 8, Troubleshooting
Fuzzy image .... Chapter 8, Troubleshooting
Display burn-in .... Chapter 8, Troubleshooting
Dead pixels .... Chapter 8, Troubleshooting
Flashing screen .... Chapter 8, Refresh Rate
Incorrect color display .... Chapter 8, Projectors
Audio issues .... Chapter 9, Installing a Sound Card
Dim image .... Chapter 13, Symptom 11
Intermittent projector shutdown .... Chapter 8, Projectors, Troubleshooting

5.5 Given a scenario, troubleshoot common issues with mobile devices.

Common symptoms
Poor battery health .... Chapter 13, Symptom 9
Swollen battery .... Chapter 13, Symptom 24; Chapter 17, Mobile Device Issues
Broken screen .... Chapter 17, Mobile Device Issues
Improper charging .... Chapter 13, Symptom 9
Poor/no connectivity .... Chapter 13, Symptom 13, Symptom 15
Liquid damage .... Chapter 13, Protective Covers
Overheating .... Chapter 13, Symptom 21; Chapter 17, Mobile Device Issues
Digitizer issues .... Chapter 7, Touch Screens, Mobile Device Display
Physically damaged ports .... Chapter 13, Troubleshooting
Malware .... Chapter 13, Security Concerns, Symptom 7
Cursor drift/touch calibration .... Chapter 13, Symptom 10, Symptom 17

5.6 Given a scenario, troubleshoot and resolve printer issues.

Common symptoms .... Chapter 12, Troubleshooting Printers
Lines down the printed pages .... Chapter 12, Vertical Lines on a Page
Garbled print .... Chapter 12, Printing Gibberish
Toner not fusing to paper .... Chapter 12, Toner Smears on Paper
Paper jams .... Chapter 12, Paper Jams
Faded print .... Chapter 12, Incorrect Inkjet Printer Settings, Pages Print Blank, Poor Print Quality
Incorrect paper size .... Chapter 12, Paper Jams
Paper not feeding .... Chapter 12, Paper Not Feeding
Multipage misfeed .... Chapter 12, Paper Jams
Multiple prints pending in queue .... Chapter 12, Print Spooling
Speckling on printed pages .... Chapter 12, Speckling on Paper
Double/echo images on the print .... Chapter 12, Ghost Images
Incorrect color settings .... Chapter 12, Incorrect Colors
Grinding noise .... Chapter 12, Grinding Noise
Finishing issues .... Chapter 12, Finishing Issues
Staple jams .... Chapter 12, Finishing Issues
Hole punch .... Chapter 12, Finishing Issues
Incorrect page orientation .... Chapter 12, Paper Jams

5.7 Given a scenario, troubleshoot problems with wired and wireless networks.

Common symptoms
- Intermittent wireless connectivity . . . Chapter 22, Intermittent Connectivity
- Slow network speeds . . . Chapter 13, Symptom 19; Chapter 22, Slow Transfer Speeds
- Limited connectivity . . . Chapter 22, Limited Connectivity
- Jitter . . . Chapter 8, Troubleshooting; Chapter 21, Basic Network Troubleshooting; Chapter 23, Other Network Problems
- Poor Voice over Internet Protocol (VoIP) quality . . . Chapter 21, Basic Network Troubleshooting
- Port flapping . . . Chapter 21, Basic Network Troubleshooting; Chapter 23, Other Network Problems
- High latency . . . Chapter 21, Basic Network Troubleshooting; Chapter 23, Other Network Problems
- External interference . . . Chapter 21, Basic Network Troubleshooting

Exam **220-1102 (Core 2)**

1.0 Operating Systems

1.1 Identify basic features of Microsoft Windows editions.

Windows 10 editions . . . Chapter 2, Windows 10 Editions
- Home . . . Chapter 2, Windows 10 Editions
- Pro . . . Chapter 2, Windows 10 Editions
- Pro for Workstations . . . Chapter 2, Windows 10 Editions
- Enterprise . . . Chapter 2, Windows 10 Editions

Feature differences
- Domain access vs. workgroup . . . Chapter 21, Peer-to-Peer Administration
- Desktop styles/user interface . . . Chapter 2, User Interface
- Availability of Remote Desktop Protocol (RDP) . . . Chapter 20, RDP
- Random-access memory (RAM) support limitations . . . Chapter 2, Windows Versions and Editions, Figure 2-26
- BitLocker . . . Chapter 2, Drive Encryption; Chapter 13, BitLocker and BitLocker To Go
- gpedit.msc . . . Chapter 15, Local Group Policy Management

Upgrade paths . . . Chapter 2, Windows Upgrade
- In-place upgrade . . . Chapter 2, Windows Upgrade

1.2 Given a scenario, use the appropriate Microsoft command-line tool.

Navigation
- cd . . . Chapter 2, Command-Line Interface, Figure 2-3
- dir . . . Chapter 2, Command-Line Interface, Figure 2-3
- md . . . Chapter 2, Figure 2-4, Figure 2-5; Chapter 18, Figure 18-7
- rmdir . . . Chapter 18, Figure 18-7
- Drive navigation inputs . . . Chapter 2, Command-Line Interface
  - C: or D: or x: . . . Chapter 2, Command-Line Interface

Command-line tools
- ipconfig . . . Chapter 22, Running Ipconfig
- ping . . . Chapter 22, Ping
- hostname . . . Chapter 22, Hostname
- netstat . . . Chapter 22, Netstat
- nslookup . . . Chapter 22, Nslookup
- chkdsk . . . Chapter 2, Command-Line Interface, Figure 2-4; Chapter 10, Chkdsk; Chapter 17, Chkdsk

net user ... Chapter 22, Figure 22-27
net use ... Chapter 21, Administrative Commands
tracert ... Chapter 22, Tracert
format ... Chapter 2, Command-Line Interface, Figure 2-4
xcopy ... Chapter 2, Command-Line Interface, Figure 2-4
copy ... Chapter 2, Command-Line Interface, Figure 2-4
gpupdate ... Chapter 2, Command-Line Interface, Figure 2-4
gpresult ... Chapter 2, Command-Line Interface, Figure 2-4
shutdown ... Chapter 2, Command-Line Interface, Figure 2-4
sfc ... Chapter 2, Command-Line Interface, Figure 2-4; Chapter 17, System File Checker
[command name] /? ... Chapter 2, Command-Line Interface
Diskpart ... Chapter 10, DiskPart Utility
Pathping ... Chapter 22, Pathping
Winver ... Chapter 2, Command-Line Interface, Figure 2-4

1.3 Given a scenario, use features and tools of the Microsoft Windows 10 operating system.

Task Manager ... Chapter 2, Task Manager; Chapter 4, Processor Affinity; Chapter 18, Task Manager
  Services ... Chapter 2, Windows Services Manager; Chapter 12, Selecting a Printer Port; Chapter 18, Microsoft System Configuration Utility, Task Manager, Figure 18-10
  Startup ... Chapter 18, Microsoft System Configuration Utility, Windows 10 Startup Settings, Windows Recovery Environment, Figure 18-4
  Performance ... Chapter 2, Task Manager; Chapter 18, Task Manager
  Processes ... Chapter 2, Task Manager; Chapter 18, Task Manager
  Users ... Chapter 2, Task Manager; Chapter 18, Task Manager
Microsoft Management Console (MMC) snap-in ... Chapter 10, Disk Management
  Event Viewer (eventvwr.msc) ... Chapter 17, Event Viewer
  Disk Management (diskmgmt.msc) ... Chapter 10, Disk Management
  Task Scheduler (taskschd.msc) ... Chapter 2, Task Scheduler
  Device Manager (devmgmt.msc) ... Chapter 3, Windows Device Manager
  Certificate Manager (certmgr.msc) ... Chapter 15, Digital Certificates
  Local Users and Groups (lusrmgr.msc) ... Chapter 15, User Accounts, Local Security Policy Management
  Performance Monitor (perfmon.msc) ... Chapter 17, Windows Performance, Resource, and Reliability Monitors
  Group Policy Editor (gpedit.msc) ... Chapter 15, Local Group Policy Management
Additional tools
  System Information (msinfo32.exe) ... Chapter 18, Microsoft System Information
  Resource Monitor (resmon.exe) ... Chapter 17, Windows Performance, Resource, and Reliability Monitors
  System Configuration (msconfig.exe) ... Chapter 18, Microsoft System Configuration Utility
  Disk Cleanup (cleanmgr.exe) ... Chapter 17, Disk Cleanup Utility
  Disk Defragment (dfrgui.exe) ... Chapter 10, Disk Defragmenter
  Registry Editor (regedit.exe) ... Chapter 2, Configuration Files

1.4 Given a scenario, use the appropriate Microsoft Windows 10 Control Panel utility.

Internet Options ... Chapter 2, Internet Options
Devices and Printers ... Chapter 12, Local Printer Installation
Programs and Features ... Chapter 2, Programs and Features
Network and Sharing Center ... Chapter 21, Network and Sharing Center; Chapter 23, Network and Sharing Center
System ... Chapter 2, System
Windows Defender Firewall ... Chapter 16, Firewall
Mail ... Chapter 2, Mail
Sound ... Chapter 9, Audio Resolution, Speakers, Sound Cards, Windows Control Panel
User Accounts ... Chapter 15, User Accounts

Device Manager .... Chapter 3, Windows Device Manager
Indexing Options .... Chapter 2, Indexing
Administrative Tools .... Chapter 3, System Resources; Chapter 12, Print Spooling; Chapter 15, User Accounts, Local Security Policy Management; Chapter 16, Firewall; Chapter 17, Windows Memory Diagnostics Tools, Component Services; Chapter 18, Windows Recovery Environment, Microsoft System Configuration Utility, Computer Management; Chapter 21, Data Sources
File Explorer Options
  Show hidden files .... Chapter 2, Control Panel
  Hide extensions .... Chapter 2, Control Panel
  General options .... Chapter 2, Control Panel
  View options .... Chapter 2, Control Panel
Power Options .... Chapter 5, Power-Management Standards; Chapter 13, Windows Power-Management Options
  Hibernate .... Chapter 13, Windows Power Management Options
  Power plans .... Chapter 5, Power-Management Standards; Chapter 13, Power Management
  Sleep/suspend .... Chapter 13, Windows Power Management Options
  Standby .... Chapter 13, Windows Power Management Options
  Choose what closing the lid does .... Chapter 13, Windows Power Management Options
  Turn on fast startup .... Chapter 13, Windows Power Management Options
  Universal Serial Bus (USB) selective suspend .... Chapter 13, Windows Power Management Options
Ease of Access .... Chapter 7, Ease of Access

1.5 Given a scenario, use the appropriate Windows settings.

Time and Language .... Chapter 2, Date and Time
Update and Security .... Chapter 2, Internet Options, Software Patch; Chapter 3, Installing Software Drivers; Chapter 15, Local Security Policy Management; Chapter 16, Windows Update, Firewall
Personalization .... Chapter 2, Personalization
Apps .... Chapter 2, Windows Apps
Privacy .... Chapter 2, Internet Options
System .... Chapter 2, System
Devices .... Chapter 2, Devices
Network and Internet .... Chapter 2, Network and Internet
Gaming .... Chapter 2, Windows Apps
Accounts .... Chapter 15, User Accounts

1.6 Given a scenario, configure Microsoft Windows networking features on a client/desktop.

Workgroup vs. domain setup .... Chapter 21, Peer-to-Peer Administration, Centralized Administration
  Shared resources .... Chapter 19, Shared Resources
  Printers .... Chapter 12, Sharing a Printer; Chapter 23, Sharing a Printer in Windows
  File servers .... Chapter 21, File Server
  Mapped drives .... Chapter 21, Administrative Commands
Local OS firewall settings .... Chapter 16, Firewall
  Application restrictions and exceptions .... Chapter 16, Firewall
  Configuration .... Chapter 16, Firewall
Client network configuration
  Internet Protocol (IP) addressing scheme .... Chapter 22, IP Addresses
  Domain Name System (DNS) settings .... Chapter 22, DNS
  Subnet mask .... Chapter 22, IPv4 Subnet Mask
  Gateway .... Chapter 22, Gateway

1.7 Given a scenario, apply application installation and configuration concepts.

1.8 Explain common OS types and their purposes.

1.9 Given a scenario, perform OS installation and upgrades in a diverse OS environment.

- Boot methods
  - USB ... Chapter 2, What Is an Operating System?
  - Optical media ... Chapter 2, What Is an Operating System?
  - Network ... Chapter 2, What Is an Operating System?
  - Solid-state/flash drives ... Chapter 2, What Is an Operating System?
  - Internet-based ... Chapter 2, What Is an Operating System?
  - External/hot-swappable drive ... Chapter 2, What Is an Operating System?
  - Internal hard drive (partition) ... Chapter 2, What Is an Operating System?
- Types of installations
  - Upgrade ... Chapter 2, Microsoft Windows Installation
  - Recovery partition ... Chapter 18, Windows Recovery Partition
  - Clean install ... Chapter 2, Microsoft Windows Installation
  - Image deployment ... Chapter 2, What Is an Operating System?
  - Repair installation ... Chapter 2, Microsoft Windows Installation
  - Remote network installation ... Chapter 2, What Is an Operating System; Chapter 21, Performing an Unattended Installation
  - Other considerations
    - Third-party drivers ... Chapter 3, Installing Software Drivers
- Partitioning ... Chapter 10, Disk Partition Systems
  - GUID [globally unique identifier] Partition Table (GPT) ... Chapter 10, Disk Partition Systems
  - Master boot record (MBR) ... Chapter 10, MBR Partitions
- Drive format ... Chapter 10, Low-Level Format, File System Formats, Formatting a Disk
- Upgrade considerations ... Chapter 2, Windows Upgrade, System Updates, Updating macOS
  - Backup files and user preferences ... Chapter 2, Scheduled Backups, 2.4 Tech Tip
  - Application and driver support/backward compatibility ... Chapter 2, Software Patch; Chapter 3, Installing Software Drivers; Chapter 16, Windows Update; Chapter 18, System Restore
  - Hardware compatibility ... Chapter 6, Factors to Consider before Upgrading Memory; Chapter 12, Conflicting Devices
- Feature updates ... Chapter 2, Windows Features and Tools Tech Tip
  - Product life cycle ... Chapter 2, What Is an Operating System? Tech Tip

1.10 Identify common features and tools of the macOS/desktop OS.

- Installation and uninstallation of applications ... Chapter 2, App Store
  - File types ... Chapter 2, App Store
    - .dmg ... Chapter 2, App Store
    - .pkg ... Chapter 2, App Store
    - .app ... Chapter 2, App Store
  - App store ... Chapter 2, App Store
  - Uninstallation process ... Chapter 2, App Store
- Apple ID and corporate restrictions ... Chapter 2, Apple Macintosh OS
- Best practices ... Chapter 2, Best Practices for Linux and macOS
  - Backups ... Chapter 2, Scheduled Backups
  - Antivirus ... Chapter 2, Antivirus and Antimalware Updates
  - Updates/patches ... Chapter 2, System Updates
- System Preferences ... Chapter 2, System Preferences
  - Displays ... Chapter 2, Displays
  - Networks ... Chapter 2, Networks
  - Printers ... Chapter 2, Printers & Scanners
  - Scanners ... Chapter 2, Printers & Scanners
  - Privacy ... Chapter 2, Privacy & Security
  - Accessibility ... Chapter 2, Accessibility

1.11 Identify common features and tools of the Linux client/desktop OS.

2.0 Security

2.1 Summarize various security measures and their purposes.

Alarm systems .... Chapter 21, Server Roles
Motion sensors .... Chapter 21, Server Roles
Door locks........ Chapter 13, Physical Locks
Equipment locks .... Chapter 13, Physical Locks; Chapter 15, Securing the Physical Area
Guards........ Chapter 15, Physical Security
Bollards........ Chapter 15, Securing the Physical Area
Fences .... Chapter 15, Securing the Physical Area

Physical security for staff
Key fobs........ Chapter 15, Radio-Frequency Identification
Smart cards .... Chapter 15, Smart Cards and Virtual Smart Cards
Keys........ Chapter 15, Securing the Physical Area
Biometrics .... Chapter 13, Biometrics
Retina scanner........ Chapter 15, Multifactor Authentication
Fingerprint scanner........ Chapter 15, Multifactor Authentication
Palm print scanner........ Chapter 15, Multifactor Authentication
Lighting........ Chapter 15, Securing the Physical Area
Magnetometers .... Chapter 15, Securing the Physical Area

Logical security
Principle of least privilege .... Chapter 15, Principle of Least Privilege
Access control lists (ACLs)........ Chapter 21, Share Permissions and Security Permissions
Multifactor authentication (MFA)........ Chapter 15, Multifactor Authentication
E-mail........ Chapter 22, Port and SSL Settings
Hard token .... Chapter 15, Radio-Frequency Identification
Soft token .... Chapter 15, Radio-Frequency Identification
Short message service (SMS)........ Chapter 15, Multifactor Authentication
Voice call........ Chapter 15, Multifactor Authentication
Authenticator application .... Chapter 13, BitLocker and BitLocker To Go; Chapter 15, BitLocker Drive Encryption

Mobile device management (MDM) .... Chapter 21, MDM Policies
Active Directory........ Chapter 21, Windows Server
Login script .... Chapter 21, Login Scripts
Domain .... Chapter 21, Domains
Group Policy/updates........ Chapter 15, Local Group Policy Management
Organizational units .... Chapter 21, Default Users and Groups
Home folder .... Chapter 21, Folder Redirection
Folder redirection .... Chapter 21, Folder Redirection
Security groups .... Chapter 15, Local Group Policy Management

2.2 Compare and contrast wireless security protocols and authentication methods.

Protocols and encryption
Wi-Fi Protected Access 2 (WPA2) .... Chapter 13, Wireless Network Security and Encryption Types
WPA3 .... Chapter 13, Wireless Network Security and Encryption Types
Temporal Key Integrity Protocol (TKIP)........ Chapter 13, Wireless Security and Encryption Types;
Advanced Encryption Standard (AES) .... Chapter 13, Wireless Security and Encryption Types

Authentication
Remote Authentication Dial-In User Service (RADIUS)........ Chapter 15, Authentication and Workstation Security; Chapter 21, RADIUS
Terminal Access Controller Access-Control System (TACACS+)........ Chapter 15, Authentication and Workstation Security; Chapter 21, TACACS
Kerberos .... Chapter 15, Kerberos
Multifactor........ Chapter 15, Multifactor Authentication

2.3 Given a scenario, detect, remove, and prevent malware using the appropriate tools and methods.

Malware.......... Chapter 16, Malicious Software
- Trojan.......... Chapter 16, Trojan Horse
- Rootkit.......... Chapter 16, Rootkit
- Virus.......... Chapter 16, Malicious Software
- Spyware.......... Chapter 16, Spyware
- Ransomware.......... Chapter 16, Ransomware
- Keylogger.......... Chapter 16, Password Virus
- Boot sector virus.......... Chapter 16, Boot Sector Virus
- Cryptominers.......... Chapter 16, Cryptominers

Tools and methods
- Recovery mode.......... Chapter 16, Malware Removal
- Antivirus.......... Chapter 16, Microsoft Malicious Software Removal Tool, Malware Prevention
- Antimalware.......... Chapter 16, Microsoft Malicious Software Removal Tool, Malware Prevention, Malware Removal
- Software firewalls.......... Chapter 16, Firewall; Chapter 23, Firewall
- Anti-phishing training.......... Chapter 16, Phishing
- User education regarding common threats.......... Chapter 15, User Security Education
- OS reinstallation.......... Chapter 18, Reinstall the Operating System

2.4 Explain common social-engineering attacks, threats, and vulnerabilities.

Social engineering.......... Chapter 15, Social Engineering
- Phishing.......... Chapter 16, Phishing
- Vishing.......... Chapter 16, Phishing
- Shoulder surfing.......... Chapter 15, Privacy Filters
- Whaling.......... Chapter 16, Phishing
- Tailgating.......... Chapter 15, Physical Security
- Impersonation.......... Chapter 15, Social Engineering
- Dumpster diving.......... Chapter 15, Dumpster Diving
- Evil twin.......... Chapter 19, Network Security

Threats
- Distributed denial of service (DDoS).......... Chapter 16, Botnet
- Denial of service (DoS).......... Chapter 16, Botnet
- Zero-day attack.......... Chapter 16, Malware Removal
- Spoofing.......... Chapter 15, User Accounts
- On-path attack.......... Chapter 16, Man-in-the-Middle (MITM)
- Brute-force attack.......... Chapter 15, Protecting Your Password
- Dictionary attack.......... Chapter 15, Protecting Your Password; Chapter 21, Account Lockout Policy
- Insider threat.......... Chapter 16, Insider Threat
- Structured Query Language (SQL) injection.......... Chapter 16, SQL Script Injection
- Cross-site scripting (XSS).......... Chapter 16, Cross-Site Scripting

Vulnerabilities
- Non-compliant systems.......... Chapter 16, Malware Prevention
- Unpatched systems.......... Chapter 2, Software Patch; Chapter 16, Windows Update
- Unprotected systems (missing antivirus/missing firewall).......... Chapter 16, Malware Prevention
- EOL OSs.......... Chapter 16, Malware Prevention
- Bring your own device (BYOD).......... Chapter 23, Using Policies to Harden Security

2.5 Given a scenario, manage and configure basic security settings in the Microsoft Windows OS.

- Defender Antivirus … Chapter 16, Firewall, Windows Defender Offline
  - Activate/deactivate… Chapter 16, Windows Security
  - Updated definitions … Chapter 16, Malicious Software
- Firewall … Chapter 16, Firewall
  - Activate/deactivate… Chapter 16, Firewall
  - Port security … Chapter 23, Firewall
  - Application security… Chapter 23, Firewall
- Users and groups … Chapter 15, User Accounts; Chapter 21, Default Users and Groups
  - Local vs. Microsoft account… Chapter 21, Local User Account
  - Standard account … Chapter 15, User Accounts; Chapter 21, Users, Default Users and Groups, Domain User Account, Administrator vs. Standard User
  - Administrator… Chapter 15, User Accounts; Chapter 21, Users, Administrator vs. Standard User
  - Guest user… Chapter 15, User Accounts; Chapter 21, Default Users and Groups
  - Power user … Chapter 21, Local Power Users
- Login OS options
  - Username and password… Chapter 15, Passwords
  - Personal identification number (PIN) … Chapter 13, Passcode Lock
  - Fingerprint… Chapter 15, Multifactor Authentication
  - Facial recognition … Chapter 13, Biometrics
  - Single sign-on (SSO) … Chapter 21, Domain User Account
- NTFS vs. share permissions… Chapter 10, NTFS; Chapter 21, Share Permissions and Security Permissions
  - File and folder attributes … Chapter 21, File Attributes
  - Inheritance… Chapter 21, Permission Propagation
- Run as administrator vs. standard user … Chapter 21, Administrator vs. Standard User
  - User Account Control (UAC) … Chapter 16, User Account Control
- BitLocker… Chapter 2, Drive Encryption; Chapter 13, BitLocker and BitLocker To Go; Chapter 15, BitLocker Drive Encryption
- BitLocker To Go … Chapter 2, Drive Encryption; Chapter 13, BitLocker and BitLocker To Go; Chapter 15, BitLocker Drive Encryption
- Encrypting File System (EFS) … Chapter 10, Encrypted File System

2.6 Given a scenario, configure a workstation to meet best practices for security.

- Data-at-rest encryption… Chapter 15, Physical Drive Encryption
- Password best practices … Chapter 15, Passwords; Chapter 21, Password Policy
  - Complexity requirements… Chapter 21, Password Policy
    - Length… Chapter 21, Password Policy
    - Character types… Chapter 21, Password Policy
  - Expiration requirements … Chapter 21, Password Policy
  - Basic input/output system (BIOS)/ Unified Extensible Firmware Interface (UEFI) passwords… Chapter 15, System Configuration Passwords
- End-user best practices
  - Use screensaver locks… Chapter 15, Screen Saver Password
  - Log off when not in use … Chapter 15, Screen Saver Password
  - Secure/protect critical hardware (e.g., laptops)… Chapter 15, User Security Education
  - Secure personally identifiable information (PII) and passwords … Chapter 24, Customer's Confidential Materials
- Account management
  - Restrict user permissions… Chapter 15, User Accounts
  - Restrict login times… Chapter 21, Time Policy
  - Disable guest account … Chapter 15, User Accounts
  - Use failed attempts lockout… Chapter 21, Account Lockout Policy
  - Use timeout/screen lock … Chapter 15, Screen Saver Password
- Change default administrator's user account/password… Chapter 23, Change Default Names

Disable AutoRun .... Chapter 11, Failure to AutoPlay Disc
Disable AutoPlay .... Chapter 11, Failure to AutoPlay Disc

2.7 Explain common methods for securing mobile and embedded devices.

Screen locks
- Facial recognition .... Chapter 13, Biometrics
- PIN codes .... Chapter 13, Passcode Lock
- Fingerprint .... Chapter 15, Multifactor Authentication
- Pattern .... Chapter 13, Patterns
- Swipe .... Chapter 13, Patterns

Remote wipes .... Chapter 13, Company Apps
Locator applications .... Chapter 13, Global Positioning System
OS updates .... Chapter 13, Mobile Device Troubleshooting
Device encryption .... Chapter 2, Drive Encryption; Chapter 13, BitLocker and BitLocker To Go; Chapter 15, BitLocker Drive Encryption
Remote backup applications .... Chapter 13, Cloud Services
Failed login attempts restrictions .... Chapter 13, Device Access Failure; Chapter 21, Account Lockout Policy
Antivirus/antimalware .... Chapter 16, Microsoft Malicious Software Removal Tool, Malware Prevention
Firewalls .... Chapter 16, Firewall
Policies and procedures
- BYOD vs. corporate owned .... Chapter 23, Using Policies to Harden Security
- Profile security requirements .... Chapter 23, Using Policies to Harden Security

Internet of Things (IoT) .... Chapter 20, Internet of Things (IoT)

2.8 Given a scenario, use common data destruction and disposal methods.

Physical destruction
- Drilling .... Chapter 15, Disposal of Computer Equipment
- Shredding .... Chapter 15, Disposal of Computer Equipment
- Degaussing .... Chapter 15, Disposal of Computer Equipment
- Incineration .... Chapter 15, Disposal of Computer Equipment

Recycling or repurposing best practices
- Erasing/wiping .... Chapter 15, Disposal of Computer Equipment
- Low-level formatting .... Chapter 10, Formatting Disk; Chapter 15, Disposal of Computer Equipment
- Standard formatting .... Chapter 10, Formatting Disk; Chapter 15, Disposal of Computer Equipment

Outsourcing concepts
- Third-party vendor .... Chapter 15, Disposal of Computer Equipment
- Certification of destruction/recycling .... Chapter 15, Disposal of Computer Equipment

2.9 Given a scenario, configure appropriate security settings on small-office/home-office (SOHO) wireless and wired networks.

Home router settings
- Change default passwords .... Chapter 22, Router; Chapter 23, Change Default Names
- IP filtering .... Chapter 15, Workstation and SOHO Security
- Firmware updates .... Chapter 11, Firmware Update
- Content filtering .... Chapter 16, Parental Controls and Family Options
- Physical placement/secure locations .... Chapter 23, Data Transfer Rates
- Dynamic Host Configuration Protocol (DHCP) reservations .... Chapter 22, Reserved IP Addresses; Chapter 23, DHCP Configuration
- Static wide-area network (WAN) IP .... Chapter 22, DHCP; Chapter 23, Port Forwarding, Single Port Forwarding
- Universal Plug and Play (UPnP) .... Chapter 20, UPnP
- Screened subnet .... Chapter 22, IPv4 Subnet Mask

Wireless specific
- Changing the service set identifier (SSID) .... Chapter 23, Change Default Names

Disabling SSID broadcast........ Chapter 23, Disable SSID Broadcast
Encryption settings .... Chapter 13, Encryption, Wireless Network Security and Encryption Types; Chapter 19, WPS; Chapter 23, Wireless
Disabling guest access........ Chapter 19, Network Security
Changing channels........ Chapter 23, Wireless

Firewall settings
Disabling unused ports........ Chapter 19, Network Security
Port forwarding/mapping .... Chapter 23, Port Forwarding, Single Port Forwarding

2.10 Given a scenario, install and configure browsers and relevant security settings.

Browser download/installation
Trusted sources .... Chapter 16, Malware Prevention, Browser Selection and Installation
Hashing........ Chapter 15, Rainbow Tables
Untrusted sources........ Chapter 16, Malware Prevention

Extensions and plug-ins
Trusted sources .... Chapter 16, Malware Prevention
Untrusted sources........ Chapter 16, Malware Prevention

Password managers .... Chapter 16, Password Managers

Secure connection/sites—valid certificates .... Chapter 15, Digital Certificates

Settings
Pop-up blocker .... Chapter 16, Adware
Clearing browsing data........ Chapter 16, Cookies
Clearing cache .... Chapter 16, Cookies
Private-browsing mode........ Chapter 16, Cookies
Sign-in/browser data synchronization........ Chapter 2, Sync Your Settings
Ad blockers........ Chapter 16, Adware

3.0 Software Troubleshooting

3.1 Given a scenario, troubleshoot common Windows OS problems.

Common symptoms
Blue screen of death (BSOD) .... Chapter 13, Symptom 4, 6; Chapter 17, Blue Screen Error
Sluggish performance .... Chapter 10, Slow Performance; Chapter 13, Symptom 19; Chapter 17, Read and Write Failure
Boot problems........ Chapter 10, Primary Partition, UEFI Specification Partition Terminology, PATA Drive Installation, Read/Write Failure
Frequent shutdowns........ Chapter 17, Symptom 8
Services not starting........ Chapter 17, Symptom 10
Applications crashing .... Chapter 17, Symptom 8
Low memory warnings .... Chapter 17, Symptom 12
USB controller resource warnings .... Chapter 17, Symptom 13
System instability .... Chapter 17, Symptom 14
No OS found........ Chapter 17, Second Stage, Symptom 2, Symptom 3, Symptom 4
Slow profile load........ Chapter 17, Symptom 11
Time drift........ Chapter 13, Mobile Device Troubleshooting

Common troubleshooting steps
Reboot .... Chapter 17, First Stage
Restart services .... Chapter 18, Task Manager
Uninstall/reinstall/update applications........ Chapter 13, Mobile Device Troubleshooting
Add resources .... Chapter 17, Windows Performance, Resource, and Reliability Monitors
Verify requirements .... Chapter 17, What Happened Last
System file check .... Chapter 17, System File Checker

Repair Windows.. Chapter 17, Second Stage, Symptom 14
Restore..Chapter 18, System Restore
Reimage..Chapter 18, Reinstall the Operating System
Roll back updates.................... Chapter 17, Verify Full System Functionality and Implement Preventive Measures
Rebuild Windows profiles ....Chapter 17, Symptom 11

3.2 Given a scenario, troubleshoot common personal computer (PC) security issues.

Common symptoms
Unable to access the network ....Chapter 23, Cannot Access Resources on the Network, Network Path Not Found Message
Desktop alerts..Chapter 16, Figure 16-17
False alerts regarding antivirus protection..Chapter 16, Figure 16-17
Altered system or personal files..Chapter 16, Figure 16-17
Missing/renamed files ....Chapter 16, Figure 16-17
Unwanted notifications within the OS ....Chapter 16, Figure 16-17
OS update failures..Chapter 16, Figure 16-17
Browser-related symptoms ....Chapter 16, Figure 16-17
Random/frequent pop-ups..Chapter 16, Figure 16-17
Certificate warnings..Chapter 16, Figure 16-17
Redirection .... Chapter 16, Figure 16-17; Chapter 21, Folder Redirection

3.3 Given a scenario, use best practice procedures for malware removal.

1. Investigate and verify malware symptoms ....Chapter 16, Malware Removal
2. Quarantine infected systems ....Chapter 16, Malware Removal
3. Disable System Restore in Windows ....Chapter 16, Malware Removal
4. Remediate infected systems ....Chapter 16, Malware Removal
   a. Update antimalware software..Chapter 16, Malware Removal
   b. Scanning and removal techniques (e.g., safe mode, pre-installation environment) ......Chapter 16, Malware Removal
5. Schedule scans and run updates..Chapter 16, Malware Removal
6. Enable System Restore and create a restore point in Windows..Chapter 16, Malware Removal
7. Educate the end user ....Chapter 16, Malware Removal

3.4 Given a scenario, troubleshoot common mobile OS and application issues.

Common symptoms
Application fails to launch.. Chapter 13, Symptom 18
Application fails to close/crashes .... Chapter 13, Mobile Device Troubleshooting
Application fails to update.. Chapter 13, Mobile Device Troubleshooting
Slow to respond .... Chapter 13, Symptom 19
Dim display .... Chapter 13, Symptom 11
OS fails to update.. Chapter 13, Symptom 27
Battery life issues.. Chapter 13, Symptom 9
Randomly reboots.. Chapter 13, Mobile Device Troubleshooting
Connectivity issues
Bluetooth ....Chapter 13, Symptom 15
Wi-Fi ....Chapter 13, Symptom 13
Near-field communication (NFC)..Chapter 13, Mobile Phone Connectivity
AirDrop..Chapter 13, Mobile Phone Connectivity
Screen does not auto-rotate.. Chapter 13, Mobile Device Troubleshooting

3.5 Given a scenario, troubleshoot mobile OS and application security issues.

Security concerns
Android package (APK) source .... Chapter 13, Security Concerns
Developer mode .... Chapter 13, Security Concerns
Root access/jailbreak..Chapter 13, Jailbreaking and Rooting

4.0 Operational Procedures

4.1 Given a scenario, implement best practices associated with documentation and support systems information management.

4.2 Given a scenario, implement basic change-management best practices

4.3 Given a scenario, implement workstation backup and recovery methods.

4.4 Given a scenario, use common safety procedures.

4.5 Summarize environmental impacts and local environmental controls.

4.6 Explain the importance of prohibited content/activity and privacy, licensing, and policy concepts.

Incident response........Chapter 24, First Response/Incident Response
Chain of custody........Chapter 24, Chain of Custody
Inform management/law enforcement as necessary........Chapter 24, Report through Proper Channels
Copy of drive (data integrity and preservation)........Chapter 24, Preservation of Data and Devices
Documentation of incident........Chapter 24, Documentation
Licensing/digital rights management (DRM)/
end-user license agreement (EULA)........Chapter 11, Digital Rights Management
Valid licenses........Chapter 11, Digital Rights Management
Non-expired licenses........Chapter 11, Digital Rights Management
Personal use license vs. corporate use license........Chapter 11, Digital Rights Management
Open-source license........Chapter 11, Digital Rights Management
Regulated data
Credit card transactions........Chapter 24, Customers' Confidential Materials
Personal government-issued information........Chapter 24, Customers' Confidential Materials
PII........Chapter 24, Customers' Confidential Materials
Healthcare data........Chapter 24, Customers' Confidential Materials
Data retention requirements........Chapter 24, Regulatory and Compliance Policy

4.7 Given a scenario, use proper communication techniques and professionalism.

Professional appearance and attire........Chapter 24, Professional Image
Match the required attire of the given environment........Chapter 24, Professional Image
Formal........Chapter 24, Professional Image
Business casual........Chapter 24, Professional Image
Use proper language and avoid jargon, acronyms, and slang, when applicable........Chapter 24, Communication Skills
Maintain a positive attitude/project confidence........Chapter 24, Attitude
Actively listen, take notes, and avoid interrupting the customer........Chapter 24, Listening Skills
Be culturally sensitive........Chapter 24, Cultural Sensitivity
Use appropriate professional titles, when applicable........Chapter 24, Cultural Sensitivity
Be on time (if late, contact the customer)........Chapter 24, Punctuality
Avoid distractions........Chapter 24, Attentiveness
Personal calls........Chapter 24, Attentiveness
Texting/social media sites........Chapter 24, Attentiveness
Personal interruptions........Chapter 24, Attentiveness
Dealing with difficult customers or situations........Chapter 24, Managing Difficult Situations
Do not argue with customers or be defensive........Chapter 24, Managing Difficult Situations, Is the Customer Always Right?
Avoid dismissing customer problems........Chapter 24, Managing Difficult Situations
Avoid being judgmental........Chapter 24, Attitude
Clarify customer statements (ask open-ended questions to narrow the scope of the problem, restate the issue, or question to verify understanding)........Chapter 24, Listening Skills
Do not disclose experience via social media outlets........Chapter 24, Customers' Confidential Materials
Set and meet expectations/time line and communicate status with the customer........Chapter 24, Your Word
Offer repair/replacement options, as needed........Chapter 24, Managing Difficult Situations
Provide proper documentation on the services provided........Chapter 24, Contracts
Follow up with customer/user at a later date to verify satisfaction........Chapter 24, Follow Up
Deal appropriate with customers' confidential and private materials........Chapter 24, Customers' Confidential Materials
Located on a computer, desktop, printer, etc..........Chapter 24, Customers' Confidential Materials

4.8 Identify the basics of scripting.

Script file types
- .bat....Appendix B, Figure B-1
- .ps1....Appendix B, Figure B-1
- .vbs....Appendix B, Figure B-1
- .sh....Appendix B, Figure B-1
- .js....Appendix B, Figure B-1
- .py....Appendix B, Figure B-1

Use cases for scripting
- Basic automation....Appendix B, Scripting Basics
- Restarting machines....Appendix B, Scripting Basics
- Remapping network drives....Appendix B, Scripting Basics
- Installation of applications....Appendix B, Scripting Basics
- Automated backups....Appendix B, Scripting Basics
- Gathering of information/data....Appendix B, Scripting Basics
- Initiating updates....Appendix B, Scripting Basics

Other considerations when using scripts
- Unintentionally introducing malware....Appendix B, Scripting Basics
- Inadvertently changing system settings....Appendix B, Scripting Basics
- Browser or system crashes due to mishandling of resources....Appendix B, Scripting Basics

4.9 Given a scenario, use remote access technologies.

Methods/tools
- RDP....Chapter 23, Remote Desktop, Figure 23-30, Figure 23-31
- VPN....Chapter 23, Virtual Private Network (VPN)
- Virtual network computer (VNC)....Chapter 23, Other Remote Access Programs
- Secure Shell (SSH)....Chapter 22, SSH
- Remote monitoring and management (RMM)....Chapter 22, Remote Troubleshooting; Chapter 23, Other Remote Access Programs
- Microsoft Remote Assistance (MSRA)....Chapter 22, Remote Troubleshooting; Chapter 23, Remote Assistance
- Third-party tools....Chapter 23, Other Remote Access Programs
  - Screen sharing software....Chapter 22, Other Cloud-Computing Tools
  - Video-conferencing software....Chapter 22, Remote Troubleshooting; Chapter 23, Other Remote Access Programs
  - File transfer software....Chapter 22, Other Cloud-Computing Tools
  - Desktop management software....Chapter 22, Virtual Desktop Infrastructure; Chapter 23, Other Remote Access Programs

Security considerations of each access method....Chapter 22, Other Cloud-Computing Tools

Appendix B

Scripting Basics

A+ 1102: 4.8

In computing, *scripting*, also called *script language*, refers to a programming language used to support scripts. *Scripts* are programs written for a specific environment to automate repetitive tasks or generate web pages. These programs are often interpreted by high-level, general-purpose languages such as Perl, PowerShell, or Python. There are many types of scripts, as shown in Figure B-1.

A+ 1102: 4.8

In scripting, the *environment* refers to the browser or program used to create and run scripts. As such, an *environment variable* is a value that affects how a running process interacts with the computer. Environment variables are dynamic objects, so they can be edited and used by multiple programs, various personal computers, and mobile operating systems. Examples in which environment variables are used include

- domain names;
- authentication keys needed for secure server applications; and
- account names for a network on Active Directory or web service.

Within the scripting environment, comments serve an important function for the programmer. A *comment* is an explanation built into the source code that makes the code easier for programmers to understand. These comments are typically ignored by the programs running, compiling, or interpreting the script. Each programming environment has different syntaxes for expressing comments. For example, C++ uses the syntax /* to denote the start of a comment and */ to denote the end of the comment, while Microsoft environments, such as VBScript, use apostrophes to show comments. Examples of comments in a Python environment beginning with the # symbol can be seen in Figure B-2. Notice in Figure B-3 that the comments do not appear once the script has been executed.

In computer programming and software development, computer programmers must generate *script constructs*, which are individual sequences of programming that initiate specific commands. A construct with multiple built-in commands is called a *nested construct*. Constructs often consist of loops and variables. A *loop* is a sequence

Figure B-1

Script Languages		
File Extension	**Script Type**	**Usage**
.bat	Windows batch file	Operates in Command Prompt to execute commands; not used as frequently as PowerShell scripts in modern computing
.ps1	PowerShell	Creates administrative framework and executes commands
.vbs	Visual Basic	Provides functionality and interaction to web pages; also used for client-side scripting and generating tools for error checking and handling
.sh	Shell	Written to command-line Interpreters similarly to batch scripts
.py	Python	General-purpose programming
.js	JavaScript	Executed in web browsers and used to create complex web pages that operate similarly top software applications

Goodheart-Willcox Publisher

that runs a repetitive series of commands or actions. Although the coding schemes of loops vary among computer programming languages, they follow a similar context. Furthermore, for these loops to operate, a computer program must have defined or measured variables. An example of loop syntax in Microsoft Visual Studio is shown in Figure B-4. A ***variable*** is an important part of scripting that refers to a group of data in memory that can be modified. Variables can be assigned any value or data type, such as text or numeric. Examples of variables are shown in Figure B-5.

The two basic data types in computer programming are integers and strings. ***Integers*** are variables in code that represent a number, while ***strings*** represent syntax that generates multiple variables together. Strings are created by placing syntax

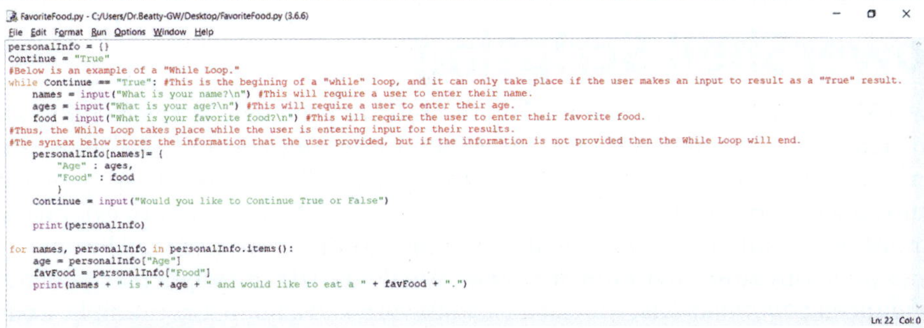

Figure B-2

Goodheart-Willcox Publisher

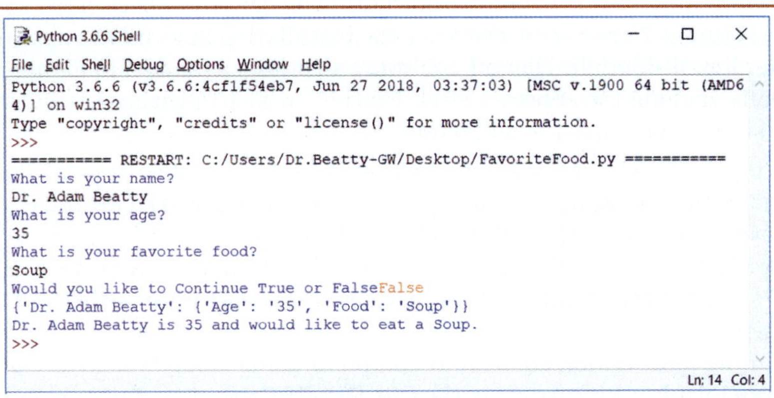

Figure B-3

Goodheart-Willcox Publisher

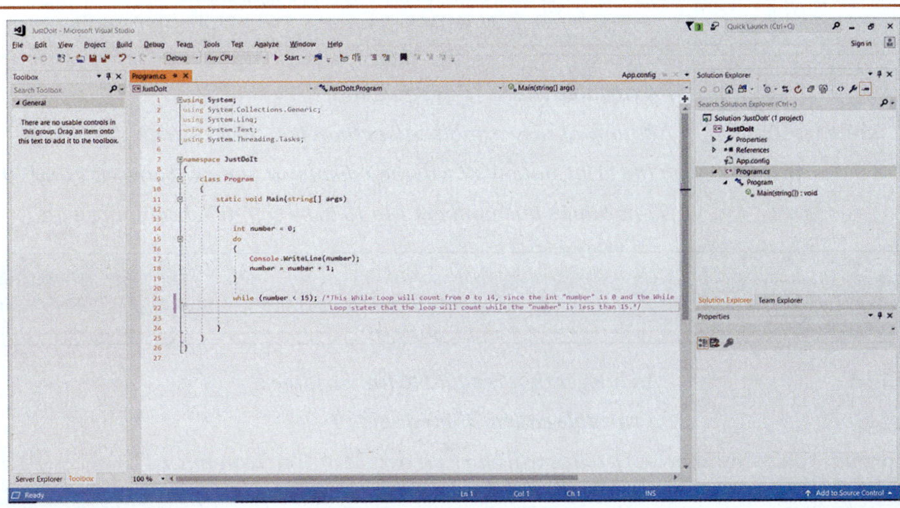

Figure B-4

Goodheart-Willcox Publisher

inside quotation marks and combining the syntax with an integer using a plus sign. Figure B-6 shows an example of an integer used inside a string. Be advised, what is placed in the quotation marks will be presented verbatim once it is printed or displayed. This can be seen in a comparison of Figure B-2 and Figure B-3.

A+ 1102: 4.8

When creating scripts, just as when programming software, it is wise to evaluate the script to ensure it is safe to run without damaging the computer or the network. Errors in a script can cause unintended consequences, such as introducing malware, inadvertently crashing system settings, or crashing the browser (or the system as a whole) due to mishandling of resources. For these reasons, it is advisable to evaluate all scripts in a sandbox environment before executing them in a live system.

PowerShell Scripting

PowerShell is a command-line interpreter and scripting environment integrated into Windows and commonly used for Windows Administrative tasks. PowerShell brings the power of the .NET Framework to command-line users and script writers by introducing powerful new concepts that enable an administrator to extend their knowledge and enhance scripts created within the Windows Command Prompt and Windows Script Host environments. PowerShell consists of scripts using ***cmdlets***, pronounced ***command-lets***, which consist of a verb and a noun. For example, a commonly used cmdlet is **get-help**.

A+ 1102: 4.8

PowerShell cmdlets enable users to perform a variety of tasks. For example, **get-psdrive** enables users to obtain information on drives connected to a system, as shown in Figure B-7. Users can also force the installation of Windows updates using the cmdlet **Install-Module-Name PSWindowsUpdate**, as shown in Figure B-8. You may have to include the **-Force** switch for this cmdlet to execute. Additional use cases for scripting include the following:

- Backing up data by entering wbAdmin-start backup -backupTarget:F: -include:C: -allCritical -quiet, where C: represents the drive being backed up and F: represents the drive where the backup will be stored
- Mapping drives using the syntax New-PSDrive -Name "DRIVER-LETTER" -PSProvider "FileSystem" -Root "\\DEVICE-NAME-OR-IP\SHARED-FOLDER" -Persist
- Obtaining information about your computer using cmdlets such as **Get-Culture** (displays culture set in the OS), **Get-PSDrive** (lists drives in current session), **Get-Process** (obtains processes running on a computer), and **Get-Service** (lists services on a computer), as shown in Figure B-9

Figure B-5

```
i = 1                    //A variable called "i" is equal to 1
  while i < 10:          //As long as the variable is less than ten, then i is true
        print (i)        //The print statement will then display a number between 1 and 10
       i + 1             //This allows the numbers 1 to 10 to be counted, beginning with 1
```

Goodheart-Willcox Publisher

Figure B-6

```
int = i                  //An integer that is equal to the variable i
i = 1                    //A variable called "i" is equal to 1
 print ("You're number" + 1) //This will show an output of "You're number 1"
```

Goodheart-Willcox Publisher

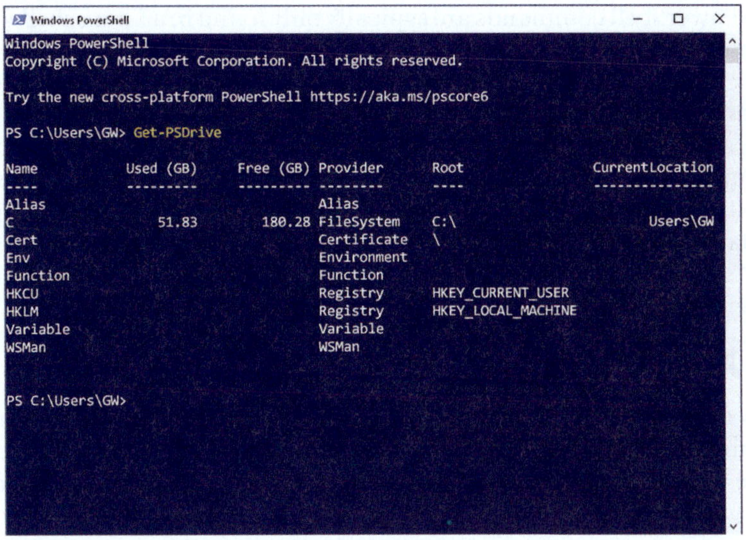

Figure B-7

Goodheart-Willcox Publisher

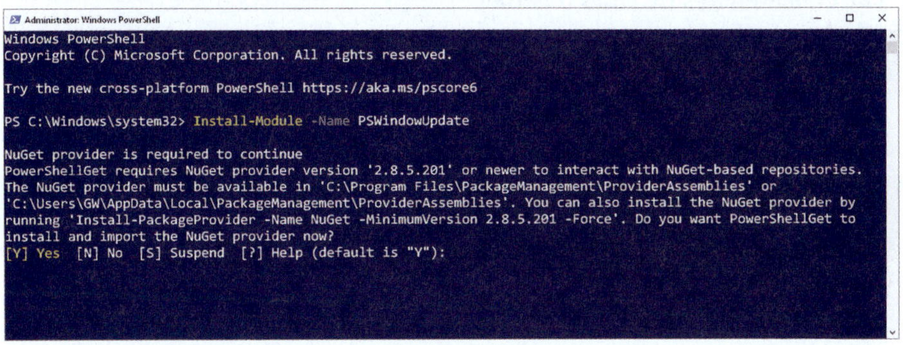

Figure B-8

Goodheart-Willcox Publisher

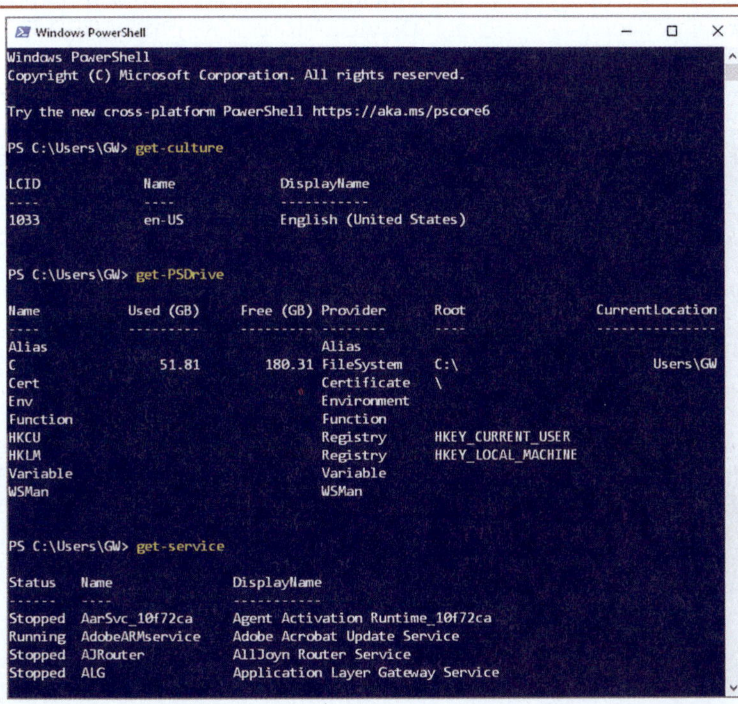

Figure B-9

Goodheart-Willcox Publisher

Some PowerShell commands are typically only found in a Linux shell. For example, the **ps** command, which lists running processes, is a Linux shell command that also exists in PowerShell. The syntax for this command is typically ps | sort-object WS-descending, as shown in Figure B-10.

The previous examples of PowerShell commands can be used in computer repair and administration, but there are many others. Entire books have been written about PowerShell, so the scope of it extends far beyond this textbook. However, a list of useful cmdlets, as well as a brief explanation of each can be found in Figure B-11.

A+ 1102: 4.8

Linux Shell Scripting

Linux has many commands that can be issued from the BASH shell, either as individual commands or as scripts. Common commands you will use frequently are listed here with a brief explanation. Some of these have associated screen captures.

A+ 1102: 4.8

- **adduser**: adds a user, as demonstrated in Figure B-12
- **apt**: refers to commands used to install software, including **apt-get install**, which installs software programs; only works in specific Linux distributions
- **cat**: concatenates two files together
- **cd**: changes file directory
- **chmod**: changes the mode for the target file and is used with scripts to make them executable
- **chown**: changes the owner of a file; requires root privileges or the user to be the current owner to execute
- **clear**: clears the screen
- **cmp**: compares different files
- **date**: sets or displays the date
- **diff**: compares two files similarly to **cmp**
- **dmesg**: displays boot messages but can fill multiple screens; output is often piped to an external file using the syntax dmesg>myfile.txt, where *myfile* is the desired file name
- **fsck**: performs a file system check; includes several related commands, such as **e2fsck**

Figure B-10

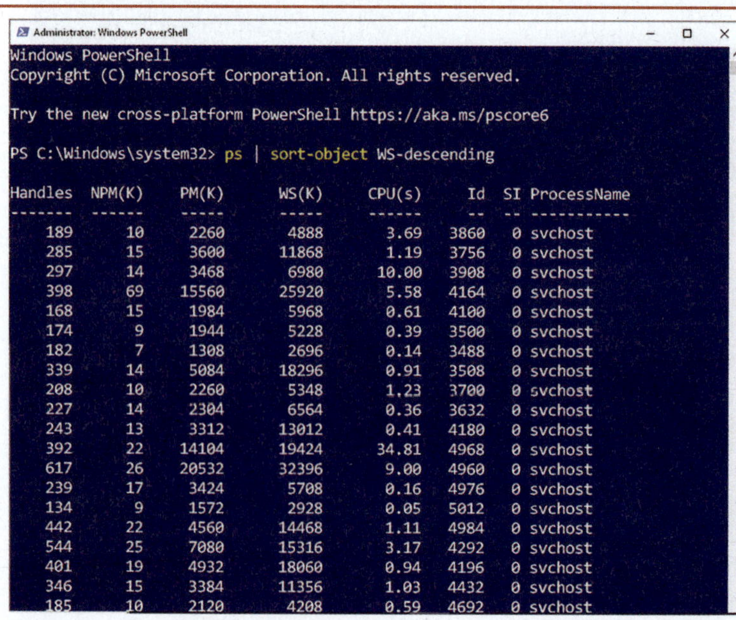

Goodheart-Willcox Publisher

Figure B-11

PowerShell Commands	
Cmdlet	**Usage**
Add-Computer	Adds local computer to a domain or workgroup
Add-PSSnapin	Adds one or more PowerShell snap-ins to the current session
Clear-EventLog	Clears all entries from specified event logs on local or remote computers
Clear-History	Deletes entries from the command history
Clear-Recyclebin	Empties the Recycle Bin on a local or remote computer
Connect-WSMAN	Connects to the WinRM service on a remote computer
Copy-Item	Copies item from one location to another
Enable-PSRemoting	Configures the computer to receive remote commands
Get-Acl	Retrieves the security descriptor for a resource such as a file or registry key
Get-ControlPanelItem	Retrieves Control Panel items
Get-Host	Retrieves an object that represents the current host program
Get-NetworkSwitchEthernetPort	Retrieves port information for a network switch
Install-Script	Installs a script
Invoke-WebRequest	Retrieves content from a web page
Net-PSDrive	Creates temporary and persistent mapped network drives
Restart-Computer	Restarts computer
Set-Service	Starts, stops, or suspends a service, or changes properties of the service
Start-Service	Starts a stopped service
Start-Process	Starts one or more processes on the local computer
Stop-Computer	Stops or shuts down local or remote computers

Goodheart-Willcox Publisher

Figure B-12

```
test@debian: ~
File  Edit  View  Terminal  Tabs  Help
debian:/home/test# adduser bsmith
Adding user `bsmith' ...
Adding new group `bsmith' (1001) ...
Adding new user `bsmith' (1001) with group `bsmith' ...
Creating home directory `/home/bsmith' ...
Copying files from `/etc/skel' ...
Enter new UNIX password:
Retype new UNIX password:
passwd: password updated successfully
Changing the user information for bsmith
Enter the new value, or press ENTER for the default
        Full Name []: bob smith
        Room Number []: 33
        Work Phone []: 214-555-5555
        Home Phone []:
        Other []:
Is the information correct? [Y/n] y
debian:/home/test#
```

Goodheart-Willcox Publisher

- **grep**: most popular search command for Linux; often used to search in files created from piped commands
- **groupadd**: adds a new group, as demonstrated in Figure B-13
- **groupdel**: deletes a group
- **groupmod**: modifies an existing group
- **head**: returns the first few lines of a specified file; often used to check multiple files for specific data
- **history**: reveals past shell commands that have been executed
- **ifconfig**: reveals or sets network card(s) settings; most commonly used network utility
- **ls**: lists the contents of the current directory; often the first command learned in Linux
- **man**: provides manual pages (help) for other commands
- **mkdir**: creates a new directory
- **mount**: mounts a new file system
- **netstat**: displays current connections to your system
- **nice**: changes the priority of a given process
- **ping**: attempts to connect to a given IP address or URL; functions like the equivalent Windows command
- **ps**: displays currently running processes for the current user, as demonstrated in Figure B-14
- **rmdir**: removes a directory
- **su**: enables super user (root) permissions in the shell; requires root password

Figure B-13

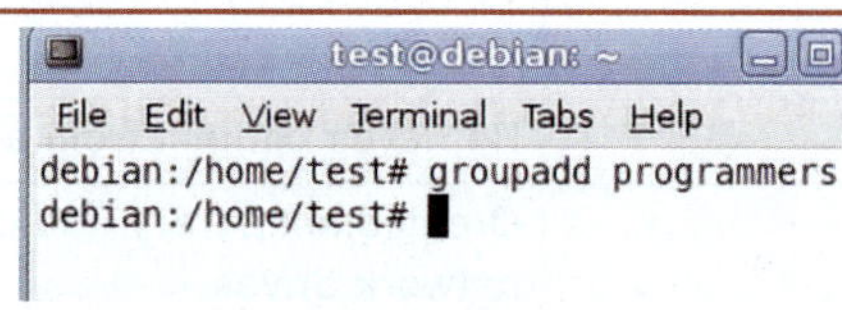

Goodheart-Willcox Publisher

Figure B-14

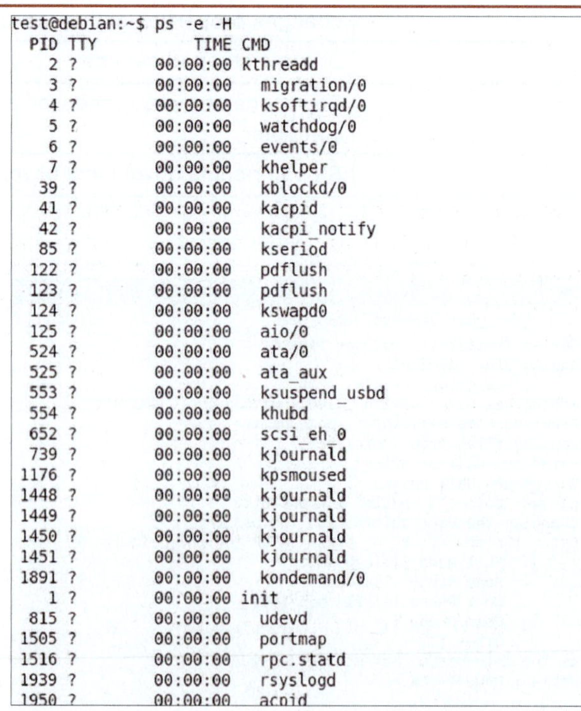

Goodheart-Willcox Publisher

- **top**: displays currently running processes but is not limited to the current user
- **touch**: changes the date and time on a file
- **traceroute**: similar to ping but displays the entire route to the target; functions like the equivalent Windows command
- **useradd**: adds new users to the system
- **userdel**: deletes a user
- **usermod**: modifies a user profile

Linux commands can be grouped into a script using any text editor, such as Notepad, but the file must be saved with a **.sh** file extension to be executable. In some distros, such as OpenSUSE, you must change the file to make it executable, which can be accomplished with the command syntax, chmod 777 myscript.sh. The three numbers represent the user who owns the file, the current group, or everyone. For example, if you wanted a specific user to be able to execute this script, the syntax would be chmod 700 myscript.sh. However, if you wanted to provide group execution access, the syntax would be chmod 070 myscript.sh. In these examples, the number 7 indicates full permission. Permission levels are designated by the following:

- 0: no permissions (---)
- 1: execute only (--x)
- 2: write only (-w-)
- 3: write and execute (-wx)
- 4: read only (r--)
- 5: read and execute (r-x)
- 6: read and write (rw-)
- 7: all permissions (rwx)

An example of a script that will execute three simple shell commands is as follows:

```
#!/bin/bash
ls; ps;who;logname;
exit 0
```

As you likely ascertained from the syntax, when executed, this script lists the contents of the current directory, displays the running processes for the logname user, then closes. In similar fashion, scripts can be used to update the system, such as in the following:

```
#!/bin/bash
# Update the system
sudo apt-get update -y
sudo apt-get upgrade -y
exit 0
```

Notice the # sign, which denotes that the line is a comment. Comments are very helpful for informing the person reading your script of what you are attempting to do. They make debugging scripts much easier, and they do not interfere with the execution of the script because BASH ignores them.

Additional uses of scripting in Linux include creating backups and removing *orphaned files*, which are files that exist in the system after their parent applications were removed or uninstalled. The syntax for creating a backup is as follows:

```
#!/bin/bash
# Create the backup
tar -zcvf /backup/$filename / --exclude=/backup
exit 0
```

The syntax for removing orphaned files is:

```
#!/bin/bash
# Check for and remove orphaned packages
sudo apt-get autoremove -y
exit 0
```

Appendix C

Binary Math

Counting and Converting Binary Numbers

Recall that in digital electronics, a circuit is either *on* or *off* or a voltage condition is *high* or *low*. For example, a digital circuit may have two distinct conditions: 5 volts present or 0 volts present. Binary math, and the binary number system, is similar and serves as an accurate representation of digital circuitry.

Binary math uses only two numbers (1 and 0) to represent an infinite range of numbers. The binary number system accomplishes this in the same basic way the decimal number system does: by placing numbers into discrete digit positions. The biggest difference between decimal and binary is that decimal uses ten numbers (0 through 9) instead of only two.

In decimal form, the first digit position is commonly referred to as the *ones* position, and the second digit position is the *tens* position. If the maximum value of 9 is entered in both these positions, the resulting number is 99 (nine tens plus nine ones). The third digit position is the *hundreds* position, followed by the *thousands*, *ten-thousands*, *hundred-thousands*, *millions*, and so on, all with maximum values of 9. Notice in Figure C-1 that each position can be expressed as an exponent of the base 10.

In Figure C-1, note that the *Range of Possible Results* column indicates the range of numbers for which the selected digit position would be the left-most digit, not the range of number that could contain that digit position. Consider the number 2,753, which contains the following:

- Two thousands = 2,000
- Seven hundreds = 700
- Five tens = 50
- Three ones = 3
- Total = 2,753

Figure C-1

Decimal Numbering System		
Digit Position	**Equivalent Exponent**	**Range of Possible Results**
Ones	10^0	0–9
Tens	10^1	10–99
Hundreds	10^2	100–999
Thousands	10^3	1,000–9,999
Ten-thousands	10^4	10,000–99,999
Hundred-thousands	10^5	100,000–999,999
Millions	10^6	1,000,000–9,999,999

Goodheart-Willcox Publisher

Binary numbers are expressed similarly, but instead of each digit position being 10 times greater than the position before it, the value of each position is double that of the position before it, as demonstrated in Figure C-2. Consider the binary number 101011000001 and compare it to Figure C-3. By adding the numbers in the *Decimal Conversion* column, you can see that 101011000001 is the binary equivalent of 2,753.

To convert a binary number to a decimal number, simply record the decimal value assigned to each position that contains a binary value of *1*. Then, add the decimal numbers together, as illustrated in Figure C-4.

Figure C-2

Binary Numbering System

Digit Position	Equivalent Exponent	Range of Possible Results
Ones	2^0	0–1
Twos	2^1	2–3
Fours	2^2	4–7
Eights	2^3	8–15
Sixteens	2^4	16–31
Thirty-twos	2^5	32–63
Sixty-fours	2^6	64–127
One-hundred twenty-eights	2^7	128–255

Goodheart-Willcox Publisher

Figure C-3

Decimal Equivalent of 101011000001

Binary Position (Value in Decimal)	Binary Value	Decimal Conversion
2^{11} (2,048)	1	2,048
2^{10} (1,024)	0	0
2^9 (512)	1	512
2^8 (256)	0	0
2^7 (128)	1	128
2^6 (64)	1	64
2^5 (32)	0	0
2^4 (16)	0	0
2^3 (8)	0	0
2^2 (4)	0	0
2^1 (2)	0	0
2^0 (1)	1	1

Goodheart-Willcox Publisher

Figure C-4

Binary Conversion

Binary Position	Binary Value	Decimal Equivalent	Total
Thirty-twos	1	32	32
Sixteens	0	0	(+0) = 32
Eights	1	8	(+8) = 40
Fours	1	4	(+4) = 44
Twos	0	0	(+0) = 44
Ones	1	1	(+1) = 45

Goodheart-Willcox Publisher

When converting a decimal number to a binary number, you simply reverse the previous operation. For example, to convert the decimal number 178 to a binary number, you must divide it by a series of powers of two. The phrase *powers of two*, or 2^n, means that you multiply a number by two to get the next number in the series before repeating the multiplication. The powers of two are 1, 2, 4, 8, 16, 32, 64, 128, 256, 512, 1,024, 2,048, and so on.

To convert the decimal number 178 to binary, start by finding the largest power of two that does not exceed 178. In this case, the largest power-of-two value that does not exceed 178 is 128. Place a 1 in the binary number position that represents 128, as shown in Figure C-5.

Subtracting 128 from 178 leaves a difference of 50. Since the number 50 is less than the next-largest power of two (64), you must insert a 0 in the *64s* position, as shown in Figure C-6.

Figure C-5

Decimal Conversion Step 1

Powers of 2	Binary Digit
128	1
64	-
32	-
16	-
8	-
4	-
2	-
1	-

Goodheart-Willcox Publisher

Figure C-6

Decimal Conversion Step 2

Powers of 2	Binary Digit
128	1
64	0
32	-
16	-
8	-
4	-
2	-
1	-

Goodheart-Willcox Publisher

Next, since 50 is larger than the next-largest power of two (32), place a 1 in the *32s* position. See Figure C-7.

Now, subtract 32 from 50. The difference is 18, which is larger than the next power-of-two value (*16*). As a result, you must place a 1 in the *16s* position. See Figure C-8.

Subtracting 16 from 18 leaves *2*, which is smaller than the next two powers of two (*8* and *4*). This means the next two positions in the binary number are both 0s. See Figure C-9.

Figure C-7

Decimal Conversion Step 3	
Powers of 2	**Binary Digit**
128	1
64	0
32	1
16	-
8	-
4	-
2	-
1	-

Goodheart-Willcox Publisher

Figure C-8

Decimal Conversion Step 4	
Powers of 2	**Binary Digit**
128	1
64	0
32	1
16	1
8	-
4	-
2	-
1	-

Goodheart-Willcox Publisher

Figure C-9

Decimal Conversion Step 5	
Powers of 2	**Binary Digit**
128	1
64	0
32	1
16	1
8	0
4	0
2	-
1	-

Goodheart-Willcox Publisher

The next power of two is *2*, and the number remaining from the last step is also 2. Therefore, a 1 goes into the *2s* position. See Figure C-10.

There are no decimal numbers remaining, so the *1s* position should be filled with 0. The binary equivalent of the decimal number 178 is 10110010, as shown in Figure C-11.

Figure C-10

Decimal Conversion Step 6	
Powers of 2	**Binary Digit**
128	1
64	0
32	1
16	1
8	0
4	0
2	1
1	-

Goodheart-Willcox Publisher

Figure C-11

Decimal Conversion Step 7	
Powers of 2	**Binary Digit**
128	1
64	0
32	1
16	1
8	0
4	0
2	1
1	0

Goodheart-Willcox Publisher

Appendix D

Number Conversion Table

Decimal, Binary, Octal, and Hexadecimal Conversion			
Decimal	Binary	Octal	Hexadecimal
0	000000	0	0
1	000001	1	1
2	000010	2	2
3	000011	3	3
4	000100	4	4
5	000101	5	5
6	000110	6	6
7	000111	7	7
8	001000	10	8
9	001001	11	9
10	001010	12	A
11	001011	13	B
12	001100	14	C
13	001101	15	D
14	001110	16	E
15	001111	17	F
16	010000	20	10
17	010001	21	11
18	010010	22	12
19	010011	23	13
20	010100	24	14
21	010101	25	15
22	010110	26	16
23	010111	27	17
24	011000	30	18
25	011001	31	19
26	011010	32	1A
27	011011	33	1B
28	011100	34	1C
29	011101	35	1D
30	011110	36	1E
31	011111	37	1F

Decimal, Binary, Octal, and Hexadecimal Conversion			
Decimal	Binary	Octal	Hexadecimal
32	100000	40	20
33	100001	41	21
34	100010	42	22
35	100011	43	23
36	100100	44	24
37	100101	45	25
38	100110	46	26
39	100111	47	27
40	101000	50	28
41	101001	51	29
42	101010	52	2A
43	101011	53	2B
44	101100	54	2C
45	101101	55	2D
46	101110	56	2E
47	101111	57	2F
48	110000	60	30
49	110001	61	31
50	110010	62	32
51	110011	63	33
52	110100	64	34
53	110101	65	35
54	110110	66	36
55	110111	67	37
56	111000	70	38
57	111001	71	39
58	111010	72	3A
59	111011	73	3B
60	111100	74	3C
61	111101	75	3D
62	111110	76	3E
63	111111	77	3F

Glossary

#

3-2-1 rule. Backup rule that states you should have three copies of your data using two different media types, with one copy being off-site. (18)

A

accelerometer. Electromechanical device that measures the force of acceleration. (13)

Access Control List (ACL). Database is used to match a user SID to the resource and then allow or deny access to it. (21)

access time. Amount of time that passes between the issue of the read command and the point in time when the actual first data bit is read after it has been located on the disc. (11)

active hub. Has a source of power connected to it and regenerates the signals it receives. (19)

active-matrix display. Display in which each pixel in the grid has its own transistor. (8)

active partition. Partition from which the operating system will boot. (10)

active tablet. Tablet that uses self-powered electronics to transmit signals. (7)

actuator arm. Device that moves the head over the disk. (10)

adapter teaming. NIC feature that allows two or more network adapters to share the network load and ensure network reliability. (19)

Address Resolution Protocol (ARP). Used to resolve IPv4 addresses to physical addresses. (22)

ad hoc network. Network formed between two or more wireless devices. (13)

administrative shares. Hidden shares on a Windows machine that have a dollar sign ($) at the end of the shared path. (21)

Advanced Access Content System (AACS). Standard designed as a digital rights management system for media content distribution. (11)

Advanced Configuration and Power Interface (ACPI). Open industry power-management standard for desktops, laptops, and servers that allows the operating system to control the power-management features. (5)

Advanced RISC Machine (ARM) processor. Processor with a microarchitecture that cannot be separated from the instruction set. (4)

Advanced Video Coding (AVC). Video compression standard used for high-definition video; also referred to as *H.264*, *MPEG-4*, and *MP4*. (9)

Advanced Video Coding High Definition (AVCHD). Proprietary specification developed jointly by Sony and Panasonic in 2006. (11)

adware. Designed to support advertisements such as pop-ups and may also gather information about the user. (16)

airplane mode. Disables wireless services so the device cannot send or receive telephone calls or text messages. (13)

alternating current (AC). Has no negative or positive markings because it is in a state of constant change or alternating polarities. (5)

alternating-frame rendering. Rendering method in which each card is responsible for rendering every other frame. (8)

American Standard Code for Information Interchange (ASCII). First attempt to standardize computer character codes among the varieties of hardware and software. (1)

amperes (A). Scale used to measure the volume of electron flow in a current. (5)

analog electronics. Those that use and produce varying voltage levels. (1)

Android. Mobile operating system owned by Google that is derived from the Linux open-source operating system. (13)

answer file. Text-based document used in conjunction with the Sysprep tool to configure the unattended destination computer. (21)

antistatic wrist strap. Device designed to create an equal static voltage level between your body and the object to which the strap is connected; also known as a *ground strap*. (1)

Anything as a Service (XaaS). Hybrid of SaaS, PaaS, and IaaS designed to meet a variety of needs. (22)

Apple picking. Act of stealing a user's mobile device while they are using it. (13)

app store. Location that provides software applications for portable devices such as smartphones and tablets. (13)

Note: The number in parentheses following each definition indicates the chapter in which the term can be found.

archive bit. Single bit within a file that indicates whether that file has been backed up. (17)

arithmetic logic unit (ALU). Performs mathematical function on data stored in the register area and performs data manipulations such as comparing two pieces of data stored in the registry unit. (4)

aspect ratio. Ratio of the display area's height and width. (8)

assembly language. One step above machine language. (4)

AT Attachment (ATA). A 16-bit data transfer system using a 40-pin cable connector that attaches to the motherboard and to the circuit board mounted on the hard drive. (10)

AT Attachment Packet Interface (ATAPI). Interface used for standard IBM PC AT and compatible systems for accessing CD devices. (11)

authentication. Process of verifying a user's identity. (15)

Automatic Medium Dependent Interface Crossover (Auto-MDIX). Electronic chip technology incorporated into the IEEE 1000BaseT (802.3ab) gigabit Ethernet standard for network devices such as switches and network adapters. (20)

Automatic Private IP Addressing (APIPA). Windows feature that allows a computer to issue an IP address to itself when a DHCP server is unavailable. (22)

B

backdoor virus. Designed to go undetected and leave a hole, or "backdoor," in the security system of a computer or network. (16)

backfeed. Refers to a common condition in which electrical power originates from a part of the circuitry. (5)

backoff interval. Random period of time taken before data is retransmitted. (20)

backplane. Circuit board with an abundance of slots along with the length of the board. (3)

bandwidth. Range or limit of frequency that a cable or device is designed to carry. (14)

bar code reader. Converts bar code images into data. (7)

basic disk. Refers to the traditional FAT16, FAT32, exFAT, and NTFS file storage system. (10)

binary number system. Numbering system that consists entirely of ones and zeros. (1)

biometrics. Science of using a person's unique physical features to confirm their identity for authentication purposes. (13)

bit. Single binary unit of either a one or zero. (1)

bitmap font. Type of font that uses a pattern of dots to represent each letter. (12)

blackout. Condition in which no voltage is present. (5)

blue screen error. Blue screen that appears with an error code and then freezes the system. (17)

Bluetooth. Standard developed for short-range radio links between portable computers, smartphones, and other mobile devices. (7)

Blu-ray Disc (BD). High-definition video and data format developed by the Blu-ray Disc Association, which was started by Sony. (11)

Blu-ray Disc Plus (BD+). Another standard used with Blu-ray Disc digital rights management systems and performs the same type of protection as DVD region codes. (11)

boot sector virus. Type of virus that infects the boot sector of the drive. (16)

boot sequence. Step-by-step process of bringing a computer to an operational state. (2)

botnet. Collection of infected computers controlled by a source computer to send spam simultaneously to millions of computers connected to the Internet; short for *robot network*. (16)

bridge. Device used to connect two dissimilar networks. (13)

brouter. Combination bridge and router and applies the best characteristics of both systems. (22)

brownout. Occurs when low voltage is present. (5)

browser hijacker. Program that changes the configuration of a browser. (16)

buffer. Used to store data temporarily before transferring it to a device. (6)

buffering. Technique used to play a downloaded file without skips or quiet spots during playback. (9)

bug. Error in programming. (2)

bus. Collection of conductors that works together for a specific purpose. (3)

bus topology. Network arrangement in which a single conductor connects to all the computers. (19)

byte. Equal to eight bits. (1)

C

cable crimper. Tool designed to crimp (squeeze) an RJ-45 connector onto the end of a twisted-pair cable, thus making the electrical connections between each of the eight conductors and the connector. (20)

cable modem. Transceiver that allows existing cable television coaxial cable to be used for Internet access. (14)

cable tester. Tool used to assess newly made and existing network cables. (20)

cable tracer. Receives the signal transmitted through a cable and produces a tone if it is near the cable. (20)

cache. Refers to a small area of temporary memory storage; pronounced *cash.* (4)

call center. Large collection of support personnel located in a common facility equipped with telephones and computer network support. (24)

campus area network (CAN). Network that spans a limited geographic area. (19)

Carrier Sense Multiple Access with Collision Avoidance (CSMA/CA). Media access method that works much like CSMA/CD but tries to avoid, rather than detect, collisions. (20)

Carrier Sense Multiple Access with Collision Detection (CSMA/CD). Media access method used to control and ensure the delivery of data. (20)

central processing unit (CPU). Brain of the computer where the actual instructions are executed. (1)

chain of custody. Method of preserving, tracking, and ensuring the integrity of evidence. (24)

change management. Refers to business or organizational guidance that prepares, equips, and supports internal employees to adopt or incorporate changes. (24)

charge-coupled device (CCD). Series of light-activated capacitors contained in a single chip. (7)

chipset. Collection of integrated circuits that connects the motherboard buses and ports that run at different speeds. (3)

Chrome OS. Linux-derived operating system merged with Google's flagship web browser, also called Chrome. (13)

circuit switching. Makes a permanent connection for the duration of the transmission, with data transmitted in a steady stream. (22)

clean install. Refers to an installation in which the operating system partition has been reformatted, thus wiping out all user data files. (18)

clean room. Environment where dust and foreign particles have been eliminated completely. (18)

client. Individual PC or workstation that accesses a server's resources and shared files. (19)

client/server network. Network model in which the network is made up of computers that are designated as either clients or servers. (19)

client-side virtualization. Software application used to create multiple operating system environments on the host machine. (22)

cluster. Refers to a file storage space that usually consists of one or more sectors. (10)

CMYK. Four-color process consisting of cyan, magenta, yellow, and a key color—most often black. (12)

coaxial cable. Network cable consisting of a core conductor surrounded by an insulator, which is covered with a shield of either a solid foil or a braided wire layer to protect the cable core from stray electromagnetic interference; also called *coax.* (20)

codec. Any hardware, software, or combination hardware and software that can compress and decompress data. (9)

Code Division Multiple Access (CDMA). Electronic technique used to encode digital information when using radio as a medium. (14)

cold boot. Refers to a boot process in which the electrical power switch is used to turn on the computer; also called a *hard boot.* (2)

collision domain. Section of a network where data collisions occur; sometimes referred to as a *contention domain.* (19)

colored books. Series of specifications that outline disc system standards. (11)

color palette. Collection of possible different colors, usually in degrees or shades, that can be displayed on a monitor. (8)

color thermal printer. Operates based on the principle of applying color by heating a special ribbon that is coated with a wax-like material. (12)

column address selection (CAS). Describes the time it takes to access the exact column location in the memory matrix after RAS; also called column address *strobe.* (6)

command-line interface (CLI). Text-based interface that allows a user to issue commands by entering text as the command prompt. (2)

community cloud. Shared infrastructure of users who share a common interest or concern. (22)

compact disc read-only memory (CD-ROM). Optical disc able to store large amounts of data. (11)

company app. Application that ensures and enforces security policies on a mobile device. (13)

compiler. Program that translates the higher-level language into machine language based on the CPU's instruction set. (4)

complex instruction set computer (CISC). CPU designed so the die can accept many machine-language commands that manipulate or process complex mathematical formulas and instruction sets. (4)

CompTIA A+ Certification Exam. Introductory computer-repair certification consisting of two tests: CompTIA A+ 220-1101 and the CompTIA A+ 220-1102. (25)

computer. Assembly of electronic modules that interact with computer programs known as *software* to create, modify, transmit, store, and display data. (1)

Computer Management. Collection of administrative tools that allows technicians to view information about a user's personal computer in a manner more detailed than the previously mentioned utilities and tools. (18)

configuration files. Contain information such as the amount of memory and the type of video adapter present in the system. (2)

constant angular velocity (CAV). Method of reading data that maintains the same rpm regardless of the data location; used by modern drives. (11)

constant linear velocity (CLV). Method of reading data that varied the speed at which the CD was spinning to keep points on the inside and outside of the disc spinning at a constant velocity and was used on early CD drives; not used by modern drives. (11)

continuity. Ability of a device or component to allow an unobstructed flow of electrical energy. (5)

control unit. Controls the overall operation of the CPU by taking instructions from the decode unit, directing command instructions to the arithmetic logic unit, and directing data to be manipulated to the register area. (4)

conventional memory. Term given to the first 640 kB of memory. (6)

cookie. Small text file used to send information about a user to a server. (16)

cooperative multitasking. Process that allows one program to dominate the CPU but will allow another program to run while it is idle. (2)

cross talk. Imposition of a signal on one pair of conductors by another pair of conductors that run parallel to it. (20)

current. Amount of electron flow. (5)

customer support. Delivery of customer assistance, training, and services. (24)

cyberbullying. Use of electronic technology to harass or threaten a person. (26)

cylinder. Vertical collection of one set of tracks. (10)

D

data miner. Gathers information about a user's web-browsing habits, which is then used for marketing purposes. (16)

Data Over Cable Service Interface Specification (DOCSIS). Standard that enforces compatibility among cable modems. (14)

data transfer rate. Measurement of how much data can be transferred from the CD to the PC RAM in a set period of time. (11)

decode unit. Decodes instructions sent to the CPU and sends the data to other areas in an understandable format. (4)

dedicated circuit. Electrical power distribution system designed to serve only computer equipment. (5)

dedicated server. Server with special functions. (19)

defense in depth. Security concept that establishes the presence of multiple, redundant levels of protection in case one of the security measures fails. (19)

defragmentation. Process of moving clusters so all files have their clusters organized sequentially. (10)

demilitarized zone (DMZ). Refers to an area of a network system that is intentionally created to be less secure than the main network system and is directly accessible from the Internet. (23)

denial-of-service (DoS). Attack in which a network server or web server is flooded with false requests to the point that it cannot fulfill legitimate requests, causing the requests to time out. (16)

deployment image. Exact copy of all the files contained on the hard disk drive of the reference computer. (21)

depot technician. Technician who performs repair work usually covered by warranty. (24)

device bay. Drive bay designed to accommodate the easy hot-swap of devices. (1)

differential backup. Backup in which all data changes since the last full backup are copied. (17)

digital camera. Takes pictures by capturing and storing images as digital data instead of on photographic film. (7)

digital citizenship. Standard of appropriate behavior when using technology. (26)

digital electronics. Those that only have two states: on or off. (1)

digital footprint. Data record of all an individual's online activities. (26)

digital rights management (DRM). Any technology that ensures copyright protection for digital media, such as digital music and video. (11)

digital subscriber line (DSL). Provides high-speed Internet access over telephone lines and has become one of the most popular methods for connecting to the Internet. (14)

digital-to-analog converter (DAC). Specialized chip that converts the digital signal from the computer to an analog signal that is displayed on the computer's monitor. (8)

digital versatile disc (DVD). Standard pushed by the motion picture industry so it could release films on discs instead of tape; also known as *digital video disc (DVD).* (11)

digitizer pad. Virtual drawing surface that allows the user to create or modify drawings or modify photos; also known as a *trackpad* or *drawing pad.* (7)

direct current (DC). Refers to electrical energy that flows in one direction, from negative to positive. (5)

direct memory access (DMA). Combination of hardware and software that allows the hard drive to transfer all data directly to memory without involving the CPU. (3)

directory. Special type of file used to group or contain other files together in a hierarchical file structure. (2)

diskless workstation. Computer that runs without a hard disk drive. (19)

disk signature. Unique identifier for a storage device that identifies the disk type and properties so the Microsoft operating system can utilize the disk. (10)

docking station. Electronic cradle that provides power for a laptop, allowing users to turn the laptop into a full-size PC when portability is not necessary. (13)

domain. Organized collection of all groups and users on the network. (21)

Domain Name Service (DNS). Service that translates domain names to IP addresses. (22)

domain user account. Provides access to network domain resources as well as resources on the workstation. (21)

dot matrix printer. Creates text and images using a pattern, or matrix, of very small dots; sometimes referred to as an *impact printer.* (12)

dot pitch. Distance measured in millimeters between two color dots on the screen. (8)

driver. Small software program written specifically for a hardware device that allows the operating system to communicate with the device properly. (1)

DSL modem. Enables high-speed Internet access over existing phone lines. (14)

dual-boot system. Arrangement in which two operating systems are installed on a single computer. (2)

dual-channel mode. Refers to an arrangement in which the DIMMs are arranged as a pair and in a specific way according to the motherboard manual; also known as *interleaved mode.* (6)

dual independent bus (DIB). Refers to a bus architecture introduced with two separate or independent bus systems incorporated into the processor chip. (4)

dual in-line memory module (DIMM). Memory module constructed much like a SIMM but has edge connectors located directly across the circuit board from each other that do not connect electrically. (6)

dumpster diving. Act of inspecting a user's or company's garbage to locate sensitive information. (15)

dye-sublimation printer. Produces near photo-quality printed images by vaporizing inks, which then solidify onto paper. (12)

dynamic addressing. Automatically assigning IP addresses. (22)

dynamic disk. First introduced with Windows 2000 Professional and provided many more disk configuration options as compared to basic disk. (10)

dynamic execution. Term coined by Intel to describe the enhanced superscalar and multiple branch prediction features associated with the Pentium II processor. (4)

Dynamic Host Configuration Protocol (DHCP). Automatically assigns IP addresses to hosts. (22)

dynamic RAM. Type of integrated circuit that uses capacitors to assist in storing data in the transistors; referred to as *DRAM* (pronounced *dee-ram*). (6)

E

EFI System Partition (ESP). Special area of the hard disk drive intended for use solely by the firmware and typically contains files and data required to boot the computer system. (10)

electrically erasable programmable read-only memory (EEPROM). Similar to EPROM in that it can be reprogrammed, but it used a high electrical charge instead of ultraviolet light to erase the chip. (6)

electromagnetic interference (EMI). Interference or damage to components caused by magnets and magnetic fields. (1)

electronic vaulting (e-vaulting). Idea of sending all changes to a file to a remote site using non-backup methods. (5)

electrophotographic process (EP). Combination of static electricity, light, dry chemical compound, pressure, and heat. (12)

electrostatic discharge (ESD). Transfer of static electrical energy from one object to another. (1)

emoticons. Pictorial representations of faces or emotions made from keyboard symbols. (24)

encrypted file system (EFS). Native encryption system used with NTFS. (10)

encryption. Act of encoding data in such a way that it cannot be converted back to meaningful words without a key. (13)

encryption key. Mathematical formula for substituting values in strings of data. (13)

erasable programmable read-only memory (EPROM). Advancement from PROM that allowed chips to be programmed, erased, and then reprogrammed. (6)

error-correction code (ECC). Not only checks for, but also corrects, most errors. (6)

Ethernet network. Computer network that communicates by broadcasting information to all the computers on the network. (20)

even parity checking. Parity checking mode in which an extra bit is included whenever there is an even number of bits in a byte being transmitted. (6)

examination objective. Outlines the required skills and knowledge needed to pass the CompTIA A+ Exams. (25)

expanded memory standard (EMS). Designed to increase the amount of data memory available for applications. (6)

expansion card. Small circuit board that can be easily installed in a computer to enhance or expand its capabilities; sometimes called an *interface card* or *host adapter*. (1)

expansion card slot. Port that allows an expansion card to connect directly to the electronic circuitry in the motherboard and communicate with other components on the motherboard or with the CPU. (3)

extended file allocation table (exFAT). Proprietary Microsoft file system designed for portable devices such as USB flash drives and flash memory cards. (10)

extended graphics array (XGA). Video standard capable of a resolution of 640 × 480 while supporting 65, 536 colors and 1024 × 768 with 256 colors. (8)

extended memory system (XMS). Includes all of the PC's memory beyond the first 1 MB when the CPU is running in real mode. (6)

F

fail-over. Process that occurs when one system fails, and another system takes over. (20)

FAT16. Used 16 bits to identify stored data and had a maximum storage of 2 GB. (10)

FAT32. Used 32 bits to identify stored data, and its upper limit for storage is theoretically 2 TB (terabytes). (10)

fault tolerance. System's ability to recover after some sort of disaster. (21)

fiber-optic cable. Contains a glass or plastic center used to carry light; often referred to as *fiber*. (20)

file system. Refers to the method of organizing files on a storage device. (2)

file table. Component of a file system used to organize files on a storage device. (2)

File Transfer Protocol (FTP). Protocol used for transmitting files across the Internet. (22)

finalizing. Process of closing the disc-burn session to prevent any additional data from being written to the disc. (11)

firewall. Hardware device or software application that protects the computer from unauthorized access or malware delivered through a network or Internet connection. (16)

firmware. Hardware-specific software required to boot the computer and support communication between the operating system and hardware devices. (1)

flag. Addition to a command that modifies its function; also referred to as a *switch*. (2)

flash BIOS. Reprogrammable BIOS stored in an electrically erasable programmable read-only memory (EEPROM) module. (3)

flash memory. Solid-state, reusable data storage device that can retain data even when the electrical power is disconnected. (6)

flash ROM. Type of ROM that behaves similarly to RAM, meaning it is possible to replace its memory contents. (6)

flex mode. Hybrid arrangement of DIMM memory modules. (6)

floating-point unit (FPU). Set of circuits incorporated into the processor that is used for mathematic computation. (4)

font. Design for a set of symbols, usually text and number characters, within a specific typeface. (12)

form factor. Physical shape or outline of a motherboard and the location of the mounting holes; also called the *footprint.* (3)

frequency response range. Range in which the human ear can detect sounds; spans from approximately 20 Hz to 20 kHz. (9)

fully qualified domain name (FQDN). Combination of the host (computer) name, the domain name, and all the higher-level domains. (23)

fuse. Cylinder shape of glass or ceramic with a metal cap on each end and a fuse link on the inside. (5)

G

game pad. Any device used as an input for a game application. (7)

gas-plasma display. Flat-panel displays that produce light when a high frequency passes through a gas to a layer of phosphor. (8)

gateway. Networking device that translates information between two networks that use different protocols to communicate. (22)

geotracking. Act of tracking the GPS location of one device with another device. (13)

global area network (GAN). WAN spread over a geographical area spanning multiple countries or continents. (19)

global positioning system (GPS). Satellite-based system developed by the Department of Defense (DoD) and provides positioning, navigation, and timing services. (13)

Global System for Mobile Communications (GSM). Originally an analog wireless communication system used for voice communications or wireless telephones that evolved into a wireless digital communication system for transmitting mobile voice and data. (14)

grandfather-father-son. Backup rotation scheme consisting of three or more backup cycles, such as daily, weekly, and monthly. (18)

graphical user interface (GUI). Visual interface that allows the user to perform functions by selecting on-screen icons rather than issuing text-based commands. (2)

grayware. Collection of malware that is not regarded as very dangerous, but rather more of a nuisance. (16)

group. Collection of users organized together by similarities in their job tasks. (21)

GUID Partition Table (GPT). Disk partitioning method in which the layout of partition tables within a storage device are identified using *globally unique identifiers (GUIDs).* (10)

gyroscope. Device that measures vertical and horizontal orientation. (13)

H

hard disk drive (HDD) password. Type of password that requests a login password from the user; also known as *drive lock password* or *hard disk drive lock password.* (15)

hard drive. Main storage device where a computer system stores programs and data; also called the *internal drive* or *hard disk drive.* (1)

hard reset. Returns the device to its original condition and removes all user data, passwords, and apps. (13)

heap. Block of allocated dynamic memory. (6)

help desk. Central point of contact that provides technical support to clients. (24)

hexadecimal number system. Number system that uses 16 characters, based on the number base 16. (1)

High-bandwidth Digital Content Protection (HDCP). Digital copy-protection system that encrypts the data sent by a high-definition content player such as Blu-ray or HD-DVD to other devices such as a television or computer monitor via a physical connection. (11)

High-Definition Multimedia Interface (HDMI). Refers to a connector used to supply video and audio in an uncompressed, all-digital signal format. (8)

high-level format. Prepares a disk to receive data in a systematic, organized manner; determines the file table type; checks the physical condition of all sectors; marks bad sectors so that they cannot be used to store data; and identifies the operating system being used. (10)

high memory area (HMA). First 64 kB of the extended memory area. (6)

High Sierra format. Standard for compact discs that was created so CDs could be read on any CD device. (11)

hive. One of five major groupings that are displayed in the left pane of the Registry Editor. (17)

hoax. False message spread about a real or unreal virus. (16)

Home Phoneline Networking Alliance (HomePNA) technology. Allows existing home telephone lines to be used as network media. (23)

HomePNA adapter. Networking device that allows every telephone jack in a building to be part of the network. (23)

HP network re-discovery port monitor. Wireless port used to support connections to a wireless printer. (12)

hub. Network device that provides a quick and easy method of connecting equipment via cables. (19)

human interface device (HID) standard. Classification of USB devices as well as a set of standards for device drivers to ensure compatibility between devices and computers. (7)

hybrid cloud. Combination of two or more of the other cloud infrastructures. (22)

hybrid topology. Mixture of star, bus, and ring topologies. (19)

Hypertext Markup Language (HTML). Programming language used to create web pages. (22)

Hypertext Transfer Protocol (HTTP). Standard protocol used to transport web page content across the Internet. (22)

hypervisor. Technical term used to identify the software that creates the virtual machine on a client device; also referred to as a *virtual machine monitor.* (22)

I

incremental backup. Operation that only backs up files that have changed since the last backup. (17)

Infrastructure as a Service (IaaS). Cloud service model that provides storage and basic networking functions, which are used by the consumer. (22)

infrastructure network. Differs from an ad hoc network in that it contains a wireless access point (WAP). (13)

inkjet printer. Uses specially designed cartridges that spray a fine mist of ink as they move horizontally in front of a sheet of paper; sometimes called a *bubble jet printer.* (12)

instructions. Commands in machine language used to process data. (4)

instruction set. Lowest language level used to program a computer, although some processors have an even lower level call *microcode.* (4)

insulation displacement connector (IDC). Electrical connector that connects to the conductor of an insulated cable by a method that forces a sharpened blade through the insulation. (20)

integrated circuit (IC). Collection of transistors, resistors, and other electronic components reduced to an unbelievably small size. (1)

Integrated Circuit Card Identification Number (ICCID). Unique code 18–22 digits in length that identifies the SIM card's country, home network, and ID number. (13)

integrated memory controller (IMC). Digital circuit built into the processor that manages data flow to and from system memory. (4)

interleave factor. Refers to the order in which sectors are laid out on a disk surface. (10)

International Mobile Station Equipment Identity (IMEI). Numeric identification number given to a mobile device. (13)

International Mobile Subscriber Identity (IMSI). A 15-digit number used by a telecommunications company to identify a SIM on its cellular network. (13)

Internet Control Message Protocol Version 6 (ICMPv6). Protocol and service for exchanging messages between neighboring network nodes on the same link. (22)

Internet Corporation for Assigned Names and Numbers (ICANN). Nonprofit organization that monitors the use of domain names, IP addresses, and related protocols. (22)

Internet Protocol (IP) address. Numeric identifier that uniquely identifies a device on a network. (22)

interpreter. Program that performs on-demand translation of higher-level language into machine language and generally runs more slowly than compiled code. (4)

intrusion detection system (IDS). System that monitors network traffic for suspicious activity or breaches and alerts a system administrator when such activities are found. (21)

intrusion prevention system (IPS). Similar to IDS as it monitors a network or certain devices for malicious traffic or activity, but it also blocks the connection where malicious traffic or activity is being generated. (21)

inverter. Electronic device that converts the low voltage (12–18 VDC) from the portable battery to a much higher voltage required by the CCFL. (8)

I/O port address. Address assigned to a device for identification and communication purposes. (3)

iOS. Apple's proprietary smartphone operating system. (13)

iPadOS. Apple's proprietary tablet operating system. (13)

IPSec. Collection of protocols that encrypt and authenticate each packet that uses an IP address over the Internet. (22)

IRQ (Interrupt Request). Signal that interrupts the processes taking place in the CPU to give attention to a device such as a keyboard or printer. (3)

ISO 9660. Update to High Sierra format that includes a file-system structure similar to FAT16, albeit with improvements; also called *CD-ROM file system (CDFS)*. (11)

ISO image. Type of disc image that serves as an exact copy of the contents by copying all sectors containing data and ignores the file system being used. (11)

J

jailbreaking. Process of overcoming the operating system's user limitations. (13)

K

kernel. Core of any operating system. (2)

keyboard-video-mouse (KVM) switch. Devices used to share a keyboard, monitor, and mouse with two or more computers or servers. (7)

L

L1 cache. Cache in the CPU and is designed to run at the same speed as the CPU. (4)

L2 cache. Used to increase the speed of data transmission to and from the processor to other parts of the motherboard. (4)

lands. Flat areas between pits that reflect the light of the laser beam. (11)

LED display. LCD screen that uses an LED backlight; also known as an *LED monitor* or *LED TV*. (8)

LED printer. Uses an array of light-emitting diodes (LEDs) to write the image to the drum. (12)

liquid-crystal display (LCD). Flat-panel display that uses liquid crystals and polarizers to produce an image. (8)

live support. Real-time support that allows a customer or client to talk directly to support personnel for technical assistance instead of using an FAQ list or web page. (24)

load balancing. Process that occurs when a computer has multiple network adapters installed and balances or divides the exchange of packets among the multiple network adapters. (20)

local area network (LAN). Small network of computers contained in a relatively small area and operates under a single management. (19)

local printer connection. Refers to a printer directly connected to a computer. (12)

local user account. Primary account configured on the workstation that controls access to resources on that specific workstation. (21)

logical drives. Separate storage areas created on a hard drive and designated by a letter. (10)

logic bomb. Destructive program that is slipped into an application and remains dormant until some event takes place. (16)

Long Term Evolution (LTE). Evolution of the GSM and UMTS standards. (14)

loopback plug. Used to assess an Ethernet network card by simulating a network. (20)

low-level format. Process that determines the type of encoding to be performed on the disk platter and the sequence in which the read/write heads will access stored data. (10)

M

macro virus. Virus created using a macro programming language and is attached to documents that use the language. (16)

magneto-optical (MO) drive. Combines magnetic and optical principles to store and retrieve data on a CD-like disc. (11)

malicious software. Software written for the express purpose of modifying a computer's configuration or causing damage to a computer system; also called *malware*. (16)

man-in-the-middle (MITM) attack. Interception of a transmission over a network; often referred to as an *on-path attack*. (16)

mantrap. Physical configuration that allows access to exactly one person at a time. (15)

Master Boot Record (MBR). Boot sector located at the beginning of a partition that identifies how and where an operating system is located so it can be booted. (10)

MBR virus. Attacks the master boot record (MBR) of a hard drive and is considered extremely destructive. (16)

Measured Boot. Works with the Trusted Platform Module (TPM) to verify the successful launch of the operating system and store the information in the TPM. (16)

media access code (MAC) address. Hexadecimal number programmed into the card's chip. (19)

memory address range. Assigned section of memory used as a temporary storage area for data before it is transferred. (3)

memory effect. Reduction in the lifespan and charge of a rechargeable battery caused by incomplete discharges. (5)

mesh topology. Network system in which each node connects directly to every other node on the network. (19)

metropolitan area network (MAN). Group of two or more interconnected LANs operating under a single management. (19)

MicroDIMM. More compact version of the standard SO-DIMM package. (6)

Microsoft Dynamic Link Library (DLL). Executable file that can be called and run by Microsoft software applications or by third-party software programs. (17)

Microsoft Reserved Partition (MSR). Data partition that reserves a portion of disk space for use by the Windows operating system and is required for GUID partition tables; also called the *System Reserved Partition.* (10)

mobile broadband. Wireless Internet connection based on mobile phone technology. (14)

mobile hotspot. Portable wireless router that allows multiple devices to share a common Internet connection. (14)

modem. Electronic device that converts a digital signal into an analog signal, and then transmits a signal across telephone lines. (14)

motherboard. Typically rectangular-shaped type of circuit board covered with many conductors that provide electrical energy paths to computer components and expansion slots. (1)

Moving Picture Experts Group (MPEG). Organization made up of professionals from all areas of the motion picture industry with the goal of developing a standard format for recording motion picture video and sound; pronounced *empeg.* (9)

multicore processor. Type of processor with two or more cores constructed on the same die. (4)

multifactor authentication. Combination of two or more authentication techniques and makes unauthorized access much more difficult. (15)

multimedia. Any file that includes interaction between audio and video. (9)

multiple-boot system. Arrangement in which more than two operating systems are installed on a single computer; also known as a *multiboot system.* (2)

multiple branch prediction. Technique that guesses what data element will be needed next rather than waiting for the next command to be issued. (4)

multiple input multiple output (MIMO). Wireless technology that uses two or more streams of data transmission to increase the data throughput and range of a wireless network. (14)

multiplexer. Special electronic device that controls the flow of data and voice over a T-carrier line. (14)

multiple zone recording (MZR). Provides twice as many sectors in the outermost tracks as compared to the innermost tracks; also called *zone bit recording.* (10)

multitasking. Ability of an operating system to simultaneously support two or more running programs. (2)

multithreading. Refers to the sharing of data and parts of a program between two or more CPUs or between the cores of a single CPU. (2)

multi-touch. Action of touching any surface-sensing device with two or more fingers. (13)

musical instrument digital interface (MIDI). File standard developed for music synthesizers. (9)

N

native resolution. Resolution that matches the pixel design of the display. (8)

network. Consists of two or more computers connected together to share data, hardware, programs, and resources, as well as communicate via e-mail and video conferencing. (19)

network administration. Use of network software packages to manage network system operations. (21)

network administrator. Person (or persons) with the highest security rating on the network. (21)

network-attached storage (NAS). Form of data storage that provides a means of centralized file sharing with little administrative overhead. (23)

network interface card (NIC). Connects media, usually twisted-pair cabling, to individual network devices such as workstations, file servers, and printers; also called *network adapter card* and *Ethernet card.* (19)

network media. Means by which an electronic signal is transmitted. (20)

network operating system (NOS). Provides communication between computers, printers, and other intelligent hardware on the network. (19)

network printer. Refers to a printer connected via a network connection. (12)

network printer connection. Refers to a printer connected by means other than a direct connection; also called a *shared printer connection.* (12)

New Technology File System (NTFS). File system designed specifically to operate with Windows NT operating systems. (10)

node. Devices connected to a network. (19)

northbridge. Chipset used to connect high-speed devices to the CPU, such as RAM and PCI slots, and was placed near the CPU. (3)

O

octet. Eight-bit binary number. (22)

odd parity checking. Mode of parity checking in which a parity bit is included whenever a transmission contains an odd number of bits. (6)

ohm. Unit of measurement for resistance; expressed with the letter *R* or the symbol omega (Ω). (5)

Open Systems Interconnection (OSI) model. Seven-layer model used to describe how hardware and software should work together to form a network communication system. (19)

operating system (OS). Underlying software that provides a computer user with all the basic services of resource management on the machine, including a file system structure for data storage and a means of communicating with all the various computer hardware. (2)

optical character recognition (OCR). Software that determines which letters, numbers, and symbols match with images taken by the scanner. (7)

optical mouse. Traces cursor movement by transmitting a light beam to a surface. (7)

Optical Network Terminal (ONT). Device that converts analog fiber-optic signals from the fiber-optic cable into digital signals. (20)

organic LED (OLED) display. Relatively new type of LED display in which the LED is constructed from carbon-based materials rather than traditional crystalline structures. (8)

overclocking. Intentional application of frequencies higher that a processor's design specification to obtain enhanced performance. (4)

P

packet. Small units of data into which larger amounts are divided for passage through a network; also called a *frame.* (20)

packet sniffer. Utility that captures packets on a network and displays their contents. (23)

packet switching. Divides data into packets, which can take a variety of routes to get to their destination. (22)

page file. Reserved portion of a hard disk divided into units called *pages*, also where virtual memory is located; sometimes called a *swap file.* (6)

paper train. Route that paper follows through a printer and consists of several rubber rollers and a paper separator pad. (12)

Parallel ATA (PATA). Interface standard for the connection of storage devices. (10)

parallel transfer. System of data transfer in which eight bits are sent side-by-side at one time. (1)

parity. The counting of either odd or even bits of the bytes transmitted. (6)

passcode lock. Typically a set of numbers used as a password; sometimes called a personal identification number or PIN. (13)

passive hub. Acts as a connection point in the topology, and transmitted digital signals from one computer are passed to all devices and networks connected to the hub. (19)

passive-matrix display. Consists of a grid of semitransparent conductors that run to each crystal. (8)

passive tablet. Tablet that uses electromagnetic induction with horizontal and vertical lines operating, transmitting, and receiving coils. (7)

passphrase. Short phrase that is not easily guessed, relevant specifically to you, memorable, and able to be made complex.

password virus. Designed to breach security and steal passwords. The passwords are stolen and redirected to another location— possibly a separate system on the Internet—so the attacker can access them later. (16)

pathname. Unique address used to identify the precise location of a specific file. (2)

PCI Express (PCIe, PCI-E). High-speed expansion bus designed to replace PCI and PCI-X. (3)

peer-to-peer network. Network model in which all the connected PCs connected are considered equal, or peers. (19)

peripheral. Optional piece of equipment used to display or input data. (1)

personal area network (PAN). Short-range network that connects devices such as a PC, smartphone, tablet, camera, and printer; sometimes called a *piconet.* (19)

personally identifiable information (PII). Data that can identify a person, including a Social Security number, credit card information, or address. (24)

pharming. Deceptive practice based on poisoning a Domain Name Service (DNS) server with an incorrect IP address for a website; also known as *DNS cache poisoning* or *DNS poisoning.* (16)

phishing. E-mail used to impersonate a legitimate company, person, or institution, thus fooling the user into believing the e-mail is from a trusted source; pronounced *fishing.* (16)

photocell. Electronic component that changes light energy into electrical energy; sometimes referred to as a photo detector. (11)

ping. Utility that is often used to verify network connections to websites by sending a packet to a distant site and then waiting for a reply. (22)

pipeline. Parallel path on which data travels to the CPU sections. (4)

pitch. Measurement for the width of a letter. (12)

pits. Holes etched into the disc to record data. (11)

pixel. Smallest unit of color in a screen display. (8)

pixel pitch. Distance between two pixels of the same color on the display area, expressed in millimeters (mm). (8)

Platform as a Service (PaaS). Cloud service model that supports programming software by enabling the consumer to deploy original applications onto the cloud using programming languages; also called *Service Platform.* (22)

plug-and-play. Automatic assignment of system resources such as DMA channels, interrupts, memory, and port assignments. (3)

points. Measurement for the height of a letter. (12)

polarized light. Light energy composed of light beams with a matching wave angle. (8)

polymorphic virus. Changes as it evolves to resist detection. (16)

port forwarding. Router configuration set to forward packets to a destination computer or server by allowing specific ports to remain open to the destination; also referred to as *port mapping.* (23)

port number. Logical address, ranging from 0 to 65,535, used by all software applications on a network system to identify the software application or service. (16)

port replicator. External device for a computer that provides additional ports to be used by a computer system. (13)

port triggering. Router configuration that monitors outbound traffic by port number. (23)

POST card. Expansion card that plugs into a motherboard and displays error codes generated during a computer's power-on self-test (POST). (17)

power. Amount of electrical energy provided or used by equipment. (5)

powerline communications (PLC). Networking technology that allows existing power lines to be used as network media. (23)

power-on password. BIOS/UEFI password entered during the POST before the operating system is loaded; also known as the *computer user password* or *boot password.* (15)

power-on self-test (POST). Simple diagnostic program that is initiated when electrical power is applied to the computer system. (2)

Power over Ethernet (PoE). Provides a means to supply small amounts of electrical power (typically 13 watts at 48 volts) to network devices such as a camera, IP phone, wireless access point, or speakers, via Ethernet connection. (20)

power supply. Electrical device that converts 120-volt AC power from the wall outlet to DC voltage levels used by the various computer components. (1)

preemptive multitasking. Process that allows multiple programs to share control of the operating system; sometimes referred to as *time slicing.* (2)

primary partition. Partition that houses the operating system as well as system files, boot files, or a combination of both. (10)

principle of least privilege (POLP). Security concept that states a user should only have enough privileges to complete their work tasks. (15)

printer. Electromechanical device that converts computer data into text or graphic images printed to paper or other presentation media. (12)

printer driver. Converts specific file types to electronic signals that control how the image or document is printed on the paper. (12)

print queue. List of print jobs waiting to be completed and their status. (12)

print spooler. Software program that temporarily stores the data in RAM or an area on the hard drive. (12)

privacy filter. Physical device that attaches to a display and limits or reduces the viewing angle; also called a *privacy screen.* (15)

private cloud. Infrastructure model typically designed for exclusive use by a single group. (22)

problem-solving. Process of choosing a course of action after evaluating available information and weighing the costs, benefits, and consequences of alternative actions. (26)

processor affinity. Ability to select the number of CPU cores to apply to a software application. (4)

processor throttling. Method of controlling processor frequency to conserve portable computer battery life. (4)

professionalism. Act of exhibiting appropriate character, judgment, and behavior by a person who is trained to perform a job. (24)

programmable read-only memory (PROM). Similar to mask ROM but is used extensively in computer program development. (6)

proprietary recovery partition. Optional partition created by the system's original equipment manufacturer (OEM); also known as the *original equipment manufacturer (OEM) partition* or *factory recovery partition*. (10)

protected health information (PHI). A person's demographic information, medical history, testing results, mental health information, and other healthcare information. (24)

protective MBR. Protects the GPT when legacy software tools are used to explore or repair the MBR. (10)

protocol. Set of rules used to govern communication between two devices. (7)

protocol suite. Combination of individual protocols, each designed for a specific purpose. (20)

proxy server. Computer server that hides all the PCs in a network from direct connection with PCs outside of it. (22)

public cloud. Infrastructure open to the general public and may be used by individuals, business organizations, or educational organizations. (22)

punch down tool. Networking tool used for inserting twisted-pair conductors into a slotted post called an insulation displacement connector (IDC). (20)

punctuality. Being on time and is essential while at work. (26)

Q

quad-channel mode. Supports four identical memory modules into the designated quad-channel slots. (6)

R

radio-frequency identification (RFID). Electronic system that uses radio waves to identify objects or people. (15)

radio frequency interference (RFI). Interference produced by electronic devices that use radio waves. (1)

rails. Electrical term used to describe the conductor paths inside the metal power supply case. (5)

rainbow table. Password-cracking method that uses a precomputed table of password hashes to search for a given hash, which yields the plaintext used to produce the hash. (15)

random access memory (RAM). Type of fast data storage where computer programs are loaded to and from the hard drive for quicker access by the CPU. (1)

ransomware. Type of malware that seizes control of your computer and demands payment to unlock it. (16)

read-only memory (ROM). Designed to store program information in a nonvolatile fashion. (6)

read/write head. Mechanism that records information to and reads information from a magnetic medium. (10)

Recovery Console. Last-resort recovery utility available in Windows often used when a problem is so severe, a technician cannot access the Safe Mode startup option. (18)

reduced instruction set computer (RISC). Type of CPU architecture that is designed for faster processing. (4)

redundant array of independent disks (RAID). System of several hard drive units arranged in such a way as to ensure recovery after a system disaster or to ensure data integrity during normal operation; also called a *redundant array of inexpensive disks*. (21)

refresh rate. Rate at which the entire image is reproduced. (8)

register. Small pocket of memory used to temporarily store data that is being processed by the CPU. (4)

registered memory. Memory module that incorporates a registry chip to drive and synchronize the memory without depending on the motherboard; sometimes called *buffered memory*. (6)

register unit. Composed of many separate storage units smaller than cache. (4)

registry. Hierarchical database that stores configuration information. (2)

registry key. Nested folder within a hive. (17)

remote wipe. Application that allows the user to wipe all user information, data, and settings if the device is stolen. (13)

repeater. Piece of equipment that regenerates a weak digital signal. (22)

Resilient File System (ReFS). Newest Microsoft file system, which builds off the enhancements made in NTFS. (10)

resistance. Opposition to the flow of electrical energy. (5)

resolution. Amount of detail a monitor can display. (8)

restore points. Backups of system settings and configurations used to correct a computer problem. (18)

ring topology. Network arrangement in which a single cable runs continuously from computer to computer. (19)

rollover cable. Ethernet cable assembly in which the pin order is completely reversed on the opposite end of the cable. (20)

root directory. Located at the top of the directory structure. (2)

rooting. Process of taking complete control of an Android device without limitations. (13)

rootkit. Collection of software programs that installs on a computer and allows an intruder to take administrative control. (16)

router. Network device used to connect to the Internet, share the Internet connection with other devices in the home or office, or support communication between different types of networks. (14)

row address selection (RAS). Describes the time it takes to start a memory read or to write the row location in the memory matrix. (6)

run-length encoding (RLE). Compression technique that replaces a series of repeated pixels with a single pixel and the length of the series (run). (8)

S

sampling. Act of measuring an analog signal at regular intervals and is required before converting an analog signal into a digital signal. (9)

sampling rate. Frequency with which samples of an audio signal are taken per second. (9)

sanitation. Removal of data from a storage media such as a hard drive. (15)

Scalable Link Interface (SLI). Proprietary video card system owned by the NVIDIA Corporation in which multiple cards work together to produce a single output. (8)

scanner. Tool that takes in an optical image and digitizes it. (7)

sectors. Physical sections of subdivided tracks. (10)

Secure Shell (SSH). Protocol that provides secure access to a remote computer; also known as *Secure Socket Shell*. (22)

Secure Sockets Layer (SSL). Protocol developed by Netscape Navigator to make HTTP-based online transactions secure. (22)

Security Accounts Manager (SAM). Registry file used to maintain the user account database on a computer. (21)

Security Identifier (SID). Identification code used to determine the assigned permissions for that user. (21)

security key. Encrypts the information that one computer sends to another computer across the network. (13)

segment. Physical or logical portion of a network. (19)

sequence number. Ensures data will be reassembled in the exact order in which it was transmitted. (20)

Serial ATA (SATA). Transport protocol that determines the amount of data that can be transferred between a motherboard and storage device. (10)

Serial Attached SCSI (SAS). Latest development for SCSI technology and is similar in design to SATA. (10)

serial presence detect (SPD). Technology that identifies the type of RAM installed on a computer. (6)

serial transfer. System of data transfer in which data is sent through a port one bit at a time in successive order over a serial cable. (1)

server. Computing device that provides a service. (19)

service. Software application that performs specific network functions. (16)

service set identifier (SSID). Broadcasted name of the wireless access point. (13)

share. Object that is distributed across the network, such as files, hard drives, optical drives, printers, and scanners, among others. (21)

shoulder surfing. Unauthorized viewing of a display to gain information. (15)

simultaneous threading. Execution of two or more threads at the same time; sometimes called *multithreading*. (4)

single-channel mode. Refers to an arrangement in which a single DIMM is installed, or multiple DIMMs of different memory capacity are installed in the motherboard memory slots. (6)

single port forwarding. Router configuration that works in similar fashion as port forwarding but only a single designated IP address is identified instead of all IP addresses in the local area network. (23)

sinkhole attack. Occurs when a compromised node on the network attacks the network by advertising a fake update of the routing table. (20)

small business service counter. Independent company that specializes in light maintenance and repair. (24)

Small Computer System Interface (SCSI). Refers to a set of standards for connecting up to seven peripheral devices, often storage devices, to a PC using an adapter board and one flat ribbon cable; pronounced *skuzzy.* (10)

small-office/home-office (SOHO) network. Simple peer-to-peer LAN used to share resources and data in a home- or small-office environment. (23)

small outline DIMM (SO-DIMM). Small-outline package of regular memory module. (6)

small outline RIMM (SO-RIMM). Small-outline package of regular memory module. (6)

smart card. Identical in size and feel to a credit card and stores information on a chip located within the body of the card. (13)

social engineering. Act of manipulating people to get them to divulge confidential information about a computer system. (15)

soft skills. Skills used to communicate and work well with others. (26)

Software as a Service (SaaS). Cloud service model that provides software applications to a user either through a web browser or thin client software application. (22)

software-defined networking (SDN). Approach to networking that uses software-based controllers or application programming interfaces (APIs) to communicate with underlying hardware infrastructure and direct traffic on a network. (20)

software driver. Small package of programs that allows proper communication between the computer and a peripheral device. (2)

software patch. Fix for operating systems and application software that have already been released. (2)

solid ink printer. Uses solid ink cartridges similar to wax. (12)

solid-state disk caching. Occurs when an SSD is used as a temporary storage location for frequently accessed files or programs. (10)

solid-state drive (SSD). Storage system designed with no moving parts and instead stores data in nonvolatile memory chips. (1)

sound. Consists of vibrations that are put into motion through a medium. (9)

southbridge. Chipset that was previously used to connect slower devices, such as the keyboard, mouse, printer, hard drive, and USB ports, and was placed farther from the CPU. (3)

spam. Unsolicited junk e-mail or newsletters and is responsible for drastically reducing the bandwidth of the Internet. (16)

spatial multiplexing (SM). Two or more streams of data transmitted in the same frequency channel. (19)

split-frame rendering. Rendering method in which each graphics card is responsible for an equal portion of the frame image, based on how many cards are used. (8)

spooling. Technique that stores data to be printed in the printer's memory so printing operations can be completed in the background while other tasks are performed by the PC without waiting for the printer to complete its job. (12)

spyware. Designed to track a user's habits such as their web-browsing tendencies. (16)

stack. Block of allocated static memory. (6)

star topology. Network arrangement in which cables run from each computer to a single point, forming a star. (19)

startup problem. Causes the computer to lock up during the boot process. (17)

static IP addressing. Manual assignment of IP addresses. (22)

static RAM. Integrated circuit technology based on digital flip-flop components; referred to as *SRAM* (pronounced *es-ram.* (6)

stealth virus. Hides from normal detection by incorporating itself into part of a known, and usually required, program for the computer. (16)

storage area network (SAN). Isolated network built entirely to handle data storage. (19)

subdirectory. File that subdivides the content of a directory. (2)

subdomain. Division of a group of networks. (22)

subnet mask. 32-bit number, usually in dotted decimal notation, used to determine the subnet to which a particular IP address refers. (22)

subscriber identity module (SIM). Integrated circuit used to securely authenticate a user's identity for a mobile device; also called a *subscriber identification module.* (13)

superscalar execution. Act of processing more than one instruction at the same time. (4)

Super VGA (SVGA). Graphics standard that supports 16 million possible colors and various resolutions. (8)

surge. Presence of higher-than-desired voltage in the electrical system. (5)

surge protector. Electrical device intended to dissipate voltage spikes to protect downstream devices. (1)

switch. Filters data packets and forwards them between network segments. (22)

switching hub. Reduces excessive data transmissions on a network by segmenting a network, which can reduce the number of frames transmitted over the entire network. (19)

synchronization. Act of matching data between multiple devices. (13)

system image. Exact replica of a hard drive partition, including all personal and operating system files. (17)

system upgrade. Refers to an installation in which only the operating system is replaced, and personal data files remain intact. (18)

T

tailgating. Occurs when an unauthorized person closely follows an authorized person into a secure area and bypasses the "gate" system. (15)

T-carrier line. Internet connection designed to carry voice and data over four wires. (14)

teamwork. Cooperative efforts by individual team members to achieve a goal. (24)

Telnet. Protocol that allows a user to log on to a remote computer and transfer files. (22)

tethering. Sharing of one device's Internet connection with another connected device that does not have an Internet connection. (14)

thin-film transistor liquid-crystal display (TFT-LCD). Consists of a matrix of thin-film transistors spread across the entire screen; often referred to as a *TFT display.* (8)

thread. Part of a software program that can be executed independently of the entire program. (4)

three-dimensional (3D) printer. Manufactures tangible objects by using code from a computer-aided drafting (CAD) file to deposit a plastic filament from a printhead onto a surface and then onto the model itself. (12)

time to live (TTL). Length of time the data in a ping packet is valid. (22)

tone generator. Attaches to one end of a cable and transmits an analog or digital signal through the cable. (20)

topology. Physical arrangement of hardware and cabling in a network. (19)

touch screen display. Computer display modified to accommodate input information by touch. (7)

traces. Electrical circuits that run across the surface of the motherboard and provide the paths between all the different components mounted on the motherboard. (3)

trackball. Mouse with a ball embedded in the top of it. (7)

tracks. Composed of a set of concentric circles where data is stored on a disk. (10)

Transmission Control Protocol/Internet Protocol (TCP/IP).
Standard default Internet protocol. (20)

triple-channel mode. Interleaved in the same way as dual-channel mode except it uses three channels to support memory access. (6)

Trojan horse. Class of malware that appears as a desirable download, but when the file is opened, the malware activates. (16)

true color. A 24-bit code that represents the actual color of the pixel image. (8)

Trusted Boot. Windows feature that checks the integrity of the operating system during the boot process and only allows digitally signed software to boot and run on the computer. (16)

Trusted Platform Module (TPM). Integrated chip incorporated into motherboards that can create and store cryptographic keys. (15)

twisted-pair cable. Consists of four pairs of conductors twisted around each other; also called *Ethernet cable.* (20)

U

Ultra High-Definition (HD) Blu-ray. Optical data storage format that supersedes Blu-ray. (11)

Ultra-Wideband (UWB) standard. Standard developed by the WiMedia Alliance to describe short-distance (10-meter) radio communication. (7)

unattended installation. Fully automated installation of a new operating system or upgrade of an existing operating system. (21)

Uniform Resource Locator (URL). Global address for websites all over the Internet. (22)

uninterruptable power supply (UPS). Electrical device designed to ensure a constant supply of equality electrical power to the computer system. (5)

Universal Disk Format (UDF). File system structure accepted for CD-RW, magneto-optical disc, and DVD technology. (11)

Universal Mobile Telecommunications System (UMTS). 3G standard developed by the 3rd Generation Partnership Project (3GPP).

Universal Serial Bus (USB). Industry standard for external serial bus ports and cables that function as connection, communication, and power for computers, peripherals, and networked devices. (3)

upper memory area (UMA). The 384 kB of memory remaining after the first 640 kB of conventional memory. (6)

USB modem. Tiny mobile broadband device that plugs into any laptop with a USB port and allows the laptop to connect to the Internet using a mobile broadband service. (14)

USB standard. Describe how different classifications of devices should communicate with a PC. (7)

user. Individual who may use the network system resources. (21)

V

vector font. Type of font that draws the outline of the letter rather than storing a separate bitmap pattern for each font; also referred to as an *outline font.* (12)

video graphics array (VGA). Baseline for video adapters. (8)

virtual hard disk (VHD). File that behaves exactly like a physical hard disk. (10)

virtual keyboard. Software-based keyboard that allows the input of data without physical keys, which can be accomplished through a touch screen or projection of light. (7)

virtual machine. Computer that runs two operating systems at the same time; also referred to as a *virtual PC.* (2)

virtual memory. Memory that supplements physical RAM. (6)

virtual printer. Software-based application installed on a computer used to create documents. (12)

virtual private network (VPN). Security configuration that creates a private tunnel between the source and destination PCs and encrypts packet contents within that tunnel to ensure data sent across the Internet is not intercepted, read, or modified. (23)

virtual smart card. Simulated card created by a combination of software and integrated circuits instead of a physical card. (15)

virus. Software that self-replicates. (16)

virus signature. Combination of characteristics that includes such things as its length, file name(s) used, mode of infection or replication, the areas of the system that are attacked, the type of software programs that are attacked, and the name or length of the file attachment. (16)

voltage. Amount of electrical pressure present in a circuit or power source. (5)

volt-amperes (VA). Alternative scale for measuring electrical power. (5)

volts (V). Scale used in measuring electrical pressure. (5)

volume mount point. NTFS file system object that allows a volume or additional hard disk drive to attach to a directory structure. (10)

Volume Table of Contents (VTOC). Data structure that tells the CD drive how the data is laid out on the disc, similar to the file table on a hard drive. (11)

W

wake-on LAN (WOL). Network adapter feature that allows the adapter to wake the computer from sleep or hibernation or power on a computer when network activity is detected; also referred to as *Remote Wake-Up (RMU).* (19)

warm boot. Refers to a boot process used to restart a computer that is already running; also called a *soft boot.* (2)

watts (W). Scale used in measuring electrical power. (5)

webcam. Peripheral device that is commonly used for video conferencing and video chatting; also referred to as a web camera. (7)

Web Services for Devices (WSD). Printer-port monitor service developed by Microsoft. (12)

wide area network (WAN). Typically a large number of computers spread over a large area and under the control of a centrally located administrator. (19)

Wi-Fi standard. Developed by the Wi-Fi Alliance to produce a specification for interfacing with 2.4-GHz networking devices and network applications. (7)

WiMAX. Wireless technology similar to Wi-Fi but has a much greater range as well as a controllable radio broadcast direction. (14)

Windows Automated Installation Kit (WAIK). Collection of tools and software applications used to make an exact copy of all content located on a computer hard disk drive and deploy that copy to other workstations. (21)

Windows Internet Naming Service (WINS). Software service that resolves a computer name to the equivalent IP address on the network. (22)

wireless access point (WAP). Device that supports communication between wireless devices and a hard-wired network system. (13)

wireless mesh network (WMN). Network system composed of wireless networking devices and base stations organized in a way so all nodes can continuously communicate with all adjacent nodes. (19)

wireless range extender. Extends the range of a wireless network by receiving the wireless signal and rebroadcasting it; sometimes called a *wireless repeater.* (19)

wireless router. Combination of a wireless access point, switch, and router; commonly used in homes and small offices as centralized distribution points for wireless and wired connections to computers and mobile devices. (19)

wireless topology. Network system that uses no cabling between the computers and instead uses either infrared light or radio transmission to communicate among devices; also called a *wireless local area network (WLAN).* (19)

Wireless USB (WUSB). Wireless standard developed by the Wireless USB Promoters Group to replace the traditional USB2 connections using radio frequencies between 3.1 GHz and 10.6 GHz. (7)

word. Total number of bytes a computer can process at one time. (1)

worm. Destructive program that contaminates files on the infected computer and spreads to other computers without prompting from the user. (16)

Z

Zero Configuration Networking. Standard developed by IEEE that recommends how to design a device that automatically detects other devices on the same network or a nearby segment without intervention by an administrator, DHCP, or DNS; also known as *Zeroconf.* (23)

zero-day attack. Attack that exploits a previously unknown vulnerability before it can be patched. (16)

zero insertion force (ZIF) socket. Type of socket for mounting a CPU that is designed not to cause stress or damage during insertion. (4)

Index

C

D

E

F

G

H

I

J

K

L

M

N

O

Q

R

S

T

U

V

W

X

Z